Less managing. More teaching. Greater learning.

INSTRUCTORS...

Would you like your **students** to show up for class **more prepared**?
(Let's face it, class is much more fun if everyone is engaged and prepared...)

Want an **easy way to assign** homework online and track student **progress**?
(Less time grading means more time teaching...)

Want an **instant view** of student or class performance?
(No more wondering if students understand...)

Need to **collect data and generate reports** required for administration or accreditation?
(Say goodbye to manually tracking student learning outcomes...)

Want to **record and post your lectures** for students to view online?
(The more students can see, hear, and experience class resources, the better they learn...)

With **McGraw-Hill's** *Connect,*™

INSTRUCTORS GET:

- Simple **assignment management,** allowing you to spend more time teaching.

- **Auto-graded** assignments, quizzes, and tests.

- **Detailed visual reporting** where student and section results can be viewed and analyzed.

- Sophisticated **online testing** capability.

- A **filtering and reporting** function that allows you to easily assign and report on materials that are correlated to learning objectives and Bloom's taxonomy.

- An easy-to-use **lecture capture** tool.

- The option to **upload course documents** for student access.

Second Canadian Edition

MANAGERIAL ACCOUNTING

Creating Value in a Dynamic Business Environment

Ronald W. Hilton
Cornell University

Michael Favere-Marchesi
Simon Fraser University

McGraw-Hill Ryerson
Connect. Learn. Succeed.

Managerial Accounting: Creating Value in a Dynamic Business Environment
Second Canadian Edition

The Internet addresses listed in the text were accurate at the time of publication. The inclusion of a website does not indicate an endorsement by the authors or McGraw-Hill Ryerson, and McGraw-Hill Ryerson does not guarantee the accuracy of the information presented at these sites.

ISBN-13: 978-0-07-105139-2
ISBN-10: 0-07-105139-2

1 2 3 4 5 6 7 8 9 10 QG 1 9 8 7 6 5 4 3

Printed and bound in the United States of America.

Care has been taken to trace ownership of copyright material contained in this text; however, the publisher will welcome any information that enables them to rectify any reference or credit for subsequent editions.

Editorial Director: *Rhondda McNabb*
Sponsoring Editor: *Keara Emmett*
Executive Marketing Manager: *Joy Armitage Taylor*
Developmental Editor: *Amy Rydzanicz*
Senior Editorial Associate: *Christine Lomas*
Supervising Editor: *Jessica Barnoski*
Photo/Permissions Researcher: *Cynthia Howard*
Copy Editor: *June Trusty*
Production Coordinator: *Scott Morrison*
Cover Design: *Katherine Strain*
Cover Images: Exercise equipment: © *Ocean/Corbis;* Trays of donuts: *Canada © Roy Ooms/All Canada Photos;* Theatre: *Ryan McVay/Getty Images;*
Automotive hi-tech: *Mark Joseph/Getty Images;* Canoes: *Wildroze/Getty Images*
Interior Design: *Katherine Strain*
Page Layout: *Aptara, Inc.*
Printer: *Quad/Graphics Versailles*

Library and Archives Canada Cataloguing in Publication

Hilton, Ronald W.
 Managerial accounting : creating value in a dynamic business environment / Ronald W. Hilton,
Michael Favere-Marchesi.—2nd Canadian ed.

Includes bibliographical references and indexes.
ISBN 978-0-07-105139-2

 1. Managerial accounting—Textbooks.
I. Favere-Marchesi, Michael II. Title.

HF5657.4.H55 2013   658.15'11   C2012-905586-7

To my wife, Meg, and our sons, Brad and Tim.

—Ronald W. Hilton

To my late beloved Brian, with forever love.

—Michael Favere-Marchesi

About the Authors

Ronald W. Hilton is a Professor of Accounting at Cornell University. With bachelor's and master's degrees in accounting from Pennsylvania State University, he received his Ph.D. from Ohio State University.

A Cornell faculty member since 1977, Professor Hilton has also taught accounting at Ohio State and the University of Florida, where he held the position of Walter J. Matherly Professor of Accounting. Prior to pursuing his doctoral studies, Hilton worked for Peat, Marwick, Mitchell & Company and served as an officer in the United States Air Force.

Professor Hilton is a member of the Institute of Management Accountants and has been active in the American Accounting Association. He has served as associate editor of *The Accounting Review* and as a member of its editorial board. Professor Hilton also has served on the editorial board of the *Journal of Management Accounting Research*. He has been a member of the resident faculties of both the Doctoral Consortium and the New Faculty Consortium sponsored by the American Accounting Association.

With wide-ranging research interests, Professor Hilton has published articles in many journals, including the *Journal of Accounting Research*, *The Accounting Review*, *Management Science*, *Decision Sciences*, *Journal of Economic Behavior and Organization*, *Contemporary Accounting Research,* and the *Journal of Mathematical Psychology.* He also has published a monograph in the *AAA Studies in Accounting Research* series, and he is a co-author of *Cost Management: Strategies for Business Decisions*, *Budgeting: Profit Planning and Control*, and *Cost Accounting: Concepts and Managerial Applications.* Professor Hilton's current research interests focus on contemporary cost management systems and international issues in managerial accounting. In recent years, he has toured manufacturing facilities and consulted with practising management accountants in North America, Europe, Asia, and Australia.

Michael Favere-Marchesi is an Associate Professor of Accounting at Simon Fraser University. With bachelor's and master's degrees in accounting from Brigham Young University, he received his Ph.D. from the University of Southern California.

A Simon Fraser faculty member since 2000, Professor Favere-Marchesi has also taught accounting at the University of Southern California, the Monterey Institute of International Studies, HEC Paris, the University of Mannheim, the Helsinki School of Economics, Chulalongkorn University, and the National Institute of Development Administration (Thailand). Prior to pursuing his doctoral studies, Professor Favere-Marchesi worked for Arthur Andersen and Mattel. He is also a reserve officer in the United States Navy.

Professor Favere-Marchesi is a licensed Certified Public Accountant (California), a Chartered Global Management Accountant, and a Certified Internal Auditor. He is a member of the American Accounting Association and the Canadian Academic Accounting Association. He is also a member of the American Institute of Certified Public Accountants, and served both on its Board of Examiners and as Chair of its International Qualification Examination committee. He has served as reviewer of *Auditing: A Journal of Practice and Theory, Behavioral Research in Accounting, The International Journal of Accounting, Advances in Accounting Behavioral Research, Journal of Accounting and Public Policy*, and *OR Spectrum: Quantitative Approaches in Management*.

With wide-ranging research interests, Professor Favere-Marchesi has published articles in several journals, including *Accounting Horizons, Auditing: A Journal of Practice and Theory, Behavioral Research in Accounting, Advances in Accounting, The International Journal of Accounting*, and *Advances in Accounting Behavioral Research*. Professor Favere-Marchesi's current research interests focus on audit judgment and decision making, audit review, fraudulent financial reporting, audit quality, and international audit environment.

Brief Contents

Contents

6 Activity Analysis, Cost Behaviour, and Cost Estimation **207**

7 Cost–Volume–Profit Analysis, Absorption and Variable Costing **248**

8 Profit Planning and Activity-Based
      Budgeting **306**

10 Cost Management Tools 433

11 Responsibility Accounting, Investment Centres, and Transfer Pricing 473

How does Hilton *Managerial Accounting* expose students to a range of businesses?

Managerial Accounting.

The world of business is changing dramatically. As a result, the role of managerial accounting is much different than it was even a decade ago. Today, management accountants serve as internal business consultants, working side by side in cross-functional teams with managers from all areas of the organization. For a thorough understanding of managerial accounting, students should not only be able to produce accounting information, but also understand how managers are likely to use and react to the information in a range of businesses.

The goal of *Managerial Accounting* is to acquaint students of business with the fundamental tools of managerial accounting and to promote their understanding of the dramatic ways in which the field is changing. The emphasis throughout the text is on using accounting information to help manage an organization.

Hilton & Favere-Marchesi *Managerial Accounting* is recognized for being:

Relevant.

Focus companies provide a powerful strategy for fostering learning, and the integration of focus companies throughout the text is unmatched by any other managerial accounting book. Each chapter introduces important managerial accounting topics within the context of a realistic company. Students see the immediate impact of managerial accounting decisions on companies and gain exposure to different types of organizations.

Balanced.

Managerial Accounting offers the most balanced coverage of manufacturing and service sector companies. Recognizing that students will work in a great variety of business environments and will benefit from exposure to diverse types of companies, *Managerial Accounting* uses a wide variety of examples from retail, service, manufacturing, and nonprofit organizations.

Contemporary.

Managerial Accounting continues to be the leader in presenting the most contemporary coverage of managerial accounting topics. The traditional tools of managerial accounting such as product costing and budgeting have been updated with current approaches. New topics such as environmental cost management and responsibility accounting continue to be featured.

Flexible.

Managerial Accounting is written in a modular format, allowing topics to be covered in the order you want. For example, Chapter 6 covers activity analysis, cost behaviour, and cost estimation. Many instructors like to cover these topics early in the course, so Chapter 6 is written so that it can be assigned right after Chapter 3, which covers product costing and cost accumulation.

How does Hilton help students learn managerial accounting in the context of business?

FOCUS COMPANIES

Students need to see the relevance of managerial accounting information in order to actively engage in learning the material. The authors have found that by using focus companies to illustrate concepts, they can help students immediately see the significance of the material and get excited about the content. *Managerial Accounting's* integration of focus companies throughout the text is unmatched by any other managerial accounting textbook. Each chapter introduces important managerial topics within the context of a realistic company.

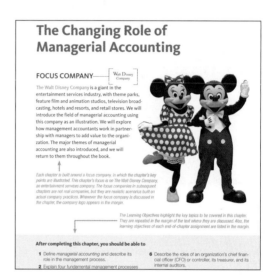

The Changing Role of Managerial Accounting

FOCUS COMPANY — Walt Disney Company

The Walt Disney Company is a giant in the entertainment services industry, with theme parks, feature film and animation studios, television broadcasting, hotels and resorts, and retail stores. We will introduce the field of managerial accounting using this company as an illustration. We will explore how management accountants work in partnership with managers to add value to the organization. The major themes of managerial accounting are also introduced, and we will return to them throughout the book.

Each chapter is built around a focus company, in which the chapter's key points are illustrated. This chapter's focus is on The Walt Disney Company, an entertainment services company. The focus companies in subsequent chapters are not real companies, but they are realistic scenarios built on actual company practices. Whenever the focus company is discussed in the chapter, the company logo appears in the margin.

The Learning Objectives highlight the key topics to be covered in this chapter. They are repeated in the margin of the text where they are discussed. Also, the learning objectives of each end-of-chapter assignment are listed in the margin.

After completing this chapter, you should be able to

1 Define *managerial accounting* and describe its role in the management process.
2 Explain four fundamental management processes.

6 Describe the roles of an organization's chief financial officer (CFO) or controller, its treasurer, and its internal auditors.

Whenever the focus company is discussed in the chapter, its logo is shown so the student sees its application to the text topic.

IN CONTRAST

In contrast to the entertainment services setting of The Walt Disney Company, we will turn our attention to Roots. This major Canadian clothing and lifestyle products retailer has more than 120 stores in Canada and the United States, and more than 40 stores in Asia. We will explore Root's value chain, which is the set of linked, value-creating activities, ranging from obtaining basic raw materials and energy to the ultimate delivery of products and services. As a retailer, Roots focuses on the design, marketing, and sales of apparel, accessories, and leather goods. All manufacturing of its clothing lines is contracted out to garment manufacturers around the world, while all leather products are made in the company's factory located in Toronto.

CONTRAST COMPANIES

A contrast company is also introduced in each chapter. In most cases, these highlight an industry different from that of the focus company. This feature allows even greater emphasis on service sector firms and other nonmanufacturing environments. The complete list of focus companies and contrast companies is featured on the front endpapers.

Real-World Examples

The text provides a variety of thought-provoking, real-world examples to focus students on managerial accounting as an essential part of the management process. Featured organizations include FedEx, WestJet Airlines, TD Canada Trust, Amazon.ca, Roots, and many others. These companies are highlighted in green in the text.

Organization Chart

A company's top management group usually consists of the board of directors, a president and chief executive officer (CEO), a chief of corporate operations, and a chief financial officer.

Line and Staff Positions   Positions on an organization chart are of two types: line positions and staff positions. Managers in **line positions** are *directly* involved in the provision of goods or services. For example, Disney's line positions include the president of Disney Consumer Products, the president of Walt Disney Studios, and the president of Walt Disney Parks and Resorts, which is the division responsible for the company's theme parks in California, Florida, France, Hong Kong, and Japan, as well as Disneyland Shanghai, slated to open in 2016. Also in line positions would be the hundreds of managers in the various operating units of the divisions. For example, the general manager of Hong Kong Disneyland, the manager of food and beverage services at the Magic Kingdom, and the manager of the Disney Store at the West Edmonton Mall in Alberta would

In Their Own Words

Quotes from both practising managers and management accountants are included in the margins throughout the text. These actual quotes show how the field of managerial accounting is changing, emphasize how the concepts are actually used, and demonstrate that management accountants are key players on most companies' management teams.

> "You've got to know how to talk to people, express yourself. And that's oral and written. You also have to be able to understand a lot of different areas, not necessarily just accounting. You've got to understand the business itself." (1)
>
> **Qwest**
> **(Currently a part of CenturyLink)**

Management accountants serve a crucial function in virtually any enterprise. As the providers of information, they interact frequently with sales staff, finance specialists, production people, and managers at all levels. To perform their duties effectively, management accountants must be knowledgeable not only in accounting but in the other major business disciplines as well. Moreover, strong oral and written communication skills are becoming increasingly important for success as a management accountant.

Professional Organizations

To keep up with new developments in their field, management accountants often belong to one or more professional organizations. Many management accountants belong to the Canadian Institute of Chartered Accountants, the Certified General Accountants Association of Canada, and/or the Society of Management Accountants of Canada. The latter

Managerial Accounting Practice

The managerial accounting practices of well-known, real-world organizations are highlighted in these boxes. They stimulate student interest and provide a springboard for classroom discussion.

MASS CUSTOMIZATION

"There is no better way to make, sell, and deliver PCs than the way Dell Inc. does it, and nobody executes that model better than Dell." The company's machines are made to order and delivered directly to customers, who get the exact machines they want cheaper than they can get them from Dell's competition. "Dell has some 24 facilities in and around Austin and employs more than 18,000 local workers. Dell is improving its earnings and gaining market share even in tough economic times. Nevertheless, Michael Dell, the company's restless founder, is constantly looking for ways to improve the company's operations."[2] In one year alone, Dell cut $1 billion out of its costs—half from manufacturing—and Dell executives vowed to cut another $1 billion.

Focus on Ethics

Focus on Ethics boxes pose an ethical dilemma and then ask tough questions that underscore the importance of ethical management. Some of these are based on real-world incidents, while others are fictional but based on well-established anecdotal evidence.

Focus on Ethics

WAS WORLDCOM'S CONTROLLER JUST FOLLOWING ORDERS?

Through a series of mergers and acquisitions, WorldCom, Inc. grew to become North America's second-largest long-distance telecommunications company. WorldCom's core communication services included network data transmission over public and private networks. Trouble arose for WorldCom because of the immense overcapacity in the telecommunications industry due to overly optimistic growth projections during the Internet boom. The combination of overcapacity, decreased demand, and high fixed costs still poses a serious problem for many of the major players in the industry.

alleged accounting scandal. The auditing firm maintained that the details of the fraud were kept from them by senior management. WorldCom's controller and its chief financial officer (CFO), who was a former KPMG employee, were fired after the alleged accounting frauds were revealed. WorldCom's CEO maintained that he knew nothing of the accounting decisions made by the CFO, but many observers question how almost $8 billion in expenses could slip by senior management.[13]

According to an Associated Press article that ran on September 27, 2002, "The former controller of Worldcom, Inc. pleaded guilty to securities fraud charges, saying he was instructed by 'senior management' to falsify records

How can my students use Hilton to master the concepts of managerial accounting?

Managerial Accounting is known for its comprehensive and reliable end-of-chapter material.

Review Problems on Cost Classifications

Problem 1

Several costs incurred by Myrtle Beach Golf Equipment, Inc. are listed below. For each cost, indicate which of the following classifications best describe(s) the cost. More than one classification may apply to the same cost item. For example, a cost may be both a variable cost and a product cost.

Cost Classifications

a. Variable

b. Fixed

c. Period

d. Product

e. Administrative

Review Problems present both a problem and a complete solution allowing students to review the entire problem-solving process.

the costs of acquiring assets or services are recognized as expenses. An **expense** is defined as the cost incurred when an asset is used up or sold for the purpose of generating revenue. The terms *product cost* and *period cost* are used to describe the timing with which various expenses are recognized.

A **product cost** is a cost assigned to goods that were either purchased or manufactured for resale. The product cost is used to value the inventory of manufactured goods or merchandise until the goods are sold. In the period of the sale, the product costs are recognized as an expense called **cost of goods sold**. The product cost of merchandise

Key Terms are boldfaced and defined in the text. The full glossary is available on Connect.

Review Questions

2–1.   Distinguish between product costs and period costs.

2–2.   Why are product costs also called *inventoriable costs*?

2–3.   What is the most important difference between a manufacturing firm and a service industry firm, with regard to the classification of costs as product costs or period costs?

2–4.   List, describe, and give an example of each of the five different types of production processes.

2–5.   "The words *mass* and *customization* in the term *mass customization* seem contradictory." Do you agree or disagree? Explain.

2–6.   Why is the cost of idle time treated as manufacturing overhead?

2–7.   Explain why an overtime premium is included in manu-

a.   Cost of medication administered

b.   Cost of overtime paid to nurses due to scheduling errors

c.   Cost of depreciation of hospital beds

2–18.   Distinguish between out-of-pocket costs and opportunity costs.

2–19.   Define the terms *sunk cost* and *differential cost*.

2–20.   Distinguish between marginal and average costs.

2–21.   Think about the process of registering for classes at your college or university.

a.   What additional information would you like to have before you register?

b.   How would it help you?

End-of-Chapter Assignment Material Each chapter includes an extensive selection of assignment material, including Review Questions, Exercises, Problems, and Cases. Our problem and case material facilitates class discussions.

Excel® Spreadsheets

Spreadsheet applications are essential to contemporary accounting practice. Students must recognize the power of spreadsheets and know how accounting data are presented in them. Excel® applications are discussed where appropriate in the text.

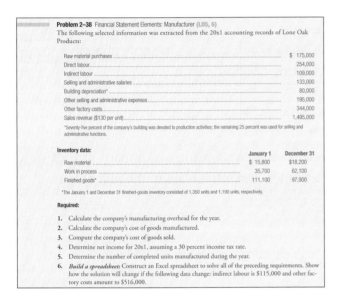

Problem 2–38 Financial Statement Elements: Manufacturer (LO5, 6)

The following selected information was extracted from the 20x1 accounting records of Lone Oak Products:

Raw material purchases	$ 175,000
Direct labour	254,000
Indirect labour	109,000
Selling and administrative salaries	133,000
Building depreciation*	80,000
Other selling and administrative expenses	195,000
Other factory costs	344,000
Sales revenue ($130 per unit)	1,495,000

*Seventy-five percent of the company's building was devoted to production activities; the remaining 25 percent was used for selling and administrative functions.

Inventory data:

	January 1	December 31
Raw material	$ 15,800	$18,200
Work in process	35,700	62,100
Finished goods*	111,100	97,900

*The January 1 and December 31 finished-goods inventory consisted of 1,350 units and 1,190 units, respectively.

Required:

1. Calculate the company's manufacturing overhead for the year.
2. Calculate the company's cost of goods manufactured.
3. Compute the company's cost of goods sold.
4. Determine net income for 20x1, assuming a 30 percent income tax rate.
5. Determine the number of completed units manufactured during the year.
6. *Build a spreadsheet:* Construct an Excel spreadsheet to solve all of the preceding requirements. Show how the solution will change if the following data change: indirect labour is $115,000 and other factory costs amount to $516,000.

Several exercises and problems in each chapter include an optional requirement for students to **Build a Spreadsheet** to develop the solution.

Required:

1. Prepare the company's schedule of cost of goods manufactured for the year.
2. Prepare the company's schedule of cost of goods sold for the year.
3. Prepare the company's income statement for the year.
4. *Build a spreadsheet:* Construct an Excel spreadsheet to solve all of the preceding requirements. Show how both cost schedules and the income statement will change if raw-material purchases amounted to $190,000 and indirect labour was $20,000.

Many problems can be solved using the Excel spreadsheet templates available on Connect. An Excel® logo appears in the margin next to these problems for easy identification.

Icons identify key business areas in the problems and cases in each chapter:

 Ethical Issues

 Group Work

 Internet Research

 International Issues

 Business Communication

 Excel Template

New to the Second Canadian Edition

Major Revisions and Reorganizations

Based on input from users and reviewers, the cost–volume–profit (CVP) analysis and absorption and variable costing coverage has been heavily reorganized and condensed into a single chapter. Chapter 7, "Cost–Volume–Profit Analysis, Absorption and Variable Costing," covers all aspects of CVP in a comprehensive focus company example, while the concepts of absorption and variable costing are illustrated using the contrast company.

In relevant chapters, a discussion of practical capacity has been added.

Many chapters include revisions of pedagogical elements, condensing and streamlining of explanations, and the addition of more current examples and references to the respected business press (e.g., *The Wall Street Journal*).

Online Chapters and Supplements

Additional chapters and supplements on special topics continue to be available on Connect. These bonus chapters and supplements include:

- Process Costing: The First-In, First-Out Method (Supplement 4A)
- Process Costing in Sequential Production Departments (Supplement 4B)
- Effect of Income Taxes on CVP Analysis (Supplement 7A) **NEW**
- Linear Programming (Supplement 12A) **NEW**
- Capital Expenditure Decisions (Chapter 14)
- Allocation of Support Activity Costs and Joint Costs (Chapter 15)

Managerial Accounting Practice

Several of the real-world examples in the Managerial Accounting Practice feature have been revised and updated for greater currency and several new examples have been added.

Emphasis on the Service Sector

As the service industry plays an increasingly greater role in the economy, even more emphasis has been placed on providing real-world service industry examples of firms using managerial accounting information.

End-of-Chapter Assignment Material

The end-of-chapter assignment material has been extensively revised. Virtually all of the quantitative exercises, problems, and cases contain new and updated data. The "Build-a-Spreadsheet" feature has been completely revised for the second edition, and several exercises and problems in each chapter include an optional requirement to build an Excel spreadsheet to solve the questions.

Chapter-by-Chapter Changes

Chapter 1:   The section on the major themes in managerial accounting has been revised, and a significant discussion of the management of capacity and capacity costs has been added. This new material includes a discussion of theoretical and practical capacity, and it provides examples of the cost of resources supplied, the cost of resources used, and the cost of resources unused (i.e., the cost of unused capacity). Also new to Chapter 1 is a revised discussion of the ethical climate of business and the role of the management accountant. A new contrast company, Roots, has been introduced.

Chapter 2:   This chapter includes a revised discussion of the use of cost information in the financial statements of WestJet, Walmart, and Caterpillar. Also revised is the discussion of mass-customization operations.

Chapter 3:   The calculation of the predetermined overhead rate is revised to include discussion of the role of practical capacity. Also revised are many end-of-chapter assignment items to account for the role of practical capacity.

Chapter 5:   The discussion of value-added costs has been revised to distinguish between customer value-added costs and business value-added costs. A discussion of practical capacity has also been added.

Chapter 6:   The discussion of whether direct labour is a variable or a fixed cost has been revised and appears in this chapter. The discussion of ethical issues surrounding the direct-labour cost classification has also been revised.

Chapter 7:   A discussion of practical capacity and its role in absorption costing has been added to this chapter. The new online supplement, "Supplement 7A: Effect of Income Taxes on CVP Analysis," discusses the impact of taxes on the CVP calculations. This section contains materials that appeared as an appendix in the previous edition.

Chapter 9:   The discussion of labour standards in the service industry has been revised.

Chapter 10:   An example of environmental costs based on the catastrophic oil spill in the Gulf of Mexico in 2010 has been added.

Chapter 11:   The discussion of "pay for performance" has been revised in this chapter.

Chapter 12:   A revised discussion of the steps in the decision-making process begins the chapter. The new online supplement, "Supplement 12A: Linear Programming," contains materials that appeared as an appendix to the chapter in the previous edition.

Teaching and Learning with Technology

Managerial Accounting's technological learning solutions complement the textbook every step of the way, giving students the extra help they need while providing instructors with tools for teaching stimulating and rewarding classes.

Connect McGraw Hill connect™

McGraw-Hill Connect™ is a web-based assignment and assessment platform that gives students the means to better connect with their coursework, with their instructors, and with the important concepts that they will need to know for success now and in the future.

With Connect, instructors can deliver assignments, quizzes, and tests online. Nearly all of the questions from the text are presented in an auto-gradeable format and all are tied to the text's learning objectives. Instructors can edit existing questions and author entirely new problems—track individual student performance, by question, assignment, or in relation to the class overall, with detailed grade reports—and integrate grade reports easily with learning management systems such as WebCT and Blackboard.

By choosing Connect, instructors are providing their students with a powerful tool for improving academic performance and truly mastering course material. Connect allows students to practise important skills at their own pace and on their own schedule. Importantly, students' assessment results and instructors' feedback are all saved online—so students can continually review their progress and plot their course to success.

Connect also provides 24/7 online access to an eBook—an online edition of the text—to aid them in successfully completing their work, wherever and whenever they choose.

Key Features

SIMPLE ASSIGNMENT MANAGEMENT

With Connect, creating assignments is easier than ever, so you can spend more time teaching and less time managing.

- Create and deliver assignments easily with selectable end-of-chapter questions and test bank material to assign online.
- Streamline lesson planning, student progress reporting, and assignment grading to make classroom management more efficient than ever.
- Go paperless with the eBook and online submission and grading of student assignments.

SMART GRADING

When it comes to studying, time is precious. Connect helps students learn more efficiently by providing feedback and practice material when they need it, where they need it.

- Automatically score assignments, giving students immediate feedback on their work and side-by-side comparisons with correct answers.
- Access and review each response; manually change grades or leave comments for students to review.
- Reinforce classroom concepts with practice tests and instant quizzes.

INSTRUCTOR LIBRARY

The Connect Instructor Library is your course creation hub. It provides all the critical resources you'll need to build your course, just how you want to teach it.

- Assign eBook readings and draw from a rich collection of textbook-specific assignments.
- Access instructor resources, including ready-made PowerPoint presentations and media to use in your lectures.
- View past assignments and resources.
- Post your own resources for students to use.

EBOOK

Connect reinvents the textbook learning experience for the modern student. Every Connect subject area is seamlessly integrated with Connect eBooks, which are designed to keep students focused on the concepts key to their success.

- Provide students with a Connect eBook, allowing for anytime, anywhere access to the textbook.
- Merge media, animation, and assessments with the text's narrative to engage students and improve learning and retention.

- Pinpoint and connect key concepts in a snap using the powerful eBook search engine.
- Manage notes, highlights, and bookmarks in one place for simple, comprehensive review.

LYRYX ASSESSMENT

Available as an option to package with the Hilton textbook at a small additional cost, Lyryx Assessment for *Managerial Accounting* contains algorithmic problems tied to the Hilton text, unlimited opportunity for students to practise, and automatic grading with extensive feedback for both students and instructors.

Services and Support

INSTRUCTOR SUPPORT

The following instructor resources are available online on Connect:

- ***Instructor's Manual:*** This comprehensive manual includes chapter outlines, summaries, and teaching overviews.
- ***Solutions Manual:*** This manual, prepared by the author, contains complete solutions to all of the text's end-of-chapter review questions, exercises, problems, and cases.
- **Computerized Test Bank:** This test bank contains multiple-choice questions, essay assignments, and short problems. Each test item is coded for level of difficulty and its related learning objective.
- **Microsoft® PowerPoint® Presentations:** These slides cover key concepts found in each chapter, using outlines, summaries, and visuals.

- **Microsoft® Excel® Templates:** These are the solutions to the Excel templates offered online.

SUPERIOR LEARNING SOLUTIONS AND SUPPORT

The McGraw-Hill Ryerson team is ready to help you assess and integrate any of our products, technology, and services into your course for optimal teaching and learning performance. Whether it's helping your students improve their grades, or putting your entire class online, the McGraw-Hill Ryerson team is here to help you do it. Contact your iLearning Sales Specialist today to learn how to maximize all of McGraw-Hill Ryerson's resources!

For more information on the latest technology and Learning Solutions offered by McGraw-Hill Ryerson and its partners, please visit us online: **www.mcgrawhill.ca/he/solutions.**

McGraw-Hill Ryerson
Connect. Learn. Succeed.

Solutions that make a difference. Technology that fits.

MH-Campus
LMS Integration

Connect
Course Management

LearnSmart
Adaptive Learning

Tegrity
Lecture Capture

Custom
Print & Digital

Acknowledgments

I am grateful . . .

I would like to express my appreciation to people who have provided assistance in the development of this textbook. First, my gratitude goes to the thousands of accounting students I have had the privilege to teach over many years. Their enthusiasm, comments, and questions have challenged me to clarify my thinking about many topics in managerial accounting.

Second, I express my sincere thanks to the following professors who provided extensive reviews for the second Canadian edition:

REVIEWERS

Dom Cianflone, *University of Toronto*

Pat Corkum, *Acadia University*

Arsineh Garabedian, *Simon Fraser University*

Hemantha Herath, *Brock University*

Sylvia Hsu, *York University*

Marg Johnson, *Thompson Rivers University*

Donna Losell, *University of Toronto*

Winston Marcellin, *George Brown College*

Debbie Musil, *Kwantlen Polytechnic University*

Pamela Quon, *Athabasca University*

Todd Rose, *College of the North Atlantic*

Frank Saccucci, *Grant MacEwan University*

Eckhard Schumann, *McMaster University*

Shu-Lun Wong, *Memorial University of Newfoundland*

I also want to thank Susan Cohlmeyer for her thorough checking of the text and solutions manual for accuracy and completeness.

The supplements are a great deal of work to prepare. I appreciate the efforts of Michael Hockenstein, Richard Michalski, Todd Rose, and Amanda Simmers for preparing them, since these valuable aids make teaching the course easier for everyone who uses the text.

I acknowledge the Institute of Management Accountants for permission to use problems from Certified Management Accountant (CMA) examinations. I also acknowledge the American Institute of Certified Public Accountants for permission to use problems from the Uniform CPA Examinations, Questions, and Unofficial Answers. I am indebted to Professors Roland Minch, David Solomons, and Michael Maher for allowing the use of their case materials in the text. The sources for the actual company information in Chapters 1 and 2 regarding The Walt Disney Company, Caterpillar, Walmart, and WestJet Airlines were the companies' published annual reports.

Finally, I wish to express my gratitude to the fine people at McGraw-Hill Ryerson who so professionally guided this book through the publication process. In particular, I wish to acknowledge Amy Rydzanicz, Keara Emmett, Rhondda McNabb, Jessica Barnoski, June Trusty, and Cynthia Howard for their hard work and commitment to the second Canadian edition.

Michael Favere-Marchesi

Second Canadian Edition

MANAGERIAL ACCOUNTING

Creating Value in a Dynamic Business Environment

CHAPTER ONE

The Changing Role of Managerial Accounting

FOCUS COMPANY ——— Walt Disney Company

The Walt Disney Company is a giant in the entertainment services industry, with theme parks, feature film and animation studios, television broadcasting, hotels and resorts, and retail stores. We will introduce the field of managerial accounting using this company as an illustration. We will explore how management accountants work in partnership with managers to add value to the organization. The major themes of managerial accounting are also introduced, and we will return to them throughout the book.

Each chapter is built around a focus company, in which the chapter's key points are illustrated. This chapter's focus is on The Walt Disney Company, an entertainment services company. The focus companies in subsequent chapters are not real companies, but they are realistic scenarios built on actual company practices. Whenever the focus company is discussed in the chapter, the company logo appears in the margin.

The Learning Objectives highlight the key topics to be covered in this chapter. They are repeated in the margin of the text where they are discussed. Also, the learning objectives of each end-of-chapter assignment are listed in the margin.

After completing this chapter, you should be able to

1 Define *managerial accounting* and describe its role in the management process.

2 Explain four fundamental management processes that help organizations to attain their goals.

3 List and describe five objectives of managerial accounting activity.

4 Explain the major differences between managerial and financial accounting.

5 Explain where management accountants are located in an organization, in terms of formal organization, deployment on cross-functional teams, and physical location.

6 Describe the roles of an organization's chief financial officer (CFO) or controller, its treasurer, and its internal auditors.

7 Briefly describe some of the major contemporary themes in managerial accounting.

8 Understand and explain the concepts of strategic cost management and the value chain.

9 Understand the ethical responsibilities of a management accountant.

10 Discuss the professional organizations, certification process, and ethical standards in the field of managerial accounting.

IN CONTRAST

In contrast to the entertainment services setting of The Walt Disney Company, we will turn our attention to Roots. This major Canadian clothing and lifestyle products retailer has more than 120 stores in Canada and the United States, and more than 40 stores in Asia. We will explore Root's value chain, which is the set of linked, value-creating activities, ranging from obtaining basic raw materials and energy to the ultimate delivery of products and services. As a retailer, Roots focuses on the design, marketing, and sales of apparel, accessories, and leather goods. All manufacturing of its clothing lines is contracted out to garment manufacturers around the world, while all leather products are made in the company's factory located in Toronto.

In Their Own Words These quotes are from both practising managers and management accountants. The quotes show how various managerial accounting concepts are actually used and how management accountants are key players in most companies. The references for these quotes appear in the "Endnotes" at the back of the book and are organized by chapter (e.g., reference [1a] relates to the first quote in Chapter 1).

Each chapter also includes a contrast company. This chapter's contrast company is Roots, a Canadian clothing and lifestyle products retailer. In most cases, the contrast company section will present a key chapter topic in an industry different from that of the focus company. The contrast companies in subsequent chapters are fictitious companies, based on actual organizations in business today. These realistic illustrations and scenarios are intended to help connect to everyday life the business and managerial accounting issues discussed in this book.

Many different kinds of organizations affect our daily lives. Manufacturers, retailers, service industry firms, agribusiness companies, nonprofit organizations, and government agencies provide us with a vast array of goods and services. All of these organizations have two things in common. First, they all have a set of *goals* or objectives. An airline, such as Cathay Pacific or WestJet Airlines, might specify profitability and customer service as its goals. The Vancouver Police Department's goals would include public safety and security, coupled with cost minimization. Second, in pursuing an organization's goals, managers need *information*. Management's information needs involve financial, production, marketing, legal, and environmental issues. Generally, the larger the organization, the greater is management's need for information.

Managerial accounting is the process of identifying, measuring, analyzing, interpreting, and communicating information in pursuit of an organization's goals. It is an integral part of the management process, and management accountants are important strategic partners on an organization's management team.

In this chapter, we will explore the role of managerial accounting within the overall management process. In the remaining chapters, we will expand our study by exploring the many concepts and tools used in managerial accounting.

Learning Objective **1**

Define *managerial accounting* and describe its role in the management process.

A Business Partnership with Management

The role of managerial accounting is very different now from what it was even a decade ago. In the past, management accountants operated in a supporting staff capacity, usually physically separated from the managers for whom they provided reports and information. Today, management accountants serve as internal business consultants, working side by side on cross-functional teams with managers from all areas of the organization. Rather than isolate management accountants in a separate accounting department, companies now tend to locate them in the operating departments, where

"We are looked upon as business advisors, more than just accountants, and that has a lot to do with the additional analysis and the forward-looking goals we are setting." (1a)

Caterpillar

they are working with other managers to make decisions and resolve operational problems. Management accountants take on leadership roles on their teams and are sought out for the valuable information they provide. Their role in leading-edge companies "has been transformed from number cruncher and financial historian to being business partner and trusted advisor."[1]

An organization's management team, on which management accountants play an integral role, seeks to create value for the organization by managing resources, activities, and people in order to achieve the organization's goals effectively.

Managing Resources, Activities, and People

The owners, directors, or trustees of an organization set its goals, often with the help of management. For example, The Walt Disney Company's goals are set by its board of directors, who are elected by the company's shareholders. According to a recent annual report, the overall goal of the company may be expressed as a commitment to creative excellence and guest service, coupled with strict financial discipline in order to maximize value for the company's shareholders.

In pursuing its goals, an organization acquires *resources*, hires *people*, and then engages in an organized set of *activities*. It is up to the management team to best use the organization's resources, activities, and people in achieving the organization's goals. The day-to-day work of the management team comprises four activities:

1. Decision making
2. Planning
3. Directing operational activities
4. Controlling

Decision Making

Several years ago, Disney's board of directors decided as one of the company's growth objectives to expand its theme park operations. However, it was not immediately clear what the best way to accomplish that goal would be. Would it be better to expand one of the company's existing theme parks—for example, the Disneyland Park in California, the Magic Kingdom and Disney Hollywood Studios in Florida, or Tokyo Disneyland? Or should the company branch out in an entirely new direction with a brand-new theme park attraction? How would each of these alternative courses of action mesh with the company's other goals of bringing the best in creative entertainment to its customers and maintaining sound financial discipline? Disney's top management team had to *make a decision* about the best way to expand the company's operations, which entailed *choosing among the available alternatives*.

Planning

Disney's top management team decided to expand the company's operations by building an entirely new theme park named Hong Kong Disneyland. Created and designed by Walt Disney's Imagineering Division, this 1.3-km² theme park would offer guests similar theme areas as the original Disneyland Park in California. Now the detailed planning phase began. How would Hong Kong Disneyland's many attractions designed by the Imagineering Division be laid out and organized? How would Chinese culture, customs, and traditions be incorporated when designing and building the resort? What food and beverage operations would be appropriate? How many employees would be needed on a day-to-day basis? What supplies would be required to run the park? How much would electricity and other utilities cost? How much would running the park during a typical year cost? Finally, how should the park's admission be priced, given predicted attendance? Disney's management team had to *plan* for running the Hong Kong Disneyland, which meant *developing a detailed financial and operational description of anticipated operations*.

Walt Disney Company

Learning Objective **2**

Explain four fundamental management processes that help organizations to attain their goals.

"The accounting people are expected to do things that are much more strategic and much more forward looking than [they] have been expected to do in the past." (1b)

Caterpillar

Directing Operational Activities

Now the theme park has been built, equipped, and staffed. How many cashiers should be on duty on Saturday morning? How much food should be ordered each day? How much cash will be needed to meet the payroll, pay the utility bills, and buy maintenance supplies next month? All of these questions fall under the general heading of *directing operational activities*, which means *running the organization on a day-to-day basis.*

Controlling

The theme park has operated for several years now. Is the company's goal being accomplished? More specifically, have the theme park's operations adhered to the plans developed by management for achieving the goal? In seeking to answer these questions, management is engaged in *control*, which means *ensuring that the organization operates in the intended manner and achieves its goals.*

Adding Value to the Organization

Managers need information for all of the activities described in the preceding section. That information comes from a variety of sources, including economists, financial experts, marketing and production staff, and the organization's managerial accounting system.

Objectives of Managerial Accounting Activity

Learning Objective   **3**

List and describe five objectives of managerial accounting activity.

Management accountants add value to an organization by pursuing five major objectives:

1. Providing information for decision making and planning, and proactively participating as part of the management team in the decision-making and planning processes
2. Assisting managers in directing and controlling operational activities
3. Motivating managers and other employees to support the organization's goals
4. Measuring and evaluating the performance of activities, subunits, managers, and other employees within the organization
5. Assessing the organization's competitive position, and working with other managers to ensure the organization's long-term competitiveness in its industry

"In five years [we will become] even more strategic. Really understanding the ins and outs of all the organizations, and really trying to be visionary—understanding what is happening to our business." (1c)
Hewlett-Packard

Today, managerial accounting analysis is considered so crucial in managing an enterprise that in most cases management accountants are integral members of the management team. Far from playing a passive role as information providers, management accountants take a proactive role in both the strategic and day-to-day decisions that confront an enterprise.

Although much of the information provided by the managerial accounting system is financial, there is a strong trend toward the presentation of substantial nonfinancial data as well. Management accountants supply many kinds of information to management and act as strategic business partners in support of management's role in decision making and managing the organization's activities. As we will see in subsequent chapters, current managerial accounting systems are increasingly focused on activities at all levels of the organization. Measuring, managing, and continuously improving operational activities are critical to an organization's success.

To illustrate the objectives of managerial accounting activity, let us continue with the example of Hong Kong Disneyland.

Providing Information for Decision Making and Planning, and Proactively Participating as Part of the Management Team in the Decision-Making and Planning Processes For virtually all major decisions, Disney's management team would rely largely on managerial accounting information. For example, the *decision* to establish the new theme park would be influenced heavily by estimates of the costs of building Hong Kong Disneyland and maintaining it throughout its life. The theme park's managers would also rely on managerial accounting data in formulating plans for the park's operations. Prominent in those *plans* would be a budget detailing the projected revenues and costs of providing entertainment.

While Disney's top management contemplated its decision about the theme park, the company's management accountants could not simply gather information and then sit on the sidelines. The management accountants were key participants in the management team as decisions were made and plans formulated for the theme park's operations.

Assisting Managers in Directing and Controlling Operational Activities Directing and controlling day-to-day operations require a variety of data about the process of providing entertainment services. For example, in *directing* operational activities, the park's management team would need data about customer food-service demand patterns in order to make sure appropriate staffing was provided in the theme park's various food venues. In *controlling* operations, management would compare actual costs incurred with those specified in the budget.

Managerial accounting information often assists management through its **attention-directing function**. Managerial accounting reports rarely solve a decision problem. However, managerial accounting information often directs managers' attention to an issue that requires their skills. To illustrate, suppose Hong Kong Disneyland incurred electricity costs that significantly exceeded the budget. This fact does not explain why the budget was exceeded, nor does it tell management what action to take, but it does direct management's attention to the situation. Suppose that on further investigation, the accounting records reveal that the local electric rates have increased substantially. This information will help management in framing the decision problem. Should steps be taken to conserve electricity? Should the park's hours be curtailed? Perhaps management should consider switching to a lower-cost method of air conditioning.

Motivating Managers and Other Employees toward the Organization's Goals Organizations have goals. However, organizations comprise people who have goals of their own. The goals of individuals are diverse, and they do not always match those of the organization. A key purpose of managerial accounting is to motivate managers and other employees to direct their efforts toward achieving the organization's goals. One means of achieving this purpose is through budgeting. In establishing a budget for Hong Kong Disneyland, top management indicates how resources are to be allocated and what activities are to be emphasized. When actual operations do not conform to the budget, the theme park's managers will be asked to explain the reasons for the deviation.

One way in which employees can be motivated toward supporting the organization's goals is through **employee empowerment**, which is the concept of encouraging and authorizing workers to take the initiative to improve operations, reduce costs, and improve product quality and customer service. At The Walt Disney Company's theme parks, for example, employees are routinely asked for suggestions about ways to improve service to the parks' millions of visitors.

Measuring the Performance of Activities, Subunits, Managers, and Other Employees within the Organization One means of motivating people toward supporting the organization's goals is to measure their performance in achieving those goals. Such measurements then can be used as the basis for rewarding performance through positive feedback, promotions, and pay raises. For example, most large corporations compensate their executives, in part, on the basis of the profit achieved by the subunits they manage. In other companies,

> "What we're seeing is less transactional and more decision support type of work. More analytical, more . . . option analysis. Looking at the whole spectrum of options in helping management make decisions." (1d)
> **Boeing**

executives are rewarded on the basis of operational measures, such as product quality, sales, or on-time delivery. At Hong Kong Disneyland, for example, management might be rewarded, in part, on the basis of growth in attendance at the theme park.

In addition to measuring the performance of people, the managerial accounting system measures the performance of an organization's subunits, such as divisions, product lines, geographical territories, and departments. These measurements help the subunits' managers to obtain the highest possible performance level in their subunits. Such measurements also help top management to decide whether a particular subunit is a viable economic investment. For example, it may turn out that a particular attraction at Hong Kong Disneyland is too costly an activity to continue, despite the efforts of a skilled management team.

Assessing the Organization's Competitive Position, and Working with Other Managers to Ensure the Organization's Long-Term Competitiveness in Its Industry   Today's business environment is changing very rapidly. These changes are reflected in global competition, rapidly advancing technology, and improved communication systems, such as the Internet. The activities that make an enterprise successful today may no longer be sufficient next year. A crucial role of managerial accounting is to continually assess how an organization measures up against the competition, with an eye toward continuously improving. Among the questions asked in assessing an organization's competitive position are the following:

- How well is the organization doing in its internal operations and business processes?
- How well is the organization doing in the eyes of its customers? Are their needs being served as well as possible?
- How well is the organization doing from the standpoint of innovation, learning, and continuously improving operations? Is the organization a trendsetter that embraces new products, new services, and new technology? Or is it falling behind?
- How well is the organization doing financially? Is the enterprise viable as a continuing entity?

Measurements along these four dimensions will form the basis of a *balanced scorecard*, a management tool that is discussed in depth in Chapter 10.

Managerial versus Financial Accounting

Learning Objective   4

Explain the major differences between managerial and financial accounting.

Take another look at the major objectives of managerial accounting activity. Notice that the focus in each of these objectives is on *managers*. So, the focus of *managerial accounting* is on the needs of managers *within* the organization, rather than interested parties outside the organization.

Financial accounting is the use of accounting information for reporting to parties outside the organization. The annual report distributed by McDonald's Corporation to its shareholders is an example of output from a financial accounting system. Users of financial accounting information include current and prospective shareholders, creditors, investment analysts, unions, consumer groups, and government agencies.

There are many similarities between managerial accounting information and financial accounting information, because they both draw on data from an organization's *accounting system*. This is the system of procedures, staff, and computers used to accumulate and store financial data in the organization. One part of the overall accounting system is the **cost accounting system**, which accumulates cost data for use in both managerial and financial accounting. For example, production cost data typically are used in helping managers set prices, which is a managerial accounting use. However, production cost data also are used to value inventory on a manufacturer's balance sheet, which is a financial accounting use.

Exhibit 1–1 depicts the relationships among an organization's accounting system, cost accounting system, managerial accounting, and financial accounting. Although similarities do exist between managerial and financial accounting, the differences are even greater. Exhibit 1–2 lists the most important differences.

Managerial Accounting in Different Types of Organizations

All organizations need information, whether they are profit-seeking or nonprofit enterprises and regardless of the activities they pursue. As a result, managerial accounting information is vital in all organizations. American Express, Bombardier, the City of Montreal, the Canadian Wildlife Federation, the Department of National Defence, Fairmont Hotels & Resorts, Manulife Financial, Simon Fraser University, and WestJet Airlines all have management accountants who provide information to management. Moreover, the five basic purposes of managerial accounting activity are relevant in each of these organizations.

> "[We are] a partner with all of the other functions in the business here. We are an equal partner with our product groups, with the engineering and manufacturing cohorts in making sure this business is a success." (1f)
> **Caterpillar**

Exhibit 1–1
Managerial Accounting, Financial Accounting, and Cost Accounting

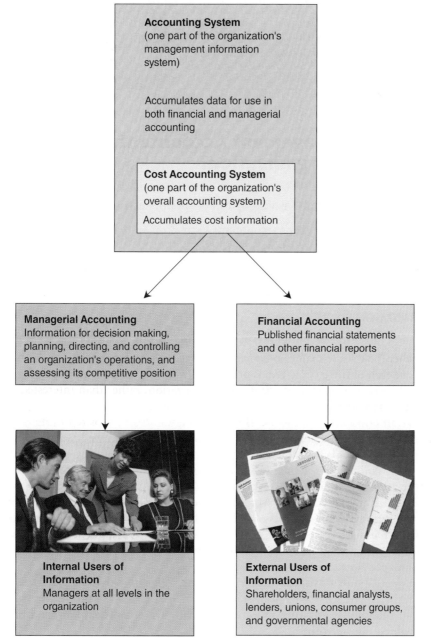

Accounting System
(one part of the organization's management information system)

Accumulates data for use in both financial and managerial accounting

Cost Accounting System
(one part of the organization's overall accounting system)

Accumulates cost information

Managerial Accounting
Information for decision making, planning, directing, and controlling an organization's operations, and assessing its competitive position

Financial Accounting
Published financial statements and other financial reports

Internal Users of Information
Managers at all levels in the organization

External Users of Information
Shareholders, financial analysts, lenders, unions, consumer groups, and governmental agencies

Exhibit 1–2
Differences between Managerial and Financial Accounting

	Managerial Accounting	**Financial Accounting**
Users of Information	Managers, *within the organization.*	Interested parties, *outside the organization.*
Regulation	*Not required* and *unregulated,* since it is intended only for management.	*Required* and must conform to generally accepted accounting principles. *Regulated* by the Accounting Standards Board of Canada and, to a lesser degree, the Canadian Securities Administrators.
Source of Data	The organization's *basic accounting system, plus various other sources,* such as rates of defective products manufactured, physical quantities of material and labour used in production, occupancy rates in hotels and hospitals, and average take-off delays in airlines.	Almost exclusively drawn from the organization's *basic accounting system,* which accumulates financial information.
Nature of Reports and Procedures	*Reports often focus on subunits* within the organization, such as departments, divisions, geographical regions, or product lines.\n\nBased on a combination of historical data, estimates, and projections of future events.	*Reports focus on the enterprise in its entirety.* Based almost exclusively on historical transaction data.

Where Are Management Accountants Located in an Organization?

Learning Objective   **5**

Explain where management accountants are located in an organization, in terms of formal organization, deployment on cross-functional teams, and physical location.

The question posed in the above heading can be interpreted in three different ways:

1. Where are management accountants located on an organization chart?
2. How are management accountants deployed?
3. In what physical location do management accountants actually do their work?

Organization Chart

A company's top management group usually consists of the board of directors, a president and chief executive officer (CEO), a chief of corporate operations, and a chief financial officer.

> "[Management accountants] need to be strongly partnered with the line management. They need to be proactive. They need to have a broad sense of business. It's not strictly accounting. It's looking at the full spectrum and range of business." (1g)
>
> **Boeing**

Line and Staff Positions   Positions on an organization chart are of two types: line positions and staff positions. Managers in **line positions** are *directly* involved in the provision of goods or services. For example, Disney's line positions include the president of Disney Consumer Products, the president of Walt Disney Studios, and the president of Walt Disney Parks and Resorts, which is the division responsible for the company's theme parks in California, Florida, France, Hong Kong, and Japan, as well as Disneyland Shanghai, slated to open in 2016. Also in line positions would be the hundreds of managers in the various operating units of the divisions. For example, the general manager of Hong Kong Disneyland, the manager of food and beverage services at the Magic Kingdom, and the manager of the Disney Store at the West Edmonton Mall in Alberta would all be in line positions.

Managers in **staff positions** supervise activities that support Disney's strategy, but they are only *indirectly* involved in operational activities. Disney's staff positions include its general counsel, the executive vice-president for government relations, and the chief financial officer, among others.

CFO or Controller   In many organizations, the designation given to the top accountant is the **chief financial officer (CFO)**. In other organizations, this individual is called or assisted by a **controller** (or sometimes a **comptroller**, particularly in nonprofit or governmental organizations). When the position of CFO and controller are split, it is usual for the controller to report to the CFO.

The controller usually is responsible for supervising the accounting staff and for preparing both managerial and financial accounting reports. As the organization's chief management accountant, the controller often interprets accounting information for line managers and participates as an integral member of the management team. Most controllers are involved in planning and decision making at all levels and across all functional areas of the enterprise. This broad role has enabled many management accountants to rise to the top of their organizations. Former accountants have served as CEO in such companies as BC Hydro, London Drugs, and Manulife Financial.

In addition to the corporate controller, most companies, including The Walt Disney Company, have divisional controllers. Thus, Disney's organization chart would show a controller each for ABC, Inc., Disneyland Paris, Walt Disney Studios, and so forth.

Treasurer   The **treasurer** typically is responsible for raising capital and safeguarding the organization's assets. In addition, the treasurer is responsible for the management of corporate investments, credit policy, and insurance coverage. The treasurer typically reports to the CFO.

Internal Auditors   Most large corporations and many governmental agencies have internal auditors. **Internal auditors** are often responsible for reviewing the accounting procedures, records, and reports in both the controller's and the treasurer's areas of responsibility. The auditors then express an opinion to top management (or in some cases to the board of directors' Audit Committee) regarding the effectiveness of the organization's accounting system. In some organizations, internal auditors also carry out a broad performance evaluation of middle and lower management.

Cross-Functional Deployment

On a formal organization chart, accountants generally are in a staff capacity, as explained in the preceding section. However, management accountants are increasingly being *deployed* in cross-functional management teams. Management accountants work with executives from top management, marketing and sales staff, design engineers, operations managers, legal experts, quality-control staff, and virtually every other specialized type of employee in an organization. Management teams are trained to make decisions, engage in planning exercises, or address operational problems from many perspectives. Since financial and other managerial accounting issues are often critically important in addressing business problems, management accountants routinely play a major role in these cross-functional teams.

Physical Location

Finally, where do management accountants actually perform their work? The answer is "just about everywhere." Management accountants are located in every part of an enterprise, from corporate headquarters to the locations where goods and services are being produced. At Disney, for example, management accountants would be present on location when a feature film is being produced, near the ABC newsroom when decisions are made about deploying journalistic resources, and in the various Disney hotels, such as the Disney Ambassador Hotel in Tokyo.

Learning Objective   **6**

Describe the roles of an organization's chief financial officer (CFO) or controller, its treasurer, and its internal auditors.

"Actually, most of the people . . . are decentralized and actually are co-located with the people that they support. That's our approach and we're moving more and more toward that and less and less toward a central group that provides information." (1h)

Boeing

Major Themes in Managerial Accounting

Learning Objective   **7**

Briefly describe some of the major contemporary themes in managerial accounting.

Several major themes influence virtually all aspects of contemporary managerial accounting. We will briefly introduce these themes now, and they will be apparent throughout the text.

Information and Incentives

The need for information is the driving force behind managerial accounting. However, managerial accounting information often serves two functions: a *decision-facilitating* function and a *decision-influencing* function. Information usually is supplied to a decision maker to assist that person or group in choosing an alternative. Often, that information is also intended to influence the person's or group's decision.

To illustrate, let us consider The Walt Disney Company's annual budget. Although the budget is prepared under the direction of the CFO, it must be approved by the CEO and, ultimately, by the board of directors. As part of the budget approval process, the CEO and the board of directors will make important decisions that determine how the company's resources will be allocated. Throughout the year, management decisions will be facilitated by the information contained in the budget. Management decisions also will be influenced by the budget, since at year-end, actual expenditures will be compared with the budgeted amounts. Explanations will then be requested for any significant deviations.

In recent years, the corporate world has moved toward sustainability and social responsibility. Managerial accounting is perfectly adept at providing the information necessary for organizations to make responsible decisions that take into account their impact on the environment and society. Environmental cost management is further discussed in Chapter 10.

Behavioural Issues

The reactions of both individuals and groups to managerial accounting information will significantly affect the course of events in an organization. How will the general manager of Hong Kong Disneyland react to a budget? How will data regarding the cost of providing entertainment services affect the way the theme park's management prices those services? How much detail should be included in the quarterly accounting reports to the general manager? If too much detail is provided, will the manager be overloaded with information and distracted from the main points?

All of these questions involve the behavioural tendencies of people and their cognitive limitations in using information. The better a management accountant's understanding of human behaviour is, the more effective he or she will be as a provider of information.

Costs and Benefits

Like other goods and services, information can be produced, purchased, and used. It can be of high or low quality, timely or late, appropriate for its intended use or utterly irrelevant. As is true of all goods and services, information entails both costs and benefits. The costs of providing managerial accounting information to the managers at Hong Kong Disneyland include the cost of compensation for the theme park's controller and Accounting Department staff, the cost of purchasing and operating computers, and the cost of the time spent by the information users to read, understand, and utilize the information. The benefits include improved decisions, more effective planning, greater efficiency of operations, and better direction and control of operations.

So, both costs and benefits are associated with managerial accounting information. The desirability of any particular managerial accounting technique or information must be determined in light of both its costs and benefits. We will reinforce this cost–benefit trade-off throughout the text by pointing out areas where managerial accounting information could be improved, but only at too great a cost.

Management of Capacity and Capacity Costs

A key objective of managerial accounting information is the management of an organization's capacity and the costs of providing that capacity. By **capacity** we mean the upper limit on the amount of goods or services that an organization can produce in a specified period of time. For example, how many iPads can Apple manufacture in a month? Or how many people can Hong Kong Disneyland effectively accommodate in a day? Or how many cellphone calls or text messages can your cellphone company process in an hour?

There are various concepts of an organization's capacity. *Theoretical capacity* refers to the upper limit on production of goods or services if everything works perfectly. (This means that no employees miss work because of illness, no machines break down, there are no unexpected interruptions such as power outages or severe storms, and so forth.) Most management accountants believe that a more useful concept of capacity is **practical capacity**, which allows for normal occurrences such as machine downtime and employee fatigue or illness.

Important questions for the managerial accounting system to address are (1) What is an organization's practical capacity? (2) What are the costs of the resources supplied to provide that capacity? and (3) How have those resources been used?

To explore these issues, let's focus on the pizza business. Suppose you have taken a job at the nearby pizza shop, making pizzas. You work the 8 to 10 p.m. shift three evenings a week, Monday, Wednesday, and Friday. In addition to the obvious fringe benefit of getting to eat the occasional slice of pizza with your favourite toppings, you receive a wage of $8 an hour. So each evening that you work, you make $16.

After some training and a little experience, you can make a pizza in about five minutes, on average. This includes picking up a premeasured lump of pizza dough, patting it out, twirling it ostentatiously over your head a few times, putting it on a baking sheet, covering it with pizza sauce, applying the cheese and other toppings, and tossing it into the oven. (The difference in the time taken to apply the toppings onto a plain cheese pizza or one with "the works" is negligible.) Also, the five-minute average time required per pizza allows for occasional mistakes, fatigue, cellphone calls, and other normal events. You have one 20-minute break during your two-hour shift, so on a busy evening, you could make as many as 20 pizzas (100 minutes available ÷ the average 5 minutes per pizza).

So, using the procedure described above, the cost of the labour resources supplied for your two-hour shift is $16, and the practical capacity of that two-hour shift is 20 completed pizzas.

Now suppose that during the first week of October, you experience very different levels of demand on your three evening shifts. Monday evening has a steady demand, and you make 20 pizzas that evening. Wednesday evening is slow, and you make just 10 pizzas. Friday evening, which is normally very busy, is unusually slow and you make just one pizza.

Now we must calculate the cost of your labour for making a pizza during each of your three shifts. One fairly simple answer is to divide your labour cost per shift by the number of pizzas you made in each shift, as follows:

Shift	Labour Cost	Pizzas Made	Cost per Pizza
Monday	$16	20	$ 0.80
Wednesday	16	10	1.60
Friday	16	1	16.00

Let's stop and think about this. Does this analysis make any sense? Most accountants and managers would argue that it does not make much sense to say that Monday's pizzas cost $0.80 each for labour, Wednesday's cost $1.60 each, and the one you made Friday cost $16.00! This result highlights the problem of confusing the cost of a resource supplied with the cost of a resource used. The cost of your labour resource supplied during each shift was $16.00, but the cost of your labour resource used varied from shift to shift due to widely different demand levels.

Many cost managers would argue that the cost of your labour resource used should be computed as shown in column (c) of the following table. Moreover, the cost of your labour resource used per pizza is a constant $0.80 per pizza, regardless of demand, as calculated in column (d). Finally, the cost of your labour resource unused (i.e., the cost of unused capacity) is calculated in column (e).

To best understand the table, start with column (a) and work across.

(a)	(b)	(c)	(d)	(e)
Shift	Cost of Labour Resource Supplied (2 hours × $8 per hour)	Cost of Labour Resource Used [$16 × (Pizzas made ÷ Pizzas in practical capacity)]	Cost of Labour Resource Used per Pizza (Cost of labour resource used ÷ Pizzas made)	Cost of Labour Resource Unused, i.e., cost of unused capacity ($16 − Cost of labour resource used)
Monday	$16	$16.00 [$16 × (20 ÷ 20)]	$0.80 ($16.00 ÷ 20)	$ 0.00
Wednesday	16	8.00 [$16 × (10 ÷ 20)]	0.80 ($8.00 ÷ 10)	8.00
Friday	16	0.80 [$16 × (1 ÷ 20)]	0.80 ($0.80 ÷ 1)	15.20

The moral of the story is that it is very important to distinguish among the cost of resources supplied (column [b] above), the cost of resources used (column [c] above), and the cost of resources unused (column [e] above), which is the same as the cost of unused capacity. An important task for any management team is to understand and manage the cost of capacity.[2]

Evolution and Adaptation in Managerial Accounting

Compared to financial accounting, managerial accounting is a young discipline. As a result, managerial accounting concepts and tools are still evolving as new ways are found to provide information that assists management. Moreover, the business environment is changing rapidly. For managerial accounting to be as useful a tool in the future as it has been in the recent past, managerial accounting information must adapt to reflect those changes. Several changes in the business environment that are especially pertinent to managerial accounting are discussed briefly here. The effect of these changes on various topics in managerial accounting will be explored in subsequent chapters.

E-Business   E-commerce, e-business, e-tailing! Our ever-expanding e-vocabulary is testimony to the rapid electronic transformation of the business environment. Many of us have gone online to order a book from Amazon.ca, an airline reservation from Expedia.ca, or possibly a computer from Dell.ca. We are all aware of the many dot-com or dot-ca companies that populate the electronic retailing landscape. We're also aware that these companies appear and often disappear at an alarming pace. Nevertheless, the electronic revolution in the marketplace is here to stay.

Perhaps what we're less aware of, though, is the depth of the e-commerce impact throughout the spectrum of the business environment. Just as we can order books or computers online in *consumer-to-business* e-commerce channels, businesses can order raw materials and supplies using *business-to-business* networks. *Supply-chain management*, which encompasses the coordination of order generation, order taking, order filling, and distribution of products and services, is increasingly an electronic, online process. *E-commerce* may be defined as buying and selling over digital media,[3] but e-business is a broader concept. In addition to encompassing e-commerce, *e-business* includes the business processes that form the engine for modern business.

Management accountants are rapidly moving toward *e-accounting* by harnessing the power of online communications to streamline the procedures of managerial accounting. For example, *e-budgeting* is now used by hundreds of companies to quickly and effectively transmit the information needed to construct a budget from business units around the globe.

E-business is here to stay, and it will affect our lives and our jobs in ways we can't even imagine today.

Service versus Manufacturing Firms   The service sector occupies a growing role in the Canadian economy. Moreover, several key service industries have been deregulated by the government—for example, telecommunications, financial services, and airlines. As more and more companies provide financial, medical, communication, transportation, consulting, and hospitality services, managerial accounting techniques must be adapted to meet the needs of managers in those industries. The key difference between service and manufacturing firms is that most services are consumed as they are produced; most services cannot be inventoried like manufactured goods. Service organizations also tend to be more labour-intensive than manufacturing firms. Many of the techniques developed for measuring costs and performance in manufacturing companies have been adapted successfully to service industry firms. Throughout the text, you will notice that roughly two-thirds of the examples of managerial accounting techniques involve service industry firms and nonprofit organizations.

Globalization   Today, the marketplace is truly a global one. A Canadian firm is just as likely to be in competition with a company in Germany or Korea as one just across town. Intense international competition is forcing companies to strive for excellence in product quality and service more than ever before.

Moreover, international economic arrangements and potential trade agreements are constantly in the news, as national economies become more and more intertwined. Organizations such as the European Union (EU) and the World Trade Organization (WTO), as well as international agreements like the North American Free Trade Agreement (NAFTA), have dramatically affected international commerce.

A *multinational* company is an organization that has operational subunits, such as manufacturing plants or sales facilities, in two or more countries. Multinational firms face several challenges that do not confront domestic companies. Political systems, accounting rules for external reporting, legal systems, and cultural norms vary widely among countries. Since income tax systems also differ among countries, managers of multinationals must take into account the different tax laws and rates in the countries where they do business.

Monetary systems also differ among countries, and multinationals must continually monitor the fluctuating values of foreign currencies. The price at which one country's currency can be converted into that of another country is called an *exchange rate*. Exchange rates can fluctuate daily, as various forces shape the world economy. As a result, managers of multinationals face challenges as they sign contracts, buy and sell goods, and conduct business operations in many countries.

Cross-Functional Teams   In past years, managers tended to stick to their own turf. Production managers focused on how best to manufacture a product or provide a service. Marketing managers concentrated on selling the product or service. Design engineers often emphasized engineering elegance rather than designing a product for manufacturability. Management accountants provided information for decision making, planning, control, and performance evaluation.

Today, a cross-functional approach has replaced this narrow managerial perspective. Cross-functional management teams bring together production and operations managers, marketing managers, purchasing and material-handling specialists, design engineers, quality management staff, and management accountants to focus their varied expertise and experience on virtually all management issues. If products are to be designed and manufactured with the customers' needs in mind, a cross-functional approach is crucial. Marketing managers have the best feel for customer needs, and production managers are up on the latest in manufacturing technology. Design engineers know how to build the functionality into a product that customers demand, and purchasing managers can acquire the materials, parts, and services necessary to get the job done.

Managerial accounting information is the glue that holds the cross-functional team together. The management accountant designs an information system and provides data ranging across all aspects of the organization's internal operations and external environment. Then the management accountant works as an integral member of

---

Managerial
Accounting
Practice

Canadian Direct
Insurance,
London Drugs,
Viewtrak
Technologies, and
PropertyGuys.com

THE INTERNET AS A LIFELINE

In a tough economic environment, the Internet can be a lifeline. "Companies in a sales squeeze are looking to the Net as a tool for cutting costs, generating new revenue streams, trimming inventories, and serving customers and employees more efficiently." Here are some examples of how companies are using the web to their advantage.

Canadian Direct Insurance

"Canadian Direct Insurance improved the delivery of its products by using 'eDelivery,' a secure way of retrieving insurance documents from its website. When quoting or purchasing a policy online at canadiandirect.com, customers are able to view and print their insurance documents online. Policy holders also have the option of renewing and paying for their policies online. These costs savings have allowed Canadian Direct Insurance to offer premiums that are substantially lower than many of its competitors' premiums."

London Drugs

"London Drugs operates 68 retail stores situated across British Columbia, Alberta, Saskatchewan, and Manitoba. Customers can go online for prescription refills, to place photo finishing orders, to purchase travel insurance, and buy online any merchandise carried in the stores."

Viewtrak Technologies

"Viewtrak Technologies in Edmonton has created a web-based software system that enables cattle breeders, producers, processors, and distributors to track an animal's production information from birth to death. As prescribed in federal legislation, the software tracks and records information about an animal's genetics, feed, production inputs, and environment. Viewtrak.com is an integrated food source management system that provides agricultural producers with the information they need to streamline production and boost earnings. As animals move along the supply chain, access to the information is provided to each stakeholder."

PropertyGuys.com

"PropertyGuys.com harnessed the power of the Internet to rival the multiple-listing web-based service provided by the Canadian Real Estate Association. The Canadian private sale company offers do-it-yourself home sellers the option to list their property, deal directly with interested parties, and gain international exposure on a website receiving 30 million hits a month, for a fee that is substantially lower than that commanded by real estate agents."[4]

the cross-functional team, interpreting information and analyzing the implications of decision alternatives. Working together, the cross-functional team creates value for the organization by meeting the customer's needs in the most effective manner possible.

Product Life Cycles and Diversity   One impact of highly automated manufacturing systems has been to enable manufacturers to produce an increasingly diverse set of products. Moreover, the rate at which technology is changing means that the life cycles of most products are becoming shorter. In the computer industry, for example, product models are used for only a few years before they are replaced by more powerful versions. To be competitive, manufacturers must keep up with the rapidly changing marketplace. Managers must have timely information about production costs and other product characteristics in order to respond quickly and effectively to the competition.

Information and Communication Technology   Although large mainframe computers still perform certain kinds of tasks, businesses make heavy use of personal computers. In most offices, almost every employee has a personal computer for such tasks as word processing, data analysis, report generation, presentation preparation, and communication. These PCs are usually linked together in a network that enables employees to electronically transfer files and reports, share data, and communicate via e-mail. Often called an *intranet*, these networked PCs are invaluable tools in the era of cross-functional management teams. Moreover, these intranets are not confined to the walls of a building, as the World Wide Web or the Internet allows computer-to-computer interface anywhere in the world.

> "The pace of change in technology is becoming much faster, and accounting and finance people are very heavy users of technology, more so than a lot of the other functions." (1i)
> **Hewlett-Packard**

Managerial accounting analyses are done on PCs using a variety of software products. Spreadsheet programs, such as Excel®,[5] are in wide use for data analysis. Software packages specifically designed for accounting applications are also widely available. Many businesses are adopting integrated business software packages, such as Systems, Applications, and Products in Data Processing (SAP) and PeopleSoft, that handle a broad range of computing needs, such as customer and supplier databases, staff and payroll functions, production scheduling and management, inventory records, and financial and managerial accounting functions. Management accountants often play significant roles in selecting software for their organizations or designing in-house software to meet the organization's unique needs.

Just-in-Time Inventory Management   In traditional manufacturing settings, inventories of raw materials and parts, partially completed goods, and finished goods were kept as a reserve against the possibility of running out of a needed item. However, large reserve inventories consume valuable resources and generate hidden costs. Consequently, many companies have completely changed their approach to production and inventory management. These manufacturers have adopted a strategy for controlling the flow of manufacturing in a multistage production process. In a **just-in-time (JIT) production system**, raw materials and parts are purchased or produced just in time to be used at each stage of the production process. This approach to inventory and production management brings considerable cost savings from reduced inventory levels.

The key to the JIT system is the "pull" approach to controlling manufacturing. To visualize this approach, look at Exhibit 1–3, which displays a simple diagram of a multistage production process. The flow of manufacturing activity is depicted by the solid arrows running across the page from one stage of production to the next. However, the signal that triggers more production activity in each stage comes from the *next* stage of production. These signals, depicted by the dashed-line arrows, run from right to left. We begin with sales at the right-hand side of the exhibit. When sales activity warrants more production of finished goods, the goods are "pulled" from production Stage III by sending a signal that more goods are needed. Similarly, when production employees in Stage

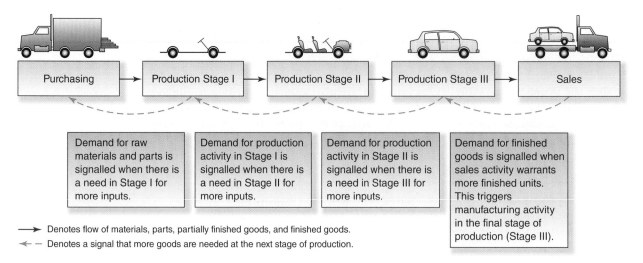

| Demand for raw materials and parts is signalled when there is a need in Stage I for more inputs. | Demand for production activity in Stage I is signalled when there is a need in Stage II for more inputs. | Demand for production activity in Stage II is signalled when there is a need in Stage III for more inputs. | Demand for finished goods is signalled when sales activity warrants more finished units. This triggers manufacturing activity in the final stage of production (Stage III). |

⟶ Denotes flow of materials, parts, partially finished goods, and finished goods.
◄ ─ Denotes a signal that more goods are needed at the next stage of production.

Exhibit 1–3
Just-in-Time (JIT) Production and Inventory Management System

III need more inputs, they send a signal back to Stage II. This triggers production activity in Stage II. Working our way back to the beginning of the process, purchases of raw materials and parts are triggered by a signal that they are needed in Stage I. This pull system of production management, which characterizes the JIT approach, results in a smooth flow of production and significantly reduced inventory levels. The result is considerable cost savings for the manufacturer.

Total Quality Management   One implication of a just-in-time inventory philosophy is the need to emphasize product quality. If a component is to be produced just in time for the next production stage, it must be "just right" for its intended purpose. One flawed component can shut down the entire production line, entailing considerable cost. Therefore, management accountants have become involved increasingly in monitoring product quality and measuring the costs of maintaining quality. This information helps companies maintain programs of **total quality management (TQM)**. This refers to the broad set of management and control processes designed to focus the entire organization and all of its employees on providing products or services that do the best possible job of satisfying the customer.

Continuous Improvement   Global competition is forcing companies to continuously improve their operations. **Continuous improvement** is the constant effort to eliminate waste, reduce response time, simplify the design of both products and processes, and improve quality and customer service. One compelling reason for the need to continuously improve is the *price down/cost down* concept. This refers to the tendency of prices to fall over the life cycle of a newly introduced product. Think, for example, about the prices of laptop computers, personal listening devices, and high-definition televisions. When each of these products was first introduced, prices were quite high. However, as manufacturers gained experience in producing them, prices fell and the products became accessible to a much wider customer pool. However, if prices are to fall over time, manufacturers must continually reduce costs as well.

One widely used approach to cost reduction is **kaizen costing**, which is the process of cost reduction during the manufacturing phase of an existing product. The Japanese word *kaizen* refers to continual and gradual improvement through small betterment activities rather than large or radical improvement made through innovation or large investments in technology. The idea is simple: Improvement is the goal and responsibility of every worker, from the CEO to the manual workers, in every activity, every day, all the time. Through the small but continual efforts of everyone, significant reductions in costs can be attained over time.

Cost Management Systems

The rapid advancement in technology, coupled with increasing worldwide competition, is forcing organizations to produce high-quality goods and services, provide outstanding customer service, and do so at the lowest possible cost. These demands are placing ever-greater requirements on the information provided by managerial accounting systems. Many companies have moved away from a historical cost accounting perspective and toward a proactive *cost management* perspective. A **cost management system** is a management planning and control system with the following objectives:

- To measure the cost of the resources consumed in performing the organization's significant *activities*.
- To identify and eliminate **non-value-added costs**. These are the costs of *activities* that can be eliminated with no deterioration of product quality, performance, or perceived value.
- To determine the efficiency and effectiveness of all major *activities* performed in the enterprise.
- To identify and evaluate new *activities* that can improve the future performance of the organization.

Notice the emphasis of a cost management system on the organization's activities. This emphasis, sometimes called **activity accounting**, is crucial to the goal of producing quality goods and services at the lowest possible cost. In keeping with the focus on activities, management accountants have developed a system for determining the cost of producing goods or services called **activity-based costing (ABC)**. In an ABC system, the costs of the organization's significant activities are accumulated and then assigned to goods or services in accordance with how resources are used in the production of those goods and services. An ABC system helps management to understand the causal linkages between activities and costs. Using an activity-based costing system to improve the operations of an organization is called **activity-based management (ABM)**. Both ABC and ABM are discussed in Chapter 5.

Strategic Cost Management and the Value Chain

How are the goods and services that we all consume created? Usually many activities are involved in obtaining basic raw materials and turning them into valuable products or services. The set of linked, value-creating activities, ranging from obtaining raw materials and energy to the ultimate delivery of products and services, is called the **value chain**. Although only one organization might be involved in a particular value chain, usually there are many.

Vancouver General Hospital's value chain, for example, would include not only the hospital but also the suppliers of pharmaceutical products and medical supplies, the manufacturers of diagnostic equipment, the physicians whose patients use the hospital, and the ambulance services that transport patients to the hospital.

The value chain for Walt Disney Studios would include *upstream* contributions such as screenwriting, film studio construction and maintenance, set design and construction, costume design and production, travel arrangements for shooting scenes on location, lighting technicians, film crews, and acting talent. Once the film has been produced, the *downstream* contributions include advertising staff; TV, radio, and print media; film distributors; theatre companies such as Cineplex Entertainment LP; cable-streaming companies such as Shaw on Demand; DVD producers; video rental outlets such as NetFlix; and DVD retailers such as Future Shop.

The major steps in the value chain for Roots are depicted in Exhibit 1–4. Established in 1973, Roots is known around the world for its quality leather goods, active

Learning Objective   **8**

Understand and explain the concepts of strategic cost management and the value chain.

Exhibit 1–4

Manufacturer's Value Chain

Roots' value chain consists of myriad activities, from securing raw materials through distribution and sales.

Obtaining raw materials, energy, and other resources   Research and development   Product design

Production   Marketing   Distribution and sales

athletic wear, yoga wear, accessories, and home furnishings. As Exhibit 1–4 shows, major steps in Roots' value chain include the following:

- Securing raw material, energy, and other resources
- Research and development
- Product design
- Production
- Marketing
- Distribution and sales

What is the role of Roots in this value chain? As the company's website explains, "For the longest while, we made most Roots products in Canada but in recent years we have shifted some of our manufacturing abroad as a result of technical, economic and capacity challenges." What Roots does is design its products, outsource the manufacturing, market the products, distribute them to retail stores where they are sold, and provide customer service. That multistage process is the company's value chain.

In order for any organization to most effectively achieve its goals, it is important for its managers to understand the *entire* value chain in which their organization participates. This understanding can help managers ask, and answer, important questions about their organization's strategy. Should the company concentrate on only a narrow link in the value chain, such as design or retailing? Or should it expand its operational scope to include securing the raw materials or manufacturing the product? Are there opportunities to form beneficial linkages with suppliers that come earlier in the value chain? Or with customers?

These questions involve fundamental, strategic issues about how an organization can best meet its goals. Although many factors affect such decisions, one important factor concerns the costs incurred in creating value in each link in the value chain. In order for a company to achieve a sustainable competitive advantage, it must either (1) perform one or more activities in the value chain at the same quality level as its competitors, but at a lower cost, or (2) perform its value chain activities at a higher quality level than its competitors, but at no greater cost. Understanding the value chain, and the factors that cause costs to be incurred in each activity in the value chain, is a crucial step in the development of a firm's strategy. These cost-causing factors are called *cost drivers*. The overall recognition of the importance of cost relationships among the activities in the value chain, and the process of managing those cost relationships to the firm's advantage, is called **strategic cost management**. Issues in strategic cost management will arise in a variety of contexts as we pursue our study of managerial accounting.

Theory of Constraints   Along with a value chain analysis, managers should carefully examine the chain of linked activities with a view toward identifying the constraints that prevent their organization from reaching a higher level of achievement. Sometimes called the **theory of constraints**, this approach seeks to find the most cost-effective ways to alleviate an organization's most limiting constraints. When binding constraints are relaxed, the organization can reach a higher level of goal attainment. For example, suppose a delay occurred in the design process for Roots' line of summer clothing because too few designers were assigned to the project. This might result in a delay in contracting for the manufacturing of the summer line, which might ultimately delay the delivery of the products to Roots' many retail outlets. In this context, the design process is a *bottleneck operation*, meaning that it slows down the progress of Roots' products through the retailer's value chain. By assigning even one or two more designers to the summer clothing line, the delay could perhaps have been avoided.

The Ethical Climate of Business and the Role of the Accountant

The seemingly endless stream of corporate scandals that have occurred over the past decade have shocked and dismayed many people. Most recent among these was the near total collapse of the U.S. and the world banking and financial systems. And the headlines keep on coming. Many of the cases involve mismanagement, some are characterized by ethical lapses, and in some instances, there is criminal behaviour. Who is to blame? According to most observers, there is plenty of blame to go around: greedy corporate executives, managers who make over-reaching business deals, lack of oversight by various companies' boards of directors (particularly the boards' audit committees), shoddy work by external auditors, lack of sufficient probing by financial analysts and the financial press, and some accountants who have been all too willing to push the envelope on aggressive accounting to (or beyond) the edge. Billions of dollars have been lost in employee pension funds, investment portfolios, and the private investment accounts of the public. It will no doubt take many years to sort out the mess. Companies have gone bankrupt, fortunes have been lost, careers have been ruined, and more of the same is yet to come. Several financial executives have filed guilty pleas on felony charges. Others have been convicted by juries. Some are serving time in prison. Several observers have wondered if the confidence of the investing public can ever be regained.

One important lesson from these scandals is that unethical behaviour in business is not only wrong in a moral sense, but it also can be disastrous from the standpoint of the economy. We cannot have businesspeople lying, stealing, perpetrating frauds, and making up accounting rules without seriously disrupting business. Ethical behaviour by businesspeople in general and accountants in particular is not a luxury or a discretionary "good thing to do"—it is an absolute necessity to the smooth functioning of the economy.

Most of the purely accounting issues in management frauds involve financial accounting (external reporting) rather than managerial accounting (internal reporting). In most companies, however, many of the same individuals are involved in both types of accounting. In the Enron case, for example, a massive fraud was perpetrated on the investing public by creating so-called related parties with names like Raptor for the sole purpose of hiding debt and overstating earnings. Yet the same fraud was perpetrated on many at Enron itself. Not all of the company's thousands of employees knew of these accounting schemes. So, ultimately, what may have been largely financial (external) accounting misstatements, almost certainly resulted in misstated managerial (internal) accounting reports as well.[6]

Learning Objective   9

Understand the ethical responsibilities of a management accountant.

For many in the accounting profession, the scandals have served as a wake-up call to concentrate more on ethical issues in practising and teaching accounting.[7] To this end, a significant *ethical issue in managerial accounting* will be addressed at the end of most chapters. The goal of these "Focus on Ethics" features is to raise the consciousness of students to the fact that legitimate ethical issues do arise in the daily practice of managerial accounting. In the last section of this chapter, we will turn our attention to managerial accounting as a profession. In the context of that discussion, the "Focus on Ethics" feature for this chapter will be a summary of The Society of Management Accountants of Ontario's code of professional ethics.

Managerial Accounting as a Career

> "You've got to know how to talk to people, express yourself. And that's oral and written. You also have to be able to understand a lot of different areas, not necessarily just accounting. You've got to understand the business itself." (1j)
>
> **Qwest**
> **(Currently a part of CenturyLink)**

Learning Objective 10

Discuss the professional organizations, certification process, and ethical standards in the field of managerial accounting.

Management accountants serve a crucial function in virtually any enterprise. As the providers of information, they interact frequently with sales staff, finance specialists, production people, and managers at all levels. To perform their duties effectively, management accountants must be knowledgeable not only in accounting but in the other major business disciplines as well. Moreover, strong oral and written communication skills are becoming increasingly important for success as a management accountant.

Professional Organizations

To keep up with new developments in their field, management accountants often belong to one or more professional organizations. Many management accountants belong to the Canadian Institute of Chartered Accountants, the Certified General Accountants Association of Canada, and/or the Society of Management Accountants of Canada. The latter publishes a journal, entitled *CMA Management* and also supports research on managerial accounting topics through the CMA Canada Research Foundation.

The primary professional association for management accountants in the United States is the Institute of Management Accountants (IMA). Great Britain's main professional organization is the Chartered Institute of Management Accountants (CIMA), and Australia's organization is the Institute of Chartered Accountants in Australia. In all, over 75 countries have professional organizations for their practising accountants.

Professional Designations

In keeping with the importance of their role and the specialized knowledge they must have, management accountants can earn a professional designation such as Chartered Accountant (CA), Certified General Accountant (CGA), or **Certified Management Accountant (CMA)**. For example, the requirements for becoming a certified management accountant include meeting specified educational requirements, passing the CMA entrance examination, and completing a two-year Strategic Leadership Program while gaining practical experience in a managerial accounting environment. In the United States, the IMA administers the CMA program. Great Britain and many other countries also have professional certification programs for their management accountants. The governing bodies of the American Institute of Certified Public Accountants and CIMA agreed on the creation of a new professional designation, the **Chartered Global Management Accountant (CGMA)**, that is a worldwide standard of professional excellence in management accounting; issuance of the new professional designation began in January 2012.

Professional Ethics

As professionals, management accountants have an obligation to themselves, their colleagues, and their organizations to adhere to high standards of ethical conduct. In recognition of this obligation, the provincial and territorial Societies/Orders of Management

Accountants have developed ethical standards for its members, who are practitioners of managerial accounting and financial management. The standards of The Society of Management Accountants of Ontario (CMA Ontario), given below, are representative.

Note: Various problems and cases at the end of each chapter in this text include ethical issues to be resolved. In addressing those issues, readers will need to refer to these ethical standards.

Focus on Ethics *These scenarios discuss ethical issues and underscore the importance of ethical behaviour in managerial accounting.*

Focus on Ethics

CODE OF PROFESSIONAL ETHICS (CMA ONTARIO)

All Members, Students, Firms, Public Accounting Firms and Professional Corporations will adhere to the following Code of Professional Ethics of CMA Ontario:

3.1 A Member, Student, Firm, Public Accounting Firm or Professional Corporation will act at all times with:
   (a) responsibility for and fidelity to public needs;
   (b) fairness and loyalty to such Member's, Student's, Firm's, Public Accounting Firm's or Professional Corporation's associates, clients and employers; and
   (c) competence through devotion to high ideals of personal honour and professional integrity.

3.2 A Member, Student, Firm, Public Accounting Firm or Professional Corporation will:
   (a) maintain at all times independence of thought and action;
   (b) not express an opinion on financial reports or statements without first assessing her, his or its relationship with her, his or its client to determine whether such Member, Student, Firm, Public Accounting Firm or Professional Corporation might expect her, his or its opinion to be considered independent, objective and unbiased by one who has knowledge of all the facts; and
   (c) when preparing financial reports or statements or expressing an opinion on financial reports or statements, disclose all material facts known to such Member, Student, Firm, Public Accounting Firm or Professional Corporation in order not to make such financial reports or statements misleading, acquire sufficient information to warrant an expression of opinion and report all material misstatements or departures from generally accepted accounting principles; and
   (d) comply with the requirements of the CMA Ontario Independence Regulation for Assurance, Audit and Review Engagements.

3.3 A Member, Student, Firm, Public Accounting Firm or Professional Corporation will:
   (a) not disclose or use any confidential information concerning the affairs of such Member's, Student's, Firm's, Public Accounting Firm's or Professional Corporation's employer or client unless authorized to do so or except when such information is required to be disclosed in the course of any defence of himself, herself or itself or any associate or employee in any lawsuit or other legal proceeding or against alleged professional misconduct by order of lawful authority of the Board or any Committee of CMA Ontario in the proper exercise of their duties but only to the extent necessary for such purpose and only as permitted by law;
   (b) obtain, at the outset of an engagement, written agreement from any party or parties to whom work is contracted not to disclose or use any confidential information concerning the affairs of such Member's, Student's, Firm's, Public Accounting Firm's or Professional Corporation's employer or client unless authorized to do so or except when such information is required to be disclosed in the course of any defence of himself, herself or itself or any associate or employee in any lawsuit or other legal proceeding or against alleged professional misconduct by order of lawful authority of the Board or any Committee of CMA Ontario in the proper exercise of their duties but only to the extent necessary for such purpose and only as permitted by law;
   (c) inform his, her or its employer or client of any business connections or interests of which such Member's, Student's, Firm's, Public Accounting Firm's or Professional Corporation's employer or client would reasonably expect to be informed;
   (d) not, in the course of exercising his, her or its duties on behalf of such Member's, Student's, Firm's, Public Accounting Firm's or Professional

Corporation's employer or client, hold, receive, bargain for or acquire any fee, remuneration or benefit without such employer's or client's knowledge and consent; and

(e) take all reasonable steps, in arranging any engagement as a consultant, to establish a clear understanding of the scope and objectives of the work before it is commenced and will furnish the client with an estimate of cost, preferably before the engagement is commenced, but in any event as soon as possible thereafter.

3.4 A Member, Student, Firm, Public Accounting Firm or Professional Corporation will:

(a) conduct himself, herself or itself toward other Members, Students, Firms, Public Accounting Firms and Professional Corporations with courtesy and good faith;

(b) not commit an act discreditable to the profession;

(c) not engage in or counsel any business or occupation which, in the opinion of CMA Ontario, is incompatible with the professional ethics of a management accountant or public accountant;

(d) not accept any engagement to review the work of another Member, Student, Firm, Public Accounting Firm or Professional Corporation for the same employer except with the knowledge of that Member, Student, Firm, Public Accounting Firm or Professional Corporation, or except where the connection of that Member, Student, Firm, Public Accounting Firm or Professional Corporation with the work has been terminated, unless the Member, Student, Firm, Public Accounting Firm or Professional Corporation reviews the work of others as a normal part of his, her or its responsibilities;

(e) not attempt to gain an advantage over other Members, Students, Firms, Public Accounting Firms and Professional Corporations by paying or accepting a commission in securing management accounting or public accounting work;

(f) uphold the principle of adequate compensation for managerial accounting and public accounting work; and

(g) not act maliciously or in any other way which may adversely reflect on the public or professional reputation or business of another Member, Student, Firm, Public Accounting Firm or Professional Corporation.

3.5 A Member, Student, Firm, Public Accounting Firm or Professional Corporation will:

(a) at all times maintain the standards of competence expressed by the Board from time to time;

(b) disseminate the knowledge upon which the profession of management accounting is based to others within the profession and generally promote the advancement of the profession;

(c) undertake only such work as he, she or it is competent to perform by virtue of his, her or its training and experience and will, where it would be in the best interests of an employer or client, engage, or advise the employer or client to engage, other specialists;

(d) expose before the proper tribunals of CMA Ontario any incompetent, unethical, illegal or unfair conduct or practice of a Member, Student, Firm, Public Accounting Firm or Professional Corporation which involves the reputation, dignity or honour of CMA Ontario; and

(e) endeavour to ensure that a professional partnership, company or individual, with which such Member, Student, Firm, Public Accounting Firm or Professional Corporation is associated as a partner, principal, director, officer, associate or employee, abides by the Code of Professional Ethics and the Rules of Professional Conduct established by CMA Ontario.

(CMA Ontario. See www.cmaontario.org.)

Chapter Summary

Each chapter's summary is built around the learning objectives, which appear at the beginning of the chapter.

LO1 Define *managerial accounting* and describe its role in the management process. Managerial accounting is the process of identifying, measuring, analyzing, interpreting, and communicating information in pursuit of an organization's goals. Managerial accounting is an integral part of the management process, and management accountants are important strategic partners on an organization's management team.

LO2 Explain four fundamental management processes that help organizations to attain their goals. In pursuing its goals, an organization acquires resources, hires employees, and then engages in an organized set of activities. It is up to the management team to make the best use of the organization's resources, employees, and activities in achieving the organization's goals. The four fundamental management processes are decision making, planning, directing operational activities, and controlling.

LO3 List and describe five objectives of managerial accounting activity. Five objectives of managerial accounting activity are (1) providing information for decision making and planning, and proactively participating as part of the management team in the decision-making and planning processes; (2) assisting managers in directing and controlling operations; (3) motivating managers and other employees to achieve the organization's goals; (4) measuring the performance of activities, subunits, managers, and other employees within the organization; and (5) assessing the organization's competitive position and working with other managers to ensure the organization's long-term competitiveness in its industry.

LO4 Explain the major differences between managerial and financial accounting. The users of managerial accounting information are managers and executives inside the organization. Managerial accounting information is not mandatory, is unregulated, and draws on data from the basic accounting system as well as other data sources. The users of financial accounting information are interested parties outside the organization. Financial accounting information is required, is regulated, and is based almost entirely on historical transaction data.

LO5 Explain where management accountants are located in an organization, in terms of formal organization, deployment on cross-functional teams, and physical location. Management accountants occupy staff positions in an organization chart. They are deployed as members of cross-functional teams, which address a variety of managerial decisions. Management accountants are physically located throughout an enterprise, alongside the managers with whom they work closely.

LO6 Describe the roles of an organization's chief financial officer (CFO) or controller, its treasurer, and its internal auditors. The organization's top management and financial accountant is called the *chief financial officer* or *controller*. The treasurer is responsible for raising capital and safeguarding the organization's assets. An organization's internal auditors are responsible for reviewing the accounting procedures, records, and reports and sometimes make a broad performance evaluation of management.

LO7 Briefly describe some of the major contemporary themes in managerial accounting. Some major themes in managerial accounting include its role in providing information and incentives, the behavioural implications of managerial accounting information, the management of capacity and capacity costs, the evolution and adaptation of the field, and the role of cost management systems. In managing capacity, it is important to distinguish between the cost of resources supplied, the cost of resources used, and the cost of resources unused (i.e., the cost of unused capacity).

LO8 Understand and explain the concepts of strategic cost management and the value chain. The value chain is the set of linked, value-creating activities, ranging from securing basic raw materials and energy to the ultimate delivery of products and services. Understanding the value chain is a crucial step in the development of an organization's strategy. Managing the cost relationships in the value chain to the organization's advantage is called *strategic cost management*.

LO9 Understand the ethical responsibilities of a management accountant. Management accountants are expected to display a commitment to ethical professional practice characterized by the fundamental principles of honesty, fairness, objectivity, and responsibility.

LO10 Discuss the professional organizations, certification process, and ethical standards in the field of managerial accounting. As professionals, management accountants must successfully complete a certification process and may enjoy the benefits of membership in one or more professional organizations, such as the Canadian Institute of Chartered Accountants, the Certified General Accountants Association of Canada, and the Certified Management Accountants of Canada. They are expected to adhere to the ethical standards of competence, confidentiality, integrity, and credibility.

Glossary

Review key terms and definitions on Connect.

Review Questions

1–1. According to some estimates, the volume of electronic commerce transactions exceeds $3 trillion in North America alone. Business-to-business transactions account for almost half of this amount. What changes do you believe are in store for managerial accounting as a result of the explosion in e-commerce?

1–2. List two plausible goals for each of these organizations: Amazon.ca, Canadian Red Cross, General Motors, Walmart, the City of Toronto, and Hertz.

1–3. List and define the four basic management activities.

1–4. Give examples of each of the four primary management activities in the context of a national fast-food chain such as Tim Hortons.

1–5. Give examples of how each of the objectives of managerial accounting activity would be important in an airline company such as WestJet.

1–6. List and describe four important differences between managerial and financial accounting.

1–7. Distinguish between cost accounting and managerial accounting.

1–8. Distinguish between line and staff positions. Give two examples of each in a university setting.

1–9. Distinguish between the following two accounting positions: controller and treasurer.

1–10. What does the following statement by a management accountant at Caterpillar imply about where in the organization the management accountants are located? "[We are] a partner with all of the other functions in the business here." (Reference [1f] in the References section at the back of this book.)

1–11. What is meant by the following statement? "Managerial accounting often serves an attention-directing role."

1–12. What is the main difference between manufacturing and service industry firms?

1–13. Explain the following terms: practical capacity, cost of resources supplied, cost of resources used, and cost of resources unused.

1–14. Explain the difference between e-business and e-commerce.

1–15. Define and explain the acronym *CMA*.

1–16. Briefly explain what is meant by each of the following ethical principles for management accountants: competence, confidentiality, integrity, and credibility.

1–17. What is meant by the term *non-value-added costs*?

1–18. Managerial accounting is an important part of any enterprise's management information system. Name two other information systems that supply information to management.

1–19. Can managerial accounting play an important role in a nonprofit organization? Explain your answer.

1–20. A large manufacturer of electronic machinery stated the following as one of its goals: "The company should become the low-cost producer in its industry." How can managerial accounting help the company achieve this goal?

1–21. What do you think it means to be a professional? In your view, are management accountants professionals?

1–22. Name several activities in the value chain of (*a*) a manufacturer of cotton shirts and (*b*) an airline.

1–23. Define the term *strategic cost management*.

Examples

Exercises

Exercise 1–24 Managerial Accounting and Decision Making **(LO2, 3)**

Give an example of managerial accounting information that could help a manager make each of the following decisions.

1. The president of Budget Rent-a-Car is deciding whether to add luxury cars to the rental car fleet.
2. The production manager in a Volvo plant is deciding whether to have routine maintenance performed on a machine weekly or biweekly.
3. The manager of a Walmart store is deciding how many security staff to employ for the purpose of reducing shoplifting.
4. The Vancouver City Council is deciding whether to build an addition onto the main public library.

Exercise 1–25 Objectives of Managerial Accounting Activity **(LO3)**

For each of the following activities, explain which of the objectives of managerial accounting activity is involved. In some cases, several objectives may be involved.

1. Developing a bonus reward system for the managers of the various offices of Flight Centre (a Canadian travel agency).
2. Comparing the actual and planned cost of a consulting project completed by an engineering firm such as Read Jones Christoffersen Ltd.
3. Determining the cost of manufacturing a tennis racquet by Wilson Sporting Goods.
4. Measuring the cost of the inventory of DVD players on hand in a Best Buy store.
5. Estimating the annual operating cost of a newly proposed TD Canada Trust branch.
6. Measuring the following costs incurred during one month in a Four Seasons hotel:
   a. Wages of table-service staff.
   b. Property taxes.
7. Comparing a Fairmont Hotel's room rate structure, occupancy rate, and restaurant patronage with industry averages.

Exercise 1–26 Contributions of Managerial Accounting; Use of the Internet (LO1, 3, 5)

Use the Internet to access the website of one of the following companies, or any other company of your choice.

This icon indicates use of the Internet.

Air Canada	www.aircanada.com
Coca-Cola	www.cocacola.com
Deere & Company	www.deere.com
IBM	www.ibm.com
Sears	www.sears.com

Required: Find the management's discussion and analysis portion of the firm's most recent online annual report. Then briefly discuss how managerial accounting can contribute to the company's financial goals.

Exercise 1–27 Value Chain; Use of the Internet (LO8)

Use the Internet to access the website for one of the following companies, or any other company of your choice.

The second icon indicates group work.

Avis Rent-a-Car	www.avis.ca
Expedia.ca	www.expedia.ca
Holland America Cruise Lines	www.hollandamerica.com
Levi Strauss & Company	www.levistrauss.com
Nokia	www.nokia.com
Cineplex Entertainment	www.cineplex.com

Required: After exploring the company's website, work as a group to list several key activities you believe would be in the company's value chain.

This icon indicates an international issue.

Problems

Problem 1–28 Managing a Retail Business; Cross-Functional Teams; E-Commerce (LO5, 6, 7)

This icon indicates a written response is required.

Dave Nelson recently retired at age 48, courtesy of numerous stock options he had been granted while president of e-Shops.com, an Internet start-up company. He soon moved to Vancouver to follow his dream of living by the sea. Nelson, always the entrepreneur, began a sporting-goods store shortly after relocating. The single store soon grew to a chain of four outlets throughout the Lower Mainland. As Nelson put it, "I can't believe how fast we've expanded. It's basically uncontrolled growth—growth that has occurred in spite of what we've done."

Although business has been profitable, the chain did have its share of problems. Store traffic was somewhat seasonal, with a slowdown occurring as winter approached. Nelson therefore added ski equipment and accessories to his product line. The need to finance required inventories, which seemed to be bulging, left cash balances at very low levels, occasionally necessitating short-term bank loans.

Part of Nelson's operation focused on canoe building and white-water rafting trips. Reports from the company's financial accounting system seemed to indicate that these operations were losing money because of increasing costs, although Nelson could not be sure. "The traditional income statement is not too useful in assessing the problem," he noted. "Also, my gut feeling is that we are not dealing with the best suppliers in terms of quality of goods, delivery reliability, and prices." Additional complications were caused by an increasingly competitive marketplace, with many former customers now buying merchandise and booking river excursions via the Internet, through catalogues received in the mail, or through businesses that advertised heavily in outdoor magazines.

Nelson's background is marketing, and he was somewhat puzzled about how to proceed. The company's chief financial officer should be an obvious asset in terms of addressing these problems but unfortunately, she knew her numbers but lacked key knowledge of general business operations. The same could be said about the other executives, who carried out their management duties in "silos"—becoming experts in a narrow facet of the company but, in general, lacking a big-picture perspective of the firm.

Required:

1. Explain how the CFO and managerial accounting could assist Nelson in addressing the company's problems.
2. Would a cross-functional team be useful here? Briefly discuss.
3. Does e-commerce appear to be a viable option for the firm? Explain, citing the difference between business-to-consumer and business-to-business channels. Which of the two channels, if either, would you recommend? Why?

The second icon indicates an ethical issue.

Problem 1–29 Quality Control; Ethical Behaviour (LO6, 9, 10)

AccuSound Corporation manufactures printed circuits for stereo amplifiers. A common product defect is a "drift" caused by failure to maintain precise heat levels during the production process. Rejects from the 100 percent testing program can be reworked to acceptable levels if the defect is drift. However, in a recent analysis of customer complaints, Marie Allen, the assistant controller, and the quality control engineer determined that normal rework does not bring the circuits up to standard. Sampling showed that about half of the reworked circuits failed after extended amplifier operation. The incidence of failure in the reworked circuits is projected to be about 10 percent over five years.

Unfortunately, there is no way to determine which reworked circuits will fail, because testing will not detect the problem. The rework process could be changed to correct the problem, but the cost–benefit analysis for the suggested change indicates that it is not economically feasible. AccuSound's marketing analyst has indicated that this problem will have a significant impact on the company's reputation and customer satisfaction. Consequently, the board of directors would interpret this problem as having serious negative implications for the company's profitability.

Allen included the circuit failure and rework problem in her report prepared for the upcoming quarterly meeting of the board of directors. Due to the potential adverse economic impact, Allen followed a long-standing practice of highlighting this information. After reviewing the reports to be presented, the plant manager and his staff complained to the controller that he should control his people better. "We can't upset the board with this kind of material. Tell Allen to tone that down. Maybe we can get it by the board in this meeting and have some time to work on it. People who buy those cheap systems and play them that loud shouldn't expect them to last forever."

The controller called Allen into his office and said, "Marie, you'll have to bury this one. The probable failure of reworks can be mentioned briefly in the oral presentation, but it should not be mentioned or highlighted in the advance material mailed to the board."

Allen feels strongly that the board will be misinformed on a potentially serious loss of income if she follows the controller's orders. Allen discussed the problem with the quality control engineer, who simply remarked, "That's your problem, Marie."

Required:

1. Discuss the ethical considerations that Marie Allen should recognize in deciding how to proceed.

2. Explain what ethical responsibilities should be accepted by (a) the controller, (b) the quality control engineer, and (c) the plant manager.

3. What should Allen do? Explain your answer.

(CMA, adapted)

Problem 1–30 Role of the Divisional Controller; Retailer (LO5, 6, 9, 10)

Urban Elite Apparel designs women's clothing and sells it through retail outlets across the country. All of the company's clothing lines are manufactured by contract manufacturers around the world. A division manager is responsible for each of the company's retail divisions. Each division's controller, assigned by the corporate controller's office, manages the division's accounting system and provides analysis of financial information for the division manager. The division manager evaluates the performance of the division controller and makes recommendations for salary increases and promotions. However, the final responsibility for promotion evaluation and salary increases rests with the corporate controller.

Each of Urban Elite Apparel's divisions is responsible for product design, sales, pricing, operating expenses, and profit. However, corporate management exercises tight control over divisional financial operations. For example, all capital expenditure above a modest amount must be approved by corporate management. The method of financial reporting from the division to corporate headquarters provides further evidence of the degree of financial control. The division manager and the division controller provide corporate headquarters with separate and independent commentary on the financial results of the division. Corporate management states that the division controller is there to provide an independent view of the division's operations, not as a spy.

Required:

1. Discuss the arrangements for line and staff reporting at Urban Elite Apparel.

2. The division controller for Urban Elite Apparel has a "dual reporting" responsibility. The division controller is responsible both to the division manager, who makes recommendations on salary and promotion, *and* to the corporate controller, who has the final say in such matters.

   a. Identify and discuss the factors that make the division controller's role difficult in this type of situation.

   b. Discuss the effect of the dual reporting relationship on the motivation of the divisional controller.

(CMA, adapted)

Case

Case 1–31 Disclosure of Confidential Information; Ethics; Software Developer **(LO1, 6, 9, 10)**

Progressive Applications Corporation, a developer and distributor of business applications software, has been in business for five years. The company's main products include programs used for list management, billing, and accounting for the mail-order shopping business. Progressive's sales have increased steadily to the current level of $25 million per year. The company has 250 employees.

Andrea Czech joined Progressive approximately one year ago as accounting manager. Czech's duties include supervision of the company's accounting operations and preparation of the company's financial statements. No one has noticed that in the past six months Progressive's sales have ceased to rise and have actually declined in the two most recent months. This unexpected downturn has resulted in cash shortages. Compounding these problems, Progressive has had to delay the introduction of a new product line due to delays in documentation preparation.

Progressive contracts most of its printing requirements to Web Graphic Inc., a small company owned by Rob Borman. Borman has dedicated a major portion of his printing capacity to Progressive's requirements because Progressive's contracts represent approximately 50 percent of Web Graphic's business. Czech has known Borman for many years; as a matter of fact, she learned of Progressive's need for an accounting manager through Borman.

While preparing Progressive's most recent financial statements, Czech became concerned about the company's ability to maintain steady payments to its suppliers; she estimated that payments to all vendors, normally made within 30 days, could exceed 75 days. Czech is particularly concerned about payments to Web Graphic; she knows that Progressive had recently placed a large order with Web Graphic for the printing of the new product documentation, and she knows that Web Graphic will soon be placing an order for the special paper required for Progressive's documentation. Czech is considering telling Borman about Progressive's cash problems, but she is aware that a delay in the printing of the documentation would jeopardize Progressive's new product.

Required:

1. Describe Czech's ethical responsibilities in this situation.

2. Independent of your answer to requirement (1), assume that Czech learns that Borman of Web Graphic has decided to postpone the special paper order required for Progressive's printing job; Czech believes Borman must have heard rumours about Progressive's financial problems from some other source, because she has not talked to Borman. Should Czech tell the appropriate Progressive officials that Borman has postponed the paper order? Explain your answer.

3. Independent of your answers to the first two requirements, assume that Borman has decided to postpone the special paper order because he has learned of Progressive's financial problems from some source other than Czech. In addition, Czech realizes that Jim Grason, Progressive's purchasing manager, knows of her friendship with Borman. Now Czech is concerned that Grason may suspect she told Borman of Progressive's financial problems when Grason finds out that Borman has postponed the order. Describe the steps Czech should take to resolve this situation.

(CMA, adapted)

Practise and learn online with Connect.

CHAPTER TWO

Basic Cost Management Concepts

FOCUS COMPANY

Cømet
Cømet.com

The Comet Computer Corporation produces computers in its Mississauga, Ontario, plant. Most of the company's sales are made online through its website at www.comet.com. This manufacturer is a mass customizer, which means that its products are combined with standardized components in different ways to produce custom-made computers to order. In this chapter, we will explore the many different issues involved in understanding the costs of running any business.

IN CONTRAST

*Fast**Car**, Inc.*

In contrast to the manufacturing setting of the Comet Computer Corporation, we explore the cost issues covered in the chapter in the context of FastCar, Inc. As the largest specialty automotive service company in North America, FastCar has more than 1,000 service locations. FastCar's management, like that of any other company, must understand its costs in order to be successful in a competitive business environment.

After completing this chapter, you should be able to

1 Explain the meaning of *cost*.

2 Distinguish among product costs, period costs, and expenses.

3 Describe the role of costs in financial statements.

4 List five types of manufacturing operations and describe one of them: mass customization.

5 Give examples of three types of manufacturing costs.

6 Prepare a schedule of cost of goods manufactured, a schedule of cost of goods sold, and an income statement for a manufacturer.

7 Understand the importance of identifying an organization's cost drivers.

8 Describe the behaviour of variable and fixed costs, in total and on a per-unit basis.

9 Distinguish among direct, indirect, controllable, and uncontrollable costs.

10 Define and give examples of an *opportunity cost*, an *out-of-pocket cost*, a *sunk cost*, a *differential cost*, a *marginal cost*, and an *average cost per unit*.

The process of management involves formulating strategy, planning, control, decision making, and directing operational activities. Managers can perform each of these functions more effectively with managerial accounting information. Much of this information focuses on the costs incurred in the organization. For example, in *formulating its overall strategy*, WestJet Airlines' management considered the cost savings that result from being a low-cost airline. In *planning* WestJet's routes and flight schedules, management must consider aircraft fuel costs, salaries of flight crews, and airport landing fees. *Controlling* the costs of manufacturing heavy equipment requires that Caterpillar's management accountants carefully measure and manage production costs. In *making decisions* about locating a new store, Walmart management needs information about the cost of building, maintaining, equipping, and staffing the store. Finally, to *direct operational activities*, managers in all three of these companies need information about the cost of salaries, utilities, security, and a host of other goods and services.

The Meaning of Cost

Each of the examples in the preceding section focuses on costs of one type or another. An important first step in studying managerial accounting is to gain an understanding of the various types of costs incurred by organizations and how those costs are actively managed.

At the most basic level, a **cost** may be defined as the sacrifice made, usually measured by the resources given up, to achieve a particular purpose. If we look more carefully, though, we find that the word *cost* can have different meanings depending on the context in which it is used. Cost data that are classified and recorded in a particular way for one purpose may be inappropriate for another use. For example, the costs incurred in producing gasoline last year are important in measuring Petro-Canada's income for the year. However, those costs may not be useful in planning the company's refinery operations for the next year if the cost of oil has changed significantly or if the methods of producing gasoline have improved.

The important point is that different cost concepts and classifications are used for different purposes. Understanding these concepts and classifications enables the management accountant to provide appropriate cost data to the managers who need it. The purpose of this chapter is to enable the users of this textbook to gain a firm grasp of the cost terminology used in managerial accounting, which will be used throughout the book.

Learning Objective **1**

Explain the meaning of *cost*.

"We are expected to say, 'Here are the costs, and this is why the costs are what they are, and this is how they compare to other things, and here are some suggestions where we could possible improve.'" (2a)

Caterpillar

Product Costs, Period Costs, and Expenses

An important issue in both managerial and financial accounting is the timing with which the costs of acquiring assets or services are recognized as expenses. An **expense** is defined as the cost incurred when an asset is used up or sold for the purpose of generating revenue. The terms *product cost* and *period cost* are used to describe the timing with which various expenses are recognized.

A **product cost** is a cost assigned to goods that were either purchased or manufactured for resale. The product cost is used to value the inventory of manufactured goods or merchandise until the goods are sold. In the period of the sale, the product costs are recognized as an expense called **cost of goods sold**. The product cost of merchandise inventory acquired by a retailer or wholesaler for resale consists of the purchase cost of the inventory plus any shipping charges. The product cost of manufactured inventory

Learning Objective **2**

Distinguish among product costs, period costs, and expenses.

includes all of the costs incurred in its manufacture. For example, the labour cost of a production employee at Comet Computer Corporation is included as a product cost of the computers manufactured. Exhibit 2–1 illustrates the relationship between product costs and cost of goods sold.

Another term for product cost is **inventoriable cost**, since a product cost is stored as the cost of inventory until the goods are sold. In addition to retailers, wholesalers, and manufacturers, the concept of product cost is relevant to other producers of inventoriable goods. Agricultural firms, lumber companies, and mining firms are examples of nonmanufacturers that produce inventoriable goods. Apples, timber, coal, and other such goods are inventoried at their product cost until the time period during which they are sold.

All costs that are not product costs are called **period costs**. These costs are identified with the period of time in which they are incurred rather than with units of purchased or produced goods. Period costs are recognized as expenses during the time period in which they are incurred. All research, selling, and administrative costs are treated as period costs. This is true in manufacturing, retail, and service industry firms.

Research costs include costs of developing new products and services. For example, the costs of running laboratories are all classified as research costs. *Selling costs* include salaries, commissions, and travel costs of salespersons and the costs of advertising and promotion. *Administrative costs* refer to all costs of running the organization as a whole. The salaries of top management and the costs of the accounting, legal, and public relations activities are examples of administrative costs.

Exhibit 2–2 illustrates the nature of period costs.

Exhibit 2–1
Product Costs and Cost of Goods Sold

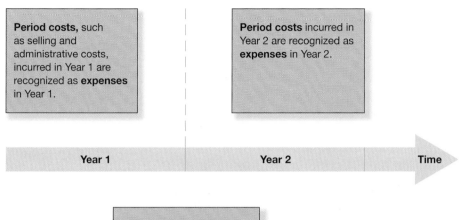

Exhibit 2–2
Period Costs

Costs on Financial Statements

The distinction between product costs and period costs is emphasized by examining the financial statements of three different types of firms.

Learning Objective **3**

Describe the role of costs in financial statements.

Income Statement

Exhibit 2–3 displays recent income statements, in highly summarized form, for WestJet Airlines Ltd., Caterpillar Inc., and Walmart Stores, Inc. These companies are in three different industries. Representing the service industry is WestJet, a major airline based in western Canada. Caterpillar is a heavy-equipment manufacturer. Walmart Stores is a large retail firm with 4,304 locations throughout the United States and 4,112 locations internationally, including 317 stores across Canada.

Selling and administrative costs are period costs on all three of the income statements shown in Exhibit 2–3. For example, Caterpillar lists $4.248 billion of selling, general, and administrative expenses.

For Caterpillar, the costs of manufactured inventory are product costs. All costs incurred in manufacturing finished products are stored in inventory until the time period when the products are sold. Then the product costs of the inventory sold become cost of goods sold, an expense, on the income statement.

Product costs for Walmart include all costs of acquiring merchandise inventory for resale. These product costs are stored in inventory until the time period during which the merchandise is sold; then these costs become cost of goods sold.

There are no inventoried product costs at WestJet Airlines. Although this firm does engage in the production of air transportation services, its service output is consumed as soon as it is produced. Service industry firms, such as TD Canada Trust, Fairmont Hotels & Resorts, Manulife Financial, and Tim Hortons, generally refer to the costs of producing services as **operating expenses**. Operating expenses are treated as period costs and are expensed during the period in which they are incurred. WestJet Airlines includes costs such as flight operations, aircraft fuel, and aircraft maintenance in operating expenses for the period.

> "What we should become in the future is a business partner who helps people understand what the financials are saying and helps them design their businesses." (2b)
>
> **Qwest**
> **(Currently a part of CenturyLink)**

Exhibit 2–3

Income statements for Three Different Industries (all figures in millions of dollars)

WESTJET AIRLINES LTD.
Income Statement for a Recent Year

Revenues:	
Guest revenues	$ 2,405
Other	204
	2,609
Expenses:	
Aircraft fuel	675
Airport operations	388
Flight operations and navigational charges	326
Marketing, general, and administration	195
Sales and distribution	256
Depreciation and amortization	133
Inflight	124
Aircraft leasing	142
Maintenance	100
Employee profit share	22
	2,361
Earnings from operations	248
Non-operating income (expenses):	
Interest income	10
Interest expense	(60)
Gain (loss) on foreign exchange	(1)
	(51)
Earnings before income taxes	197
Income tax expense	(60)
Net earnings	$ 137

CATERPILLAR®

Value measured by product costs →

CATERPILLAR INC.
Income Statement for a Recent Year

Sales revenue	$42,588
Less: Cost of goods sold	30,367
Gross profit	12,221
Less: Operating costs:	
Selling, general, and administrative expenses	4,248
Research and development expenses	1,905
Other operating expenses	2,105
Total operating costs	8,258
Operating profit	3,963
Interest expense	(343)
Other income (expense)	130
Profit before taxes	3,750
Provision for income taxes	(968)
Equity in profit (loss) of affiliated companies	(24)
Minority interest	(58)
Profit	$ 2,700

(continued)

WALMART STORES, INC.
Income Statement for a Recent Year

Value measured by product costs →

Sales revenue	$421,849
Less: Cost of goods sold	315,287
Gross profit	106,562
Less: Selling, general, and administrative expenses	81,020
Operating income	25,542
Less: Interest, net	2,004
Income before income taxes	23,538
Provision for income taxes	(7,579)
Minority interest	(604)
Income (loss) from discontinued operations, net of tax	1,034
Net income	$ 16,389

Balance Sheet

Since retailers, wholesalers, and manufacturers sell inventoriable products, their balance sheets are also affected by product costs. Exhibit 2–4 displays the current assets section of recent Caterpillar and Walmart balance sheets, which include inventory. Manufacturers, such as Caterpillar, have three types of inventory: **Raw-material inventory** includes all materials before they are placed into production. **Work-in-process inventory** refers to manufactured products that are only partially completed at the date when the balance sheet is prepared. **Finished-goods inventory** refers to manufactured goods that are complete and ready for sale. The values of the work-in-process and finished-goods inventories are measured by their product costs.

On the Walmart balance sheet, the cost of acquiring merchandise is listed as the value of the merchandise inventories.

> "Now the accountants are not only the interpreters. They drive management toward the proper response to what the numbers are telling us." (2c)
> **ITT Automotive**

CATERPILLAR INC.
Partial Balance Sheet at the End of a Recent Year

Current assets:

Value measured by product costs →

Cash and short-term investments	$ 3,592
Receivables	16,792
Inventories	9,587
Other current assets	1,839
Total current assets	$31,810

WALMART STORES, INC.
Partial Balance Sheet at the End of a Recent Year

Current assets:

Value measured by product costs →

Cash and cash equivalents	$ 7,395
Receivables (net)	5,089
Inventories	36,318
Prepaid expenses and other current assets	3,091
Total current assets	$51,893

Exhibit 2–4

Partial Balance Sheets for a Manufacturer and a Retailer (all figures in millions of dollars)

CATERPILLAR®

Manufacturing Operations and Costs

Learning Objective **4**

List five types of manufacturing operations and describe one of them: mass customization.

Although there are thousands of manufacturing firms, their basic production processes can be classified into five generic types. The nature of the manufacturing process can affect the manufacturing costs incurred; therefore, the management team is in a better position to manage these costs if the relationship of the production process to the types of costs incurred is understood. Exhibit 2–5 defines and describes the five generic manufacturing processes.[1]

We will study the role of managerial accounting and cost management in four of these manufacturing processes. This chapter will focus on mass-customization operations, similar to that used by Dell Inc. Chapter 3 will examine managerial accounting techniques used in job-shop and batch-production operations. Chapter 4 will focus on the cost accumulation and cost management processes in a continuous-flow manufacturing environment.

Mass-Customization Operations

In **mass customization**, many standardized components are combined in different ways to produce custom-made products to customer order. Dell Inc. is a prime example of mass customizers. Such companies are characterized by high production volume and often use a direct-sales approach, in which the consumer orders directly from the manufacturer, often via the Internet.

Exhibit 2–5
Types of Production Processes

Type of Production Process	Description of Process	Example of Manufacturer
Job Shop	Low production volume; little standardization; one-of-a-kind products. Major film studios, such as 20th Century Fox (a scene from the box office hit *Avatar*).	
Batch	Multiple products; low volume. Caterpillar (batch production of heavy equipment).	
Assembly Line	A few major products; higher volume. Ford (automobile assembly line).	
Mass Customization	High production volume; many standardized components; customized combination of components. Dell Inc. (Computer products).	
Continuous Flow	High production volume; highly standardized commodity products. ExxonMobil (production of gasoline, a continuous-flow product).	

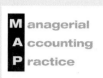

MASS CUSTOMIZATION

"There is no better way to make, sell, and deliver PCs than the way Dell Inc. does it, and nobody executes that model better than Dell." The company's machines are made to order and delivered directly to customers, who get the exact machines they want cheaper than they can get them from Dell's competition. "Dell has some 24 facilities in and around Austin and employs more than 18,000 local workers. Dell is improving its earnings and gaining market share even in tough economic times. Nevertheless, Michael Dell, the company's restless founder, is constantly looking for ways to improve the company's operations."[2] In one year alone, Dell cut $1 billion out of its costs—half from manufacturing—and Dell executives vowed to cut another $1 billion.

At the Topfer Manufacturing Center in Austin, workers "scuttle about in the 200,000-square-foot plant like ants on a hot plate. Gathered in cramped six-person 'cells,' they assemble computers from batches of parts that arrive via a computer-directed conveyor system overhead. If a worker encounters a problem, that batch can instantly be shifted to another cell, avoiding the stoppages that plague conventional assembly lines. Dell is constantly tinkering with factory layout and product design to move computers through at a higher velocity."

In spite of the ups and downs of the computer technology industry, most observers believe that Dell's business model will continue to be successful. However, the company has recently acknowledged that it needs to upgrade its tech support services in order to better serve its customers.[3]

Michael Dell has charted a change in course for Dell, by seeking to acquire companies that can help Dell compete more effectively with rivals Apple and HP. Through structured acquisitions, Dell hopes to better position itself as "the center of the tech industry has shifted from the PC to the Internet."[4]

To illustrate a mass-customization environment, let's focus on Comet Computer Corporation, a manufacturer of computers and peripheral devices.[5] Comet purchases parts such as motherboards, computer chips, and power units and then assembles these parts into customized PCs to customer specifications. A finished computer is then packaged with the monitor, keyboard, printer, and cables ordered by the customer, all of which are purchased by Comet.

Comet uses the direct-sales model, which was popularized by Dell Inc. Ninety percent of Comet's orders are placed on the company's website at comet.com, and 10 percent are taken on a toll-free phone number. No sales are made through retail channels.

Comet's production process is triggered when a customer places an order. The customer specifies every aspect of the desired computer system, including the processor type and the amount of memory on the hard drive, the monitor size and the printer type, and any preinstalled software. A sales representative transmits the order electronically to the appropriate production cell module.[6] A production cell module, or *mod*, is responsible for manufacturing a particular product line, such as desktops, laptops, or servers.

When the order is received in the appropriate mod, the assembly process begins. Memory and processor chips are installed on the motherboard, which is then mounted on the chassis. Next, components such as the hard drive, DVD drive, and power supply are placed into the chassis. After all of the components are mounted, the computer's cover is installed, and the finished unit moves to a test and inspection mod. After the unit checks out for reliability, it goes to the software installation mod, where the software ordered by the customer is preinstalled. From the software mod, the unit goes to the

"[Management accountants] will be more analytical . . . and more of a partner with the operational side of the business." (2d)
ITT Automotive

shipping mod, where it is boxed and prepared for shipping. Comet strives to ship every customer order within six days.

Before we discuss Comet's production process further, let's turn our attention to the types of manufacturing costs incurred by Comet and other manufacturers.

Manufacturing Costs

Learning Objective   **5**

Give examples of three types of manufacturing costs.

To assist managers in planning, decision making, and cost management, management accountants classify costs by the functional area of the organization to which costs relate. Some examples of functional areas are research and development, manufacturing, marketing, and administration. Manufacturing costs are further classified into the following three categories: direct material, direct labour, and manufacturing overhead.

Direct Material   Raw material used in the manufacturing process that is physically incorporated into the finished product and can be easily traced to the product is called **direct material**. Examples include the sheet metal in a Volkswagen automobile and the semiconductors in a Comet computer.

Some confusion can be caused by the seemingly interchangeable use of the terms *raw material* and *direct material*. However, there is a difference in the meaning of these terms: Before material is entered into the production process, it is called *raw material*. *After* it enters production, it becomes *direct material*.

Direct Labour   The cost of wages and benefits for employees who work *directly* on the manufactured products is called **direct labour**. Examples include wages of employees who assemble Comet computers and of those who operate the equipment in a Petro-Canada refinery. The cost of benefits for direct-labour employees, such as employer-paid dental insurance premiums and the employer's pension contributions, also are classified as direct-labour costs.

Manufacturing Overhead   All other manufacturing costs are classified as **manufacturing overhead**, which includes three types of costs: indirect material, indirect labour, and other manufacturing costs.

- **Indirect material**   The cost of materials that are required for the production process but do not become an integral part of the finished product are classified as **indirect material** costs. An example is the cost of drill bits used in a Volkswagen metal-fabrication department. The drill bits wear out and are discarded, but they do not become part of the product. Materials that become an integral part of the finished product but are insignificant in cost are also classified as indirect material. Materials such as glue or paint may be so inexpensive that it is not worth tracing their costs to specific products as direct materials.

- **Indirect labour**   The wages, salaries, and benefits of employees who do not work directly on the product, but whose services are necessary for the manufacturing process, are classified as **indirect labour**. Such employees include production department supervisors, custodial employees, and security guards.

- **Other manufacturing costs**   All other manufacturing costs that are neither direct material nor direct labour costs are classified as manufacturing overhead. These costs include depreciation of plant and equipment, property taxes, insurance, and utilities for the manufacturing facilities, as well as the costs of operating service departments. **Service departments** or **support departments** are those that do not work directly on manufacturing products but are necessary for the manufacturing process to occur. Examples include the equipment-maintenance department and the computer-aided-design (CAD) department. In some manufacturing firms, departments are referred to as *work centres*.

"If you just simply have [an employee] performing an [assembly] operation, that's direct labor. But when you put in a robot to do the job, which we're all doing, then you've got to have an engineer to make sure the [robot] is programmed right. So now it becomes indirect labor." (2e)

Chrysler

Other manufacturing-overhead costs include overtime premiums and the cost of idle time. An **overtime premium** is the *extra* compensation above the regular compensation that is paid to an employee who works beyond the time normally scheduled. Suppose a technician assembling Comet computers earns $16 per hour. The technician works 48 hours during a week instead of the scheduled 40 hours. The overtime pay scale is time-and-a-half, or 150 percent of the regular wage. The technician's compensation for the week amounts to $832 [($16 × 40 hours) + ($24 × 8 hours)] and is classified as follows:

Direct-labour cost ($16 × 48 hours)	$768
Overhead (overtime premium: ½ × $16 × 8 hours)	64
Total compensation paid	$832

Only the *extra* compensation of $8 per hour is classified as overtime premium. The regular wage of $16 per hour is treated as direct labour, even for the eight overtime hours.

Idle time is time not spent productively by an employee due to such events as equipment breakdowns or new setups of production runs. Such idle time is an unavoidable feature of most manufacturing processes. The cost of an employee's idle time is classified as overhead so that it can be spread across all production jobs. Suppose that during one 40-hour shift, a machine breakdown results in idle time of 1½ hours and a power failure idles workers for an additional ½ hour. If an employee earns $14 per hour, the employee's wages for the week will be classified as follows:

Direct-labour cost ($14 × 38 hours)	$532
Overhead (idle time $14 × 2 hours)	28
Total compensation paid	$560

Both overtime premium and the cost of idle time are classified as manufacturing overhead, rather than associated with a specific production job, because idle time or overtime occurs randomly. Suppose several production jobs are scheduled during an eight-hour shift, and the last job remains unfinished at the end of the shift. The overtime necessary to finish the last job is caused by all of the jobs scheduled during the shift, not just the last one. Similarly, if a power failure occurs during one of several production jobs, the resulting idle time is not due to the job that happens to be in process at the time. The power failure is a random event, and the resulting cost should be treated as a cost of all of the department's production.

To summarize, manufacturing costs include direct material, direct labour, and manufacturing overhead. Direct labour and overhead are often called **conversion costs**, since they are the costs of "converting" raw material into finished products. Direct material and direct labour are often referred to as **prime costs**.

Manufacturing Cost Flows

As discussed previously, direct material, direct labour, and manufacturing overhead are the three types of production costs incurred by manufacturers. These costs are product costs because they are stored in inventory until the time period when the products are sold. Manufacturers use product-costing systems to keep track of the flow of these costs from the time production begins until products are sold. This flow of manufacturing costs is depicted in Exhibit 2–6. As direct material is used in production, its cost is added to the work-in-process inventory. Similarly, the costs of direct labour and manufacturing overhead are accumulated in the work-in-process inventory.

Exhibit 2–6
Flow of Manufacturing Costs

C(o)met.com

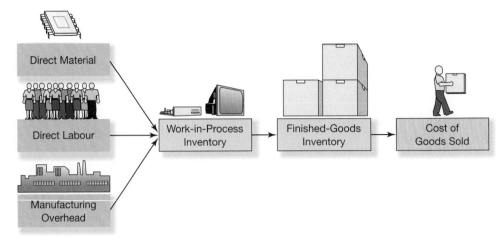

Product costs . . .   . . . are stored in inventory . . .   . . . until the products are sold.

When products are finished, their costs (direct material, direct labour, and manufacturing overhead) are transferred from the work-in-process inventory to the finished-goods inventory. The total of these transferred costs is called the **cost of goods manufactured**, and these costs are kept in the finished-goods inventory until the time period when the products are sold. At that time, these product costs are transferred from the finished-goods inventory to the cost of goods sold, which is an expense of the period when the sale is made. Exhibit 2–6 focuses on the flow of manufacturing costs, which is the basis of a product-costing system. The detailed procedures and accounts used to keep track of product costs are covered in Chapters 3 and 4.

Learning Objective 6

Prepare a schedule of cost of goods manufactured, a schedule of cost of goods sold, and an income statement for a manufacturer.

Manufacturers generally prepare a **schedule of cost of goods manufactured** and a **schedule of cost of goods sold** to summarize the flow of manufacturing costs during an accounting period. These schedules are intended only for internal use by management. Exhibit 2–7 shows these two schedules, along with an income statement for Comet Computer Corporation. Notice the extremely low inventories of raw material, finished goods, and work in process in these schedules. With annual sales of $700 million, Comet's year-end inventory of raw material is only $5,020,000, which is less than 1 percent of sales. Work-in-process inventory ($100,000) and finished-goods inventory ($190,000) are even lower. These low inventories, relative to sales volume, are characteristic of mass customizers using the direct-sales approach.

Production Costs in Service Firms and Nonprofit Organizations

Service firms and many nonprofit organizations are also engaged in production. What distinguishes these organizations from manufacturers is that a service is used as it is produced, whereas a manufactured product can be stored as inventory. Businesses such as Fairmont Hotels & Resorts, TD Canada Trust, WestJet, and the Canucks are in the business of producing services. Similarly, nonprofit organizations such as the Royal Winnipeg Ballet School and the Canadian Red Cross also are engaged in service production. While less commonly observed in service firms, the same cost classifications used in manufacturing companies can be applied. For example, Air Canada produces air transportation services. Direct material includes such items as jet fuel, aircraft parts, and food and beverages. Direct labour includes the salaries of the flight crew and the wages of aircraft-maintenance employees. Overhead costs include depreciation of baggage-handling equipment, insurance, and airport landing fees.

The process of recording and classifying costs is important in service firms and nonprofit organizations for the same reasons as in manufacturing firms. Cost analysis is used in pricing banking and insurance services, positioning travel and car-rental agencies,

Exhibit 2–7
Manufacturing Cost
Schedules

Comet.com

COMET COMPUTER CORPORATION
Schedule of Cost of Goods Manufactured
For the Year Ended December 31, 20x2
(in thousands)

Direct material:

Raw-material inventory, January 1	$ 6,000	
Add: Purchases of raw material	134,000	
Raw material available for use	$140,000	
Deduct: Raw-material inventory, December 31	5,020	
Raw material used		$134,980
Direct labour		50,000

Manufacturing overhead:

Indirect material	$ 10,000	
Indirect labour	40,000	
Depreciation on factory	90,000	
Depreciation on equipment	70,000	
Utilities	15,000	
Insurance	5,000	
Total manufacturing overhead		230,000
Total manufacturing costs		$414,980
Add: Work-in-process (WIP) inventory, January 1		120
Subtotal		$415,100
Deduct: Work-in-process inventory, December 31		100
Cost of goods manufactured*		$415,000

*Formula used to compute cost of goods manufactured:
Beg. WIP inventory + Total manufacturing costs − End WIP inventory = Cost of goods manufactured

COMET COMPUTER CORPORATION
Schedule of Cost of Goods Sold
For the Year Ended December 31, 20x2
(in Thousands)

Finished-goods inventory, January 1	$ 200
Add: Cost of goods manufactured*	415,000
Cost of goods available for sale	$415,200
Finished-goods (FG) inventory, December 31	190
Cost of goods sold†	$415,010

*From the Schedule of Cost of Goods Manufactured.
†Formula used to compute cost of goods sold:
Beg. FG inventory + Cost of goods manufactured − End FG inventory = Cost of goods sold

COMET COMPUTER CORPORATION
Income Statement
For the Year Ended December 31, 20x2
(in thousands)

Sales revenue	$700,000
Less: Cost of goods sold*	415,010
Gross margin	$284,990
Selling and administrative expenses	174,490
Income before taxes	$110,500
Income tax expense	30,000
Net Income	$ 80,500

*From the Schedule of Cost of Goods Sold.

setting enrolment targets in universities, and determining cost reimbursements in hospitals. As such organizations occupy an ever-growing role in our economy, applying managerial accounting to their activities will take on ever-greater importance.

Basic Cost Management: Different Costs for Different Purposes

An understanding of cost concepts is absolutely critical to cost management. Moreover, different perspectives on costs are important in different managerial situations. The phrase *different costs for different purposes* is often used to convey the fact that an understanding of the different characteristics of costs can be important in a variety of managerial circumstances. In this section, we will briefly discuss the work of several cross-functional management teams at Comet Computer Corporation, each of which is focusing on a particular management challenge. Through our discussion of these cost management teams' work, we will explore some of the key cost terms and concepts used in managerial accounting and cost management.

The Cost Driver Team

Learning Objective   **7**

Understand the importance of identifying an organization's cost drivers.

One of the most important cost classifications involves the way a cost changes in relation to changes in the activity of the organization. **Activity** refers to a measure of the organization's output of products or services. The number of automobiles manufactured by Audi, the number of days of patient care provided by Saskatoon City Hospital, and the number of insurance claims settled by Canadian Direct Insurance are all measures of activity. The activities that cause costs to be incurred are also called *cost drivers*.

One of Comet Computer Corporation's cost management teams was formed to examine the various costs incurred by Comet. The team consisted of an engineer, a production manager, a purchasing manager, and a management accountant. After identifying the costs incurred by Comet, the team was charged to identify the cost drivers on which various types of costs depend.[7] A **cost driver** is a characteristic of an activity or event that causes costs to be incurred by that activity or event. In most organizations, different types of costs respond to widely differing cost drivers. For example, in a manufacturing firm, the cost of

Cost drivers in the airline industry are complex. The capacity of an airplane and its passenger load drive costs, but so do a variety of other factors related to the airline's operations.

assembly labour would be driven by the quantity of products manufactured as well as the number of parts in each product. In contrast, the cost of machine-setup labour would be driven by the number of production runs. The cost of material-handling labour would be driven by material-related factors such as the quantity and cost of raw material used, the number of parts in various products, and the number of raw-material shipments received.

In identifying a cost driver, the management accountant should consider the extent to which a cost or pool of costs varies in accordance with the cost driver. The higher the correlation between the cost and the cost driver, the more accurate will be the resulting understanding of cost behaviour. Another important consideration is the cost of measuring the cost driver. Thus, there is a cost–benefit trade-off in the identification of cost drivers. As the number of cost drivers increases, the accuracy of the resulting information will increase. However, the cost of the information will also increase. The concept of a cost driver will be an important aspect of many of the topics discussed in subsequent chapters.

Variable and Fixed Costs

After identifying costs and cost drivers for Comet Computer Corporation's operations, the cost driver team examined the relationship of various costs to the activities performed. Such a relationship is referred to as *cost behaviour* and will be the focus of Chapter 6. At this juncture, though, let's look at two types of cost behaviour identified at Comet: *variable* and *fixed costs*.

Learning Objective 8

Describe the behaviour of variable and fixed costs, in total and on a per-unit basis.

Variable Costs   A **variable cost** changes *in total* in direct proportion to a change in the level of activity (or cost driver). If activity increases by 20 percent, total variable cost increases by 20 percent also. For example, the cost of sheet metal used by Volkswagen will increase by approximately 5 percent if automobile production increases by 5 percent. The cost of cups and other paper products at Tim Hortons will increase by nearly 10 percent if the number of customers increases by 10 percent.

At Comet Computer Corporation, the cost management team identified direct material as a variable cost. One purchased component, a power bus assembly, costs $100 per computer manufactured. The cost behaviour for this direct material cost is graphed and tabulated in Exhibit 2–8. Panel A of Exhibit 2–8 displays a graph of this variable cost. As this graph shows, *total* variable cost increases proportionately with activity. When activity doubles, from 10 to 20 units, total variable cost doubles, from $1,000 to $2,000. However, the variable cost *per unit* remains the same as activity changes. The variable cost associated with each unit of activity is $100, whether it is the first unit, the fourth, or the eighteenth (the variable cost per unit represents the slope of the straight line). The table in panel B of Exhibit 2–8 illustrates this point.

To summarize, as activity changes, *total* variable cost increases or decreases proportionately with the activity change, but *unit* variable cost remains the same.

A. Graph of Total Variable Cost

Total variable cost (power bus assemblies)

Exhibit 2–8

Variable Cost

Comet.com

$3,000

$2,000

$1,000

10   20   30

Activity (or cost driver): units produced

B. Tabulation of Variable Cost

Activity (or cost driver)	Variable Cost per Unit	Total Variable Cost
1	$100	$ 100
4	100	400
18	100	1,800
30	100	3,000

Fixed Costs   A **fixed cost** remains unchanged in total as the level of activity (or cost driver) varies. If activity increases or decreases by 20 percent, total fixed cost remains the same. Examples of fixed costs include depreciation of plant and equipment at a Nike factory, the cost of property taxes at a Fairmont Hotel, and the salary of a pilot employed by WestJet.

Comet Computer Corporation identified the salary of the manager of web sales operations as a fixed cost. Her $150,000 annual salary does not vary with the number of units produced or sold. This fixed cost is graphed in panel A of Exhibit 2–9. From the graph in Exhibit 2–9, it is apparent that *total* fixed cost remains unchanged as activity changes. When activity triples, from 10 to 30 units, total fixed cost remains constant at $150,000. However, the fixed cost *per unit* does change as activity changes. If the activity level is only 1 unit, then the fixed cost per unit is $150,000 per unit ($150,000 ÷ 1). If the activity level is 10 units, then the fixed cost per unit declines to $15,000 per unit ($150,000 ÷ 10). The behaviour of total fixed cost and unit fixed cost is illustrated in panel B of Exhibit 2–9.

Another way of viewing the change in unit fixed cost as activity changes is in a graph, as shown in panel C of Exhibit 2–9. Unit fixed cost declines steadily as activity increases. Notice that the decrease in unit fixed cost when activity changes from 1 to 2 units is much larger than the decrease in unit fixed cost when activity changes from 10 to 11 units or from 20 to 21 units. Thus, the amount of the change in unit fixed cost declines as the activity level increases.

To summarize, as the activity level increases, *total* fixed cost remains constant but *unit* fixed cost declines. As you will see in subsequent chapters, it is vital in managerial accounting to thoroughly understand the behaviour of both total fixed costs and unit fixed costs.

The Cost Management and Control Team

An important objective of managerial accounting is to assist managers in managing and controlling costs. Sometimes cost management is facilitated by tracing costs to the department or work centre in which the cost was incurred. Such tracing of costs to departments is known as *responsibility accounting*.

Comet Computer Corporation formed a cost management and control team to refine the company's responsibility accounting system. The team consisted of an engineer, the production scheduling manager, the assistant manager of quality control, the manager of human resources, and a management accountant. The ultimate objective of the team was to develop a responsibility accounting system that would assist management in managing and controlling costs as well as reducing costs whenever possible. We will study cost management systems and cost reduction in considerable detail in Chapter 5 and responsibility accounting is covered in Chapter 11. For now, let's focus on a couple of cost concepts that are useful in these areas of managerial accounting.

Learning Objective   **9**

Distinguish among direct, indirect, controllable, and uncontrollable costs.

Direct and Indirect Costs   A product, service, or department, to which a cost is assigned, is called a **cost object**. A cost that can be traced to one specific cost object is called a **direct cost** of that cost object.

For example, the salary of an auto mechanic is a direct cost of the automotive service department in a Canadian Tire store. The cost of paint used in the painting department of a Bombardier plant is a direct cost of the painting department.

A cost that is not directly traceable to a specific cost object is called an **indirect cost** of that cost object. For example, the costs of national advertising for Fairmont Hotels & Resorts are indirect costs for each of the hotel and resort properties. The salary of a Honda plant manager is an indirect cost of each of the plant's production departments. The plant manager's duties are important to the smooth functioning of each of the plant's departments, but there is no way to trace a portion of the plant manager's salary cost to each department.

43

A. Graph of Total Fixed Cost

Total fixed cost (web sales manager's salary)

Exhibit 2–9
Fixed Cost

C⊙met

C⊙met.com

$150,000

Activity (or cost driver): units produced

10   20   30

B. Tabulation of Fixed Cost

Activity (or cost driver)	Fixed Cost per Unit	Total Fixed Cost
1	$150,000	$150,000
2	75,000	150,000
5	30,000	150,000
10	15,000	150,000
11	13,636*	150,000
20	7,500	150,000
21	7,143*	150,000
30	5,000	150,000

*Rounded.

C. Graph of Unit Fixed Cost

Managerial
Accounting
Practice

WestJet, Southwest,
Air Canada, AirTran,
JetBlue, United

AIRLINE INDUSTRY: COST STRUCTURE, COST DRIVERS, AND A SHIFTING BUSINESS MODEL[8]

North American business has changed its flying habits, possibly forever. The bottom line: Business travel is being taken over by low-cost operators. Just as Walmart Stores did in retailing, the discounters of the air—WestJet Airlines, Southwest Airlines and others—are proving that even some of the most finicky corporate fliers can't resist a bargain.

"WestJet was started in 1996—single fleet, low cost, highly productive, good utilization . . . a seating configuration that provides a cost advantage over other operators of similar aircraft." Low-cost carriers account for an increasing share of Canadian domestic air capacity. "In the past ten years, WestJet has made significant gains in domestic market share against Air Canada. In 2000, it held only 7% to Air Canada's 77%, though by the end of 2009, WestJet had risen to 38%, against Air Canada's 55%.

"A second force behind the fundamental shift in airline economics is the Internet, which has given travelers, travel agents, and corporate travel managers powerful tools to find and take advantage of deeply discounted fares.

"The shift is dire news for the big airlines, the full-service retailers of flight. The carriers, which are bleeding red ink, have massive fixed costs that aren't easy to scale back. Most of them have built expensive hub-and-spoke route systems and signed costly labor contracts that they had hoped to finance by charging high-margin business fares.

"It isn't easy for major airlines to cut their costs. Consider the current advantages low-fare carriers have over full-service rivals. They tend to have younger fleets, which require less maintenance, and younger labor forces that aren't tied to complicated, inefficient labor contracts. That's why labor costs are equivalent to just 25 percent of revenue at discounters AirTran Airways . . . and Jet Blue and 30 percent at Southwest. At United . . ., labor costs exceed 40 percent of revenue. Moreover, low-fare carriers typically stick to one airplane model, thus minimizing maintenance, operating, and training costs." WestJet and Southwest exclusively fly 737s. Many of the biggest carriers still fly six or seven types of aircraft.

The bottom line is that the airline industry is undergoing a sea change in its business model, and it is driven by the very different cost structures that characterize the largest carriers as against their smaller discount competitors. The discounters are more flexible and have proportionately lower fixed costs. An understanding of the cost drivers in the industry will be crucial to the survival of the big airlines.

"The flight crew's salaries on a flight, say from Atlanta to St. Louis, would be considered a direct cost of that flight. The salaries of the flight scheduling folks, on the other hand, would be an indirect cost of any given flight." (2g)

Delta Air Lines

Whether a cost is a direct cost or an indirect cost of a department often depends on which department is under consideration. A cost can be a direct cost of one department or subunit in the organization but an indirect cost of other departments. While the salary of a Honda Company plant manager is an *indirect* cost of the plant's departments, the manager's salary is a *direct* cost of the plant.

Comet Computer Corporation's cost management and control team determined that many of the company's costs were traceable to various departments or to specific activities of those departments. In the purchasing department, for example, costs were traced not just to the department, but also to the specific activities of identifying vendors, qualifying vendors, securing design specifications from the engineering design department, negotiating prices, placing orders, expediting orders, receiving materials and components, inspecting materials, and releasing materials to the material-handling operation.

An important objective of a cost management system is to trace as many costs as possible directly to the activities that cause them to be incurred. Sometimes called *activity accounting*, this process is vital to management's objective of eliminating *non-value-added costs*. These are costs of activities that can be eliminated without deterioration of product quality, performance, or perceived value. (We will study the elimination of non-value-added costs in greater detail in Chapter 5.)

Controllable and Uncontrollable Costs   Another cost classification that can be helpful in cost control involves the controllability of a cost item by a particular manager. If a manager can control or heavily influence the level of a cost, then that cost is classified as a **controllable cost** of that manager. Costs that a manager cannot influence significantly are classified as **uncontrollable costs** of that manager. Many costs are not completely under the control of any individual. In classifying costs as controllable or uncontrollable, management accountants generally focus on a manager's ability to influence costs. The question is not "Who controls the cost?" but "Who is in the best position to influence the level of a cost item?" Exhibit 2–10 lists several cost items along with their typical classification as controllable or uncontrollable.

Comet Computer was able to designate many of its costs as controllable or uncontrollable by various managers. Take the cost of raw materials and components: The *quantity* of materials used was largely controllable by the production supervisor, but the *price* of the materials was influenced more by the purchasing manager.

The Outsourcing Action Team

Another of Comet Computer Corporation's interdisciplinary management teams was formed to take a close look at which of the raw materials and components used in Comet's products should be manufactured by Comet and which ones should be outsourced (purchased from outside vendors).[9] This team consisted of the assistant manager of purchasing, a product design engineer, a product group sales manager, and a management accountant. As the team pursued its assignment, its members soon found that they were once again dealing with several different cost concepts.

In addition to accounting cost classifications, such as product costs and period costs, the team's members also found themselves using economic concepts in classifying costs. Such concepts are often useful in helping management accountants decide what cost information is relevant to the decisions faced by the organization's managers. Several of the most important economic cost concepts are discussed next.

Learning Objective **10**

Define and give examples of an *opportunity cost*, an *out-of-pocket cost*, a *sunk cost*, a *differential cost*, a *marginal cost*, and an *average cost per unit*.

Opportunity Costs   An **opportunity cost** is defined as the benefit sacrificed when the choice of one action precludes taking an alternative action.

Cost Item	Manager	Classification
Cost of raw material used to produce computer chips in an Intel factory	Supervisor of the production department for computer chips	Controllable (The production supervisor can exercise some control over the quantity of material used by ensuring that waste and defective units are minimized.)
Cost of food used in a Subway restaurant	Restaurant manager	Controllable (The restaurant manager exercises some control over the quantity of food used by scheduling production to ensure that excess food is not produced and wasted.)
Cost of national advertising for the Avis car rental company	Manager of the Avis rental agency at the Vancouver airport	Uncontrollable
Cost of national accounting and data processing operations for Future Shop	Manager of a Future Shop store in Coquitlam, BC	Uncontrollable

Exhibit 2–10
Controllable and Uncontrollable Costs

Opportunity costs arise in many business decisions. For example, suppose a sports equipment manufacturer receives a special order for basketballs from the recreation department of a university. If the firm accepts the order, it will not have enough productive capacity (labour and machine time) to produce its usual output of basketballs for sale to a large chain of sporting-goods stores. The opportunity cost of accepting the order is the foregone benefit from the basketball production that cannot be achieved. This foregone benefit is measured by the potential revenue from the basketball sales minus the cost of manufacturing the basketballs.

Opportunity costs also arise in personal decisions. The opportunity cost of a student's university education includes the income that is foregone as a result of not taking a full-time job during the student's years in university.

From an economic perspective, a dollar of opportunity cost associated with an action should be treated as equivalent to a dollar of out-of-pocket cost. **Out-of-pocket costs** are those that require the payment of cash or other assets as a result of their incurrence. The out-of-pocket costs associated with the basketball order consist of the manufacturing costs required to produce the basketballs. In making the decision to accept or reject the order, the firm's management should consider *both* the out-of-pocket costs and the opportunity cost of the order.

Studies by behavioural scientists and economists have shown that many people have a tendency to ignore or downplay the importance of opportunity costs. For example, in one study people were asked if they would pay $500 for two tickets to the Super Bowl.[10] Most people responded that they would not. However, many of the same people said that they would not sell the Super Bowl tickets for $500 if they were given the tickets free of charge. These people refused to incur the $500 *out-of-pocket cost* of buying the Super Bowl tickets, but they were willing to incur the $500 *opportunity cost* of going to the game rather than sell the tickets. In each case, a couple that attends the game ends up $500 poorer than a couple that does not attend the game.

Behaviour such as that illustrated in the Super Bowl example is economically inconsistent. Ignoring or downplaying the importance of opportunity costs can result in inconsistent and faulty business decisions.

Comet Computer's outsourcing action team found that the opportunity cost of using constrained production resources (such as space, machine time, and employee time) to produce a computer component in-house was an important factor to consider in deciding whether to outsource the component.[11]

Sunk Costs **Sunk costs** are costs that have been incurred in the past. Consequently, they do not affect future costs and cannot be changed by any current or future action. Examples of such costs include the acquisition cost of equipment previously purchased and the manufacturing cost of inventory on hand. Regardless of the current usefulness of the equipment or the inventory, the costs of acquiring it cannot be changed by any prospective action. Hence, these costs are irrelevant to all future decisions.

Suppose, for example, that a college's parking department purchased a desktop computer to assist in the vehicle registration process. A year has passed, the computer's warranty has expired, and the computer is not working well. An investigation reveals that this brand of computer is very sensitive to humidity and temperature changes. The parking department is located in an old building with poor heating and no air conditioning. As a result, the computer works only intermittently, repair bills have been high, and the office staff is fed up. The office manager requests that the department director junk the computer and instruct the staff to return to the old manual registration system. The director responds by insisting, "We can't afford to junk the computer! We paid $3,400 for it."

This illustration is a typical example of the inappropriate attention paid to sunk costs. The $3,400 paid for the computer is sunk. No future decision about the computer or the office's procedures can affect that cost. Future decisions should be based on future costs, such as the computer repair bills or the costs of upgrading the building's heating and air-conditioning systems.

Although it is incorrect, from an economic perspective, to allow sunk costs to affect future decisions, people often do so. It is human nature to attempt to justify past decisions. When there is a perceived need to demonstrate competence, either to themselves or to others, managers may seek to justify their decisions. The response of the parking department director that "We can't afford to junk the computer!" may represent the director's need to justify the past decision to purchase the computer. It is important for management accountants to be aware of these behavioural tendencies. Such an awareness enables the accountant to prepare the most relevant data for managers' decisions and, sometimes, to assist the managers in using the information.

Comet Computer's outsourcing action team encountered a sunk cost as it considered outsourcing production of a component called a *monitor interface unit* (MIU). The team discovered that the robot used to insert components into the MIU was difficult to maintain and expensive to operate. Nevertheless, the department supervisor was inclined to keep the robot and continue in-house production of the MIU, because, as he put it, "Comet paid an arm and a leg for this robot." The team was able to demonstrate that the robot's acquisition cost was a sunk cost and was irrelevant to the outsourcing decision. We will explore sunk costs in more detail in Chapter 12.

Differential Costs   A **differential cost** is the amount by which the cost differs under two alternative actions. Suppose, for example, that a city is considering two competing sites for a new landfill. If the northern site is chosen, the annual cost of transporting waste to the site is projected at $85,000. If the southern site is selected, annual transportation charges are expected to be $70,000. The annual differential cost of transporting waste is calculated as follows:

Annual cost of transporting waste to northern site	$85,000
Annual cost of transporting waste to southern site	70,000
Annual differential cost	$15,000

The increase in cost from one alternative to another is called an **incremental cost**. In the landfill example, the annual incremental cost of waste transportation is $15,000 if the site is moved from the southern location to the northern location. Differential or incremental costs are found in a variety of economic decisions. The additional cost incurred by a travel agency in locating a new office in the suburbs is the incremental cost of the new business location. The difference in the total cost incurred by the travel agency with or without the suburban location is the differential cost of the decision whether to establish the new office. Decisions about establishing new airline routes, adding additional shifts in a manufacturing firm, or increasing the nursing staff in a hospital all involve differential costs.

At Comet Computer, the outsourcing action team estimated that the differential cost between outsourcing the production of the MIU and producing it in-house would be $200,000 annually in favour of outsourcing, on the basis of current projections of annual production.

Marginal Costs and Average Costs   A special case of the differential-cost concept is the **marginal cost**, which is the extra cost incurred when one additional unit is produced. The additional cost incurred by Comet Computer when one additional high-performance laptop computer is made is the marginal cost of manufacturing the computer. The table in Exhibit 2–11 shows how marginal cost can change across different ranges of production quantities.

Marginal costs typically differ across different ranges of production quantities because the efficiency of the production process changes. At Comet Computer, the marginal cost of producing a laptop computer declines as output increases. It is much more efficient for the company to manufacture 101 computers than to make only one.

Exhibit 2–11

Marginal Cost of Producing
Laptop Computers at Comet
Computer Corporation

C☄met.com

Number of Laptop Computers Produced	Total Cost of Producing Laptops	Marginal Cost of Producing a Laptop	
1	$ 2,000	Difference is $1,900 ⟶	Marginal cost of 2nd laptop is $1,900.
2	3,900		
10	18,000	Difference is $1,690 ⟶	Marginal cost of 11th laptop is $1,690.
11	19,690		
100	150,000	Difference is $995 ⟶	Marginal cost of 101st laptop is $995.
101	150,995		

It is important to distinguish between *marginal costs* and *average costs*. In the Comet Computer example, the marginal cost of the second computer is $1,900. However, the average cost per unit when two laptops are manufactured is $3,900 divided by 2, or $1,950. Similarly, the marginal cost of the eleventh laptop is $1,690, but the average cost per unit when 11 laptops are produced is $1,790 (calculated by dividing $19,690 by 11). What is the marginal cost of the 101st laptop computer? The average cost per unit when 101 laptops are manufactured?[12]

To summarize, the marginal cost of production is the extra cost incurred when one more unit is produced. The **average cost per unit** is the total cost, for whatever quantity is manufactured, divided by the number of units manufactured. Marginal costs and average costs arise in a variety of economic situations. An administrator at Simon Fraser University might be interested in the marginal cost of educating one additional student, and a Ford executive might want to know the marginal cost of producing one more truck. A Greyhound route manager might be interested in the average cost per kilometre on the Winnipeg to Calgary route.

Costs and Benefits of Information

"If you can't communicate information to the individual, then the information is . . . lost. So, your communication skills are very important." (2h)

Abbott Labs

Many different cost concepts have been explored in this chapter. An important task of the management accountant is to determine which of these cost concepts is most appropriate in each situation. The accountant then strives to *communicate* the cost information to the user in the most effective manner possible. The accountant attempts to structure the organization's accounting information system to record data that will be useful for a variety of purposes. The benefits of measuring and classifying costs in a particular way are realized through the improvements in planning, control, and decision making that the information facilitates.

Another important task of the management accountant is to weigh the benefits of providing information against the costs of generating, communicating, and using that information. Some accountants, eager to show that they have not overlooked anything, tend to provide too much information. But when managers receive more data than they can utilize effectively, *information overload* occurs. Struggling to process large amounts of information, managers may be unable to recognize the most important facts. In deciding how much and what type of information to provide, management accountants should consider these human limitations.

Costs in the Service Industry

The cost terms and concepts that we have studied in this chapter are just as relevant in the service industry as in a manufacturing firm like Comet Computer Corporation. Here we will explore those cost issues in the context of an automotive service company.

FastCar, Inc. is a very large specialty automotive service company, with more than 1,000 service locations. It has established relationships with automobile parts vendors, which distribute their products directly to the service locations.

A typical FastCar service location has approximately 370 m² of floor space and six service bays. It is usually staffed by a manager, an assistant manager, and three to four automotive service technicians. FastCar supports the service locations with 30 district managers and six regional managers. Each district manager covers approximately 58 service locations and assists managers with operations, retail initiatives, and training.

Now let's think about a typical FastCar service location to explore the various cost issues in a service-industry environment.

Product and Period Costs   FastCar purchases auto parts and supplies, such as exhaust pipes, brake pads, oil filters, and engine oil, from vendors. These costs are stored in inventory as *product costs* (or *inventoriable costs*) until the time period when they are consumed in the repair process. At that time, these *product costs* become part of *cost of goods sold*, an *expense*. All of FastCar's other costs are *period costs*, and they are expensed as *operating expenses* during the period they are incurred. Examples of these period costs include employee salaries and wages, utilities, and depreciation on equipment and facilities.

Variable and Fixed Costs   The costs incurred in the FastCar service location that vary directly with activity are *variable costs*. For example, the cost of lubricant, engine oil, and oil filters is a variable cost, because it varies in proportion to the number of lube–oil–filter (LOF) jobs the service location provides. Thus, a likely *cost driver* for this cost would be the number of LOF jobs performed. In contrast, any costs that do not tend to vary with service activity are *fixed costs*. Examples include the service location's managerial salaries, depreciation on equipment and facilities, insurance, and property taxes.

Direct and Indirect Costs   Consider a typical service and repair job. The customer has requested a routine LOF job and an exhaust system repair, which requires a new muffler. The *direct costs* of this service and repair job (the *cost object*) include the parts and supplies used (lubricant, engine oil, oil filter, and a new muffler) and the wages of the automotive service technician for the time spent on this job. The many *indirect costs* of this service job include the service location manager's salary, the depreciation on the building, and the cost of utilities.

Now consider a different cost object—this FastCar service location. For this cost object, the manager's salary is a direct cost of the service location. However, the FastCar CEO's salary is an indirect cost of this particular service location.

Controllable and Uncontrollable Costs   Costs that are *controllable* by the manager of this service location include local advertising, assuming the manager is responsible for such local ad buys. A cost that is partially controllable by the manager might include heating costs. Although the manager has little control over electricity or heating oil prices, the manager can ensure that the service location's heating system is properly maintained and the windows and doors have the proper weatherstripping. Many of the service location's costs are largely *uncontrollable* by the manager. The depreciation, insurance, and property taxes on the building, for example, are the result of decisions made higher up in the organization.

Opportunity, Out-of-Pocket, and Sunk Costs   These cost types all are represented in the FastCar auto service business. Suppose the manager decides to shut down one of the service bays on a particular day to inspect and maintain the lift and other equipment. Any customer business that is lost that day due to a shortage of service bays would be an *opportunity cost* of the shutdown decision. (Note that such an opportunity cost does not necessarily mean the shutdown decision was a poor one. The opportunity cost of any lost business could well be exceeded by the additional operating costs that could be incurred if the service bay was not properly maintained.) The wages paid to service technicians and utility costs are examples of *out-of-pocket costs*. The money spent last year to replace an auto lift is an example of a *sunk cost*.

Differential, Marginal, and Average Costs   Suppose the service location owns a small van that makes runs to pick up auto parts needed on short notice. The van needs to be replaced, and two vehicles are under consideration. The difference in the cost of these two alternative vehicles is a *differential cost* of the vehicle replacement decision. The cost of performing one additional LOF job in a given time period is the *marginal cost* of that type of service. The total cost of all LOF jobs in a time period, divided by the number of jobs, is the average cost of an LOF job.

To summarize, although manufacturers, like Bombardier and Research In Motion, and service firms, like WestJet Airlines and Fairmont Hotels & Resorts, are in very different businesses, they all must understand their costs in order to be successful in a competitive environment.

Focus on Ethics

WAS WORLDCOM'S CONTROLLER JUST FOLLOWING ORDERS?

Through a series of mergers and acquisitions, WorldCom, Inc. grew to become North America's second-largest long-distance telecommunications company. WorldCom's core communication services included network data transmission over public and private networks. Trouble arose for WorldCom because of the immense overcapacity in the telecommunications industry due to overly optimistic growth projections during the Internet boom. The combination of overcapacity, decreased demand, and high fixed costs still poses a serious problem for many of the major players in the industry.

In June 2002, the company disclosed that it had overstated earnings for 2001 and the first quarter of 2002 to the tune of $3.8 billion. The overstatement arose because the company incorrectly classified period expenses as capital expenditures. This manoeuvre had two major effects on the company's financial statements: The company's assets were artificially inflated and the capitalization allowed the company to spread the recognition of its expenses into the future, which increased net income in the current period. The expenses in question related to line costs—the fees that WorldCom pays outside providers for access to their communications networks. In addition, the company announced in July 2002 that it had also manipulated reserve accounts, which affected another $3.8 billion in earnings in 1999 and 2000.

The problems at WorldCom were discovered during an internal audit and brought to the attention of the company's new auditors, KPMG. Arthur Andersen served as WorldCom's auditors during the period covered by the alleged accounting scandal. The auditing firm maintained that the details of the fraud were kept from them by senior management. WorldCom's controller and its chief financial officer (CFO), who was a former KPMG employee, were fired after the alleged accounting frauds were revealed. WorldCom's CEO maintained that he knew nothing of the accounting decisions made by the CFO, but many observers question how almost $8 billion in expenses could slip by senior management.[13]

According to an Associated Press article that ran on September 27, 2002, "The former controller of Worldcom, Inc. pleaded guilty to securities fraud charges, saying he was instructed by 'senior management' to falsify records in what became the largest corporate accounting scandal in U.S. history. His plea was the first admission of guilt in the multibillion dollar scandal."[14] Subsequently, WorldCom's CFO pleaded guilty to his part in the accounting scandal.[15] In March of 2005, the company's CEO was convicted by a jury of nine criminal counts in the accounting fraud, including conspiracy and securities fraud.[16]

The CFO and controller were the top two financial and management accountants in the WorldCom organization. They were ultimately responsible for all of the company's financial and managerial accounting reports. (Note that this case also involves the alleged intentional misclassification of period costs.)

What ethical issues are involved here? What do you make of the controller's assertion that he was just following orders given by senior management? What steps should WorldCom's controller have taken? (Review the Code of Professional Ethics of CMA Ontario in Chapter 1.)

Chapter Summary

LO1 Explain the meaning of *cost*. The word *cost* can have a variety of meanings in different situations. In general, a cost is the sacrifice made, usually measured by the resources given up, to achieve a particular purpose.

LO2 Distinguish among product costs, period costs, and expenses. A product cost is a cost assigned to manufactured or purchased goods. Period costs are those associated with the period of time in which they are incurred. An expense is the cost incurred when an asset is used up for the purpose of generating revenue.

LO3 Describe the role of costs in financial statements. The cost of goods sold is an expense on the income statement. Inventory on the balance sheet is measured at its cost, as are all assets.

LO4 List five types of manufacturing operations and describe one of them: mass customization. The five basic types of manufacturing operations are job shop, batch, assembly line, mass customization, and continuous flow. In a mass-customization production environment, many standardized components are used to manufacture customized products to customer order.

LO5 Give examples of three types of manufacturing costs. Manufacturing costs are categorized as direct material, direct labour, and manufacturing overhead.

LO6 Prepare a schedule of cost of goods manufactured, a schedule of cost of goods sold, and an income statement for a manufacturer. These accounting schedules, which are illustrated in the chapter, provide information to management about the costs incurred in a production operation.

LO7 Understand the importance of identifying an organization's cost drivers. A cost driver is any activity or event that causes costs to be incurred. Understanding the cost drivers in an organization is an essential component of managing those costs.

LO8 Describe the behaviour of variable and fixed costs, in total and on a per-unit basis. As activity in an organization increases, a variable cost increases proportionately to activity in total, but remains constant on a per-unit basis. In contrast, as activity in an organization increases, a fixed cost remains constant in total but decreases on a per-unit basis.

LO9 Distinguish among direct, indirect, controllable, and uncontrollable costs. Direct and indirect costs refer to the ability of the accountant to trace costs to various departments in the organization. The terms *controllable* and *uncontrollable* are used to describe the extent to which a manager can influence a cost.

LO10 Define and give examples of an *opportunity cost*, an *out-of-pocket cost*, a *sunk cost*, a *differential cost*, a *marginal cost*, and an *average cost per unit*. An opportunity cost is the benefit foregone because the choice of one action precludes another action. An out-of-pocket cost requires the payment of cash or other assets. Sunk costs are costs incurred in the past that cannot be altered by a current or future decision. A differential (or incremental) cost refers to the difference in the costs incurred under two alternative actions. A marginal cost is the cost of producing one additional unit. Finally, the average cost per unit is the total cost for whatever quantity is produced, divided by the number of units produced.

Review Problems on Cost Classifications

Problem 1

Several costs incurred by Myrtle Beach Golf Equipment, Inc. are listed below. For each cost, indicate which of the following classifications best describe(s) the cost. More than one classification may apply to the same cost item. For example, a cost may be both a variable cost and a product cost.

Cost Classifications

a. Variable

b. Fixed

c. Period

d. Product

e. Administrative

f. Selling

g. Manufacturing

h. Research and development

i. Direct material

j. Direct labour

k. Manufacturing overhead

Cost Items

1. Metal used in golf clubs

2. Salary of the plant manager

3. Cost of natural gas used to heat the factory

4. Commissions paid to salespersons

5. Wages paid to employees who assemble golf bags

6. Salary of an engineer who is working on a prototype of a new solar-powered golf cart

7. Depreciation on the computer used by the secretary of the company's president

Problem 2

Listed below are several costs incurred in the loan department of Atlantic Coast Savings. For each cost, indicate which of the following classifications best describe(s) the cost. More than one classification may apply to the same cost item.

Cost Classifications

a. Controllable by the loan department manager

b. Uncontrollable by the loan department manager

c. Direct cost of the loan department

d. Indirect cost of the loan department

e. Differential cost

f. Marginal cost

g. Opportunity cost

h. Sunk cost

i. Out-of-pocket cost

Cost Items

1. Salary of the loan department manager

2. Cost of office supplies used in the loan department

3. Cost of the department's personal computers purchased by the loan department manager last year

4. Cost of general advertising by the bank, which is allocated to the loan department

5. Revenue that the loan department would have generated for the bank if a branch loan office had been located downtown instead of in the suburbs

6. Difference in the cost incurred by the bank when one additional loan application is processed

Solutions to Review Problems
Problem 1

1. a, d, g, i	**2.** b, d, g, k	**3.** a, d, g, k	**4.** a, c, f	**5.** a, d, g, j
6. b, c, h	**7.** b, c, e			

Problem 2

1. b, c, i	**2.** a, c, i	**3.** a, c, h	**4.** b, d, i	**5.** g	**6.** e, f

Glossary

Review key terms and definitions on Connect.

Review Questions

2–1. Distinguish between product costs and period costs.

2–2. Why are product costs also called *inventoriable costs*?

2–3. What is the most important difference between a manufacturing firm and a service industry firm, with regard to the classification of costs as product costs or period costs?

2–4. List, describe, and give an example of each of the five different types of production processes.

2–5. "The words *mass* and *customization* in the term *mass customization* seem contradictory." Do you agree or disagree? Explain.

2–6. Why is the cost of idle time treated as manufacturing overhead?

2–7. Explain why an overtime premium is included in manufacturing overhead.

2–8. What is meant by the phrase "different costs for different purposes"?

2–9. Give examples to illustrate how a city could use cost information in planning, controlling costs, and making decisions.

2–10. Distinguish between fixed costs and variable costs.

2–11. How does the fixed cost per unit change as the level of activity (or cost driver) increases? Why?

2–12. How does the variable cost per unit change as the level of activity (or cost driver) increases? Why?

2–13. Distinguish between volume-based and operations-based cost drivers in the airline industry.

2–14. Would each of the following characteristics be a volume-based or an operations-based cost driver in a college or university: (*a*) number of students, (*b*) number of disciplines offered for study, and (*c*) urban versus rural location?

2–15. List three direct costs of the food and beverage department in a hotel. List three indirect costs of the department.

2–16. List three costs that are likely to be controllable by a city's airport manager. List three costs that are likely to be uncontrollable by the manager.

2–17. Which of the following costs are likely to be controllable by the chief of nursing in a hospital?

a. Cost of medication administered

b. Cost of overtime paid to nurses due to scheduling errors

c. Cost of depreciation of hospital beds

2–18. Distinguish between out-of-pocket costs and opportunity costs.

2–19. Define the terms *sunk cost* and *differential cost*.

2–20. Distinguish between marginal and average costs.

2–21. Think about the process of registering for classes at your college or university.

a. What additional information would you like to have before you register?

b. How would it help you?

c. What sort of information might create information overload for you?

2–22. Two years ago, the manager of a large department store purchased new bar-code scanners costing $39,000. A salesperson recently tried to sell the manager a new computer-integrated checkout system for the store. The new system would save the store a substantial amount of money each year. The recently purchased scanners could be sold in the second-hand market for $19,000. The store manager refused to listen to the salesperson, saying, "I just bought those scanners. I can't get rid of them until I get my money's worth out of them."

a. What type of cost is the cost of purchasing the old bar-code scanners?

b. What common behavioural tendency is the manager exhibiting?

2–23. Indicate whether each of the following costs is a direct cost or an indirect cost of the restaurant in a hotel.

a. Cost of food served

b. Chef's salary and fringe benefits

c. Part of the cost of maintaining the grounds around the hotel, which is allocated to the restaurant

d. Part of the cost of advertising the hotel, which is allocated to the restaurant

Exercises

Exercise 2–24 Cost of Goods Manufactured and Sold: Missing Data (LO1, 3, 6)

For each case below, find the missing amount.

	Case I	Case II	Case III
Beginning inventory of finished goods	?	$12,000	$ 7,000
Cost of goods manufactured during period	$419,000	$95,000	?
Ending inventory of finished goods	98,000	8,000	21,000
Cost of goods sold	405,000	?	304,000

Exercise 2–25 Idle Time (LO5)

A foundry employee worked a normal 40-hour shift, but four hours were idle due to a small fire in the plant. The employee earns $18 per hour.

Required:

1. Calculate the employee's total compensation for the week.
2. How much of this compensation is a direct-labour cost? How much is overhead?

Exercise 2–26 Overtime Cost (LO5)

A loom operator in a textiles factory earns $16 per hour. The employee earns $20 for overtime hours. The operator worked 45 hours during the first week of May, instead of the usual 40 hours.

Required:

1. Compute the loom operator's compensation for the week.
2. Calculate the employee's total overtime premium for the week.
3. How much of the employee's total compensation for the week is direct-labour cost? How much is overhead?

Exercise 2–27 Mass Customization: Use of the Internet (LO4)

Go to Dell Inc.'s website: www.dell.com

Required: Read on the company's website about how Dell operates and serves its customers. Then briefly explain whether you believe mass customization to be the best type of manufacturing process for Dell.

Exercise 2–28 Cost Classifications (LO2, 8, 9)

Consider the following costs that were incurred during the current year:

1. Tire costs incurred by Ford Motor Company
2. Sales commissions paid to the sales force of Dell Inc.
3. Wood glue consumed in the manufacture of Palliser Furniture Upholstery Ltd.
4. Hourly wages of refinery security guards employed by Petro-Canada
5. The salary of a financial vice-president of Sony Canada
6. Advertising costs of Coca-Cola
7. Straight-line depreciation on factory machinery of Bombardier Corporation
8. Wages of assembly-line employees of Whirlpool Canada
9. Delivery costs on customer shipments of Chapman's Ice Cream
10. Newsprint consumed in printing *The Globe and Mail*
11. Plant insurance costs of Research In Motion
12. Glass costs incurred in light-bulb manufacturing of Sylvania

Required: Evaluate each of the preceding and determine whether the cost is (*a*) a product cost or a period cost, (*b*) variable or fixed in terms of behaviour, and (*c*) for the product costs only, whether the cost is properly classified as direct material, direct labour, or manufacturing overhead. Item 1 is done as an example:

Tire costs: Product cost, variable, direct material

Exercise 2–29 Schedules of Cost of Goods Manufactured and Sold; Income Statement (LO1, 3, 6)

Alexandra Aluminum Company, a manufacturer of recyclable soda cans, had the following inventory balances at the beginning and end of 20x1.

Inventory Classification	January 1, 20x1	December 31, 20x1
Raw material	$ 60,000	$ 70,000
Work in process	120,000	115,000
Finished goods	150,000	165,000

During 20x1, the company purchased $250,000 of raw material and spent $400,000 on direct labour. Manufacturing-overhead costs were as follows:

Indirect material	$ 10,000
Indirect labour	25,000
Depreciation on plant and equipment	100,000
Utilities	25,000
Other	30,000

Sales revenue was $1,105,000 for the year. Selling and administrative expenses for the year amounted to $110,000. The firm's tax rate is 40 percent.

Required:

1. Prepare a schedule of cost of goods manufactured.
2. Prepare a schedule of cost of goods sold.
3. Prepare an income statement.
4. *Build a spreadsheet:* Construct an Excel spreadsheet to handle all of the preceding requirements. Show how both cost schedules and the income statement will change if the following data change: direct labour is $390,000 and utilities cost $35,000.

Exercise 2–30 Fixed and Variable Costs: Automobile Service; Missing Data (LO1, 8)

Mighty Muffler, Inc. operates an automobile service facility that specializes in replacing mufflers on compact cars. The following table shows the costs incurred during a month when 600 mufflers were replaced.

	Muffler Replacements		
	500	600	700
Total costs:			
Fixed costs	a	$42,000	b
Variable costs	c	30,000	d
Total costs	e	$72,000	f
Cost per muffler replacement:			
Fixed cost	g	h	i
Variable cost	j	k	l
Total cost per muffler replacement	m	n	o

Required: Fill in the missing amounts, labelled (a) through (o), in the table.

Exercise 2–31 Fixed, Variable, Marginal, and Average Costs: Hotel (LO1, 8, 10)

A hotel pays the phone company $100 per month plus $0.25 for each call made. During January, 6,000 calls were made. In February, 5,000 calls were made.

Required:

1. Calculate the hotel's phone bills for January and February.
2. Calculate the cost per phone call in January and in February.
3. Separate the January phone bill into its fixed and variable components.
4. What is the marginal cost of one additional phone call in January?
5. What was the average cost of a phone call in January?

Exercise 2–32 Economic Characteristics of Costs (LO1, 10)

Martin Shrood purchased a vacant lot outside of London for £13,500, because he heard that a shopping mall was going to be built on the other side of the road. He figured that he could make a bundle by putting in a fast-food outlet on the site. As it turned out, the rumour was false. A sanitary landfill was located on the other side of the road, and the land was worthless. (£ denotes the British monetary unit, pounds sterling.)

Required: What type of cost is the £13,500 that Martin paid for the vacant lot?

Exercise 2–33 Differential Cost (LO1, 10)

Orbital Communications, Inc. manufactures communications satellites used in TV signal transmission. The firm currently purchases one component for its satellites from a European firm. An Orbital Communications engineering team has found a way to use the company's own component, Part A200, instead of the European component. However, the Orbital Communications component must be modified at a cost of $500 per part. The European component costs $8,900 per part. Orbital Communications' Part A200 costs $5,100 before it is modified. Orbital Communications currently uses 10 of the European components per year.

Required: Calculate the annual differential cost between Orbital Communications' two production alternatives.

Exercise 2–34 Computing Costs: Government Agency **(LO1, 9, 10)**

A province's Ministry of Education owns a computer system, which its employees use for word processing and keeping track of education statistics. The premier's office recently began using this computer system, also. As a result of the increased usage, the demands on the computer system soon exceeded its capacity. The director of Management Services for the Ministry of Education was soon forced to lease several personal computers to meet the computing needs of her employees. The annual cost of leasing the equipment is $14,000.

Required:

1. Is this $14,000 an opportunity cost? Why or why not?
2. Should this cost be associated with the premier's office or the Ministry of Education? Why?

Exercise 2–35 Economic Characteristics of Costs **(LO1, 10)**

Suppose you paid $60 for a ticket to see your city's hockey team compete in a championship game. Someone offered to buy your ticket for $100, but you decided to go to the game.

Required:

1. What did it really cost you to see the game?
2. What type of cost is this?

Exercise 2–36 Marginal Costs **(LO1, 10)**

List the costs that would likely be included in each of the following marginal cost calculations:

1. The marginal cost of one additional passenger on an Air Canada flight
2. The marginal cost of serving one additional customer in a White Spot restaurant
3. The marginal cost of WestJet adding a flight from Toronto to Vancouver
4. The marginal cost of keeping a branch of a TD Canada Trust branch open one additional hour on Saturdays
5. The marginal cost of manufacturing one additional BRP Ski-Doo

Problems

Problem 2–37 Content of Financial Statements and Reports; Mass Customization **(LO3, 4)**

Consider the following cost items:

1. Salaries of players on the Vancouver Canucks team
2. Year-end completed goods of Roots pants
3. Executive compensation costs at Home Depot
4. Advertising costs for Sony
5. Costs incurred to insure a Ford plant against fire and flood losses
6. Current year's depreciation on an S-Class ship owned by BC Ferries
7. The cost of chemicals and paper used by Kodak
8. Assembly-line wage cost incurred by Rocky Mountain Bicycles
9. Year-end production in process at Dell Inc.
10. The cost of products sold to customers at The Bay
11. The cost of products sold to authorized Apple resellers

Required:

1. Evaluate the costs just cited, and determine whether the associated dollar amounts would be found on the firm's balance sheet, income statement, or schedule of cost of goods manufactured. (*Note:* In some cases, more than one answer will apply.)
2. What major asset will normally be insignificant for service enterprises and relatively substantial for retailers, wholesalers, and manufacturers? Briefly discuss.
3. Briefly explain the major differences between income statements of service enterprises versus those of retailers, wholesalers, and manufacturers.

4. Picture the operations of a firm such as Dell Inc., one that is involved in direct sales and mass customization of products. What would be the major difference in the balance sheet of this type of organization versus the balance sheet of a company that engages in more traditional manufacturing activities, that is, producing goods and waiting for customer orders to arrive?

Problem 2–38 Financial Statement Elements: Manufacturer **(LO5, 6)**

The following selected information was extracted from the 20x1 accounting records of Lone Oak Products:

Raw material purchases	$ 175,000
Direct labour	254,000
Indirect labour	109,000
Selling and administrative salaries	133,000
Building depreciation*	80,000
Other selling and administrative expenses	195,000
Other factory costs	344,000
Sales revenue ($130 per unit)	1,495,000

*Seventy-five percent of the company's building was devoted to production activities; the remaining 25 percent was used for selling and administrative functions.

Inventory data:

	January 1	December 31
Raw material	$ 15,800	$18,200
Work in process	35,700	62,100
Finished goods*	111,100	97,900

*The January 1 and December 31 finished-goods inventory consisted of 1,350 units and 1,190 units, respectively.

Required:

1. Calculate the company's manufacturing overhead for the year.
2. Calculate the company's cost of goods manufactured.
3. Compute the company's cost of goods sold.
4. Determine net income for 20x1, assuming a 30 percent income tax rate.
5. Determine the number of completed units manufactured during the year.
6. *Build a spreadsheet:* Construct an Excel spreadsheet to solve all of the preceding requirements. Show how the solution will change if the following data change: indirect labour is $115,000 and other factory costs amount to $516,000.

2. Cost of goods manufactured: $913,200
4. Net income: $154,420

For most problems, selected key figures from the solution appear in the margin.

eXcel

Problem 2–39 Inventory Estimates: Partial Data **(LO5, 6)**

On April 12, after the close of business, Singh & Sons had a devastating fire that destroyed the company's work-in-process and finished-goods inventories. Fortunately, all raw materials escaped damage, because materials owned by the firm were stored in another warehouse. The following information is available:

Direct material used: $40,000

Sales revenue through April 12	$330,000
Income before taxes through April 12	68,000
Direct labour through April 12	120,000
Cost of goods available for sale, April 12	275,000
Work-in-process inventory, January 1	21,000
Finished-goods inventory, January 1	37,000
Gross margin	30% of sales

The firm's accountants determined that the cost of direct materials used normally averages 25 percent of prime costs (i.e., direct material plus direct labour). In addition, manufacturing overhead is 50 percent of the firm's total production costs.

Required: The company is in the process of negotiating a settlement with its insurance company. Prepare an estimate of the cost of work-in-process and finished-goods inventories that were destroyed by the fire.

Problem 2–40 Financial Statement Elements; Cost Behaviour (LO5, 6, 8)

2. Net income: $168,000

Mason Corporation began operations at the beginning of the current year. One of the company's products, a refrigeration element, sells for $185 per unit. Information related to the current year's activities follows.

Variable costs per unit:		
Direct material..	$	20
Direct labour		37
Manufacturing overhead		48
Annual fixed costs:		
Manufacturing overhead		$600,000
Selling and administrative		860,000
Sales and production activity:		
Sales (units)..		20,000
Production (units)...		24,000

Mason carries its finished-goods inventory at the average unit cost of production and is subject to a 30 percent income tax rate. There was no work in process at year-end.

Required:

1. Determine the cost of the December 31 finished-goods inventory.
2. Compute Mason's net income for the current year ended December 31.
3. If next year's production decreases to 23,000 units and general cost behaviour patterns do not change, what is the likely effect on
    a. The direct-labour cost of $37 per unit? Why?
    b. The fixed manufacturing-overhead cost of $600,000? Why?
    c. The fixed selling and administrative cost of $860,000? Why?
    d. The average unit cost of production? Why?

Problem 2–41 Incomplete Data: Manufacturing Costs (LO2, 5)

Net income,
Case A: $110,000

Determine the missing amounts in each of the following independent cases.

	Case A	Case B	Case C
Beginning inventory, raw material..	?	20,000	15,000
Ending inventory, raw material...	90,000	?	30,000
Purchases of raw material..	100,000	85,000	?
Direct material used	70,000	95,000	?
Direct labour	?	100,000	125,000
Manufacturing overhead	250,000	?	160,000
Total manufacturing costs	520,000	345,000	340,000
Beginning inventory, work in process	35,000	20,000	?
Ending inventory, work in process	?	35,000	5,000
Cost of goods manufactured	525,000	?	350,000
Beginning inventory, finished goods	50,000	40,000	?
Cost of goods available for sale	?	?	370,000
Ending inventory, finished goods	?	?	25,000
Cost of goods sold	545,000	330,000	?
Sales	$?	$?	$480,000
Gross margin...	255,000	170,000	?
Selling and administrative expenses	?	75,000	?
Income before taxes	150,000	?	90,000
Income tax expense	40,000	45,000	?
Net income	?	?	55,000

Problem 2–42 Cost Terminology (LO2, 5, 10)

The following cost data for the year just ended pertain to Sentiments, Inc., a greeting card manufacturer:

Direct material	$2,100,000
Advertising expense	99,000
Depreciation on factory building	115,000
Direct labour: Wages	485,000
Cost of finished-goods inventory at year-end	115,000
Indirect labour: Wages	140,000
Production supervisor's salary	45,000
Service department costs*	100,000
Direct labour: Fringe benefits	95,000
Indirect labour: Fringe benefits	30,000
Fringe benefits for production supervisor	9,000
Total overtime premiums paid	55,000
Cost of idle time: Production employees†	40,000
Administrative costs	150,000
Rental of office space for salespersons§	15,000
Sales commissions	5,000
Product promotion costs	10,000

*All services are provided to manufacturing departments.

†Cost of idle time is an overhead item; it is not included in the direct-labour wages given above.

§The rental of sales space was made necessary when the sales offices were converted to storage space for raw material.

Required:

1. Compute each of the following costs for the year just ended: (*a*) total prime costs, (*b*) total manufacturing-overhead costs, (*c*) total conversion costs, (*d*) total product costs, and (*e*) total period costs.
2. One of the costs listed above is an opportunity cost. Identify this cost, and explain why it is an opportunity cost.

Problem 2–43 Schedules of Cost of Goods Manufactured and Sold; Income Statement **(LO1, 3, 5, 6)**

The following data are for Atelier Alexandre for the year 20x2:

Sales revenue	$950,000
Work-in-process inventory, December 31	30,000
Work-in-process inventory, January 1	40,000
Selling and administrative expenses	150,000
Income tax expense	90,000
Purchases of raw material	180,000
Raw-material inventory, December 31	25,000
Raw-material inventory, January 1	40,000
Direct labour	200,000
Utilities: Plant	40,000
Depreciation: Plant and equipment	60,000
Finished-goods inventory, December 31	50,000
Finished-goods inventory, January 1	20,000
Indirect material	10,000
Indirect labour	15,000
Other manufacturing overhead	80,000

Required:

1. Prepare the company's schedule of cost of goods manufactured for the year.
2. Prepare the company's schedule of cost of goods sold for the year.
3. Prepare the company's income statement for the year.
4. *Build a spreadsheet:* Construct an Excel spreadsheet to solve all of the preceding requirements. Show how both cost schedules and the income statement will change if raw-material purchases amounted to $190,000 and indirect labour was $20,000.

2. Total cost of wages: $608

Problem 2–44   Direct and Indirect Labour **(LO1, 5, 9)**

Highlander Cutlery manufactures kitchen knives. One of the employees, whose job is to cut out wooden knife handles, worked 48 hours during a week in January. The employee earns $12 per hour for a 40-hour week. For additional hours, the employee is paid an overtime rate of $16 per hour. The employee's time was spent as follows:

Regular duties involving cutting out knife handles	38 hours
General shop cleanup duties	9 hours
Idle time due to power outage	1 hours

Required:

1. Calculate the total cost of the employee's wages during the week described above.

2. Determine the portion of this cost to be classified in each of the following categories:

    a.   Direct labour

    b.   Manufacturing overhead (idle time)

    c.   Manufacturing overhead (overtime premium)

    d.   Manufacturing overhead (indirect labour)

Problem 2–45   Cost Classifications **(LO5, 8, 9)**

Cape Breton Shirt Shop manufactures T-shirts and decorates them with custom designs for retail sale on the premises. Several costs incurred by the company are listed below. For each cost, indicate which of the following classifications best describe(s) the cost. More than one classification may apply to the same cost item.

Cost Classifications

a. Variable

b. Fixed

c. Period

d. Product

e. Administrative

f. Selling

g. Manufacturing

h. Research and development

i. Direct material

j. Direct labour

k. Manufacturing overhead

Cost Items

1. Cost of fabric used in T-shirts

2. Wages of shirtmakers

3. Cost of new sign in front of retail T-shirt shop

4. Wages of the employee who repairs the firm's sewing machines

5. Cost of electricity used in the sewing department

6. Wages of T-shirt designers and painters

7. Wages of salespersons

8. Depreciation on sewing machines

9. Rent on the building. Part of the building's first floor is used to make and paint T-shirts. Part of it is used for the retail sales shop. The second floor is used for administrative offices and storage of raw material and finished goods.

10. Cost of daily advertisements in local media

11. Wages of designers who experiment with new fabrics, paints, and T-shirt designs

12. Cost of hiring a pilot to fly along the beach pulling a banner advertising the shop

13. Salary of the owner's secretary

14. Cost of repairing the gas furnace

15. Cost of insurance for the production employees

Problem 2–46 Overtime Premiums and Fringe Benefit Costs: Airline (LO1, 3, 5, 9, 10)

Heartland Airways operates commuter flights in several provinces. Due to a political convention held in Toronto, the airline added several extra flights during a two-week period. Additional cabin crews were hired on a temporary basis. However, rather than hiring additional flight attendants, the airline used its current attendants on overtime. Monica Gaines worked the following schedule on August 10. All of Gaines's flights on that day were extra flights that the airline would not normally fly.

> Regular time: 2 round-trip flights between Toronto and Ottawa (4 hours)
> Overtime: 1 one-way flight from Toronto to Thunder Bay (1.5 hours)

Gaines earns $12 per hour plus time and a half for overtime. Fringe benefits cost the airline $3 per hour for any hour worked, regardless of whether it is a regular or overtime hour.

Required:

1. Compute the direct cost of compensating Gaines for her services on the flight from Toronto to Thunder Bay.
2. Compute the cost of Gaines' services that is an indirect cost.
3. How should the cost computed in requirement (2) be treated for cost accounting purposes?
4. Gaines ended her workday on August 10 in Thunder Bay. However, her next scheduled flight departed Toronto at 11 a.m. on August 11. This required Gaines to "deadhead" back to Toronto on an early-morning flight. This means she travelled from Thunder Bay to Toronto as a passenger, rather than as a working flight attendant. Since the morning flight from Thunder Bay to Toronto was full, Gaines displaced a paying customer. The revenue lost by the airline was $82. What type of cost is the $82? To what flight, if any, is it chargeable? Why?

Problem 2–47 Variable Costs: Graphical and Tabular Analyses (LO8)

Richmond Sheet Metal Corp. incurs a variable cost of $40 per kilogram for raw material to produce a special alloy used in manufacturing aircraft.

Required:

1. Draw a graph of the firm's raw-material cost, showing the total cost at the following production levels: 10,000 kilograms, 20,000 kilograms, and 30,000 kilograms.
2. Prepare a table that shows the unit cost and total cost of raw material at the following production levels: 1 kilograms, 10 kilograms, and 1,000 kilograms.

Problem 2–48 Fixed Costs: Graphical and Tabular Analyses (LO8)

Hightide Upholstery Company manufactures a special fabric used to upholster the seats in power boats. The company's annual fixed production cost is $100,000.

Required:

1. Draw a graph of the company's fixed production cost showing the total cost at the following production levels of the fabric: 10,000 metres, 20,000 metres, 30,000 metres, and 40,000 metres.
2. Prepare a table that shows the unit cost and the total cost for the firm's fixed production costs at the following production levels: 1 metre, 10 metres, 10,000 metres, and 40,000 metres.
3. Prepare a graph that shows the unit cost for the company's fixed production cost at the following production levels: 10,000 metres, 20,000 metres, 30,000 metres, and 40,000 metres.

Problem 2–49 Direct, Indirect, Controllable, and Uncontrollable Costs (LO1, 9)

For each of the following costs, indicate whether the amount is a direct or indirect cost of the equipment-maintenance department. Also indicate whether each cost is at least partially controllable by the department supervisor.

1. Cost of plant manager's salary, which is allocated to the maintenance department
2. Cost of property taxes allocated to the maintenance department
3. Cost of electricity used in the maintenance department
4. Depreciation on the building space occupied by the maintenance department
5. Idle time of maintenance department employees

Problem 2–50 Product Costs and Period Costs **(LO1, 2, 3)**

Indicate for each of the following costs whether it is a product cost or a period cost.

1. Wages of aircraft mechanics employed by an airline
2. Wages of drill-press operators in a manufacturing plant
3. Cost of food in a microwaveable dinner
4. Cost incurred by a department store chain to transport merchandise to its stores
5. Cost of grapes purchased by a winery
6. Depreciation on pizza ovens in a pizza restaurant
7. Cost of plant manager's salary in a computer production facility
8. Wages of security guards in a department store
9. Cost of utilities in a manufacturing facility

Problem 2–51 Fixed and Variable Costs; Forecasting **(LO7, 8)**

Warner Technology incurred the following costs during 20x1. The company sold all of its products manufactured during the year.

Direct material, 20X2
forecast: $3,600,000

Direct material	$3,000,000
Direct labour	2,200,000
Manufacturing overhead:	
Utilities (primarily electricity)	140,000
Depreciation on plant and equipment	230,000
Insurance	160,000
Supervisory salaries	300,000
Property taxes	210,000
Selling costs:	
Advertising	195,000
Sales commissions	90,000
Administrative costs:	
Salaries of top management and staff	372,000
Office supplies	40,000
Depreciation on building and equipment	80,000

During 20x1, the company operated at about half of its capacity, due to a slowdown in the economy. Prospects for 20x2 are slightly better. Jared Lazinsky, the marketing manager, forecasts a 20 percent growth in sales over the 20x1 level.

Required: Categorize each of the costs listed above as to whether it is most likely variable or fixed. Forecast the 20x2 cost amount for each of the cost items listed above.

Problem 2–52 Economic Characteristics of Costs **(LO4, 10)**

The following terms are used to describe various economic characteristics of costs.

a. Opportunity cost
b. Out-of-pocket cost
c. Sunk cost
d. Differential cost
e. Marginal cost
f. Average cost

Required: Choose one of the terms listed above to characterize each of the amounts described below.

1. The cost of feeding 500 children in a public school cafeteria is $800 per day, or $1.60 per child per day. What economic term describes this $1.60 cost?
2. The cost of including one extra child in a daycare centre
3. The cost of merchandise inventory purchased two years ago, which is now obsolete
4. The management of a high-rise office building uses 2,500 m² of space in the building for its own management functions. This space could be rented for $250,000. What economic term describes this $250,000 in lost rental revenue?
5. The cost of building an automated assembly line in a factory is $800,000. The cost of building a manually operated assembly line is $375,000. What economic term is used to describe the difference between these two amounts?
6. Referring to the preceding question, what economic term is used to describe the $800,000 cost of building the automated assembly line?

7. The cost incurred by a mass customizer such as Dell Inc. to produce one more unit in its most popular line of laptop computers?

Problem 2–53 Cost Classifications: Hotel (L01, 3, 9, 10)
Several costs incurred by Bayview Hotel and Restaurant are given in the following list. For each cost, indicate which of the following classifications best describe(s) the cost. More than one classification may apply to the same cost item.

Cost Classifications

a. Direct cost of the food and beverage department
b. Indirect cost of the food and beverage department
c. Controllable by the kitchen manager
d. Uncontrollable by the kitchen manager
e. Controllable by the hotel general manager
f. Uncontrollable by the hotel general manager
g. Differential cost
h. Marginal cost
i. Opportunity cost
j. Sunk cost
k. Out-of-pocket cost

Cost Items

1. The cost of general advertising by the hotel, which is allocated to the food and beverage department
2. The cost of food used in the kitchen
3. The difference in the total cost incurred by the hotel when one additional guest is registered
4. The cost of space (depreciation) occupied by the kitchen
5. The cost of space (depreciation) occupied by a sauna next to the pool, space that could otherwise have been used for a newsstand
6. The profit that would have been earned in a newsstand, if the hotel had one
7. The discount on room rates given as a special offer for a "Labour Day Getaway Special"
8. The wages earned by food and beverage servers
9. The salary of the kitchen manager
10. The cost of the refrigerator purchased 13 months ago. The unit was covered by a warranty for 12 months, during which time it worked perfectly. It stopped working after 13 months, despite an original estimate that it would last five years.
11. The hotel has two options for obtaining fresh pies, cakes, and pastries. The goodies can be purchased from a local bakery for approximately $1,600 per month, or they can be made in the hotel's kitchen. To make the pastries on the premises, the hotel will have to hire a part-time pastry chef. This will cost $600 per month. The cost of ingredients will amount to roughly $700 per month. Thus, the savings from making the goods in the hotel's kitchen amount to $300 per month.
12. The cost of dishes broken by kitchen employees
13. The cost of leasing a computer used for reservations, payroll, and general hotel accounting
14. The cost of a pool service that cleans and maintains the hotel's swimming pool
15. The wages of the hotel's maintenance employees, who spent 11 hours (at $14 per hour) repairing the dishwasher in the kitchen

Problem 2–54 Interpretation of Accounting Reports (L01, 3)
Refer to Exhibit 2–3, and answer the following questions.

Required:

1. List the major differences between the income statements shown for WestJet, Caterpillar, and Walmart.
2. Explain how cost accounting data were used to prepare these income statements.
3. On the income statement for WestJet, where would the ticket agents' salaries be shown? Where would the costs of the computer equipment used to keep track of reservations be included on the statement?
4. On the income statement for Walmart, where would the cost of newspaper advertising be shown? How about the cost of merchandise?

5. Refer to the income statement for Caterpillar. Where would the salary of the brand manager who plans advertising for Caterpillar equipment be shown? How about the salary of a production employee? Where would the cost of the raw materials used in the company's products be included on the statement?

Problem 2–55 Marginal Costs and Average Costs (LO7, 10)

Roberta Coy makes custom mooring covers for boats. Each mooring cover is hand-sewn to fit a particular boat. If covers are made for two or more identical boats, each successive cover generally requires less time to make. Coy has been approached by a local boat dealer to make mooring covers for all of the boats sold by the dealer. Coy has developed the following cost schedule for mooring covers made to fit outboard power boats.

6. $370

Mooring Covers Made	Total Cost of Covers
1	$ 450
2	850
3	1,210
4	1,540
5	1,850

Required: Compute the following:

1. Marginal cost of second mooring cover
2. Marginal cost of fourth mooring cover
3. Marginal cost of fifth mooring cover
4. Average cost if two mooring covers are made
5. Average cost if four mooring covers are made
6. Average cost if five mooring covers are made

Problem 2–56 Cost Classifications: Government Agency (LO 8, 9, 10)

A Parks and Recreation division is responsible for maintaining the province's parks and forest lands, and generally overseeing the protection of the environment. Several costs incurred by the agency are listed below. For each cost, indicate which of the following classifications best describe(s) the cost. More than one classification may apply to the same cost item.

Cost Classifications

a. Variable
b. Fixed
c. Controllable by the Parks director
d. Uncontrollable by the Parks director
e. Differential cost
f. Marginal cost
g. Opportunity cost
h. Sunk cost
i. Out-of-pocket cost
j. Direct cost of the agency
k. Indirect cost of the agency
l. Direct cost of providing a particular service
m. Indirect cost of providing a particular service

Cost Items

1. Cost of the automobiles used by Parks rangers. These cars were purchased by the province and they would otherwise have been used by the Sheriff Services
2. Cost of live-trapping and moving beavers that were creating a nuisance in recreational lakes
3. The agency director's salary
4. Cost of containing naturally caused forest fires, which are threatening private property
5. Cost of maintaining recreational trails in the various provincial parks
6. The difference between (a) the cost of maintaining recreational trails by staff in the various provincial parks and (b) the cost of contracting out the maintenance of recreational trails

7. Cost of producing literature that describes the agency's role in environmental protection and is mailed free, on request, to schools, local governments, libraries, and private citizens

8. Cost of sending the agency's hydro engineers to inspect one additional dam for stability and safety

9. Cost of operating the provincial computer services department, a portion of which is allocated to the Parks and Recreation division

10. Cost of administrative supplies used in the agency's head office

11. Cost of providing a toll-free number for the province's residents to report environmental problems

12. Cost of replacing batteries in sophisticated monitoring equipment used to evaluate the effects of acid rain on the province's lakes

13. Cost of a ranger's salary, when the ranger is giving a talk about environmental protection to elementary-school children

14. Cost of direct-mailing to 1 million residents a brochure explaining the benefits of voluntarily recycling cans and bottles

15. The cost of producing a TV show to be aired on public television whose purpose is to educate people on how to spot and properly dispose of hazardous waste

Problem 2–57 Unit Costs; Profit-Maximizing Output (LO7, 8, 10)

The controller for Canandaigua Vineyards has predicted the following costs at various levels of wine output.

2. Output of 20,000, profit: $26,000

	Wine Output (0.75-litre bottles)		
	10,000 Bottles	**15,000 Bottles**	**20,000 Bottles**
Variable production costs	$ 37,000	$ 55,500	$ 74,000
Fixed production costs	100,000	100,000	100,000
Fixed selling and administrative costs	40,000	40,000	40,000
Total	$177,000	$195,500	$214,000

The company's marketing manager has predicted the following prices for the firm's fine wines at various levels of sales.

	Wine Sales		
	10,000 Bottles	**15,000 Bottles**	**20,000 Bottles**
Sales price per 0.75-litre bottle	$18.00	$15.00	$12.00

Required:

1. Calculate the unit costs of wine production at each level of output. At what level of output is the unit cost minimized?

2. Calculate the company's profit at each level of production. Assume that the company will sell all of its output. At what production level is profit maximized?

3. Which of the three output levels is best for the company profitwise?

4. Why does the unit cost of wine decrease as the output level increases?

Problem 2–58 Variable and Fixed Costs; Make or Buy a Component (LO8, 10)

Langley Industries currently manufactures 30,000 units of Part MR24 every month for use in production of several of its products. The facilities now used to produce Part MR24 have a fixed monthly cost of $150,000 and a capacity to produce 84,000 units per month. If the company was to buy Part MR24 from an outside supplier, the facilities would be idle, but its fixed costs would continue at 40 percent of their present amount. The variable production costs of Part MR24 are $11 per unit.

Required:

1. If Langley Industries continues to use 30,000 units of Part MR24 each month, it would realize a net benefit by purchasing Part MR24 from an outside supplier only if the supplier's unit price is less than what amount?

2. If Langley Industries is able to obtain Part MR24 from an outside supplier at a unit purchase price of $12.875, what is the monthly usage at which it will be indifferent between purchasing and making Part MR24?

(CMA, adapted)

Cases

Case 2–59 Economic Characteristics of Costs; Closing a Department; Ethics (LO1, 9, 10)

CompTech Company Limited manufactures printers for use with home computer systems. The firm currently manufactures both the electronic components for its printers and the plastic cases in which the devices are enclosed. Jim Cassanitti, the production manager, recently received a proposal from Universal Plastics Corporation to manufacture the cases for CompTech's printers. If the cases are purchased outside, CompTech will be able to close down its Printer Case Department. To help decide whether to accept the bid from Universal Plastics Corporation, Cassanitti asked CompTech's controller to prepare an analysis of the costs that would be saved if the Printer Case Department was closed. Included in the controller's list of annual cost savings were the following items:

Building rental (The Printer Case Department occupies one-sixth of the factory building, which CompTech rents for $177,000 per year.)	$29,500
Salary of the Printer Case Department supervisor	$50,000

In a lunchtime conversation with the controller, Cassanitti learned that CompTech was currently renting space in a warehouse for $39,000. The space is used to store completed printers. If the Printer Case Department was discontinued, the entire storage operation could be moved into the factory building and occupy the space vacated by the closed department. Cassanitti also learned that the supervisor of the Printer Case Department would be retained by CompTech even if the department was closed. The supervisor would be assigned the job of managing the assembly department, whose supervisor recently gave notice of his retirement. All of CompTech's department supervisors earn the same salary.

Required:

1. You have been hired as a consultant by Cassanitti to advise him in making his decision. Write a memo to Cassanitti commenting on the costs of space and supervisory salaries included in the controller's cost analysis. Explain in your memo about the "real" costs of the space occupied by the Printer Case Department and the supervisor's salary. What types of costs are these?

2. Independently of your response to requirement (1), suppose that CompTech's controller had been approached by his friend Jack McGinty, the assistant supervisor of the Printer Case Department. McGinty is worried that he will be laid off if the Printer Case Department is closed down.

   McGinty has asked his friend to understate the cost savings from closing the department in order to slant the production manager's decision toward keeping the department in operation. Comment on the controller's ethical responsibilities.

Case 2–60 Understanding Cost Concepts (LO7, 8, 10)

You just started a summer internship with the successful management consulting firm of Kirk, Spock, and McCoy. Your first day on the job was a busy one, as the following problems were presented to you.

Required: Supply the requested comments in each of the following independent situations.

1(a) 60,000 copies

1. SpeedyQ Company, a specialist in printing, has established 500 convenience copying centres throughout the country. In order to upgrade its services, the company is considering three new models of laser copying machines for use in producing high-quality copies. This copy production would be added to the growing list of services offered in the SpeedyQ shops. The selling price to the customer for each laser copy would be the same, no matter which machine is installed in the shop. The three models of laser copying machines under consideration are 1024S, a small-volume model; 1024M, a medium-volume model; and 1024G, a large-volume model. The annual rental costs and the operating costs vary with the size of each machine. The machine capacities and costs are as follows:

	Copier Model		
	1024S	**1024M**	**1024G**
Annual capacity (copies)	100,000	350,000	800,000
Costs:			
Annual machine rental	$ 8,000	$ 11,000	$ 20,000
Direct material and direct labour	0.02	0.02	0.02
Variable overhead costs	0.12	0.07	0.03

   a. Calculate the volume level in copies where SpeedyQ Company would be indifferent to acquiring either the small-volume model laser copier, 1024S, or the medium-volume model laser copier, 1024M.

   b. The management of SpeedyQ Company is able to estimate the number of copies to be sold at each establishment. Present a decision rule that would enable SpeedyQ Company to select the most profitable machine without having to make a separate cost calculation for each establishment. (*Hint:* To specify a decision rule, determine the volume at which SpeedyQ would be indifferent between the small and medium copiers. Then determine the volume at which SpeedyQ would be indifferent between the medium and large copiers.)

2. Alderon Enterprises is evaluating a special order it has received for a ceramic fixture to be used in aircraft engines. Alderon has recently been operating at less than full capacity, so the firm's management will accept the order if the price offered exceeds the costs that will be incurred in producing it. You have been asked for advice on how to determine the cost of two raw materials that would be required to produce the order.

   a. The special order will require 9,800 litres of endor, a highly perishable material that is purchased as needed. Alderon currently has 1,200 litres of endor on hand, since the material is used in virtually all of the company's products. The last time endor was purchased, Alderon paid $5 per litre. However, the average price paid for the endor in stock was only $4.75. The market price for endor is quite volatile, with the current price being $5.50. If the special order is accepted, Alderon will have to place a new order next week to replace the 800 litres of endor used. By then the price is expected to have reached $5.75 per litre.

       Using the cost terminology introduced in this chapter, comment on each of the cost figures mentioned in the preceding discussion. What is the real cost of endor if the special order is produced?

   b. The special order also would require 1,500 kilograms of tatooine, a material not normally required in any of Alderon's regular products. The company does happen to have 2,000 kilograms of tatooine on hand, since it formerly manufactured a ceramic product that used the material. Alderon recently received an offer of $14,000 from Solo Industries for its entire supply of tatooine. However, Solo Industries is not interested in buying any quantity less than Alderon's entire 2,000-kilogram stock. Alderon's management is unenthusiastic about Solo's offer, since Alderon paid $20,000 for the tatooine. Moreover, if the tatooine were purchased at today's market price, it would cost $11 per kilogram. Due to the volatility of tatooine, Alderon will need to get rid of its entire supply one way or another. If the material is not used in production or sold, Alderon will have to pay $1,000 for every 500 kilograms transported away and disposed of in a hazardous waste disposal site.

       Using the cost terminology introduced in this chapter, comment on each of the cost figures mentioned in the preceding discussion. What is the real cost of tatooine to be used in the special order?

3. A local TV station has decided to produce a TV series on state-of-the-art manufacturing. The director of the TV series, Justin Tyme, is currently attempting to analyze some of the projected costs for the series. Tyme intends to take a TV production crew on location to shoot various manufacturing scenes as they occur. If the four-week series is shown in the 8–9 p.m. prime-time slot, the station will have to cancel a currently scheduled wildlife show. Management projects a 10 percent viewing audience for the wildlife show, and each 1 percent is expected to bring in advertising revenues of $10,000. In contrast, the manufacturing show is expected to be watched by 15 percent of the viewing audience. However, each 1 percent of the viewership will likely generate only $5,000 in advertising revenues. If the wildlife show is cancelled, it can be sold to network television for $25,000.

       Using the cost terminology introduced in this chapter, comment on each of the financial amounts mentioned in the preceding discussion. What are the relative merits of the two shows regarding the projected revenue to the station?

(CMA, adapted)

 Practise and learn online with Connect.

CHAPTER THREE

Product Costing and Cost Accumulation

FOCUS COMPANY

Rocky Lake Outfitters, a small manufacturer of canoes near Lake Lucid, Alberta, uses job-order costing to accumulate the costs of each of its products. Job-order costing is well-suited to companies like Rocky Lake Outfitters that manufacture relatively small numbers of distinct products. In a job-order costing system, direct material, direct labour, and manufacturing overhead are first assigned to each production job, such as a set number of canoes of a particular type. Then the cost of the production job is averaged across the number of units in the job.

IN CONTRAST

In contrast to the manufacturing setting of Rocky Lake Outfitters, we explore job-order costing in a service industry environment. Metro Advertising Agency is a small firm in Saskatoon. The ad agency has two managing partners, six artistic staff, and one office support staff. Metro Advertising Agency calculates predetermined overhead rates based on two cost drivers: partner direct professional labour and artistic staff direct professional labour. The ad agency's cost of completing the work for an advertising contract with Super Scoop Ice Cream Company includes direct material, direct professional labour for both partner and artistic staff time, and applied overhead.

After completing this chapter, you should be able to

1   Discuss the role of product and service costing in manufacturing and nonmanufacturing firms.

2   Diagram and explain the flow of costs through the manufacturing accounts used in product costing.

3   Distinguish between job-order costing and process costing.

4   Compute a predetermined overhead rate and explain its use in job-order costing for job-shop and batch-production environments.

5   Prepare journal entries to record the costs of direct material, direct labour, and manufacturing overhead in a job-order costing system.

6   Prepare a schedule of cost of goods manufactured, a schedule of cost of goods sold, and an income statement for a manufacturer, using a normal costing system.

7   Describe the two-stage allocation process used to assign manufacturing-overhead costs to production jobs.

8   Describe the process of project costing used in service industry firms and nonprofit organizations.

Product and Service Costing

A **product-costing system** accumulates the costs incurred in a production process and assigns those costs to the final products. Product costs are needed for a variety of purposes in financial accounting, managerial accounting, cost management, and reporting to interested organizations.

Learning Objective ▮ **1**

Discuss the role of product and service costing in manufacturing and nonmanufacturing firms.

Use in Financial Accounting   In financial accounting, product costs are needed to value inventory on the balance sheet and to compute cost of goods sold on the income statement. Under generally accepted accounting principles, inventory is usually valued at its cost until it is sold. Then the cost of the inventory becomes an expense of the period in which it is sold.

Use in Managerial Accounting   In managerial accounting, product costs are needed to help managers with planning and to provide them with data for decision making. Decisions about product prices, the mix of products to be produced, and the quantity of output to be manufactured are among those for which product cost information is needed.

Use in Cost Management   It is hard to imagine how management can control or reduce production costs if it does not have a clear idea of the product costs. Thus, product costs provide important data for a variety of cost management purposes. Many of the uses of product-costing information will be covered throughout this book.

Use in Reporting to Interested Organizations   In addition to financial statement preparation and internal decision making, there is an ever-growing need for product cost information in relationships between firms and various outside organizations. Public utilities, such as electric and gas companies, record product costs to justify rate increases that must be approved by regulatory bodies. Hospitals keep track of the costs of medical procedures that are reimbursed by the provincial health authorities. Manufacturing firms often sign cost-plus contracts with the government, where the contract price depends on the cost of manufacturing the product.

"We recognized that our key competitors were overseas. We realized that in order to compete, we had to be extremely cost conscious." (3a)
MiCRUS
(Joint venture of IBM and Cirrus Logic)

Product Costing in Nonmanufacturing Firms

The need for product costs is not limited to manufacturing firms. Merchandising companies include the costs of buying and transporting merchandise in their product costs. Producers of inventoriable goods, such as mining products, petroleum, and agricultural products also record the costs of producing their goods. The role of product costs in these companies is identical to that in manufacturing firms. For example, the pineapples grown and sold by Dole are inventoried at their product cost until they are sold. Then the product cost becomes cost of goods sold.

Service Firms and Nonprofit Organizations   The production output of service firms and nonprofit organizations consists of services that are consumed as they are produced. Since services cannot be stored and sold later like manufactured goods, there are no inventoriable costs in service industry firms and nonprofit organizations. However, such organizations need information about the costs of producing services. Banks, insurance companies, restaurants, airlines, law firms, hospitals, and city governments all record the costs of producing various services for the purposes of planning, cost control, and decision making. For example, in making a decision about adding a flight from Toronto to Winnipeg, Air Canada's management needs to know the cost of flying the proposed route. Before building a new branch bank, BMO's management would want to know the cost of maintaining the branch, as well as the additional revenue to be generated. A City of Halifax manager can make a better decision as to whether the city government should begin a drug counselling program if the cost of providing similar, existing services is known.

"The closer we get to the client physically, the more likely it is that we're going to have an opportunity to participate in what's going on in the business. The more remote you are from where the business decision makers are, the less likely they are to think about you." (3b)
Qwest
(Currently a part of CenturyLink)

Manufacturing Cost Flows

Manufacturing costs consist of direct material, direct labour, and manufacturing overhead. The product-costing systems used by manufacturing firms employ several manufacturing accounts. As production takes place, all manufacturing costs are added to the *work-in-process inventory* account. Work in process represents partially completed inventory. A debit to the account increases the cost-based valuation of the asset represented by the unfinished products. As soon as products are completed, their costs are transferred from work-in-process inventory to *finished-goods inventory*. This is accomplished with a credit to work in process and a debit to finished goods. During the time period when products are sold, the cost of the inventory sold is removed from finished goods and added to *cost of goods sold*, which is an expense of the period in which the sale occurred. A credit to finished goods and a debit to cost of goods sold completes this step. Exhibit 3–1 depicts the flow of costs through the manufacturing accounts.

Exhibit 3–1
Flow of Costs through
Manufacturing Accounts

Example of Manufacturing Cost Flows   Suppose that the Bradley Paper Company incurred the following manufacturing costs during 20x1.

Direct material	$30,000
Direct labour	20,000
Manufacturing overhead	40,000

During 20x1, products costing $60,000 were finished and products costing $25,000 were sold for $32,000. Exhibit 3–2 shows the flow of costs through the Bradley Paper Company's manufacturing accounts and the effect of the product costs on the company's balance sheet and income statement.

Product-Costing Systems

The detailed accounting procedures used in product-costing systems depend on the type of industry involved. Two basic product-costing systems are used: job-order costing and process costing.

Job-Order Costing System

Job-order costing is used by companies with *job-shop* operations or *batch-production* operations. In a job-shop environment, products are manufactured in very low volumes or one at a time. Examples of a job-shop environment include movie production, customized

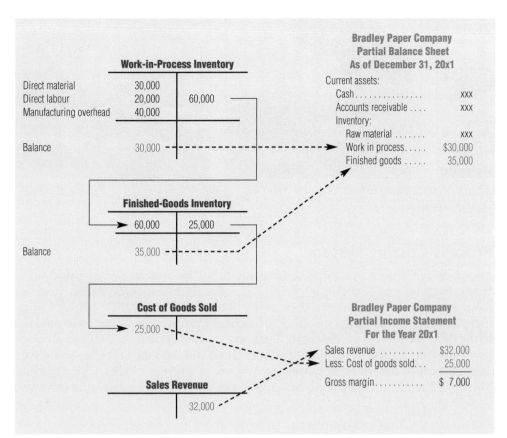

Exhibit 3–2

Example of Manufacturing
Cost Flows for Bradley Paper
Company

house building, ship building, aircraft manufacturing, and customized machining operations. In a batch-production environment, multiple products are produced in batches of
relatively small quantities. Examples include furniture manufacturing, printing, agricultural equipment manufacturing, and pleasure boat production.

In **job-order costing**, each distinct batch of production is called a *job* or *job order*.
The accounting procedures are designed to assign costs to each job. The costs assigned to
each job are averaged over the units produced in the job to obtain an average cost per
unit. For example, suppose that AccuPrint worked on two printing jobs during October,
and the following costs were incurred.

	Job A27 (1,000 campaign posters)	Job B39 (100 wedding invitations)
Direct material	$100	$ 36
Direct labour	250	40
Manufacturing overhead	150	24
Total manufacturing cost	$500	$100

The cost per campaign poster is $0.50 per poster ($500 ÷ 1,000 posters) and the
cost per wedding invitation is $1 ($100 ÷ 100 invitations).

Procedures similar to those used in job-order costing are also used in many service
industry firms, although these firms have no work-in-process or finished-goods inventories. In a law firm, for example, costs are assigned to clients in much the same way they
are assigned to a batch of products by a furniture manufacturer. Similar procedures are
used to assign costs to "patients" in health-care facilities, to "programs" in government
agencies, to research "projects" in universities, and to "contracts" in consulting and architectural firms.

"We have to be the best
in cost throughout the
world." (3c)

MiCRUS

**(Joint venture of IBM and
Cirrus Logic)**

The accounting system keeps track of production costs as they flow from work-in-process inventory through the finished-goods inventory and into cost of goods sold.

Process-Costing System

Process costing is used by companies that produce large numbers of identical units. Firms that produce chemicals, microchips, gasoline, beer, fertilizer, textiles, processed food, and electricity are among those using process costing. In these kinds of firms, there is no need to trace costs to specific batches of production, because the products in the different batches are identical. A **process-costing system** accumulates all of the production costs for a large number of units of output, and then these costs are averaged over all of the units. For example, suppose the Ottawa Valley Company produced 40,000 microchips during November. The following manufacturing costs were incurred in November.

Direct material	$1,000
Direct labour	2,000
Manufacturing overhead	3,000
Total manufacturing cost	$6,000

The cost per microchip is $0.15 (total manufacturing cost of $6,000 ÷ 40,000 units produced).

Summary of Alternative Product-Costing Systems

The distinction between job-order and process costing hinges on the type of production process involved. Job-order costing systems assign costs to significantly different production jobs. An average cost is then computed for each unit of product in each job. Process-costing systems average costs over a large number of identical (or very similar) units of product. Exhibit 3–3 summarizes the differences between these two product-costing systems.

The remainder of this chapter examines the details of job-order costing. The next chapter covers process costing.

Exhibit 3–3
Comparison of Product-Costing Systems

Job-Order Costing System	Process-Costing System
Used for production of large, unique, high-cost items.	Used for production of small, identical, low-cost items.
Built to order rather than mass-produced.	Mass-produced in automated continuous production process.
• *Job-shop operations.* Products manufactured in very low volumes or one at a time.	
• *Batch-production operations.* Multiple products in batches of relatively small quantities.	
Many costs can be directly traced to each job.	Costs cannot be directly traced to each unit of product.
Typical applications are special-order printing, building construction, hospitals, law firms.	Typical applications are in a petrochemical refinery, paint manufacturer, paper mill.

Cost Accumulation in a Job-Order Costing System

To illustrate job-order costing, we will focus on Rocky Lake Outfitters Inc. In a job-order costing system, direct-material, direct-labour, and manufacturing-overhead costs are assigned to each production job. These costs are the *inputs* of the product-costing *system*. As costs are incurred, they are added to the work-in-process inventory account. To keep track of the manufacturing costs assigned to *each job*, a subsidiary record is maintained. The subsidiary record of each job is a document called a **job-cost record**.

Job-Cost Record

An example of a job-cost record is displayed in Exhibit 3–4. For now, focus only on the major sections and headings, which are printed in blue.

Exhibit 3–4

Job-Cost Record: Rocky Lake Outfitters Inc.

JOB-COST RECORD

Job Number	F16	**Description**	80 deluxe aluminum canoes
Date Started	Nov. 1, 20x1	**Date Completed**	Nov. 22, 20x1
		Number of Units Completed	80

Direct Material

Date	Requisition Number	Quantity	Unit Price	Cost
11/1	803	7,200 m²	$2.50	$18,000

Direct Labour

Date	Time Card Number	Hours	Rate	Cost
Various dates	Various time cards	600	$20	$12,000

Manufacturing Overhead

Date	Cost Driver (Activity Base)	Quantity	Application Rate	Cost
11/30	Machine hours	2,000	$9.00	$18,000

Cost Summary

Cost Item	Amount
Total direct material	$18,000
Total direct labour	12,000
Total manufacturing overhead	18,000
Total cost	$48,000
Unit cost	$600

Shipping Summary

Date	Units Shipped	Units Remaining in Inventory	Cost Balance
11/30	60	20	$12,000

This job-cost record is for Job F16 consisting of 80 deluxe aluminum canoes, which were produced during November 20x1. Three major sections on the job-cost record are used to accumulate the costs of direct material, direct labour, and manufacturing overhead assigned to the job. The other two sections are used to record the total cost and average unit cost for the job, and to keep track of units shipped to customers. A job-cost record may be a paper document on which the entries for direct material, direct labour, and manufacturing overhead are written, or a computer file where entries are made.

The procedures used to accumulate the costs of direct material, direct labour, and manufacturing overhead for a job constitute the *set of activities* performed by the job-order costing *system*. These procedures are discussed next.

Direct-Material Costs

As raw materials are needed for the production process, they are transferred from the warehouse to the production department. To authorize the release of materials, the production department completes a **material-requisition form**, which is given to the warehouse; a copy goes to the accounting department and is used as the basis for transferring the cost of the requisitioned material from the raw-material inventory account to the work-in-process inventory account, and for entering the direct-material cost on the job-cost record for the production job in process. A document, such as the material-requisition form, which is used as the basis for an accounting entry, is called a **source document**. Exhibit 3–5 shows an example of a material-requisition form.

In many factories, the production department enters directly into a computer the material requisitions, which are then electronically transmitted to the warehouse and to the accounting department. Such automation reduces paperwork, minimizes clerical errors, and speeds up the product-costing process.

Direct-Labour Costs

The assignment of direct-labour costs to jobs is based on time records filled out by employees. A **time record** details the amount of time an employee spends on each production job. The time record is the source document used as the basis for adding direct-labour costs to work-in-process inventory and to the job-cost records for the various jobs in process. The time record often consists of a computerized time-clock system. Employees enter the time they begin and stop work on each job into the time clock. The time clock is connected to a computer that records the time spent on various jobs and transmits the information to the accounting department.

Exhibit 3–6 displays an example of a time record. As the example shows, most of the employee's time was spent working on two different production jobs. The time spent on each job will be multiplied by the employee's wage rate, and the cost will be recorded in work-in-process inventory and on the appropriate job-cost records. The employee also spent one-half hour on shop cleanup duties. This time will be classified as indirect labour, and its cost will be included in manufacturing overhead.

Exhibit 3–5
Material-Requisition Form

ROCKY LAKE
OUTFITTERS

| Material-Requisition Number ____352____   Date ____1/28/x1____ |
| Job Number to Be Charged ____J621____   Department ____Painting____ |
| Department Supervisor ____Timothy Williams____ |

Item	Quantity	Unit Cost	Amount
White enamel paint	35 L	$3.20	$112
Clear lacquer	8 L	2.75	22

Exhibit 3–6
Time Record

| Employee Name | Ron Bradley | | Date | 12/19/x1 |
| Employee Number | 12 | | Department | Painting |

Time Started	Time Stopped	Job Number
8:00	11:30	A267
11:30	12:00	Shop cleanup
1:00	5:00	J122

Manufacturing-Overhead Costs

It is relatively simple to trace direct-material and direct-labour costs to production jobs, but manufacturing overhead is not easily traced to jobs. By definition, manufacturing overhead is a diverse pool of indirect production costs, such as indirect material, indirect labour, utility costs, and depreciation. These costs often bear no obvious direct relationship to individual jobs or units of product, but they must be incurred for production to take place. Therefore, it is necessary to assign manufacturing-overhead costs to jobs in order to have a complete picture of product costs. This process of assigning manufacturing-overhead costs to production jobs is called **overhead application** (or sometimes **overhead absorption**).

Overhead Application   For product-costing information to be useful, it must be provided to managers on a timely basis. Suppose the accounting department waited until the end of an accounting period so that the *actual* costs of manufacturing overhead could be determined before applying overhead costs to the firm's products. The result would be very accurate overhead application. However, the information might be useless because it was not available to managers for planning, control, and decision making during the period.

Predetermined Overhead Rate   The solution to this problem is to apply overhead to products on the basis of estimates made at the beginning of the accounting period. The accounting department chooses some measure of productive activity to use as the basis for overhead application. In traditional product-costing systems, this measure is usually some **volume-based cost driver** (or **activity base**), such as direct-labour hours, direct-labour cost, or machine hours. An *estimate* is made of (1) the amount of manufacturing overhead that will be incurred during a specified period of time and (2) the amount of the cost driver that will be used or incurred during the same time period. Then a **predetermined overhead rate** is computed as follows:

Learning Objective **4**

Compute a predetermined overhead rate and explain its use in job-order costing for job-shop and batch-production environments.

$$\frac{\text{Predetermined}}{\text{overhead rate}} = \frac{\text{Budgeted manufacturing-overhead cost}}{\text{Budgeted amount of cost driver (or activity base)}}$$

For example, Rocky Lake Outfitters has chosen machine hours as its cost driver. For the Year 20x1, the firm estimates that overhead cost will amount to $360,000 and a total of 40,000 machine hours used will be required. The 40,000 budgeted machine hours represent the company's practical capacity for production. This means that 40,000 machine hours are expected to be available for production under normal operating conditions. Recall from the discussion in Chapter 1 (Management of Capacity and Capacity Costs) that normal operating conditions allow for such issues as routine machine maintenance, employee fatigue, and so forth. The predetermined overhead rate is computed as follows:

$$\frac{\text{Predetermined}}{\text{overhead rate}} = \frac{\$360,000}{40,000 \text{ hours}} = \$9 \text{ per machine hour}$$

In our discussion of the predetermined overhead rate, we have emphasized the term *cost driver*, because increasingly this term is replacing the more traditional term *activity base*. Furthermore, we have emphasized that *traditional* product-costing systems tend to rely on a *single, volume-based cost driver*. We will discuss more elaborate product-costing systems based on multiple cost drivers later in this chapter. This topic is examined in even greater detail in Chapter 5.

Applying Overhead Costs   The predetermined overhead rate is used to apply manufacturing overhead costs to production jobs. The quantity of the cost driver required by a particular job is multiplied by the predetermined overhead rate to determine the amount of overhead cost applied to the job. For example, suppose Rocky Lake Outfitters' Job D22 requires 30 machine hours. The overhead applied to the job is computed as follows:

Predetermined overhead rate	$ 9
Machine hours required by Job D22	× 30
Overhead applied to Job D22	$270

The $270 of applied overhead will be added to work-in-process inventory and recorded on the job-cost record for Job D22. The accounting entries to add manufacturing overhead to work-in-process inventory may be made daily, weekly, or monthly, depending on the time required to process production jobs. Before the end of an accounting period, entries should be made to record all manufacturing costs incurred to date in work-in-process inventory. This is necessary to properly value work-in-process inventory on the balance sheet.

Job-Order Costing Illustrated

Now let's examine the accounting entries made by Rocky Lake Outfitters Inc. during November 20x1. The company worked on two production jobs:

Job C12   80 deluxe wooden canoes
Job F16   80 deluxe aluminum canoes

The events of November are described below, along with the associated accounting entries.

Material Purchase

The purchase on account of 4,000 m² of rolled aluminum sheet metal for $10,000 is recorded with the following journal entry.

(1)	Raw-material inventory	10,000	
	Accounts payable		10,000

The postings of this entry and all subsequent journal entries to the ledger are shown in Exhibit 3–11, later in this chapter.

Direct Material

On November 1, the following material requisitions were submitted.

Requisition 802 (for Job C12)   8,000 board metres of lumber, at $2 per board metre, for a total of $16,000

Requisition 803 (for Job F16)   7,200 square metres of aluminum sheet metal, at $2.50 per square metre, for a total of $18,000

The following journal entry records the transfer of these raw materials to production:

(2)	Work-in-process inventory..	34,000	
	Raw-material inventory		34,000

These direct-material costs are also recorded on the job-cost record for each job. The job-cost record for Job F16 is displayed in Exhibit 3–4. Since the job-cost record for Job C12 is similar, it is not shown.

Direct Labour

At the end of November, the accounting department uses the labour time records filed during the month to determine the following direct-labour costs of each job:

Direct labour: Job C12	$ 9,000
Direct labour: Job F16	12,000
Total direct labour	$21,000

The journal entry to record these costs is as follows:

This small production facility records the cost of manufacturing canoes and other boats, which are manufactured in small batches. Direct-material, direct-labour, and manufacturing-overhead costs are tracked.

(3)	Work-in-process inventory..	21,000	
	Wages payable		21,000

These direct-labour costs also are recorded on the job-cost record for each job. The job-cost record for Job F16 is displayed in Exhibit 3–4. Only one direct-labour entry is shown on the job-cost record. In practice, there would be numerous entries made on different dates at a variety of wage rates for different employees.

Actual Manufacturing Overhead

The following information relates to indirect-material, indirect-labour, and other manufacturing-overhead costs incurred in the month of November.

Indirect Material   On November 15, the following material requisition was submitted.

Requisition 804:   5 litres of bonding glue, at $10 per litre, for a total
cost of $50

Small amounts of bonding glue are used in the production of all canoes manufactured by Rocky Lake Outfitters. Since the cost incurred is small, no attempt is made to trace the cost of glue to specific jobs. Instead, glue is considered to be an indirect material, and its cost is included in manufacturing overhead. The company accumulates all manufacturing-overhead costs in a *manufacturing overhead account*. All actual overhead costs are recorded by debiting this account when indirect materials are requisitioned, indirect-labour costs are incurred, utility bills are paid, depreciation is recorded on manufacturing equipment, and so forth. The journal entry made to record the usage of glue is as follows:

(4)	Manufacturing overhead..	50	
	Manufacturing supplies inventory		50

No entry is made on any job-cost record for the usage of glue, since its cost is not traced to individual production jobs.

Indirect Labour The analysis of labour time records on November 30 also revealed the following incurrence of indirect labour:

Indirect labour: Not charged to any particular job $14,000

This cost is made up of the production supervisor's salary and the wages of various employees who spent some of their time on maintenance and general cleanup duties during November. The following journal entry is made to add indirect-labour costs to manufacturing overhead:

(5)	Manufacturing Overhead	14,000	
	Wages Payable		14,000

No entry is made on any job-cost record, since indirect-labour costs are not traceable to any particular job.

Other Manufacturing Overhead In addition to indirect materials and indirect labour, the following manufacturing-overhead costs were incurred during November:

Manufacturing overhead:	
Rent on factory building (prepaid)	$ 3,000
Depreciation on equipment	5,000
Utilities (electricity and natural gas)	4,000
Property taxes	2,000
Insurance (prepaid)	1,000
Total	$15,000

The following compound journal entry is made on November 30 to record these costs:

(6)	Manufacturing Overhead	15,000	
	Prepaid Rent		3,000
	Accumulated Depreciation—Equipment		5,000
	Accounts Payable (utilities and property taxes)		6,000
	Prepaid Insurance		1,000

No entry is made on any job-cost record, since manufacturing-overhead costs are not traceable to any particular job.

Applied Manufacturing Overhead

As shown above, several actual manufacturing-overhead costs were incurred during November and recorded as debits to the manufacturing overhead account. However, no manufacturing-overhead costs have yet been added to work-in-process inventory or recorded on the job-cost records. Recall that the application of manufacturing overhead to products is based on a predetermined overhead rate. This rate was computed by the accounting department at the beginning of 20x1 as follows:

$$\text{Predetermined overhead rate} = \frac{\text{Budgeted total manufacturing overhead for 20x1}}{\text{Budgeted total machine hours for 20x1}}$$

$$= \frac{\$360,000}{40,000} = \$9 \text{ per machine hour}$$

Factory records indicate that the following machine hours were used during November:

Job C12	1,200 hours
Job F16	2,000 hours
Total machine hours	3,200 hours

The total manufacturing overhead applied to work-in-process inventory during November is calculated as follows:

	Machine Hours		Predetermined Overhead Rate		Manufacturing Overhead Applied
Job C12	1,200	×	$9	=	$10,800
Job F16	2,000	×	$9	=	18,000
Total manufacturing overhead applied					$28,800

The following journal entry is made to add **applied manufacturing overhead** to work-in-process inventory:

(7)	Work-in-process inventory	28,800	
	Manufacturing overhead		28,800

The manufacturing overhead applied to Job F16 is entered on the job-cost record in Exhibit 3–4.

Summary of Accounting for Manufacturing Overhead

As the following time line shows, three concepts are used in accounting for overhead. Overhead is *budgeted* at the *beginning* of the accounting period, it is *applied during* the period, and *actual* overhead is measured at the *end* of the period.

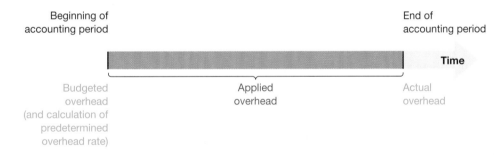

Exhibit 3–7 summarizes the accounting for manufacturing overhead. The left side of the manufacturing overhead account is used to record the costs of **actual manufacturing overhead** as they are incurred throughout the accounting period. The actual costs incurred for indirect material, indirect labour, factory rental, equipment depreciation, utilities, property taxes, and insurance are recorded as debits to the account.

The right side of the manufacturing overhead account is used to record manufacturing overhead *applied* to work-in-process inventory. It is important to note that actual overhead costs are not charged to jobs and thus do not appear in the work-in-process account. Only the applied overhead costs, based on the predetermined overhead rate, appear in the work-in-process account.

The manufacturing overhead account is a temporary (clearing) account containing costs or amounts, the balance of which is to be transferred to another account. While the left side of the manufacturing overhead account records *actual* overhead costs, the right side records *applied* overhead costs using the predetermined overhead rate, based on *estimated*

Exhibit 3–7
Manufacturing Overhead
Account

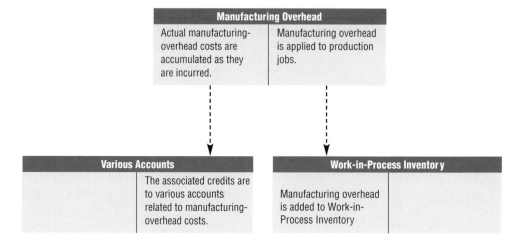

overhead costs. The estimates used to calculate the predetermined overhead rate at the beginning of the period will generally prove to be inaccurate to some degree. Consequently, there will usually be a balance in the manufacturing overhead account at the end of the year. This balance is usually relatively small, and its disposition is covered later in this illustration.

Selling and Administrative Costs

During November, Rocky Lake Outfitters incurred selling and administrative costs as follows:

Rental of sales and administrative offices	$ 1,500
Salaries of sales staff	4,000
Salaries of management	8,000
Advertising	1,000
Office supplies used	300
Total	$14,800

Since these are not manufacturing costs, they are not added to work-in-process inventory. Selling and administrative costs are period costs, not product costs. They are treated as expenses of the accounting period in which they are incurred. The following journal entry is made:

(8)	Selling and administrative expenses	14,800	
	Wages payable		12,000
	Accounts payable		1,000
	Prepaid rent		1,500
	Offices supplies inventory		300

Completion of a Production Job

Job F16 was completed during November, whereas Job C12 remained in process. As the job-cost record in Exhibit 3–4 indicates, the total cost of Job F16 was $48,000. The following journal entry records the transfer of this cost from work-in-process inventory to finished-goods inventory.

(9)	Finished-goods inventory	48,000	
	Work-in-process inventory		48,000

Sale of Goods

Sixty deluxe aluminum canoes manufactured in Job F16 were sold for $900 each during November. The cost of each unit sold was $600, as shown on the job-cost record in Exhibit 3–4. The following journal entries are made:

(10) Accounts receivable	54,000	
Sales revenue		54,000

(11) Cost of goods sold	36,000	
Finished-goods inventory		36,000

The remainder of the manufacturing costs for Job F16 stays in the finished-goods inventory until some subsequent accounting period when the units are sold. Therefore, the cost balance for Job F16 remaining in inventory is $12,000 (20 units remaining times $600 per unit). This balance is shown on the job-cost record in Exhibit 3–4.

Underapplied and Overapplied Manufacturing Overhead

During November, Rocky Lake Outfitters incurred total *actual* manufacturing-overhead costs of $29,050, but only $28,800 of overhead was *applied* to work-in-process inventory. The amount by which actual overhead exceeds applied overhead is called **underapplied overhead** and is calculated as shown below.

Actual manufacturing overhead*	$29,050
Applied manufacturing overhead†	28,800
Underapplied manufacturing overhead	$ 250

*Sum of debit entries in the manufacturing overhead account: $50 + $14,000 + $15,000 = $29,050. See Exhibit 3–11.

†Applied overhead: $9 per machine hour × 3,200 machine hours.

If actual overhead had been less than applied overhead, the difference would have been called **overapplied overhead**. Underapplied (or overapplied) overhead is caused by underestimation (or overestimation) of overhead costs and activity used to compute the predetermined overhead rate at the beginning of the accounting period. In this illustration, Rocky Lake Outfitters' predetermined rate was underestimated by a small amount.

Disposition of Underapplied or Overapplied Overhead   At the end of an accounting period, there are two alternatives to dispose of the underapplied or overapplied overhead. If the balance in the manufacturing overhead account is small, the underapplied or overapplied overhead is closed into cost of goods sold. This is the method used by Rocky Lake Outfitters, and the required journal entry is shown below:

(12) Cost of goods sold	250	
Manufacturing overhead		250

This entry reduces the balance in the manufacturing overhead account down to zero. The account is then clear to record both actual and applied manufacturing overhead in the next accounting period.

Journal entry (12) has the effect of increasing cost of goods sold. This reflects the fact that the cost of the units sold had been underestimated due to the small underestimation of the predetermined overhead rate. Most companies use this approach because it is simple and the amount of underapplied or overapplied overhead is usually small. Moreover, most firms wait until the end of the year to close underapplied or overapplied overhead into cost of goods sold, rather than making the entry monthly as in this illustration.

Some companies use a more accurate procedure to dispose of underapplied or over-applied overhead. This approach recognizes that underestimation or overestimation of the predetermined overhead rate affects not only cost of goods sold, but also work-in-process inventory and finished-goods inventory. As the following diagram shows, applied overhead passes through all three of these accounts. Therefore, all three accounts are affected by any inaccuracy in the predetermined overhead rate.

When underapplied or overapplied overhead is allocated among the three accounts shown above, the process is called **proration**. The amount of the current period's applied manufacturing overhead, which remains in each of the three accounts, is the basis for the proration procedure. In the Rocky Lake Outfitters example, the amounts of applied overhead remaining in the three accounts on November 30 are determined as follows:

	Applied Overhead Remaining in Each Account on November 30				
Account	**Explanation**	**Amount**	**Percentage***		**Calculation of Percentages**
Work in Process	Job C12 only	$10,800	37%		$10,800 ÷ $28,800
Finished Goods	¼ of units in Job F16	4,500	16%		$4,500 ÷ $28,800
Cost of Goods Sold	¾ of units in Job F16	13,500	47%		$13,500 ÷ $28,800
Total overhead applied in November		$28,800	100%		

*Rounded.

Using the percentages calculated above, the proration of Rocky Lake Outfitters' underapplied overhead is determined as follows:

Account	**Underapplied Overhead**	×	**Percentage**	=	**Amount Added to Account**
Work in Process	$250	×	37%	=	$ 92.50
Finished Goods	250	×	16%	=	40.00
Cost of Goods Sold	250	×	47%	=	117.50
Total underapplied overhead prorated					$250.00

If Rocky Lake Outfitters had chosen to prorate underapplied overhead, the following journal entry would have been made:

Work-in-process inventory	92.50	
Finished-goods inventory	40.00	
Cost of goods sold	117.50	
Manufacturing overhead		250.00

Since this is *not* the method used by Rocky Lake Outfitters in our continuing illustration, this entry is *not* posted to the ledger in Exhibit 3–11.

Schedule of Cost of Goods Manufactured

Exhibit 3–8 displays the November schedule of cost of goods manufactured for Rocky Lake Outfitters. The schedule details the costs of direct material, direct labour, and manufacturing overhead *applied* to work in process during November and shows the change in work-in-process inventory. The cost of goods manufactured, shown in the last line of the schedule, is $48,000. This is the amount transferred from work-in-process inventory to the finished-goods inventory during November, as recorded in journal entry number (9).

Learning Objective   **6**

Prepare a schedule of cost of goods manufactured, a schedule of cost of goods sold, and an income statement for a manufacturer, using a normal costing system.

Exhibit 3–8
Schedule of Cost of Goods Manufactured

ROCKY LAKE
OUTFITTERS

ROCKY LAKE OUTFITTERS INC.
Schedule of Cost of Goods Manufactured
For the Month of November, 20x1

Direct material:		
Raw-material inventory, November 1...	$30,000	
Add: November purchases of raw material..	10,000	
Raw material available for use...	40,000	
Deduct: Raw-material inventory, November 30	6,000	
Raw material used		$34,000
Direct labour...		21,000
Manufacturing overhead:		
Indirect material..	$ 50	
Indirect labour	14,000	
Rent on factory building	3,000	
Depreciation on equipment..	5,000	
Utilities..	4,000	
Property taxes	2,000	
Insurance...	1,000	
Total *actual* manufacturing overhead..	29,050	
Deduct: Underapplied overhead*..	250	
Overhead *applied* to work in process..		28,800
Total manufacturing costs		83,800
Add: Work-in-process inventory, November 1...		4,000
Subtotal		87,800
Deduct: Work-in-process inventory, November 30...		39,800
Cost of goods manufactured...		$48,000

*The schedule of cost of goods manufactured lists the manufacturing costs *applied* to work in process. Therefore, the underapplied overhead, $250, must be deducted from total actual overhead to arrive at the amount of overhead *applied* to work in process during November. If there had been overapplied overhead, the balance would have been *added* to total actual manufacturing overhead.

Schedule of Cost of Goods Sold

A schedule of cost of goods sold for Rocky Lake Outfitters is displayed in Exhibit 3–9. This schedule shows the November cost of goods sold and details the changes in finished-goods inventory during the month. Exhibit 3–10 shows the company's November income statement. As the income statement shows, income before taxes is $2,950, from which income tax expense of $885 is subtracted, yielding net income of $2,065.

Exhibit 3–9
Schedule of Cost of Goods Sold

ROCKY LAKE OUTFITTERS INC.
Schedule of Cost of Goods Sold
For the Month of November, 20x1

Finished-goods, inventory, November 1	$12,000
Add: Cost of goods manufactured*	48,000
Cost of goods available for sale	60,000
Deduct: Finished-goods inventory, November 30	24,000
Cost of goods sold	36,000
Add: Underapplied overhead†	250
Cost of goods sold (adjusted for underapplied overhead)	$36,250

*From the schedule of cost of goods manufactured in Exhibit 3–8.
†The company closes underapplied or overapplied overhead into cost of goods sold. Hence, the $250 balance in underapplied overhead is added to the cost of goods sold for the month.

Exhibit 3–10
Income Statement

ROCKY LAKE OUTFITTERS INC.
Income Statement
For the Month of November, 20x1

Sales revenue	$54,000
Less: Cost of goods sold*	36,250
Gross margin	17,750
Selling and administrative expenses	14,800
Income before taxes	2,950
Income tax expense	885
Net income	$ 2,065

*From the schedule of cost of goods sold in Exhibit 3–9.

Posting Journal Entries to the Ledger

All of the journal entries in the Rocky Lake Outfitters example are posted to the ledger in Exhibit 3–11. An examination of these T-accounts provides a summary of the cost flows discussed throughout the illustration.

Further Aspects of Overhead Application

Actual and Normal Costing

"We use an actual costing system for the costs incurred in producing a feature film." (3e)
The Walt Disney Company

Most firms use a predetermined overhead rate, based on overhead and activity estimates for a relatively long time period. When direct material and direct labour are added to work-in-process inventory at their actual amounts, but overhead is applied to work-in-process inventory using a *predetermined overhead rate*, the product-costing process is referred to as **normal costing**. This approach takes its name from the use of an overhead

Accounts Receivable		
Bal.	11,000	
(10)	54,000	

Accounts Payable		
	3,000	Bal.
	10,000	(1)
	6,000	(6)
	1,000	(8)

Prepaid Insurance		
Bal.	2,000	1,000 (6)

Wages Payable		
	10,000	Bal.
	21,000	(4)
	14,000	(5)
	12,000	(8)

Prepaid Rent		
Bal.	5,000	3,000 (6)
		1,500 (8)

Office Supplies Inventory		
Bal.	900	300 (8)

Manufacturing Supplies Inventory		
Bal.	750	50 (3)

Accumulated Depreciation: Equipment		
	105,000	Bal.
	5,000	(6)

Raw-Material Inventory		
Bal.	30,000	34,000 (2)
(1)	10,000	

Manufacturing Overhead		
(3)	50	28,800 (7)
(5)	14,000	250 (12)
(6)	15,000	

Work-in-Process Inventory		
Bal.	4,000	48,000
(2)	34,000	
(4)	21,000	
(7)	28,800	

Cost of Goods Sold		
(11)	36,000	
(12)	250	

Finished-Goods Inventory		
Bal.	12,000	36,000
(9)	48,000	

Selling and Administrative Expenses		
(8)	14,800	

Sales Revenue		
	54,000	(10)

Exhibit 3–11
Ledger Accounts for Rocky Lake Outfitters Illustration*

*The numbers in parentheses relate T-account entries to the associated journal entries. The numbers in colour are the November 1 account balances.

rate that is normalized over a fairly long period. A **normalized overhead rate** is used in the Rocky Lake Outfitters example.

A few companies use **actual costing**, a system in which direct material and direct labour are added to work in process at their actual amounts, and actual overhead is allocated to work in process using an **actual overhead rate** computed at the *end* of each accounting period. Note that even though an actual overhead rate is used, the amount of overhead assigned to each production job is still an allocated amount. Overhead costs, which are by definition indirect costs, cannot be traced easily to individual production jobs. Actual and normal costing may be summarized as follows:

ACTUAL COSTING Work-in-Process Inventory	
Actual direct- material costs	
Actual direct- labour costs	
Overhead allocated:	
Actual overhead rate (computed at *end of* period) ×	Actual amount of cost driver used (e.g., direct-labour hours)

NORMAL COSTING Work-in-Process Inventory	
Actual direct- material costs	
Actual direct- labour costs	
Overhead applied:	
Predetermined overhead rate (computed at *beginning* of period) ×	Actual amount of cost driver used (e.g., direct-labour hours)

Choosing a Cost Driver for Overhead Application

Manufacturing overhead includes various indirect manufacturing costs that vary greatly in their relationship to the production process. If a single, volume-based cost driver is used in calculating the predetermined overhead rate, it should be some productive input that is common across all of the firm's products. If, for example, all of the firm's products require direct labour but only some products require machine time, direct-labour hours would be a preferable cost driver. If machine time was used as a cost driver, products not requiring machine time would not be assigned any overhead cost.

In selecting a volume-based cost driver, the goal is to choose an input that varies in a pattern that is most similar to the pattern with which overhead costs vary. Products that indirectly cause large amounts of overhead costs also should require large amounts of the cost driver, and vice versa. During periods when the cost driver is at a low level, the overhead costs incurred should be low. Thus, there should be a correlation between the incurrence of overhead costs and use of the cost driver.

> "As we continue to automate our production processes, direct labour is becoming less and less appropriate as a basis for the application of manufacturing overhead." (3f)
> **Chrysler**

Limitation of Direct Labour as a Cost Driver   In traditional product-costing systems, the most common volume-based cost drivers are direct-labour hours and direct-labour cost. However, there is a trend away from using direct labour as the overhead cost driver. Many production processes have become automated through the use of robotics and computer-integrated manufacturing systems. Increased automation brings two results. First, manufacturing-overhead costs represent a larger proportion of total production costs. Second, direct labour decreases in importance as a factor of production. As direct labour declines in importance as a productive input, it becomes less appropriate as a cost driver. For this reason, some firms have switched to machine hours, process time, or throughput time as cost drivers that better reflect the pattern of overhead cost incurrence. **Throughput time** (or **cycle time**) is the average amount of time required to convert raw materials into finished goods ready to be shipped to customers. Throughput time includes the time required for material handling, production processing, inspection, and packaging.

Departmental Overhead Rates

In the Rocky Lake Outfitters example presented earlier in this chapter, all of the firm's manufacturing overhead was combined into a single cost pool. The overhead was then applied to products using a single predetermined overhead rate based on machine hours. Since only one overhead rate is used, it is known as a **plantwide overhead rate**. In some production processes, the relationship between overhead costs and the firm's products differs substantially across production departments. In such cases, the firm may use **departmental overhead rates**, which differ across production departments. This usually results in a more accurate assignment of overhead costs to the firm's products. An even more detailed allocation of overhead costs can be achieved with *activity-based costing (ABC)*, which is covered in Chapter 5.

Two-Stage Cost Allocation

When a company uses departmental overhead rates, the allocation of manufacturing-overhead costs to production jobs is accomplished in two stages, a process called **two-stage cost allocation**. In the first stage, all manufacturing-overhead costs are allocated to the production departments, such as machining and assembly. In the second stage, the overhead costs that have been allocated to each production department are applied to the production jobs that pass through the department. Let's examine this process in more detail.

Learning Objective **7**

Describe the two-stage allocation process used to assign manufacturing-overhead costs to production jobs.

- *Stage 1.* In the first stage, all manufacturing-overhead costs are allocated to the firm's production departments. However, Stage 1 often involves two different types of allocation processes. First, all manufacturing-overhead costs are allocated to **departmental overhead centres**. This step is called **cost distribution** (or sometimes **cost allocation**). For example, the costs of heating a factory with natural gas would be distributed among all of the departments in the factory, possibly in proportion to the cubic metres of space in each department. In the cost distribution step, manufacturing-overhead costs are allocated to *both* production departments and service departments. Service departments, such as equipment-maintenance and material-handling departments, are departments that do not work directly on the firm's products but are necessary for production to take place.

  Second, all service department costs are reassigned to the production departments through a process called **service department cost allocation**. In this step, an attempt is made to allocate service department costs on the basis of the relative proportion of each service department's output that is used by the various production departments. For example, production departments with more equipment would be allocated a larger share of the maintenance department's costs.

  At the conclusion of Stage 1, all manufacturing-overhead costs have been assigned to the production departments.
- *Stage 2.* In the second stage, all of the manufacturing-overhead costs accumulated in each production department are assigned to the production jobs on which the department has worked. This process is called *overhead application* (or sometimes *overhead absorption*). In Stage 2, each production department has its own predetermined overhead rate. These rates often are based on different cost drivers.

The two-stage process of assigning overhead costs to production jobs is portrayed in Exhibit 3–12. Notice the roles of cost distribution, service department cost allocation, and overhead application in the exhibit. The techniques of overhead distribution and service department cost allocation will be covered later in Chapter 15, available on Connect. In this chapter, we are focusing primarily on the process of overhead application.[1]

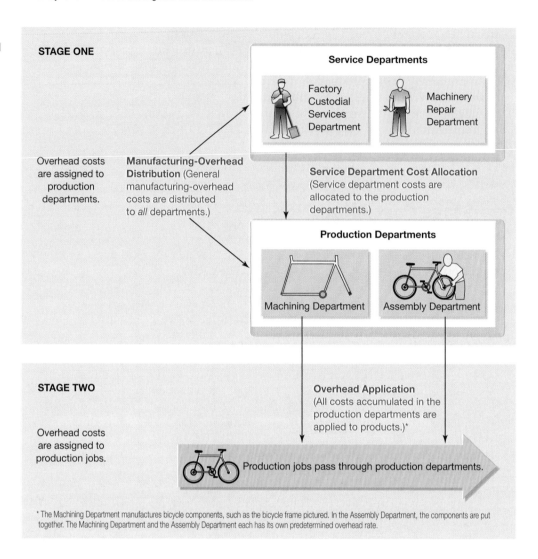

Different Product Costs under Plantwide and Departmental Costing Systems

The accuracy of a product-costing system is affected by the number of cost drivers and overhead rates. A single, plantwide overhead rate based on only one volume-related cost driver is the simplest but generally least accurate method to apply manufacturing overhead to the products. The two-stage allocation process previously discussed will result in multiple departmental overhead rates and will typically improve the accuracy of the product-costing system. This is particularly true when the production technology differs markedly among the departments. If, for example, one department relies chiefly on manual labour, while another department makes heavy use of machinery, departmental overhead rates with different cost drivers generally will increase product-costing accuracy.

Let's examine the effects of two alternative product-costing methods at Apex Controls Corporation, which manufactures two types of control valves used in the food-processing industry. Valve A has been Apex's main product for 15 years; it is used to control the flow of milk in various food-processing operations, such as the production of cookies. Valve B, a more recently introduced product, is a specialty valve used to control the flow of thicker foods, such as jelly. The basic data for our examination of the effects of the two alternative product-costing methods follow:

	Valve A	Valve B
Annual production and sales..	30,000 units	5,000 units
Direct material...	$ 140	$ 140
Direct labour:		
Machining Department..	30 (1.5 hrs. @ $20)	30 (1.5 hrs. @ $20)
Assembly Department...	30 (1.5 hrs. @ $20)	30 (1.5 hrs. @ $20)
Total prime costs	$ 200	$ 200
Machine time in Machining Department	1 h	3 h
Budgeted overhead costs:		
Machining Department..	$630,000	
Assembly Department...	315,000	
Total	$945,000	

Now let's compute the applied overhead cost per valve under two alternative product-costing methods.

Plantwide Overhead Rate

Using a single, plantwide overhead rate based on direct-labour hours (DLH), each product is allocated $27 of overhead per unit.

	Valve A	Valve B
Applied overhead per unit*	$27 (3 DLH @ $9 per DLH)	$27 (3 DLH @ $9 per DLH)

*Total budgeted DLH = (30,000 units of A) $\times$ (3 DLH per unit) + (5,000 units of B) $\times$ (3 DLH per unit) = 105,000 DLH.

$$\text{Predetermined overhead rate} = \frac{\text{Total budgeted overhead}}{\text{Total budgeted DLH}} = \frac{\$945,000}{105,000} = \$9 \text{ per DLH}$$

Adding the $200 of prime costs for each valve, we have product costs of $227 per unit for each type of valve.

Departmental Overhead Rates

Now suppose we use departmental overhead rates. The Machining Department rate is based on machine hours (MH), whereas the Assembly Department rate is based on direct-labour hours (DLH). This approach yields allocated overhead costs of $23 per unit of Valve A and $51 per unit of Valve B.

	Valve A	Valve B
Applied overhead per unit:		
Machining Department*	$14 (1 MH @ $14 per MH)	$42 (3 MH @ $14 per MH)
Assembly Department†	9 (1.5 DLH @ $6 per DLH)	9 (1.5 DLH @ $6 per DLH)
Total	$23	$51

*Total budgeted MH = (30,000 units of A) $\times$ (1 MH per unit) + (5,000 units of B) $\times$ (3 MH per unit) = 45,000 MH.

$$\text{Machining Department overhead rate} = \frac{\text{Machining Department overhead}}{\text{Budgeted MH}} = \frac{\$630,000}{45,000} = \$14 \text{ per MH}$$

†Total budgeted DLH in Assembly Department = (30,000 units of A) $\times$ (1.5 DLH) + (5,000 units of B) $\times$ (1.5 DLH) = 52,500 DLH.

$$\text{Assembly Department overhead rate} = \frac{\text{Assembly Department overhead}}{\text{Budgeted DLH}} = \frac{\$315,000}{52,500} = \$6 \text{ per DLH}$$

Adding the $200 of prime costs for each valve, we have product costs of $223 for each unit of Valve A and $251 for each unit of Valve B. Valve A, which spends considerably less time in the more costly Machining Department than Valve B, is now allocated a lower portion of overhead cost than it was when a plantwide overhead rate was used. In contrast, Valve B's allocated overhead cost has increased.

Summary

The following table compares the total reported product costs of each product under the two alternative product-costing methods.

	Valve A	Valve B
Plantwide overhead rate	$227	$227
Departmental overhead rates	223	251

The use of departmental overhead rates yields a more accurate product cost for each valve. Notice that the use of a plantwide overhead rate overcosts the high-volume and relatively simple Valve A, and undercosts the low-volume and complex Valve B. This latter method results in a cost distortion. The following table compares the total overhead costs assigned to each product under both methods.

	Valve A	Valve B	Total
Plantwide overhead rate	$810,000	$135,000	$945,000
	($27 × 30,000)	($27 × 5,0000)	
Departmental overhead rates	$690,000	$255,000	$945,000
	($23 × 30,000)	($51 × 5,000)	

The cost distortion is obvious in the following graph, which shows the total overhead costs of $945,000 assigned to Valve A and Valve B under both methods.

Project Costing: Job-Order Costing in Nonmanufacturing Organizations

Learning Objective   **8**

Describe the process of project costing used in service industry firms and nonprofit organizations.

Job-order costing also is used in service industry companies and other nonmanufacturing organizations. However, rather than referring to production "jobs," such organizations use terminology that reflects their operations. For example, hospitals such as the Vancouver Children's Hospital assign costs to "cases," and consulting firms like McKinsey & Company track "contract" costs. Law firms assign costs to cases, while government agencies typically refer to "programs" or "missions." The need for cost accumulation exists in these and similar organizations for the same reasons found in manufacturing firms. For example, a mission to launch a commercial satellite by NASA is assigned a cost for the purposes of planning, cost control, and pricing of the launch service.

To illustrate the cost accumulation system used in a service industry firm, let's turn our attention to Metro Advertising Agency in Saskatoon. This small ad agency has two managing partners who pay themselves annual salaries of $100,000 each, and an artistic staff of six people who each earns $50,000 per year. Fringe benefits for these professionals average 40 percent of their compensation. So Metro Advertising Agency's direct professional labour budget is as follows:

METRO
ADVERTISING

Partner salaries	$200,000
Partner benefits (40%)	80,000
Total partner compensation	$280,000
Artistic staff salaries	$300,000
Artistic staff benefits (40%)	120,000
Total artistic staff compensation	$420,000

The ad agency's annual overhead budget, which totals $756,000, appears in Exhibit 3–13. The overhead budget includes the costs of the support staff, artistic and photographic supplies, office operation, utilities, rent, insurance, advertising, vehicle maintenance, and depreciation. Metro's accountant has estimated that one-third of the budgeted overhead cost is incurred to support the ad agency's two partners, and two-thirds of it goes to support the artistic staff. Thus, the following two overhead rates are calculated:

"SFU seeks to recover indirect costs on research funded under grant and contract agreements. Researchers must budget overhead in applications for research funding using the rates appropriate to the funding mechanism and sponsor's guidelines." (3h)
Simon Fraser University

$$\frac{\text{Budgeted annual partner support overhead}}{\text{Budgeted annual partner compensation}} = \frac{\$756,000 \times \frac{1}{3}}{\$280,000} = 90\%$$

$$\frac{\text{Budgeted annual artistic staff support overhead}}{\text{Budgeted annual artistic staff compensation}} = \frac{\$756,000 \times \frac{2}{3}}{\$420,000} = 120\%$$

Overhead is assigned to each ad contract at the rate of 90 percent of partner direct professional labour plus 120 percent of artistic staff direct professional labour. During May, Metro Advertising Agency completed an advertising project for Super Scoop Ice Cream Company. The contract required $1,800 in direct material, $1,200 of partner direct professional labour, and $2,000 of artistic staff direct professional labour. The total cost of the contract is computed as follows:

Contract MJH0207: Advertising Program for Super Scoop Ice Cream Company	
Direct material	$1,800
Direct professional labour (partner)	1,200
Direct professional labour (artistic staff)	2,000
Applied overhead:	
Partner support ($1,200 × 90%)	1,080
Artistic staff support ($2,000 × 120%)	2,400
Total cost	$8,480

The total contract cost of $8,480 includes actual direct-material and direct professional labour costs, and applied overhead based on the predetermined overhead rates for partner support costs and artistic staff support costs. The contract cost can be used by the firm in controlling costs, for planning cash flows and operations, and as one informational input in

Exhibit 3–13
Metro Advertising Agency:
Annual Overhead Budget

METRO ADVERTISING AGENCY Annual Overhead Budget For the Year 20x6	
Support staff:	
Receptionist	$ 32,000
Secretarial	70,000
Accounting	40,000
Custodial	29,000
Support staff benefits	68,400
Artistic supplies	160,000
Photographic supplies	120,000
Office:	
Computer	20,000
Photocopying	15,000
Office supplies	18,000
Postage	2,100
Utilities:	
Electricity	13,000
Heat/air conditioning	16,000
Internet access	1,500
Cable TV	2,000
Telephone	3,100
Trash collection	2,400
Other	2,500
Building rent	50,000
Insurance	15,000
Advertising	20,000
Vehicle maintenance	4,000
Depreciation:	
Equipment	12,000
Vehicles	20,000
Other	20,000
Total overhead	$756,000

its contract-pricing decisions. In addition to the contract cost, the firm also should consider the demand for its advertising services and the prices charged by its competitors.

The discussion above provides only a brief overview of cost accumulation procedures in service industry and nonprofit organizations. The main point is that job-order costing systems are used in a wide variety of organizations, and these systems provide important information to managers for planning, decision making, and control.

Changing Technology in Manufacturing Operations

The technology of manufacturing is changing rapidly and often affects the managerial accounting procedures used to collect data and transmit information to the intended users. Three such technological changes are electronic data interchange (EDI), Extensible Markup Language (XML), and the use of bar codes.

EDI and XML

Electronic data interchange (EDI) is the direct exchange of data between organizations via a computer-to-computer interface. EDI is used to transmit such documents as purchase orders, shipping notices, receiving notices, invoices, and a host of other production-related data. This eliminates the need for paperwork, speeding up the flow of information and substantially reducing errors. EDI is now in widespread use. For example, Walmart places most of its merchandise orders to its suppliers using this information technology.

An alternative to EDI is *Extensible Markup Language (XML)*, which is web-based and less expensive to implement than EDI. Its purpose is to allow users to share structured data (e.g., product order lists or price data) via the Internet. XML allows its users to define "tags" that the computer then interprets as a particular type of information. For example, a tag might indicate a product's in-stock date or price. See www.xml.com for a primer on this web-based data-sharing tool.

Use of Bar Codes

We have all seen bar codes used to record inventory and sales information in retail stores. This efficient means of recording data also is becoming widely used in recording important events in manufacturing processes. Production employees can record the time they begin working on a particular job order by scanning the bar code on their employee ID badge and a bar code assigned to the production job order. Raw materials and partially completed components are assigned bar codes, and their movement throughout the production process is efficiently recorded. For example, raw materials may be requisitioned by a production employee simply by scanning the bar code assigned to the needed raw materials. When the materials are sent from the warehouse to the requisitioning production department, the bar code is scanned again. Inventory records are updated instantly. Bar codes represent one more instance where technology is changing both the production environment and the procedures used in accounting for production operations.

> "Each production job, from beginning to end, can take several weeks. Bar code technology is used extensively. The container that carries the work in process is bar-coded, and we use that to track each job." (3i)
>
> **MiCRUS**
> **(Joint venture of IBM and Cirrus Logic)**

Managerial **A**ccounting **P**ractice

Walmart,
U.S. Department
of Defense,
Bell Canada,
and CN

RADIO FREQUENCY IDENTIFICATION SYSTEMS

In some places, bar codes are being replaced by radio frequency identification systems (RFID). Unlike bar codes, which can be read by a scanner only when visible, the RFID system allows the information to be read from longer distances and without visibility. For example, a raw-material shipment that embeds the RFID system could be identified while still unpacked or in a delivery truck. Among the benefits attributed to RFID systems are reduced labour costs, fewer supply delays, and a reduction of waste in the supply chain.

Leading the move toward RFID systems are Walmart and the U.S. Department of Defense. "Both organizations have mandated that their suppliers comply with their RFID guidelines." The Bell Canada RFID-enabled asset management solution allows CN, the Canadian National Railway Company, to accurately manage incoming and outgoing truck chassis wirelessly, resulting in an increase in supply chain efficiency, productivity, and cost savings.[2]

Focus on Ethics

DID BOEING EXPLOIT ACCOUNTING RULES TO CONCEAL COST OVERRUNS AND PRODUCTION DELAYS?[3]

Aircraft manufacturers use job-order costing to determine the cost of an airplane. Supply-chain management and production controls are also important tools used by manufacturers to manage production costs. As *BusinessWeek* reported, however, things don't always go according to plan.

For three years, Boeing's top management had been seeking a merger with McDonnell Douglas Corporation, whose board of directors was reluctant to approve the deal. Finally, the deal went through, and the world's largest aerospace company was born—"the first manufacturer ever with the ability to build everything that flies, from helicopters and fighter jets to space stations."

Unfortunately, "a disaster was quietly unfolding inside Boeing's sprawling factories—one that would ultimately wind up costing billions of dollars, cause several executives to lose their jobs, and lead to claims of accounting fraud. Facing an unprecedented surge in orders because of a booming economy, workers were toiling around the clock, pushing the assembly line to the breaking point. At the same time, the company was struggling to overhaul outdated production methods. These pressures were building up to what was, in essence, a manufacturing nervous breakdown. In the weeks after the merger announcement, parts shortages and overtime approached all-time highs. As costs went through the roof, the profitability of airliners such as the 777 crumpled. A special team formed to study the crisis issued a report with a blunt conclusion: 'Our production system is broken.'"

Had investors "understood the scope of the problems, the stock would probably have tumbled and the McDonnell deal—a stock swap that hinged on Boeing's ability to maintain a lofty share price—would have been jeopardized."

In May of 2002, *BusinessWeek* reported the results of its three-month investigation, which "reconstructed this hidden chapter in the company's history—and analyzed its current implications." The *BusinessWeek* article alleged that "new details supplied by several inside witnesses indicate that Boeing did more than simply fail to tell investors about its production disaster. It also engaged in a wide variety of aggressive accounting techniques that papered over the mess. Critics say the company should have taken charges for the assembly-line disaster in the first half of 1997, even if it meant jeopardizing the McDonnell merger. They also claim that Boeing took advantage of the unusual flexibility provided by *program accounting*—a system that allows the huge upfront expense of building a plane to be spread out over several years—to cover up cost overruns and to book savings from efficiency initiatives that never panned out. 'Boeing managed its earnings to the point where it got caught,' says Debra A. Smith, a partner at Constraints Management, a Seattle-area manufacturing consultancy, and a former senior auditor at Deloitte & Touche who worked on the company's account during the early 1980s. 'Boeing basically decided in the short run that [managing earnings] was a lesser evil than losing the merger,' adds Smith. At a time when investors are asking themselves how far Corporate America can be trusted, the Boeing saga provides rich new evidence that companies have much greater leeway to manipulate their numbers than most people suspect."

Boeing allegedly used program accounting to spread its huge cost overruns across several years, propping up earnings and the company's share price. After the merger, however, the truth came out in the form of much lower earnings.

What is your view of how Boeing handled its cost overruns, production problems, and the merger? Did the company's top executives act ethically? How about its accountants?

Chapter Summary

LO1 Discuss the role of product and service costing in manufacturing and nonmanufacturing firms.
Product costing is the process of accumulating the costs of a production process and assigning them to the firm's products. Product costs are needed for three major purposes: (1) to value inventory and cost of goods sold in financial accounting; (2) to provide managerial accounting information to managers for planning, cost control, and decision making; and (3) to provide cost data to various organizations outside the firm.

LO2 Diagram and explain the flow of costs through the manufacturing accounts used in product costing.
The costs of direct material, direct labour, and manufacturing overhead are first entered into the work-in-process

inventory account. When goods are completed, the accumulated manufacturing costs are transferred from work-in-process inventory to finished-goods inventory. Finally, these product costs are transferred from finished-goods inventory to cost of goods sold when sales occur.

LO3 Distinguish between job-order costing and process costing. Job-order costing is used by firms that engage in either job-shop or batch-production operations. Such firms produce relatively small numbers of dissimilar products. Process costing is used by companies that produce relatively large numbers of nearly identical products.

LO4 Compute a predetermined overhead rate and explain its use in job-order costing for job-shop and batch-production environments. Overhead is applied to production jobs using a predetermined overhead rate, which is based on estimates of manufacturing overhead (in the numerator) and the level of some cost driver or activity base (in the denominator).

LO5 Prepare journal entries to record the costs of direct material, direct labour, and manufacturing overhead in a job-order costing system. Journal entries, as illustrated in the chapter, are used to track the flow of manufacturing costs through the various accounts, such as raw-material inventory, work-in-process inventory, finished-goods inventory, and cost of goods sold.

LO6 Prepare a schedule of cost of goods manufactured, a schedule of cost of goods sold, and an income statement for a manufacturer, using a normal costing system. These accounting schedules, which are illustrated in the chapter, provide information to management about the costs incurred in a production operation.

LO7 Describe the two-stage allocation process used to assign manufacturing-overhead costs to production jobs. In Stage 1, cost distribution and service department cost allocation are used to assign all manufacturing-overhead costs to production departments. In Stage 2, cost application is used to assign overhead costs from production departments to production jobs using a predetermined overhead rate.

LO8 Describe the process of project costing used in service industry firms and nonprofit organizations. Job-order costing methods are used in a variety of service industry firms and nonprofit organizations. Accumulating costs of projects, contracts, cases, programs, or missions provides important information to managers in such organizations as hospitals, law firms, and government agencies.

Review Problem on Job-Order Costing

Pryor Paint Company uses a job-order costing system, and the company had two jobs in process at the beginning of the current year. Job JY65 currently has a cost of $134,400 assigned to it, and Job DC66 currently has a cost of $85,600 assigned to it. The following additional information is available:

- The company applies manufacturing overhead on the basis of machine hours. Budgeted overhead and machine activity for the year were anticipated to be $1,344,000 and 16,000 hours, respectively.
- The company worked on four jobs during the first quarter. Direct materials used, direct labour incurred, and machine hours consumed were as follows:

Job No.	Direct Material	Direct Labour	Machine Hours
JY65	$33,600	$ 56,000	1,200
DC66	—	35,200	700
SG78	70,400	104,000	2,000
RG82	24,000	14,080	500

- Manufacturing overhead during the first quarter included charges for depreciation ($54,400), indirect labour ($96,000), indirect materials ($8,000), and other factory costs ($223,200).
- Pryor Paint Company completed Job JY65 and Job DC66. Job DC66 was sold on account, producing a profit of $55,520 for the firm.

Required:

1. Determine Pryor Paint Company's predetermined overhead application rate.
2. Prepare journal entries as of March 31 to record the following. (*Note:* Use summary entries where appropriate by combining individual job data.)
    a. The issuance of direct material to production and the direct labour incurred
    b. The manufacturing overhead incurred during the quarter

    c. The application of manufacturing overhead to production

    d. The completion of Jobs JY65 and DC66

    e. The sale of Job DC66

3. Determine the cost of the jobs still in production as of March 31.

4. Did the finished-goods inventory increase or decrease during the first quarter? By how much?

5. Was manufacturing overhead under- or overapplied for the first quarter of the year? By how much?

Solution to Review Problem

1. Predetermined overhead rate = Budgeted overhead ÷ Budgeted machine hours

$$= \$1,344,000 \div 16,000 = \$84 \text{ per machine hour}$$

2. *(a)*

Work-in-process inventory	128,000*	
Raw-material inventory		128,000
Work-in-process inventory	209,280†	
Wages payable		209,280

    *$33,600 + $70,400 + $24,000 = $128,000

    † $56,000 + $35,200 + $104,000 + $14,080 = $209,280

    (b)

Manufacturing overhead	381,600	
Accumulated depreciation		54,400
Wages payable		96,000
Manufacturing supplies inventory		8,000
Miscellaneous accounts		223,200

    (c)

Work-in-process inventory	369,600*	
Manufacturing overhead		369,600

    *(1,200 + 700 + 2,000 + 500) × $84 = $369,600.

    (d)

Finished-goods inventory	504,400*	
Work-in-process inventory		504,400

    *Job JY65: $134,400 + $33,600 + $56,000 + (1,200 × $84) = $324,800

    Job DC66: $85,600 + $35,200 + (700 × $84) = $179,600

    $324,800 + $179,600 = $504,400

    (e)

Accounts receivable	235,120*	
Sales revenue		235,120

    *$179,600 + $55,520 = $235,120.

Cost of goods sold	179,600	
Finished-goods inventory		179,600

3. Jobs SG78 and RG82 are in production as of March 31:

Job SG78: $70,400 + $104,000 + (2,000 × $84)	$342,400
Job RG82: $24,000 + $14,080 + (500 × $84)	80,080
Total	$422,480

4. Finished-goods inventory increased by $324,800 ($504,400 − $179,600).

5. The company's actual overhead amounted to $381,600, whereas applied overhead totalled $369,600. Thus, overhead was underapplied by $12,000.

Glossary

Review key terms and definitions on Connect.

Review Questions

3–1. List and explain four purposes of product costing.

3–2. Explain the difference between job-order and process costing.

3–3. How is the concept of product costing applied in service industry firms?

3–4. What are the purposes of the following documents: (*a*) material requisition form, (*b*) labour time record, and (*c*) job-cost record.

3–5. Why is manufacturing overhead applied to products when product costs are used in making pricing decisions?

3–6. Explain the benefits of using a predetermined overhead rate instead of an actual overhead rate.

3–7. Describe one advantage and one disadvantage of prorating overapplied or underapplied overhead.

3–8. Describe an important cost–benefit issue involving accuracy versus timeliness in accounting for overhead.

3–9. Explain the difference between actual and normal costing.

3–10. When a single, volume-based cost driver (or activity base) is used to apply manufacturing overhead, what is the management accountant's primary objective in selecting the cost driver?

3–11. Describe some costs and benefits of using multiple overhead rates instead of a plantwide overhead rate.

3–12. Describe the process of two-stage cost allocation in the development of departmental overhead rates.

3–13. Define each of the following terms, and explain the relationship among them: (*a*) overhead cost distribution,

(*b*) service department cost allocation, and (*c*) overhead application.

3–14. Describe how job-order costing concepts are used in professional service firms, such as law practices and consulting firms.

3–15. What is meant by the term *cost driver*? What is a *volume-based cost driver*?

3–16. Describe the flow of costs through a product-costing system. What special accounts are involved, and how are they used?

3–17. Give an example of how a hospital might use job-order costing concepts.

3–18. Why are some manufacturing firms switching from direct-labour hours to machine hours or throughput time as the basis for overhead application?

3–19. What is the cause of overapplied or underapplied overhead?

3–20. Briefly describe two ways of closing out overapplied or underapplied overhead at the end of an accounting period.

3-21. Describe how a large retailer such as Walmart could use EDI.

3-22. Explain how an engineer might use bar-code technology to record the time she spends on various activities.

Exercises

Exercise 3–23 Job-Order versus Process Costing (LO1, 3)

For each of the following companies, indicate whether job-order or process costing is more appropriate.

1. Manufacturer of swimming pool chemicals
2. Manufacturer of custom hot tubs and spas
3. Architectural firm
4. Manufacturer of ceramic tile
5. Producer of yogurt
6. Manufacturer of custom tool sheds
7. Manufacturer of paper clips
8. Engineering consulting firm
9. Manufacturer of balloons
10. Manufacturer of custom emergency rescue vehicles

Exercise 3–24 Fixed and Variable Costs; Overhead Rate: Agribusiness (LO1, 4)

The controller for Tender Bird Poultry, Inc. estimates that the company's fixed overhead is $100,000 per year. She also has determined that the variable overhead is approximately $0.10 per chicken raised and sold. Since the firm has a single product, overhead is applied on the basis of output units: chickens raised and sold.

Required:

1. Calculate the predetermined overhead rate under each of the following output predictions: 200,000 chickens, 300,000 chickens, and 400,000 chickens.
2. Does the predetermined overhead rate change in proportion to the change in predicted production? Why?

Exercise 3–25 Basic Journal Entries in Job-Order Costing (LO5)

Finley Educational Products started and finished Job B67 during June. The job required $4,600 of direct material and 40 hours of direct labour at $17 per hour. The predetermined overhead rate is $5 per direct-labour hour.

Required: Prepare journal entries to record the incurrence of production costs and the completion of Job B67.

Exercise 3–26 Job-Order Costing: Movie Production; Use of the Internet (LO1, 3)

Visit the website of a film producer, such as Disney, MGM, or Warner Brothers.

Walt Disney Studios	www.disney.com
MGM	www.mgm.com
Warner Brothers	www.warnerbros.com

Required: Read about one of the company's recent (or upcoming) movie releases. Then discuss why or why not job-order costing would be an appropriate costing method for movie production. Would your answer be any different depending on the type of movie being produced (e.g., animation in a studio versus filming on location in Timbuktu)?

Exercise 3–27 Job-Order Costing Basics (LO2, 4, 6)

Bodin Company manufactures finger splints for kids who get tendonitis from playing video games. The firm had the following inventories at the beginning and end of the month of January:

	January 1	January 31
Finished goods	$125,000	$117,000
Work in process	235,000	251,000
Raw material	134,000	124,000

The following additional data pertain to January operations.

Raw material purchased	$191,000
Direct labour	300,000
Actual manufacturing overhead	175,000
Actual selling and administrative expenses	115,000

The company applies manufacturing overhead at the rate of 60 percent of direct-labour cost. Any over-applied or underapplied manufacturing-overhead is accumulated until the end of the year.

Required: Compute the following amounts.

1. The company's prime cost for January
2. The total manufacturing cost for January
3. The cost of goods manufactured for January
4. The cost of goods sold for January
5. The balance in the manufacturing-overhead account on January 31. Debit or credit?

(CMA, adapted)

Exercise 3–28 Cost Relationships: Normal Costing System (LO2, 4, 6)

McAllister Ltd. employs a normal costing system. The following information pertains to the year just ended:

- Total manufacturing costs were $2,500,000.
- Cost of goods manufactured was $2,425,000.
- Applied manufacturing overhead was 30 percent of total manufacturing costs.
- Manufacturing overhead was applied to production at a rate of 80 percent of direct-labour cost.
- Work-in-process inventory on January 1 was 75 percent of work-in-process inventory on December 31.

Required:

1. Compute the total direct-labour cost for the year.
2. Calculate the total cost of direct material used during the year.
3. Compute the value of the company's work-in-process inventory on December 31.

(CMA, adapted)

Exercise 3–29 Job-Cost Record (LO2, 4)

Garrett Toy Company incurred the following costs to produce Job TB78, which consisted of 1,000 teddy bears that can walk, talk, and play cards. The job was started on 4/1/x0 and completed on 4/15/x0.

Direct material:

    4/1/x0 Requisition 101: 400 metres of fabric at $0.80 per metre

    4/5/x0 Requisition 108: 500 cubic metres of stuffing at $0.30 per cubic metre

Direct labour:

    From employee time cards for 4/1/x0 through 4/8/x0: 500 hours at $12 per hour

Manufacturing overhead:

    Applied on the basis of direct-labour hours at $2 per hour on completion date of the job.

On April 30, 700 of the bears were shipped to a local toy store.

Required: Prepare a job-cost record using the information given above. (Use Exhibit 3–4 as a guide.)

Exercise 3–30 Schedule of Cost of Goods Manufactured (LO2, 4, 6)

Crunchem Cereal Company incurred the following actual costs during 20x1:

Direct material used	$275,000
Direct labour	120,000
Manufacturing overhead	252,000

The firm's predetermined overhead rate is 210 percent of direct-labour cost. The January 1 inventory balances were as follows:

Raw material	$30,000
Work in process	39,000
Finished goods	42,000

Each of these inventory balances was 10 percent higher at the end of the year.

Required:

1. Prepare a schedule of cost of goods manufactured for 20x1.
2. What was the cost of goods sold for the year?
3. *Build a spreadsheet:* Construct an Excel spreadsheet to solve all of the preceding requirements. Show how the solution will change if the following data change: Direct material used amounted to $281,000 and raw-material inventory on December 31 was $28,000.

Exercise 3–31 Manufacturing Cost Flows (LO2, 5, 6)

Reimel Furniture Company, Inc. incurred the following costs during 20x2:

Direct material used	$174,000
Direct labour	324,000
Manufacturing overhead applied	180,000

During 20x2, products costing $120,000 were finished, and products costing $132,000 were sold on account for $195,000. There were no purchases of raw material during the year. The beginning balances in the firm's inventory accounts are as follows:

Raw material	$227,000
Work in process	18,000
Finished goods	30,000

Required:

1. Prepare T-accounts to show the flow of costs through the company's manufacturing accounts during 20x2.
2. Prepare a partial balance sheet and a partial income statement to reflect the information given above. (*Hint:* See Exhibit 3–2.)

Exercise 3–32 Basic Manufacturing Cost Flows (LO2, 6)

Selected data concerning the past year's operations of the Yukon Manufacturing Company are as follows:

	Inventories	
	Beginning	Ending
Raw material	$71,000	$ 81,000
Work in process	80,000	30,000
Finished goods	90,000	110,000
Other data:		
Direct material used		$326,000
Total manufacturing costs charged to production during the year (includes direct material, direct labour, and manufacturing overhead applied at a rate of 60% of direct-labour cost)		686,000
Cost of goods available for sale		826,000
Selling and administrative expenses		31,500

Required:

1. What was the cost of raw materials purchased during the year?
2. What was the direct-labour cost charged to production during the year?
3. What was the cost of goods manufactured during the year?
4. What was the cost of goods sold during the year?

(CMA, adapted)

Exercise 3–33 Proration of Underapplied Overhead (L05)

Sweet Tooth Confectionary incurred $157,000 of manufacturing-overhead costs during the year just ended. However, only $141,000 of overhead was applied to production. At the conclusion of the year, the following amounts of the year's applied overhead remained in the various manufacturing accounts.

	Applied Overhead Remaining in Account on December 31
Work-in-process inventory	$35,250
Finished-goods inventory	49,350
Cost of goods sold	56,400

Required: Prepare a journal entry to close out the balance in the manufacturing-overhead account and prorate the balance to the three manufacturing accounts.

Exercise 3–34 Overapplied or Underapplied Overhead (L04, 5)

The following information pertains to Trenton Glass Works for the year just ended:

Budgeted direct-labour cost	75,000 hours (practical capacity) at $16 per hour
Actual direct-labour cost	80,000 hours at $17.50 per hour
Budgeted manufacturing overhead	$997,500
Budgeted selling and administrative expenses	435,000
Actual manufacturing overhead:	
Depreciation	$231,000
Property taxes	21,000
Indirect labour	82,000
Supervisory salaries	200,000
Utilities	59,000
Insurance	30,000
Rental of space	300,000
Indirect material (see data below)	79,000
Indirect material:	
Beginning inventory, January 1	48,000
Purchases during the year	94,000
Ending inventory, December 31	63,000

Required:

1. Compute the firm's predetermined overhead rate, which is based on direct-labour hours.
2. Calculate the overapplied or underapplied overhead for the year.
3. Prepare a journal entry to close out the manufacturing overhead account into cost of goods sold.
4. *Build a spreadsheet:* Construct an Excel spreadsheet to solve requirements (1) and (2) above. Show how the solution will change if the following data change: Budgeted manufacturing overhead was $990,000, property taxes were $25,000, and purchases of indirect material amounted to $97,000.

Exercise 3–35 Predetermined Overhead Rate; Various Cost Drivers **(LO4)**

The following data pertain to the Oneida Restaurant Supply Company for the year just ended:

Budgeted sales revenue	$205,000
Actual manufacturing overhead	340,000
Budgeted machine hours	10,000
Budgeted direct-labour hours (based on practical capacity)	20,000
Budgeted direct-labour rate	$14
Budgeted manufacturing overhead	364,000
Actual machine hours	11,000
Actual direct-labour hours	18,000
Actual direct-labour rate	$15

Required:

1. Compute the firm's predetermined overhead rate for the year using each of the following common cost drivers: (*a*) machine hours, (*b*) direct-labour hours, and (*c*) direct-labour dollars.
2. Calculate the overapplied or underapplied overhead for the year using each of the cost drivers listed above.

Exercise 3–36 Actual versus Normal Costing **(LO4, 5)**

Refer to the data in the preceding exercise for Oneida Restaurant Supply Company. Prepare a journal entry to add to work-in-process inventory the total manufacturing-overhead cost for the year, assuming that

1. The firm uses actual costing.
2. The firm uses normal costing, with a predetermined overhead rate based on machine hours.

Exercise 3–37 Project Costing: Interior Decorating **(LO8)**

Design Arts is an interior decorating firm in Berlin. The following costs were incurred in the firm's contract to redecorate the mayor's offices (€ is the symbol for the euro):

Direct material used	€3,500
Direct professional labour	€6,000

The firm's budget for the year included the following estimates:

Budgeted overhead	€400,000
Budgeted direct professional labour	€250,000

Overhead is applied to contracts using a predetermined overhead rate calculated annually. The rate is based on direct professional labour cost.

Required: Calculate the total cost of the firm's contract to redecorate the mayor's offices. (Remember to express your answer in euros.)

Exercise 3–38 Choice of a Cost Driver for Overhead Application **(LO1, 4)**

Suppose you are the controller for a company that produces handmade glassware.

1. Choose a volume-based cost driver on which to base the application of overhead. Write a memo to the company president explaining your choice.
2. Now you have changed jobs. You are the controller of a microchip manufacturer that uses a highly automated production process. Repeat the same requirements stated above.

Exercise 3–39 Cost Drivers: Different Production Methods (LO4, 5)

Foothills Leatherworks, which manufactures saddles and other leather goods, has three departments. The Assembly Department manufactures various leather products, such as belts, purses, and saddlebags, using an automated production process. The Saddle Department produces handmade saddles and uses very little machinery. The Tanning Department produces leather. The tanning process requires little in the way of labour or machinery, but it does require space and process time. Due to the different production processes in the three departments, the company uses three different cost drivers for the application of manufacturing overhead. The cost drivers and overhead rates are as follows:

	Cost Driver	Predetermined Overhead Rate
Tanning Department	Square metres of leather	$3 per square metre
Assembly Department	Machine time	$9 per machine hour
Saddle Department	Direct-labour time	$4 per direct-labour hour

The company's deluxe saddle and accessory set consists of a handmade saddle, two saddlebags, a belt, and a vest, all coordinated to match. The entire set uses 100 square metres of leather from the Tanning Department, 3 machine hours in the Assembly Department, and 40 direct-labour hours in the Saddle Department.

Required: Job DS-20 consisted of 20 deluxe saddle and accessory sets. Prepare journal entries to record applied manufacturing overhead in the work-in-process inventory account for each department.

Exercise 3–40 Two-Stage Allocation (LO1, 7)

Refer to Exhibit 3–12, which portrays the three types of allocation procedures used in two-stage allocation. Give an example of each of these allocation procedures in a hospital setting. The ultimate cost object is a patient-day of hospital care. This is one day of care for one patient. (*Hint:* First think about the various departments in a hospital. Which departments deal directly with patients? Which ones are service departments and do not deal directly with patients? What kinds of costs does a hospital incur that should be distributed among all of the hospital's departments? Correct hospital terminology is not important here. Focus on the *concepts* of cost allocation portrayed in Exhibit 3–12.)

Exercise 3–41 Overhead Application in a Service Industry Firm (LO8)

Refer to the example of overhead application in the Metro Advertising Agency in the section in this chapter entitled "Project Costing: Job-Order Costing in Nonmanufacturing Organizations." Suppose the firm used a single cost driver, total staff compensation, to apply overhead costs to each ad contract.

Required:

1. Compute the total budgeted staff compensation—both partner and artistic staff compensation.
2. Compute Metro's overhead rate on the basis of this single cost driver.
3. Recalculate the applied overhead for the Super Scoop Ice Cream Company contract.
4. Compare the applied overhead using the single cost driver with the applied overhead computed using the two cost drivers used in the text example.

Problems

Problem 3–42 Schedule of Cost of Goods Manufactured and Sold; Income Statement (LO6)

The following data refer to Twisto Pretzel Corp. for the year 20x1:

1. Total manufacturing costs: $175,100

3. Net income: $7,100

Work-in-process inventory, 12/31/x0	$ 8,100	Utilities for sales and administrative offices	$ 2,500
Selling and administrative salaries	13,800	Other selling and administrative expenses	4,000
Insurance on factory and equipment	3,600	Indirect-labour cost incurred	29,000
Work-in-process inventory, 12/31/x1	8,300	Depreciation on factory building	3,800
Finished-goods inventory, 12/31/x0	14,000	Depreciation on cars used by sales staff	1,200
Cash balance, 12/31/x1	6,000	Direct-labour cost incurred	79,000
Indirect material used	4,900	Raw-material inventory, 12/31/x1	11,000
Depreciation on factory equipment	2,100	Accounts receivable, 12/31/x1	4,100
Raw-material inventory, 12/31/x0	10,100	Rental for warehouse space to store raw material	3,100
Property taxes on factory	2,400	Rental of space for company president's office	1,700
Finished-goods inventory, 12/31/x1	15,400	Applied manufacturing overhead	58,000
Purchases of raw material in 20x1	39,000	Sales revenue	205,800
Utilities for factory	6,000	Income tax expense	5,100

Required:

1. Prepare the company's schedule of cost of goods manufactured for 20x1.
2. Prepare the company's schedule of cost of goods sold for 20x1. The company closes overapplied or underapplied overhead into cost of goods sold.
3. Prepare the company's income statement for 20x1.

Problem 3–43 Basic Job-Order Costing; Journal Entries (LO4, 5)

1. Predetermined overhead rate: $12 per hour

Burlington Clock Works manufactures fine handcrafted clocks. The firm uses a job-order costing system, and manufacturing overhead is applied on the basis of direct-labour hours. Estimated manufacturing overhead for the year is $240,000. The firm employs 10 master clockmakers, who constitute the direct-labour force. Each of these employees is expected to work 2,000 hours during the year. The following events occurred during October:

a. The firm purchased 3,000 board metres of mahogany veneer at $11 per board metre.

b. Twenty brass counterweights were requisitioned for production. Each weight cost $23.

c. Five litres of glue were requisitioned for production. The glue cost $20 per litre. Glue is treated as an indirect material.

d. Depreciation on Burlington's building for October was $8,000.

e. A $400 utility bill was paid in cash.

f. Time cards showed the following usage of labour:

    Job G60:   12 grandfather clocks; 1,000 hours of direct labour

    Job C81:   20 cuckoo clocks; 700 hours of direct labour

The master clockmakers (direct-labour staff) earn $20 per hour.

g. The October property tax bill for $910 was received but has not yet been paid in cash.

h. The firm employs labourers who perform various tasks such as material handling and shop cleanup. Their wages for October amounted to $2,500.

i. Job G60, which was started in July, was finished in October. The total cost of the job was $14,400.

j. Nine of the grandfather clocks from Job G60 were sold in October for $1,500 each.

Required:

1. Calculate the firm's predetermined overhead rate for the year.
2. Prepare journal entries to record the events described above.

Problem 3–44 Manufacturing Cost Flows; Analysis of T-Accounts (LO2, 5)

Perfecto Pizza Company produces microwaveable pizzas. The following accounts appeared in the ledger as of December 31.

Raw-Material Inventory			
Bal. 1/1	21,000		
Bal. 12/31	?	?	
	36,000		

Accounts Payable			
		2,500	Bal. 1/1
	136,500	?	
		1,000	Bal. 12/31

Work-in-Process Inventory			
Bal. 1/1	17,000		
Direct material	?	?	
Direct labour	?		
Manufacturing overhead	?		
Bal. 12/31	19,000		

Finished-Goods Inventory			
Bal. 1/1	12,000		
	?	?	
Bal. 12/31	20,000		

Manufacturing Overhead		
	?	?

Cost of Goods Sold	
710,000	

Wages Payable		
	2,000	Bal. 1/1
147,000	?	
	5,000	Bal. 12/31

Sales Revenue	
	?

Accounts Receivable			
Bal. 1/1	11,000		
		?	806,000
Bal. 12/31	15,000		

Additional information:

a. Accounts payable is used only for direct-material purchases.

b. Underapplied overhead of $2,500 for the year has not yet been closed into cost of goods sold.

Required: Complete the T-accounts by computing the amounts indicated by a question mark.

Problem 3–45 Job-Order Costing; Journal Entries (LO2, 4, 5)

Stellar Sound Inc., which uses a job-order costing system, had two jobs in process at the start of 20x1: Job 64 ($84,000) and Job 65 ($53,500). The following information is available:

a. The company applies manufacturing overhead on the basis of machine hours (based on practical capacity). Budgeted overhead and machine activity for the year were anticipated to be $840,000, and 16,000 hours, respectively.

b. The company worked on four jobs during the first quarter. Direct materials used, direct labour incurred, and machine hours consumed were as follows:

Job Number	Direct Material	Direct Labour	Machine Hours
64	$21,000	$35,000	1,200
65	—	22,000	700
66	44,000	65,000	2,000
67	15,000	8,800	500

c. Manufacturing overhead during the first quarter included charges for depreciation ($34,000), indirect labour ($60,000), indirect materials used ($5,000), and other factory costs ($139,500).

d. Stellar Sound completed Job 64 and Job 65. Job 65 was sold on account, producing a profit of $34,700 for the firm.

Required:

1. Determine the company's predetermined overhead application rate.

2. Prepare journal entries as of March 31 to record the following. (*Note:* Use summary entries where appropriate by combining individual job data.)

    a. The issuance of direct material to production and the direct labour incurred

    b. The manufacturing overhead incurred during the quarter

    c. The application of manufacturing overhead to production

    d. The completion of Jobs 64 and 65

    e. The sale of Job 65

3. Determine the cost of the jobs still in production as of March 31.

4. Did the finished-goods inventory increase or decrease during the first quarter? By how much?

5. Was manufacturing overhead under- or overapplied for the first quarter of the year? By how much?

Problem 3–46 Job-Order Costing; Focus on Manufacturing Overhead (LO2, 4, 5)

Finlon Upholstery uses a job-order costing system to accumulate manufacturing costs. The company's work-in-process on December 31, 20x1, consisted of one job (Job 2077), which was carried on the year-end balance sheet at $156,800. There was no finished-goods inventory on this date.

Finlon applies manufacturing overhead to production on the basis of direct-labour cost. Budgeted totals for 20x2 for direct labour and manufacturing overhead are $4,200,000 and $5,460,000, respectively. Actual results for the year follow:

1. Predetermined overhead rate: 130% of direct labour cost
6. Cost of goods sold: $15,309,300

Direct material used	$ 5,600,000
Direct labour	4,350,000
Indirect material used	65,000
Indirect labour	2,860,000
Factory depreciation	1,740,000
Factory insurance	59,000
Factory utilities	830,000
Selling and administrative expenses	2,160,000
Total	$17,664,000

Job 2077 was completed in January 20x2; there was no work in process at year-end. All jobs produced during 20x2 were sold with the exception of Job 2143, which contained direct-material costs of $156,000 and direct-labour charges of $85,000. The company charges any under- or overapplied overhead to cost of goods sold.

Required:

1. Determine the company's predetermined overhead application rate.
2. Determine the additions to the work-in-process inventory account for direct material used, direct labour, and manufacturing overhead.
3. Compute the amount that the company would disclose as finished-goods inventory on the December 31, 20x2, balance sheet.
4. Prepare the journal entry needed to record the year's completed production.
5. Compute the amount of under- or overapplied overhead at year-end, and prepare the necessary journal entry to record its disposition.
6. Determine the company's 20x2 cost of goods sold.
7. Would it be appropriate to include selling and administrative expenses in either manufacturing overhead or cost of goods sold? Briefly explain.

Problem 3–47 Job-Order Costing in a Consulting Firm (LO1, 2, 4, 8)

1. Traceable costs: $2,500,000

JLR Enterprises provides consulting services and uses a job-order costing system to accumulate the cost of client projects. Traceable costs are charged directly to individual clients; in contrast, other costs incurred by JLR, but not identifiable with specific clients, are charged to jobs by using a predetermined overhead application rate. Clients are billed for directly chargeable costs, overhead, and a markup.

JLR's director of cost management, Michel DeLoire, anticipates the following costs for the upcoming year:

	Cost	Percentage of Cost Directly Traceable to Clients
Professional staff salaries	$2,500,000	80%
Administrative support staff	300,000	60%
Photocopying	50,000	90%
Travel	250,000	90%
Other operating costs	100,000	50%
Total	$3,200,000	

The firm's partners want to make a $640,000 profit for the firm and plan to add a percentage markup on total cost to achieve that figure.

On March 10, JLR completed work on a project for Martinsky Manufacturing. The following costs were incurred: professional staff salaries, $41,000; administrative support staff, $2,600; photocopying, $500; travel, $4,500; and other operating costs, $1,400.

Required:

1. Determine JLR's total traceable costs for the upcoming year and the firm's total anticipated overhead.
2. Calculate the predetermined overhead rate. The rate is based on total costs traceable to client jobs.

3. What percentage of cost will JLR add to each job to achieve its profit target?

4. Determine the total cost of the Martinsky Manufacturing project. How much would Martinsky be billed for services performed?

5. Notice that only 50 percent of JLR's other operating cost is directly traceable to specific client projects. Cite several costs that would be included in this category and difficult to trace to clients.

6. Notice that 80 percent of the professional staff cost is directly traceable to specific client projects. Cite several reasons that would explain why this figure isn't 100 percent.

Problem 3–48   Job-Order Costing; Focus on Overhead and Cost Drivers (LO2, 4, 5, 7)

2. Ending work-in-process inventory cost: $153,530

Garcia, Inc. uses a job-order costing system for its products, which pass from the Machining Department, to the Assembly Department, to finished-goods inventory. The Machining Department is heavily automated; in contrast, the Assembly Department performs a number of manual-assembly activities. The company applies manufacturing overhead by the use of machine hours in the Machining Department and direct-labour cost in the Assembly Department. The following information relates to the year just ended:

	Machining Department	Assembly Department
Budgeted manufacturing overhead...	$4,000,000	$3,080,000
Actual manufacturing overhead	4,260,000	3,050,000
Budgeted direct-labour cost (based on practical capacity).............	1,500,000	5,600,000
Actual direct-labour cost	1,450,000	5,780,000
Budgeted machine hours (based on practical capacity).................	400,000	100,000
Actual machine hours	425,000	110,000

The data that follow pertain to Job 775, the only job in production at year-end.

	Machining Department	Assembly Department
Direct material..	$24,500	$ 6,700
Direct labour..	27,900	58,600
Machine hours..	360	150

Selling and administrative expense amounted to $2,500,000.

Required:

1. Assuming the use of normal costing, determine the predetermined overhead rates used in the Machining Department and the Assembly Department.

2. Compute the cost of the company's year-end work-in-process inventory.

3. Determine whether overhead was under- or overapplied during the year in the Machining Department.

4. Repeat requirement (3) for the Assembly Department.

5. If the company disposes of under- or overapplied overhead as an adjustment to cost of goods sold, would the company's cost of goods sold account increase or decrease? Explain.

6. How much overhead would have been charged to the company's work-in-process account during the year?

7. Comment on the appropriateness of the company's cost drivers (i.e., the use of machine hours in Machining and direct-labour cost in Assembly).

Problem 3–49   Journal Entries in Job-Order Costing (LO4, 5)

1. Predetermined overhead rate: $20 per machine hour

MarineCo manufactures outboard motors and an assortment of other marine equipment. The company uses a job-order costing system. Normal costing is used, and manufacturing overhead is applied on the basis of machine hours. Estimated manufacturing overhead for the year is $1,464,000, and management estimates the firm's practical capacity at 73,200 machine hours.

Required:

1. Calculate the company's predetermined overhead rate for the year.

2. Prepare journal entries to record the following events, which occurred during April:

   a. The firm purchased marine propellers from Peninsula Marine Corporation for $7,850 on account.

   b. A requisition was filed by the Gauge Department for 300 kilograms of clear plastic. The material cost $0.60 per kilogram when it was purchased.

c. The Motor Testing Department requisitioned 300 metres of electrical wire, which is considered to be an indirect material. The wire cost $0.10 per metre when it was purchased.

d. An electric utility bill of $800 was paid in cash.

e. Direct-labour costs incurred in April were $75,000.

f. April's insurance cost was $1,800 for insurance on the cars driven by sales staff. The policy had been prepaid in March.

g. Metal tubing costing $3,000 was purchased on account.

h. A cash payment of $1,700 was made on outstanding accounts payable.

i. Indirect-labour costs of $21,000 were incurred during April.

j. Depreciation on equipment for April amounted to $7,000.

k. Job G22, consisting of 50 tachometers, was finished during April. The total cost of the job was $1,100.

l. During April, 7,000 machine hours were used.

m. Sales on account for April amounted to $176,000. The cost of goods sold in April was $139,000.

Problem 3–50 Schedules of Cost of Goods Manufactured and Sold; Income Statement **(LO6)**

The following data refer to Huron Corporation for the year 20x2:

Sales revenue	$2,105,000		Indirect material used	$ 45,000
Raw-material inventory, 12/31/x1	89,000		Depreciation on factory equipment	60,000
Purchases of raw material in 20x2	731,000		Insurance on factory and equipment	40,000
Raw-material inventory, 12/31/x2	59,000		Utilities for factory	70,000
Direct-labour cost incurred	474,000		Work-in-process inventory, 12/31/x1	—
Selling and administrative expenses	269,000		Work-in-process inventory, 12/31/x2	40,000
Indirect labour cost incurred	150,000		Finished-goods inventory, 12/31/x1	35,000
Property taxes on factory	90,000		Finished-goods inventory, 12/31/x2	40,000
Depreciation on factory building	125,000		Applied manufacturing overhead	577,500
Income tax expense	25,000			

2. Cost of goods sold (adjusted for underapplied overhead): $1,770,000

Required:

1. Prepare the company's schedule of cost of goods manufactured for 20x2.

2. Prepare the company's schedule of cost of goods sold for 20x2. The company closes overapplied or underapplied overhead into cost of goods sold.

3. Prepare the company's income statement for 20x2.

4. *Build a spreadsheet:* Construct an Excel spreadsheet to solve all of the preceding requirements. Show how the solution will change if the following data change: Sales revenue was $2,115,000, applied manufacturing overhead was $580,000, and utilities amounted to $78,000.

eXcel

Problem 3–51 Interpreting the Schedule of Cost of Goods Manufactured **(LO2, 6)**

Refer to the schedule of cost of goods manufactured prepared for Huron Corporation in the preceding problem.

Required:

1. How much of the manufacturing costs incurred during 20x2 remained associated with the work-in-process inventory on December 31, 20x2?

2. Suppose the company had increased its production in 20x2 by 20 percent. Would the direct-material cost shown on the schedule have been larger or the same? Why?

3. Answer the same question as in requirement (2) for depreciation on the factory building.

4. Suppose only half of the $60,000 in depreciation on equipment had been related to factory machinery, and the other half was related to selling and administrative equipment. How would this have changed the schedule of cost of goods manufactured?

Problem 3–52 Cost of Goods Manufactured; Prime and Conversion Costs **(LO2, 6)**

1. Cost of goods manufactured: $348,000

Marco Polo Map Company's cost of goods sold for March was $345,000. The March 31 work-in-process inventory was 90 percent of the March 1 work-in-process inventory. Manufacturing overhead applied was

50 percent of direct-labour cost. Other information pertaining to the company's inventories and production for the month of March is as follows:

Beginning inventories, March 1:	
Raw material	$ 17,000
Work in process..	40,000
Finished goods	102,000
Purchases of raw material during March	113,000
Ending inventories, March 31:	
Raw material	26,000
Work in process..	?
Finished goods	105,000

Required:

1. Prepare a schedule of cost of goods manufactured for the month of March.
2. Prepare a schedule to compute the prime costs (direct material and direct labour) incurred during March.
3. Prepare a schedule to compute the conversion costs (direct labour and manufacturing overhead) charged to work in process during March.

(CMA, adapted)

Problem 3–53 Proration of Overapplied or Underapplied Overhead (LO2, 4, 5, 6)

3. Underapplied overhead: $6,000

Midnight Sun Apparel Company uses normal costing, and manufacturing overhead is applied to work-in-process on the basis of machine hours. On January 1 of the current year, there were no balances in work-in-process or finished-goods inventories. The following estimates were included in the current year's budget:

Total budgeted manufacturing overhead	$235,000
Total budgeted machine hours	47,000

During January, the firm began the following production jobs:

A79	1,000 machine hours
N08	2,500 machine hours
P82	500 machine hours

During January, Jobs A79 and N08 were completed, and Job A79 was sold. The actual manufacturing overhead incurred during January was $26,000.

Required:

1. Compute the company's predetermined overhead rate for the current year.
2. How much manufacturing overhead was applied to production during January?
3. Calculate the overapplied or underapplied overhead for January.
4. Prepare a journal entry to close the balance calculated in requirement (3) into cost of goods sold.
5. Prepare a journal entry to prorate the balance calculated in requirement (3) among the work-in-process inventory, finished-goods inventory, and cost of goods sold accounts.

Problem 3–54 Ethical Issues; Underapplication of Manufacturing Overhead (LO1, 2, 4, 6)

Marc Jackson has recently been hired as a cost accountant by Offset Press Company, a privately held company that produces a line of offset printing presses and lithograph machines. During his first few months on the job, Jackson discovered that Offset has been underapplying factory overhead to the work-in-process inventory account, while overstating expenses through the general and administrative expense account. This practice has been going on since the start of the company, which is in its sixth year of operation. The effect in each year has been favourable, having a material impact on the company's tax position. No internal audit function exists at Offset, and the external auditors have not yet discovered the underapplied factory overhead.

Prior to the sixth-year audit, Jackson had pointed out the practice and its effect to Ayita Bena, the corporate controller, and had asked her to let him make the necessary adjustments. Bena directed him not to make the adjustments, but to wait until the external auditors had completed their work and see what they uncovered.

The sixth-year audit has now been completed, and the external auditors have once again failed to discover the underapplication of factory overhead. Jackson again asked Bena if he could make the required adjustments and was again told not to make them. Jackson, however, believes that the adjustments should be made and that the external auditors should be informed of the situation.

Since there are no established policies at Offset Press Company for resolving ethical conflicts, Jackson is considering one of the following three alternative courses of action:

1. Follow Bena's directive and do nothing further.
2. Attempt to convince Bena to make the proper adjustments and to advise the external auditors of her actions.
3. Tell the Audit Committee of the board of directors about the problem and give the committee the appropriate accounting data.

Required:

1. For each of the three alternative courses of action that Jackson is considering, explain whether the action is appropriate.
2. Independent of your answer to requirement (1), assume that Jackson again approaches Bena to make the necessary adjustments and is unsuccessful. Describe the steps that Jackson should take in proceeding to resolve this situation.

(CMA, adapted)

Problem 3–55 Predetermined Overhead Rate; Different Time Periods; Pricing (LO4)

Troy Electronics Company calculates its predetermined overhead rate on a quarterly basis. The following estimates were made for the current year:

4. Predetermined rate: $4.44 per hour (rounded)

	Estimated Manufacturing Overhead	Estimated Direct-Labour Hours	Quarterly Predetermined Overhead Rate (per direct-labour hour)
First quarter	$100,000	25,000	?
Second quarter	80,000	16,000	?
Third quarter	50,000	12,500	?
Fourth quarter	70,000	14,000	?
Total	$300,000	67,500	

The firm's main product, Part A200, requires $100 of direct material and 20 hours of direct labour per unit. The labour rate is $15 per hour.

Required:

1. Calculate the firm's *quarterly* predetermined overhead rate for each quarter.
2. Determine the cost of one unit of Part A200 if it is manufactured in January versus April.
3. Suppose the company's pricing policy calls for a 10 percent markup over cost. Calculate the price to be charged for a unit of Part A200 if it is produced in January versus April.
4. Calculate the company's predetermined overhead rate for the year if the rate is calculated *annually*.
5. Based on your answer to requirement (4), what is the cost of a unit of Part A200 if it is manufactured in January? In April?
6. What is the price of a unit of Part A200 if the predetermined overhead rate is calculated annually?

Problem 3–56 Overhead Application Using a Predetermined Overhead Rate (LO2, 4, 6)

Tiana Shar, the controller for Bondi Furniture Company, is in the process of analyzing the overhead costs for the month of November. She has gathered the following data for the month:

2. Cost of Job 77: $200,675
6. Underapplied overhead for November: $4,575

Labour

Direct-labour hours:

Job 77	3,500
Job 78	3,000
Job 79	2,000

(continued)

Labour costs:

Direct-labour wages	$204,000
Indirect-labour wages	15,000
Supervisory salaries	6,000

Material

Inventories, November 1:

Raw material and supplies	$ 10,500
Work in process (Job 77)	54,000
Finished goods	112,500

Purchases of raw material and supplies:

Raw material	$135,000
Supplies (indirect material)	15,000

Direct material and supplies requisitioned for production:

Job 77	$ 45,000
Job 78	37,500
Job 79	25,500
Supplies (indirect material)	12,000
Total	$120,000

Other

Building occupancy costs (heat, light, depreciation, etc.):

Factory facilities	$ 6,400
Sales offices	1,600
Administrative offices	1,000
Total	$ 9,000

Production equipment costs:

Power	$ 4,100
Repairs and maintenance	1,500
Depreciation	1,500
Other	1,000
Total	$ 8,100

The firm's job-order costing system uses direct-labour hours (measured at practical capacity) as the cost driver for overhead application. In December of the preceding year, Shar had prepared the following budget for direct-labour and manufacturing-overhead costs for the current year. The plant is capable of operating at 150,000 direct-labour hours per year. However, Shar estimates that the practical capacity is 120,000 hours in a typical year.

	Manufacturing Overhead	
Direct-Labour Hours	**Variable**	**Fixed**
100,000	$325,000	$216,000
120,000	390,000	216,000
140,000	455,000	216,000

During November the following jobs were completed:

Job 77	Side chairs
Job 78	End tables

Required: Assist Shar by making the following calculations:

1. Calculate the predetermined overhead rate for the current year.
2. Calculate the total cost of Job 77.
3. Compute the amount of manufacturing overhead applied to Job 79 during November.
4. What was the total amount of manufacturing overhead applied during November?
5. Compute the actual manufacturing overhead incurred during November.
6. Calculate the overapplied or underapplied overhead for November.

(CMA, adapted)

1. Predetermined overhead rate: $21 per direct-labour hour
4. Total actual overhead: $33,900
7. Income (loss): $(1,625)

Problem 3–57 Comprehensive Job-Order Costing Problem (LO2, 4, 5, 6)

Scholastic Brass Corporation manufactures brass musical instruments for use by secondary school students. The company uses a normal costing system, in which manufacturing overhead is applied on the basis of direct-labour hours. The company's budget for the current year included the following predictions:

Budgeted total manufacturing overhead	$426,300
Budgeted total direct-labour hours	20,300

During March, the firm worked on the following two production jobs:

Job T81, consisting of 76 trombones
Job C40, consisting of 110 cornets

The events of March are described as follows:

a. Rolled brass sheet metal purchased on account for $5,000: 1,000 m².

b. Brass tubing purchased on account for $4,000: 400 kg.

c. The following requisitions were submitted on March 5:

Requisition 112: 250 m² of brass sheet metal at $5 per square metre (for Job T81)
Requisition 113: 1,000 kg of brass tubing, at $10 per kilogram (for job C40)
Requisition 114: 10 L of valve lubricant, at $10 per litre

All brass used in production is treated as direct material. Valve lubricant is an indirect material.

d. An analysis of labour time cards revealed the following labour usage for March:

Direct labour: Job T81, 800 hours at $20 per hour
Direct labour: Job C40, 900 hours at $20 per hour
Indirect labour: General factory cleanup, $4,000
Indirect labour: Factory supervisory salaries, $9,000

e. Depreciation of the factory building and equipment during March amounted to $12,000.

f. Rent paid in cash for warehouse space used during March was $1,200.

g. Utility costs incurred during March amounted to $2,100. The invoices for these costs were received, but the bills were not paid in March.

h. March property taxes on the factory were paid in cash: $2,400.

i. The insurance cost covering factory operations for the month of March was $3,100. The insurance policy had been prepaid.

j. The costs of salaries and fringe benefits for sales and administrative staff paid in cash during March amounted to $8,000.

k. Depreciation on administrative office equipment and space amounted to $4,000.

l. Other selling and administrative expenses paid in cash during March amounted to $1,000.

m. Job T81 was completed on March 20.

n. Half of the trombones in Job T81 were sold on account during March for $700 each.

The March 1 balances in selected accounts are as follows:

Cash	$ 10,000
Accounts receivable	21,000
Prepaid insurance	5,000
Raw-material inventory	149,000
Manufacturing supplies inventory	500
Work-in-process inventory	91,000
Finished-goods inventory	220,000
Accumulated depreciation: Buildings and equipment	102,000
Accounts payable	13,000
Wages payable	8,000

Required:

1. Calculate the company's predetermined overhead rate for the year.
2. Prepare journal entries to record the events in March.
3. Set up T-accounts, and post the journal entries made in requirement (2).
4. Calculate the overapplied or underapplied overhead for March. Prepare a journal entry to close this balance into cost of goods sold.
5. Prepare a schedule of cost of goods manufactured for March.
6. Prepare a schedule of cost of goods sold for March.
7. Prepare an income statement for March.

Problem 3–58 Job-Cost Record; Continuation of Preceding Problem **(LO2, 4, 6)**

Total cost of Job T81: $34,050

Refer to the preceding problem regarding Scholastic Brass Corporation. Complete the following job-cost record for Job T81.

SCHOLASTIC BRASS CORPORATION:
JOB-COST RECORD

Job Number _____ T81 _____   **Description** _____
Date Started _____   **Date Completed** _____
                                        Number of Units Completed _____

Direct Material

Date	Requisition Number	Quantity	Unit Price	Cost

Direct Labour

Date	Time Card Number	Hours	Rate	Cost
3/8 to 3/12	3–08 through 3–12			

Manufacturing Overhead

Date	Cost Driver (Activity Base)	Quantity	Application Rate	Cost
3/8 to 3/12				

Cost Summary

Cost Item	Amount
Total direct material	
Total direct labour	
Total manufacturing overhead	
Total cost	
Unit cost	

Shipping Summary

Date	Units Shipped	Units Remaining in Inventory	Cost Balance

Problem 3–59 Flow of Manufacturing Costs; Incomplete Data (LO2, 4, 5)   5. $80,000

Conundrum Corporation manufactures furniture. Due to a fire in the administrative offices, the accounting records for November of the current year were partially destroyed. You have been able to piece together the following information from the ledger:

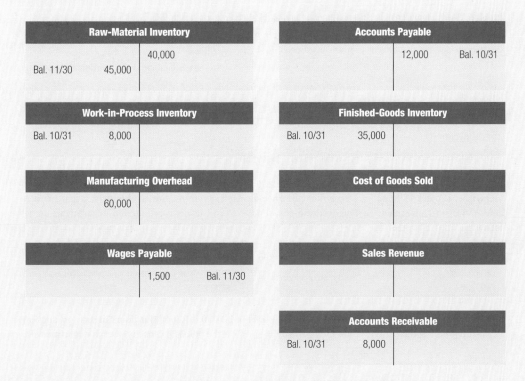

Raw-Material Inventory		
	40,000	
Bal. 11/30	45,000	

Accounts Payable		
	12,000	Bal. 10/31

Work-in-Process Inventory		
Bal. 10/31	8,000	

Finished-Goods Inventory		
Bal. 10/31	35,000	

Manufacturing Overhead		
	60,000	

Cost of Goods Sold		

Wages Payable		
	1,500	Bal. 11/30

Sales Revenue		

Accounts Receivable		
Bal. 10/31	8,000	

By examining various source documents and interviewing several employees, you were able to gather the following additional information:

a. Collections of accounts receivable during November amounted to $205,000.

b. Sales revenue in November was 120 percent of cost of goods sold. All sales are on account.

c. Overhead is applied using an annual predetermined overhead rate based on direct-labour hours (based on practical capacity).

d. The budgeted overhead for the current year is $720,000.

e. Budgeted direct-labour cost for the current year is $960,000. The direct-labour rate is $20 per hour.

f. The accounts payable balance on November 30 was $1,000. Only purchases of raw material are credited to accounts payable. A payment of $81,000 was made on November 15.

g. November's cost of goods sold amounted to $180,000.

h. The November 30 balance in finished-goods inventory was $5,000.

i. Payments of $79,500 were made to direct-labour employees during November. The October 31 balance in the wages payable account was $1,000.

j. The *actual* manufacturing overhead for November was $60,000.

k. An analysis of the furniture still in process on November 30 revealed that so far these items have required 500 hours of direct labour and $20,500 of direct material.

Required:

Calculate the following amounts. Then complete the T-accounts given in the problem.

1. Sales revenue for November

2. November 30 balance in accounts receivable

3. Cost of raw material purchased during November

4. November 30 balance in work-in-process inventory

5. Direct labour added to work in process during November

6. Applied overhead for November

7. Cost of goods completed during November
8. Raw material used during November
9. October 31 balance in raw-material inventory
10. Overapplied or underapplied overhead for November

Problem 3–60 Plantwide versus Departmental Overhead Rates; Product Pricing (LO1, 4, 7)

TeleTech Corporation manufactures two different fax machines for the business market. Cost estimates for the two models for the current year are as follows:

	Basic System	Advanced System
Direct material	$ 400	$ 800
Direct labour (20 hours at $16 per hour)	300	300
Manufacturing overhead*	400	400
Total	$1,100	$1,500

*The predetermined overhead rate is $20 per direct-labour hour.

Each model of fax machine requires 20 hours of direct labour. The basic system requires 5 hours in Department A and 15 hours in Department B. The advanced system requires 15 hours in Department A and 5 hours in Department B. The overhead costs budgeted in these two production departments are as follows:

	Department A	Department B
Variable cost	$16 per direct-labour hour	$4 per direct-labour hour
Fixed cost	$200,000	$200,000

The firm's management expects to operate at a level of 20,000 direct-labour hours in each production department during the current year. (This estimate is based on the practical capacity of each department.)

Required:

1. Show how the company's predetermined overhead rate was calculated.
2. If the firm prices each model of fax machine at 10 percent over its cost, what will be the price of each model?
3. Suppose the company was to use departmental predetermined overhead rates. Calculate the rate for each of the two production departments.
4. Compute the product cost of each model using the departmental overhead rates calculated in requirement (3).
5. Compute the price to be charged for each model, assuming the company continues to price each product at 10 percent above cost. Use the revised product costs calculated in requirement (4).
6. Write a memo to the president of TeleTech Corporation making a recommendation as to whether the firm should use a plantwide overhead rate or departmental rates. Consider the potential implications of the overhead rates and the firm's pricing policy. How might these considerations affect the firm's ability to compete in the marketplace?

Cases

Case 3–61 Interpreting Information from a Job-Order Costing System (LO2, 3, 4, 6, 7)

CompuFurn Inc. manufactures furniture for computer workstations. The company uses a job-order costing system and absorption costing. The company's work-in-process inventory on November 30 consisted of the following jobs:

Job Number	Description	Units	Accumulated Cost
CC723	Computer caddy	20,000	$ 900,000
CH291	Chair	15,000	431,000
PS812	Printer stand	25,000	250,000
Total			$1,581,000

On November 30, the company's finished-goods inventory, which is valued using the first-in, first-out (FIFO) method, consisted of four items:

Item	Quantity and Unit Cost	Accumulated Cost
Computer caddy	7,500 units @ $64 each	$ 480,000
Chair	19,400 units @ $35 each	679,000
Printer stand	21,000 units @ $56 each	1,176,000
Desk	11,200 units @ $102 each	1,142,400
Total		$3,477,400

At the end of November, the balance in the materials inventory account, which includes both raw materials and purchased parts, was $668,000. Additions to and requisitions from the materials inventory during the month of December included the following:

Additions/Requisitions	Raw Materials	Purchased Parts
Additions	$242,000	$396,000
Requisitions:		
Job CC723	51,000	104,000
Job CH291	3,000	10,800
Job PS812	124,000	87,000
Job DS444 (5,000 desks)	65,000	187,000

Manufacturing overhead is applied on the basis of machine hours. The company's overhead budget for the year totalled $4,500,000. The company planned to use 900,000 machine hours during this period, which is the firm's estimated practical capacity. Through the first 11 months of the year, a total of 830,000 machine hours were used, and total overhead amounted to $4,140,000.

During the month of December, machine hours and labour hours consisted of the following:

Account	Machine Hours	Labour Hours	Labour Cost
CC723	12,000	11,600	$122,400
CH291	4,400	3,600	43,200
PS812	19,500	14,300	200,500
DS444	14,000	12,500	138,000
Indirect labour	—	3,000	29,400
Supervision	—	—	57,600
Total	49,900	45,000	$591,100

The jobs completed in December and the unit sales for that month are as follows:

	Production			Sales	
Job Number	Items	Quantity Completed		Items	Quantity Shipped
CC723	Computer caddy	20,000		Computer caddy	17,500
CH291	Chair	15,000		Chair	21,000
DS444	Desk	5,000		Desk	6,000
				Printer stand	18,000

Required:

1. Explain when it is appropriate for a company to use a job-order costing system.
2. Calculate the balance in the work-in-process inventory account as of December 31.
3. Calculate the cost of the chairs in the finished-goods inventory as of December 31.
4. Actual manufacturing overhead incurred in December amounted to $252,000. Calculate the overapplied or underapplied overhead for the year.
5. Explain two alternative accounting treatments for overapplied or underapplied overhead balances when using a job-order costing system.

(CMA, adapted)

3. Manufacturing overhead
applied in December: $90,000
6. Cost of goods manufactured:
$2,976,300

Case 3–62 Cost Flows in a Job-Order Costing System; Schedule of Cost of Goods Manufactured; Automation (LO2, 3, 4, 5, 6)

FibreCom, Inc., a manufacturer of fibre optic communications equipment, uses a job-order costing system. Since the production process is heavily automated, manufacturing overhead is applied on the basis of machine hours, using a predetermined overhead rate. The current annual rate of $15 per machine hour is based on budgeted manufacturing-overhead costs of $4,200,000 and a budgeted activity level of 80,000 machine hours, the company's estimated practical capacity. Operations for the year have been completed, and all of the accounting entries have been made for the year except the application of manufacturing overhead to the jobs worked on during December, the transfer of costs from work in process to finished goods for the jobs completed in December, and the transfer of costs from finished goods to cost of goods sold for the jobs that have been sold during December. Summarized data as of November 30 and for the month of December are presented in the following table. Jobs T11-007, N11-013, and N11-015 were completed during December. All completed jobs except Job N11-013 had been turned over to customers by the close of business on December 31.

Work-in-Process		December Activity		
Job No.	Balance November 30	Direct Material	Direct Labour	Machine Hours
T11-007	$ 87,000	$ 1,500	$ 4,500	300
N11-013	55,000	4,000	12,000	1,000
N11-015	—	25,600	26,700	1,400
D12-002	—	37,900	20,000	2,500
D12-003	—	26,000	16,800	800
Total	$142,000	$95,000	$80,000	6,000

Operating Activity	Activity through November 30	December Activity
Actual manufacturing overhead incurred:		
Indirect material	$ 125,000	$ 9,000
Indirect labour	345,000	30,000
Utilities	245,000	22,000
Depreciation	385,000	35,000
Total overhead	$1,100,000	$96,000
Other data:		
Raw-material purchases*	$965,000	$98,000
Direct-labour costs	$845,000	$80,000
Machine hours	73,000	6,000

Account Balances at Beginning of Year	January 1
Raw-material inventory*	$105,000
Work-in-process inventory	60,000
Finished-goods inventory	125,000

*Raw-material purchases and raw-material inventory consist of both direct and indirect materials. The balance of the raw-material inventory account as of December 31 of the year just completed is $85,000.

Required:

1. Explain why manufacturers use a predetermined overhead rate to apply manufacturing overhead to their jobs.

2. How much manufacturing overhead would the company have applied to jobs through November 30 of the year just completed?

3. How much manufacturing overhead would have been applied to jobs during December of the year just completed?

4. Determine the amount by which manufacturing overhead is overapplied or underapplied as of December 31 of the year just completed.

5. Determine the balance in the finished-goods inventory account on December 31 of the year just completed.

6. Prepare a schedule of cost of goods manufactured for the year just completed. (*Hint:* In computing the cost of direct material used, remember that FibreCom includes both direct and indirect material in its raw-material inventory account.)

(CMA, adapted)

Practise and learn online with Connect.

CHAPTER FOUR

Process Costing and Hybrid Product-Costing Systems

FOCUS COMPANY

The MVP Sports Equipment Company's Alberta Division manufactures ski gloves in its Calgary plant. Each glove requires work in two departments: the Cutting Department and the Stitching Department. The Alberta Division uses a product-costing method called *process costing*. Under process costing, direct-material and conversion costs (direct labour and manufacturing overhead) are first assigned to each process (or department) used in the manufacturing operation. The costs of each process (or department) are then assigned to the units on which each department worked. Process costing is used by manufacturing companies that produce relatively large numbers of similar products.

IN CONTRAST

In contrast to the process-costing system used by the Alberta Division, we explore a different product-costing system in the company's Ontario Division. This division manufactures two types of basketballs in its Kingston plant. The professional basketballs are covered with genuine leather, whereas the scholastic basketballs are covered with imitation leather. Except for the different exterior material, each basketball requires the same production steps. The Ontario Division uses a hybrid product-costing system called *operation costing*, which is well suited to its production environment. Operation costing is used only by manufacturing companies.

After completing this chapter, you should be able to

1 List and explain the similarities and differences between job-order and process costing.

2 Prepare journal entries to record the flow of costs in a process-costing system with sequential production departments.

3 Prepare a table of equivalent units using weighted-average process costing.

4 Compute the cost per equivalent unit using weighted-average process costing.

5 Analyze the total production costs for a department using weighted-average process costing.

6 Prepare a departmental production report using weighted-average process costing.

7 Describe how an operation costing system accumulates and assigns the costs of direct material and conversion activity in a batch-manufacturing process.

Two primary functions are performed by a product-costing system:

1. The accumulation of production costs
2. The assignment of those costs to the firm's products

Product costs are needed for the purposes of planning, cost management, decision making, and reporting to various outside organizations, such as government regulatory agencies.

As described in Chapter 3, a job-order costing system is used when relatively small numbers of products are produced in distinct batches (or job orders) and these products differ significantly from each other. This chapter covers process-costing systems, which are used in **repetitive production environments** where large numbers of identical or very similar products are manufactured in a continuous flow. Industries using process costing include paper, petroleum, chemicals, textiles, food processing, lumber, and electronics.

Comparison of Job-Order Costing and Process Costing

In many ways, job-order costing and process costing are similar. Both product-costing systems have the same ultimate purpose—assignment of production costs to units of output. Furthermore, the flow of costs through the manufacturing accounts is the same in the two systems.

Flow of Costs

Learning Objective ▮1

List and explain the similarities and differences between job-order and process costing.

Exhibit 4–1 illustrates the flow of costs in two process-costing situations: one with a single production department and one with two production departments used in sequence. The accounts in this process-costing illustration are the same as those used in the job-order costing described in Chapter 3. As the illustration shows, direct-material, direct-labour, and manufacturing-overhead costs are added to a work-in-process inventory account. As goods are finished, costs are transferred to a finished-goods inventory. During the period when goods are sold, the product costs are transferred to cost of goods sold. In the two-department case, when goods are finished in Department A, costs accumulated in the work-in-process inventory account of Department A are transferred to the work-in-process inventory account of Department B, which will incur direct-labour and manufacturing-overhead costs (and possibly additional direct-material costs) in finishing the goods.

Learning Objective ▮2

Prepare journal entries to record the flow of costs in a process-costing system with sequential production departments.

The journal entries for the case of two sequential production departments, illustrated in Exhibit 4–1, are as follows. The numbers used in the journal entries are assumed for the purpose of showing the form of the entries and it is assumed that this is the first year of operations (no beginning inventories).

1. As direct-material ($50,000) and direct-labour ($20,000) costs are incurred in Department A, they are added to the work-in-process inventory account of Department A. Overhead ($30,000) is applied using a predetermined overhead rate, which is computed in the same way in both job-order and process costing.

Work-in-process inventory: Department A	100,000	
Raw-material inventory		50,000
Wages payable		20,000
Manufacturing overhead		30,000

2. When units are completed in Department A, they are transferred to Department B for further work. The costs assigned to these units are transferred from the work-in-process inventory account of Department A to the work-in-process inventory account of Department B. These costs assigned to the partially completed units transferred to Department B are called **transferred-in costs**. In

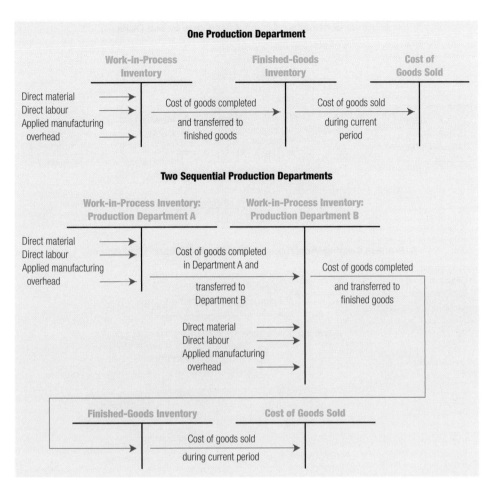

Exhibit 4–1
Flow of Costs in Process-Costing Systems

this illustration, of the $100,000 accumulated in the work-in-process inventory account of Department A, the cost of goods transferred to Department B is $80,000, while the cost of goods still in process in Department A is $20,000.

Work-in-process inventory: Production Department B	80,000	
Work-in-process inventory: Production Department A		80,000

3. Additional direct-material ($40,000) and direct-labour ($15,000) costs are also incurred in Department B, and manufacturing overhead ($20,000) is applied using a predetermined overhead rate.

Work-in-process inventory: Department B	75,000	
Raw-material inventory		40,000
Wages payable		15,000
Manufacturing overhead		20,000

4. Goods completed in Department B are transferred to the finished-goods warehouse. In this example, of the $155,000 ($80,000 + $75,000) accumulated in Department B's work-in-process inventory account, the cost of goods transferred to the finished-goods inventory is $130,000, while the cost of goods still in process in Department B is $25,000.

Finished-goods inventory	130,000	
Work-in-process inventory: Department B		130,000

Exhibit 4–2

Comparison of Job-Order and
Process Costing

A. Job-Order Costing: Accumulates Costs by Job Order

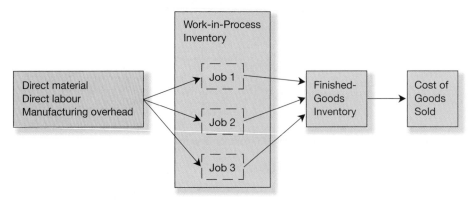

B. Process Costing: Accumulates Costs by Production Department

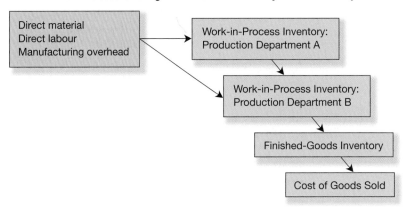

5. Goods are sold. In this example, of the $130,000 accumulated in the finished-goods inventory account, the cost of goods transferred to the cost of goods sold is $125,000, while the cost of goods remaining in the finished-goods inventory is $5,000.

Cost of goods sold	125,000	
Finished-goods inventory		125,000

Differences between Job-Order and Process Costing

In job-order costing, *costs are accumulated by batch (job order)* and recorded on job-cost records. The cost of each unit in a particular batch is computed by dividing the total costs of the batch by the number of units in the batch.

In process costing, *costs are accumulated by department*, rather than by batch. The cost per unit is computed by averaging the total costs incurred over the units produced. Exhibit 4–2 summarizes this key difference.

Equivalent Units: A Key Concept

Material, labour, and overhead costs often are incurred at different rates in a production process. Direct material is usually placed into production at one or more specific points in the process. In contrast, direct labour and manufacturing overhead, called *conversion costs*, are usually incurred continuously throughout the process. When an accounting

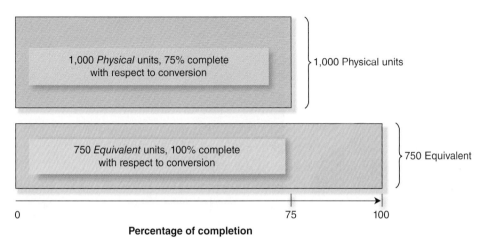

Exhibit 4–3
Conversion Activity in a
Typical Production Process

period ends, the partially completed units that remain in process generally are at different stages of completion in relation to material and conversion activity. For example, the in-process units may be 75 percent complete in relation to conversion, but they may already include all of their direct materials. This situation is portrayed in Exhibit 4–3.

Equivalent Units

The graphical illustration in Exhibit 4–3 supposes there are 1,000 physical units in process at the end of an accounting period. Each of the physical units is 75 percent complete in relation to conversion (direct labour and manufacturing overhead). How much conversion activity has been applied to these partially completed units? Conversion activity occurs uniformly throughout the production process. Therefore, the amount of conversion activity required to do 75 percent of the conversion on 1,000 units is *equivalent* to the amount of conversion activity required to do all of the conversion on 750 units. This number is computed as follows:

$$\begin{array}{ccc} \text{1,000 partially completed} \\ \text{physical units in process} \end{array} \times \begin{array}{c} \text{75\% complete in} \\ \text{relation to conversion} \end{array} = \text{750 equivalent units}$$

To verify this is the case, look at the area of the two rectangles in Exhibit 4–3. The height of the rectangles represents the number of units and their width represents the percentage of completion. The area of a rectangle is the product of its height and its width (Area = Height × Width). Specifically, the green rectangle has a height of 3 cm (representing 1,000 physical units) and a width of 9 cm (75% complete), while the orange rectangle has a height of 2.25 cm (representing 750 equivalent units) and a width of 12 cm (100% complete). The area of the orange rectangle is 27 cm² (2.25 cm × 12 cm), which is *equivalent* to the area of the green rectangle (3 cm × 9 cm = 27 cm²). Hence, 1,000 units, 75% complete in relation to conversion, is equivalent to 750 units, 100% complete in relation to conversion.

The term **equivalent units** is used in process costing to refer to the amount of manufacturing activity that has been applied to a batch of physical units. The *1,000 physical units* in process represent *750 equivalent units* of conversion activity.

The term *equivalent units* is also used to measure the quantity of direct materials represented by the partially completed goods. Since direct materials are added at the beginning of the production process, the *1,000 physical units* represent *1,000 equivalent units of direct material* (1,000 physical units × 100% complete in relation to direct materials).

The most important feature of process costing is that the costs of direct material and conversion are assigned to equivalent units rather than to physical units. Refer again to Exhibit 4–3. For simplicity, suppose that the only production activity of the current accounting period was to start work on the 1,000 physical units and complete 75 percent of the required conversion activity. Assume that the costs incurred were $5,000 for direct

Learning Objective **3**

Prepare a table of equivalent units using weighted-average process costing.

"Operations [managers] have a keen interest in cost management. To truly manage costs, you must look at the processes involved." (4b)
John Deere Health Care, Inc.

Process costing is used in the wine industry. First, raw material (in this case, grapes) is harvested and entered into production. Then conversion costs are incurred in the production process. At the end of the accounting period, partially completed units of wine remain in process as the wine ages.

material and \$1,500 for conversion (direct labour and manufacturing overhead). These costs would then be assigned as follows:

$$\frac{\$5,000 \text{ direct-material cost}}{1,000 \text{ equivalent units of direct material}} = \frac{\$5 \text{ per equivalent unit}}{\text{for direct material}}$$

$$\frac{\$1,500 \text{ conversion cost}}{750 \text{ equivalent units of conversion}} = \frac{\$2 \text{ per equivalent unit}}{\text{for conversion}}$$

This is a highly simplified example because there is no work-in-process inventory at the beginning of the accounting period and no goods were completed during the period. Nevertheless, it illustrates the important concept that, under process costing, costs are assigned to equivalent units rather than physical units.

Process Costing Illustrated

The key document in a typical process-costing system is the **departmental production report**, prepared for each production department at the end of every accounting period. This report replaces the job-cost record, which is used to accumulate costs by job in a job-order costing system. The departmental production report summarizes the flow of production quantities through the department, and it shows the amount of production cost transferred out of the department's work-in-process inventory account during the period. The following four steps are used in preparing a departmental production report:

1. Analysis of physical flow of units
2. Calculation of equivalent units (for direct material and conversion activity)
3. Computation of unit costs (i.e., the cost per equivalent unit for direct material and conversion)
4. Analysis of total costs (determine the cost to be removed from work in process and transferred either to the next production department or to finished goods)

The method of process costing that will be the focus of this chapter is called the **weighted-average method**. *This method is almost always used in practice* by companies using process costing. There is another process-costing method called the *first-in, first-out (FIFO) method*. Except for raw material prices, the differences in results between FIFO and weighted-average methods are usually insignificant. Although this method is covered in some cost accounting courses, it is rarely used in practice.[1]

Work in Process, March 1—20,000 units
(100% complete, direct material; 10% complete, conversion)

Direct material	$ 50,000
Conversion	7,200
Total work in process*	$ 57,200

Units started during March	30,000	units
Units completed during March and transferred to Stitching Department	40,000	units
Work in process, March 31	10,000	units
Direct material: 100% complete		
Conversion: 50% complete		

Costs incurred during March:

Direct material	$ 90,000
Conversion costs:	
Direct labour	$ 86,000
Applied manufacturing overhead†	107,500
Total conversion costs	$193,500

*These costs were incurred during the prior month, February.

†Direct labour cost × Predetermined overhead rate = $86,000 × 125% = $107,500.

Exhibit 4–4
Basic Data for Illustration—
Cutting Department

Basic Data for Illustration

The Alberta Division of MVP Sports Equipment Company manufactures ski gloves in its Calgary plant. Two production departments are used in sequence: the Cutting Department and the Stitching Department. In the Cutting Department, direct material is placed into production at the beginning of the process. Direct-labour and manufacturing-overhead costs are incurred uniformly throughout the process. The material is cut into the pieces needed to produce gloves. The predetermined overhead rate used in the Cutting Department is 125 percent of direct-labour *cost*.

The data in Exhibit 4–4 present a summary of the activity and costs in the Cutting Department during March. The direct-material and conversion costs for the March 1 work-in-process consist of costs that were incurred in February. These costs were assigned to the units remaining in process at the end of February.

Based on the data in Exhibit 4–4, the Cutting Department's work-in-process inventory account has the following balance on March 1:

Work-in-Process Inventory: Cutting Department	
March 1 balance 57,200	

The following journal entry is made during March to add the costs of direct material, direct labour, and manufacturing overhead to the Work-in-Process Inventory.

Work-in-process inventory: Cutting Department	283,500	
Raw-material inventory		90,000
Wages payable		86,000
Manufacturing overhead		107,500

BRITISH COLUMBIA WINE INDUSTRY

British Columbia is the second-largest wine producer in Canada, after Ontario. Known as the "Napa Valley of the North," the Okanagan Valley in central British Columbia boasts about 2,400 hectares of vineyards and over seven dozen wineries. Some of the most notable wineries are Mission Hill (the largest and most elaborate), Summerhill Pyramid Winery (with bottles aged inside a four-storey-high pyramid), Sumac Ridge, and Quails' Gate Estate. British Columbia's wineries constitute the fastest-growing segment of the province's tourism industry. Wine production provides an excellent example of process costing. The processes used in a typical Okanagan vineyard are as follows:[2]

- *Trimming.* At the end of a growing season, the vines are trimmed, which helps prepare them for the next harvest.
- *Tying.* The vines are also tied onto wires at the end of the season, to help protect them from the weather.
- *Hilling.* Dirt is piled up around the roots to protect them.
- *Conditioning.* In the spring, the dirt is levelled back from the roots.
- *Untying.* The vines are untied from the wires to allow them freedom to grow during the spring and summer months.
- *Chemical spraying.* The vines are sprayed in the spring to protect them from disease and insects.
- *Harvesting.* The highest-quality grapes are picked by hand to minimize damage.
- *Stemming and crushing.* Batches of grapes are loaded into a machine, which gently removes the stems and mildly crushes the grapes.
- *Pressing.* After removal from the stemmer/crusher, the juice runs freely from the grapes when they are pressed.
- *Filtering.* Filtering separates the skins and other solid matter from the liquid.
- *Fermentation.* This process varies, depending on the type of wine. For example, Riesling grape juice is placed in stainless-steel tanks for fermentation. Chardonnay grape juice undergoes a two-stage fermentation process in oak barrels.
- *Aging.* Again, this process varies. Riesling wines are aged in the stainless-steel tanks for approximately a year. Chardonnays are aged in the oak barrels for about two years.
- *Bottling.* A machine bottles the wine and corks the bottles.
- *Labelling.* Each bottle is labelled with the name of the vintner, vintage, and variety.
- *Packing.* The bottles are packed into 12-bottle cases.
- *Case labelling.* The cases are stamped with the same information as is on the bottles.
- *Shipping.* The wine is shipped to wine distributors and retailers.

Weighted-Average Method

The four steps used to prepare a departmental production report using weighted-average process costing are as follows:

Step 1: Analysis of Physical Flow of Units   The first step is to prepare a table summarizing the physical flow of production units during March. The table is shown in Exhibit 4–5 and reflects the following inventory formula:

$$\begin{pmatrix} \text{Physical units} \\ \text{in beginning} \\ \text{work in process} \end{pmatrix} + \begin{pmatrix} \text{Physical} \\ \text{units} \\ \text{started} \end{pmatrix} - \begin{pmatrix} \text{Physical units} \\ \text{completed and} \\ \text{transferred out} \end{pmatrix} = \begin{pmatrix} \text{Physical units} \\ \text{in ending work} \\ \text{in process} \end{pmatrix}$$

Step 2: Calculation of Equivalent Units The second step in the process-costing procedure is to calculate the equivalent units of direct material and conversion activity. A table of equivalent units, displayed in Exhibit 4–6, is based on the table of physical flows prepared in Step 1. The 40,000 physical units that were completed and transferred out of the Cutting Department were 100 percent complete. Thus, they represent 40,000 equivalent units for both direct material and conversion. The 10,000 units in the ending work-in-process inventory are complete with respect to direct material and represent 10,000 equivalent units of direct material. However, they are only 50 percent complete with respect to conversion. Therefore, the ending work-in-process inventory represents 5,000 equivalent units of conversion activity (10,000 physical units × 50% complete). As Exhibit 4–6 indicates, the total number of equivalent units is calculated:

$$\begin{pmatrix} \text{Equivalent units of} \\ \text{activity in units completed} \\ \text{and transferred out} \end{pmatrix} + \begin{pmatrix} \text{Equivalent units of} \\ \text{activity in ending} \\ \text{work in process} \end{pmatrix} = \begin{pmatrix} \text{Total} \\ \text{equivalent units} \\ \text{of activity} \end{pmatrix}$$

Note that the total equivalent units of activity, for both direct material (50,000) and conversion (45,000), exceeds the activity accomplished in the current period alone. Since only 30,000 physical product units were started during March and direct material is added at the beginning of the process, only 30,000 equivalent units of direct material were actually placed into production during March. However, the total number of equivalent units of direct material used for weighted-average process costing is 50,000. The other 20,000 equivalent units of direct material were actually entered into production

	Physical Units
Work in process, March 1	20,000
Units started during March	30,000
Total units to account for	**50,000**
Units completed and transferred out during March	40,000
Work in process, March 31	10,000
Total units accounted for	**50,000**

Exhibit 4–5
Step 1: Analysis of Physical Flow of Units—Cutting Department

	Physical Units (from Exhibit 4–5)	Percentage of Completion with Respect to Conversion	Equivalent Units	
			Direct Material	Conversion
Work in process, March 1	20,000	10%		
Units started during March	30,000			
Total units to account for	**50,000**			
Units completed and transferred out during March	40,000	100%	40,000	40,000
Work in process, March 31	10,000	50%	10,000	5,000
Total units accounted for	**50,000**			
Total equivalent units			50,000	45,000

Exhibit 4–6
Step 2: Calculation of Equivalent Units—Cutting Department (weighted-average method)

Exhibit 4–7
Step 3: Computation of Unit
Costs—Cutting Department
(weighted-average method)

	Direct Material	Conversion	Total
Work in process, March 1 (from Exhibit 4–4)	$ 50,000	$ 7,200	$ 57,200
Costs incurred during March (from Exhibit 4–4)	90,000	193,500	283,500
Total costs to account for	$140,000	$200,700	$340,700
Equivalent units (from Exhibit 4–6)	50,000	45,000	
Costs per equivalent unit	**$ 2.80**	**$ 4.46**	**$ 7.26**
	$\frac{\$140,000}{50,000}$	$\frac{\$200,700}{45,000}$	$2.80 + $4.46

during the preceding month. *This is the key feature of the weighted-average method. The number of equivalent units of activity is calculated without making a distinction as to whether the activity occurred in the current or the preceding accounting period.*

Learning Objective   **4**

Compute the cost per equivalent
unit using weighted-average
process costing.

Step 3: Computation of Unit Costs   The third step in the process-costing procedure, calculating the cost per equivalent unit for both direct material and conversion activity, is presented in Exhibit 4–7. The cost per equivalent unit for direct material is computed by dividing the total direct-material cost, including the cost of the beginning work in process *and* the cost incurred during March, by the total equivalent units (from Step 2, Exhibit 4–6). A similar procedure is used for conversion costs.

Learning Objective   **5**

Analyze the total production costs
for a department using weighted-
average process costing.

Step 4: Analysis of Total Costs   Now we can complete the process-costing procedure by determining the total cost to be transferred out of the Cutting Department's work-in-process inventory account and into the Stitching Department's work-in-process inventory account. Exhibit 4–8 provides the required calculations. For convenience, the computations in

Exhibit 4–8
Step 4: Analysis of Total
Costs—Cutting Department
(weighted-average method)

	Direct Material	Conversion	Total
Work in process, March 1 (from Exhibit 4–4)	$ 50,000	$ 7,200	$ 57,200
Costs incurred during March (from Exhibit 4–4)	90,000	193,500	283,500
Total costs to account for	$140,000	$200,700	**$340,700** ◄
Equivalent units (from Exhibit 4–6)	50,000	45,000	
Costs per equivalent unit	**$ 2.80**	**$ 4.46**	**$ 7.26**
	$\frac{\$140,000}{50,000}$	$\frac{\$200,700}{45,000}$	$2.80 + $4.46

Cost of goods completed and transferred out of the Cutting Department during March:

$\left(\begin{array}{c}\text{Number of units}\\\text{transferred out}\end{array}\right) \times \left(\begin{array}{c}\text{Total cost per}\\\text{equivalent unit}\end{array}\right)$ 40,000 × $7.26 $290,400

Cost remaining in March 31 work-in-process inventory in the Cutting Department:

Direct material:

$\left(\begin{array}{c}\text{Number of equivalent}\\\text{units of direct material}\end{array}\right) \times \left(\begin{array}{c}\text{Cost per equivalent}\\\text{unit of direct material}\end{array}\right)$ 10,000 × $2.80 $ 28,000

Conversion:

$\left(\begin{array}{c}\text{Number of equivalent}\\\text{units of conversion}\end{array}\right) \times \left(\begin{array}{c}\text{Cost per equivalent}\\\text{unit of conversion}\end{array}\right)$ 5,000 × $4.46   22,300

Total cost of March 31 work in process $ 50,300

Check: Cost of goods completed and transferred out $290,400

Cost of March 31 work-in-process inventory   50,300

Total costs accounted for   **$340,700** ◄

Step 3 are repeated in Exhibit 4–8. At the bottom of Exhibit 4–8, a check is made to be sure that the total costs of $340,700 have been fully accounted for in the cost of goods completed and transferred out, and the balance remaining in the work-in-process inventory.

The calculations in Exhibit 4–8 are used as the basis for the following journal entry to transfer the cost of goods completed and transferred out to the Stitching Department

Work-in-process inventory: Stitching Department	290,400	
Work-in-process inventory: Cutting Department		290,400

On March 31, the Cutting Department's work-in-process inventory account appears as follows. The March 31 balance in the account agrees with that calculated in Exhibit 4–8.

Work-in-Process Inventory: Cutting Department			
March 1 balance	57,200		
March cost of direct material, direct labour, and applied manufacturing overhead	283,500	290,400	Cost of goods completed and transferred to Stitching Department
March 31 balance	50,300		

Departmental Production Report   We have now completed all four steps necessary to prepare a production report for the Cutting Department. The report, which is displayed in Exhibit 4–9, simply combines the tables presented in Exhibits 4–6 and 4–8. The report provides a convenient summary of all of the process-costing calculations made under the weighted-average method.

Learning Objective **6**

Prepare a departmental production report using weighted-average process costing.

Exhibit 4–9
Production Report: Cutting Department (weighted-average method)

MVP SPORTS EQUIPMENT COMPANY
Production Report: Cutting Department

	Physical Units	Percentage of Completion with Respect to Conversion	Equivalent Units — Direct Material	Equivalent Units — Conversion
Work in process, March 1	20,000	10%		
Units started during March	30,000			
Total units to account for	**50,000**			
Units completed and transferred out during March	40,000	100%	40,000	40,000
Work in process, March 31	10,000	50%	10,000	5,000
Total units accounted for	**50,000**			
Total equivalent units			50,000	45,000

	Direct Material	Conversion	Total
Work in process, March 1	$ 50,000	$ 7,200	$ 57,200
Costs incurred during March	90,000	193,500	283,500
Total costs to account for	$140,000	$200,700	**$340,700**
Equivalent units	50,000	45,000	
Costs per equivalent unit	$ 2.80	$ 4.46	$ 7.26
Cost of goods completed and transferred out during March			$290,400
Cost in March 31 work-in-process inventory:			
Direct material			$ 28,000
Conversion			22,300
Total cost of March 31 work in process			$ 50,300
Total costs accounted for			**$340,700**

Steps 1 & 2 · Step 3 · Step 4

Why is this process-costing method called the *weighted-average* method? Because the cost per equivalent unit for March, for both direct material and conversion activity, is computed as a weighted average of the costs incurred during two different accounting periods, February and March. To demonstrate this fact, we will focus on direct material. Since direct material is placed into production at the beginning of the process, the 20,000 physical units in the March 1 work in process already have their direct material. The direct-material cost per equivalent unit in the March 1 work in process is $2.50 ($50,000 ÷ 20,000, from Exhibit 4–4). This cost was actually incurred in *February*.

In March, 30,000 physical units were entered into work in process and received their direct material. The direct-material cost incurred in March was $90,000. Thus, the direct-material cost per equivalent unit experienced in *March* was $3 ($90,000 ÷ 30,000, from Exhibit 4–4).

Under the weighted-average method of process costing, the cost per equivalent unit for direct material was calculated in Exhibit 4–7 to be $2.80. *This $2.80 unit-cost figure is a weighted average*, as the following calculation shows.

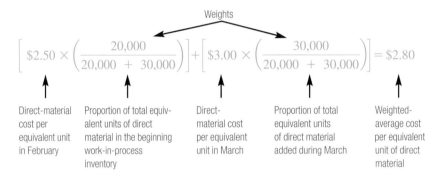

The point of this demonstration is that under weighted-average process costing, unit-cost figures are weighted averages of costs incurred over two or more accounting periods.

Other Issues in Process Costing

Several other issues related to process costing are worth discussing.

Normal and Abnormal Spoilage

Spoilage refers to unacceptable units that do not meet the specifications required for good units and thus must be discarded or sold at reduced prices. **Normal spoilage** occurs under normal operating conditions; it is uncontrollable in the short term and is considered a normal part of production and product cost. Thus, the cost of *normal spoilage* units is absorbed by the cost of *good units* produced. **Abnormal spoilage** is in excess of the amount of normal spoilage expected under normal operating conditions; it is controllable and results from inefficient operations. The cost of ab*normal spoilage* units is recorded in a *Loss from abnormal spoilage* account, in the period in which the spoilage is identified. Hence, while normal spoilage is considered to be a product cost, abnormal spoilage cost is a period cost.

The spoiled units are included in the computation of equivalent production up to the point at which they were removed from production (usually the point of inspection). Once the cost is recognized, it can be further allocated between normal and abnormal spoilage.

Referring to the data in Exhibit 4-9, let's assume that only 35,000 units were transferred out of the Cutting Department and that 5,000 units were identified as spoiled (with a normal spoilage rate of 10% of the units transferred out). Thus, normal spoilage amounted to 3,500 units (35,000 units × 10%), with the remaining 1,500 units considered

	Physical Units (from Exhibit 4–5)	Percentage of Completion with Respect to Conversion	Equivalent Units	
			Direct Material	Conversion
Work in process, March 1	20,000	10%		
Units started during March	30,000			
Total units to account for	**50,000**			
Units completed and transferred out during March	35,000	100%	35,000	35,000
Normal spoilage (35,000 × 10%)	3,500	100%	3,500	3,500
Abnormal spoilage (5,000 – 3,500)	1,500	100%	1,500	1,500
Work in process, March 31	10,000	50%	10,000	5,000
Total units accounted for	**50,000**			
Total equivalent units			50,000	45,000

Exhibit 4–10
Calculation of Equivalent Units (with spoiled units)—Cutting Department (weighted-average method)

abnormal spoilage. Since the inspection point is at the end of the production process, the spoiled units were 100% complete with regards to direct material and conversion activity. Exhibit 4-10 shows the calculation of equivalent units in the Cutting Department.

Note that the cost per equivalent unit would remain the same as previously calculated: $2.80 for direct material and $4.46 for conversion (Exhibit 4-7). The analysis of total cost is shown in Exhibit 4-11.

The calculations in Exhibit 4–11 are used as the basis for the following journal entry to transfer the cost of goods completed and transferred out to the Stitching Department.

Work-in-process inventory: Stitching Department	279,510	
Loss from abnormal spoilage	10,890	
Work-in-process inventory: Cutting Department		290,400

Actual versus Normal Costing

Our example of process costing assumed that *normal costing* was used. As explained in Chapter 3, in a normal-costing system, direct material and direct labour are applied to work-in-process inventory at their *actual* amounts, but manufacturing overhead is

	Direct Material	Conversion	Total
Work in process, March 1	$ 50,000	$ 7,200	$ 57,200
Costs incurred during March	90,000	193,500	283,500
Total costs to account for	**$140,000**	**$200,700**	**$340,700**
Equivalent units	50,000	45,000	
Costs per equivalent unit	$ 2.80	$ 4.46	$ 7.26
Good units completed and transferred out (35,000 units)			
Cost before adding normal spoilage (35,000 × $7.26)			$254,100
Normal spoilage (3,500 × $7.26)			25,410
Total costs of good units completed and transferred out			279,510
Abnormal spoilage (1,500 × $7.26)			10,890
Cost in March 31 work-in-process inventory:			
Direct material			$ 28,000
Conversion			22,300
Total cost of March 31 work in process			$ 50,300
Total costs accounted for			**$340,700**

Exhibit 4–11
Analysis of Total Costs (with spoiled units)—Cutting Department (weighted-average method)

applied to work-in-process inventory using a predetermined overhead rate. In contrast, under an *actual-costing* system, the actual costs of direct material, direct labour, *and manufacturing overhead* are entered into work-in-process inventory.

Either actual or normal costing may be used in conjunction with a process-costing system. Our example used normal costing since a predetermined overhead rate was used to compute applied manufacturing overhead in Exhibit 4–4. This resulted in applied overhead for March of $107,500 (125% × $86,000). If actual costing had been used, the manufacturing-overhead cost for March would have been the actual overhead cost incurred instead of the applied overhead amount given in Exhibit 4–4. In all other ways, the process-costing procedures used under actual and normal costing are identical.

When normal costing is used, there may be overapplied or underapplied overhead at the end of the period. This amount is either closed into cost of goods sold or prorated, as explained in Chapter 3.

Other Cost Drivers for Overhead Application

Our example used a predetermined overhead rate based on direct-labour cost. Since the application of manufacturing overhead was based on direct-labour cost, direct labour and manufacturing overhead were combined into the single cost element: *conversion cost*. This procedure is quite common in practice. If some cost driver (or activity base) other than direct labour had been used to apply manufacturing overhead, then overhead costs would be accounted for separately from direct-labour costs in the process-costing calculations.

Suppose, for example, that manufacturing overhead is applied on the basis of machine hours. A group of 100 physical units is 100 percent complete as to direct material, 60 percent complete as to direct labour, and 40 percent complete as to machine time. This situation could arise in a production process that is labour-intensive in its early stages but more automated in its later stages. In this case, the 100 physical units represent the following quantities of equivalent units:

	Equivalent Units		
Physical Units	**Direct Material**	**Direct Labour**	**Manufacturing Overhead**
100	100	60	40
	↑	↑	↑
	100 × 100%	100 × 60%	100 × 40%

Throughout the process-costing procedure, there will now be three cost elements (direct material, direct labour, and manufacturing overhead) instead of only two (direct material and conversion). In all other respects, the process-costing calculations will be identical to those illustrated earlier in the chapter.

Subsequent Production Departments

In our example, production requires two sequential production operations: cutting and stitching. Although the process-costing procedures for the second department are similar to those illustrated for the first, there is one additional complication. The cost of goods completed and transferred out of the Cutting Department must remain assigned to the partially completed product units as they undergo further processing in the Stitching Department.[3]

Hybrid Product-Costing Systems: Operation Costing in Batch-Manufacturing Processes

Job-order and process costing represent the polar extremes of product-costing systems. But some production processes exhibit characteristics of both job-order and process-costing environments. Examples of such production processes include some clothing and food-processing operations. In these production processes, the conversion activities may be very similar or identical across all of the firm's product lines, even though the direct materials may differ significantly. Different clothing lines require significantly different direct materials, such as cotton, wool, or polyester. However, the conversion of these materials, involving direct labour and manufacturing overhead, may not differ much across product types. In the food industry, production of economy-grade or premium applesauce differs with regard to the quality and cost of the direct-material input: apples. However, the cooking, straining, and canning operations for these two product lines are similar.

Operation Costing for Batch-Manufacturing Processes

Learning Objective   7

Describe how an operation-costing system accumulates and assigns the costs of direct material and conversion activity in a batch-manufacturing process.

The production processes previously described often are referred to as **batch-manufacturing processes**. Such processes are characterized by high-volume production of several product lines that differ in some important ways but are nearly identical in others. Since batch-manufacturing operations have characteristics of both job-order costing and process-costing environments, a **hybrid product-costing system** is required. One common approach is called **operation costing**. This product-costing system is used when conversion activities are very similar across product lines, but the direct materials differ significantly. *Conversion costs* are accumulated by *department*, and process-costing methods are used to assign these costs to products. In contrast, *direct-material costs* are accumulated by *job order or batch*, and job-order costing is used to assign material costs to products.

The main features of operation costing are illustrated in Exhibit 4–12. Notice in the exhibit that products pass sequentially through Production Departments A and B. Direct-material costs are traced directly to each batch of goods, but conversion costs are applied on a departmental basis. Direct labour and manufacturing overhead are combined in a single cost category called *conversion costs*, rather than separately identifying direct labour. Moreover, under operation costing, conversion costs are applied to products

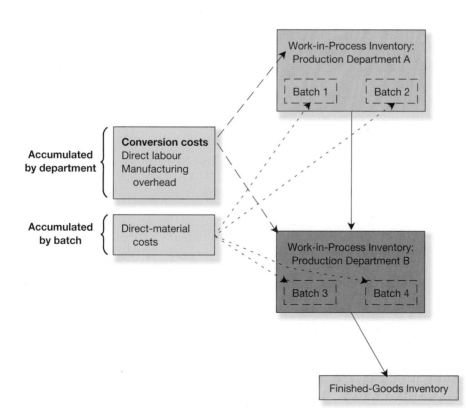

Exhibit 4–12
Operation Costing

using a predetermined application rate. This predetermined rate is based on budgeted conversion costs, as follows:[4]

$$\text{Predetermined application rate for conversion costs} = \frac{\text{Budgeted conversion costs (direct labour and manufacturing overhead)}}{\text{Budgeted cost driver (or activity base)}}$$

As an illustration of operation costing, we will focus on the Ontario Division of MVP Sports Equipment Company. This division manufactures two different grades of basketballs: professional balls, which have genuine leather exteriors, and scholastic balls, which use imitation leather. The cutting and stitching operations for the two different products are identical. Scholastic balls are sold without special packaging, but professional balls are packaged in an attractive cardboard box.

During October, two batches were entered into production and finished. There was no beginning or ending inventory of work in process for October. Cost and production data are given in Exhibit 4-13. Notice that the direct-material costs are identified by *batch*. The conversion costs, however, are associated with the two production departments and the Packaging Department.

Exhibit 4–13
Basic Data for the Operation-Costing Example

Operation-Costing Data		
Direct-material costs:		
Batch P19 (1,000 professional basketballs)	$20,000	(Includes $1,000 for packaging material)
Batch S28 (3,000 scholastic basketballs)	30,000	
Total direct-material costs	$50,000	
Conversion costs (budgeted):		
Preparation Department		$ 30,000
Finishing Department		24,000
Packaging Department		500
Total		$ 54,500
Total costs:		
Direct material		50,000
Conversion: Preparation	$ 30,000	
Finishing	24,000	
Packaging	500	
Total conversion costs		54,500
Total		$104,500

Predetermined application rates for conversion costs:*

  Preparation Department:

$$\frac{\text{Budgeted conversion costs}}{\text{Budgeted production}} = \frac{\$30,000}{4,000 \text{ units}} = \$7.50 \text{ per unit}$$

  Finishing Department:

$$\frac{\text{Budgeted conversion costs}}{\text{Budgeted production}} = \frac{\$24,000}{4,000 \text{ units}} = \$6.00 \text{ per unit}$$

  Packaging Department:

$$\frac{\text{Budgeted conversion costs}}{\text{Budgeted units packaged}} = \frac{\$500}{1,000 \text{ units}} = \$0.50 \text{ per unit}$$

*The cost driver (or activity base) is the number of units processed.

The product cost for each of the basketballs is computed as follows:

	Professional	Scholastic
Direct material:		
Batch P19 ($20,000 ÷ 1,000)..	$20.00	
Batch S28 ($30,000 ÷ 3,000)..		$10.00
Conversion: Preparation Department		
(conversion costs of $30,000 ÷ 4,000 units produced)*	7.50	7.50
Conversion: Finishing Department		
(conversion costs of $24,000 ÷ 4,000 units produced)*	6.00	6.00
Conversion: Packaging Department		
(conversion costs of $500 ÷ 1,000 units packaged)*...	.50	–0–
Total product cost	$34.00	$23.50

*The two production departments each worked on a total of 4,000 balls, but the Packaging Department handled only the 1,000 professional balls.

Notice in the preceding display that each ball receives the same conversion costs in the Preparation Department and the Finishing Department, since these operations are identical for the two products. Direct-material costs and packaging costs, though, differ for the products. The total costs of $104,500 are accounted for in the product costs, as shown below.

Professional balls: 1,000 × $34.00	$ 34,000
Scholastic balls: 3,000 × $23.50	70,500
Total	$104,500

The following journal entries are made to record the Ontario Division's flow of costs. The first entry is made to record the requisition of raw material by the Preparation Department, when Batch P19 is entered into production. (This amount excludes the $1,000 in packaging costs to be incurred subsequently for Batch P19.)

Work-in-process inventory: Preparation Department	19,000	
Raw-material inventory		19,000

The following entry is made to record the requisition of raw material by the Preparation Department, when Batch S28 is entered into production:

Work-in-process inventory: Preparation Department	30,000	
Raw-material inventory		30,000

Conversion costs are applied in the Preparation Department with the following journal entry:

Work-in-process inventory: Preparation Department	30,000	
Applied conversion costs		30,000

The following entry records the transfer of the partially completed professional and scholastic basketballs to the Finishing Department:

Work-in-process inventory: Finishing Department	79,000	
Work-in-process inventory: Preparation Department		79,000

The conversion costs applied in the Finishing Department are recorded as follows:

Work-in-process inventory: Finishing Department	24,000	
Applied conversion costs		24,000

Next, the professional balls are transferred to the Packaging Department, and the scholastic balls are transferred to finished goods:

Work-in-process inventory: Packaging Department	32,500	
Finished-goods inventory	70,500	
Work-in-process inventory: Finishing Department		103,000

Raw-material (packaging) costs and conversion costs are recorded in the Packaging Department as follows:

Work-in-process inventory: Packaging Department	1,500	
Raw-material inventory		1,000
Applied conversion costs		500

Finally, the professional basketballs are transferred to finished goods:

Finished-goods inventory	34,000	
Work-in-process inventory: Packaging Department		34,000

Suppose that at the end of an accounting period, applied conversion costs differ from the actual conversion costs incurred. Then the difference, called *overapplied* or *underapplied conversion costs*, would be closed into cost of goods sold. This accounting treatment is similar to that described in Chapter 3 for overapplied or underapplied overhead.

Chapter Summary

LO1 List and explain the similarities and differences between job-order and process costing. Process costing is used in production processes where relatively large numbers of nearly identical products are manufactured. The purpose of a process-costing system is the same as that of a job-order costing system—to accumulate costs and assign these costs to units of product. Job-order costing is used by firms that produce relatively small numbers of dissimilar products.

LO2 Prepare journal entries to record the flow of costs in a process-costing system with sequential production departments. Costs of direct material, direct labour, and manufacturing overhead are added to a work-in-process inventory account. Direct labour and manufacturing overhead often are combined into a single cost category termed *conversion costs*. When products are completed, the costs assigned to them are transferred either to finished-goods inventory or to the next production department's work-in-process inventory account. Finally, when goods are sold, their costs are transferred to the expense account called *cost of goods sold*.

LO3 Prepare a table of equivalent units using weighted-average process costing. The table of equivalent units, illustrated in the chapter, computes the equivalent units of activity for the period for both direct material and conversion costs.

LO4 Compute the cost per equivalent unit using weighted-average process costing. The cost per equivalent unit, for both direct material and conversion, is calculated as shown in the chapter. For each factor input, direct material and conversion, the cost of that input is divided by the number of equivalent units for that input.

LO5 Analyze the total production costs for a department using weighted-average process costing. The total production costs incurred during the period, for both direct material and conversion, are assigned to either ending work-in-process inventory or to the cost of goods completed and transferred out.

LO6 Prepare a departmental production report using weighted-average process costing. As illustrated in the chapter, there are four steps in preparing a departmental production report: (1) Analyze the physical flow of units, (2) calculate the equivalent units, (3) compute the cost per equivalent unit, and (4) analyze the total costs of the department. In the weighted-average method of process costing, the cost per equivalent unit, for each cost category, is a weighted average of (1) the costs assigned to the beginning work-in-process inventory and (2) the costs incurred during the current period.

LO7 Describe how an operation-costing system accumulates and assigns the costs of direct material and conversion activity in a batch-manufacturing process. Operation costing is a hybrid of job-order and process costing. It is designed for production processes in which the direct material differs significantly among product lines, but the conversion activities are essentially the same. Direct-material costs are accumulated by batches of products using job-order costing methods. Conversion costs are accumulated by production departments and are assigned to product units using process-costing methods.

Review Problem on Process Costing

The following data have been compiled for MVP's Cutting Department for the month of June. Direct material is placed into production at the beginning of the process. Conversion activity occurs uniformly throughout the production process.

Work in process, June 1—25,000 units:	
Direct material: 100% complete, cost of	$ 73,750
Conversion: 40% complete, cost of	46,000
Balance in work in process, June 1	$119,750
Units started during June	40,000
Units completed during June and transferred out	60,000
Work in process, June 30:	
Direct material: 100% complete	
Conversion: 60% complete	
Costs incurred during June:	
Direct material	$121,250
Conversion costs: direct labour and applied manufacturing overhead	$237,500

Required: Prepare the Cutting Department's June production report using weighted-average process costing. (*Hint:* Follow the format of Exhibit 4–9).

Solution to Review Problem

The Cutting Department's June production report is displayed in Exhibit 4–13.

MVP SPORTS EQUIPMENT COMPANY
June Production Report: Cutting Department

	Physical Units	Percentage of Completion with Respect to Conversion	Equivalent Units Direct Material	Equivalent Units Conversion
Work in process, June 1	25,000	40%		
Units started during June	40,000			
Total units to account for	65,000			
Units completed and transferred out during June	60,000	100%	60,000	60,000
Work in process, June 30	5,000	60%	5,000	3,000
Total units accounted for	65,000			
Total equivalent units			65,000	63,000

Exhibit 4–13
June Production Report: Cutting Department (weighted-average method)

(*continued*)

Exhibit 4–13
(*concluded*)

	Direct Material	Conversion	Total
Work in process, June 1	$ 73,750	$ 46,000	$119,750
Costs incurred during June	121,250	237,500	358,750
Total costs to account for	$195,000	$283,500	$478,500
Equivalent units	65,000	63,000	
Costs per equivalent unit	$ 3.00	$ 4.50	$ 7.50

$$\frac{\$195,000}{65,000} \qquad \frac{\$283,500}{63,000} \qquad \$3.00 + \$4.50$$

Cost of goods completed and transferred out of the Cutting Department during June:

$\left(\begin{array}{c}\text{Number of units}\\\text{transferred out}\end{array}\right) \times \left(\begin{array}{c}\text{Total cost per}\\\text{equivalent unit}\end{array}\right)$ .... 60,000 × $7.50 .... $450,000

Cost remaining in June 30 work-in-process inventory in the Cutting Department:

Direct material:

$\left(\begin{array}{c}\text{Number of equivalent}\\\text{units of direct material}\end{array}\right) \times \left(\begin{array}{c}\text{Cost per equivalent}\\\text{unit of direct material}\end{array}\right)$ .... 5,000 × $3.00 .... $ 15,000

Conversion:

$\left(\begin{array}{c}\text{Number of equivalent}\\\text{units of conversion}\end{array}\right) \times \left(\begin{array}{c}\text{Cost per equivalent}\\\text{unit of conversion}\end{array}\right)$ .... 3,000 × $4.50 13,500

Total cost of June 30 work in process .... $ 28,500

Check: Cost of goods completed and transferred out $450,000

Cost of June 30 work-in-process inventory 28,500

Total costs accounted for $478,500

Glossary

Review key terms and definitions on Connect.

Review Questions

4–1. Explain the primary differences between job-order and process costing.

4–2. List five types of manufacturing in which process costing would be an appropriate product-costing system. What is the key characteristic of these products that makes process costing a good choice?

4–3. List three nonmanufacturing businesses in which process costing could be used. For example, a public accounting firm could use process costing to accumulate the costs of processing clients' tax returns.

4–4. What are the purposes of a product-costing system?

4–5. Define the term *equivalent unit* and explain how the concept is used in process costing.

4–6. List and briefly describe the purpose of each of the four process-costing steps.

4–7. (*a*) Show how to prepare a journal entry to enter direct-material costs into the work-in-process inventory account for the first department in a sequential production process. (*b*) Show how to prepare the journal entry recording the transfer of goods from the first to the second department in the sequence.

4–8. What are transferred-in costs?

4–9. A food-processing company has two sequential production departments: mixing and cooking. The cost of the January 1 work in process in the cooking department is detailed as follows:

Direct material	$ 79,000
Conversion	30,000
Transferred-in costs	182,000

During what time period and in what department were the $182,000 of costs listed above incurred? Explain your answer.

4–10. Explain the reasoning underlying the name of the *weighted-average method*.

4–11. How does process costing differ under normal or actual costing?

4–12. How would the process-costing computations differ from those illustrated in the chapter if overhead was applied on some activity base other than direct labour?

4–13. Explain the concept of *operation costing*. How does it differ from process or job-order costing? Why is operation costing well suited for batch-manufacturing processes?

4–14. What is the purpose of a departmental production report prepared using process costing?

Exercises

Exercise 4–15 Physical Flow of Units **(L03)**

In each case below, fill in the missing amount.

1. | Work in process, September 1 | 9,000 tonnes |
    |---|---|
    | Units started during September | ? |
    | Units completed during September | 19,000 tonnes |
    | Work in process, September 30 | 2,000 tonnes |

2. | Work in process, February 1 | 13,000 kilograms |
    |---|---|
    | Units started during February | 1,500 kilograms |
    | Units completed during February | 9,200 kilograms |
    | Work in process, February 28 | ? |

3. | Work in process, January 1 | 100,000 litres |
    |---|---|
    | Units started during the year | 850,000 litres |
    | Units completed during the year | ? |
    | Work in process, December 31 | 200,000 litres |

Exercise 4–16 Process Costing; Use of Internet **(L01)**

Use the Internet to access the website for Canfor (www.canfor.com), Domtar (www.domtar.com), or Boise Cascade (www.bc.com).

Required: Skim over the information presented on the website about the company's products and operations. Then discuss why process costing is an appropriate product-costing method for this company.

Exercise 4–17 Equivalent Units; Weighted Average **(L03)**

Rainbow Glass Company manufactures decorative glass products. The firm uses a process-costing system for its manufacturing operations. All direct materials are added at the beginning of the process, and conversion costs are incurred uniformly throughout the process. The company's production schedule for August follows:

	Units
Work in process on October 1 (60% complete as to conversion)	1,000
Units started during October	5,000
Total units to account for	6,000
Units from beginning work in process, which were completed and transferred out during October	1,000
Units started and completed during October	3,000
Work in process on October 31 (20% complete as to conversion)	2,000
Total units accounted for	6,000

Required: Calculate each of the following amounts using weighted-average process costing:

1. Equivalent units of direct material during October.
2. Equivalent units of conversion activity during October.

(CMA, adapted)

Exercise 4–18 Equivalent Units; Weighted Average **(L03)**

Terra Energy Company refines a variety of petrochemical products. The following data are from the firm's Lodi plant for the month of November.

Work in process, November 1	2,000,000 litres
Direct material	100% complete
Conversion	25% complete
Units started in process during November	7,950,000 litres
Work in process, November 30	2,240,000 litres
Direct material	100% complete
Conversion	80% complete

Required: Compute the equivalent units of direct material and conversion for the month of November. Use the weighted-average method of process costing.

Exercise 4–19 Physical Flow and Equivalent Units; Weighted Average (L03)

The Edmonton plant of Fit-For-Life Foods Corporation produces low-fat salad dressing. The following data pertain to the year just ended:

		Percentage of Completion	
	Units	**Direct Material**	**Conversion**
Work in process, January 1	20,000 kilograms	80%	60%
Work in process, December 31	15,000 kilograms	70%	30%

During the year, the company started 120,000 kilograms of material in production.

Required: Prepare a schedule analyzing the physical flow of units and computing the equivalent units of both direct material and conversion for the year. Use weighted-average process costing.

Exercise 4–20 Cost per Equivalent Unit; Weighted Average (L03, 4)

Quebec Lumber Company grows, harvests, and processes timber for use in construction. The following data pertain to the firm's sawmill during November:

Work in process, November 1:	
Direct material...	$ 65,000
Conversion..	180,000
Costs incurred during November:	
Direct material...	$425,000
Conversion..	690,000

The equivalent units of activity for November were as follows: 7,000 equivalent units of direct material and 1,740 equivalent units of conversion activity.

Required: Calculate the cost per equivalent unit, for both direct material and conversion, during November. Use weighted-average process costing.

Exercise 4–21 Cost per Equivalent Unit; Weighted Average (L03, 4)

Otsego Glass Company manufactures window glass for automobiles. The following data pertain to the Plate Glass Department.

Work in process, June 1:	
Direct material...	$ 37,000
Conversion..	36,750
Costs incurred during June:	
Direct material...	$150,000
Conversion..	230,000

The equivalent units of activity for June were as follows: 17,000 equivalent units of direct material and 48,500 equivalent units of conversion activity.

Required: Calculate the cost per equivalent unit, for both direct material and conversion, during June. Use weighted-average process costing.

Exercise 4–22 Analysis of Total Costs; Weighted Average (L05)

Yorkton Textiles Company manufactures a variety of natural fabrics for the clothing industry. The following data pertain to the Weaving Department for the month of September:

Equivalent units of direct material (weighted-average method)...	60,000
Equivalent units of conversion (weighted-average method)	52,000
Units completed and transferred out during September	50,000

The cost data for September are as follows:

Work in process, September 1:	
Direct material	$ 94,000
Conversion	44,400
Costs incurred during September:	
Direct material	$164,000
Conversion	272,800

There were 20,000 units in process in the Weaving Department on September 1 (100% complete as to direct material and 40% complete as to conversion).

Required: Compute each of the following amounts using weighted-average process costing:

1. Cost of goods completed and transferred out of the Weaving Department
2. Cost of the September 30 work-in-process inventory in the Weaving Department
3. *Build a spreadsheet.* Construct an Excel spreadsheet to solve all of the preceding requirements. Show how the solution will change if the following data change: the costs incurred in September were $328,000 for direct material and $818,400 for conversion.

Exercise 4–23 Analysis of Total Costs; Weighted Average (LO5)

The following data pertain to Thomas Paperboard Company, a manufacturer of cardboard boxes:

Work in process, February 1	10,000 units*
Direct material	$ 5,500
Conversion	17,000
Costs incurred during February:	
Direct material	$110,000
Conversion	171,600

*100 percent complete as to direct material; 40 percent complete as to conversion.

The equivalent units of activity for February were as follows:

Direct material (weighted-average method)	110,000
Conversion (weighted-average method)	92,000
Units completed and transferred out	90,000

Required: Compute the following amounts using weighted-average process costing.

1. Cost of goods completed and transferred out during February
2. Cost of the February 28 work-in-process inventory

Exercise 4–24 Operation Costing (LO2,7)

The November production of MVP's Ontario Division consisted of Batch P25 (2,000 professional basketballs) and Batch S33 (4,000 scholastic basketballs). Each batch was started and finished during November, and there was no beginning or ending work in process. Costs incurred were as follows.

Direct Material:

Batch P25, $42,000, including $2,500 for packaging material; Batch S33, $45,000.

Conversion Costs:

Preparation Department, predetermined rate of $7.50 per unit; Finishing Department, predetermined rate of $6 per unit; Packaging Department, predetermined rate of $.50 per unit. (Only the professional balls are packaged.)

Required:

1. Draw a diagram depicting the division's batch manufacturing process. Refer to Exhibit 4–12 for guidance.
2. Compute the November product cost for each type of basketball.
3. Prepare journal entries to record the cost flows during November.

Problems

Problem 4–25 Step-by-Step Weighted-Average Process Costing **(LO3, 4, 5)**

3. Cost per equivalent unit, total: $4.77

Timing Technology manufactures timing devices. During 20x1, 900,000 units were completed and transferred to finished-goods inventory. On December 31, 20x1, 300,000 units were in work in process. These units were 50 percent complete as to conversion and 100 percent complete as to direct material. Finished-goods inventory consisted of 200,000 units. Materials are added to production at the beginning of the manufacturing process, and overhead is applied to each product at the rate of 60 percent of direct-labour costs. There was no finished-goods inventory on January 1, 20x1. A review of the inventory cost records disclosed the following information:

		Costs	
	Units	Materials	Labour
Work in process, January 1, 20x1 (80% complete as to conversion)	200,000	$ 200,000	$ 315,000
Units started in production	1,000,000		
Direct-material costs		$1,300,000	
Direct-labour costs			$1,995,000

Required: Prepare schedules as of December 31, 20x1, to compute the following:

1. Physical flow of units
2. Equivalent units of production using the weighted-average method
3. Costs per equivalent unit for material and conversion
4. Cost of the December 31, 20x1, finished-goods inventory and work-in-process inventory

(CMA, adapted)

Problem 4–26 Straightforward Weighted-Average Process Costing, Step-by-Step Approach **(LO3, 4, 5)**

2. Total equivalent units, conversion: 226,000

Scotian Plastics Company manufactures a highly specialized plastic that is used extensively in the automobile industry. The following data have been compiled for the month of June. Direct material is added at the beginning of the production process. Conversion activity occurs uniformly throughout the production process:

Work in process, June 1—50,000 units:	
Direct material: 100% complete cost of	$120,000
Conversion: 40% complete, cost of	34,400
Balance in work in process, June 1	$154,400
Units started during June	200,000
Units completed during June and transferred out to finished-goods inventory	190,000
Work in process, June 30:	
Direct material: 100% complete	
Conversion: 60% complete	
Costs incurred during June:	
Direct material	$492,500
Conversion costs:	
Direct labour	$ 87,450
Applied manufacturing overhead	262,350
Total conversion costs	$349,800

Required: Prepare schedules to accomplish each of the following process-costing steps for the month of June. Use the weighted-average method of process costing.

1. Analysis of physical flow of units
2. Calculation of equivalent units
3. Computation of unit costs
4. Analysis of total costs

Problem 4–27 Missing Data; Production Report; Weighted Average (LO4, 5, 6)

The following data pertain to the Vesuvius Tile Company for July:

Cost remaining in ending work-in-process inventory, direct material: $123,750

Work in process, July 1 (in units)	20,000
Units started during July	?
Total units to account for	65,000
Units completed and transferred out during July	?
Work in process, July 31 (in units)	15,000
Total equivalent units: Direct material	65,000
Total equivalent units: Conversion	?
Work in process, July 1: Direct material	$164,400
Work in process, July 1: Conversion	?
Costs incurred during July: Direct material	?
Costs incurred during July: Conversion	659,400
Work in process, July 1: Total cost	244,200
Total costs incurred during July	1,031,250
Total costs to account for	1,275,450
Cost per equivalent unit: Direct material	8.25
Cost per equivalent unit: Conversion	?
Total cost per equivalent unit	21.45
Cost of goods completed and transferred out during July	?
Cost remaining in ending work-in-process inventory: Direct material	?
Cost remaining in ending work-in-process inventory: Conversion	79,200
Total cost of July 31 work in process	202,950

Additional Information:

a. Direct material is added at the beginning of the production process, and conversion activity occurs uniformly throughout the process.

b. The company uses weighted-average process costing.

c. The July 1 work in process was 30 percent complete as to conversion.

d. The July 31 work in process was 40 percent complete as to conversion.

Required: Compute the missing amounts, and prepare the firm's July production report.

Problem 4–28 Partial Production Report; Journal Entries; Weighted-Average Method (LO2, 3, 4, 5)

1(b). Cost per equivalent unit, direct material: $5.60

Triangle Fastener Limited accumulates costs for its single product using process costing. Direct material is added at the beginning of the production process, and conversion activity occurs uniformly throughout the process. A partially completed production report for the month of May follows.

Production Report
For the Month of May

	Physical Units	Percentage of Completion with Respect to Conversion	Equivalent Units Direct Material	Conversion
Work in process, May 1	25,000	40%		
Units started during May	30,000			
Total units to account for	55,000			
Units completed and transferred out during May	35,000	100%	35,000	35,000
Work in process, May 31	20,000	80%	20,000	16,000
Total units accounted for	55,000			

	Direct Material	Conversion	Total
Work in process, May 1	$143,000	$ 474,700	$ 617,700
Costs incurred during May	165,000	2,009,000	2,174,000
Total costs to account for	$308,000	$2,483,700	$2,791,700

Required:

1. Complete each of the following process-costing steps using the weighted-average method:
   a. Calculation of equivalent units
   b. Computation of unit costs
   c. Analysis of total costs
2. Prepare a journal entry to record the transfer of the cost of goods completed and transferred out during May.

Problem 4–29 Straightforward Weighted-Average Process Costing; Step-by-Step Approach (LO3, 4, 5)

Natimany Company processes and packages cream cheese. The following data have been compiled for the month of April. Conversion activity occurs uniformly throughout the production process.

Work in process, April 1—10,000 units:	
Direct material: 100% complete, cost of	$ 22,000
Conversion: 20% complete, cost of	4,500
Balance in work in process, April 1	$ 26,500
Units started during April...	100,000
Units completed during April and transferred out to finished-goods inventory..............................	80,000
Work in process, April 30:	
Direct material: 100% complete	
Conversion: 33 1/3% complete	
Costs incurred during April:	
Direct material...	$198,000
Conversion costs:	
Direct labour..	$ 52,800
Applied manufacturing overhead	105,600
Total conversion costs...	$158,400

Required: Prepare schedules to accomplish each of the following process-costing steps for the month of April. Use the weighted-average method of process costing.

1. Analysis of physical flow of units
2. Calculation of equivalent units
3. Computation of unit costs
4. Analysis of total costs

5. *Build a spreadsheet:* Construct an Excel spreadsheet to solve all of the preceding requirements. Show how the solution will change if the following data change: The April 1 work-in-process costs were $66,000 for direct material and $18,000 for conversion.

Problem 4–30 Partial Production Report; Journal Entries; Weighted-Average Method (LO2, 3, 4, 5)

Albany Company accumulates costs for its product using process costing. Direct material is added at the beginning of the production process, and conversion activity occurs uniformly throughout the process.

Production Report
For August 20x1

	Physical Units	Percentage of Completion with Respect to Conversion
Work in process, August 1	40,000	80%
Units started during August	80,000	
Total units to account for	120,000	
Units completed and transferred out during August	100,000	100%
Work in process, August 31	20,000	30%
Total units accounted for	120,000	

	Direct Material	Conversion	Total
Work in process, August 1	$ 42,000	$ 305,280	$ 347,280
Costs incurred during August	96,000	784,400	880,400
Total costs to account for	$138,000	$1,089,680	$1,227,680

Required: Use weighted-average process costing in completing the following requirements:

1. Prepare a schedule of equivalent units.
2. Compute the costs per equivalent unit.
3. Compute the cost of goods completed and transferred out during August.
4. Compute the cost remaining in the work-in-process inventory on August 31.
5. Prepare a journal entry to record the transfer of the cost of goods completed and transferred out.

Problem 4–31 Determination of Production Costs; Analysis of Equivalent Units **(LO3, 4, 5)**

Flaherty Corporation assembles various components used in the telecommunications industry. The company's major product, a relay switch, is the result of assembling three parts: XY634, AA788, and GU321. The following information relates to activities of April:

- Beginning work-in-process inventory: 4,000 units, 75 percent complete as to conversion; cost, $286,000 (direct materials, $220,000; conversion cost, $66,000)
- Production started: 25,000 units
- Production completed: 24,000 units
- Ending work-in-process inventory: 5,000 units, 40 percent complete as to conversion
- Direct materials used: XY634, $267,000; AA788, $689,000; GU321, $448,000
- Hourly wage of direct labourers, $20; total direct-labour payroll, $126,500
- Overhead application rate: $60 per direct-labour hour

1. Overhead applied: $379,500

3. Cost of ending work-in-process inventory: $324,000

All parts are introduced at the beginning of the manufacturing process; conversion cost is incurred uniformly throughout production.

Required:

1. Calculate the total cost of direct material and conversion during April.
2. Determine the cost of goods completed during the month.
3. Determine the cost of the work-in-process inventory on April 30.
4. With regard to the ending work-in-process inventory on April 30:
   a. How much direct-material cost would be added to these units in May?
   b. What percentage of conversion would be performed on these units in May?
5. Assume that the disk drive required the addition of another part (HH887) at the 70-percent stage of completion. How many equivalent units with respect to Part HH887 would be represented in April's ending work-in-process inventory?

Problem 4–32 Analysis of Work-in-Process Inventory Account **(LO2, 3, 4, 5)**

A-1 Products manufactures wooden furniture using an assembly-line process. All direct materials are introduced at the start of the process, and conversion cost is incurred evenly throughout manufacturing. An examination of the company's work-in-process inventory account for June revealed the following selected information:

3. Cost of June 30 work-in-process inventory: $34,600

Debit side:

    June 1 balance: 300 units, 30% complete as to conversion, cost $21,300*

    Production started: 900 units

    Direct material used during June: $45,000

    June conversion cost: $25,700

Credit side:

    Production completed: 700 units

*Supplementary records revealed direct-material cost of $15,000 and conversion cost of $6,300.

Conversations with manufacturing personnel revealed that the ending work in process was 60 percent complete as to conversion.

Required:

1. Determine the number of units in the June 30 work-in-process inventory.
2. Calculate the cost of goods completed during June and prepare the appropriate journal entry to record completed production.
3. Determine the cost of the June 30 work-in-process inventory.
4. Briefly explain the meaning of equivalent units. Why are equivalent units needed to properly allocate costs between completed production and production in process?

Problem 4–33   Missing Data; Production Report; Weighted Average **(LO4, 5, 6)**

The following data pertain to the Hercules Tire and Rubber Company for May:

Work in process, May 1 (in units)	?
Units started during May	60,000
Total units to account for	75,000
Units completed and transferred out during May	?
Work in process, May 31 (in units)	10,000
Total equivalent units: Direct material	75,000
Total equivalent units: Conversion	?
Work in process, May 1: Direct material	$135,000
Work in process, May 1: Conversion	?
Costs incurred during May: Direct material	?
Costs incurred during May: Conversion	832,250
Work in process, May 1: Total cost	172,500
Total costs incurred during May	1,402,250
Total costs to account for	1,574,750
Cost per equivalent unit: Direct material	9.40
Cost per equivalent unit: Conversion	?
Total cost per equivalent unit	21.65
Cost of goods completed and transferred out during May	?
Cost remaining in ending work-in-process inventory: Direct material	?
Cost remaining in ending work-in-process inventory: Conversion	73,500
Total cost of May 31 work in process	167,500

Additional Information:

a. Direct material is added at the beginning of the production process, and conversion activity occurs uniformly throughout the process.
b. Hercules uses weighted-average process costing.
c. The May 1 work in process was 20 percent complete as to conversion.
d. The May 31 work in process was 60 percent complete as to conversion.

Required: Compute the missing amounts, and prepare the firm's May production report.

Problem 4–34   Process Costing in a British Public Accounting Firm **(LO3, 4, 5)**

Donlevy and Price, a public accounting firm in London, is engaged in the preparation of income tax returns for individuals. The firm uses the weighted-average method of process costing for internal reporting. The following information pertains to February. (£ denotes the British monetary unit, pounds.*)

Returns in process, February 1	
(25% complete)	200
Returns started in February	825
Returns in process, February 28	
(80% complete)	125

Total equivalent units,
conversion: 71,000
Cost remaining in ending
work-in-process inventory:
Direct material: $94,000

2. Total cost of returns in process, February 28: £14,250

Returns in process, February 1:	
Labour...	£6,000
Overhead..	2,500
Labour, February (4,000 hours)..	89,000
Overhead, February	45,000

*Although the euro is used in most European markets, business in the United Kingdom continues to be conducted in British pounds.

Required:

1. Compute the following amounts for labour and for overhead:
   a. Equivalent units of activity
   b. Cost per equivalent unit (remember to express your answer in terms of British pounds, denoted by £)
2. Compute the cost of returns in process as of February 28.

(CMA, adapted)

Problem 4–35 Process Costing; Production Report; Journal Entries; Weighted-Average Method **(LO2, 3, 4, 5, 6)**
GroFast Company manufactures a high-quality fertilizer, which is used primarily by commercial vegetable growers. Two departments are involved in the production process. In the Mixing Department, various chemicals are entered into production. After processing, the Mixing Department transfers a chemical called Chemgro to the Finishing Department. There the product is completed, packaged, and shipped under the brand name Vegegro.

Cost of goods completed and transferred out, November: $306,300

In the Mixing Department, the raw material is added at the beginning of the process. Labour and overhead are applied continuously throughout the process. All direct departmental overhead is traced to the departments, and plant overhead is allocated to the departments on the basis of direct labour. The plant overhead rate for 20x2 is $0.40 per direct-labour dollar.

The following information relates to production during November 20x2 in the Mixing Department:

a. Work in process, November 1 (4,000 kilograms, 75% complete as to conversion):

Raw material	$22,800
Direct labour...	24,650
Departmental overhead	12,000
Allocated plant overhead	9,860

b. Raw material:

Inventory, November 1, 2,000 kilograms...	$10,000
Purchases, November 3, 10,000 kilograms	51,000
Purchases, November 18, 10,000 kilograms	51,500
Released to production during November, 16,000 kilograms	

c. Direct-labour cost, $103,350
d. Direct departmental overhead costs, $52,000
e. Transferred to Finishing Department, 15,000 kilograms
f. Work in process, November 30, 5,000 kilograms, 20 percent complete

The company uses weighted-average process costing to accumulate product costs. However, for raw-material inventories, the firm uses the FIFO inventory method.

Required:

1. Prepare a production report for the Mixing Department for November 20x2. The report should show:
   a. Equivalent units of production by cost factor (i.e., direct material and conversion)
   b. Cost per equivalent unit for each cost factor (round your answers to the nearest cent)
   c. Cost of Chemgro transferred to the Finishing Department
   d. Cost of the work-in-process inventory on November 30, 20x2, in the Mixing Department

2. Prepare journal entries to record the following events:

   a. Release of direct material to production during November

   b. Incurrence of direct-labour costs in November

   c. Application of overhead costs for the Mixing Department (direct departmental and allocated plant overhead costs)

   d. Transfer of Chemgro out of the Mixing Department

(CMA, adapted)

Problem 4–36 Operation Costing; Unit Costs; Journal Entries (L07)

1. Total product cost, deluxe model: $207,900

Plasto Corporation manufactures a variety of plastic products including a series of moulded chairs. The three models of moulded chairs, which are all variations of the same design, are Standard (can be stacked), Deluxe (with arms), and Executive (with arms and padding). The company uses batch manufacturing and has an operation-costing system. The production process includes an extrusion operation and subsequent operations to form, trim, and finish the chairs. Plastic sheets are produced by the extrusion operation, some of which are sold directly to other manufacturers. During the forming operation, the remaining plastic sheets are moulded into chair seats and the legs are added; the Standard model is sold after this operation. During the trim operation, the arms are added to the Deluxe and Executive models and the chair edges are smoothed. Only the Executive model enters the finish operation where the padding is added. All of the units produced receive the same steps within each operation. The May production run had a total manufacturing cost of $898,000. The units of production and direct-material costs incurred were as follows:

	Units Produced	Extrusion Materials	Form Materials	Trim Materials	Finish Materials
Plastic sheets	5,000	$ 60,000			
Standard model	6,000	72,000	$24,000		
Deluxe model	3,000	36,000	12,000	$ 9,000	
Executive model	2,000	24,000	8,000	6,000	$12,000
Total	16,000	$192,000	$44,000	$15,000	$12,000

Manufacturing costs applied during the month of May were as follows:

	Extrusion Operation	Form Operation	Trim Operation	Finish Operation
Direct labour	$152,000	$60,000	$30,000	$18,000
Manufacturing overhead	240,000	72,000	39,000	24,000

Required:

1. For each product produced by Plasto Corporation during the month of May, determine the (a) unit cost and (b) total cost. Be sure to account for all costs incurred during the month.

2. Prepare journal entries to record the flow of production costs during May.

(CMA, adapted)

Problem 4–37 Operation Costing; Unit Costs; Journal Entries (L07)

2. Conversion cost per unit, Department II: $10.00

5. Cost of etched, coloured glass sheet: $76.25 per sheet

Glass Glow Company manufactures a variety of glass windows in its Egalton plant. In Department I, clear glass sheets are produced, and some of these sheets are sold as finished goods. Other sheets made in Department I have metallic oxides added in Department II to form coloured glass sheets. Some of these coloured sheets are sold; others are moved to Department III for etching and then are sold. The company uses operation costing.

Glass Glow Company's production costs applied to products in May are given in the following table. There was no beginning or ending inventory of work in process for May.

Cost Category	Dept. I	Dept. II	Dept. III
Direct material	$450,000	$72,000	—
Direct labour	38,000	22,000	$38,000
Manufacturing overhead	230,000	68,000	73,750

Products	Units	Dept. I Dir. Mat.	Dept. II Dir. Mat.
Clear glass, sold after Dept. I	11,000	$247,500	—
Unetched coloured glass, sold after Dept. II	4,000	90,000	$32,000
Etched coloured glass, sold after Dept. III	5,000	112,500	40,000

Each sheet of glass requires the same steps within each operation.

Required: Compute each of the following amounts:

1. The conversion cost per unit in Department I
2. The conversion cost per unit in Department II
3. The cost of a clear glass sheet
4. The cost of an unetched coloured glass sheet
5. The cost of an etched coloured glass sheet

Problem 4–38 Operation Costing; Unit Cost; Cost Flow; Journal Entries **(LO7)**

Orbital Industries, Inc. manufactures a variety of materials and equipment for the aerospace industry. A team of R&D engineers in the firm's Brandon plant has developed a new material that will be useful for a variety of purposes in orbiting satellites and spacecraft. Trade-named Ceralam, the material combines some of the best properties of both ceramics and laminated plastics. Ceralam is already being used for a variety of housings in satellites produced in three different countries. Ceralam sheets are produced in an operation called "rolling," in which the various materials are rolled together to form a multilayer laminate. Orbital Industries sells many of these Ceralam sheets just after the rolling operation to aerospace firms worldwide. However, Orbital also processes many of the sheets further. After rolling, they are sent to the moulding operation, where they are formed into various shapes used to house a variety of instruments. After moulding, the sheets are sent to the punching operation, where holes are punched in the moulded sheets to accommodate protruding instruments, electrical conduits, and so forth. Some of these sheets are then sold. The remaining units are sent to the dipping operation, in which the moulded sheets are dipped into a special chemical mixture to give them a reflective surface.

During the month of March, the following products were manufactured. The direct-material costs are also shown.

2. Unit cost, reflective
Ceralam housing: $200.00

	Units	Direct Materials Used in Ceralam Sheets	Direct Materials Used in Dipping
Ceralam sheets (sold after the rolling operation)	12,000	$480,000	
Nonreflective housings (sold after the punching operation)	5,000	200,000	
Reflective housings (sold after the dipping operation)	3,000	120,000	$30,000
Total	20,000	$800,000	$30,000

The costs incurred in producing the various Ceralam products during March are shown in the following table. Manufacturing overhead is applied on the basis of direct-labour dollars at the rate of 150 percent.

	Rolling	Moulding	Punching	Dipping
Direct material	$ 800,000	—	—	$ 30,000
Direct labour	300,000	$112,000	$128,000	45,000
Manufacturing overhead	450,000	168,000	192,000	67,500
Total	$1,550,000	$280,000	$320,000	$142,500

Orbital Industries uses operation costing for its Ceralam operations.

Required:

1. Prepare a table that includes the following information *for each of the four operations.*
   - Total conversion costs
   - Units manufactured
   - Conversion cost per unit

2. Prepare a second table that includes the following information *for each product* (i.e., rolled Ceralam sheets, nonreflective Ceralam housings, and reflective Ceralam housings).

   - Total manufacturing costs
   - Units manufactured
   - Total cost per unit

3. Prepare journal entries to record the flow of all manufacturing costs through the Ceralam operations during March. (Ignore the journal entries to record sales revenue.)

4. *Build a spreadsheet:* Construct an Excel spreadsheet to solve requirements (1) and (2) above. Show how the solution will change if the following data change: The cost of direct material used in dipping was $45,000 and the overhead application rate is 200 percent of direct-labour cost.

Case

4. Weighted-average unit cost of completed leather belts: $6.10
Total cost of October 31 work in process: $4,700

Case 4–39 Weighted-Average Process Costing; Ethics (LO3, 4, 5, 6)

Laredo Leather Company manufactures high-quality leather goods in Quebec. The company's profits have declined during the past nine months. In an attempt to isolate the causes of poor profit performance, management is investigating the manufacturing operations of each of its products.

One of the company's main products is leather belts. The belts are produced in a single, continuous process in the Montreal plant. During the process, leather strips are sewn, punched, and dyed. The belts then enter a final finishing stage to conclude the process. Labour and overhead are applied continuously during the manufacturing process. All materials, leather strips, and buckles are introduced at the beginning of the process. The firm uses the weighted-average method to calculate its unit costs.

The leather belts are sold wholesale for $9.95 each. Management wants to compare the current manufacturing costs per unit with the market prices for leather belts. Top management has asked the plant controller to submit data on the cost of manufacturing the leather belts for the month of October. These cost data will be used to determine whether modifications in the production process should be initiated or whether an increase in the selling price of the belts is justified. The cost per belt used for planning and control is $5.35.

The work-in-process inventory consisted of 400 partially completed units on October 1. The belts were 25 percent complete as to conversion. The costs included in the inventory on October 1 were as follows:

Leather strips	$ 990
Buckles	260
Conversion costs	300
Total	$1,550

During October, 7,600 leather strips and buckles were put into production. A total of 7,000 leather belts were completed. The work-in-process inventory on October 31 consisted of 1,000 belts, which were 50 percent complete as to conversion.

The costs charged to production during October were as follows:

Leather strips	$19,900
Buckles	5,250
Conversion costs	20,700
Total	$45,850

Required: In order to provide cost data regarding the manufacture of leather belts to top management, compute the following amounts for the month of October:

1. The equivalent units for material and conversion
2. The cost per equivalent unit of material and conversion
3. The assignment of production costs to the October 31 work-in-process inventory and to goods transferred out
4. The weighted-average unit cost of leather belts completed and transferred to finished goods. Comment on the company's cost per belt used for planning and control.

5. The production manager, Gerard Langlois, has been under pressure from the company president to reduce the cost of conversion. In spite of several attempts to reduce conversion costs, they have remained more or less constant. Now Langlois is faced with an upcoming meeting with the company president, at which he will have to explain why he has failed to reduce conversion costs. Langlois has approached his friend, Monique Bedard, who is the corporate controller, with the following request: "Monique, I'm under pressure to reduce costs in the production process. There is no way to reduce material cost, so I've got to get the conversion costs down. If I can show just a little progress in next week's meeting with the president, then I can buy a little time to try some other cost-cutting measures I've been considering. I want you to do me a favour. If we raise the estimate of the percentage of completion of October's inventory to 60 percent, that will increase the number of equivalent units. Then the unit conversion cost will be a little lower." By how much would Langlois' suggested manipulation lower the unit conversion cost? What should Bedard do? Discuss this situation, citing specific ethical standards for managerial accountants.

(CMA, adapted)

ONLINE SUPPLEMENT 4A Process Costing: The First-In, First-Out Method

 See Connect for supplements to this chapter.

ONLINE SUPPLEMENT 4B Process Costing In Sequential Production Departments

 See Connect for supplements to this chapter.

 Practise and learn online with Connect.

CHAPTER FIVE

Activity-Based Costing and Management

FOCUS COMPANY

The Patio Grill Company manufactures high-end gas barbeque grills in its Mississauga plant. The company has recently experienced intense competition in its two high-volume product lines, forcing management to drop these products' prices below their target levels. A careful study of this situation revealed that Patio Grill Company's traditional product-costing system distorted product costs by assigning too much cost to the high-volume gas-grill lines and not enough cost to the low-volume complex line of grills. Management then implemented a new costing system, called *activity-based costing* (ABC), which assigns product costs more accurately than traditional product-costing systems. With the cost insights from the ABC system, management was able to change its pricing structure to compete more effectively in the gas-grill market.

IN CONTRAST

In contrast to the manufacturing setting of the Patio Grill Company, we explore the use of ABC by the Pacific Children's Hospital. ABC is used in this health-care facility to assign treatment costs to categories of patient visits, such as routine, extended, and complex visits, as well as new and continuing patients.

After completing this chapter, you should be able to

1 Compute product costs under a traditional volume-based product-costing system.

2 Explain how activity-based costing (ABC) operates, including the use of a two-stage procedure for cost assignment, the identification of activity cost pools, and the selection of cost drivers.

3 Explain the concept of cost levels, including unit-level, batch-level, product-sustaining-level, and facility-level costs.

4 Compute product costs under an ABC system.

5 Explain why traditional volume-based costing systems tend to distort product costs.

6 Explain three criteria for selecting cost drivers.

7 Discuss several key issues in ABC, including data collection and storyboarding.

8 Explain the concept of activity-based management (ABM) and two-dimensional ABC.

9 Explain and execute a customer-profitability analysis.

10 Understand and discuss how ABC is used in service organizations.

11 List and explain eight important features of just-in-time inventory and production management systems (Appendix to Chapter 5).

The growth of international competition, the rapid pace of technological innovation, and amazing advances in computerized systems have all created a new environment for manufacturers around the globe. Some manufacturers have emerged as world-class producers, while others have fallen by the wayside. World-class companies such as Caterpillar, Coca-Cola, Johnson & Johnson, and Pfizer are among the many manufacturers that have changed key business processes to compete effectively in the 21st century.

The service sector also is undergoing extraordinary transformation. The growth of the Internet, the trend toward a service economy, and the willingness of businesses to outsource critical service functions have caused many service organizations to reinvent the way they do business. Among the service firms that have adapted most successfully to the changing business environment are American Express, TD Canada Trust, FedEx, Google, and WestJet Airlines.

What is the role of managerial accounting in this rapidly changing environment? To explore these issues, we will review recent events in the life of Patio Grill Company, a manufacturer of barbeque grills and accessories. The company's Mississauga plant manufactures three product lines, all high-end gas barbeque grills. The plant's three gas-grill lines are the Patio Standard (STD), the Deluxe (DEL), and the Ultimate (ULT).

Traditional Volume-Based Product-Costing System

Until recently, Patio Grill Company used a job-order product-costing system similar to the one described in Chapter 3 for Rocky Lake Outfitters. The cost of each product was the sum of its actual direct-material cost, actual direct-labour cost, and applied manufacturing overhead. Overhead was applied using a predetermined overhead rate based on direct-labour hours. Exhibit 5–1 provides the basic data on which the traditional costing system was based.

Learning Objective **1**

Compute product costs under a traditional volume-based product-costing system.

The Excel spreadsheet in Exhibit 5–2 shows the calculation of the product cost for each of three gas-grill lines (STD, DEL, and ULT). Overhead is applied to the products at the rate of $24 per direct-labour hour. Notice that all of the plant's budgeted manufacturing-overhead costs are lumped together in a single cost pool. This total budgeted overhead amount ($4,896,000) then is divided by the total budgeted direct-labour hours (204,000 hours).

Patio Grill Company's labour-hour-based product-costing system is typical of many manufacturing companies. Labour hours are related closely to the volume of activity in the factory, which sometimes is referred to as *throughput*. Consequently, these traditional product-costing systems often are said to be **volume-based** (or **throughput-based**) **costing systems**.

	Standard Grill (STD)	Deluxe Grill (DEL)	Ultimate Grill (ULT)
Planned annual production:			
Volume in units..................	10,000	8,000	2,000
Production runs.................	80 runs of 125 units each	80 runs of 100 units each	40 runs of 50 units each
Direct material	$100	$120	$180
Direct labour (not including setup time)........	$180 (9 hours @ $20 per hour)	$220 (11 hours @ $20 per hour)	$260 (13 hours @ $20 per hour)
Machine hours (MH) per product unit..................	10 MH	12 MH	17 MH
Total machine hours consumed by product line	100,000 (10 MH × 10,000 units)	96,000 (12 MH × 8,000 units)	34,000 (17 MH × 2,000 units)

Exhibit 5–1
Basic Production and Cost Data: Patio Grill Company

Exhibit 5–2
Product Costs from Traditional
Volume-Based Product-Costing
System: Patio Grill Company

	A	B	C	D	E	F	G	H
1			STD		DEL		ULT	
2								
3	Direct material		$ 100.00		$ 120.00		$ 180.00	
4	Direct labour							
5	(not including setup time)		180.00	(9 hr. @ $20)	220.00	(11 hr. @ $20)	260.00	(13 hr. @ $20)
6	Manufacturing overhead*		216.00	(9 hr. @ $24)	264.00	(11 hr. @ $24)	312.00	(13 hr. @ $24)
7	Total		$ 496.00		$ 604.00		$ 752.00	
8								
9								
10	*Calculation of predetermined-overhead rate:							
11								
12	Budgeted manufacturing overhead			$4,896,000				
13								
14	Direct labour, budgeted hours:							
15	STD: 10,000 units x 9 hours			90,000				
16	DEL: 8,000 units x 11 hours			88,000				
17	ULT: 2,000 units x 13 hours			26,000				
18	Total direct-labour hours			204,000	hours			
19								
20	Predetermined overhead rate:							
21	(Budgeted manufacturing overhead / Budgeted direct-labour hours) = $4,896,000 / 204,000 = $24 per hour							

Trouble in Mississauga

The profitability of Patio Grill Company's Mississauga operation has been faltering in recent years. The company's pricing policy has been to set a target price for each grill equal to 120 percent of the full product cost. Thus, the prices were determined as shown in Exhibit 5–3. Also shown are the actual prices that Patio Grill Company has been obtaining for its products.

Due to price competition from other manufacturers, Standard (STD) grills were selling at $585, approximately $10 below their target price of $595.20. Moreover, Patio Grill Company's competition had forced management to reduce the price of the Deluxe grill (DEL) to $705, almost $20 below its target price of $724.80. Even at this lower price, the sales team was having difficulty getting orders for its planned volume of DEL production. Fortunately, the disappointing profitability of the STD and DEL grills was partially offset by greater-than expected profits on the Ultimate (ULT) line of grills. Patio Grill Company's sales staff had discovered that the company was swamped with orders when charging the ULT grill's target price of $902.40. Consequently, management had raised the price on the ULT grills several times, and eventually the product was selling for $940. Even at this price, customers did not seem to hesitate to place orders. Moreover, the company's competitors did not mount a challenge in the market for the ULT line of grills. Management was pleased to have a strong position in the ULT grill market. The ULT grill appeared to be a highly profitable, low-volume specialty product. Nevertheless, concern continued to mount about the difficulty in the STD and DEL grill markets. After all, these were the Mississauga plant's bread-and-butter products, with projected annual sales of 10,000 STD grills and 8,000 DEL grills.

Exhibit 5–3
Target and Actual Selling
Prices: Patio Grill Company

	Standard Grill STD	Deluxe Grill DEL	Ultimate Grill ULT
Production cost under traditional volume-based system (Exhibit 5–2)	$496.00	$604.00	$752.00
Target selling price (Cost × 120%)	595.20	724.80	902.40
Actual current selling price	585.00	705.00	940.00

Activity-Based Costing (ABC) System

Patio Grill Company's director of cost management, Hamilton Burger, had been thinking for some time about refining the plant's product-costing system. He wondered if the traditional volume-based system was providing management with accurate data about product costs. Burger had read about activity-based costing (ABC) systems, which follow a two-stage procedure to assign overhead costs to products. The first stage identifies significant activities in the production of the products and assigns overhead costs to each activity in accordance with the cost of the organization's resources used by the activity. The overhead costs assigned to each activity make up the **activity cost pools**.

After assigning overhead costs to activity cost pools in Stage One, cost drivers appropriate for each cost pool are identified in Stage Two. Then, using **pool rates**, the overhead costs are allocated from each activity cost pool to each product line in proportion to the amount of the cost driver consumed by the product line.

The two-stage cost assignment process of ABC is depicted in Exhibit 5–4.

Burger discussed ABC with Antonia Palermo, the assistant director of cost management. Together they met with all of the department supervisors to discuss development of an ABC system. After initial discussion, an ABC proposal was made to and approved by the company's top management. An ABC project team was formed, which included Burger, Palermo, and representatives of various departments. Through several months of careful data collection and analysis, the project team was able to gather the information necessary to implement an ABC system.

ABC Stage One

The ABC project team identified eight activity cost pools, which fall into four broad categories:

- *Unit level.* These activities happen for each unit of products. For example, the machine-related activity cost pool represents a **unit-level activity** since every unit of products requires machine time.

Exhibit 5–4
ABC System

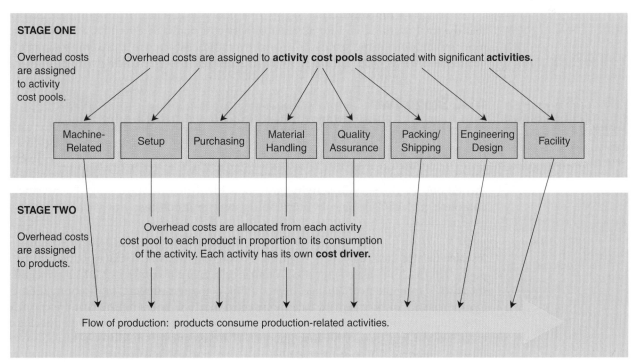

STAGE ONE

Overhead costs are assigned to activity cost pools.

Overhead costs are assigned to **activity cost pools** associated with significant **activities.**

| Machine-Related | Setup | Purchasing | Material Handling | Quality Assurance | Packing/Shipping | Engineering Design | Facility |

STAGE TWO

Overhead costs are assigned to products.

Overhead costs are allocated from each activity cost pool to each product in proportion to its consumption of the activity. Each activity has its own **cost driver.**

Flow of production: products consume production-related activities.

The forklift operator is engaged in material-handling, which is usually a batch-level activity in an ABC system. The engineer using this computer-aided-design (CAD) system is engaged in the product-sustaining-level activity of product design.

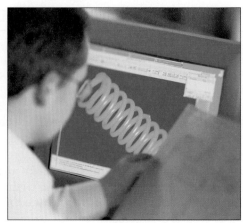

- *Batch level.* These activities must be performed for each batch of products, rather than for each unit. Patio Grill Company's **batch-level activities** include the setup, purchasing, material-handling, quality-assurance, and packing/shipping activity cost pools.
- *Product-sustaining level.* This category includes activities that are needed to support an entire product line but are not performed every time a new unit or batch of products is produced. Patio Grill Company's project team identified engineering design costs as a **product-sustaining-level activity** cost pool.
- *Facility-level (or general operations-level).* **Facility-level (or general operations-level) activities** are required in order for the entire production process to occur. Examples of such activity costs include plant management salaries, plant depreciation, property taxes, plant maintenance, and insurance.

This classification of activities into unit-level, batch-level, product-sustaining-level, and facility-level activities is called a **cost hierarchy**.

Patio Grill Company's eight activity cost pools are depicted in Exhibit 5–5. Notice that the total overhead cost for all eight activity cost pools, $4,896,000, is shown at the top. This amount is the same as the total overhead cost shown in Exhibit 5–2, which details the product costs calculated under a traditional product-costing system.

ABC Stage Two

Learning Objective **4**

Compute product costs under an ABC system.

In Stage Two of the ABC project, Burger and Palermo identified cost drivers for each activity cost pool. They then used a three-step process to compute unit activity costs for each of the three product lines and for each of the eight activity cost pools. In the following sections, we will discuss in detail how Stage Two of the ABC project was carried out for the various activity cost pools identified in Stage One. Then we will complete the ABC project by developing new product costs for each of the grill product lines.

Machine-Related Cost Pool   Let's begin by focusing on only one of the eight activity cost pools. The machine-related cost pool, a unit-level activity, totals $1,242,000 and includes the costs of machine maintenance, depreciation, computer support, lubrication, electricity, and calibration. Burger and Palermo selected machine hours for the cost driver, since a product that uses more machine hours should bear a larger share of machine-related costs. Exhibit 5–6 shows how machinery costs are assigned to products in Stage Two of the ABC analysis. This exhibit includes only a portion of the larger spreadsheet that we

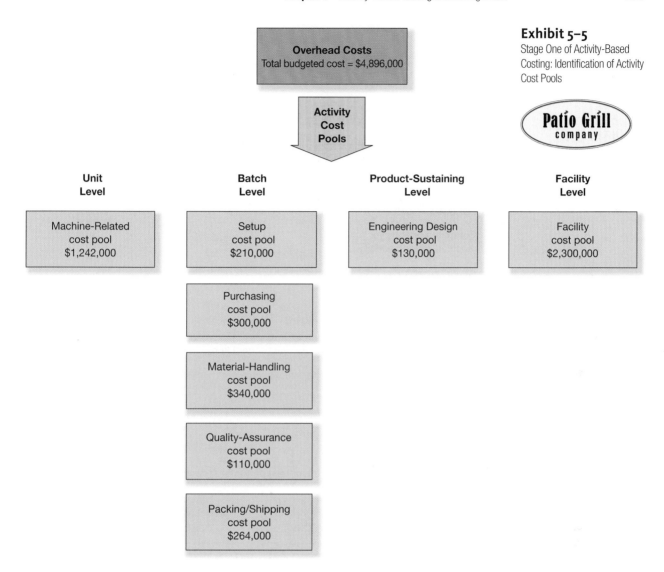

Exhibit 5–5
Stage One of Activity-Based
Costing: Identification of Activity
Cost Pools

Patio Grill
company

will examine later. The spreadsheet rows focus just on the machine-related activity cost pool. Most of the columns in the exhibit contain ABC data that were collected by the ABC project team. We will learn later in this chapter about how this type of information is collected. For now, take this information as a given.

Data Collected by ABC Project Team (Exhibit 5–6)

Column A   Activity: Machine-related

Column B   Activity cost pool: $1,242,000 (from Exhibit 5–5)

Column C   Cost driver: Machine hours

Column D   Cost driver quantity: 230,000 machine hours (total of machine hours for the three products lines in column G)[1]

Column F   Product lines: STD, DEL, ULT

Column G   Cost driver quantity for each product line (from Exhibit 5–1):
               STD 100,000 machine hours
               DEL 96,000 machine hours
               ULT 34,000 machine hours

Column I   Product line production volume (from Exhibit 5–1):
               STD 10,000 units
               DEL 8,000 units
               ULT 2,000 units

Exhibit 5–6

ABC Data and Calculations for the Machine-Related Cost Pool: Patio Grill Company

**INFORMATION SUPPLIED
BY ABC PROJECT TEAM**

	A	B	C	D	E	F	G	H	I	J
1							Cost	Activity	Product	Activity
2		Activity		Cost			Driver	Cost for	Line	Cost
3		Cost	Cost	Driver	Pool	Product	Quantity for	Product	Production	per Unit
4	Activity	Pool	Driver	Quantity	Rate	Line	Product Line	Line	Volume	of Product
5										
6	Machine	$1,242,000	Machine	230,000	$5.40	STD	100,000	$540,000	10,000	$ 54.00
7	Related		Hours			DEL	96,000	518,400	8,000	64.80
8						ULT	34,000	183,600	2,000	91.80
9						Total	230,000	1,242,000		

ABC CALCULATIONS

**1 Compute pool rate for
machine-related activity**

$$\underset{\text{(Col. B)}}{\underset{\text{cost pool}}{\text{Activity}}} \div \underset{\text{(Col. D)}}{\underset{\text{quantity}}{\underset{\text{driver}}{\text{Cost}}}} = \underset{\text{(Col. E)}}{\underset{\text{rate}}{\text{Pool}}}$$

$1,242,000 \div 230,000 = \$5.40$

2 Compute total activity cost for each product line

Product line (Col. F)	Pool rate (Col. E)	×	Cost driver quantity for each product line (Col. G)	=	Activity cost for each product line (Col. H)
STD	$5.40	×	100,000	=	$540,000
DEL	5.40	×	96,000	=	518,400
ULT	5.40	×	34,000	=	183,600

3 Compute product cost per unit for each product line

Product line (Col. F)	Activity cost for each product line (Col. H)	÷	Product line production volume (Col. I)	=	Activity cost per unit of product (Col. J)
STD	$540,000	÷	10,000	=	$54.00
DEL	518,400	÷	8,000	=	64.80
ULT	183,600	÷	2,000	=	91.80

Notice that only three columns in Exhibit 5–6 remain: columns E, H, and J. These columns contain the *amounts that are computed* during the ABC calculations, and they appear in red in Exhibit 5–6.

Amounts Computed during ABC Calculations (Exhibit 5–6)

Column E   Pool rate

Column H   Activity cost for each product line

Column J   Activity cost per unit of product for each product line

Exhibit 5–6, below the spreadsheet excerpt, shows in detail how each of these amounts (shown in red) is computed. Take time to examine the exhibit carefully, in order to understand how these amounts are computed in the ABC calculations.

Now we have seen the type of data that the ABC project team must supply for the machine-related cost pool. In addition, we have studied how the ABC calculations are carried out in order to determine the machine-related activity cost per unit of each type of product (STD, DEL, and ULT). The final conclusion of the ABC analysis *for the machine-related cost pool only* is given in column J of Exhibit 5–6. So, under ABC, the following machine-related costs per product unit should be assigned to each of the three product lines:

STD: $54.00 of machine-related cost per grill

DEL: $64.80 of machine-related cost per grill

ULT: $91.80 of machine-related cost per grill

Completing the ABC Calculations Now that we have studied the ABC data requirements and calculations for the machine-related cost pool, we can complete the ABC calculations for all eight activity cost pools (Exhibit 5-5). The entire Excel spreadsheet for Patio Grill Company's ABC project is displayed in Exhibit 5–7. There is good news and bad news. The bad news is that the spreadsheet contains eight times as many rows as the one we just examined in detail for the machine-related cost pool (Exhibit 5-6). The good news is that the ABC data requirements and calculations are conceptually *identical* for each of the eight activity cost pools. In other words, the same type of ABC data is supplied for each activity cost pool, and the three steps of ABC computations are performed for each activity cost pool in exactly the same manner as they were for the machine-related cost pool. So if we understand the computations for the machine-related costs, we will understand the computations for all eight activity cost pools. (The *computed* amounts in Exhibit 5–7 are shown in red.)

Examine Exhibit 5–7 carefully and select an activity other than the machine-related activity. Verify the computations of the pool rate in column E, the activity cost for each product line in column H, and the ABC overhead cost per unit of product in column J.

Now that we have the activity cost per unit of product for each activity cost pool and each product line, it is straightforward to compute the total unit product cost for each type of grill. To do so, we need only to add the direct-material and direct-labour costs for each grill type (given in Exhibit 5–1) to the ABC activity costs calculated in Exhibit 5–7. We do this in the Excel spreadsheet displayed as Exhibit 5–8.

	A	B	C	D	E	F	G	H	I	J
1							Cost	Activity	Product	Activity
2		Activity		Cost			Driver	Cost for	Line	Cost
3		Cost	Cost	Driver	Pool	Product	Quantity for	Product	Production	per Unit
4	Activity	Pool	Driver	Quantity	Rate	Line	Product Line	Line	Volume	of Product
5										
6	Machine	$ 1,242,000	Machine	230,000	$ 5.40	STD	100,000	$ 540,000	10,000	$ 54.00
7	Related		Hours			DEL	96,000	518,400	8,000	64.80
8						ULT	34,000	183,600	2,000	91.80
9						Total	230,000	1,242,000		
10	Setup	210,000	Production	200	1,050.00	STD	80	84,000	10,000	8.40
11			Runs			DEL	80	84,000	8,000	10.50
12						ULT	40	42,000	2,000	21.00
13						Total	200	210,000		
14	Purchasing	300,000	Purchase	600	500.00	STD	200	100,000	10,000	10.00
15			Orders			DEL	192	96,000	8,000	12.00
16						ULT	208	104,000	2,000	52.00
17						Total	600	300,000		
18	Material	340,000	Production	200	1,700.00	STD	80	136,000	10,000	13.60
19	Handling		Runs			DEL	80	136,000	8,000	17.00
20						ULT	40	68,000	2,000	34.00
21						Total	200	340,000		
22	Quality	110,000	Inspection	2,200	50.00	STD	800	40,000	10,000	4.00
23	Assurance		Hours			DEL	800	40,000	8,000	5.00
24						ULT	600	30,000	2,000	15.00
25						Total	2,200	110,000		
26	Packing/	264,000	Shipments	2,200	120.00	STD	1,000	120,000	10,000	12.00
27	Shipping					DEL	800	96,000	8,000	12.00
28						ULT	400	48,000	2,000	24.00
29						Total	2,200	264,000		
30	Engineering	130,000	Engineering	1,300	100.00	STD	500	50,000	10,000	5.00
31	Design		Hours			DEL	400	40,000	8,000	5.00
32						ULT	400	40,000	2,000	20.00
33						Total	1,300	130,000		
34	Facility	2,300,000	Machine	230,000	10.00	STD	100,000	1,000,000	10,000	100.00
35			Hours			DEL	96,000	960,000	8,000	120.00
36						ULT	34,000	340,000	2,000	170.00
37						Total	230,000	2,300,000		
38										
39	Grand Total	$ 4,896,000				Grand Total		$ 4,896,000		

Exhibit 5–7

ABC Data and Calculations: Patio Grill Company

Exhibit 5–8

Product Costs from ABC System: Patio Grill Company

	A	B	C	D	E	F	G	H
1			STD		DEL		ULT	
2								
3	Direct material		$100.00		$120.00		$180.00	
4	Direct labour							
5	(not including setup time)		180.00	(9 hr. @ $20)	220.00	(11 hr. @ $20)	260.00	(13 hr. @ $20)
6	Total direct costs per unit		$280.00		$340.00		$440.00	
7								
8	Manufacturing overhead (based on ABC):*							
9	Machine-related		$54.00		$64.80		$91.80	
10	Setup		8.40		10.50		21.00	
11	Purchasing		10.00		12.00		52.00	
12	Material handling		13.60		17.00		34.00	
13	Quality assurance		4.00		5.00		15.00	
14	Packing/shipping		12.00		12.00		24.00	
15	Engineering design		5.00		5.00		20.00	
16	Facility		100.00		120.00		170.00	
17	Total ABC overhead cost per unit		$207.00		$246.30		$427.80	
18	Total product cost per unit		$487.00		$586.30		$867.80	
19								
20	*ABC overhead costs from Exhibit 5-7.							

Interpreting the ABC Product Costs

Hamilton Burger was amazed to see the product costs reported under the ABC system. Both the STD and the DEL grills exhibited lower product costs under the ABC system than under the traditional system. This might explain the price competition Patio Grill Company faced on its STD and DEL grills. Patio Grill Company's competitors might sell their comparable standard and deluxe grills at a lower price because they realized it cost less to produce these grills than Patio Grill Company's traditional costing system had indicated. However, as Burger scanned the new product costs, he was alarmed by the substantial increase in the reported cost of an ULT grill. The cost of an ULT grill had risen by more than $100 above the company's original estimate. The complexity of the ULT grills, and its impact on costs, was hidden by the traditional volume-based costing system.

To compare the results of the two alternative costing systems, Burger prepared Exhibit 5–9. The STD grills emerged as a profitable product, selling for approximately 120 percent of their reported cost under the ABC system ($585 ÷ $487). The DEL grills were also selling at approximately 120 percent of their new reported product cost ($705 ÷ $586.30). "No wonder we couldn't sell the Deluxe grills at the old target price of $724.80," said Burger to Palermo, as they looked over the data. "Our competitors probably knew their deluxe grills cost around $586, and they priced them accordingly." When he got to the ULT column in Exhibit 5–9, Burger was appalled. "We thought those Ultimate grills were a winner," lamented Burger, "but we've been selling them at a price that is just about 8 percent over their cost!" (Burger had made this calculation: Actual current selling price of $940 ÷ ABC product cost of $867.80.) "And worse yet," Burger continued, "we've

Exhibit 5–9

Comparison of Product Costs and Target Prices from Alternative Product-Costing Systems: Patio Grill Company

	STD	DEL	ULT
Reported unit *overhead* cost:			
Traditional volume-based costing system (Exhibit 5–2)............................	$216.00	$264.00	$312.00
ABC system (Exhibit 5–8)	207.00	246.30	427.80
Reported unit *product* cost (direct material, direct labour, and overhead):			
Traditional volume-based costing system (Exhibit 5–2)............................	496.00	604.00	752.00
ABC system (Exhibit 5–8)..	487.00	586.30	867.80
Sales price data:			
Original target price (120% of product cost based on traditional volume-based costing system (Exhibit 5–3)..	595.20	724.80	902.40
New target price (120% of product cost based on ABC system	584.40	703.56	1,041.36
Actual current selling price (Exhibit 5–3)..	585.00	705.00	940.00

been selling the Ultimate grills for $940, which is more than a hundred dollars below the new target price of $1,041.36." After looking over the data, Burger made a beeline for the president's office. "We've got to get this operation straightened out," he thought.

Burger also realized that the comparison of the two product-costing systems was even more striking when he focused on just the reported *overhead* costs. He commented to Palermo, "The direct-material and direct-labour costs for each product line don't change under ABC. They're the same under both costing systems. Since these are direct costs, it's straightforward to trace these costs to each product with considerable accuracy. It's the overhead costs that cause the problem." To see what Burger was saying, look again at Exhibit 5–9 and focus on the top two rows. The overhead cost of an STD grill dropped from the old reported cost of $216 to $207 under ABC. Similarly, the overhead cost of a DEL grill dropped from the old reported cost of $264 to $246.30 under ABC. Now look at the ULT column, though. Here the overhead cost rose from the old reported cost of $312 to $427.80 under ABC! This represents an increase of more than a third. ($427.80 ÷ $312.00 is a little over 137 percent, which yields an *increase* of over 37 percent.)

The Punch Line

Learning Objective **5**

Explain why traditional volume-based costing systems tend to distort product costs.

What has happened at Patio Grill Company's plant? The essence of the problem is that the traditional volume-based costing system was overcosting the high-volume product lines (STD and DEL) and undercosting the complex, relatively low-volume product line (ULT). The high-volume products basically subsidized the low-volume line. The ABC system revealed this problem by more accurately assigning overhead costs to the three product lines.

Exhibit 5–10 summarizes the effects of the cost distortion under the traditional product-costing system. The traditional system *overcosted* each STD grill by $9, for a total of $90,000 for the STD product line on a volume of 10,000 units. Each DEL grill was *overcosted* by $17.70, for a total of $141,600 on a volume of 8,000 units. These excess costs had to come from somewhere, and that place was the ULT product line. Each ULT grill was *undercosted* by $115.80, for a total of $231,600 on a volume of 2,000 units. Notice that the *total* amount by which the STD and DEL grill lines were overcosted equals the *total* amount by which the ULT grill line was undercosted. This cost distortion can easily be seen in the graph below, which compares the total product costs for each of the grills under both systems.

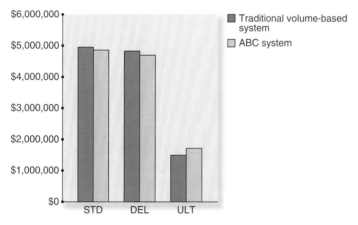

Cost Distortions with Traditional Volume-Based Costing Systems

Why did Patio Grill Company's traditional product-costing system distort its product costs? The answer lies in the use of a single volume-based cost driver. The old costing system assigned overhead to products on the basis of their relative usage of direct labour. Since the STD and DEL grill lines use substantially more direct labour than the ULT grill line, *in total*, the traditional system assigned them more overhead costs.

	STD	DEL	ULT
Traditional volume-based costing system: reported product cost	$496.00	$604.00	$ 752.00
Activity-based costing system: reported product cost	487.00	586.30	867.80
Amount of cost distortion per unit	$ 9.00	$ 17.70	$(115.80)

Traditional system overcosts STD grills by $9.00 per unit.

Traditional system overcosts DEL grills by $17.70 per unit.

Traditional system undercosts ULT grills by ($115.80) per unit.

× Production volume	× 10,000	× 8,000	× 2,000
Total amount of cost distortion for entire product line	$90,000	$141,600	$(231,600)

Sum of these three amounts is zero.

STD   DEL   ULT

Traditional system shifts costs from ULT product line to STD and DEL product lines.

Exhibit 5–10

Cost Distortion under Patio Grill Company's Traditional Product-Costing System

The problem with this result is that for every one of Patio Grill Company's overhead activities, the proportion of the activity actually consumed by the ULT grill line is far greater than its low volume would suggest. The ULT grill line has a budgeted production volume of just 2,000 units, which is only 10 percent of the total budgeted production volume of 20,000 units. (20,000 units = 10,000 STD units + 8,000 DEL units + 2,000 ULT units.) Now examine the ABC calculations in Exhibit 5–7. Focus on column G, which details the consumption of the cost driver by each product line for each activity cost pool. Notice that for every one of the overhead activities, the ULT grill line consumes much more than a 10 percent share of the activity, even though the ULT line accounts for only 10 percent of budgeted production volume. The relatively heavy consumption of overhead activities by the ULT product line is due to its greater complexity and small production runs. We must conclude, therefore, that direct labour is not a suitable cost driver for overhead costs. Usage of direct labour does not drive most overhead costs in this company.

There are actually two factors working against the old product-costing system. First, many of the activities that result in overhead costs are *not unit-level activities*. Second, the company manufactures a *diverse set of products*.

Non-Unit-Level Overhead Costs   When the project team designed the ABC system, only the machine-related overhead cost pool was classified as a unit-level activity. All of the other activities were classified as batch-level, product-sustaining-level, or facility-level activities. This means that many overhead costs are not incurred every time a unit is produced. Instead, they are related to starting new production batches, supporting a product line, or running the entire operation. Since direct labour is a unit-level cost driver, it fails to capture the forces that drive these other types of costs. In the ABC system, cost drivers that were appropriate for each activity cost pool were selected. For example, since setting up machinery for a new production run is a batch-level activity, the number of production runs is an appropriate batch-level cost driver.

Product Diversity   Although all three products are gas barbeque grills, the grills are quite different. The STD and DEL grills are high-volume, relatively simple products. The ULT grills constitute a considerably more complex, and relatively low-volume, product line. As a result of this *product line diversity*, the three product lines consume overhead activities in different proportions. For example, compare the *consumption ratios* for the purchasing and material-handling activity cost pools shown below. The **consumption ratio** is the proportion of an activity consumed by a particular product.

	Consumption Ratios*		
Activity Cost Pool	STD	DEL	ULT
Purchasing activity (Cost driver: Purchase orders or POs)	200 POs (33%)	192 POs (32%)	208 POs (35%)
Material-handling activity (Cost driver: Production runs)	80 runs (40%)	80 runs (40%)	40 runs (20%)

*The purchase order and production run data come from Exhibit 5–7.

These widely varying consumption ratios result from product line diversity. A single cost driver will not capture the widely differing usage of these activities by the three products. The ABC system uses two different cost drivers to assign these costs to the company's diverse products.

Two Key Points   To summarize, either of the following characteristics will undermine the ability of a volume-based product-costing system to assign overhead costs accurately.

- *A large proportion of non-unit-level activities.* A unit-level cost driver, such as direct labour, machine hours, or throughput, will not be able to assign the costs of non-unit-level activities accurately.
- *Product diversity.* When the consumption ratios differ widely between activities, no single cost driver will accurately assign the resulting overhead costs.

When either of these characteristics is present, a volume-based product-costing system is likely to distort product costs.

Does the sort of product-cost distortion experienced by Patio Grill Company occur in other companies? The answer is yes, as illustrated by the following example of DHL International, the express transport service.

Managerial Accounting Practice

DHL International

COST DISTORTION AT DHL

DHL International, the express transport company, ships a billion packages to 220 countries and territories throughout the world. Management at DHL found that its cost accounting system had distorted costs between the various types of express transport services the firm provided. Before implementation of a full ABC system at DHL, express transport services provided to banks appeared to be unprofitable, whereas transport services provided to heavy manufacturers appeared to be highly profitable. "This was bad news because we [DHL] had a lot more banking customers than heavy manufacturing customers." After fully implementing ABC, however, management found that the previous costing system had used cost drivers that failed to account for package weights, thereby distorting costs between services to banks and services to heavy manufacturers. The ABC analysis revealed that express transport services to banks were actually quite profitable after all.[2]

ABC: Key Issues

Patio Grill Company's movement toward ABC is typical of changes experienced by many companies. Added domestic and foreign competition is forcing manufacturers to strive for a better understanding of their cost structures. Moreover, the cost structures of many manufacturers have changed significantly over the past decade. Years ago, a typical manufacturer produced a relatively small number of products that did not differ much in the amount and types of manufacturing support they required. Labour was the dominant element in such a firm's cost structure. Nowadays, products are more numerous and more complicated, and vary more in their production requirements. Perhaps most important, labour is becoming an ever-smaller component of total production costs. All these factors mean manufacturers must take a close look at their traditional volume-based costing systems and consider a move toward ABC. Among the many well-known manufacturers that have benefited from ABC are Caterpillar, Coca-Cola, Hewlett-Packard, Vale Inco, John Deere, Johnson & Johnson, Magna International, and Pfizer, to name a few.

The service sector has also undergone dynamic change in recent years. Increasing competition, outsourcing of key business processes, and the growth of the Internet have changed many service companies' business models. As their business environment changes, many service organizations have made use of ABC. Service companies benefiting from ABC include American Express, BC Hydro, FedEx, Purolator Courier Ltd., Sun Life Insurance, TELUS, and WestJet Airlines, among many others. Among the government units that have benefited from ABC are such diverse organizations as the Canadian Navy, the Royal Canadian Mounted Police, BC Health Authority Shared Services Organization, the City of Toronto, and several agencies of the federal government, including the Canadian Human Rights Commission, the Department of National Defence, Fisheries and Oceans Canada, Health Canada, and the Treasury Board of Canada.

An important factor in the move toward ABC systems is related to the information requirements of such systems. The data required for ABC are more readily available than in the past. Increasing automation, coupled with sophisticated real-time information systems, provides the kind of data necessary to implement highly accurate product-costing systems. Some key issues related to ABC systems are discussed in the following sections.

Cost Drivers

A cost driver is a characteristic of an event or activity that results in the incurrence of costs. In ABC systems, the most significant cost drivers are identified. A database is then created that shows how these cost drivers are distributed across products. Three factors are important in selecting appropriate cost drivers.

1. *Degree of correlation.* The central concept of an ABC system is to assign the costs of each activity to product lines on the basis of how each product line consumes the cost driver identified for that activity. The idea is to *infer* how each product line consumes the activity by *observing* how each line consumes the cost driver. Therefore, the accuracy of the resulting cost assignments depends on the *degree of correlation* between consumption of the activity and consumption of the cost driver.

    Assume that inspection cost is selected as an activity cost pool. The objective of the ABC system is to assign inspection costs to product lines on the basis of their consumption of the inspection activity. There are two potential cost drivers: (1) number of inspections and (2) hours of inspection time. If every inspection requires the same amount of time for all products, then the number of inspections on a product line will be highly correlated with the consumption of inspection activity by that product line. On the other hand, if inspections vary significantly in the time required, then simply recording the number of inspections will not adequately portray the consumption of inspection activity. In this case, hours of inspection time would be more highly correlated with the actual consumption of the inspection activity.

2. *Cost of measurement.* Designing any information system entails cost–benefit trade-offs. The more activity cost pools there are in an ABC system, the greater will be the accuracy of the cost assignments. However, more activity cost pools also entail more cost drivers, which results in greater costs of implementing and maintaining the system.

   Similarly, the higher the correlation between a cost driver and the actual consumption of the associated activity, the greater the accuracy of the cost assignments. However, it may also be more costly to measure the more highly correlated cost driver. Returning to our example of the inspection activity, it may be that inspection hours make a more accurate cost driver than the number of inspections. It is likely, however, that inspection hours will also be more costly to measure and track over time.

3. *Behavioural effects.* Information systems have the potential not only to facilitate decisions but also to influence the behaviour of decision makers. This can be good or bad, depending on the behavioural effects. In identifying cost drivers, an ABC analyst should consider the possible behavioural consequences. For example, in a just-in-time (JIT) production environment, a key goal is to reduce inventories and material-handling activities to the absolute minimum level possible. The number of material moves may be the most accurate measure of the consumption of the material-handling activity for cost assignment purposes. It also may have a desirable behavioural effect of inducing managers to reduce the number of times materials are moved, thereby reducing material-handling costs.

   Dysfunctional behavioural effects are also possible. For example, the number of vendor contacts may be a cost driver for the purchasing activity of vendor selection. This could induce purchasing managers to contact fewer vendors, which might result in the failure to identify the lowest-cost or highest-quality vendor.

> "ABC is not a magic bullet, but it is a tool to help you understand your business better." (5b)
> **Braas Company**

> "After the initial run-through, we completed a separate analysis detailing how many times a [cost] driver was used. We performed a sort of cost–benefit analysis. We gave each [cost] driver a grade, such as how easy would the driver be to collect." (5c)
> **John Deere Health Care, Inc.**

Collecting ABC Data

The output of an organization's various departments consists of the activities performed by employees or machines in those departments. Activities usually result in paperwork or the generation of computer documents. For example, engineering departments typically deal with documents such as specification sheets and engineering change orders. Purchasing departments handle requisitions and orders, which may be either hard-copy or computer documents. In an ABC system, analysis of documents such as these can be used to assign the costs of activities to product lines on the basis of the amount of activity generated by each product.

Interviews and Paper Trails   The information used in Patio Grill Company's ABC system came initially from extensive interviews with key employees in each of the organization's support departments and a careful review of each department's records. In the engineering area, for example, ABC project team members interviewed each engineer to determine the breakdown of time spent on each of the three products. They also examined every engineering change order completed in the past two years. The team concluded that engineering costs were driven largely by engineering hours and that the breakdown was 500 hours for the STD grill line, 400 hours for the DEL grill line, and 400 hours for the ULT grill line.

> **Learning Objective   7**
> Discuss several key issues in ABC, including data collection and storyboarding .

> "We were negotiating fees, and the customer was under the impression that they were paying more than they should. . . . To make this customer comfortable with the pricing, we needed a [more accurate] costing system." (5d)
> **Dana Commercial Credit Corporation**

Storyboarding   As Patio Grill Company's project team probed further into the ABC analysis, it made considerable use of another technique for collecting activity data. **Storyboarding** is a procedure used to develop a detailed process flow chart, which visually represents activities and the relationships among the activities. A storyboarding session involves all or most of the employees who participate in the activities oriented toward achieving a specific objective. A facilitator helps the employees identify the key activities involved in their jobs. These activities are written on small cards and placed on a large board in the order they are accomplished. Relationships among the activities are shown by the order and proximity of the cards. Other information about the activities is recorded on the cards, such as the amount of time and other resources that are expended on each activity and the events that trigger the activity. After several storyboarding sessions, a completed storyboard emerges, recording key activity information vital to the ABC project. Historically, storyboards have been used by Walt Disney and other film producers in the development of plots for animated films. Storyboarding is also used by advertising agencies in developing event sequences for TV commercials.

Storyboarding provides a powerful tool for collecting and organizing the data needed in an ABC project. Patio Grill Company's ABC project team used storyboarding very effectively to study each of the firm's activity cost pools. The team concluded that purchasing costs were driven by the number of purchase orders. Material-handling costs were driven by the number of production runs. Quality-assurance costs were driven by the number of inspection hours devoted to each product line. Packaging and shipping costs were driven by the number of shipments made.

In summary, the ABC project team conducted a thorough and lengthy analysis involving many employee interviews, examination of hundreds of documents, and storyboarding sessions. The final result was the data used in the ABC calculations displayed in Exhibits 5–7 and 5–8. This in-depth analysis is normally conducted only at the implementation phase of a new ABC system; once implemented, data needed for ABC is captured by the product-costing system.

Interviews with department staff and storyboarding sessions are often used by ABC project teams to accumulate the data needed for an ABC study. In the interview sessions, an ABC project team member asks department employees to detail their activities, as well as the time and other resources consumed by the activities. Storyboards, like the one shown here, depict the relationships between the activities performed in an organization.

Multidisciplinary ABC Project Teams   Collecting ABC data is difficult and costly. In order to gather information from all facets of an organization's operations, it is essential to involve staff from a variety of functional areas. A typical ABC project team includes accounting and finance people as well as engineers, marketing staff, production and operations managers, and so forth. Hence, ABC should be seen as a companywide initiative, not simply an accounting project. A multidisciplinary project team not only designs a better ABC system but also helps in gaining credibility for the new system throughout the organization. Senior management commitment and support is also crucial to the successful implementation of ABC.

Activity Dictionary and Bill of Activities

Many ABC teams compile an **activity dictionary**, which is a complete listing of the activities identified and used in the ABC analysis. An activity dictionary helps in the implementation of ABC across several divisions of an organization, because it provides for consistency in the ABC system terminology and the complexity of the ABC analyses in the various divisions.

A **bill of activities** is another commonly used element in an ABC analysis. A bill of activities for a product or service is a complete listing of the activities required for the product or service to be produced. As a familiar analogy, think about a recipe for chocolate chip cookies. The *bill of materials* for the cookies is the list of ingredients provided in the recipe. The *bill of activities* is the list of steps given in the recipe for making the cookies (e.g., combine ingredients in a bowl, stir in chocolate chips, place spoon-size lumps of dough on greased cookie sheet, bake at 375° for 10 minutes or until done).

> "Having a plant-level activity dictionary allows the plant to manage its activities locally and serves as a standard reference that employees can use to see which activities roll up into which processes." (5e)
> **Navistar International Corporation**

Activity-Based Management

Learning Objective　**8**

Explain the concept of activity-based management (ABM) and two-dimensional ABC.

Using ABC information to support organizational strategy, improve operations, and manage costs is called *activity-based management (ABM)*, as discussed in Chapter 1. We have already seen a little of ABM in the previous sections, where Patio Grill Company used ABC information to better understand its product-pricing decisions. Management discovered through ABC analysis that some products were overcosted and others undercosted by their traditional product-costing system. They realized that, as a result of this cost distortion, they were setting some prices too high to be competitive and other products were being priced too low. This important insight presented management with the opportunity to revise its product pricing in order to reflect the more accurate product costs provided by the ABC analysis. When management followed up on this product-pricing opportunity, it was engaging in ABM. However, ABM is a much broader concept than this. ABM involves any use of ABC information to support the organization's strategy, improve operations, or manage activities and their resulting costs.

Two-Dimensional ABC

One way of picturing the relationship between ABC and ABM is in terms of the **two-dimensional ABC model** depicted in Exhibit 5–11.[3] The vertical dimension of the model depicts the cost assignment view of an ABC system. From the *cost assignment viewpoint*, the ABC system uses two-stage cost allocation to *assign* the costs of resources to the firm's cost objects. These cost objects could be products manufactured, services provided, or customers served.

Now focus on the horizontal dimension of the model. Depicted here is the *process view* of an ABC system. The emphasis now is on the activities themselves, the various processes by which work is accomplished in the organization. The left-hand side of Exhibit 5–11 depicts **activity analysis**, which is the detailed identification and description of the activities conducted in the enterprise. Activity analysis entails identification

Exhibit 5–11
Two-Dimensional ABC Model

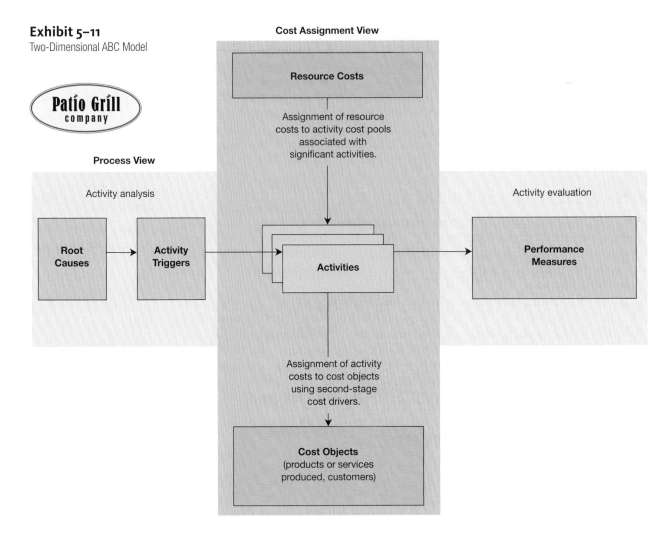

not only of the activities but also of their *root causes*, the events that *trigger* activities, and the *linkages* among activities. The right-hand side of Exhibit 5–11 depicts the evaluation of activities through performance measures. It is these processes of *activity analysis and evaluation* that make up ABM. Notice that the *activities*, which appear in the centre of both dimensions, are the focal point of ABC and ABM.

Using ABM to Identify Non-Value-Added Activities and Costs

An important goal of ABM is to identify and eliminate non-value-added activities and costs. **Non-value-added activities** are operations that are either (1) unnecessary and dispensable or (2) necessary but inefficient and improvable.[4] Non-value-added costs, which result from such activities, are the costs of activities that can be eliminated without deterioration of product quality, performance, or perceived value. The following five steps provide a strategy for eliminating non-value-added costs in both manufacturing and service firms.

Identifying Activities   The first step is activity analysis, which identifies all of the organization's significant activities. The resulting activity list should be broken down to the most fundamental level that is practical. For example, rather than listing purchasing as an activity, the list should break down the purchasing operation into its component activities, such as obtaining part specifications, compiling vendor lists, selecting vendors, negotiating prices, ordering, and expediting.

Identifying Non-Value-Added Activities   Three criteria for determining whether an activity adds value are as follows:

1. *Is the activity necessary?* If it is a duplicate or nonessential operation, it is non-value-added.
2. *Is the activity efficiently performed?* In answering this question, it is helpful to compare the actual performance of the activity to a value-added baseline established using budgets, targets, or external benchmarks.
3. *Is the activity sometimes value-added and sometimes non-value-added?* For example, it may be necessary to move work-in-process units between production operations, but unnecessary to move raw materials around while in storage.

> "Putting a spotlight on non-value-added activities, such as [correcting] errors in procurement, provided the focus for ultimately implementing process improvements." (5f)
> **GTE Supply (currently part of Verizon)**

Understanding Activity Linkages, Root Causes, and Triggers   In identifying non-value-added activities, it is critical to understand the ways in which activities are linked together. The following chain of activities provides an example:

The rework of defective units is a non-value-added activity. The rework is *triggered* by the identification of defective products during inspection. The *root cause* of the rework, however, might lie in any one of many preceding activities. Perhaps the part specifications were in error or an unreliable vendor was selected. Maybe the wrong parts were received or the production activity is to blame.

A set of linked activities (such as that depicted above) is called a **process**. Sometimes activity analysis is referred to as **process value analysis (PVA)**.

Establishing Performance Measures   By continually measuring the performance of all activities, and comparing performance with benchmarks, management's attention may be directed to unnecessary or inefficient activities. We will explore performance measurement extensively in Chapter 8.

Reporting Non-Value-Added Costs   Non-value-added costs should be highlighted in activity centre cost reports. By identifying non-value-added activities and reporting their costs, management can strive toward the ongoing goals of process improvement and elimination of non-value-added costs.

One approach that cost-management analysts find helpful in identifying non-value-added activities is to categorize the ways in which time is spent in a production process. Let's return to our illustration of Patio Grill Company's Mississauga plant. How is time spent in the plant between the arrival of raw material and shipment of a grill to a customer? As in most manufacturing operations, time is spent in the following five ways:

1. *Process time.* The time during which a product is undergoing conversion activity
2. *Inspection time.* The amount of time spent ensuring that the product is of high quality
3. *Move time.* The time spent moving raw materials, work in process, or finished goods between operations
4. *Waiting time.* The amount of time that raw materials or work in process spend waiting for the next operation
5. *Storage time.* The time during which raw materials, partially completed products, or finished goods are held in stock before further processing or shipment to customers

Thinking about the production operation in these terms allows management to ask: "Does the time spent in all of these activities add value to the product? Will the customer pay for it? Can the time spent on inspection be reduced without diminishing product quality? Can production efficiency be improved by reducing the number of times that raw materials or work-in-process or finished goods are moved from one place to another? Can production be scheduled so that partially completed products spend less time just waiting for the next operation? Can storage time be reduced by ordering raw materials and producing products only as they are needed?" If reductions can be made in any of these time-consuming activities, without diminishing product quality or functionality, management has a real opportunity to reduce non-value-added costs.

Customer-Profitability Analysis

Learning Objective   9

Explain and execute a customer-profitability analysis.

It is quite possible for a company to have profitable products and, at the same time, incur customer-related costs that make certain customer relationships unprofitable. **Customer-profitability analysis** uses ABC to determine the activities, costs, and profit associated with serving particular customers. Suppose, for example, that Customer X frequently changes its orders after they are placed, but Customer Y typically does not. Then the costs incurred in updating sales orders for changes should be recorded in a manner that reflects the fact that Customer X is more responsible for those activities and costs than is Customer Y. An effective cost management system should allow managers to derive such cost details.

Many factors can result in some customers being more profitable than others. Customers that order in small quantities, order frequently, often change their orders, require special packaging or handling, demand faster delivery, or need special parts or engineering design generally are less profitable than customers who demand less in terms of customized services. If managers have a good understanding of which customers are generating the greatest profit, they can make more-informed decisions about customer service. Moreover, this allows customers to be educated as to the costs they are causing when demanding special services. In many cases, customers' behaviour can be changed in a way that reduces costs to the supplier. These cost savings can then be shared by the supplier and the customer.

The task of assigning costs to customers is a challenge. A system must be in place that enables the company to identify which customers are using customer support services and how frequently they do so. How much time must the company spend on a customer to make the sale and to provide ongoing support services? These costs are in addition to the cost of manufacturing the product or initially providing a service for the customer.

Customer-Profitability Analysis Example

To illustrate customer-profitability analysis, let's focus again on Patio Grill Company. Two more years have passed and the company has successfully implemented an ABC system in its Mississauga plant. At a recent strategy meeting with the senior management team, Patio Grill Company's president and CEO expressed interest in assessing the profitability of the entire company's various customer relationships. He found support for the idea from the director of cost management, who had been reading about customer-profitability analysis in professional journals. The marketing manager also expressed interest in customer-profitability analysis, since he was concerned about the profitability of two customers in particular. "We have a few customers who seem to want the moon and the stars when it comes to customer service," he complained. "I know the customer is always right and all, but you really have to wonder if we're making any money from a couple of these customers, what with all the extra design and packaging they demand. And some of our other customers seem to require an awful lot of extra attention in sales calls, order processing, and billing. If we had a better idea of each customer's profitability, it would help our marketing and sales staffs to focus their efforts."

The controller soon had his cost management staff working on the customer-profitability analysis that the president had requested. The first step required an ABC analysis of certain *customer-related costs* that could seriously affect a customer's profitability. Recall that ABC analysis relies on a cost hierarchy with cost levels, such as unit-level, batch-level, product-line-level, customer-level, and facility-level or general operations-level costs. In this use of ABC, the cost management team is focusing on the customer-related costs. After an extensive analysis and several interviews with staff throughout the company, the cost management team came up with the ABC analysis in Exhibit 5–12.[5]

Based on the ABC information, the cost management team assessed the profitability of each of Patio Grill Company's customer relationships. Detailed information from that analysis for five of these customers appears in the Excel spreadsheet in Exhibit 5–13. These five customers were singled out because three of them are key customers (i.e., Customers 106, 112, and 113), and two of them (107 and 119) were suspected by the marketing manager to be at best marginally profitable. As it turned out, suspicions about Customers 107 and 119 were well founded. Both customers were found to be unprofitable; in fact, Customer 119 had caused a loss of almost $120,000 during the year.

> "When we saw what some of our customers were costing us, we were quite surprised. We shared this information with them, and they were also surprised to see how much work went into servicing them. At this point, we negotiated with them to eliminate certain discounts they were receiving." (5g)
> **Pfizer**

Customer-Related Activities	Cost Driver Base	Cost Driver Rate
Order processing	Purchase orders	$ 150
Sales contacts (phone calls, faxes, etc.)	Contacts	100
Sales visits	Visits	1,000
Shipment processing	Shipments	200
Billing and collection	Invoices	160
Design/engineering change orders	Engineering/design changes	4,000
Special packaging	Units packaged	40
Special handling	Units handled	60

Exhibit 5–12
ABC Analysis for Customer-Related Costs: Patio Grill Company

	A	B	C	D	E	F
1		Designated Customers (By 3-Digit Customer Code)				
2		Customer 106	Customer 107	Customer 112	Customer 113	Customer 119
3						
4	Sales revenue	$ 4,320,000	$ 3,480,000	$ 6,500,000	$ 4,490,000	$ 1,960,000
5	Cost of goods sold	3,220,000	2,810,000	4,890,000	3,380,000	1,480,000
6	Gross margin	$ 1,100,000	$ 670,000	$ 1,610,000	$ 1,110,000	$ 480,000
7	Selling and administrative costs:					
8	General selling costs	$ 362,000	$ 220,000	$ 530,000	$ 366,000	$ 160,000
9	General administrative costs	181,000	110,000	265,000	183,000	80,000
10	Customer-related costs					
11	Order processing	11,100	80,250	16,050	22,200	38,400
12	Sales contacts	22,000	13,400	32,000	24,100	28,800
13	Sales visits	44,000	20,000	47,000	38,000	32,000
14	Shipment processing	33,000	27,800	64,200	44,600	19,200
15	Billing and collection	33,600	14,000	80,480	22,400	9,600
16	Design/engineering changes	93,000	96,000	84,000	112,000	68,000
17	Special packaging	88,000	27,200	64,440	44,480	76,800
18	Special handling	33,000	80,400	48,300	33,300	86,400
19	Total selling and administrative cost	$ 900,700	$ 689,050	$ 1,231,470	$ 890,080	$ 599,200
20	Operating income	$ 199,300	$ (19,050)	$ 378,530	$ 219,920	$ (119,200)

Exhibit 5–13
Customer-Profitability Analysis for Five Designated Customers: Patio Grill Company

A complete customer-profitability analysis for all of Patio Grill Company's customers appears in the spreadsheet in Exhibit 5–14. This exhibit reveals several interesting aspects of the customer-profitability scenario. Of 20 customers, 17 are profitable. The three unprofitable customers (107, 134, and 119) accounted for losses of over $240,000 in operating income in a single year! Notice that over 25 percent of the company's profit is generated by its top three customers. Almost half of the profit

> "Almost any person in any organization that implements ABM has some real surprises when they start seeing the data about customer profitability and product profitability." (5h)
> **Shiloh Industries, Inc.**

CUSTOMER PROFITABILITY ANALYSIS AT BANK ONE CORP.

Managerial
Accounting
Practice

Bank One Corp

The Wall Street Journal described how Bank One Corp. (now part of JPMorgan Chase Bank) used customer-profitability analysis to guide decisions about customer service.

At Bank One Corp., at the time one of the largest banks, "the line in the sand between preferred and nonpreferred customers has become strikingly obvious." The bank was redesigning its 218 branches in Louisiana so that its "Premier One" customers could be whisked away to a special teller window with no wait or to the desk of an appropriate bank officer. "Customers qualify by keeping at least $2,500 in a checking account or a total of $25,000 in a combination of certain bank accounts," or by paying a $17 monthly fee. "Management estimates that the extra attention will go only to the top 20 percent of its customers."[6]

Insights into Canadian Banking reported that "as they strive to meet the evolving needs and expectations of their customers, banks need to work toward a customer profitability measure that effectively balances traditional costing methods, a complex operating environment and an ever-evolving consumer landscape."[7]

Changes at TD Canada Trust, such as online statements and dedicated tellers for business customers, are the direct results of customer-profitability analysis.

comes from its top six customers, and fully three-quarters of its profit is generated by half of its customers. This sort of customer-profitability scenario is quite typical for manufacturers. The biggest share of most companies' profits come from a handful of their customers. Such an insight is important for management, as it determines where to devote the company's resources in serving customers.[8]

A graphical portrayal of the complete customer-profitability analysis is given in Exhibit 5–15. This graph is called a **customer-profitability profile**, and it is a common and useful way of presenting a customer-profitability analysis to management.

Exhibit 5–14
Customer-Profitability Analysis
with Customers Ranked
by Operating Income:
Patio Grill Company

	A	B	C	D	E	F
1						Cumulative Operating
2	3-Digit	Customer	Customer	Customer	Cumulative	Income as a
3	Customer	Sales	Gross	Operating	Operating	Percentage of Total
4	Code	Revenue	Margin	Income	Income	Operating Income
5						
6	112	$ 6,500,000	$ 1,610,000	$ 378,530	$ 378,530	8.8%
7	108	6,964,000	1,570,000	370,000	748,530	17.3%
8	114	6,694,000	1,484,300	351,000	1,099,530	25.5%
9	116	5,846,000	1,461,600	340,000	1,439,530	33.4%
10	110	5,602,000	1,430,000	336,070	1,775,600	41.1%
11	121	5,400,000	1,413,000	331,000	2,106,600	48.8%
12	124	5,601,000	1,405,520	330,000	2,436,600	56.5%
13	127	5,090,000	1,280,020	300,000	2,736,600	63.4%
14	128	4,760,000	1,160,200	281,400	3,018,000	69.9%
15	125	5,000,200	1,181,000	276,000	3,294,000	76.3%
16	135	4,431,000	1,150,000	270,000	3,564,000	82.6%
17	133	4,008,000	1,059,800	251,400	3,815,400	88.4%
18	113	4,490,000	1,110,000	219,920	4,035,320	93.5%
19	111	4,200,000	875,220	205,000	4,240,320	98.2%
20	106	4,320,000	1,100,000	199,300	4,439,620	102.9%
21	136	1,920,000	351,200	82,000	4,521,620	104.8%
22	137	1,641,000	139,400	35,600	4,557,220	105.6%
23	107	3,480,000	670,000	(19,050)	4,538,170	105.1%
24	134	2,820,000	582,000	(102,600)	4,435,570	102.8%
25	119	1,960,000	480,000	(119,200)	4,316,370	100.0%

Cumulative Operating Income as a
Percentage of Total Operating Income

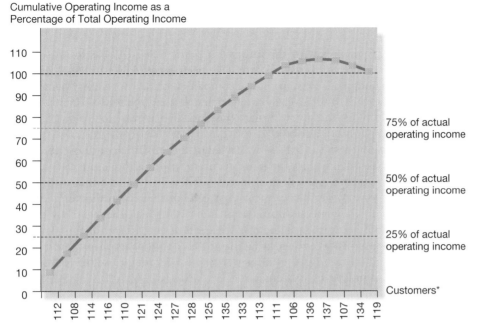

75% of actual
operating income

50% of actual
operating income

25% of actual
operating income

Customers*

*Customers ranked by operating income.

Exhibit 5–15

Customer-Profitability Profile
in Terms of Cumulative
Operating Income as a
Percentage of Total Operating
Income: Patio Grill Company

Managerial
Accounting
Practice

Best Buy

CUSTOMER-PROFITABILITY ANALYSIS AT BEST BUY

Best Buy, with over $45 billion in annual revenue, is the largest U.S. consumer electronics retailer.[9] Best Buy's CEO "is embracing a heretical notion for a retailer. He wants to separate the best customers among the 1.5 million people who visit Best Buy's stores every day from the worst customers." Best Buy's preferred customers "boost profits at the consumer electronics giant by snapping up high-definition televisions, portable electronics, and newly released DVDs without waiting for mark-downs or rebates."[10] The retailer's worst customers, on the other hand, "buy products, apply for rebates, return the purchases, and then buy them back at returned-merchandise discounts. They load up on loss-leaders, severely discounted merchandise designed to boost store traffic, then 'flip' the goods at a profit on eBay. They slap down rock-bottom price quotes from Web sites and demand that Best Buy make good on its lowest-price pledge." According to Best Buy's CEO, these customers "can wreak enormous economic havoc." The company estimates "that as many as 100 million of its 500 million customer visits each year are undesirable." And Best Buy's CEO "wants to be rid of these customers." The company's new approach "upends what has long been standard practice for mass merchants. Most chains use their advertising budgets chiefly to maximize customer traffic." Best Buy's new plan is to "rate its customers according to profitability, and then dump the up to 20 percent that are unprofitable." Best Buy is rolling out its new strategy in about 100 of its 670 stores. Best Buy "is examining its sales records and demographic data and sleuthing through computer databases to identify good and bad customers. To lure the high spenders, it is stocking more merchandise and providing more appealing service. To deter the undesirables, it is cutting back on promotions and sales tactics that tend to draw them, and culling them from marketing lists."[11]

ABC in the Service Sector

Learning Objective **10**

Understand and discuss how ABC is used in service organizations.

We conclude this chapter with the important point that ABC has found widespread usage in the service sector as well. There have been many ABC success stories in such diverse organizations as airlines, insurance companies, banks, hospitals, financial services firms, hotels, railroads, and government agencies. Among the service organizations that use ABC are the BC Ministry of Health, the Canadian Forces, the Canadian National Railway Company, and the Royal Bank of Canada.

The overall objectives of ABC for service firms are similar to those for manufacturing companies. Managers want more accurate information about the cost of providing the services they are selling. Moreover, they want to use this information to improve operations and to better meet the needs of their customers in a more cost-effective manner. The general approach of identifying activities, activity cost pools, and cost drivers is also similar. The classification of activities into unit-level, batch-level, product-sustaining-level, and facility-level activities applies as well in service settings. For example, a private auto insurance provider might use the following activity classifications in its ABC system:[12]

"BMO implemented new funds transfer pricing and cost methodologies. The new funds transfer pricing methodology is matched-maturity based, and the cost system is activity based. These enhancements provide more detailed profitability information." (5i)

BMO Financial Group

- *Unit level.* Entering initial claim data into the computer (for each claim received)
- *Batch level.* Moving a batch of claims from one processing step to the next
- *Product-sustaining level.* Maintenance of the repair facility provider network (i.e., maintaining relationships with body shops providing repairs to claimants)
- *Facility (general operations) level.* General administration of the claims business unit

ABC at Pacific Children's Hospital

To see how management can use ABC in a service setting, let's explore how ABC is used at Pacific Children's Hospital (PCH).[13] PCH provides expert care for the most seriously ill or injured children, including newborns and adolescents. The hospital's services range from ambulatory clinics to more specialized services, such as pediatric surgery, transplants, and oncology. The asthma clinic, dermatology clinic, and diabetes clinic are examples of the many clinics that fall under the umbrella of specialized pediatrics. All of the clinics have implemented ABC to determine how much it costs to serve patients in various categories. The clinics classify patient appointments as routine, extended, or complex, depending on the appointment length and complexity. In addition, each appointment is classified as either a new-patient appointment or a continuing-patient appointment. Thus, every patient appointment is one of the following six types:

	Routine	Extended	Complex
New patient	New patient; routine appointment	New patient; extended appointment	New patient; complex appointment
Continuing patient	Continuing patient; routine appointment	Continuing patient; extended appointment	Continuing patient; complex appointment

Every patient appointment involves a registered nurse who takes vital signs and prepares the patient for the primary health-care professional. Then, every patient is seen by one primary health-care professional, which can be a physician, a resident, or an intern.[14] The hospital's ABC project team designated the following activities and cost drivers:

Activity	Cost Driver
Physician time	Physician minutes with patient
Intern or resident time	Intern or resident minutes with patient
Registered nurse time	Registered nurse minutes with patient
Clerical time: New patients	New patient visits
Clerical time: Continuing patients	Continuing patient visits
Billing	Billing lines (i.e., number of line items on bill)
Facility	Patient visits (both new and continuing)

The ABC analysis for the dermatology clinic is displayed in Exhibit 5–16. Notice that this ABC spreadsheet has a format that is identical to the ABC spreadsheet prepared for Patio Grill Company (Exhibit 5–7). The column headings are different, because the clinic provides medical services to patients, whereas Patio Grill Company manufactures barbeque grills. Conceptually and computationally, however, the two Excel spreadsheets are identical. *The ABC computations* are in columns E, H, and J and are shown in red.

Interpreting the PCH Dermatology Clinic's ABC Information

The hospital administration can use the ABC information in Exhibit 5–16 to determine the cost of each of the clinic's six types of patient appointments discussed earlier.

Exhibit 5–16
Activity-Based Costing Analysis: PCH Dermatology Clinic

Microsoft Excel - Activity-Based Costing Analysis - PCH Dermatology Clinic

E6 =B6/D6

	A	B	C	D	E	F	G	H	I	J
1							Cost Driver	Activity	Patient	Activity
2		Activity		Cost		Patient	Quantity for	Cost for	Type	Cost per
3		Cost	Cost	Driver	Pool	Visit	Patient	Patient	Visit	Patient of
4	Activity	Pool	Driver	Quantity	Rate	Type	Visit Type	Type	Volume	Each Type
5										
6	Physician	$ 960,000	Physician	240,000	$4.00	Routine	80,000	$ 320,000	8,000	$ 40.00
7	Time		Minutes			Extended	100,000	400,000	5,000	80.00
8			With Patient			Complex	60,000	240,000	2,000	120.00
9						Total	240,000	960,000		
10	Intern or	412,500	I/R	125,000	3.30	Routine	40,000	132,000	4,000	33.00
11	Resident		Minutes			Extended	50,000	165,000	2,500	66.00
12	(I/R) Time		With Patient			Complex	35,000	115,500	1,000	115.50
13						Total	125,000	412,500		
14	Registered	281,980	RN	245,200	1.15	Routine	132,000	151,800	13,200	11.50
15	Nurse		Minutes			Extended	80,000	92,000	8,000	11.50
16	(RN) Time		With Patient			Complex	33,200	38,180	3,320	11.50
17						Total	245,200	281,980		
18	Clerical Time	135,300	New	12,300	11.00	Routine	7,200	79,200	7,200	11.00
19	New		Patient			Extended	3,000	33,000	3,000	11.00
20	Patients		Visits			Complex	2,100	23,100	2,100	11.00
21						Total	12,300	135,300		
22	Clerical Time	61,100	Continuing	12,220	5.00	Routine	6,000	30,000	6,000	5.00
23	Continuing		Patient			Extended	5,000	25,000	5,000	5.00
24	Patients		Visits			Complex	1,220	6,100	1,220	5.00
25						Total	12,220	61,100		
26	Billing	38,480	Billing	76,960	0.50	Routine	26,400	13,200	13,200	1.00
27			Lines			Extended	24,000	12,000	8,000	1.50
28						Complex	26,560	13,280	3,320	4.00
29						Total	76,960	38,480		
30	Facility	245,200	Patient	24,520	10.00	Routine	13,200	132,000	13,200	10.00
31			Visits			Extended	8,000	80,000	8,000	10.00
32			(Both New &			Complex	3,320	33,200	3,320	10.00
33			Continuing)			Total	24,520	245,200		
34										
35	Grand Total	$2,134,560				Grand Total		$2,134,560		

Sheet1 / Sheet2 / Sheet3 /

Ready

Notice, though, that there is an important conceptual difference in the interpretation of the clinic's ABC data versus that of Patio Grill Company's ABC data (Exhibit 5–7). In the Patio Grill Company manufacturing example *all eight of the activities* identified in the ABC analysis were required by each line of barbeque grills manufactured. However, that is not true in the dermatology clinic example. In this health-care services setting, each patient sees *either* a physician, *or* a resident, *or* an intern—not all three. Moreover, each patient is *either* a new patient *or* a continuing patient—not both. Therefore, to compute the cost of a particular type of appointment, we must *select only one of the primary health-care professionals*, which are highlighted by the red bar on the right-hand side of Exhibit 5–16. Moreover, we select *just one of the two categories for clerical time*, new patient or continuing patient, which are highlighted by the green bar. Finally, since every patient appointment involves a registered nurse, *and* billing, *and* use of the clinic facility, *all* of these activities, highlighted by the yellow bars, must be included in the cost calculation.

Let's compute the cost of an extended appointment in which a new patient sees a resident:

Activity	Cost (spreadsheet cell)
Resident time	$ 66.00 (cell J11)
Registered nurse time	11.50 (cell J15)
Clerical time: New patients	11.00 (cell J19)
Billing	1.50 (cell J27)
Facility	10.00 (cell J31)
Total	$100.00

Now let's compute the cost of a routine appointment in which a continuing patient sees a physician:

Activity	Cost (spreadsheet cell)
Physician time	$40.00 (cell J6)
Registered nurse time	11.50 (cell J14)
Clerical time: Continuing patients	5.00 (cell J22)
Billing	1.00 (cell J26)
Facility	10.00 (cell J30)
Total	$67.50

With a good understanding of how much it costs the clinic to provide various types of patient appointments, the hospital's administration is in a much better position to make decisions. Determining appropriate charges for appointments, justifying third-party reimbursements from insurance companies and government agencies, and adding or discontinuing services are among the types of decisions that will be enhanced by the ABC information.

Focus on Ethics

ETHICAL ISSUES SURROUNDING ABC

Xavier Auto Parts, Inc. manufactures a wide range of auto parts, which it sells to auto manufacturers, primarily in the United States and Canada.[15] The company's Engine Parts Division operated three plants in South Carolina and specialized in engine parts. The division's Charlotte plant manufactured some 6,500 different parts.

Trouble Brewing

Both the Engine Parts Division and, in particular, the Charlotte plant had shown satisfactory profitability through the 1980s and 1990s. In 2000, however, the Charlotte plant's profitability took a sharp downward turn, in spite of rising sales. The trend continued through the next several years. Management at both the division and the plant level took note of the plant's declining profits and held several strategy meetings as a result.

Division Strategy

The Engine Parts Division had always positioned itself as the industry's full-line producer. If a customer wanted a product, the division would make it. Although occasionally very low-volume products were discontinued due to lack of consistent orders, the division's product line remained a full line of engine parts. As part of its strategy review, division management did two things. First, an ABC study was initiated in the Charlotte plant in order to give management a better picture of each product line's profitability. Second, a high-level review was undertaken to determine whether the full-line-producer strategy continued to make sense.

ABC Astonishing Revelations

An ABC project team was formed, and a successful pilot study was conducted on two of the Charlotte plant's product lines. Then the ABC project was extended to the entire Charlotte operation. Management was astonished to find that fully a quarter of the plant's products were selling at a loss. Moreover, the ABC project highlighted the extent of the product-line proliferation at the Charlotte plant. It turned out that in many instances, unprofitable products had been dropped only to creep back into the product lineup after a customer requested it and a salesperson acquiesced. It became a joke around the plant that the only way to be sure a dropped product was really gone was to burn the engineering drawings and destroy the special tools required to make it.

ABC Team Recommendations

The ABC project team made sweeping recommendations to division management, which suggested that the Charlotte plant's product lines be pruned and that roughly 20 percent of its products be dropped. New emphasis would then be devoted to increasing the profitability of the remaining 80 percent of the Charlotte plant's products. Attention would be given to identifying inefficient processes, and process improvements would be evaluated.

Top Management Response

Top management balked at the recommendations of the ABC project team. Some did not believe the ABC results. It just seemed impossible to them that so many of the Charlotte plant's products were losers. Other members of the management team largely accepted the validity of the ABC study, but they, too, hesitated to drop so many products. To do so would most likely have meant massive layoffs and even the possibility of closing the Charlotte plant altogether, while shifting its remaining production to the division's other two plants. Some members of the ABC project team quietly speculated that some of the division's managers were more concerned about their own pay and perks than they were about the well-being of the division. In the final analysis, only a handful of products were dropped, and then only if they were suspected to be unprofitable before the ABC study was undertaken.

Aftermath

The Charlotte plant's profits continued to deteriorate, as did the Engine Parts Division's profitability. Eventually, Xavier's corporate management cut its losses by selling off the Engine Parts Division to a competitor at bargain-basement prices. The division's new owners closed the Charlotte plant and changed the division's focus to be a boutique producer of high-quality engine parts, which was more in line with its own corporate strategy.

What ethical issues do you see in this scenario? How would you resolve them?

Chapter Summary

LO1 Compute product costs under a traditional volume-based product-costing system. Traditional product-costing systems are structured on single volume-based cost drivers, such as direct labour or machine hours. Overhead is applied to production jobs using a predetermined overhead rate, which is based on estimates of manufacturing overhead (in the numerator) and the level of some cost driver (in the denominator).

LO2 Explain how activity-based costing (ABC) operates, including the use of a two-stage procedure for cost assignment, the identification of activity cost pools, and the selection of cost drivers. In the first stage of ABC, resource costs are identified and divided into activity cost pools. In the second stage, a cost driver is selected for each activity cost pool and the costs in each pool are assigned to cost objects, such as products, services, product lines, customers, and so forth.

LO3 Explain the concept of cost levels, including unit-level, batch-level, product-sustaining-level, and facility-level costs. Unit-level costs are incurred for each unit produced. Batch-level costs are incurred once for each batch of products (i.e., one production run). Product-sustaining-level costs are incurred once for each product line. Facility-level costs are incurred to keep the overall facility in operation.

LO4 Compute product costs under an ABC system. A product's cost is the sum of its direct-material cost, its direct-labour cost, and its overhead cost, which is the accumulation of all the resource costs driven to the product by the various cost drivers selected for the ABC system.

LO5 Explain why traditional volume-based costing systems tend to distort product costs. Traditional volume-based costing systems tend to distort product costs because of two factors: (1) product-line diversity and (2) non-unit-level overhead costs. No single cost driver can capture the complex relationships between products and the myriad activities necessary to produce and sell them.

LO6 Explain three criteria for selecting cost drivers. Three criteria for selecting cost drivers are: (1) the degree of correlation between the cost driver and the incurrence of costs in the activity cost pool associated with the cost driver; (2) the cost of measurement of the cost driver; and (3) the behavioural effects that might result from the selection of a cost driver.

LO7 Discuss several key issues in ABC, including data collection and storyboarding. Collecting ABC data is difficult and costly. Techniques for data collection include interviews, examination of work product and other documentation, and sometimes storyboarding, which is a detailed map of the processes used in the organization.

LO8 Explain the concept of activity-based management and two-dimensional ABC. Activity-based management (ABM) is the use of ABC information to improve operations and eliminate non-value-added costs. One way of depicting ABM is the two-dimensional ABC model. This model combines the cost assignment role of ABC with the process and activity evaluation view of an ABC system.

LO9 Explain and execute a customer-profitability analysis. Customer profitability analysis is an application of ABM in which management determines the cost drivers for customer-related costs. The resulting ABC information is then used to assess the profitability of key customer relationships.

LO10 Understand and discuss how ABC is used in service organizations. ABC has found widespread successful implementation in the service industry. The application of ABC in the service industry is similar to that in manufacturing, wherein a two-stage costing model is used that first assigns resource costs to activity cost pools and then uses cost drivers to assign the costs in these pools to the various services provided and customers served.

Many service-industry firms are implementing ABC and ABM systems to better meet the needs of management.

Review Problem on Cost Drivers and Product-Cost Distortion

Edgeworth Box Corporation manufactures a variety of special packaging boxes used in the pharmaceutical industry. The company's plant is semiautomated, but the special nature of the boxes requires some manual labour. The controller has chosen the following activity cost pools, cost drivers, and pool rates for the plant's product-costing system.

Activity Cost Pool	Overhead Cost	Cost Driver	Budgeted Level for Cost Driver	Pool Rate
Purchasing, storage, and material-handling........	$ 200,000	Raw-material costs	$1,000,000	20% of material cost
Engineering and product design	100,000	Hours in design department	5,000 hrs.	$20.00/hr.
Machine setup costs	70,000	Production runs	1,000 runs	$70.00/run
Machine depreciation and maintenance...............	300,000	Machine hours	100,000 hrs.	$3.00/hr.
Factory depreciation, taxes, insurance, and utilities	200,000	Machine hours	100,000 hrs.	$2.00/hr.
Other manufacturing-overhead costs	150,000	Machine hours	100,000 hrs.	$1.50/hr.
Total	$1,020,000			

Two recent production orders had the following requirements:

	20,000 Units of Box C52	10,000 Units of Box W29
Direct-labour hours	42 hrs.	21 hrs.
Raw-material cost	$40,000	$35,000
Hours in design department	10	25
Production runs	2	4
Machine hours	24	20

Required:

1. Compute the total overhead that should be assigned to each of the two production orders, C52 and W29.

2. Compute the overhead cost per box in each order.

3. Suppose the plant was to use a single predetermined overhead rate based on direct-labour hours. The direct-labour budget calls for 4,000 hours.

   a. Compute the predetermined overhead rate per direct-labour hour.

   b. Compute the total overhead cost that would be assigned to the order for Box C52 and the order for Box W29.

   c. Compute the overhead cost per box in each order.

4. Why do the two product-costing systems yield such widely differing overhead costs per box?

Solution to Review Problem

1.

	Box C52	Box W29
Purchasing, storage, and material-handling	$8,000 (20% × $40,000)	$7,000 (20% × $35,000)
Engineering and product design	200 (10 × $20/hr.)	500 (25 × $20/hr.)
Machine setup costs	140 (2 × $70/run)	280 (4 × $70/run)
Machine depreciation and maintenance	72 (24 × $3/hr.)	60 (20 × $3/hr.)
Factory depreciation, taxes, insurance, and utilities	48 (24 × $2/hr.)	40 (20 × $2/hr.)
Other manufacturing overhead costs	36 (24 × $1.50/hr.)	30 (20 × $1.50/hr.)
Total overhead assigned to production order	$8,496	$7,910

2. Overhead cost per box: $0.425 each for Box C52 $\left(\dfrac{\$8,496}{20,000}\right)$ and $0.791 each for Box W29 $\left(\dfrac{\$7,910}{10,000}\right)$

3. Computations based on a single predetermined overhead rate based on direct-labour hours:

   a. $\dfrac{\text{Total budgeted over head}}{\text{Total budgeted directt-labour hours}} = \dfrac{\$1,020,000}{4,000} = \$255 \text{ per hour}$

b. Total overhead assigned to each order:

Box C52 order: 42 direct-labour hours $\times$ \$255/hr. = \$10,710

Box W29 order: 21 direct-labour hours $\times$ \$255/hr. = \$5,355

c. Overhead cost per box:

Box C52:   \$10,710 $\div$ 20,000 = \$0.5355 per box

Box W29:   \$5,355 $\div$ 10,000 = \$0.5355 per box

4. The widely differing overhead costs are assigned as a result of the inherent inaccuracy of the single volume-based overhead rate. The relative usage of direct labour by the two production orders does not reflect their relative usage of other manufacturing support services.

Glossary

Review key terms and definitions on Connect.

APPENDIX TO CHAPTER 5

Just-in-Time Inventory and Production Management

Learning Objective   11

List and explain eight important features of just-in-time inventory and production management systems.

A cost management tool that is widely used in manufacturing is the *just-in-time* (or JIT) system. As discussed previously, a just-in-time (JIT) inventory and production management system is a comprehensive inventory and manufacturing control system in which no materials are purchased and no products are manufactured until they are needed. Raw materials and parts are purchased only as they are needed in some phase of the production process. Component parts and subassemblies are not manufactured in any stage of production until they are required in the next stage. Finished goods are manufactured only as they are needed to fill customer orders. A primary goal of a JIT production system is to reduce or eliminate inventories at every stage of production, from raw materials to finished goods. The JIT philosophy, made famous by Toyota, has been credited with the success of many of the world's leading manufacturers. Tremendous cost savings have been realized by many companies that have adopted the JIT approach.

How does a JIT system achieve its vast reductions in inventory and associated cost savings? A production-systems expert lists the following key features of the JIT approach:[16]

1. *A smooth, uniform production rate.* An important goal of a JIT system is to establish a smooth production flow, beginning with the arrival of materials from suppliers and ending with the delivery of goods to customers.

2. *A pull method of coordinating steps in the production process.* Most manufacturing processes occur in multiple stages. Under the **pull method**, goods are produced in each manufacturing stage only as they are needed at the next stage. This approach reduces or eliminates work-in-process inventory between production steps. The result is a reduction in waiting time and its associated non-value-added cost.

    The pull method of production begins at the last stage of the manufacturing process.[17] When additional materials and parts are needed for final assembly, a message is sent to the immediately preceding work centre to send the amount of materials and parts that will be needed over the next few hours. Often this message is in the form of a **withdrawal Kanban**,[18] a card indicating the number and type of parts requested from the preceding work centre. The receipt of the withdrawal Kanban in the preceding work centre triggers the release of a **production Kanban**, which is another card specifying the number of parts to be manufactured in that work centre. Thus, the parts are "pulled" from a particular work centre by a need for parts in the subsequent work centre. This *pull approach* to production is repeated all the way back through the manufacturing sequence toward the beginning. Nothing is manufactured at any stage until its need is signalled from the subsequent process via a Kanban.

3. *Purchase of materials and manufacture of subassemblies and products in small lot sizes.* This is an outgrowth of the pull method of production planning. Materials are purchased and goods are produced only as required, rather than for the sake of building up stocks.

4. *Quick and inexpensive setups of production machinery.* In order to produce in small lot sizes, a manufacturer must be able to set up production runs quickly. Advanced manufacturing technology aids in this process, as more and more machines are computer-controlled.

5. *High quality levels for raw materials and finished products.* If raw materials and parts are to arrive "just in time" for production, they must be "just right" for their intended purpose. Otherwise, the production line will be shut down and significant non-value-added costs of waiting will result. Moreover, if very small stocks of finished goods are to be maintained, then finished products must be of uniform high quality. For this reason, a **total quality control (TQC)** program often accompanies a just-in-time production environment.

6. *Effective preventive maintenance of equipment.* If goods are to be manufactured just in time to meet customer orders, a manufacturer cannot afford significant production delays. By strictly adhering to routine maintenance schedules, the firm can avoid costly downtime from machine breakdowns.

7. *An atmosphere of teamwork to improve the production system.* A company can maintain a competitive edge in today's worldwide market only if it is constantly seeking ways to improve its product or service, achieve more efficient operations, and eliminate non-value-added costs. Any coach will tell you that a team must improve from one week to the next. Otherwise the team will get worse, because it rarely will stay at the same level. So it goes in business as well. If a company's employees are not constantly seeking ways to improve the firm's performance, before long its competitors will pass it by.

8. *Multiskilled workers and flexible facilities.* To facilitate just-in-time production, manufacturing equipment must be flexible enough to produce a variety of components and products. Otherwise, if a particular production line can produce only one item, bottlenecks may result. A bottleneck can hold up production in subsequent manufacturing stages and result in the non-value-added costs associated with waiting time.

JIT Purchasing   Along with a JIT production approach, many companies implement *JIT purchasing*. Under this approach, materials and parts are purchased from outside vendors only as they are needed. This avoids the costly and wasteful buildup of raw-material inventories. The following are five key features of **JIT purchasing**.

1. *Only a few suppliers.* This results in less time spent on vendor relations. Only highly reliable vendors, who can invariably deliver high-quality goods on time, are used.

2. *Long-term contracts negotiated with suppliers.* This eliminates costly paperwork and negotiations with each individual transaction. The need for delivery can be communicated via a telephone call or computer message. The long-term contracts state the price, quality, and delivery terms of the goods.

3. *Materials and parts delivered in small lot sizes immediately before they are needed.* This is the essence of the just-in-time approach. Costly inventories are avoided by having supplies arrive "just-in-time" to be placed into production.

4. *Only minimal inspection of delivered materials and parts.* The long-term contracts clearly state the quality of material required. Vendors are selected on the basis of their reliability in meeting these stringent standards and in delivering the correct amount of materials on time.

5. *Grouped payments to each vendor.* Instead of paying for each delivery, payments are made for batches of deliveries according to the terms of the contract. This reduces costly paperwork for both the vendor and the purchaser.

JIT purchasing is widely used in a variety of organizations. In manufacturing firms, it goes hand in hand with JIT production. In retail and service industry firms, JIT purchasing reduces costly warehouse inventories and streamlines the purchasing function.

Appendix to Chapter 5 Summary

LO11 List and explain eight important features of just-in-time inventory and production management systems. The key features of JIT systems are (1) a smooth, uniform production rate; (2) a pull method of coordinating steps in the production process; (3) purchase and manufacturing in small lot sizes; (4) quick and inexpensive machine setups; (5) high quality levels for raw materials and finished products; (6) effective preventive maintenance of equipment; (7) an atmosphere of teamwork to improve the production process; and (8) multiskilled workers and flexible facilities.

Review Questions

5–1. Briefly explain how a traditional volume-based product-costing system operates.

5–2. Why was Patio Grill Company's management being misled by the traditional product-costing system? What mistakes were being made?

5–3. Explain how an ABC system operates.

5–4. What are cost drivers? What is their role in an ABC system?

5–5. List and briefly describe the four broad categories of activities identified in Stage One of an ABC system.

5–6. How can an ABC system alleviate the problems that Patio Grill Company's management was having under its traditional volume-based product-costing system?

5–7. Why do product-costing systems based on a single volume-based cost driver tend to overcost high-volume products? What undesirable strategic effects can such distortion of product costs have?

5–8. How is the distinction between direct and indirect costs handled differently under volume-based versus activity-based costing systems?

5–9. Explain the concept of a *pool rate* in ABC. (Refer to Exhibit 5–6).

5–10. Briefly explain two factors that tend to result in product-cost distortion under traditional volume-based product-costing systems.

5–11. List three factors that are important in selecting cost drivers for an ABC system.

5–12. What is the role of an *activity dictionary* in an ABC project?

5–13. Explain why a new product-costing system may be needed when line managers suggest that an apparently profitable product should be dropped.

5–14. Explain why a manufacturer with diverse product lines may benefit from an ABC system.

5–15. Are ABC systems appropriate for the service sector? Explain.

5–16. Explain why the maintenance of a network is treated as a product-sustaining-level activity by PCH.

5–17. How could the PCH administration use the ABC information developed by the ABC project team?

5–18. Explain a key difference in the interpretation of the ABC data in Exhibit 5–7 (Patio Grill Company) and Exhibit 5–16 (PCH's dermatology clinic).

5–19. Explain the concept of *two-dimensional ABC.* Support your explanation with a diagram.

5–20. What is meant by the term *activity analysis*? Give three criteria for determining whether an activity adds value.

5–21. Distinguish between an activity's *trigger* and its *root cause*. Give an example of each.

5–22. What is meant by *customer-profitability analysis*? Give an example of an activity that might be performed more commonly for one customer than for another.

5–23. Explain the relationship between customer-profitability analysis and ABC.

5–24. What is a customer-profitability profile?

5-25. (Appendix) Explain in words and then draw a diagram depicting the pull method of coordinating steps in a JIT system.

Exercises

Exercise 5–26 Volume-Based Cost Driver versus ABC (LO1, 2, 4)

Tioga Company manufactures sophisticated lenses and mirrors used in large optical telescopes. The company is now preparing its annual profit plan. As part of its analysis of the profitability of individual products, the controller estimates the amount of overhead that should be allocated to the individual product lines from the following information:

	Lenses	Mirrors
Units produced	25	25
Material moves per product line	5	15
Direct-labour hours per unit	200	200

The total budgeted material-handling cost is $50,000.

Required:

1. Under a costing system that allocates overhead on the basis of direct-labour hours, the material-handling costs allocated to one lens would be what amount?
2. Answer the same question as in requirement (1), but for lenses.
3. Under ABC, the material-handling costs allocated to one mirror would be what amount? The cost driver for the material-handling activity is the number of material moves.
4. Answer the same question as in requirement (3), but for lenses.

(CMA, adapted)

Exercise 5–27 ABC; Quality-Control Costs (LO1, 2, 4)

Urban Elite Cosmetics has used a traditional cost accounting system to apply quality-control costs uniformly to all products at a rate of 14.5 percent of direct-labour cost. Monthly direct-labour cost for Satin Sheen makeup is $27,500. In an attempt to more equitably distribute quality-control costs, management is considering ABC. The monthly data shown in the following chart have been gathered for Satin Sheen makeup:

Activity Cost Pool	Cost Driver	Pool Rates	Quantity of Driver for Satin Sheen
Incoming material inspection	Type of material	$11.50 per type	12 types
In-process inspection	Number of units	0.14 per unit	17,500 units
Product certification	Per order	77 per order	25 orders

Required:

1. Calculate the monthly quality-control cost to be assigned to the Satin Sheen product line under each of the following product-costing systems. (Round to the nearest dollar)
   a. Traditional system, which assigns overhead on the basis of direct-labour cost
   b. ABC
2. Does the traditional product-costing system overcost or undercost the Satin Sheen product line with respect to quality-control costs? By what amount?

(CMA, adapted)

Exercise 5–28   Cost Drivers; Activity Cost Pools (LO2, 3)

Kentaro Corporation manufactures Blu-ray players in its Tokyo plant. The following costs are budgeted for January. (The *yen* is the Japanese monetary unit.)

Raw materials and components	2,950,000 yen
Insurance, plant	600,000
Electricity, machinery	120,000
Electricity, light	60,000
Engineering design	610,000
Depreciation, plant	700,000
Depreciation, machinery	1,400,000
Custodial wages, plant	40,000
Equipment maintenance, wages	150,000
Equipment maintenance, parts	30,000
Setup wages	40,000
Inspection of finished goods	30,000
Property taxes	120,000
Natural gas, heating	30,000

Required: Divide these costs into activity cost pools, and identify a cost driver for assigning each pool of costs to products. Calculate the total cost in each activity cost pool.

Exercise 5–29   Categorizing Activity Cost Pools (LO2, 3)

Refer to the information given in the preceding exercise. For each of the activity cost pools identified, indicate whether it represents a unit-level, batch-level, product-sustaining-level, or facility-level activity.

Exercise 5–30   ABC in a Government Agency; Use of the Internet (LO2, 7, 10)

Visit the website of a municipal, territorial, or provincial government of your choosing.

Required: Read about the services offered to the public by this government. Then discuss how ABC could be used effectively by this government to determine the cost of providing these services.

Exercise 5–31   Distortion of Product Costs (LO2, 5)

Wheelco, Inc. manufactures automobile and truck wheels. The company produces four basic, high-volume wheels used by each of the large automobile and pickup truck manufacturers. Wheelco also has two specialty wheel lines. These are fancy, complicated wheels used in expensive sports cars.

Lately, Wheelco's profits have been declining. Foreign competitors have been undercutting Wheelco's prices in three of its bread-and-butter product lines, and Wheelco's sales volume and market share have declined. In contrast, Wheelco's specialty wheels have been selling steadily, although in relatively small numbers, in spite of three recent price increases. At a recent staff meeting. Wheelco's president made the following remarks: "Our profits are going down the tubes, folks. It costs us $29 to manufacture our A22 wheel. That's our best seller, with a volume last year of 17,000 units. But our chief competitor is selling basically the same wheel for $27. I don't see how that company can do it. I think it's just one more example of foreign dumping. I'm going to write my MP about it! Thank goodness for our specialty wheels. I think we've got to get our salespeople to push those wheels more and more. Take the D52 model, for example. It's a complicated thing to make, and we don't sell many. But look at the profit margin. Those wheels cost us $49 to make and we're selling them for $105 each."

Required: What do you think is behind the problems faced by Wheelco? Comment on the president's remarks. Do you think his strategy is a good one? What do you recommend, and why?

Exercise 5–32   Key Features of ABC (LO2, 5, 7)

Refer to the description given for Wheelco, Inc. in the preceding exercise. Suppose the firm's president has decided to implement an ABC system.

Required:

1. List and briefly describe the key features that Wheelco's new product-costing system should have.
2. What impact will the new system be likely to have on the company's situation?
3. What strategic options would you expect to be suggested by the product-costing results from the new system?

Exercise 5–33 Winery: Classification of Activities (LO2, 3, 7)

Finger Lakes Winery is a small family-run operation in Ontario. The winery produces two varieties of wine: Riesling and Chardonnay. Among the activities engaged in by the winery are the following:

1.	*Trimming*	At the end of a growing season, the vines are trimmed, which helps prepare them for the next harvest.
2.	*Tying*	The vines are tied onto wires to help protect them from the cold. (This also occurs at the end of the season.)
3.	*Hilling*	Dirt is piled up around the roots to help protect them from frost.
4.	*Conditioning*	After the snow melts in the spring, the dirt is levelled back from the roots.
5.	*Untying*	The vines are untied from the wires to allow them freedom to grow during the spring and summer months.
6.	*Chemical spraying*	The vines are sprayed in the spring to protect them from disease and insects.
7.	*Harvesting*	All of the grapes of both varieties are picked by hand to minimize damage.
8.	*Stemming and crushing*	Batches of grapes are hand-loaded into a machine, which gently removes the stems and mildly crushes the grapes.
9.	*Pressing*	After removal from the stemmer/crusher, the juice runs freely from the grapes when they are mechanically pressed.
10.	*Filtering*	Filtering separates the skins and other solid matter from the liquid.
11.	*Fermentation.*	The Riesling grape juice is placed in stainless steel tanks for fermentation. The Chardonnay grape juice undergoes a two-stage fermentation process in oak barrels.
12.	*Aging*	The Riesling wines are aged in the stainless steel tanks for approximately a year. The Chardonnays are aged in the oak barrels for about two years.
13.	*Bottling*	A machine bottles the wine and corks the bottles.
14.	*Labelling*	Each bottle is manually labelled with the name of the vintner, vintage, and variety.
15.	*Packing*	The bottles are manually packed in 12-bottle cases.
16.	*Case labelling*	The cases are hand-stamped with the same information that the bottles received.
17.	*Shipping*	The wine is shipped to wine distributors and retailers. Generally, about 100 cases are shipped at a time.
18.	*Building maintenance*	This is done during the slow winter months.
19.	*Equipment maintenance*	Preventive maintenance is done on a routine basis; otherwise, work on equipment is done when required.

Required: Classify each of the activities listed as a unit-, batch-, product-sustaining-, or facility-level activity.

Exercise 5–34 Classification of Activities (LO2, 3, 7)

The following table shows 27 activities and eight accounts, along with the classification determined by the ABC project team.

Name of Activity or Account	Classification by Activity Level	Name of Activity or Account	Classification by Activity Level
Acquiring material	Batch	General management	Facility
Inspecting incoming materials	Batch	Maintaining facilities	Facility
Moving materials	Batch	Managing the environment	Facility
Planning production	Batch	Assuring quality	Product-sustaining
Processing special orders	Batch	Expediting	Product-sustaining
Processing supplier invoices	Batch	Maintaining tools and dies	Product-sustaining
Receiving material	Batch	Maintaining/improving production processes	Product-sustaining
Scheduling production	Batch	Managing human resources	Product-sustaining
Inspecting production processes	Batch	Managing waste disposal	Product-sustaining
Processing purchase orders	Batch	Processing payroll	Product-sustaining
Building occupancy	Facility		
Depreciation	Facility		

Name of Activity or Account	Classification by Activity Level	Name of Activity or Account	Classification by Activity Level
Processing production information	Product-sustaining	Direct-labour allowances	Unit
Providing product cost	Product-sustaining	Direct-labour fringes	Unit
Setting manufacturing methods	Product-sustaining	Utilities (equipment)	Unit
Supervising production	Product-sustaining	Overtime (hourly)	Unit
Accounting	Product-sustaining	Rework	Unit
Maintaining production equipment	Product-sustaining	Shift differential	Unit
		Spoilage	Unit

Required: Choose two activities or accounts from each of the four classifications and explain why you agree or disagree with the ABC project team's classification.

Exercise 5–35 ABC: Selling Costs (LO2, 4)

Redwood Company sells craft kits and supplies to retail outlets and through its catalogue. Some of the items are manufactured by Redwood, while others are purchased for resale. For the products it manufactures, the company currently bases its selling prices on a product-costing system that accounts for direct material, direct labour, and the associated overhead costs. In addition to these product costs, Redwood incurs substantial selling costs, and Roger Jackson, controller, has suggested that these selling costs should be included in the product pricing structure.

After studying the costs incurred over the past two years for one of its products (skeins of knitting yarn), Jackson has selected four categories of selling costs and chosen cost drivers for each of these costs. The selling costs actually incurred during the past year and the cost drivers are as follows:

Cost Category	Amount	Cost Driver
Sales commissions	$ 675,000	Boxes of yarn sold to retail stores
Catalogues	295,400	Catalogues distributed
Cost of catalogue sales	105,000	Skeins sold through catalogue
Credit and collection	60,000	Number of retail orders
Total selling costs	$1,135,400	

The knitting yarn is sold to retail outlets in boxes, each containing 12 skeins of yarn. The sale of partial boxes is not permitted. Commissions are paid on sales to retail outlets but not on catalogue sales. The cost of catalogue sales includes telephone costs and the wages of staff who take the catalogue orders. Jackson believes that the selling costs vary significantly with the size of the order. Order sizes are divided into three categories as follows:

Order Size	Catalogue Sales	Retail Sales
Small	1–10 skeins	1–10 boxes
Medium	11–20 skeins	11–20 boxes
Large	Over 20 skeins	Over 20 boxes

An analysis of the previous year's records produced the following statistics:

	Order Size			
	Small	**Medium**	**Large**	**Total**
Retail sales in boxes (12 skeins per box)	2,000	45,000	178,000	225,000
Catalogue sales in skeins	79,000	52,000	44,000	175,000
Number of retail orders	485	2,415	3,100	6,000
Catalogues distributed	254,300	211,300	125,200	590,800

Required:

1. Prepare a schedule showing Redwood Company's total selling cost for each order size and the per-skein selling cost within each order size.

2. Explain how the analysis of the selling costs for skeins of knitting yarn is likely to impact future pricing and product decisions at Redwood Company.

(CMA, adapted)

Exercise 5–36 Classification of Activities at a University; Cost Drivers (LO2, 3, 6, 7, 10)

As a group, discuss the activities at your school (e.g., admission, registration). List as many activities as you can.

Required: Make a presentation to your class that includes the following:

1. Your list of activities
2. The classification of each activity (e.g., unit-level)
3. An appropriate cost driver for each activity

Exercise 5–37 Non-Value-Added Costs (LO8)

Non-value-added costs occur in nonmanufacturing organizations, just as they do in manufacturing firms.

Required: Identify four potential non-value-added costs in (1) an airline, (2) a bank, and (3) a hotel.

Exercise 5–38 Design Your Own Production Process; Non-Value-Added Costs (LO8)

Since you have always wanted to be an industrial baron, invent your own product and describe at least five steps used in its production.

Required: Explain how you would go about identifying non-value-added costs in the production process.

Exercise 5–39 Performance Measures in Two-Dimensional ABC; ABM (LO8, 10)

List five activities performed by the employees of an airline *on the ground*. For each of these activities, suggest a performance measure that could be used in ABM.

Exercise 5–40 Activity Analysis; Non-Value-Added Activities (LO8, 10)

Visit a restaurant for a meal or think carefully about a recent visit to a restaurant. List as many activities as you can think of that would be performed by the restaurant's employees for its customers.

Required: For each activity on your list, indicate the following:

1. Value-added or non-value-added
2. The trigger of the activity
3. The possible root causes of the activity

Exercise 5–41 University or College Registration: Activity Analysis (LO8, 10)

As a group, think carefully about the various activities and steps involved in the course registration process at your university or college.

Required:

1. List the steps in the registration process in the sequence in which they occur.
2. Prepare an activity analysis of the registration process. Discuss the activity linkages, triggers, and root causes.
3. Redesign your institution's course registration process with these goals in mind:
   a. Improve the convenience and effectiveness of the process for a student registering.
   b. Improve the effectiveness and cost efficiency of the process from the standpoint of the institution.

Exercise 5–42 Customer-Profitability Analysis: Customers Ranked by Sales Revenue (LO9)

The customer-profitability analysis for Patio Grill Company, which is displayed in Exhibit 5–14, ranks customers by operating income. An alternative, often-used approach is to rank customers by sales *revenue*.

Required:

1. List the customer numbers in the left-hand column of Exhibit 5–14 by sales revenue, from highest to lowest. Is the ranking different from that in Exhibit 5–14?
2. Patio Grill Company's smallest customers, in terms of sales revenue, are last in the listing done for requirement (1). Are these customers the company's least profitable?
3. Would the customer-profitability profile in Exhibit 5–15 be different if the customers were ranked by sales revenue instead of operating income? Explain.
4. What factors could cause a larger customer (in terms of sales revenue) to be less profitable than a smaller customer?

Exercise 5–43 Customer-Profitability Graph (LO9)

Big Apple Design Company specializes in designing commercial office space in Winnipeg. The firm's president recently reviewed the following income statement and noticed that operating profits were below her expectations. She had a hunch that certain customers were not profitable for the company and asked the controller to perform a customer-profitability analysis showing profitability by customer for the month of March.

BIG APPLE DESIGN COMPANY	
Income Statement	
For the Month Ended March 31	
Sales revenue...	$300,000
Cost of services billed	255,000
Gross margin...	45,000
Marketing and administrative costs..	30,000
Operating profit..	$ 15,000

The controller provided the following customer-profitability graph:

Required: Put yourself in the position of Big Apple's controller and write a memo to the president to accompany the customer-profitability graph. Comment on the implications of the customer-profitability analysis and discuss four or more courses of action that could be taken by the firm's management team.

Exercise 5–44 ABC (LO2, 3, 10)

Service industry firms can make effective use of ABC systems as well as manufacturers. For each of the following businesses, list five key activities that are important in the provision of a firm's service. For each activity cost pool, suggest an appropriate cost driver to use in assigning costs from the activity cost pool to the services provided to customers.

1. Air Canada
2. Tim Hortons
3. Hamilton Health & Fitness Club
4. BMO branch
5. Four Seasons Hotel
6. Toronto General Hospital

Problems

Problem 5–45 Overhead Application; ABC (LO1, 2, 7)

Borealis Manufacturing has just completed a major change in its quality control (QC) process. Previously, products were reviewed by QC inspectors at the end of each major process, and the company's 10 QC inspectors were charged as direct labour to the operation or job. In an effort to improve efficiency and quality, a computerized video QC system was purchased for $250,000. The system consists of a minicomputer, 15 video cameras, other peripheral hardware, and software. The new system uses cameras stationed by QC engineers at key points in the production process. Each time an operation changes or there is a new operation, the cameras are moved, and a new master picture is loaded into the computer by a QC engineer. The camera takes pictures of the units in process, and the computer compares them to the picture of a "good" unit. Any differences are sent to a QC engineer, who removes the bad units and discusses the flaws with the production supervisors. The new system has replaced the 10 QC inspectors with two QC engineers.

The operating costs of the new QC system, including the salaries of the QC engineers, have been included as factory overhead in calculating the company's plantwide manufacturing-overhead rate, which is based on direct-labour dollars. The company's president is confused. His vice-president of production has told him how efficient the new system is. Yet there is a large increase in the overhead rate. The computation of the rate before and after automation is as follows:

	Before	After
Budgeted manufacturing overhead..	$1,900,000	$2,100,000
Budgeted direct-labour cost	1,000,000	700,000
Budgeted overhead rate	190%	300%

"Three hundred percent," lamented the president. "How can we compete with such a high overhead rate?"

Required:

1. *a.* Define *manufacturing overhead* and cite three examples of typical costs that would be included in manufacturing overhead.
   b. Explain why companies develop predetermined overhead rates.
2. Explain why the increase in the overhead rate should not have a negative financial impact on Borealis Manufacturing.
3. Explain how Borealis Manufacturing could change its overhead application system to eliminate confusion over product costs.
4. Discuss how an ABC system might benefit Borealis Manufacturing.

(CMA, adapted)

Problem 5–46 ABC; Cost Analysis (LO1, 2, 4, 5, 7)

Ontario, Inc. manufactures two types of medical devices, Standard and Enhanced, and applies overhead on the basis of direct-labour hours. Anticipated overhead and direct-labour time for the upcoming accounting period are $800,000 and 25,000 hours, respectively. Information about the company's products follows.

Standard:
   Estimated production volume, 3,000 units
   Direct-material cost, $25 per unit
   Direct labour per unit, 3 hours at $12 per hour

Enhanced:
   Estimated production volume, 4,000 units
   Direct-material cost, $40 per unit
   Direct labour per unit, 4 hours at $12 per hour

1. Total cost, Standard unit: $157
2. Manufactured cost, Standard unit: $181

Ontario, Inc.'s overhead of $800,000 can be identified with three major activities: order processing ($150,000), machine processing ($560,000), and product inspection ($90,000). These activities are driven by the number of orders processed, machine hours worked, and inspection hours, respectively. Data relevant to these activities follow.

	Orders Processed	Machine Hours Worked	Inspection Hours
Standard	300	18,000	2,000
Enhanced...	200	22,000	8,000
Total..	500	40,000	10,000

Top management is very concerned about declining profitability despite a healthy increase in sales volume. The decrease in income is especially puzzling because the company recently undertook a massive plant renovation during which new, highly automated machinery was installed—machinery that was expected to produce significant operating efficiencies.

Required:

1. Assuming use of direct-labour hours to apply overhead to production, compute the unit manufacturing costs of the Standard and Enhanced products if the expected manufacturing volume is attained.

2. Assuming use of ABC, compute the unit manufacturing costs of the Standard and Enhanced products if the expected manufacturing volume is attained.

3. Ontario, Inc.'s selling prices are based heavily on cost.

    a. By using direct-labour hours as an application base, which product is overcosted and which product is undercosted? Calculate the amount of the cost distortion for each product.

    b. Is it possible that overcosting and undercosting (i.e., cost distortion) and the subsequent determination of selling prices are contributing to the company's profit woes? Explain.

4. *Build a spreadsheet:* Construct an Excel spreadsheet to solve requirements 1, 2, and 3(a) above. Show how the solution will change if the following data change: The overhead associated with order processing is $300,000 and the overhead associated with product inspection is $270,000.

2. Machine-related costs for REG line: $135,000
3. Total cost per unit, under ABC, for GMT line: $663.90
5. Cost distortion per unit for ADV line: Overcosted by $8.85

Problem 5–47 Straightforward ABC calculations (LO1, 2, 4, 5)

Kitchen King's Windsor plant manufactures three product lines, all multi-burner ceramic cook tops. The plant's three product models are the Regular (REG), the Advanced (ADV), and the Gourmet (GMT). Until recently, the plant used a job-order product-costing system, with manufacturing overhead applied on the basis of direct-labour hours. The following table displays the basic data on which the traditional costing system was based.

	REG	ADV	GMT
Planned annual production:			
Volume in units.............	5,000	4,000	1,000
Production runs............	40 runs of 125 units	40 runs of 100 units	20 runs of 50 units
Direct material..................	$129	$151	$203
Direct labour			
(not including setup)	$171 (9 hrs. @ $19 per hr.)	$209 (11 hrs. @ $19 per hr.)	$247 (13 hrs. @ $19 per hr.)
Machine hours (MH)			
per product unit............	10 MH	12 MH	17 MH
Total machine hours consumed by product line in a year.....................	50,000 (10 MH × 5,000)	48,000 (12 MH × 4,000)	17,000 (17 MH × 1,000)

The annual budgeted overhead is $1,224,000, and the company's predetermined overhead rate is $12 per direct-labour hour. The product costs for the three product models, as reported under the plant's traditional costing system, are shown in the following table.

	REG	ADV	GMT
Direct material..................	$129.00	$151.00	$203.00
Direct labour (not including setup time).....	171.00 (9 hrs. @ $19 per hr.)	209.00 (11 hrs. @ $19 per hr.)	247.00 (13 hrs. @ $19 per hr.)
Manufacturing overhead....	108.00 (9 hrs. @ $12 per hr.)	132.00 (11 hrs. @ $12 per hr.)	156.00 (13 hrs. @ $12 per hr.)
Total................................	$408.00	$492.00	$606.00

Kitchen King's pricing policy is to set a target price for each product equal to 130 percent of the full product cost. Due to price competition from other appliance manufacturers, REG units were selling at $525, and ADV units were selling for $628. These prices were somewhat below the firm's target prices. However, these results were partially offset by greater-than-expected profits on the GMT product line. Management had raised the price on the GMT model to $800, which was higher than the original target price. Even at this price, Kitchen King's customers did not seem to hesitate to place orders. Moreover, the company's competitors did not mount a challenge in the market for the GMT product line. Nevertheless, concern continued to mount in at the Windsor plant about the difficulty in the REG and ADV markets. After all, these were the plant's bread-and-butter products, with projected annual sales of 5,000 REG units and 4,000 ADV units.

Kitchen King's director of cost management, Angela Ramirez, had been thinking for some time about a refinement in the Windsor plant's product-costing system. Ramirez wondered if the traditional volume-based system was providing management with accurate data about product costs. She had read about ABC, and wondered if ABC would be an improvement to the plant's product-costing system. After some discussion, an ABC proposal was made to the company's top management, and approval was obtained. The data collected for the new ABC system are displayed in the following table.

Activity	Activity Cost Pool	Cost Driver	Product Line	Cost Driver Quantity for Product Line
Machine-related	$310,500	Machine hours	REG	50,000
			ADV	48,000
			GMT	17,000
			Total	115,000
Material-handling	$ 52,500	Production runs	REG	40
			ADV	40
			GMT	20
			Total	100
Purchasing	$ 75,000	Purchase orders	REG	100
			ADV	96
			GMT	104
			Total	300
Setup	$ 85,000	Production runs	REG	40
			ADV	40
			GMT	20
			Total	100
Inspection	$ 27,500	Inspection hours	REG	400
			ADV	400
			GMT	300
			Total	1,100
Shipping	$ 66,000	Shipments	REG	500
			ADV	400
			GMT	200
			Total	1,100
Engineering	$ 32,500	Engineering hours	REG	250
			ADV	200
			GMT	200
			Total	650
Facility	$575,000	Machine hours	REG	50,000
			ADV	48,000
			GMT	17,000
			Total	115,000

Required:

1. Show how the company's overhead rate of $12 per direct-labour hour was calculated.

2. Complete an ABC analysis for Kitchen King's three product lines. Display the results of your ABC analysis in a table similar to Exhibit 5–7 in the text.

3. Prepare a table similar to Exhibit 5–8, which computes the new product cost for each product line under ABC.

4. Prepare a table similar to Exhibit 5–9, which compares the overhead cost, total product cost, and target price for each product line under the two alternative costing systems.

5. Was each of Kitchen King's three product lines overcosted or undercosted? By how much per unit?

6. *Build a spreadsheet:* Construct an Excel spreadsheet to solve requirement (2) above. Show how the solution would change if the machine-related cost pool was $621,000, and the facility cost pool was $1,150,000.

Problem 5–48 Continuation of Preceding Problem: Explaining ABC (LO2, 4)

Refer to your solution to requirement (2) of the preceding problem.

Required: Prepare an exhibit similar to Exhibit 5–6 in the text to explain the ABC calculations for the material-handling activity. Use your exhibit to explain ABC to a person who is not a business student.

Problem 5–49 ABC; Cost Distortion; Product Promotion (LO1, 2, 4, 5)

Masey & Sons manufactures two types of storage cabinets—Type A and Type B—and applies manufacturing overhead to all units at the rate of $80 per machine hour. Production information follows.

	Type A	Type B
Anticipated volume (units)	8,000	15,000
Direct-material cost per unit	$35	$60
Direct-labour cost per unit	$20	$20

The controller, who is studying the use of ABC, has determined that the firm's overhead can be identified with three activities: manufacturing setups, machine processing, and product shipping. Data on the number of setups, machine hours, and outgoing shipments, which are the activities' three respective cost drivers, follow:

	Type A	Type B	Total
Setups	50	30	80
Machine hours	16,000	22,500	38,500
Outgoing shipments	100	75	175

The firm's total overhead of $3,080,000 is subdivided as follows: manufacturing setups, $672,000; machine processing, $1,848,000; and product shipping, $560,000.

Required:

1. Compute the unit manufacturing cost of Type A and Type B storage cabinets by using the company's current overhead costing procedures.
2. Compute the unit manufacturing cost of Type A and Type B storage cabinets by using ABC.
3. Is the cost of the Type A storage cabinet overstated or understated (i.e., distorted) by the use of machine hours to allocate total manufacturing overhead to production? By how much?
4. Assume that the current selling price of a Type A storage cabinet is $260 and the marketing manager is contemplating a $30 discount to stimulate volume. Is this discount advisable? Briefly discuss.

Problem 5–50 ABC; Analysis of Operations (LO1, 2, 4, 7, 10)

Grady and Associates performs a variety of activities related to information systems and e-commerce consulting in Vancouver. The firm, which bills $125 per hour for services performed, is in a very tight local labour market and is having difficulty finding quality help for its overworked professional staff. The cost per hour for professional staff time is $45. Selected information follows:

- Billable hours to clients for the year totalled 5,000, consisting of information systems services, 3,100; e-commerce consulting, 1,900.
- Administrative cost of $342,000 was (and continues to be) allocated to both services based on billable hours. These costs consist of staff support, $180,000; in-house computing, $136,400; and miscellaneous office charges, $25,600.

A recent analysis of staff support costs found a correlation with the number of clients served. In-house computing and miscellaneous office charges varied directly with the number of computer hours logged and number of client transactions, respectively. A tabulation revealed the following data:

	Information Systems Services	E-Commerce Consulting	Total
Number of clients	200	50	250
Number of computer hours	2,600	1,800	4,400
Number of client transactions	400	600	1,000

1. Type A manufacturing overhead cost: $160 per unit
2. Manufactured cost of Type A cabinet: $243.50

2. E-commerce consulting, income: $22,040
3. Activity-based application rate, staff support: $720 per client
Billings, information systems services: $387,500

Required:

1. ABC is said to result in improved costing accuracy when compared with traditional costing procedures. Briefly explain how this improved accuracy is attained.

2. Assume that the firm uses traditional costing procedures, allocating total costs on the basis of billable hours. Determine the profitability of the firm's information systems and e-commerce activities, expressing your answer both in dollars and as a percentage of activity revenue.

3. Repeat requirement (2), using ABC.

4. Jeffrey Grady, one of the firm's partners, doesn't care where his professionals spend their time because, as he notes, "many clients have come to expect both services and we need both to stay in business. Also, information systems and e-commerce professionals are paid the same hourly rate." Should Grady's attitude change? Explain.

5. Is an aggressive expansion of either service currently desirable? Briefly discuss.

Problem 5–51   Automation; Robotics; Overhead Application, ABC **(LO1, 2, 5, 8)**

John Patrick has recently been hired as controller of Valdosta Vinyl Company (VVC), a manufacturer of vinyl siding used in residential construction. VVC has been in the vinyl siding business for many years and is currently investigating ways to modernize its manufacturing process. At the first staff meeting Patrick attended, Jack Kielshesky, chief engineer, presented a proposal for automating the Moulding Department. Kielshesky recommended that the company purchase two robots that would have the capability of replacing the eight direct-labour employees in the department. The cost savings outlined in the proposal include the elimination of direct-labour cost in the Moulding Department plus a reduction to zero of manufacturing-overhead cost in the department, because VVC charges manufacturing overhead on the basis of direct-labour dollars, using a plantwide rate. The president of VVC was puzzled by Kielshesky's explanation: "This just doesn't make any sense. How can a department's overhead rate drop to zero by adding expensive, high-tech manufacturing equipment? If anything, it seems like the rate ought to go up."

Kielshesky responded by saying "I'm an engineer, not an accountant. But if we're charging overhead on the basis of direct labour, and we eliminate the labour, then we eliminate the overhead."

Patrick agreed with the president. He explained that, as firms become more automated, they should rethink their product-costing systems. The president then asked Patrick to look into the matter and prepare a report for the next staff meeting. Patrick gathered the following data on the manufacturing-overhead rates experienced by VVC over the years. Patrick also wanted to have some departmental data to present at the meeting and, by using VVC's accounting records, he was able to estimate the following annual averages for each manufacturing department over the five decades since VVC's formation.

Historical Plantwide Data

Decade	Average Annual Manufacturing-Overhead Cost	Average Annual Direct-Labour Cost	Average Manufacturing-Overhead Application Rate
1st	$ 2,200,000	$2,000,000	110%
3rd	13,600,000	4,000,000	340
4th	24,600,000	6,000,000	410
5th	38,710,000	7,900,000	490

Annual Averages during Recent Years

	Cutting Department	Finishing Department	Moulding Department
Manufacturing overhead	$22,000,000	$14,000,000	$4,000,000
Direct labour	4,000,000	3,500,000	500,000

Required:

1. Disregarding the proposed use of robots in the Moulding Department, describe the shortcomings of the system for applying overhead that is currently used by Valdosta Vinyl Company.

2. Explain the misconceptions underlying Kielshesky's statement that the manufacturing-overhead cost in the Moulding Department will be reduced to zero if the automation proposal is implemented.

3. Recommend ways to improve VVC's method for applying overhead by describing how it should revise its product-costing system for each of the following departments:
   a. In the Cutting and Finishing Departments.
   b. To accommodate automation in the Moulding Department.

(CMA, adapted)

3. Predetermined overhead
rate: $31.25 per machine hr.

Problem 5–52 Activity Cost Pools; Cost Drivers; Pool Rates (LO1, 2, 3, 4, 5, 7)

The controller for Tulsa Photographic Supply Company has established the following activity cost pools and cost drivers:

Activity Cost Pool	Budgeted Overhead Cost	Cost Driver	Budgeted Level for Cost Driver	Pool Rate
Machine setups	$250,000	Number of setups	125	$2,000 per setup
Material-handling	75,000	Weight of raw material	37,500 kg	$2 per kg
Hazardous waste control	25,000	Weight of hazardous chemicals used	5,000 kg	$5 per kg
Quality control	75,000	Number of inspections	1,000	$75 per inspection
Other overhead costs	200,000	Machine hours	20,000	$10 per machine hour
Total..................................	$625,000			

An order for 1,000 boxes of film-developing chemicals has the following production requirements.

Machine setups	5
Raw material	10,000 kilograms
Hazardous materials	2,000 kilograms
Inspections..	10
Machine hours...	500 machine hours

Required:

1. Compute the total overhead that should be assigned to the developing chemicals order.
2. What is the overhead cost per box of chemicals?
3. Suppose Tulsa Photographic Supply Company was to use a single predetermined overhead rate based on machine hours. Compute the rate per hour.
4. Under the approach in requirement (3), how much overhead would be assigned to the developing chemical order:
   a. In total?
   b. Per box of chemicals?
5. Explain why these two product-costing systems result in such widely differing costs. Which system do you recommend? Why?
6. *Build a spreadsheet:* Construct an Excel spreadsheet to solve requirements (1), (2), (3), and (4) above. Show how the solution will change if the following data change. The overhead associated with machine setups is $375,000, and there are 500 inspections budgeted.

Problem 5–53 Overhead Cost Drivers (LO2, 3, 4)

Refer to the original data given in the preceding problem for Tulsa Photographic Supply Company

1. Unit cost per plate:
$260.25

Required:

1. Calculate the unit cost of a production order for 100 specially coated plates used in film developing. In addition to direct material costing $120 per plate and direct labour costing $40 per plate, the order requires the following:

Machine setups..	3
Raw material..	900 kilograms
Hazardous materials..	300 kilograms
Inspections	3
Machine hours	50

2. *Build a spreadsheet:* Construct an Excel spreadsheet to solve the preceding requirement. (This will be an extension of the spreadsheet constructed for the preceding problem.) Show how the solution will change if the data *given in the preceding problem* change as follows: The overhead associated with machine setups is $375,000, and there are 500 inspections budgeted.

Problem 5–54 ABC; ABM (LO2, 3, 4, 5, 7)

Montreal Electronics Company manufactures two large-screen television models: the Nova, which has been produced for 3 years and sells for $900, and the Royal, a new model introduced in early 20x0, which sells for $1,140. Based on the following income statement for 20x1, a decision has been made to concentrate Montreal's marketing resources on the Royal model and to begin to phase out the Nova model.

2. Total cost, Royal: $4,431,900

MONTREAL ELECTRONICS COMPANY
Income Statement
For the Year Ended December 31, 20x1

	Royal	Nova	Total
Sales	$4,560,000	$19,800,000	$24,360,000
Cost of goods sold	3,192,000	12,540,000	15,732,000
Gross margin	1,368,000	7,260,000	8,628,000
Selling and administrative expense	978,000	5,830,000	6,808,000
Net income	$ 390,000	$ 1,430,000	$ 1,820,000
Units produced and sold	4,000	22,000	
Net income per unit sold	$97.50	$65.00	

The standard unit costs for the Royal and Nova models are as follows:

	Royal	Nova
Direct material	$584	$208
Direct labour:		
Royal (3.5 hrs. × $12)	42	
Nova (1.5 hrs. × $12)		18
Machine usage:		
Royal (4 hrs. × $18)	72	
Nova (8 hrs. × $18)		144
Manufacturing overhead*	100	200
Standard cost	$798	$570

*Manufacturing overhead was applied on the basis of machine hours at a predetermined rate of $25 per hour.

Montreal Electronics Company's controller is advocating the use of ABC and ABM and has gathered the following information about the company's manufacturing-overhead costs for 20x1.

Activity Centre (cost driver)	Traceable Costs	Number of Events		
		Royal	Nova	Total
Soldering (number of solder joints)	$ 942,000	385,000	1,185,000	1,570,000
Shipments (number of shipments)	860,000	3,800	16,200	20,000
Quality control (number of inspections)	1,240,000	21,300	56,200	77,500
Purchase orders (number of orders)	950,400	109,980	80,100	190,080
Machine power (machine hours)	57,600	16,000	176,000	192,000
Machine setups (number of setups)	750,000	14,000	16,000	30,000
Total traceable costs	$4,800,000			

Required:

1. Briefly explain how an ABC system operates.
2. Using ABC, determine if Montreal Electronics should continue to emphasize the Royal model and phase out the Nova model.

(CMA, adapted)

2. Total contribution margin
for PC boards: $2,360,000

3. Using ABC, total contribution margin from TV board:
$2,557,100

Problem 5–55 ABC (LO1, 2, 4, 5)

Manchester Technology manufactures several different types of printed circuit boards; however, two of the boards account for the majority of the company's sales. The first of these boards, a television circuit board, has been a standard in the industry for several years. The market for this type of board is competitive and price-sensitive. Manchester Technology plans to sell 65,000 of the TV boards in 20x1 at a price of $150 per unit. The second high-volume product, a personal computer circuit board, is a recent addition to Manchester Technology's product line. Because the PC board incorporates the latest technology, it can be sold at a premium price. The 20x1 plans include the sale of 40,000 PC boards at $300 per unit.

Manchester Technology's management group is meeting to discuss how to spend the sales and promotion dollars for 20x1. The sales manager believes that the market share for the TV board could be expanded by concentrating Manchester Technology's promotional efforts in this area. In response to this suggestion, the production manager said, "Why don't you go after a bigger market for the PC board? The cost sheets that I get show that the contribution from the PC board is more than double the contribution from the TV board. I know we get a premium price for the PC board. Selling it should help overall profitability."

The cost accounting system shows that the following costs apply to the PC and TV boards:

	PC Board	TV Board
Direct material	$140	$80
Direct labour	4.0 hrs.	1.5 hrs.
Machine time	1.5 hrs.	0.5 hrs.

Variable manufacturing overhead is applied on the basis of direct-labour hours. For 20x1, variable overhead is budgeted at $1,120,000, and direct-labour hours are estimated at 280,000. The hourly rates for machine time and direct labour are $10 and $14, respectively. The company applies a material-handling charge at 10 percent of material cost. This material-handling charge is not included in variable manufacturing overhead. Total 20x1 expenditures for direct material are budgeted at $10,800,000.

Andrew Fulton, Manchester Technology's controller, believes that before the management group proceeds with the discussion about allocating sales and promotional dollars to individual products, it might be worthwhile to look at these products on the basis of the activities involved in their production. Fulton has prepared the following schedule to help the management group understand this concept.

"Using this information," Fulton explained, "we can calculate an activity-based cost for each TV board and each PC board and then compare it to the standard cost we have been using. The only cost that remains the same for both cost methods is the cost of direct material. The cost drivers will replace the direct labour, machine time, and overhead costs in the old standard cost figures."

	Budgeted Cost	Cost Driver	Budgeted Annual Activity for Cost Driver
Procurement	$ 400,000	Number of parts	4,000,000 parts
Production scheduling	220,000	Number of boards	110,000 boards
Packaging and shipping	440,000	Number of boards	110,000 boards
Total	$1,060,000		
Machine setup	$ 446,000	Number of setups	278,750 setups
Hazardous waste disposal	48,000	Kilograms of waste	16,000 kg
Quality control	560,000	Number of inspections	160,000 inspections
General supplies	66,000	Number of boards	110,000 boards
Total	$1,120,000		
Machine insertion	$1,200,000	Number of parts	3,000,000 parts
Manual insertion	4,000,000	Number of parts	1,000,000 parts
Wave-soldering	132,000	Number of boards	110,000 boards
Total	$5,332,000		

	Required per Unit	
	PC Board	**TV Board**
Parts:	55	25
Machine insertions	35	24
Manual insertions	20	1
Machine setups	3	2
Hazardous waste disposal	0.35 kg	0.02 kg
Inspections	2	1

Required:

1. Identify at least four general advantages associated with ABC.

2. On the basis of Manchester Technology's unit cost data given in the problem, calculate the total amount that each of the two product lines will contribute toward covering fixed costs and profit in 20x1. (In other words, for each product line, calculate the total sales revenue minus the total *variable* costs. This amount is often referred to as a product's total *contribution margin*.)

3. Repeat requirement (2) but now use the cost data from the ABC system.

4. Explain how a comparison of the results of the two costing methods may impact the decisions made by Manchester Technology's management group.

(CMA, adapted)

Problem 5–56 ABC **(LO1, 2, 4, 5, 7)**

World Gourmet Coffee Company (WGCC) is a distributor and processor of different blends of coffee. The company buys coffee beans from around the world and roasts, blends, and packages them for resale. WGCC currently has 15 different coffees that it offers to gourmet shops in one-kilogram bags. The major cost is raw materials; however, there is a substantial amount of manufacturing overhead in the predominantly automated roasting and packing process. The company uses relatively little direct labour.

2. New product cost, under ABC: $7.46 per kilogram of Kona

Some of the coffees are very popular and sell in large volumes, while a few of the newer blends have very low volumes. WGCC prices its coffee at full product cost, including allocated overhead, plus a markup of 30 percent. If prices for certain coffees are significantly higher than market, adjustments are made. The company competes primarily on the quality of its products, but customers are price-conscious as well.

Data for the 20x1 budget include manufacturing overhead of $3,000,000, which has been allocated on the basis of each product's direct-labour cost. The budgeted direct-labour cost for 20x1 totals $600,000. Based on the sales budget and raw-material budget, purchases and use of raw materials (mostly coffee beans) will total $6,000,000.

The expected prime costs for one-kilogram bags of two of the company's products are as follows:

	Kona	Malaysian
Direct material	$3.20	$4.20
Direct labour	0.30	0.30

WGCC's controller believes the traditional product-costing system may be providing misleading cost information. She has developed an analysis of the 20x1 budgeted manufacturing-overhead costs shown in the following chart.

Activity	Cost Driver	Budgeted Activity	Budgeted Cost
Purchasing	Purchase orders	1,158	$ 579,000
Material-handling	Setups	1,800	720,000
Quality control	Batches	720	144,000
Roasting	Roasting hours	96,100	961,000
Blending	Blending hours	33,600	336,000
Packaging	Packaging hours	26,000	260,000
Total manufacturing-overhead cost			$3,000,000

Data regarding the 20x1 production of Kona and Malaysian coffee are shown in the following table. There will be no raw-material inventory for either of these coffees at the beginning of the year.

	Kona	Malaysian
Budgeted sales	2,000 kg	100,000 kg
Batch size	500 kg	10,000 kg
Setups	3 per batch	3 per batch
Purchase order size	500 kg	25,000 kg
Roasting time	1 hr. per 100 kg	1 hr. per 100 kg
Blending time	0.5 hr. per 100 kg	0.5 hr. per 100 kg
Packaging time	0.1 hr. per 100 kg	0.1 hr. per 100 kg

Required:

1. Using WGCC's current product-costing system:
   a. Determine the company's predetermined overhead rate using direct-labour cost as the single cost driver.
   b. Determine the full product costs and selling prices of one kilogram of Kona coffee and one kilogram of Malaysian coffee.
2. Develop a new product cost, using an ABC approach, for one kilogram of Kona coffee and one kilogram of Malaysian coffee.
3. What are the implications of the ABC system with respect to
   a. The use of direct labour as a basis for applying overhead to products?
   b. The use of the existing product-costing system as the basis for pricing?

(CMA, adapted)

Problem 5–57   ABC; Activity Cost Pools; Pool Rates; Calculation of Product Costs; Cost Distortion (LO1, 2, 3, 4, 5)

Knickknack, Inc. manufactures two products: odds and ends. The firm uses a single plantwide overhead rate based on direct-labour hours. Production and product-costing data are as follows:

2. Pool rate, plant-related costs: $50 per m²
5. New target price: odds: $605.16

	Odds	Ends
Production quantity	1,000 units	5,000 units
Direct material	$ 40	$ 60
Direct labour (not including setup time)	30 (2 hrs. @ $15 per hr.)	45 (3 hrs. @ $15 per hr.)
Manufacturing overhead*	96 (2 hrs. @ $48 per hr.)	144 (3 hrs. @ $48 per hr.)
Total cost per unit	$ 166	$249

*Calculation of predetermined overhead rate:

Manufacturing-overhead budget:

Machine-related costs	$450,000
Setup and inspection	180,000
Engineering	90,000
Plant-related costs	96,000
Total	$816,000

Predetermined overhead rate:

$$\frac{\text{Budgeted manufacturing overhead}}{\text{Budgeted direct-labour hours}} = \frac{\$816,000}{(1,000)(2) + (5,000)(3)} = \$48 \text{ per direct-labour hour}$$

Knickknack prices its products at 120 percent of cost, which yields target prices of $199.20 for odds and $298.80 for ends. Recently, however, Knickknack has been challenged in the market for ends by a European competitor, Bricabrac Corporation. A new entrant in this market, Bricabrac has been selling ends for $220 each. Knickknack's president is puzzled by Bricabrac's ability to sell ends at such a low cost. She has asked you (the controller) to look into the matter. You have decided that Knickknack's traditional volume-based product-costing system may be causing cost distortion between the firm's two products. Ends are a high-volume, relatively simple product. Odds, on the other hand, are quite complex and exhibit a much lower volume. As a result, you have begun work on an ABC system.

Required:

1. Let each of the overhead categories in the budget represent an activity cost pool. Categorize each in terms of the type of activity (e.g., unit-level activity).
2. The following cost drivers have been identified for the four activity cost pools:

Activity Cost Pool	Cost Driver	Budgeted Level of Cost Driver
Machine-related costs	Machine hours	9,000 hrs.
Setup and inspection	Number of production runs	40 runs
Engineering	Engineering change orders	100 change orders
Plant-related costs	Square metres of space	1,920 m²

You have gathered the following additional information:

- Each odd requires 4 machine hours, whereas each end requires 1 machine hour.
- Odds are manufactured in production runs of 50 units each. Ends are manufactured in 250-unit batches.
- Three-quarters of the engineering activity, as measured in terms of change orders, is related to odds.
- The plant has 1,920 m² of space, 80 percent of which is used in the production of odds.

For each activity cost pool, compute a pool rate.

3. Determine the unit cost, for each activity cost pool, for odds and ends.

4. Compute the new product cost per unit for odds and ends, using the ABC system.

5. Using the same pricing policy as in the past, compute prices for odds and ends. Use the product costs determined by the ABC system.

6. Show that the ABC system fully assigns the total budgeted manufacturing-overhead costs of $816,000.

7. Show how Knickknack's traditional volume-based costing system distorted its product costs. (Refer to Exhibit 5–10 for guidance.)

Problem 5–58 ABC; Forecasting; Ethics (LO1, 2, 4, 5)

Northwest Aircraft Industries (NAI) was founded 45 years ago by Jay Preston as a small machine shop producing machined parts for the military. By the end of its first decade, NAI's annual sales had reached $15 million, almost exclusively under government contracts. The next 30 years brought slow but steady growth, as cost-reimbursement government contracts continued to be the main source of revenue. Realizing that NAI could not depend on government contracts for long-term growth and stability, Drew Preston, son of the founder and now president of the company, began planning for diversified commercial growth. As a result of these efforts, three years ago NAI had succeeded in reducing the ratio of government contract sales to 50 percent of total sales.

Traditionally, the costs of the Material-Handling Department have been allocated to direct material as a percentage of direct-material dollar value. This was adequate when the majority of the manufacturing was homogeneous and related to government contracts. Recently, however, government auditors have rejected some proposals, stating that "the amount of Material-Handling Department costs allocated to these proposals is disproportionate to the total effort involved."

Kara Lindley, the newly hired cost accounting manager, was asked by the manager of the Government Contracts Unit, Paul Anderson, to find a more equitable method of allocating Material-Handling Department costs to the user departments. Her review has revealed the following information:

- The majority of the direct-material purchases for government contracts are high-dollar, low-volume purchases, while commercial materials represent low-dollar, high-volume purchases.
- Administrative departments such as marketing, finance and administration, human resources, and maintenance also use the services of the Material-Handling Department on a limited basis but have never been charged in the past for material-handling costs.
- One purchasing agent with a direct phone line is assigned exclusively to purchasing high-dollar, low-volume material for government contracts at an annual salary of $36,000. Employee benefits are estimated to be 20 percent of the annual salary. The annual dedicated phone line costs are $2,800.

The components of the Material-Handling Department's budget for 20x1, as proposed by Lindley's predecessor, are as follows:

Payroll	$ 180,000
Employee benefits	36,000
Telephone	38,000
Other utilities	22,000
Materials and supplies	6,000
Depreciation	6,000
Direct-material budget:	
Government contracts	2,006,000
Commercial products	874,000

1. Total Material-Handling Department costs: $288,000

3. Reduction in material-handling costs allocated to government contracts: $74,600

4. Cumulative impact of recommended change in allocating Material-Handling Department costs: $234,346

Lindley has estimated the number of purchase orders to be processed in 20x1 to be as follows:

Government contracts*	80,000
Commercial products	156,000
Marketing	1,800
Finance and administration	2,700
Human resources	500
Maintenance	1,000
Total	242,000

*Exclusive of high-dollar, low-volume materials.

Lindley recommended to Anderson that material-handling costs be allocated on a per-purchase-order basis. Anderson realizes and accepts that the company has been allocating to government contracts more material-handling costs than can be justified. However, the implication of Lindley's analysis could be a decrease in his unit's earnings and, consequently, a cut in his annual bonus. Anderson told Lindley to "adjust" her numbers and modify her recommendation so that the results will be more favourable to the Government Contracts Unit.

Being new in her position, Lindley is not sure how to proceed. She feels ambivalent about Anderson's instructions and suspects his motivation. To complicate matters for Lindley, Preston has asked her to prepare a three-year forecast of the Government Contracts Unit's results, and she believes that the newly recommended allocation method would provide the most accurate data. However, this would put her in direct opposition to Anderson's directives.

Lindley has assembled the following data to project the material-handling costs:

- Total direct-material costs increase 2.5 percent per year.
- Material-handling costs remain the same percentage of direct-material costs.
- Direct government costs (payroll, employee benefits, and direct phone line) remain constant.
- The number of purchase orders increases 5 percent per year.
- The ratio of government purchase orders to total purchase orders remains at 33 percent.
- In addition, she has assumed that government material in the future will be 70 percent of total material.

Required:

1. Calculate the material-handling rate that would have been used by Kara Lindley's predecessor at Northwest Aircraft Industries.

2. *a.* Calculate the revised material-handling costs to be allocated on a per-purchase-order basis.

   b. Discuss why purchase orders might be a more reliable cost driver than the dollar amount of direct material.

3. Calculate the difference due to the change to the new method of allocating material-handling costs to government contracts.

4. Prepare a forecast of the cumulative dollar impact over a three-year period from 20x1 through 20x3 of Kara Lindley's recommended change for allocating Material-Handling Department costs to the Government Contracts Unit. Round all calculations to the nearest whole number.

5. Referring to the standards of ethical conduct for management accountants:

   a. Discuss why Kara Lindley has an ethical conflict.

   b. Identify several steps that Lindley could take to resolve the ethical conflict.

(CMA, adapted)

Problem 5–59 ABC; Production and Pricing Decisions (LO1, 2, 3, 4, 5)

Marconi Manufacturing produces two items in its Surrey Plant: Tuff Stuff and Ruff Stuff. Since inception, Marconi has used only one manufacturing-overhead cost pool to accumulate costs. Overhead has been allocated to products based on direct-labour hours. Until recently, Marconi was the sole producer of Ruff Stuff and was able to dictate the selling price. However, last year Marvella Products began marketing a comparable product at a price below the cost assigned by Marconi. Market share has declined rapidly, and Marconi must now decide whether to meet the competitive price or to discontinue the product line. Recognizing that discontinuing the product line would place an additional burden on its remaining product, Tuff Stuff, management is using ABC to determine if this method would show a different cost structure for the two products.

The two major indirect costs for manufacturing the products are power usage and setup costs. Most of the power is used in fabricating, while most of the setup costs are required in assembly. The setup costs are predominantly related to the Tuff Stuff product line.

1(b). Tuff Stuff unit cost: $28.00

3. Fabricating cost per unit, Tuff Stuff: $4.93 per unit (rounded)

A decision was made to separate the Manufacturing Department costs into two activity cost pools as follows:

Fabricating: Machine hours will be the cost driver.
Assembly: Number of setups will be the cost driver.

The controller has gathered the following information:

MANUFACTURING DEPARTMENT
Annual Budget before Separation of Overhead

		Product Line	
	Total	Tuff Stuff	Ruff Stuff
Number of units...		20,000	20,000
Direct-labour hours*..		2 hours per unit	3 hours per unit
Total direct-labour cost....................................	$800,000		
Direct material..		$5 per unit	$3 per unit
Budgeted overhead:...			
Indirect labour	24,000		
Fringe benefits	5,000		
Indirect material..	31,000		
Power	180,000		
Setup..	75,000		
Quality assurance	10,000		
Other utilities..	10,000		
Depreciation..	15,000		

*Direct-labour hourly rate is the same in both departments.

MANUFACTURING DEPARTMENT
Cost Structure after Separation of Overhead into Activity Cost Pools

	Fabrication	Assembly
Direct-labour cost	75%	25%
Direct material (no change)...	100%	0%
Indirect labour	75%	25%
Fringe benefits...	80%	20%
Indirect material...	$ 20,000	$11,000
Power	$160,000	$20,000
Setup	$ 5,000	$70,000
Quality assurance	80%	20%
Other utilities...	50%	50%
Depreciation...	80%	20%

	Product Line	
Cost driver:	Tuff Stuff	Ruff Stuff
Machine-hours per unit..	4.4	6.0
Setups	1,000	272

Required:

1. Assigning overhead based on direct-labour hours, calculate the following:
   a. Total budgeted cost of the Manufacturing Department
   b. Unit cost of Tuff Stuff and Ruff Stuff
2. After separation of overhead into activity cost pools, compute the total budgeted cost of each department: fabricating and assembly.
3. Using ABC, calculate the unit costs for each product. (In computing the pool rates for the fabricating and assembly activity cost pools, round to the nearest cent. Then, in computing unit product costs, round to the nearest cent.)

4. Discuss how a decision regarding the production and pricing of Ruff Stuff will be affected by the results of your calculations in the preceding requirements.

(CMA, adapted)

Problem 5–60 Traditional versus ABC Systems (LO1, 2, 3, 4, 5)

Gigabyte, Inc. manufactures three products for the computer industry:

Gismos (Product G): Annual sales, 8,000 units

Thingamajigs (Product T): Annual sales, 15,000 units

Whatchamacallits (Product W): Annual sales, 4,000 units

The company uses a traditional, volume-based product-costing system with manufacturing overhead applied on the basis of direct-labour dollars. The product costs have been computed as follows:

	Product G	Product T	Product W
Direct material	$ 35.00	$ 52.50	$17.50
Direct labour	16.00 (0.8 hrs. @ $20/hr.)	12.00 (0.6 hrs. @ $20/hr.)	8.00 (0.4 hrs. @ $20/hr.)
Manufacturing overhead*	140.00	105.00	70.00
Total cost per unit	$191.00	$169.50	$95.50

*Calculation of predetermined overhead rate:

Manufacturing-overhead budget:

Machine setup	$ 5,250
Machinery	1,225,000
Inspection	525,000
Material-handling	875,000
Engineering	344,750
Total	$2,975,000

Direct-labour budget (based on budgeted annual sales):

Product G	8,000 × $16	=	$128,000
Product T direct labour	15,000 × $12	=	180,000
Product W Manufacturing overhead	4,000 × $8	=	32,000
Total			$340,000

$$\text{Predetermined overhead rate} = \frac{\text{Budgeted overhead}}{\text{Budgeted direct labour}} = 875\%$$

Gigabyte's pricing method has been to set a target price equal to 150 percent of full product cost. However, only the thingamajigs have been selling at their target price. The target and actual current prices for all three products are the following:

	Product G	Product T	Product W
Product cost	$191.00	$169.50	$ 95.50
Target price	286.50	254.25	143.25
Actual current selling price	213.00	254.25	200.00

Gigabyte has been forced to lower the price of gismos in order to get orders. In contrast, Gigabyte has raised the price of whatchamacallits several times, but there has been no apparent loss of sales. The company has been under increasing pressure to reduce the price even further on gismos. In contrast, Gigabyte's competitors do not seem to be interested in the market for whatchamacallits. Gigabyte apparently has this market to itself.

Required:

1. Which product is the company's least profitable product under the current costing method?
2. Which product is most profitable for Gigabyte under the current costing method?

3. Comment on the reactions of Gigabyte's competitors to the firm's pricing strategy. What dangers does Gigabyte face?

4. Gigabyte's controller, Nan O'Second, recently attended a conference at which ABC systems were discussed. She became convinced that such a system would help Gigabyte's management to understand its product costs better. She got top management's approval to design an ABC system, and an ABC project team was formed. In Stage One of the ABC project, each of the overhead items listed in the overhead budget was placed into its own activity cost pool. Then a cost driver was identified for each activity cost pool. Finally, the ABC project team compiled data showing the percentage of each cost driver that was consumed by each of Gigabyte's product lines. These data are summarized as follows:

Activity Cost Pool	Cost Driver	Product G	Product T	Product W
Machine setup	Number of setup	20%	30%	50%
Machinery	Machine hours	25%	50%	25%
Inspection	Number of inspections	15%	45%	40%
Material-handling	Raw-material costs	25%	69%	6%
Engineering	Number of change orders	35%	10%	55%

Show how the controller determined the percentages given above for raw-material costs. (Round to the nearest whole percentage.)

5. Develop product costs for the three products on the basis of an activity-based costing system. (Round to the nearest cent.)

6. Calculate a target price for each product, using Gigabyte's pricing formula. Compare the new target prices with the current actual selling prices and previously reported product costs.

7. *Build a spreadsheet:* Construct an Excel spreadsheet to solve requirements (5) and (6) above. Show how the solution will change if the inspection activity is divided among the three products in the following manner: Product G, 20%; Product T, 40%; and Product W, 40%.

Problem 5–61 Strategic Cost Analysis; Continuation of Preceding Problem (LO2, 5, 7)

Refer to the new target prices for Gigabyte's three products, based on the new ABC system calculated in the preceding problem.

Required: Write a memo to the company president commenting on the situation that Gigabyte, Inc. has been facing regarding the market for its products and the actions of its competitors. Discuss the strategic options available to management. What do you recommend, and why?

Problem 5–62 Cost Distortion; Continuation of Problem 5-60 (LO2, 5)

Refer to the product costs developed in requirement (5) of Problem 5–60. Prepare a table showing how Gigabyte's traditional volume-based product-costing system distorts the product costs of gismos, thingamajigs, and whatchamacallits. (You may wish to refer to Exhibit 5–10 for guidance. Because of rounding in the calculation of the product costs, there will be a small rounding error in this cost distortion analysis as well.)

Traditional system undercosts Product W by $120.25 per unit

Problem 5–63 Basic Elements of a Production Process; Non-Value-Added Costs (LO7, 8, 10)

Better Bagels, Inc. bakes a variety of bagels, which are frozen and sold in grocery stores. The production process consists of the following steps.

1. Ingredients, such as flour and raisins, are received and inspected. Then they are stored until needed.

2. Ingredients are carried on hand carts to the mixing room.

3. Dough is mixed in 40-kilogram batches in four heavy-duty mixers.

4. Dough is stored on large boards in the mixing room until a bagel machine is free.

5. A board of dough is carried into the bagel room. The board is tipped, and the dough slides into the hopper of a bagel machine. This machine pulls off a small piece of dough, rolls it into a cylindrical shape, and then squeezes it into a doughnut shape. The bagel machines can be adjusted in a setup procedure to accommodate different sizes and styles of bagels. Workers remove the uncooked bagels and place them on a tray, where they are kept until a boiling vat is free.

6. Next the trays of uncooked bagels are carried into an adjoining room, which houses three 50-litre vats of boiling water. The bagels are boiled for approximately one minute.

7. Bagels are removed from the vats with a long-handled strainer and placed on a wooden board. The boards of bagels are carried to the oven room, where they are kept until an oven rack is free. The two ovens contain eight racks that rotate but remain upright, much like the seats on a Ferris wheel. A rack of bagels is finished baking after one complete revolution in the oven. When a rack of bagels is

removed from the oven, a fresh rack replaces it. The oven door is opened and closed as each rack completes a revolution in the oven.

8. After the bagels are removed from the oven, they are placed into wire baskets for cooling.

9. While the bagels are cooling, they are inspected. Misshapen bagels are removed and set aside. (Most "rejects" are eaten by the staff.)

10. After the bagels are cool, the wire baskets are carried to the packaging department. Here the bagels are dumped into the hopper of a bagging machine. This machine packages a half-dozen bagels in each bag and seals the bag with a twist tie.

11. Then the packaged bagels are placed in cardboard boxes, each holding 24 bags. The boxes are placed on a forklift and are driven to the freezer, where the bagels are frozen and stored for shipment.

Required:

1. Identify the steps in the bagel-production process that fall into each of the following categories: process time, inspection time, move time, waiting time, storage time.

2. List the steps in the production process that could be candidates for non-value-added activities.

Problem 5–64 Key Features of JIT Production Systems (Appendix) **(LO11)**

Refer to the information given in the preceding problem for Better Bagels, Inc..

Required:

Redesign the bagel production process so that it adheres to the JIT philosophy. Explain how the eight key features of JIT systems would be present in the new production process. What new equipment would the company need to purchase in order to implement the JIT approach fully?

Problem 5–65 Two-Dimensional ABC; Activity Analysis; ABM **(LO8)**

Home Furnishings Corporation (HFC) manufactures a variety of housewares for the consumer market. The company's three major product lines are cooking utensils, tableware, and flatware. HFC implemented ABC four years ago and now has a well-developed ABC system in place for determining product costs. Only recently, however, has the ABC system been systematically used for the purposes of ABM. As a pilot project, HFC's controller asked the ABC project team to do a detailed activity analysis of the purchasing activity. The following specific activities were identified:

1. Receipt of parts specifications from the Design Engineering Department

2. Follow-up with design engineers to answer any questions

3. Vendor (supplier) identification

4. Vendor consultations (by phone or in person)

5. Price negotiation

6. Vendor selection

7. Ordering (by phone or mail)

8. Order follow-up

9. Expediting (attempting to speed up delivery)

10. Order receiving

11. Inspection of parts

12. Return of parts not meeting specifications

13. Consultation with design engineers and production staff if parts do not satisfy intended purpose

14. Further consultation and/or negotiation with vendor if necessary

15. Ship parts back to vendor if necessary

16. If satisfactory, move parts to storage

Required:

1. Draw a diagram to depict HFC's two-dimensional ABC efforts. The diagram should include the following:
    a. The cost assignment role of ABC, with the cost pools, activities, and product lines represented
    b. The process view of ABC, with the purchasing activities displayed. Also indicated here will be the linkages among the activities. (To save space, indicate the activities by their numbers.)
    c. The activity evaluation phase of two-dimensional ABC

2. Identify the triggers for each of the following activities in HFC's purchasing activity analysis:
    Follow-up with design engineers (Activity 2)

Expediting (Activity 9)

Inspection of parts (Activity 11)

Return of parts (Activity 12)

Consultation with design engineers and production staff (Activity 13)

3. For each of the activities listed in requirement (2), identify the possible root causes.

4. Choose four activities in HFC's purchasing function, and suggest a performance measure for each of these activities.

Problem 5–66 Customer-Profitability Analysis; ABC **(LO9)**

1. Operating income, Trace Telecom: $7,000

Fibre Optics, Inc. manufactures fibre-optic cables for the computer and telecommunications industries. At the request of the company vice-president of marketing, the cost management staff has recently completed a customer-profitability study. The following ABC information was the basis for the analysis:

Customer-Related Activities	Cost Driver Base	Cost Driver Rate
Sales activity	Sales visits	$1,000
Order taking	Purchase orders	200
Special handling	Units handled	50
Special shipping	Shipments	500

Cost driver data for two of Fibre Optics' customers for the most recent year are

Customer-Related Activities	Trace Telecom	Caltex Computer
Sales activity	8 visits	6 visits
Order taking	15 orders	20 orders
Special handling	800 units handled	600 units handled
Special shipping	18 shipments	20 shipments

The following additional information has been compiled for Fibre Optics for Trace Telecom and Caltex Computer for the most recent year:

	Trace Telecom	Caltex Computer
Sales revenue	$190,000	$123,800
Cost of goods sold	80,000	62,000
General selling costs	24,000	18,000
General administrative costs	19,000	16,000

Required:

1. Prepare a customer-profitability analysis for Trace Telecom and Caltex Computer. (*Hint:* Refer to Exhibit 5–13 for guidance.)

2. *Build a spreadsheet:* Construct an Excel spreadsheet to solve requirement (1) above. Show how the solution will change if the following information changes: Trace Telecom's sales revenue was $185,000 and Caltex Computer's cost of goods sold was $59,000.

Problem 5–67 Customer-Profitability Profile; Continuation of Preceding Problem **(LO9)**

Refer to the information given in the preceding problem for Fibre Optics and two of its customers, Trace Telecom and Caltex Computer. Additional information for six of Fibre Optics' other customers for the most recent year follows:

Customer	Operating Income
Golden Gate Service Associates	$71,000
Tele-Install, Inc.	(18,000)
Graydon Computer Company	60,000
Atlantic Computing Company	42,000
Network-All, Inc.	93,000
The Ontario Group	6,000

Required:

1. Prepare Fibre Optics' customer-profitability profile for the most recent year.

2. As Fibre Optics' director of cost management, write a memo to the company's vice-president of marketing that will accompany the customer-profitability profile. Include a brief explanation of the methodology used and comment on the results.

Cases

3. Total cost, JR-14, estimated
20x2 product cost:
$1,540,000
4. Gross margin, RM-13:
$(113,000)

Case 5–68 ABC; Budgeted Operating Margin (LO1, 2, 4, 5, 7)

Whitestone Company produces two subassemblies, JR-14 and RM-13, used in manufacturing trucks. The company is currently using an absorption costing system that applies overhead based on direct-labour hours. The budget for the current year ending December 31, 20x1 is as follows:

WHITESTONE COMPANY
Budgeted Statement of Gross Margin for 20x1

	JR-14	RM-13	TOTAL
Sales in units	5,000	5,000	10,000
Sales revenue	$1,700,000	$2,200,000	$3,900,000
Cost of goods manufactured and sold:			
Beginning finished-goods inventory	$ 240,000	$ 300,000	$ 540,000
Add: Direct material	1,000,000	1,750,000	2,750,000
Direct labour	185,185	92,593	277,778
Applied manufacturing overhead*	544,025	272,013	816,038
Cost of goods available for sale	1,969,210	2,414,606	4,383,816
Less: Ending finished-goods inventory	240,000	300,000	540,000
Cost of goods sold	1,729,210	2,114,606	3,843,816
Gross margin	$ (29,210)	$ 85,394	$ 56,184

*Applied on the basis of direct-labour hours:

Machining	$424,528
Assembly	216,981
Material-handling	56,604
Inspection	117,925
Total	$816,038

Mark Ward, Whitestone's president, has been reading about a costing method called *ABC*. Ward is convinced that ABC will cast a new light on future profits. As a result, Brian Walters, the company's director of cost management, has accumulated cost pool information for this year shown in the following chart. This information is based on a product mix of 5,000 units of JR-14 and 5,000 units of RM-13.

Cost Pool Information for 20x1

Cost Pool	Activity	JR-14	RM-13
Direct labour	Direct-labour hours	10,000	5,000
Machining	Machine hours	15,000	30,000
Assembly	Assembly hours	6,000	5,500
Material-handling	Number of parts	5	10
Inspection	inspection hours	5,000	7,500

In addition, the following information is projected for the next calendar year, 20x2:

	JR-14	RM-13
Sales (in units)	5,100	4,900
Beginning inventory, finished goods (in units)	800	600
Ending inventory, finished goods (in units)	700	700

On January 1, 20x2, Ward is planning to increase the prices of JR-14 to $355 and RM-13 to $455. Material costs are not expected to increase in 20x2, but direct labour will increase by 8 percent, and all manufacturing overhead costs will increase by 6 percent. Due to the nature of the manufacturing process, the company does not have any beginning or ending work-in-process inventories.

Whitestone Company has materials delivered to the production facility directly from the vendors. The raw-material inventory both at the beginning and the end of the month is immaterial and can be ignored for the purposes of a budgeted income statement. The company uses the first-in, first-out (FIFO) inventory method.

Required:

1. Explain how ABC differs from traditional product-costing methods.

2. Using ABC, calculate the total cost for 20x2 for the following activity cost pools: machining, assembly, material-handling, and inspection. (For the total costs, round to the nearest dollar.) Then, calculate the pool rate per unit of the appropriate cost driver for each of the four activities. (*Hint*: Refer to Exhibit 5–6 regarding calculation of the pool rate.)

3. Prepare a table showing for each product line the estimated 20x2 cost for each of the following cost elements: direct material, direct-labour, machining, assembly, material-handling, and inspection. (Round to the nearest dollar.)

4. Prepare a budgeted statement showing the gross margin for Whitestone Company for 20x2, using ABC. The statement should show each product and a total for the company. Be sure to include detailed calculations for the cost of goods manufactured and sold. (Round each amount in the statement to the nearest dollar.)

(CMA, adapted)

Case 5–69   Traditional versus ABC Systems (LO1, 2, 3, 4, 5)

Morelli Electric Pump Corporation manufactures electric pumps for commercial use. The company produces three models, designated as standard, deluxe, and heavy-duty. The company uses a job-order cost accounting system with manufacturing overhead applied on the basis of direct-labour hours. The system has been in place with little change for 25 years. Product costs and annual sales data are as follows:

2. Product costs with ABC, Standard Model: $437.75
3. New target price, Heavy-Duty Model: $248.73

	Standard Model	Deluxe Model	Heavy-Duty Model
Annual sales (units)	20,000	1,000	10,000
Product costs:			
Raw material	$ 10	$ 25	$ 42
Direct labour	10 (0.5 hr. @ $20 per hr.)	20 (1 hr. @ $20 per hr.)	20 (1 hr. @ $20 per hr.)
Manufacturing overhead*	85	170	170
Total product cost	$105	$215	$232

*Calculation of predetermined overhead rate:

Manufacturing-overhead budget:

Depreciation, machinery	$1,480,000
Maintenance, machinery	120,000
Depreciation, taxes, and insurance for factory	300,000
Engineering	350,000
Purchasing, receiving and shipping	250,000
Inspection and repair of defects	375,000
Material-handling	400,000
Miscellaneous manufacturing-overhead costs	295,000
Total	$3,570,000

Direct-labour budget:

Standard model	10,000 hours
Deluxe model	1,000 hours
Heavy-duty model	10,000 hours
Total	21,000 hours

Predetermined overhead rate: $\dfrac{\text{Budgeted overhead}}{\text{Budgeted direct-labour hours}} = \dfrac{\$3,570,000}{21,000 \text{ hours}} = \$170 \text{ per hour}$

For the past 10 years, the company's pricing formula has been to set each product's target price at 110 percent of its full product cost. Recently, however, the standard-model motor has come under increasing price pressure from offshore competitors. The result was that the price on the standard model has been lowered to $110.

The company president recently asked the controller, "Why can't we compete with these other companies? They're selling pumps just like our standard model for $106. That's only two dollars more than our production cost. Are we really that inefficient? What gives?"

The controller responded by saying, "I think this is due to an outmoded product-costing system. As you may remember, I raised a red flag about our system when I came on board last year. But the decision was to keep our current system in place. In my judgment, our product-costing system is distorting our product costs. Let me run a few numbers to demonstrate what I mean."

Getting the president's go-ahead, the controller compiled the basic data needed to implement an ABC system. These data are displayed in the following table. The percentages are the proportion of each cost driver consumed by each product line.

Activity Cost Pool	Cost Driver	Product Lines		
		Standard Model	Deluxe Model	Heavy-Duty Model
I: Depreciation, machinery	Machine time	40%	13%	47%
Maintenance, machinery				
II: Engineering	Engineering hours	47%	6%	47%
Inspection and repair of defects				
III: Purchasing, receiving, and shipping	Number of material orders	47%	8%	45%
Material-handling				
IV: Depreciation, taxes, and insurance for factory	Factory space usage	42%	15%	43%
Miscellaneous manufacturing overhead				

Required:

1. Compute the target prices for the three models, based on the traditional volume-based product-costing system.

2. Compute new product costs for the three products, based on the new data collected by the controller. Round to the nearest cent.

3. Calculate a new target price for the three products, based on the ABC system. Compare the new target price with the current actual selling price for the standard model pump.

4. Write a memo to the company president explaining what has been happening as a result of the firm's traditional volume-based product-costing system.

5. What strategic options does management have? What do you recommend, and why?

Case 5–70 Cost Distortion; Continuation of Preceding Case **(LO2, 5)**

Traditional system undercosts Deluxe Model by $222.75 per unit

Refer to the product costs developed in requirement (2) of the preceding problem. Prepare a table showing how Morelli Electric Pump Corporation's traditional volume-based product-costing system distorts the product costs of the standard, deluxe, and heavy-duty models. (You might want to refer to Exhibit 5–10 for guidance. Because of rounding in the calculation of the product costs, there will be a small rounding error in this cost distortion analysis as well.)

Case 5–71 Ethical Issues Related to Product-Cost Distortion; ABC; Continuation of Case 5–69 **(LO2, 5, 7)**

Morelli Electric Pump Corporation's controller, Erin Jackson, developed new product costs for the three pump models using ABC. It was apparent that the firm's traditional product-costing system had been undercosting the deluxe-model electric pump by a significant amount. This was due largely to the low volume of the deluxe model. Before she could report back to the president, Jackson received a phone call from her friend, Alan Tyler. He was the production manager for the deluxe-model electric motor. Tyler was upset, and he let Jackson know it. "Erin, I've heard about your new product-cost analysis. There's no way the deluxe model costs anywhere near what your numbers say. For years and years, this line has been highly profitable, and its reported product cost was low. Now you're telling us it costs more than twice what we thought. I just don't buy it."

Jackson briefly explained to her friend about the principles of ABC and why it resulted in more accurate product costs. "Alan, the deluxe model is really losing money. It simply has too low a volume to be manufactured efficiently."

Tyler was even more upset now. "Erin, if you report these new product costs to the president, he's going to discontinue the deluxe model. My job's on the line, Erin! How about massaging those numbers a little bit. Who's going to know?"

"I'll know, Alan. And you'll know," responded Jackson. "Look, I'll go over my analysis again, just to make sure I haven't made an error."

Required:
Discuss the ethical issues involved in this scenario:

1. Is the controller, Erin Jackson, acting ethically?

2. Is the production manager, Alan Tyler, acting ethically?

3. What are Jackson's ethical obligations? To the president? To her friend?

Practise and learn online with Connect.

CHAPTER SIX

Activity Analysis, Cost Behaviour, and Cost Estimation

FOCUS COMPANY

Tasty Donuts, Inc. is a chain of 10 donut shops in Toronto. Using Tasty Donuts as an example, we explore cost behaviour, cost estimation, and cost prediction. *Cost behaviour* refers to the relationship between cost and activity. Variable and fixed costs, which we introduced in Chapter 2, are two examples of the many types of cost behaviour. *Cost estimation* is the process of determining cost behaviour, often relying on historical cost data. *Cost prediction* means using our knowledge of cost behaviour to forecast the cost to be incurred at a particular level of activity. *Cost analysis* helps Tasty Donuts' management to plan for the costs to be incurred at various levels of donut sales activity.

IN CONTRAST

In contrast to the service industry setting of Tasty Donuts, we turn to a manufacturing environment to explore the effect of the learning curve on cost behaviour. In many production processes, production efficiency increases with experience. As cumulative production output increases, unit variable costs decrease. For example, as the labour time declines, labour cost decreases as well. This phenomenon is called the *learning curve*. To illustrate the concept, we explore its use by Cosmos Communications Technology (CCT), a manufacturer of sophisticated communications satellites. CCT's management has found that the learning curve applies to the labour-intensive assembly operation for each new satellite design.

After completing this chapter, you should be able to

1 Explain the relationships among cost estimation, cost behaviour, and cost prediction.

2 Define and describe the behaviour of the following types of costs: variable, step-variable, fixed, step-fixed, mixed, and curvilinear.

3 Explain the importance of the relevant range in using a cost behaviour pattern for cost prediction.

4 Define and give examples of engineered costs, committed costs, and discretionary costs.

5 Describe and use the following cost-estimation methods: account classification, visual fit, high–low, and least-squares regression.

6 Describe the multiple regression and engineering approaches to cost estimation.

7 Describe some problems often encountered in collecting data for cost estimation.

8 Describe the effect of learning on cost behaviour.

9 Perform and interpret a least-squares regression analysis with a single independent variable (Appendix to Chapter 6).

Learning Objective **1**

Explain the relationships among cost estimation, cost behaviour, and cost prediction.

Managers in almost all organizations want to know how costs will be affected by changes in the organization's activity. The relationship between cost and activity, called **cost behaviour**, is relevant to the management functions of planning, control, and decision making. In order to *plan* operations and prepare a budget, managers at McCain Foods need to predict the costs that will be incurred at different levels of production and sales. To *control* the costs of providing commercial-loan services at TD Canada Trust, executives need to have a feel for the costs that the bank should incur at various levels of commercial-loan activity. In *deciding* whether to add a new intensive care unit, hospital administrators need to predict the cost of operating the new unit at various levels of patient demand. In each of these situations, knowledge of *cost behaviour* will help the manager to make the desired **cost prediction**—a forecast of cost at a particular level of activity. In the first half of this chapter, we will study cost behaviour patterns and their use in making cost predictions.

How does a management accountant determine the cost behaviour pattern for a particular cost item? The determination of cost behaviour, which is often called *cost estimation*, can be accomplished in a number of ways. One way is to analyze historical data concerning costs and activity levels. Cost estimation is covered later in this chapter.

The following diagram summarizes the key points in the preceding discussion.

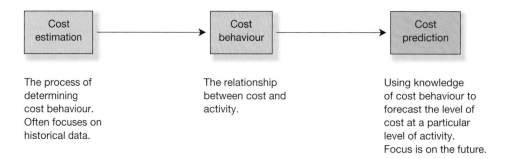

Cost estimation	Cost behaviour	Cost prediction
The process of determining cost behaviour. Often focuses on historical data.	The relationship between cost and activity.	Using knowledge of cost behaviour to forecast the level of cost at a particular level of activity. Focus is on the future.

Cost Behaviour Patterns

Our discussion of cost behaviour patterns, also called *cost functions*, will be set in the context of a restaurant business. Tasty Donuts, Inc. operates a chain of 10 donut shops in Toronto. Each shop sells a variety of donuts, muffins, and sweet rolls as well as various beverages. Beverages, such as coffee and fruit juices, are prepared in each donut shop, but all of the company's donuts and baked products are made in a centrally located bakery. The company leases several small delivery trucks to transport the bakery items to its shops. Use of a central bakery is more cost-efficient. Moreover, this approach allows the firm to smooth out fluctuations in demand for each type of product. For example, the demand for glazed donuts may change from day to day in each donut shop, but these fluctuations tend to cancel each other out when the total demand is aggregated across all 10 shops.

The corporate controller for Tasty Donuts has recently completed a study of the company's cost behaviour to use in preparing the firm's budget for the coming year. The controller studied the following costs:

- *Direct material:* Ingredients for donuts, muffins, and sweet rolls; beverages; paper products, such as napkins and disposable cups
- *Direct labour:* Wages and fringe benefits of bakers, shop sales staff, and delivery-truck drivers
- *Overhead:*

    Facilities costs. Property taxes; depreciation on bakery building, donut shops, and equipment; salaries and fringe benefits of maintenance staff

Indirect labour. Salaries and fringe benefits of managers and assistant managers for bakery and shops

Delivery trucks. Rental payments under lease contract; costs of gasoline, oil, tires, and maintenance

Utilities. Electricity, telephone, and trash collection

In studying the behaviour of each of these costs, the controller measured company *activity* in terms of *dozens of bakery items sold*. Thus, dozens of bakery items sold is the *cost driver* for each of the costs studied. A bakery item is one donut, muffin, or sweet roll. The costs to make each of these products are nearly identical. The number of bakery items sold each day is roughly the same as the number produced, since bakery goods are produced to keep pace with demand as reported by the company's shop managers.

Variable Costs

A variable cost changes *in total* in direct proportion to a change in the activity level (or cost driver). Tasty Donuts' direct-material cost is a variable cost. As the company sells more donuts, muffins, and sweet rolls, the *total* cost of the ingredients for these goods increases in direct proportion to the number of items sold. Moreover, the quantities of beverages sold and paper products used by customers also increase in direct proportion to the number of bakery items sold. As a result, the costs of beverages and paper products are also variable costs.

Panel A of Exhibit 6–1 displays a graph of Tasty Donuts' direct-material cost. As the graph shows, *total* variable cost increases in proportion to the activity level. For example,

Learning Objective   **2**

Define and describe the behaviour of the following types of costs: variable, step-variable, fixed, step-fixed, mixed, and curvilinear.

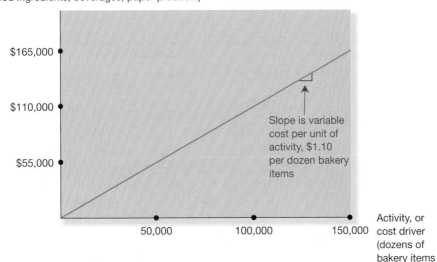

A. Graph of Total Direct-Material Cost

Total direct-material cost
(food ingredients, beverages, paper products)

Exhibit 6–1

Variable Cost: Direct-Material Cost—Tasty Donuts, Inc.

B. Tabulation of Direct-Material Cost

Activity (or cost driver)	Direct-Material Cost per Dozen Bakery Items Sold	Total Direct-Material Cost
50,000	$1.10	$ 55,000
100,000	1.10	110,000
150,000	1.10	165,000

when activity (on the *X*-axis) doubles from 50,000 dozen items to 100,000 dozen items, total direct-material costs (on the *Y*-axis) also doubles from $55,000 to $110,000. However, the variable cost *per unit* remains the same as activity changes. The total direct-material cost incurred *per dozen* items sold is constant at $1.10 per dozen. The table in panel B of Exhibit 6–1 illustrates this point. The variable cost per unit is also represented on the graph in panel A of Exhibit 6–1 as the slope of the variable cost line.

To summarize, as activity changes, *total* variable cost increases in direct proportion to the change in activity level, but the variable *cost per unit* remains constant.

Step-Variable Costs

Some costs are nearly variable, but they increase in small steps rather than continuously. Such costs, called **step-variable costs**, represent inputs that are purchased and used in relatively small increments. At Tasty Donuts, the direct-labour cost of bakers, shop counter-service staff, and delivery-truck drivers is a step-variable cost. Many of these employees are part-time workers, called on for relatively small increments of time, such as a few hours. On a typical day, for example, Tasty Donuts may have 35 employees at work in the bakery and the donut shops. If activity increases slightly, these employees can handle the extra work. However, if activity increases substantially, the bakery manager or various shop managers may call on additional help. Exhibit 6–2, a graph of Tasty Donuts' monthly direct-labour cost, shows that this cost remains constant within an activity range of about 5,000 dozen bakery items per month. When monthly activity increases beyond this narrow range, direct-labour costs increase.

Approximating a Step-Variable Cost   If the steps in a step-variable cost behaviour pattern are small, the step-variable cost function may be approximated by a variable cost function without much loss in accuracy. Exhibit 6–3 shows such an approximation for Tasty Donuts' direct-labour cost.

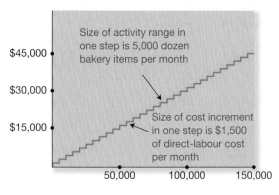

Total direct-labour cost (wages and fringe benefits of bakers, sales personnel, and delivery-truck drivers)

Total direct-labour cost (wages and fringe benefits of bakers, sales personnel, and delivery-truck drivers)

Exhibit 6–2
Step-Variable Cost: Direct-Labour Cost—Tasty Donuts

Exhibit 6–3
Approximating a Step-Variable Cost—Tasty Donuts

Fixed Costs

A fixed cost remains unchanged *in total* as the activity level (or cost driver) varies. Facilities costs, which include property taxes, depreciation on buildings and equipment, and the salaries of maintenance staff, are fixed costs for Tasty Donuts, Inc. These fixed costs are graphed in panel A of Exhibit 6–4. This graph shows that the *total* monthly cost of property taxes, depreciation, and maintenance staff is $200,000, regardless of how many dozen bakery items are produced and sold during the month.

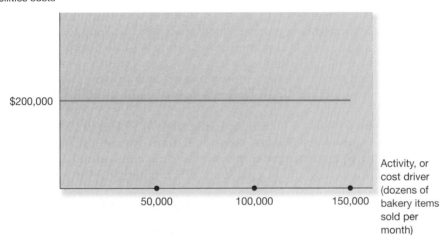

A. Graph of Total Monthly Fixed Costs: Facilities Costs

Total monthly fixed costs:
facilities costs

$200,000

Activity, or cost driver (dozens of bakery items sold per month)

50,000   100,000   150,000

Exhibit 6–4

Fixed Cost: Facilities Costs—Tasty Donuts, Inc.

B. Tabulation of Monthly Fixed Costs: Facilities Costs

Activity (or cost driver)	Cost of Facilities per Dozen Bakery Items Sold	Total Monthly Cost of Facilities
50,000	$4.00	$200,000
100,000	2.00	200,000
150,000	1.33*	200,000

*Rounded.

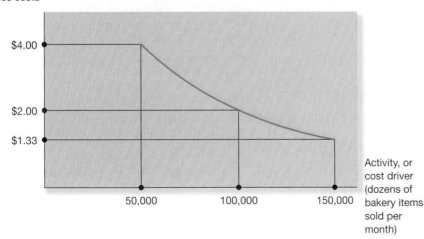

C. Graph of Unit Fixed Costs: Cost of Facilities per Dozen Bakery Items Sold

Unit fixed cost:
facilities costs

$4.00

$2.00

$1.33

Activity, or cost driver (dozens of bakery items sold per month)

50,000   100,000   150,000

The fixed cost *per unit* does change as activity varies. Exhibit 6–4 (panel B) shows that the company's facilities cost per dozen bakery items is $4 when 50,000 dozen items are produced and sold. However, this unit cost decreases to $2 when 100,000 dozen items are produced and sold. If activity increases to 150,000 dozen items, the unit fixed cost will decrease further, to about $1.33. Panel C of Exhibit 6–4 displays a graph of Tasty Donuts' fixed costs *per dozen bakery items*. As the graph shows, the fixed cost per dozen bakery items decreases steadily as activity increases.

To summarize, as the activity level increases, total fixed cost does not change, but unit fixed cost decreases. For this reason, it is preferable in any cost analysis to work with total fixed cost rather than fixed cost per unit.

Step-Fixed Costs

> "By understanding the costs and workload associated with the real business activities we undertake . . . we are better positioned to understand where value is created. . . . From this information, we can then make better decisions as to the management and direction of the business." (6b)
>
> **Transco**

Some costs remain fixed over a wide range of activity but jump to a different amount for activity levels outside that range. Such costs are called **step-fixed costs**. Tasty Donuts' cost of indirect labour is a step-fixed cost. Indirect-labour cost consists of the salaries and fringe benefits for the managers and assistant managers of the company's bakery and shops. Tasty Donuts' monthly indirect-labour cost is graphed in Exhibit 6–5.

As Exhibit 6–5 shows, for activity in the range of 50,000 to 100,000 dozen bakery items per month, Tasty Donuts' monthly indirect-labour cost is $35,000. For this range of activity, the company employs a full-time manager and a full-time assistant manager in the bakery and in each shop. When monthly activity exceeds this range during the summer tourist season, the company employs additional part-time assistant managers in the bakery and in its busiest donut shops. The company hires college students who are majoring in hospitality management for these summer positions. Their salaries boost the monthly indirect-labour cost to $45,000. Tasty Donuts has not experienced demand of less than 50,000 dozen bakery items per month. However, the controller anticipates that if such a decrease in demand were to occur, the company would reduce the daily operating hours for its donut shops. This would allow the firm to operate each shop with only a full-time manager and no assistant manager. As the

Exhibit 6–5

Step-Fixed Cost: Indirect-Labour Cost—Tasty Donuts, Inc.

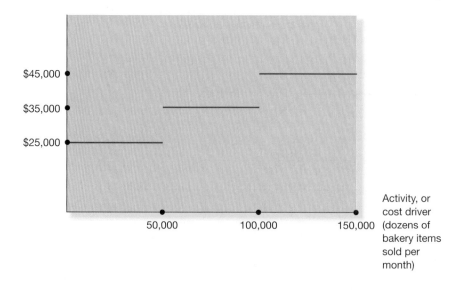

graph in Exhibit 6–5 indicates, such a decrease in managerial staff would reduce monthly indirect-labour cost to $25,000.

Mixed Costs

A **mixed cost** has both a fixed and a variable component. The cost of operating delivery trucks is a mixed cost for Tasty Donuts, Inc. These costs are graphed in Exhibit 6–6. As the graph shows, the company's delivery-truck costs have two components. The fixed-cost component is $3,000 per month, which is the monthly rental payment paid under the lease contract for the delivery trucks. The monthly rental payment is constant, regardless of the level of activity (or cost driver). The variable-cost component consists of the costs of gasoline, oil, routine maintenance, and tires. These costs vary with activity, since greater activity levels result in more deliveries. The distance between the fixed-cost line (dashed line) and the total cost line in Exhibit 6–6 is the amount of variable cost. For example, at an activity level of 100,000 dozen bakery items, the total variable-cost component is $10,000.

The slope of the total cost line is the variable cost per unit of activity. For Tasty Donuts, the variable cost of operating its delivery trucks is $0.10 per dozen bakery items sold.

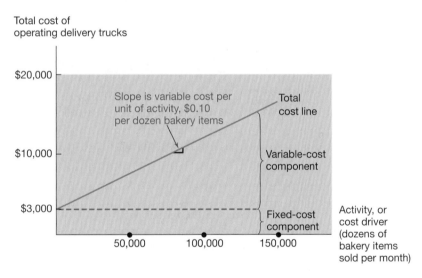

Exhibit 6–6

Mixed Cost: Cost of Operating Delivery Trucks— Tasty Donuts, Inc.

Curvilinear Cost

The graphs of all of the cost behaviour patterns examined so far consist of either straight lines or several straight-line sections. A **curvilinear cost** is a relationship between cost and activity that is indicated by a curved line. Tasty Donuts' utilities cost, depicted as the *solid curve* in Exhibit 6–7, is a curvilinear cost. For low levels of activity, this cost exhibits *decreasing marginal costs*. As the discussion in Chapter 2 indicated, a marginal cost is the cost of producing the next unit, in this case, the next dozen bakery items. As the graph in Exhibit 6–7 shows, the marginal utilities cost of producing the next dozen bakery items decreases as activity increases in the range of zero to 100,000 dozen items per month. For activity greater than 100,000 dozen bakery items per month, the graph in Exhibit 6–7 shows *increasing marginal costs*.

Tasty Donuts' utilities cost includes electricity, telephone, and trash collection costs. The utilities cost is curvilinear as a result of the company's pattern of electricity usage in the bakery. If the demand in a particular month is less than 100,000 dozen bakery items,

Exhibit 6–7
Curvilinear Cost: Utilities
Cost—Tasty Donuts, Inc.

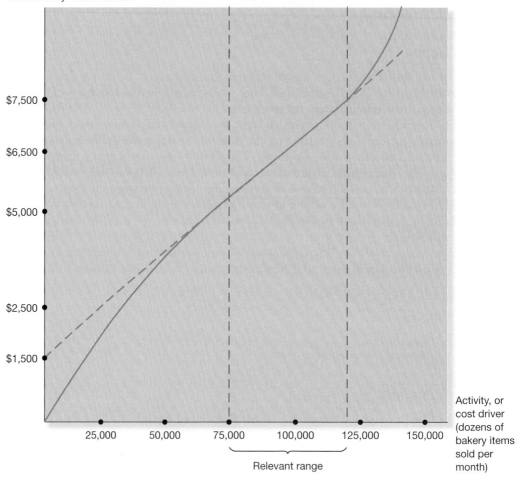

the goods can be produced entirely in the modernized section of the bakery. This section uses recently purchased deep-fat fryers and ovens that are very energy-efficient. As long as the bakery operates only the modernized section, the utilities cost per dozen items declines as production increases.

During the summer tourist months, when Tasty Donuts' sales exceed 100,000 dozen items per month, the older section of the bakery also must be used. This section uses much older cooking equipment that is less energy-efficient. As a result, the marginal utilities cost per dozen bakery items rises as monthly activity increases in the range above 100,000 dozen items per month.

Learning Objective   **3**

Explain the importance of the relevant range in using a cost behaviour pattern for cost prediction.

Relevant Range   The cost behaviour graphed in Exhibit 6–7 is very different at low activity levels (below 50,000) and at high activity levels (above 125,000). However, management need not concern itself with these extreme levels of activity if it is unlikely that Tasty Donuts, Inc. will operate at those activity levels. Management is interested in cost behaviour within the company's **relevant range**, the range of activity within which management expects the company to operate. Tasty Donuts' management believes the firm's relevant range to be 75,000 to 120,000 dozen bakery items per month. Based on past experience and sales projections, management does not expect the firm to operate outside that range of monthly activity. Tasty Donuts' relevant range is shown in Exhibit 6–7 as the section of the graph between the dashed lines.

Nestlé, Boeing, and
Hilton Hotels

IS DIRECT LABOUR A VARIABLE OR A FIXED COST?

Are direct-labour costs variable or fixed? The answer is "It depends." What it depends on is the ability and willingness of a company's management to continually fine-tune the size of its workforce. If union labour contracts make it difficult to lay off workers during an economic downturn, or if top management adopts a policy of maintaining a stable workforce, direct-labour costs will tend to be largely fixed (or step-fixed). However, if management is able *and willing* to reduce the labour force when activity declines, then labour cost will be a variable (or step-variable) cost.

The current trend in many companies seems to be toward adjusting the workforce to conform to current needs. Here are some cases in point.

Nestlé

"Nestlé's prepared foods unit has built an in-house roster of part-time workers in Cherokee County, South Carolina, who stick by the telephone to hear if they should report on a given day to assemble frozen chicken dinners. The county job-placement office sends Nestlé lists of 'call-ins': people available to work when Nestlé phones them. The workers usually get a day's notice. Some agree to stay by the phone in the morning, in case the company is short for the afternoon shift. They typically work two to six days a week and earn slightly more than $11 an hour, which is considered good part-time pay in the area."

The head of human resources for the prepared-foods division says demand for its Lean Cuisine glazed-chicken entrees and Stouffers creamed-spinach side dishes is fairly steady. The company still hires some people full-time. But the Nestlé executive says it is still hard to predict labour needs, because schedules for producing certain meals vary, and each product requires a different number of people to make. "'We don't need the same number of people every day,' he says. 'They work as we need them.'"[1]

Boeing

Boeing typifies the companies that are taking advantage of flexibility. In 2009, it cut 1,500 contingent workers from its commercial division. Says spokesman Jim Proulx: "The first imperative was to reduce all of the contract and contingent labor that we possibly could to shield our regular employees from those layoffs." Boeing says less than 3 percent of its workforce is contingent. It has also reduced its dependence on costly permanent staff in the United States by making new hires abroad. Last March, it announced a research and development centre in Bangalore that will "coordinate the work of more than 1,500 technologists, including 100 advanced technology researchers, from across India."[2]

Hilton Hotels

"Many employers, wary of losing valued workers altogether, are reducing the workweek rather than the workforce. Officials of Hilton Hotels Corp. in Beverly Hills, California, boast that they have laid off relatively few workers. However, Hilton says workweek reductions are widespread among its 77,000 workers."[3]

By relying more on part-time workers and daily call-ins, cross-training and frequently moving employees to new jobs, and shortening the workweek, Nestlé and Hilton Hotels are moving toward direct-labour costs that are much more variable than in the past. Other companies trending toward a "just-in-time workforce" are Walmart, Taco Bell, Starbucks, and U-Haul, among others. This is "all part of the larger development in corporate America of transforming labor from a fixed to a more flexible cost."[4]

Approximating a Curvilinear Cost within the Relevant Range   The straight dashed line in Exhibit 6–7 may be used to approximate Tasty Donuts' utilities cost. Notice that the approximation is quite accurate for activity levels within the relevant range. However, as the activity level gets farther away from the boundary of the relevant range, the approximation declines in accuracy. For monthly activity levels of 25,000 or 150,000, for example, the approximation is very poor.

The straight dashed line used to approximate Tasty Donuts' utilities cost *within the relevant range* represents a mixed-cost behaviour pattern. This straight-line graph has a slope of $0.05, which represents a unit variable-cost component of $0.05 per dozen bakery items. The line intersects the vertical axis of the graph at $1,500, which represents a fixed-cost component of $1,500 per month. Management accountants often use a mixed-cost behaviour pattern to approximate a curvilinear cost. However, it is important to limit this approximation to the range of activity in which its accuracy is acceptable.

Using Cost Behaviour Patterns to Predict Costs

How can Tasty Donuts' corporate controller use the cost behaviour patterns identified in the cost study to help in the budgeting process? First, a sales forecast is made for each month during the budget year. Suppose management expects Tasty Donuts' activity level to be 110,000 dozen bakery items during the month of June. Second, a *cost prediction* is made for each of the firm's cost items. The following cost predictions are based on the cost behaviour patterns discussed earlier. (Try to verify these cost predictions by referring to the graphs in Exhibits 6–1 through 6–7.)

Cost Item	Cost Prediction for June (110,000 dozen bakery items per month)
Direct material	$121,000
Direct labour	33,000
Overhead:	
Facilities costs	200,000
Indirect labour	45,000
Delivery trucks	14,000
Utilities	7,000

The preparation of a complete budget involves much more analysis and detailed planning than is shown here.[5] The point is that cost prediction is an important part of the planning process. The cost behaviour patterns discussed in this chapter make those cost predictions possible.

Engineered, Committed, and Discretionary Costs

In the process of budgeting costs, it is often useful for management to make a distinction between engineered, committed, and discretionary costs. An **engineered cost** bears a definitive physical relationship to the activity measure. Tasty Donuts' direct-material cost is an engineered cost. It is impossible to produce more donuts without incurring greater material cost for food ingredients.

A **committed cost** results from an organization's ownership or use of facilities and its basic organization structure. Property taxes, depreciation on buildings and equipment, costs of renting facilities or equipment, and the salaries of management staff are examples of committed fixed costs. Tasty Donuts' facilities cost is a committed fixed cost.

A **discretionary cost** arises as a result of a *management decision* to spend a particular amount of money for some purpose. Examples of discretionary costs include amounts spent on research and development, advertising and promotion, management development programs, and contributions to charitable organizations. For example,

Learning Objective   4

Define and give examples of engineered costs, committed costs, and discretionary costs.

suppose Tasty Donuts' management decided to spend $12,400 each month on promotion and advertising.

The distinction between committed and discretionary costs is an important one. Management can change committed costs only through relatively major decisions that have long-term implications. Decisions to build a new production facility, lease a fleet of vehicles, or add more management staff to oversee a new division are examples of such decisions. These decisions will generally influence costs incurred over a long period of time. In contrast, discretionary costs can be changed in the short run much more easily. Management can be flexible about expenditures for advertising, promotion, employee training, or research and development. This does not imply that such programs are unimportant, but simply that management can alter them over time. For example, the management of a manufacturing firm may decide to spend $100,000 on research and development in the current year, but cut back to $60,000 in the next year because of an anticipated economic downturn.

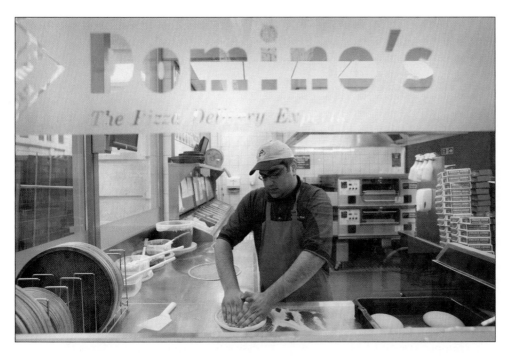

The raw material (ingredients) in these Domino's pizzas represents an engineered cost. The depreciation on the equipment is a committed cost. Expenditures on advertising and promotion are discretionary costs.

Cost Behaviour in Other Industries

We have illustrated a variety of cost behaviour patterns for Tasty Donuts' business. The same cost behaviour patterns are used in other industries. The cost behaviour pattern appropriate for a particular cost item depends on the organization and the activity base (or cost driver). In manufacturing firms, production quantity, direct-labour hours, and machine hours are common cost drivers. Direct-material and direct-labour costs are usually considered variable costs. Other variable costs include some manufacturing-overhead costs, such as indirect material and indirect labour. Fixed manufacturing costs are generally the costs of creating production capacity. Examples include depreciation on plant and equipment, property taxes, and the plant manager's salary. Such overhead costs as utilities and equipment maintenance are usually mixed or curvilinear costs. A mixed-cost behaviour pattern is generally used to approximate a curvilinear cost within the relevant range. Supervisory salaries are usually step-fixed costs, since one person can supervise production over a range of activity. When activity increases beyond that range, such as when a new shift is added, an additional supervisor is added.

In merchandising firms, such as Chapters, the activity base (or cost driver) usually is sales revenue. The cost of merchandise sold is a variable cost. Most labour costs are fixed or step-fixed costs, since a particular number of sales and stock staff can generally handle sales activity over a fairly wide range of sales. Store facility costs, such as rent, depreciation on buildings and furnishings, and property taxes, are fixed costs.

In some industries, the choice of the cost driver is not obvious, and the cost behaviour pattern can depend on the cost driver selected. At WestJet Airlines, for instance, the cost driver might be air miles flown, passengers flown, or passenger miles flown. A passenger mile is the transportation of one passenger for one mile. Fuel costs are variable with respect to air miles travelled, but are not necessarily variable with respect to passenger miles flown. An airplane uses more fuel in flying from Toronto to Vancouver than from Toronto to Montreal. However, a plane does not require significantly more fuel to fly 200 people from one city to another than to fly 190 people the same distance. In contrast, an airport landing fee is a fixed cost for a particular number of aircraft arrivals, regardless of how far the planes have flown or how many people were transported. The point of this discussion is that both the organization and the cost driver are crucial determinants of the cost behaviour for each cost item. Conclusions drawn about cost behaviour in one industry are not necessarily transferable to another industry.

Cost Estimation

Learning Objective **5**

Describe and use the following cost-estimation methods: account classification, visual fit, high–low, and least-squares regression.

As the preceding discussion indicates, different costs exhibit a variety of behaviour patterns. **Cost estimation** is the process of determining how a particular cost behaves. Several methods are commonly used to estimate the relationship between cost and activity. Some of these methods are simple, while some are more complex. In some firms, managers use more than one method of cost estimation. The results of the different methods are then combined by the cost analyst on the basis of experience and judgment. We will examine some methods of cost estimation.

Account-Classification Method

The **account-classification method** of cost estimation, also called **account analysis**, involves a careful examination of the organization's accounts. The cost analyst classifies each cost item as a variable, fixed, or mixed cost. The classification is based on the analyst's knowledge of the organization's activities and on experience with the organization's costs. For example, it may be obvious to the analyst going through the accounts that direct-material cost is variable, building depreciation is fixed, and utility costs are mixed.

Once the costs have been classified, the cost analyst estimates cost amounts by examining job-cost records, paid bills, labour time cards, or other source documents. A property-tax bill, for example, will provide the cost analyst with the information needed to estimate this fixed cost. This examination of historical source documents is combined with other knowledge that may affect costs in the future. For example, the municipal government may have recently enacted a 10 percent property tax increase, which takes effect the following year.

For some costs, particularly those classified as mixed, the cost analyst may use one of several more systematic methods of incorporating historical data in the cost estimate. These methods are discussed next.

Visual-Fit Method

When a cost has been classified as mixed, or when the analyst has no clear idea about the behaviour of a cost item, it is helpful to use the **visual-fit method** to plot recent observations of the cost at various activity levels. The resulting **scatter diagram** helps the analyst to visualize the relationship between cost and the level of activity (or cost driver). To illustrate, suppose Tasty Donuts' controller has compiled the following historical data for the company's utility costs.

Month	Utility Cost for Month	Activity or Cost Driver (dozens of bakery items sold per month)
January	$5,100	75,000
February	5,300	78,000
March	5,650	80,000
April	6,300	92,000
May	6,400	98,000
June	6,700	108,000
July	7,035	118,000
August	7,000	112,000
September	6,200	95,000
October	6,100	90,000
November	5,600	85,000
December	5,900	90,000

The scatter diagram of these data is shown in Exhibit 6–8. The cost analyst can *visually fit a line* to these data by laying a ruler on the plotted points. The line is positioned so that a roughly equal number of plotted points lie above and below the line. Just a glance at the visually fit cost line reveals that utilities cost is a mixed cost *within the relevant range*. The scatter diagram provides little or no information about the cost relationship outside the relevant range. Recall from the discussion of utilities cost (see Exhibit 6–7) that the controller believes the cost behaviour pattern to be curvilinear over the *entire range* of activity. This judgment is based on the knowledge of the firm's facilities and an understanding of electricity usage by the modern bakery equipment and the older bakery equipment. As Exhibit 6–7 shows, however, the curvilinear utilities cost can be approximated closely by a mixed cost *within the relevant range*. The data plotted in the scatter diagram lie within the relevant range. Consequently, the data provide a sound basis for the approximation that the controller has chosen to use.

Exhibit 6–8

Scatter Diagram of Cost Data with Visually Fit Cost Line— Tasty Donuts, Inc.

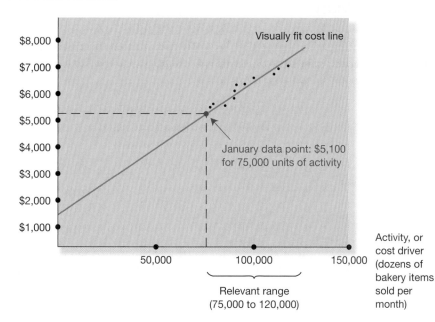

The visually fit cost line in Exhibit 6–8 intercepts the vertical axis at $1,500. Thus, $1,500 is the estimate of the fixed-cost component in the mixed-cost approximation. To determine the variable cost per unit, subtract the fixed cost from the total cost at any activity level. The remainder is the total variable cost for that activity level. For example, the total utilities cost in January was $5,100 at an activity level of 75,000 dozen items sold. Therefore, the total utilities variable cost for an activity level of 75,000 dozen items is $3,600 (total cost of $5,100 minus fixed cost of $1,500). This yields a variable cost of approximately $0.05 per dozen bakery items ($3,600 ÷ 75,000 ≈ $0.05). These estimates are valid only *within the relevant range*.

Evaluation of Visual-Fit Method The scatter diagram and visually fit cost line provide a valuable first step in the analysis of any cost item suspected to be mixed or curvilinear. The method is easy to use and to explain to others, and it provides a useful view of the overall cost behaviour pattern.

The visual-fit method also enables an experienced cost analyst to spot *outliers* in the data. An **outlier** is a data point that falls far away from the other points in the scatter diagram and is not representative of the data. Suppose, for example, that the data point for January had been $6,000 for 75,000 units of activity. Exhibit 6–8 reveals that such a data point would be way out of line with the rest of the data. The cost analyst would follow up on such a cost observation to discover the reasons behind it. The data point might be in error. Perhaps a utility bill was misread when the data were compiled, or possibly the billing itself was in error. Another possibility is that the cost observation is correct but due to unusual circumstances. Perhaps Toronto experienced a record cold wave during January that required the company's donut shops to use unusually high amounts of electric heat. Perhaps an oven in the bakery had a broken thermostat during January that caused the oven to overheat consistently until discovered and repaired. An outlier can result from many causes. If the outlier is due to an error or very unusual circumstances, the data point should be eliminated in the cost analysis.

The primary drawback of the visual-fit method is its lack of objectivity. Two cost analysts may draw two different visually fit cost lines. This is not usually a serious problem, however, particularly if the visual-fit method is combined with other, more objective methods.

High–Low Method

In the **high–low method**, the mixed-cost approximation is computed using exactly two data points. The high and low *activity levels* are chosen from the available data set. These activity levels, together with their associated cost levels, are used to compute the variable and fixed cost components as follows:

$$\frac{\text{Variable cost per}}{\text{dozen bakery items}} = \frac{\text{Difference between the } \textit{costs} \text{ corresponding to the highest and lowest activity levels}}{\text{Difference between the highest and lowest } \textit{activity} \text{ levels}}$$

$$= \frac{\$7,035 - \$5,100}{118,000 - 75,000} = \frac{\$1,935}{43,000}$$

$$= \$0.045 \text{ per dozen items}$$

Now we can compute the total variable cost at either the high or low activity level. At the low activity of 75,000 dozen items, the total variable cost is $3,375 ($0.045 × 75,000). Subtracting the total variable cost from the total cost at the 75,000 dozen activity level, we obtain the fixed-cost estimate of $1,725 ($5,100 − $3,375). Notice that the high and low *activity* levels are used to choose the two data points. In general, these two points need not necessarily coincide with the high and low cost levels in the data set.

Exhibit 6–9 presents a graph of the utilities cost, which is based on the high–low method of cost estimation. As in any cost-estimation method, this estimate of the cost behaviour pattern should be *restricted to the relevant range*.

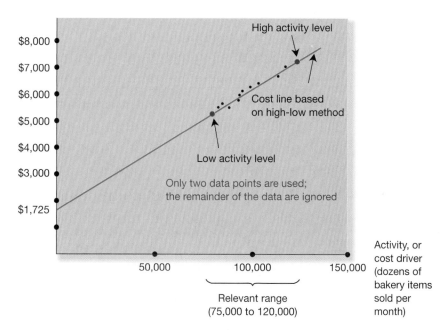

Utilities cost (for one month)

Exhibit 6–9
Graph of Utilities Cost Using
High–Low Method—Tasty
Donuts, Inc.

Evaluation of High–Low Method   The high–low method is more objective than the visual-fit method, since it leaves no room for the cost analyst's judgment. However, the high–low method suffers from a major weakness. Only two data points are used to estimate the cost behaviour pattern; the remainder of the data points are ignored. In this regard, the visual-fit method is superior to the high–low method, since the former approach uses all of the available data.

Least-Squares Regression Method

Statistical techniques may be used to estimate objectively a cost behaviour pattern using all of the available data. The most common of these methods is called *least-squares regression*. To understand this method, examine Exhibit 6–10, which repeats the scatter diagram of the utilities cost data. The exhibit also includes a cost line that has been drawn through the plotted data points. Since the data points do not lie along a perfectly straight line, any cost line drawn through this scatter diagram will miss some or most of the data points. The objective is to draw the cost line so as to make the sum of the deviations between the cost line and the data points as small as possible.

In the **least-squares regression method**, the cost line is positioned so as to *minimize* the sum of the *squared deviations* between the cost line and the data points. The inset in Exhibit 6–10 depicts this technique graphically. Note that the deviations between the cost line and the data points are measured vertically on the graph rather than perpendicular to the line. The cost line fit to the data using least-squares regression is called a *least-squares regression line* (or simply a **regression line**). As always, the least-squares regression estimate of the cost behaviour pattern should be restricted to the relevant range.

Utilities cost (for one month)

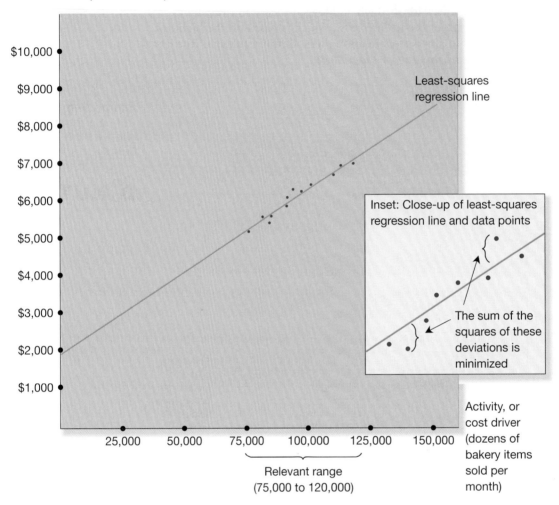

Exhibit 6–10
Graph of Utilities Cost Using
Least-Squares Regression
Method—Tasty Donuts, Inc.

Equation Form of Least-Squares Regression Line   The least-squares regression line shown in Exhibit 6–10 may be represented by the equation of a straight line. In the following equation, X denotes the activity level for a month, and Y denotes the estimated utilities cost for that level of activity. The intercept of the line on the vertical axis is denoted by a, and the slope of the line is denoted by b. *Within the relevant range, a is interpreted as an estimate of the fixed-cost component, and b is interpreted as an estimate of the variable cost per unit of activity.*

$$Y = a + bX \tag{1}$$

In regression analysis, X is referred to as the **independent variable**, since it is the variable upon which the estimate is based. Y is called the **dependent variable**, since its estimate depends on the independent variable.

The least-squares regression line for utilities cost is shown below in equation form.

$$Y \quad = \quad 1{,}920 \quad + \quad 0.0448X$$

Estimated utilities
cost for one month

Activity level
for one month

Within the relevant range of activity, the regression estimate of the fixed-cost component is $1,920 per month, and the regression estimate of the variable-cost component is $0.0448 per dozen bakery items.

Evaluation of Least-Squares Regression Method   The least-squares regression is an objective method of cost estimation that makes use of all available data. Moreover, the regression line has desirable statistical properties for making cost predictions and drawing inferences about the relationship between cost and activity. The method requires more computation than either the visual-fit or high–low method. However, computer programs are readily available to perform least-squares regression. The appendix to this chapter shows the computation of these estimates using Microsoft® Excel.

Evaluating a Particular Least-Squares Regression Line   We have seen the benefits of least-squares regression *in general*. How does a cost analyst evaluate a *particular* regression line based on a specific set of data? A number of criteria may be used, including *economic plausibility* and *goodness of fit*.

The cost analyst should always evaluate a regression line from the perspective of *economic plausibility*. Does the regression line make economic sense? Is it intuitively plausible to the cost analyst? If not, the analyst should reconsider using the regression line to make cost predictions. It may be that the chosen independent variable is not a good predictor of the cost behaviour being analyzed. Perhaps another independent variable should be considered. Alternatively, there may be errors in the data on which the regression is based. Rechecking the data will resolve this issue. It could be that fundamental assumptions that underlie the regression method have been violated. In this case, the analyst may have to resort to some other method of cost estimation.

Another criterion commonly used to evaluate a particular regression line is to assess its **goodness of fit**. Statistical methods can be used to determine objectively how well a regression line fits the data on which it is based. If a regression line fits the data well, a large proportion of the variation in the dependent variable will be explained by the variation in the independent variable. One frequently used measure of goodness of fit is the *coefficient of determination*, commonly denoted R^2. This measure is defined as the percentage of the variability of the dependent variable about its mean that is explained by the variability of the independent variable about its mean. The higher the R^2, the better the regression line fits the data. The interpretation for a high R^2 is that the independent variable is a good predictor of the behaviour of the dependent variable. In cost estimation, a high R^2 means that the cost analyst can be relatively confident in the cost predictions based on the estimated cost behaviour pattern.

Multiple Regression

In each of the cost-estimation methods discussed so far, we have based the estimate on a single independent variable. Moreover, all of Tasty Donuts' cost behaviour patterns were specified with respect to a single activity (or cost driver): dozens of bakery items produced and sold. However, there may be two or more independent variables that are important predictors of cost behaviour.

To illustrate, we will continue our analysis of the utilities costs. The company uses electricity for two primary purposes: operating cooking equipment, such as deep-fat fryers and ovens, and heating the bakery and donut shops. The cost of electricity for food production is a function of the firm's activity, as measured in dozens of bakery items produced and sold. However, the cost of electricity for shop heating is related more closely to the number of customers than to the number of bakery items sold. A shop's heating costs go up each time the door is opened, resulting in loss of heat. Two customers purchasing half a dozen donuts each result in greater heating cost than one customer buying a dozen donuts.

Learning Objective   **6**

Describe the multiple regression and engineering approaches to cost estimation.

Suppose the controller wants to estimate a cost behaviour pattern for utilities cost that is based on both units of sales and number of customers. The method of *multiple regression* may be used for this purpose. **Multiple regression** is a statistical method that estimates a linear (straight-line) relationship between one dependent variable and two or more independent variables. In Tasty Donuts' case, the following regression equation would be estimated:

$$Y = a + b_1 X_1 + b_2 X_2 \tag{2}$$

where Y denotes the dependent variable: utilities cost

X_1 denotes the first independent variable: dozens of bakery items sold

X_2 denotes the second independent variable: number of customers served

In regression equation (2), a denotes the regression estimate of the fixed-cost component, b_1 denotes the regression estimate of the variable utilities cost per dozen bakery items, and b_2 denotes the regression estimate of the variable utilities cost per customer served. The multiple-regression equation will likely enable the controller to make more accurate cost predictions than could be made with **simple regression**, which is based on just one independent variable.

Engineering Method

All of the methods of cost estimation examined so far are based on historical data. Each method estimates the relationship between cost and activity by studying the relationship observed in the past. A completely different method of cost estimation is to study the process that results in cost incurrence. This approach is called the **engineering method**. In a manufacturing firm, for example, a detailed study is made of the production technology, materials, and labour used in the manufacturing process. Rather than asking what the cost of material was last period, the engineering approach is to ask how much material should be needed and how much it should cost. Industrial engineers sometimes perform *time and motion studies*, which determine the steps required for people to perform the manual tasks that are part of the production process. Cost behaviour patterns for various types of costs are then estimated on the basis of the engineering analysis. Engineering cost studies are time-consuming and expensive, but they often provide highly accurate estimates of cost behaviour. Moreover, in rapidly evolving, high-technology industries, there may not be any historical data on which to base cost estimates. Such industries as genetic engineering, superconductivity, and electronics are evolving so rapidly that historical data are often irrelevant in estimating costs.

Data Collection Problems

Learning Objective   7

Describe some problems often encountered in collecting data for cost estimation.

Regardless of the method used, the resulting cost estimation will be only as good as the data on which it is based. The collection of data appropriate for cost estimation requires a skilled and experienced cost analyst. Six problems frequently complicate the process of data collection:

1. *Missing data.* Misplaced source documents or failure to record a transaction can result in missing data.

2. *Outliers.* We have discussed these extreme observations of cost–activity relationships. If outliers are determined to represent errors or highly unusual circumstances, they should be eliminated from the data set.

3. *Mismatched time periods.* The units of time for which the dependent and independent variables are measured may not match. For example, production activity may be recorded daily, but costs may be recorded monthly. A common solution is to aggregate the production data to get monthly totals.

4. *Trade-offs in choosing the time period.* In choosing the length of the time period for which data are collected, there are conflicting objectives. One objective is to obtain as many data points as possible, which implies a short time period. Another objective is to choose a long enough time period to ensure that the accounting system has accurately associated costs with time periods. If, for example, a cost that resulted from production activity in one period is recorded in a later period, the cost and activity data will not be matched properly. Longer time periods result in fewer recording lags in the data.

5. *Allocated and discretionary costs.* Fixed costs are often *allocated* on a per-unit-of-activity basis. For example, fixed manufacturing-overhead costs such as depreciation are allocated to units of production. As a result, such costs may appear to be variable in the cost records. *Discretionary costs* often are budgeted in a manner that makes them appear variable. A cost such as advertising, for example, may be fixed once management decides on the level of advertising. If management's policy is to budget advertising on the basis of sales dollars, however, the cost will appear to be variable to the cost analyst. An experienced analyst will be wary of such costs and take steps to learn how their amounts are determined.

6. *Inflation.* During periods of inflation, historical cost data may not reflect future cost behaviour. One solution is to choose historical data from a period of low inflation and then factor in the current inflation rate. Other, more sophisticated approaches are also available, and they are covered in cost accounting texts.

Costs and Benefits of Information

We have discussed a variety of cost-estimation methods, ranging from the simple visual-fit approach to sophisticated techniques such as regression. Which of these methods is best? In general, the more sophisticated methods will yield more accurate cost estimates than the simpler methods. However, even a sophisticated method still yields only an imperfect estimate of an unknown cost behaviour pattern.

All cost-estimation methods are based on simplifying assumptions. The two most important assumptions are as follows:

1. Except for the multiple-regression technique, all of the methods assume that cost behaviour depends on *one activity variable*. Even multiple regression uses only a small number of independent variables. In reality, however, costs are affected by a host of factors, including the weather, the mood of the employees, and the quality of the raw materials used.

2. Another simplifying assumption usually made in cost estimation is that cost behaviour patterns are linear (straight lines) within the relevant range.

The cost analyst must consider on a case-by-case basis whether these assumptions are reasonable. The analyst also must decide when it is important to use a more sophisticated, and more costly, cost-estimation method and when it is acceptable to use a simpler approach. As in any choice among managerial accounting methods, the costs and benefits of the various cost-estimation techniques must be weighed.

Effect of Learning on Cost Behaviour

In many production processes, production efficiency increases with experience. As cumulative production output increases, the average labour time required per unit declines. As the labour time declines, labour cost declines as well. This phenomenon is called the **learning curve**. First documented by aeronautical engineer P. T. Wright in the 1930s,

Learning Objective **8**

Describe the effect of learning on cost behaviour.

B. Tabular Presentation of Learning Curve

Cumulative Output (in units)	Average Labour Time per Unit (hours)	Total Labour Time (hours)
5	100.00	500.0
10	80.00	800.0
20	64.00	1,280.0
40	51.20	2,048.0

the learning-curve concept was popularized by the Boston Consulting Group (BCG) in the 1970s. BCG broadened the learning-curve idea to include costs other than direct labour and named this phenomenon the **experience curve**. The learning-curve and experience-curve concepts have been applied primarily to complex, labour-intensive manufacturing operations, such as aircraft assembly and ship building. Boeing and Airbus, for example, make extensive use of the learning- and experience-curve concepts when budgeting the cost for a new aircraft design. However, the learning curve has also seen some application in the health-care services industry, mainly focusing on complex surgical procedures.

To illustrate the learning-curve concept, let's explore its use by Cosmos Communications Technology (CCT), a manufacturer of sophisticated communications satellites. The company's satellites transmit voice and data communications around the world. CCT's management has found that the learning curve applies to the labour-intensive assembly operation for each new satellite design. A graphical portrayal of CCT's learning curve is shown in panel A of Exhibit 6–11. On this learning curve, when cumulative output doubles, the average labour time per unit declines by 20 percent. Panel B displays the total labour time and average labour time per unit for various levels of cumulative output. As cumulative output doubles from 5 to 10 units, for example, the average labour time per unit declines by 20 percent, from 100 hours per unit to 80 hours per unit. As CCT gains experience with a new satellite design, estimates of the cost of direct labour should be adjusted downward to take this learning effect into account.

When the learning-curve concept is applied to a broader set of costs than just labour costs, it is referred to as an *experience curve*. Suppose, for example, that all labour and variable overhead costs are observed to decline by 20 percent every time cumulative output doubles. Then we would change the vertical axis of Exhibit 6–11 to *labour and variable overhead costs*. The graph would then be called an *experience curve*.

Exhibit 6–11

Learning Curve

A. Graphical Presentation of Learning Curve

Average labour time per unit (hours)

Focus on Ethics

CISCO SYSTEMS, WALMART, TACO BELL, STARBUCKS, U-HAUL, AND GENERAL DYNAMICS: IS DIRECT LABOUR A VARIABLE COST?[6]

The question as to whether direct labour is a variable cost is interesting from a cost-estimation perspective, but it also presents an interesting ethical issue.

Direct material is always a variable cost. At the other extreme, depreciation on fixed facilities and infrastructure typically is not. What about direct labour? Here it depends on the ability and willingness of management to adjust the labour force to current needs. If management is able *and willing* to hire workers as needed and lay them off when activity declines, direct labour would be a variable cost. The contemporary trend at many companies seems to be in this direction. "Companies are looking first to bring in contract workers that they can quickly tap and zap without paying any benefits or severance." In fact, the temps have recently been the fastest-growing sector of employment. "And they aren't accounted for as regular employees.

This helps companies that use a lot of them, like Cisco Systems Inc., to drive up revenue per employee."

"The growing use of the *just-in-time workforce* is not the only means by which companies are priming the productivity pump. Workers complain that many employers are taking advantage of outdated labour laws by misclassifying them as salaried-exempt so they can skirt overtime pay. Walmart, Taco Bell, Starbucks, and U-Haul, among others, have been slapped with class-action lawsuits. In the case of General Dynamics Corp., this resulted in a $100 million award to current and former employees. Some employers are so worried about the issue that they are now doing wage-and-hour audits."

Is it ethical to "tap and zap" employees? Is it ethical to classify hourly (variable cost) labour staff as salaried (fixed cost) employees, thus exempt from overtime, in order contain labour costs? What do you think? (For more on this issue, see the Managerial Accounting Practice feature in this chapter.)

Chapter Summary

LO1 Explain the relationships among cost estimation, cost behaviour, and cost prediction. Cost behaviour is the relationship between cost and activity. Cost estimation refers to the determination of a cost's behaviour. A cost prediction is a forecast of a cost at a particular level of activity.

LO2 Define and describe the behaviour of the following types of costs: variable, step-variable, fixed, step-fixed, mixed, and curvilinear. A variable cost changes in total in direct proportion to a change in the activity level (or cost driver). A step-variable cost is nearly variable, but increases in small steps instead of continuously. A fixed cost remains unchanged in total as the activity level (or cost driver) varies. A step-fixed cost remains constant over a wide range of activity but jumps to a different amount for activity levels outside that range. A mixed cost has both a variable and a fixed component. A curvilinear cost behaviour pattern has a curved graph.

LO3 Explain the importance of the relevant range in using a cost behaviour pattern for cost prediction. Cost predictions should be confined to the relevant range, which is the range of activity expected for the organization. If the organization operates at an activity level outside the relevant range, any cost predictions based on data from the relevant range may not be very accurate.

LO4 Define and give examples of engineered costs, committed costs, and discretionary costs. An engineered cost bears a definitive physical relationship to the activity measured. Direct-material cost is an example. A committed cost results from an organization's ownership or use of facilities and its basic organization structure. Examples include property taxes and depreciation on buildings and equipment. A discretionary cost arises as a result of a management decision to spend a particular amount of money for some purpose. Examples include research and development, advertising, and promotion.

LO5 Describe and use the following cost-estimation methods: account classification, visual fit, high–low, and least-squares regression. The account-classification, visual-fit, high–low, and least-squares regression methods of cost estimation are all based on an analysis of historical cost data observed at a variety of activity levels. The account-classification method involves a careful examination of an organization's accounts. In the visual-fit method, a cost analyst plots recent observations of cost at various activity levels. In the high–low method, a mixed cost is estimated using only two data points: the high and the low activity levels. In the least-squares regression method, the cost line is estimated so as to minimize the sum of the squared deviations between the cost line and the data points.

LO6 Describe the multiple regression and engineering approaches to cost estimation. Multiple regression is a statistical method that estimates a linear (straight-line) relationship between one dependent variable and two or more independent variables. The engineering method of cost estimation is based on a detailed analysis of the process that results in cost incurrence.

LO7 Describe some problems often encountered in collecting data for cost estimation. Some common data-collection problems include missing data, outliers (highly unusual observations), mismatched time periods, and cost inflation. Allocated and discretionary costs create other challenges in data collection and cost estimation.

LO8 Describe the effect of learning on cost behaviour. In many production processes, production efficiency increases with experience. As cumulative production output increases, the average labour time required per unit declines. As the labour time declines, labour cost declines as well. This phenomenon is called the *learning curve*. Under the learning-curve approach, the labour cost is estimated by studying the relationship between the cumulative production quantity and the average labour time required per unit. When this approach is applied to costs other than labour, it is referred to as the *experience-curve approach*.

Review Problems on Cost Behaviour and Estimation

Problem 1

Erie Hardware, Inc. operates a chain of four retail stores. Data on the company's maintenance costs for its store buildings and furnishings are as follows:

Month	Maintenance Cost	Sales
January	$53,000	$600,000
February	55,000	700,000
March	47,000	550,000
April	51,000	650,000
May	45,000	500,000
June	49,000	610,000

Using the high-low method, estimate and graph the cost behaviour for the firm's maintenance costs.

Problem 2

The *Keystone Sentinel* is a weekly newspaper. The following costs were incurred by its publisher during a week when circulation was 100,000 newspapers: total variable costs, $40,000; total fixed costs, $66,000. Fill in your predictions for the following cost amounts.

	Circulation	
	110,000 Newspapers	**120,000 Newspapers**
Total variable cost	_____	_____
Variable cost per unit	_____	_____
Total fixed cost	_____	_____
Fixed cost per unit	_____	_____

Solutions to Review Problems
Problem 1

	Sales	Cost
At high activity	$700,000	$55,000
At low activity	500,000	45,000
Difference	$200,000	$10,000

$$\text{Variable cost per sales dollar} = \frac{\$10,000}{\$200,000} = \$0.05 \text{ per sales dollar}$$

Total cost at $700,000 of sales	$55,000
Total variable cost at $700,000 of sales (700,000 × $0.05)	35,000
Difference is total fixed cost	$20,000

The company's maintenance cost may be expressed by the following equation:

Total maintenance cost = $20,000 + $0.05 (sales dollars)

Alternatively, the maintenance cost can be expressed in the following graph:

Maintenance cost

$60,000

$40,000

$20,000

Fixed-cost component

Slope of $0.05 per sales dollar represents the variable-cost component

Sales

$200,000 $400,000 $600,000

Problem 2

	Circulation	
	110,000 Newspapers	**120,000 Newspapers**
Total variable cost	$40,000 × ($\frac{110,000}{100,000}$) = $44,000	$40,000 × ($\frac{120,000}{100,000}$) = $48,000
Variable cost per unit	$44,000 ÷ 110,000 = $0.40	$48,000 ÷ 120,000 = $0.40
Total fixed cost	$66,000	$66,000
Fixed cost per unit	$66,000 ÷ 110,000 = $0.60	$66,000 ÷ 120,000 = $0.55

Glossary

Review key terms and definitions on Connect.

APPENDIX TO CHAPTER 6

Finding the Least-Squares Regression Estimates

The least-squares regression line, which is shown below in equation form, includes two estimates. These estimates, which are called *parameters*, are the intercept (denoted by *a*) and the slope coefficient (denoted by *b*).

Learning Objective   **9**

Perform and interpret a least-squares regression analysis with a single independent variable (Appendix).

$$Y = a + bX \qquad\qquad (3)$$

where X denotes the independent variable (activity level for one month)

Y denotes the dependent variable (cost for one month)

Calculating the intercept (a) and the slope coefficient (b) is very laborious to do manually. There are many statistical software programs available to do the regression calculations. Alternatively, Microsoft® Excel can calculate the regression estimates, as the next section demonstrates.

Using Microsoft® Excel to Calculate the Regression Parameters

A cost analyst can use commands in Microsoft® Excel to easily calculate the regression estimate for the intercept (a) and the slope (b). All the analyst needs to do is input the data into a spreadsheet. The spreadsheet in Exhibit 6–12 displays the data used to compute Tasty Donuts' utilities cost. The dependent variable (utilities cost) is in column B, and the independent variable (activity) is in column C. Then the Excel functions INTERCEPT and SLOPE are used to compute the parameters. To use each command, the analyst specifies the range of cells in the spreadsheet in which the values of the dependent variable reside and the range of cells in which the values of the independent variable reside. This is illustrated in the Excel worksheet in Exhibit 6–12 as follows:

Cell B24 contains the following formula: = INTERCEPT(B7:B18,C7:C18)

Cell B25 contains the following formula: = SLOPE(B7:B18,C7:C18)

In these formulas, B7:B18 specifies the range of cells where the values of the dependent variable reside, and C7:C18 specifies the range of cells where the values of the independent variable reside.

As the Excel calculations show in Exhibit 6–12, the regression estimates are as follows:

Intercept: $a = 1,920$

Slope: $b = 0.0448$

So the regression equation is the following:

$$Y \qquad = \quad 1,920 \quad + \quad 0.0448X$$

Estimated utilities cost for one month   Activity level for one month

Goodness of Fit

The goodness of fit for the regression line may be measured by the **coefficient of determination**, commonly denoted R^2. This measure is defined as the percentage of the variability of the dependent variable about its mean that is explained by the variability of the independent variable about its mean. The higher the R^2, the better the regression line fits the data. The interpretation for a high R^2 is that the independent variable is a good predictor of the behaviour of the dependent variable. In cost estimation, a high R^2 means

	A	B	C
1		Utility	
2	Month	Cost	Activity
3	of	for	during
4	Preceding	Month	Month
5	Year	Y	X
6			
7	January	5,100	75,000
8	February	5,300	78,000
9	March	5,650	80,000
10	April	6,300	92,000
11	May	6,400	98,000
12	June	6,700	108,000
13	July	7,035	118,000
14	August	7,000	112,000
15	September	6,200	95,000
16	October	6,100	90,000
17	November	5,600	85,000
18	December	5,900	90,000
19	Total	73,285	1,121,000
20			
21	Computation of Regression Parameters		
22	Using Spreadsheet Functions		
23			
24	Intercept	1,920	
25	Slope	0.0448	
26	R^2	0.949	

Exhibit 6–12

Using Microsoft® Excel to Compute the Least-Squares Regression Estimates

that the cost analyst can be relatively confident in the cost predictions based on the estimated cost behaviour pattern.

Excel can be used to calculate the R^2. The analyst simply uses the RSQ command in Excel. As shown in cell B26 of the Excel worksheet in Exhibit 6–12, the R^2 is 0.949.

Cell B26 contains the following formula: = RSQ(B7:B18,C7:C18)

This is a high value for R^2, and Tasty Donuts' controller may be quite confident in the resulting cost predictions. As always, these predictions should be confined to the relevant range.

Appendix to Chapter 6 Summary

LO9 Perform and interpret a least-squares regression analysis with a single independent variable (Appendix). In the least-squares regression method, the cost line is estimated so as to minimize the sum of the squared deviations between the cost line and the data points. The resulting regression line has an intercept on the vertical (cost) axis and a slope, which measures how steeply the cost line rises as activity increases.

Review Questions

6–1. Describe the importance of cost behaviour patterns in planning, control, and decision making.

6–2. Define the following terms, and explain the relationship among them: (*a*) cost estimation, (*b*) cost behaviour, and (*c*) cost prediction.

6–3. Suggest an appropriate activity base (or cost driver) for each of the following organizations: (*a*) hotel, (*b*) hospital, (*c*) computer manufacturer, (*d*) computer sales

store, (*e*) computer repair service, and (*f*) public accounting firm.

6–4. Draw a simple graph of each of the following types of cost behaviour patterns: (*a*) variable, (*b*) step-variable, (*c*) fixed, (*d*) step-fixed, (*e*) mixed, and (*f*) curvilinear.

6–5. Explain the impact of an increase in the level of activity (or cost driver) on (*a*) total fixed cost and (*b*) fixed cost per unit of activity.

6–6. Explain why a manufacturer's cost of supervising production might be a step-fixed cost.

6–7. Explain the impact of an increase in the level of activity (or cost driver) on (*a*) total variable cost and (*b*) variable cost per unit.

6–8. Using graphs, show how a mixed-cost behaviour pattern can be used to approximate (*a*) a step-variable cost and (*b*) a curvilinear cost.

6–9. Indicate which of the following descriptions is most likely to describe each cost listed below:

Description: (*a*) Engineered cost; (*b*) committed cost; (*c*) discretionary cost

Description	Costs
	Annual cost of maintaining a highway
	Cost of ingredients in a breakfast cereal
	Cost of advertising for a credit card company
	Depreciation on an insurance company's computer
	Cost of charitable donations that are budgeted as 1 percent of sales revenue
	Research and development costs, which have been budgeted at $45,000 per year

6–10. A cost analyst showed the company president a graph that portrayed the firm's utility cost as mixed. The president criticized the graph by saying, "This fixed-cost component doesn't look right to me. If we shut down the plant for six months, we wouldn't incur half of these costs." How should the cost analyst respond?

6–11. What is meant by a *learning curve*? Explain its role in cost estimation.

6–12. Suggest an appropriate independent variable to use in predicting the costs of the following tasks:
a. Handling materials at a loading dock
b. Registering vehicles at a provincial motor vehicle office
c. Picking oranges
d. Inspecting computer components in an electronics firm

6–13. What is an *outlier*? List some possible causes of outliers. How should outliers be handled in cost estimation?

6–14. Explain the cost-estimation problem caused by allocated and discretionary costs.

6–15. Describe the visual-fit method of cost estimation. What are the main strengths and weaknesses of this method?

6–16. What is the main drawback of the high–low method of cost estimation? What problem might an outlier cause if the high–low method was used?

6–17. Explain the meaning of the term *least squares* in the least-squares regression method of cost estimation.

6–18. Use an equation to express a least-squares regression line. Interpret each term in the equation.

6–19. Distinguish between simple regression and multiple regression.

6–20. List several possible cost drivers that could be used by a cruise line.

6–21. Briefly describe two methods that can be used to evaluate a particular least-squares regression line.

Exercises

Exercise 6–22 Graphing Cost Behaviour Patterns: Hospital **(LO1, 2)**

Draw a graph of the cost behaviour for each of the following costs incurred by the Mountain Summit Hospital. The hospital measures monthly activity in patient days. Label both axes and the cost line in each graph.

1. The cost of food varies in proportion to the number of patient days of activity. In January, the hospital provided 3,000 patient days of care, and food costs amounted to $24,000.

2. The cost of salaries and fringe benefits for the administrative staff totals $12,000 per month.

3. The hospital's laboratory costs include two components: (*a*) $40,000 per month for compensation of staff and depreciation on equipment and (*b*) $10 per patient day for chemicals and other materials used in performing the tests.

4. The cost of utilities depends on how many wards the hospital needs to use during a particular month. During months with activity under 2,000 patient days of care, two wards are used, resulting in utility costs of $10,000. During months with greater than 2,000 patient days of care, three wards are used, and utility costs total $15,000.

5. Many of the hospital's nurses are part-time employees. As a result, the hours of nursing care provided can be easily adjusted to the amount required at any particular time. The cost of wages and fringe benefits for nurses is approximately $2,500 for each block of 200 patient days of care provided during a month. For example, nursing costs total $2,500 for 1 to 200 patient days, $5,000 for 201 to 400 patient days, $7,500 for 401 to 600 patient days, and so forth.

Exercise 6–23 Approximating a Curvilinear Cost: School District **(LO1, 2, 3)**

The behaviour of the annual maintenance and repair cost in the Bus Transportation Department of the Coquitlam School District is shown by the solid line in the following graph. The dashed line depicts a mixed-cost approximation of the department's repair and maintenance cost.

Required:

1. What is the actual (curvilinear) and estimated (mixed) cost shown by the graph for each of the following activity levels?

	Actual	Estimated
a. 20,000 kilometres		
b. 40,000 kilometres		
c. 60,000 kilometres		
d. 90,000 kilometres		

2. How good an approximation does the mixed-cost pattern provide if the department's relevant range is 40,000 to 60,000 kilometres per month? What if the relevant range is 20,000 to 90,000 kilometres per month?

Exercise 6–24 Behaviour of Fixed and Variable Costs: Television Station **(LO1, 2)**

WMEJ is an independent television station. The station's broadcast hours vary during the year. The station's production crew and supervisory costs are as follows for July and September.

Cost Item	Cost Behaviour	Cost Amount	Broadcast Hours during Month
Production crew..	Variable		
July...		$4,875	390
September		8,000	640
Supervisory employees..	Fixed		
July...		5,000	390
September		5,000	640

Required:

1. Compute the cost per broadcast hour during July and September for each of these cost items.
2. What will be the total amount incurred for each of these costs during December, when the station's activity will be 420 broadcast hours?
3. What will be the cost per broadcast hour in December for each of the cost items?

Exercise 6–25 Estimating Cost Behaviour: High–Low Method (LO1, 2, 5)

Jonathan Macintosh is a highly successful apple grower who has formed his own company to produce and package applesauce. Apples can be stored for several months in cold storage, so applesauce production is relatively uniform throughout the year. The recently hired controller for the firm is about to apply the high–low method in estimating the company's energy cost behaviour. The following costs were incurred during the past 12 months:

Month	Litres of Applesauce Produced	Energy Cost
January	35,000	$23,400
February	21,000	22,100
March	22,000	22,000
April	24,000	22,450
May	30,000	22,900
June	32,000	23,350
July	40,000	28,000
August	30,000	22,800
September	30,000	23,000
October	28,000	22,700
November	41,000	24,100
December	39,000	24,950

Required:

1. Use the high–low method to estimate the company's energy cost behaviour and express it in equation form.
2. Predict the energy cost for a month in which 26,000 litres of applesauce are produced.

Exercise 6–26 Estimating Cost Behaviour: Visual-Fit Method (LO1, 2, 5)

Refer to the data in the preceding exercise.

Required:

1. Draw a scatter diagram and graph the company's energy cost behaviour using the visual-fit method.
2. Predict the energy cost for a month in which 26,000 litres of applesauce are produced.
3. What peculiarity is apparent from the scatter diagram? What should the cost analyst do?

Exercise 6–27 Cost Behaviour; Use of Internet (LO2)

Visit the website of one of the following companies, or a different company of your choosing:

Boeing	www.boeing.com
Dell Inc.	www.dell.com
Ford	www.ford.com
General Electric	www.ge.com
Shaw	www.shaw.ca
McDonald's	www.mcdonalds.com
Tim Hortons	www.timhortons.com

Required: Read about the company's products and operations. Then list five costs that the company would incur and explain what type of cost behaviour you believe would be appropriate for each of these cost items.

Exercise 6–28 Visual-Fit Method: Veterinary Laboratory (LO1, 2, 5)

The West Vancouver Veterinary Laboratory performs a variety of diagnostic tests on commercial and domestic animals. The lab has incurred the following costs over the past year:

March's costs consisted of machine supplies ($102,000), depreciation ($15,000), and plant maintenance ($469,000). These costs exhibit the following respective behaviour: variable, fixed, and mixed.

The manufacturing overhead figures presented in the preceding table do not include Manitoba's supervisory labour cost, which is step-fixed in nature. For volume levels of less than 15,000 hours, supervisory labour amounts to $45,000. The cost is $90,000 from 15,000 to 29,999 hours, and $135,000 when activity reaches 30,000 hours or more.

Required:

1. Determine both the machine supplies cost and depreciation for January.
2. Using the high–low method, analyze Manitoba's plant maintenance cost and calculate the monthly fixed portion and the variable cost per direct-labour hour.
3. Assume that the present cost behaviour patterns continue into the latter half of the year. Estimate the *total* amount of manufacturing overhead the company can expect in November if 29,500 direct-labour hours are worked.
4. Briefly explain the difference between a fixed cost and a step-fixed cost.
5. Assume that a company has a step-fixed cost. Generally speaking, where on a step should the firm attempt to operate if it desires to achieve a maximum return on its investment?

Problem 6–37 Cost Behaviour and Analysis: High–Low Method (LO2, 4, 5)

2. Total cost for 1,650 tonnes: $823,500

Antioch Extraction, which mines ore in Alberta, uses a calendar year for both financial reporting and tax purposes. The following selected costs were incurred in December, the low point of activity, when 1,500 tonnes of ore were extracted:

Straight-line depreciation	$25,000	Royalties	$135,000
Charitable contributions*	11,000	Trucking and hauling	275,000
Mining labour/fringe benefits	345,000		

*Incurred only in December.

Peak activity of 2,600 tonnes occurred in June, resulting in mining labour/fringe benefit costs of $598,000, royalties of $201,000, and trucking and hauling outlays of $325,000. The trucking and hauling outlays exhibit the following behaviour:

Less than 1,500 tonnes	$250,000
From 1,500 to 1,899 tonnes	275,000
From 1,900 to 2,299 tonnes	300,000
From 2,300 to 2,699 tonnes	325,000

Antioch uses the high–low method to analyze costs.

Required:

1. Classify the five costs listed in terms of their behaviour: variable, step-variable, committed fixed, discretionary fixed, step-fixed, or mixed. Show calculations to support your answers for mining labour/fringe benefits and royalties.
2. Calculate the total cost for next February when 1,650 tonnes are expected to be extracted.
3. Comment on the cost-effectiveness of hauling 1,500 tonnes with respect to Antioch's trucking/hauling cost behaviour. Can the company's effectiveness be improved? How?
4. Distinguish between committed and discretionary fixed costs. If the company was to experience severe economic difficulties, which of the two types of fixed costs should management try to cut? Why?
5. Speculate as to why the company's charitable contribution cost arises only in December.

Problem 6–38 High-Low Method: Fitness Centres (LO1, 2, 5)

3. Cost prediction at 590 hours of activity, maintenance cost: $4,995

Capital Fitness, Inc. operates a chain of fitness centres in the Ottawa area. The firm's controller is accumulating data to be used in preparing its annual profit plan for the coming year. The cost behaviour pattern of the firm's equipment maintenance costs must be determined. The accounting staff has suggested the use of an equation, in the form of $Y = a + bX$, for maintenance costs. Data regarding the maintenance hours and costs for last year are as follows:

Month	Hours of Maintenance Service	Maintenance Costs
January	520	$ 4,470
February	490	4,260
March	300	2,820
April	500	4,250
May	310	2,960
June	480	4,200
July	320	3,000
August	400	3,600
September	470	4,050
October	350	3,300
November	340	3,160
December	320	3,030
Total	4,800	$43,100
Average	400	$ 3,600

Required:

1. Using the high–low method of cost estimation, estimate the behaviour of the maintenance costs incurred by Capital Fitness. Express the cost behaviour pattern in equation form.

2. Using your answer to requirement (1), what is the variable component of the maintenance cost?

3. Compute the predicted maintenance cost at 590 hours of activity.

4. Compute the variable cost per hour and the fixed cost per hour at 600 hours of activity. Explain why the fixed cost per hour could be misleading.

(CMA, adapted)

Problem 6–39 Account-Classification Method: Private School (LO1, 2, 5)

The Regina School of Music has hired you as a consultant to help in analyzing the behaviour of the school's costs. Use the account-classification method of cost estimation to classify each of the following costs as variable, fixed, or mixed. Before classifying the costs, choose an appropriate measure for the school's activity.

1. Salaries and fringe benefits of the school's full-time teachers.

2. Salaries and fringe benefits of the school's full-time administrative staff.

3. Cost of buying books, sheet music, and other academic materials that are supplied to the students by the school.

4. Repairs on musical instruments. The school employs a full-time repair technician. Repair jobs that are beyond the technician's capability are taken to a local musical instrument dealer for repairs.

5. Fee charged by a local public accounting firm to audit the school's accounting records.

6. Wages of the school's part-time assistant recital instructors. These employees are hired on a temporary basis. For each student enrolled in the school's music programs, four hours of assistant instructor time are needed per week.

7. Depreciation on the school's musical instruments

8. Rent for the building in which the school operates

9. Electricity for the school. The school pays a fixed monthly charge plus $0.11 per kilowatt-hour of electricity.

Problem 6–40 Approximating a Step-Variable Cost; Visual-Fit Method: Golf Course (LO1, 2, 5)

3. Fixed-cost component: $12,010

Rolling Hills Golf Association is a nonprofit, private organization that operates three 18-hole golf courses. The organization's financial director has just analyzed the course maintenance costs incurred by the golf association during recent summers. The courses are maintained by a full-time crew of four people, who are assisted by part-time employees. These employees are typically college students on summer vacation. The course maintenance costs vary with the number of people using the course. Since a large part of the maintenance work is done by part-time employees, the maintenance crew size can easily be adjusted to reflect current needs. The financial director's analysis revealed that the course maintenance cost includes two components:

1. A fixed component of $12,000 per month (when the courses are open)
2. A step-variable cost component. For each additional 1 to 10 people teeing off in one day, $20 in costs are incurred. So, if 101 to 110 people tee off, $220 of additional cost will be incurred. If 111 to 120 people tee off, $240 of additional cost will be incurred.

Required:

1. Draw a graph of Rolling Hills Golf Association's course maintenance costs. Show on the graph the fixed-cost component and the step-variable cost component. Label each clearly.
2. Use a mixed-cost behaviour pattern to approximate the golf association's course maintenance cost behaviour. Visually fit the mixed-cost line to your graph.
3. Using your graph, estimate the variable- and fixed-cost components included in your mixed approximation. Express this approximate cost behaviour pattern in equation form.
4. Fill in the following table of cost predictions:

	Predicted Course Maintenance Costs	
	Using Fixed-Cost Coupled with Step-Variable Cost Behaviour Pattern	Using Mixed-Cost Approximation
150 people tee off	?	?
158 people tee off	?	?

Problem 6–41 Work Measurement; Cost Estimation with Different Methods: Wholesaler **(LO1, 2, 5, 6)**

(*Note:* Instructors who want to cover all three cost-estimation methods with the same data set may assign this problem in conjunction with the next one.) Victoria Marine Supply is a wholesaler for a large variety of boating and fishing equipment. The company's controller, Mathew Knight, recently completed a cost study of the firm's Material-Handling Department in which he used work measurement to quantify the department's activity. The control factor unit used in the work-measurement study was hundreds of kilograms of equipment unloaded or loaded at the company's loading dock. Knight compiled the following data:

3. Variable cost per unit of activity: $1

Month	Units of Activity (hundreds of kilograms of equipment loaded or unloaded)	Material-Handling Department Costs
January	1,400	$11,350
February	1,200	11,350
March	1,100	11,050
April	2,600	12,120
May	1,800	11,400
June	2,000	12,000
July	2,400	12,550
August	2,200	11,100
September	1,000	10,200
October	1,300	11,250
November	1,600	11,300
December	1,800	11,700

Required:

1. Draw a scatter diagram of the cost data for the Material-Handling Department.
2. Visually fit a cost line to the scatter diagram.
3. Estimate the variable and fixed components of the department's cost behaviour pattern using the visually fit cost line.
4. Using your estimate from requirement (3), specify an equation to express the department's cost behaviour.
5. Estimate the Material-Handling Department's cost behaviour using the high–low method. Use an equation to express the results of this estimation method.
6. Write a brief memo to the company's president explaining why the cost estimates developed in requirements (4) and (5) differ.
7. Predict the company's material-handling costs for a month when 2,300 units of activity are recorded. Use each of your cost equations to make the prediction. Which prediction would you prefer to use? Why?

Problem 6–42 Continuation of Preceding Problem; Computing Least-Squares Regression Estimates; Comparing Multiple Methods (Appendix) (LO1, 2, 5, 6, 9)

Refer to the original data in the preceding problem for Victoria Marine Supply.

Required:

1. *Build a spreadsheet:* Construct an Excel spreadsheet and use the Excel commands to perform a least-squares regression. Estimate the variable- and fixed-cost components in the company's Material-Handling Department costs.
2. Write the least-squares regression equation for the department's costs.
3. Predict the firm's Material-Handling Department's costs for a month when 2,300 units of activity are recorded.
4. Why do the three cost predictions computed in this and the preceding problem differ? Which method do you recommend? Why?
5. *Build a spreadsheet:* Use your Excel spreadsheet from requirement (1) to compute the R^2 value for the regression. Interpret the R^2 value.

Problem 6–43 Cost-Estimation Methods; Cost Analysis; E-Commerce (LO2, 5)

Shortly after being hired as an analyst with Global Airlines, Kim Williams was asked to prepare a report that focused on passenger ticketing cost. The airline writes most of its own tickets (largely through reservations staff), makes little use of travel agents, and has seen an ever-increasing passenger interest in e-ticketing (i.e., electronic reservations and tickets handled over the Internet).

After some discussion, Williams thought it would be beneficial to begin her report with an overview of three different cost-estimation tools: scatter diagrams, least-squares regression, and the high–low method. She would then present the results of her analysis of the past year's monthly ticketing cost, which was driven largely by the number of tickets written. These results would be presented in the form of algebraic equations that were derived by the three tools just cited. The equations follow. (*C* denotes ticketing cost, and *PT* denotes number of passenger tickets written.)

Scatter diagram: $C = \$320,000 + \$2.15PT$

Least-squares regression: $C = \$312,000 + \$2.30PT$

High–low method: $C = \$295,000 + \$2.55PT$

Williams had analyzed data over the past 12 months and built equations on these data, purposely including the slowest month of the year (February) and the busiest month (October) so that things would "tend to average out." She observed that October was especially busy because of Thanksgiving, passengers purchasing tickets for upcoming holiday travel in December, and the effects of a strike by National Airlines, Global's chief competitor. The lengthy strike resulted in many of National's passengers being rerouted on Global flights.

Required:

1. Prepare a bullet-point list suitable for use in Williams's report that describes the features of scatter diagrams, least-squares regression, and the high–low method. Determine which of the three tools will typically produce the most accurate results.
2. Will the three cost-estimation tools normally result in different equations? Why?
3. Assuming the use of least-squares regression, explain what the $312,000 and $2.30 figures represent.
4. Assuming the use of a scatter diagram, predict the cost of an upcoming month when Global expects to write 580,000 tickets.
5. Did Williams make a mistake in constructing the equations on data of the past 12 months? Briefly explain.
6. Assume that over the next few years, more of Global's passengers will take advantage of e-ticketing over the Internet. What will likely happen to the airline's cost structure in terms of variable and fixed cost incurred?

Problem 6–44 Comparing Regression and High–Low Estimates: Manufacturer **(LO1, 2, 5, 7)**

5. Fixed cost: $150

The controller of Mirabel Chain Company believes that the identification of the variable and fixed components of the firm's costs will enable the firm to make better planning and control decisions. Among the costs the controller is concerned about is the behaviour of indirect-materials cost. She believes there is a correlation between machine hours and the amount of indirect materials used.

A member of the controller's staff has suggested that least-squares regression be used to determine the cost behaviour of indirect materials. The regression equation shown below was developed from 40 pairs of observations:

$$S = \$200 + \$4H$$

where S = Total monthly cost of indirect materials

H = Machine hours per month

Required:

1. Explain the meaning of 200 and 4 in the regression equation $S = \$200 + \$4H$.
2. Calculate the estimated cost of indirect materials if 900 machine hours are to be used during a month.
3. To determine the validity of the cost estimate computed in requirement (2), what question would you ask the controller about the data used for the regression?
4. The high and low activity levels during the past four years, as measured by machine hours, occurred during April and August, respectively. Data concerning machine hours and indirect-material usage follow:

	April	August
Machine hours..	1,100	800
Indirect supplies:		
Beginning inventory..	$1,200	$ 950
Ending inventory..	1,550	2,900
Purchases...	6,000	6,100

Determine the cost of indirect materials used during April and August.

5. Use the high–low method to estimate the behaviour of the company's indirect-material cost. Express the cost behaviour pattern in equation form.
6. Which cost estimate would you recommend to the controller, the regression estimate or the high–low estimate? Why?

(CMA, adapted)

Problem 6–45 Interpreting Regression Analysis in Cost Estimation **(LO1, 2, 5)**

3. Minimum bid for 250-person cocktail party: $5,500

Dana Rand owns a catering company that prepares banquets and parties for both individual and business functions throughout the year. Her business is seasonal, with a heavy schedule during the summer months and the year-end holidays and a light schedule at other times. During peak periods, there are extra costs; however, even during nonpeak periods, she must work more to cover her expenses.

One of the major events her customers request is a cocktail party. She offers a standard cocktail party and has developed the following cost structure on a per-person basis:

Food and beverages	$15
Labour (0.5 hrs. @ $10 per hr.)	5
Overhead (0.5 hrs. @ $14 per hr.)	7
Total cost per person	$27

When bidding on cocktail parties, Rand adds a 15 percent markup to this cost structure as a profit margin. She is quite certain about her estimates of the prime costs but is not as comfortable with the overhead estimate. This estimate was based on the actual data for the past 12 months presented in the following table. These data indicate that overhead expenses vary with the direct-labour hours expended. The $14 per hour overhead estimate was determined by dividing total overhead expended for the 12 months ($805,000) by total labour hours (57,600) and rounding to the nearest dollar.

Month	Labour Hours	Overhead Expenses
January	2,500	$55,000
February	2,800	59,000
March	3,000	60,000
April	4,200	64,000
May	4,500	67,000
June	5,500	71,000
July	6,500	74,000
August	7,500	77,000
September	7,000	75,000
October	4,500	68,000
November	3,100	62,000
December	6,500	73,000
Total	57,600	$805,000

Rand recently attended a meeting of the local Chamber of Commerce and heard a business consultant discuss regression analysis and its business applications. After the meeting, she decided to do a regression analysis of the overhead data she had collected. The following results were obtained:

Intercept (*a*)	48,000
Coefficient (*b*)	4

Required:

1. Explain the difference between the overhead rate originally estimated by Rand and the overhead rate developed from the regression method.

2. Using data from the regression analysis, develop the following cost estimates per person for a cocktail party:

   a. Variable cost per person

   b. Absorption (full) cost per person (includes both variable and fixed cost per person)

   Assume that the level of activity remains within the relevant range.

3. Rand has been asked to prepare a bid for a 250-person cocktail party to be given next month. Determine the minimum bid price that she should be willing to submit.

4. What other factors should Rand consider in developing the bid price for the cocktail party?

(CMA, adapted)

Problem 6–46 Computing Least-Squares Regression Estimates (Appendix): Airport Costs (LO1, 2, 5, 9)

Langley Airport handles several daily commuter flights and many private flights. The budget officer has compiled the following data regarding airport costs and activity over the past year:

2. Variable: $6.77 per flight
2. Fixed: $11,796 per month
4. Cost prediction, 1,600
flights: $22,628

Month	Flights Originating at Langley Airport	Airport Costs
January	1,100	$20,000
February	800	17,000
March	1,400	19,000
April	900	18,000
May	1,000	19,000
June	1,200	20,000
July	1,100	18,000
August	1,400	24,000
September	1,000	19,000
October	1,200	21,000
November	900	17,000
December	1,500	21,000

Required:

1. Draw a scatter diagram of the airport costs shown above.

eXcel

2. *Build a spreadsheet:* Construct an Excel spreadsheet and use the Excel commands to perform a least-squares regression. Estimate the variable- and fixed-cost components in the airport's cost behaviour pattern.

3. Write the least-squares regression equation for the airport's costs.
4. Predict the airport's costs during a month when 1,600 flights originate at the airport.
5. Using the Excel spreadsheet prepared for requirement (2), compute the coefficient of determination (R^2) for the regression equation. Briefly interpret R^2.

Cases

Case 6–47 Interpreting Least-Squares Regression: Landscaping Service; Activity-Based Costing **(LO1, 2, 5)**

Earth and Artistry, Inc. provides commercial landscaping services. Sasha Cairns, the firm's owner, wants to develop cost estimates that he can use to prepare bids on jobs. After analyzing the firm's costs, he has developed the following preliminary cost estimates for each 1,000 m² of landscaping:

2. Total variable cost per 1,000 m²: $496.25
5(b). Total incremental variable overhead: $3,285

Direct material	$400
Direct labour (5 direct-labour hours at $10 per hour)	50
Overhead (at $18 per direct-labour hour)	90
Total cost per 1,000 m²	$540

Cairns is quite certain about the estimates for direct material and direct labour. However, he is not as comfortable with the overhead estimate. The estimate for overhead is based on the overhead costs that were incurred during the past 12 months as presented in the following schedule. The estimate of $18 per direct-labour hour was determined by dividing the total overhead costs for the 12-month period ($648,000) by the total direct-labour hours (36,000).

	Total Overhead	Regular Direct-Labour Hours	Overtime Direct-Labour Hours*	Total Direct-Labour Hours
January.............	$ 54,000	2,910	190	3,100
February	47,000	2,380	20	2,400
March	48,000	2,210	40	2,250
April..................	56,000	2,590	210	2,800
May	57,000	3,030	470	3,500
June	65,000	3,240	760	4,000
July...................	64,000	3,380	620	4,000
August	56,000	3,050	350	3,400
September	53,000	2,760	40	2,800
October.............	47,000	2,770	30	2,800
November	47,000	2,120	30	2,150
December	54,000	2,560	240	2,800
Total.............	$648,000	33,000	3,000	36,000

*The overtime premium is 50 percent of the direct-labour wage rate.

Cairns believes that overhead is affected by total monthly direct-labour hours. He decided to perform a least-squares regression of overhead (OH) on total direct-labour hours (DLH). The following regression formula was obtained.

$OH = \$26,200 + 9.25DLH$

Required:

1. The overhead rate developed from the least-squares regression is different from Sasha's preliminary estimate of $18 per direct-labour hour. Explain the difference in the two overhead rates.
2. Using the overhead formula that was derived from the least-squares regression, determine a total variable-cost estimate for each 1,000 m² of landscaping.
3. Cairns has been asked to submit a bid on a landscaping project for the city government consisting of 60,000 m². He estimates that 40 percent of the direct-labour hours required for the project will be on overtime. Calculate the incremental costs that should be included in any bid that he would submit on this project. Use the overhead formula derived from the least-squares regression.
4. Should Cairns rely on the overhead formula derived from the least-squares regression as the basis for the variable overhead component of its cost estimate? Explain your answer.

5. After attending a seminar on activity-based costing, Cairns decided to further analyze the company's activities and costs. He discovered that a more accurate portrayal of the firm's cost behaviour could be achieved by dividing overhead into three separate pools, each with its own cost driver. Separate regression equations were estimated for each of the cost pools, with the following results:

$$OH_1 = \$10,000 + \$4.10DLH$$

where *DLH* denotes direct-labour hours

$$OH_2 = \$9,100 + \$13.50SMS$$

where *SMS* denotes the number of square metres of turf seeded (in thousands)

$$OH_3 = \$8,000 + \$6.60PL$$

where *PL* denotes the number of individual plantings (e.g., trees and shrubs)

Assume that five direct-labour hours will be needed to landscape each 1,000 m², regardless of the specific planting material used.

   a. Suppose the landscaping project for the city will involve seeding all 60,000 m² of turf and planting 80 trees and shrubs. Calculate the incremental *variable overhead* cost that Cairns should include in the bid.

   b. Recompute the incremental variable overhead cost for the city's landscaping project assuming half of the 60,000-m² landscaping area will be seeded and there will be 250 individual plantings. The plantings will cover the entire 60,000-m² area.

   c. Briefly explain, using concepts from activity-based costing, why the incremental costs differ in requirements (*a*) and (*b*).

(CMA, adapted)

6. Administrative cost = $7,000 + $3X, where X denotes number of patients

Case 6–48   Approximating a Curvilinear Cost; Visual-Fit Method: Pediatrics Clinic (LO1, 2, 5)

(*Note:* Instructors who want to cover all three cost-estimation methods with the same data set may assign this case in conjunction with the following case.) "I don't understand this cost report at all," exclaimed Jeff Mahoney, the newly appointed administrator of Mountainview General Hospital. "Our administrative costs in the new pediatrics clinic are all over the map. One month the report shows $8,300, and the next month it's $16,100. What's going on?"

Mahoney's question was posed to Megan McDonough, the hospital's director of cost management. "The main problem is that the clinic has experienced some widely varying patient loads in its first year of operation. There seems to be some confusion in the public's mind about what services we offer in the clinic. When do they come to the clinic? When do they go to the emergency room? That sort of thing. As the patient load has varied, we've frequently changed our clinic administrative staffing."

Mahoney continued to puzzle over the report. "Could you pull some data together, Megan, so we can see how this cost behaves over a range of patient loads?"

"You'll have it this afternoon," McDonough responded. Later that morning, she gathered the following data:

Month	Patient Load	Administrative Cost
January	1,400	$ 13,900
February	500	7,000
March	400	6,000
April	1,000	10,000
May	1,300	11,900
June	900	9,200
July	1,100	10,200
August	300	4,100
September	700	9,400
October	1,200	11,100
November	600	8,300
December	1,500	16,100

McDonough does not believe the first year's widely fluctuating patient load will be experienced again in the future. She has estimated that the clinic's relevant range of monthly activity in the future will be 600 to 1,200 patients.

Required:

1. Draw a scatter diagram of the clinic's administrative costs during its first year of operation.
2. Visually fit a curvilinear cost line to the plotted data.
3. Mark the clinic's relevant range of activity on the scatter diagram.
4. Visually fit a mixed-cost line to approximate the curvilinear cost behaviour pattern within the clinic's relevant range.
5. Estimate the fixed- and variable-cost components of the visually fit mixed-cost line.
6. Use an equation to express the mixed-cost approximation of the clinic's administrative costs.
7. What is your prediction of the clinic's administrative cost during a month when 800 patients visit the clinic? When 300 patients visit? Which one of your visually fit cost lines did you use to make each of these predictions? Why?

Case 6–49 Comparing Multiple Cost-Estimation Methods; Ethics (Appendix) **(LO1, 2, 3, 5, 9)**
Refer to the data and accompanying information in the preceding case.

1. High–low method, variable administrative cost per patient: $10
2. Total monthly administrative cost = $2,671 + $7.81X, where X denotes number of patients per month

Required:

1. Use the high–low method to estimate the cost behaviour for the clinic's administrative costs. Express the cost behaviour in formula form ($Y = a + bX$). What is the variable cost per patient?
2. *Build a spreadsheet:* Construct an Excel spreadsheet and use the Excel commands to perform a least-squares regression and estimate the administrative cost behaviour. Express the cost behaviour in formula form. What is the variable cost per patient? Compute and interpret the R^2 value for the regression.
3. Write a memo to the hospital administrator comparing the cost estimates using (*a*) least-squares regression, (*b*) the high–low method, and (*c*) the scatter diagram and visually fit mixed-cost line from the preceding case (requirement 4). Make a recommendation as to which estimate should be used, and support your recommendation. Make any other suggestions you feel are appropriate.
4. After receiving the memo comparing the three cost estimates, Mahoney called McDonough to discuss the matter. The following exchange occurred:

   Mahoney: As you know, Megan, I was never in favour of this clinic. It's going to be a drag on our administrative staff, and we'd have been far better off keeping the pediatrics operation here in the hospital.

   McDonough: I was aware that you felt the clinic was a mistake. Of course, the board of trustees had other issues to consider. I believe the board felt the clinic should be built to make pediatric care more accessible to the economically depressed area on the other side of the city.

   Mahoney: That's true, but the board doesn't realize how difficult it's going to make life for us here in the hospital. In any case, I called to tell you that when you and I report to the board next week, I'm going to recommend that the clinic be shut down. I want you to support my recommendation with one of your cost estimates showing that administrative costs will soar at high activity levels.

   McDonough: But that estimate was based on the high–low method. It's not an appropriate method for this situation.

   Mahoney: It *is* an estimate, Megan, and it's based on a well-known estimation method. This is just the ammunition I need to make the board see things my way.

   McDonough: I don't know, Jeff. I just don't think I can go along with that.

   Mahoney: Be a team player, Megan. I've got a meeting now. Got to run.

   That night McDonough called her best friend, you, to discuss the matter. How would you advise McDonough?

CHAPTER SEVEN

Cost–Volume–Profit Analysis, Absorption and Variable Costing

FOCUS COMPANY

The Toronto Contemporary Theatre, a nonprofit enterprise, was formed to bring contemporary drama to the Toronto area. It operates in a historic theatre building owned by the City of Toronto, for which it pays the City a fixed monthly rental charge and a portion of the price of each ticket sold. The theatre has to cover its operating expenses with ticket revenue in order to break even. Using the Toronto Contemporary Theatre as an illustration, we will explore a technique called *cost–volume–profit* (*CVP*) analysis, which the theatre's managing director and business manager use to better understand the relationships among the theatre's costs, ticket sales volume, and revenue.

IN CONTRAST

In contrast to the nonprofit, entertainment-service setting of the Toronto Contemporary Theatre, we examine the use of cost–volume–profit

---

After completing this chapter, you should be able to

1 Compute a break-even point using the contribution-margin approach and the equation approach.

2 Compute the contribution-margin ratio and use it to find the break-even point in sales dollars.

3 Prepare a cost–volume–profit (CVP) graph and explain how it is used.

4 Apply CVP analysis to determine the effect on profit of changes in fixed expenses, variable expenses, sales prices, and sales volume.

5 Compute the break-even point for a multiproduct enterprise.

6 Prepare an income statement under absorption and variable costing, and reconcile the difference in reporting income.

7 Explain the implications of absorption and variable costing for CVP, and evaluate both product-costing systems.

8 Explain throughput costing and prepare an income statement using this costing approach.

9 Explain the role of cost structure and operating leverage in CVP relationships.

10 Understand the implications of activity-based costing (ABC) for CVP analysis.

11 Be aware of the effects of advanced manufacturing technology on CVP relationships.

analysis by Qui**kmath**.com, a manufacturer of hand-held calculators and other electronic gadgetry. Qui**kmath** specializes in all levels of the school market, and virtually all of its sales are web-based. We explore two product-costing systems called *absorption costing* and *variable costing*. Under absorption costing, all manufacturing costs, including fixed manufacturing overhead, are assigned as product costs and stored in inventory until the products are sold. Under variable costing, fixed manufacturing overhead is not included in inventory as a product cost. Instead, fixed manufacturing overhead is treated as a period cost, and it is expensed during the period in which it is incurred. The choice between these two product-costing systems arises only in manufacturing firms.

The company's management also analyzes the firm's cost structure, which refers to the relative proportion of fixed and variable costs. *Throughput costing*, an alternative to absorption and variable costing, assigns only the unit-level spending for direct costs as the cost of a product.

What effect on profit can WestJet Airlines expect if it adds a flight on the Calgary to Toronto route? How will CBC's profit change if the ratings increase for its evening news program? How many patient days of care must Whitehorse General Hospital provide to break even for the year? What happens to this break-even patient load if the hospital leases a new computerized system for patient records?

Each of these questions concerns the effects on costs and revenues when the organization's activity changes. The analytical technique used by management accountants to address these questions is called **cost–volume–profit analysis**, or **CVP analysis**. This technique summarizes the effects of changes in an organization's *volume* of activity on its *costs*, revenue, and *profit*.[1] CVP analysis can be extended to cover the effects on profit of changes in selling prices, service fees, costs, income tax rates, and the organization's mix of products or services. What will happen to profit, for example, if the Montreal Canadiens raise ticket prices for stadium seats? In short, CVP analysis provides management with a comprehensive overview of the effects on revenue and costs of all kinds of short-run financial changes.

Although the word *profit* appears in the term, use of CVP analysis is not confined to profit-seeking enterprises. Managers in nonprofit organizations also routinely use CVP analysis to examine the effects of activity and other short-run changes on revenue and costs. For example, as the city of Surrey (the second-largest city in British Columbia) gains nearly 10,000 new residents per year, the city must analyze the effects of this change on property-tax revenues and the cost of providing services, such as mass transit and police protection. Managers at such diverse nonprofit institutions as Vancouver General Hospital, Simon Fraser University, and the Terry Fox Foundation all use CVP analysis as a routine operational tool.

Cost–Volume–Profit Analysis Illustrated

To illustrate the various analytical techniques used in CVP analysis, we will focus on a performing arts organization. The Toronto Contemporary Theatre was recently formed as a nonprofit organization to bring contemporary drama to the Toronto area. The organization has a part-time, unpaid board of trustees made up of local professional people who are avid theatre fans. The board has hired the following full-time employees.

- *Managing director.* Responsibilities include overall management of the organization; direction of six plays per year.
- *Artistic director.* Responsibilities include hiring of actors and production crews for each play; direction of six plays per year.
- *Business manager and producer.* Responsibilities include managing the organization's business functions and ticket sales; direction of the production crews, who handle staging, lighting, costuming, and makeup.

The board of trustees has negotiated an agreement with the City of Toronto to hold performances in a historic theatre owned by the City. The theatre has not been used for 30 years, but the City has agreed to refurbish it and to provide lighting and sound equipment. In return, the City will receive a rental charge of $10,000 per month plus $8 for each theatre ticket sold.

Projected Expenses and Revenue

The theatre's business manager and producer, Andrew Lloyd, has made the following projections for the first few years of operation:

Fixed expenses per month:	
Theatre rental	$10,000
Employees' salaries and fringe benefits	8,000
Actors' wages	15,000
(to be supplemented with local volunteer talent)	
Production crew's wages	5,600
(to be supplemented with local volunteers)	
Playwrights' royalties for use of plays	5,000
Insurance	1,000
Utilities: Fixed portion	1,400
Advertising and promotion	800
Administrative expenses	1,200
Total fixed expenses per month	$48,000
Variable expenses per ticket sold:	
City's charge per ticket for use of theatre	$ 8
Other: Miscellaneous expenses (e.g., printing of playbills and tickets,	
variable portion of utilities)	2
Total variable cost per ticket sold	$10
Revenue:	
Price per ticket	$16

Importance of Cost Behaviour   Notice that the theatre's expenses have been categorized according to their cost behaviour: fixed or variable. Analyzing an organization's cost behaviour, the topic of Chapter 6, is a necessary first step in any CVP analysis. As we proceed through this chapter, the data pertaining to the Toronto Contemporary Theatre will be an important part of our CVP analysis.

The Break-Even Point

As the first step in the CVP analysis for the Toronto Contemporary Theatre, we will find the **break-even point**—the volume of activity at which the organization's revenues and expenses are equal. At this amount of sales, the organization has no profit or loss; it *breaks even.*

Whether running a small business or a worldwide enterprise, understanding CVP relationships is crucial in managing any organization.

Suppose the Toronto Contemporary Theatre sells 8,000 tickets during a play's one-month run. The following income statement shows that the profit for the month will be zero; thus, the theatre will break even.

Sales revenue (8,000 × $16)	$128,000
Less variable expenses (8,000 × 10)	80,000
Total contribution margin	$ 48,000
Less fixed expenses	48,000
Profit	$ 0

Notice that this income statement highlights the distinction between variable and fixed expenses. The statement also shows the **total contribution margin**, which is defined as total sales revenue less total variable expenses. This is the amount of revenue that is available to *contribute* toward paying fixed expenses after all variable expenses have been covered. The contribution income statement will be covered in more depth later in the chapter. At this point, it provides a useful way to think about the meaning of breaking even.

How could we compute the Toronto Contemporary Theatre's break-even point if we did not already know that it is 8,000 tickets per month? This is the question to which we turn our attention next.

> "Break-even analyses figure prominently in any discussion of new programs. Although we have programs that operate at a loss because of their importance educationally, overall our cash inflows have to be sufficient to support our total program." (7b)
> **Cornell University**

Contribution-Margin Approach

The Toronto Contemporary Theatre will break even when the organization's revenue from ticket sales is equal to its expenses. How many tickets must be sold during one month (one play's run) for the organization to break even?

Each ticket sells for $16, but $10 of this is used to cover the variable expense per ticket. This leaves $6 per ticket to *contribute* toward paying the fixed expenses of $48,000. When enough tickets have been sold in one month so that these $6 contributions per ticket add up to $48,000, the organization will break even for the month. So we can compute the break-even volume of tickets as follows:

$$\frac{\text{Fixed expenses}}{\text{Contribution of each ticket toward covering fixed expenses}} = \frac{\$48,000}{\$6} = 8,000$$

The Toronto Contemporary Theatre must sell 8,000 tickets during a play's one-month run to break even for the month.

The $6 amount that remains of each ticket's price, after the variable expenses are covered, is called the **unit contribution margin**. The general formula for computing the break-even sales volume in units is given below:

$$\frac{\text{Fixed expenses}}{\text{Unit contribution margin}} = \text{Break-even point (in units)} \qquad (1)$$

Contribution-Margin Ratio   Sometimes management prefers that the break-even point be expressed in sales *dollars* rather than *units*. The Toronto Contemporary Theatre's break-even point in sales dollars is computed as follows:

Break-even point in units (tickets)	8,000
Sales price per unit	× $16
Break-even point in sales dollars	$128,000

The following computation provides an alternative way to determine the break-even point in sales dollars.

$$\frac{\text{Fixed expenses}}{\underset{\text{Unit sales price}}{\text{Unit contribution margin}}} = \frac{\$48,000}{\dfrac{\$6}{\$16}} = \frac{\$48,000}{0.375} = \$128,000$$

The unit contribution margin divided by the unit sales price is called the **contribution-margin ratio**. This ratio also can be expressed as a percentage, in which case it is called the *contribution-margin percentage*. The Toronto Contemporary Theatre's contribution-margin ratio is 0.375 (in percentage form, 37.5 percent). So the organization's break-even point in sales dollars can be found by dividing its fixed expenses by its contribution-margin ratio. The logic behind this approach is that 37.5 percent of each sales dollar is available to make a contribution toward covering fixed expenses. The general formula is given below:

$$\frac{\text{Fixed expenses}}{\text{Contribution-margin ratio}} = \text{Break-even point in sales dollars} \qquad (2)$$

Equation Approach

An alternative approach to finding the break-even point is based on the profit equation. Income (or profit) is equal to sales revenue minus expenses. If expenses are separated into variable and fixed expenses, the essence of the income (profit) statement is captured by the following equation:

$$\text{Sales revenue} - \text{Variable expenses} - \text{Fixed expenses} = \text{Profit}$$

The equation can be restated as follows:

$$\left[\left(\begin{array}{c} \text{Unit} \\ \text{sales} \\ \text{price} \end{array} \right) \times \left(\begin{array}{c} \text{Sales} \\ \text{volume} \\ \text{in units} \end{array} \right) \right] - \left[\left(\begin{array}{c} \text{Unit} \\ \text{variable} \\ \text{expense} \end{array} \right) \times \left(\begin{array}{c} \text{Sales} \\ \text{volume} \\ \text{in units} \end{array} \right) \right] - \left(\begin{array}{c} \text{Fixed} \\ \text{expenses} \end{array} \right) = \text{Profit} \qquad (3)$$

To find the Toronto Contemporary Theatre's break-even volume of ticket sales per month, we define profit in equation (3) to be zero.

$$(\$16 \times X) - (\$10 \times X) - \$48,000 = 0$$

$$\left[\left(\begin{array}{c} \text{Unit} \\ \text{sales} \\ \text{price} \end{array} \right) \times \left(\begin{array}{c} \text{Sales} \\ \text{volume} \\ \text{in units} \end{array} \right) \right] - \left[\left(\begin{array}{c} \text{Unit} \\ \text{variable} \\ \text{expense} \end{array} \right) \times \left(\begin{array}{c} \text{Sales} \\ \text{volume} \\ \text{in units} \end{array} \right) \right] - \left(\begin{array}{c} \text{Fixed} \\ \text{expenses} \end{array} \right) = \text{Break-even point (zero)} \qquad (4)$$

where X denotes the number of sales units (tickets) required to break even.

Equation (4) can be solved for X as shown below.

$$\$16X - \$10X - \$48,000 = 0$$
$$\$6X = \$48,000$$
$$X = \frac{\$48,000}{\$6} = 8,000$$

Using the equation approach, we have arrived at the same general formula for computing the break-even sales volume; see formula (1).

The contribution-margin and equation approaches are two equivalent techniques for finding the break-even point. Both methods reach the same conclusion, so personal preference dictates which approach should be used.

Graphing Cost–Volume–Profit Relationships

While the break-even point conveys useful information to management, it does not show how profit changes when activity changes. To capture the relationship between the profit and volume of an activity, a **CVP graph** is commonly used. The following steps are used to prepare a CVP graph for the Toronto Contemporary Theatre. The graph is displayed in Exhibit 7–1. Notice that the graph shows the *relevant range,* which is the range of activity within which management expects the theatre to operate.

Learning Objective 3

Prepare a cost–volume–profit (CVP) graph and explain how it is used.

> **Step 1:** Draw the axes of the graph. Label the vertical axis in dollars and the horizontal axis in units of sales (tickets).
>
> **Step 2:** Draw the fixed-expense line. It is parallel to the horizontal axis, since fixed expenses do not change with activity.
>
> **Step 3:** Compute *total* expense at any convenient volume. For example, select a volume of 6,000 tickets.

Variable expenses (6,000 × $10 per ticket)	$ 60,000
Fixed expenses	48,000
Total expenses (at 6,000 tickets)	$108,000

> Plot this point ($108,000 at 6,000 tickets) on the graph. See point A on the graph in Exhibit 7–1.
>
> **Step 4:** Draw the total expense line. This line passes through the point plotted in Step 3 (point A) and the intercept of the fixed-expense line on the vertical axis ($48,000).
>
> **Step 5:** Compute total sales revenue at any convenient volume. We will choose 6,000 tickets again. Total revenue is $96,000 (6,000 × $16 per ticket). Plot this point ($96,000 at 6,000 tickets) on the graph. See point B on the graph in Exhibit 7–1.
>
> **Step 6:** Draw the total revenue line. This line passes through the point plotted in Step 5 (point B) and the origin.
>
> **Step 7:** Label the graph as shown in Exhibit 7–1.

Interpreting the CVP Graph

Several conclusions can be drawn from the CVP graph in Exhibit 7–1.

Break-Even Point The break-even point is determined by the intersection of the total-revenue line and the total-expense line. The Toronto Contemporary Theatre breaks even

Exhibit 7–1

CVP Graph: Toronto
Contemporary Theatre

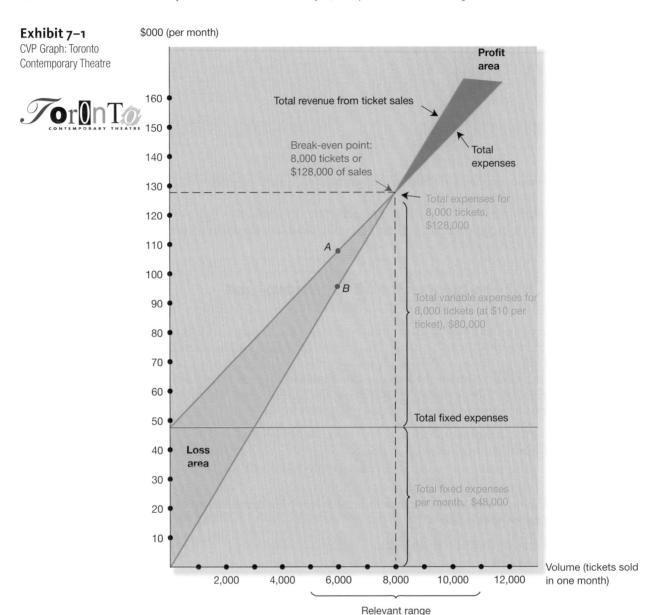

for the month at 8,000 tickets, or $128,000 of ticket sales. This agrees with our calculations in the preceding section.

Profit and Loss Areas   The CVP graph discloses more information than the break-even calculation. From the graph, a manager can see the effects on profit of changes in volume. The vertical distance between the lines on the graph represents the profit or loss at a particular sales volume. If the Toronto Contemporary Theatre sells fewer than 8,000 tickets in a month, the organization will suffer a loss. The magnitude of the loss increases as ticket sales decline. The theatre organization will have a profit if sales exceed 8,000 tickets in a month.

Implications of the Break-Even Point   The position of the break-even point within an organization's relevant range of activity provides important information to management. The Toronto Contemporary Theatre building seats 450 people. The agreement with the City of Toronto calls for 20 performances during each play's one-month run. So the maximum number of tickets that can be sold each month is 9,000 (450 seats × 20 performances).

The organization's break-even point is quite close to the maximum possible sales volume. This could be cause for concern in a nonprofit organization operating on limited resources.

What might management do to improve this situation? One possibility is to renegotiate with the City to schedule additional performances. However, this might not be feasible, because the actors need some rest each week. Also, additional performances would likely entail additional costs, such as increased theatre-rental expenses and increased compensation for the actors and production crew. Other possible solutions are to raise ticket prices or reduce costs. These kinds of issues will be explored later in the chapter.

The CVP graph will not resolve this potential problem for the management of the Toronto Contemporary Theatre. However, the graph will *direct management's attention* to the situation.

Alternative Format for the CVP Graph

An alternative format for the CVP graph, preferred by some managers, is displayed in Exhibit 7–2. The key difference is that fixed expenses are graphed above (and parallel to) variable expenses, instead of the reverse as they were in Exhibit 7–1.

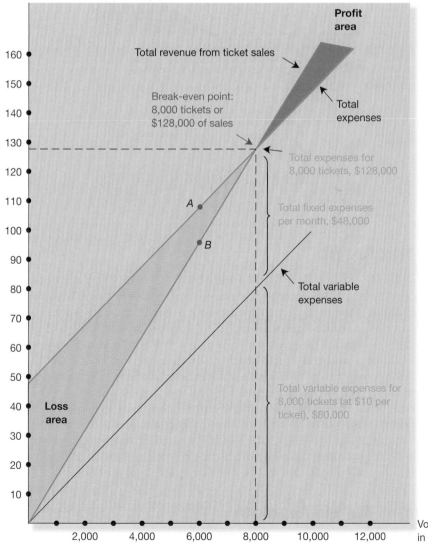

Exhibit 7–2

Alternative Format for CVP Graph: Toronto Contemporary Theatre

Profit–Volume Graph

Yet another approach to graphing CVP relationships is displayed in Exhibit 7–3. This format is called a **profit–volume graph**, since it highlights the amount of profit or loss. Notice that the graph intercepts the vertical axis at the amount equal to fixed expenses at the zero activity level. The graph crosses the horizontal axis at the break-even point. The vertical distance between the horizontal axis and the profit line, at a particular level of sales volume, is the profit or loss at that volume.

Exhibit 7–3

Profit–Volume Graph:
Toronto Contemporary
Theatre

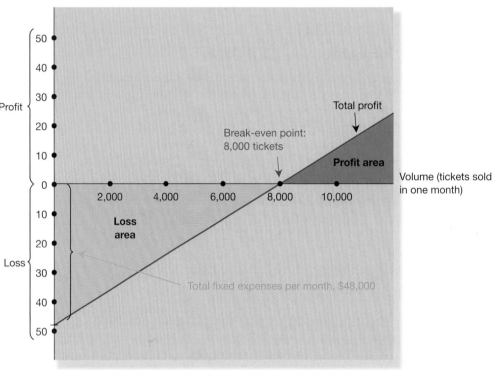

[**Target Net Profit**]

The board of trustees for the Toronto Contemporary Theatre would like to run free workshops and classes for young actors and aspiring playwrights. This program would cost $3,600 per month in fixed expenses, including teachers' salaries and rental of space at a local college. No variable expenses would be incurred. If the Toronto Contemporary Theatre could make a profit of $3,600 per month on its performances, the Toronto Drama Workshop could be opened. The board has asked Andrew Lloyd, the organization's business manager and producer, to determine how many theatre tickets must be sold during each play's one-month run to make a profit of $3,600.

The desired profit level of $3,600 is called a **target net profit** (or **income**). The problem of computing the volume of sales required to earn a particular target net profit is very similar to the problem of finding the break-even point. After all, the break-even point is the number of units of sales required to earn a target net profit of zero.

Contribution-Margin Approach

Each ticket sold by the Toronto Contemporary Theatre has a unit contribution margin of $6 (sales price of $16 minus unit variable expense of $10). Eight thousand of these $6 contributions will contribute just enough to cover fixed expenses of $48,000. *Each* *additional ticket sold will contribute $6 toward profit.* So we can modify formula (1), given earlier in this chapter, as follows:

$$\frac{\text{Fixed expenses} + \text{Target net profit}}{\text{Unit contribution margin}} = \begin{array}{c}\text{Number of sales units required}\\ \text{to earn target net profit}\end{array} \qquad (5)$$

$$\frac{\$48,000 + \$3,600}{\$6} = 8,600 \text{ tickets}$$

If the Toronto Contemporary Theatre sells 8,600 tickets during each play's one-month run, the organization will make a monthly profit of $3,600 on its performances. This profit can be used to fund the Toronto Drama Workshop. The total dollar sales required to earn a target net profit is found by modifying formula (2) given previously:

$$\frac{\text{Fixed expenses} + \text{Target net profit}}{\text{Contribution-margin ratio}} = \begin{array}{c}\text{Dollar sales required to earn}\\ \text{target net profit}\end{array} \qquad (6)$$

$$\frac{\$48,000 + \$3,600}{0.375} = \$137,600$$

where the contribution margin ratio $= \dfrac{\$6}{\$16} = 0.375$

This dollar sales figure also can be found by multiplying the required sales of 8,600 tickets by the ticket price of $16 (8,600 × $16 = $137,600).

Equation Approach

The equation approach also can be used to find the units of sales required to earn a target net profit. We can modify the profit equation given previously as follows:

$$\left[\begin{pmatrix}\text{Unit}\\ \text{sales}\\ \text{price}\end{pmatrix} \times \begin{pmatrix}\text{Sales volume}\\ \text{required to}\\ \text{earn target}\\ \text{net profit}\end{pmatrix}\right] - \left[\begin{pmatrix}\text{Unit}\\ \text{variable}\\ \text{expense}\end{pmatrix} \times \begin{pmatrix}\text{Sales volume}\\ \text{required to}\\ \text{earn target}\\ \text{net profit}\end{pmatrix}\right]$$

$$- \begin{pmatrix}\text{Fixed}\\ \text{expenses}\end{pmatrix} = \text{Target net profit}$$

Filling in the values for the Toronto Contemporary Theatre, we have the following equation:

$$(\$16 \times X) - (\$10 \times X) - \$48,000 = \$3,600 \qquad (7)$$

where X denotes the sales volume required to earn the target net profit.

Equation (7) can be solved for X as follows:

$$\$16X - \$10X - \$48,000 = \$3,600$$

$$\$6X = \$51,600$$

$$X = \frac{\$51,600}{\$6} = 8,600$$

Graphical Approach

The profit–volume graph in Exhibit 7–3 also can be used to find the sales volume required to earn a target net profit. First, locate the Toronto Contemporary Theatre's target net profit of $3,600 on the vertical axis. Then move horizontally until the profit line is reached. Finally, move down from the profit line to the horizontal axis to determine the required sales volume.

Applying CVP Analysis

The CVP relationships that underlie break-even calculations and CVP graphs have wide-ranging applications in management. We will look at several common applications illustrated by the Toronto Contemporary Theatre.

Safety Margin

The **safety margin** is the difference between the budgeted sales revenue and the break-even sales revenue. Suppose the Toronto Contemporary Theatre's business manager expects every performance of each play to be sold out. Then budgeted monthly sales revenue is $144,000 (450 seats × 20 performances of each play × $16 per ticket). Since break-even sales revenue is $128,000, the organization's safety margin is $16,000 ($144,000 − $128,000). The safety margin gives management a feel for how close the projected operations are to the organization's break-even point. We will further discuss the safety margin concept later in the chapter.

Changes in Fixed Expenses

What would happen to the Toronto Contemporary Theatre's break-even point if fixed expenses change? Suppose the business manager is concerned that the estimate for fixed utilities expenses, $1,400 per month, is too low. What would happen to the break-even point if fixed utilities expenses prove to be $2,600 instead? The break-even calculations for both the original and the new estimate of fixed utilities expenses are as follows:

	Original Estimate	New Estimate
Fixed utilities expenses..	$ 1,400	$ 2,600
Total fixed expenses..	$48,000	$49,200
Break-even calculation...	$48,000	$49,200
(Fixed expenses ÷ Unit contribution margin)	$6	$6
Break-even point (units)	8,000 tickets	8,200 tickets
Break-even point (dollars)..	$128,000	$131,200

The estimate of fixed expenses has increased by 2.5 percent, since $1,200 ($49,200 − $48,000) is 2.5 percent of $48,000. Notice that the break-even point also increased by 2.5 percent (200 additional tickets represent 2.5 percent of 8,000 tickets). This relationship will always exist.

$$\frac{\text{Fixed expenses}}{\text{Unit contribution margin}} = \text{Break-even point (in units)}$$

$$\frac{\text{Fixed expenses} \times 1.025}{\text{Unit contribution margin}} = (\text{Break-even point in units}) \times 1.025$$

Donations to Offset Fixed Expenses   Nonprofit organizations often receive cash donations from people or organizations that want to support a worthy cause. A donation is equivalent to a reduction in fixed expenses, and it reduces the organization's break-even point.

In our original set of data, the Toronto Contemporary Theatre's monthly fixed expenses total $48,000. Suppose that various people pledge donations amounting to $6,000 per month. The new break-even point is computed as follows:

$$\frac{\text{Fixed expenses} - \text{Donations}}{\text{Unit contribution margin}} = \text{Break-even point (in units)}$$

$$\frac{\$48,000 - \$6,000}{\$6} = 7,000 \text{ tickets}$$

Changes in the Unit Contribution Margin

What would happen to the Toronto Contemporary Theatre's break-even point if miscellaneous variable expenses were $3 per ticket instead of $2? Alternatively, what would be the effect of raising the ticket price to $18?

Change in Unit Variable Expenses　If the theatre organization's miscellaneous variable expenses increase from $2 to $3 per ticket, the unit contribution margin will decrease from $6 to $5. The original and new break-even points are computed as follows:

	Original Estimate	New Estimate
Miscellaneous variable expenses	$2 per ticket	$ 3 per ticket
Unit contribution margin	$6	$5
Break-even calculation	$48,000	$48,000
(Fixed expenses ÷ Unit contribution margin)	$6	$5
Break-even point (units)	8,000 tickets	9,600 tickets
Break-even point (dollars)	$128,000	$153,600

If this change in unit variable expenses actually occurs, it will no longer be possible for the organization to break even. Only 9,000 tickets are available for each play's one-month run (450 seats × 20 performances), but 9,600 tickets would have to be sold to break even. Once again, CVP analysis will not solve this problem for management, but it will direct management's attention to potentially serious difficulties.

Change in Sales Price　Changing the unit sales price will also alter the unit contribution margin. Suppose the ticket price is raised from $16 to $18. This change will increase the unit contribution margin from $6 to $8. The new break-even point will be 6,000 tickets ($48,000 ÷ $8).

A $2 increase in the ticket price will lower the break-even point from 8,000 tickets to 6,000 tickets. Is this change desirable? A lower break-even point decreases the risk of operating with a loss if sales are sluggish. However, the organization may be more likely to at least break even with a $16 ticket price than with an $18 ticket price. The reason is that the lower ticket price encourages more people to attend the theatre's performances. It could be that break-even sales of 8,000 tickets at $16 are more likely than break-even sales of 6,000 tickets at $18. Ultimately, the desirability of the ticket price increase depends on management's assessment of the likely reaction of theatre patrons.

Management's decision about the ticket price increase also will reflect the fundamental goals of the Toronto Contemporary Theatre. This nonprofit drama organization was formed to bring contemporary drama to the people of Toronto. The lower the ticket price, the more accessible the theatre's productions will be to people at all income levels.

The point of this discussion is that CVP analysis provides valuable information, but it is only one of several elements that influence management's decisions.

Predicting Profit Given Expected Volume

So far, we have focused on finding the required sales volume to break even or achieve a particular target net profit. So we have posed the following problem:

Given: $\left\{\begin{array}{l}\text{Fixed expenses} \\ \text{Unit contribution margin} \\ \text{Target net profit}\end{array}\right\}$ Find: {Required sales volume}

We also can use CVP analysis to turn this problem around:

Given: $\left\{\begin{array}{l}\text{Fixed expenses} \\ \text{Unit contribution margin} \\ \text{Expected sales volume}\end{array}\right\}$ Find: {Expected profit}

Suppose the management of the Toronto Contemporary Theatre expects fixed monthly expenses of $48,000 and unit variable expenses of $10 per ticket. The organization's board of trustees is considering two different ticket prices, and the business manager has forecast monthly demand at each price:

Ticket Price	Forecast Monthly Demand
$16	9,000
$20	6,000

Expected profit may be calculated at each price as shown in the following table. In these profit calculations, the *total contribution margin* is the difference between *total* sales revenue and *total* variable expenses. This use of the term *contribution margin* is a "total" concept rather than the "per-unit" concept used earlier in the chapter. The *total contribution margin* is the *total* amount left to contribute to covering fixed expenses after *total* variable expenses have been covered.

	Ticket Price	
	$16	**$20**
Sales revenue:		
9,000 × $16	$144,000	
6,000 × $20		$120,000
Less variable expenses:		
9,000 × $10	90,000	
6,000 × $10		60,000
Total contribution margin	$ 54,000	$ 60,000
Less fixed expenses	48,000	48,000
Profit	$ 6,000	$ 12,000

The difference in expected profit at the two ticket prices is due to two factors:

1. A different *unit* contribution margin, defined previously as *unit* sales price minus *unit* variable expenses
2. A different sales volume

Incremental Approach   Rather than presenting the entire income statement under each ticket price alternative, we can use a simpler incremental approach. This analysis focuses only on the difference in the total contribution margin under the two prices. So the combined effect of the change in unit contribution margin and the change in sales volume is as follows:

Expected *total* contribution margin at a $20 ticket price:	
6.000 × ($20 − $10)	$60,000
Expected *total* contribution margin at a $16 ticket price:	
9.000 × ($16 − $10)	54,000
Difference in *total* contribution margin...	$ 6,000

The $6,000 difference in expected profit, at the two ticket prices, is due to a $6,000 difference in the total contribution margin. The board of trustees will consider these projected profits as it decides which ticket price is best. Even though the Toronto Contemporary Theatre is a nonprofit organization, it may still have legitimate reasons for attempting to make a profit on its theatre performances. For example, the board might use these profits to fund a free drama workshop, provide scholarships for local young people to study drama in college, or produce a free outdoor play for Toronto's residents.

Interdependent Changes in Key Variables

Sometimes a change in one key variable will cause a change in another key variable. Suppose the board of trustees is choosing between ticket prices of $16 and $20, and the business manager has projected demand as shown in the preceding section. A famous retired actress who lives in Toronto has offered to donate $10,000 per month to the Toronto Contemporary Theatre if the board will set the ticket price at $16. The actress is interested in making the theatre's performances affordable for as many people as possible. The facts are now as follows:

Ticket Price	Unit Contribution Margin	Forecast Monthly Demand	Net Fixed Expenses (after subtracting donation)
$16	$ 6	9,000	$38,000 ($48,000 − $10,000)
20	10	6,000	48,000

The organization's expected profit at each price is computed as follows:

	Ticket Price	
	$16	**$20**
Sales revenue:		
9,000 × $16...	$144,000	
6,000 × $20...		$120,000
Less variable expenses:		
9,000 × $10...	90,000	
6,000 × $10...		60,000
Total contribution margin..	$ 54,000	$ 60,000
Less fixed expenses..	38,000	48,000
Profit...	$ 16,000	$ 12,000

Now the difference in expected profit at the two ticket prices is due to three factors:

1. A different *unit* contribution margin
2. A different sales volume
3. A difference in the *net* fixed expenses, after deducting the donation

Incremental Approach   The combined effect of these factors is shown in the following analysis, which focuses on the effects of the price alternatives on the total contribution margin and the net fixed expenses:

Expected *total* contribution margin at $20 ticket price:	
6,000 × ($20 − $10)	$60,000
Expected *total* contribution margin at $16 ticket price:	
9,000 × ($16 − $10)	54,000
Difference in *total* contribution margin (higher with $20 ticket price)	$ 6,000
Net fixed expenses at $20 ticket price..	$48,000
Net fixed expenses at $16 ticket price..	38,000
Difference in net fixed expenses (higher with $20 ticket price)	$10,000

The expected total contribution margin is $6,000 higher with the $20 ticket price, but net fixed expenses are $10,000 higher. So the Toronto Contemporary Theatre will make $4,000 more in profit at the $16 price ($10,000 − $6,000).

Indifference Point

CVP analysis can compare alternative cost structures or selling prices and determine the point at which management would be indifferent between the alternatives. An **indifference point** is the level of activity at which equal cost or profit occurs across two or more alternatives. Using the previous example and keeping in mind that only 9,000 tickets are available for each play's one-month run, let's compute the level of activity at which the Toronto Contemporary Theatre would be indifferent between the two proposed ticket prices. Q denotes such level of activity (number of tickets to be sold) and UCM stands for *unit contribution margin*.

Option 1 $20 tickets		Option 2 $16 tickets
Profit	=	Profit
$UCM \times Q$ – Fixed costs	=	$UCM \times Q$ – Fixed costs
($20 − $10) × Q − $48,000	=	($16 – $10) × Q − $38,000
10Q$ − $48,000	=	6Q$ – $38,000

So the indifference point Q can be computed as follows:

Q ($10 − $6)	=	$48,000 − $38,000
4Q$	=	$10,000
Q	=	2,500 tickets

We can also verify this level of activity using a profit–volume graph. Notice that, at a level of 2,500 tickets, both options will result in a loss of $23,000 ($10 × 2,500 − $48,000). Beyond this level, the profit of option 1 ($20 ticket) will rise faster than that of option 2.

Fixed cost

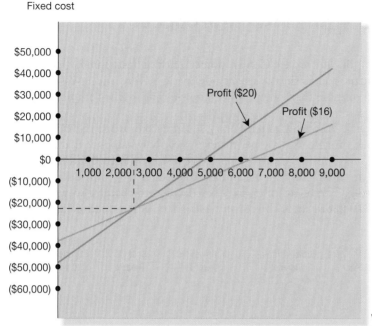

Volume (tickets sold in one month)

CVP Information in Annual Reports

CVP relationships are so important to understanding an organization's operations that some companies disclose CVP information in their published annual reports. The Managerial Accounting Practice feature here is from the airline industry.

Managerial Accounting Practice

British Airways, JetBlue, Air France, and Sabena

AIRLINES KEEP A CLOSE EYE ON BREAK-EVEN LOAD FACTORS[2, 3]

Airlines generally disclose their systemwide break-even load factors in their annual reports. British Airways, for example, listed its break-even load factor as 64 percent in an annual report. The large airlines, like British Airways, usually fill a smaller percentage of their seats than the upstart, discount airlines. JetBlue is a good example. "The low-fare, low-cost carrier . . . now operates more than 100 flights a day to 18 cities in nine states." Its load factor, or percentage of seats filled, is 76 percent.

"Air France has been able to make up for cutting Dallas and Miami flights with more flights and larger planes to African cities. The airline has also expanded its service to many French-speaking former destinations in the Caribbean and the Indian Ocean. Together with Africa, the former colonies should account for almost the same amount of Air France's revenue this year as North America, analysts say. Still, the operating costs of flying to Africa are 50 percent higher for Air France than flying to the U.S., and the logistical problems are much more challenging."

In past years, "Sabena [the former Belgian Airlines operating as Brussels Airlines since 2006] lost at least 8 percent on its flights to the U.S., but had margins above 10 percent on routes to its former colonies Congo, Rwanda, and Burundi, according to an internal Sabena study. That kind of difference in profit margins is common. Across the busy North Atlantic, where competition and seasonal variation force heavy discounting, all airlines are lucky to break even with a plane 75 percent full. For Kinshasa and other parts of Africa, where traffic is steadier, European carriers can break even with their planes barely 60 percent full, and planes often fly 85 percent full."

CVP Analysis with Multiple Products

Our CVP illustration for the Toronto Contemporary Theatre has assumed that the organization has only one product: a theatre seat at a dramatic performance. Most firms have a *sales mix* consisting of more than one product, and this adds some complexity to their CVP analyses.

As we have seen, the Toronto Contemporary Theatre's monthly fixed expenses total $48,000, and the unit variable expense per ticket is $10. Now suppose that the City of Toronto has agreed to refurbish 10 theatre boxes in the historic theatre building. Each box has five seats, which are more comfortable and afford a better view of the stage than the theatre's general seating. The board of trustees has decided to charge $16 per ticket for general seating and $20 per ticket for box seats. These facts are summarized as follows:

Seat Type	Ticket Price	Unit Variable Expense	Unit Contribution Margin	Seats in Theatre	Seats Available per Month (20 performances)
Regular	$16	$10	$ 6	450	9,000
Box	20	10	10	50	1,000

Notice that 90 percent of the available seats are regular seats, and 10 percent are box seats. The business manager estimates that tickets for each type of seat will be sold in the same proportion as the number of seats available. If, for example, 5,000 tickets are sold during a month, sales will be as follows:

Regular seats:	90% × 5,000	4,500
Box seats:	10% × 5,000	500
Total		5,000

For any organization selling multiple products, the relative proportion of each type of product *sold* is called the **sales mix**. The business manager's estimate of the Toronto Contemporary Theatre's *sales mix* is 90 percent regular seats and 10 percent box seats.

The sales mix is an important assumption in multiproduct CVP analysis. The sales mix is used to compute a **weighted-average unit contribution margin**. This is the *average* of the several products' *unit contribution margins, weighted* by the relative sales proportion of each product. The Toronto Contemporary Theatre's weighted-average unit contribution margin is computed as follows:

$$\text{Weighted-average unit contribution margin} = (\$6 \times 90\%) + (\$10 \times 10\%) = \$6.40$$

The organization's break-even point in units is computed using the following formula:

$$\text{Break-even point} = \frac{\text{Fixed expenses}}{\text{Weighted-average unit contribution margin}} \qquad (8)$$

$$= \frac{\$48,000}{\$6.40} = 7,500 \text{ tickets}$$

The break-even point of 7,500 tickets must be interpreted in light of the sales mix. The Toronto Contemporary Theatre will break even for the month if it sells 7,500 tickets as follows:

Break-even sales in units	Regular seats: 7,500 × 90%	6,750 tickets
	Box seats: 7,500 × 10%	750 tickets
	Total	7,500 tickets

The following income calculation verifies the break-even point:

Sales revenue:	
Regular seats: 6,750 × $16	$108,000
Box seats: 750 × $20	15,000
Total Revenue: 7,500 seats in total	$123,000
Less variable expenses: 7,500 × $10	75,000
Total contribution margin	$ 48,000
Less fixed expenses	48,000
Profit	$ 0

The break-even point of 7,500 tickets per month is *valid only for the sales mix assumed* in computing the weighted-average unit contribution margin. If 7,500 tickets are sold in any other mix of regular and box seats, the organization will not break even.

Notice that break-even formula (8) is a modification of formula (1) given earlier. The only difference is that formula (8) uses the weighted-average unit contribution margin.

The Toronto Contemporary Theatre's business manager has constructed the profit–volume graph in Exhibit 7–4. The PV graph shows the organization's profit at any level of total monthly sales, assuming the sales mix of 90 percent regular seats and 10 percent box seats. For example, if 9,000 tickets are sold in total, at the assumed sales mix, the PV graph indicates that profit will be $9,600.

With multiproduct CVP analysis, a management accountant can investigate the impact on profit of changes in sales volume, prices, variable costs, fixed costs, or the sales mix itself. For example, what would be the effect on the Toronto Contemporary Theatre's break-even point if the sales mix was 95 percent regular seats and 5 percent box seats? With this sales mix, the weighted-average unit contribution margin is computed as follows:

$$\text{Weighted-average unit contribution margin} = (\$6 \times 95\%) + (\$10 \times 5\%) = \$6.20$$

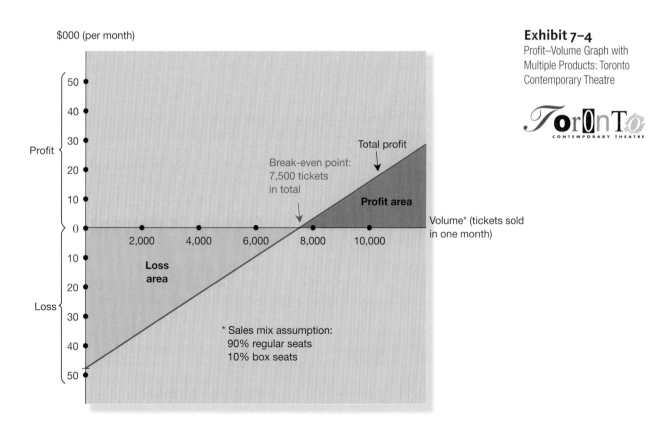

Exhibit 7–4
Profit–Volume Graph with Multiple Products: Toronto Contemporary Theatre

The break-even point increases from 7,500 tickets to approximately 7,742 tickets as a result of the lower proportion of expensive seats in the sales mix:

$$\text{Break-even point} = \frac{\text{Fixed expenses}}{\text{Weighted-average unit contribution margin}}$$

$$= \frac{\$48,000}{\$6.20} = 7,742 \text{ tickets*}$$

*Rounded.

Assumptions of CVP Analysis

For any CVP analysis to be valid, the following important assumptions must be reasonably satisfied *within the relevant range*:

1. The behaviour of total revenue is linear (straight-line). This implies that the price of the product or service will not change as sales volume varies within the relevant range.
2. The behaviour of total expenses is linear (straight-line) over the relevant range. This implies the following more specific assumptions:
   a. Expenses can be categorized as fixed, variable, or mixed. *Total* fixed expenses remain constant as activity changes, and the *unit* variable expense remains unchanged as activity varies.
   b. The efficiency and productivity of the production process and workers remain constant.
3. In multiproduct organizations, the sales mix remains constant over the relevant range.
4. In manufacturing firms, the inventory levels at the beginning and end of the period are the same. This implies that the number of units produced during the period equals the number of units sold.

CVP analysis is based on the four general assumptions listed above as well as on specific estimates of all the variables used in the analysis. Since these variables are rarely known with certainty, it is helpful to run a CVP analysis many times with different combinations of estimates. For example, the Toronto Contemporary Theatre's business manager might do the CVP analysis using different estimates for the ticket prices, sales mix for regular and box seats, unit variable expenses, and fixed expenses. This approach is called **sensitivity analysis**, since it provides the analyst with a feel for how sensitive the analysis is to the estimates on which it is based. The widespread availability of personal computers and electronic spreadsheet software has made sensitivity analysis relatively easy to do.

CVP Relationships and the Income Statement

Learning Objective **6**

Prepare an income statement under absorption and variable costing, and reconcile the difference in reporting income.

The management functions of planning, control, and decision making all are facilitated by an understanding of CVP relationships. These relationships are important enough to operating managers that some businesses prepare income statements in a way that highlights CVP issues.

Income is one of many important measures used to evaluate the performance of companies and segments of companies. There are two commonly used methods for determining product costs and reporting income in a manufacturing firm, depending on the accounting treatment of fixed manufacturing overhead. We will examine these two income-reporting alternatives, called *absorption costing* and *variable costing*. In addition, we will study a third alternative for product costing and income reporting, called *throughput costing*.

Product Costs

In the product-costing systems we have studied so far, manufacturing overhead is applied to work-in-process inventory as a product cost along with direct material and direct labour. When the manufactured goods are finished, these product costs flow from work-in-process inventory into finished-goods inventory. Finally, during the accounting period when the goods are sold, the product costs flow from finished-goods inventory into cost of goods sold, an expense account. The following diagram summarizes this flow of costs.

Since the costs of production are stored in inventory accounts until the goods are sold, these costs are said to be *inventoried costs*.

Fixed Manufacturing Overhead: The Key   In our study of product-costing systems, we have included both variable and fixed manufacturing overhead in the product costs that flow through the manufacturing accounts. This approach to product costing is called **absorption costing** (or **full costing**), because *all* manufacturing-overhead costs are applied to (or absorbed by) manufactured goods. An alternative approach to product costing is called **variable costing** (or **direct costing**), in which only variable manufacturing overhead is applied to work-in-process inventory as a product cost.

The distinction between absorption and variable costing is summarized in Exhibit 7–5. Notice that the distinction involves the timing with which fixed manufacturing overhead becomes an expense. Eventually, fixed overhead is expensed under both product-costing

Exhibit 7–5
Absorption versus Variable Costing

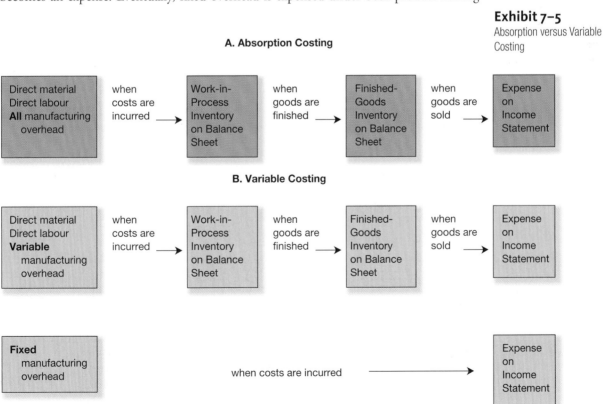

systems. Under variable costing, however, fixed overhead is expensed immediately, as it is incurred. Under absorption costing, fixed overhead is inventoried until the accounting period during which the manufactured goods are sold.

Absorption and Variable Costing Illustrated

Quik**math**.com began operations on January 1, 20x0, to manufacture hand-held electronic calculators. Cost, production, and sales data for the first three years of Quik**math**'s operations are given in Exhibit 7–6. Comparative income statements for 20x0, 20x1, and 20x2 are presented in Exhibit 7–7, using both absorption and variable costing.

Absorption-Costing Income Statements

Examine the absorption-costing income statements in the upper half of Exhibit 7–7. Two features of these income statements are particularly worth noting. First, notice that the

cost of goods sold expense for each year is determined by multiplying the year's sales by the absorption manufacturing cost per unit, $9. Included in the $9 cost per unit is the predetermined fixed manufacturing-overhead cost of $3 per unit. Second, notice that on Quik**math**'s absorption-costing income statements, the only period expenses are the selling and administrative expenses. There is no deduction of fixed-overhead costs as a lump-sum period expense at the bottom of each income statement. As mentioned above, fixed manufacturing-overhead costs are included in cost of goods sold on these absorption-costing income statements.

The fixed costs of operating this truck manufacturing plant include such costs as the depreciation on plant and equipment, property taxes, insurance, and the salary of the plant manager. Fixed manufacturing costs are incurred in order to generate production capacity. Under absorption costing, these costs are treated as product costs and included in the cost of inventory. Under variable costing, they are expensed during the period in which they are incurred.

Variable-Costing Income Statements

Now examine the income statements based on variable costing in the lower half of Exhibit 7–7. Notice that the format of the statements is different from the format used in the absorption-costing statements. In the variable-costing statements, the contribution format is used to highlight the separation of variable and fixed costs. Let's focus on the same two aspects of the variable-costing statements that we discussed for the absorption-costing statements. First, the manufacturing expenses subtracted from sales revenue each year include only the variable costs, which amount to $6 per unit. Second, fixed manufacturing overhead is subtracted as a lump-sum period expense at the bottom of each year's income statement.

Reconciling Income under Absorption and Variable Costing

Examination of Exhibit 7–7 reveals that the income reported under absorption and variable costing is sometimes different. Although income is the same for the two product-costing methods in 20x0, it is different in 20x1 and 20x2. Let's figure out why these results occur.

No Change in Inventory   In 20x0 there is no change in inventory over the course of the year. Beginning and ending inventory are the same, because actual production and sales

	20x0	20x1	20x2
Production and Inventory Data			
Planned production (in units)	50,000	50,000	50,000
Finished-goods inventory (in units), January 1	–0–	–0–	15,000
Actual production (in units)	50,000	50,000	50,000
Sales (in units)	50,000	35,000	65,000
Finished-goods inventory (in units), December 31	–0–	15,000	–0–
Revenue and Cost Data, All Three Years			
Sales price per unit			$12
Manufacturing costs per unit:			
Direct material			$ 3
Direct labour			2
Variable manufacturing overhead			1
Total variable cost per unit			$ 6

Used only under absorption costing
$$\left\{\begin{array}{l}\text{Fixed manufacturing overhead:}\\ \dfrac{\text{Budgeted annual fixed overhead}}{\text{Planned annual production*}}\;\; \dfrac{\$150{,}000}{50{,}000}\\ \text{Total absorption cost per unit}\end{array}\right.$$

			3
			$ 9
Variable selling and administrative cost per unit			$ 1
Fixed selling and administrative cost per year			$25,000

Exhibit 7–6
Data for Quik**math**.com Example

Quik**math**.com

*Planned annual production of 50,000 units is management's estimate of the company's practical capacity for production.

QUIKMATH.COM
Absorption-Costing Income Statement

	20x0	20x1	20x2
Sales revenue (at $12 per unit)	$600,000	$420,000	$780,000
Less: Cost of goods sold (at absorption cost of $9 per unit)	450,000	315,000	585,000
Gross margin	$150,000	$105,000	$195,000
Less: Selling and administrative expenses:			
Variable (at $1 per unit)	50,000	35,000	65,000
Fixed	25,000	25,000	25,000
Net income	$ 75,000	$ 45,000	$105,000

QUIKMATH.COM
Variable-Costing Income Statement

	20x0	20x1	20x2
Sales revenue (at $12 per unit)	$600,000	$420,000	$780,000
Less: Variable expenses:			
Variable manufacturing costs (at variable cost of $6 per unit)	300,000	210,000	390,000
Variable selling and administrative costs (at $1 per unit)	50,000	35,000	65,000
Contribution margin	$250,000	$175,000	$325,000
Less: Fixed expenses:			
Fixed manufacturing overhead	150,000	150,000	150,000
Fixed selling and administrative expenses	25,000	25,000	25,000
Net income	$ 75,000	$ 0	$150,000

Exhibit 7–7
Income Statements under Absorption and Variable Costing

Quik**math**.com

are the same. Think about the implications of the stable inventory level for the treatment of fixed manufacturing overhead. On the variable-costing statement, the $150,000 of fixed manufacturing overhead incurred during 20x0 is an expense in 20x0. Under absorption costing, however, fixed manufacturing overhead was applied to production at the predetermined rate of $3 per unit. Since all of the units produced in 20x0 were also sold in 20x0, all of the fixed manufacturing-overhead cost flowed through into cost of goods sold. So $150,000 of fixed manufacturing overhead was expensed in 20x0 under absorption costing also.

The 20x0 column of Exhibit 7–8 reconciles the 20x0 net income reported under absorption and variable costing. The reconciliation focuses on the two places in the income statements where differences occur between absorption and variable costing.

Exhibit 7–8
Reconciliation of Income under Absorption and Variable Costing: Quik**math**.com

Quik**math**.com

	20x0	20x1	20x2
Cost of goods sold under absorption costing	$450,000	$315,000	$585,000
Variable manufacturing costs under variable costing	300,000	210,000	390,000
Subtotal	$150,000	$105,000	$195,000
Fixed manufacturing overhead as period expense under variable costing	150,000	150,000	150,000
Total	$ 0	$ (45,000)	$ 45,000
Net income under variable costing	$ 75,000	$ 0	$150,000
Net income under absorption costing	75,000	45,000	105,000
Difference in net income	$ 0	$ (45,000)	$ 45,000

Increase in Inventory   In 20x1, inventory increased from zero on January 1 to 15,000 units on December 31. The increase in inventory was the result of production exceeding sales. Under variable costing, the $150,000 of fixed overhead cost incurred in 20x1 is expensed, just as it was in 20x0. Under absorption costing, however, only a portion of the 20x1 fixed manufacturing overhead is expensed in 20x1. Since the fixed overhead is inventoried under absorption costing, some of this cost *remains in inventory* at the end of 20x1.

The 20x1 column of Exhibit 7–8 reconciles the 20x1 net income reported under absorption and variable costing. As before, the reconciliation focuses on the two places in the income statements where differences occur between absorption and variable costing.

Decrease in Inventory   In 20x2, inventory decreased from 15,000 units to zero. Sales during the year exceeded production. As in 20x0 and 20x1, under variable costing, the $150,000 of fixed manufacturing overhead incurred in 20x2 is expensed in 20x2. Under absorption costing, however, *more than* $150,000 of fixed overhead is expensed in 20x2. Why? Because some of the fixed overhead incurred during the prior year, which was inventoried then, is now expensed in 20x2 as the goods are sold.

The 20x2 column of Exhibit 7–8 reconciles the 20x2 income under absorption and variable costing.

A Shortcut to Reconciling Income   When inventory increases or decreases during the year, reported income differs under absorption and variable costing. This results from the fixed overhead that is inventoried under absorption costing but expensed immediately under variable costing. The following formula may be used to compute the difference in the amount of fixed overhead expensed in a given time period under the two product-costing methods:[4]

$$\begin{pmatrix} \text{Difference in fixed overhead} \\ \text{expensed under absorption} \\ \text{and variable costing} \end{pmatrix} = \begin{pmatrix} \text{Change in} \\ \text{inventory,} \\ \text{in units} \end{pmatrix} \times \begin{pmatrix} \text{Predetermined} \\ \text{fixed-overhead} \\ \text{rate per unit} \end{pmatrix}$$

As the following table shows, this difference in the amount of fixed overhead expensed explains the difference in reported income under absorption and variable costing:

Year	Change in Inventory (in units)		Predetermined Fixed-Overhead Rate		Difference in Fixed-Overhead Expensed		Absorption-Costing Income Minus Variable-Costing Income
20x0	—	×	$3	=	—	=	—
20x1	15,000 increase	×	$3	=	$45,000	=	$45,000
20x2	15,000 decrease	×	$3	=	$(45,000)	=	$(45,000)

Length of Time Period   The discrepancies between absorption-costing and variable costing income in Exhibit 7–7 occur because of the changes in inventory levels during 20x1 and 20x2. It is common for production and sales to differ over the course of a week, month, or year. Therefore, the income measured for those time periods often will differ between absorption and variable costing. This discrepancy is likely to be smaller over longer time periods. Over the course of a decade, for example, Quik**math**.com cannot sell much more or less than it produces. So the income amounts under the two product-costing methods, when added together over a lengthy time period, will be approximately equal under absorption and variable costing.

Notice in Exhibit 7–7 that Quik**math**.com's total income over the three-year period is $225,000 under *both* absorption and variable costing. This results from the fact that the company produced and sold the same total amount over the three-year period.

Cost–Volume–Profit Analysis

Learning Objective   **7**

Explain the implications of absorption and variable costing for CVP, and evaluate both product-costing systems.

Quik**math**.com's break-even point in units can be computed as follows:

$$\text{Break-even point} = \frac{\text{Fixed costs}}{\text{Unit contribution margin}} = \frac{\$150,000 + \$25,000}{\$12 - \$6 - \$1}$$

$$= \frac{\$175,000}{\$5} = 35,000 \text{ units}$$

If Quik**math**.com sells 35,000 calculators, net income should be zero, as Exhibit 7–9 confirms.

Exhibit 7–9
Break-Even Graph:
Quik**math**.com

Quik**math**.com

Now return to Exhibit 7–7 and examine the 20x1 income statements under absorption and variable costing. In 20x1 Quik**math**.com sold 35,000 units, the break-even volume. This fact is confirmed on the variable-costing income statement, since net income is zero. On the absorption-costing income statement, however, the 20x1 net income is $45,000. What has happened here?

The answer to this inconsistency lies in the different treatment of fixed manufacturing overhead under absorption and variable costing. Variable costing highlights the separation between fixed and variable costs, as do CVP analysis and break-even calculations. Both of these techniques account for fixed manufacturing overhead as a lump sum. In contrast, *absorption costing is inconsistent with CVP analysis*, because fixed overhead is applied to goods as a product cost on a per-unit basis.

Evaluation of Absorption and Variable Costing

Some managers find the inconsistency between absorption costing and CVP analysis troubling enough to warrant using variable costing for internal income reporting. Variable costing dovetails much more closely than absorption costing with any operational analyses that require a separation between fixed and variable costs.

Pricing Decisions   Many managers prefer to use absorption-costing data in cost-based pricing decisions. They argue that fixed manufacturing overhead is a necessary cost incurred in the production process. To exclude this fixed cost from the inventoried cost of a product, as is done under variable costing, is to understate the cost of the product. For this reason, most companies that use cost-based pricing set up their prices on absorption-costing data.

Proponents of variable costing argue that a product's variable cost provides a better basis for the pricing decision. They point out that any price above a product's variable cost makes a positive contribution to covering fixed cost and profit.

Definition of an Asset   Another controversy about absorption and variable costing hinges on the definition of an asset. An *asset* is a thing of value with future service potential that is owned by the organization. By accounting convention, assets are valued at their cost. Since fixed costs make up part of the cost of production, advocates of absorption costing argue that inventory (an asset) should be valued at its full (absorption) cost of production. Moreover, they argue that these costs have future service potential since the inventory can be sold in the future to generate sales revenue.

Proponents of variable costing argue that the fixed-cost component of a product's absorption-costing value has no future service potential. Their reasoning is that the fixed manufacturing-overhead costs during the current period will not prevent these costs from having to be incurred again next period. Fixed-overhead costs will be incurred every period, regardless of production levels. In contrast, the incurrence of variable costs in manufacturing a product does allow the firm to avoid incurring these costs again.

To illustrate, Quik**math**.com produced 15,000 more calculators in 20x1 than it sold. These units will be carried in inventory until they are sold in some future year. Quik**math**.com will never again have to incur the costs of direct material, direct labour, and variable overhead incurred in 20x1 to produce those calculators. Yet Quik**math**.com will have to incur approximately $150,000 of fixed-overhead costs every year, even though the firm has the 15,000 units from 20x1 in inventory.

External Reporting   For external reporting purposes, generally accepted accounting principles require that income reporting be based on absorption costing. Tax laws allow either direct costing or absorption costing as acceptable methods of inventory costing in reporting income for tax purposes.[5]

Why Not Both?   In the age of computerized accounting systems, it is straightforward for a company to prepare income statements under both absorption and variable costing.

Since absorption-costing statements are required for external reporting, managers will want to keep an eye on the effects of their decisions on financial reports to outsiders. Yet the superiority of variable-costing income reporting as a method for dovetailing with operational analyses cannot be denied. Preparation of both absorption-costing and variable-costing data is perhaps the best solution to the controversy.

JIT Manufacturing Environment   In a just-in-time inventory and production management system, all inventories are kept very low. Since finished-goods inventories are minimal, there is little change in inventory from period to period. So in a JIT environment, the income differences under absorption and variable costing generally will be insignificant.

Throughput Costing

Learning Objective   **8**

Explain throughput costing and prepare an income statement using this costing approach.

Some managers advocate *throughput costing* as an alternative to either absorption or variable costing for product costing and income reporting. **Throughput costing** assigns *only* the unit-level *spending* for direct costs as the cost of products or services. A unit-level cost is one that is incurred every time a unit of product is manufactured and that will *not* be incurred if another unit is not manufactured.[6] Advocates of throughput costing argue that classifying any other past or committed cost as a product cost creates an incentive to drive down the average cost per unit simply by manufacturing more units on nonbottleneck processes.

Suppose Quik**math**.com's management team decided that only direct material qualified as a throughput cost. This implies that Quik**math**.com's management has *committed*, at least for the time being, to provide *all* other resources (i.e., direct labour and all manufacturing support costs included in manufacturing overhead) regardless of how many calculators and other devices Quik**math**.com produces. Under throughput costing, then, Quik**math**.com's income statements for the three years in our example would appear as in the Excel spreadsheet shown in Exhibit 7–10. Notice that all costs other than the throughput cost (only direct material in this hypothetical example) are considered to be operating costs of the period.

Exhibit 7–10

Income Statements under Throughput Costing

Quik**math**.com

	A	B	C	D	E
1	QUIKMATH.COM				
2	Throughput-Costing Income Statement				
3					
4			20x0	20x1	20x2
5					
6	Sales revenue (at $12 per unit)		$ 600,000	$ 420,000	$ 780,000
7	Less: Cost of goods sold (at throughput cost:				
8	standard direct-material cost)[a]		150,000	105,000	195,000
9	Gross margin		$ 450,000	$ 315,000	$ 585,000
10	Less: Operating costs:				
11	Direct labour[b]		$ 100,000	$ 100,000	$ 100,000
12	Variable manufacturing overhead[c]		50,000	50,000	50,000
13	Fixed manufacturing overhead[c]		150,000	150,000	150,000
14	Variable selling and administrative costs[d]		50,000	35,000	65,000
15	Fixed selling and administrative costs[d]		25,000	25,000	25,000
16	Total operating costs		$ 375,000	$ 360,000	$ 390,000
17	Net income		$ 75,000	$ (45,000)	$ 195,000
18					
19	[a]Standard direct-material cost per unit of $3 multiplied by sales volume in units.				
20					
21	[b]Assumes management has committed to direct labour sufficient to produce the planned annual production				
22	volume of 50,000; direct-labour cost is used at a rate of $2 per unit produced.				
23					
24	[c]Assumes management has committed to support resources sufficient to produce the planned annual				
25	production volume of 50,000 units; variable-overhead cost is used at a rate of $1 per unit produced. Fixed				
26	overhead is $150,000 per year.				
27					
28	[d]Variable selling and administrative costs used amount to $1 per unit sold. Fixed selling and				
29	administrative costs are $25,000 per year.				

A comparison of the reported income under throughput costing with the reported income under either variable or absorption costing reveals substantial differences in the "bottom line" under the three methods for each year. Proponents of throughput costing argue that this method alone eliminates the incentive to produce excess inventory simply to reduce unit costs by spreading *committed* resource costs (i.e., direct labour and variable and fixed manufacturing overhead) across more units. The incentive for such overproduction disappears under throughput costing, because all nonthroughput costs (direct labour and manufacturing overhead in our example) will be expensed as period costs regardless of how many units are produced.

Cost Structure and Operating Leverage

Learning Objective   **9**

Explain the role of cost structure and operating leverage in CVP relationships.

The **cost structure** of an organization is the relative proportion of its fixed and variable costs. Cost structures differ widely among industries and among firms within an industry. A company using a computer-integrated manufacturing system has a large investment in plant and equipment, which results in a cost structure dominated by fixed costs. In contrast, a cleaning service firm's cost structure has a much higher proportion of variable costs. The highly automated manufacturing firm is capital-intensive, whereas the service firm is labour-intensive.

An organization's cost structure has a significant effect on the sensitivity of its profit to changes in volume. A convenient way to portray a firm's cost structure is shown in the Excel spreadsheet in Exhibit 7–11.[7] The variable-costing income statement for AccuTime Company (Company A), a manufacturer of digital clocks, is presented along with those of two other companies. Although these three firms have the same sales revenue ($500,000) and net income ($50,000), they have very different cost structures. Company B's production process is largely manual, and its cost structure is dominated by variable costs. It has a low contribution-margin ratio of only 20 percent. In contrast, Company C uses a highly automated production process, and its cost structure is dominated by fixed costs. The firm's contribution-margin ratio is 90 percent. Company A falls between these two extremes, with a contribution-margin ratio of 40 percent.

Suppose sales revenue increases by 10 percent, or $50,000, in each company. The resulting increase in each company's profit is calculated in Exhibit 7–12. Notice that Company B, with its high variable expenses and low contribution-margin ratio, shows a relatively low *percentage* increase in profit. In contrast, the high fixed expenses and large contribution-margin ratio of Company C result in a relatively high *percentage* increase in profit. Company A falls between these two extremes. So, the greater the proportion of fixed costs in a firm's cost structure, the greater the impact on profit will be from a given percentage change in sales revenue.

Exhibit 7–11

Comparison of
Cost Structures

AccuTime

	A	B	C	D	E	F	G
1		Company A		Company B		Company C	
2		(AccuTime Company)		(Manual System)		(Automated System)	
3							
4		Amount	%	Amount	%	Amount	%
5							
6	Sales	$ 500,000	100	$ 500,000	100	$ 500,000	100
7	Variable expenses	300,000	60	400,000	80	50,000	10
8	Contribution margin	$ 200,000	40	$ 100,000	20	$ 450,000	90
9	Fixed expenses	150,000	30	50,000	10	400,000	80
10	Net income	$ 50,000	10	$ 50,000	10	$ 50,000	10

	$$\begin{pmatrix}\text{Increase}\\\text{In Sales}\\\text{Revenue}\end{pmatrix}$$	×	$$\begin{pmatrix}\text{Contribution}\\\text{Margin}\\\text{Ratio}\end{pmatrix}$$	=	$$\begin{pmatrix}\text{Increase}\\\text{In Net}\\\text{Income}\end{pmatrix}$$	Percentage Increase in Net Income
Company A (AccuTime)	$50,000	×	40%	=	$20,000	40% ($20,000 ÷ $50,000)
Company B (high variable expenses) ...	$50,000	×	20%	=	$10,000	20% ($10,000 ÷ $50,000)
Company C (high fixed expenses)	$50,000	×	90%	=	$45,000	90% ($45,000 ÷ $50,000)

Exhibit 7–12
Effect on Profit of Increase in Sales Revenue

Using the profit–volume graph shown below, we can easily observe that all three companies will make a profit of $50,000 with a sales level of $500,000. However, the slopes of the profit lines are all different. Company B is the first one to reach the break-even point but, with the lowest slope, any movement either above or below the break-even point does not generate great profit or loss, respectively. In contrast, Company C is the last one to reach break-even point but, having the steepest slope, any movement either above or below the break-even point will generate much larger profit and greater loss, respectively, when compared to the other two companies.

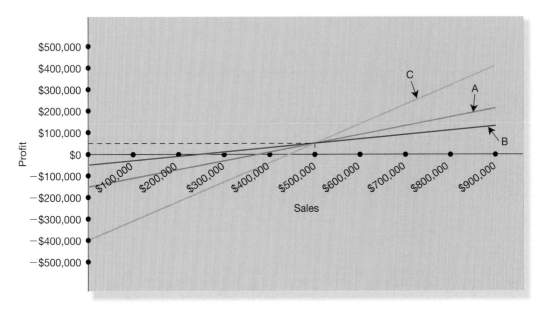

Operating Leverage

The extent to which an organization uses fixed costs in its cost structure is called **operating leverage**. The operating leverage is greatest in firms with a large proportion of fixed costs, low proportion of variable costs, and the resulting high contribution-margin ratio. Refer back to Exhibit 7–11, which shows that Company B has low operating leverage, Company C has high operating leverage, and Company A falls in between. To a physical scientist, *leverage* refers to the ability of a small force to move a heavy weight. To the management accountant, *operating leverage* refers to the ability of the firm to generate an increase in net income when sales revenue increases.

Measuring Operating Leverage   The management accountant can measure a firm's operating leverage, *at a particular sales volume*, using the **operating leverage factor**:

$$\text{Operating leverage factor} = \frac{\text{Contribution margin}}{\text{Net income}}$$

Using the data in Exhibit 7–11, the operating leverage factors of Companies A, B, and C are computed as follows:

	$\left(\begin{array}{c}\text{Contribution}\\\text{Margin}\end{array}\right)$	÷	$\left(\begin{array}{c}\text{Net}\\\text{Income}\end{array}\right)$	=	$\left(\begin{array}{c}\text{Operating}\\\text{Leverage}\\\text{Factor}\end{array}\right)$
Company A (AccuTime)	$200,000	÷	$50,000	=	4
Company B (high variable expenses)	$100,000	÷	$50,000	=	2
Company C (high fixed expenses)	$450,000	÷	$50,000	=	9

The operating leverage factor is a measure, at a particular level of sales, of the *percentage* impact on net income of a given *percentage* change in sales revenue. Multiplying the *percentage* change in sales revenue by the operating leverage factor yields the *percentage* change in net income.

	$\left(\begin{array}{c}\text{Percentage}\\\text{Increase in}\\\text{Sales Revenue}\end{array}\right)$	×	$\left(\begin{array}{c}\text{Operating}\\\text{Leverage}\\\text{Factor}\end{array}\right)$	=	$\left(\begin{array}{c}\text{Percentage}\\\text{Change in}\\\text{Net Income}\end{array}\right)$
Company A (AccuTime)	10%	×	4	=	40%
Company B (high variable expenses)	10%	×	2	=	20%
Company C (high fixed expenses)	10%	×	9	=	90%

The percentage change in net income shown above for each company can be verified by re-examining Exhibit 7–12.

Break-Even Point and Safety Margin A firm's operating leverage affects its break-even point as well. Since a firm with relatively high operating leverage has proportionally high fixed expenses, the firm's break-even point will be relatively high. This fact is illustrated using the data from Exhibit 7–11 and was shown in the profit–volume graph on the previous page.

	$\left(\begin{array}{c}\text{Fixed}\\\text{Expenses}\end{array}\right)$	÷	$\left(\begin{array}{c}\text{Contribution}\\\text{Margin Ratio}\end{array}\right)$	=	$\left(\begin{array}{c}\text{Break-Even}\\\text{Sales Revenue}\end{array}\right)$
Company A (AccuTime)	$150,000	÷	40%	=	$375,000
Company B (high variable expenses)	$ 50,000	÷	20%	=	$250,000
Company C (high fixed expenses)	$400,000	÷	90%	=	$444,444*

*Rounded.

The safety margin is also affected by a firm's operating leverage. Suppose the budgeted sales revenue for each of the three companies is $500,000. Then the safety margin, defined as budgeted sales revenue minus break-even sales revenue, is calculated as follows:

	Budgeted Sales Revenue	Break-Even Sales Revenue	Safety Margin
Company A (AccuTime)	$500,000	$375,000	$125,000
Company B (high variable expenses)	500,000	250,000	250,000
Company C (high fixed expenses)	500,000	444,444	55,556

To summarize, Company C's high fixed expenses result in a high break-even point and low safety margin. Company B displays the opposite characteristics, and Company A falls in between the two extremes.

Labour-Intensive Production Processes versus Advanced Manufacturing Systems The effects of labour-intensive (manual) production processes and highly automated,

	Budgeted Sales Revenue	Break-Even Sales Revenue	Safety Margin
Company A (AccuTime)	$500,000	$375,000	$125,000
Company B (high variable expenses)	500,000	250,000	250,000
Company C (high fixed expenses)	500,000	444,444	55,555

advanced manufacturing systems illustrated by companies A, B, and C are typical. As Exhibit 7–13 shows, a movement toward an advanced manufacturing environment often results in a higher break-even point, lower safety margin, and higher operating leverage. However, high-technology manufacturing systems generally have greater throughput, thus allowing greater potential for profitability. Along with the increased potential for profitability comes increased risk. In an economic recession, for example, a highly automated company with high fixed costs will be less able to adapt to lower consumer demand than will a firm with a more labour-intensive production process.

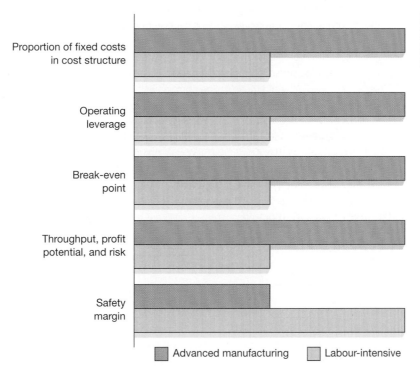

Exhibit 7–13
Labour-Intensive Production Processes versus Advanced Manufacturing Systems

Cost Structure and Operating Leverage: A Cost–Benefit Issue

An organization's cost structure plays an important role in determining its CVP relationships. A firm with proportionately high fixed costs has relatively high operating leverage. The result of high operating leverage is that the firm can generate a large percentage increase in net income from a relatively small percentage increase in sales revenue. On the other hand, a firm with high operating leverage has a relatively high break-even point. This entails some risk to the firm.

The optimal cost structure for an organization involves a trade-off. Management must weigh the benefits of high operating leverage against the risks of large committed fixed costs and the associated high break-even point.

OPERATING LEVERAGE HELPS THESE WEB COMPANIES BECOME PROFITABLE[8]

Overture Services, eBay, Hotels.com, and Expedia

"Four Web companies made a . . . ranking of the Info Tech One Hundred: search engine Overture Services, auctioneer eBay, discount-hotel broker Hotels.com, and travel site Expedia." That's up from only one, and all of them are profitable. "The leaders of the Web pack are starting to show that once they turn profitable, they can quickly become big moneymakers. The reason is operating leverage. That's accounting-speak for a simple concept: Once you invest enough to build a Web site and your basic operations, you don't need to spend much money as sales rise. After you cover your fixed costs, the expense of processing each sale is so little that profits grow faster than revenues. That philosophy made for big Internet losses early on." The payoff, however, is at hand.

"Online travel agency Expedia, Inc. is a textbook example of leverage in action." In one quarter alone, "Expedia doubled its sales, to $116 million. Yet its overhead, including administrative and marketing costs, rose only 8 percent, to $63 million. One big reason is that the company already had paid for the computing gear it needed to handle the higher volume of ticket sales."

Just a few years after the boom in e-commerce IPOs, "a clear pecking order of profitability has emerged. The biggest moneymakers: online travel, software, and financial-services firms." Why did these online companies turn profitable first? "Because software, financial services, and travel reservations are pure information products, without a physical widget to store or ship. Once overhead costs are covered, the expense in providing the service to one more customer is close to zero. Online retailers are making slower, yet tangible, progress toward profitability. What's holding Amazon.com Inc. and other e-tailers back is simple: Every time someone buys a book on Amazon, the company has to buy a new copy from the publisher. The upshot is that Amazon's gross margins are around 26 percent, compared with 70 percent at Expedia."

Every year, Web business writes a different story, "but now it's past the point where predictions of profitability are written in sand. Some Web businesses do work. The proof is in the black ink."

CVP Analysis, ABC, and Advanced Manufacturing Systems

Learning Objective 10

Understand the implications of activity-based costing (ABC) for CVP analysis.

Traditional CVP analysis focuses on the number of units sold as the only cost and revenue driver. Sales revenue is assumed to be linear in units sold. Moreover, costs are categorized as fixed or variable, with respect to the number of units sold, within the relevant range. This approach is consistent with traditional product-costing systems, in which cost assignment is based on a single volume-related cost driver. In CVP analysis, as in product costing, the traditional approach can be misleading or provide less than adequate information for various management purposes. An ABC system can provide a much more complete picture of CVP relationships and thus provide better information to managers.

To illustrate the potential impact of ABC on CVP analysis, we will use the following information from AccuTime Company, a manufacturer of digital clocks:

Sales volume	20,000 units
Sales price	$25
Unit variable costs:	
Variable manufacturing	$14
Variable selling and administrative	1
Total unit variable cost	$15
Unit contribution margin	$10
Fixed costs:	
Fixed manufacturing	$100,000
Fixed selling and administrative	50,000
Total fixed costs	$150,000

These data are adequate for a traditional CVP analysis of various questions management may ask. For example, the break-even point is easily calculated as 15,000 units, as the following analysis shows:

$$\text{Break-even point} = \frac{\text{Fixed costs}}{\text{Unit contribution margin}} = \frac{\$150,000}{\$10} = 15,000 \text{ units}$$

Alternatively, management may determine how many clocks must be sold to earn a target net profit of $200,000, as the following calculation demonstrates:

$$\text{Sales volume required to earn target net profit of \$200,000} = \frac{\text{Fixed costs} + \text{Target net profit}}{\text{Unit contribution margin}}$$

$$= \frac{\$150,000 + \$200,000}{\$10} = 35,000 \text{ units}$$

What do these questions have in common? They both focus on *sales volume* as the sole revenue and cost driver. The CVP analysis depends on a distinction between costs that are fixed and costs that are variable *with respect to sales volume*.

"ABC was critical to the organization in helping us gain a better understanding of our costs. It provided us with a foundation for managing expenses better." (7f)
BlueCross and BlueShield of North Carolina

Pictured here is a production cell in a flexible manufacturing system engaged in the production of disks for computer hard disk drives. In such a high-tech manufacturing environment, setups are quicker and more frequent, and production runs are smaller. An activity-based costing CVP analysis will give management a better understanding of CVP relationships.

A Move toward JIT and Flexible Manufacturing

Learning Objective   **11**

Be aware of the effects of advanced manufacturing technology on CVP relationships.

Now let's examine another question that AccuTime's management might face. Suppose management is considering the installation of a *flexible manufacturing system* and a move toward just-in-time (JIT) production. A flexible manufacturing system uses highly automated material-handling and production equipment to manufacture a variety of similar products. In the new production process, setups would be quicker and more frequent and production runs would be smaller. Fewer inspections would be required, due to the total quality control (TQC) philosophy that often accompanies JIT. Variable manufacturing costs would be lower, due to savings in direct labour. Finally, general factory overhead costs would increase, due to the greater depreciation charges on the new production equipment.

Suppose management wants to answer the same two questions addressed previously, under the assumption that the production process changes are adopted. To properly address this issue, we need a much more detailed understanding of the impact of other, *non-volume-based cost drivers* on AccuTime's costs. This type of detail is the hallmark of an activity-based costing system. Suppose AccuTime's controller completes an ABC analysis of the company's 20x1 activity before the new equipment is installed. The results are shown in Exhibit 7–14.

There is a subtle but important point to realize about the cost behaviour depicted in Exhibit 7–14. Setup, inspection, and material handling are listed as fixed costs. *They are largely fixed with respect to sales volume.* However, they are *not* fixed with respect to *other cost drivers,* such as the number of setups, inspections, and hours of material handling. This is the fundamental distinction between a traditional CVP analysis and an activity-based costing CVP analysis. The traditional CVP analysis recognizes a single volume-based cost driver, namely, sales volume. The activity-based costing CVP analysis recognizes multiple cost drivers. As a result, some costs viewed as fixed under the traditional analysis are considered variable (with respect to the appropriate cost drivers) under the ABC approach.

Now let's return to management's decision regarding the installation of a flexible manufacturing system and the adoption of the JIT and TQC philosophies. The ABC analysis of the proposed production technology is displayed in Exhibit 7–15. Due to the decreased use of direct labour, the unit variable manufacturing cost has declined from $14 to $9, bringing the total unit variable cost down to $10. This results in an increase in the unit contribution margin to $15. The installation of sophisticated new manufacturing equipment has more than tripled general factory overhead, from $60,000 to $184,000. Under the proposed JIT approach, setups will be daily instead of weekly; each setup will be quicker and less expensive.

Exhibit 7–14
Activity-Based Costing Data under Current Production Process (20x1)

Sales price	$25
Unit variable costs:	
Variable manufacturing	$14
Variable selling and administrative	1
Total unit variable costs	$15
Unit contribution margin	$10
Fixed costs (fixed with respect to sales volume):	
General factory overhead (including depreciation on plant and equipment)	$ 60,000
Setup (52 setups at $100 per setup)*	5,200
Inspection (52 × 21 inspections at $20 per inspection)†	21,840
Material handling (1,080 hours at $12 per hour)	12,960
Total fixed manufacturing costs	$100,000
Fixed selling and administrative costs	50,000
Total fixed costs	$150,000

*One setup per week.

†Three inspections per day, seven days a week (52 weeks per year).

Sales price	$25
Unit variable costs:	
Variable manufacturing	$9
Variable selling and administrative	1
Total unit variable costs	$10
Unit contribution margin	$15
Fixed costs (fixed with respect to sales volume):	
General factory overhead (including depreciation on plant and equipment)	$184,000
Setup (365 setups at $30 per setup)	10,950
Inspection (365 inspections at $10 per inspection)	3,650
Material handling (100 hours at $14 per hour)	1,400
Total fixed manufacturing costs	$200,000
Fixed selling and administrative costs	50,000
Total fixed costs	$250,000

Exhibit 7–15
Activity-Based Costing Data under Proposed Production Technology

 AccuTime

As a result of the emphasis on total quality control, only one inspection per day will be necessary, instead of three as before. Moreover, each inspection will be less expensive. Finally, the amount of material-handling activity will decline dramatically, although there will be a slight increase in the cost per hour. This is due to the higher skill grade of labour required to operate the new automated material-handling system.

Using the ABC data in Exhibit 7–10, we can answer the two CVP questions posed by management. If the new production technology is adopted, the following CVP computations will be appropriate:

$$\text{Break-even point} = \frac{\text{Fixed costs}}{\text{Unit contribution margin}} = \frac{\$250,000}{\$15} = 16,667 \text{ units (rounded)}$$

$$\begin{aligned}\text{Sales volume required to earn target net profit of } \$200,000 &= \frac{\text{Fixed costs} + \text{Target net profit}}{\text{Unit contribution margin}} \\ &= \frac{\$250,000 + \$200,000}{\$15} = 30,000 \text{ units}\end{aligned}$$

Notice that AccuTime's break-even point increased with the introduction of the advanced manufacturing system (from 15,000 to 16,667 units). However, the number of sales units required to earn a target net profit of $200,000 declined (from 35,000 to 30,000 units). These kinds of CVP changes are typical when firms install an advanced manufacturing system. Typically, the cost structure of an advanced manufacturing environment is characterized by a lower proportion of variable costs and a larger proportion of costs that are fixed (with respect to sales volume).

ABC Provides a Richer Understanding of Cost Behaviour and CVP Relationships The point in this section is that ABC provides a richer description of a company's cost behaviour. AccuTime's traditional costing system treated setup, inspection, and material handling as fixed costs. However, the ABC analysis showed that while these costs are largely fixed with respect to sales volume, they are not fixed with respect to other appropriate cost drivers. In analyzing the CVP implications of the proposed changes in manufacturing technology, it was crucial to have an understanding of how these costs would change with respect to such cost drivers as the number of setups, number of inspections, and amount of material-handling activity.

Just as ABC can improve an organization's product-costing system, it also can facilitate a deeper understanding of cost behaviour and CVP relationships.

Focus on Ethics

INCENTIVE TO OVERPRODUCE INVENTORY

This classic case is based on an actual company's experience.[9] Brandolino Company uses an actual cost system to apply all production costs to units produced. The plant has a maximum production capacity of 40 million units but produced and sold only 10 million units during Year 1. There were no beginning or ending inventories. The company's absorption-costing income statement for Year 1 follows:

BRANDOLINO COMPANY
Income Statement
For Year 1

Sales (10,000,000 units at $6)		$ 60,000,000
Cost of goods sold:		
Direct costs (material and labour)		
(10,000,000 at $2)	$20,000,000	
Manufacturing overhead	48,000,000	68,000,000
Gross margin		(8,000,000)
Selling and administrative costs		10,000,000
Operating profit (loss)		$(18,000,000)

The board of directors is upset about the $18 million loss. A consultant approached the board with the following offer: "I agree to become president for no fixed salary. But I insist on a year-end bonus of 10 percent of operating profit (before considering the bonus)." The board of directors agreed to these terms and hired the consultant as Brandolino's new president. The new president promptly stepped up production to an annual rate of 30 million units. Sales for Year 2 remained at 10 million units. The resulting absorption-costing income statement for Year 2 is displayed in the right-hand column.

The day after the Year 2 statement was verified, the president took his cheque for $1,400,000 and resigned to take a job with another corporation. He remarked, "I enjoy challenges. Now that Brandolino Company is in the black,

I'd prefer tackling another challenging situation." (His contract with his new employer is similar to the one he had with Brandolino Company.)

BRANDOLINO COMPANY
Income Statement
For Year 2

Sales (10,000,000 units at $6)		$60,000,000
Cost of goods sold:		
Costs of goods manufactured:		
Direct costs (material and labour)		
(30,000,000 at $2)	$ 60,000,000	
Manufacturing overhead	48,000,000	
Total cost of goods		
manufactured	108,000,000	
Less: Ending inventory:		
Direct costs (material and labour)		
(20,000,000 at $2)	40,000,000	
Manufacturing overhead		
(20/30 × $48,000,000) ..	32,000,000	
Total ending inventory costs	72,000,000	
Cost of goods sold		36,000,000
Gross margin		24,000,000
Selling and administrative costs		10,000,000
Operating profit before bonus		14,000,000
Bonus		1,400,000
Operating profit after bonus		$12,600,000

What do you think is going on here? How would you evaluate the company's Year 2 performance? Using variable costing, what would operating profit be for Year 1? For Year 2? (Assume that all selling and administrative costs are committed and unchanged.) Compare those results with the absorption-costing statements. Comment on the ethical issues in this scenario.

Chapter Summary

LO1 Compute a break-even point using the contribution-margin approach and the equation approach.
These two approaches result in the same general formula for computing the break-even point (in units). Under the equation approach, the profit equation is specified as follows: Sales revenue – Variable expense – Fixed expenses = Profit. When this equation is manipulated, the contribution-margin approach to the break-even point results, as follows: Break-even point (in units) = Fixed expenses ÷ Unit contribution margin.

LO2 Compute the contribution-margin ratio and use it to find the break-even point in sales dollars.
The contribution-margin ratio is defined as follows: Unit contribution margin ÷ Unit sales price. The break-even point (in sales dollars) can be computed as follows: Fixed expenses ÷ Contribution-margin ratio.

LO3 Prepare a cost–volume–profit (CVP) graph and explain how it is used. A CVP graph shows the break-even point (in sales dollars) as the intersection of the total revenue line and the total expense line. The graph can be used to help management understand how changes in the volume of activity affect cost and profit.

LO4 Apply CVP analysis to determine the effect on profit of changes in fixed expenses, variable expenses, sales prices, and sales volume. Management can use the break-even equation to predict the effects on the break-even point of changes in any component of the equation, e.g., sales price, unit variable cost, fixed cost, and so forth. Such prediction can help management in making a variety of operational decisions.

LO5 Compute the break-even point for a multiproduct enterprise. Break-even analysis in a multiproduct firm is accomplished by computing a weighted-average contribution margin, which is based on the expected sales mix. The same break-even formulas are used as in a single-product analysis, except that the unit contribution margin is replaced by the weighted-average contribution margin. This analysis is limited by the assumption of a constant sales mix across the range of total sales volume.

LO6 Prepare an income statement under absorption and variable costing, and reconcile the difference in reported income. On an absorption-costing income statement, the cost of goods sold is measured at absorption cost (i.e., includes direct material, direct labour, and both variable and fixed manufacturing overhead) and, therefore, fixed overhead is not a period cost. On a variable-costing income statement, the cost of goods sold is measured at variable cost (i.e., includes direct material, direct labour, and only variable manufacturing overhead), and fixed overhead is treated as a period cost. Income reported under absorption and variable costing can be reconciled by focusing on the effects of the two places where the two statements differ: (1) calculation of cost of goods sold and (2) period costs.

LO7 Explain the implications of absorption and variable costing for CVP, and evaluate both product-costing systems. Variable costing highlights the separation between fixed and variable costs, as do CVP analysis and break-even calculations. Both of these techniques account for fixed manufacturing overhead as a lump-sum period cost. In contrast, absorption costing is inconsistent with CVP analysis, because fixed overhead is applied to goods as a product cost on a per-unit basis. There are pros and cons to both costing methods. Variable costing dovetails much more closely than absorption costing with any operational analysis that requires a separation between fixed and variable costs (e.g., CVP analysis). On the other hand, variable costing understates a product's cost, because it excludes fixed manufacturing overhead from the unit cost calculation. In contrast, absorption costing alleviates that objection by including fixed overhead on a per-unit basis in a product's cost. However, this distorts the cost behaviour of fixed costs, which do not in fact vary with production activity.

LO8 Explain throughput costing and prepare an income statement using this approach. Some accountants and managers advocate throughput costing, in which only throughput costs are inventoried as product costs. They argue that throughput costing reduces the incentives for management to produce excess inventory simply for the purpose of spreading committed (non-throughput) costs across a larger number of units produced.

LO9 Explain the role of cost structure and operating leverage in CVP relationships. An organization's cost structure is the relative proportions of its fixed and variable costs. The extent to which an organization uses fixed costs in its cost structure is called *operating leverage*. Firms with high operating leverage tend to have higher break-even points, other things being equal.

LO10 Understand the implications of activity-based costing (ABC) for CVP analysis. ABC provides a richer description of an organization's cost behaviour and CVP relationships than is provided by a traditional costing system. An ABC cost–volume–profit analysis recognizes that some costs that are fixed with respect to sales volume may not be fixed with respect to other important cost drivers. In many cases, management can benefit substantially from such an improved understanding of cost behaviour and CVP relationships.

LO11 Be aware of the effects of advanced manufacturing technology on CVP relationships. Companies with advanced manufacturing technology tend to have higher fixed costs, lower variable costs, and higher break-even points.

Review Problem on CVP Analysis

Overlook Inn is a small bed-and-breakfast located on Vancouver Island. The charge is $50 per person for one night's lodging and a full breakfast in the morning. The retired couple who own and manage the B&B estimate that the variable expense per person is $20. This includes such expenses as food, maid service, and utilities. The B&B's fixed expenses total $42,000 per year. The B&B can accommodate 10 guests each night.

Required: Compute the following:

1. Contribution margin per unit of service (a unit of service is one night's lodging for one guest)
2. Contribution-margin ratio
3. Annual break-even point in units of service and in dollars of service revenue
4. The number of units of service required to earn a target net profit of $60,000 for the year (ignore income taxes)

Solution to Review Problem

1. Contribution margin per unit of service = Nightly room charge − Variable expense per person

$$\$30 \quad = \quad \$50 \quad - \quad \$20$$

2. Contribution-margin ratio $= \dfrac{\text{Contribution margin per unit}}{\text{Nightly room charge}}$

$$0.60 \quad = \frac{\$30}{\$50}$$

3. $\dfrac{\text{Break-even point}}{\text{in units of service}} = \dfrac{\text{Fixed expenses}}{\text{Contribution margin per unit}}$

$$1,400 = \frac{\$42,000}{\$30}$$

$\dfrac{\text{Break-even point in}}{\text{dollars of revenue}} = \dfrac{\text{Fixed expenses}}{\text{Contribution-margin ratio}}$

$$\$70,000 \quad = \frac{\$42,000}{0.60}$$

4. $\dfrac{\text{Number of units of service}}{\text{required to earn target net profit}} = \dfrac{\text{Fixed expenses} + \text{Target net profit}}{\text{Contribution margin per unit of service}}$

$$3,400 \quad = \frac{\$42,000 + \$60,000}{\$30}$$

Review Problem on Absorption and Variable Costing

ScholasticPak Company manufactures backpacks used by students. A typical backpack has the following price and variable costs:

Sales price	$45
Direct material	15
Direct labour	6
Variable overhead	9

Budgeted fixed overhead in the company's first year of operations, was $900,000. Actual production was 150,000 units, of which 125,000 were sold. ScholasticPak incurred the following selling and administrative expenses.

Fixed	$150,000 for the year
Variable	$3 per unit sold

Required:

1. Compute the product cost per backpack under (*a*) variable costing and (*b*) absorption costing.
2. Prepare income statements for the year using (*a*) variable costing and (*b*) absorption costing.
3. Reconcile the income reported under the two methods by analyzing the two key places where the income statements differ.

Solution to Review Problem

1. $\text{Predetermined fixed overhead rate} = \dfrac{\text{Budgeted fixed overhead}}{\text{Budgeted production}}$

$$= \dfrac{\$900,000}{150,000} = \$6 \text{ per unit}$$

Product Cost per Unit

Direct material	$15
Direct labour	6
Variable overhead	9
a. Cost per unit under variable costing	$30
Fixed overhead per unit under absorption costing	6
b. Cost per unit under absorption costing	$36

2. *a.* **Variable-Costing Income Statement**

Sales revenue (125,000 units sold at $45 per unit)	$5,625,000
Less: Variable expenses:	
Variable manufacturing costs (at variable cost of $30 per unit)	3,750,000
Variable selling and administrative costs (at $3 per unit × 125,000 units sold)	375,000
Contribution margin	1,500,000
Less: Fixed expenses:	
Fixed manufacturing overhead	900,000
Fixed selling and administrative expenses	150,000
Net income	$ 450,000

b. **Absorption-Costing Income Statement**

Sales revenue (125,000 units sold at $45 per unit)	$5,625,000
Less: Cost of goods sold	
(at absorption cost of $36 per unit)	4,500,000
Gross margin	1,125,000
Less: Selling and administrative expenses:	
Variable (at $3 per unit × 125,000 units sold)	375,000
Fixed	150,000
Net income	$ 600,000

3.

Cost of goods sold under absorption costing	$4,500,000
Less: Variable manufacturing costs under variable costing	3,750,000
Subtotal	750,000
Less: Fixed manufacturing overhead as period expense under variable costing	900,000
Total	$ (150,000)
Net income under variable costing	$ 450,000
Less: Net income under absorption costing	600,000
Difference in net income	$ (150,000)

Glossary

Review key terms and definitions on Connect.

McGraw Hill **connect**

Review Questions

7–1. Briefly explain each of the following methods of computing a break-even point in units: (*a*) contribution-margin approach, (*b*) equation approach, and (*c*) graphical approach.

7–2. What is the meaning of the term *unit contribution margin*? Contribution to what?

7–3. What information is conveyed by a CVP graph in addition to a company's break-even point?

7–4. What does the term *safety margin* mean?

7–5. Suppose the fixed expenses of a travel agency increase. What will happen to its break-even point, measured in number of clients served?

7–6. Delmarva Oyster Company has been able to decrease its variable expenses per kilogram of oysters harvested. How will this affect the firm's break-even sales volume?

7–7. In a strategy meeting, a manufacturing company's president said, "If we raise the price of our product, the company's break-even point will be lower." The financial vice-president responded by saying, "Then we should raise our price. The company will be less likely to incur a loss." Do you agree with the president? Why? Do you agree with the vice-president? Why?

7–8. What will happen to a company's break-even point if the sales price and unit variable cost of its only product increase by the same dollar amount?

7–9. An art museum covers its operating expenses by charging a small admission fee. The objective of the nonprofit organization is to break even. A local arts enthusiast has just pledged an annual donation of $10,000 to the museum. How will the donation affect the museum's break-even attendance level?

7–10. How can a profit–volume graph be used to predict a company's profit for a particular sales volume?

7–11. Why do many operating managers prefer a contribution income statement instead of a traditional income statement?

7–12. What is the difference between a manufacturing company's *gross margin* and its total *contribution margin*?

7–13. Briefly explain the difference between absorption costing and variable costing.

7–14. Timing is the key in distinguishing between absorption and variable costing. Explain this statement.

7–15. "The term *direct costing* is a misnomer. *Variable costing* is a better term for the product-costing method." Do you agree or disagree? Why?

7–16. When inventory increases, will absorption-costing or variable-costing income be greater? Why?

7–17. Explain how throughput costing differs from absorption and variable costing.

7–18. Explain why some management accountants believe that absorption costing may provide an incentive for managers to overproduce inventory. How does throughput costing avoid this problem?

7–19. Will variable and absorption costing result in significantly different income measures in a JIT setting? Why?

7–20. Why do proponents of absorption costing argue that absorption costing is preferable as the basis for pricing decisions?

7–21. Why do proponents of variable costing prefer variable costing when making pricing decisions?

7–22. Which is more consistent with cost–volume–profit analysis, variable costing or absorption costing? Why?

7–23. East Company manufactures DVDs using a completely automated production process. West Company also manufactures DVDs, but its products are assembled manually. How will these two firms' cost structures differ? Which company will have a higher operating leverage factor?

7–24. When sales volume increases, which company will experience a larger percentage increase in profit: Company X, which has mostly fixed expenses, or Company Y, which has mostly variable expenses?

7–25. What does the term *sales mix* mean? How is a *weighted-average unit contribution margin* computed?

7–26. How can a hotel's management use CVP analysis to help in deciding on room rates?

7–27. Two companies have identical fixed expenses, unit variable expenses, and profits. Yet one company has set a much lower price for its product. Explain how this can happen.

7–28. A company with an advanced manufacturing environment typically will have a higher break-even point, greater operating leverage, and larger safety margin than a labour-intensive firm. True or false? Explain.

7–29. Explain briefly how activity-based costing (ABC) affects CVP analysis.

Exercises

Exercise 7–30 Fill in the Blanks: Basic CVP Relationships **(LO1, 2)**

Fill in the missing data for each of the following independent cases. (Ignore income taxes.)

	Sales Revenue	Variable Expenses	Total Contribution Margin	Fixed Expenses	Net Income	Break-Even Sales Revenue
1.	?	$40,000	?	$30,000	?	$40,000
2.	$80,000	?	$15,000	?	?	80,000
3.	?	40,000	$80,000	?	$50,000	?
4.	110,000	22,000	?	?	38,000	?

Exercise 7–31 Basic CVP Analysis: Pizza Delivery Business (LO1, 2, 4)

University Pizza delivers pizzas to the dormitories and apartments near a major university. The company's annual fixed expenses are $40,000. The sales price of a pizza is $10, and it costs the company $5 to make and deliver each pizza. (In the following requirements, ignore income taxes.)

Required:

1. Using the contribution-margin approach, compute the company's break-even point in units (pizzas).
2. What is the contribution-margin ratio?
3. Compute the break-even sales revenue. Use the contribution-margin ratio in your calculation.
4. How many pizzas must the company sell to earn a target net profit of $65,000? Use the equation method.

Exercise 7–32 Using CVP Analysis: Manufacturing (LO1, 4)

Rosario Company, which is located in Buenos Aires, Argentina, manufactures a component used in farm machinery. The firm's fixed costs are 4,000,000 pesos (p) per year. The variable cost of each component is 2,000 p, and the components are sold for 3,000 p each. The company sold 5,000 components during the prior year. (p denotes the peso, Argentina's national currency. Several countries use the peso as their monetary unit. On the day this exercise was written, Argentina's peso was worth 0.314 Canadian dollar. In the following requirements, ignore income taxes.)

Required: Answer requirements (1) through (4) independently.

1. Compute the break-even point in units.
2. What will the new break-even point be if fixed costs increase by 10 percent?
3. What was the company's net income for the prior year?
4. The sales manager believes that a reduction in the sales price to 2,500 p will result in orders for 1,200 more components each year. What will the break-even point be if the price is changed?
5. Should the price change discussed in requirement (4) be made?

Exercise 7–33 CVP Graph: Sports Franchise (LO3, 4)

A minor-league hockey team plays its weekly games in a small stadium just outside of Richmond. The stadium holds 10,000 people and tickets sell for $10 each. The franchise owner estimates that the team's annual fixed expenses are $180,000, and the variable expense per ticket sold is $1. (In the following requirements, ignore income taxes.)

Required:

1. Draw a CVP graph for the sports franchise. Label the axes, break-even point, profit and loss areas, fixed expenses, variable expenses, total expense line, and total revenue line.
2. If the stadium is two-thirds full for each game, how many games must the team play to break even?

Exercise 7–34 Continuation of Preceding Exercise; Profit–Volume Graph; Safety Margin (LO3, 4)

Refer to the data given in the preceding exercise. (Ignore income taxes.)

Required:

1. Prepare a fully labelled profit–volume graph for the hockey team.
2. What is the safety margin for the hockey franchise if the team plays a 12-game season and the team owner expects the stadium to be 30 percent full for each game?
3. If the stadium is half full for each game, what ticket price would the team have to charge in order to break even?

Exercise 7–35 CVP Analysis with Multiple Products: Retail (LO1, 2, 5)

Tim's Bicycle Shop sells 21-speed bicycles. For purposes of a CVP analysis, the shop owner has divided sales into two categories, as follows:

Product Type	Sales Price	Invoice Cost	Sales Commission
High-quality	$500	$275	$25
Medium-quality	300	135	15

Three-quarters of the shop's sales are medium-quality bikes. The shop's annual fixed expenses are $65,000. (In the following requirements, ignore income taxes.)

Required:

1. Compute the unit contribution margin for each product type.
2. What is the shop's sales mix?
3. Compute the weighted-average unit contribution margin, assuming a constant sales mix.
4. What is the shop's break-even sales volume in dollars? Assume a constant sales mix.
5. How many bicycles of each type must be sold to earn a target net income of $48,750? Assume a constant sales mix.

Exercise 7–36 Difference in Income under Absorption and Variable Costing (LO6)

Manta Ray Company manufactures diving masks with a variable cost of $25. The masks sell for $34. Budgeted fixed manufacturing overhead for the most recent year was $792,000. Actual production was equal to planned production.

Required: Under each of the following conditions, state (*a*) whether income is higher under variable or absorption costing and (*b*) the amount of the difference in reported income under the two methods. Treat each condition as an independent case.

1.	Production	110,000 units
	Sales	108,000 units
2.	Production	90,000 units
	Sales	95,000 units
3.	Production	79,200 units
	Sales	79,200 units

Exercise 7–37 Absorption versus Variable Costing (LO6, 8)

Information taken from Tuscarora Paper Company's records for the most recent year is as follows:

Direct material used	$290,000
Direct labour	100,000
Variable manufacturing overhead	50,000
Fixed manufacturing overhead	80,000
Variable selling and administrative costs	40,000
Fixed selling and administrative costs	20,000

Required:

1. Assuming Tuscarora Paper Company uses variable costing, compute the inventoriable costs for the year.
2. Compute the year's inventoriable costs using absorption costing.
3. Now assume that Tuscarora Paper Company uses throughput costing, and the company has committed to spending for direct labour, variable overhead, and fixed overhead in the amounts given in the problem. Under this scenario, compute the company's inventoriable costs for the year.

(CMA, adapted)

Exercise 7–38 Absorption and Variable Costing (LO6)

Easton Pump Company's planned production for the year just ended was 20,000 units. This production level was achieved, and 21,000 units were sold. Other data follow:

Direct material used..	$600,000
Direct labour incurred	$300,000
Fixed manufacturing overhead...	$420,000
Variable manufacturing overhead...	$200,000
Fixed selling and administrative expenses	$350,000
Variable selling and administrative expenses	$105,000
Finished-goods inventory, January 1	2,000 units

There were no work-in-process inventories at the beginning or end of the year.

Required:

1. What would be Easton Pump Company's finished-goods inventory cost on December 31 under the variable-costing method?

2. Which costing method, absorption or variable costing, would show a higher operating income for the year? By what amount?

(CMA, adapted)

Exercise 7–39 Absorption, Variable, and Throughput Costing (LO6, 8)

Pandora Pillow Company's planned production for the year just ended was 10,000 units. This production level was achieved, but only 9,000 units were sold. Other data follow:

Direct material used...	$40,000
Direct labour incurred	20,000
Fixed manufacturing overhead..	25,000
Variable manufacturing overhead..	12,000
Fixed selling and administrative expenses	30,000
Variable selling and administrative expenses	4,500
Finished-goods inventory, January 1	None

There were no work-in-process inventories at the beginning or end of the year.

Required:

1. What would be Pandora Pillow Company's finished-goods inventory cost on December 31 under the variable-costing method?

2. Which costing method, absorption or variable costing, would show a higher operating income for the year? By what amount?

3. Suppose Pandora Pillow Company uses throughput costing, and direct material is its only unit-level cost. What would be Pandora's finished-goods inventory on December 31?

(CMA, adapted)

Exercise 7–40 Difference in Income under Absorption and Variable Costing (LO6)

Bianca Bicycle Company manufactures mountain bikes with a standard variable cost of $200. The bicycles sell for $350 each. Budgeted fixed manufacturing overhead for the most recent year was $2,200,000. Planned and actual production for the year were the same.

Required: Under each of the following conditions, state (*a*) whether income is higher under variable or absorption costing and (*b*) the amount of the difference in reported income under the two methods. Treat each condition as an independent case.

1.	Production	20,000 units
	Sales	23,000 units
2.	Production	10,000 units
	Sales	10,000 units
3.	Production	11,000 units
	Sales	9,000 units

Exercise 7–41 Variable Costing and Cost–Volume–Profit Analysis (LO6)

Refer to the data given in the preceding exercise for Bianca Bicycle Company

Required:

1. Prepare a cost–volume–profit graph for the company. (Scale the vertical axis in millions of dollars, and draw the CVP graph up through 15,000 units on the horizontal axis.)

2. Calculate Bianca Bicycle Company's break-even point in units, and show the break-even point on the CVP graph.

3. Explain why variable costing is more compatible with your CVP graph than absorption costing would be.

Exercise 7–42 Absorption, Variable, and Throughput Costing; Use of the Internet (LO6)

Visit the website of one of the following companies, or of a different company of your choosing.

Bombardier	www.bombardier.com
Corby Distilleries Limited	www.corby.ca
Goodyear Canada	www.goodyear.ca
Magna International	www.magna.com
Research In Motion	www.rim.com
Xerox Corporation	www.xerox.com

Required: Read about the company's products and operations. Discuss the pros and cons of absorption, variable, and throughput costing as the basis for product costing if the firm uses cost-based pricing.

Exercise 7–43 Cost Structure and Operating Leverage: Hotel and Restaurant (LO8)

A contribution income statement for the Nantucket Hotel is shown below. (Ignore income taxes.)

Revenue	$500,000
Less: Variable expenses	300,000
Contribution margin	$200,000
Less: Fixed expenses	150,000
Net income	$ 50,000

Required:

1. Show the hotel's cost structure by indicating the percentage of the hotel's revenue represented by each item on the income statement.
2. Suppose the hotel's revenue declines by 15 percent. Use the contribution-margin percentage to calculate the resulting decrease in net income.
3. What is the hotel's operating leverage factor when revenue is $500,000?
4. Use the operating leverage factor to calculate the increase in net income resulting from a 20 percent increase in sales revenue.

Problems

Problem 7–44 Basic CVP Relationships: Retailer (LO1, 2, 4)

2. Net income: $280,000

Disk City, Inc. is a retailer of DVDs. The projected net income for the current year is $200,000 based on a sales volume of 200,000 DVDs. Disk City has been selling the DVDs for $16 each. The variable costs consist of the $10 unit purchase price of the DVDs and a handling cost of $2 per DVD. Disk City's annual fixed costs are $600,000.

Management is planning for the coming year, when it expects that the unit purchase price of the DVDs will increase 30 percent. (Ignore income taxes.)

Required:

1. Calculate Disk City's break-even point for the *current year* in number of DVDs.
2. What will be the company's net income for the *current year* if there is a 10 percent increase in projected unit sales volume?
3. What volume of sales (in dollars) must Disk City achieve in the *coming year* to maintain the same net income as projected for the current year if the unit selling price remains at $16,?
4. In order to cover a 30 percent increase in the DVD's purchase price for the *coming year* and still maintain the current contribution-margin ratio, what selling price per DVD must Disk City establish for the coming year?

5. *Build a spreadsheet:* Construct an Excel spreadsheet to solve requirements (1), (2), and (3) above. Show how the solution will change if the following information changes: The selling price is $17 and the annual fixed costs are $640,000.

(CMA, adapted)

Problem 7–45 Basic CVP Computations (LO1, 2, 4)

CollegePak Company produced and sold 60,000 backpacks during the year just ended at an average price of $20 per unit. Variable manufacturing costs were $8 per unit, and variable marketing costs were $4 per unit sold. Fixed costs amounted to $180,000 for manufacturing and $72,000 for marketing. There was no year-end work-in-process inventory. (Ignore income taxes.)

2. Sales units required for $180,000 income: 54,000 units

Required:

1. Compute CollegePak's break-even point in sales dollars for the year.
2. Compute the number of sales units required to earn a net income of $180,000 during the year.
3. CollegePak's variable manufacturing costs are expected to increase by 10 percent in the coming year. Compute the firm's break-even point in sales dollars for the coming year.
4. If CollegePak's variable manufacturing costs do increase by 10 percent, compute the selling price that would yield the same contribution-margin ratio in the coming year.

(CMA, adapted)

Problem 7–46 CVP Relationships; Indifference Point (LO1, 4)

Corrigan Enterprises is studying the acquisition of two electrical component insertion systems for producing its sole product, the universal gismo. Data relevant to the systems follow.

2. Net income, Model 4399: $1,094,400

Model 6754:
    Variable costs, $16 per unit
    Annual fixed costs, $985,000
Model 4399:
    Variable costs, $12.80 per unit
    Annual fixed costs, $1,113,600

Corrigan's selling price is $64 per unit for the universal gismo, which is subject to a 5 percent sales commission. (In the following requirements, ignore income taxes.)

Required:

1. How many units must the company sell to break even if Model 6754 is selected?
2. Which of the two systems would be more profitable if sales and production are expected to average 46,000 units per year?
3. Assume Model 4399 requires the purchase of additional equipment that is not reflected in the preceding figures. The equipment will cost $450,000 and will be depreciated over a five-year life by the straight-line method. How many units must Corrigan sell to earn $956,400 of income if Model 4399 is selected? As in requirement (2), sales and production are expected to average 46,000 units.
4. Ignoring the information presented in requirement (3), at what volume level will management be indifferent between the acquisition of Model 6754 and Model 4399? In other words, at what volume level will the annual total cost of each system be equal? (*Hint:* At any given sales volume, sales commissions will be the same amount, regardless of which model is selected.)

Problem 7–47 CVP Analysis; Impact of Operating Changes (LO1, 4)

Advanced Electronics manufactures audio speakers for desktop computers. The following data relate to the period just ended when the company produced and sold 42,000 speaker sets:

2. Break-even point: 32,000 units

Sales	$3,360,000
Variable costs	840,000
Fixed costs	2,280,000

Management is considering relocating its manufacturing facilities to Mexico to reduce costs. Variable costs are expected to average $18 per set; annual fixed costs are anticipated to be $1,984,000. (In the following requirements, ignore income taxes.)

Required:

1. Calculate the company's current income and determine the level of dollar sales needed to double that figure, assuming that manufacturing operations remain in Canada.
2. Determine the break-even point in speaker sets if operations are shifted to Mexico.

3. Assume that management desires to achieve the Mexican break-even point; however, operations will remain in Canada.

   a. If variable costs remain constant, what must management do to fixed costs? By how much must fixed costs change?

   b. If fixed costs remain constant, what must management do to the variable cost per unit? By how much must unit variable cost change?

4. Determine the impact (increase, decrease, or no effect) of the following operating changes.

   a. Effect of an increase in direct material costs on the break-even point

   b. Effect of an increase in fixed administrative costs on the unit contribution margin

   c. Effect of an increase in the unit contribution margin on net income

   d. Effect of a decrease in the number of units sold on the break-even point

2(c). Commissions, total: $535,600

Problem 7–48 Sales Mix and Employee Compensation; Operating Changes **(LO4, 5)**

Lawrence Corporation sells two ceiling fans, Deluxe and Basic. Current sales total 60,000 units, consisting of 39,000 Deluxe units and 21,000 Basic units. Selling price and variable cost information follow.

	Deluxe	Basic
Selling price	$86	$74
Variable cost	65	41

Salespeople currently receive flat salaries that total $400,000. Management is contemplating a change to a compensation plan that is based on commissions in an effort to boost the company's presence in the marketplace. Two plans are under consideration:

Plan A: 10% commission computed on gross dollar sales. Deluxe sales are expected to total 45,500 units; Basic sales are anticipated to be 19,500 units.

Plan B: 30% commission computed on the basis of production contribution margins. Deluxe sales are anticipated to be 26,000 units; Basic sales are expected to total 39,000 units.

Required:

1. Define the term *sales mix*.

2. Comparing Plan A to the current compensation arrangement:

   a. Will Plan A achieve management's objective of an increased presence in the marketplace? Briefly explain.

   b. From a sales mix perspective, will the salespeople be promoting the product that one would logically expect? Briefly discuss.

   c. Will the sales force likely be satisfied with the results of Plan A? Why?

   d. Will Lawrence likely be satisfied with the resulting impact of Plan A on company profitability? Why?

3. Assume that Plan B is under consideration.

   a. Compare Plan A and Plan B with respect to total units sold and the sales mix. Comment on the results.

   b. In comparison with flat salaries, is Plan B more attractive to the sales force? To the company? Show calculations to support your answers.

1. Plan B break-even point: 2,200 units
3. Operating leverage factor, Plan A: 1.2

Problem 7–49 Leverage; Analysis of Operating Change **(LO4, 8)**

Consolidated Industries is studying the addition of a new valve to its product line. The valve would be used by manufacturers of irrigation equipment. The company anticipates starting with a relatively low sales volume and then boosting demand over the next several years. A new salesperson must be hired because Consolidated's current sales force is working at capacity. Two compensation plans are under consideration:

Plan A: An annual salary of $22,000 plus a 10% commission based on gross dollar sales.
Plan B: An annual salary of $66,000 and no commission.

Consolidated Industries will purchase the valve for $50 and sell it for $80. Anticipated demand during the first year is 6,000 units. (In the following requirements, ignore income taxes.)

Required:

1. Compute the break-even point for Plan A and Plan B.

2. What is meant by the term *operating leverage*?

3. Analyze the cost structures of both plans at the anticipated demand of 6,000 units. Which of the two plans is more highly leveraged? Why

4. Assume that a general economic downturn occurred during Year 2, with product demand falling from 6,000 to 5,000 units. Determine the percentage decrease in company net income if Consolidated had adopted Plan A.

5. Repeat requirement (4) for Plan B. Compare Plan A and Plan B, and explain a major factor that underlies any resulting differences.

6. Briefly discuss the likely profitability impact of an economic recession for highly automated manufacturers. What can you say about the risk associated with these firms?

Problem 7–50 Basic CVP Relationships (L01, 2, 4)

Serendipity Sound, Inc. manufactures and sells CDs. Price and cost data are as follows:

Selling price per unit (package of two CDs)	$	25.00
Variable costs per unit:		
Direct material	$	10.50
Direct labour		5.00
Manufacturing overhead		3.00
Selling expenses		1.30
Total variable costs per unit	$	19.80
Annual fixed costs:		
Manufacturing overhead	$	192,000
Selling and administrative		276,000
Total fixed costs	$	468,000
Forecasted annual sales volume (120,000 units)	$3,000,000	

3. Sales units required for target net profit: 140,000 units
6. Old contribution-margin ratio: 0.208

In the following requirements, ignore income taxes.

Required:

1. What is Serendipity Sound's break-even point in units?
2. What is the company's break-even point in sales dollars?
3. How many units would Serendipity Sound have to sell in order to earn $260,000?
4. What is the firm's margin of safety?
5. Management estimates that direct-labour costs will increase by 8 percent next year. How many units will the company have to sell next year to reach its break-even point?
6. If the company's direct-labour costs do increase by 8 percent, what selling price per unit of product must it charge to maintain the same contribution-margin ratio?

(CMA, adapted)

Problem 7–51 Variable-Costing and Absorption-Costing Income Statements; Reconciling Reported Income (L06)

Skinny Dippers, Inc. produces nonfat frozen yogurt. The product is sold wholesale in 5-L commercial containers, which have the following price and variable costs.

2(a). Net income: $200,000
3. Cost of goods sold under absorption costing: $1,500,000

Sales price	$15
Direct material	5
Direct labour	2
Variable overhead	3

Budgeted fixed overhead in 20x1, the company's first year of operations, was $300,000. Actual production was 150,000 5-L containers, of which 125,000 were sold. Skinny Dippers, Inc. incurred the following selling and administrative expenses.

Fixed	$50,000 for the year
Variable	$1 per container sold

Required:

1. Compute the product cost per container of frozen yogurt under (*a*) variable costing and (*b*) absorption costing.

2. Prepare income statements for 20x1 using (*a*) absorption costing and (*b*) variable costing.

3. Reconcile the income reported under the two methods by listing the two key places where the income statements differ.

4. Reconcile the income reported under the two methods using the shortcut method.

5. *Build a spreadsheet:* Construct an Excel spreadsheet to solve all of the preceding requirements. Show how the solution will change if the following information changes: The selling price and direct-material cost per unit are $16 and $4.50, respectively.

Problem 7–52 Straightforward Problem on Throughput Costing (LO6)

2. Net income: $25,000

Refer to the information given in the preceding problem for Skinny Dippers, Inc. Assume that the company has *committed* spending for direct labour and manufacturing overhead; direct material is the only unit-level production cost.

Required:

1. Compute the cost of Skinny Dippers' year-end finished-goods inventory using throughput costing.

2. Prepare an income statement for 20x1 using throughput costing.

3. Briefly explain the difference between gross margin computed under absorption costing and gross margin computed under throughput costing.

4. *Build a spreadsheet:* Construct an Excel spreadsheet to solve requirement (2) above. Show how the solution will change if the following information changes: The selling price and direct-material cost per unit are $16 and $4.50, respectively.

Problem 7–53 Absorption and Variable Costing; CVP Analysis (LO6)

1. Total contribution margin: $320,000

2. Break-even point: 25,000 units

Yellowstone Company began operations on January 1 to produce a single product. It used an absorption costing system with a planned production volume of 100,000 units. During its first year of operations, the planned production volume was achieved, and there were no fixed selling or administrative expenses. Inventory on December 31 was 20,000 units, and net income for the year was $240,000.

Required:

1. If Yellowstone Company had used variable costing, its net income would have been $220,000. Compute the break-even point in units under variable costing.

2. Draw a profit–volume graph for Yellowstone Company. (Use variable costing.)

Problem 7–54 Variable versus Absorption Costing; JIT (LO7)

2. Budgeted variable manu-facturing costs: $3,500,000

3. Increase in inventory (in units): 5,000 units

Outback Corporation manufactures rechargeable flashlights in Brisbane, Australia. The firm uses an absorption costing system for internal reporting purposes; however, the company is considering using variable costing. Data regarding Outback's planned and actual operations for 20x1 follow:

	Budgeted Costs		
	Per Unit	**Total**	**Actual Costs**
Direct material	$12.00	$1,680,000	$1,560,000
Direct labour	9.00	1,260,000	1,170,000
Variable manufacturing overhead	4.00	560,000	520,000
Fixed manufacturing overhead	5.00	700,000	715,000
Variable selling expenses	8.00	1,120,000	1,000,000
Fixed selling expenses	7.00	980,000	980,000
Variable administrative expenses	2.00	280,000	250,000
Fixed administrative expenses	3.00	420,000	425,500
Total	$50.00	$7,000,000	$6,620,000

	Planned Activity	**Actual Activity**
Beginning finished-goods inventory in units	35,000	35,000
Sales in units	140,000	125,000
Production in units	140,000	130,000

The budgeted per-unit cost figures were based on Outback producing and selling 140,000 units in 20x1. Outback uses a predetermined overhead rate for applying manufacturing overhead to its product. A total manufacturing overhead rate of $9 per unit was employed for absorption costing purposes in 20x1. Any overapplied or underapplied manufacturing overhead is closed to the cost of goods sold account at the end of the year. The 20x1 beginning finished-goods inventory for absorption costing purposes was valued at the 20x0 budgeted unit manufacturing cost, which was the same as the 20x1 budgeted unit manufacturing cost. There are no work-in-process inventories at either the beginning or the end of the year. The planned and actual unit selling price for 20x1 was $70 per unit.

Required:

1. Was Outback's 20x1 income higher under absorption costing or variable costing? Why? Compute the following amounts.
    a. The value of Outback Corporation's 20x1 ending finished-goods inventory under absorption costing.
    b. The value of Outback Corporation's 20x1 ending finished-goods inventory under variable costing.
    c. The difference between Outback Corporation's 20x1 reported income calculated under absorption costing and calculated under variable costing.

2. Suppose Outback Corporation had introduced a JIT production and inventory management system at the beginning of 20x1.
    a. What would likely be different about the scenario as described in the problem?
    b. Would reported income under variable and absorption costing differ by the magnitude you found in requirement (3)? Explain.

(CMA, adapted)

Problem 7–55 Variable-Costing and Absorption-Costing Income Statements; FMS; JIT **(LO6, 7)**

Great Outdoze, Inc. manufactures high-quality sleeping bags, which sell for $65 each. The variable costs of production are as follows:

Direct material	$20
Direct labour	11
Variable manufacturing overhead	8

1. Total variable cost: $39

2(b). Net income: $320,000

Budgeted fixed overhead in 20x1 was $200,000 and budgeted production was 25,000 sleeping bags. The year's actual production was 25,000 units, of which 22,000 were sold. Variable selling and administrative costs were $1 per unit sold; fixed selling and administrative costs were $30,000. The firm does not prorate variances.

Required:

1. Calculate the product cost per sleeping bag under (*a*) absorption costing and (*b*) variable costing.
2. Prepare income statements for the year using (*a*) absorption costing and (*b*) variable costing.
3. Reconcile reported income under the two methods using the shortcut method.
4. Suppose that Great Outdoze, Inc. implemented a JIT inventory and production management system at the beginning of 20x1. In addition, the firm installed a flexible manufacturing system. Would you expect reported income under variable and absorption costing to be different by as great a magnitude as you found in requirement (3)? Explain.

Problem 7–56 Throughput Costing **(LO7)**

Refer to the information given in the preceding problem for Great Outdoze, Inc. Assume that direct material is the only unit-level manufacturing cost. The company has committed its spending for direct labour and overhead (variable and fixed).

2. Net income: $263,000

Required:

1. Calculate the product cost per sleeping bag under throughput costing.
2. Prepare an income statement for the year 20x1 using throughput costing.
3. Give an argument for and against throughput costing.

Problem 7–57 Variable and Absorption Costing **(LO6)**

Dayton Lighting Company had net income for the first 10 months of the current year of $200,000. One hundred thousand units were manufactured during this period (the same as the planned production), and all

2*a*. Contribution margin per unit: $22

2*b*. Projected net income for the year under absorption costing: $178,000 were sold. Fixed manufacturing overhead was $2,000,000 over the 10-month period (i.e., $300,000 per month). There are no selling and administrative expenses for Dayton Lighting Company. Both variable and fixed costs are expected to continue at the same rates for the balance of the year (i.e., fixed costs at $200,000 per month and variable costs at the same variable cost per unit). Over the last two months of the current year, 20,000 are to be produced and 19,000 units are to be sold in total. Assume that the unit variable cost is the same in the current year as in the previous year. (*Hint:* You cannot calculate revenue or cost of goods sold; you must work directly with contribution margin or gross margin.)

Required:

1. If operations proceed as described, will net income be higher under variable or absorption costing for the current year in total? Why?

2. If operations proceed as described, what will net income for the year in total be under (*a*) variable costing and (*b*) absorption costing? (Ignore income taxes.)

3. Discuss the advantages and disadvantages of absorption and variable costing.

Problem 7–58 Throughput Costing, Absorption Costing, and Variable Costing **(LO6, 7)**

Emerson Corporation, which uses throughput costing, just completed its first year of operations. Planned and actual production equalled 10,000 units, and sales totalled 9,600 units at $72 per unit. Cost data for the year are as follows:

Direct material (per unit)	$12
Conversion cost:	
Direct labour	45,000
Variable manufacturing overhead	65,000
Fixed manufacturing overhead	220,000
Selling and administrative costs:	
Variable (per unit)	8
Fixed	118,000

The company classifies only direct material as a throughput cost.

Required:

1. Compute the company's total cost for the year assuming that variable manufacturing costs are driven by the number of units produced, and variable selling and administrative costs are driven by the number of units sold.

2. How much of this cost would be held in year-end inventory under (*a*) absorption costing, (*b*) variable costing, and (*c*) throughput costing?

3. How much of the company's total cost for the year would be included as an expense on the period's income statement under (*a*) absorption costing, (*b*) variable costing, and (*c*) throughput costing?

4. Prepare Emerson's throughput-costing income statement.

5. *Build a spreadsheet:* Construct an Excel spreadsheet to solve requirements (1) and (2) above. Show how the solution will change if the following information changes: The direct-material cost is $11 per unit, and the total direct-labour cost is $46,000.

Problem 7–59 Variable-Costing and Absorption-Costing Income Statements; Reconciling Reported Income **(LO6)**

Chataqua Can Company manufactures metal cans used in the food-processing industry. A case of cans sells for $50. The variable costs of production for one case of cans are as follows:

Direct material	$15
Direct labour	5
Variable manufacturing overhead	12
Total variable manufacturing cost per case	$32

Variable selling and administrative costs amount to $1 per case. Budgeted fixed manufacturing overhead is $800,000 per year, and fixed selling and administrative cost is $75,000 per year. The following data pertain to the company's first three years of operation.

	Year 1	Year 2	Year 3
Planned production (in units)	80,000	80,000	80,000
Finished-goods inventory (in units), January 1	0	0	20,000
Actual production (in units)	80,000	80,000	80,000
Sales (in units)	80,000	60,000	90,000
Finished-goods inventory (in units), December 31	0	20,000	10,000

Actual costs were the same as the budgeted costs.

Required:

1. Prepare operating income statements for Chataqua Can Company for its first three years of operations using:
   a. Absorption costing
   b. Variable costing
2. Reconcile Chataqua Can Company's operating income reported under absorption and variable costing for each of its first three years of operation. Use the shortcut method.
3. Suppose that during Chataqua's fourth year of operation actual production equals planned production, actual costs are equal to budgeted or standard costs, and the company ends the year with no inventory on hand.
   a. What will be the difference between absorption-costing income and variable-costing income in Year 4?
   b. What will be the relationship between total operating income for the four-year period as reported under absorption and variable costing? Explain.

Problem 7–60 Throughput Costing (LO7)

Refer to the information in the preceding problem for Chataqua Can Company. Assume that direct material is the *only unit-level* manufacturing cost.

Required: Prepare income statements for all three years using throughput costing.

Net income, Year 1: $485,000

Problem 7–61 CVP Graph; Cost Structure; Operating Leverage (LO6, 8)

Athletico, Inc. manufactures warm-up suits. The company's projected income for the coming year, based on sales of 160,000 units, is as follows:

3. Margin of safety: $4,000,000

Sales		$8,000,000
Operating expenses:		
Variable expenses	$2,000,000	
Fixed expenses	3,000,000	
Total expenses		5,000,000
Net income		$3,000,000

Required: In completing the following requirements, ignore income taxes.

1. Prepare a CVP graph for Athletico, Inc. for the coming year.
2. Calculate the firm's break-even point for the year in sales dollars.
3. What is the company's margin of safety for the year?
4. Compute Athletico's operating leverage factor, based on the budgeted sales volume for the year.
5. Compute Athletico's required sales in dollars in order to earn income of $9,000,000 in the coming year.
6. Describe the firm's cost structure. Calculate the percentage relationships between variable and fixed expenses and sales revenue.

(CMA, adapted)

Problem 7–62 Break-Even Point; Safety Margin: Law Firm (LO1, 4)

Terry Smith and two of his colleagues are considering opening a law office in a large metropolitan area. They plan to make inexpensive legal services available to those who could not otherwise afford the services. The intent is to provide easy access for their clients by having the office open 360 days per year, 16 hours each day from 7:00 a.m. to 11:00 p.m. The office would be staffed by a lawyer, paralegal, legal secretary, and clerk-receptionist for each of the two eight-hour shifts.

In order to determine the feasibility of the project, Smith hired a marketing consultant to assist with market projections. The results of this study show that if the firm spends $490,000 on advertising the first

1. Total fixed expenses: $1,491,980
2. Safety margin: $1,167,000

year, the number of new clients expected each day will be 50. Smith and his associates believe this number is reasonable and are prepared to spend the $490,000 on advertising. Other pertinent information about the operation of the office follows:

- The only charge to each new client would be $30 for the initial consultation. All cases that warrant further legal work will be accepted on a contingency basis, with the firm earning 30 percent of any favourable settlements or judgments. Smith estimates that 20 percent of new client consultations will result in favourable settlements or judgments averaging $2,000 each. It is not expected that there will be repeat clients during the first year of operations.

- The hourly wages of the staff are projected to be $25 for the lawyer, $20 for the paralegal, $15 for the legal secretary, and $10 for the clerk-receptionist. Fringe benefit expense will be 40 percent of the wages paid. A total of 400 hours of overtime is expected for the year; this will be divided equally between the legal secretary and the clerk-receptionist positions. Overtime will be paid at one and one-half times the regular wage, and the fringe benefit expense will apply to the full wage.

- Smith has located 6,000 m² of suitable office space that rents for $28 per square metre annually. Associated expenses will be $27,000 for property insurance and $37,000 for utilities.

- It will be necessary for the group to purchase malpractice insurance, which is expected to cost $180,000 annually.

- The initial investment in the office equipment will be $60,000. This equipment has an estimated useful life of four years.

- The cost of office supplies has been estimated to be $4 per expected new client consultation.

Required:

1. Determine how many new clients must visit the law office being considered by Terry Smith and his colleagues in order for the venture to break even during its first year of operations.

2. Compute the law firm's safety margin.

(CMA, adapted)

Problem 7–63   Break-Even Analysis; Operating Leverage: New Manufacturing Environment **(LO1, 4, 10)**

1(a). Computer-assisted manufacturing system, break-even point: 210,000 units

Celestial Products, Inc. has decided to introduce a new product that can be manufactured by either a computer-assisted manufacturing system or a labour-intensive production system. The manufacturing method will not affect the quality of the product. The estimated manufacturing costs by the two methods are as follows:

	Computer-Assisted Manufacturing System		Labour-Intensive Production System	
Direct material		$5.00		$5.60
Direct labour (DLH denotes direct-labour hours)	0.5 DLH @ $12	6.00	0.8 DLH @ $9	7.20
Variable overhead	0.5 DLH @ $6	3.00	0.8 DLH @ $6	4.80
Fixed overhead*		$2,440,000		$1,320,000

*These costs are directly traceable to the new product line. They would not be incurred if the new product was not produced.

The company's marketing research department has recommended an introductory unit sales price of $30. Selling expenses are estimated to be $500,000 annually plus $2 for each unit sold. (Ignore income taxes.)

Required:

1. Calculate the estimated break-even point in annual unit sales of the new product if the company uses the (*a*) labour-intensive production system; (*b*) computer-assisted manufacturing system

2. Determine the annual unit sales volume at which the firm would be indifferent between the two manufacturing methods.

3. Management must decide which manufacturing method to employ. One factor it should consider is operating leverage. Explain the concept of operating leverage. How is this concept related to Celestial Products' decision?

4. Describe the circumstances under which the firm should employ each of the two manufacturing methods.

5. Identify some business factors other than operating leverage that management should consider before selecting the manufacturing method.

(CMA, adapted)

Problem 7–64 Break-Even Analysis; Profit-Volume Graph: Movie Theatres (LO1, 3, 4)

Silver Screen, Inc. owns and operates a nationwide chain of movie theatres. The 500 properties in the Silver Screen chain vary from low-volume, small-town, single-screen theatres to high-volume, urban, multiscreen theatres. The firm's management is considering installing popcorn machines, which would allow the theatres to sell freshly popped corn rather than pre-popped corn. This new feature would be advertised to increase patronage at the company's theatres. The fresh popcorn will be sold for $1.75 per tub. The annual rental costs and the operating costs vary with the size of the popcorn machines. The machine capacities and costs are shown below. (Ignore income taxes.)

1. Break-even sales volume, regular model: 27,500 tubs
3. Volume at which both machines produce the same profit: 37,500 tubs

	Popper Model		
	Economy	**Regular**	**Super**
Annual capacity	45,000 tubs	90,000 tubs	140,000 tubs
Costs:			
Annual machine rental	$8,000	$11,000	$20,000
Popcorn cost per tub	0.13	0.13	0.13
Other costs per tub	1.22	1.14	1.05
Cost of each tub	0.08	0.08	0.08

Required:

1. Calculate each theatre's break-even sales volume (measured in tubs of popcorn) for each model of popcorn popper.
2. Prepare a profit–volume graph for one theatre, assuming that the Super Popper is purchased.
3. Calculate the volume (in tubs) at which the Economy Popper and the Regular Popper earn the same profit or loss in each movie theatre.

(CMA, adapted)

Problem 7–65 CVP Analysis of Changes in Sales Prices and Costs (LO1, 4)

Jupiter Game Company manufactures pocket electronic games. Last year Jupiter sold 25,000 games at $25 each. Total costs amounted to $525,000, of which $150,000 were considered fixed.

In an attempt to improve its product, the company is considering replacing a component part that has a cost of $2.50 with a new and better part costing $4.50 per unit in the coming year. A new machine also would be needed to increase plant capacity. The machine would cost $18,000 with a useful life of six years and no salvage value. The company uses straight-line depreciation on all plant assets. (Ignore income taxes.)

3. New break-even point: 19,125 units
5. New contribution-margin ratio: 0.40 (rounded)

Required:

1. What was Jupiter's break-even point in number of units last year?
2. How many units of product would the company have had to sell in the last year to earn $140,000?
3. If management holds the sales price constant and makes the suggested changes, how many units of product must be sold in the coming year to break even?
4. If the firm holds the sales price constant and makes the suggested changes, how many units of product will the company have to sell to make the same net income as last year?
5. If Jupiter Game Company wishes to maintain the same contribution-margin ratio, what selling price per unit of product must it charge next year to cover the increased direct-material cost?

(CMA, adapted)

Problem 7–66 Continuation of Preceding Problem; Activity-Based Costing; Advanced Manufacturing Systems; Ethical Issues (LO4, 9, 10)

Refer to the original data given for Jupiter Game Company in the preceding problem. An activity-based costing study has revealed that Jupiter's $150,000 of fixed costs include the following components:

2. Break-even point: 17,000 units

Setup (40 setups at $400 per setup)	$ 16,000
Engineering (500 hours at $25 per hour)	12,500
Inspection (1,000 inspections at $30 per inspection)	30,000
General factory overhead	61,500
Total	$120,000
Fixed selling and administrative costs	30,000
Total fixed costs	$150,000

Management is considering the installation of new, highly automated manufacturing equipment that would significantly alter the production process. In addition, management plans a move toward just-in-time inventory and production management. If the new equipment is installed, setups will be quicker and less expensive. Under the proposed JIT approach, there would be 300 setups per year at $50 per setup. Since a total quality control program would accompany the move toward JIT, only 100 inspections would be anticipated annually, at a cost of $45 each. After the installation of the new production system, 800 hours of engineering would be required, at a cost of $28 per hour. General factory overhead would increase to $166,100. However, the automated equipment would allow Jupiter to cut its unit variable cost by 20 percent. Moreover, the more consistent product quality anticipated would allow management to raise the price of electronic games to $26 per unit. (Ignore income taxes.)

Required:

1. On seeing the ABC analysis given in the problem, Jupiter's vice-president of manufacturing exclaimed to the controller, "I thought you told me this $150,000 cost was fixed. These don't look like fixed costs at all. What you're telling me now is that setup costs us $800 every time we set up a production run. What gives?"

   As Jupiter's controller, write a short memo explaining to the vice-president what is going on.

2. Compute Jupiter's new break-even point if the proposed automated equipment is installed.

3. Determine how many units Jupiter will have to sell to show a profit of $140,000, assuming the new technology is adopted.

4. If Jupiter adopts the new manufacturing technology, will its break-even point be higher or lower? Will the number of sales units required to earn a profit of $140,000 be higher or lower? (Refer to your answers for the first two requirements of the preceding problem.) Are the results in this case consistent with what you would typically expect to find? Explain.

5. The decision as to whether to purchase the automated manufacturing equipment will be made by Jupiter's board of directors. In order to support the proposed acquisition, the vice-president of manufacturing asked the controller to prepare a report on the financial implications of the decision. As part of the report, the vice-president asked the controller to compute the new break-even point, assuming the installation of the equipment. The controller complied, as in requirement (2) of this problem.

   When the vice-president of manufacturing saw that the break-even point would increase, he asked the controller to delete the break-even analysis from the report. What should the controller do? Which ethical standards for management accountants are involved here?

Problem 7–67 CVP Relationships: Retail (LO1, 4)

2. Decrease in operating income: $(1,400)

Condensed monthly income data for Thurber Book Stores are presented in the following table for November 20x1. (Ignore income taxes.)

	Mall Store	Downtown Store	Total
Sales	$80,000	$120,000	$200,000
Less: Variable expenses	32,000	84,000	116,000
Contribution margin	$48,000	$ 36,000	$ 84,000
Less: Fixed expenses	20,000	40,000	60,000
Operating income	$28,000	$ (4,000)	$ 24,000

Additional Information:

- Management estimates that closing the downtown store would result in a 10 percent decrease in mall store sales, while closing the mall store would not affect downtown store sales.

- One-fourth of each store's fixed expenses would continue through December 31, 20x2, if either store was closed.

- The operating results for November 20x1 are representative of all months.

Required:

1. Calculate the increase or decrease in Thurber's monthly operating income during 20x2 if the downtown store is closed.

2. The management of Thurber is considering a promotional campaign at the downtown store that would not affect the mall store. Annual promotional expenses at the downtown store would be increased by $60,000 in order to increase downtown store sales by 10 percent. What would be the effect of this promotional campaign on the company's monthly operating income during 20x2?

3. One-half of the downtown store's dollar sales are from items sold at their variable cost to attract customers to the store. Thurber's management is considering the deletion of these items, a move that would reduce the downtown store's direct fixed expenses by 15 percent and result in the loss of 20 percent of the remaining downtown store's sales volume. This change would not affect the mall store. What would be the effect on Thurber's monthly operating income if the items sold at their variable cost are eliminated?

4. *Build a spreadsheet:* Construct an Excel spreadsheet to solve all of the preceding requirements. Show how the solution will change if the following information changes: The downtown store's sales amounted to $126,000 and its variable expenses were $86,000.

(CMA, adapted)

Problem 7–68 CVP; Multiple Products; Changes in Costs and Sales Mix **(LO4, 5)**

Coquitlam Tool Company (CTC) manufactures a line of electric garden tools that are sold in general hardware stores. The company's controller, Will Fulton, has just received the sales forecast for the coming year for CTC's three products: line trimmers, hedge clippers, and leaf blowers. CTC has experienced considerable variations in sales volumes and variable costs over the past two years, and Fulton believes the forecast should be carefully evaluated from a CVP viewpoint. The preliminary budget information for 20x2 follows:

2. Total sales to break even: 162,500 units

3. Weighted-average unit contribution margin: $13.00

	Line Trimmers	Hedge Clippers	Leaf Blowers
Unit sales	50,000	50,000	100,000
Unit selling price	$28	$36	$48
Variable manufacturing cost per unit	13	12	25
Variable selling cost per unit	5	4	6

For 20x2, CTC's fixed manufacturing overhead is budgeted at $2,000,000, and the company's fixed selling and administrative expenses are forecasted to be $600,000. CTC has a tax rate of 40 percent.

Required:

1. Determine CTC's budgeted net income for 20x2.

2. Assuming the sales mix remains as budgeted, determine how many units of each product CTC must sell in order to break even in 20x2.

3. After preparing the original estimates, management determined that its variable manufacturing cost of leaf blowers would increase by 20 percent, and the variable selling cost of hedge clippers could be expected to increase by $1 per unit. However, management has decided not to change the selling price of either product. In addition, management has learned that its leaf blower has been perceived as the best value on the market, and it can expect to sell three times as many leaf blowers as each of its other products. Under these circumstances, determine how many units of each product CTC would have to sell in order to break even in 20x2.

(CMA, adapted)

Problem 7–69 CVP Relationships; International Business; Automation **(LO1, 4, 10)**

The Limestone Company produces thin limestone sheets used for cosmetic facing on buildings. The following income statement represents the operating results for the year just ended. The company had sales of 1,800 tonnes during the year. The manufacturing capacity of the firm's facilities is 3,000 tonnes per year. (Ignore income taxes.)

1. Break-even volume in tonnes: 1,100

5. Break-even point in tonnes: 1,224

THE LIMESTONE COMPANY
Income Statement
For the Year Ended December 31, 20x1

Sales	$900,000
Variable costs:	
Manufacturing	315,000
Selling costs	180,000
Total variable costs	495,000
Contribution margin	405,000
Fixed costs:	
Manufacturing	100,000
Selling	107,500
Administrative	40,000
Total fixed costs	247,500
Net income	$157,500

Required:

1. Calculate the company's break-even volume in tonnes for 20x1.

2. If the sales volume is estimated to be 2,100 tonnes in the next year, and if the prices and costs stay at the same levels and amounts, what is the net income that management can expect for 20x2?

3. Limestone has been trying for years to get a foothold in the European market. The company has a potential German customer that has offered to buy 1,500 tonnes at $450 per tonne. Assume that all of the firm's costs would be at the same levels and rates as in 20x1. What net income would the firm earn if it took this order and rejected some business from regular customers so as not to exceed capacity?

4. Limestone plans to market its product in a new territory. Management estimates that an advertising and promotion program costing $61,500 annually would be needed for the next two or three years. In addition, a $25 per tonne sales commission to the sales force in the new territory, over and above the current commission, would be required. How many tonnes would have to be sold in the new territory to maintain the firm's current net income? Assume that sales and costs will continue as in 20x1 in the firm's established territories.

5. Management is considering replacing its labour-intensive process with an automated production system. This would result in an increase of $58,500 annually in fixed manufacturing costs. The variable manufacturing costs would decrease by $25 per tonne. Compute the new break-even volume in tonnes and in sales dollars.

6. Ignore the facts presented in requirement (5). Assume that management estimates that the selling price per tonne would decline by 10 percent next year. Variable costs would increase by $40 per tonne, and fixed costs would not change. What sales volume in dollars would be required to earn a net income of $94,500 next year?

(CMA, adapted)

Cases

Case 7–70 Break-Even Analysis; Hospital CVP Relationships (LO1,4)

Seattle Medical Centre operates a general hospital. The medical centre also rents space and beds to separately owned entities rendering specialized services, such as pediatrics and psychiatric care. Seattle Medical Centre charges each separate entity for common services, such as patients' meals and laundry, and for administrative services, such as billings and collections. Space and bed rentals are fixed charges for the year, based on bed capacity rented to each entity. Seattle Medical Centre charged the following costs to Pediatrics for the year ended June 30, 20x1:

	Patient Days (variable)	Bed Capacity (fixed)
Dietary	$ 600,000	—
Janitorial	—	$ 70,000
Laundry	300,000	—
Laboratory	450,000	—
Pharmacy	350,000	—
Repairs and maintenance	—	30,000
General and administrative	—	1,300,000
Rent	—	1,500,000
Billings and collections	300,000	—
Total	$2,000,000	$2,900,000

During the year ended June 30, 20x1, Pediatrics charged each patient an average of $300 per day, had a capacity of 60 beds, and had revenue of $6 million for 365 days. In addition, Pediatrics directly employed personnel with the following annual salary costs per employee: supervising nurses, $25,000; nurses, $20,000; and aides, $9,000.

Seattle Medical Centre has the following minimum departmental personnel requirements, based on total annual patient days:

Annual Patient Days	Aides	Nurses	Supervising Nurse
Up to 22,000	20	10	4
22,001 to 26,000	25	14	5
26,001 to 29,200	31	16	5

Pediatrics always employs only the minimum number of required personnel. Salaries of supervising nurses, nurses, and aides are therefore fixed within ranges of annual patient days.

Pediatrics operated at 100 percent capacity on 90 days during the year ended June 30, 20x1. Administrators estimate that on these 90 days, Pediatrics could have filled another 20 beds above capacity. Seattle Medical Centre has an additional 20 beds available for rent for the year ending June 30, 20x2. Such additional rental would increase Pediatrics' fixed charges based on bed capacity. (In the following requirements, ignore income taxes.)

Required:

1. Calculate the minimum number of patient days required for Pediatrics to break even for the year ending June 30, 20x2, if the additional 20 beds are not rented. Patient demand is unknown, but assume that revenue per patient day, cost per patient day, cost per bed, and salary rates will remain the same as for the year ended June 30, 20x1.

2. Assume that patient demand, revenue per patient day, cost per patient day, cost per bed, and salary rates for the year ending June 30, 20x1, remain the same as for the year ended June 30, 20x2. Prepare a schedule of Pediatrics' increase in revenue and increase in costs for the year ending June 30, 20x1. Determine the net increase or decrease in Pediatrics' earnings from the additional 20 beds if Pediatrics rents this extra capacity from Seattle Medical Centre.

(CPA, adapted)

Case 7–71 Comparison of Absorption and Variable Costing; Actual Costing **(LO2, 3, 4)**

The Lehighton Chalk Company manufactures blackboard chalk for educational uses. The company's product is sold by the box at $50 per unit. Lehighton uses an actual costing system, which means that the actual costs of direct material, direct labour, and manufacturing overhead are entered into work-in-process inventory. The actual application rate for manufacturing overhead is computed each year; actual manufacturing overhead is divided by actual production (in units) to compute the application rate. Information for Lehighton's first two years of operation is as follows:

1. Operating income, Year 1: $27,500

2. Operating income, Year 2: $20,500

	Year 1	Year 2
Sales (in units)	2,500	2,500
Production (in units)	3,000	2,000
Production costs:		
Variable manufacturing costs	$21,000	$14,000
Fixed manufacturing overhead	42,000	42,000
Selling and administrative costs:		
Variable	25,000	25,000
Fixed	20,000	20,000

Required: The Lehighton Chalk Company had no beginning or ending work-in-process inventories for either year.

1. Prepare operating income statements for both years based on absorption costing.
2. Prepare operating income statements for both years based on variable costing.
3. Prepare a numerical reconciliation of the difference in income reported under the two costing methods used in requirements (1) and (2).

Case 7–72 Continuation of Preceding Case; Analysis of Differences in Absorption-Costing and Variable-Costing Income Statements **(LO1, 4)**

Refer to the information given in the preceding problem for the Lehighton Chalk Company.

Required:

1. Reconcile Lehighton's income reported under absorption and variable costing, during each year, by comparing the following two amounts on each income statement:
   - Cost of goods sold
   - Fixed cost (expensed as a period expense)
2. What was Lehighton's total income across both years under absorption costing and under variable costing?
3. What was the total sales revenue across both years under absorption costing and under variable costing?
4. What was the total of all costs expensed on the income statements across both years under absorption costing and under variable costing?
5. Subtract the total costs expensed across both years (requirement [4]) from the total sales revenue across both years (requirement [3]): (*a*) under absorption costing and (*b*) under variable costing.
6. Comment on the results obtained in requirements (1), (2), (3), and (4) in light of the following assertion: *Timing is the key in distinguishing between absorption and variable costing.*

Case 7–73 Continuation of Preceding Case; Absorption and Variable Costing; Effect on the Balance Sheet **(LO1, 4)**

Refer to the information given in Case 7–71 for Lehighton Chalk Company. Selected information from Lehighton's year-end balance sheets for its first two years of operation is as follows:

LEHIGHTON CHALK COMPANY
Selected Balance Sheet Information

Based on Absorption Costing	End of Year 1	End of Year 2
Finished-goods inventory	$10,500	$ 0
Retained earnings	16,500	24,600
Based on Variable Costing	**End of Year 1**	**End of Year 2**
Finished-goods inventory	$ 3,500	$ 0
Retained earnings	9,500	24,600

Required:

1. Why is the Year 1 ending balance in finished-goods inventory higher if absorption costing is used than if variable costing is used?
2. Why is the Year 2 ending balance in finished-goods inventory the same under absorption and variable costing?
3. Notice that the ending balance of finished-goods inventory under absorption costing is greater than or equal to the ending finished-goods inventory balance under variable costing *for both Years 1 and 2.* Will this relationship always hold true at any balance sheet date? Explain.
4. Compute the amount by which the year-end balance in finished-goods inventory declined during Year 2 (i.e., between December 31 of Year 1 and December 31 of Year 2):
   - Using the data from the balance sheet prepared under absorption costing
   - Using the data from the balance sheet prepared under variable costing

5. Refer to your calculations from requirement (4). Compute the difference in the amount by which the year-end balances in finished-goods inventory declined under absorption versus variable costing. Then compare the amount of this difference with the difference in the company's reported income for Year 2 under absorption versus variable costing. (Refer to the income statements prepared in Case 7–71.)

6. Notice that the retained earnings balance at the end of both Years 1 and 2 on the balance sheet prepared under absorption costing is greater than or equal to the corresponding retained earnings balance on the statement prepared under variable costing. Will this relationship hold true at any balance sheet date? Explain.

ONLINE SUPPLEMENT 7A Effect of Income Taxes on CVP Analysis

   See Connect for a supplement to this chapter.

   Practise and learn online with Connect.

CHAPTER EIGHT

Profit Planning and Activity-Based Budgeting

FOCUS COMPANY

This chapter's focus is on CozyCamp Company, a manufacturer of backpacking tents based in Port Moody, BC. CozyCamp uses a highly automated manufacturing process to produce its tents, and 75 percent of its sales are made through its website: cozycamp.ca. In this chapter, we will explore how CozyCamp develops its annual budget. A budget is a detailed plan, expressed in quantitative terms, that specifies how resources will be acquired and used during a specific period of time. CozyCamp's management uses a budget for many purposes, including planning, communication, resource allocation, control of operations, and evaluation of performance and provision of incentives.

IN CONTRAST

In contrast to the manufacturing setting of CozyCamp, we explore budgeting at the Canadian Fitness Cooperative. As the name suggests, this service organization operates as a cooperative. The members elect a board of directors that hires a manager and assistant manager to run the fitness club. The Cooperative does not seek to make a profit. Every year, membership fees are adjusted with the intention of bringing in just enough revenue to cover projected expenses. The club's budget is an important part of that process.

After completing this chapter, you should be able to

1. List and explain five purposes of budgeting systems.

2. Describe the similarities and differences in the operational budgets prepared by manufacturers, service industry firms, merchandisers, and nonprofit organizations.

3. Explain the concept of activity-based budgeting and the benefits it brings to the budgeting process.

4. Prepare each of the budget schedules that make up the master budget.

5. Discuss the role of assumptions and predictions in budgeting.

6. Describe a typical organization's process of budget administration.

7. Understand the importance of budgeting product life-cycle costs.

8. Discuss the behavioural implications of budgetary slack and participative budgeting.

Developing a budget is a critical step in planning any economic activity. This is true for businesses, for government agencies, and for individuals. We all have to budget our money to meet day-to-day expenses and to plan for major expenditures, such as buying a car or paying college or university tuition fees. Similarly, businesses of all types and government units at every level have to make financial plans to carry out routine operations, plan for major expenditures, and help in making financial decisions.

Purposes of Budgeting Systems

A **budget** is a detailed plan, expressed in quantitative terms, that specifies how resources will be acquired and used during a specified period of time. The procedures used to develop a budget constitute a **budgeting system**. Budgeting systems have five primary purposes: to force formulation of a plan of action; to facilitate communication and coordination; to identify the best allocation of resources; to set a benchmark for measurement of profit and operations; and to evaluate performance and provide incentives.

Learning Objective 1

List and explain five purposes of budgeting systems.

Planning   The most obvious purpose of a budget is to develop a plan of action. The budgeting process forces the individuals who make up an organization to plan ahead. The development of a quarterly budget for a Fairmont Hotel, for example, forces the hotel manager, the reservation manager, and the food and beverage manager to plan for the staffing and supplies needed to meet anticipated demand for the hotel's services.

Facilitating Communication and Coordination   For any organization to be effective, every manager in the organization must be aware of the plans made by other managers. In order to plan reservations and ticket sales effectively, the reservations manager for WestJet Airlines must know the flight schedules developed by the airline's route manager. The budgeting process pulls together the plans of each manager in an organization.

Allocating Resources   Generally, an organization's resources are limited, and budgets provide one means of allocating resources among competing uses. The City of Port Moody, for example, must allocate its revenue among basic life services (such as police and fire protection), maintenance of property and equipment (such as city streets, parks, and vehicles), and other community services (such as child-care services and programs to prevent alcohol and drug abuse).

Controlling Profit and Operations   A budget is a plan, and plans are subject to change. Nevertheless, a budget serves as a useful benchmark against which actual results can be compared. For example, Manulife Financial can compare its actual sales of insurance policies for a year against its budgeted sales. Such a comparison can help managers evaluate the firm's effectiveness in selling insurance.

Evaluating Performance and Providing Incentives   Comparing actual results with budgeted results also helps managers to evaluate the performance of individuals, departments, divisions, or entire companies. Since budgets are used to evaluate performance, they also can be used to provide incentives for people to perform well. For example, General Motors Corporation, like many other companies, provides incentives for managers to improve profits by awarding bonuses to managers who meet or exceed their budgeted profit goals.

> "Budgeting is used extensively for cost control. Each plant manager develops a plant budget, and then each department supervisor is responsible for his or her own cost center. . . . There are budgets for every department in the company." (8a)
> **Best Foods (A subsidiary of Unilever)**

Types of Budgets

Different types of budgets serve different purposes. A **master budget**, or **profit plan**, is a comprehensive set of budgets covering all phases of an organization's operations for a specified period of time. We will examine a master budget in detail later in this chapter.

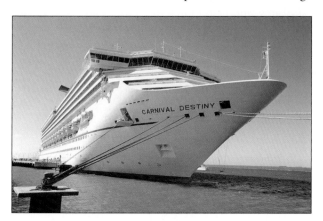

Diverse organizations use budgets for a variety of reasons. A cruise line, such as Carnival, uses budgets to plan for meeting the payroll and operating expenses and to coordinate operations by matching staffing with projected cruise demand. Carnival also uses its budgeting process to allocate capital improvement funds among competing projects, such as expanding its fleet or improving land-side facilities.

Budgeted financial statements, often called **pro forma financial statements**, show how the financial statements will appear at a specified time if operations proceed according to plan. Budgeted financial statements include a *budgeted income statement, a budgeted balance sheet,* and *a budgeted statement of cash flows.*

A **capital budget** is a plan for the acquisition of capital assets, such as buildings and equipment. A **financial budget** is a plan that shows how the organization will acquire its financial resources, such as through the issuance of stock or incurrence of debt.

Budgets are developed for specific time periods. *Short-range budgets* cover a year, a quarter, or a month, whereas *long-range budgets* cover periods longer than a year. **Rolling budgets** are continually updated by periodically adding a new incremental time period, such as a quarter, and dropping the period just completed. Rolling budgets are also called **revolving budgets** or **continuous budgets**.

The Master Budget: A Planning Tool

The master budget, the main output of a budgeting system, is a comprehensive profit plan that ties together all phases of an organization's operations. The master budget comprises many separate budgets, or schedules, that are interdependent. Exhibit 8–1 portrays these interrelationships in a flow chart.

Sales of Goods or Services

The starting point for any master budget is a sales revenue budget based on a sales forecast for goods or services. Airlines forecast the number of passengers on each of their routes. Financial institutions forecast the number and dollar amount of consumer loans and home mortgages to be provided. Hotels forecast the number of rooms that will be occupied during various seasons. Manufacturing and merchandising companies forecast sales of their goods. Some companies sell both goods and services. For example, Canadian Tire is a large merchandising company, but its Auto Service Centres provide the firm with substantial service revenue.

Sales Forecasting

All companies recognize two things when it comes to forecasting sales of goods or services—**sales forecasting** is a critical step in the budgeting process, and it is very difficult to do accurately.

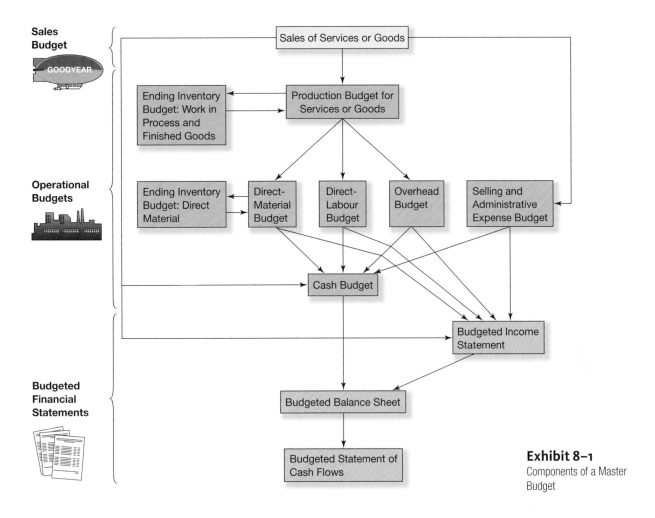

Sales Budget

Operational Budgets

Budgeted Financial Statements

Exhibit 8–1
Components of a Master Budget

Various procedures are used in sales forecasting, and the final forecast usually combines information from many different sources. Many firms have a top management-level market research staff whose job is to coordinate the company's sales forecasting efforts. Typically, everyone from key executives to the firm's sales personnel will be asked to contribute sales projections.

Major factors considered when forecasting sales include

1. Past sales levels and trends
    a. For the firm developing the forecast (e.g., Petro-Canada)
    b. For the entire industry (e.g., the petroleum industry)
2. General economic trends. (Is the economy growing? How fast? Is a recession or economic slowdown expected?)
3. Economic trends in the company's industry. (In the petroleum industry, for example, is personal travel likely to increase, thereby implying increased demand for gasoline?)
4. Other factors expected to affect sales in the industry. (Is an unusually cold winter expected, which would result in increased demand for home heating oil?)
5. Political and legal events. (e.g., is any legislation pending that would affect the demand for petroleum, such as tax incentives to use alternative energy sources?)

"Sales forecasting is difficult in every industry, but it's especially difficult in a highly competitive industry such as ours. Sales forecasting relies on several areas for input—market research, sales and marketing. We forecast the size of the market for each product, and then we forecast our share of that market." (8b)
Best Foods
(A subsidiary of Unilever)

6. The intended pricing policy of the company
7. Planned advertising and product promotion
8. Expected actions of competitors
9. New products contemplated by the company or other firms (e.g., automobile manufacturers are continuing to develop hybrids, which run on a combination of gasoline and battery power, thereby reducing the demand for gasoline.)
10. Market research studies

The starting point in the sales forecasting process is generally the sales level of the prior year. Then the market research staff considers the information discussed above along with input from key executives and sales personnel. In many firms, elaborate *econometric models* are built to incorporate all of the available information systematically. (*Econometric* means *economic measurement*.) Statistical methods, such as regression analysis and probability distributions for sales, are often used. A great deal of effort generally goes into the sales forecast, since it is such a critical step in the budgeting process. Making a sales forecast is like shooting an arrow. If the archer's aim is off by only a fraction of a centimetre, the arrow will go farther and farther astray and miss the bull's eye by a wide margin. Similarly, a slightly inaccurate sales forecast, coming at the very beginning of the budgeting process, will throw off all of the other schedules in the master budget.

Operational Budgets

Based on the sales budget, a company develops a set of **operational budgets** that specify how its operations will be carried out to meet the demand for its goods or services. The budgets constituting this operational portion of the master budget are depicted in the middle portion of Exhibit 8–1.

Manufacturing Firms   A manufacturing company develops a *production budget*, which shows the number of product units to be manufactured. Coupled with the production budget are *ending-inventory budgets* for raw material, work in process, and finished goods. Manufacturers plan to have some inventory on hand at all times to meet peak demand, while keeping production at a stable level. From the production budget, a manufacturer develops budgets for the direct materials, direct labour, and overhead that will be required in the production process. A budget for selling and administrative expenses is also prepared.

Merchandising Firms   The operational portion of the master budget is similar in a merchandising firm, but instead of a production budget for goods, a merchandiser develops a budget for merchandise purchases. A merchandising firm will not have a budget for direct material, because it does not engage in production. However, the merchandiser will develop budgets for labour (or human resources), overhead, and selling and administrative expenses.

Service Industry Firms   Based on the sales budget for its services, a service industry firm develops a set of budgets that show how the demand for those services will be met. An airline, for example, prepares the following operational budgets: a budget of planned air miles to be flown; material budgets for spare aircraft parts, aircraft fuel, and in-flight food; labour budgets for flight crews and maintenance staff; and an overhead budget.

Cash Budget   Every business prepares a cash budget. This budget shows expected cash receipts, as a result of selling goods or services, and planned cash disbursements, to pay expenses incurred by the firm.

Summary of Operational Budgets Operational budgets differ since they are adapted to the operations of individual companies in various industries. However, operational budgets are also similar in important ways. In each firm, they encompass a detailed plan for using the basic factors of production—material, labour, and overhead—to produce a product or provide a service.

Budgeted Financial Statements

The final portion of the master budget, depicted in Exhibit 8–1, includes a budgeted income statement, a budgeted balance sheet, and a budgeted statement of cash flows. These budgeted financial statements show the overall financial results of the organization's planned operations for the budget period.

Nonprofit Organizations

The master budget for a nonprofit organization includes many of the components shown in Exhibit 8–1. However, there are important differences. Many nonprofit organizations provide services free of charge, so there is no sales budget as shown in Exhibit 8–1. However, such organizations do begin their budgeting process with a budget that shows the level of services to be provided. For example, the budget for the City of Moncton would show the planned levels of various public services, such as the hours of operation for libraries and parks.

Nonprofit organizations also prepare budgets showing their anticipated funding. The City of Moncton budgets for such revenue sources as city taxes and provincial and federal revenue sharing.

In summary, all organizations begin the budgeting process with plans for (1) the goods or services to be provided and (2) the revenue to be available, whether from sales or from other funding sources.

Activity-Based Budgeting

The process of constructing a master budget can be significantly enhanced if the concepts of activity-based costing (ABC) are applied.[1] ABC uses a two-stage cost-assignment process. In Stage One, overhead costs are assigned to cost pools that represent the most significant *activities* of the production process. The activities identified vary across manufacturers, but such activities as engineering design, material handling, machine setup, production scheduling, inspection, quality control, and purchasing provide examples.

After assigning costs to the activity cost pools in Stage One, cost drivers are identified that are appropriate for each cost pool. Then, in Stage Two, the overhead costs are allocated from each activity cost pool to cost objects (e.g., products, services, and customers) in proportion to the amount of activity consumed.

Exhibit 8–2 portrays the two-stage allocation process used in ABC systems.

Applying ABC concepts to the budgeting process yields **activity-based budgeting (ABB)**.[2] Under ABB, the first step is to specify the products or services to be produced and the customers to be served. The activities that are necessary to produce these products and services are then determined. Finally, the resources necessary to perform the specified activities are quantified. Conceptually, ABB takes the ABC model and reverses the flow of the analysis. As portrayed in Exhibit 8–3, ABC assigns resource costs to activities, and then it assigns activity costs to products and services produced and customers served. ABB, on the other hand, begins by forecasting the demand for

Learning Objective **3**

Explain the concept of activity-based budgeting and the benefits it brings to the budgeting process.

Commenting on how the company's ABC and activity-based management (ABM) initiatives led to activity-based budgeting: "We are using ABM as a means to execute our strategic management process." (8d)
Paradyne Corporation

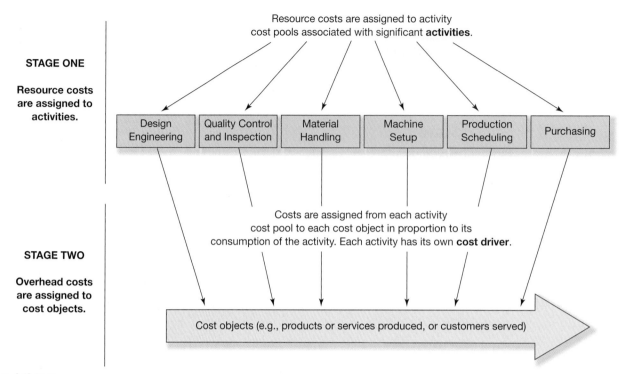

Exhibit 8–2
Activity-Based Costing System

products and services as well as the customers to be served. These forecasts are then used to plan the activities for the budget period and budget the resources necessary to carry out the activities.

In the next section of this chapter, we will illustrate the process of constructing a master budget. Notice how the conceptual ABB model is used in the budgeting process. In the context of the master budget illustration, we will explore the benefits and implications of the ABB approach.

Exhibit 8–3
Activity-Based Costing versus
Activity-Based Budgeting

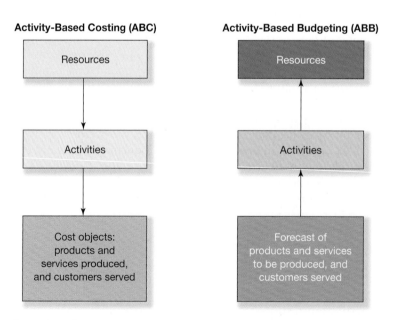

Source: Robert S. Kaplan and Robin Cooper, *Cost and Effect* (Boston: Harvard Business School Press, 1998), p. 303.

ACTIVITY-BASED BUDGETING (ABB) AT AMERICAN EXPRESS AND PARADYNE

American Express has successfully used ABB for its travel-related services in its New York operations. This system has been used for several years to identify and implement cost-reduction and process-improvement initiatives. Then, an activity-by-activity analysis of each department has allowed process-improvement savings to be factored into the forecasted costs for each department in the next budget cycle.[3]

Paradyne Corporation designs and produces medium-and high-speed data communications equipment, which provides an interface between telephone networks and computers. The company's activity-based costing project ultimately led to activity-based budgeting. As ABM and ABB matured at Paradyne, the company experienced a culture change. A key lesson learned in this case was that linking activity-based costing to the budgeting process and performance evaluation led to the integration of ABC into the management of the company.[4]

Preparing the Master Budget

To illustrate the steps in developing a master budget, we will focus on CozyCamp, a manufacturer of backpacking tents. The company is wholly owned by Mary Edwards, who started the company in her basement 15 years ago. After a difficult two to three years, success came quickly for the company, and Edwards eventually built a production facility. The manufacturing process is highly automated, using several machines to cut out pieces of tent fabric and sew them together to form a lightweight but durable backpacking tent. Production of the aluminum tent poles is outsourced to a company nearby, and the poles are purchased on a just-in-time basis so they can be packaged with the finished tents just before they are shipped. Initially, sales were made to regional retailers in western Canada using a traditional sales approach. Three years ago, however, the company moved into the world of Internet sales and almost 75 percent of CozyCamp's sales are now made through its website. Although CozyCamp retained several of its sales staff to handle the traditional sales to area retailers, new staff had to be hired to handle the company's Internet sales environment. Tents are shipped to Internet customers via Canada Post, Purolator, UPS, FedEx, and other express delivery services.

The 20x2 master budget for CozyCamp has just been completed. It contains the following schedules, which are displayed and explained in the following pages:

Learning Objective **4**

Prepare each of the budget schedules that make up the master budget.

CozyCamp Company

Schedule	Title of Schedule
1	Sales Budget
2	Cash Receipts Budget
3	Production Budget
4	Direct-Material Budget
5	Direct-Labour Budget
6	Manufacturing-Overhead Budget
7	Selling, General, and Administrative Expense Budget
8	Cash Disbursements Budget
9	Cash Budget

Schedule	Title of Schedule
10	Budgeted Schedule of Cost of Goods Manufactured and Sold
11	Budgeted Income Statement
12	Budgeted Statement of Cash Flows
13	Budgeted Balance Sheet

Sales Budget

The first step in developing CozyCamp's 20x2 master budget is to prepare the **sales budget**, which is shown as Schedule 1. This budget displays the projected sales in units for each quarter and then multiplies the unit sales by the sales price to determine sales revenue. Notice that there is a significant seasonal pattern in the sales forecast, with the bulk of the sales in the spring and summer.

Schedule 1

CozyCamp Company

COZYCAMP COMPANY
Sales Budget
For the Year Ending December 31, 20x2

	Quarter				
	1st	2nd	3rd	4th	Year
Sales in units	5,000	15,000	20,000	10,000	50,000
Unit sales price	× $225	× $225	× $225	× $225	× $225
Total sales revenue	$1,125,000	$3,375,000	$4,500,000	$2,250,000	$11,250,000

Cash Receipts Budget

The **cash receipts budget** details the expected cash collections during a budget period. CozyCamp's cash receipts budget is shown as Schedule 2. The firm collects 80 percent of its sales during the same quarter in which the sale is made, and another 18 percent in the following quarter. Two percent of each quarter's sales are expected to be uncollectable.

Schedule 2

CozyCamp Company

COZYCAMP COMPANY
Cash Receipts Budget
For the Year Ending December 31, 20x2

	Quarter				
	1st	2nd	3rd	4th	Year
Sales revenue (Schedule 1)	$1,125,000	$3,375,000	$4,500,000	$2,250,000	$11,250,000
Collections in quarter of sale (80% of sales)	$ 900,000	$2,700,000	$3,600,000	$1,800,000	$ 9,000,000
Collections in quarter following sale (18% of prior quarter's sales)*	405,000†	202,500	607,500	810,000	2,025,000
Total cash receipts	$1,305,000	$2,902,500	$4,207,500	$2,610,000	$11,025,000

*Two percent of each quarter's sales are expected to be uncollectable, as shown in the table below.
†The sales revenue in the prior quarter (i.e., the 4th quarter of 20x1) is assumed to be $2,250,000. Therefore, $405,000 is 18% of $2,250,000.

	Quarter				
	1st	2nd	3rd	4th	Year
Uncollectible accounts	$22,500	$67,500	$90,000	$45,000	$225,000

How to Budget Cash Receipts   To understand how the cash receipts budget is prepared, let's focus on the second quarter column, which is shaded. The $3,375,000 of total revenue comes directly from Schedule 1, the sales budget (second column, last row). Since most of CozyCamp's sales are on account, not all of the second quarter's revenue will be collected during the second quarter. The cash that the firm will collect during the second quarter has two parts, as depicted in the following diagram.

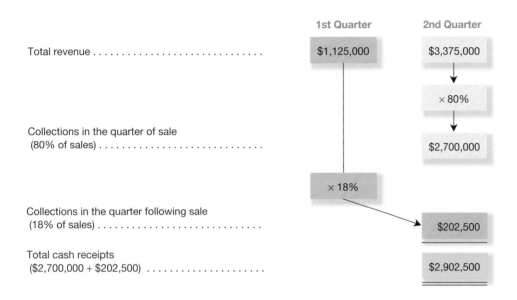

The second quarter's total cash receipts are the sum of $2,700,000 (80 percent of second quarter sales) and $202,500 (18 percent of first quarter sales).

One final point to notice is that 2 percent of each quarter's sales are not expected to be collected. Thus, the $67,500 of second quarter uncollectable accounts amounts to 2 percent of the second quarter's revenue ($67,500 = 2% × $3,375,000). Almost all of CozyCamp's uncollectable accounts relate to the company's traditional sales, not to website sales.

Production Budget

The **production budget** shows the number of units of goods (or services) that are to be produced (or rendered) during a budget period. CozyCamp's production budget, displayed as Schedule 3, determines the number of tents to be produced each quarter based on the quarterly sales projections in the sales budget. Schedule 3 is based on the following formula:

$$\text{Sales in units} + \text{Desired ending inventory of finished goods} = \text{Total units required}$$

$$\text{Total units required} - \text{Expected beginning inventory of finished goods} = \text{Units to be produced}$$

Focus on the shaded second quarter column in Schedule 3. Expected sales are 15,000 tents, and the company wants to have 2,000 finished units on hand at the end of the quarter (10 percent of the expected sales for the third quarter). However, 1,500 tents are expected to be available at the beginning of the second quarter, so only 15,500 tents need to be produced.

Schedule 3

CozyCamp Company

	COZYCAMP COMPANY				
	Production Budget				
	For the Year Ending December 31, 20x2				
		Quarter			
	1st	**2nd**	**3rd**	**4th**	**Year**
Sales in units (Schedule 1)	5,000	15,000	20,000	10,000	50,000
Add desired ending inventory of finished goods*	1,500	2,000	1,000	500†	500
Total units required	6,500	17,000	21,000	10,500	50,500
Less expected beginning inventory of finished goods	500	1,500	2,000	1,000	500
Units to be produced.	6,000	15,500	19,000	9,500	50,000

*Ten percent of the next quarter's expected sales.

†Ten percent of the expected sales for the first quarter of the next year, 20x3, which is predicted to be 5,000 units.

Direct-Material Budget

The **direct-material budget** shows the number of units and the cost of material to be purchased and used during a budget period. CozyCamp's direct-material budget, displayed as Schedule 4, has two sections: one for tent fabric and one for tent poles. As is true for almost all manufacturers, CozyCamp's direct-material cost is a unit-level cost.[5] Each tent requires 12 metres of fabric and one tent pole kit. The tent poles required for each tent are prepackaged in a kit by the outside vendor and delivered to CozyCamp on a just-in-time basis.[6] The shaded top portion of Schedule 4 shows the total amount of tent fabric *needed* to make tents during each quarter and the amount of tent fabric to be *purchased* each quarter. This part of the schedule is based on the following formula.

$$\begin{matrix} \text{Raw} \\ \text{material} \\ \text{required} \\ \text{for} \\ \text{production} \end{matrix} + \begin{matrix} \text{Desired} \\ \text{ending} \\ \text{inventory} \\ \text{of raw} \\ \text{material} \end{matrix} = \begin{matrix} \text{Total raw} \\ \text{material} \\ \text{required} \end{matrix}$$

$$\begin{matrix} \text{Total raw} \\ \text{material} \\ \text{required} \end{matrix} - \begin{matrix} \text{Expected beginning} \\ \text{inventory of} \\ \text{raw material} \end{matrix} = \begin{matrix} \text{Raw material} \\ \text{to be} \\ \text{purchased} \end{matrix}$$

The lower portion of Schedule 4 calculates the quantity and cost of tent pole kits to be purchased each quarter.

Finally, the last row totals the cost of tent fabric and tent pole kits to show the total cost of raw material to be purchased each quarter.

Schedule 4

CozyCamp Company

COZYCAMP COMPANY
Direct-Material Budget
For the Year Ending December 31, 20x2

| | Quarter | | | | |
	1st	2nd	3rd	4th	Year
Tent fabric:					
Tents to be produced (Schedule 3)	6,000	15,500	19,000	9,500	50,000
Raw material required per unit (metres of fabric)	× 12	× 12	× 12	× 12	× 12
Raw material required for production (metres)	72,000	186,000	228,000	114,000	600,000
Add desired ending inventory of raw material (metres)*	18,600	22,800	11,400	7,200†	7,200
Total raw material required	90,600	208,800	239,400	121,200	607,200
Less expected beginning inventory of raw material (metres).	7,200	18,600	22,800	11,400	7,200
Raw material to be purchased (metres)	83,400	190,200	216,600	109,800	600,000
Cost per metre	× $9	× $9	× $9	× $9	× $9
Total cost of tent fabric purchases	$750,600	$1,711,800	$1,949,400	$ 988,200	$5,400,000
Tent poles:					
Tents to be produced (Schedule 3)	6,000	15,500	19,000	9,500	50,000
Tent pole kits required per tent	× 1	× 1	× 1	× 1	× 1
Tent pole kits to be purchased‡	6,000	15,500	19,000	9,500	50,000
Cost per tent pole kit	× $20	× $20	× $20	× $20	× $20
Total cost of tent pole kit purchases	$120,000	$ 310,000	$ 380,000	$ 190,000	$1,000,000
Total cost of raw material purchases (fabric and poles)	$870,600	$2,021,800	$2,329,400	$1,178,200	$6,400,000

*Ten percent of the next quarter's expected raw material requirements.

†Ten percent of the expected raw material requirements for the first quarter of the next year, 20x3, which is assumed to be 72,000 metres. (Sales, and therefore production, are predicted to be the same in each quarter of 20x3 as in the corresponding quarter of 20x2.)

‡Since the tent pole kits are prepackaged by the vendor and delivered on a just-in-time basis, there is no need for inventory. So the number of tent pole kits purchased each quarter is the same as the number needed each quarter.

Production and Purchasing: An Important Link Notice the important link between planned production and purchases of raw material. This link is obvious in Schedule 4, and it is also emphasized in the formula preceding the schedule. Let's focus on the second quarter. Since 15,500 tents are to be produced, 186,000 metres of material will be needed (15,500 tents × 12 metres per tent). In addition, the company wants to have 22,800 metres of material in inventory at the end of the quarter.[7] Total needs therefore are 208,800 metres. Does CozyCamp need to purchase this much raw material? No, it does not, because 18,600 metres will be in inventory at the beginning of the quarter. Therefore, the firm needs to purchase only 190,200 metres of material during the quarter (208,800 metres needed less 18,600 metres in the beginning inventory).

Inventory Management   The linkage between planned production and raw material purchases is a particularly critical one in manufacturing firms, so considerable effort is devoted to careful inventory planning and management. How did the company decide how much raw material to have in inventory at the end of each quarter? Schedule 4 shows that each quarter's desired ending inventory of raw material is 10 percent of the *material needed for production* in the next quarter. For example, 22,800 metres of raw material will be in inventory at the end of the second quarter, because 228,000 metres will be needed for production in the third quarter (22,800 = 10% × 228,000). The effect of this approach is to have a larger ending inventory when the next quarter's planned production is greater. Inventories are drawn down when the subsequent quarter's planned production is lower.[8]

Direct-Labour Budget

The **direct-labour budget** shows the number of hours and the cost of the direct labour during the budget period. CozyCamp's direct-labour budget is shown as Schedule 5. Based on each quarter's planned production, this schedule computes the amount of direct labour needed each quarter and the cost of the required labour. CozyCamp is a relatively small company, and owner Mary Edwards hires all of her direct-labour production employees on a part-time basis only. This allows CozyCamp to meet the labour demands of a given time period, which vary significantly with the seasonal pattern of demand and production. Thus, CozyCamp's direct labour may be adjusted up or down to meet short-term needs. As a result, direct labour for this company is a unit-level cost. Each manufactured tent requires half an hour of direct labour.

A Note on Direct Labour and the Cost Hierarchy   Where direct labour belongs in the cost hierarchy depends on management's ability to adjust the organization's labour force to match short-term requirements, as well as management's attitude about making such adjustments.[9] Either for strategic business reasons or due to ethical concerns, many companies strive to maintain a relatively stable labour force. If production employees are retained when production declines, then direct labour will not be a unit-level cost. In the extreme case, where employees are virtually never laid off, direct labour becomes a facility-level or general-operations-level cost. CozyCamp's ability to easily adjust the total hours of its part-time workforce results in a unit-level designation for direct-labour cost in this situation.

Schedule 5

CozyCamp Company

	COZYCAMP COMPANY Direct-Labour Budget For the Year Ending December 31, 20x2				
	Quarter				
	1st	**2nd**	**3rd**	**4th**	**Year**
Units to be produced (Schedule 3)	6,000	15,500	19,000	9,500	50,000
Direct-labour required per unit (hours)..........	× 0.5	× 0.5	× 0.5	× 0.5	× 0.5
Total direct-labour hours required	3,000	7,750	9,500	4,750	25,000
Direct-labour cost per hour........................	× $15	× $15	× $15	× $15	× $15
Total direct-labour cost.............................	$45,000	$116,250	$142,500	$71,250	$375,000

Manufacturing-Overhead Budget

The **manufacturing-overhead budget** shows the cost of overhead expected to be incurred in the production process during the budget period. CozyCamp's manufacturing-overhead budget, displayed as Schedule 6, lists the expected cost of each overhead item by quarter. At the bottom of the schedule, the total budgeted overhead for each quarter is shown. Importantly, then each quarter's *depreciation is subtracted* to determine the total cash disbursements to be expected for overhead during each quarter. This cash disbursement information will be needed later in the budgeting process when the cash disbursements budget is constructed (Schedule 8).

Activity-Based Budgeting and the Cost Hierarchy   CozyCamp uses an activity-based budgeting (ABB) approach in the construction of the manufacturing-overhead budget. This budget explicitly uses ABC information, so the budgeted cost for various overhead items is based on the expected quantity of the appropriate cost driver. For example, the cost driver used to budget setup costs is the number of production runs.

In CozyCamp's cost hierarchy, unit-level costs include indirect material and electricity used to run the production machinery.[10] Batch-level costs include machine setup, purchasing and material handling, and quality control and inspection. The cost driver for these costs is the number of production runs. A run typically produces 500 tents. CozyCamp's only product-level cost is design engineering. The company typically develops one new tent design each quarter. Each new design costs $1,200. The remaining overhead costs in Schedule 6 are costs incurred at the facility, or general-operations, level.

Benefits of ABB   Proponents of ABB believe that real, sustainable payoffs from ABC and activity-based management will not be forthcoming until an organization's budgeting process embraces the ABM approach. Using ABC information in the budgeting process provides solid reasoning for budgeting costs at particular levels, since the underlying ABC information is based explicitly on the relationships among cost drivers, activities, and resources consumed. Moreover, the resulting budget is more useful to management, because it reveals how cost levels will change if the predicted quantities of the cost drivers change. For example, what will happen to CozyCamp's setup costs in the first quarter if the quantity produced is 6,000 units as reflected in the budget (Schedule 6), but 15 production runs are used to produce these 6,000 units instead of 12 runs as specified in the budget? According to Schedule 6, setup cost is $400 per production run ($4,800/12 runs). Therefore, 15 runs would result in $6,000 of setup cost in the first quarter, instead of $4,800 as forecast in the budget. This will be true even if 6,000 units are produced as forecast in the budget.

Traditional budgeting processes often classify as *fixed* costs such costs as setup, purchasing and material handling, quality control and inspection, or design engineering, since they do not vary with the number of units produced. The ABB approach, however, recognizes that these costs are really *variable* if the budget analyst is careful to identify the appropriate cost driver with which each of these costs varies.

Learning Objective   **3**

Explain the concept of activity-based budgeting and the benefits it brings to the budgeting process.

> "Activity-based budgets are more actionable and understandable." (8e)
> **James A. Brimson and John Antos (Presidents of management consulting firms)**[11]

Selling, General, and Administrative (SG&A) Expense Budget

The **selling, general, and administrative (SG&A) expense budget**, displayed as Schedule 7, shows the planned amounts of expenditures to administer the firm and sell its product during the budget period.

Activity-Based Budgeting and the Cost Hierarchy   Similarly to the manufacturing-overhead budget, CozyCamp's SG&A expense budget reflects the ABB approach. ABC information

Schedule 6

CozyCamp Company

	COZYCAMP COMPANY Manufacturing-Overhead Budget For the Year Ending December 31, 20x2				
	Quarter				
	1st	2nd	3rd	4th	Year
Unit-level costs:					
Units	*6,000*	*15,500*	*19,000*	*9,500*	*50,000*
Indirect material	$ 18,000	$ 46,500	$ 57,000	$ 28,500	$ 150,000
Electricity (for machinery)	6,000	15,500	19,000	9,500	50,000
Total unit-level costs	$ 24,000	$ 62,000	$ 76,000	$ 38,000	$ 200,000
Batch-level costs:					
Production runs	*12*	*31*	*38*	*19*	*100*
Setup	$ 4,800	$ 12,400	$ 15,200	$ 7,600	$ 40,000
Purchasing and material handling	7,200	18,600	22,800	11,400	60,000
Quality control and inspection	6,000	15,500	19,000	9,500	50,000
Total batch-level costs	$ 18,000	$ 46,500	$ 57,000	$ 28,500	$ 150,000
Product-level costs:					
New tent designs	*1*	*1*	*1*	*1*	*4*
Design engineering	$ 1,200	$ 1,200	$ 1,200	$ 1,200	$ 4,800
Total product-level costs	$ 1,200	$ 1,200	$ 1,200	$ 1,200	$ 4,800
Facility-level and general-operations-level costs:					
Supervisory salaries	$ 52,500	$ 52,500	$ 52,500	$ 52,500	$ 210,000
Insurance and property taxes	11,300	11,300	11,300	11,300	45,200
Maintenance	47,500	47,500	47,500	47,500	190,000
Utilities	40,000	40,000	40,000	40,000	160,000
Depreciation	110,000	110,000	110,000	110,000	440,000
Total facility-level and general-operations-level costs	$261,300	$261,300	$261,300	$261,300	$1,045,200
Total overhead	$304,500	$371,000	$395,500	$329,000	$1,400,000
Less *depreciation*	110,000	110,000	110,000	110,000	440,000
Total cash disbursements for overhead	$194,500	$261,000	$285,500	$219,000	$ 960,000

was used to develop this budget. For example, the cost driver used to budget sales commissions (for sales in the firm's traditional market) is the number of units sold.

In CozyCamp's cost hierarchy, the only unit-level marketing expenses consist of sales commissions. For CozyCamp's traditional sales through regional retail outlets, sales staff are paid commissions based on the number of units sold. The SG&A budget reflects a $5 commission paid on each tent sold through traditional outlets, which account for 25 percent of CozyCamp's sales. In the second quarter, for example, sales commissions are predicted to be $18,750 (15,000 tents × 25% traditional sales × $5).

The customer-level expenses incurred by CozyCamp are the sales staff salaries, which differ depending on whether the customers are traditional regional retailers or Internet shoppers. To sell its tents in the traditional marketplace, CozyCamp employs sales staff who travel to the retailers in the area to personally take orders, and who receive both a salary and sales commission. (The sales commissions are unit-level expenses, as noted above.) To serve its Internet customers, CozyCamp employs computer operators to update the company's website and a couple of telephone operators to provide customer service over the phone. For example, some Internet customers are hesitant to give their credit card numbers to CozyCamp online, so they place their orders online and then phone in to an authorized telephone number to submit their credit card information.

The remainder of CozyCamp's SG&A expenses are incurred at the facility- or general-operations-level.

Schedule 7

CozyCamp Company

	Quarter				
	1st	2nd	3rd	4th	Year
Unit-level expenses:					
Units	*5,000*	*15,000*	*20,000*	*10,000*	*50,000*
Sales commissions (traditional market) ...	$ 6,250	$ 18,750	$ 25,000	$ 12,500	$ 62,500
Total unit-level expenses	$ 6,250	$ 18,750	$ 25,000	$ 12,500	$ 62,500
Customer-level expenses:					
Sales personnel salaries (traditional market)	$ 16,000	$ 16,000	$ 16,000	$ 16,000	$ 64,000
Computer operator salaries	18,000	18,000	18,000	18,000	72,000
Telephone operator salaries	6,000	6,000	6,000	6,000	24,000
Total customer-level expenses	$ 40,000	$ 40,000	$ 40,000	$ 40,000	$ 160,000
Facility- and general-operations-level expenses:					
Sales manager's salary	$ 15,000	$ 15,000	$ 15,000	$ 15,000	$ 60,000
Media advertising	61,000	61,000	61,000	61,000	244,000
Administrative salaries	220,000	220,000	220,000	220,000	880,000
Depreciation.................................	10,000	10,000	10,000	10,000	40,000
Total facility- and general operations-level expenses	$306,000	$306,000	$306,000	$306,000	$1,224,000
Total SG&A	$352,250	$364,750	$371,000	$358,500	$1,446,500
Less *depreciation*	10,000	10,000	10,000	10,000	40,000
Total cash disbursements for SG&A	$342,250	$354,750	$361,000	$348,500	$1,406,500

COZYCAMP COMPANY
Selling, General, and Administrative Expense Budget
For the Year Ending December 31, 20x2

Cash Disbursements Budget

The **cash disbursements budget** details the expected cash payments during a budget period. Schedule 8 displays CozyCamp's cash disbursements budget. The shaded top portion shows the schedule of cash payments for raw material purchases, which are all made on account (from Schedule 4). The company pays for 60 percent of its purchases during the quarter in which the purchase is made. The remaining 40 percent of each quarter's purchases are paid for during the quarter following the purchase.

The lower portion of Schedule 8 shows all of CozyCamp's direct-labour, manufacturing-overhead, and SG&A expenditures.

How to Budget Cash Disbursements   CozyCamp purchases raw material, direct labour, and various services. The raw-material purchases are made on account, which means payment is not made in cash at the time of the purchase. The shaded top portion of Schedule 8 shows the purchases on account. Let's focus on the second quarter column.

Schedule 8

CozyCamp Company

	Quarter				
COZYCAMP COMPANY Cash Disbursements Budget For the Year Ending December 31, 20x2	1st	2nd	3rd	4th	Year
Cost of raw material purchases (Schedule 4)	$ 870,600	$2,021,800	$2,329,400	$1,178,200	$6,400,000
Cash payments for purchases made during the quarter (60% of current quarter's purchases)	$ 522,360	$1,213,080	$1,397,640	$ 706,920	$3,840,000
Cash payments for prior quarter's purchases (40% of prior quarter's purchases)	471,280*	348,240	808,720	931,760	2,560,000
Total cash payments for raw material purchases	$ 993,640	$1,561,320	$2,206,360	$1,638,680	$6,400,000
Other cash disbursements:					
Direct labour (Schedule 5)	$ 45,000	$ 116,250	$ 142,500	$ 71,250	$ 375,000
Manufacturing overhead (Schedule 6)	194,500	261,000	285,500	219,000	960,000
SG&A expenses (Schedule 7)	342,250	354,750	361,000	348,500	1,406,500
Total of other cash disbursements	$ 581,750	$ 732,000	$ 789,000	$ 638,750	$2,741,500
Total cash disbursements	$1,575,390	$2,293,320	$2,995,360	$2,277,430	$9,141,500

*Forty percent of the purchases in the fourth quarter of the prior year, 20x1, which is assumed to be $1,178,200.

The second quarter's raw-material purchases on account amount to $2,021,800. Does the company pay for all of the $2,021,800 purchases on account during the same quarter? No, it does not. As the following diagram shows, the second quarter's actual cash payment for purchases made on account is in two parts.

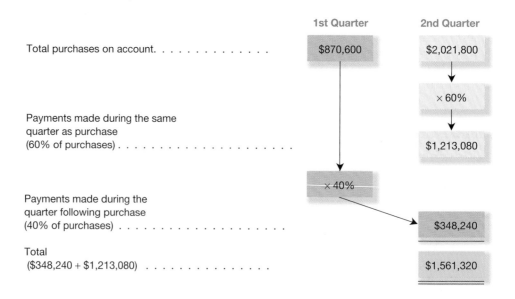

The second quarter's total cash payments *for purchases made on account* are the sum of $1,213,080 (which relates to second quarter purchases on account) and $348,240 (which relates to first quarter purchases on account).

We are not finished with the second quarter's cash disbursements yet, because CozyCamp *also pays for some of its purchases in cash at the time of purchase.* These cash expenditures are detailed in the lightly shaded lower portion of Schedule 8. The amounts are drawn from Schedules 5, 6, and 7, which detail expenditures for direct-labour, manufacturing-overhead, and SG&A expenses, respectively. For example, Schedule 5 lists $116,250 for direct labour in the second quarter; Schedule 6 lists $261,000 for cash expenditures on manufacturing-overhead costs; and Schedule 7 lists $354,750 for SG&A expenditures.

Finally, the last row in the cash disbursements budget (Schedule 8) shows the total cash disbursements during each quarter. Thus, the $2,293,320 total payment in the second quarter is the sum of $1,561,320 (for raw-material purchases on account) and $732,000 for other purchases made in cash.

Cash Budget: Combining Receipts and Disbursements

The **cash budget** details the expected cash receipts and disbursements during a budget period. CozyCamp's completed cash budget is displayed as Schedule 9. The shaded top portion pulls together the cash receipts and cash disbursements detailed in Schedules 2 and 8. The lower portion of Schedule 9 discloses the company's plans to take out a short-term bank loan on January 2, 20x2, for the purpose of building an addition to its production facility. The pattern of construction payments reflects high outlays early in the year as the major construction takes place. The high payment in the fourth quarter is due to the costs of reconfiguring the production line after the addition is finished. The company will repay the loan (with interest) in four equal instalments on the last day of each quarter in 20x2. The funds for this repayment will come from excess cash generated from operations during 20x2.

Also shown in Schedule 9 are the interest payments on the short-term bank loan.

Budgeted Schedule of Cost of Goods Manufactured and Sold

The **budgeted schedule of cost of goods manufactured and sold** details the direct-material, direct-labour, and manufacturing-overhead costs to be incurred, and shows the cost of the goods to be sold during the budget period. Schedule 10 shows CozyCamp's budgeted schedule of cost of goods manufactured and sold. The following Excel spreadsheet shows how the absorption cost per unit of the beginning and ending inventories of finished goods in Schedule 10 is determined.

	A	B
1	Type of Manufacturing Cost	Amount
2		
3	Direct material, tent fabric (12 metres x $9 per metre)	$108.000
4	Direct material, tent poles (1 tent pole kit x $20 per kit)	20.000
5	Direct labour (.5 hour x $15 per hour)	7.500
6	Unit-level manufacturing overhead ($200,000/50,000 units)	4.000
7	Batch-level manufacturing overhead ($150,000/50,000 units)	3.000
8	Product-level manufacturing overhead ($4,800/50,000 units)	0.096
9	Facility-level manufacturing overhead ($1,045,200/50,000 units)	20.904
10		
11	Total absorption cost per unit	$163.500

Recall that the *absorption* cost includes the direct-material and direct-labour costs and an allocation of all manufacturing-overhead costs (i.e., overhead at the unit, batch, product, and facility or general-operations, levels). The direct-material cost per unit consists of $108 for the tent fabric and $20 for the pole kit, or a total of $128 (Schedule 4), and the unit direct-labour cost is $7.50 (Schedule 5). The overhead cost

Schedule 9

CozyCamp Company

	COZYCAMP COMPANY Cash Budget For the Year Ending December 31, 20x2				
	Quarter				
	1st	2nd	3rd	4th	Year
Cash receipts (Schedule 2)	$1,305,000	$2,902,500	$4,207,500	$2,610,000	$11,025,000
Less cash disbursements (Schedule 8)	(1,575,390)	(2,293,320)	(2,995,360)	(2,277,430)	(9,141,500)
Change in cash balance during quarter due to operations	$ (270,390)	$ 609,180	$1,212,140	$ 332,570	$ 1,883,500
Proceeds from bank loan (1/2/x2)	1,000,000				1,000,000
Payments for construction of plant addition	(500,000)	(120,000)	(80,000)	(300,000)	(1,000,000)
Repayment of principal on bank loan (at the end of each quarter)	(250,000)	(250,000)	(250,000)	(250,000)	(1,000,000)
Interest on bank loan (at 10% per year)*	(25,000)	(18,750)	(12,500)	(6,250)	(62,500)
Change in cash balance during the year					$ 821,000
Cash balance 1/1/x2					10,000
Cash balance 12/31/x2					$ 831,000

*Interest computations:

Quarter	Unpaid Principal during the Quarter	Annual Interest Rate	Portion of Year	Interest Payment†
1st	$1,000,000	10%	1/4	$25,000‡
2nd	750,000	10%	1/4	18,750
3rd	500,000	10%	1/4	12,500
4th	250,000	10%	1/4	6,250

†Unpaid principal × Annual interest rate × 1/4

‡$1,000,000 × 0.10 × 1/4 = $25,000

data come from Schedule 6. So the absorption manufacturing cost for one unit of product is $163.50. In Schedule 3, we see that the expected beginning and ending inventories of finished goods for 20x2 both consist of 500 units. Therefore, the cost of the beginning and ending inventories of finished goods in 20x2 is $81,750 (500 units × $163.50 per unit).

Budgeted Income Statement

The **budgeted income statement** shows the expected revenue and expenses for the budget period, assuming that planned operations are carried out. CozyCamp's budgeted income statement is displayed as Schedule 11.

Budgeted Statement of Cash Flows

The **budgeted statement of cash flows** provides information about the expected sources and uses of cash for operating activities, investing activities, and financing activities during a particular period of time. CozyCamp's budgeted statement of cash flows for 20x2 is displayed as Schedule 12. Notice that the format used in the budgeted statement of cash flows reflects the *direct method* of preparing the statement, which is recommended by Canadian accounting standards and *International Financial Reporting Standards* (IFRS).[12] The format used in the statement of cash flows, which is a statement prepared by companies for *external* reporting purposes, generally

Schedule 10

CozyCamp Company

COZYCAMP COMPANY
Budgeted Schedule of Cost of Goods Manufactured and Sold
For the Year Ending December 31, 20x2

Direct material (Schedule 4):		
Raw-material inventory, January 1	$ 64,800*	
Add: Purchases of raw material	6,400,000†	
Raw material available for use	6,464,800	
Deduct: Raw-material inventory, December 31	64,800*	
Direct material used		$6,400,000
Direct labour (Schedule 5).		375,000
Manufacturing overhead (Schedule 6)		1,400,000
Total manufacturing costs		8,175,000
Add: Work-in-process inventory, January 1		0‡
Subtotal		8,175,000
Deduct: Work-in-process inventory, December 31		0‡
Cost of goods manufactured		8,175,000
Add: Finished-goods inventory, January 1		81,750§
Cost of goods available for sale		8,256,750
Deduct: Finished-goods inventory, December 31		81,750§
Cost of goods sold		$8,175,000

*From Schedule 4: 7,200 metres of tent fabric × $9 per metre, and zero inventory of tent pole kits.
†From Schedule 4: $5,400,000 for tent fabric + $1,000,000 for tent pole kits.
‡The company's production cycle is short enough that there is no work-in-process inventory at any time.
§From Schedule 3: 500 units × $163.50 per unit, which is the absorption manufacturing cost per unit.

Schedule 11

CozyCamp Company

COZYCAMP COMPANY
Budgeted Income Statement
For the Year Ending December 31, 20x2

Sales revenue (Schedule 1)		$11,250,000
Less: Cost of goods sold (Schedule 10)		8,175,000
Gross margin		3,075,000
Other expenses:		
Selling, general, and administrative expenses (Schedule 7)	$1,446,500	
Uncollectable accounts expense (Schedule 2)	225,000	
Interest expense (Schedule 9)	62,500	
Total other expenses		1,734,000
Net income		$ 1,341,000

reflects the *indirect method* and differs from the format used in the cash receipts and cash disbursements budgets, which are prepared for *internal* use by management. Notice the differences in the format of Schedule 12 when compared with Schedules 2, 8, and 9. Notice also the greater detail in Schedules 2, 8, and 9, which are designed for internal managerial use.

Schedule 12

CozyCamp Company

COZYCAMP COMPANY Budgeted Statement of Cash Flows For the Year Ending December 31, 20x2		
Cash flows from operating activities:		
Cash receipts from customers (Schedule 2)		$11,025,000
Cash payments:		
To suppliers of raw material (Schedule 8)	$6,400,000	
For direct labour (Schedule 8)	375,000	
For manufacturing-overhead expenditures (Schedule 8)	960,000	
For selling, general, and administrative expenses (Schedule 8)	1,406,500	
For interest (Schedule 9)	62,500	
Total cash payments		9,204,000
Net cash flow from operating activities		$ 1,821,000
Cash flows from investing activities:		
Construction of building addition (Schedule 9)	(1,000,000)	
Net cash from investing activities		(1,000,000)
Cash flows from financing activities:		
Principal of bank loan (Schedule 9)	$1,000,000	
Repayment of bank loan (Schedule 9)	(1,000,000)	
Net cash from financing activities		0
Net increase in cash and cash equivalents		$ 821,000
Balance in cash and cash equivalents, beginning of year		10,000
Balance in cash and cash equivalents, end of year		$ 831,000

Budgeted Balance Sheet

The **budgeted balance sheet** shows the expected end-of-period balances for the company's assets, liabilities, and owner's equity, assuming that planned operations are carried out. CozyCamp's budgeted balance sheet for December 31, 20x2, is displayed as Schedule 13. To construct this budgeted balance sheet, we start with the firm's balance sheet projected for the *beginning* of the budget year (Exhibit 8–4) and adjust each account balance for the changes expected during 20x2. These expected changes are reflected in the various 20x2 budget schedules.

Balance sheet December 31, 20x1 (see Exhibit 8–4) → Expected changes in account balances during 20x2 → Balance sheet December 31, 20x2 (Schedule 13)

Explanations for the account balances on the budgeted balance sheet for December 31, 20x2, are given at the bottom of Schedule 13. Examine these explanations carefully. Notice how the budgeted balance sheet pulls together information from most of the schedules constituting the master budget.

COZYCAMP COMPANY
Balance Sheet
December 31, 20x1

Assets

Current assets:

Cash		$ 10,000
Accounts receivable (net of allowance for uncollectable accounts)		405,000
Inventory:		
Raw material	$ 64,800	
Finished goods	81,750	
Supplies	42,000	
Total inventory		188,550
Total current assets		603,550
Long-lived assets:		
Building	$8,200,000	
Equipment	2,280,000	
Less accumulated depreciation on building and equipment	(1,883,550)	
Building and equipment, net of accumulated depreciation		8,596,450
Total assets		$9,200,000

Liabilities and Owner's Equity

Current liabilities:

Accounts payable	$ 471,280
Total current liabilities	471,280
Long-term liabilities:	
Note payable (non-interest-bearing; due on December 31, 20x4)	4,100,000
Total liabilities	4,571,280
Owner's equity	4,628,720
Total liabilities and owner's equity	$9,200,000

Exhibit 8–4
Balance Sheet for
December 31, 20x1

CozyCamp Company

Assumptions and Predictions Underlying the Master Budget

A master budget is based on many assumptions and estimates of unknown parameters. Some estimates tend to be quite accurate, while other predictions are much more difficult to make accurately. To explore the role of assumptions and predictions in the budgeting process, consider the budget prepared for Canadian Fitness Cooperative. This service organization operates as a cooperative. The members elect a board of directors that hires a manager and assistant manager to run the club. Canadian Fitness Cooperative does not seek to make a profit. Each year, the membership fees are adjusted with the intention of bringing in just enough revenue to cover projected expenses. The budget is an important part of that process.

Canadian Fitness Cooperative's annual budget is displayed in Exhibit 8–5. The Cooperative sells individual adult, family, and youth/student memberships. The individual adult and the family memberships can be monthly or annual, with a significant price break offered on the annual memberships. The Cooperative also allows licensed massage therapists and nutritionists to meet clients in the club's facilities and charges a

Learning Objective **5**

Discuss the role of assumptions and predictions in budgeting.

Schedule 13

CozyCamp Company

COZYCAMP COMPANY
Budgeted Balance Sheet
December 31, 20x2

Assets

Current assets:

Cash (Schedule 12) .... | | $ 831,000
Accounts receivable (net of allowance for uncollectable accounts) .... | | 405,000*

Inventory:

Raw material (Schedule 10)	$ 64,800	
Finished goods (Schedule 10)	81,750	
Supplies	42,000†	

Total inventory .... | | 188,550

Total current assets .... | | 1,424,550

Long-lived assets:

Building	$9,200,000‡	
Equipment	2,280,000	
Less accumulated depreciation on building and equipment	(2,363,550)§	

Building and equipment, net of accumulated depreciation .... | | 9,116,450

Total assets .... | | $10,541,000

*From Schedule 2: Fourth quarter sales of $2,250,000 × 18% = $405,000.

†Assuming no change in supplies inventory between 20x1 and 20x2.

‡Balance in the Building account on the December 31, 20x1, balance sheet, plus the $1,000,000 cost of the building construction project in 20x2 (Schedule 9).

§Balance in the Accumulated Depreciation account on the December 31, 20x1, balance sheet, plus the $440,000 (Schedule 6) and $40,000 (Schedule 8) in depreciation during 20x2.

Liabilities and Owner's Equity

Current liabilities:

Accounts payable .... | | $ 471,280*

Total current liabilities .... | | 471,280

Long-term liabilities:

Note payable (non-interest-bearing; due on December 31, 20x4) .... | | 4,100,000

Total liabilities .... | | 4,571,280

Owner's equity .... | | 5,969,720†

Total liabilities and owner's equity .... | | $10,541,000

*From Schedule 8: Fourth quarter raw-material purchases of $1,178,200 × 40% = $471,280.

†Balance in Owner's Equity on the December 31, 20x1, balance sheet, plus the 20x2 budgeted net income of $1,341,000 (Schedule 11).

---

fee to the professional offering the service. Employees include a manager and assistant manager to administer the operation; various part-time instructors who teach classes such as yoga, Pilates, aerobic exercise, weight training, and proper use of the fitness equipment; reception and cashier staff; and custodians. Other operating expenses include such items as utilities, insurance, supplies, maintenance, property taxes, advertising, and depreciation.

Notice the differences and similarities between the budgets for CozyCamp and Canadian Fitness Cooperative. CozyCamp's budgeted income statement (Schedule 11) subtracts cost of goods sold from sales revenue to calculate the gross margin. In contrast, the Cooperative does not show cost of goods sold, because the Cooperative does not sell

	A	B	C	D	E	F
1		CANADIAN FITNESS COOPERATIVE				
2		ANNUAL BUDGET				
3		For the Year 20x6				
4						
5						
6		1st Quarter	2nd Quarter	3rd Quarter	4th Quarter	Year
7						
8	Revenue:					
9	Membership revenue:					
10	Individual adult memberships					
11	Monthly	$ 52,200	$ 36,000	$ 14,400	$ 52,200	$ 154,800
12	Annual	30,000	30,000	30,000	30,000	120,000
13	Family memberships					
14	Monthly	22,500	18,000	3,000	22,500	66,000
15	Annual	48,750	48,750	48,750	48,750	195,000
16	Youth/student memberships	9,000	8,100	900	9,000	27,000
17	Fees for professional space:					
18	Massage therapists	5,460	5,460	1,820	5,460	18,200
19	Nutritionists	3,640	3,640	1,300	3,640	12,220
20	Total revenue	$ 171,550	$ 149,950	$ 100,170	$ 171,550	$ 593,220
21						
22	Operating expenses:					
23	Salaries and wages:					
24	Administration	$ 20,000	$ 20,000	$ 20,000	$ 20,000	$ 80,000
25	Yoga/pilates instruction	14,700	13,200	4,200	14,700	46,800
26	Aerobics instruction	14,700	13,200	4,200	14,700	46,800
27	Weight training/fitness instruction	9,600	6,400	2,200	9,600	27,800
28	Personal trainers	6,400	4,200	1,200	6,400	18,200
29	Other instruction (e.g., racquetball)	5,400	3,400	800	5,400	15,000
30	Reception/cashier	13,650	13,650	7,800	13,650	48,750
31	Maintenance/custodial	13,000	13,000	13,000	13,000	52,000
32	Employee fringe benefits	29,235	26,115	16,020	29,235	100,605
33	Utilities:					
34	Electricity	3,000	3,000	1,800	3,000	10,800
35	Heat/air conditioning	2,500	2,500	2,500	2,500	10,000
36	Telephone	600	600	600	600	2,400
37	Satellite TV	450	450	450	450	1,800
38	Trash collection	200	200	200	200	800
39	Other	1,000	1,000	1,000	1,000	4,000
40	Insurance	3,200	3,200	3,200	3,200	12,800
41	Supplies	900	700	450	900	2,950
42	Administrative	800	800	800	800	3,200
43	Maintenance/repair	2,500	2,500	4,000	2,500	11,500
44	Property taxes	9,000	9,000	9,000	9,000	36,000
45	Advertising	1,100	1,100	500	1,100	3,800
46	Depreciation:					
47	Building	10,000	10,000	10,000	10,000	40,000
48	Equipment	2,500	2,500	2,500	2,500	10,000
49	Other	1,300	1,300	1,300	1,300	5,200
50	Total operating expenses	$ 165,735	$ 152,015	$ 107,720	$ 165,735	$ 591,205
51						
52	Revenue less operating expenses	$ 5,815	$ (2,065)	$ (7,550)	$ 5,815	$ 2,015

Exhibit 8–5

Annual Budget: Canadian
Fitness Cooperative

a physical product. Nor does it show a gross margin. The Cooperative budget shows revenue from membership dues and fees for professional space, and operating expenses. While CozyCamp's budget shows *net income*, the Cooperative's budget refers to *revenue less operating expenses*. This emphasizes the Cooperative's status as a nonprofit enterprise.

There are also similarities between these two budgets. For example, both businesses experience significant seasonality in activity. CozyCamp sells more tents in the second and third quarters than in the first and fourth quarters. Canadian Fitness Cooperative sells more monthly memberships in the cold months (first and fourth quarters) than in the warmer months (second and third quarters). During quarters with increased sales activity, both businesses show correspondingly higher expenses.

Now let's briefly discuss some of the assumptions and predictions that are reflected in the Cooperative's budget. First, the fitness club's manager has assumed that people will continue to use the club more in the colder months of the year than in the warmer months as they have in the past. Second, the manager has also assumed that the split between monthly and annual memberships for both individuals and families will be about the same as in the past. Based on these assumptions, the manager has predicted membership sales for each quarter. For example, the budget reflects the following predictions for memberships and prices in the first and second quarters. Notice that the monthly memberships decline in the second quarter, whereas the annual memberships are constant across the entire year.

Membership Type	1st Quarter	2nd Quarter
Individual adult, monthly	290 @ $60 per month	200 @ $60 per month
Individual adult, annual	200 @ $600 per year	200 @ $600 per year
Family, monthly	50 @ $150 per month	40 @ $150 per month
Family, annual	130 @ $1,500 per year	130 @ $1,500 per year
Youth/student	100 @ $30 per month	90 @ $30 per month

The Cooperative budget includes many other predictions, such as salaries, wage rates, electric and other utility rates, insurance and property tax rates, and so forth. Some of these predictions—property tax rates, for example—would likely be quite accurate. Other predictions would be more difficult, as, for example, the cost of natural gas for heating purposes due to its dependence on the weather.

Financial Planning Models

Managers have to make assumptions and predictions in preparing budgets, because organizations operate in a world of uncertainty. One way of coping with that uncertainty is to supplement the budgeting process with a *financial planning model*. A **financial planning model** is a set of mathematical relationships that express the interactions among the various operational, financial, and environmental events, which determine the overall results of an organization's activities. A financial planning model is a mathematical expression of all the relationships shown in the flow chart in Exhibit 8–1.

To illustrate this concept, focus on the following equation, which is used to budget the Cooperative's employee fringe benefits:

$$(\text{Employee fringe benefits}) = 0.30 \times (\text{Total salaries and wages})$$

However, suppose the cooperative's manager is uncertain about this 30 percent estimate. A financial planning model might include the following equation instead:

$$(\text{Employee fringe benefits}) = p \times (\text{Total salaries and wages})$$

$$\text{where } 0 \leq p \leq 1.0$$

The financial planning model can be run as many times as desired on a computer, using a different value for p each time. Perhaps the following values would be tried: 0.29, 0.30, and 0.31. Now the manager can answer the question: What if employee fringe benefits cost 29 percent of salaries and wages?

In a fully developed financial planning model, all of the key estimates and assumptions are expressed as general mathematical relationships. Then the model is run many times to determine the impact of different combinations of these unknown variables. This approach is reminiscent of the *sensitivity analysis* used in CVP relationships, which was discussed in the previous chapter. "What if" questions can be answered about such unknown variables as inflation, interest rates, demand, competitors' actions, union demands in forthcoming wage negotiations, and a host of other factors. The widespread availability of personal computers and electronic-spreadsheet software has made financial planning models a common management tool.

Budget Administration

In small organizations, the procedures used to gather information and construct a master budget are usually informal. In contrast, larger organizations use a formal process to collect data and prepare the master budget. Such organizations usually designate a **budget director** or **chief budget officer**. This role is often filled by the organization's controller. The budget director specifies the process by which budget data will be gathered, collects the information, and prepares the master budget. To communicate budget procedures and deadlines to employees throughout the organization, the budget director often develops and disseminates a **budget manual**. The budget manual states who is responsible for providing various types of information, when the information is required, and what form the information is to take. For example, the budget manual for

Learning Objective   **6**

Describe a typical organization's process of budget administration.

M anagerial
A ccounting
P ractice

Simon Fraser
University (SFU)

BUDGET ADMINISTRATION AT SIMON FRASER UNIVERSITY

Simon Fraser University's annual budget covers the period from April 1 through the following March 31. The budgeting process begins in October, when the university president consults with the academic community at all levels. The deans and vice-presidents have meetings to discuss the programs the university will conduct during the following budget year. The university's priorities in educational, research, and public service programs are established during these meetings. In early October, a set of assumptions to be used during the remainder of the budgeting process is distributed to the vice-presidents. These assumptions include such key forecasts as the next year's inflation rate, interest rates, and tuition levels. Based on these assumptions, the dean of each of SFU's faculties must develop a detailed budget for salaries and general expenses. These detailed budgets are prepared during November and December by the financial staff in each faculty. In February, the university president reviews these budgets with the vice-presidents. After any needed revisions have been made, the budgets for the faculties are consolidated by the university's budget office into a master budget. This budget is presented to the university's board of governors in March for final approval.

As many companies operate globally, the Internet plays an ever-greater role in the budgeting process. E-budgeting is an increasingly popular, Internet-based budgeting tool that can help streamline and speed up an organization's budgeting process. The *e* in **e-budgeting** stands for both *electronic* and *enterprise-wide*; employees throughout an organization, at all levels and around the world, can submit and retrieve budget information electronically via the Internet. Budgeting software is used and made available on the web, so that budget information electronically submitted from any location is in a consistent companywide format. Managers in organizations using e-budgeting have found that it greatly streamlines the entire budgeting process. In the past, these organizations compiled their master budgets on hundreds of spreadsheets, which had to be collected and integrated by the corporate controller's office. One result of this cumbersome approach was that a disproportionate amount of time was spent compiling and verifying data from multiple sources. Under e-budgeting, both the submission of budget information and its compilation are accomplished electronically by the web-based budgeting software. E-budgeting is just one more area where the Internet has transformed how the workplace operates in the era of e-business.[13]

a manufacturing firm might specify that each regional sales director is to send an estimate of the following year's sales, by product line, to the budget director by September 1. The budget manual also states who should receive each schedule when the master budget is complete.

A **budget committee**, consisting of key senior executives, is often appointed to advise the budget director during the preparation of the budget. The authority to give final approval to the master budget usually belongs to the board of directors, or a board of trustees in many nonprofit organizations. Usually the board has a subcommittee whose task is to examine the proposed budget carefully and recommend approval or any changes deemed necessary. By exercising its authority to make changes in the budget and grant final approval, the board of directors, or trustees, can wield considerable influence on the overall direction the organization takes.

International Aspects of Budgeting

As the economies and cultures of countries throughout the world become intertwined, many companies are multinational in their operations. Firms with international operations face a variety of additional challenges in preparing their budgets. First, a multinational firm's budget must reflect the conversion of foreign currencies into the local currency. Since almost all of the world's other currencies fluctuate in their values relative to the local currency, budgeting for those conversions is difficult. Although multinationals have sophisticated financial ways of protecting themselves against such currency fluctuations, the budgeting task is still quite challenging. Second, it is difficult to prepare budgets when inflation is high or unpredictable. While Canada has experienced periods of inflation, some foreign countries have experienced hyperinflation, sometimes with annual inflation rates well over 100 percent. Predicting such high inflation rates is difficult and further complicates a multinational's budgeting process. Finally, the economies of all countries fluctuate in terms of consumer demand, availability of skilled labour, the effects of laws affecting commerce, and so forth. Companies with overseas operations face the task of anticipating such changing conditions in their budgeting processes.

As this photo from Bangkok, Thailand, shows, McDonald's operates throughout the world. Multinational companies face special challenges in preparing their budgets.

Budgeting Product Life-Cycle Costs

Learning Objective **7**

Understand the importance of budgeting product life-cycle costs.

A relatively recent focus of the budgeting process is to plan for all of the costs that will be incurred throughout a product's life cycle, before a commitment is made to the product.[14] Product life-cycle costs encompass the following five phases in a product's life cycle:

1. Product planning and concept design
2. Preliminary design
3. Detailed design and testing
4. Production
5. Distribution and customer service

To justify a product's introduction, the sales revenues it will generate over its lifetime have to cover all of these costs, so planning these life-cycle costs is a crucial step in making a decision about the introduction of a new product. This is particularly true for firms with very short product life cycles, such as some products in the computer and electronics industries. When product life cycles are as short as a year or two, the firm does not have time to adjust its pricing strategy or production methods to ensure that the product turns a profit. Management must be fairly certain before a commitment is made to the product that its life-cycle costs will be covered. As Exhibit 8–6 shows, most of a product's life-cycle costs are committed rather early in the product's life. By the time the planning, design, and testing phases are complete, roughly 85 percent of this product's life-cycle costs have been committed, while only about 5 percent actually have been incurred.

Given the early commitment that must be made to significant downstream costs in a product's life cycle, it is crucial to budget these costs as early as possible. Exhibit 8–7 displays a product life-cycle cost budget for a peripheral computer device with an anticipated five-year life cycle.

Behavioural Impact of Budgets

One of the underlying themes stressed in this text is the behavioural impact of managerial accounting practices. There is no other area where the behavioural implications are more important than in the budgeting area. A budget affects virtually everyone in an organization: those who prepare the budget, those who use the budget to facilitate decision making, and those who are evaluated using the budget. People's reactions to

Learning Objective   **8**

Discuss the behavioural implications of budgetary slack and participative budgeting.

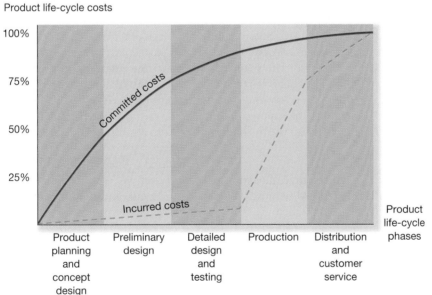

Exhibit 8–6
Product Life-Cycle Costs and Cost Commitment for a Typical Product

Exhibit 8–7
Product Life-Cycle Cost Budget

Life-Cycle Phase	Year				
	20x1	20x2	20x3	20x4	20x5
Product planning and concept design	$300,000				
Preliminary design	100,000				
Detail design and testing		$600,000			
Production		300,000	$2,000,000	$2,700,000	$1,200,000
Distribution and customer service		50,000	750,000	1,000,000	1,000,000

the budgeting process can have considerable influence on an organization's overall effectiveness.

A great deal of study has been devoted to the behavioural effects of budgets. We will briefly consider two important issues: budgetary slack and participative budgeting.

Budgetary Slack: Padding the Budget

The information on which a budget is based comes mainly from people throughout an organization. For example, the sales forecast relies on market research and analysis but also incorporates projections made by sales staff. If a territorial sales manager's performance is evaluated on the basis of whether the sales budget for the territory is exceeded, what is the incentive for the sales manager in projecting sales? The incentive is to give a conservative, or cautiously low, sales estimate. The sales manager's performance will look much better in the eyes of top management when a conservative estimate is exceeded than when an ambitious estimate is not met. At least that is the *perception* of many sales managers, and, in the behavioural area, perceptions are what count most.

When a supervisor provides a departmental cost projection for budgetary purposes, there is an incentive to overestimate costs. When the actual cost incurred in the department proves to be less than the inflated cost projection, the supervisor appears to have managed in a cost-effective way.

These illustrations are examples of **padding the budget**. Budget padding means underestimating revenue and/or overestimating costs. The difference between the revenue or cost projection that a person provides and a realistic estimate of the revenue or cost is called **budgetary slack**. For example, if a manager believes the annual utilities cost will be $18,000, but gives a budgetary projection of $20,000, the manager has built $2,000 of slack into the budget.

Why do people pad budgets with budgetary slack? There are three primary reasons. First, people often *perceive* that their performance will look better in their superiors' eyes if they can "beat the budget." Second, budgetary slack often is used to cope with uncertainty. A departmental supervisor may feel confident in the cost projections for 10 cost items. However, the supervisor also may feel that some unforeseen event during the budgetary period could result in unanticipated costs. For example, an unexpected machine break-down could occur. One way of dealing with that unforeseen event is to pad the budget. If nothing goes wrong, the supervisor can beat the cost budget. If some negative event does occur, the supervisor can use the budgetary slack to absorb the impact of the event and still meet the cost budget.

The third reason why cost budgets are padded is that budgetary cost projections are often cut in the resource-allocation process. Thus, we have a vicious circle. Budgetary projections are padded because they will likely be cut, and they are cut because they are likely to have been padded.

How does an organization solve the problem of budgetary slack? First, it can avoid relying on the budget as a negative evaluation tool. If a departmental supervisor is penalized by the budget director or some other top manager every time a budgetary cost projection is exceeded, the likely behavioural response will be to pad the budget. In contrast, if the supervisor is allowed some managerial discretion to exceed the budget when necessary, there will be less tendency toward budgetary padding. Second, managers can be given incentives not only to achieve budgetary projections but also to *provide accurate projections*. This can be accomplished by asking managers to justify all or some of their projections and by rewarding managers who consistently provide accurate estimates.

Participative Budgeting

Most people will perform better and make greater attempts to achieve a goal if they have been consulted in setting the goal. The idea of **participative budgeting** is to involve employees throughout an organization in the budgetary process. Such participation can give employees the feeling that "This is our budget," rather than the all-too-common feeling that "This is the budget you imposed on us."

While participative budgeting can be very effective, it also can have shortcomings. Too much participation and discussion can lead to indecision and delay. Also, when those involved in the budgeting process disagree in significant and irreconcilable ways, the process of participation can accentuate those differences. Finally, the problem of budget padding can be severe unless incentives for accurate projections are provided.

Focus on Ethics

IS PADDING THE BUDGET UNETHICAL?

A departmental or divisional budget often is used as the basis for evaluating a manager's performance. Actual results are compared with budgeted performance levels, and those who outperform the budget often are rewarded with promotions or salary increases. In many cases, bonuses are tied explicitly to performance relative to a budget. For example, the top management of a division may receive a bonus if divisional profit exceeds budgeted profit by a certain percentage.

Serious ethical issues can arise in situations where a budget is the basis for rewarding managers. For example, suppose a division's top management will split a bonus equal to 10 percent of the amount by which actual divisional profit exceeds the budget. This may create an incentive for the divisional budget officer, or other managers supplying data, to pad the divisional profit budget. Such padding would make the budget easier to achieve, thus increasing the chance of a bonus. Alternatively, there may be an incentive to manipulate the actual divisional results

in order to maximize management's bonus. For example, year-end sales could be shifted between years to increase reported revenue in a particular year. Budget staff could have such incentives for either of two reasons: (1) they might share in the bonus or (2) they might feel pressure from the managers who would share in the bonus.

Put yourself in the position of the division controller. Your bonus, and that of your boss, the division vice-president, will be determined in part by the division's income in comparison to the budget. When your division has submitted budgets in the past, the corporate management has usually cut your budgeted expenses, thereby increasing the division's budgeted profit. This, of course, makes it more difficult for your division to achieve the budgeted profit. Moreover, it makes it less likely that you and your divisional colleagues will earn a bonus.

Now your boss is pressuring you to pad the expense budget, because "The budgeted expenses will just be cut anyway at the corporate level." Is padding the budget ethical under these circumstances? What do you think?

Chapter Summary

LO1 List and explain five purposes of budgeting systems. The budget is a key tool for planning, control, and decision making in virtually every organization. The five purposes of budgeting systems are: to force planning, to facilitate communication and coordination, to identify the best allocation of resources, to set a benchmark for measurement of profit and operations, and to evaluate performance and provide incentives.

LO2 Describe the similarities and differences in the operational budgets prepared by manufacturers, service industry firms, merchandisers, and nonprofit organizations. The key difference in the operational budgets of manufacturers and merchandisers versus service industry and nonprofit organizations is that the operational budgets of manufacturers and merchandisers must account for the production or purchase and holding of inventory. In contrast, the budgets of service industry and nonprofit organizations generally do not have inventories of manufactured or purchased inventories.

LO3 Explain the concept of activity-based budgeting and the benefits it brings to the budgeting process. Activity-based budgeting (ABB) applies the concepts of activity-based costing (ABC) to the budgeting process. Utilizing ABC information in the budgeting process through ABB provides sound information for budgeting costs, because the underlying ABC information is based explicitly on the relationships among cost drivers, activities, and resources consumed.

LO4 Prepare each of the budget schedules that make up the master budget. The master budget includes the following key budget schedules: sales; cash receipts; production; direct material; direct labour; manufacturing overhead; selling, general, and administrative expense; cash disbursements; cash; and the cost of goods manufactured and sold. Also included are the following budgeted financial statements: income statement; statement of cash flows; and balance sheet.

LO5 Discuss the role of assumptions and predictions in budgeting. A master budget is based on many assumptions and predictions of unknown parameters. Some estimates tend to be quite accurate, while other predictions are much more difficult to make and might prove to be inaccurate.

LO6 Describe a typical organization's process of budget administration. Most organizations have a well-defined process by which budget data are collected and the budget is prepared. This administrative process often involves a budget director or chief budget officer, a budget manual, and a budgeting committee.

LO7 Understand the importance of budgeting product life-cycle costs. A relatively recent focus of the budgeting process is to plan for product life-cycle costs. A large portion of these costs often are committed early in a product's life cycle. It is important for management to be fairly certain that the revenue to be generated by a product will cover all of its life-cycle costs.

LO8 Discuss the behavioural implications of budgetary slack and participative budgeting. A common problem in budgeting is the tendency of people to pad budgets. The resulting budgetary slack makes the budget less useful because the padded budget does not present an accurate picture of expected revenue and expenses. Participative budgeting is the process of allowing employees throughout the organization to have a significant role in developing the budget. Participative budgeting can result in greater commitment to meet the budget by those who participated in the process.

Review Problem on Preparing Master Budget Schedules

SolarTech, Inc. manufactures a special ceramic tile used as a component in residential solar energy systems. Sales are seasonal due to the seasonality of the home-building industry.

- The expected pattern of sales for the next year (20x8) is as follows:

| | Quarter | | | | |
	1st	2nd	3rd	4th	Year
Sales in units	2,000	6,000	8,000	4,000	20,000

- Each tile sells for $25. All sales are on account, and SolarTech's experience with cash collections is that 60 percent of each quarter's sales are collected during the same quarter as the sale. The remaining 40 percent of sales is collected in the quarter after the sale. SolarTech experiences negligible bad debts, so this is ignored in the budgeting process. Sales in the 4th quarter of 20x7 are expected to be $100,000 (4,000 units).
- SolarTech wants to have 10 percent of the following quarter's sales needs in finished-goods inventory at the end of each quarter. (On December 31, 20x7, SolarTech expects to have 200 units in inventory.)
- Each tile requires two kilograms of raw material. SolarTech wants to have 10 percent of the next quarter's raw material in inventory at the end of each quarter. (On December 31, 20x7, SolarTech expects to have 480 kilograms of raw material in inventory.)
- The raw-material price is $5 per kilogram. The company buys its raw material on account and pays 70 percent of the resulting accounts payable during the quarter of the purchase. The remaining 30 percent is paid during the following quarter. (The raw-material purchases in the 4th quarter of 20x7 are expected to be $36,600.)

Required: Prepare the following budget schedules for 20x8. Include a column for each quarter and for the year.

1. Sales budget (in units and dollars)
2. Cash receipts budget
3. Production budget
4. Direct-material budget (*Hint:* The desired ending inventory in the 4th quarter is 480 kilograms.)
5. Cash disbursements budget for raw-material purchases

Solution to Review Problem

1. Sales budget for 20x8:

		Quarter			
	1st	2nd	3rd	4th	Year
Sales in units	2,000	6,000	8,000	4,000	20,000
Unit sales price	$ 25	$ 25	$ 25	$ 25	$ 25
Total sales revenue	$50,000	$150,000	$200,000	$100,000	$500,000

2. Cash receipts budget for 20x8:

		Quarter			
	1st	2nd	3rd	4th	Year
Sales revenue (from sales budget)	$50,000	$150,000	$200,000	$100,000	$500,000
Collections in quarter of sale (60% of revenue)	$30,000	$ 90,000	$120,000	$ 60,000	$300,000
Collections in quarter after sale (40% of prior quarter's revenue)*	40,000*	20,000	60,000	80,000	200,000
Total cash receipts	$70,000	$110,000	$180,000	$140,000	$500,000

*Forty percent of sales revenue from the fourth quarter of 20x7, which was given at $100,000.

3. Production budget for 20x8:

		Quarter			
	1st	2nd	3rd	4th	Year
Sales in units (from sales budget)	2,000	6,000	8,000	4,000	20,000
Add desired ending inventory of finished goods*	600	800	400	200†	2,000
Total units required	2,600	6,800	8,400	4,200	22,000
Less expected beginning inventory of finished goods	200	600	800	400	2,000
Units to be produced	2,400	6,200	7,600	3,800	20,000

*Ten percent of the next quarter's expected sales.
†Ten percent of the expected sales for the first quarter of the next year 20x9, which is predicted to be 2,000 units.

4. Direct-material budget for 20x8:

		Quarter			
	1st	2nd	3rd	4th	Year
Units to be produced (from production budget)	2,400	6,200	7,600	3,800	20,000
Raw material required per unit (kilograms)	× 2	× 2	× 2	× 2	× 2
Raw material required for production (kilograms)	4,800	12,400	15,200	7,600	40,000
Add desired ending inventory of raw material (kilograms)*	1,240	1,520	760	480†	4,000
Total raw material required	6,040	13,920	15,960	8,080	44,000
Less expected beginning inventory of raw material (kilograms)	480‡	1,240	1,520	760	4,000
Raw material to be purchased (kilograms)	5,560	12,680	14,440	7,320	40,000
Cost per pound	× $5	× $5	× $5	× $5	× $5
Total cost of raw-material purchases	$27,800	$63,400	$72,200	$36,600	$200,000

*Ten percent of the next quarter's raw-material requirements.
†The desired ending raw-material inventory for the fourth quarter of 20x8 is given at 480 kilograms. However, it can also be computed independently by noting that the expected sales pattern for 20x9 is the same as that for 20x8. Therefore, the first quarter budgets for 20x9 will be the same as those for the first quarter of 20x8. So the desired ending raw-material inventory for the fourth quarter of 20x8 is 480 kilograms (10% × 4,800 kilograms required for production in the first quarter of 20x9).
‡Given in problem.

5. Cash disbursements budget for raw material purchases for 20x8:

	Quarter				
	1st	2nd	3rd	4th	Year
Cost of raw-material purchases (from direct-material budget)	$27,800	$63,400	$72,200	$36,600	$200,000
Cash payments for purchases made during the quarter (70% of current quarter's purchases)	$19,460	$44,380	$50,540	$25,620	$140,000
Cash payments for prior quarter's purchases (30% of prior quarter's purchases)	10,980*	8,340	19,020	21,660	60,000
Total cash payments for raw-material purchases	$30,440	$52,720	$69,560	$47,280	$200,000

*Purchases in the fourth quarter of 20x7 were given at $36,600.

Glossary

Review key terms and definitions on Connect.

Review Questions

8–1. Explain how a budget facilitates communication and coordination.

8–2. Use an example to explain how a budget could be used to allocate resources in a university or college.

8–3. Explain what a *master budget* is, and list five of its parts.

8–4. For a service station, draw a flow chart that is similar to the one in Exhibit 8–1. The service station provides automotive maintenance services in addition to selling gasoline and other vehicle-related products.

8–5. Give an example of how general economic trends would affect sales forecasting in the airline industry.

8–6. What is meant by the term *operational budgets*? List three operational budgets that would be prepared by a hospital.

8–7. How does activity-based budgeting differ from more traditional budgeting methods?

8–8. How does e-budgeting make use of the Internet?

8–9. Give three examples of how a city could use a budget for planning purposes.

8–10. Describe the role of a *budget director*.

8–11. What is the purpose of a *budget manual*?

8–12. How can a company's board of directors use the budget to influence the future direction of the firm?

8–13. Discuss the importance of predictions and assumptions in the budgeting process.

8–14. Define the term *budgetary slack*, and briefly describe a problem it can cause.

8–15. How can an organization help to reduce the problems caused by budgetary slack?

8–16. Why is participative budgeting often an effective management tool?

8–17. Discuss this comment by a small-business owner: "Budgeting is a waste of time. I've been running this business for 40 years. I don't need to plan."

8–18. List the steps you would go through in developing a budget to meet your school expenses.

8–19. Briefly describe three issues that create special challenges for multinational firms in preparing their budgets.

8–20. List five phases in a product's *life cycle*, and explain why it is important to budget the costs in each of these phases.

Exercises

Exercise 8–21 Missing Amounts; Various Types of Budgets **(LO4)**

Fill in the missing amounts in the following schedules:

	July	August	September
1. Sales*	$80,000	$60,000	$?
Cash receipts:			
From cash sales	$?	$?	$45,000
From sales on account†	?	34,000	?
Total cash receipts	$?	$?	$?

*Half of each month's sales are on account. June sales amounted to $60,000.

†60% of credit sales is collected in the month of sale; 40% is collected in the following month.

2. Accounts payable, 12/31/x0	300,000
Purchase of goods and services on account during 20x1	1,200,000
Payments of accounts payable during 20x1	?
Accounts payable, 12/31/x1	400,000
3. Accounts receivable, 12/31/x0	$ 340,000
Sales on account during 20x1	900,000
Collections of accounts receivable during 20x1	780,000
Accounts receivable, 12/31/x1	?
4. Accumulated depreciation, 12/31/x0	$ 810,000
Depreciation expense during 20x1	150,000
Accumulated depreciation, 12/31/x1	?
5. Retained earnings, 12/31/x0	$2,050,000
Net income for 20x1	400,000
Dividends paid in 20x1	–0–
Retained earnings, 12/31/x1	?

Exercise 8–22 City or Provincial Budget; Use of Internet **(LO1, 2)**

Choose a city or province, and use the Internet to explore the annual budget of the governmental unit you selected. For example, you could check out the budget for the City of Vancouver at http://vancouver.ca/fs/budgetServices/index.htm#operating.

Required: List three items in the budget that you found surprising or particularly interesting, and explain why.

Exercise 8–23 Budgeting Production and Direct-Material Purchases **(LO4)**

Bodin Company budgets on an annual basis. The following beginning and ending inventory levels (in units) are planned for the year 20x1. Two units of raw material are required to produce each unit of finished product.

	January 1	December 31
Raw material	35,000	45,000
Work in process	12,000	12,000
Finished goods	80,000	50,000

Required:

1. If Bodin Company plans to sell 480,000 units during the year, compute the number of units the firm would have to manufacture during the year.

2. If 500,000 finished units were to be manufactured by Bodin Company during the year, determine the amount of raw material to be purchased.

(CMA, adapted)

Exercise 8–24 Cash Collections **(LO4)**

Coyote Loco, Inc., a manufacturer of salsa, has the following historical collection pattern for its credit sales:

- 70 percent collected in the month of sale
- 15 percent collected in the first month after sale
- 10 percent collected in the second month after sale
- 4 percent collected in the third month after sale
- 1 percent uncollectable

The sales on account have been budgeted for the last seven months as follows:

June	$ 49,000
July	60,000
August	70,000
September	80,000
October	90,000
November	100,000
December	85,000

Required:

1. Compute the estimated total cash collections during October from credit sales.
2. Compute the estimated total cash collections during the fourth quarter from sales made on account during the fourth quarter.

3. *Build a spreadsheet:* Construct an Excel spreadsheet to solve both of the preceding requirements. Show how the solution will change if the following information changes: sales in June and July were $50,000 and $65,000, respectively.

(CMA, adapted)

Exercise 8–25 Budgeting Production and Raw-Material Purchases (LO4)

Greener Grass Fertilizer Company plans to sell 200,000 units of finished product in July and anticipates a growth rate in sales of 5 percent per month. The desired monthly ending inventory in units of finished product is 80 percent of the next month's estimated sales. There are 160,000 finished units in inventory on June 30. Each unit of finished product requires four kilograms of raw material at a cost of $1.15 per kilogram. There are 700,000 kilograms of raw material in inventory on June 30.

Required:

1. Compute the company's total required production in units of finished product for the entire three-month period ending September 30.
2. Independent of your answer to requirement (1), assume the company plans to produce 600,000 units of finished product in the three-month period ending September 30, and to have raw-material inventory on hand at the end of the three-month period equal to 25 percent of the use in that period. Compute the total estimated cost of raw-material purchases for the entire three-month period ending September 30.

(CMA, adapted)

Exercise 8–26 Cash Budgeting (LO4)

The following information is from Binghamton Film Corporation's financial records.

Month	Sales	Purchases
April	$72,000	$42,000
May	66,000	48,000
June	60,000	36,000
July	78,000	54,000

Collections from customers are normally 70 percent in the month of sale, 20 percent in the month following the sale, and 9 percent in the second month following the sale. The balance is expected to be uncollectable. All purchases are on account. Management takes full advantage of the 2 percent discount allowed on purchases paid for by the tenth of the following month. Purchases for August are budgeted at $60,000, and sales for August are forecasted at $66,000. Cash disbursements for expenses are expected to be $14,400 for the month of August. The company's cash balance on August 1 was $22,000.

Required: Prepare the following schedules:

1. Expected cash collections during August
2. Expected cash disbursements during August
3. Expected cash balance on August 31

Exercise 8–27 Budgetary Slack: Bank (LO8)

Tanya Williams is the bank's new-accounts manager at Coast Mountain Bank. She has just been asked to project how many new bank accounts she will generate during 20x2. The economy of the region in which the bank operates has been growing, and the bank has experienced a 10 percent increase in its number of bank accounts over each of the past five years. In 20x1, the bank had 10,000 accounts.

The new-accounts manager is paid a salary plus a bonus of $15 for every new account she generates above the budgeted amount. So, if the annual budget calls for 500 new accounts and 540 new accounts are obtained, Williams's bonus will be $600 (40 × $15).

Williams believes the economy of the region will continue to grow at the same rate in 20x2 as it has in recent years. She has decided to submit a budgetary projection of 700 new accounts for 20x2.

Required: Your consulting firm has been hired by the bank president to make recommendations for improving its operations. Write a memorandum to the president defining and explaining the negative consequences of budgetary slack. Also discuss the bank's bonus system for the new-accounts manager and how the bonus program tends to encourage budgetary slack.

Exercise 8–28 Using Budgets for Financial Planning (LO1, 4, 5)

Sound Investments, Inc. is a large retailer of stereo equipment. The controller is about to prepare the budget for the first quarter of 20x2. Past experience has indicated that 75 percent of the store's sales are cash sales. The collection experience for the sales on account is as follows:

- 80 percent during month of sale
- 15 percent during month following sale
- 5 percent uncollectable

The total sales for December 20x1 are expected to be $190,000. The controller feels that sales in January 20x2 could range from $100,000 to $160,000.

Required:

1. Demonstrate how financial planning can be used to project cash receipts in January of 20x2 for three different levels of January sales. Use the following columnar format:

	Total Sales in January 20x2		
	$100,000	**$130,000**	**$160,000**
Cash receipts in January 20x2:			
From December sales on account	$	$	$
From January cash sales			
From January sales on account			
Total cash receipts	$	$	$

2. How could the controller of Sound Investments, Inc. use this financial planning approach to help in planning operations for January?

Exercise 8–29 Budgeted Financial Statements: Retailer (LO4)

Handy Hardware is a retail hardware store. Information about the store's operations follows:

- November 20x1 sales amounted to $200,000.
- Sales are budgeted at $220,000 for December 20x1 and $200,000 for January 20x2.
- Collections are expected to be 60 percent in the month of sale and 38 percent in the month following the sale. Two percent of sales are expected to be uncollectable. Bad debts expense is recognized monthly.
- The store's gross margin is 25 percent of its sales revenue.
- A total of 80 percent of the merchandise for resale is purchased in the month prior to the month of sale, and 20 percent is purchased in the month of sale. Payment for merchandise is made in the month following the purchase.
- Other monthly expenses paid in cash amount to $22,600.
- Annual depreciation is $216,000.

The company's balance sheet as of November 30, 20x1, is as follows:

HANDY HARDWARE, INC.
Balance Sheet
November 30, 20x1

ASSETS

Cash	$ 22,000
Accounts receivable (net of $3,500 allowance for uncollectable accounts)	76,000
Inventory	140,000
Property, plant, and equipment (net of $590,000 accumulated depreciation)	862,000
Total assets	$1,100,000

LIABILITIES AND SHAREHOLDERS' EQUITY

Accounts payable	$ 162,000
Common shares	795,000
Retained earnings	143,000
Total liabilities and shareholders' equity	$1,100,000

Required: Compute the following amounts:

1. The budgeted cash collections for December 20x1
2. The budgeted income (loss) before income taxes for December 20x1
3. The projected balance in accounts payable on December 31, 20x1

(CMA, adapted)

Exercise 8–30   Professional Services Budget for a Dental Practice; Activity-Based Budgeting (LO2, 3, 4)

Metropolitan Dental Associates is a large dental practice. The firm's controller is preparing the budget for the next year. The controller projects a total of 48,000 office visits, to be evenly distributed throughout the year. Eighty percent of the visits will be half-hour appointments, and the remainder will be one-hour visits. The average rates for professional dental services are $40 for half-hour appointments and $70 for one-hour office visits. Ninety percent of each month's professional service revenue is collected during the month when services are rendered, and the remainder is collected the month following service. Uncollectable billings are negligible. Metropolitan's dental associates earn $60 per hour.

Metropolitan uses activity-based budgeting to budget office overhead and administrative expenses. Two cost drivers are used: office visits and direct professional labour. The cost driver rates are as follows:

Patient registration and records	$2.00 per office visit (of any length)
All other overhead and administrative expenses	$5.00 per direct professional labour-hour

Required: Prepare the following budget schedules:

1. Direct professional labour budget for the month of June
2. Cash collections during June for professional services rendered during May and June
3. Overhead and administrative expense budget for the month of June
4. *Build a spreadsheet:* Construct an Excel spreadsheet to handle all of the preceding requirements. Show how the results will change if the following information changes: a total of 54,000 office visits are expected for the year and 70 percent of the office visits are half-hour appointments.

Problems

Problem 8–31   Production and Direct-Labour Budgets; Activity-Based Overhead Budget (LO3, 4)

1. Total direct-labour cost for the quarter: $470,155

Spiffy Shades Corporation manufactures artistic frames for sunglasses. Talia Demarest, controller, is responsible for preparing the company's master budget. In compiling the budget data for 20x1, Demarest has learned that new automated production equipment will be installed on March 1. This will reduce the direct labour per frame from 1 hour to 0.75 hour.

Labour-related costs include pension contributions of $0.50 per hour, Workers' Compensation insurance of $0.20 per hour, employee medical insurance of $0.80 per hour, and other benefits equal to 7 percent of direct-labour wages. The cost of employee benefits paid by the company for its employees is treated as a direct-labour cost. Spiffy Shades Corporation has a labour contract that calls for a wage increase to $18 per hour on April 1, 20x1. Management expects to have 16,000 frames on hand at December 31, 20x0, and has a policy of carrying an end-of-month inventory of 100 percent of the following month's sales plus 50 percent of the second following month's sales.

These and other data compiled by Demarest are summarized in the following table:

	January	February	March	April	May
Direct-labour hours per unit	1.0	1.0	0.75	0.75	0.75
Wage per direct-labour hour	$16.00	$16.00	$16.00	$18.00	$18.00
Estimated unit sales	10,000	12,000	8,000	9,000	9,000
Sales price per unit	$50.00	$47.50	$47.50	$47.50	$47.50
Manufacturing overhead:					
Shipping and handling (per unit sold)	$2.00	$2.00	$2.00	$2.00	$2.00
Purchasing, material handling, and inspection (per unit produced)	$3.00	$3.00	$3.00	$3.00	$3.00
Other manufacturing overhead (per direct-labour hour)	$7.00	$7.00	$7.00	$7.00	$7.00

Required:

1. Prepare a production budget and a direct-labour budget for Spiffy Shades Corporation by month and for the first quarter of 20x1. Both budgets may be combined into one schedule. The direct-labour budget should include direct-labour hours and show the detail for each direct-labour cost category.

2. For each item used in the firm's production budget and direct-labour budget, identify the other components of the master budget that also would use these data.

3. Prepare a manufacturing-overhead budget for each month and for the first quarter.

(CMA, adapted)

Problem 8–32 Revenue and Labour Budgeting for a University; Budget Linkages (LO4, 6)

2. Faculty needed: 672

Western University (WU) is preparing its master budget for the upcoming academic year. Currently, 8,000 students are enrolled on campus; however, the admissions office is forecasting a 5 percent growth in the student body despite a tuition hike to $75 per credit hour. The following additional information has been gathered from an examination of university records and conversations with university officials:

*   WU is planning to award 120 tuition-free scholarships.
*   The average class has 25 students, and the typical student takes 15 credit hours each semester. Each class is three credit hours. WU operates two semesters per year and has no summer term.
*   WU's faculty members are evaluated on the basis of teaching, research, and university and community service. Each faculty member teaches five classes during the academic year.

Required:

1. Prepare a tuition revenue budget for the upcoming academic year.
2. Determine the number of faculty members needed to cover classes.
3. Assume there is a shortage of full-time faculty members. List at least five actions that WU might take to accommodate the growing student body.
4. You have been requested by the university's administrative vice-president (AVP) to construct budgets for other areas of operation (e.g., the library, grounds, dormitories, and maintenance). The AVP noted: "The most important resource of the university is its faculty. Now that you know the number of faculty needed, you can prepare the other budgets. Faculty members are indeed the key driver—without them we don't operate." Does the administrative vice-president really understand the linkages within the budgeting process? Explain.

Problem 8–33 Cash Budgeting (LO4)

2. Total cash disbursements in February: $121,000

Mary and Kay, Inc., a distributor of cosmetics, is in the process of assembling a cash budget for the first quarter of 20x1. The following information has been extracted from the company's accounting records:

*   All sales are on account. Sixty percent of customer accounts are collected in the month of sale; 35 percent are collected in the following month. Uncollectables amounting to 5 percent of sales are anticipated, and management believes that only 20 percent of the accounts outstanding on December 31, 20x0, will be recovered and that the recovery will be in January 20x1.
*   Seventy percent of the merchandise purchases are paid for in the month of purchase; the remaining 30 percent are paid for in the month after acquisition.
*   The December 31, 20x0, balance sheet disclosed the following selected figures: cash, $20,000; accounts receivable, $55,000; and accounts payable, $22,000.
*   Mary and Kay, Inc. maintains a $20,000 minimum cash balance at all times. Financing is available (and retired) in $1,000 multiples at an 8 percent interest rate, with borrowings taking place at the beginning of the month and repayments occurring at the end of the month. Interest is paid at the time of repaying principal and computed on the portion of principal repaid at that time.

Additional data:

	January	February	March
Sales revenue	$150,000	$180,000	$185,000
Merchandise purchases	90,000	100,000	140,000
Cash operating costs	31,000	24,000	45,000
Proceeds from sale of equipment	—	—	5,000

Required:

1. Prepare a schedule that discloses the firm's total cash collections for January through March.
2. Prepare a schedule that discloses the firm's total cash disbursements for January through March.
3. Prepare a schedule that discloses the firm's cash needs, if any, for January through March. The schedule should present the following information in the order cited: beginning cash balance, total receipts (from requirement [1]), total payments (from requirement [2]), the cash excess (deficiency) before financing, borrowing needed to maintain minimum balance, loan principal repaid, loan interest paid, and ending cash balance.

Problem 8–34   Relationships of the Master Budget Components **(LO4)**

5. December 31 inventory:
1,900 units

Badlands, Inc. manufactures a household fan that sells for $40 per unit. All sales are on account, with 40 percent of sales collected in the month of sale and 60 percent collected in the following month. The data that follow were extracted from the company's accounting records.

- Badlands maintains a minimum cash balance of $30,000. Total payments in January 20x1 are budgeted at $390,000.
- A schedule of cash collections for January and February of 20x1 revealed the following receipts for the period:

	Cash Receipts	
	January	**February**
From December 31 accounts receivable..	$216,000	
From January sales...	152,000	$228,000
From February sales		156,800

- March 20x1 sales are expected to total 10,000 units.
- Finished-goods inventories are maintained at 20 percent of the following month's sales.
- The December 31, 20x0, balance sheet revealed the following selected figures: cash, $45,000; accounts receivable, $216,000; and finished goods, $44,700.

Required:

1. Determine the number of units that Badlands sold in December 20x0.
2. Compute the sales revenue for March 20x1.
3. Compute the total sales revenue to be reported on Badlands' budgeted income statement for the first quarter of 20x1.
4. Determine the accounts receivable balance to be reported on the March 31, 20x1, budgeted balance sheet.
5. Calculate the number of units in the December 31, 20x0, finished-goods inventory.
6. Calculate the number of units of finished goods to be manufactured in January 20x1.
7. Calculate the financing required in January, if any, to maintain the firm's minimum cash balance.

Problem 8–35   Cash Budget: Wholesaler **(LO1, 4)**

1. Total cash disbursements,
April: $9,785,000
Ending cash balance, June:
$2,605,000

Alpha-Tech, a rapidly growing distributor of electronic components, is formulating its plans for 20x5. Carol Jones, the firm's marketing director, has completed the following sales forecast.

ALPHA-TECH 20x5 Forecasted Sales (in thousands)			
Month	**Sales**	**Month**	**Sales**
January	$ 9,000	July	$15,000
February	10,000	August	15,000
March	9,000	September	16,000
April	11,500	October	16,000
May	12,500	November	15,000
June	14,000	December	17,000

Phillip Smith, an accountant in the Planning and Budgeting Department, is responsible for preparing the cash flow projection. The following information will be used in preparing the cash flow projection.

- Alpha-Tech's excellent record in accounts receivable collection is expected to continue. Sixty percent of billings are collected the month after the sale, and the remaining 40 percent two months after.

- The purchase of electronic components is Alpha-Tech's largest expenditure, and each month's cost of goods sold is estimated to be 40 percent of sales. Seventy percent of the parts are received by Alpha-Tech one month prior to sale, and 30 percent are received during the month of sale.

- Historically, 75 percent of accounts payable has been paid one month after receipt of the purchased components, and the remaining 25 percent has been paid two months after receipt.

- Hourly wages and fringe benefits, estimated to be 30 percent of the current month's sales, are paid in the month incurred.

- General and administrative expenses are projected to be $15,620,000 for the year. The breakdown of these expenses is presented in the following schedule. All cash expenditures are paid uniformly throughout the year, except the property taxes, which are paid in four equal instalments at the end of each quarter.

20x5 Forecasted General and Administrative Costs (in thousands)	
Salaries and fringe benefits	$ 3,200
Promotion	3,800
Property taxes	1,360
Insurance	2,000
Utilities	1,800
Depreciation	3,460
Total	$15,620

- Income tax payments are made at the beginning of each calendar quarter based on the income of the prior quarter. Alpha-Tech is subject to an income tax rate of 40 percent. Alpha-Tech's operating income for the first quarter of 20x5 is projected to be $3,200,000. The company pays 100 percent of the estimated tax payment.

- Alpha-Tech maintains a minimum cash balance of $500,000. If the cash balance is less than $500,000 at the end of each month, the company borrows amounts necessary to maintain this balance. All amounts borrowed are repaid out of the subsequent positive cash flow. The projected April 1, 20x5, opening balance is $500,000.

- Alpha-Tech has no short-term debt as of April 1, 20x5.

- Alpha-Tech uses a calendar year for both financial reporting and tax purposes.

Required:

1. Prepare a cash budget for Alpha-Tech by month for the second quarter of 20x5. For simplicity, ignore any interest expense associated with borrowing.

2. Discuss why cash budgeting is important for Alpha-Tech.

(CMA, adapted)

Problem 8–36 Ethics; Budgetary Pressure; Management Bonuses; Budgetary Constraints (LO4, 5, 7)

Tulsa Chemical Company (TCC) produces and distributes industrial chemicals. TCC's earnings increased sharply in 20x1, and bonuses were paid to the management staff for the first time in several years. Bonuses are based in part on the amount by which reported income exceeds budgeted income.

Jim Kern, vice-president of finance, was pleased with TCC's 20x1 earnings and thought that the pressure to show financial results would ease. However, Ellen North, TCC's president, told Kern that she saw no reason why the 20x2 bonuses should not be double those of 20x1. As a result, Kern felt pressure to increase reported income in order to exceed budgeted income by an even greater amount. This would assure increased bonuses.

Kern met with Bill Keller of Pristeel, Inc., a primary vendor of TCC's manufacturing supplies and equipment. Kern and Keller have been close business contacts for many years. Kern asked Keller to identify all of TCC's purchases of perishable supplies as equipment on Pristeel's sales invoices. The reason Kern gave for his request was that TCC's president had imposed stringent budget constraints on operating expenses but not on capital expenditures. Kern planned to capitalize the purchase of perishable supplies, and include them with the Equipment account on the balance sheet. In this way Kern could defer the expense recognition for these items to a later year. This procedure would increase reported earnings, leading to increased bonuses. Keller agreed to do as Kern had asked.

While analyzing the second quarter financial statements, Gary Wood, TCC's controller, noticed a large decrease in supplies expense from one year ago. Wood reviewed the Supplies Expense account and noticed that only equipment and no supplies had been purchased from Pristeel, a major source for supplies. Wood, who reports to Kern, immediately brought this to Kern's attention.

Kern told Wood of North's high expectations and of the arrangement made with Keller of Pristeel. Wood told Kern that his action was an improper accounting treatment for the supplies purchased from Pristeel. Wood requested that he be allowed to correct the accounts and urged that the arrangement with Pristeel be discontinued. Kern refused the request and told Wood not to become involved in the arrangement with Pristeel.

After clarifying the situation in a confidential discussion with an objective and qualified peer within TCC, Wood arranged to meet with North, TCC's president. At the meeting, Wood disclosed the arrangement Kern had made with Pristeel.

Required:

1. Explain why the use of alternative accounting methods to manipulate reported earnings is unethical.
2. Is Gary Wood, TCC's controller, correct in saying that the supplies purchased from Pristeel Inc. were accounted for improperly? Explain your answer.
3. Assuming that Jim Kern's arrangement with Pristeel Inc. was in violation of the standards of ethical conduct for management accountants, discuss whether the actions of Wood were appropriate or inappropriate. (The standards are given in Chapter 1.)

(CMA, adapted)

Problem 8–37 Completion of Budget Schedules (LO2, 4)

2. Planned production, June: 15,000 sets
4. Planned direct-labour cost, May: $378,000

Scholastic Furniture, Inc. manufactures a variety of desks, chairs, tables, and shelf units that are sold to public school districts. The controller of the company's Desk Division is currently preparing a budget for the second quarter of the year. The following sales forecast has been made by the division's sales manager:

April	10,000 desk-and-chair sets
May	12,000 desk-and-chair sets
June	15,000 desk-and-chair sets

Each desk-and-chair set requires 10 board metres of pine planks and 1.5 hours of direct labour. Each set sells for $50. Pine planks cost $0.50 per board metre, and the division ends each month with enough wood to cover 10 percent of the next month's production requirements. The division incurs a cost of $20 per hour for direct-labour wages and fringe benefits. The division ends each month with enough finished-goods inventory to cover 20 percent of the next month's sales.

Required: Complete the following budget schedules.

1. Sales budget:

	April	May	September
Sales (in sets)	10,000		
Sales price per set	× $50		
Sales revenue	$500,000		

2. Production budget (in sets):

	April	May	September
Sales	10,000		
Add: Desired ending inventory	2,400		3,000
Total requirements	12,400		
Less: Projected beginning inventory	2,000		
Planned production	10,400		

3. Raw-material purchases:

	April	May	September
Planned production (sets)	10,400		
Raw material required per set (board metres)	× 10		
Raw material required for production (board metres)	104,000		
Add: Desired ending inventory of raw material, in board metres (10% of next month's requirement)	12,600		16,000
Total requirements	116,600		
Less: Projected beginning inventory of raw material, in board metres (10% of current month's requirement)	10,400		
Planned purchases of raw material (board metres)	106,200		
Cost per board metre	× $.50		
Planned purchases of raw material (dollars)	$53,100		

4. Direct-labour budget:

	April	May	June
Planned production (sets)	10,400		
Direct-labour hours per set	× 1.5		
Direct-labour hours required	15,600		
Cost per hour	× $20		
Planned direct-labour cost	$312,000		

5. *Build a spreadsheet:* Construct an Excel spreadsheet to solve all of the preceding requirements. Show how the solution will change if the following information changes: Each set sells for $55 and direct-labour cost per hour is $21.

Problem 8–38 Production and Materials Budgets **(LO4)**

Empire Chemical Company produces three products using three different continuous processes. The products are Yarex, Darol, and Norex. Projected sales in litres for the three products for the years 20x2 and 20x3 are as follows:

	20x2	20x3
Yarex	60,000	65,000
Darol	40,000	35,000
Norex	25,000	30,000

2. Conversion cost budget: $245,040

4. Increase in cost of raw material: $100,820

- Inventories are planned for each product so that the projected finished-goods inventory at the beginning of each year is equal to 8 percent of that year's projected sales.
- Because of the continuous nature of Empire's processes, work-in-process inventory for each of the products remains constant throughout the year.
- The conversion requirements in hours per litre for the three products are Yarex, 0.07 hours; Darol, 0.10 hours; and Norex, 0.16 hours. The conversion cost of $20 per hour is considered 100 percent variable.
- The raw-material requirements of the three products are shown in the following chart:

Raw Material	Units	Unit Price	Yarex	Darol	Norex
Gamma	Kilograms	$ 8	0.2	0.4	—
Murad	Kilograms	6	0.4	—	0.5
Islin	Litres	5	1.0	0.7	0.5
Tarden	Litres	10	—	0.3	0.5

- Raw-material inventories are planned so that each raw material's projected inventory at the beginning of a year is equal to 10 percent of the previous year's usage of that raw material.

Required:

1. Determine Empire Chemical Company's production budget (in litres) for the three products for 20x2.
2. Determine Empire Chemical Company's conversion cost budget for 20x2.
3. Assuming the 20x1 usage of Islin is 100,000 litres, determine the company's raw-material purchases budget (in dollars) for Islin for 20x2.
4. Assume that for 20x2 production, Empire Chemical Company could replace the raw material Islin with the raw material Philin. The usage of Philin would be the same as the usage of Islin. However, Philin would cost 20 percent more than Islin and would cut production times on all three products by 10 percent. Determine whether management should use Philin or Islin for the 20x2 production, supporting your decision with appropriate calculations. For this requirement, ignore any impact of beginning and ending inventory balances.

(CMA, adapted)

Problem 8–39   Sales, Production, and Purchases Budgets; Activity-Based Overhead Budget **(LO3, 4)**

Vista Electronics, Inc. manufactures two different types of coils used in electric motors. In the fall of the current year, the controller compiled the following data.

2. Production required (units), heavy coils: 41,000

6. Manufacturing overhead budget for 20x0, total manufacturing overhead: $1,464,250

-   Sales forecast for 20x0 (all units to be shipped in 20x0):

Product	Units	Price
Light coil	60,000	$120
Heavy coil	40,000	170

-   Raw-material prices and inventory levels:

Raw Material	Expected Inventories, January 1, 20x0	Desired Inventories, December 31, 20x0	Anticipated Purchase Price
Sheet metal	32,000 kilograms	36,000 kilograms	$8
Copper wire	29,000 kilograms	32,000 kilograms	5
Platform	6,000 units	7,000 units	3

-   Use of raw material:

Raw Material	Amount Used per Unit	
	Light Coil	Heavy Coil
Sheet metal	4 kilograms	5 kilograms
Copper wire	2 kilograms	3 kilograms
Platform		1 unit

-   Direct-labour requirements and rates:

Product	Hours per Unit	Rate per Hour
Light coil	2	$15
Heavy coil	3	20

-   Finished-goods inventories (in units):

Product	Expected January 1, 20x0	Desired December 31, 20x0
Light coil	20,000	25,000
Heavy coil	8,000	9,000

• Manufacturing overhead:

Overhead Cost Item	Activity-Based Budget Rate
Purchasing and material handling	$0.25 per kilogram of sheet metal and copper wire purchased
Depreciation, utilities, and inspection	$4.00 per coil produced (either type)
Shipping	$1.00 per coil shipped (either type)
General manufacturing overhead	$3.00 per direct-labour hour

Required: Prepare the following budgets for 20x0:

1. Sales budget (in dollars)
2. Production budget (in units)
3. Raw-material purchases budget (in quantities)
4. Raw-material purchases budget (in dollars)
5. Direct-labour budget (in dollars)
6. Manufacturing-overhead budget (in dollars)

(CPA, adapted)

Problem 8–40 Interrelationships between Components of a Master Budget **(LO1, 2, 4, 6)**

United Security Systems, Inc. (USSI) manufactures and sells security systems. The company started by installing photoelectric security systems in offices and has expanded into the private-home market. USSI has a basic security system that has been developed into three standard products, each of which can be adapted to meet the specific needs of customers. The manufacturing operation is moderate in size, as the bulk of the component manufacturing is completed by independent contractors. The security systems are approximately 85 percent complete when received from contractors and require only final assembly in the USSI plant. Each product passes through at least one of three assembly operations.

USSI operates in a rapidly growing community. There is evidence that a great deal of new commercial construction will take place in the near future, and management has decided to pursue this new market. In order to be competitive, the firm will have to expand its operations.

In view of the expected increase in business, Sandra Feldman, the controller, believes that USSI should implement a complete budgeting system. Feldman has decided to make a formal presentation to the company's president explaining the benefits of a budgeting system and outlining the budget schedules and reports that would be necessary.

Required:

1. Explain the benefits that USSI would gain from implementing a budgeting system.
2. If Sandra Feldman develops a master budget:
   a. Identify, in order, the schedules that will have to be prepared.
   b. Identify the subsequent schedules that would be based on the schedules identified above. Use the following format for your answer.

Schedule	Subsequent Schedule

(CMA, adapted)

Problem 8–41 Revised Operating Budget: Consulting Firm **(LO1, 4, 5)**

1. Operating income: $179,600

Total compensation, management consulting: $245,000

Toronto Business Associates, a division of Maple Leaf Services Corporation, offers management and computer consulting services to clients throughout Canada and the northwestern United States. The division specializes in website development and other Internet applications. The corporate management at Maple Leaf Services is pleased with the performance of Toronto Business Associates for the first nine months of the current year and has recommended that the division manager, Richard Howell, submit a revised forecast for the remaining quarter, as the division has exceeded the annual plan year-to-date forecast by 20 percent of operating income. An unexpected increase in billed hour volume over the original plan is the main reason for this increase in income. The original operating budget for the first three quarters for Toronto Business Associates follows.

TORONTO BUSINESS ASSOCIATES
20X1 OPERATING BUDGET

	1st Quarter	2nd Quarter	3rd Quarter	Total for First Three Quarters
Revenue:				
Consulting fees:				
Computer system consulting	$ 421,875	$ 421,875	$ 421,875	$1,265,625
Management consulting	315,000	315,000	315,000	945,000
Total consulting fees	736,875	736,875	736,875	2,210,625
Other revenue	10,000	10,000	10,000	30,000
Total revenue	746,875	746,875	746,875	2,240,625
Expenses:				
Consultant salary expenses	386,750	386,750	386,750	1,160,250
Travel and related expenses	45,625	45,625	45,625	136,875
General and administrative expenses	100,000	100,000	100,000	300,000
Depreciation expense	40,000	40,000	40,000	120,000
Corporate expense allocation	50,000	50,000	50,000	150,000
Total expenses	622,375	622,375	622,375	1,867,125
Operating income	$ 124,500	$ 124,500	$ 124,500	$ 373,500

Howell will reflect the following information in his revised forecast for the fourth quarter.

- Toronto Business Associates currently has 25 consultants on staff, 10 for management consulting and 15 for computer systems consulting. Three additional management consultants have been hired to start work at the beginning of the fourth quarter in order to meet the increased client demand.
- The hourly billing rate for consulting revenue will remain at $90 per hour for each management consultant and $75 per hour for each computer consultant. However, due to the favourable increase in billing hour volume when compared to the plan, the hours for each consultant will be increased by 50 hours per quarter.
- The budgeted annual salaries and actual annual salaries, paid monthly, are the same: $50,000 for a management consultant and $46,000 for a computer consultant. Corporate management has approved a merit increase of 10 percent at the beginning of the fourth quarter for all 25 existing consultants, while the new consultants will be compensated at the planned rate.
- The planned salary expense includes a provision for employee fringe benefits amounting to 30 percent of the annual salaries. However, the improvement of some corporatewide employee programs will increase the fringe benefits to 40 percent.
- The original plan assumes a fixed hourly rate for travel and other related expenses for each billing hour of consulting. These are expenses that are not reimbursed by the client, and the previously determined hourly rate has proven to be adequate to cover these costs.
- Other revenue is derived from temporary rentals and interest income and remains unchanged for the fourth quarter.
- General and administrative expenses have been favourable at 7 percent below the plan; this 7 percent savings on fourth quarter expenses will be reflected in the revised plan.
- Depreciation of office equipment and personal computers will stay constant at the projected straight-line rate.
- Due to the favourable experience for the first three quarters and the division's increased ability to absorb costs, the corporate management at Maple Leaf Services has increased the corporate expense allocation by 50 percent.

Required:

1. Prepare a revised operating budget for the fourth quarter for Toronto Business Associates that Richard Howell will present to corporate management.
2. Discuss the reasons why an organization would prepare a revised operating budget.

(CMA, adapted)

Problem 8–42 Preparation of Master Budget **(LO4)**

FreshPak Corporation manufactures two types of cardboard boxes used in shipping canned food, fruit, and vegetables. The canned food box (Type C) and the perishable food box (Type P) have the following material and labour requirements.

	Type of Box	
	C	P
Direct material required per 100 boxes:		
Paperboard ($0.20 per kg)	30 kg	70 kg
Corrugating medium ($0.10 per kg)	20 kg	30 kg
Direct labour required per 100 boxes ($12 per hour)	0.25 hour	0.50 hour

The following manufacturing-overhead costs are anticipated for the next year. The predetermined overhead rate is based on a production volume of 495,000 units for each type of box. Manufacturing overhead is applied on the basis of direct-labour hours.

Indirect material....................	$ 10,500
Indirect labour	50,000
Utilities....................	25,000
Property taxes	18,000
Insurance....................	16,000
Depreciation....................	29,000
Total	$148,500

The following selling and administrative expenses are anticipated for the next year:

Salaries and fringe benefits of sales personnel	$ 75,000
Advertising	15,000
Management salaries and fringe benefits	90,000
Clerical wages and fringe benefits	26,000
Miscellaneous administrative expenses	4,000
Total	$210,000

The sales forecast for the next year is as follows:

	Sales Volume	Sales Price
Box Type C	500,000 boxes	$90 per hundred boxes
Box Type P	500,000 boxes	130 per hundred boxes

The following inventory information is available for the next year:

	Expected Inventory, January 1	Desired Ending Inventory, December 31
Finished goods:		
Box Type C	10,000 boxes	5,000 boxes
Box Type P	20,000 boxes	15,000 boxes
Raw material:		
Paperboard	15,000 kg	5,000 kg
Corrugating medium	5,000 kg	10,000 kg

Required: Prepare a master budget for FreshPak Corporation for the next year. Assume an income tax rate of 35 percent. Include the following schedules:

1. Sales budget
2. Production budget
3. Direct-material budget
4. Direct-labour budget
5. Manufacturing-overhead budget
6. Selling and administrative expense budget
7. Budgeted income statement (*Hint:* To determine cost of goods sold, first compute the manufacturing cost per unit for each type of box. Include applied manufacturing overhead in the cost. Carry these calculations to three decimal places.)

2. Increase in sales: 11.5%

Problem 8–43 Budgeting; Financial Objectives; Ethics **(L01, 2, 5)**

Healthful Foods Inc., a manufacturer of breakfast cereals and snack bars, has experienced several years of steady growth in sales, profits, and dividends while maintaining a relatively low level of debt. The board of directors has adopted a long-run strategy to maximize the value of the shareholders' investment. In order to achieve this goal, the board of directors established the following five-year financial objectives:

- Increase sales by 12 percent per year.
- Increase income before taxes by 15 percent per year.
- Maintain long-term debt at a maximum of 16 percent of assets.

These financial objectives have been attained for the past three years. At the beginning of last year, the president of Healthful Foods, Andrea Donis, added a fourth financial objective of maintaining cost of goods sold at a maximum of 70 percent of sales. This goal also was attained last year.

The company's budgeting process is to be directed toward attaining these goals for the forthcoming year, a difficult task with the economy in a prolonged recession. In addition, the increased emphasis on eating healthful foods has driven up the price of ingredients used by the company significantly faster than the expected rate of inflation. John Winslow, cost accountant at Healthful Foods, has responsibility for preparation of the profit plan for next year. Winslow assured Donis that he could present a budget that achieved all of the financial objectives. Winslow believed that he could overestimate the ending inventory and reclassify fruit and grain inspection costs as administrative rather than manufacturing costs to attain the desired objective. The actual statements for 20x1 and the budgeted statements for 20x2 that Winslow prepared are as follows:

HEALTHFUL FOODS INC.
Income Statement

	20x1 Actual	20x2 Budgeted
Sales	$850,000	$947,750
Less: Variable costs:		
Cost of goods sold	510,000	574,725
Selling and administrative	90,000	87,500
Contribution margin	250,000	285,525
Less: Fixed costs:		
Manufacturing	85,000	94,775
Selling and administrative	60,000	70,000
Income before taxes	$105,000	$120,750

HEALTHFUL FOODS INC
Balance Sheet

	20x1 Actual	20x2 Budgeted
Assets:		
Cash	$ 10,000	$ 17,000
Accounts receivable	60,000	68,000
Inventory	300,000	365,000
Plant and equipment (net of accumulated depreciation)	1,630,000	1,600,000
Total	$2,000,000	$2,050,000
Liabilities:		
Accounts payable	$ 110,000	$ 122,000
Long-term debt	320,000	308,000
Shareholders' equity:		
Common shares	400,000	400,000
Retained earnings	1,170,000	1,220,000
Total	$2,000,000	$2,050,000

The company paid dividends of $27,720 in 20x1, and the expected tax rate for 20x2 is 34 percent.

Required:

1. Describe the role of budgeting in a firm's strategic planning.

2. For each of the financial objectives established by the board of directors and the president of Healthful Foods Inc., determine whether John Winslow's budget attains these objectives. Support your conclusion in each case by presenting appropriate calculations, and use the following format for your answer.

Objective	Attained/Not Attained	Calculations

3. Explain why the adjustments contemplated by John Winslow are unethical, citing specific standards of ethical conduct for management accountants.

(CMA, adapted)

Problem 8–44 Comprehensive Master Budget; Borrowing; Acquisition of Automated Material-Handling System
(LO1, 4)

"We really need to get this new material-handling equipment in operation just after the new year begins. I hope we can finance it largely with cash and marketable securities, but if necessary we can get a short-term loan from Metro Bank." This statement by Beth Davies-Lowry, president of Intercoastal Electronics Company, concluded a meeting she had called with the firm's top management. Intercoastal is a small, rapidly growing wholesaler of consumer electronic products. The firm's main product lines are small kitchen appliances and power tools. Marcia Wilcox, Intercoastal Electronics' general manager of marketing, has recently completed a sales forecast. She believes the company's sales during the first quarter of 20x1 will increase by 10 percent each month over the previous month's sales. Then Wilcox expects sales to remain constant for several months. Intercoastal's projected balance sheet as of December 31, 20x0, is as follows:

2. Total cash receipts, first quarter: $1,367,030

4. Total cash disbursements, first quarter: $1,213,576

6. Required short-term borrowing: $(100,000)

7. Net income: $160,656

Cash	$ 35,000
Accounts receivable	270,000
Marketable securities	15,000
Inventory	154,000
Buildings and equipment (net of accumulated depreciation)	626,000
Total assets	$1,100,000
Accounts payable	$ 176,400
Bond interest payable	12,500
Property taxes payable	3,600
Bonds payable (10%; due in 20x6)	300,000
Common shares	500,000
Retained earnings	107,500
Total liabilities and shareholders' equity	$1,100,000

Jack Hanson, the assistant controller, is now preparing a monthly budget for the first quarter of 20x1. In the process, the following information has been accumulated:

1. Projected sales for December of 20x0 are $400,000. Credit sales typically are 75 percent of total sales. Intercoastal's credit experience indicates that 10 percent of the credit sales are collected during the month of sale, and the remainder are collected during the following month.

2. Intercoastal Electronics' cost of goods sold generally runs at 70 percent of sales. Inventory is purchased on account, and 40 percent of each month's purchases are paid during the month of purchase. The remainder is paid during the following month. In order to have adequate stocks of inventory on hand, the firm attempts to have inventory at the end of each month equal to half of the next month's projected cost of goods sold.

3. Hanson has estimated that Intercoastal's other monthly expenses will be as follows:

Sales salaries	$21,000
Advertising and promotion	16,000
Administrative salaries	21,000
Depreciation	25,000
Interest on bonds	2,500
Property taxes	900

In addition, sales commissions run at the rate of 1 percent of sales.

4. Intercoastal Electronics' president, Davies-Lowry, has indicated that the firm should invest $125,000 in an automated inventory-handling system to control the movement of inventory in the firm's warehouse just after the new year begins. These equipment purchases will be financed primarily from the firm's cash and marketable securities. However, Davies-Lowry believes that the company needs to keep a minimum cash balance of $25,000. If necessary, the remainder of the equipment purchases will be financed using short-term credit from a local bank. The minimum period for such a loan is three months. Hanson believes short-term interest rates will be 10 percent per year at the time of the equipment purchases. If a loan is necessary, Davies-Lowry has decided it should be paid off by the end of the first quarter if possible.

5. Intercoastal Electronics' board of directors has indicated an intention to declare and pay dividends of $50,000 on the last day of each quarter.

6. The interest on any short-term borrowing will be paid when the loan is repaid. Interest on Intercoastal Electronics' bonds is paid semiannually on January 31 and July 31 for the preceding six-month period.

7. Property taxes are paid semiannually on February 28 and August 31 for the preceding six-month period.

Required: Prepare Intercoastal Electronics Company's master budget for the first quarter of 20x1 by completing the following schedules and statements:

1. Sales budget:

	20x0	20x1			
	December	January	February	March	1st Quarter
Total sales					
Cash sales					
Sales on account					

2. Cash receipts budget:

	20x1			
	January	February	March	1st Quarter
Cash sales				
Cash collections from credit sales made during current month				
Cash collections from credit sales made during preceding month				
Total cash receipts				

3. Purchases budget:

	20x0	20x1			
	December	January	February	March	1st Quarter
Budgeted cost of goods sold					
Add: Desired ending inventory					
Total goods needed					
Less: Expected beginning inventory					
Purchases					

4. Cash disbursements budget:

	20x1			
	January	February	March	1st Quarter
Inventory purchases:				
Cash payments for purchases during the current month*				
Cash payments for purchases during the preceding month†				
Total cash payments for inventory purchases				
Other expenses:				
Sales salaries				
Advertising and promotion				
Administrative salaries				
Interest on bonds‡				
Property taxes‡				
Sales commissions				
Total cash payments for other expenses				
Total cash disbursements				

*40% of the current month's purchases (Schedule 3).

†60% of the prior month's purchases (Schedule 3).

‡Bond interest is paid every six months, on January 31 and July 31. Property taxes also are paid every six months, on February 28 and August 31.

5. Complete the first three lines of the following summary cash budget. Then do the analysis of short-term financing needs in requirement (6). Then finish requirement (5).

	20x1			
	January	February	March	1st Quarter
Cash receipts (from Schedule 2)				
Less: Cash disbursements (from Schedule 4)				
Change in cash balance during period due to operations				
Sale of marketable securities (1/2/x1)				
Proceeds from bank loan (1/2/x1)				
Purchase of equipment				
Repayment of bank loan (3/31/x1)				
Interest on bank loan				
Payment of dividends				
Change in cash balance during first quarter ..				
Cash balance, 1/1/x1				
Cash balance, 3/31/x1				

6. Analysis of short-term financing needs:

Projected cash balance as of December 31, 20x0	$
Less: Minimum cash balance	
Cash available for equipment purchases	$
Projected proceeds from sale of marketable securities	
Cash available	$
Less: Cost of investment in equipment	
Required short-term borrowing	$

7. Prepare Intercoastal Electronics' budgeted income statement for the first quarter of 20x1. (Ignore income taxes.)

8. Prepare Intercoastal Electronics' budgeted statement of retained earnings for the first quarter of 20x1.

9. Prepare Intercoastal Electronics' budgeted balance sheet as of March 31, 20x1. (*Hint:* On March 31, 20x1, Bond Interest Payable is $5,000 and Property Taxes Payable is $900.)

Cases

Case 8–45 Using Budgets to Evaluate Business Decisions (LO1, 2, 5)

City Racquetball Club (CRC) offers racquetball and other physical fitness facilities to its members. There are four of these clubs in the metropolitan area. Each club has between 1,800 and 2,500 members. Revenue is derived from annual membership fees and hourly court fees. The annual membership fees are as follows:

Individual	$40
Student	25
Family	95

The hourly court fees vary from $6 to $10 depending on the season and the time of day (prime time versus non-prime time).

The peak racquetball season is considered to run from September through April. During this period, court usage averages 90 to 100 percent of capacity during prime time (5–9 p.m.) and 50 to 60 percent of capacity during the remaining hours. Daily court usage during the off-season (i.e., summer) averages only 20 to 40 percent of capacity.

Most of CRC's memberships have September expirations. A substantial amount of the cash receipts is collected during the early part of the racquetball season due to the renewal of the annual membership fees and heavy court usage. However, cash receipts are not as large in the spring and drop significantly in the summer months.

CRC is considering changing its membership and fee structure in an attempt to change its cash receipts. Under the new membership plan, only an annual membership fee would be charged, rather than a membership fee plus hourly court fees. There would be two classes of membership as follows:

Individual	$250
Family	400

The annual fee would be collected in advance at the time the membership application is completed. Members would be allowed to use the racquetball courts as often as they want during the year under the new plan.

All future memberships would be sold under these new terms. Current memberships would be honoured on the old basis until they expired. However, a special promotional campaign would be instituted to attract new members and to encourage current members to convert to the new membership plan immediately.

The annual fees for individual and family memberships would be reduced to $200 and $350, respectively, during the two-month promotional campaign. In addition, all memberships sold or renewed during this period would be for 15 months rather than the normal one-year period. Current members also would be given a credit toward the annual fee for the unexpired portion of their membership fee, and for all prepaid hourly court fees for league play that have not yet been used.

CRC's management estimates that 60 to 70 percent of the present membership would continue with the club. The most active members (45 percent of the present membership) would convert immediately to the new plan, while the remaining members who continue would wait until their current memberships expire. Those members who would not continue are not considered active (i.e., they play five or less times during the year). Management estimates that the loss of members would be offset fully by new members within six months of instituting the new plan. Furthermore, many of the new members would be individuals who would play during non-prime time. Management estimates that adequate court time will be available for all members under the new plan.

If the new membership plan is adopted, it would be instituted on February 1, well before the summer season. The special promotional campaign would be conducted during March and April. Once the plan is implemented, annual renewal of memberships and payment of fees would take place as each individual or family membership expires.

Required: Your consulting firm has been hired to help CRC evaluate its new fee structure. Write a letter to the club's president that addresses the following items:

1. Will City Racquetball Club's new membership plan and fee structure improve its ability to plan its cash receipts? Explain your answer.

2. City Racquetball Club should evaluate the new membership plan and fee structure completely before it decides to adopt or reject it.

   a. Identify the key factors that CRC should consider in its evaluation.

   b. Explain what type of financial analyses CRC should prepare in order to make a complete evaluation.

3. Explain how City Racquetball Club's cash management would differ from the present if the new membership plan and fee structure were adopted.

(CMA, adapted)

Case 8–46 Participative Budgeting (L01, 2, 8)

Patricia Eklund, controller of the social services division for the province, recognizes the importance of the budgetary process for planning, control, and motivational purposes. She believes that a properly implemented participative budgetary process for planning purposes and an evaluation procedure will motivate the managers to improve productivity in their particular departments. Based on this philosophy, Eklund has implemented the following budgetary procedures:

- An appropriation target figure is given to each department manager. This amount is the maximum funding that each department can expect to receive in the next year.
- Department managers develop their individual budgets within the following spending constraints as directed by the controller's staff:
  - Expenditure requests cannot exceed the appropriation target.
  - All fixed expenditures should be included in the budget. Fixed expenditures would include such items as contracts and salaries at current levels.
  - All government projects directed by a higher authority should be included in the budget in their entirety.
- The controller's staff consolidates the budget requests from the various departments into a master budget submission for the entire division.
- Once the final budget has been approved by the legislature, the controller's staff allocates the appropriation to the various departments as instructed by the division manager. However, a specified percentage of each department's appropriation is held back in anticipation of potential budget cuts and special funding needs. The amount and use of this contingency fund is left to the discretion of the division manager.
- Each department is allowed to adjust its budget when necessary to operate within the reduced appropriation level. However, as stated in the original directive, specific projects authorized by a higher authority must remain intact.
- The final budget is used as the basis of control. Excessive expenditures for each department are highlighted by account on a monthly basis. Department managers are expected to account for all expenditures over budget. Fiscal responsibility is an important factor in the overall performance evaluation of department managers.

Eklund believes her policy of allowing the department managers to participate in the budgetary process and then holding them accountable for their performance is essential, especially during times of limited resources. She further believes that the department managers will be positively motivated to increase the efficiency and effectiveness of their departments because they have provided input into the initial budgetary process and are required to justify any unfavourable performances.

Required:

1. Describe several operational and behavioural benefits that are generally attributed to a participative budgetary process.

2. Identify at least four deficiencies in Patricia Eklund's participative policy for planning and performance evaluation purposes. For each deficiency identified, recommend how it can be corrected.

(CMA, adapted)

Case 8–47 Comprehensive Master Budget; Short-Term Financing; Acquisition of Robotic Equipment (LO1, 2, 4)

Jeffrey Vaughn, president of Frame-It Company, was just concluding a budget meeting with his senior staff. It was November of 20x0 and the group was discussing preparation of the firm's master budget for 20x1. "I've decided to go ahead and purchase the industrial robot we've been talking about. We'll make the acquisition on January 2 of next year, and I expect it will take most of the year to train the personnel and reorganize the production process to take full advantage of the new equipment."

In response to a question about financing the acquisition, Vaughn replied as follows: "The robot will cost $1,000,000. We'll finance this purchase with a one-year $1,000,000 loan from Shark Bank and Trust Company. I've negotiated a repayment schedule of four equal instalments on the last day of each quarter. The interest rate will be 10 percent, and interest payments will be quarterly as well." With that the meeting broke up, and the budget process was on.

Frame-It Company is a manufacturer of metal picture frames. The firm's two product lines are designated as S (small frames) and L (large frames). The primary raw materials are flexible metal strips and glass sheets. Each S frame requires two metal strips; an L frame requires three strips. Allowing for normal breakage and scrap glass, Frame-It can get either four S frames or two L frames out of a glass sheet. Other raw materials, such as cardboard backing, are insignificant in cost and are treated as indirect materials. Emily Jackson, Frame-It's controller, is in charge of preparing the master budget for 20x1. She has gathered the following information:

1. Sales in the fourth quarter of 20x0 are expected to be 50,000 S frames and 40,000 L frames. The sales manager predicts that over the next two years, sales in each product line will grow by 5,000 units each quarter over the previous quarter. For example, S frame sales in the first quarter of 20x1 are expected to be 55,000 units.

2. Frame-It's sales history indicates that 60 percent of all sales are on credit, with the remainder of the sales in cash. The company's collection experience shows that 80 percent of the credit sales are collected during the quarter in which the sale is made, while the remaining 20 percent is collected in the following quarter. (For simplicity, assume the company is able to collect 100 percent of its accounts receivable.)

3. The S frame sells for $10, and the L frame sells for $15. These prices are expected to hold constant throughout 20x1.

4. Frame-It's production manager attempts to end each quarter with enough finished-goods inventory in each product line to cover 20 percent of the following quarter's sales. Moreover, an attempt is made to end each quarter with 20 percent of the glass sheets needed for the following quarter's production. Since metal strips are purchased locally, Frame-It buys them on a just-in-time basis; inventory is negligible.

5. All of Frame-It's direct-material purchases are made on account, and 80 percent of each quarter's purchases are paid in cash during the same quarter as the purchase. The other 20 percent is paid in the next quarter.

6. Indirect materials are purchased as needed and paid for in cash. Work-in-process inventory is negligible.

7. Projected manufacturing costs in 20x1 are as follows:

	S Frame	L Frame
Direct material:		
Metal strips:		
S: 2 @ $1 per strip	$2	
L: 3 @ $1 per strip		$ 3
Glass sheets:		
S: ¼ sheet @ $8 per sheet	2	
L: ½ sheet @ $8 per sheet		4
Direct labour:		
0.1 hour @ $20 per hour	2	2
Manufacturing overhead:		
0.1 direct-labour hour × $10 per hour	1	1
Total manufacturing cost per unit	$7	$10

8. The predetermined overhead rate is $10 per direct-labour hour. The following manufacturing overhead costs are budgeted for 20x1:

	1st Quarter	2nd Quarter	3rd Quarter	4th Quarter	Entire Year
Indirect material	$ 10,200	$ 11,200	$ 12,200	$ 13,200	$ 46,800
Indirect labour	40,800	44,800	48,800	52,800	187,200
Other overhead	31,000	36,000	41,000	46,000	154,000
Depreciation	20,000	20,000	20,000	20,000	80,000
Total overhead	$102,000	$112,000	$122,000	$132,000	$468,000

All of these costs will be paid in cash during the quarter incurred except for the depreciation charges.

9. Frame-It's quarterly selling and administrative expenses are $100,000, paid in cash.

10. Jackson anticipates that dividends of $50,000 will be declared and paid in cash each quarter.

11. Frame-It's projected balance sheet as of December 31, 20x0, follows:

Cash..	$ 95,000
Accounts receivable..	132,000
Inventory:	
Raw material...	59,200
Finished goods..	167,000
Plant and equipment (net of accumulated depreciation)...	8,000,000
Total assets..	$8,453,200
Accounts payable	$ 99,400
Common shares	5,000,000
Retained earnings...	3,353,800
Total liabilities and shareholders' equity...	$8,453,200

Required: Prepare Frame-It Company's master budget for 20x1 by completing the following schedules and statements.

1. Sales budget:

	20x0		20x1				
	4th Quarter	1st Quarter	2nd Quarter	3rd Quarter	4th Quarter	Entire Year
S frame unit sales						
× S sales price						
S frame sales revenue						
L frame unit sales						
× L sales price						
L frame sales revenue						
Total sales revenue						
Cash sales*						
Sales on account†						

*40% of total sales.
†60% of total sales.

2. Cash receipts budget:

	20x1				
	1st Quarter	2nd Quarter	3rd Quarter	4th Quarter	Entire Year
Cash sales					
Cash collections from credit sales made during current quarter*					
Cash collections from credit sales made during previous quarter†					
Total cash receipts					

*80% of current quarter's credit sales.
†20% of previous quarter's credit sales.

3. Production budget:

	20x0	20x1				
	4th Quarter	1st Quarter	2nd Quarter	3rd Quarter	4th Quarter	Entire Year
S frames:						
Sales (in units)						
Add: Desired ending inventory						
Total units needed						
Less: Expected beginning inventory						
Units to be produced						
L frames:						
Sales (in units)						
Add: Desired ending inventory						
Total units needed........................						
Less: Expected beginning inventory						
Units to be produced						

4. Direct-material budget:

	20x0	20x1				
	4th Quarter	1st Quarter	2nd Quarter	3rd Quarter	4th Quarter	Entire Year
Metal strips:						
S frames to be produced						
×Metal strips per unit						
Needed for S frame production						
L frames to be produced						
× Metal strips per unit						
Needed for L frame production						
Total metal strips needed for production; to be purchased						
× Price per strip						
Cost of metal strips to be purchased						
Glass sheets:						
S frames to be produced (sheets) ..						
× Glass quantity per unit						
Needed for S frame production						
L frames to be produced (sheets)...						
× Glass quantity per unit						
Needed for L frame production						
Total glass needed for production (sheets)						
Add: Desired ending inventory						10,400	10,400
Total glass needs						
Less: Expected beginning inventory.....................						
Glass to be purchased.....................						
× Price per glass sheet						
Cost of glass to be purchased						
Total raw-material purchases (metal and glass)						

5. Cash disbursements budget:

	20x1				
	1st Quarter	2nd Quarter	3rd Quarter	4th Quarter	Entire Year
Raw-material purchases:					
Cash payments for purchases during the current quarter					
Cash payments for purchases during the preceding quarter					
Total cash payments for raw-material purchases					
Direct labour:					
Frames produced (S and L)					
Direct-labour hours per frame					
Direct-labour hours to be used					
Rate per direct-labour hour					
Total cash payments for direct labour..............					
Manufacturing overhead:					
Indirect material...					
Indirect labour					
Other					
Total cash payments for manufacturing overhead					
Cash payments for selling and administrative expenses.............................					
Total cash disbursements					

6. Summary cash budget:

	20x1				
	1st Quarter	2nd Quarter	3rd Quarter	4th Quarter	Entire Year
Cash receipts (from Schedule 2)					
Less: Cash disbursements (from Schedule 5)					
Change in cash balance due to operations					
Payment of dividends					
Proceeds from bank loan (1/2/x1)					
Purchase of equipment					
Quarterly instalment on loan principal					
Quarterly interest payment					
Change in cash balance during the period					
Cash balance, beginning of period					
Cash balance, end of period					

7. Prepare a budgeted schedule of cost of goods manufactured and sold for the year 20x1. (*Hint:* In the budget, actual and applied overhead will be equal.)

8. Prepare Frame-It's budgeted income statement for 20x1. (Ignore income taxes.)

9. Prepare Frame-It's budgeted statement of retained earnings for 20x1.

10. Prepare Frame-It's budgeted balance sheet as of December 31, 20x1.

 Practise and learn online with Connect.

CHAPTER NINE

Standard Costing and Flexible Budgeting

FOCUS COMPANY

This chapter's focus company is DCdesserts, which supplies fancy desserts to a variety of restaurants, caterers, and upscale food stores. The company's order-taking system is entirely web-based. Every day, DCdesserts posts its dessert menu on its website, and orders are accepted via the Internet. In this chapter, we explore the use of standard costing by DCdesserts. A standard-costing system sets predetermined (or standard) costs for each of a product's inputs, such as direct material and direct labour. Then the actual costs to produce the product are compared with the standard costs that should have been incurred. The management of DCdesserts uses a standard-costing system to help control the production costs.

We also explore the use of flexible budgeting by DCdesserts to plan for and control overhead costs. A flexible budget allows for a variety of levels of activity. As activity increases, the costs in the flexible budget rise as well. This tool enables management to compare the actual overhead costs incurred with the costs that should have been incurred, given the actual level of production activity.

After completing this chapter, you should be able to

1 Explain how standard costing is used to help manage costs, and describe ways to set standards.

2 Compute and interpret the direct-material and direct-labour variances.

3 Distinguish between static and flexible budgets, and explain the advantages of a flexible-overhead budget.

4 Prepare a flexible-overhead budget and explain how overhead is applied to work-in-process inventory.

5 Explain some important issues in choosing an activity measure for overhead budgeting and application.

6 Compute and interpret the variable-overhead and fixed-overhead variances.

7 Prepare an overhead cost performance report.

8 Explain how an activity-based flexible budget differs from a conventional flexible budget.

9 Explain several methods for determining the significance of cost variances.

10 Describe some behavioural effects of standard costing.

11 Explain how standard costs are used in product costing, and summarize some advantages and some criticisms of standard costing.

12 Prepare journal entries to record and close out cost variances (Appendix A to Chapter 9).

13 Compute and interpret the sales-price and sales-volume variances (Appendix B to Chapter 9).

IN CONTRAST — **Tri-Cities** AUTO RENTALS

In contrast to the food-processing setting of DCdesserts, we will turn our attention to flexible budgeting in the service industry. Tri-Cities Auto Rentals is a small automobile rental company with locations in Coquitlam, Port Coquitlam, and Port Moody. The company specializes in short-term car rentals, primarily for local use when a customer's car is in the repair shop. The company's flexible budget uses two cost drivers: the number of kilometres driven in its rental cars and the number of customer contracts.

A budget provides a plan for managers to follow in making decisions and directing an organization's activities. At the end of a budget period, managers use the budget as a benchmark against which to compare the results of actual operations. Did the company make as much profit as anticipated in the budget? Were costs greater or less than expected? These questions involve issues of cost management and control. In this chapter, we will study one of the tools used by accountants to assist managers in controlling an organization's operations and costs—standard costing.

Managing Costs

How can managers use a control system as a cost management tool? Any control system has three basic parts: a predetermined or *standard* performance level, a measure of *actual* performance, and a *comparison* between standard and actual performance. A thermostat is a control system with which we are all familiar. First, a thermostat has a predetermined or standard temperature that can be set at any desired level. If you want the temperature in a room to be 20°C, you set the thermostat at the *standard* of 20°C. Second, the thermostat has a thermometer, which measures the *actual* temperature in the room. Third, the thermostat *compares* the preset or standard temperature with the actual room temperature. If the actual temperature falls below the preset or standard temperature, the thermostat activates a heating device. The three features of a control system are depicted in Exhibit 9–1.

A budgetary-control system works like a thermostat. First, a predetermined or **standard cost** is set. In essence, a standard cost is a budget for the production of one unit of product or service. It is the cost chosen to serve as the benchmark in the budgetary-control system. When the firm produces many units, the standard unit cost is used to

Learning Objective 1

Explain how standard costing is used to help manage costs, and describe ways to set standards.

1. **Predetermined or standard performance** (The thermostat is set to a standard temperature.)

2. **Measure of actual performance** (The thermometer measures the actual room temperature.)

3. **Comparison of actual and standard performance** (The thermostat compares the preset or standard temperature with the actual temperature.)

Exhibit 9–1

Control System: A Thermostat

determine the total standard or budgeted cost of production. For example, suppose the standard direct-material cost for one unit of product is $5 and 100 units are manufactured. The total standard or budgeted direct-material cost, given an actual output of 100 units, is $500 ($5 × 100).

Second, the management accountant measures the actual cost incurred in the production process.

Third, the management accountant compares the actual cost with the budgeted or standard cost. Any difference between the two is called a **cost variance**. Cost variances are then used in controlling costs.

Management by Exception

Managers do not have time to look into the causes of every variance between actual and standard costs. However, they investigate the causes of significant cost variances. This process of following up on only significant cost variances is called **management by exception**. When operations are going along as planned, actual costs and profit will typically be close to the budgeted amounts. However, if there are significant departures from planned operations, such effects will show up as significant cost variances. Managers investigate these variances to determine their causes, if possible, and take corrective action when indicated.

What constitutes a significant variance? No precise answer can be given to this question, since it depends on the size and type of the organization and its production process. We will consider this issue later in the chapter when we discuss common methods for determining the significance of cost variances. First, however, we will turn our attention to the process of setting standards.

Setting Standards

Methods for Setting Standards

Management accountants typically use one of two methods for setting cost standards: analysis of historical data or task analysis. Often, a combination of both is used.

Analysis of Historical Data   One indicator of future costs is historical cost data. In a mature production process, where the firm has a lot of production experience, historical costs can provide a good basis for predicting future costs. The methods for analyzing cost behaviour that we studied in Chapter 6 are used in making cost predictions. The management accountant often will need to adjust these predictions to reflect movements in price levels or technological changes in the production process. For example, the amount of rubber required to manufacture a particular type of tire will likely be the same this year as last year, unless there has been a significant change in the process used to manufacture tires. However, the price of rubber is likely to be different this year than last, and this fact must be reflected in the new standard cost of a tire.

Despite the relevance of historical cost data in setting cost standards, management accountants must guard against relying on them excessively. Even a seemingly minor change in the way a product is manufactured may make historical data almost totally irrelevant. Moreover, new products also require new cost standards. For new products, such as genetically engineered medicines, there are no historical cost data on which to base standards. In such cases, the management accountant must turn to another approach.

Task Analysis   Another way to set cost standards is to analyze the process of manufacturing a product to determine what it *should* cost. The emphasis shifts from what the product *did* cost in the past to what it *should* cost in the future. In using **task analysis**, the management accountant typically works with engineers who are intimately familiar with the production process. Together they conduct studies to determine exactly how much direct material should be required and how labour and machinery should be used in the production process. Time and motion studies are conducted to determine how long each step performed should take.

A Combined Approach Management accountants often apply both historical cost analysis and task analysis in setting cost standards. It may be, for example, that the technology has changed for only one step in the production process. In such a case, the management accountant would work with engineers to set cost standards for the technologically changed part of the production process. However, the accountant would likely rely on the less expensive method of analyzing historical cost data to update the cost standards for the remainder of the production process.

Participation in Setting Standards

Standards should not be determined by the management accountant alone. People generally will be more committed to meeting standards if they are allowed to participate in setting them. For example, production supervisors should have a role in setting production cost standards, and sales managers should be involved in setting targets for sales prices and volume. In addition, knowledgeable staff personnel should participate in the standard-setting process. For example, task analysis should be carried out by a team consisting of production engineers and supervisors, and management accountants.

Perfection versus Practical Standards: A Behavioural Issue

How difficult should it be to attain standard costs? Should standards be set so that actual costs rarely exceed standard costs? Or should it be so hard to attain standards that actual costs frequently exceed them? The answers to these questions depend on the purpose for which standards will be used and how standards affect behaviour.

Perfection Standards A **perfection** (or **ideal**) **standard** is one that can be attained only under nearly perfect operating conditions. Such standards assume peak efficiency, the lowest possible input prices, the best-quality materials obtainable, and no disruptions in production due to such causes as machine breakdowns or power failures. Some managers believe that perfection standards motivate employees to achieve the lowest cost possible. They claim that since the standard is theoretically attainable, employees will have an incentive to come as close as possible to achieving it.

Other managers and many behavioural scientists disagree. They feel that perfection standards discourage employees, since they are so unlikely to be attained. Moreover, setting unrealistically difficult standards may encourage employees to sacrifice product quality to achieve lower costs. By skimping on raw-material quality or the attention given to manual production tasks, employees may be able to lower the production cost. However, this lower cost may come at the expense of a higher rate of defective units. Thus, the firm ultimately may incur higher costs than necessary, as defective products are returned by customers or scrapped on inspection.

Practical Standards Standards that are as tight as practical, but still are expected to be attained, are called **practical** (or **attainable**) **standards**. Such standards assume a production process that is as efficient as practical under normal operating conditions. Practical standards allow for such occurrences as occasional machine breakdowns

"At Best Foods, standard costs are set at attainable levels." (9a)
Best Foods (A subsidiary of Unilever)

and normal amounts of raw-material waste. Attaining a practical standard keeps employees on their toes without demanding miracles. Most behavioural theorists believe that practical standards encourage more positive and productive employee attitudes than do perfection standards.

Use of Standards by Service Organizations

Many service industry firms, nonprofit organizations, and government units make use of standards. For example, FedEx allows its crews 18 minutes to unload the 9 to 12 containers of packages from a Boeing 727. A delay of over a minute must be explained at a daily 5 a.m. meeting. Burger King sets a standard for the amount of meat in a hamburger. Airlines such as WestJet and Air Canada set standards for fuel and maintenance costs. Insurance companies such as Manulife Financial and Pacific Blue Cross set standards for the amount of time to process an insurance claim. Even a provincial licensing office may have a standard for the number of days required to process and return an application for a licence. These and similar organizations use standards in budgeting and cost control in much the same way that manufacturers use standards.

Cost Variance Analysis: Direct Material and Direct Labour

Learning Objective **2**

Compute and interpret the direct-material and direct-labour variances.

To illustrate the use of standards in managing costs, we will focus on DCdesserts, a supplier of fresh and frozen fancy desserts to a variety of restaurants, caterers, and upscale food stores. The company's order-taking system is entirely web-based. DCdesserts posts its menu of fresh dessert products for each day on its website four days in advance of the delivery date. Orders are accepted via the Internet three days in advance of delivery. For example, the menu of desserts to be available for delivery on Friday afternoon is posted onto the company's website on Monday, and orders are accepted up to midnight on Tuesday. The company places orders for ingredients on Wednesday and accepts their delivery on Thursday. The ordering is also done largely via the Internet. Production then takes place throughout the day on Friday, and the desserts are delivered Friday afternoon. Independent delivery services are used to deliver its dessert products.

DCdesserts also produces frozen dessert products for upscale grocery stores. Unlike the fresh desserts, which vary daily, the frozen desserts are stock items that are varied less frequently. Like the fresh desserts, however, the frozen dessert menu is posted on the company's website, and orders are accepted entirely via the Internet. The company produces its fresh and frozen desserts in two different production facilities.

The production process for the fresh desserts involves a combination of semiautomated equipment and manual labour. The making of fancy desserts involves considerable direct labour. In the words of the company's founder and owner, "Making a Black Forest cake or a linzer torte is not the same as making your basic pumpkin pie. There's a lot of touch labour by skilled people in doing these fancy desserts." The basic steps in the production process are much as you might expect. These steps include selecting ingredients, mixing, baking, cooling, and finishing. The finishing work, of course, involves the most skilled direct labour. In making a six-layer chocolate raspberry cake, for example, each individual cake layer must be sliced into two pieces, and then fillings and icings are applied to each layer. The cake's top is finished artistically, and any additional toppings are carefully applied.

The controller has set standards for direct material and direct labour as follows for a category of dessert products generically referred to as *multilayer fancy cakes*.

Direct-Material Standards

The standard quantity and price of ingredients for one multilayer fancy cake, such as a Black Forest cake, are shown in the following:

Standard quantity:	
Ingredients in finished product..	4.75 kilograms
Allowance for normal waste..	0.25 kilogram
Total standard quantity required per multilayer fancy cake..	5.00 kilograms
Standard price:	
Purchase price per kilogram of ingredients (net of purchase discounts)...................................	$1.30
Transportation cost per kilogram..	0.10
Total standard price per kilogram of ingredients...	$1.40

The standard quantity of ingredients needed to produce one cake is 5 kilograms, even though only 4.75 kilograms actually remain in the finished product. One-quarter kilogram of ingredients is wasted as a normal result of the production process. Therefore, the entire amount of ingredients needed to produce a fancy cake is included in the standard quantity of material.

The standard cost of ingredients reflects all of the costs incurred to acquire the material and transport it to the production facility. Any purchase discounts would be subtracted from the purchase cost to obtain a net cost.

To summarize, the **standard direct-material quantity** is the total amount of direct material normally required to produce a finished product, including allowances for normal waste or inefficiency. The **standard direct-material price** is the total delivered cost, after subtracting any purchase discounts.

Direct-Labour Standards

The standard quantity and rate for direct labour for the production of one multilayer fancy cake are as follows:

Standard quantity:	
Direct labour required per multilayer fancy cake	0.5 hour
Standard rate:	
Hourly wage rate	$16
Fringe benefits (25% of wages)	4
Total standard rate per hour	$20

The **standard direct-labour quantity** is the number of direct-labour hours normally needed to manufacture one unit of product. The **standard direct-labour rate** is the total hourly cost of compensation, including fringe benefits.

Standard Costs Given Actual Output

During September, DCdesserts produced 2,000 multilayer fancy cakes. The total standard or budgeted costs for direct material and direct labour are computed as follows:

Direct material:		
Standard direct-material cost per cake (5 kilograms × $1.40 per kilogram).............................	$	7
Actual output..	×	2,000
Total standard direct-material cost..		$ 14,000
Direct labour:		
Direct-labour cost per cake (0.5 hour × $20 per hour)...	$	10
Actual output..	×	2,000
Total standard direct-labour cost..		$ 20,000

Notice that the total standard cost for the direct-material and direct-labour inputs is based on the actual *output*. The company should incur total costs of $34,000 for direct material and direct labour, *given that it produced 2,000 multilayer fancy cakes*. The total standard costs for direct material and direct labour serve as the management accountant's benchmarks against which to compare actual costs. This comparison then serves as the basis for controlling direct-material and direct-labour costs.

Analysis of Cost Variances

During September, DCdesserts incurred the following actual costs for direct material and direct labour in the production of 2,000 multilayer fancy cakes:

Direct material purchased: Actual cost 12,500 kilograms at $1.42 per kilogram	$17,750
Direct material used: Actual cost 10,250 kilograms at $1.42 per kilogram	$14,555
Direct labour: Actual cost 980 hours at $21 per hour	$20,580

Compare these actual expenditures with the total standard costs for the production of the 2,000 multilayer fancy cakes. DCdesserts spent more than the budgeted amount for both direct material and direct labour. But why were these excess costs incurred? Is there any further analysis the management accountant can provide to help answer this question?

Direct-Material Variances

What caused the company to spend more than the anticipated amount on direct material? First, the company purchased ingredients at a higher price ($1.42 per kilogram) than the standard price ($1.40 per kilogram). Second, the company used more ingredients than the standard amount. The amount actually used was 10,250 kilograms instead of the standard amount of 10,000 kilograms, which is based on actual output of 2,000 multilayer fancy cakes (2,000 cakes × 5 kilograms per cake). The management accountant can show both of these deviations from standards by computing a **direct-material price variance** (or **purchase price variance**) and a **direct-material quantity variance**. The computation of these variances is depicted in Exhibit 9–2.

Exhibit 9–2
Direct-Material Price and Quantity Variances: DCdesserts

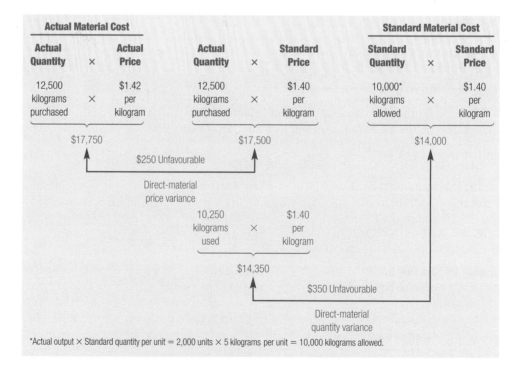

The formula for the direct-material price variance is as follows:

Direct-material price variance = $(AQ_p \times AP) - (AQ_p \times SP)$

where

AQ_p = Actual quantity purchased
AP = Actual price
SP = Standard price

The direct-material price variance for September's production of multilayer fancy cakes is computed as follows:

$$
\begin{aligned}
\text{Direct-material price variance} &= AQ_p \times (AP - SP) \\
&= 12{,}500 \times (\$1.42 - \$1.40) \\
&= \$250 \text{ Unfavourable}
\end{aligned}
$$

This variance is unfavourable, because the actual purchase price ($1.42) exceeded the standard price ($1.40). Notice that the price variance is based on the actual quantity of material *purchased* (AQ_p), not the quantity actually used in production.

As Exhibit 9–2 shows, the following formula defines the direct-material quantity variance:

Direct-material quantity variance = $(AQ_u \times SP) - (SQ \times SP)$

where

AQ_u = Actual quantity used
SQ = Standard quantity allowed

The direct-material quantity variance for September's production of multilayer fancy cakes is computed as follows:

$$
\begin{aligned}
\text{Direct-material quantity variance} &= SP \times (AQ_u - SQ) \\
&= \$1.40 \times (10{,}250 - 10{,}000) \\
&= \$350 \text{ Unfavourable}
\end{aligned}
$$

This variance is unfavourable, because the actual quantity of direct material used (10,250) in September exceeded the standard quantity allowed (10,000), *given the actual September output* of 2,000 multilayer fancy cakes. The quantity variance is based on the quantity of material actually *used* in production (AQ_u).

Quantity Purchased versus Quantity Used   As stated above, the direct-material price variance is based on the quantity purchased (AQ_p). This makes sense, because deviations between the actual and standard price, which are highlighted by the price variance, relate to the *purchasing* function in the firm. Timely action to follow up a significant price variance will be facilitated by calculating this variance as soon as possible after the material is *purchased*.

In contrast, the direct-material quantity variance is based on the amount of material *used* in production. The quantity variance highlights deviations between the quantity of material actually used (AQ_u) and the standard quantity allowed (SQ). Thus, it makes sense to compute this variance at the time the material is *used* in production.

Basing the Quantity Variance on Actual Output   Notice that the standard quantity of material must be based on the actual production output in order for the quantity variance to be meaningful. It would not make any sense to compare standard or budgeted material usage at one level of output (e.g., 1,000 multilayer fancy cakes) with the actual material usage at a *different* level of output (e.g., 2,000 multilayer fancy cakes). Everyone would expect more direct material to be used in the production of 2,000 cakes than in the

> "The folks that have had the opportunity to engage as a real business partner are really excited by it, and we are doing some exciting things about our material [purchasing] organization, and finance, what we call vendor cost analysis folks." (9b)
>
> **Boeing**

production of 1,000 cakes. For the direct-material quantity variance to provide helpful information for management, the standard or budgeted quantity must be based on *actual output*. Then the quantity variance compares the following two quantities.

Actual quantity used in the production of *actual output*

Standard quantity allowed, given *actual output*

Comparison of these quantities is the basis of the **direct-material quantity variance.**

Direct-Labour Variances

Why did DCdesserts spend more than the anticipated amount on direct labour during September? The company incurred a cost of $21 per hour for direct labour instead of the standard amount of $20 per hour. However, this increase in rate was partially offset by using only 980 hours of direct labour, which is less than the standard quantity of 1,000 hours, given actual output of 2,000 multilayer fancy cakes. The management accountant analyzes direct-labour costs by computing a **direct-labour rate variance** and a **direct-labour efficiency variance**. Exhibit 9–3 depicts the computation of these variances.

The formula for the direct-labour rate variance is

$$\text{Direct-labour rate variance} = (AH \times AR) - (AH \times SR)$$

where

AH = Actual hours used
AR = Actual rate per hour
SR = Standard rate per hour

The direct-labour rate variance for September's production of multilayer fancy cakes is computed as follows:

$$
\begin{aligned}
\text{Direct-labour rate variance} &= AH \times (AR - SR) \\
&= 980 \times (\$21 - \$20) \\
&= \$980 \text{ Unfavourable}
\end{aligned}
$$

This variance is unfavourable because the actual rate ($21) exceeded the standard rate ($20) during September.

As Exhibit 9–3 shows, the formula for the direct-labour efficiency variance is as follows:

$$\text{Direct-labour efficiency variance} = (AH \times SR) - (SH \times SR)$$

where

SH = Standard hours allowed

The direct-labour efficiency variance for September is computed as follows:

$$
\begin{aligned}
\text{Direct-labour efficiency variance} &= SR \times (AH - SH) \\
&= \$20 \times (980 - 1000) \\
&= \$400 \text{ Favourable}
\end{aligned}
$$

Actual Labour Cost						Standard Labour Cost			
Actual Hours	×	**Actual Rate**		**Actual Hours**	×	**Standard Rate**		**Standard Hours**	×	**Standard Rate**

Exhibit 9–3
Direct-Labour Rate and Efficiency Variances: DCdesserts

980 hours used	×	$21 per hour		980 hours used	×	$20 per hour		1,000* hours allowed	×	$20 per hour

$20,580 $19,600 $20,000

$980 Unfavourable $400 Favourable

Direct-labour
rate variance

Direct-labour
efficiency variance

$580 Unfavourable

Direct-labour variance

*Actual output × Standard hours per unit = 2,000 units × .5 hour per unit = 1,000 hours allowed.

This variance is favourable because the actual direct-labour hours used (900) in September were less than the standard hours allowed (1,000), *given actual September output of 2,000* multilayer fancy cakes.

Notice that the direct-labour rate and efficiency variances add up to the total direct-labour variance. The rate and efficiency variances have opposite signs, since one variance is unfavourable and the other favourable.

Direct-labour rate variance	$980 Unfavourable
Direct-labour efficiency variance	400 Favourable
Direct-labour variance	$580 Unfavourable

} Different signs of variances cancel just as plus and minus signs cancel in arithmetic.

Basing the Efficiency Variance on Actual Output   The number of standard hours of direct labour allowed is based on the *actual* production output. It would not be meaningful to compare standard or budgeted labour usage at one level of output with the actual hours used at a different level of output.

Allowing for Spoilage or Defects

In some manufacturing processes, a certain amount of spoilage or defective production is normal. This must be taken into account when the standard quantity of material is computed. To illustrate, suppose that 100 litres of chemicals are normally required in a chemical process in order to obtain 80 litres of good output. If total good output in January is 500 litres, what is the standard allowed quantity of input?

	Good output quantity	= 80% × Input quantity
Dividing both sides of the equation by 80%	$\dfrac{\text{Good output quantity}}{80\%}$	= Input quantity allowed
Using the numbers in the example	$\dfrac{500 \text{ litres of good output}}{80\%}$	= 625 litres of input allowed

The total standard allowed input is 625 litres, given 500 litres of good output.

PARKER HANNIFIN CORPORATION'S BRASS PRODUCTS DIVISION

Parker Hannifin Corporation's Brass Products Division, a world-class manufacturer of brass fittings, valves, and tubing, is a standard-costing success story.[1] "Parker Brass uses its standard-costing system and variance analyses as important business tools to target problem areas so it can develop solutions for continuous improvement. Variances are reported for each product line, and if any production variance exceeds 5 percent of product-line sales, the product-line manager is required to provide an explanation. Also required is a plan to correct the problems underlying any unfavourable variances. Variance reports, which are generated within one day of the completion of a job order, are distributed to managers and production schedulers. A variance database is kept, which can be accessed by product-line managers, to provide variance data by part number, by job-order number, or by dollar amount."

From the perspective of Parker Brass's management, the division has modified its standard-costing system to provide disaggregated and timely cost information to enable timely corrective action in a rapidly changing business environment.

Overhead Budgets

How do service industry companies, such as Manulife Financial, Tim Hortons, TD Canada Trust, Fairmont Hotels and Resorts, and WestJet Airlines, control the overhead costs they incur in producing their services? Similarly, how do manufacturing firms such as General Motors, Hewlett-Packard, and Bombardier control the many overhead costs incurred in their production processes? Unlike direct material and direct labour, overhead costs are not traceable to individual products. Moreover, overhead is a pool of many different kinds of costs. Indirect material, indirect labour, and other indirect production costs often exhibit different relationships to productive activity. Some overhead costs are variable, and some are fixed. Moreover, different individuals in an organization are responsible for different types of overhead costs. Considering all of these issues together, controlling overhead presents a challenge for management.

Since direct material and direct labour are traceable to products, it is straightforward to determine standard costs for these inputs. If a table requires 20 board metres of oak lumber at $4 per board metre, the standard direct-material cost for the table is $80. But how much electricity does it take to produce a table? How much supervisory time, equipment depreciation, or machinery repair services does the table require? Since all of these overhead costs are indirect costs of production, we cannot set overhead cost standards for the oak table. If standard costs do not provide the answer to controlling overhead, what does?

Flexible Budgets

The tool used by most companies to control overhead costs is called a **flexible budget**. A flexible budget resembles the budgets we studied in Chapter 8, with one important difference: *A flexible budget is not based on only one level of activity.* Instead, it covers a range of activity within which the firm may operate. A *flexible-overhead budget* is defined as a detailed plan for controlling overhead costs that is valid in the firm's relevant range of activity. In contrast, a **static budget** is based on a particular planned level of activity.

At DCdesserts, the measure of activity used for flexible budgeting purposes is process time. The process time for a dessert is the total amount of time the product is in process, including selecting ingredients, mixing, baking, cooling, assembly and finishing, and packaging. The controller estimates that the average process time required for fancy desserts is three hours.

To illustrate the flexible budgeting concept, suppose that electricity is a variable cost, incurred at the rate of $0.50 per hour of process time. Two different budgets for electricity cost are shown in Exhibit 9–4. The static budget is based on management's predicted level of activity for September—7,500 hours of process time. This estimate is based on planned production of 2,500 multilayer fancy cakes, in which each cake requires three hours of total process time. The flexible budget includes three different production activity levels within the relevant range: 6,000, 7,500, and 9,000 hours of process time.

Advantages of Flexible Budgets

Why is the distinction between static and flexible budgets so important? Suppose DCdesserts produced 2,000 multilayer fancy cakes during September, used 6,000 hours of process time, and incurred electricity costs of $3,200. Does this constitute good control or poor control of electricity costs? Which budget in Exhibit 9–4 is more useful in answering this question?

A manager using the static budget makes the following comparison:

Actual Electricity Cost	Budgeted Electricity Cost (Static Budget)	Cost Variance
$3,200	$3,750	$550 Favourable

This comparison suggests that operating staff maintained excellent control over electricity costs during September, generating a favourable variance of $550. Is this a valid analysis and conclusion?

The fault with this analysis is that the manager is comparing the electricity cost incurred at the *actual* activity level (2,000 multilayer fancy cakes) with the budgeted electricity cost at the *planned* activity level (2,500 multilayer fancy cakes). Since these activity levels are different, we should expect the electricity cost to be different.

A more sensible approach is to compare the actual electricity cost incurred with the cost that should be incurred when 2,000 multilayer fancy cakes are produced. At this production level, 6,000 process hours should be used (3 hours per cake). The flexible

Static Budget		Flexible Budget			
Activity (process hours)*	7,500	Activity (process hours)	6,000	7,500	9,000
Budgeted electricity cost	$3,750	Budgeted electricity cost	$3,000	$3,750	$4,500

Static budget: Based on only one anticipated activity level.

Flexible budget: Includes several possible activity levels.

*Based on planned September production of 2,500 multilayer fancy cakes, at three hours of process time per cake.

Exhibit 9–4
Static Budget versus Flexible Budget: DCdesserts

DC desserts

budget in Exhibit 9–4 shows that the manager should expect $3,000 of electricity cost at the 6,000 process-hour level of activity. Therefore, an analysis based on the flexible budget gives the following comparison:

Actual Electricity Cost	Budgeted Electricity Cost (Flexible Budget)	Cost Variance
$3,200	$3,000	$200 Unfavourable

Now the manager's conclusion is different; the revised analysis indicates an unfavourable variance. Electricity cost was greater than it should have been, given the actual level of output. The flexible budget provides the correct basis for comparison between actual and expected costs, given actual activity.

The Activity Measure

Notice that the flexible budget for electricity cost in Exhibit 9–4 is based on hours of process time, which is an input in the production process. The process-hour activity levels shown in the flexible budget are the standard allowed process hours given various levels of output. If 2,000 multilayer fancy cakes are produced, and the standard allowance per cake is 3 process hours, then the standard allowed number of process hours is 6,000.

Why are the activity levels in the flexible budget based on process hours, an *input* measure, instead of the number of multilayer fancy cakes produced, an *output* measure? When only a single product is manufactured, it makes no difference whether the flexible budget is based on input or output. In our example, either of the flexible budgets shown in Exhibit 9–5 could be used.

Now suppose that during August, DCdesserts produced three different products: 1,000 multilayer fancy cakes, 1,500 single-layer sheet cakes, and 600 specialty cakes (such as wedding cakes). The following standards have been assigned to these products:

	Standard Process Product Hours per Unit
Multilayer fancy cakes..	3
Single-layer sheet cakes	2
Specialty cakes..	6

During August, the company's production output was 3,100 cakes. Is 3,100 cakes a meaningful output measure? Adding numbers of multilayer fancy cakes, sheet cakes, and specialty cakes, which require different amounts of productive inputs, is like adding apples and oranges. It would not make sense to base a flexible budget for electricity cost on units of output when the output consists of different products with different electricity requirements. In this case, the flexible budget must be based on an *input* measure.

Exhibit 9–5
Flexible Budgets: Input versus Output: DCdesserts

Flexible Budget (based on input)			
Activity: Standard allowed process hours	6,000	7,500	9,000
Budgeted electricity cost	$3,000	$3,750	$4,500
Flexible Budget (based on output)			
Activity: Multilayer fancy cakes produced	2,000	2,500	3,000
Budgeted electricity cost	$3,000	$3,750	$4,500

3 standard allowed process hours per multilayer fancy cake

The standard allowed number of process hours for the August production is computed as follows:

Product	Units Produced	Standard Process Hours per Unit	Total Standard Allowed Process Hours
Multilayer fancy cakes	1,000	3	3,000
Single-layer sheet cakes	1,500	2	3,000
Specialty cakes	600	6	3,600
Total			9,600

Recall that the controller estimates electricity cost at $0.50 per process hour, so the flexible-budget cost of electricity during August is computed as follows:

Standard allowed process hours given August output	9,600
Electricity cost per process hour	$ 0.50
Flexible budget for electricity cost	$4,800

The important point is that *units of output* usually is not a meaningful measure in a multiproduct firm, because it would require us to add numbers of unlike products. To avoid this problem, output is measured in terms of the *standard allowed input, given actual output*. The flexible-overhead budget is then based on this standard input measure.

Flexible-Overhead Budget Illustrated

DCdesserts' monthly flexible-overhead budget is shown in the Excel spreadsheet in Exhibit 9–6. The overhead costs in the flexible budget are divided into variable and fixed costs. The total budgeted variable cost increases proportionately with increases in the activity. So, when the number of process hours increases by 50 percent, from 6,000 hours to 9,000 hours, the total budgeted variable-overhead cost also increases by 50 percent, from $30,000 to $45,000. In contrast, the total budgeted fixed overhead does not change with increases in activity; it remains constant at $15,000 per month.

When overhead costs can be divided into variable and fixed categories, we can express the flexible-overhead budget differently. The format used in Exhibit 9–6 is called a *columnar flexible budget*. The budgeted overhead cost for each overhead item is listed in a column under a particular activity level. Notice that the columnar format allows for only a limited number of activity levels. DCdesserts' flexible budget shows only three.

A more general format for expressing a flexible budget is called a *formula flexible budget*. In this format, the management accountant expresses the relationship between activity and total budgeted overhead cost by the following formula:

$$\text{Total budgeted monthly overhead cost} = \left(\text{Budgeted variable-overhead cost per activity unit} \times \text{Total activity units} \right) + \text{Budgeted fixed-overhead cost per month}$$

To use this formula for DCdesserts, we first need to compute the budgeted variable-overhead cost per process hour. Dividing total budgeted variable-overhead cost by the associated activity level yields a budgeted variable-overhead rate of $5 per process hour. Notice that we can use any activity level in Exhibit 9–6 to compute this rate:

$$\frac{\$30,000}{6,000} = \frac{\$37,500}{7,500} = \frac{\$45,000}{9,000} = \$5 \text{ per process hour}$$

Learning Objective **4**

Prepare a flexible-overhead budget and explain how overhead is applied to work-in-process inventory.

Exhibit 9–6

Flexible-Overhead Budget: DCdesserts

	A	B	C	D	E	F	G
1	DCdesserts						
2	Monthly Flexible Overhead Budget						
3							
4					Process Hours		
5							
6					6,000	7,500	9,000
7	Budgeted costs:						
8							
9	Variable costs:						
10	Indirect material:						
11	Nonstick cooking spray				$ 12,000	$ 15,000	$ 18,000
12	Waxed paper				2,000	2,500	3,000
13	Other paper products				2,000	2,500	3,000
14	Miscellaneous supplies				6,000	7,500	9,000
15	Indirect labour: Maintenance				4,000	5,000	6,000
16	Utilities						
17	Electricity				3,000	3,750	4,500
18	Natural gas				1,000	1,250	1,500
19	Total variable cost				$ 30,000	$ 37,500	$ 45,000
20							
21							
22	Fixed costs:						
23	Indirect labour:						
24	Inspection				$ 2,200	$ 2,200	$ 2,200
25	Production supervisors				6,000	6,000	6,000
26	Setup				3,000	3,000	3,000
27	Material handling				2,000	2,000	2,000
28	Depreciation: Plant and equipment				500	500	500
29	Insurance and property taxes				100	100	100
30	Test kitchen				1,200	1,200	1,200
31	Total fixed cost				$ 15,000	$ 15,000	$ 15,000
32	Total overhead cost				$ 45,000	$ 52,500	$ 60,000

DCdesserts' formula flexible-overhead budget is shown below:

$$\text{Total budgeted monthly overhead cost} = (\$5 \times \text{Total process hours}) + \$15{,}000$$

To check the accuracy of the formula, compute the total budgeted overhead cost at each of the activity levels shown in Exhibit 9–6.

Activity (process hours)	Formula Flexible-Overhead Budget		Budgeted Monthly Overhead Cost
6,000	$5 × 6,000 + $15,000	=	$45,000
7,500	$5 × 7,500 + $15,000	=	$52,500
9,000	$5 × 9,000 + $15,000	=	$60,000

The budgeted monthly overhead cost computed above is the same as that shown in Exhibit 9–6 for each activity level.

The formula flexible budget is more general than the columnar flexible budget, because the formula allows the management accountant to compute budgeted overhead costs at any activity level. Then the flexible-budgeted overhead cost can be used at the end of the period as a benchmark against which to compare the actual overhead costs incurred.

"It's critical to understand variable and fixed-overhead costs. When activity levels change, what costs will change and how?" (9d)

A. T. Kearney, Inc.

Overhead Application in a Standard-Costing System

Learning Objective 4

Prepare a flexible-overhead budget and explain how overhead is applied to work-in-process inventory.

Recall that *overhead application* refers to the addition of overhead cost to the work-in-process inventory account as a product cost. In the normal-costing system, described in Chapter 3, overhead is applied as shown in the top panel of Exhibit 9–7. Overhead application is based on *actual* hours. In a standard-costing system, overhead application is based on standard hours allowed, given actual output. This system is depicted in the bottom panel of Exhibit 9–7. The difference between normal costing and standard costing, insofar as overhead is concerned, lies in the quantity of hours used.

Both normal-costing and standard-costing systems use a predetermined overhead rate. In a standard-costing system, the predetermined overhead rate is also referred to as the *standard overhead rate*. DCdesserts calculates its predetermined or standard overhead rate annually. The rate for the current year, computed in Exhibit 9–8, is based on *planned* activity of 7,500 process hours per month. DCdesserts breaks its predetermined overhead rate into a variable rate and a fixed rate.

Exhibit 9–7
Overhead Application

Normal Costing

Manufacturing Overhead		Work-in-Process Inventory	
Actual overhead	Applied overhead: **Actual hours** × Predetermined overhead rate	Applied overhead: **Actual hours** × Predetermined overhead rate	

Difference lies in the quantity of hours used.

Standard Costing

Manufacturing Overhead		Work-in-Process Inventory	
Actual overhead	Applied overhead: **Standard allowed hours** × Predetermined (or standard) rate	Applied overhead: **Standard allowed hours** × Predetermined (or standard) rate	

Exhibit 9–8
Predetermined Overhead Rate: DCdesserts

	Budgeted Overhead	Planned Monthly Activity	Predetermined Overhead Rate
Variable	$37,500*	7,500 process hours	$5.00 per process hour
Fixed	15,000*	7,500 process hours	2.00 per process hour
Total	$52,500	7,500 process hours	$7.00 per process hour

*From the flexible budget (Exhibit 9–6) for planned monthly activity of 7,500 process hours.

Choice of Activity Measure

Learning Objective 5

Explain some important issues in choosing an activity measure for overhead budgeting and application.

DCdesserts' flexible-overhead budget is based on process hours. A variety of activity measures are used in practice. Machine hours, direct-labour hours, direct-labour cost, total process time, and direct-material cost are among the most common measures. Choosing the appropriate activity measure for the flexible-overhead budget is important, because the flexible budget is the chief tool for managing overhead costs.

As manufacturing has become increasingly automated, direct labour is becoming less appropriate as an activity measure in flexible budgeting. Moreover, computer-integrated manufacturing entails a shift in the cost structure away from direct-labour costs and toward greater overhead costs. Left, cutting and sewing is a labour-intensive process for these textile workers. Right, automated equipment like that used in producing these washing machines is commonplace in high-tech manufacturing.

Criteria for Choosing the Activity Measure

How should the management accountant select the activity measure for the flexible budget? The activity measure should be one that varies in a similar pattern to the way that variable overhead varies. As productive activity increases, both variable-overhead cost and the activity measure should increase in roughly the same proportion. As productive activity declines, both variable-overhead cost and the activity measure should decline in roughly the same proportion. In short, variable-overhead cost and the activity measure should *move together* as overall productive activity changes.

Changing Manufacturing Technology: Computer-Integrated Manufacturing   Direct labour time has traditionally been the most popular activity measure in manufacturing firms. However, as automation increases, more and more firms are switching to such measures as machine hours or process time for their flexible-overhead budgets. Machine hours and process time are linked more closely than direct-labour hours to the robotic technology and computer-integrated manufacturing systems common in today's manufacturing environment.

Cost Drivers   As we discussed in Chapter 5, some companies have refined their cost management systems even further. *Cost drivers* are identified as the most significant factors affecting overhead costs. Then multiple overhead rates based on these cost drivers are used to compute product costs and control overhead expenditures. A relentless search for *non-value-added* costs is an integral part of such a cost management system. We will discuss the role of *activity-based costing* (ABC) in flexible budgeting later in the chapter.

Beware of Dollar Measures   Dollar measures, such as direct-labour cost or raw-material cost, are often used as the basis for flexible-overhead budgeting. However, such measures have significant drawbacks, and they should be avoided. Dollar measures are subject to price-level changes and fluctuate more than physical measures. For example, the direct-labour *hours* required to produce a fancy dessert will be relatively stable over time. However, the direct-labour *cost* will vary as wage levels and fringe benefit costs change with inflation and conditions in the labour market.

Cost Variance Analysis: Manufacturing-Overhead Costs

The flexible-overhead budget is one of the primary tools for control of manufacturing-overhead costs. At the end of each accounting period, the management accountant uses the flexible-overhead budget to determine the level of overhead cost that should have been incurred, given the actual level of activity. Then the accountant compares the overhead cost in the flexible budget with the actual overhead cost incurred. The management accountant then computes four separate overhead variances, each of which conveys information useful in controlling overhead costs.

Learning Objective 6

Compute and interpret the variable-overhead and fixed-overhead variances.

To illustrate overhead variance analysis, we will continue our DCdesserts example.

Flexible Budget   DCdesserts' monthly flexible-overhead budget, displayed in Exhibit 9–6, shows budgeted variable and fixed manufacturing-overhead costs at three levels of production activity. During September, DCdesserts produced 2,000 multilayered fancy cakes. Since production standards allow three process hours per cake, the total standard allowed number of process hours is 6,000 hours.

Actual production output	2,000 multilayered fancy cakes
Standard allowed process hours per multilayered fancy cake	× 3
Total standard allowed process hours	6,000 process hours

From the 6,000 process-hour column in Exhibit 9–6, the budgeted overhead cost for September is as follows:

	Budgeted Overhead Cost for September
Variable overhead	$30,000
Fixed overhead	15,000

From the cost accounting records, DCdesserts' controller determined that the following overhead costs were actually incurred during September:

	Actual Cost for September
Variable overhead	$34,650
Fixed overhead	16,100
Total overhead	$50,750

The production supervisor's records indicate that the actual total process time in September was as follows:

Actual process hours for September	6,300

Notice that the actual number of process hours used (6,300) exceeds the standard allowed number of process hours (6,000), given actual production output.

We now have assembled all of the information necessary to compute DCdesserts' overhead variances for September.

Variable Overhead

DCdesserts' total variable-overhead variance for September is computed below:

Actual variable overhead	$34,650
Budgeted variable overhead	30,000
Total variable-overhead variance	$ 4,650 Unfavourable

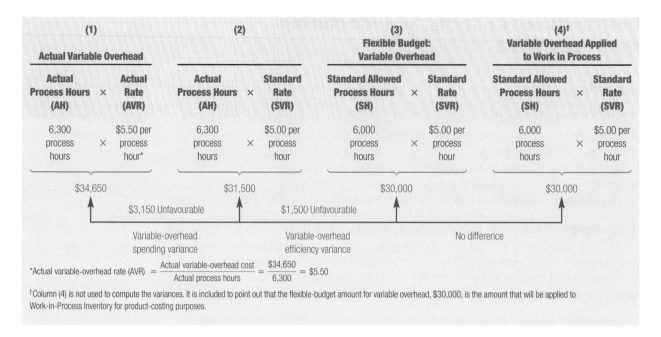

(1)		(2)		(3) **Flexible Budget:** **Variable Overhead**		(4)† **Variable Overhead Applied** **to Work in Process**	
Actual Variable Overhead							
Actual **Process Hours** **(AH)**	**Actual** **Rate** **(AVR)**	**Actual** **Process Hours** **(AH)**	**Standard** **Rate** **(SVR)**	**Standard Allowed** **Process Hours** **(SH)**	**Standard** **Rate** **(SVR)**	**Standard Allowed** **Process Hours** **(SH)**	**Standard** **Rate** **(SVR)**
6,300 process hours	× $5.50 per process hour*	6,300 process hours	× $5.00 per process hour	6,000 process hours	× $5.00 per process hour	6,000 process hours	× $5.00 per process hour
$34,650		$31,500		$30,000		$30,000	

$3,150 Unfavourable $1,500 Unfavourable   No difference

Variable-overhead   Variable-overhead
spending variance   efficiency variance

*Actual variable-overhead rate (AVR) $= \dfrac{\text{Actual variable-overhead cost}}{\text{Actual process hours}} = \dfrac{\$34,650}{6,300} = \$5.50$

†Column (4) is not used to compute the variances. It is included to point out that the flexible-budget amount for variable overhead, $30,000, is the amount that will be applied to Work-in-Process Inventory for product-costing purposes.

Exhibit 9–9

Variable-Overhead Spending
and Efficiency Variances:
DCdesserts

What caused the company to spend $4,650 more than the budgeted amount on variable overhead? To discover the reasons behind this performance, the management accountant computes a **variable-overhead spending variance** and a **variable-overhead efficiency variance**. The computation of these variances is depicted in Exhibit 9–9.

The equivalent formula for the variable-overhead spending variance is shown below.

$$\text{Variable-overhead spending variance} = \text{Actual variable overhead} - (AH \times SVR)$$

where   AH denotes actual process hours
        SVR denotes standard variable-overhead rate

The variable-overhead spending variance for September is computed as follows:

$$
\begin{aligned}
\text{Variable-overhead spending variance} &= \text{Actual variable overhead} - (AH \times SVR), \\
&= \$34,650 - (6,300 \times \$5) \\
&= \$3,150 \text{ Unfavourable}
\end{aligned}
$$

This variance is unfavourable because the actual variable-overhead cost exceeded the expected amount, after adjusting that expectation for the actual number of process hours used.

As Exhibit 9–9 shows, the following formula defines the variable-overhead efficiency variance:

$$\text{Variable-overhead efficiency variance} = (AH \times SVR) - (SH \times SVR) = SVR \times (AH - SH)$$

where   SH denotes standard process hours

The variable-overhead efficiency variance for September is computed as follows:

$$
\begin{aligned}
\text{Variable-overhead efficiency variance} &= SVR(AH - SH) \\
&= \$5(6,300 - 6,000) \\
&= \$1,500 \text{ Unfavourable}
\end{aligned}
$$

Key:
Total variable-overhead variance: blue areas
Variable-overhead spending variance: dark blue area
Variable-overhead efficiency variance: light blue area

This variance is unfavourable because actual process hours exceeded standard allowed process hours, given actual output.

Product Costing versus Cost Management   Columns (1), (2), and (3) in Exhibit 9–9 are used to compute the variances for *cost management purposes*. Column (4) in the exhibit shows the variable overhead applied to work in process for the *product-costing purpose*. Notice that the variable-overhead cost in the flexible budget, $30,000, is the same as the amount applied to work in process.

Graphing Variable-Overhead Variances   Exhibit 9–10 provides a graphical analysis of the variable-overhead variances for September. The graph shows the variable-overhead rate per process hour on the vertical axis. The standard rate is $5 per process hour, while the actual rate is $5.50 per process hour (actual variable-overhead cost of $34,650 divided by actual process hours of 6,300). Process hours are shown on the horizontal axis.

The green area of the graph represents the flexible-budget amount for variable over-head, given actual September output of 2,000 multilayered fancy cakes. The large area of the graph enclosed by red-coloured lines on the top and right-hand side represents actual variable-overhead cost. The blue-coloured area in between, representing the total vari-able-overhead variance, is divided into the spending and efficiency variances.

Managerial Interpretation of Variable-Overhead Variances   What do the variable-overhead variances mean? What information do they convey to management? The formulas for computing the variable-overhead variances resemble those used to compute the direct-labour variances. To see this, compare Exhibit 9–9 (variable overhead) with Exhibit 9–3 (direct labour).

Despite the similar formulas, the interpretation of the variable-overhead variances is quite different from that applicable to the direct-labour variances.

Spending Variance   An unfavourable direct-labour rate variance is straightforward to interpret; the actual labour rate *per hour* exceeds the standard rate. Although the formula for computing the variable-overhead spending variance is similar to that for the direct-labour rate variance, its interpretation is quite different.

An unfavourable spending variance simply means that the total actual cost of variable overhead is greater than expected, after adjusting for the actual quantity of process hours used. An unfavourable spending variance could result from paying a higher-than-expected price per unit for variable-overhead items. Or the variance could result from using more of the variable-overhead items than expected.

Suppose, for example, that electricity was the only variable-overhead cost item. An unfavourable variable-overhead spending variance could result from paying a higher-than-expected price per kilowatt-hour for electricity, from using more than the expected amount of electricity, or from both.

Efficiency Variance   Recall that an unfavourable direct-labour efficiency variance results when more direct labour is used than the standard allowed quantity. So, direct labour has been used inefficiently, relative to the standard. However, that is not the proper interpretation of an unfavourable variable-overhead efficiency variance. DCdesserts' variable-overhead efficiency variance did *not* result from using more of the variable-overhead items, such as electricity and indirect material, than the standard allowed amount. Instead, this variance resulted when the division used *more process hours* than the standard quantity, given actual output. Recall that the company's controller has found that variable-overhead cost varies in a pattern similar to that with which process hours vary. Since 300 more process hours were used than the standard quantity, management should expect that variable-overhead costs will be greater. Thus, the variable-overhead efficiency variance has nothing to do with efficient or inefficient usage of electricity, indirect material, and other variable-overhead items. This variance simply reflects an adjustment in the expectation about variable-overhead cost, because the company used more than the standard quantity of process hours.

What is the important difference between direct labour and variable overhead that causes this different interpretation of the efficiency variance? Direct labour is a traceable cost and is budgeted on the basis of direct-labour hours. Variable overhead, on the other hand, is a pool of *indirect* costs that are budgeted on the basis of *process hours*. The indirect nature of variable-overhead costs causes the different interpretation.

Management of Variable-Overhead Costs   Since the variable-overhead efficiency variance says nothing about efficient or inefficient usage of variable overhead, the spending variance is the real control variance for variable overhead. Managers can use the spending variance to alert them if variable-overhead costs are out of line with expectations.

Fixed Overhead

To analyze performance with regard to fixed overhead, the management accountant calculates two fixed-overhead variances.

Fixed-Overhead Budget Variance   The variance used by managers to control fixed overhead is called the **fixed-overhead budget variance**. It is defined as follows:

$$\text{Fixed-overhead budget variance} = \text{Actual fixed overhead} - \text{Budgeted fixed overhead}$$

DCdesserts' fixed-overhead budget variance for September is as follows:

$$
\begin{aligned}
\text{Fixed-overhead budget variance} &= \text{Actual fixed overhead} - \text{Budgeted fixed overhead} \\
&= \quad \$16{,}100 \quad - \quad \$15{,}000^* \\
&= \$1{,}100 \text{ Unfavourable}
\end{aligned}
$$

*From the flexible budget (Exhibit 9–6).

The fixed-overhead budget variance is unfavourable because the company spent more than the budgeted amount on fixed overhead. Notice that we do not need to specify an activity level to determine budgeted fixed overhead. All three columns in the flexible budget (Exhibit 9–6) specify $15,000 as budgeted fixed overhead.

Fixed-Overhead Volume Variance The **fixed-overhead volume variance** is defined as follows:

$$\text{Fixed-overhead volume variance} = \text{Budgeted fixed overhead} - \text{Applied fixed overhead}$$

DCdesserts' applied fixed overhead for September is $12,000:

$$
\begin{aligned}
\text{Applied fixed overhead} &= \text{Predetermined fixed overhead rate} \times \text{Standard allowed hours}\\
&= \$2 \text{ per process hour} \times 6{,}000 \text{ process hours}\\
&= \$12{,}0000
\end{aligned}
$$

The $2 predetermined fixed-overhead rate was calculated in Exhibit 9–8. The 6,000 standard allowed process hours are based on actual September production of 2,000 multi-layered fancy cakes, each with a standard allowance of three process hours. DCdesserts' fixed-overhead volume variance is calculated below:

$$
\begin{aligned}
\text{Fixed-overhead volume variance} &= \text{Budgeted fixed overhead} - \text{Applied fixed overhead}\\
&= \$15{,}000 - \$12{,}000\\
&= \$3{,}000 \text{ Unfavourable}
\end{aligned}
$$

Managerial Interpretation of Fixed-Overhead Variances Exhibit 9–11 shows DCdesserts' two fixed-overhead variances for September. The budget variance is the real control variance for fixed overhead, because it compares actual expenditures with budgeted fixed-overhead costs.

Exhibit 9–11
Fixed-Overhead Budget and Volume Variances: DCdesserts

*Consistently with our discussion of the fixed-overhead volume variance, some management accountants would designate a positive va riance as "unfavourable."

Exhibit 9–12
Budgeted versus Applied
Fixed Overhead: DCdesserts

Fixed overhead

Applied fixed overhead ($2.00 per standard allowed process hour)

Budgeted fixed overhead — $15,000

Applied fixed overhead in September — $12,000

Volume variance $3,000

Budgeted fixed overhead

6,000 — Standard allowed hours, given actual output

7,500 — Planned monthly activity, expressed in hours

Process hours

The volume variance provides a way of reconciling two different purposes of the cost management system. For the *control purpose*, the system recognizes that fixed overhead does not change as production activity varies; therefore, budgeted fixed overhead is the same at all activity levels in the flexible budget (see Exhibit 9–6). Budgeted fixed overhead is the basis for controlling fixed overhead, because it provides the benchmark against which actual expenditures are compared.

For *product-costing purposes*, budgeted fixed overhead is divided by planned activity to obtain a predetermined (or standard) fixed-overhead rate. For DCdesserts, this rate is $2 per process hour (budgeted fixed overhead of $15,000 divided by planned activity of 7,500 process hours). This predetermined rate is then used to apply fixed overhead to the work-in-process inventory. During any period in which the standard allowed number of process hours, given actual output, differs from the planned level of process hours, the budgeted fixed overhead differs from applied fixed overhead.

Exhibit 9–12 illustrates this point graphically. Budgeted fixed overhead is constant at $15,000 for all levels of activity. However, applied fixed overhead increases with activity, since fixed overhead is applied to the work-in-process inventory at the rate of $2 per standard allowed process hour. Notice that budgeted and applied fixed overhead are equal *only* if the number of standard allowed hours equals the planned activity level of 7,500 process hours. When this happens, there is no fixed-overhead volume variance. DCdesserts has a $3,000 volume variance in September because the standard allowed hours and planned hours are different.

Capacity Utilization   A common, but faulty, interpretation of a positive volume variance is that it measures the cost of underutilizing productive capacity. Some firms even designate a positive volume variance as unfavourable. The reasoning behind this view is that the planned activity level used to compute the predetermined fixed-overhead rate is a measure of normal capacity utilization. Moreover, fixed-overhead costs, such as depreciation and property taxes, are costs incurred to create productive capacity. Therefore, the predetermined fixed-overhead rate measures the cost of providing an hour of productive capacity. If 7,500 process hours are planned, but output is such that only 6,000 standard process hours are allowed, then capacity has been underutilized by 1,500 hours. Since each hour costs $2 (DCdesserts' predetermined fixed-overhead rate), the cost of underutilization is $3,000 (1,500 × $2), which is DCdesserts' volume variance.

The fault with this interpretation of the volume variance is that it ignores the real cost of underutilizing productive capacity. The real cost is due to the lost contribution margins of the products that are not produced when capacity is underutilized. Moreover, this interpretation fails to recognize that underutilizing capacity and reducing inventory may be a wise managerial response to slackening demand.

For this reason, many management accountants interpret the volume variance merely as a way of reconciling the two purposes of the cost management system. Moreover, they would choose not to designate the volume variance as either favourable or unfavourable. However, some accountants designate a positive volume variance as *unfavourable*. Their reasoning is that when the volume variance is closed into cost of goods sold expense at the end of the accounting period, the effect is to increase cost of goods sold, which in turn has an *unfavourable* effect on income. In contrast, other accountants argue that no sign (favourable or unfavourable) should be assigned to the fixed-overhead volume variance.

Overhead Cost Performance Report

The variable-overhead spending and efficiency variances, as well as the fixed-overhead budget variance, can be computed for each overhead cost item in the flexible budget. When these itemized variances are presented along with actual and budgeted costs for each overhead item, the result is an **overhead cost performance report,** as displayed in Exhibit 9–13. This report would be used by management to exercise control over each of the division's overhead costs.

Notice that the performance report includes spending and efficiency variances for the variable items, but only a budget variance for the fixed items. On receiving this report, a manager might investigate the relatively large variances for indirect maintenance labour, electricity, and production supervisory labour.

Learning Objective **7**

Prepare an overhead cost performance report.

Andreas Stihl AG & Co. KG

COST MANAGEMENT SYSTEMS IN GERMANY

Throughout the world, flexible budgeting is found in cost management systems as a means of controlling overhead costs. In Germany, for example, *grenzplankostenrechnung* (or *flexible standard costing*) exhibits many of the features illustrated in this chapter. Under the German approach, "Each cost center distinguishes between variable costs (e.g., energy) and fixed costs (e.g., a manager's salary)." The number of machine hours is a common activity measure. "For purposes of cost planning and control, companies budget each cost center's expenses and then distribute the expenses to each month of the budget year. The budgeted costs are standards for efficient resource consumption. . . ." The cost and performance information "allows for effective discussions about productivity improvement" among department managers, management accountants, and plant managers.

Among the companies using the flexible standard-costing system is Andreas Stihl AG & Co. KG, a well-known German manufacturer of chain saws and other landscaping equipment.[2]

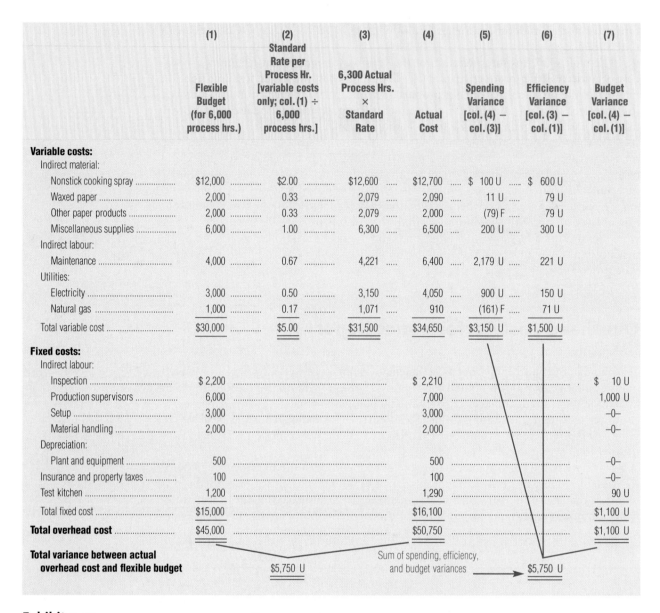

	(1) Flexible Budget (for 6,000 process hrs.)	(2) Standard Rate per Process Hr. [variable costs only; col. (1) ÷ 6,000 process hrs.]	(3) 6,300 Actual Process Hrs. × Standard Rate	(4) Actual Cost	(5) Spending Variance [col. (4) − col. (3)]	(6) Efficiency Variance [col. (3) − col. (1)]	(7) Budget Variance [col. (4) − col. (1)]
Variable costs:							
Indirect material:							
Nonstick cooking spray	$12,000	$2.00	$12,600	$12,700	$ 100 U	$ 600 U	
Waxed paper	2,000	0.33	2,079	2,090	11 U	79 U	
Other paper products	2,000	0.33	2,079	2,000	(79) F	79 U	
Miscellaneous supplies	6,000	1.00	6,300	6,500	200 U	300 U	
Indirect labour:							
Maintenance	4,000	0.67	4,221	6,400	2,179 U	221 U	
Utilities:							
Electricity	3,000	0.50	3,150	4,050	900 U	150 U	
Natural gas	1,000	0.17	1,071	910	(161) F	71 U	
Total variable cost	$30,000	$5.00	$31,500	$34,650	$3,150 U	$1,500 U	
Fixed costs:							
Indirect labour:							
Inspection	$ 2,200			$ 2,210			$ 10 U
Production supervisors	6,000			7,000			1,000 U
Setup	3,000			3,000			–0–
Material handling	2,000			2,000			–0–
Depreciation:							
Plant and equipment	500			500			–0–
Insurance and property taxes	100			100			–0–
Test kitchen	1,200			1,290			90 U
Total fixed cost	$15,000			$16,100			$1,100 U
Total overhead cost	$45,000			$50,750			$1,100 U
Total variance between actual overhead cost and flexible budget		$5,750 U	Sum of spending, efficiency, and budget variances ⟶				$5,750 U

Exhibit 9–13
Overhead Cost Performance
Report: DCdesserts

Activity-Based Flexible Budget

Learning Objective 8

Explain how an activity-based flexible budget differs from a conventional flexible budget.

The flexible budget shown in Exhibit 9–6, which underlies our variance analysis for DCdesserts, is based on a single cost driver. Overhead costs that vary with respect to *process hours* are categorized as variable; all other overhead costs are treated as fixed. This approach is consistent with traditional, volume-based product-costing systems.

Under the more accurate product-costing method called *activity-based costing* (ABC), several cost drivers are identified.[3] Costs that may appear fixed with respect to a single volume-based cost driver, such as process hours, may be variable with respect to some other cost driver. The activity-based costing approach also can be used as the

DCdesserts Monthly Flexible-Overhead Budget			
Budgeted Cost	**Level of Activity**		
Cost Pool I (Cost driver: Process hours)	**6,000**	**7,500**	**9,000**
Indirect material:			
Nonstick cooking spray	$ 12,000	$ 15,000	$ 18,000
Waxed paper	2,000	2,500	3,000
Other paper products	2,000	2,500	3,000
Miscellaneous supplies	6,000	7,500	9,000
Indirect labour: Maintenance	4,000	5,000	6,000
Utilities:			
Electricity	3,000	3,750	4,500
Natural gas	1,000	1,250	1,500
Total of Cost Pool I	$ 30,000	$ 37,500	$ 45,000
Cost Pool II (Cost driver: Production runs)	**8**	**12**	**16**
Indirect labour:			
Inspection	$ 2,200	$ 3,300	$ 4,400
Setup	3,000	4,500	6,000
Total of Cost Pool II	$ 5,200	$ 7,800	$ 10,400
Cost Pool III (Cost driver: New products tested)	**20**	**30**	**40**
Test kitchen	$ 1,200	$ 1,800	$ 2,400
Total of Cost Pool III	$ 1,200	$ 1,800	$ 2,400
Cost Pool IV (Cost driver: Kilograms of material handled)	**20,000**	**30,000**	**40,000**
Material handling	$ 2,000	$ 3,000	$ 4,000
Total of Cost Pool IV	$ 2,000	$ 3,000	$ 4,000
Cost Pool V (facility level costs)			
Indirect labour: Production supervisors	$ 6,000	$ 6,000	$ 6,000
Depreciation: Plant and equipment	500	500	500
Insurance and property taxes	100	100	100
Total of Cost Pool V	$ 6,600	$ 6,600	$ 6,600
Total overhead cost	**$45,000**	**$56,700**	**$ 68,400**

Exhibit 9–14
Activity-Based Flexible
Budget: DCdesserts

basis for a flexible budget for planning and cost management purposes. Exhibit 9–14 displays an **activity-based flexible budget** for DCdesserts, using the same data as Exhibit 9–6.

Compare the conventional flexible budget (Exhibit 9–6) and the activity-based flexible budget (Exhibit 9–14). The key difference lies in the costs that were categorized as fixed in the conventional flexible budget. These costs are fixed with respect to process hours but are not fixed with respect to other more appropriate cost drivers. For example, Cost Pool II includes inspection and setup costs, which vary in relation to the number of production runs.

Effect on Performance Reporting The activity-based flexible budget provides a more accurate prediction (and benchmark) of overhead costs. For example, suppose that activity in December is as follows:

December activity		
	Process hours	6,000
	Production runs	12
	New products tested	40
	Direct material handled (kilograms)	30,000

The following table compares the budgeted cost levels for several overhead items on the conventional and activity-based flexible budgets:

Overhead Cost Item	Conventional Flexible Budget	Activity-Based Flexible Budget
Electricity	$3,000	$3,000
Inspection	2,200	3,300
Setup	3,000	4,500
Test kitchen	1,200	2,400
Material handling	2,000	3,000
Insurance and property taxes	100	100

> "ABC has enhanced our clients' ability to manage overhead costs through flexible budgeting systems." (9g)
>
> **A. T. Kearney, Inc.**

The budgeted electricity cost is the same in both budgets, because both use the same cost driver (process hours). Insurance and property taxes are also the same, because both budgets recognize these as facility-level fixed costs. However, the other overhead costs are budgeted at different levels, because the conventional and activity-based flexible budgets use *different cost drivers* for these items. While the conventional budget treats inspection, setup, test kitchen, and material-handling costs as fixed, the activity-based flexible budget shows that they are all variable in relation to the appropriate cost driver.

These differences are important for performance reporting. The activity-based flexible budget provides a more accurate benchmark against which to compare actual costs. Suppose the actual inspection cost in December is $3,000. Using the conventional flexible budget would result in an unfavourable variance of $800 ($3,000 − $2,200). However, the activity-based flexible budget yields a favourable variance of $300 ($3,000 − $3,300).

To summarize, activity-based flexible budgeting provides a richer view of cost behaviour and the underlying cost drivers, and it provides a valuable tool for cost management.

Flexible Budgeting in the Service Industry

An activity-based flexible budget is based on many cost drivers. Think about the costs that are incurred at your school. The cost of staffing the faculty, for example, depends on factors such as the number of students enrolled, the number of courses offered, and the average class size. The cost of operating the admissions department depends in part on the number of applicants.[4]

All kinds of organizations benefit from the concept of a flexible budget. Like manufacturing firms, service industry organizations incur overhead costs that vary with appropriately chosen cost drivers. At York University, for example, the cost of operating the admissions department depends in part on the number of applicants. At Pacific Blue Cross Insurance Company, the cost of administering the claims department depends in part on the number of claims. At Vancouver General Hospital, the cost of operating the patient records department depends in part on the number of patients.

Let's briefly turn our attention to Tri-Cities Auto Rentals, a small automobile rental company with rental locations in Coquitlam, Port Coquitlam, and Port Moody, which specializes in short-term car rentals, primarily for local use when a customer's car is in the repair shop. Tri-Cities Auto Rentals' flexible budget is displayed in Exhibit 9–15. Notice that unlike DCdesserts' flexible-overhead budget, Tri-Cities' flexible budget lists its operating expenses. All of this service industry firm's costs are operating expenses. Tri-Cities' management has chosen two cost drivers for its activity-based flexible budget: the number of kilometres driven and the number of customer contracts.

Some operating expenses (Cost Pool I in the flexible budget) vary with the number of kilometres driven in the rental cars. Automobile maintenance and tire replacement expenses increase as the cars are driven more kilometres. Similarly, such operating

	A	B	C	D
1	TRI– CITIES AUTO RENTALS			
2	Annual Flexible Budget: Operating Expenses			
3				
4	Budgeted Operating Expenses		Level of Activity	
5				
6	Cost Pool I (cost driver: kilometres driven)	750,000	1,000,000	1,250,000
7	Automobile maintenance	$ 240,000	$ 320,000	$ 400,000
8	Tire replacement	6,000	8,000	10,000
9	Automobile insurance	27,000	36,000	45,000
10	British Columbia registration and inspection	900	1,200	1,500
11	Leasing costs	36,000	48,000	60,000
12	Total of Cost Pool I	$ 309,900	$ 413,200	$ 516,500
13				
14	Cost Pool II (cost driver: customer contracts)	3,000	6,000	9,000
15	Reservations	$ 16,000	$ 32,000	$ 48,000
16	Registration of contract information	18,000	36,000	54,000
17	Inspection of vehicle by employee/customer	8,000	16,000	24,000
18	Employee commissions	20,000	40,000	60,000
19	Cleaning/washing automobile	17,000	34,000	51,000
20	Total of Cost Pool II	$ 79,000	$ 158,000	$ 237,000
21				
22	Cost Pool III (overall organization: fixed costs)			
23	Office managers' salaries	240,000	240,000	240,000
24	Rent: Buildings	36,000	36,000	36,000
25	Utilities: Buildings	13,000	13,000	13,000
26	Liability insurance: Rental offices	12,000	12,000	12,000
27	Depreciation: Equipment	11,000	11,000	11,000
28	Total of Cost Pool III	$ 312,000	$ 312,000	$ 312,000
29				
30	Total operating expenses	$ 700,900	$ 883,200	$1,065,500

Exhibit 9–15

Flexible Budget: Tri-Cities Auto Rentals

expenses as insurance and leasing costs increase with the number of kilometres driven, because the company needs to have more cars on hand. Other operating expenses (Cost Pool II) vary with the number of customer contracts, regardless of how many kilometres each customer drives a rental car. Such expenses as rental reservations, filling out contracts, and cleaning up a rental car on its return depend on the number of times the cars are rented. Finally, some fixed operating expenses (Cost Pool III), such as the office managers' salaries and rental charges on the office locations, do not vary with any cost driver.

Tri-Cities Auto Rentals' management can use this flexible budget to predict operating expenses at varying levels of activity, as measured by the two cost drivers.

Focus on Ethics

MISSTATED STANDARDS AFFECT ACCURACY OF REPORTS

The scenario described here, while placed in the context of a fictitious enterprise, is based on an actual situation that occurred at NuTone Housing Group, which at the time was a subsidiary of Scoville Inc.[5]

To set the stage, consider these facts about the standard-costing system in place at Shrood Division, a subsidiary of Gigantic Enterprises, Inc. Shrood Division manufactures a wide range of electric household products, such as lighting, fans, water pumps, and security systems.

The division manufactures approximately 10,000 products, made from over 70,000 components. Tom Cleverly has run the division in what he calls a hands-on manner for over a quarter of a century. When Shrood was acquired by Gigantic a decade ago, Cleverly was at first unhappy with the merger, but it soon became apparent that Gigantic's top management would let him run the business the way he was used to running it. Three aspects of Cleverly's management style are noteworthy. First, he insists on being involved in all major pricing decisions; he's not a delegator. Second, he has developed a second-level management that is loyal and supportive of his approach. Third, he has refused to lower the direct-labour time standards for years, even though many productivity improvements have been made. At present, the actual direct-labour times are on average only about a third of the standard times. Moreover, since manufacturing overhead is applied on the basis of direct labour, both the standard direct-labour and the standard overhead costs are inflated relative to actual costs.

The implications of this practice are that huge favourable variances are experienced all year long in both direct labour and overhead. Cleverly has used these favourable variances to "manage the quarterly earnings" reported by Shrood Division to corporate. Cleverly has instructed his manager of accounting, Evan Twixt, to release just enough of the favourable variances into the cost of goods sold (CGS) account on a quarterly basis to ensure that Shrood Division just meets its earnings target in the budget. Then, at the end of the year, the remainder of this large favourable variance is released into CGS, with the result that Shrood ends each year with fourth-quarter earnings far in excess of the target. Like a knight in shining white armour, Shrood Division saves the day for Gigantic Enterprises year after year. Shrood has come to be known in corporate circles as "the jewel in the crown of Gigantic."

Now for the conflict. Gigantic has hired a new corporate controller, Jeffrey Fixit, whose mandate is to introduce more consistency in the reporting methods of Gigantic's various divisions. When Fixit visited Shrood Division and discovered what was going on, he tried to get Tom Cleverly to instruct Evan Twixt to correct the direct-labour standards to reflect attainable results (i.e., reality). Cleverly has refused, though, and Fixit doesn't have the power to force him to do so. Meanwhile, poor Twixt is caught in the middle.

Here is what each of them had to say about the situation.

Cleverly (division manager): I've been running this business for 25 years. And you know what? We've been profitable for 25 years! The high labour standards help me make sure that neither I nor my salespeople shave prices too much. It's like setting the clock 10 minutes ahead to make sure you're not late. We always make budget. We always report the highest profits in the company. And we are, in fact, the "jewel in the crown."

Fixit (corporate controller): This is a really bad situation. Shrood is reporting fictitious numbers to corporate on a quarterly basis, which then get rolled up into Gigantic's quarterly results. Then these numbers get published to the shareholders. We're misleading them. I don't have the authority to get Tom Cleverly to fix the problem. I can, however, go to the board of directors and explain to them that they need to get Cleverly to do what needs to be done.

Twixt (Shrood's accounting manager): I'm caught in the middle. We basically have two sets of books: the ones based on Mr. Cleverly's labour standards, and the ones based on the more accurate results that Mr. Fixit wants. I can report either set of results. I feel like I'm serving two gods—and so far I'm getting away with it.

What do you make of this situation? Can a company that keeps two sets of books be well managed? What ethical issues do you see here? What actions should Cleverly, Twixt, and Fixit take?

Significance of Cost Variances

Learning Objective

Explain several methods for determining the significance of cost variances.

Managers do not have time to investigate the causes of every cost variance. Management by exception enables managers to look into the causes of only significant variances. But what constitutes an exception? How does the manager know when to follow up on a cost variance and when to ignore it?

These questions are difficult to answer because, to some extent, the answers are part of the art of management. A manager applies judgment and experience in making guesses, pursuing hunches, and relying on intuition to determine when a variance should be investigated. Nevertheless, there are guidelines and rules of thumb that managers often apply.

Size of Variances The absolute size of a variance is one consideration. Managers are more likely to follow up on large variances than on small ones. The relative size of the

	Amount		Percentage of Standard Cost
Direct material			
Standard cost, given actual output	$14,000		
Direct-material price variance	250	Unfavourable	1.79%
Direct-material quantity variance	350	Unfavourable	2.50%
Direct labour			
Standard cost, given actual output	$20,000		
Direct-labour rate variance	980	Unfavourable	4.9%
Direct-labour efficiency variance	400	Favourable	(2.0%)

Exhibit 9–16

Cost Variance Report for September: DCdesserts

variance is probably even more important. A manager is more likely to investigate a $20,000 material quantity variance that is 20 percent of the standard direct-material cost of $100,000 than a $50,000 labour efficiency variance that is only 2 percent of the standard direct-labour cost of $2,500,000. The *relative* magnitude of the $20,000 material quantity variance (20%) is greater than the *relative* magnitude of the $50,000 labour efficiency variance (2%). For this reason, management accountants often show the relative magnitude of variances in their cost variance reports. For example, the September cost variance report for DCdesserts' production of multilayer fancy cakes is shown in Exhibit 9–16.

Managers often apply a rule of thumb that takes into account both the absolute and the relative magnitudes of a variance. An example of such a rule is the following: Investigate variances that are either greater than $10,000 or greater than 10 percent of standard cost.

Recurring Variances Another consideration in deciding when to investigate a variance is whether the variance occurs repeatedly or only infrequently. Suppose a manager uses the rule of thumb stated above and direct-material quantity variances occur as shown in the following Excel spreadsheet:

	A	B	C	D	E
1		Standard	Direct-Material		Percentage
2		Direct-Material	Quantity		of Standard
3	Month	Cost	Variance		Cost
4					
5	January	$ 50,000	$ 3,000 F*		6.0%
6	February	50,000	3,200 F		6.4%
7	March	50,000	1,800 F		3.6%
8	April	50,000	3,100 F		6.2%
9					
10	*F denotes a favourable variance.				

A strict adherence to the rule of thumb indicates no investigation, since none of the monthly variances is greater than $10,000 or 10 percent of standard cost. Nevertheless, the manager might investigate this variance in April, since it has *recurred* at a reasonably high level for several consecutive months. In this case, the consistency of the variance triggers an investigation, not its absolute or relative magnitude.

Trends A trend in a variance also may call for investigation. Suppose a manager observes the direct-labour efficiency variances shown in the following Excel spreadsheet. None of these variances is large enough to trigger an investigation if the manager uses the "$10,000 or 10 percent" rule of thumb. However, the four-month *trend* is worrisome. An alert manager will likely follow up on this unfavourable trend to determine its causes before costs get out of hand.

	A	B	C	D	E
1		Standard	Direct-Labour		Percentage
2		Direct-Labour	Efficiency		of Standard
3	Month	Cost	Variance		Cost
4					
5	January	$ 100,000	$ 100	U*	0.10%
6	February	100,000	550	U	0.55%
7	March	100,000	3,000	U	3.00%
8	April	100,000	9,100	U	9.10%
9					
10	*U denotes an unfavourable variance.				

Controllability   Another important consideration in deciding when to look into the causes of a variance is the manager's view of the **controllability** of the cost item. A manager is more likely to investigate the variance for a cost that is controllable by someone in the organization than one that is not. For example, there may be little point to investigating a material price variance if the organization has no control over the price. This could happen, for example, if the firm has a long-term contract with a supplier of the material at a price determined on the international market. In contrast, the manager is likely to follow up on a variance that should be controllable, such as a direct-labour efficiency variance or a direct-material quantity variance.

Favourable Variances   It is just as important to investigate significant favourable variances as significant unfavourable variances. For example, a favourable direct-labour efficiency variance may indicate that employees have developed a more efficient way of performing a production task. By investigating the variance, management can learn about the improved method. It may be possible to use a similar approach elsewhere in the organization.

Costs and Benefits of Investigation   The decision whether to investigate a cost variance is a cost–benefit decision. The costs of investigation include the time spent by the manager and the employees in the department where the investigation occurs. Other potential costs include disruption of the production process as the investigation is conducted, and corrective actions taken to eliminate the cause of a variance. The benefits of a variance investigation include reduced future production costs if the cause of an unfavourable variance is eliminated. Another potential benefit is the cost saving associated with the lowering of cost standards when the cause of a favourable variance is discovered.

Weighing these considerations takes the judgment of skilful and experienced managers. Key to this judgment is an intimate understanding of the organization's production process and day-to-day contact with its operations.

Behavioural Impact of Standard Costing

Learning Objective **10**

Describe some behavioural effects of standard costing.

Standard costs and variance analysis are useful in diagnosing organizational performance. These tools help managers discern "the story behind the story"—the details of operations that underlie reported cost and profit numbers. Standard costs, budgets, and variances are also used to evaluate the performance of individuals and departments. The performance of individuals, relative to standards or budgets, often is used to help determine salary increases, bonuses, and promotions. When standards and variances affect employee reward structures, they can profoundly influence behaviour.

For example, suppose the manager of a hotel's Food and Beverage Department earns a bonus when food and beverage costs are below the budgeted amount, given actual sales. This reward structure will provide a concrete incentive for the manager to keep food and beverage costs under control. But such an incentive can have either positive or negative effects. The bonus may induce the manager to seek the most economical suppliers and to watch more carefully for employee theft and waste. However, the bonus also could persuade the manager to buy cheaper but less tender steaks for the restaurant. This could ultimately result in lost patronage for the restaurant and the hotel. One aspect of skilful management is knowing how to use standards, budgets, and variances to get the most out of an organization's employees. Unfortunately, there are no simple answers or formulas for success in this area. Despite such difficulties, standards, budgets, and variances are used in the executive compensation schemes of many well-known companies.

Controllability of Variances

Cost control is accomplished through the efforts of individual managers in an organization. By determining which managers are in the best position to influence each cost variance, the management accountant can assist managers in deriving the greatest benefit from cost variance analysis.

Who is responsible for the direct-material price and quantity variances? The direct-labour rate and efficiency variances? Answering these questions is often difficult, because it is rare that any one person completely controls any event. Nevertheless, it is often possible to identify the manager who is *most able to influence* a particular variance, even if he or she does not exercise complete control over the outcome.

> "We designate variances as controllable or uncontrollable. Plant managers are held accountable for the controllable variances." (9h)
> **Best Foods (A subsidiary of Unilever)**

Direct-Material Price Variance   The purchasing manager is generally in the best position to influence material price variances. Through skilful purchasing practices, an expert purchasing manager can get the best prices available for purchased goods and services. To achieve this goal, the purchasing manager uses such practices as buying in quantity, negotiating purchase contracts, comparing prices among vendors, and global sourcing.

Despite these purchasing skills, the purchasing manager is not in complete control of prices. The need to purchase component parts with precise engineering specifications, the all-too-frequent rush requests from the production department, and worldwide shortages of critical materials all contribute to the challenges faced by the purchasing manager.

Direct-Material Quantity Variance   The production supervisor is usually in the best position to influence material quantity variances. Skilful supervision and motivation of production employees, coupled with the careful use and handling of materials, contribute to minimal waste. Production engineers are also partially responsible for material quantity variances, since they determine the grade and technical specifications of materials and component parts. In some cases, using a low-grade material may result in greater waste than using a high-grade material.

Direct-Labour Rate Variance   Direct-labour rate variances generally result from using a different mix of employees than that anticipated when the standards were set. Wage rates differ among employees due to their skill levels and their seniority with the organization. Using a higher proportion of more senior or more highly skilled employees than a task requires can result in unfavourable direct-labour rate variances. The production supervisor is generally in the best position to influence the work schedules of employees.

Direct-Labour Efficiency Variance   Once again, the production supervisor is usually most responsible for the efficient use of employee time. Through motivation toward production goals and effective work schedules, the efficiency of employees can be maximized.

Interaction among Variances

Interactions among variances often occur, making it even more difficult to determine the responsibility for a particular variance. To illustrate, consider the following anecdote from a manufacturer of brass musical instruments. The purchasing manager obtained a special price on brass alloy from a new supplier. When the material was placed into production, it turned out to be a lower grade of material than the production employees were used to. The alloy was of a slightly different composition, which made the material bend less easily during the formation of brass instruments. The company could have returned the material to the supplier, but that would have interrupted production and kept the division from filling its orders on time. Since using the off-standard material would not affect the quality of the company's finished products, the division manager decided to keep the material and make the best of the situation.

The ultimate result was that the company incurred four interrelated variances during May. The material was less expensive than normal, so the direct-material price variance was favourable. However, the employees had difficulty using the material, which resulted in more waste than expected, so the division incurred an unfavourable direct-material quantity variance.

What were the labour implications of the off-standard material? Due to the difficulty in working with the metal alloy, the employees required more than the standard amount of time to form the instruments. This resulted in an unfavourable direct-labour efficiency variance. Finally, the production supervisor had to use his most senior employees to work with the off-standard material. Since these people earned relatively high wages, the direct-labour rate variance was also unfavourable.

To summarize, the purchase of off-standard material resulted in the following interrelated variances:

Purchase of off-standard material $\longrightarrow$
$\begin{cases}
\text{Favourable direct-material price variance} \\
\text{Unfavourable direct-material quantity variance} \\
\text{Unfavourable direct-labour rate variance} \\
\text{Unfavourable direct-labour efficiency variance}
\end{cases}$

Such interactions of variances make it more difficult to assign responsibility for any particular variance.

Trade-Offs among Variances   Does the incident described above mean that the decision to buy and use the off-standard material was a poor one? Not necessarily. Perhaps these variances were anticipated, and a conscious decision was made to buy the material anyway. How could this be a wise decision? Suppose the amounts of the variances were as follows:

$(8,500)	Favourable direct-material price variance
1,000	Unfavourable direct-material quantity variance
2,000	Unfavourable direct-labour rate variance
1,500	Unfavourable direct-labour efficiency variance
$(4,000)	Favourable net overall variance

The company saved money overall on the decision to use a different grade of brass alloy. Given that the quality of the final product was not affected, the company's management acted wisely.

Standard Costs and Product Costing

Learning Objective   **11**

Explain how standard costs are used in product costing, and summarize some advantages and some criticisms of standard costing.

Our discussion of standard costing has focused on its use in controlling costs. But firms that use standard costs for control also use them for product costing. Recall from Chapter 3 that *product costing* is the process of accumulating the costs of a production process and assigning them to the completed products. Product costs are used for various purposes in both financial and managerial accounting.

As production takes place, product costs are added to the work-in-process inventory account. The flow of product costs through a firm's manufacturing accounts is depicted in Exhibit 9–17.

Exhibit 9–17
Flow of Product Costs through
Manufacturing Accounts

*Cost of goods sold is an expense. Although it is more descriptive, the term *cost of goods sold expense* is not used as much in practice as the simpler term *cost of goods sold*.

Different types of product-costing systems are distinguished by the type of costs that are entered into work-in-process inventory. In Chapter 3, we studied *actual costing* and *normal* costing systems. In these product-costing systems, the *actual* costs of direct material and direct labour are charged to work-in-process inventory. In a **standard-costing system**, the *standard* costs of direct material and direct labour are entered into work-in-process inventory.

Evaluation of Standard Costing

Standard costing has been the predominant accounting system in manufacturing companies, for both cost control and product-costing purposes, for several decades. This remains true today, and the use of standard costing is spreading to nonmanufacturing firms as well. The widespread use of standard costing over such a long time period suggests that it has traditionally been perceived as offering several advantages. However, today's manufacturing environment is changing dramatically. Some managers are calling into question the usefulness of the traditional standard-costing approach. They argue that the role of standard-costing systems must change.

Advantages of Standard Costing

Some advantages traditionally attributed to standard costing include the following:

- Standard costs provide a basis for *sensible cost comparisons*. As we discussed earlier, it would make no sense to compare budgeted costs at one (planned) activity level with actual costs incurred at a different (actual) activity level. Standard costs enable the management accountant to compute the standard allowed cost, given actual output, which then serves as a sensible benchmark to compare with the actual cost.
- Computation of standard costs and cost variances facilitates *management by exception*. This approach conserves valuable management time.
- Variances provide a means of *performance evaluation* and rewards for employees.
- Since the variances are used in performance evaluation, they provide *motivation* for employees to adhere to standards.
- Use of standard costs in product costing results in *more stable product costs* than if actual production costs are used. Actual costs often fluctuate erratically, whereas standard costs are changed only periodically.
- A standard-costing system is usually *less expensive* than an actual or normal product-costing system.

COST OF OWNERSHIP

Texas Instruments has developed a supplier rating system referred to as CETRAQ, which stands for cost, environmental responsibility, technology, responsiveness, assurance of supply, and quality. The company's vendors are regularly measured on these six criteria.

The Northrop Grumman Aircraft Division tracks various elements of the total cost of ownership (TCO)* through its cost-based Supplier Performance Rating System (SPRS). Among the cost factors measured by the SPRS are the costs Northrop incurs due to suppliers' hardware, paperwork, or delivery deficiencies. Any "non-conformance event is assigned a standard cost based on industrial engineering studies of the hours required to resolve the problem."

This Texas Instruments manufacturing facility relies on its suppliers for high-quality raw materials delivered on a timely basis. Texas Instruments, like many other companies, uses a sophisticated supplier rating system to measure the performance of its vendors.

At a Spennymore, England, plant owned by Black & Decker, the company "has integrated the cost-of-ownership concept into its activity-based costing system." Among the TCO issues included are quality, delivery, flexibility, and customer service. Also considered is a supplier's billing reliability. One Spennymore manager noted, "You can be dealing with the best company in the world in terms of quality, but if they can't get their invoices right, you're going to have trouble doing business with them."

*The total cost of ownership includes all costs incurred in order to have materials in place and ready for use in production, including the purchase price; transportation cost; and costs of ordering, receiving, inspecting, and storing the materials."[6]

Like any tool, a standard-costing system can be misused. When employees are criticized for every cost variance, the positive motivational effects will quickly vanish. Moreover, if standards are not revised often enough, they will become outdated. Then the benefits of cost benchmarks and product costing will disappear.

Criticisms of Standard Costing

Listed below are several drawbacks attributed to standard costing in an advanced manufacturing setting:[7]

- Some accountants argue that traditional standard costing is out of step with the philosophy of *activity-based management*. A production process comprises many activities, which result in costs. By focusing on the activities that cause costs to be incurred, by eliminating non-value-added activities, and by continually improving performance in value-added activities, costs will be minimized and profit maximized.[8]

- Traditional cost variances are also too aggregate in the sense that they are not tied to specific product lines or production batches. The aggregate nature of the variances makes it difficult for managers to determine the causes of the variances.

- Traditional standard-costing systems focus too much on the cost and efficiency of direct labour, which is rapidly becoming a relatively unimportant factor of production.

- An important condition for the successful use of standard costing is a stable production process. Yet the introduction of flexible manufacturing systems has reduced this stability, with frequent switching among products on the same production line.

- Traditional standard costs are not defined broadly enough to capture various important aspects of performance. For example, the standard direct-material price does not capture all of the *costs of ownership*. In addition to the purchase price and transportation costs, the *cost of ownership* includes the costs of ordering, paying bills, scheduling delivery, receiving, inspecting, handling and storing, and any production-line disruptions resulting from untimely or incorrect delivery.[9]

- Traditional standard-costing systems tend to focus too much on cost minimization, rather than on increasing product quality or improving customer service. For example, buying the least expensive materials of a given quality, in order to avoid a material price variance, may result in using a vendor whose delivery capabilities are not consistent with just-in-time (JIT) system requirements.

Focus on Ethics

SACRIFICING QUALITY TO CUT STANDARD COSTS

Pressures to control costs, coupled with bonus systems based on adherence to standards, can present the opportunity to engage in ethical lapses. The following hypothetical scenario describes such a situation.

Keystone Company manufactures small wooden household items such as cutting boards and knife racks. Keystone's controller, Marc Rigas, recently completed the installation of a new standard-costing system, which has been in place now for six months. Jack Smith, the purchasing manager, is about to place an order for wood to be used in Keystone's cutting boards. Smith has found a supplier that will furnish the necessary wood at $2 per board metre, rather than the standard cost of $3. This is very appealing to Smith, since his annual bonus is influenced by any favourable price variances he is able to obtain. Smith is due to be transferred at the end of the year to Keystone's Medicine Hat Division, which manufactures metal kitchen utensils. The transfer is a promotion for Smith.

After further discussions with the potential supplier, Smith realized that the wood being offered would not be well suited for cutting boards. Although the wood would seem fine in the manufacturing process, and it would result in an attractive product, it would not hold up well. After repeated cycles of getting wet and drying out, it would tend to crack. Smith figured that it might take about a year for the boards to deteriorate, and then Keystone Company would be beset with customer complaints.

Smith mulled over the situation for a while and then decided to accept the new supplier's offer. The $2 price would help him get a nice annual bonus, which he could use to help with the down payment on a new home. By the time the boards cracked and customers started to complain, he would be long gone. Someone else could worry about it then, he reasoned. After all, he thought, people shouldn't expect a cutting board to last forever.

Several weeks later, when the invoice for the first shipment of wood came through, Rigas noticed the large, favourable price variance. When he ran into Smith on the golf course, Rigas congratulated Smith on the purchase. The following conversation resulted:

Rigas: "That was quite a price break on that wood, Jack. How'd you swing it?"

Smith: "Hard-ball negotiating, Marc. It's as simple as that."

Rigas: "Is it good wood? And how about the supplier, Jack? Will they deliver on time?"

Smith: "This supplier is very timely in their deliveries. I made sure of that."

Rigas: "How about the quality, Jack? Did you check into that?"

Smith: "Sure I did, Marc. Hey, what is this? An interrogation? I thought we were here to play golf."

Rigas was left feeling puzzled and disconcerted by Smith's evasiveness. The next day, Rigas talked to the production manager, Amy Wilcox, about his concerns. Later that day, Wilcox raised the issue with Smith. After a lengthy and sometimes heated exchange, the story came out.

Discuss the ethical issues involved in this scenario. Did the purchasing manager, Jack Smith, act

ethically? Did the controller, Marc Rigas, act ethically when he asked Smith about the quality of the wood? Did Rigas act ethically when he went to the production manager with his concerns? What should the controller do now?

Chapter Summary

LO1 Explain how standard costing is used to help manage costs, and describe ways to set standards. The management accountant works with others in the organization to set standard costs for direct material, direct labour, and manufacturing overhead through either historical cost analysis, task analysis, or a combination of the two methods. The accountant then uses the standard cost as a benchmark against which to compare actual costs incurred. Managers use management by exception to determine the causes of significant cost variances.

LO2 Compute and interpret the direct-material price and direct-labour variances. The direct-material price variance calculates the effect on production cost of deviations between actual and standard direct-material prices. The direct-material quantity variance calculates the effect on production cost of deviations between actual and standard direct-material quantities allowed, given actual production output. The direct-labour rate variance calculates the effect on production cost of deviations between actual and standard direct-labour rates. The direct-labour efficiency variance calculates the effect on production cost of deviations between actual and standard direct-labour hours allowed, given actual production output.

LO3 Distinguish between static and flexible budgets, and explain the advantages of a flexible-overhead budget. A static budget is based on a single, predicted volume of production activity. A flexible budget allows for many possible activity levels. The flexible-overhead budget is based on some activity measure that varies in a pattern similar to that of variable overhead. The management accountant uses the amount of overhead cost specified by the flexible budget, given actual output, as a benchmark against which to compare actual overhead costs.

LO4 Prepare a flexible-overhead budget and explain how overhead is applied to work-in-process inventory. A columnar flexible budget is based on several distinct activity levels, while a formula flexible budget is valid for a continuous range of activity. The flexible-overhead budget is based on some activity measure that varies in a pattern similar to that of variable overhead.

LO5 Explain some important issues in choosing an activity measure for overhead budgeting and application. The flexible-overhead budget is based on some activity measure that varies in a pattern similar to that of variable overhead. Machine hours, process time, and direct-labour hours are common activity bases.

LO6 Compute and interpret the variable-overhead and fixed-overhead variances. The variable-overhead spending variance calculates the effect on production cost of deviations between the actual and standard variable-overhead rates. The variable-overhead efficiency variance calculates the effect on production cost of deviations between actual and standard amounts of the cost driver, multiplied by the standard variable-overhead rate. The fixed-overhead budget variance calculates the effect on production cost of deviations between actual and budgeted fixed overhead. The fixed-overhead volume variance calculates the effect of deviations between budgeted and applied fixed overhead.

LO7 Prepare an overhead cost performance report. The overhead cost performance report shows the actual and budgeted costs for each overhead item, along with the four overhead variances: the variable-overhead spending and efficiency variances, and the fixed-overhead budget and volume variances. These variances help management to control overhead costs.

LO8 Explain how an activity-based flexible budget differs from a conventional flexible budget. In an activity-based flexible budget, each overhead item may have a different cost driver identified on which the flexible-overhead budget for that cost item is based. Such a flexible budget is more accurate than conventional flexible budgets, because multiple cost drivers are identified to explain the behaviour of overhead costs.

LO9 Explain several methods for determining the significance of cost variances. Managers determine the significance of cost variances through judgment and rules of thumb. The absolute and relative sizes of variances, recurrence of variances, variance trends, and controllability of variances are all considered in deciding whether variances warrant investigation. In some cases a statistical control chart can help determine the significance of cost variances.

LO10 Describe some behavioural effects of standard costing. Variances that affect employees' reward structures, such as pay increases or promotions, can significantly affect employee behaviour. For example, an unfavourable direct-material price variance may cause a purchasing manager to purchase a lower quality of material than is specified or needed.

LO11 Explain how standard costs are used in product costing, and summarize some advantages and some criticisms of standard costing. The management accountant achieves the product-costing purpose of the standard-costing system by entering the standard cost of production into work-in-process inventory as a product cost. This standard cost then flows through the finished-goods inventory account and into the cost of goods sold account. Standard-costing systems offer an organization many advantages. Among these are sensible cost comparisons, management by exception, performance evaluation, employee motivation, and more stable product costs. Some common criticisms of standard costing include too high a level of aggregation exhibited by variances, untimely reporting of variances, excessive focus on direct labour, inconsistency with flexible manufacturing systems, quick outdating of standards, narrow focus of standard costs, such as ignoring the total cost of ownership, and an excessive focus on cost minimization.

Review Problem on Standard Costing

In November, DCdesserts produced 3,000 multilayered fancy cakes, used 9,100 hours of process time, and incurred the following actual costs for direct material, direct labour, and manufacturing overhead:

Purchased 16,500 kilograms of ingredients at $1.44 per kilogram.

Used 15,500 kilograms of ingredients at $1.44 per kilogram.

Used 1,520 hours of direct labour at $22 per hour.

Variable overhead $45,955

Fixed overhead $15,800

The standard costs for production of multilayer fancy cakes were the same in November as those given in Exhibit 9–6.

Compute DCdesserts' direct-material and direct-labour variances for November using the format shown in Exhibits 9–2 and 9–3, and the variable-overhead and fixed-overhead variances using the format shown in Exhibits 9–9 and 9–11.

Solutions to Review Problem

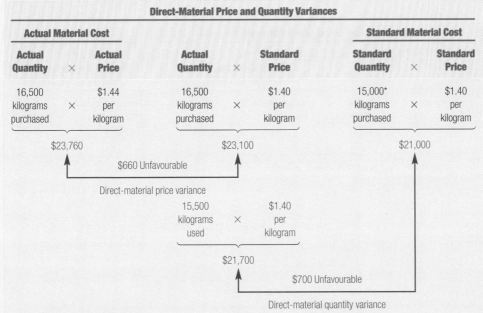

*Actual output × Standard quantity per unit = 3,000 units × 5 kilograms per unit = 15,000 kilograms allowed.

Using Formulas

$$\text{Direct-material price variance} = AQ_p \times (AP - SP)$$
$$= 16{,}500 \times (\$1.44 - \$1.40)$$
$$= \$660 \text{ Unfavourable}$$

$$\text{Direct-material quantity variance} = SP \times (AQ_u - SQ)$$
$$= \$1.40 \times (15{,}500 - 15{,}000)$$
$$= \$700 \text{ Unfavourable}$$

Direct-Labour Rate and Efficiency Variances

Actual Labour Cost				**Standard Labour Cost**	
Actual Hours × **Actual Rate**		**Actual Hours** × **Standard Rate**		**Standard Hours** × **Standard Rate**	
1,520 hours used × $22 per hour		1,520 hours used × $20 per hour		1,500* hours used × $20 per hour	
$33,440		$30,400		$30,000	
	$3,040 Unfavourable		$400 Unfavourable		
	Direct-labour rate variance		Direct-labour efficiency variance		

*Actual output × Standard quantity per unit = 3,000 units × 0.5 hour per unit = 1,500 hours allowed.

Using Formulas

$$\text{Direct-labour rate variance} = AH \times (AR - SR)$$
$$= 1{,}520 \times (\$22 - \$20)$$
$$= \$3{,}040 \text{ Unfavourable}$$

$$\text{Direct-labour efficiency variance} = SR \times (AH - SH)$$
$$= \$20 \times (1{,}520 - 1{,}500)$$
$$= \$400 \text{ Unfavourable}$$

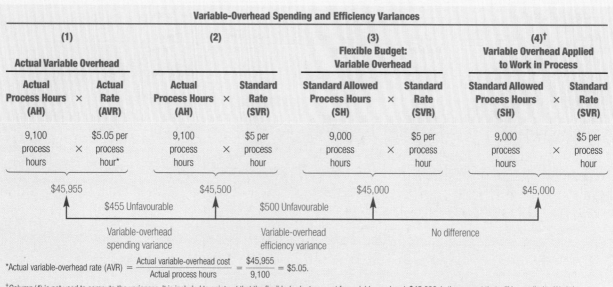

Variable-Overhead Spending and Efficiency Variances

(1)		(2)		(3)		(4)†	
Actual Variable Overhead				**Flexible Budget: Variable Overhead**		**Variable Overhead Applied to Work in Process**	
Actual Process Hours (AH) × **Actual Rate (AVR)**		**Actual Process Hours (AH)** × **Standard Rate (SVR)**		**Standard Allowed Process Hours (SH)** × **Standard Rate (SVR)**		**Standard Allowed Process Hours (SH)** × **Standard Rate (SVR)**	
9,100 process hours × $5.05 per process hour*		9,100 process hours × $5 per process hour		9,000 process hours × $5 per process hour		9,000 process hours × $5 per process hour	
$45,955		$45,500		$45,000		$45,000	
	$455 Unfavourable		$500 Unfavourable				
	Variable-overhead spending variance		Variable-overhead efficiency variance		No difference		

*Actual variable-overhead rate (AVR) = $\dfrac{\text{Actual variable-overhead cost}}{\text{Actual process hours}} = \dfrac{\$45{,}955}{9{,}100} = \$5.05.$

†Column (4) is not used to compute the variances. It is included to point out that the flexible-budget amount for variable overhead, $45,000, is the amount that will be applied to Work-in-Process Inventory for product-costing purposes.

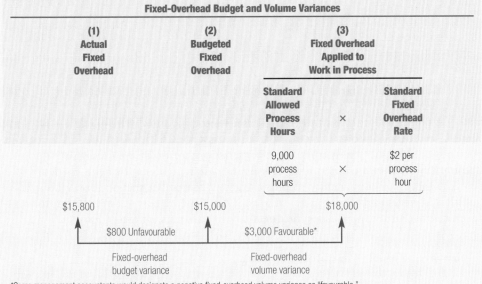

Fixed-Overhead Budget and Volume Variances

(1) Actual Fixed Overhead	(2) Budgeted Fixed Overhead	(3) Fixed Overhead Applied to Work in Process	
		Standard Allowed Process Hours	Standard Fixed Overhead Rate
		$\times$	
		9,000 process hours	$2 per process hour
		$\times$	
$15,800	$15,000	$18,000	

$800 Unfavourable $3,000 Favourable*

Fixed-overhead   Fixed-overhead
budget variance   volume variance

*Some management accountants would designate a negative fixed-overhead volume variance as "favourable."

Glossary ———————————————————————————

Review key terms and definitions on Connect.

APPENDIX A TO CHAPTER 9

Standard Costs and Product Costing

In a standard-costing system, the standard costs are used for product costing as well as for cost control. The costs of direct material, direct labour, and manufacturing overhead are all entered into work-in-process inventory at their standard costs. (Review Exhibit 9–7.)

Learning Objective **12**

Prepare journal entries to record and close out cost variances.

DC desserts

[Journal Entries under Standard Costing]

To illustrate the use of standard costs in product costing, we will continue our DCdesserts example. The following journal entries record the information shown in Exhibit 9–2 and isolate the direct-material price and quantity variances:

Raw-material inventory	17,500	
Direct-material price variance	250	
Accounts payable		17,750
To record the purchase of raw material and the incurrence of an unfavourable price variance.		

Work-in-process inventory	14,000	
Direct-material quantity variance	350	
Raw-material inventory		14,350
To record the use of direct material in production and the incurrence of an unfavourable quantity variance.		

Notice that the material purchase is recorded in the raw-material inventory account at its standard price ($17,500 = 12,500 kilograms purchased × $1.40 per kilogram). The $14,000 debit entry to work-in-process inventory adds only the standard cost of the material to work-in-process inventory as a product cost ($14,000 = 10,000 kilograms allowed × $1.40 per kilogram). The two variances are isolated in their own variance accounts. Since they are both unfavourable, they are represented by debit entries.

The following journal entry records the actual September cost of direct labour, as an addition to wages payable. The entry also adds the standard cost of direct labour to work-in-process inventory and isolates the direct-labour variances, shown in Exhibit 9–3.

Work-in-process inventory	20,000	
Direct-labour rate variance	980	
Direct-labour efficiency variance		400
Wages payable		20,580
To record the usage of direct labour and the direct-labour variances for September.		

Since the direct-labour efficiency variance is favourable, it is recorded as a credit entry.

For September's production of multilayer fancy cakes, the company incurred actual manufacturing-overhead costs of $50,750, which includes $34,650 of variable overhead and $16,100 of fixed overhead. A summary journal entry to record these actual expenditures follows:

Manufacturing overhead	50,750	
Indirect-material inventory		23,290*
Wages payable		20,610*
Utilities payable		4,960
Accumulated depreciation		500
Prepaid insurance and property taxes		100
Test kitchen salaries payable		1,290

*The credit amounts can be verified in column (4) of Exhibit 9–13. For example, indirect-material costs amounted to $23,290 ($12,700 + $2,090 + $2,000 + $6,500). The credit to wages payable is for indirect-labour costs, which amounted to $20,610 ($6,400 + $2,210 + $7,000 + $3,000 + $2,000).

The application of manufacturing overhead to work-in-process inventory is based on a predetermined overhead rate of $7 per process hour (the total of the variable and the fixed rates) and 6,000 standard allowed process hours, given an actual output of 2,000 multilayered fancy cakes. The summary journal entry is as follows:

Work-in-process inventory	42,000	
Manufacturing overhead		42,000*

*Applied overhead = $7 × 6,000 = $42,000

Now the manufacturing-overhead account appears as follows:

Manufacturing Overhead			
Actual	$50,750	$42,000	Applied

The *underapplied overhead* for September is $8,750 ($50,750 − $42,000). This means that the overhead applied to work-in-process inventory in September was $8,750 less than the actual overhead cost incurred. Notice that the underapplied overhead is equal to the sum of the four overhead variances for September, shown in

Exhibits 9–9 and 9–11. The total of the four overhead variances will always be equal to the overapplied or underapplied overhead for the accounting period.

Variable-overhead spending variance	$3,150 Unfavourable
Variable-overhead efficiency variance	$1,500 Unfavourable
Fixed-overhead budget variance	$1,100 Unfavourable
Fixed-overhead volume variance	$3,000 Unfavourable
Underapplied overhead	$8,750

Disposition of Variances

Variances are temporary accounts and most companies close them directly into cost of goods sold at the end of each accounting period. The journal entry required to close out the September variances is as follows:

Cost of goods sold	9,930	
Direct-labour efficiency variance	400	
Direct-material price variance		250
Direct-material quantity variance		350
Direct-labour rate variance		980
Manufacturing overhead		8,750

The journal entry to dispose of the variances and close out underapplied or overapplied overhead typically is made annually, rather than monthly.

An alternative accounting treatment is to prorate the variances and the underapplied or overapplied overhead among work-in-process inventory, finished-goods inventory, and cost of goods sold.

Cost Flow under Standard Costing

In a standard-costing system, since standard costs are entered into work-in-process inventory, all of the product costs flowing through the accounts are standard costs. To illustrate, suppose DCdesserts produced 2,000 multilayer fancy cakes in September and sold all 2,000 of them. The journal entries to record the flow of standard costs are shown below:

Finished-goods inventory	76,000*	
Work-in-process inventory		76,000

*Total standard cost of direct material, direct labour, and variable and fixed overhead: $76,000 = $14,000 + $20,000 + $30,000 + $12,000.

Cost of goods sold	76,000*	
Finished-goods inventory		76,000

*All 2,000 multilayer fancy cakes were sold.

A Note on Perishable Products and JIT Production Management Systems

Traditional manufacturing systems typically exhibit the cost flows explained in this section. Direct-material, direct-labour, and manufacturing-overhead costs are entered in work-in-process inventory, from which they flow into finished-goods inventory when the goods are finished, and then on into cost of goods sold. Since DCdesserts produces perishable goods, which are produced and sold on the same day, a simpler procedure might be used. In DCdesserts' case, the *standard* costs of direct material, direct labour, and manufacturing overhead might be entered directly into cost of goods sold as they are incurred. This simplification is feasible because the production process is very short and the goods are sold immediately, and thus there is never any work-in-process inventory or finished-goods inventory on hand. Such situations are common with producers of perishable goods.

An analogous situation occurs with manufacturers that employ a just-in-time (JIT) production and inventory control system. In such an environment, raw materials are delivered just in time to be entered into production, and parts or components are manufactured in each stage of the production process just in time for the next stage. So, as in the case of perishable goods, there is little or no work-in-process or finished-goods inventory at any given time. For this reason, many manufacturers that use the JIT approach make use of highly simplified cost accounting procedures similar to those just explained for DCdesserts.

APPENDIX A SUMMARY

LO12 Prepare journal entries to record and close out cost variances. The management accountant prepares journal entries: to enter the standard cost of production into work-in-process inventory as a product cost; to transfer the standard production cost to finished-goods inventory; and to close the standard production cost into cost of goods sold.

APPENDIX B TO CHAPTER 9

Sales Variances

Learning Objective 13

Compute and interpret the sales-price and sales-volume variances.

The variances discussed in this chapter focus on production costs. Management accountants also compute variances to help management analyze the firm's sales performance. To illustrate two commonly used sales variances, we will continue our discussion of DCdesserts. The expected sales price and standard variable cost for a multilayered fancy cake are as follows:

Budgeted sales price	$38
Standard variable costs:	
Direct material (1.4 kilograms × $5 per kilogram)..	$ 7
Direct labour (0.5 hour × $20 per hour)...	10
Variable overhead (3 process hours at $5 per hour)	15
Total unit variable cost	$32

During October, management expects to sell 1,500 multilayered fancy cakes. Based on this sales forecast, the controller computed the following budgeted **total contribution margin**:

Budgeted sales revenue (1,500 multilayered fancy cakes × $38)	$57,000
Budgeted variable costs (1,500 multilayered fancy cakes × $32)	48,000
Budgeted total contribution margin (1,500 multilayered fancy cakes × $6)	$ 9,000

The *actual* results for October were as follows:

Actual sales volume	1,600 cakes
Actual sales price	$37
Actual unit variable cost	$32

Using these actual results, the actual total contribution margin for October is as follows:

Actual sales revenue (1,600 multilayered fancy cakes × $37)	$59,200
Actual variable costs (1,600 multilayered fancy cakes × $32)	51,200
Actual total contribution margin (1,600 multilayered fancy cakes × $5)	$ 8,000

DCdesserts' actual and budgeted results for October are summarized in the following table. Notice that actual sales revenue exceeded budgeted sales revenue by $2,200. However, this favourable variance was more than offset by the additional $3,200 in variable costs resulting from actual sales volume exceeding budgeted sales volume. So the actual total contribution margin was $1,000 less than the budgeted total contribution margin, as this table shows:

	Budget	Actual	Variance
Revenue	$57,000	$59,200	$2,200 F
Variable costs	48,000	51,200	3,200 U
Contribution margin	$ 9,000	$ 8,000	$1,000 U

The management accountant computes two sales variances to explain the $2,200 favourable variance in sales revenue. These variances are defined and computed as follows:

$$\text{Sales-price variance} = \left(\begin{array}{ccc} \text{Actual} & & \text{Budgeted} \\ \text{sales} & - & \text{sales} \\ \text{price} & & \text{price} \end{array} \right) \times \text{Actual sales volume}$$

$$= \quad (\$37 \quad - \quad \$38) \quad \times \quad 1,600$$

$$= \quad \$1,600 \text{ Unfavourable}$$

$$\text{Sales-volume variance} = \left(\begin{array}{ccc} \text{Actual} & & \text{Budgeted} \\ \text{sales} & - & \text{sales} \\ \text{volume} & & \text{volume} \end{array} \right) \times \text{Budgeted sales price}$$

$$= \quad (1,600 \quad - \quad 1,500) \quad \times \quad \$38$$

$$= \quad \$3,800 \text{ Favourable}$$

Together, the **sales-price variance** and **sales-volume variance** explain the $2,200 favourable variance between actual and budgeted sales revenue.

Sales-price variance	$1,600 Unfavourable
Sales-volume variance	3,800 Favourable
Variance between actual and budgeted sales revenue	$2,200 Favourable

With information about the market, the sales-volume variance can be further broken down into a **market-share variance** and a **market-volume variance**. The market-share variance represents the effect on sales revenue of DCdesserts' market share being different from what was expected at the beginning of the year. The market-volume variance represents the effect on sales revenue of the total market size being different from what was expected at the beginning of the year. Let us assume that the actual market volume and the expected (budgeted) market volume for multilayered fancy cakes are as follows:

	Market Volume
Actual	16,000 cakes
Budget	18,750 cakes

The management accountant computes the following two sales variances to explain the $3,800 favourable sales-volume variance. These variances are defined and computed as follows:

$$\text{Market-share variance} = \begin{pmatrix} \text{Actual} \\ \text{sales} \\ \text{volume} \end{pmatrix} - \begin{pmatrix} \text{Actual} \\ \text{market} \times \frac{\text{Budgeted}}{\text{market}} \\ \text{volume} \quad \text{share} \end{pmatrix} \times \text{Budgeted sales price}$$

$$= 1,600 - [16,000 \times (1,500 \div 18,750)] \times \$38$$
$$= 1,600 - [16,000 \times 8\%] \times \$38$$
$$= \$12,160 \text{ Favourable}$$

$$\text{Market-volume variance} = \begin{pmatrix} \text{Actual} \\ \text{market} - \frac{\text{Budgeted}}{\text{market}} \\ \text{volume} \quad \text{volume} \end{pmatrix} \times \begin{pmatrix} \text{Budgeted} \\ \text{market} \\ \text{share} \end{pmatrix} \times \text{Budgeted sales price}$$

$$= (16,000 - 18,750) \times (1,500 \div 18,750) \times \$38$$
$$= -2,750 \times 8\% \times \$38$$
$$= \$8,360 \text{ Unfavourable}$$

Together, the market-share and market-volume variances explain the $3,800 favourable sales-volume variance.

Market-share variance	$12,160 Favourable
Market-volume variance	8,360 Unfavourable
Sales-volume variance	$3,800 Favourable

So, while the actual market size (16,000 cakes) was smaller than expected at the beginning of the year (18,750 cakes), DCdesserts captured a larger market share (10% = 1,600 ÷ 16,000) than budgeted at the beginning of the year (8%), allowing for a favourable sales-volume variance.

APPENDIX B SUMMARY

LO13 Compute and interpret the sales-price and sales-volume variances. The sales-price variance is the difference between the actual and budgeted sales prices multiplied by the actual sales volume. This variance measures the effect on sales revenue of sales-price deviations. The sales-volume variance is the difference between the actual and budgeted sales volumes multiplied by the budgeted sales price. This variance measures the effect on sales revenue of deviations in sales volume.

Review Questions

9–1. List the three parts of a control system, and explain how such a system works.

9–2. What is meant by the phrase *management by exception*?

9–3. Describe two methods of setting standards.

9–4. Distinguish between perfection and practical standards. Which type of standard is likely to produce the best motivational effects?

9–5. Explain how standard material prices and quantities are set.

9–6. What is the interpretation of the direct-material price variance? What manager is usually in the best position to influence the direct-material price variance?

9–7. What is the interpretation of the direct-material quantity variance? What manager is usually in the best position to influence the direct-material quantity variance?

9–8. Explain why the quantity purchased (AQ_p) is used in computing the direct-material price variance, but the actual quantity consumed (AQ_u) is used in computing the direct-material quantity variance.

9–9. What is the interpretation of the direct-labour rate variance? What are some possible causes? What manager is generally in the best position to influence the direct-labour rate variance?

9–10. What is the interpretation of the direct-labour efficiency variance? What manager is generally in the best position to influence the direct-labour efficiency variance?

9–11. Distinguish between static and flexible budgets. Explain the advantage of using a flexible budget.

9–12. Why are flexible-overhead budgets based on an activity measure, such as hours of process time, machine time, or direct-labour hours?

9–13. What is the interpretation of the variable-overhead spending variance?

9–14. Jeffries Company's only variable-overhead cost is electricity. Does an unfavourable variable-overhead spending variance imply that the company paid more than the anticipated rate per kilowatt-hour?

9–15. What is the interpretation of the variable-overhead efficiency variance? Distinguish between the interpretations of the direct labour and variable-overhead efficiency variances.

9–16. What is the fixed-overhead budget variance? What is the correct interpretation of the fixed-overhead volume variance?

9–17. Describe a common but misleading interpretation of the fixed-overhead volume variance. Why is this interpretation misleading?

9–18. What types of organizations use flexible budgets?

9–19. Distinguish between the control purpose and the product-costing purpose of standard costing and flexible budgeting.

9–20. Why are fixed-overhead costs sometimes called *capacity-producing costs*?

9–21. Give one example of a plausible activity base to use in flexible budgeting for each of the following organizations: an insurance company, an express delivery service, a restaurant, and the Canada Revenue Agency (CRA).

9–22. Explain how an activity-based flexible budget differs from a conventional flexible budget.

Exercises

Exercise 9–23 Straightforward Computation of Variances (L02)

Saskatchewan Can Company manufactures recyclable soft-drink cans. A unit of production is a case of 12 dozen cans. The following standards have been set by the production-engineering staff and the controller:

Direct labour:	Direct material:
Quantity, 0.25 hour	Quantity, 4 kilograms
Rate, $16 per hour	Price, $0.80 per kilogram

Actual material purchases amounted to 240,000 kilograms at $0.81 per kilogram. Actual costs incurred in the production of 50,000 units were as follows:

Direct labour	$211,900 for 13,000 hours
Direct material	$170,180 for 210,000 kilograms

Required:

1. Use the variance formulas to compute the direct-material price and quantity variances and the direct labour rate and efficiency variances. Indicate whether each variance is favourable or unfavourable.

2. *Build a spreadsheet:* Construct an Excel spreadsheet to solve the preceding requirement. Show how the solution will change if the following information changes: The standard direct-labour rate is $15 per hour, and the standard direct-material price is $0.79 per kilogram.

Exercise 9–24 Determination of Variances Using Diagrams (L02)

Refer to the data in the preceding exercise. Use diagrams similar to those in Exhibits 9–2 and 9–3 to determine the direct-material and direct-labour variances. Indicate whether each variance is favourable or unfavourable.

Exercise 9–25 Developing Standards for New Products: Use of the Internet (L01)

Choose one of the following manufacturers (or any manufacturer of your choosing), and use the Internet to gather information about any new products the company has recently introduced or plans to introduce.

Boeing	www.boeing.com	Kodak	www.kodak.com
Caterpillar	www.caterpillar.com	Pfizer	www.pfizer.com
Ford	www.ford.com	Xerox	www.xerox.com

Required: Discuss the steps you think the company would have to take to establish standard costs for its new products.

Exercise 9–26 Computing Standard Direct-Material Cost (L02)

Cayuga Hardwoods produces handcrafted jewellery boxes. A standard-size box requires 8 board metres of hardwood in the finished product. In addition, 2 board metres of scrap lumber are normally left from the production of one box. Hardwood costs $4 per board metre, plus $1.50 in transportation charges per board metre.

Required: Compute the standard direct-material cost of a jewellery box.

Exercise 9–27 Straightforward Calculation of Variances (LO2)

During June, Danby Company's material purchases amounted to 6,000 kilograms at a price of $7.30 per kilogram. Actual costs incurred in the production of 2,000 units were as follows:

Direct labour: $116,745 ($18.10 per hour)
Direct material: $30,660 ($7.30 per kilogram)

The standards for one unit of Danby Company's product are as follows:

Direct labour:
   Quantity, 3 hours per unit
   Rate, $18 per hour
Direct material:
   Quantity, 2 kilograms per unit
    Price, $7 per kilogram

Required: Compute the direct-material price and quantity variances and the direct-labour rate and efficiency variances. Indicate whether each variance is favourable or unfavourable.

Exercise 9–28 Diagramming Direct-Material and Direct-Labour Variances (LO2)

Refer to the data in the preceding exercise. Draw diagrams depicting the direct-material and direct-labour variances similar to the diagrams in Exhibits 9–2 and 9–3.

Exercise 9–29 Standard Allowed Input (LO2)

Due to evaporation during production, Plano Plastics Company requires 8 kilograms of material input for every 7 kilograms of good plastic sheets manufactured. During May, the company produced 4,200 kilograms of good sheets.

Required: Compute the total standard allowed input quantity, given the good output produced.

Exercise 9–30 Reconstructing Standard-Cost Information from Partial Data (LO2)

Part of your company's accounting database was destroyed when Godzilla attacked the city. You have been able to gather the following data from your files. Reconstruct the remaining information using the available data. All of the raw material purchased during the period was used in production. (*Hint:* It is helpful to solve for the unknowns in the order indicated by the letters in the following table.)

	Direct Material	Direct Labour
Standard price or rate per unit of input	$8 per kilogram	e
Standard quantity per unit of output	c	f
Actual quantity used per unit of output	a	3.5 hours
Actual price or rate per unit of input	$7 per kilogram	$21 per hour
Actual output	10,000 units	10,000 units
Direct-material price variance	$30,000 F	—
Direct-material quantity variance	b	—
Total of direct-material variances	$10,000 F	—
Direct-labour rate variance	—	d
Direct-labour efficiency variance	—	$100,000 Favourable
Total of direct-labour variances	—	$65,000 Favourable

Exercise 9–31 Straightforward Computation of Overhead Variances (LO6)

Crystal Glassware Company has the following standards and flexible-budget data:

Standard variable-overhead rate	$6.00 per direct-labour hour
Standard quantity of direct labour	2 hours per unit of output
Budgeted fixed overhead	$100,000
Budgeted output	25,000 units

Actual results for April are as follows:

Actual output	20,000 units
Actual variable overhead	$320,000
Actual fixed overhead	$97,000
Actual direct labour	50,000 hours

Required:

1. Use the variance formulas to compute the following variances. Indicate whether each variance is favourable or unfavourable, where appropriate.
   a. Variable-overhead spending variance
   b. Variable-overhead efficiency variance
   c. Fixed-overhead budget variance
   d. Fixed-overhead volume variance

Exercise 9–32 Diagram of Overhead Variances (LO6)

Refer to the data in the preceding exercise. Use diagrams similar to those in Exhibits 9–9 and 9–11 to compute the variable-overhead spending and efficiency variances, and the fixed-overhead budget and volume variances.

Exercise 9–33 Graphing Overhead Variances (LO6)

Refer to the data in Exercise 9–31 for Crystal Glassware Company. Draw graphs similar to those in Exhibit 9–10 (variable overhead) and Exhibit 9–12 (fixed overhead) to depict the overhead variances.

Exercise 9–34 Straightforward Computation of Overhead Variances (LO6)

The following data are the actual results for Marvellous Marshmallow Company for October:

Actual output	9,000 cases
Actual variable overhead	$405,000
Actual fixed overhead	$122,000
Actual machine time	40,500 machine hours

Standard cost and budget information for Marvellous Marshmallow Company follows:

Standard variable-overhead rate	$9 per machine hour
Standard quantity of machine hours	4 hours per case of marshmallows
Budgeted fixed overhead	$120,000 per month
Budgeted output	10,000 cases per month

Required:

1. Use any of the methods explained in the chapter to compute the following variances. Indicate whether each variance is favourable or unfavourable, where appropriate.
   a. Variable-overhead spending variance
   b. Variable-overhead efficiency variance
   c. Fixed-overhead budget variance
   d. Fixed-overhead volume variance

2. *Build a spreadsheet:* Construct an Excel spreadsheet to solve the preceding requirement. Show how the solution will change based on the following information changes: Actual output was 9,100 cases, and actual variable overhead was $395,000.

Exercise 9–35 Standard Hours Allowed; Flexible Budgeting: Multiple Products (LO3, 4)

Outdoor Optics Company produces binoculars of two quality levels: field and professional. The field model requires four direct-labour hours, while the professional binoculars require six hours. The firm uses direct-labour hours for flexible budgeting.

Required:

1. How many standard hours are allowed in May, when 200 field models and 300 professional binoculars are manufactured?

2. Suppose the company based its flexible-overhead budget for May on the number of binoculars manufactured, which is 500. What difficulties would this approach cause?

Exercise 9–36 Construct a Flexible-Overhead Budget: Hospital (LO4)

The controller for Rainbow Children's Hospital, located in Munich, Germany, estimates that the hospital uses 30 kilowatt-hours of electricity per patient-day, and that the electric rate will be 0.10 euros per kilowatt-hour. The hospital also pays a fixed monthly charge of 1,000 euros to the electric utility to rent emergency backup electric generators.

Required: Construct a flexible budget for the hospital's electricity costs using each of the following techniques:

1. Formula flexible budget.
2. Columnar flexible budget for 30,000, 40,000 and 50,000 patient-days of activity. List variable and fixed electricity costs separately.

Exercise 9–37 Interpretation of Variable-Overhead Efficiency Variance (LO6)

You recently received the following note from the production supervisor of the company where you work as controller. "I don't understand these crazy variable-overhead efficiency variances. My employees are very careful in their use of electricity and manufacturing supplies, and we use very little indirect labour. What are we supposed to do?" Write a brief memo responding to the production supervisor's concern.

Exercise 9–38 Reconstruct Missing Information from Partial Data (LO3, 6)

You brought your work home one evening, and your nephew spilled his chocolate milkshake on the variance report you were preparing. Fortunately, you were able to reconstruct the obliterated information from the remaining data. Fill in the missing numbers below. (*Hint:* It is helpful to solve for the unknowns in the order indicated by the letters in the following table.)

Budgeted fixed overhead	$50,000
Actual fixed overhead	a
Budgeted production in units	25,000
Actual production in units	c
Standard machine hours per unit of output	4 hours
Standard variable-overhead rate per machine hour	$8
Actual variable-overhead rate per machine hour	b
Actual machine hours per unit of output	d
Variable-overhead spending variance	$ 72,000 Unfavourable
Variable-overhead efficiency variance	$ 192,000 Favourable
Fixed-overhead budget variance	$ 15,000 Unfavourable
Fixed-overhead volume variance	g
Total actual overhead	$713,000
Total budgeted overhead (flexible budget)	e
Total budgeted overhead (static budget)	f
Total applied overhead	$816,000

Exercise 9–39 Overhead Variances (LO6)

Montoursville Control Company, which manufactures electrical switches, uses a standard-costing system. The standard manufacturing-overhead costs per switch are based on direct-labour hours and are as follows:

Variable overhead (5 hrs. @ $8 per hr.)	$ 40
Fixed overhead (5 hrs. @ $12 per hr.)*	60
Total overhead	$100

*Based on capacity of 300,000 direct-labour hours per month.

The following information is available for the month of October:

- Variable-overhead costs were $2,340,000.
- Fixed-overhead costs were $3,750,000.
- 56,000 switches were produced, although 60,000 switches were scheduled to be produced.
- 275,000 direct-labour hours were worked at a total cost of $2,550,000.

Required: Compute the variable-overhead spending and efficiency variances and the fixed-overhead budget and volume variances for October. Indicate whether a variance is favourable or unfavourable where appropriate.

(CMA, adapted)

Exercise 9–40 Activity-Based Flexible Budget (LO8)

Refer to DCdesserts' activity-based flexible budget in Exhibit 9–14. Suppose that the company's activity in June is described as follows:

Process hours	7,500
Production runs	16
New products tested	30
Direct material handled (kilograms)	40,000

Required:

1. Determine the flexible budgeted cost for each of the following:
   - a. Indirect material
   - b. Utilities
   - c. Inspection
   - d. Test kitchen
   - e. Material handling
   - f. Total overhead cost

2. Compute the variance for setup cost during the month, assuming that the actual setup cost was $3,000:
   - a. Using the activity-based flexible budget.
   - b. Using DCdesserts' conventional flexible budget (Exhibit 9–6).

Exercise 9–41 Journal Entries under Standard Costing (Appendix A) (LO12)

Refer to the data in Exercise 9–23, regarding Saskatchewan Can Company. Prepare journal entries to

1. Record the purchase of direct material on account.
2. Add direct-material and direct-labour cost to work-in-process inventory.
3. Record the direct-material and direct-labour variances.
4. Close these variances into cost of goods sold.

Exercise 9–42 Posting Journal Entries for Variances (Appendix A) (LO12)

Refer to your answer for Exercise 9–41. Set up T-accounts, and post the journal entries to the general ledger.

Exercise 9–43 Journal Entries for Overhead (Appendix A) (LO12)

Refer to the data in Exercise 9–31 for Crystal Glassware Company. Prepare journal entries to

- Record the incurrence of actual variable overhead and actual fixed overhead.
- Add variable and fixed overhead to work-in-process inventory.
- Close underapplied or overapplied overhead into cost of goods sold.

Exercise 9–44 Sales Variances (Appendix B) (LO13)

The following data pertain to Alexis Electronics for the month of February:

	Static Budget	Actual
Units sold	10,000	9,000
Sales revenue	$ 120,000	$103,500
Variable manufacturing cost	$ 40,000	$ 36,000
Fixed manufacturing cost	$ 20,000	$ 20,000
Variable selling and administrative cost	$ 10,000	$ 9,000
Fixed selling and administrative cost	$ 10,000	$ 10,000

Required: Compute the sales-price and sales-volume variances for February.

Problems

Problem 9–45 Direct-Material and Direct-Labour Variances (LO2)

Jersey Valve Company manufactured 7,800 units during January of a control valve used by milk processors in its plant. Records indicated the following:

2. Direct-material quantity variance: $750 Favourable

Direct labour	40,100 hrs. @ $14.60 per hr.
Direct material purchased	25,000 kg @ $2.60 per kg
Direct material used	23,100 kg

The control valve has the following standard prime costs:

Direct material:	3 kg @ $2.50 per kg	$ 7.50
Direct labour:	5 hrs. @ $15.00 per hr.	75.00
Standard prime cost per unit		$82.50

Required:

1. Prepare a schedule of standard production costs for January, based on actual production of 7,800 units.
2. For the month of January, compute the following variances, indicating whether each is favourable or unfavourable:
    a. Direct-material price variance
    b. Direct-material quantity variance
    c. Direct-labour rate variance
    d. Direct-labour efficiency variance

3. *Build a spreadsheet:* Construct an Excel spreadsheet to solve all of the preceding requirements. Show how the solution will change if the following information changes: The standard direct-labour rate is $16 per hour, and the standard direct-material price is $2.60 per kilogram.

Problem 9–46 Determining Standard Material Cost **(LO2)**

South Atlantic Chemical Company manufactures industrial chemicals in Rio de Janeiro, Brazil. The company plans to introduce a new chemical solution and needs to develop a standard product cost. The new chemical solution is made by combining a chemical compound (nyclyn) and a solution (salex), heating the mixture, adding a second compound (protet), and bottling the resulting solution in 10-litre containers. The initial mix, which is 11 litres in volume, consists of 12 kilograms of nyclyn and 9.6 litres of salex. A 1-litre reduction in volume occurs during the boiling process. The solution is cooled slightly before 5 kilograms of protet are added. The addition of protet does not affect the total liquid volume.

The purchase price of the direct materials used in the manufacture of this new chemical solution are given below. (The *real* is Brazil's national currency. On the day this problem was written, the real was equivalent to C$0.602.)

Nyclyn	1.45 real per kilogram
Salex	1.80 real per litre
Protet	2.40 real per kilogram

Required:

Determine the standard material cost of a 10-litre container of the new product. (Remember to express your answer in terms of the real, the Brazilian national currency.)

(CMA, adapted)

Problem 9–47 Direct-Material and Direct-Labour Variances **(LO2)**

1. Direct-material price variance: $540 unfavourable

During May, Joliet Fabrics Corporation manufactured 500 units of a special multilayer fabric with the trade name Stylex. The following information from the Stylex production department also pertains to May.

Direct material purchased: 18,000 metres at $1.38 per metre	$24,840
Direct material used: 9,500 metres at $1.38 per metre	13,110
Direct labour: 2,100 hours at $9.15 per hour	19,215

The standard prime costs for one unit of Stylex are as follows:

Direct material: 20 metres at $1.35 per metre	$27
Direct labour: 4 hours at $9.00 per hour	36
Total standard prime cost per unit of output	$63

Required: Compute the following variances for the month of May, indicating whether each variance is favourable or unfavourable.

1. Direct-material price variance.
2. Direct-material quantity variance.
3. Direct-labour rate variance.
4. Direct-labour efficiency variance.

Problem 9–48 Variance Calculation; Analysis: Service Business **(LO1, 2)**

2. Direct-labour efficiency
variance: $495.00 favourable
4. Total material and labour
variances: $902.50
favourable

Sal Amato operates a residential landscaping business. In an effort to provide quality service, he has concentrated solely on the design and installation of upscale landscaping plans (e.g., trees, shrubs, fountains, and lighting). With his clients continually requesting additional services, Sal recently expanded into lawn maintenance, including fertilization.

The following data relate to his first year's experience with 55 fertilization clients. Each client required six applications throughout the year and was billed $40 per application.

- Two applications involved Type I fertilizer, which contains a special ingredient for weed control. The remaining four applications involved Type II fertilizer.

- Wolfe purchased 5,000 kilograms of Type I fertilizer at $0.53 per kilogram and 10,000 kilograms of Type II fertilizer at $0.40 per kilogram. Actual usage amounted to 3,700 kilograms of Type I and 7,800 kilograms of Type II.

- A new, part-time employee was hired to spread the fertilizer. Wolfe had to pay premium wages of $11.50 per hour because of a very tight labour market; the employee logged a total of 165 hours at client residences.

- Based on previous knowledge of the operation, articles in trade journals, and conversations with other landscapers, Sal established the following standards:

Fertilizer purchase price per kilogram	Type I, $0.50; Type II, $0.42
Fertilizer usage	40 kilograms per application
Typical hourly wage rate of landscape personnel	$9
Labour time per application	40 minutes

Unfortunately, Sal's new lawn fertilization service did not go as smoothly as planned, with customer complaints actually much higher than expected.

Required:

1. Compute Sal's direct-material variances of each type of fertilizer.

2. Compute the direct-labour variances.

3. Compute the actual cost of the client applications. (*Note:* Exclude any fertilizer in inventory, as remaining fertilizer can be used next year.) Was the new service a financial success? Explain.

4. Analyze the variances that you computed in requirements (1) and (2).

   a. Was the new service a success from an overall cost control perspective? Briefly discuss.

   b. What seems to have happened that would give rise to customer complaints?

5. In view of the complaints, should the fertilizer service be continued next year? Why or why not?

Problem 9–49 Analysis of Performance and Responsibility; Computing Variances **(LO1, 2)**

2. Direct-labour rate variance:
$47,025 Unfavourable

Santa Rosa Industries uses a standard-costing system to assist in the evaluation of operations. The company has had considerable trouble in recent months with suppliers and employees, so much so that management hired a new production supervisor, Frank Schmidt. The new supervisor has been on the job for five months and has seemingly brought order to an otherwise chaotic situation.

The vice-president of manufacturing recently commented that "Schmidt has really done the trick. The change to a new direct-material supplier and Schmidt's team-building/morale-boosting training exercises have truly brought things under control." The VP's comments were based on both a plant tour, where he observed a contented workforce, and a review of the following data, which were taken from a performance report:

Direct-material variances	$4,620 Favourable
Direct-labour variances	$6,175 Favourable

These variances are especially outstanding, given that the amounts are favourable and small. (Santa Rosa's budgeted material and labour costs generally average about $350,000 each for similar periods.) Additional data follow:

- The company purchased and consumed 45,000 kilograms of direct materials at $7.70 per kilogram, and paid $16.25 per hour for 20,900 direct-labour hours of activity. Total completed production amounted to 9,500 units.

- A review of the firm's standard cost records found that each completed unit requires 4.2 kilograms of direct material at $8.80 per kilogram and 2.6 direct-labour hours at $14 per hour.

Required:

1. On the basis of the information contained in the performance report, should Santa Rosa's management be concerned about its variances? Why?

2. Calculate the company's direct-material variances and direct-labour variances.

3. On the basis of your answers to requirement (2), should Santa Rosa's management be concerned about its variances? Why?

4. Are things going as smoothly as the vice-president believes? Evaluate the company's variances and determine whether the change to a new supplier and Schmidt's team-building/morale-boosting training exercises appear to be working. Explain.

5. Is it possible that some of the company's current problems lie outside Schmidt's area of responsibility? Explain.

Problem 9–50 Direct-Material and Direct-Labour Variances **(LO2)**

2. Direct-material quantity variance: $16,625 Favourable

Orion Corporation has established the following standards for the prime costs of one unit of its chief product, dartboards.

	Standard Quantity	Standard Price or Rate	Standard Cost
Direct material	8 kilograms	$1.75 per kilogram	$14.00
Direct labour	0.25 hour	$8.00 per hour	2.00
Total			$16.00

During June, Orion purchased 160,000 kilograms of direct material at a total cost of $304,000. The total wages for June were $42,000, 90 percent of which were for direct labour. Orion manufactured 19,000 dartboards during June, using 142,500 kilograms of direct material and 5,000 direct-labour hours.

Required: Compute the following variances for June, and indicate whether each is favourable or unfavourable.

1. The direct-material price variance.

2. The direct-material quantity variance.

3. The direct-labour rate variance.

4. The direct-labour efficiency variance.

(CMA, adapted)

Problem 9–51 Direct-Labour Variances **(LO1, 2)**

1(b). Direct-labour efficiency variance, Labour Class III: $800 Unfavourable

The controller for Portland Instrument Corporation compares each month's actual results with a monthly plan. The standard direct-labour rates for the year just ended and the standard hours allowed, given the actual output in April, are shown in the following schedule:

	Standard Direct-Labour Rate per Hour	Standard Direct-Labour Hours Allowed, Given April Output
Labour Class III	$16.00	500
Labour Class II	14.00	500
Labour Class I	10.00	500

A new union contract negotiated in March resulted in actual wage rates that differed from the standard rates. The actual direct-labour hours worked and the actual direct-labour rates per hour experienced for the month of April were as follows:

	Actual Direct-Labour Rate per Hour	Actual Direct-Labour Hours
Labour class III	$17.20	550
Labour class II	15.00	650
Labour class I	10.80	375

Required:

1. Compute the following variances for April. Indicate whether each is favourable or unfavourable:

   a. Direct-labour rate variance for *each* labour class

   b. Direct-labour efficiency variance for *each* labour class

2. Discuss the advantages and disadvantages of a standard-costing system in which the standard direct-labour rates are not changed during the year to reflect such events as a new labour contract.

3. *Build a spreadsheet:* Construct an Excel spreadsheet to solve requirement (1) above. Show how the solution will change based on the following information changes: The actual labour rates were $16.95, $15.10, and $10.60 for Labour Classes III, II, and I, respectively.

(CMA, adapted)

Problem 9–52 Development of Standard Costs; Ethics **(LO1, 10)**

1. Total standard unit cost: $8.62

Ogwood Company's Johnstown Division is a small manufacturer of wooden household items. Al Rivkin, division controller, plans to implement a standard-costing system. Rivkin has collected information from several co-workers that will assist him in developing standards. One of the Johnstown Division's products is a wooden cutting board. Each cutting board requires 1.25 board metres of lumber and 12 minutes of direct-labour time to prepare and cut the lumber. The cutting boards are inspected after they are cut. Because the cutting boards are made of a natural material that has imperfections, one board is normally rejected for each five that are accepted. Four rubber foot pads are attached to each good cutting board. A total of 15 minutes of direct-labour time is required to attach all four foot pads and finish each cutting board. The lumber for the cutting boards cost $3 per board metre, and each foot pad costs $0.05. Direct labour is paid at the rate of $8 per hour.

Required:

1. Develop the standard cost for direct material and direct labour of a cutting board.

2. Explain the role of each of the following people in developing standards:

   a. Purchasing manager

   b. Industrial engineer

   c. Management accountant

3. The production manager complained that the standards are unrealistic, stifle motivation by concentrating only on unfavourable variances, and are out of date too quickly. He noted that his recent switch to cherry for the cutting boards has resulted in higher material costs but decreased labour hours. The net result was no increase in the total cost to produce the product. The monthly reports continue to show an unfavourable material variance and a favourable labour variance despite indications that the workers are slowing down.

   a. Explain why a standard-costing system can strengthen cost management.

   b. Give at least two reasons to explain why a standard-costing system could negatively impact the motivation of production employees.

Problem 9–53 Determining Standard Costs; Ethics **(LO1, 2, 10)**

1. Total standard cost per 10-gallon batch: $30.20

Quincy Farms, located in central California, produces items made from local farm products that are distributed to supermarkets. For many years, Quincy's products have had strong regional sales on the basis of brand recognition; however, other companies have begun marketing similar products in the area, and price competition has become increasingly important. Doug Gilbert, the company's controller, is planning to implement a standard cost system for Quincy and has gathered considerable information from his co-workers on production and material requirements for Quincy's products. Gilbert believes that the use of standard costing will allow Quincy to improve cost control and make better pricing decisions.

Quincy's most popular product is strawberry jam. The jam is produced in 10-gallon batches, and each batch requires six quarts of good strawberries (1 gallon is approximately 4.55 litres and there are 4 quarts in a gallon). The fresh strawberries are sorted by hand before entering the production process. Because of imperfections in the strawberries and normal spoilage, one quart of berries is discarded for every four quarts of acceptable berries. Three minutes is the standard direct-labour time for sorting required to obtain one quart of acceptable strawberries. The acceptable strawberries are then blended with the other ingredients. Blending requires 12 minutes of direct-labour time per batch. After blending, the jam is packaged in quart containers. Gilbert has gathered the following information from Joe Adams, Quincy's cost accountant:

- Quincy purchases strawberries at a cost of $0.80 per quart. All other ingredients cost a total of $0.45 per gallon.

- Direct labour is paid at the rate of $9 per hour.

- The total cost of material and labour required to package the jam is $0.38 per quart.

Adams has a friend who owns a strawberry farm that has been losing money in recent years. Because of good crops, there has been an oversupply of strawberries, and prices have dropped to $0.50 per quart. Adams has arranged for Quincy to purchase strawberries from his friend and hopes that $0.80 per quart will help his friend's farm become profitable again.

Required:

1. Develop the standard cost for the direct-cost components of a 10-gallon batch of strawberry jam. The standard cost should identify the following amounts for each direct-cost component of a batch of strawberry jam: (*a*) standard quantity, (*b*) standard price or rate, and (*c*) standard cost per batch.

2. Citing the specific ethical standards of competence, confidentiality, integrity, and credibility for management accountants, explain why Joe Adams' behaviour regarding the cost information provided to Doug Gilbert is unethical.

3. As part of the implementation of a standard-costing system at Quincy Farms, Doug Gilbert plans to train those responsible for maintaining the standards in the use of variance analysis. Gilbert is particularly concerned with the causes of unfavourable variances. Discuss the possible causes of the following unfavourable variances and identify the individual(s) who should be held responsible: (*a*) direct-material price variance and (*b*) direct-labour efficiency variance.

(CMA, adapted)

Problem 9–54 Straightforward Overhead Variances **(LO6)**

Actual variable-overhead rate: $3.10 per hour

Calgary Paper Company produces paper for photocopiers. The company has developed standard overhead rates based on a monthly capacity of 180,000 direct-labour hours as follows:
Standard costs per unit (one box of paper):

Variable overhead (2 hrs. @ $3 per hr.)	$6
Fixed overhead (2 hrs. @ $5 per hr.)	10
Total	$16

During April, 90,000 units were scheduled for production; however, only 80,000 units were actually produced. The following data relate to April.

1. Actual direct-labour cost incurred was $1,567,500 for 165,000 actual hours of work.

2. Actual overhead incurred totalled $1,371,500, of which $511,500 was variable and $860,000 was fixed.

Required: Prepare two exhibits similar to Exhibits 9–9 and 9–11 in the chapter, which show the following variances. State whether each variance is favourable or unfavourable, where appropriate.

1. Variable-overhead spending variance
2. Variable-overhead efficiency variance
3. Fixed-overhead budget variance
4. Fixed-overhead volume variance

(CMA, adapted)

Problem 9–55 Standard Hours Allowed; Flexible Budget; Multiple Products: Insurance Company **(LO3, 4, 5)**

4. Budgeted overhead cost for July: $11,800

Gibraltar Insurance Company uses a flexible-overhead budget for its application-processing department. The firm offers five types of policies, with the following standard hours allowed for clerical processing:

Automobile.	1 hour
Renter's	1 hours
Homeowner's	2 hours
Health	2 hours
Life	5 hours

The following numbers of insurance applications were processed during July:

Automobile.	250
Renter's	200
Homeowner's	100
Health	400
Life	200

The controller estimates that the variable-overhead rate in the application-processing department is $4 per hour, and that fixed-overhead costs will amount to $2,000 per month.

Required:

1. How many standard clerical hours are allowed in July, given actual application activity?
2. Why would it not be sensible to base the company's flexible budget on the number of applications processed instead of the number of clerical hours allowed?
3. Construct a formula flexible-overhead budget for the company.
4. What is the flexible budget for total overhead cost in July?

Problem 9–56 Graphing Budgeted and Applied Overhead: Recording Studio (LO3, 4)

Countrytime Studios is a recording studio in Nashville. The studio budgets and applies overhead costs on the basis of production time. Countrytime's controller anticipates 10,000 hours of production time to be available during the year. The following overhead amounts have been budgeted for the year:

Variable overhead	$40,000
Fixed overhead	90,000

Required:

1. Draw two graphs, one for variable overhead and one for fixed overhead. The variable on the horizontal axis of each graph should be production time, in hours, ranging from 5,000 to 15,000 hours. The variable on the vertical axis of each graph should be overhead cost (variable or fixed). Each graph should include two lines, one for the flexible-budget amount of overhead and one for applied overhead.
2. Write a brief memo to Countrytime Studio's general manager, explaining the graph so that she will understand the concepts of budgeted and applied overhead.

Problem 9–57 Overhead Variances (LO6)

Newark Plastics Corporation developed its overhead application rate from the annual budget. The budget is based on an expected total output of 720,000 units requiring 3,600,000 machine hours. The company is able to schedule production uniformly throughout the year.

A total of 66,000 units requiring 315,000 machine hours were produced during May. Actual overhead costs for May amounted to $375,000. The actual costs, as compared to the annual budget and to one-twelfth of the annual budget, are as follows:

1 *(d).* Variable-overhead efficiency variance: $8,850 F

NEWARK PLASTICS CORPORATION Annual Budget					
	Total Amount	Per Unit	Per Machine Hour	Monthly Budget	Actual Costs for May
Variable overhead:					
Indirect material	$1,224,000	$ 1.70	$ 0.34	$102,000	$111,000
Indirect labour	900,000	1.25	0.25	75,000	75,000
Fixed overhead:					
Supervision	648,000	0.90	0.18	54,000	51,000
Utilities	540,000	0.75	0.15	45,000	54,000
Depreciation	1,008,000	1.40	0.28	84,000	84,000
Total	$4,320,000	$6.00	$1.20	$360,000	$375,000

Required:

1. Prepare a schedule showing the following amounts for Newark Plastics Corporation for May:
   a. Applied overhead costs
   b. Variable-overhead spending variance
   c. Fixed-overhead budget variance
   d. Variable-overhead efficiency variance
   e. Fixed-overhead volume variance

   Where appropriate, be sure to indicate whether each variance is favourable or unfavourable.

2. Draw a graph similar to Exhibit 9–10 to depict the variable-overhead variances.

3. Why does your graph differ from Exhibit 9–10, other than the fact that the numbers differ?

(CMA, adapted)

3. Direct material used: $20 per unit; variable manufacturing overhead: $6.25 per unit; supervisory salaries: $36,000 per month.

Problem 9–58 Budgets and Performance Evaluation (LO3, 7)

Johnson Electrical produces industrial ventilation fans. The company plans to manufacture 72,000 fans evenly over the next quarter at the following costs: direct material, $1,440,000; direct labour, $360,000; variable manufacturing overhead, $450,000; and fixed manufacturing overhead, $900,000. The last amount includes $72,000 of straight-line depreciation and $108,000 of supervisory salaries.

Shortly after the conclusion of the quarter's first month, Johnson reported the following costs:

Direct material	$ 432,500
Direct labour	110,600
Variable manufacturing overhead	152,000
Depreciation	24,000
Supervisory salaries	37,800
Other fixed manufacturing overhead	239,000
Total	$ 995,900

Dave Kellerman and his crews produced 20,000 fans during the month—a remarkable feat given that the firm's manufacturing plant was closed for several days because of storm damage and flooding.

Kellerman was especially pleased with the fact that overall financial performance for the period was favourable when compared with the budget. His pleasure, however, was very short-lived, as Johnson's general manager issued a stern warning that performance must improve, and improve quickly, if Kellerman had any hopes of keeping his job.

Required:

1. Explain the difference between a static budget and a flexible budget.

2. Which of the two budgets would be more useful when planning the company's cash needs over a range of activity?

3. Prepare a performance report that compares budgeted and actual costs for the period just ended (i.e., the report that Kellerman likely used when assessing his performance).

4. Prepare a performance report that compares budgeted and actual costs for the period just ended (i.e., the report that the general manager likely used when assessing Kellerman's performance).

5. Which of the two reports is preferred? Should Kellerman be praised for outstanding performance or is the general manager's warning appropriate? Explain, citing any apparent problems for the firm.

Problem 9–59 Linkages between the Flexible Budget and Variances (LO3, 4, 6)

1. Medical assistants, budget: $11,060
Medical assistants, actual: $13,020
3. Variable-overhead spending variance: $20,856 F

Fall City Hospital has an outpatient clinic. Jeffrey Harper, the hospital's chief administrator, is very concerned about cost control and has asked that performance reports be prepared that compare budgeted and actual amounts for medical assistants, clinic supplies, and lab tests. Past financial studies have shown that the cost of clinic supplies used is driven by the number of medical assistant labour hours worked, whereas lab tests are highly correlated with the number of patients served.

The following information is available for June:

-   *Medical assistants.* Fall City's standard wage rate is $14 per hour, and each assistant is expected to spend 30 minutes with a patient. Assistants totalled 840 hours in helping the 1,580 patients seen, at an average pay rate of $15.50 per hour.

-   *Clinic supplies.* The cost of clinic supplies used is budgeted at $12 per labour hour, and the actual cost of supplies used was $9,150.

-   *Lab tests.* Each patient is anticipated to have three lab tests, at an average budgeted cost of $65 per test. Actual lab tests for June cost $318,054 and averaged 3.3 per patient.

Required:

1. Prepare a report that shows budgeted and actual costs for the 1,580 patients served during June. Compute the differences (variances) between these amounts and label them as favourable or unfavourable.

2. On the basis of your answer to requirement (1), determine whether Fall City Hospital has any significant problems with respect to clinic supplies and lab tests. Briefly discuss your findings.

3. By performing a detailed analysis, determine the spending and efficiency variances for lab tests. Does it appear that Fall City Hospital has any significant problems with the cost of its lab tests? Briefly explain. (*Hint:* In applying the overhead variance formulas, think of the number of tests as analogous to the number of hours, and think of the cost per test as analogous to the variable-overhead rate.)

4. Compare the lab test variance computed in requirement (1), a flexible-budget variance, with the sum of the variances in requirement (3). Discuss your findings and explain the relationship of flexible-budget variances and standard-cost variances for variable overhead.

Problem 9–60 Overhead Calculations; Variance Interpretation (LO6)

Maxwell Company uses a standard-cost accounting system and applies manufacturing overhead to products on the basis of machine hours. The following information is available for the year just ended:

Standard variable-overhead rate per hour	$2.50
Standard fixed-overhead rate per hour	$4
Planned activity during the period	20,000 machine hours
Actual production	10,700 finished units
Machine-hour standard	Two completed units per machine hour
Actual variable overhead	$55,440
Actual total overhead	$155,900
Actual machine hours worked	23,100

2. Variable-overhead spending variance: $2,310 Favourable

5. Variable-overhead is underapplied by $42,065

Required:

1. Calculate the budgeted fixed overhead for the year.
2. Compute the variable-overhead spending variance.
3. Calculate the company's fixed-overhead volume variance.
4. Did the company spend more or less than anticipated for fixed overhead? How much?
5. Was variable overhead underapplied or overapplied during the year? By how much?
6. On the basis of the data presented, does it appear that the company suffered a lengthy strike during the year by its production workers? Briefly explain.

Problem 9–61 Flexible Budget; Performance Report (LO3, 7)

Mark Fletcher, president of SoftGro, Inc., was looking forward to seeing the performance reports for November because he knew the company's sales for the month had exceeded budget by a considerable margin. SoftGro, a distributor of educational software packages, had been growing steadily for approximately two years. Fletcher's biggest challenge at this point was to ensure that the company did not lose control of expenses during this growth period. When Fletcher received the November reports, he was dismayed to see the large unfavourable variance in the company's *Monthly Selling Expense Report*, below. ("F" denotes favourable variance; "U" denotes unfavourable variance.)

2. Advertising, flexible budget: $1,650,000

SOFTGRO, INC.
Monthly Selling Expense Report
For the Month of November

	Annual Budget	November Budget	November Actual	November Variance
Unit sales	2,000,000	280,000	310,000	30,000
Dollar sales	$80,000,000	$11,200,000	$12,400,000	$1,200,000
Orders processed	54,000	6,500	5,800	(700)
Sales personnel per month	90	90	96	(6)
Advertising	$19,800,000	$1,650,000	$1,660,000	$10,000 U
Staff salaries	1,500,000	125,000	125,000	—
Sales salaries	1,296,000	108,000	115,400	7,400 U
Commissions	3,200,000	448,000	496,000	48,000 U
Per diem expense	1,782,000	148,500	162,600	14,100 U
Office expenses	4,080,000	340,000	358,400	18,400 U
Shipping expenses	6,750,000	902,500	976,500	74,000 U
Total expenses	$38,408,000	$3,722,000	$3,893,900	$171,900 U

Fletcher called in the company's new controller, Susan Porter, to discuss the implications of the variances reported for November and to plan a strategy for improving performance. Porter suggested that the company's reporting format might not be giving Fletcher a true picture of the company's operations. She proposed that SoftGro implement flexible budgeting. Porter offered to redo the *Monthly Selling Expense Report* for November using flexible budgeting so that Fletcher could compare the two reports and see the advantages of flexible budgeting.

Porter discovered the following information about the behaviour of SoftGro's selling expenses:

- The total compensation paid to the sales force consists of a monthly base salary and a commission; the commission varies with sales dollars.
- Sales office expense is a mixed cost, with the variable portion related to the number of orders processed. The fixed portion of office expense is $3,000,000 annually and is incurred uniformly throughout the year.
- Subsequent to the adoption of the annual budget for the current year, SoftGro decided to open a new sales territory. As a consequence, approval was given to hire six additional salespeople effective November 1. Porter decided that these additional six people should be recognized in her revised report.
- Per diem reimbursement to the sales force, while a fixed amount per day, is variable with the number of sales personnel and the number of days spent travelling. SoftGro's original budget was based on an average sales force of 90 people throughout the year, with each salesperson travelling 15 days per month.
- The company's shipping expense is a mixed cost, with the variable portion, $3 per unit, dependent on the number of units sold. The fixed portion is incurred uniformly throughout the year.

Required:

1. Citing the benefits of flexible budgeting, explain why Susan Porter would propose that SoftGro use flexible budgeting in this situation.
2. Prepare a revised *Monthly Selling Expense Report* for November that would permit Mark Fletcher to more clearly evaluate SoftGro's control over selling expenses. The report should have a line for each selling expense item showing the appropriate budgeted amount, the actual selling expense, and the monthly dollar variance.

(CMA, adapted)

---

1. Operating income: $122,400

2. Operating income, flexible-budget variance: $45,400 U

Problem 9–62   Flexible Budgeting; Variances; Impact on Behaviour **(LO3, 4, 6)**

LawnMate Company manufactures power mowers that are sold throughout Canada and the United States. The company uses a comprehensive budgeting process and compares actual results to budgeted amounts on a monthly basis. Each month, LawnMate's accounting department prepares a variance analysis and distributes the report to all responsible parties. Al Richmond, production manager, is upset about the results for May. Richmond, who is responsible for the cost of goods manufactured, has implemented several cost-cutting measures in the manufacturing area and is discouraged by the unfavourable variance in variable costs. ("F" denotes favourable variance; "U" denotes unfavourable variance.)

LAWNMATE COMPANY Operating Results For the Month of May			
	Master Budget	Actual	Variance
Units sold	5,000	4,800	200 U
Revenue	$1,200,000	$1,152,000	48,000 U
Variable cost	760,000	780,000	20,000 U
Contribution margin	$ 440,000	372,000	68,000 U
Fixed overhead	180,000	180,000	—
Fixed general and administrative cost	120,000	115,000	5,000 F
Operating income	$ 140,000	$ 77,000	$63,000 U

When the master budget was prepared, LawnMate's cost accountant, Joan Ballard, supplied the following unit costs: direct material, $60; direct labour, $44; variable overhead, $36; and variable selling, $12.

The total variable costs of $780,000 for May include $320,000 for direct material, $192,000 for direct labour, $176,000 for variable overhead, and $92,000 for variable selling expenses. Ballard believes that LawnMate's monthly reports would be more meaningful to everyone if the company adopted flexible budgeting and prepared more detailed analyses.

Required:

1. Prepare a flexible budget for LawnMate Company for the month of May that includes separate variable-cost budgets for each type of cost (direct material, etc.).

2. Determine the variance between the flexible budget and actual cost for each cost item.

3. Discuss how the revised budget and variance data are likely to impact the behaviour of Al Richmond, the production manager.

4. *Build a spreadsheet:* Construct an Excel spreadsheet to solve requirements (1) and (2) above. Show how the solution will change if the following information changes: Actual sales amounted to 4,700 units, and actual fixed overhead was $179,000.

(CMA, adapted)

Problem 9–63 Finding Missing Data; Overhead Accounting **(LO3, 6)**

For each of the following independent cases, fill in the missing information. The company budgets and applies manufacturing-overhead costs on the basis of direct-labour hours.

2. Case A: $7 per hour
5. Case B: $18,000
14. Case B: 1,000 UNITS

	Case A	Case B
1. Standard variable-overhead rate	$2.50 per hour	? per hour
2. Standard fixed-overhead rate	? per hour	? per hour
3. Total standard overhead rate	? per hour	$13 per hour
4. Flexible budget for variable overhead	$90,000	?
5. Flexible budget for fixed overhead	$210,000	?
6. Actual variable overhead	?	?
7. Actual fixed overhead	$207,000	?
8. Variable-overhead spending variance	$5,550 U	$2,000 U
9. Variable-overhead efficiency variance	?	$400 F
10. Fixed-overhead budget variance	?	$1,080 U
11. Fixed-overhead volume variance	?	$3,600 U
12. Underapplied or overapplied variable overhead	?	?
13. Underapplied or overapplied fixed overhead	?	?
14. Budgeted production (in units)	5,000 units	?
15. Standard direct-labour hours per unit	6 hours per unit	2 hours per unit
16. Actual production (in units)	?	?
17. Standard direct-labour hours allowed, given actual production	36,000 hours	1,600 hours
18. Actual direct-labour hours	37,000 hours	1,500 hours
19. Applied variable overhead	?	?
20. Applied fixed overhead	?	?

Problem 9–64 Preparing and Using a Columnar Flexible Budget: Tour Company; Ethical Issues **(LO3, 4, 7)**

Flaming Foliage Sky Tours is a small sightseeing tour company in Quebec. The firm specializes in aerial tours of the countryside during September and October, when the fall colours are at their peak. Until recently, the company had not had an accounting department. Routine bookkeeping tasks, such as billing, had been handled by an individual who had little formal training in accounting. As the business began to grow, however, the owner recognized the need for more formal accounting procedures. Jacqueline Frost has recently been hired as the new controller, and she will have the authority to hire an assistant.

During her first week on the job, Frost was given the following performance report. The report was prepared by Red Leif, the company's manager of aircraft operations, who was planning to present it to the owner the next morning. "Look at these favourable variances for fuel and so forth," Leif pointed out, as he

Total variable expenses, activity level (air miles), 38,000: $93,100
4. Total variable expenses, flexible budget: $78,400

showed the report to Frost. "My operations people are really doing a great job." Later that day, Frost looked at the performance report more carefully. She immediately realized that it was improperly prepared and would be misleading to the company's owner.

	Formula Flexible Budget (per air mile)	Actual (32,000 air miles)	Static Budget (35,000 air miles)	Variance
FLAMING FOLIAGE SKY TOURS				
Performance Report				
For the Month of September				
Passenger revenue	$ 3.50	$112,000	$122,500	$10,500 U
Less: Variable expenses:				
Fuel	0.50	17,000	17,500	500 F
Aircraft maintenance	0.75	23,500	26,250	2,750 F
Flight crew salaries	0.40	13,100	14,000	900 F
Selling and administrative	0.80	24,900	28,000	3,100 F
Total variable expenses	2.45	78,500	85,750	7,250 F
Contribution margin	$ 1.05	33,500	36,750	3,250 U
Less: Fixed expenses:	**Per Month**			
Depreciation on aircraft	$ 2,900	2,900	2,900	$0
Landing fees	900	1,000	900	100 U
Supervisory salaries	9,000	8,600	9,000	400 F
Selling and administrative	11,000	12,400	11,000	1,400 U
Total fixed expenses	$23,800	24,900	23,800	1,100 U
Net income		$ 8,600	$ 12,950	$ 4,350 U

Required:

1. Prepare a columnar flexible budget for Flaming Foliage Sky Tours' expenses, based on the following activity levels: 32,000 air miles, 35,000 air miles, and 38,000 air miles.

2. In spite of several favourable expense variances shown in the report above, the company's September net income was only about two-thirds of the expected level. Why?

3. Write a brief memo to the manager of aircraft operations explaining why the original variance report is misleading.

4. Prepare a revised expense variance report for September, which is based on the flexible budget prepared in requirement (1).

5. Jacqueline Frost presented the revised expense report to Leif, along with the memo explaining why the original performance report was misleading. Leif did not take it well. He complained of Frost's "interference" and pointed out that the company had been doing just fine without her. "I'm taking my report to the owner tomorrow," Leif insisted. "Yours just makes us look bad." What are Frost's ethical obligations in this matter? What should she do?

Problem 9–65 Interactions between Variances; Flexible Manufacturing System (LO6)

Eastern Auto Parts Company manufactures replacement parts for automobile repair. The company recently installed a flexible manufacturing system (FMS), which has significantly changed the production process. The installation of the new FMS was not anticipated when the current year's budget and cost structure were developed. The installation of the new equipment was hastened by several major breakdowns in the company's old production machinery.

The new equipment was very expensive, but management expects it to cut the labour time required by a substantial amount. Management also expects the new equipment to allow a reduction in direct-material waste. On the negative side, the FMS requires a more highly skilled labour force to operate it than the company's old equipment.

The following cost variance report was prepared for the month of July, the first full month after the equipment was installed:

EASTERN AUTO PARTS COMPANY
Cost Variance Report
For the Month of July

Direct material:	
Standard cost	$602,450
Actual cost	598,700
Direct-material price variance	150 U*
Direct-material quantity variance	3,900 F
Direct labour:	
Standard cost	393,000
Actual cost	383,800
Direct-labour rate variance	4,800 U
Direct-labour efficiency variance	14,000 F
Manufacturing overhead:	
Applied to work in process	400,000
Actual cost	408,000
Variable-overhead spending variance	8,000 U
Variable-overhead efficiency variance	10,000 F
Fixed-overhead budget variance	30,000 U
Fixed-overhead volume variance	(20,000)†

*"F" denotes favourable variance; "U" denotes unfavourable variance.

†The sign of the volume variance is negative; applied fixed overhead exceeded budgeted fixed overhead.

Required: Comment on the possible interactions between the variances listed in the report. Which ones are likely to have been caused by the purchase of the new production equipment? The company budgets and applies manufacturing overhead on the basis of direct-labour hours.

Problem 9–66 Flexible Budget; Improved Performance Report; Behavioural Issues (LO3, 7)

WoodCrafts, Inc. is a manufacturer of furniture for specialty shops and has an annual sales volume of $12 million. The company has four major product lines: bookcases, magazine racks, end tables, and barstools. Each line is managed by a production manager. Since production is spread fairly evenly over the 12 months of operation, Sara McKinley, WoodCrafts' controller, has prepared an annual budget divided into 12 periods for monthly reporting purposes.

WoodCrafts uses a standard-costing system and applies variable overhead on the basis of process hours. Fixed production cost is allocated on the basis of square metre occupied, using a predetermined plantwide rate; the size of the space occupied varies considerably across the product lines. All other costs are assigned on the basis of revenue dollars earned. At the monthly meeting to review November performance, Steve Clark, manager of the bookcase line, received the following report:

Contribution margin, actual: $59,400

WOODCRAFTS, INC.
Bookcase Production Performance Report
For the Month of November

	Actual	Budget	Variance
Units	3,000	2,500	500 F
Revenue	$161,000	$137,500	$23,500 F
Variable production costs:			
Direct material	23,100	20,000	3,100 U
Direct labour	18,300	15,000	3,300 U
Machine time	19,200	16,250	2,950 U
Manufacturing overhead	41,000	35,000	6,000 U
Fixed production costs:			
Indirect labour	9,400	6,000	3,400 U
Depreciation	5,500	5,500	—
Property taxes	2,400	2,300	100 U
Insurance	4,500	4,500	—
Administrative expenses	12,000	9,000	3,000 U
Marketing expenses	8,300	7,000	1,300 U
Research and development	6,000	4,500	1,500 U
Total expenses	149,700	125,050	24,650 U
Operating income	$ 11,300	$ 12,450	$ 1,150 U

While distributing the monthly reports at the meeting, McKinley remarked to Clark, "We need to talk about getting your division back on track. Be sure to see me after the meeting."

Clark had been so convinced that his division did well in November that McKinley's remark was a real surprise. He spent the balance of the meeting avoiding the looks of the other managers and trying to figure out what could have gone wrong. The monthly performance report was no help.

Required:

1. *a.* Identify three weaknesses in WoodCrafts, Inc.'s monthly *Bookcase Production Performance Report*.

   b. Discuss the behavioural implications of Sara McKinley's remarks to Steve Clark during the meeting.

2. WoodCrafts, Inc. could do a better job of reporting monthly performance to the production managers.

   a. Recommend how the report could be improved to eliminate weaknesses, and revise it accordingly.

   b. Discuss how the recommended changes in reporting are likely to affect Steve Clark's behaviour.

(CMA, adapted)

Problem 9–67 Using a Flexible Budget (LO3, 4, 6)

Rutherford Wheel and Axle, Inc. has an automated production process, and production activity is quantified in terms of process hours. A standard-costing system is used. The annual static budget for 20x1 called for 6,000 units to be produced, requiring 30,000 machine hours. The standard overhead rate for the year was computed using this planned level of production. The 20x1 manufacturing cost report follows.

RUTHERFORD WHEEL AND AXLE, INC.
Manufacturing Cost Report for 20x1
(in thousands of dollars)

Cost Item	Static Budget	Flexible Budget		Actual Cost
	30,000 Machine Hours	31,000 Machine Hours	32,000 Machine Hours	
Direct material:				
G27 aluminum	$ 252.0	$ 260.4	$ 268.8	$ 270.0
M14 steel alloy	78.0	80.6	83.2	83.0
Direct labour:				
Assembler	273.0	282.1	291.2	287.0
Grinder	234.0	241.8	249.6	250.0
Manufacturing overhead:				
Maintenance	24.0	24.8	25.6	25.0
Supplies	129.0	133.3	137.6	130.0
Supervision	80.0	82.0	84.0	81.0
Inspection	144.0	147.0	150.0	147.0
Insurance	50.0	50.0	50.0	50.0
Depreciation	200.0	200.0	200.0	200.0
Total cost	$1,464.0	$1,502.0	$1,540.0	$1,523.0

Rutherford develops flexible budgets for different levels of activity for use in evaluating performance. A total of 6,200 units was produced during 20x1, requiring 32,000 machine hours. The preceding manufacturing cost report compares the company's actual cost for the year with the static budget and the flexible budget for two different activity levels.

Required: Compute the following amounts. For variances, indicate whether favourable or unfavourable where appropriate. Answers should be rounded to two decimal places when necessary.

1. The standard number of machine hours allowed to produce one unit of product

2. The actual cost of direct material used in one unit of product

3. The cost of material that should be processed per machine hour

4. The standard direct-labour cost for each unit produced

5. The variable-overhead rate per machine hour in a flexible-budget formula. (*Hint:* Use the high–low method to estimate cost behaviour.)

6. The standard fixed-overhead rate per machine hour used for product costing

7. The variable-overhead spending variance. (Assume management has determined that the actual fixed-overhead cost in 20x1 amounted to $324,000.)

8. The variable-overhead efficiency variance

9. The fixed-overhead budget variance

10. The fixed-overhead volume variance. (Make the same assumption as in requirement [7].)

11. The total budgeted manufacturing cost (in thousands of dollars) for an output of 6,050 units. (*Hint:* Use the flexible-budget formula.)

(CMA, adapted)

Problem 9–68 Complete Analysis of Cost Variances (LO2, 5, 6)

Chillco Corporation produces containers of frozen food. During April, Chillco produced 1,450 cases of food and incurred the following actual costs:

Direct-labour efficiency variance: $13,500 unfavourable; Fixed-overhead budget variance: $1,000 unfavourable

Variable overhead	$ 11,000
Fixed overhead	26,000
Actual labour cost (8,000 direct-labour hours)	151,200
Actual material cost (30,000 kilograms purchased and used)	66,000

Standard cost and annual budget information are as follows:

Standard Costs per Case

Direct labour (5 hrs. @ $18 per hr.)	$ 90.00
Direct material (20 kg @ $2 per kg)	40.00
Variable overhead (5 hrs. @ $1.50 per hr.)	7.50
Fixed overhead (5 hrs. @ $3 per hr.)	15.00
Total	$152.50

Annual Budget Information

Variable overhead	$150,000
Fixed overhead	$300,000
Planned activity for year	100,000 direct-labour hours

Required:

1. Prepare as complete an analysis of cost variances as is possible from the available data.

2. *Build a spreadsheet:* Construct an Excel spreadsheet to solve the preceding requirement. Show how the solution will change if the following information changes: The standard rates were $17.50 per hour for direct labour and $1.60 per direct-labour hour for variable overhead.

Problem 9–69 Investigating Cost Variances (LO9)

Schiffer Corporation manufactures agricultural machinery. At a recent staff meeting, the following direct-labour variance report for the year just ended was presented by the controller:

SCHIFFER CORPORATION
Direct-Labour Variance Report

	Direct-Labour Rate Variance		Direct-Labour Efficiency Variance	
	Amount	Standard Cost, %	Amount	Standard Cost, %
January	$ 800 F	0.16%	$ 5,000 U	1.00%
February	4,900 F	0.98%	7,500 U	1.50%
March	100 U	0.02%	9,700 U	1.94%
April	2,000 U	0.40%	12,800 U	2.56%
May	3,800 F	0.76%	20,100 U	4.02%
June	3,900 F	0.78%	17,000 U	3.40%
July	4,200 F	0.84%	28,500 U	5.70%
August	5,100 F	1.02%	38,000 U	7.60%
September	4,800 F	0.96%	37,000 U	7.40%
October	5,700 F	1.14%	42,000 U	8.40%
November	4,200 F	0.84%	60,000 U	12.00%
December	4,300 F	0.86%	52,000 U	10.40%

Schiffer's controller uses the following rule of thumb: Investigate all variances equal to or greater than $30,000, which is 6 percent of standard cost.

Required:

1. Which variances would have been investigated during the year? (Indicate month and type of variance.)

2. What characteristics of the variance pattern shown in the report should draw the controller's attention, regardless of the usual investigation rule? Explain. Given these considerations, which variances would you have investigated? Why?

3. Is it important to follow up on favourable variances, such as those shown in the report? Why or why not?

Problem 9–70 Comprehensive Problem on Variance Analysis (LO2, 5, 6)

Springsteen Company manufactures guitars. The company uses a standard, job-order cost accounting system in two production departments. In the Construction Department, the wooden guitars are built by highly skilled craftsmen and coated with several layers of lacquer. Then the units are transferred to the Finishing Department, where the bridge of the guitar is attached and the strings are installed. The guitars are also tuned and inspected in the Finishing Department. The diagram below depicts the production process.

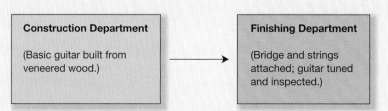

Each finished guitar contains seven kilograms of veneered wood. In addition, one kilogram of wood is typically wasted in the production process. The veneered wood used in the guitars has a standard price of $12 per kilogram. The other parts needed to complete each guitar, such as the bridge and strings, cost $15 per guitar. The labour standards for Springsteen's two production departments are as follows:

Construction Department	6 hours of direct labour at $20 per hour
Finishing Department	3 hours of direct labour at $15 per hour

The following pertains to the month of July:

1. There were no beginning or ending work-in-process inventories in either production department.

2. There was no beginning finished-goods inventory.

3. Actual production was 500 guitars, and 300 guitars were sold on account for $400 each.

4. The company purchased 6,000 kilograms of veneered wood at a price of $12.50 per kilogram.

5. Actual usage of veneered wood was 4,500 kilograms.

6. Enough parts (bridges and strings) to finish 600 guitars were purchased at a cost of $9,000.

7. The Construction Department used 2,850 direct-labour hours. The total direct-labour cost in the Construction Department was $54,150.

8. The Finishing Department used 1,570 direct-labour hours. The total direct-labour cost in that department was $25,120.

9. There were no direct-material variances in the Finishing Department.

Required:

1. Prepare a schedule that computes the standard costs of direct material and direct labour in each production department.

2. Prepare three exhibits that compute the July direct-material and direct-labour variances in the Construction Department and the July direct-labour variances in the Finishing Department. (Refer to Exhibits 9–2 and 9–3 for guidance.)

3. Prepare a cost variance report for July similar to that shown in Exhibit 9–16.

Problem 9–71 Journal Entries under Standard Costing; Continuation of Preceding Problem (Appendix A) **(LO12)**
Refer to your solution for the preceding problem regarding Springsteen Company.

To close variances into cost of goods sold (CGS): $5.770 (debit to CGS)

Required:

1. Prepare journal entries to record all of the events listed for Springsteen Company during July. Specifically, these journal entries should reflect the following events.

    a. Purchase of direct material.

    b. Use of direct material.

    c. Incurrence of direct-labour costs.

    d. Addition of production costs to the work-in-process inventory account for each department.

    e. Incurrence of all variances.

    f. Completion of 500 guitars.

    g. Sale of 300 guitars.

    h. Closing of all variance accounts into cost of goods sold.

2. Draw T-accounts, and post the journal entries prepared in requirement (1). Assume the beginning balance in all accounts is zero.

Problem 9–72 Overhead Variances; Journal Entries (Appendix A) **(LO6, 12)**
Montreal Scholastic Supply Company uses a standard-costing system. The firm estimates that it will operate its manufacturing facilities at 800,000 machine hours for the year. The estimate for total budgeted overhead is $2,000,000. The standard variable-overhead rate is estimated to be $2 per machine hour or $6 per unit. The actual data for the year are presented below.

1(a). Variable-overhead spending variance: $173,000 unfavourable
2. Cost of goods sold (debit): $218,000

Actual finished units	250,000
Actual machine hours	764,000
Actual variable overhead	$1,701,000
Actual fixed overhead	$ 392,000

Required:

1. Compute the following variances. Indicate whether each is favourable or unfavourable, where appropriate.

    a. Variable-overhead spending variance.

    b. Variable-overhead efficiency variance.

    c. Fixed-overhead budget variance.

    d. Fixed-overhead volume variance.

2. Prepare journal entries to

- Record the incurrence of actual variable overhead and actual fixed overhead.
- Add variable and fixed overhead to work-in-process inventory.
- Close underapplied or overapplied overhead into cost of goods sold.

(CMA, adapted)

2. Sales volume variance:
$50,000 unfavourable

Problem 9–73 Sales Variances (Appendix B) (LO13)

White Mountain Sled Company manufactures children's snow sleds. The company's performance report for November is as follows:

	Actual	Budget
Sleds sold	5,000	6,000
Sales	$240,000	$300,000
Variable costs	150,000	180,000
Contribution margin	$ 90,000	$120,000
Fixed costs	84,000	80,000
Operating income	$ 6,000	$ 40,000

The company uses sales variance analysis to explain the difference between budgeted and actual sales revenue.

Required: Compute the following variances and indicate whether each is favourable or unfavourable.

1. November sales-price variance.
2. November sales-volume variance.

Cases

1. Actual output (in drums):
1,000 drums
2. Direct material, quantity
variance, A: $2,500 U
3. Direct labour, actual hours
(mixers): 2,000 hrs.
4. Total of all variances for the
month: $1,510 F

Case 9–74 Missing Data; Variances, Ledger Accounts (Appendix A) (LO2, 6, 12)

MacGyver Corporation manufactures a product called Miracle Goo, which comes in handy for just about anything. The thick, tarry substance is sold in six-litre drums. Two raw materials are used, referred to as "A" and "B" by people in the business. Two types of labour are required also: "mixers" (Labour Class I) and "packers" (Labour Class II). You were recently hired by the company president, Pete Thorn, to be the controller. You soon learned that MacGyver uses a standard-costing system. Variances are computed and closed into cost of goods sold monthly. After your first month on the job, you gathered the necessary data to compute the month's variances for direct material and direct labour. You finished everything up by 5 p.m. on the 31st, including the credit to cost of goods sold for the sum of the variances. You decided to take all your notes home to review them prior to your formal presentation to Thorn first thing in the morning. As an afterthought, you grabbed a drum of Miracle Goo as well, thinking it could prove useful in some unanticipated way.

You spent the evening boning up on the data for your report and were ready to call it a night. As luck would have it, though, you knocked over the Miracle Goo as you rose from the kitchen table. The stuff splattered everywhere, and, most unfortunately, obliterated most of your notes. All that remained legible was the following information:

Direct Material A: Quantity Variance	
2,500	

Direct Material B: Price Variance	
1,200	

Direct Labour I: Rate Variance	
600	

Direct Labour II: Efficiency Variance	
1,200	

Cost of Goods Sold	
143,000	
	1,510

Accounts Payable		
	1,500	Beg. bal.
70,000	73,200	
	4,700	End. bal.

Other assorted data gleaned from your notes:

- The standards for each drum of Miracle Goo include 10 kilograms of Material A at a standard price of $5 per kilogram.
- The standard cost of Material B is $15 for each drum of Miracle Goo.
- Purchases of Material A were 12,000 kilograms at $4.50 per kilogram.
- Given the actual output for the month, the standard allowed quantity of Material A was 10,000 kilograms. The standard allowed quantity of Material B was 5,000 litres.
- Although 6,000 litres of B were purchased, only 4,800 litres were used.
- The standard wage rate for mixers is $15 per hour. The standard labour cost per drum of product for mixers is $30 per drum.
- The standards allow 4 hours of direct-labour II (packers) per drum of Miracle Goo. The standard labour cost per drum of product for packers is $48 per drum.
- Packers were paid $11.90 per hour during the month.

You happened to remember two additional facts. There were no beginning or ending inventories of either work in process or finished goods for the month. The increase in accounts payable relates to direct-material purchases only.

Required: Now you've got a major problem. Somehow you've got to reconstruct all the missing data in order to be ready for your meeting with the president. You start by making the following list of the facts you want to use in your presentation. Before getting down to business, you need a brief walk to clear your head. Out to the trash you go, and toss the remaining Miracle Goo.

Fill in the missing amounts in this list, using the available facts:

1. Actual output (in drums):_____

2. Direct material:	A	B
a. Standard quantity per drum	_____	_____
b. Standard price	_____	_____
c. Standard cost per drum	_____	_____
d. Standard quantity allowed, given actual output	_____	_____
e. Actual quantity purchased	_____	_____
f. Actual price	_____	_____
g. Actual quantity used	_____	_____
h. Price variance	_____	_____
i. Quantity variance	_____	_____

3. Direct labour:	I (mixers)	II (packers)
a. Standard hours per drum	_____	_____
b. Standard rate per hour	_____	_____
c. Standard cost per drum	_____	_____
d. Standard quantity allowed, given actual output	_____	_____
e. Actual rate per hour	_____	_____
f. Actual hours	_____	_____
g. Rate variance	_____	_____
h. Efficiency variance	_____	_____

4. Total of all variances for the month:_____

Case 9–75 Integrative; Drawing Conclusion from Missing Data **(LO3, 4, 6)**

Your next-door neighbour recently began a new job as assistant controller for Conundrum Corporation. As her first assignment, she prepared a performance report for January. She was scheduled to present the report to management the next morning, so she brought it home to review. Unfortunately, her dog thought the report was an object to be fetched. The pup made a flying leap and got a firm grip on the report. After chasing the dog around the house, she managed to wrest the report from its teeth. Needless to say, it was torn to bits. Only certain data are legible on the report. This information follows:

3. Actual fixed overhead: $43,250

7. Actual variable-overhead rate: $6.30 per hr.

10. Applied fixed overhead: $36,000

CONUNDRUM CORPORATION
Performance Report for the Month of January

	Direct Material	Direct Labour	Variable Overhead	Fixed Overhead
Standard allowed cost given actual output	?	?		
	(? kilograms at $12 per kilogram)	(2 hours at $14 per hour)		
Flexible-overhead budget			?	$40,000
Actual cost	$189,000	?	?	?
	(14,000 kilograms at $13.50 per kilogram)	(8,800 hours at ? per hour)		
Direct-material price variance	?			
Direct-material quantity variance........................	$6,000 U			
Direct-labour rate variance		$8,800 U		
Direct-labour efficiency variance		2,800 F		
Variable-overhead spending variance			$2,640 U	
Variable-overhead efficiency variance			1,200 F	
Fixed-overhead budget variance				$3,250 U
Fixed-overhead volume variance				?

In addition to the fragmentary data still legible on the performance report, your neighbour happened to remember the following facts:

- Planned production of Conundrum's sole product was 500 units more than the actual production.
- All of the direct material purchased in January was used in production.
- There were no beginning or ending inventories.
- Variable and fixed overhead are applied on the basis of direct-labour hours. The fixed-overhead rate is $4 per hour.

Required: Your neighbour needs to reconstruct the following facts, which will be necessary for her presentation:

1. Planned production (in units)
2. Actual production (in units)
3. Actual fixed overhead
4. Total standard allowed direct-labour hours
5. Actual direct-labour rate
6. Standard variable-overhead rate
7. Actual variable-overhead rate
8. Standard direct-material quantity per unit
9. Direct-material price variance
10. Applied fixed overhead
11. Fixed-overhead volume variance

Case 9–76 Comprehensive Variance Analysis Used to Explain Operational Results; Activity-Based Costing (Appendix B) **(L03, 4, 6, 8, 13)**
Aunt Molly's Old Fashioned Cookies bakes cookies for retail stores. The company's best-selling cookie is chocolate nut supreme, which is marketed as a gourmet cookie and regularly sells for $8.00 per dozen. The standard cost per dozen of chocolate nut supreme, based on Aunt Molly's normal monthly production of 400,000 dozen, is as follows:

Cost Item	Quantity	Standard Unit Cost	Total Cost
Direct materials:			
Cookie mix	10 grams	$ 0.02 per gram	$ 0.20
Milk chocolate	5 grams	0.15 per gram	0.75
Almonds	1 grams	0.50 per gram	0.50
			$ 1.45
Direct labour:*			
Mixing	1 min.	14.40 per hr.	$ 0.24
Baking	2 min.	18.00 per hr.	0.60
			$ 0.84
Variable overhead†	3 min.	32.40 per hr.	$ 1.62
Total standard cost per dozen cookies			$ 3.91

*Direct-labour rates include employee benefits.
†Applied on the basis of direct-labour hours.

4(a). Direct-material price variance, total: $133,000 U
4(e). Variable-overhead spending variance: $75,000 U
4(g). Sales-price variance: $45,000 U

Aunt Molly's management accountant, Karen Blair, prepares monthly budget reports based on these standard costs. April's contribution report, which compares budgeted and actual performance, is shown in the following schedule.

Contribution Report for April

	Static Budget	Actual	Variance
Units (in dozens)	400,000	450,000	50,000 F
Revenue	$3,200,000	$3,555,000	$355,000 F
Direct material	$ 580,000	$ 865,000	$285,000 U
Direct labour	336,000	348,000	12,000 U
Variable overhead	648,000	750,000	102,000 U
Total variable costs	$1,564,000	$1,963,000	$399,000 U
Contribution margin	$1,636,000	$1,592,000	$ 44,000 U

Justine Madison, president of the company, is disappointed with the results. Despite a sizable increase in the number of cookies sold, the product's expected contribution to the overall profitability of the firm decreased. Madison has asked Blair to identify the reason why the contribution margin decreased. Blair has gathered the following information to help in her analysis of the decrease.

Usage Report for February

Cost Item	Quantity	Actual Cost
Direct materials:		
Cookie mix	4,650,000 grams	$ 93,000
Milk chocolate	2,660,000 grams	532,000
Almonds	480,000 grams	240,000
Direct labour:		
Mixing	450,000 min.	108,000
Baking	800,000 min.	240,000
Variable overhead		750,000
Total variable costs		$1,963,000

Required:

1. Prepare a new contribution report for April, in which
   - The static-budget column in the contribution report is replaced with a flexible-budget column.
   - The variances in the contribution report are recomputed as the difference between the flexible budget and actual columns.

2. What is the total contribution margin in the flexible-budget column of the new report prepared for requirement (1)?

3. Explain (i.e., interpret) the meaning of the total contribution margin in the flexible-budget column of the new report prepared for requirement (1).

4. What is the total variance between the flexible-budget contribution margin and the actual contribution margin in the new report prepared for requirement (1)? Explain this total contribution-margin variance by computing the following variances. (Assume that all materials are used in the month of purchase.)

   a. Direct-material price variance.

   b. Direct-material quantity variance.

   c. Direct-labour rate variance.

   d. Direct-labour efficiency variance.

   e. Variable-overhead spending variance.

   f. Variable-overhead efficiency variance.

   g. Sales–price variance.

5. a. Explain the problems that might arise in using direct-labour hours as the basis for applying overhead.

   b. How might activity-based costing (ABC) solve the problems described in requirement (5a)?

(CMA, adapted)

 Practise and learn online with Connect.

CHAPTER TEN

Cost Management Tools

FOCUS COMPANY

 CANADIAN PACIFIC BANK

This chapter's focus company is Canadian Pacific Bank (CPB), a chartered bank headquartered in Vancouver with principal operations in western Canada. CPB's use of the balanced scorecard helps management and employees focus on the customers, internal operations, and learning and growth areas of the business, so that ultimately the bank's long-term financial goals will be attained.

IN CONTRAST — Handico

In contrast to the financial-services industry, we will turn our attention to a manufacturing company in order to explore the management of product quality and environmental costs. Handico manufactures cordless telephones.

Using Handico as an example, we will explore various types of quality-related costs incurred in manufacturing companies. We also will discuss how companies try to identify and manage a variety of environmental costs.

After completing this chapter, you should be able to

1 Describe the balanced scorecard concept and explain the reasoning behind it.

2 Describe the operational performance measures appropriate for today's manufacturing environment.

3 Define and give an example of target costing.

4 Explain the concept of kaizen costing and prepare a kaizen costing chart.

5 Briefly explain the concepts of benchmarking, reengineering, and the theory of constraints.

6 Prepare a quality-cost report.

7 Discuss the traditional and contemporary views of the optimal level of product quality.

8 Understand the different types of environmental costs and discuss environmental cost management.

9 Calculate the economic order quantity (EOQ) using the EOQ decision model (Appendix to Chapter 10).

10 Understand the differences between the EOQ and just-in-time (JIT) approaches to inventory management (Appendix to Chapter 10).

Managers of the most successful organizations do not rely on either financial or nonfinancial performance measures alone. They recognize that financial performance measures summarize the results of past actions. These measures are important to a firm's owners, creditors, employees, and so forth. Thus, they must be watched carefully by management as well. Nonfinancial performance measures concentrate on *current* activities, which will be the drivers of *future* financial performance. Thus, effective management requires a balanced perspective on performance measurement, a viewpoint called the *balanced scorecard* perspective.

In the present manufacturing environment, operational measures are also being developed to control key aspects of the production process. A just-in-time (JIT) philosophy demands adherence to strict quality standards for raw materials, manufactured components, and finished products. Nonfinancial data are vital for assessing a manufacturer's effectiveness in maintaining product quality.

The Balanced Scorecard

Learning Objective **1**

Describe the balanced scorecard concept and explain the reasoning behind it.

The **balanced scorecard** is a model of business performance evaluation that balances measures of financial performance, internal operations, learning and growth, and customer satisfaction.[1]

Managerial Accounting Practice

United Parcel Service (UPS)

THE BALANCED SCORECARD

For many companies, the balanced scorecard plays a key role in formulating strategy. According to a survey by Bain & Company, approximately 50 percent of Fortune 1000 companies in North America and roughly 40 percent in Europe use some version of the balanced scorecard (often abbreviated BSC). Among them are both manufacturers and service industry companies.[2]

Managers at United Parcel Service (UPS) believe that its balanced scorecard has played a critical strategic role in moving the organization forward. The company's scorecard was widely accepted by its employees, who felt that the BSC helped them link their jobs to the big picture of overall company success. UPS includes the following key measures in the four perspectives of its balanced scorecard.[3]

Financial

- Profit
- Revenue
- Cost
- Volume

Internal Operations

- Quality (e.g., timeliness of delivery, care in handling parcels)
- Operations (i.e., operational efficiency)

Customer

- Customer claims (e.g., lost parcels)
- Customer concerns
- Data integrity (e.g., accuracy of the parcel tracking process)

People*

- Employee injuries
- Employee retention
- Employee relation index

*This section is entitled "Learning and Growth" or "Innovation and Learning" in some versions of the balanced scorecard.

"The balanced scorecard is a communication, information, and learning system. Building a scorecard helps managers link today's actions with the achievement of today's priorities." (10a)

City of Charlotte, North Carolina

If an organization is to remain viable in a changing and competitive business environment, its managers need to continually ask the questions emphasized in the balanced scorecard. A management team must be concerned with the cost-effectiveness of their company's business processes as well as its products and/or services. Management must continually monitor the needs of its customers and assess their level of satisfaction with the products sold and/or services provided. The company's overall financial strength also must be prominent in management's thinking. Finally, are the company's products keeping up with the times in terms of technology? Are the company's employees providing the innovation critical to the company's future success?

Let's think about the goals and measures that top management might consider for the balanced scorecard depicted in Exhibit 10–1. For many companies, their primary financial goals are to maximize earnings and cash flow, and to allocate capital profitably toward growth initiatives that will drive long-term shareholder value. So the *financial perspective* would include such measures as earnings, earnings per share, and cash flow.

Now the question is, for any company to achieve its *financial goals* in *the future*, what does it need to be doing *now* in the balanced scorecard's *other three perspectives*? For its *customer perspective*, a company might use surveys to assess customer satisfaction with its products, as well as collect more objective data such as the number of customer claims or product returns. For the *learning and growth perspective*, a company might focus on the percentage of sales obtained from new products and services, and the average time from initial design to production. For its *internal operations perspective*, a company might focus on measures such as the percentage reduction in scrap/waste, the percentage improvement in labour productivity, the number of defects, and number of items reworked, and

> "[We are] a partner with all of the other functions in the business here. We are an equal partner with our product groups, with the engineering and manufacturing cohorts in making sure this business is a success." (10b)
> **Caterpillar**

Exhibit 10–1
Hypothetical Balanced Scorecard

How do we look to the company's owners?

How do our customers view our products?

In which activities must we excel?

How can we continually improve and create value?

so forth. The key point of the balanced scorecard concept is that by focusing on measures of performance *now* in these three key perspectives, a company can achieve its financial goals in the *future*.

To illustrate the balanced scorecard, we will explore its use by Canadian Pacific Bank (CPB). The bank's balanced scorecard, depicted in Exhibit 10–2, integrates performance measures in four key areas: financial, internal operations, customer, and learning and growth.[4] What is the rationale behind CPB's scorecard? The bank's dominant, long-term goal is financial growth. This goal will be assessed by the following financial measures: profit growth percentage, revenue growth percentage, and return on assets.

This raises the question, though, of what CPB has to do right now to ensure its long-term financial goals are met. Management has decided on several key goals that have to be achieved in the near term for this to happen.

Let's first look at the customer perspective in the balanced scorecard. The question for CPB's management is "How do the bank's customers see us?" Management has

Exhibit 10–2

Balanced Scorecard: Canadian Pacific Bank

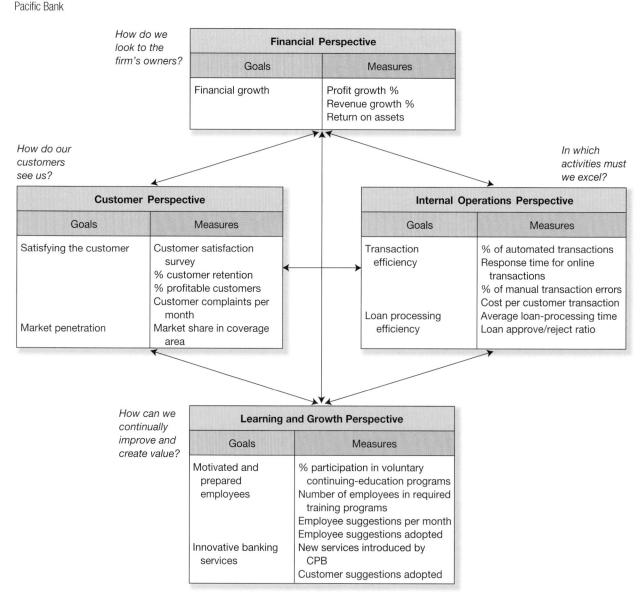

expressed its customer-perspective goal as "Satisfying the customer." How, then, can management measure progress on this short-term, day-to-day objective? Management has chosen five measures:

1. A customer satisfaction survey is conducted annually among all the bank's customers. Moreover, a more detailed customer satisfaction survey is aimed at the bank's key customers, which account for about 20 percent of the customer base.

2. CPB's management keeps track of the percentage of its customers that it retains from one year to the next. The assumption is that a customer who stays with CPB is largely satisfied with the service.

3. Not all of CPB's customers are profitable. (This is true of almost all banks.) For example, customers that keep low account balances, pay off their credit cards each month, and avoid service charges tend to be unprofitable. Therefore, the percentage of profitable customers is a very important measure. A trend in the wrong direction here would almost certainly spell trouble for the bank's financial goals in the future.

4. CPB's management has found that a particularly sensitive customer satisfaction measure is the number of complaints received in a month. If something is going awry in CPB's customer interface, customers are not shy about letting the bank know about it—and quickly.

5. Finally, CPB's market share in its coverage area is a key measure of market penetration. Increasing this key measure would most likely translate into revenue and profit growth in the future.

What about Canadian Pacific Bank's internal operations? In what business processes must CPB excel in order to achieve its long-term financial goals? Management has decided to focus on two important goals: completing routine bank transactions efficiently and processing loan applications efficiently. For routine bank transactions (e.g., making deposits, withdrawals, or loan payments), CPB's management focuses on three key measures:

1. Customers can complete automated transactions in three ways. They can bank online, use an ATM, or use a touch-tone telephone to make phone-automated inquiries. CPB's management believes that the greater the percentage of automated transactions, as opposed to transactions involving a bank teller, the more efficient will be the bank's transaction operations.

2. Another measure of transaction efficiency is the average time that it takes a customer to complete an online transaction. The smaller this time interval is, CPB's management believes, the more likely customers will be to use online banking.

3. As far as manual, teller-assisted transactions go, CPB's management keeps track of the percentage of these transactions that exhibit errors.

On the loan side of CPB's internal operations, management tracks two measures of loan-processing efficiency:

1. The average time to process a loan application is a key indicator of how smoothly this aspect of the bank's operations is running.

2. CPB's management also believes that the higher the ratio of approved-to-rejected loans, the more successful the bank has been in communicating its loan criteria to the bank's customer base.

Finally, let's look at the learning and growth perspective in Canadian Pacific Bank's balanced scorecard. Management has highlighted two goals: motivated and prepared

> "The overall big picture reason we designed the balanced scorecard for performance management at CIBC was to facilitate the deployment of strategic goals through the organization, and we needed a common framework to do this. It was important that every employee had ownership for the goals that they were expected to achieve, and understood what their contribution was to the goals of the overall business." (10c)
> **CIBC**

employees and innovative banking services. To assess the goal of motivated and prepared employees, CPB's management has established three measures:

1. The bank's human resource management team believes that the percentage of employees participating in voluntary continuing-education programs is an indicator of both employee motivation and preparation.

2. On the other hand, the number of employees in required training programs speaks to both the company's training program offerings as well as employee preparation.

3. The number of employee suggestions per month, as well as the number of those suggestions adopted, also speaks to both employee motivation and preparation. A motivated employee is more likely to submit a suggestion, and a well-prepared employee is more likely to make an adoptable suggestion.

The second goal under learning and growth on CPB's scorecard involves innovative banking services.

1. The number of new banking services first offered by CPB in its coverage area, as opposed to those first offered by competing banks, is a measure of just how innovative CPB's management is.

2. When the bank is able to act positively on a customer suggestion, this too speaks to CPB's ability to learn from its customer base.

All in all, CPB's management team believes that if the bank meets its current goals for its customer, internal operations, and learning and growth perspectives, the bank will ultimately be successful in achieving its long-term goal of financial growth.

Lead and Lag Measures: The Key to the Balanced Scorecard

Key to understanding the balanced scorecard is the distinction between lead and lag indicators of performance. *Lead indicators* of performance are measures of nonfinancial and financial outcomes that guide management in making current decisions that will result in desirable results in the future. In other words, lead indicators guide management to take actions *now* that will have positive effects on enterprise performance *later*. For example, Canadian Pacific Bank's scorecard includes the bank's market share in its coverage area as an indicator of future market growth, which will ultimately translate into growth of the bank's profitability. By including this key lead indicator in its scorecard, management is directed to take actions now that will increase the bank's market share.

Rockwater, which is owned by Halliburton, is a global undersea oil services company headquartered in Aberdeen, Scotland. Doing the undersea engineering and construction for drilling rigs such as the one pictured here requires diverse technical operations, both onshore and offshore. Rockwater's management found the balanced scorecard to be an invaluable tool in clarifying the company's goals and communicating them to the employees. Among the measures in Rockwater's balanced scorecard are the following: cash flow and project profitability (financial); safety index and hours spent with customers on new work (internal); project pricing and customer satisfaction (customer); percentage of revenue from new services and number of employee suggestions (learning and growth).[5]

Lag indicators are measures of the final outcomes of earlier management decisions. Examples of lag indicators are a company's profit and cash flow. These key financial measures, while important, improve only in later time periods, well after management has taken important actions to affect key operational results.

The whole idea of the balanced scorecard is to *use lead indicators to communicate with, motivate, and evaluate individuals* with the expectation that their current actions will result in improvements in the company's important lag measures (e.g., profitability) in the future. Exhibit 10–3 gives examples of several key lead and lag measures used in a variety of organizations' balanced scorecards.

Many companies, in all types of industries, have developed a balanced scorecard to help management and employees understand the important lead indicators of performance that will ultimately bring success on the company's key long-term goals. Among the many service industry firms that have developed a balanced scorecard are CIBC, Toronto's Hospital for Sick Children, Rogers Wireless Communications, Bank of Nova Scotia, and UPS. Retailers too have made use of the balanced scorecard. Among them are Best Buy, The Gap, and IKEA.

Among the well-known manufacturers making use of the balanced scorecard concept are Apple Computer, Caterpillar, Cisco Systems, General Motors, Microsoft, Motorola, Nissan Canada, and Phillips Electronics. Finally, government units have benefited from a balanced scorecard, among them the Royal Canadian Air Force, the Ontario Ministry of Health and Long-Term Care, and Vancouver Coastal Health.

> "Because of the balanced scorecard, the nature of the monthly financial meetings changed from a focus on the things Pitney Bowes is doing well to the three things we need to improve, with the emphasis on an appropriate action plan." (10d)
> **Pitney Bowes**

Exhibit 10–3
Selected Performance Measures Used in Balanced Scorecards

Financial Perspective

Earnings	Cash flow
Earnings per share	Cash flow from operations

Customer Perspective

Customer contacts	Customer satisfaction (surveyed)
Repeat customers	Customer complaints
New customers	Market share

Learning and Growth Perspective

Employee training hours	New processes
Employee promotion rate	Employee suggestions
New products or services	Employee retention

Internal Operations Perspective

Product quality/defect rates	Finished products per day per employee
Number of vendors	Floor space per finished product
Cycle time	Cost of inventories held
Throughput	Number of common parts
Machine downtime	Number of part numbers

Linking the Balanced Scorecard to Organizational Strategy

A key to making successful use of the balanced scorecard is linking the scorecard's lead and lag measures to the organization's strategy. As depicted in the diagram in Exhibit 10–4, the organization's vision and strategy drive the specification of both goals and metrics in the scorecard's financial, customer, internal operations, and learning and growth perspectives.[6]

Exhibit 10–4

Linkage between the
Balanced Scorecard and
Organizational Strategy

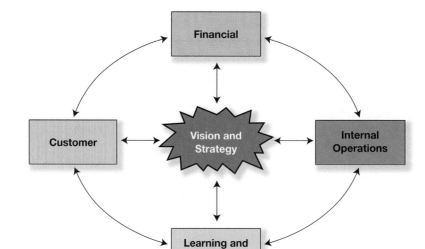

The precise form of the linkage between strategy and the goals and measures in the balanced scorecard will, of course, depend on the nature of the organization and its strategy. The following Managerial Accounting Practice feature explores this linkage for Dell Computer Corporation. (See also the Managerial Accounting Practice feature on Dell, "Mass Customization," in Chapter 2.)

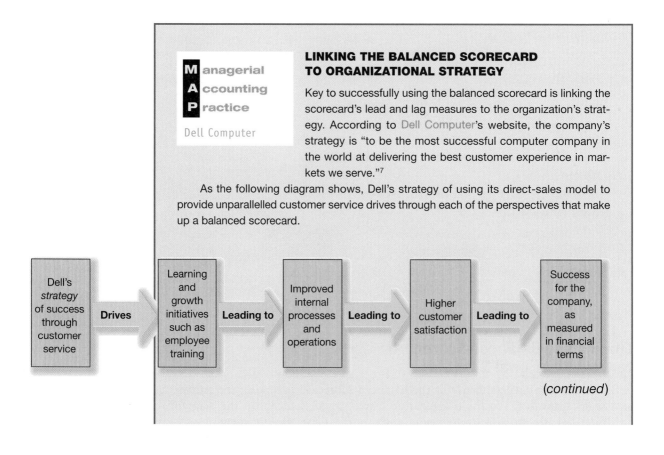

Managerial
Accounting
Practice

Dell Computer

LINKING THE BALANCED SCORECARD TO ORGANIZATIONAL STRATEGY

Key to successfully using the balanced scorecard is linking the scorecard's lead and lag measures to the organization's strategy. According to Dell Computer's website, the company's strategy is "to be the most successful computer company in the world at delivering the best customer experience in markets we serve."[7]

As the following diagram shows, Dell's strategy of using its direct-sales model to provide unparallelled customer service drives through each of the perspectives that make up a balanced scorecard.

Dell's *strategy* of success through customer service **Drives** Learning and growth initiatives such as employee training **Leading to** Improved internal processes and operations **Leading to** Higher customer satisfaction **Leading to** Success for the company, as measured in financial terms

(continued)

The following selected balanced scorecard measures are among those relevant for Dell Computer to successfully implement its strategy. Notice the frequency of the words *customer* and *sales* in these measures. Dell's strategy and its relevant balanced scorecard measures are dominated by its customer-focused direct-sales business model.

| **Financial** | Profit (in relation to assets invested)
Cash flow
Revenue growth by customer segment
Gross margin by customer segment |

| **Customer** | Customer perception of value (i.e., product quality relative to cost)
Customer retention
Customer perception of ease of interacting with Dell
Customer perception of customer response by Dell |

| **Internal processes and operations** | Defect rate within Dell's manufacturing operations
Defect rate by Dell's suppliers
Order-to-delivery cycle time
Time spent in contact with customers
Number of customer-focused process innovations |

| **Learning and growth** | Training expenditures per full-time employees
Number of customer-initiated product innovations
Number of patents that improve Dell's direct-sales business model
Number of emerging technologies evaluated |

Dell's vision and strategy

Operational Performance Measures in Today's Manufacturing Environment

Learning Objective **2**

Describe the operational performance measures appropriate for today's manufacturing environment.

In today's advanced manufacturing environment, operational performance measures are taking on ever-greater importance.[8] Under the philosophy of *activity-based management*, the goal is to focus on continually improving each activity. As a result, the emerging operational control measures focus on the key *activities* in which the organization engages. Exhibit 10–5 lists some commonly used operational performance measures. The list is representative, but not exhaustive, of those used in practice. In using these measures to control operations, management emphasizes trends over time. The goal is to continually improve all aspects of the plant's operations.

Exhibit 10–5
Operational Performance Measures for an Advanced Manufacturing Environment

Raw Material and Scrap   Raw material continues to be a significant cost element in any manufacturing process, whether labour-intensive or highly automated. Worldwide material sourcing and international competition have resulted in the purchasing function taking on greater importance in many firms. As a result, purchasing performance has

---

Raw Material and Scrap

Number of vendors
Number of unique parts
Number of common parts
Raw material as a percentage of total cost
Lead time for material delivery
Percentage of orders received on time
Total raw-material cost
Deviations between actual and budgeted raw-material prices
Scrap as a percentage of raw-material cost
Cost of scrap
Quality of raw material

Inventory

Average value of inventory
Average amount of time various inventory items are held
Ratio of inventory value to sales revenue
Number of inventoried parts

Machinery

Hours of machine downtime
Percentage of machine downtime
Percentage of machine availability
Bottleneck machine downtime
Percentage of bottleneck machine downtime
Percentage of bottleneck machine availability
Detailed maintenance records
Percentage of on-time routine maintenance procedures
Setup time
Machine flexibility:
  Product switchover times in a flexible manufacturing system (FMS) cell
  Number of different products manufactured in an FMS cell

Product Quality

Customer acceptance measures:
  Number of customer complaints
  Number of warranty claims
  Number of products returned
  Cost of repairing returned products
In-process quality measures:
  Number of defects found
  Cost of rework
Quality costs

Production and Delivery

Manufacturing cycle time
Velocity
Manufacturing cycle efficiency
Percentage of on-time deliveries
Percentage of orders filled
Delivery cycle time

Productivity

Financial measures:
  Aggregate or total productivity (Output in dollars ÷ Total input in dollars)
  Partial or component productivity (Output in dollars ÷ A particular input in dollars)
Operational (physical) measures:
  Partial or component productivity measures. These measures express
    relationships between inputs and outputs, in physical terms. For example:
    Finished products produced per day per employee
    Square metres of floor space required per finished product per day
    Electricity required per finished product

Learning and Growth

New products:
  Percentage of sales from new products
  New products introduced by this firm versus introductions by competitors
Process improvements:
  Number of process improvements made
  Cost savings from process improvements

become an important area of measurement; criteria include total raw-material cost, deviations between actual and budgeted material prices, the quality of raw materials, and the delivery performance of vendors.

The cost of scrap is highlighted as a separate item, rather than being included in the standard direct-material cost as a normal production cost. The objective is to reduce scrap to the absolute minimum.

Inventory The essence of the just-in-time production environment is low inventories at every stage of production. Thus, inventory control is of paramount importance in achieving the benefits of the JIT philosophy. Inventory control measures include the average value of inventory, the average amount of time various inventory items are held, and other inventory turnover measures, such as the ratio of inventory value to sales revenue.

Machinery If inventories are to be kept low, as the JIT philosophy demands, then the production process must be capable of producing goods quickly. This goal requires that production machinery must work when it is needed, which means that routine maintenance schedules must be adhered to scrupulously. Performance controls in this area include measures of machine downtime and machine availability, and detailed maintenance records. Some manufacturers make a distinction between *bottleneck machinery* and nonbottleneck machinery. A bottleneck operation is one that limits the production capacity of the entire facility. It is vital that the machinery in bottleneck operations be available 100 percent of the time, excluding time for routine required maintenance. In an advanced manufacturing environment, based on JIT and FMS, the investment in machinery is extremely large. To obtain the anticipated return from this investment, through the benefits of JIT and FMS, the machinery has to be kept running. This emphasis on bottleneck operations is consistent with the management philosophy known as the *theory of constraints*. This approach stresses the importance of identifying and easing the organization's constraints, which are the phenomena that limit the organization's productive capacity.[9]

Setup time also is highlighted as a machinery performance measure, and the objective in a JIT/FMS setting is to minimize this non-value-added activity. Machine flexibility measures emphasize the value of producing many different products in the same FMS cell.

Product Quality A JIT philosophy demands adherence to strict quality standards for raw materials, manufactured components, and finished products. Various nonfinancial data are vital for assessing a manufacturer's effectiveness in maintaining product quality. **Customer-acceptance measures** focus on the extent to which a firm's customers perceive its product to be of high quality. Typical performance measures include the number of customer complaints, the number of warranty claims, the number of products returned, and the cost of repairing returned products. **In-process quality controls** refer to procedures designed to assess product quality before production is completed. For example, in a *quality audit program*, partially completed products are randomly inspected at various stages of production. Defect rates are measured, and corrective actions are suggested. A third area of quality measurement relates to *raw-material quality*. Suppliers are rated on the basis of the quality of their materials as well as customer service.

Some companies routinely prepare a *quality-cost report*, which details the costs incurred in assuring product quality. We will discuss quality costs in a later section.

Production and Delivery A company will achieve little success if it manufactures a great product but delivers it to the customer a week late. World-class manufacturers are striving toward a goal of filling 100 percent of their orders on time. Common measures of product delivery performance include the percentage of on-time deliveries and the percentage of orders filled. Another measure is **delivery cycle time**, the average time between the receipt of a customer order and delivery of the goods.

Delivering goods on time requires that they be produced on time. Various operational performance measures have been developed to assess the timeliness of the production

"We have to be the best in cost throughout the world. And cycle time is also very important." (10e)
MiCRUS (Joint venture of IBM and Cirrus Logic)

process. **Manufacturing cycle time** is the total amount of production time (or through-put time) required per unit. It can be computed by dividing the total time required to produce a batch by the number of units in the batch. **Velocity** is defined as the number of units produced in a given time period. Perhaps an even more important operational measure is the **manufacturing cycle efficiency (MCE)**, defined as follows:

$$\text{Manufacturing cycle efficiency} = \frac{\text{Processing time}}{\text{Processing time} + \text{Inspection time} + \text{Waiting time} + \text{Move time}}$$

The value of the MCE measure lies in its comparison between value-added time (processing) and non-value-added time (inspection, waiting, and moving). In many manufacturing companies, MCE is less than 10 percent. Firms with advanced manufacturing systems strive for as high an MCE measure as possible.

Productivity   Global competitiveness has forced virtually all manufacturers to strive for greater productivity. One *financial* productivity measure is **aggregate** (or **total**) **productivity**, defined as total output divided by total input. A firm's total output is measured as the sum, across all of the goods and services produced, of those products and services times their sales prices. Total input is the sum of the direct-material, direct-labour, and overhead costs incurred in production. Another financial measure is a **partial** (or **component**) **productivity** measure, in which total output (in dollars) is divided by the cost of a particular input.

A preferable approach to productivity measurement is to record multiple physical measures that capture the most important determinants of a company's productivity. These *operational* (or *physical*) measures are also partial productivity measures, since each one focuses on a particular input. For example, a large automobile manufacturer routinely records the following data for one of its plants: the number of engines produced per day per employee and the number of square metres of floor space required per engine produced in a day. A large chemical company keeps track of the amount of energy (in British thermal units, Btu, or about 1,055 joules) required to convert a kilogram of raw chemicals into a kilogram of finished product. Data such as these convey more information to management than a summary financial measure such as aggregate productivity.

Learning and Growth   Global competition requires that companies continually improve and innovate. New products must be developed and introduced to replace those that become obsolete. New processes must continually be developed to make production more efficient. In a world-class manufacturer or service firm, the one thing that is most constant is change.

To summarize, nonfinancial measures are being used increasingly. These operational performance measures assist management in its goal of continuous process improvement. To be most effective, operational controls should be tied to the strategic objectives of the organization. Specific improvement targets can be set for various measures to provide motivation for improvement in the areas deemed most important by management.

Gain-Sharing Plans

One widely used method of providing incentives to employees to improve their performance on various operational control measures is gain sharing. A **gain-sharing plan** is an incentive system that specifies a formula by which cost or productivity gains achieved by a company are shared with the workers who helped accomplish the improvements. For example, suppose an electronics manufacturer reduced its defect rate in the Manual Insertion Department by 2 percent for a saving of $100,000. A gain-sharing formula might call for 25 percent of the savings to be shared with the employees in that department.

Other Management Tools

To remain competitive in today's global market, businesses must continually improve. Moreover, this continuous improvement needs to apply across the spectrum of business activity: from product design and quality, through production operations and cost management, to customer service. *Continuous improvement* may be defined as the constant effort to eliminate waste, reduce response time, simplify the design of both products and processes, and improve quality and customer service. One compelling reason for the need for continuous improvement is the *price down/cost down concept*. This refers to the tendency of prices to fall over the life cycle of a newly introduced product. Think, for example, about the prices of hand-held calculators, DVD players, personal listening devices, and HDTVs. When each of these products was first introduced, prices were quite high. However, as manufacturers gained experience in producing them, prices fell and the products became accessible to a much wider customer pool. However, if prices are to fall over time, manufacturers have to continually reduce costs as well.

Two approaches to continuous improvement (i.e., reduction) in production costs are now in widespread use. These techniques are called *target costing* and *kaizen costing*.

> "The idea of continuous improvement is just paramount. People have a sense of purpose. They have a real sense of 'I'm adding value to the company by reducing this waste.'" (10f)
>
> **Caterpillar**

Target Costing

Target costing refers to the design of a product and the processes used to produce it, so that ultimately the product can be manufactured at a cost that will enable the firm to make a profit when the product is sold at an estimated market-driven price. This estimated price is called the *target price*, the desired profit margin is called the *target profit*, and the cost at which the product must be manufactured is called the *target cost*.

To illustrate, suppose the design engineers of the Patio Grill Company we used as an example in Chapter 5 have designed a new built-in poolside barbeque grill to be sold under the brand name Poolside Grill. The company's management estimates that after a few years on the market, assuming the firm's competitors come out with comparable products, the Poolside Grill will sell for approximately $2,100. Moreover, management wants a target profit on its new Poolside Grill of $250. The target cost, then, for the manufacture of a Poolside Grill is $1,850 ($2,100 − $250). The task faced by Patio Grill Company's design engineers now is to refine the Poolside Grill's product design, and the processes that will be used to manufacture it, so that ultimately it will cost no more than $1,850 to produce.

Since target costing is closely related to the pricing process, it is explored more extensively in Chapter 13, which covers pricing decisions.

Learning Objective 3

Define and give an example of target costing.

Kaizen Costing

Target costing applies to the *design* of a new product or model and the *design* of its production process. In contrast, kaizen costing is the process of cost reduction during the manufacturing phase of an existing product. The Japanese word *kaizen* refers to continual and gradual improvement through small betterment activities, rather than large or radical improvement made through innovation or large investments in technology. The idea is simple: Improvement is the goal and responsibility of every worker, from the CEO to the manual labourers, in every activity, every day, all the time! Through the small but continual efforts of everyone, significant reductions in costs can be attained over time.

To help achieve the continuous cost reduction implied by the kaizen costing concept, an annual (or monthly) *kaizen cost goal* is established. Then, actual costs are tracked over time and compared to the kaizen goal. A kaizen costing chart used by Daihatsu (a Japanese auto manufacturer owned in part by Toyota) is shown in Exhibit 10–6.[10] Notice that the cost base or reference point is the actual cost performance at the end of the prior

Learning Objective 4

Explain the concept of kaizen costing and prepare a kaizen costing chart.

Exhibit 10–6

Kaizen Costing Chart Used by
Daihatsu Motor Company
(Osaka. Japan)

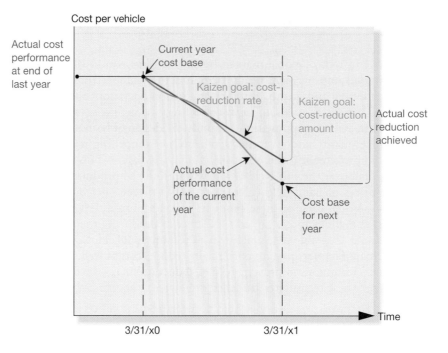

year. A kaizen goal is established for the cost-reduction rate and amount during the current year. Actual cost performance throughout the year is compared with the kaizen goal. At the end of the current year, the current actual cost becomes the cost base or reference point for the next year. Then, a new (lower) kaizen goal is established, and the cost-reduction effort continues.

How are kaizen costing goals met? The continual and relentless reduction of non-value-added activities and costs, the elimination of waste, and improvements in manufacturing cycle time all contribute to the effort. In addition, the improvement suggestions and kaizen efforts of all employees are taken seriously and implemented when appropriate. The result is a continually more efficient and cost-effective production process.

A good example of the successful use of both target costing and kaizen costing in bringing about continuous improvement is provided by Toyota, as the next section illustrates.

Toyota: Target Costing and Kaizen Costing in Action

Toyota Motor Corporation, the world's largest automaker, uses both target costing and kaizen costing to maintain its strong competitive position. "Cost planning at Toyota is mainly an effort to reduce cost at the design stage. Toyota sets goals for cost reduction, and then seeks to achieve those goals through design changes. To correctly assess the gains made, the exact amount of cost reduction through redesign is measured. Setting goals and assessing the results based on cost differences between old and new models constitute the essence of cost control at Toyota."[11]

Toyota also has achieved significant cost reduction through the redesign of production processes. For example, "over a five-year period, Toyota reduced the setup time for its 800-ton (1 ton = 0.90718474 tonnes) stamping presses from more than one hour to under 12 minutes."[12] Time savings such as this significantly reduce costs.

In addition to the cost savings realized in the design phase, Toyota aggressively pursues kaizen costing to reduce costs in the manufacturing phase. "In July and January, plant managers submit six-month plans for attaining their kaizen goals. Methods for achieving these goals include cutting material costs per unit and improvements in standard operating procedures. These are pursued based on employee suggestions. For improvements involving industrial engineering or value engineering, employees often receive support from the technical staff. To draw up a kaizen plan after kaizen goals have been set by top management, employees look for ways to contribute to kaizen in their daily work. About two million suggestions were received from Toyota employees in one recent year alone (roughly 35 suggestions per employee). Ninety-seven percent of them were adopted."[13] This is a prime example of the concept of employee empowerment, in which workers are encouraged to take the initiative in improving operations, reducing costs, and improving product quality and customer service.

Benchmarking

Benchmarking (also called **competitive benchmarking**) is the continual search for the most effective method of accomplishing a task, by comparing existing methods and performance levels with those of other organizations or with other subunits within the same organization. The most effective methods of accomplishing various tasks in a particular industry, often discovered through benchmarking, are referred to as **best practices**. Xerox Corporation is often credited with originating the benchmarking concept, but now the idea is widely used by organizations throughout the world. Benchmarking provides one more tool for companies to use in identifying non-value-added activities and pursuing continuous improvement.

Learning Objective **5**

Briefly explain the concepts of benchmarking, reengineering, and the theory of constraints.

Reengineering

In contrast to the concept of kaizen, which involves small, incremental steps toward gradual improvement, reengineering involves a giant leap. **Reengineering** is the complete redesign of a process, with an emphasis on finding creative new ways to accomplish an objective. Reengineering has sometimes been described as taking a blank piece of paper and starting from scratch to redesign a business process. Rather than searching continually for minute improvements, reengineering involves a radical shift in thinking about how an objective should be met. In the words of one reengineering consultant: "Reengineering prescribes radical, quick and significant change. Admittedly, this can entail high risks, but it can also bring big rewards. These benefits are most dramatic when new models are discovered for conducting business."[14]

Theory of Constraints

The theory of constraints (or TOC) is another contemporary management tool that supports continuous improvement and cost management programs. The theory of constraints is a management approach that seeks to maximize long-run profit through proper management of organizational bottlenecks or constrained resources.[15] The key idea in TOC is to identify the constraints in a system that are preventing the organization from achieving a higher level of success, then to seek to relieve or relax those constraints. Moreover, TOC recommends subordinating all other management goals to the objective of solving the constraint problems. For example, if limited capacity in a particular machining operation is increasing cycle time, reducing throughput, and reducing profits, then management would concentrate much of its efforts on expanding the capacity of that bottleneck operation.

Total Quality Management

For many companies, quality is at the forefront of the areas in which nonfinancial performance is critically important. The quality of the product or service that an organization provides can spell the difference between future profitability and disaster. Quality is equally important in the service and manufacturing industries. For Canadian Pacific Bank, the quality of service includes the convenience of branch locations, the customer support provided for online banking, the expediency of loan approvals, the friendliness of the bank tellers, and so forth. Bank customers are increasingly discriminating as they assess the overall quality of service and then select their banks accordingly. Similar comments apply to the airlines, long-distance telecommunications companies, hotels, car rental firms, and financial investment firms.

In the manufacturing industry, product quality has become a key factor in determining a firm's success or failure in the global marketplace. Advanced, highly reliable manufacturing methods have made it possible to achieve very high standards of product quality. As a result, more and more firms are making product quality a keystone of their competitive strategy.

Measuring and Reporting Quality Costs

Recognizing the importance of maintaining high product quality, companies often measure and report the costs of doing so. Before we examine the costs that companies incur to maintain high product quality, let's consider what product quality means.

Product Quality   What is meant by a high-quality product? There are two concepts of quality that determine a product's degree of excellence or the product's ultimate fitness for its intended use. A product's **grade** refers to the extent of its capability in performing its intended purpose in relation to other products with the same functional use. For example, a computer monitor that displays 65,536 colours is of a higher grade than a monitor that displays only 256 colours. A product's **quality of design** refers to how well it is conceived or designed for its intended use. For example, a coffee mug designed with a handle that is too small for the user's fingers is a poorly designed mug. The **quality of conformance** refers to the extent to which a product meets the specifications of its design. A coffee mug with an appropriately sized handle might be well designed, but if the handle breaks off due to shoddy manufacturing, it will be useless. This mug fails to conform to its design specifications. Both quality of design and quality of conformance are required in order to achieve a high-quality finished product.

Learning Objective   6
Prepare a quality-cost report.

Costs of Quality   Due to the increasing importance of maintaining high product quality, many companies routinely measure and report the costs of ensuring high quality. Four types of costs are monitored.

First are **prevention costs**, the costs of preventing defects. Second are **appraisal costs**, the costs of determining whether defects exist. The third type of costs are **internal failure costs**, those costs of repairing defects found prior to product sale. The last type of costs are **external failure costs**, those costs incurred when defective products have been sold.

Handic⊚

Exhibit 10–7 shows a quality-cost report prepared by Handico, Inc., a manufacturer of cordless telephones.[16] As is always true in cost monitoring, quality-cost reporting is most useful when cost trends are examined over a period of time. Through trend analysis, management can see where improvement is occurring and where difficulties exist. Goals can be set to achieve a particular cost target in an area of concern. For example, Handico's management might strive to reduce warranty costs to zero by a certain date.

Observable versus Hidden Quality Costs   The quality costs discussed in the preceding section are *observable*. They can be measured and reported, often on the basis of

Exhibit 10–7
Quality-Cost Report: Handico

Handic◎

	Current Month's Cost	Percentage of Total
Prevention costs		
Quality training	$ 2,000	1.3
Reliability engineering	10,000	6.5
Pilot studies	5,000	3.3
Systems development	8,000	5.2
Total prevention costs	$ 25,000	16.3
Appraisal costs		
Materials inspection	$ 6,000	3.9
Supplies inspection	3,000	2.0
Reliability testing	5,000	3.3
Metallurgical laboratory	25,000	16.3
Total appraisal costs	$ 39,000	25.5
Internal failure costs		
Scrap	$ 15,000	9.8
Repair	18,000	11.8
Rework	12,000	7.8
Downtime	6,000	3.9
Total internal failure costs	$ 51,000	33.3
External failure costs		
Warranty costs	$ 14,000	9.2
Out-of-warranty repairs and replacement	6,000	3.9
Customer complaints	3,000	2.0
Product liability	10,000	6.5
Transportation losses	5,000	3.3
Total external failure costs	$ 38,000	24.9
Total quality costs	$ 153,000	100.0

information in the accounting records. In addition to these observable quality costs, however, companies incur *hidden* quality costs. When products of inferior quality make it to market, customers are dissatisfied. Their dissatisfaction can result in decreased sales and a tarnished reputation for the company. Not only does the company experience lost sales for the inferior products but it will also likely experience lost sales in its other product lines. The opportunity cost of these lost sales and decreased market share can represent a significant hidden cost. Such hidden costs are difficult to estimate or report.

Changing Views of Optimal Product Quality

One way to express product quality is in the percentage of products that fail to conform to their specifications, that is, the percentage of defects. Given this perspective, what is the optimal level of product quality?[17]

Learning Objective   7

Discuss the traditional and contemporary views of the optimal level of product quality.

Traditional Perspective   The traditional viewpoint holds that finding the optimal level of product quality is a balancing act between incurring costs of prevention and appraisal on one hand and incurring costs of failure on the other. Panel A of Exhibit 10–8 depicts this trade-off. As the percentage of defective products decreases, the costs of prevention

Exhibit 10–8

Quality Costs and the Optimal Level of Product Quality

and appraisal increase. However, the costs of internal and external failure decrease. Adding the costs of prevention, appraisal, and internal and external failure yields total quality costs. The optimal product quality level is the point that minimizes total quality costs.

Contemporary Perspective   Due largely to the influence of Japanese product quality expert Genichi Taguchi, the contemporary viewpoint of optimal product quality differs from the traditional perspective. The contemporary view is that if both observable and hidden costs of quality are considered, *any* deviation from a product's target specifications results in the incurrence of increasing quality costs. Under the contemporary viewpoint, as depicted in panel B of Exhibit 10–8, the optimal level of product quality occurs at the *zero-defect level*. As panel B shows, the observable and hidden costs of internal and external failure increase as the percentage of defective products increases. The observable and hidden costs of prevention and appraisal increase slightly and then decrease as the percentage of defects increases. The most important point, though, is that the total costs of quality are minimized at the zero-defect level.

Whether the traditional or contemporary view of optimal product quality is most accurate is still being debated by quality-control experts. Moreover, the exact shape of the cost functions in Exhibit 10–8 is largely an empirical question, and the cost functions probably differ across industries and product types. One thing is certain, though: To compete successfully in today's global market, any company must pay very close attention to achieving a very high level of product quality.

Total Quality Management   Monitoring product quality coupled with measuring and reporting quality costs helps companies maintain programs of total quality management, or TQM. This refers to the broad set of management and control processes designed to focus the entire organization and all of its employees on providing products or services that do the best possible job of satisfying the customer. Among the tools used in total quality management is the **Six Sigma** program, an analytical method that aims at achieving near-perfect results in a production process. (See the following Managerial Accounting Practice feature for details.)

Identifying Quality-Control Problems   An effective TQM program includes methods for identifying quality-control problems. One method of identifying quality problems is the

Managerial
Accounting
Practice

Motorola,
General Electric,
Dell Computer,
Walmart,
Dow Chemical,
Allied Signal, and
Honeywell

SIX SIGMA FOR QUALITY MANAGEMENT AND COST REDUCTION

"Originally conceived by Motorola Inc. as a quality-improvement device" two decades ago, "Six Sigma soon morphed into a cost-cutting utensil for manufacturers of all stripes. Now, it's fast becoming the Swiss army knife of the business world. Goods producers still make up the bulk of users, who typically rely on statistics to uncover and then reduce product variance in order to boost quality and efficiency. But increasingly, manufacturers are applying Six Sigma to functions as varied as accounts receivable, sales, and research and development. And their success in these nonfactory domains has inspired Six Sigma projects at financial institutions, retailers, health-care concerns, and in other areas of the service sector."

Six Sigma is "an analytical method aimed at achieving *near-perfect results* in a production process. In statistics, the Greek letter *sigma* denotes variation in a standard bell curve. One sigma equals 690,000 defects per 1 million. Most companies do no better than three sigma, or 66,000 errors per million. Six Sigma reduces that count to *3.4 defects per million*. That saves money by preventing waste."

Six Sigma "achieves results by reducing subjective errors in the assessment of problems. First, auditors *define* a process where results are subpar. Then they *measure* the process to determine current performance, *analyze* this information to pinpoint where things are going wrong, and *improve* the process and eliminate the error. Last, *controls* are set up to prevent future bugs."

"In the world of manufacturing, Six Sigma has become something akin to a religion." When General Electric's former chairman Jack Welch embraced Six Sigma, for example, "he quickly assembled an unprecedented army of employees to pinpoint and fix problems throughout GE" using their Six Sigma training. "The results were awesome: In three years alone, these troops saved the company $8 billion, according to GE." Now "GE is sending out its Six Sigma squads to customers such as Dell Computer and Walmart stores to help them root out what GE estimates to be more than $1 billion in inefficiencies and waste—and help GE win more business."[18]

Dow Chemical has initiated several Six Sigma projects, each of which has saved an average of a half million dollars in its first year alone.[19] Allied Signal, which uses activity-based costing in conjunction with its Six Sigma program, saved over $500 million in the program's first year.[20] Honeywell is using the Six Sigma approach, in conjunction with other productivity improvements, with a goal of over a billion dollars in cost savings.[21]

"Employees charged with Six Sigma duties generally have what's called a *black belt*." At Allied Signal, for example, "it's awarded to those employees who complete four separate weeks of classroom study. In between those weeks of class, black-belt candidates must use what they've learned to focus on a project within the company and show some cost savings achieved by using Six Sigma."[22]

cause-and-effect diagram (also called an *Ishikawa* or *fishbone diagram*). Exhibit 10–9 displays such a diagram used by Xerox Corporation to identify the causes of errors in its customer billing process. As can be seen, the quality improvement team has identified a wide range of possible causes for billing errors. After identifying possible causes for billing errors, the Xerox team, nicknamed the Billing Bloopers Team, might take systematic steps to eliminate the root causes of the errors.

"Six Sigma might be the maturation of everything we've learned over the past 100 years about quality." (10g)
President, American Society for Quality

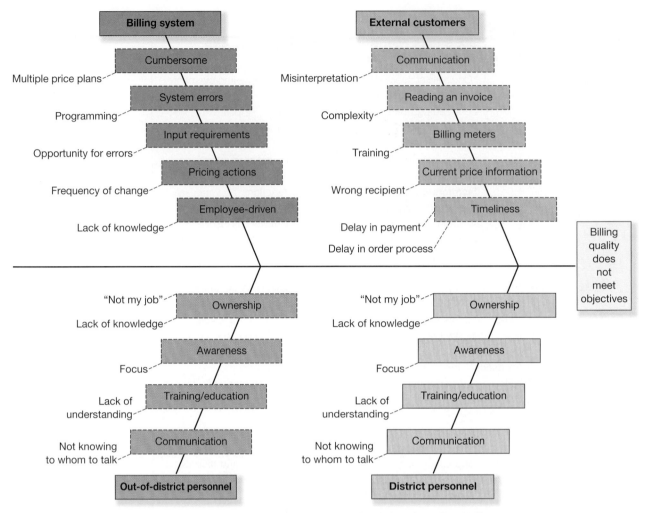

Source: David M. Buehlman and Donald Stover, "How Xerox Solves Quality Problems," *Management Accounting 75*/3 (September 1993), pp. 33–36.

Exhibit 10–9
Cause-and-Effect Diagram:
Billing Quality at Xerox
Corporation

Another helpful tool in quality improvement programs is the *Pareto diagram*, depicted in Exhibit 10–10. This one shows graphically the frequency with which various quality-control problems are observed for a particular model of cordless telephone. The diagram helps the TQM team visualize and communicate to others what the most serious types of defects are. Steps can then be taken to attack the most serious and most frequent problems first.

ISO 9000 Standards

A key factor in determining the quality of a company's products is its quality-control system. The organizational structure, personnel, procedures, and policies that are in place to monitor product quality will greatly affect a firm's ability to achieve high quality standards. In 1987, the International Organization for Standardization (ISO), based in Geneva, Switzerland, issued a set of quality-control standards for companies selling products in Europe. The ISO 9000 standards, as they have come to be known, focus on a manufacturer's quality-control system. The ISO 9000 standards basically require that a manufacturer have a well-defined quality-control system in place, and that the target level of product quality be maintained consistently. Moreover, the ISO 9000 standards require a manufacturer to prepare extensive

Number of
defective units

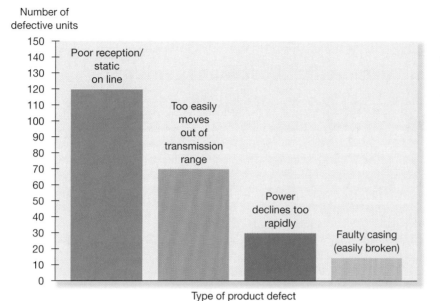

Handico

documentation of all aspects of the quality-control system. The first standard, ISO 9000, lists three objectives:

1. The company should sustain the quality of its product or service at a level that continually meets the purchaser's stated or implied needs.
2. The quality-control system should be sufficient to give the supplier's own management confidence that the intended quality is being maintained.
3. The supplying company should give the purchaser confidence that the intended quality is consistently achieved in the delivered product or service.

The ISO 9000 standards have been adopted in Canada as well. In fact, as early as 1972, Canada held a seat on ISO's governing Council; the Standards Council of Canada (SCC) manages Canada's participation in the ISO. The Canadian government and many large companies are more and more inclined to require their suppliers to have ISO 9000 certification.

The ISO 9000 standards consist of five major parts. ISO 9000 states the objectives of the standards, defines a quality-related vocabulary, and provides a guide to the other standards in the series. ISO 9001 provides a model for quality assurance in design, development, production, installation, and servicing. ISO 9002 focuses more narrowly on quality assurance in production and installation. ISO 9003 addresses quality assurance in final inspection and testing. Finally, ISO 9004 provides guidelines for the design of a quality management system.

Implications for Managerial Accounting   The ISO 9000 standards have several implications for management accountants. First, the standards require extensive documentation of the quality-control system. This task often falls to the controller's office. In fact, several of the largest public accounting firms are offering assurance services in helping companies meet the ISO documentation requirements. Second, the ISO standards require that the costs and benefits of the quality-control system be measured and documented. This means that management accountants will be responsible for measuring and reporting product life-cycle costs, quality costs, and the effectiveness of efforts at continuous improvement.

To summarize, the ISO 9000 standards are having a global impact on the way companies approach their quality-assurance objectives. The standards will affect virtually every area within a firm subject to its guidelines. Management accountants will be integrally involved in the informational and documentation aspects of the ISO 9000 program.[23]

Environmental Cost Management

As the world's population grows, business activity expands, and the globe seemingly shrinks, millions of people the world over are more aware than ever of the critical need to preserve our environment for ourselves and for posterity. Issues like air and water quality, hidden carcinogens, global warming, and the overconsumption of nonrenewable energy sources are in the headlines every day. Business leaders talk about the desirability of **sustainable development**, which means business activity that produces the goods and services needed in the present without limiting the ability of future generations to meet their needs. Many companies are striving for greater *ecoefficiency*, which means increasing their production of goods and services while at the same time decreasing the deleterious effects on the environment of that production. Unfortunately, not all companies are striving equally hard toward these desirable goals. To force companies to pay attention to environmental issues, in Canada we have environmental laws, such as the *Canadian Environmental Protection Act, 1999*, and the *Canadian Environmental Assessment Act*, as well as a federal agency, Environment Canada, which uses regulations to place strict controls on areas governed by these Acts. On a global scale, there are environmental initiatives as well, such as the Kyoto Protocol, which seeks to reduce emissions of greenhouse gases that many scientists believe contribute to climate change.

In 2010, Enbridge Inc. completed expansion of its solar energy facility in Sarnia, Ontario, to create the world's largest photovoltaic solar farm. The facility comprises 1.3 million solar modules across 943,000 square metres and generates enough energy to power more than 12,000 homes.

So, besides being a very important issue to all of us due to the clear health and quality-of-life implications, what does any of this have to do with managerial accounting? The answer is that the *costs* of dealing with environmental issues in one way or another are enormous. These **environmental costs** take many forms, such as installing scrubbers on a smokestack to comply with environmental regulations, improving a production process to reduce or eliminate certain pollutants, or cleaning up a contaminated river. In the next section, we will systematically explore these costs with the goal of having a better understanding of how to manage them.

Classifying Environmental Costs

There are many types of environmental costs—private and social, both visible and hidden.

Learning Objective **8**

Understand the different types of environmental costs and discuss environmental cost management.

Private versus Social Environmental Costs One important distinction is between private costs and social (or public) costs. *Private environmental costs* are those borne by a company or individual. Examples would be costs incurred by a company to comply with environmental regulations or to clean up a polluted lake. *Social environmental costs* are those borne by the public at large. Examples of these include costs borne by the taxpayers to staff Environment Canada; costs borne by the taxpayers to clean up a polluted lake or river; costs borne by individuals, insurance companies, and Medicare due to health problems caused by pollutants; and the unquantifiable quality-of-life costs we all bear from a degraded environment.

The tragic oil spill in the Gulf of Mexico stemming from an explosion at the Deepwater Horizon oil rig provides an unfortunate example of both social and private environmental costs. The social environmental costs associated with this disaster, which will be borne for years to come, include such costs as cleaning up fouled beaches and fragile wetlands, severe harm to the gulf states' recreational and fishing industries, and possible human health hazards from the hydrocarbons contaminating the Gulf's waters, marshes, and beaches. Huge private environmental costs will be borne by the companies involved in Deepwater Horizon's drilling operations, such as BP and its partners. While these social environmental costs are of great importance to all of us, we will focus our attention here on **environmental cost management**, which is the systematic attempt to measure and control or reduce the private environmental costs borne by a company or other organization.[24]

Visible versus Hidden Environmental Costs Both social and private environmental costs can be *visible* or *hidden*. *Visible social environmental costs* are those that are known and clearly identified as tied to environmental issues, such as the taxpayers' costs of staffing Environment Canada or cleaning up a polluted lake. *Hidden social environmental costs* include those that are caused by environmental issues but have not been so identified, such as the costs borne by individuals, insurance companies, or Medicare due to cancers caused by pollutants but not clearly identified as such. For example, is melanoma (a serious type of skin cancer) caused by a familial tendency, failure to use sun block, or a thinning of the ozone layer resulting from industrial emissions of chlorofluorocarbons? No one knows for sure.

Managing Private Environmental Costs

Let's focus our attention now on environmental cost management, or the measuring and control or reduction of private environmental costs.

Visible versus Hidden Private Environmental Costs Once again, we need to distinguish between visible and hidden costs. *Visible private environmental costs* are those that are measurable and have been clearly identified as tied to environmental issues. *Hidden private environmental costs* are those that are caused by environmental issues but have not been so identified by the accounting system.[25] Exhibit 10–11 provides examples of both visible and hidden private environmental costs.[26] Notice that the visible and the hidden costs listed in Exhibit 10–11 are further classified as follows:

- *Monitoring costs.* Costs of monitoring the production process to determine if pollution is being generated (e.g., costs of testing waste water for contaminants)
- *Abatement costs.* Costs incurred to reduce or eliminate pollution (e.g., changing a product's design to use more expensive materials that do not result in environmental contamination)

Exhibit 10–11
Private Environmental Costs

	Visible Costs	**Hidden Costs***
Monitoring	Inspecting products for contamination	Inspection of products
	Measuring contamination of processes or machinery	Incremental costs of procurement staff to ensure vendor compliance with environmental standards
	Verifying vendor compliance with environmental standards	
Abatement	Qualifying vendors for environmental compliance	Incremental material costs incurred to use less-polluting materials
	Recycling materials, containers, or water	Incremental direct-labour costs incurred to perform duties related to reducing pollution
	Designing products and processes to reduce or eliminate negative environmental impacts	Incremental costs of more expensive processes installed all or in part to reduce pollution
	Doing environmental impact analyses	Incremental costs of purchasing hybrid (electric and gasoline-powered) vehicles to reduce air pollution
Remediation		
On-site	Installing pollution reduction or elimination devices	Incremental direct-labour costs incurred to maintain remediation equipment
	Disposing of toxic waste in an environmentally sound manner	Incremental energy or other overhead costs incurred to operate remediation equipment
	Treating toxic waste	
Off-site	Cleaning up polluted sites (e.g., water, soil, or buildings)	Incremental direct-labour costs for workers used to perform environmental cleanup tasks
	Defending or settling environmental lawsuits	Foregone contribution margins on lost sales due to an unfavourable environmental record or reputation
	Paying regulatory fines	

*Each of the costs listed in the *Hidden Costs* column is included under the assumption that although these costs are caused by environmental concerns, the accounting system has not identified them as such. A study by Joshi and his colleagues provides evidence for the plausibility of this assumption. See Satish Joshi, Ranjani Krishnan, and Lester Lave, "Estimating the Hidden Costs of Environmental Regulation," *The Accounting Review 76*/2 (April 2001), pp. 171–198.

- *Remediation costs.* Cleanup costs
- *On-site remediation.* Costs of reducing or preventing the discharge into the environment of pollutants that have been generated in the production process (e.g., cost of installing scrubbers on a smokestack to remove certain air pollutants in the smoke)
- *Off-site remediation.* Costs of reducing or eliminating pollutants from the environment after they have been discharged (e.g., cost of cleaning up a river polluted by a company's operations)

The distinction between the visible and hidden costs listed in Exhibit 10–11 is an important but subtle one. Consider, for example, the incremental cost of using a more expensive material because it causes less (or no) negative environmental impact. Is this a visible or a hidden cost? The answer is *it depends on whether the accounting system has measured this cost and identified it as an environmental cost.* Studies show that many environmental costs are hidden, because the accounting system does not measure and identify them as environmental costs. "Most accounting systems accumulate visible costs into environmental cost pools, separate from other overhead cost pools. . . . For example, many steel mills compile separate cost pools for wastewater treatment, remediation, hazardous waste disposal, pollution-abatement capital expenditures, and depreciation on pollution abatement equipment."[27] However, a steel mill's incremental material costs caused by changing from sinters to less-polluting pellets in response to more stringent environmental regulations is typically not separately reported by the accounting system as an environmental cost.[28] Hence, it remains a *hidden* environmental cost.

Why is this point about visible versus hidden costs so important? Because many observers believe that the visible costs reported by most accounting systems may be only a small proportion of the hidden costs. A steel industry study, for example, concluded that the hidden costs were nearly 10 times the visible costs!

Environmental Cost Strategies

We have only scratched the surface in our discussion of environmental costs, and it is an area certain to receive much greater attention in the future—both in practice and in academia. Let's conclude our discussion with a brief mention of three strategies for managing environmental costs.[29]

1. *End-of-pipe strategy.* Under this approach, companies produce the waste or pollutant, and then clean it up before it is discharged into the environment. Smokestack scrubbers, waste water treatment, and carbon air filters are examples of end-of-pipe strategies.

2. *Process improvement strategy.* Under this approach, companies modify products and production processes to produce little or no pollutants, or find ways to recycle wastes internally.

3. *Prevention strategy.* "The ultimate strategy for maximizing the value of pollution-related activities involves . . . not producing any pollutants in the first place. With this strategy, companies avoid all problems with regulatory authorities and, in many cases, generate significant profit improvements."[30]

ISO 14000 Standards

The ISO 14000 standards address "environmental management." This means what the organization does to minimize harmful effects on the environment caused by its activities, and to achieve continual improvement of its environmental performance. The very first two standards deal with environmental management systems (EMS). ISO 14001 provides the requirements for an EMS and ISO 14004 gives general EMS guidelines. The other standards and guidelines address specific environmental aspects, including labelling, performance evaluation, life cycle analysis, communication and auditing.

An ISO 14001-based EMS is a management tool enabling an organization of any size or type to

- Identify and control the *environmental impact* of its activities, products, or services
- *Improve* its environmental performance continually
- Implement a *systematic approach* to setting environmental objectives and targets, to achieving these, and to demonstrating that they have been achieved

The Standards Council of Canada accredits certification bodies that assess and certify environmental management systems to the international standard ISO 14001. In addition, SCC manages various sector programs. For example, the use of forestry standards by Canadian producers enables them to move toward sustainable practices and ensure a renewable supply of raw materials. The Canadian national standard, *CAN/CSA Z809-2002 Sustainable Forest Management* and the *Sustainable Forestry Initiative (SFI) 2005–2009* standard, outline the principal requirements of conformance. These standards support continued marketplace acceptance, both domestically and internationally, of forestry products by environmentally conscious consumers. Certification to ISO 14001, CAN/CSA Z809, and SFI 2005–2009 provide significant contributions to the verification of sustainable forestry management practices. Organizations that achieve this certification from a body accredited by the SCC are showing their dedication to corporate social responsibility and continuous improvement.

Chapter Summary

LO1 Describe the balanced scorecard concept and explain the reasoning behind it. The balanced scorecard is an important tool designed to focus management's attention on key current goals, which, if achieved, will facilitate the attainment of the organization's long-term goals. By achieving current goals in the customer, internal operations, and learning and growth perspectives, the company will ultimately achieve its long-term financial goals.

LO2 Describe the operational performance measures appropriate for today's manufacturing environment. Nonfinancial measures of operational performance are widely used to augment the control information provided by standard costing. These measures typically focus on raw material and scrap, inventory, machinery, product quality, production and delivery, productivity, and learning and growth.

LO3 Define and give an example of target costing. *Target costing* refers to the design of a product and the processes used to produce it, so that ultimately the product can be manufactured at a cost that will enable the firm to make a profit when the product is sold at an estimated market-driven price.

LO4 Explain the concept of kaizen costing and prepare a kaizen costing chart. Kaizen costing is the process of cost reduction during the manufacturing phase of an existing product.

LO5 Briefly explain the concepts of benchmarking, reengineering, and the theory of constraints. Management tools that are consistent with continuous improvement efforts include benchmarking, reengineering, and the theory of constraints. Benchmarking is the continual search for the most effective method of accomplishing a task, by comparing existing methods and performance levels with those of other organizations or with other subunits within the same organization. Reengineering is the complete redesign of a process, with an emphasis on finding creative new ways to accomplish an objective. The theory of constraints is a management approach that seeks to maximize long-run profit through proper management of organizational bottlenecks or constrained resources.

LO6 Prepare a quality-cost report. As product quality becomes increasingly important, many firms are beginning to carefully monitor the costs of maintaining product quality. Quality costs often are categorized as follows: prevention costs, appraisal costs, internal failure costs, and external failure costs. These quality costs are periodically listed in a quality-cost report, which is used by management as it seeks to ensure quality products and services and manage the costs of providing them.

LO7 Discuss the traditional and contemporary views of the optimal level of product quality. In addition to observable quality costs, companies experience hidden quality costs, such as the opportunity cost associated with lost market share. The contemporary perspective on product quality holds that if both observable and hidden costs of product quality are considered, the optimal level of product quality occurs at the zero defect level. In contrast, the traditional viewpoint holds that the optimal level of product quality occurs at the minimum point on the total quality cost curve, which typically is above the zero-defect level.

LO8 Understand the different types of environmental costs and discuss environmental cost management. Companies incur a variety of environmental costs. These costs include private versus social environmental costs, and the private environmental costs include some visible and some hidden costs. These visible and hidden environmental costs include the costs of monitoring, abatement, and both on-site and off-site remediation.

Review Problem on Operational Performance Measures

Tuscarora Door Company manufactures high-quality wooden doors used in home construction. The following information pertains to operations during April.

Processing time (average per batch)	6 hours
Inspection time (average per batch)	1 hour
Waiting time (average per batch)	4 hours
Move time (average per batch)	5 hours
Units per batch	40 units

Compute the following operational measures: (1) average value-added time per batch; (2) average non-value-added time per batch; (3) manufacturing cycle efficiency; (4) manufacturing cycle time; (5) velocity.

Solutions to Review Problem

1. Average value-added time per batch = Processing time = 6 hours

2. Average non-value-added time per batch = Inspection time + Waiting time + Move time

$$= 10 \text{ hours}$$

3. Manufacturing cycle efficiency $= \dfrac{\text{Processing time}}{\substack{\text{Processing time} + \text{Inspection time} \\ + \text{ Waiting time } + \text{ Move time}}}$

$$= \dfrac{6 \text{ hours}}{6 \text{ hours} + 1 \text{ hour} + 4 \text{hours} + 5 \text{ hours}} = 37.5\%$$

4. Manufacturing cycle time $= \dfrac{\text{Total production time per batch}}{\text{Units per batch}}$

$$= \dfrac{16 \text{ hours}}{40 \text{ units per batch}} = 0.4 \text{ hour or 24 minutes) per unit}$$

5. Velocity $= \dfrac{\text{Units per batch}}{\text{Total production time per batch}}$

$$= \dfrac{40 \text{ units}}{16 \text{ hours}} = 2.5 \text{ units per hour}$$

Glossary

Review key terms and definitions on Connect.

APPENDIX TO CHAPTER 10

Inventory Management

A key decision in manufacturing, retail, and some service industry firms is how much inventory to keep on hand. Once inventory levels are established, they become an important input to the budgeting system. Inventory decisions involve a delicate balance between three classes of costs: ordering costs, holding costs, and shortage costs. Examples of costs in each of these categories are given in Exhibit 10–12.

Learning Objective 9

Calculate the economic order quantity (EOQ) using the EOQ decision model.

Exhibit 10–12
Inventory Ordering, Holding, and Shortage Costs

Ordering Costs

Clerical costs of preparing purchase orders

Time spent finding suppliers and expediting orders

Transportation costs

Receiving costs (e.g., unloading and inspection)

Holding Costs

Costs of storage space (e.g., warehouse depreciation)

Security

Insurance

Foregone interest on working capital tied up in inventory

Deterioration, theft, spoilage, or obsolescence

Shortage Costs

Disrupted production when raw materials are unavailable:

Idle workers

Extra machinery setups

Lost sales resulting in dissatisfied customers

Loss of quantity discounts on purchases

The following example of an outdoor equipment manufacturer emphasizes the benefits of a sound inventory policy.

Calculating Economic Order Quantity

An outdoor equipment manufacturer has recently expanded its product line into winter sports equipment. The company's newest product is a fibreglass snowboard. One of the raw materials is a special resin used to bind the fibreglass in the moulding phase of production. The production manager, Hi Mogul, uses an **economic order quantity (EOQ)** decision model to determine the size and frequency with which resin is ordered. The EOQ model is a mathematical tool for determining the order quantity that minimizes the costs of ordering and holding inventory.

Resin is purchased in 50-litre drums, and 9,600 drums are used each year. Each drum costs $400. The controller estimates that the cost of placing and receiving a typical resin order is $225. The controller's estimate of the annual cost of carrying resin in inventory is $3 per drum.

Tabular Approach

Suppose Mogul orders 800 drums of resin in each order placed during the year. The total annual cost of ordering and holding resin in inventory is calculated as follows:

$$\frac{\text{Annual requirement}}{\text{Quantity per order}} = \frac{9,600}{800} = 12 = \text{Number of orders}$$

$$\text{Annual ordering cost} = 12 \text{ orders} \times \$225 \text{ per order} = \$2,700$$

$$\text{Average quantity in inventory} = \frac{\text{Quantity per order}}{2} = \frac{800}{2} = 400 \text{ drums}$$

$$\text{Annual holding cost} = (\text{Average quantity in inventory}) \times (\text{Annual carrying cost per drum})$$
$$= 400 \times \$3 = \$1,200$$

$$\frac{\text{Total annual cost}}{\text{of inventory policy}} = \text{Ordering cost} + \text{Holding cost} = \$2,700 + \$1,200 = \$3,900$$

Notice that the $3,900 cost does not include the purchase cost of the resin at $400 per drum. We are focusing only on the costs of *ordering* and *holding* resin inventory.

Can Mogul do any better than $3,900 for the annual cost of his resin inventory policy? Exhibit 10–13, which tabulates the inventory costs for various order quantities, indicates that Mogul can lower the costs of ordering and holding resin inventory. Of the five order quantities listed, the 1,200-drum order quantity yields the lowest total annual cost. Unfortunately, this tabular method for finding the least-cost order quantity is cumbersome. Moreover, it does not necessarily result in the optimal order quantity. It is possible that some order quantity other than those listed in Exhibit 10–13 is the least-cost order quantity.

Equation Approach

The total annual cost of ordering and holding inventory is given by the following equation:

$$\text{Total annual cost} = \left(\frac{\text{Annual requirement}}{\text{Order quantity}}\right)\left(\begin{array}{c}\text{Cost per}\\\text{order}\end{array}\right)$$
$$+ \left(\frac{\text{Order quantity}}{2}\right)\left(\begin{array}{c}\text{Annual holding}\\\text{cost per unit}\end{array}\right)$$

Exhibit 10–13
Tabulation of Inventory
Ordering and Holding Costs

Order size..	800	960	1,200	1,600	2,400
Number of orders (9,600 ÷ Order size).....................	12	10	8	6	4
Ordering costs ($225 × Number of orders)...............	$2,700	$2,250	$1,800	$1,350	$ 900
Average inventory (Order size ÷ 2)...........................	400	480	600	800	1,200
Holding costs ($3 × Average inventory).....................	$1,200	$1,440	$1,800	$2,400	$3,600
Total annual cost (Ordering cost + Holding cost).........	$3,900	$3,690	$3,600	$3,750	$4,500

↑
Minimum

The following formula for the least-cost order quantity or EOQ has been developed using calculus:

$$\text{Economic order quantity} = \sqrt{\frac{(2)(\text{Annual requirement})(\text{Cost per order})}{(\text{Annual holding cost per unit})}}$$

The EOQ formula in this example yields the following EOQ for resin:

$$\text{EOQ} = \sqrt{\frac{(2)(9,600)(225)}{3}} = 1,200$$

Graphical Approach

Another method for solving the EOQ problem is the graphical method, which is presented in Exhibit 10–14. Notice that the ordering-cost line slants down to the right. This indicates a decline in these costs as the order size increases and the order frequency

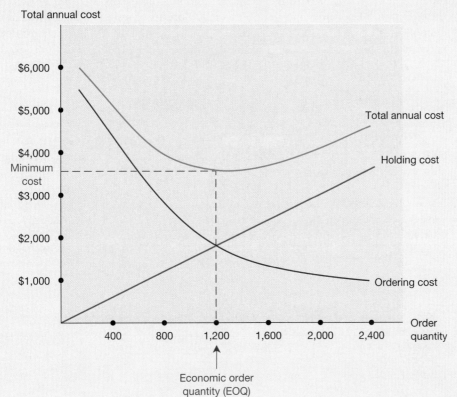

Exhibit 10–14
Graphical Solution to Economic
Order Quantity Decision

decreases. However, as the order size increases, so does the average inventory on hand. This results in an increase in holding costs, as indicated by the positive slope of the holding-cost line. The EOQ falls at 1,200 units, where the best balance is struck between these two costs. Total costs are minimized at $3,600.

Timing of Orders

The EOQ model helps management decide how much to order at a time. Another important decision is when to order. This decision depends on the **lead time**, which is the length of time it takes for the material to be received after an order is placed. Suppose the lead time for resin is one month. Since the company uses 9,600 drums of resin per year and the production rate is constant throughout the year, the implication is that 800 drums are used each month. Production manager Mogul should order resin, in the economic order quantity of 1,200 drums, when the inventory falls to 800 drums. By the time the new order arrives, one month later, the 800 drums in inventory will have been used in production. Exhibit 10–15 depicts this pattern of ordering and using inventory. By placing an order early enough to avoid a stockout, management takes into account the potential costs of shortages.

Safety Stock

Our example assumed that the usage of resin is constant at 800 drums per month. Suppose instead that monthly usage fluctuates between 600 and 1,000 drums. Although average monthly usage still is 800 drums, there is the potential for an excess usage of 200 drums in any particular month. In light of this uncertainty, management might want to keep a safety stock of resin equal to the potential excess monthly usage of 200 drums. With a safety stock of 200 drums, the reorder point is 1,000 drums. Thus, Mogul should order the EOQ of 1,200 drums whenever resin inventory falls to 1,000 drums. During the one-month lead time, another 600 to 1,000 drums of resin will be consumed in production. Although a safety stock will increase inventory holding costs, it will minimize the potential costs caused by shortages.

Exhibit 10–15

Ordering, Lead Time, and Usage of Inventory

JIT Inventory Management: Implications for EOQ

The EOQ model minimizes the total cost of ordering and holding purchased inventory. Thus, this inventory management approach seeks to balance the cost of ordering against the cost of storing inventory. Under the JIT philosophy, the goal is to keep *all* inventories as low as possible. *Any* inventory holding costs are seen as inefficient and wasteful. Moreover, under JIT purchasing, ordering costs are minimized by reducing the number of vendors, negotiating long-term supply agreements, making less frequent payments, and eliminating inspections. The implication of the JIT philosophy is that inventories should be minimized by more frequent deliveries in smaller quantities. This result can be demonstrated using the EOQ formula, as shown in Exhibit 10–16. As the cost of holding inventory increases, the EOQ decreases. Moreover, as the cost of placing an order declines, the EOQ decreases.

The economics underlying the EOQ model support the JIT viewpoint that inventory should be purchased or produced in small quantities, and inventories should be kept to an absolute minimum. However, the basic philosophies of JIT and EOQ are quite different. The EOQ approach takes the view that some inventory is necessary, and the goal is to optimize the order quantity in order to balance the cost of ordering against the cost of holding inventory. In contrast, the JIT philosophy argues that holding costs tend to be higher than is apparent because of the inefficiency and waste of storing inventory. Thus, inventory should be minimized, or even eliminated completely if possible. Moreover, under the JIT approach, orders will typically vary in size, depending on needs. The EOQ model, in contrast, results in a constant order quantity.

Learning Objective   10

Understand the differences between the EOQ and just-in-time (JIT) approaches to inventory management.

Holding Costs per Unit	Ordering Costs per Order				
	$225	**$150**	**$100**	**$50**	
$3	1,200*	980	800	566	EOQ declines
4	1,039	849	693	490	
5	930	759	620	438	
6	849	693	566	400	
	EOQ declines				

Exhibit 10–16
Economic Order Quantity with Different Ordering and Holding Costs

*The annual requirement is assumed to be 9,600 units for each case in this table. This was the annual requirement for drums of resin in the example. (Several of the EOQs in the table are rounded.)

Appendix to Chapter 10 Summary

LO9 Calculate the economic order quantity (EOQ) using the EOQ decision model. The EOQ model is a mathematical tool for determining the order quantity that minimizes the costs of ordering and holding inventory.

LO10 Understand the differences between the EOQ and just-in-time (JIT) approaches to inventory management. The EOQ approach takes the view that some inventory is necessary, and the goal is to optimize the order quantity in order to balance the cost of ordering against the cost of holding inventory. In contrast, the JIT philosophy argues that holding costs tend to be higher than is apparent because of the inefficiency and waste of storing inventory.

Review Questions

10–1. Suggest two performance measures in each of the four balanced scorecard categories for a service industry firm of your choice. Using these measures as examples, explain the difference between lead and lag measures.

10–2. List seven areas in which nonfinancial, operational performance measures are receiving increased emphasis in today's manufacturing environment.

10–3. Define the term *manufacturing cycle efficiency*.

10–4. List four examples of customer acceptance measures.

10–5. What is meant by *aggregate productivity*, and what are its limitations?

10–6. Give an example of a gain-sharing plan that could be implemented by an airline.

10–7. What is meant by the following terms: continuous improvement, price down/cost down concept, target costing, target price, target cost, target profit, value engineering, and kaizen costing?

10–8. Which of the following terms is most consistent with the old saying "Slow and steady wins the race": target costing, kaizen costing, or reengineering? Explain.

10–9. What is meant by *employee empowerment, benchmarking, best practices*, and *reengineering*?

10–10. Explain how the concepts of *continuous improvement* and the *theory of constraints* are related.

10–11. Elimination of production bottleneck activities is an example of what management concept?

10–12. List and define four types of product quality costs.

10–13. Explain the difference between observable and hidden quality costs.

10–14. Distinguish between a product's quality of design and its quality of conformance.

10–15. What is meant by a product's *grade*, as a characteristic of quality? Give an example in the service industry.

10–16. "An ounce of prevention is worth a pound of cure." Interpret this old saying in the light of Exhibit 10–7.

10–17. Briefly explain the purpose of a cause-and-effect (or fishbone) diagram.

10–18. Define the following types of environmental costs: private, social, visible, hidden, monitoring, abatement, and both on-site and off-site remediation.

10–19. Explain three strategies of environmental cost management.

10-20. (Appendix) Define and give examples of *inventory ordering, holding*, and *shortage costs*.

10–21. (Appendix) Explain the differences in the basic philosophies underlying the JIT and EOQ approaches to inventory management.

Exercises

Exercise 10–22 Balanced Scorecard: Educational Institution **(LO1)**

Think carefully about the overall mission and goals of your college or university.

Required:

1. How does the task of building a balanced scorecard for an educational institution differ from that for a profit-seeking enterprise?

2. Design a simple balanced scorecard for your school, with a minimum of two measures in each of the scorecard's perspectives.

Exercise 10–23 Operational Performance Measures **(LO2)**

Hiawatha Hydrant Company manufactures fire hydrants in London, Ontario. The following information pertains to operations during May.

Processing time (average per batch)	8.5 hours
Inspection time (average per batch)	0.5 hour
Waiting time (average per batch)	0.5 hour
Move time (average per batch)	0.5 hour
Units per batch	20 units

Required: Compute the following operational measures: (1) manufacturing cycle efficiency; (2) manufacturing cycle time; (3) velocity.

Exercise 10–24 Performance Measures for Production and Delivery **(LO2)**

Data Screen Corporation is a highly automated manufacturing firm. The vice-president of finance has decided that traditional standards are inappropriate for performance measures in an automated environment. Labour is insignificant in terms of the total cost of production and tends to be fixed, material quality is considered more important than minimizing material cost, and customer satisfaction is the number-one priority. As a result, production and delivery performance measures have been chosen to evaluate performance. The following information is considered typical of the time involved to complete and ship orders.

Waiting time:

From order being placed to start of production	8 days
From start of production to completion	7 days
Inspection time	1.5 days
Processing time	3 days
Move time	2.5 days

Required:

1. Calculate the manufacturing cycle efficiency.
2. Calculate the delivery cycle time.

(CMA, adapted)

Exercise 10–25 Productivity Measurement (LO2)

Managerial accounting procedures developed for the manufacturing industry often are applied in nonmanufacturing settings also. Ontario Bank and Trust Company's total output of financial services during the year just ended was valued at $10 million. The total cost of the firm's inputs, primarily direct labour and overhead, was $8 million.

Required:

1. Compute Ontario Bank and Trust's aggregate (or total) productivity for the year.
2. Do you believe this is a useful measure? Why? Suggest an alternative approach that Ontario Bank and Trust might use to measure productivity.

Exercise 10–26 Target Costing (LO3)

Suppose you have just started a business to manufacture your newest invention, the photon gismo. Let's say you believe that after a few years on the market, photon gismos will sell for about $125. This allows for the introduction of similar devices by your competitors. Furthermore, let's say you want to make a profit of $25 on each gismo sold.

Required:

1. What is the target cost for the photon gismo?
2. What is the target profit?
3. What is the target price?
4. Suppose your engineers and cost accountants conclude that your design of the photon gismo will result in a unit cost of $115. How can you use the concept of target costing to help achieve your objective?

Exercise 10–27 Benchmarking (LO5)

The continual search for the most effective method of accomplishing a task through comparison of existing methods and performance levels with those of other organizations or with other subunits within the same organization is called *benchmarking*. Sometimes organizations benchmark their operations against similar organizations, including their competitors. In other cases, organizations benchmark against a completely different type of organization. For example, a telecommunications company benchmarked its customer service operations against a NASCAR pit crew. The idea was to see how the telecommunications company's customer service unit could improve its response time by learning from the NASCAR crew. The pit crew, of course, had honed its procedures meticulously to get the necessary service accomplished in the least time possible. This type of benchmarking study is sometimes referred to as benchmarking "outside the box."

Required:

1. How could your college or university benefit from benchmarking against a similar institution of higher education? What departments, operations, or procedures might be appropriate for the focus of such a benchmarking study?
2. How could your school benefit from benchmarking outside the box? What departments, operations, or procedures might benefit from such a study? What noneducational organizations might be chosen for the benchmarking study?

Exercise 10–28 Quality Costs (LO6)

The following costs were incurred by Osaka Metals Company to maintain the quality of its products. (*Yen* is the national currency of Japan.)

1. Operating an X-ray machine to detect faulty welds, 110,000 yen
2. Repairs of products sold last year, 116,000 yen
3. Cost of rewelding faulty joints, 17,000 yen
4. Cost of sending machine operators to a three-week training program so they could learn to use new production equipment with a lower defect rate, 18,100 yen

Required: Classify each of these costs as a prevention, appraisal, internal failure, or external failure cost.

Exercise 10–29 Quality-Cost Report (LO6)

Coquitlam Circuitry manufactures electrical instruments for a variety of purposes. The following costs related to maintaining product quality were incurred in May.

Training of quality-control inspectors	$21,000
Tests of instruments before sale	30,000
Inspection of electrical components purchased from outside suppliers	12,000
Costs of rework on faulty instruments	9,000
Replacement of instruments already sold, which were still covered by warranty	16,500
Costs of defective parts that cannot be salvaged	6,100

Required: Prepare a quality-cost report similar to the report shown in Exhibit 10–7.

Exercise 10–30 Costs of Quality: Airline (LO6)

List three observable and three hidden quality costs that could occur in the airline industry related to the quality of service provided.

Exercise 10–31 Environmental Cost Management; Internet (LO8)

Visit the website of TransAlta, Inc. at www.transalta.com and find the company's report on sustainability.

Required: What are TransAlta's products? Describe the company's efforts toward sustainable development.

Exercise 10–32 Economic Order Quantity (Appendix) (LO9)

For each of the following independent cases, use the equation method to compute the economic order for quantity.

	Case A	Case B	Case C
Annual requirement (in units)	13,230	1,681	560
Cost per order	$250	$40	$10
Annual holding cost per unit	6	20	7

Exercise 10–33 Lead Time and Safety Stock (Appendix) (LO9)

Andrew and Fulton, Inc. uses 780 tonnes of a chemical bonding agent each year. Monthly demand fluctuates between 50 and 80 tonnes. The lead time for each order is one month, and the economic order quantity is 130 tonnes.

Required:

1. Determine the safety stock appropriate for the chemical bonding agent.
2. At what order point, in terms of tonnes remaining in inventory, should Andrew and Fulton, Inc. order the bonding agent?

Exercise 10–34 Economic Order Quantity: Equation Approach; JIT Purchasing (Appendix) (LO9, 10)

Fibre Technology, Inc. manufactures glass fibres used in the communications industry. The company's materials and parts manager is currently revising the inventory policy for XL-20, one of the chemicals used in the production process. The chemical is purchased in 10-kilogram canisters for $95 each. The firm uses 4,800 canisters per year. The controller estimates that it costs $150 to place and receive a typical order of XL-20. The annual cost of storing XL-20 is $4 per canister.

Required:

1. Write the formula for the total annual cost of ordering and storing XL-20.

2. Use the EOQ formula to determine the optimal order quantity.

3. What is the total annual cost of ordering and storing XL-20 at the economic order quantity?

4. How many orders will be placed per year?

5. Fibre Technology's controller, Jay Turnbull, recently attended a seminar on JIT purchasing. Afterward he analyzed the cost of storing XL-20, including the costs of wasted space and inefficiency. He was shocked when he concluded that the real annual holding cost was $19.20 per canister. Turnbull then met with Doug Kaplan, Fibre Technology's purchasing manager. Together they contacted Reno Industries, the supplier of XL-20, about a JIT purchasing arrangement. After some discussion and negotiation, Kaplan concluded that the cost of placing an order for XL-20 could be reduced to just $20. Using these new cost estimates, Turnbull computed the new EOQ for XL-20.

   a. Use the equation approach to compute the new EOQ.

   b. How many orders will be placed per year?

Exercise 10–35 Economic Order Quantity: Tabular Approach (Appendix) **(LO9)**
Refer to the *original* data given in the preceding exercise for Fibre Technology, Inc.

Required:

1. Prepare a table showing the total annual cost of ordering and storing XL-20 for each of the following order quantities: 400, 600, and 800 canisters.

2. What are the weaknesses in the tabular approach?

Exercise 10–36 Economic Order Quantity: Graphical Approach (Appendix) **(LO9)**
Refer to the *original* data given in Exercise 10–34 for Fibre Technology, Inc.

Required: Prepare a graphical analysis of the economic order quantity decision for XL-20, assuming order quantities of 400, 600, and 800 canisters.

Exercise 10–37 Economic Order Quantity; Lead Time and Safety Stock (Appendix) **(LO9)**
Refer to the *original* data given in Exercise 10–34 for Fibre Technology, Inc. The lead time required to receive an order of XL-20 is one month.

Required:

1. Assuming stable usage of XL-20 each month, determine the reorder point for XL-20.

2. Draw a graph showing the usage, lead time, and reorder point for XL-20.

3. Suppose that monthly usage of XL-20 fluctuates between 300 and 500 canisters, although annual demand remains constant at 4,800 canisters. What level of safety stock should the materials and parts manager keep on hand for XL-20? What is the new reorder point for the chemical?

Problems

Problem 10–38 Balanced Scorecard: Banking; Use of Internet **(LO1)**
Visit the website of a major bank, for example, TD Canada Trust at www.tdcanadatrust.com. Explore the site to learn about the bank's services and operations.

Required:

1. What do you think the bank's overall, long-term goals are?

2. Develop a balanced scorecard for the bank. Include two to five measures in each of the scorecard's four perspectives.

3. How would the balanced scorecard affect the way managers develop the bank's strategy?

4. Explain the concept of lead and lag measures in the context of the scorecard you have developed.

Problem 10–39 Manufacturing Performance Measurement **(LO2)**
MedTech, Inc. manufactures diagnostic testing equipment used in hospitals. The company practises just-in-time inventory management and has a state-of-the-art manufacturing system. The following nonfinancial data were collected biweekly in the Surrey plant during the first quarter of the current year.

Biweekly Measurement Period

	1	2	3	4	5	6
Cycle time (days)	1.5	1.3	1.3	1.2	1.2	1.1
Number of defective finished products	4	4	3	4	3	3
Manufacturing cycle efficiency	94%	94%	96%	96%	97%	96%
Customer complaints	6	7	6	5	7	8
Unresolved complaints	2	1	0	0	0	0
Products returned	3	3	2	2	1	1
Warranty claims	2	2	2	0	1	0
In-process products rejected	5	5	7	9	10	10
Aggregate productivity	1.5	1.5	1.5	1.5	1.4	1.5
Number of units produced per day per employee	410	405	412	415	415	420
Percentage of on-time deliveries	94%	95%	95%	97%	100%	100%
Percentage of orders filled	100%	100%	100%	98%	100%	100%
Inventory value/sales revenue	2%	2%	2%	1.5%	2%	1.5%
Machine downtime (minutes)	80	80	120	80	70	75
Bottleneck machine downtime (minutes)	25	20	15	0	60	10
Overtime (minutes) per employee	20	0	0	10	20	10
Average setup time (minutes)	120	120	115	112	108	101

Required:

1. For each nonfinancial performance measure, indicate which of the following areas of manufacturing performance is involved: (*a*) production processing, (*b*) product quality, (*c*) customer acceptance, (*d*) in-process quality control, (*e*) productivity, (*f*) delivery performance, (*g*) raw material and scrap, (*h*) inventory, (*i*) machine maintenance. Some measures may relate to more than one area.

2. Write a memo to management commenting on the performance data collected for the Surrey plant. Be sure to note any trends or other important results you see in the data. Evaluate the Surrey plant in each of the areas listed in requirement (1).

Problem 10–40 Production Efficiency Report; Operational Performance Measures (L02)

Montreal Plastics Corporation manufactures a range of moulded plastic products, such as kitchen utensils and desk accessories. The production process in the Mirabel plant uses a just-in-time inventory and production management system. Every month, the controller prepares a production efficiency report, which is sent to corporate headquarters. The data compiled in these reports, for the first six months of the year, are as follows:

PRODUCTION EFFICIENCY REPORT
MONTREAL PLASTICS CORPORATION
Mirabel Plant
January through June

	Jan.	Feb.	Mar.	Apr.	May	June	Average
Overtime hours	60	70	75	80	85	105	79.2
Total setup time	70	70	65	64	62	62	65.5
Cycle time (average in hours)	20	20	19	18	19	17	18.8
Manufacturing cycle efficiency	95%	94%	96%	90%	89%	90%	92.3%
Percentage of orders filled	100%	100%	100%	100%	100%	100%	100%
Percentage of on-time deliveries	99%	98%	99%	100%	96%	94%	97.7%
Inventory value/sales revenue	5%	5%	5%	4%	5%	5%	4.8%
Number of defective units, finished goods	80	82	75	40	25	22	54
Number of defective units, in process	10	30	35	40	60	60	39.2
Number of raw-material shipments with defective materials	3	3	2	0	0	0	1.3
Number of products returned	0	0	0	0	0	0	0
Aggregate productivity	1.3	1.3	1.2	1.25	1.2	1.15	1.23
Power consumption (thousands of kilowatt-hours)	800	795	802	801	800	800	800
Machine downtime (hours)	30	25	25	20	20	10	21.7
Bottleneck machine downtime	0	0	2	0	15	2	3.2
Number of unscheduled machine maintenance calls	0	0	1	0	2	3	1

Required:

1. Write a memo to the company president evaluating the Mirabel plant's performance. Structure your report by dividing it into the following parts: (*a*) production processing and productivity; (*b*) product quality and customer acceptance; (*c*) delivery performance; (*d*) raw material, scrap, and inventory; and (*e*) machine maintenance.

2. If you identify any areas of concern in your memo, indicate an appropriate action for management.

Problem 10–41 Gain-Sharing; Operational Performance Measures (LO2)

1. Cloverdale Division, total bonus awarded for the year: $6,600

MedLine Equipment Corporation specializes in the manufacture of medical equipment, a field that has become increasingly competitive. Approximately two years ago, Ben Harrington, president of Med-Line, became concerned that the company's bonus plan, which focused on division profitability, was not helping MedLine remain competitive. Harrington decided to implement a gain-sharing plan that would encourage employees to focus on operational areas that were important to customers and that added value without increasing cost. In addition to a profitability incentive, the revised plan also includes incentives for reduced rework costs, reduced sales returns, and on-time deliveries. Bonuses are calculated and awarded semiannually to the relevant employees according to a formula developed by the division manager:

- *Profitability.* Two percent of operating income.
- *Rework.* Costs in excess of 2 percent of operating income are deducted from the bonus amount.
- *On-time delivery.* $5,000 if over 98 percent of deliveries are on time, $2,000 if 96 to 98 percent of deliveries are on time, and no increment if on-time deliveries are below 96 percent.
- *Sales returns.* $3,000 if returns are less than 1.5 percent of sales. Fifty percent of any amount in excess of 1.5 percent of sales is deducted from the bonus amount.
- If the calculation of the bonus results in a negative amount for a particular period, there is no bonus, and the negative amount is not carried forward to the next period.

The revised bonus plan was implemented on January 1, 20x1. Presented in the following table are the results for MedLine's Cloverdale and Vernon Divisions for the first year under the new bonus plan. Both of these divisions had similar sales and operating income results for the prior year, when the old bonus plan was in effect. Based on the 20x0 results, the employees of the Cloverdale Division earned a bonus of $27,060, while the employees of the Vernon Division earned $22,440.

	Cloverdale Division		Vernon Division	
	January 20x1–June 20x1	July 20x1–December 20x1	January 20x1–June 20x1	July 20x1–December 20x1
Sales	$4,200,000	$4,400,000	$2,850,000	$2,900,000
Operating income	$462,000	$440,000	$342,000	$406,000
On-time delivery	95.4%	97.3%	98.2%	94.6%
Rework costs	$11,500	$11,000	$6,000	$8,000
Sales returns	$84,000	$70,000	$44,750	$42,500

Required:

1. For the Cloverdale Division:
   a. Compute the semiannual instalments and total bonus awarded for 20x1.
   b. Discuss the likely behaviour of the Cloverdale Division employees under the revised bonus plan.
2. For the Vernon Division:
   a. Compute the semiannual instalments and total bonus awarded for 20x1.
   b. Discuss the likely behaviour of the Vernon Division employees under the revised bonus plan.
3. Citing specific examples, evaluate whether Harrington's revisions to the bonus plan at MedLine Equipment Corporation have achieved the desired results, and recommend any changes that might improve the plan.

(CMA, adapted)

Problem 10–42 Kaizen Costing Chart (LO4)

Queensland Television Corporation (QTC) manufactures TV sets in Australia, largely for the domestic market. QTC recently implemented a kaizen costing program, with the goal of reducing the manufacturing cost per television set by 10 percent during 20x1, the first year of the kaizen effort. The cost per TV set at the end of 20x0 was $500. The following table shows the average cost per television set estimated during each month of 20x1. (The day this problem was written, the Australian dollar was valued at $0.74 in Canadian dollars.)

Month	Cost per Set	Month	Cost per Set
January	$500	July	$485
February	500	August	470
March	495	September	460
April	492	October	460
May	490	November	450
June	485	December	440

Required: Prepare a kaizen costing chart for 20x1 to show the results of Queensland Television Corporation's first year of kaizen costing. In developing the chart, use the following steps:

1. Draw and label the axes of the kaizen costing chart.

2. Indicate the current year cost base and the kaizen goal (cost-reduction rate) on the chart.

3. Label the horizontal axis with the months of 20x1, and the vertical axis with dollar amounts in the appropriate range.

4. Plot the 12 monthly estimates of the average cost per TV set. Then draw a line connecting the cost points that were plotted.

5. Complete the chart with any further labelling necessary.

6. Briefly explain the purpose of kaizen costing. How could a continuous-quality-improvement program, coupled with the kaizen costing effort implemented by Queensland Television Corporation, help the firm to begin competing in the worldwide market?

Problem 10–43   Quality Costs: Identification and Analysis **(LO6)**

2. & 3. Total quality costs, No. 165: $439,900

Advanced Technologies (AT) produces two compression machines that are popular with manufacturers of plastics: No. 165 and No. 172. Machine No. 165 has an average selling price of $60,000, whereas No. 172 typically sells for approximately $55,000. The company is very concerned about quality and has provided the following information:

	No. 165	No. 172
Number of machines produced and sold	80	100
Warranty costs:		
Average repair cost per unit	$1,200	$400
Percentage of units needing repair	70%	10%
Reliability engineering at $150 per hour	1,600 hours	2,000 hours
Rework at AT's manufacturing plant:		
Average rework cost per unit	$1,900	$1,600
Percentage of units needing rework	35%	25%
Manufacturing inspection at $50 per hour	300 hours	500 hours
Transportation costs to customer sites to fix problems	$29,500	$15,000
Quality training for employees	$35,000	$50,000

Required:

1. Classify the preceding costs as prevention, appraisal, internal failure, or external failure.

2. Using the classifications in requirement (1), compute AT's quality costs for machine No. 165 in dollars and as a percentage of sales revenues. Also calculate prevention, appraisal, internal failure, and external failure costs as a percentage of total quality costs.

3. Repeat requirement (2) for machine No. 172.

4. Comment on your findings, noting whether the company is "investing" its quality expenditures differently for the two machines.

5. Quality costs can be classified as observable or hidden. What are hidden quality costs, and how do these costs differ from observable costs?

Problem 10–44 Quality-Improvement Programs and Quality Costs **(L06)**

Laser News Technology, Inc. manufactures computerized laser printing equipment used by newspaper publishers throughout North America. In recent years, the company's market share has been eroded by stiff competition from Asian and European competitors. Price and product quality are the two key areas in which companies compete in this market.

Ben McDonough, Laser News Technology's president, decided to devote more resources to the improvement of product quality after learning that his company's products had been ranked fourth in product quality in a recent survey of newspaper publishers. He believed that the company could no longer afford to ignore the importance of product quality. McDonough set up a task force that he headed to implement a formal quality-improvement program. Included on the task force were representatives from engineering, sales, customer service, production, and accounting, as McDonough believed this was a companywide program and all employees should share the responsibility for its success.

After the first meeting of the task force, Sheila Hayes, manager of sales, asked Tony Reese, the production manager, what he thought of the proposed program. Reese replied, "I have reservations. Quality is too abstract to be attaching costs to it and then to be holding you and me responsible for cost improvements. I like to work with goals that I can see and count! I don't like my annual income to be based on a decrease in quality costs; there are too many variables that we have no control over!"

Laser News Technology's quality-improvement program has now been in operation for 18 months, and the following quality-cost report has recently been issued. As they were reviewing the report, Hayes asked Reese what he thought of the quality program now. "The work is really moving through the Production Department," replied Reese. "We used to spend time helping the Customer Service Department solve their problems, but they are leaving us alone these days. I have no complaints so far. I'll be anxious to see how much the program increases our bonuses."

LASER NEWS TECHNOLOGY, INC.
Cost of Quality Report
(in thousands)

	Quarter Ended:					
	6/30/x0	9/30/x0	12/31/x0	3/31/x1	6/30/x1	9/30/x1
Prevention costs:						
Design review	$ 20	$ 102	$ 111	$ 100	$ 104	$ 95
Machine maintenance	215	215	202	190	170	160
Training suppliers	5	45	25	20	20	15
Total	$ 240	$ 362	$ 338	$ 310	$ 294	$ 270
Appraisal costs:						
Incoming inspection	$ 45	$ 53	$ 57	$ 36	$ 34	$ 22
Final testing	160	160	154	140	115	94
Total	$ 205	$ 213	$ 211	$ 176	$ 149	$ 116
Internal failure costs:						
Rework	$ 120	$ 106	$ 114	$ 88	$ 78	$ 62
Scrap	68	64	53	42	40	40
Total	$ 188	$ 170	$ 167	$ 130	$ 118	$ 102
External failure costs:						
Warranty repairs	$ 69	$ 31	$ 24	$ 25	$ 23	$ 23
Customer returns	262	251	122	116	87	80
Total	$ 331	$ 282	$ 146	$ 141	$ 110	$ 103
Total quality cost	$ 964	$1,027	$ 862	$ 757	$ 671	$ 591
Total production cost	$4,120	$4,540	$4,380	$4,650	$4,580	$4,510

Required:

1. Identify at least three factors that should be present for an organization to successfully implement a quality-improvement program.

2. By analyzing the cost of quality report presented, determine if Laser News Technology's quality-improvement program has been successful. List specific evidence to support your answer.

3. Discuss why Tony Reese's current reaction to the quality-improvement program is more favourable than his initial reaction.

4. Laser News Technology's president believed that the quality-improvement program was essential and that the firm could no longer afford to ignore the importance of product quality. Discuss how the company could measure the opportunity cost of not implementing the quality-improvement program.

(CMA, adapted)

Problem 10–45 Environmental Cost Management (L08)

As a group, take a walking tour of your campus and the surrounding community. Make a list of all of the environmental costs of which you see evidence.

Required: Make a presentation to the class about your findings. List and categorize the environmental costs you noted either for your school or for businesses in the community. (You might consider writing a letter to your campus newspaper regarding these environmental issues and their costs.)

  Practise and learn online with Connect.

CHAPTER ELEVEN

Responsibility Accounting, Investment Centres, and Transfer Pricing

FOCUS COMPANY

This chapter's focus company is Aloha Hotels and Resorts, Inc., a chain of luxury hotels and resorts in Hawaii. Here we will explore this company's responsibility-accounting system. *Responsibility accounting* refers to the various concepts and tools used to measure the performance of both people and departments in an organization. The management of Aloha Hotels and Resorts uses detailed performance reports about the company's divisions, hotels, and departments to help ensure that everyone in the organization is working toward the same overall corporate goals.

IN CONTRAST

In contrast to the hospitality-services setting of Aloha Hotels and Resorts, we will turn to Suncoast Food Centres, a chain of retail grocery stores on the Sunshine Coast of British Columbia. The company has three divisions. The Lower Sunshine Coast and Upper Sunshine Coast Divisions operate individual grocery stores in six coastal cities. The Food Processing Division operates dairy plants, bakeries, and meat-processing facilities that supply the grocery stores with fresh food products.

After completing this chapter, you should be able to

1. Explain the role of responsibility accounting in fostering goal congruence.

2. Define and give an example of a cost centre, a revenue centre, a profit centre, and an investment centre.

3. Prepare a performance report and explain the relationships among the performance reports for various responsibility centres.

4. Use a cost allocation base to allocate costs.

5. Prepare a segmented income statement.

6. Compute an investment centre's return on investment (ROI), residual income (RI), and economic value added (EVA).

7. Explain how a manager can improve ROI.

8. Describe some advantages and disadvantages of both ROI and residual income as divisional performance measures.

9. Explain how to measure a division's income and invested capital.

10. Use the general economic rule to set an optimal transfer price.

11. Explain how to base a transfer price on market prices, costs, or negotiations.

We will explore how companies evaluate the performance of investment centres, such as Suncoast's three divisions. In addition to the evaluation of investment centre performance, we will also discuss transfer pricing, the amount charged when one division of a company sells products or services to another division. In our Suncoast Food Centres example, the Food Processing Division sells its dairy, bakery, and meat products to the Suncoast grocery stores at a transfer price. We will explore different ways to set such transfer prices.

Learning Objective 1

Explain the role of responsibility accounting in fostering goal congruence.

Most organizations are divided into smaller units, each of which is assigned particular responsibilities. These units are called by various names, including *divisions, segments, business units,* and *departments*. Each department is composed of individuals who are responsible for particular tasks or managerial functions. The managers of an organization should ensure that the people in each department are striving toward the same overall goals. **Goal congruence** results when the managers of subunits throughout an organization strive to achieve the goals set by top management.

How can an organization's managerial accounting system promote goal congruence? *Responsibility accounting* refers to the various concepts and tools used by management accountants to measure the performance of people and departments in order to foster goal congruence.

Responsibility Centres

Learning Objective 2

Define and give an example of a cost centre, a revenue centre, a profit centre, and an investment centre.

The basis of a responsibility-accounting system is the designation of each subunit in the organization as a particular type of *responsibility centre*. A **responsibility centre** is a subunit in an organization whose manager is held accountable for specified financial results of the subunit's activities. There are four common types of responsibility centres.

Cost Centre   A **cost centre** is an organizational subunit, such as a department or division, whose manager is held accountable for the costs incurred in the subunit. The Painting Department in an automobile plant is an example of a cost centre.

Revenue Centre   The manager of a **revenue centre** is held accountable for the revenue attributed to the subunit. The Reservations Department of an airline and the Sales Department of a manufacturer are revenue centres.

Profit Centre   A **profit centre** is an organizational subunit whose manager is held accountable for profit. Since profit is equal to revenue minus expenses, profit centre managers are held accountable for both the revenue and expenses attributed to their subunits. An example of a profit centre is a company-owned restaurant in a fast-food chain.

Investment Centre   The manager of an **investment centre** is held accountable for the subunit's profit *and the invested capital* used by the subunit to generate its profit. A division of a large corporation is typically designated as an investment centre.[1]

Responsibility Accounting Illustrated

To illustrate the concepts used in responsibility accounting, we will focus on a hotel chain. Aloha Hotels and Resorts operates luxury hotels in the state of Hawaii. The company is divided into the Maui Division, which operates seven hotels on the island of Maui, and the Oahu Division, with three properties on the island of Oahu. Exhibit 11–1 shows the company's organization chart, and Exhibit 11–2 depicts the responsibility-accounting system.

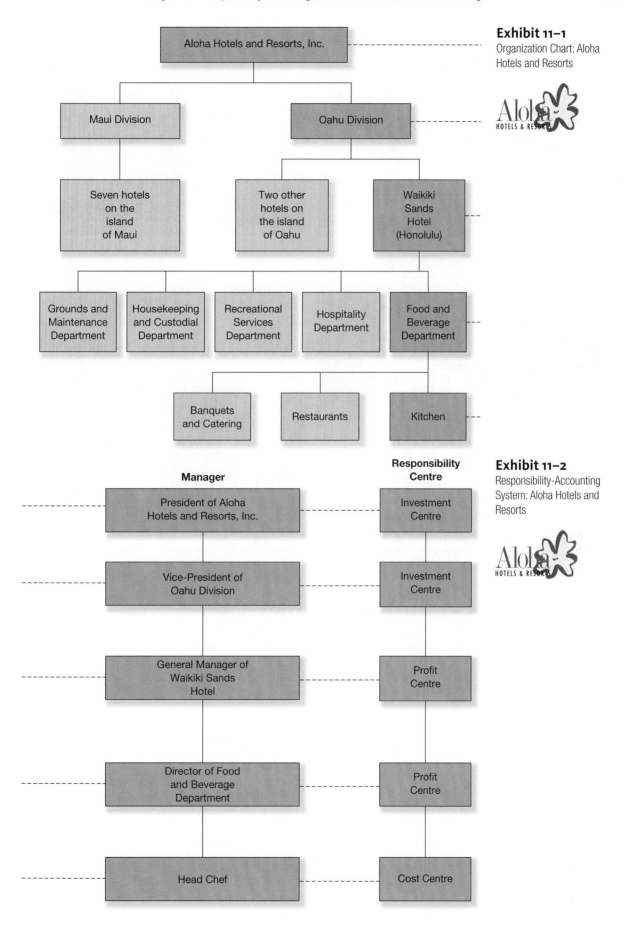

Exhibit 11–1
Organization Chart: Aloha Hotels and Resorts

Exhibit 11–2
Responsibility-Accounting System: Aloha Hotels and Resorts

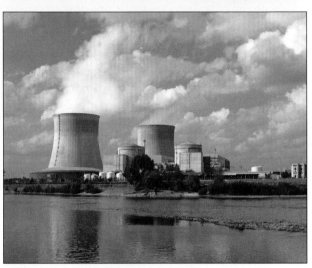

This aircraft maintenance department is a cost centre. The telemarketing operation shown here is a revenue centre. This Applebee's is a profit centre. The power plant in the Loire Valley, France, is an investment centre. What sort of responsibility centre designation would be appropriate for your local car wash, hair salon, and laundromat?

Corporate Level   The chief executive officer (CEO) of Aloha Hotels and Resorts, Inc. is the company's president. The president, who is responsible to the company's shareholders, is accountable for corporate profit in relation to the capital (assets) invested in the company. Therefore, the entire company is an *investment centre*. The president has the autonomy to make significant decisions that affect the company's profit and invested capital. For example, the final decision to add a new luxury tower to any of the company's resort properties would be made by the president.

Division Level   The vice-president of the Oahu Division is accountable for the profit earned by the three resort hotels on Oahu in relation to the capital invested in those properties, so the Oahu Division is also an *investment centre*. The vice-president has the authority to make major investment decisions regarding the properties on Oahu, up to a limit of $300,000. For example, he or she might decide to install a new swimming pool at one of the Oahu resort hotels, but could not decide to add a new wing.

"Responsibility accounting is an integral part of our reporting process in this company. Always has been. Always will." (11a)

Chrysler

Hotel Level   The Waikiki Sands Hotel in Honolulu is one of the properties in the Oahu Division. The general manager of the Waikiki Sands Hotel is accountable for the profit earned by the hotel. The general manager does not have the authority to make major investment decisions, but is responsible for operational decisions. For example, the general manager hires all of the hotel's departmental managers, sets wage rates, determines procedures and standards for operations, approves decorating decisions, and generally oversees the hotel's operation. Since the hotel's general manager has no authority to make major investment decisions, she is held accountable only for the hotel's profit, not the capital invested in the property. So the Waikiki Sands Hotel is a *profit centre*.

Departmental Level   The Waikiki Sands Hotel has five departments, as shown in Exhibit 11–1. The Grounds and Maintenance Department includes landscaping, building and equipment maintenance, and hotel security. The Housekeeping and Custodial Department covers laundry and janitorial services. These two departments are called *service departments*, since they provide services to the hotel's other departments but do not deal directly with hotel guests. The Recreational Services Department operates the hotel's swimming pools, saunas, video arcade, and tennis courts. The Hospitality Department is responsible for the hotel's reservations desk, room allocation, bell staff, and shopping facilities. Finally, the Food and Beverage Department operates the resort's restaurants, coffee shop, lounges, poolside snack bar, banquet operations, and catering service.

The director of the Food and Beverage Department is accountable for the profit earned on all food and beverage operations. Therefore, this department is a *profit centre*. The director has the authority to approve the menu, set food and beverage prices, hire the wait staff, schedule entertainers, and generally oversee all food and beverage operations.

Food and Beverage Subunits   The Food and Beverage Department is divided further into Banquets and Catering, Restaurants, and Kitchen subunits.

The head chef manages the kitchen and is accountable for the costs incurred there, so the Kitchen subunit is a *cost centre*. The head chef hires the kitchen staff, orders food supplies, and oversees all food preparation. The head chef is responsible for providing high-quality food at the lowest possible cost.

Performance Reporting

The performance of each responsibility centre is summarized periodically on a *performance report*. A **performance report** shows the budgeted and actual amounts, and the variances between these amounts, of key financial results appropriate for the type of responsibility centre involved. For example, a cost centre's performance report concentrates on budgeted and actual amounts for various cost items attributable to the cost centre. Performance reports also typically show the variance between budgeted and actual amounts for the financial results conveyed in the report. The data in a performance report help managers to use *management by exception* to control an organization's operations effectively.

The performance report for the kitchen of the Waikiki Sands Hotel for February is shown in the Excel spreadsheet in Exhibit 11–3.

> "But you have to wear the hat of the management team you are on to help them achieve the goals. You also have to wear the corporate finance hat to recognize that you have a duty to the corporate finance function, to do things right and do them correctly, to stand up for what has to be done, and to say no when no is the appropriate thing to say." (11b)
> **Abbott Laboratories**

Learning Objective 3

Prepare a performance report and explain the relationships among the performance reports for various responsibility centres.

Exhibit 11–3
Performance Report for February: Kitchen, Waikiki Sands Hotel

	A	B	C	D	E	F	G	H	I
1		Flexible Budget		Actual Results		Variance*			
2		February	Year to Date	February	Year to Date	February		Year to Date	
3									
4	Kitchen staff wages	$ 80,000	$ 168,000	$ 78,000	$ 169,000	$ 2,000	F	$ 1,000	U
5	Food	675,000	1,420,000	678,000	1,421,000	3,000	U	1,000	U
6	Paper products	120,000	250,000	115,000	248,000	5,000	F	2,000	F
7	Variable overhead	70,000	150,000	71,000	154,000	1,000	U	4,000	U
8	Fixed overhead	85,000	180,000	83,000	181,000	2,000	F	1,000	U
9	Total expense	$ 1,030,000	$ 2,168,000	$ 1,025,000	$ 2,173,000	$ 5,000	F	$ 5,000	U
10									
11	*F denotes favourable variance, U denotes unfavourable variance.								

As the organization chart in Exhibit 11–1 shows, Aloha Hotels and Resorts is a *hierarchy*. Each subunit manager reports to one higher-level manager, from the head chef all the way up to the president. In such an organization, there is also a hierarchy of performance reports, since the performance of each subunit constitutes part of the performance of the next higher-level subunit. For example, the cost performance in the kitchen of the Waikiki Sands Hotel constitutes part of the profit performance of the hotel's Food and Beverage Department.

Exhibit 11–4 shows the relationships among the February performance reports for several subunits of Aloha Hotels and Resorts. Notice that the numbers for the Grounds and Maintenance Department, the Housekeeping and Custodial Department, and the Kitchen subunit are in parentheses. These departments and the Kitchen subunit are cost centres, so the numbers shown are expenses. All of the other subunits shown in Exhibit 11–4 are either profit centres or investment centres. The numbers shown for these subunits are profits, so they are not enclosed in parentheses. In addition to the profit figures shown, the performance reports for the investment centres should include data about invested capital. The Maui Division, the Oahu Division, and the

Exhibit 11–4

Performance Reports for February: Selected Subunits of Aloha Hotels and Resorts

	Flexible Budget*		Actual Results*		Variance†	
	February	**Year to Date**	**February**	**Year to Date**	**February**	**Year to Date**
Company	$30,660	$64,567	$30,716	$64,570	$56 F	$ 3 F
Maui Division	$18,400	$38,620	$18,470	$38,630	$70 F	$10 F
Oahu Division	12,260	25,947	12,246	25,940	14 U	7 U
Total profit	$30,660	$64,567	$30,716	$64,570	$56 F	$ 3 F
Oahu Division						
Waimea Beach Resort	$ 6,050	$12,700	$ 6,060	$12,740	$10 F	$40 F
Diamond Head Lodge	2,100	4,500	2,050	4,430	50 U	70 U
Waikiki Sands Hotel	4,110	8,747	4,136	8,770	26 F	23 F
Total profit	$12,260	$25,947	$12,246	$25,940	$14 U	$ 7 U
Waikiki Sands Hotel						
Grounds and Maintenance	$ (45)	$ (90)	$ (44)	$ (90)	$ 1 F	—
Housekeeping and Custodial	(40)	(90)	(41)	(90)	1 U	—
Recreational Services	40	85	41	88	1 F	$ 3 F
Hospitality	2,800	6,000	2,840	6,030	40 F	30 F
Food and Beverage	1,355	2,842	1,340	2,832	15 U	10 U
Total profit	$ 4,110	$ 8,747	$ 4,136	$ 8,770	$26 F	$23 F
Food and Beverage Department						
Banquets and Catering	$ 600	$ 1,260	$ 605	$ 1,265	$ 5 F	$ 5 F
Restaurants	1,785	3,750	1,760	3,740	25 U	10 U
Kitchen	(1,030)	(2,168)	(1,025)	(2,173)	5 F	5 U
Total profit	$ 1,355	$ 2,842	$ 1,340	$ 2,832	$15 U	$10 U
Kitchen						
Kitchen staff wages	$ (80)	$ (168)	$ (78)	$ (169)	$ 2 F	$ 1 U
Food	(675)	(1,420)	(678)	(1,421)	3 U	1 U
Paper products	(120)	(250)	(115)	(248)	5 F	2 F
Variable overhead	(70)	(150)	(71)	(154)	1 U	4 U
Fixed overhead	(85)	(180)	(83)	(181)	2 F	1 U
Total expense	$ (1,030)	$ (2,168)	$ (1,025)	$ (2,173)	$ 5 F	$ 5 U

*Numbers without parentheses denote profit; numbers with parentheses denote expenses. The numbers are in thousands.

†F denotes favourable variance; U denotes unfavourable variance.

company as a whole are investment centres. Performance evaluation in investment centres is covered later in the chapter.

The kitchen is the lowest-level subunit shown in Exhibit 11–4, and its performance report is the same as that displayed in Exhibit 11–3. The *total expense* line from the kitchen performance report is included as one line in the performance report for the Food and Beverage Department. Also included are the total profit figures for the department's other two subunits: Banquets and Catering, and Restaurants. How is the *total profit* line for the Food and Beverage Department used in the performance report for the Waikiki Sands Hotel? Follow the relationships emphasized with arrows in Exhibit 11–4.

The hierarchy of performance reports starts at the bottom and builds toward the top, just like the organization structure depicted in Exhibit 11–1 builds from the bottom upward. Each manager in the organization receives the performance report for his or her own subunit in addition to the performance reports for the major subunits in the next lower level. For example, the general manager of the Waikiki Sands Hotel receives the reports for the hotel, and each of its departments: Grounds and Maintenance, Housekeeping and Custodial, Recreational Services, Hospitality, and Food and Beverage. With these reports, the hotel's general manager can evaluate her subordinates as well as her own performance. This will help the general manager in improving the hotel's performance, motivating employees, and planning future operations.

Budgets, Variance Analysis, and Responsibility Accounting

Notice that the performance reports in Exhibit 11–4 make heavy use of budgets and variance analysis. Thus, the topics of budgeting, variance analysis, and responsibility accounting are closely interrelated. The flexible budget provides the benchmark against which actual revenues, expenses, and profits are compared. As you saw in Chapter 9, it is important to use a flexible budget so that appropriate comparisons can be made. It would make no sense, for example, to compare the actual costs incurred in the kitchen at Waikiki Sands Hotel with budgeted costs established for a different level of hotel occupancy.

The performance reports in Exhibit 11–4 also show variances between budgeted and actual performance. These variances are often broken down into smaller components to help management pinpoint responsibility and diagnose performance. Variance analysis, which was discussed in detail in Chapter 9, is an important tool in a responsibility-accounting system.

Cost Allocation and Allocation Bases

Many costs incurred by an organization are the joint result of several subunits' activities. For example, the property taxes and utility costs incurred by Aloha Hotels and Resorts for the Waikiki Sands Hotel are the joint result of all of the hotel's activities. One function of a responsibility-accounting system is to assign all of an organization's costs to the subunits that cause them to be incurred.

A collection of costs to be assigned is called a **cost pool**. At the Waikiki Sands Hotel, for example, all utility costs are combined into a *utility cost pool*, which includes the costs of electricity, water, sewer, trash collection, television cable, and telephone. The responsibility centres, products, or services to which costs are to be assigned are called *cost objects*. The Waikiki Sands' cost objects are its major departments. (See the organization chart in Exhibit 11–1.) The process of assigning the costs in the *cost pool* to the *cost objects* is called **cost allocation** or **cost distribution**.

Allocation Bases and Budgets

To distribute (or allocate) costs to responsibility centres, the management accountant chooses an *allocation base* for each cost pool. An **allocation base** is a measure of activity, physical characteristic, or economic characteristic that is associated with the responsibility

Learning Objective **4**

Use a cost allocation base to allocate costs.

centres, which are the cost objects in the allocation process. The allocation base chosen for a cost pool should reflect some characteristic of the various responsibility centres that is related to the incurrence of costs. An allocation base also may be referred to as a *cost driver*.

Exhibit 11–5 shows the Waikiki Sands Hotel's February cost distribution for selected cost pools. Each cost pool is distributed to each responsibility centre in proportion to that centre's relative amount of the allocation base. For example, the Food and Beverage Department receives 30 percent of the total administrative costs, $25,000, because that department's 36 employees constitute 30 percent of the hotel's employees. Notice that no marketing costs are allocated to either the Grounds and Maintenance Department or the Housekeeping and Custodial Department. Neither of these responsibility centres generates any sales revenue.

At the Waikiki Sands Hotel, administrative and marketing costs are distributed on the basis of *budgeted* amounts of the relevant allocation bases, rather than *actual* amounts. The management accountant should design an allocation procedure so that the behaviour of one responsibility centre does not affect the costs allocated to other responsibility centres.

Suppose, for example, that the budgeted and actual February sales revenues for the hotel were as shown in Exhibit 11–6. Notice that the Hospitality Department's actual sales revenue is close to the budget. However, the actual sales of the Recreational Services Department and the Food and Beverage Department are substantially below the budget. If the distribution of marketing costs is based on actual sales instead of budgeted sales, then the cost distributed to the Hospitality Department jumps from $40,000 to $45,000, an increase of 12.5 percent. Why does this happen? As a result of a sales performance substantially below the budget for the *other two departments*, the Hospitality Department is penalized with a hefty increase in its cost distribution. This is misleading and unfair to the Hospitality Department manager. A preferable cost distribution procedure is to use budgeted sales revenue as the allocation base, rather than actual sales revenue. Then the marketing costs distributed to each department do not depend on the performance in the other two departments.

Exhibit 11–5
Cost Distribution to Responsibility Centres: Waikiki Sands Hotel

Cost Pool	Responsibility Centre	Allocation Base	Percentage of Total	Costs Distributed
Administration	Grounds and Maintenance	12 employees	10.0%	$ 2,500
	Housekeeping and Custodial	24 employees	20.0	5,000
	Recreational Services	12 employees	10.0	2,500
	Hospitality	36 employees	30.0	7,500
	Food and Beverage	36 employees	30.0	7,500
	Total	120 employees	100.0%	$25,000
Facilities	Grounds and Maintenance	2,000 m²	1.0%	$ 300
	Housekeeping and Custodial	2,000 m²	1.0	300
	Recreational Services	5,000 m²	2.5	750
	Hospitality	175,000 m²	87.5	26,250
	Food and Beverage	16,000 m²	8.0	2,400
	Total	200,000 m²	100.0%	$30,000
Marketing	Grounds and Maintenance	—	—	—
	Housekeeping and Custodial	—	—	—
	Recreational Services	$ 20,000 of sales	4.0%	$ 2,000
	Hospitality	400,000 of sales	80.0	40,000
	Food and Beverage	80,000 of sales	16.0	8,000
	Total	$500,000 of sales	100.0%	$50,000

Responsibility Centre	Budgeted Sales Revenue	Actual Sales Revenue	Marketing Cost Distribution	
			Based on Budget	Based on Actual
Recreational Services	$ 20,000 (4%)*	$ 4,500 (1%)*	$ 2,000	$ 500
Hospitality	400,000 (80%)	405,000 (90%)	40,000	45,000
Food and Beverage	80,000 (16%)	40,500 (9%)	8,000	4,500
Total	$ 500,000	$450,000	$50,000	$50,000

*Percentage of column total.

Exhibit 11–6
Cost Distribution Alternative for the Responsibility Centres: Budgeted versus Actual Allocation Bases

Activity-Based Responsibility Accounting

Traditional responsibility-accounting systems tend to focus on the financial performance measures of cost, revenue, and profit for the *subunits* of an organization. Contemporary cost management systems, however, are beginning to focus more and more on *activities*. Costs are incurred in organizations and their subunits because of activities. *Activity-based costing (ABC)* systems associate costs with the activities that drive those costs. The database created by an ABC system, coupled with nonfinancial measures of operational performance for each activity, enables management to use **activity-based responsibility accounting**. Under this approach, management's attention is directed not only to the cost incurred in an activity but also to the activity itself. Is the activity necessary? Does it add value to the organization's product or service? Can the activity be improved? By seeking answers to these questions, managers can eliminate non-value-added activities and increase the cost-effectiveness of the activities that do add value.[2]

Behavioural Effects of Responsibility Accounting

Responsibility-accounting systems can influence behaviour significantly. Whether the behavioural effects are positive or negative, however, depends on how responsibility accounting is implemented.

Information versus Blame

The proper focus of a responsibility-accounting system is *information*. The system should identify the individual in the organization who is in the best position to explain each particular event or financial result. The emphasis should be on providing that individual and higher-level managers with information to help them understand the reasons behind the organization's performance. When properly used, a responsibility-accounting system *does not emphasize blame*. If managers feel they are beaten over the head with criticism and rebukes when unfavourable variances occur, they are unlikely to respond in a positive way. Instead, they will tend to undermine the system and view it with skepticism. But when the responsibility-accounting system emphasizes its informational role, managers tend to react constructively, and strive for improved performance.

Controllability

Some organizations use performance reports that distinguish between controllable and uncontrollable costs or revenues. For example, the head chef at the Waikiki Sands Hotel can influence the hours and efficiency of the kitchen staff, but he probably cannot

"Distinguishing between controllable and uncontrollable costs can increase the effectiveness of a cost management system, if it's done from the perspective of helping a client department understand where the opportunities for cost reduction are." (11d)
American Management Systems (Currently a part of CGI)

change the wage rates. A performance report that distinguishes between the financial results influenced by the head chef and those he does not influence has the advantage of providing complete information to the head chef. Yet the report recognizes that certain results are beyond his control.

Identifying costs as controllable or uncontrollable is not always easy. Many cost items are influenced by more than one person. The time frame also may be important in determining controllability. Some costs are controllable over a long time frame, but not within a short time period. To illustrate, suppose the Waikiki Sands' head chef has signed a one-year contract with a local seafood supplier. The cost of seafood can be influenced by the head chef if the time period is a year or more, but the cost cannot be controlled on a weekly basis.

Motivating Desired Behaviour

Management accountants often use the responsibility-accounting system to motivate actions considered desirable by upper-level management. Sometimes the responsibility-accounting system can solve behavioural problems as well. As a case in point, consider the problem of rush orders. To accept or reject a rush order is a cost–benefit decision:

Costs of Accepting Rush Order	**Benefits of Accepting Rush Order**
Disrupted production	Satisfied customers
More setups	Greater future sales
Higher costs	

The following real-world example involving rush orders provides a case in point.

The production scheduler in a manufacturing firm was frequently asked to interrupt production of one product with a rush order for another product. Rush orders typically resulted in greater costs because more product setups were required. Since the production scheduler was evaluated on the basis of costs, he was reluctant to accept rush orders. The sales manager, on the other hand, was evaluated on the basis of sales revenue. By agreeing to customers' demands for rush orders, the sales manager satisfied his customers. This resulted in more future sales and favourable performance ratings for the sales manager.

As the rush orders became more and more frequent, the production manager began to object. The sales manager responded by asking if the production scheduler wanted to take the responsibility for losing a customer by refusing a rush order. The production scheduler did not want to be blamed for lost sales, so he grudgingly accepted the rush orders. However, considerable ill will developed between the sales manager and production scheduler.

The company's management accountant came to the rescue by redesigning the responsibility-accounting system. The system was modified to accumulate the extra costs associated with rush orders and charge them to the sales manager's responsibility centre, rather than the production scheduler's centre. The ultimate result was that the sales manager chose more carefully which rush-order requests to make, and the production manager accepted them gracefully.

The problem described in the preceding illustration developed because two different managers were considering the costs and benefits of the rush-order decision. The production manager was looking only at the costs, while the sales manager was looking only at the benefits. The modified responsibility-accounting system made the sales manager look at *both the costs and the benefits* associated with each rush order. Then the sales manager could make the necessary trade-off between costs and benefits in considering each rush order. Some rush orders were rejected, because the sales manager decided the costs exceeded the benefits. Other rush orders were accepted, when the importance of the customer and potential future sales justified it.

This example illustrates how a well-designed responsibility-accounting system can make an organization run more smoothly and achieve higher performance.

Segmented Reporting

Learning Objective **5**

Prepare a segmented income statement.

Subunits of an organization are often called *segments*. *Segmented reporting* refers to the preparation of accounting reports by segment and for the organization as a whole. Many organizations prepare **segmented income statements**, which show the income for major segments and for the entire enterprise.

In preparing segmented income statements, the management accountant must decide how to treat costs that are incurred to benefit more than one segment. Such costs are called **common costs**. The salary of the president of Aloha Hotels and Resorts is a common cost. The president manages the entire company. Some of her time is spent on matters related specifically to the Maui Division or the Oahu Division, but much of it is spent on tasks that are not traced easily to either division. The president works with the company's board of directors, develops strategic plans for the company, and helps set policy and goals for the entire enterprise. So her compensation is a common cost, not easily related to any particular segment's activities.

Many management accountants believe that it is misleading to allocate common costs to an organization's segments. Since these costs are not traceable to the activities of segments, they can be allocated to segments only on the basis of some highly arbitrary allocation. Consider the salary of Aloha Hotels and Resorts' president. What allocation base would you choose to reflect the contribution of the president's managerial efforts to the company's two divisions? The possible allocation bases include budgeted divisional sales revenue, the number of hotels or employees in each division, or some measure of divisional size, such as total assets. However, all of these allocation bases would yield arbitrary cost allocations and possibly misleading segment profit information. For this reason, many organizations choose not to allocate common costs on segmented income statements.

Exhibit 11–7 shows February's segmented income statement (on a budgeted basis) for Aloha Hotels and Resorts. Each segment's income statement is presented in the *contribution format* discussed in Chapter 7. Notice that Exhibit 11–7 shows income statements for the following segments:

> "Senior management wants to know yesterday. So the pace has quickened and there's more pressure to get information much sooner and at the same time there is so much more information there." (11e)
>
> **Qwest (Currently a part of CenturyLink)**

Aloha Hotels and Resorts ⎰ Maui Division ⎱ Oahu Division { Waimea Beach Resort, Diamond Head Lodge, Waikiki Sands Hotel

Three numbers in Exhibit 11–7 require special emphasis. First, the $10,000,000 of common fixed expenses in the left-hand column is not allocated to the company's two divisions. Included in this figure are such costs as the company president's salary. These costs cannot be allocated to the divisions, except in some arbitrary manner.

Second, $1,000,000 of controllable fixed expense in the right-hand column constitutes part of the Oahu Division's $9,000,000 of controllable fixed expense. All $9,000,000 of expense is controllable by the vice-president of the Oahu Division. However, $1,000,000 of these expenses cannot be traced to the division's three hotels, except on an arbitrary basis. For example, this $1,000,000 of expense includes the salary of the Oahu Division's vice-president. Therefore, the $1,000,000 of expense is *not allocated* among the division's three hotels. This procedure illustrates an important point. Costs that are traceable to segments at one level in an organization may become common costs at a lower level in the organization. The vice-president's salary is traceable to the Oahu Division, but it cannot be allocated among the division's three hotels except arbitrarily.

		Segment of Company		Segment of Oahu Division			
	Aloha Hotels and Resorts	Maui Division	Oahu Division	Waimea Beach Resort	Diamond Head Lodge	Waikiki Sands Hotel	Not Allocated
Sales revenue............................	$2,500,000	$1,600,000	$900,000	$450,000	$150,000	$300,000	—
Variable operating expenses:							
Personnel............................	820,900	510,400	310,500	155,500	50,000	105,000	—
Food, beverages, and supplies ...	738,000	458,600	279,400	139,700	46,400	93,300	—
Other	83,000	58,000	25,000	12,500	4,000	8,500	—
Total....................................	1,641,900	1,027,000	614,900	307,700	100,400	206,800	—
Segment contribution margin.......	858,100	573,000	285,100	142,300	49,600	93,200	—
Less: Fixed expenses controllable by segment manager..............	30,000	21,000	9,000	4,000	1,000	3,000	$ 1,000
Profit margin controllable by segment manager..............	828,100	552,000	276,100	138,300	48,600	90,200	(1,000)
Less: Fixed expenses, traceable to segment, but controllable by others...........................	750,000	500,000	250,000	26,000	8,000	16,000	200,000
Segment profit margin	78,100	$ 52,000	$ 26,100	$112,300	$ 40,600	$ 74,200	$(201,000)
Less: Common fixed expenses.....	10,000						
Income before taxes...................	68,100						
Less: Income tax expense...........	37,440						
Net income...............................	$ 30,660						

Exhibit 11–7
Segmented Income Statements: Aloha Hotels and Resorts (in thousands)

Thus, the vice-president's salary is a traceable cost at the divisional level, but it becomes a common cost at the hotel level.

Third, the $200,000,000 of fixed expenses controllable by others in the right-hand column constitutes part of the Oahu Division's $250,000,000 of fixed expenses controllable by others. However, the $200,000,000 portion cannot be allocated among the division's three hotels, except arbitrarily.

Segments versus Segment Managers

One advantage of segmented reports like the one in Exhibit 11–7 is that they make a distinction between segments and segment managers. Some costs that are traceable to a segment may be completely beyond the influence of the segment manager. Property taxes on the Waikiki Sands Hotel, for example, are traceable to the hotel, but the hotel's general manager cannot influence them. To properly evaluate the *Waikiki Sands Hotel as an investment* of the company's resources, the property taxes should be included in the hotel's costs. However, in evaluating the general manager's performance, the property tax cost should be *excluded*, since the manager has no control over it.

Key Features of Segmented Reporting

To summarize, Exhibit 11–7 illustrates three important characteristics of segmented reporting:

1. *Contribution format.* These income statements use the contribution format. The statements subtract variable expenses from sales revenue to obtain the *contribution margin.*
2. *Controllable versus uncontrollable expenses.* The income statements in Exhibit 11–7 highlight the costs that can be controlled, or heavily influenced,

by each segment manager. This approach is consistent with *responsibility accounting.*

3. *Segmented income statement. Segmented reporting* shows income statements for the company as a whole and for its major segments.

Performance Evaluation

How do the top managers of large companies such as General Electric and Procter & Gamble evaluate their divisions and other major subunits? The largest subunits within these and similar organizations usually are designated as investment centres. The manager of this type of *responsibility centre* is held accountable not only for the investment centre's *profit* but also for the *capital invested* to earn that profit. *Invested capital* refers to assets, such as buildings and equipment, used in a subunit's operations.

Learning Objective   **6**

Compute an investment centre's return on investment (ROI), residual income (RI), and economic value added (EVA).

Measuring Performance in Investment Centres

In our study of investment centre performance evaluation, we will focus on Suncoast Food Centres. This chain of retail grocery stores has three divisions, as shown in the organization chart in Exhibit 11–8.

The Lower Sunshine Coast and Upper Sunshine Coast divisions consist of individual grocery stores located in six coastal cities. The company's Food Processing Division operates dairy plants, bakeries, and meat processing plants in Gibsons and Powell River. These facilities provide all Suncoast Food Centres with milk, ice cream, yogurt, cheese, breads and desserts, and packaged meat. These Suncoast-brand food products are transferred to the company's Lower Sunshine Coast and Upper Sunshine Coast divisions at transfer prices established by the corporate controller's office.

Suncoast Food Centres' three divisions are investment centres. This responsibility centre designation is appropriate, because each division manager has the authority to make decisions that affect both profit and invested capital. For example, the Lower Sunshine Coast Division manager approves the overall pricing policies in the Lower Sunshine Coast Division's stores, and also has the autonomy to sign contracts to buy food and other products for resale. These actions influence the division's profit. In addition, the Lower Sunshine Coast Division manager has the authority to build new Suncoast Food Centres, rent space in shopping centres, or close existing stores. These decisions affect the amount of capital invested in the division.

"Accounting is changing. You're no longer sitting behind a desk just working on a computer, just crunching the numbers. You're actually getting to be a part of the day-to-day functions of the business." (11f)
Abbott Laboratories

Exhibit 11–8
Organization Chart: Suncoast Food Centres

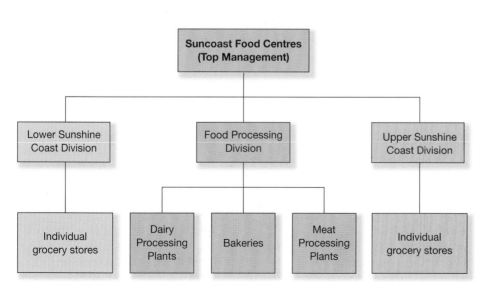

The primary goals of any profit-making enterprise include maximizing its profitability and using its invested capital as effectively as possible. Management accountants use three different measures to evaluate the performance of investment centres: return on investment (ROI), residual income (RI), and economic value added (EVA®). (EVA® is a registered trademark of Stern Stewart & Co.) We will illustrate each of these measures for Suncoast Food Centres.

Return on Investment

The most common investment centre performance measure is **return on investment**, or **ROI**, which is defined as follows:

$$\text{Return on investment (ROI)} = \frac{\text{Income}}{\text{Invested capital}}$$

The most recent year's ROI calculations for Suncoast Food Centres' three divisions are

	$\dfrac{\text{Income}}{\text{Invested capital}}$ =	Return on investment (ROI)
Lower Sunshine Coast Division	$\dfrac{\$3,000,000}{\$20,000,000}$ =	15%
Food Processing Division	$\dfrac{\$3,600,000}{\$18,000,000}$ =	20%
Upper Sunshine Coast Division	$\dfrac{\$6,750,000}{\$45,000,000}$ =	15%

Notice how the ROI calculation for each division takes into account *both divisional income and the capital invested* in the division. Why is this important? Suppose each division was evaluated only on the basis of its divisional profit. The Upper Sunshine Coast Division reported a higher divisional profit than the Lower Sunshine Coast Division. Does this mean that the Upper Sunshine Coast Division performed better than the Lower Sunshine Coast Division? The answer is no. Although the Upper Sunshine Coast Division's profit exceeded the Lower Sunshine Coast Division's profit, the Upper Sunshine Coast Division used a much larger amount of invested capital to earn its profit. The Upper Sunshine Coast Division's assets are more than two times the assets of the Lower Sunshine Coast Division so, considering the relative size of the two divisions, we should expect the Upper Sunshine Coast Division to earn a larger profit than the Lower Sunshine Coast Division. The important question is not how much profit each division earned, but rather how effectively each division used its invested capital to earn a profit.

Factors Underlying ROI We can rewrite the ROI formula as follows:

$$\text{Return on investment} = \frac{\text{Income}}{\text{Invested capital}} = \frac{\text{Income}}{\text{Sales revenue}} \times \frac{\text{Sales revenue}}{\text{Invested capital}}$$

Notice that the *sales revenue* term cancels out in the denominator and numerator when the two right-hand fractions are multiplied.

Writing the ROI formula in this way highlights the factors that determine a division's return on investment. Income divided by sales revenue is called the **sales margin**. This term measures the percentage of each sales dollar that remains as profit after all expenses are covered. Sales revenue divided by invested capital is called the **capital turnover**. This term focuses on the number of sales dollars generated by every dollar of invested capital.

The sales margin and capital turnover for Suncoast Food Centres' three divisions are calculated below for the most recent year.

	Sales margin	$\times$	Capital turnover	= ROI
	$\dfrac{\text{Income}}{\text{Sales revenue}}$	$\times$	$\dfrac{\text{Sales revenue}}{\text{Invested capital}}$	= ROI
Lower Sunshine Coast Division	$\dfrac{\$3,000,000}{\$60,000,000}$	$\times$	$\dfrac{\$60,000,000}{\$20,000,000}$	= 15%
Food Processing Division	$\dfrac{\$3,600,000}{\$9,000,000}$	$\times$	$\dfrac{\$9,000,000}{\$18,000,000}$	= 20%
Upper Sunshine Coast Division	$\dfrac{\$6,750,000}{\$135,000,000}$	$\times$	$\dfrac{\$135,000,000}{\$45,000,000}$	= 15%

The Lower Sunshine Coast Division's sales margin is 5 percent ($3,000,000 of profit ÷ $60,000,000 of sales revenue). Thus, each dollar of divisional sales resulted in a five-cent profit. The division's capital turnover was 3 ($60,000,000 of sales revenue ÷ $20,000,000 of invested capital). Thus, three dollars of sales revenue were generated by each dollar of capital invested in the division's assets, such as store buildings, display shelves, checkout equipment, and inventory.

Improving ROI How could the Lower Sunshine Coast Division manager improve the division's return on investment? Since ROI is the product of the sales margin and the capital turnover, ROI can be improved by increasing either or both of its components. For example, if the Lower Sunshine Coast Division manager increased the division's sales margin to 6 percent while holding the capital turnover constant at 3, the division's ROI would climb from 15 percent to 18 percent, as follows:

Learning Objective **7**

Explain how a manager can improve ROI.

Lower Sunshine Coast Division's improved ROI	=	Improved sales margin	$\times$	Same capital turnover	
	=	6%	$\times$	3	= 18%

To bring about the improved sales margin, the Lower Sunshine Coast Division manager would need to increase divisional profit to $3,600,000 on sales of $60,000,000 ($3,600,000 ÷ $60,000,000 = 6%). How could profit be increased without changing total sales revenue? There are two possibilities: Increase sales prices while selling less quantity or decrease expenses. Neither of these is necessarily easy to do. In increasing sales prices, the division manager must be careful not to lose sales to the extent that total sales revenue declines. Similarly, reducing the expenses must not diminish product quality, customer service, or overall store atmosphere. Any of these changes could also result in lost sales revenue.

An alternative way of increasing the Lower Sunshine Coast Division's ROI would be to increase its capital turnover. Suppose the Lower Sunshine Coast Division manager increased the division's capital turnover to 4 while holding the sales margin constant at 5 percent. The division's ROI would climb from 15 percent to 20 percent:

Lower Sunshine Coast Division's improved ROI	=	Same sales margin	$\times$	Improved capital turnover	
	=	5%	$\times$	4	= 20%

To obtain the improved capital turnover, the Lower Sunshine Division manager would need to either increase sales revenue or reduce the division's invested capital. For example, the improved ROI could be achieved by reducing invested capital to $15,000,000 while maintaining sales revenue of $60,000,000. This would be a very tall order. The division manager can lower invested capital somewhat by reducing inventories and can increase sales revenue by using store space more effectively. But reducing inventories may lead to stockouts and lost sales, and crowded aisles may drive customers away.

Improving ROI is a balancing act that requires all the skills of an effective manager. The ROI analysis above merely shows the arena in which the balancing act is performed.

Residual Income

Although ROI is the most popular investment centre performance measure, it has one major drawback. To illustrate, suppose Suncoast's Food Processing Division manager can buy a new food-processing machine for $500,000, which will save $80,000 in operating expenses and thereby raise divisional profit by $80,000. The return on this investment in new equipment is 16 percent:

$$\frac{\text{Return on investment}}{\text{in new equipment}} = \frac{\text{Increase in divisional profit}}{\text{Increase in invested capital}} = \frac{\$80,000}{\$500,000} = 16\%$$

Now suppose it costs Suncoast Food Centres 12 cents of interest for each dollar of capital borrowed to invest in operational assets. What is the optimal decision for the Food Processing Division manager to make, *viewed from the perspective of the company as a whole*? Since it costs Suncoast Food Centres 12 percent for every dollar of capital borrowed, and the return on investment in new equipment is 16 percent, the equipment should be purchased. For goal congruence, the autonomous division manager should decide to buy the new equipment.

Now consider what is likely to happen. The Food Processing Division manager's performance is evaluated on the basis of his division's ROI. Without the new equipment, the divisional ROI is 20 percent ($3,600,000 of divisional profit ÷ $18,000,000 of invested capital). If he purchases the new equipment, his divisional ROI will decline:

Food Processing Division's Return on Investment

Without Investment in New Equipment	With Investment in New Equipment
$\dfrac{\$3,600,000}{\$18,000,000} = 20\%$	$\dfrac{\$3,600,000 + \$80,000}{\$18,000,000 + \$500,000} < 20\%$

Why did this happen? Even though the investment in new equipment earns a return of 16 percent, which is greater than the company's cost of raising capital (12 percent), the return is less than the division's ROI without the equipment (20 percent). Averaging the new investment with those already in place in the Food Processing Division merely reduces the division's ROI. Since the division manager is evaluated using ROI, he will be reluctant to decide in favour of acquiring the new equipment.

The problem is that the ROI measure leaves out an important piece of information: it ignores the firm's cost of raising investment capital. For this reason, many managers prefer to use a different investment centre performance measure instead of ROI.

Computing Residual Income   An investment centre's **residual income** is defined as follows:

$$\frac{\text{Residual}}{\text{income}} = \frac{\text{Investment centre's}}{\text{profit}} - \left(\frac{\text{Investment centre's}}{\text{invested capital}} \times \frac{\text{Imputed}}{\text{interest rate}}\right)$$

where the imputed interest rate is the firm's cost of acquiring investment capital.

Residual income is a dollar amount, not a ratio like ROI. It is the amount of an investment centre's profit that remains (as a residual) after subtracting an imputed interest charge.

The term *imputed* means that the interest charge is estimated. This charge reflects the firm's minimum required rate of return on invested capital. In some firms, the imputed interest rate depends on the riskiness of the investment for which the funds will be used. So, divisions that have different levels of risk sometimes are assigned different *imputed* interest rates.

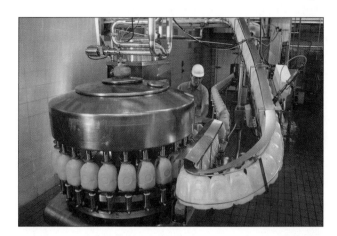

ROI and residual income are common performance measures for investment centres. Both measures relate the profit earned from selling the final product to the capital required to carry out production operations. Here the product is orange juice, and this bottling equipment represents a capital investment.

The residual income of Suncoast's Food Processing Division is computed below, both with and without the investment in the new equipment. The imputed interest rate is 12 percent.

	Food Processing Division's Residual Income			
	Without Investment in New Equipment		**With Investment in New Equipment**	
Divisional profit		$3,600,000		$3,680,000
Less imputed interest charge:				
Invested capital	$18,000,000		$18,500,000	
× Imputed interest rate	× 0.12		× 0.12	
Imputed interest charge		2,160,000		2,220,000
Residual income		$1,440,000		$1,460,000

Investment in new equipment
raises residual income by
$20,000

Notice that the Food Processing Division's residual income will *increase* if the new equipment is purchased. What will be the division manager's incentive if he is evaluated on the basis of residual income instead of ROI? He will want to make the investment because that decision will increase his division's residual income. Thus, goal congruence is achieved when the management accountant uses residual income to measure divisional performance.

Why does residual income facilitate goal congruence while ROI does not? Because the residual-income formula incorporates an important piece of data that is excluded from the ROI formula: the firm's minimum required rate of return on invested capital. To summarize, ROI and residual income are compared as shown in the following diagram:

$$\text{ROI} = \frac{\text{Investment centre's profit}}{\text{Investment centre's invested capital}} \longleftarrow \begin{array}{l}\text{Two pieces}\\ \text{of data}\end{array}$$

$$\begin{array}{l}\text{Residual}\\ \text{income}\end{array} = \begin{array}{l}\text{Investment centre's}\\ \text{profit}\end{array} - \left(\begin{array}{l}\text{Investment centre's}\\ \text{invested capital}\end{array} \times \begin{array}{l}\text{Imputed}\\ \text{interest rate}\end{array}\right)$$

Three pieces
of data

Unfortunately, residual income also has a serious drawback: It should not be used to compare the performance of different-sized investment centres because it incorporates a bias in favour of the larger investment centre. To illustrate, the following table compares the residual income of Suncoast Food Centres' Lower Sunshine Coast and Upper Sunshine Coast divisions. Notice that the Upper Sunshine Coast Division's residual income is considerably higher than the Lower Sunshine Coast Division's. This is entirely due to the much greater size of the Upper Sunshine Coast Division, as evidenced in the following table by its far greater invested capital.

	Comparison of Residual Income: Two Divisions	
	Lower Sunshine Coast Division	**Upper Sunshine Coast Division**
Divisional profit	$3,000,000	$6,750,000
Less imputed interest charge:		
Invested capital	$20,000,000	$45,000,000
× Imputed interest rate	× 0.12	× 0.12
Imputed interest charge	2,400,000	5,400,000
Residual income	$ 600,000	$1,350,000

In short, neither ROI nor residual income provides a perfect measure of investment centre performance. ROI can undermine goal congruence. Residual income distorts comparisons between investment centres of different sizes. As a result, some companies routinely use both measures for divisional performance evaluation.

Shareholder Value Analysis Some companies apply the residual income concept to individual product lines. **Shareholder value analysis** calculates the residual income for a major product line, with the objective of determining how the product line affects the firm's value to the shareholders. Suppose, for example, that Suncoast Food Centres offers in-store, one-hour film development in selected stores. Let's say that the company's investment in this service is $200,000 and the annual profit is $40,000. Then the residual income on one-hour film development is $16,000 [$40,000 − ($200,000 × 12%)].

Economic Value Added

The most contemporary measure of investment centre performance is **economic value added (EVA)**, which is defined as follows:

$$\begin{matrix} \text{Economic} \\ \text{value} \\ \text{added} \end{matrix} = \begin{matrix} \text{Investment} \\ \text{centre's after-tax} \\ \text{operating income} \end{matrix} - \left[\left(\begin{matrix} \text{Investment} \\ \text{centre's} \\ \text{total assets} \end{matrix} - \begin{matrix} \text{Investment} \\ \text{centre's current} \\ \text{liabilities} \end{matrix} \right) \times \begin{matrix} \text{Weighted-} \\ \text{average cost} \\ \text{of capital} \end{matrix} \right]$$

Like residual income, the economic value added is a dollar amount. However, it differs from residual income in two important ways. First, an investment centre's current liabilities are subtracted from its total assets. Second, the weighted-average cost of capital is used in the calculation.

Weighted-Average Cost of Capital Suncoast Food Centres has two sources of long-term capital: debt and equity. The cost to Suncoast of issuing debt is the after-tax cost of the interest payments on the debt, taking account of the fact that the interest payments are tax-deductible. The cost of Suncoast's equity capital is the investment opportunity rate of Suncoast Food Centres' investors, that is, the rate they could earn on investments of similar risk to that of investing in Suncoast Food Centres. The **weighted-average cost of capital (WACC)** is defined as follows:

$$\text{Weighted-average} \atop \text{cost of capital} = \frac{\left(\begin{matrix}\text{After-tax cost}\\\text{of debt}\\\text{capital}\end{matrix}\right)\left(\begin{matrix}\text{Market}\\\text{value}\\\text{of debt}\end{matrix}\right) + \left(\begin{matrix}\text{Cost of}\\\text{equity}\\\text{capital}\end{matrix}\right)\left(\begin{matrix}\text{Market}\\\text{value}\\\text{of equity}\end{matrix}\right)}{\begin{matrix}\text{Market} & \text{Market}\\\text{value} + \text{value}\\\text{of debt} & \text{of equity}\end{matrix}}$$

The interest rate on Suncoast Food Centres' $40 million of debt is 9 percent, and the company's tax rate is 30 percent. Therefore, Suncoast's after-tax cost of debt is 6.3 percent [9% × (1 − 30%)]. Let's assume that the cost of Suncoast's equity capital is 12 percent. Moreover, the market value of the company's equity is $60 million.[3] The following calculation shows that Suncoast Food Centres' WACC is 9.72 percent:

$$\text{Weighted-average} \atop \text{cost of capital} = \frac{(0.063)(\$40{,}000{,}000) + (0.12)(\$60{,}000{,}000)}{\$40{,}000{,}000 + \$60{,}000{,}000} = 0.0972$$

Finally, Suncoast Food Centres had an average balance of $2 million in current liabilities, distributed as follows:

Division	Current Liabilities
Lower Sunshine Coast Division	$ 400,000
Food Processing Division	1,000,000
Upper Sunshine Coast Division	600,000

Now we can compute the economic value added (or EVA) for each of Suncoast's three divisions.

Division	After-tax operating income (in millions)	−	[(Total assets (in millions)	−	Current liabilities (in millions))	× WACC]	=	Economic value added
Lower Sunshine Coast	$3.00 × (1 − 0.30) −		[($20	−	$0.4)	× 0.0972]	=	$194,880
Food Processing	$3.60 × (1 − 0.30) −		[($18	−	$1.0)	× 0.0972]	=	867,600
Upper Sunshine Coast	$6.75 × (1 − 0.30) −		[($45	−	$0.6)	× 0.0972]	=	409,320

The EVA analysis reveals that all three of Suncoast Food Centres' divisions are contributing substantially to the company's economic value.

What does an EVA analysis tell us? EVA indicates how much shareholder wealth is being created, as Roberto Goizueta, Coca-Cola's former CEO, explained: "We raise capital to make concentrate and sell it at an operating profit. Then we pay the cost of that capital. Shareholders pocket the difference (EVA amount)."

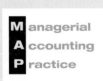

M anagerial
A ccounting
P ractice

Siemens,
Royal Bank of
Canada

PAY FOR PERFORMANCE BASED ON EVA

In the wake of the excesses in top management compensation over the past few years, pay for performance is back in vogue at many companies. Top executives earn hefty bonuses when times are good, but are expected to share in the pain during a decline in business.

Siemens, a global electronics firm, links the compensation of its top 500 managers to their business units' economic value added (EVA) measure. Similarly, the Royal Bank of Canada, upon observing that its lower-level managers were not acting in accordance with the bank's overall strategy, began linking their compensation to the bank's EVA and revenue growth.[4]

Measuring Income and Invested Capital

Learning Objective **9**

Explain how to measure a division's income and invested capital.

The ROI, residual-income, and economic value added (EVA) measures of investment centre performance all use profit and invested capital in their formulas. This raises the question of how to measure divisional profit and invested capital. This section will illustrate various approaches to resolving these measurement issues.

Invested Capital

We will focus on Suncoast Food Centres' Food Processing Division to illustrate several alternative approaches to measuring an investment centre's capital. Exhibit 11–9 lists the assets and liabilities associated with the Food Processing Division. Notice that Exhibit 11–9 does not constitute a complete balance sheet. First, there are no long-term liabilities, such as bonds payable, associated with the Food Processing Division. Although Suncoast Food Centres may have such long-term debt, it would not be meaningful to assign portions of that debt to the company's individual divisions. Second, there is no shareholders' equity associated with the Food Processing Division. The owners of the company own shares in Suncoast Food Centres, not in its individual divisions.

Average Balances ROI, residual income, and EVA are computed for a period of time, such as a year or a month. Asset balances, on the other hand, are measured at a point in time, such as December 31. Since divisional asset balances generally will change over time, we use average balances in calculating ROI, residual income, and EVA. For example, if the Food Processing Division's balance in invested capital was $19,000,000 on January 1 and $17,000,000 on December 31, we would use the year's average invested capital of $18,000,000 in the ROI, residual income, and EVA calculations.

Should Total Assets Be Used? Exhibit 11–9 shows that the Food Processing Division had average balances during the year of $2,000,000 in current assets, $15,000,000 in long-lived assets, and $1,000,000 tied up in a plant under construction. (Suncoast Food Centres is building a new high-tech dairy plant in Gibsons to produce its innovative zero-calorie ice cream.) In addition, Exhibit 11–9 discloses that the Food Processing Division's average balance of current liabilities was $1,000,000.

What is the division's invested capital? Several possibilities exist:

- ***Total assets.*** The management of Suncoast Food Centres has decided to use *average total assets* for the year in measuring each division's invested capital. Thus, $18,000,000 is the amount used in the ROI, residual-income, and EVA

Exhibit 11–9
Assets and Liabilities Associated with the Food Processing Division

Suncoast
FOOD CENTRES

Assets*		
Current assets (cash, accounts receivable, inventories, etc.)		$ 2,000,000
Long-lived assets (land, buildings, equipment, vehicles, etc.):		
Gross book value (acquisition cost)	$19,000,000	
Less: Accumulated depreciation..	4,000,000	
Net book value		15,000,000
Plant under construction...		1,000,000
Total assets		$18,000,000

Liabilities		
Current liabilities (accounts payable, salaries payable, etc.).........................		$ 1,000,000

*This is not a balance sheet, but rather a listing of certain assets and liabilities associated with the Food Processing Division.

calculations discussed earlier in this chapter. This measure of invested capital is appropriate if the division manager has considerable authority in making decisions about *all* of the division's assets, *including nonproductive assets*. In this case, the Food Processing Division's partially completed dairy plant is a nonproductive asset. Since the division manager had considerable influence in deciding to build the new plant and he is responsible for overseeing the project, average total assets provides an appropriate measure.

- *Total productive assets.* In other companies, division managers are directed by top management to hold on to nonproductive assets, such as vacant land or construction in progress. In such cases, it is appropriate to exclude nonproductive assets from the measure of invested capital. Then *average total productive assets* is used to measure invested capital. If Suncoast Food Centres had chosen this alternative, $17,000,000 would have been used in the ROI, residual-income, and EVA calculations (total assets of $18,000,000 less $1,000,000 for the plant under construction).

- *Total assets less current liabilities.* Some companies allow division managers to secure short-term bank loans and other short-term credit. In such cases, invested capital often is measured by *average total assets less average current liabilities*. This approach encourages investment centre managers to minimize resources tied up in assets and maximize the use of short-term credit to finance operations. If this approach had been used by Suncoast Food Centres, the Food Processing Division's invested capital would have been $17,000,000: total assets of $18,000,000 less current liabilities of $1,000,000. (Note that current liabilities are always subtracted from total assets for the measure of invested capital used in the EVA measure.)

Gross or Net Book Value Another decision to make in choosing a measure of invested capital is whether to use the *gross book value (acquisition cost)* or the *net book value* of long-lived assets. (Net book value is the acquisition cost less accumulated depreciation.) Suncoast Food Centres' management has decided to use the average net book value of $15,000,000 to value the Food Processing Division's long-lived assets. If gross book value had been used instead, the division's measure of invested capital would have been $22,000,000, as the following calculation shows:

Current assets	$ 2,000,000
Long-lived assets (at gross book value)	19,000,000
Plant under construction	1,000,000
Total assets (at gross book value)	$22,000,000

There are advantages and disadvantages associated with both gross and net book value as a measure of invested capital:

- Using net book value maintains consistency with the balance sheet prepared for external reporting purposes. This allows for more meaningful comparisons of return-on-investment measures across different companies.
- Using net book value to measure invested capital is also more consistent with the definition of income, which is the numerator in ROI calculations. In computing income, the current period's depreciation on long-lived assets is deducted as an expense.

The following two advantages are often associated with using gross book value:

1. The usual methods of computing depreciation, such as the straight-line and the declining-balance methods, are arbitrary. Hence, they should not be allowed to affect ROI, residual-income, or EVA calculations.
2. When long-lived assets are depreciated, their net book value declines over time. This results in a misleading increase in ROI, residual income, and EVA

across time. Exhibit 11–10 provides an illustration of this phenomenon for the ROI calculated on an equipment purchase under consideration by the Food Processing Division manager. Notice that the ROI rises steadily across the five-year horizon if invested capital is measured by net book value. However, using gross book value eliminates this problem. If an accelerated depreciation method was used instead of the straight-line method, the increasing trend in ROI would be even more pronounced.

Exhibit 11–10

Increase in ROI over Time (when net book value is used)

Suncoast
FOOD CENTRES

Acquisition cost of equipment	$500,000
Useful life	5 years
Residual value at end of useful life	0
Annual straight-line depreciation	$100,000
Annual income generated by asset (before deducting depreciation)	$150,000

Year	Income before Depreciation	Annual Depreciation	Income Net of Depreciation	Average Net Book Value*	ROI Based on Net Book Value†	Average Gross Book Value	ROI Based on Gross Book Value
1	$150,000	$100,000	$50,000	$450,000	11.1%	$500,000	10%
2	150,000	100,000	50,000	350,000	14.3	500,000	10
3	150,000	100,000	50,000	250,000	20.0	500,000	10
4	150,000	100,000	50,000	150,000	33.3	500,000	10
5	150,000	100,000	50,000	50,000	100.0	500,000	10

*Average net book value is the average of the beginning and ending balances for the year in net book value. In Year 1, for example, the average net book value is:

$$\frac{\$500,000}{2} = \$400,000$$

†ROI rounded to nearest one-tenth of 1 percent.

A Behavioural Problem   The tendency for net book value to produce a misleading increase in ROI over time can have a serious effect on the incentives of investment centre managers. Investment centres with old assets will show much higher ROIs than investment centres with relatively new assets. This can discourage investment centre managers from investing in new equipment. If this behavioural tendency persists, a division's assets can become obsolete, making the division uncompetitive.

Allocating Assets to Investment Centres   Some companies control certain assets centrally, although these assets are needed to carry on operations in the divisions. Common examples are cash and accounts receivable. Divisions need cash in order to operate, but many companies control cash balances centrally in order to minimize their total cash holdings. Some large retail firms manage accounts receivable centrally. A credit customer of some national department store chains can make a payment at the local store, mail the payment to corporate headquarters, or make the payment online.

When certain assets are controlled centrally, some allocation basis generally is chosen to allocate these asset balances to investment centres for the purpose of measuring invested capital. For example, cash may be allocated based on the budgeted cash needs in each division or on the basis of divisional sales. Accounts receivable usually are allocated on the basis of divisional sales. Divisions with less stringent credit terms are allocated proportionately larger balances of accounts receivable.

Learning Objective **9**

Explain how to measure a division's income and invested capital.

Measuring Investment Centre Income

In addition to choosing a measure of investment centre capital, an accountant must also decide how to measure a centre's income. The key issue is controllability; the choice involves the extent to which uncontrollable items are allowed to influence the income measure. The spreadsheet in Exhibit 11–11 illustrates several different possibilities for measuring the income of Suncoast Food Centres' Food Processing Division.

Suncoast Food Centres' top management uses the *profit margin controllable by division manager*, $3,600,000, to evaluate the Food Processing Division manager. This profit measure is used in calculating ROI, residual income, or EVA. Some fixed costs traceable to the division have not been deducted from this $3,600,000 amount, but the division manager cannot control or significantly influence these costs, so they are excluded from the ROI calculation in evaluating the division manager. In calculating EVA, the $3,600,000 profit margin amount is converted to an after-tax basis by multiplying by 1 minus the tax rate of 30 percent.

Pay for Performance   Some companies reward investment centre managers with **cash bonuses** if they meet a predetermined target on a specified performance criterion, such as residual income, ROI, or EVA. Such payments often are referred to as **pay for performance**, **merit pay**, or **incentive compensation**. These cash bonuses generally are single payments, independent of a manager's base salary.

Managers versus Investment Centres   It is important to make a distinction between an investment centre and its manager. In evaluating the *manager's* performance, only revenues and costs that the manager can control or significantly influence should be included in the profit measure. Remember that the overall objective of the performance measure is to provide incentives for goal-congruent behaviour. No performance measure can motivate a manager to make decisions about costs that he or she cannot control. This explains why Suncoast Food Centres' top management relies on the profit margin controllable by division manager to compute the manager's ROI performance measure.

Evaluating the Food Processing Division as a viable economic investment is a different matter altogether. In this evaluation, traceability of costs, rather than controllability, is the issue. For this purpose, Suncoast Food Centres' top management uses the profit margin traceable to division to compute the divisional ROI, residual income, or EVA. As Exhibit 11–11 shows, this amount is $2,400,000.

Other Profit Measures   The other measures of divisional profit shown in Exhibit 11–11 (lines 4, 5, and 6) also are used by some companies. The rationale behind these divisional income measures is that all corporate costs have to be covered by the operations of the divisions. Allocating corporate costs, interest, and income taxes to the divisions makes division managers aware of these costs.

		A	B	C	D	E	F	G	H
1					FOOD PROCESSING DIVISION				
2					Divisional Income Statement				
3									
4			Sales revenue						$9,000,000
5			Variable expenses						3,800,000
6	(1)		Divisional contribution margin						$5,200,000
7			Fixed expenses controllable by division manager						1,600,000
8	(2)		Profit margin controllable by division manager						$3,600,000
9			Fixed expenses, traceable to division, but controlled by others						1,200,000
10	(3)		Profit margin traceable to division						$2,400,000
11			Common fixed expenses, allocated from corporate headquarters						400,000
12	(4)		Divisional income before interest and taxes						$2,000,000
13			Interest expense allocated from corporate headquarters						250,000
14	(5)		Divisional income before taxes						$1,750,000
15			Income taxes allocated from corporate headquarters						525,000
16	(6)		Divisional net income						$1,225,000

Exhibit 11–11

Divisional Income Statement:
Food Processing Division

Suncoast
FOOD CENTRES

Transfer Pricing

Measuring performance in profit centres or investment centres is made more complicated by transfers of goods or services between responsibility centres. The amount charged when one division sells goods or services to another division is called a **transfer price**.

Transfer pricing is widely used in all kinds of businesses. When the chassis for this Ford Mustang convertible was transferred from the manufacturing division to the assembly division, a transfer price was specified.

This price affects the profit measurement for both the selling division and the buying division. A high transfer price results in high profit for the selling division and low profit for the buying division. A low transfer price has the opposite effect. Consequently, the transfer pricing policy *can* affect the *incentives* of autonomous division managers as they decide whether to make the transfer. Exhibit 11–12 depicts this scenario.

Goal Congruence

What should be management's goal in setting transfer prices for internally transferred goods or services? In a decentralized organization, the managers of profit centres and investment centres often have considerable autonomy in deciding whether to accept or reject orders and whether to buy inputs from inside the organization or from outside. For

Exhibit 11–12
The Transfer Pricing Scenario

Assuming the transfer is made, the transfer price will not affect the company's overall profit;* however, it does affect the profit associated with each division. As a consequence, the transfer pricing policy can affect the decisions of autonomous divison managers who are deciding whether to make the transfer.

*Assumes no tax complexities involving multinational companies. This issue is addressed later in the chapter.

example, a large manufacturer of farm equipment allows its Assembly Division managers to buy parts either from another division of the company or from independent manufacturers. The goal in setting transfer prices is to establish incentives for autonomous division managers to make decisions that support the overall goals of the organization.

Suppose it is in the best interests of Suncoast Food Centres for the baked goods produced by the Food Processing Division's Gibsons Bakery to be transferred to the Lower Sunshine Coast Division's stores in the Sechelt Bay area. So, if the firm was centralized, bakery products would be transferred from the Food Processing Division to the Lower Sunshine Coast Division. However, Suncoast Food Centres is a decentralized company, and the Lower Sunshine Coast Division manager is free to buy baked goods either from the Food Processing Division or from an outside bakery company. Similarly, the Food Processing Division manager is free to accept or reject an order for baked goods, at any given price, from the Lower Sunshine Coast Division. The goal of the company's controller in setting the transfer price is to provide incentives for each of these division managers to act in the company's best interests. The transfer price should be chosen so that each division manager, when striving to maximize her or his own division's profit, makes the decision that maximizes the company's profit.

General Transfer Pricing Rule

Management's objective in setting a transfer price is to encourage goal congruence among the division managers involved in the transfer. A general rule that will ensure goal congruence is given below.

Learning Objective **10**

Use the general economic rule to set an optimal transfer price.

$$\text{Transfer price} = \begin{array}{c} \text{Additional } \textit{outlay cost} \\ \text{per unit incurred because} \\ \text{goods are transferred} \end{array} + \begin{array}{c} \textit{Opportunity cost } \text{per unit} \\ \text{to the organization} \\ \text{because of the transfer} \end{array}$$

The general rule specifies the transfer price as the sum of two cost components. The first component is the outlay cost incurred by the division that produces the goods or services to be transferred. Outlay costs will include the direct variable costs of the product or service and any other outlay costs that are incurred only as a result of the transfer. The second component in the general transfer pricing rule is the opportunity cost incurred by the organization as a whole because of the transfer. Recall from Chapter 2 that an *opportunity cost* is a benefit that is foregone as a result of taking a particular action.

We will illustrate the general transfer pricing rule for Suncoast Food Centres. The company's Food Processing Division produces bread in its Gibsons Bakery. The division transfers some of its products to the company's Lower Sunshine Coast and Lower Sunshine Coast divisions, and sells some of its products to other companies in the *external market* under different labels.

Bread is transported to stores in racks containing one dozen loaves of packaged bread. In the Gibsons bakery, the following diagram shows the variable costs that are incurred to produce bread and transport it to a buyer:

Production:
    Standard variable cost per rack (including packaging) $7.00
Transportation:
    Standard variable cost per rack to transport bread 0.25

In applying the general transfer pricing rule, we will distinguish between the following two different scenarios.

Scenario I: No Excess Capacity Suppose the Food Processing Division can sell all of the bread it can produce to outside buyers at a market price of $11 per rack. Since the division

"Transfer pricing is a business issue as well as a tax issue that should be considered in the board-room." (11h)

Ernst & Young

can sell all of its production, it has *no excess capacity*. *Excess capacity* exists only when more goods can be produced than the producer is able to sell, due to low demand for the product.

What transfer price does the general rule yield under this scenario of no excess capacity? The transfer price is determined as follows:

Outlay cost:

Standard variable cost of production	$ 7.00 per rack
Standard variable cost of transportation	0.25 per rack
Total outlay cost...	$ 7.25 per rack

Opportunity cost:

Selling price per unit in external market	$11.00 per rack
Less: Variable cost of production and transportation..	7.25 per rack
Opportunity cost (foregone contribution margin)...	$ 3.75 per rack

General transfer pricing rule:

Transfer price	=	Outlay cost	+	Opportunity cost
$11.00	=	$7.25	+	$3.75

The *outlay cost* incurred by the Food Processing Division in order to transfer a rack of bread includes the standard variable production cost of $7 and the standard variable transportation cost of $0.25. The *opportunity cost* incurred by Suncoast Food Centres when its Food Processing Division transfers a rack of bread to the Lower Sunshine Coast Division instead of selling it in the external market is the foregone contribution margin from the lost sale, equal to $3.75. Why does the company lose a sale in the external market for every rack of bread transferred to the Lower Sunshine Coast Division? The sale is lost because there is *no excess capacity* in the Food Processing Division. Every rack of bread transferred to another company division results in one less rack of bread sold in the external market.

How does the general transfer pricing rule promote goal congruence? Suppose the Lower Sunshine Coast Division's grocery stores can sell a loaf of bread for $1.50, or $18 for a rack of 12 loaves ($18 = 12 × $1.50). What is the best way for Suncoast Food Centres to use the limited production capacity in the Food Processing Division's Gibsons bakery? The answer is determined as follows:

Contribution to Suncoast Food Centres from Sale in External Market		**Contribution to Suncoast Food Centres from Transfer to Lower Sunshine Coast Division**	
Wholesale selling price per rack......................	$11.00	Retail selling price per rack............................	$18.00
Less: Variable costs..	7.25	Less: Variable costs..	7.25
Contribution margin	$ 3.75	Contribution margin	$10.75

The best use of the bakery's limited production capacity is to produce bread for transfer to the Lower Sunshine Coast Division. If the transfer price is set at $11, as the general rule specifies, goal congruence is maintained. The Food Processing Division manager is willing to transfer bread to the Lower Sunshine Coast Division, because the transfer price of $11 is equal to the external market price. The Lower Sunshine Coast Division manager is willing to buy the bread, because her division will have a contribution margin of $7 on each rack of bread transferred ($18 sales price minus the $11 transfer price).

Now consider a different situation. Suppose a local organization makes a special offer to the Lower Sunshine Coast Division manager to buy several hundred loaves of bread to sell in a promotional campaign. The organization offers to pay $0.80 per loaf, which is $9.60 per rack of a dozen loaves. What will the Lower Sunshine Coast Division manager do? She must pay a transfer price of $11 per rack, so the Lower Sunshine Coast Division would lose $1.40 per rack if the special offer was accepted ($11 − $9.60 = $1.40). The Lower Sunshine Coast Division manager will decline the special offer. Is this decision in the best interests of Suncoast Food Centres as a whole? If the offer was accepted, the company as a whole would make a positive contribution of $2.35 per rack, as shown below.

Contribution to Suncoast Food Centres If Special Offer Is Accepted

Special price per rack	$9.60 per rack
Less: Variable cost to company	7.25 per rack
Contribution to company, per rack..	$2.35 per rack

However, the company can make even more if its Food Processing Division sells bread directly in its external market. Then the contribution to the company is $3.75, as we have just seen. (The external market price of $11 per rack minus a variable cost of $7.25 per rack equals $3.75 per rack.) Thus, Suncoast Food Centres is better off, as a whole, if the Lower Sunshine Coast Division's special offer is rejected. Once again, the general transfer pricing rule results in goal-congruent decision making.

Scenario II: Excess Capacity   Now let's change our basic assumption and suppose the Food Processing Division's Gibsons bakery has excess production capacity. This means that the total demand for its bread from all sources, including the Lower Sunshine Coast and Upper Sunshine Coast divisions and the external market, is less than the bakery's production capacity. Under this scenario of excess capacity, what does the general rule specify for a transfer price?

$$\text{Transfer price} = \text{Outlay cost} + \text{Opportunity cost}$$
$$\$7.25 \quad = \quad \$7.25 \quad + \quad 0$$

The *outlay cost* in the Food Processing Division's Gibsons bakery is still $7.25, since it does not depend on whether there is idle capacity or not. The *opportunity cost*, however, is now zero. There is no opportunity cost to the company when a rack of bread is transferred to the Lower Sunshine Coast Division, because the Food Processing Division can still satisfy all of its external demand for bread. Thus, the general rule specifies a transfer price of $7.25, the total standard variable cost of production and transportation.

Let's reconsider what will happen when the Lower Sunshine Coast Division manager receives the local organization's special offer to buy bread at $9.60 per rack. The Lower Sunshine Coast Division will now show a positive contribution of $2.35 per rack on the special order.

Special price per rack	$9.60 per rack
Less: Transfer price paid by Lower Sunshine Coast Division	7.25 per rack
Contribution to Lower Sunshine Coast Division..	$2.35 per rack

The Lower Sunshine Coast Division manager will accept the special offer. This decision is also in the best interests of Suncoast Food Centres. The company, as a whole, also will make a contribution of $2.35 per rack on every rack transferred to the Lower Sunshine Coast Division to satisfy the special order. Once again, the general transfer pricing rule maintains goal-congruent decision-making behaviour.

Notice that the general rule yields a transfer price that leaves the Food Processing Division manager indifferent as to whether the transfer will be made. At a transfer price of $7.25, the contribution to the Food Processing Division will be zero (transfer price of $7.25 less variable cost of $7.25). To avoid this problem, we can view the general rule as providing a lower bound on the transfer price. Some companies allow the producing division to add a markup to this lower bound in order to provide a positive contribution margin. This in turn provides a positive incentive to make the transfer.

Difficulty in Implementing the General Rule   The general transfer pricing rule will always promote goal-congruent decision making *if the rule can be implemented*. However,

> "It is difficult for people 'doing the business' to stop and consult about the transfer pricing implications of their moves, but they have to." (11i)
>
> **Respondent, Ernst & Young survey**

the rule is often difficult or impossible to implement due to the difficulty of measuring opportunity costs. Such a cost-measurement problem can arise for a number of reasons. One reason is that the external market may not be perfectly competitive. Under **perfect competition**, the market price does not depend on the quantity sold by any one producer. Under **imperfect competition**, a single producer or group of producers can affect the market price by varying the amount of product available in the market. In such cases, the external market price depends on the production decisions of the producer. This in turn means that the opportunity cost incurred by the company as a result of internal transfers depends on the quantity sold externally. These interactions may make it impossible to measure accurately the opportunity cost caused by a product transfer.

Other reasons for difficulty in measuring the opportunity cost associated with a product transfer include uniqueness of the transferred goods or services, a need for the producing division to invest in special equipment in order to produce the transferred goods, and interdependencies among several transferred products or services. For example, the producing division may provide design services as well as production of the goods for a buying division. What is the opportunity cost associated with each of these related outputs of the producing division? In many such cases, it is difficult to sort out the opportunity costs.

The general transfer pricing rule provides a good conceptual model for the management accountant to use in setting transfer prices. Moreover, in many cases, it can be implemented. When the general rule cannot be implemented, organizations turn to other transfer pricing methods, as we will see next.

Transfers Based on the External Market Price

Learning Objective   **11**

Explain how to base a transfer price on market prices, costs, or negotiations.

A common approach is to set the transfer price equal to the price in the external market. In the Suncoast Food Centres example, the Food Processing Division would set the transfer price for bread at $11 per rack, since that is the price the division can obtain in its external market. When the producing division has no excess capacity and perfect competition prevails, where no single producer can affect the market price, the general transfer pricing rule and the external market price yield the same transfer price. This fact is illustrated for Suncoast Food Centres as follows:

General Transfer Pricing Rule

$$
\begin{aligned}
\text{Transfer price} &= \quad \text{Outlay cost} \quad + \quad \text{Opportunity cost} \\[4pt]
&= \begin{array}{c} \text{Variable cost of} \\ \text{production and} \\ \text{transportation} \end{array} + \begin{array}{c} \text{Foregone contribution} \\ \text{margin of an external} \\ \text{sale} \end{array} \\[4pt]
&= \quad\quad \$7.25 \quad\quad + \quad (\$11.00 - \$7.25) = \$11.00
\end{aligned}
$$

Market Price

$$\text{Transfer price} = \text{External market price} = \$11.00$$

If the producing division has excess capacity or the external market is imperfectly competitive, the general rule and the external market price will not yield the same transfer price.

If the transfer price is set at the market price, the producing division should have the option of either producing goods for internal transfer or selling in the external market. The buying division should be required to purchase goods from inside its organization if the producing division's goods meet the product specifications. Otherwise, the buying division should have the autonomy to buy from a supplier outside its own organization. To handle pricing disputes that may arise, an arbitration process should be established.

Transfer prices based on market prices are consistent with the responsibility-accounting concepts of profit centres and investment centres. In addition to encouraging division managers to focus on divisional profitability, market-based transfer prices help to show the contribution of each division to overall company profit. Suppose the Food

Processing Division of Suncoast Food Centres transfers bread to the Lower Sunshine Coast Division at a market-based transfer price of $11 per rack. The following contribution margins will be earned by the two divisions and the company as a whole:

Food Processing Division		Lower Sunshine Coast Division	
Transfer price	$11.00 per rack	Retail sales price	$18.00 per rack
Less: Variable costs	7.25 per rack	Less: Transfer price	11.00 per rack
Contribution margin	$ 3.75 per rack	Contribution margin	$ 7.00 per rack

Suncoast Food Centres	
Retail sales price	$18.00 per rack
Less: Variable costs	7.25 per rack
Contribution margin	$10.75 per rack

When aggregate divisional profits are determined for the year, and ROI and residual income are computed, the use of a market-based transfer price helps to assess the contributions of each division to overall corporate profits.

Distress Market Prices

Occasionally an industry will experience a period of significant excess capacity and extremely low prices. For example, when gasoline prices soared, the market prices for recreational vehicles and power boats fell temporarily to very low levels.

Under such extreme conditions, basing transfer prices on market prices can lead to decisions that are not in the best interests of the overall company. Basing transfer prices on artificially *low distress market prices* could lead the producing division to sell or close the productive resources devoted to producing the product for transfer. Under distress market prices, the producing division manager might prefer to move the division into a more profitable product line. While such a decision might improve the division's profit in the short run, it could be contrary to the best interests of the company overall. It might be better for the company as a whole to avoid divesting itself of any productive resources and to ride out the period of market distress. To encourage an autonomous division manager to act in this fashion, some companies set the transfer price equal to the long-run average external market price, rather than the current (possibly depressed) market price.

Negotiated Transfer Prices

Many companies use negotiated transfer prices. Division managers or their representatives actually negotiate the price at which transfers will be made. Sometimes they start with the external market price and then make adjustments for various reasons. For example, the producing division may enjoy some cost savings on internal transfers that are not obtained on external sales. Commissions may not have to be paid to sales personnel on internally transferred products. In such cases, a negotiated transfer price may split the cost savings between the producing and buying divisions.

In other instances, a negotiated transfer price may be used because no external market exists for the transferred product.

Two drawbacks sometimes characterize negotiated transfer prices. First, negotiations can lead to divisiveness and competition between participating division managers. This can undermine the spirit of cooperation and unity that is desirable throughout an organization. Second, although negotiating skill is a valuable managerial talent, it should not be the sole or dominant factor in evaluating a division manager. If, for example, the producing division's manager is a better negotiator than the buying division's manager, then the producing division's profit may look better than it should, simply because of its manager's superior negotiating ability.

Cost-Based Transfer Prices

Organizations that do not base prices on market prices or negotiations often turn to a cost-based transfer pricing approach.

Variable Cost   One approach is to set the transfer price equal to the standard variable cost. The problem with this approach is that even when the producing division has excess capacity, it is not allowed to show any contribution margin on the transferred products or services. To illustrate, suppose the Food Processing Division has excess capacity and the transfer price is set at the standard variable cost of $7.25 per rack of bread. There is no positive incentive for the division to produce and transfer bread to the Lower Sunshine Coast Division. The Food Processing Division's contribution margin from a transfer will be zero (transfer price of $7.25 minus variable costs of $7.25 equals zero). Some companies avoid this problem by setting the transfer price at standard variable cost plus a markup to allow the producing division a positive contribution margin.

Full Cost   An alternative is to set the transfer price equal to the *full cost* of the transferred product or service. **Full** (or **absorption**) **cost** is equal to the product's variable cost plus an allocated portion of fixed overhead.

Suppose the Food Processing Division's Gibsons bakery has budgeted annual fixed overhead of $500,000 and budgeted annual production of 200,000 racks of bread. The full cost of the bakery's product is computed as follows:

$$
\begin{aligned}
\text{Full cost} &= \text{Variable cost} + \text{Allocated fixed overhead} \\[2mm]
&= \$7.25 \text{ per rack} + \frac{\$500,000 \text{ budgeted fixed overhead}}{200,000 \text{ budgeted racks of bread}} \\[2mm]
&= \quad \$7.25 \quad + \quad\quad\quad\quad \$2.50 \\[2mm]
&= \$9.75 \text{ per rack}
\end{aligned}
$$

Under this approach, the transfer price is set at $9.75 per rack of bread.

Dysfunctional Decision-Making Behaviour   Basing transfer prices on full cost entails a serious risk of causing dysfunctional decision-making behaviour. Full cost-based transfer prices lead the buying division to view costs that are fixed for the company as a whole as variable costs to the buying division. This can cause faulty decision making.

To illustrate, suppose the Food Processing Division has excess capacity, and the transfer price of bread is equal to the full cost of $9.75 per rack. What will happen if the Lower Sunshine Coast Division receives the special offer discussed previously, where it can sell bread to a local organization at a special price of $9.60 per rack? The Lower Sunshine Coast Division manager will reject the special order, since otherwise her division would incur a loss of $0.15 per rack:

Special price per rack	$ 9.60 per rack
Less: Transfer price based on full cost	9.75 per rack
Loss	$ 0.15 per rack

What is in the best interests of the company as a whole? Suncoast Food Centres would make a positive contribution of $2.35 per rack on the bread sold in the special order:

Special price per rack	$9.60 per rack
Less: Variable cost in Food Processing Division	7.25 per rack
Contribution to company as a whole	$2.35 per rack

What has happened here? Setting the transfer price equal to the full cost of $9.75 has turned a cost that is fixed in the Food Processing Division, and hence is fixed for the company as a whole, into a variable cost from the viewpoint of the Lower Sunshine Coast Division manager. The manager would tend to reject the special offer, even though accepting it would benefit the company as a whole.

Although the practice is common, transfer prices should not be based on full cost. The risk is too great that the cost behaviour in the producing division will be obscured. This can all too easily result in poor decisions in the buying division.

Standard versus Actual Costs

Throughout our discussion of transfer prices, we have used standard costs rather than actual costs. This was true in our discussion of the general transfer pricing rule as well as for cost-based transfer prices. Transfer prices should not be based on actual costs, because such a practice would allow an inefficient producing division to pass its excess production costs on to the buying division in the transfer price. When standard costs are used in transfer pricing formulas, the buying division is not forced to pick up the tab for the producer's inefficiency. Moreover, the producing division is given an incentive to control its costs, since any costs of inefficiency cannot be passed on.

Undermining Divisional Autonomy

Suppose the manager of Suncoast Food Centres' Food Processing Division has excess capacity but insists on a transfer price of $9.75, based on full cost. The Lower Sunshine Coast Division manager is faced with the special offer for bread at $9.60 per rack. She regrets that she will have to decline the offer because it would cause her division's profit to decline, even though the company's interests would be best served by accepting the special order. The Lower Sunshine Coast Division manager calls the company president and explains the situation. She asks the president to intervene and force the Food Processing Division manager to lower his transfer price.

As the company president, what would you do? If you stay out of the controversy, your company will lose the contribution on the special order. If you intervene, you will run the risk of undermining the autonomy of your division managers. You established a decentralized organization structure for Suncoast Centres and hired competent managers because you believed in the benefits of decentralized decision making.

There is no obvious answer to this dilemma. In practice, central managers are reluctant to intervene in such disputes unless the negative financial consequences to the organization are quite large. Most managers believe the benefits of decentralized decision making are important to protect, even if it means an occasional dysfunctional decision.

> "[Transfer pricing] affects nearly every aspect of multi-national operations—R&D, manufacturing, marketing and distribution, after-sale services." (11j)
> **Ernst & Young**

An International Perspective

Two international issues arise in the case of multinational firms setting transfer prices between divisions in different countries.

Income Tax Rates   Multinational companies often consider domestic and foreign income tax rates when setting transfer prices. For example, suppose a company based in Europe also has a division in Asia. A European division produces a subassembly, which is transferred to the Asian division for assembly and sale of the final product. Suppose also that the income tax rate for the company's European division is higher than the rate in the Asian division's country. How would these different tax rates affect the transfer price for the subassembly?

The company's management has an incentive to set a low transfer price for the subassembly. This will result in relatively low profits for the company's European division

TRANSFER PRICING AND TAX ISSUES

Ernst & Young, Canada Revenue Agency

According to a survey by Ernst & Young, "Transfer pricing is the top tax issue facing multinational corporations." Of the international tax directors at 582 multinational organizations polled in the survey, 75 percent expected their company to face a transfer pricing audit within the following two years. Respondents cited related-party transactions (including the intercompany transfer of goods, services, properties, loans, and leases) involving administrative and management services as the most likely to be audited. Moreover, there has been an increase in transfer pricing audit activity in recent years.[5]

"The Canada Revenue Agency (CRA) is concerned that companies could use transfer prices to shift profits between related entities through cost of goods sold. Thus, transfer pricing manipulation could be used by taxpayers to shift income from high-tax jurisdictions like Canada to low-tax jurisdictions. The right price from the CRA's perspective is the market value price. Because it's difficult to prove that the transfer price was equal to the market price, companies often find themselves in disputes with the CRA. But now there's help. The CRA's Advance Pricing Arrangement program provides companies with an opportunity to avoid costly audits and litigation by allowing them to negotiate a prospective agreement with the CRA regarding the facts, the transfer pricing methodology, and an acceptable range of results. The program is aimed at multinational corporations interested in avoiding penalties, managing risk, and determining their tax liability with certainty."[6]

and a relatively high income for the Asian division. Since the tax rate is lower in the Asian country, the overall company will save on income tax. By setting a low transfer price, the company will shift a portion of its income to a country with a lower tax rate. Tax laws vary among countries with regard to flexibility in setting transfer prices. Some countries' tax laws prohibit the behaviour described in our example, while other countries' laws permit it.

Import Duties Another international issue that can affect a firm's transfer pricing policy is the imposition of import duties, or tariffs. These are fees charged to an importer, generally on the basis of the reported value of the goods being imported. Consider again the example of a firm with divisions in Europe and Asia. If the Asian country imposes an import duty on goods transferred in from the European division, the company has an incentive to set a relatively low transfer price on the transferred goods. This will minimize the duty to be paid and maximize the overall profit for the company as a whole. As in the case of taxation, countries sometimes pass laws to limit a multinational firm's flexibility in setting transfer prices for the purpose of minimizing import duties.

> "Transfer pricing has become the most difficult area of international taxation." (11k)
>
> **Ernst & Young**

Transfer Pricing in the Service Industry

Service industry firms and nonprofit organizations also use transfer pricing when services are transferred between responsibility centres. In banks, for example, the interest rate at which depositors' funds are transferred to the loan department is a form of transfer price. At Simon Fraser University, Document Solutions manages up to 2,000 print jobs per month, servicing the other administrative and academic units of the university. When a print job is completed, a transfer price based on market prices is charged to the unit that ordered the job and is reflected as a fund transfer between the two units in the university's financial system.

Behavioural Issues: Risk Aversion and Incentives

The designer of a performance evaluation system for responsibility centre managers has to consider many factors. Trade-offs often have to be made between competing objectives. The overall objective is to achieve goal congruence by providing *incentives* for managers to act in the best interests of the organization as a whole. Financial performance measures such as divisional income, ROI, and residual income go a long way toward achieving this objective. However, these measures do have the disadvantage of imposing *risk* on a manager, because the measures also are affected by factors beyond the manager's control. For example, the income of an apple-growing division of an agricultural company will be affected not only by the manager's diligence and ability, but also by the weather and insect infestations.

Transfer prices are used in the service industry as well as in manufacturing. Simon Fraser University, *for example, charges a project fee when Facilities Management undertakes a major maintenance project for any of the administrative or academic units of the university.*

Since most people exhibit *risk aversion*, managers must be compensated for the risk they must bear. This compensation comes in the form of higher salaries or bonuses. Thus, the design of a managerial performance evaluation and reward system involves a trade-off between the following two factors:

Evaluation of a manager on the basis of financial performance measures, which provide incentives for the manager to act in the organization's interests

Imposition of risk on a manager who exhibits risk aversion, because financial performance measures are controllable only partially by the manager

Trade-offs in designing
managerial performance
evaluation and reward system

Achieving the optimal trade-off between risk and incentives is a delicate balancing act that requires the skill and experience of top management.

Chapter Summary

LO1 Explain the role of responsibility accounting in fostering goal congruence. Responsibility-accounting systems are designed to foster goal congruence among the managers in decentralized organizations by specifying the performance measures on which managers of various organizational subunits will be evaluated.

LO2 Define and give an example of a cost centre, a revenue centre, a profit centre, and an investment centre. A cost centre is an organizational subunit, the manager of which is held accountable for the subunit's costs. Examples include the assembly department of an auto manufacturer and the maintenance department of a hotel. A revenue centre is an organizational subunit, the manager of which is held accountable for the subunit's revenue. Examples include the sales departments of a cruise line or an insurance company. A profit centre is an organizational subunit, the manager of which is held accountable for the subunit's profit. Examples include an individual branch bank or an individual fast-food restaurant. An investment centre is an organizational subunit, the manager of which is held accountable for the relationship between the subunit's profit and its invested capital. A division of a large corporation (manufacturing, service, or retail) is usually designated as an investment centre.

LO3 Prepare a performance report and explain the relationships among the performance reports for various responsibility centres. The performance of each of an organization's responsibility-accounting centres is summarized periodically on a performance report. This report shows the budgeted and actual performance results for a specified time period for each responsibility-accounting centre.

LO4 Use a cost allocation base to allocate costs. A cost allocation base is a measure of activity, physical characteristic, or economic characteristic associated with a group of organizational subunits or activities, which is the basis for allocating costs among those subunits or activities.

LO5 Prepare a segmented income statement. Segmented income statements often are included in a responsibility-accounting system to show the performance of the organization and its various segments. To be most effective, such reports should distinguish between the performance of segments and segment managers.

LO6 Compute an investment centre's return on investment (ROI), residual income (RI), and economic value added (EVA). An investment centre's ROI is equal to its income divided by its invested capital. The investment centre's RI is equal to its profit minus the product of its invested capital and an imputed interest rate. The investment centre's EVA is computed as follows: After-tax operating income [(Total assets − Current liabilities) × Weighted-average cost of capital].

LO7 Explain how a manager can improve ROI. An investment centre's ROI equals sales margin multiplied by capital turnover. Therefore, a manager can improve ROI by increasing either the sales margin or capital turnover.

LO8 Describe some advantages and disadvantages of both ROI and residual income as divisional performance measures. Each of these performance measures relates an investment centre's income to the capital invested to earn it. However, residual income and EVA have the additional advantage of incorporating the organization's cost of acquiring capital into the performance measure.

LO9 Explain how to measure a division's income and invested capital. There are several ways that investment centres' invested capital is measured in practice. Among the commonly observed measures are total assets, total productive assets, and total assets less current liabilities. Similarly, several measures of investment centre income are observed in practice. As explained in the chapter, these income measures differ in the degree to which certain expenses are controllable at the investment centre level.

LO10 Use the general economic rule to set an optimal transfer price. The general rule states that the transfer price should be equal to the outlay cost incurred to make the transfer plus the organization's opportunity cost associated with the transfer.

LO11 Explain how to base a transfer price on market prices, costs, or negotiations. Due to difficulties in implementing the general transfer pricing rule, most companies base transfer prices on external market prices, costs, or negotiations. Market prices may be the best practical measure, as long as an external market for the transferred product exists. Alternatively, transfer prices may be based on full, absorption product costs or variable product costs. Negotiation, although widely used in setting transfer prices, can be time-consuming and divisive.

Review Problems on Responsibility Accounting, Investment Centres, and Transfer Pricing

Problem 1

The North Shore Credit Union has a division for each of the two cities in which it operates, North Vancouver and West Vancouver. Each divisional vice-president is held accountable for both profit and invested capital. Each division consists of two branches. Each branch manager is responsible for that bank's profit. The North Vancouver Division's Deep Cove Branch has a Deposit Department, a Loan Department, and an Administrative Services Department. The department supervisors of the Loan and Deposit Departments are accountable for departmental revenues; the Administrative Services Department supervisor is accountable for costs.

All of the North Shore Credit Union's advertising and promotion is done centrally. The advertising and promotion cost pool for the year just ended, which amounted to $40,000, is allocated across the four branches on the basis of budgeted branch revenue. Budgeted revenue for the year is shown below.

North Vancouver Division:	Londsdale Branch	$400,000
	Deep Cove Branch	200,000
West Vancouver Division:	Howe Sound Branch	250,000
	Capilano Branch	150,000

Required:

1. Draw an organization chart for the North Shore Credit Union that shows each subunit described above, its manager's title, and its designation as a responsibility centre.

2. Distribute (allocate) the bank's advertising cost pool to the four branches.

Problem 2

Stellar Systems Company manufactures guidance systems for rockets used to launch commercial satellites. The company's Software Division reported the following results for 20x7.

Income	$ 300,000
Sales revenue	2,000,000
Invested capital (total assets)	3,000,000
Average balance in current liabilities	20,000

Stellar Systems' weighted-average cost of capital (WACC) is 9 percent, and the company's tax rate is 40 percent. Moreover, the company's required rate of return on invested capital is 9 percent.

Required:

1. Compute the Software Division's (*a*) sales margin, (*b*) capital turnover, (*c*) return on investment (ROI), (*d*) residual income (RI), and (*e*) economic value added (EVA) for 20x7.

2. If income and sales remain the same in 20x8, but the division's capital turnover improves to 80 percent, compute the following for 20x8: (*a*) invested capital and (*b*) ROI.

Problem 3

Stellar Systems Company's Microprocessor Division sells a computer module to the company's Guidance Assembly Division, which assembles completed guidance systems. The Microprocessor Division has no excess capacity. The computer module costs $10,000 to manufacture, and it can be sold in the external market to companies in the computer industry for $13,500.

Required: Compute the transfer price for the computer module using the general transfer pricing rule.

Solutions to Review Problems
Problem 1

1. Organization chart (subunits, managers, responsibility centre designation) is shown below.

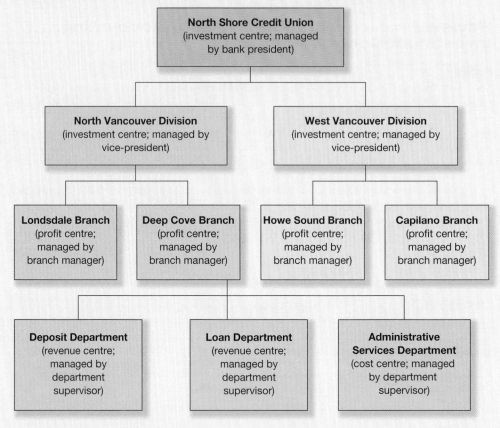

2. Cost distribution (or allocation):

Cost Pool	Responsibility Centre	Allocation Base: Revenue	Percentage of Total*	Costs Distributed
Advertising	North Vancouver, Londsdale Branch	$ 400,000	40%	$16,000
and	North Vancouver, Deep Cove Branch	200,000	20	8,000
Promotion	West Vancouver, Howe Sound Branch...........	250,000	25	10,000
Costs	West Vancouver, Capilano Branch...	150,000	15	6,000
	Total..	$1,000,000	100%	$40,000

*Branch revenue as a percentage of total revenue: $1,000,000.

Problem 2

1. *a.* Sales margin $= \dfrac{\text{Income}}{\text{Sales revenue}} = \dfrac{\$300,000}{\$2,000,000} = 15\%$

   b. Capital turnover $= \dfrac{\text{Sales revenue}}{\text{Invested capital}} = \dfrac{\$2,000,000}{\$3,000,000} = 67\%$

   c. Return on investment $= \dfrac{\text{Income}}{\text{Invested capital}} = \dfrac{\$300,000}{\$3,000,000} = 10\%$

   d. Residual income:

Divisional income...		$300,000
Less: Imputed interest charge:		
Invested capital	$3,000,000	
× Imputed interest rate	× 0.09	
Imputed interest charge		270,000
Residual income		$ 30,000

e. Economic value added (EVA):

$$\text{EVA} = \begin{array}{c}\text{Investment centre's}\\ \text{after-tax}\\ \text{operating income}\end{array} - \left[\left(\begin{array}{c}\text{Investment centre's}\\ \text{total assets}\end{array} - \begin{array}{c}\text{Investment centre's}\\ \text{current liabilities}\end{array}\right) \times \begin{array}{c}\text{Weighted-average}\\ \text{cost of capital}\end{array}\right]$$

$$= \$300,000\,(1-0.40) - [(\quad \$3,000,000 \quad - \quad \$20,000 \quad) \times \quad 0.09 \quad]$$

$$= \$(88,200)$$

2. *a.* Capital turnover $= \dfrac{\text{Sales revenue}}{\text{Invested capital}} = \dfrac{\$2,000,000}{?} = 80\%$

Therefore: Invested capital $= \dfrac{\$2,000,000}{0.80} = \$2,500,000$

b. New ROI $= 15\% \times 80\% = 12\%$

Problem 3

Transfer price = Outlay cost + Opportunity cost

$$= \$10,000 \quad + (\$13,500 - \$10,000)$$

$$= \$13,500$$

The $3,500 opportunity cost of a transfer is the contribution margin that will be foregone if a computer module is transferred instead of sold in the external market.

Glossary

Review key terms and definitions on Connect.

Review Questions

11–1. Why is goal congruence important to an organization's success? How does a responsibility-accounting system foster goal congruence?

11–2. Define and give examples of the following terms: cost centre, revenue centre, profit centre, and investment centre.

11–3. Under what circumstances would it be appropriate to change the Waikiki Sands Hotel from a profit centre to an investment centre?

11–4. Explain the relationship between performance reports and flexible budgeting.

11–5. What is the key feature of activity-based responsibility accounting? Briefly explain.

11–6. Explain how to get positive behavioural effects from a responsibility-accounting system.

11–7. "Performance reports based on controllability are impossible. Nobody really *controls* anything in an organization!" Do you agree or disagree? Explain your answer.

11–8. Explain how and why cost allocation might be used to assign the costs of a mainframe computer system used for research purposes in a university.

11–9. Define the term *cost allocation base*. What would be a sensible allocation base for assigning advertising costs to the various components of a large theme park?

11–10. Referring to Exhibit 12–5, why are marketing costs distributed to the Waikiki Sands Hotel's departments on the basis of *budgeted* sales dollars?

11–11. Explain what is meant by a *segmented income statement*.

11–12. Why do some management accountants choose not to allocate common costs in segmented reports?

11–13. Why is it important in responsibility accounting to distinguish between segments and segment managers?

11–14. List and explain three key features of the segmented income statement shown in Exhibit 12–7.

11–15. Can a common cost for one segment be a traceable cost for another segment? Explain your answer.

11–16. Describe the managerial approach known as *management by objectives* or MBO.

11–17. Write the formula for ROI, showing sales margin and capital turnover as its components.

11–18. Explain how the manager of the Automobile Division of an insurance company could improve her division's ROI.

11–19. Make up an example showing how residual income is calculated. What information is used in computing residual income that is not used in computing ROI?

11–20. What is the main disadvantage of ROI as an investment centre performance measure? How does the residual income measure eliminate this disadvantage?

11–21. Define the term *economic value added*. How does it differ from residual income?

11–22. Distinguish between the following measures of invested capital, and briefly explain when each should be used: (a) total assets, (b) total productive assets, and (c) total assets less current liabilities.

11–23. Why do some companies use gross book value instead of net book value to measure a division's invested capital?

11–24. Explain why it is important in performance evaluation to distinguish between investment centres and their managers.

11–25. How do organizations use pay for performance to motivate managers?

11–26. Describe an alternative to using ROI or residual income to measure investment centre performance.

11–27. Identify and explain the management accountant's primary objective in choosing a transfer pricing policy.

11–28. Describe four methods by which transfer prices may be set.

11–29. Explain the significance of excess capacity in the transferring division when transfer prices are set using the general transfer pricing rule.

11–30. Why might income tax laws affect the transfer-pricing policies of multinational companies?

11–31. Explain the role of import duties, or tariffs, in affecting the transfer pricing policies of multinational companies.

Exercises

Exercise 11–32 Assigning Responsibility for Skilled Employees' Wages (LO1)

Saddle River Electronics Company manufactures complex circuit boards for the aerospace industry. Demand for the company's products has fallen in recent months, and the firm has cut its production significantly. Many unskilled workers have been temporarily laid off. Top management has made a decision, however, not to lay off any highly skilled employees, such as inspectors and machinery operators. Management was concerned that these highly skilled employees would easily find new jobs elsewhere and not return when production returned to normal levels.

To occupy the skilled employees during the production cutback, they have been reassigned temporarily to the Maintenance Department. Here they are performing general maintenance tasks, such as repainting the interior of the factory, repairing the loading dock, and building wooden storage racks for the warehouse. The skilled employees continued to receive their normal wages, which average $22 per hour. However, the normal wages for Maintenance Department employees average $12 per hour.

The supervisor of the Maintenance Department recently received the March performance report, which indicated that his department's labour cost exceeded the budget by $19,360. The department's actual labour cost was approximately 90 percent over the budget. The department supervisor complained to the controller.

Required:

1. As the controller, how would you respond?

2. Would you make any modification in Saddle River's responsibility-accounting system? If so, list the changes you would make. Explain your reasoning. If not, explain your reasoning.

Exercise 11–33 Designating Responsibility Centres (LO2)

For each of the following organizational subunits, indicate the type of responsibility centre that is most appropriate:

1. A movie theatre in a company that operates a chain of theatres.
2. A radio station owned by a large broadcasting network.
3. The claims department in an insurance company.
4. The ticket sales division of a major airline.
5. A bottling plant of a soft drink company.
6. An orange juice factory operated by a large orange grower.
7. The Faculty of Engineering at a large university.
8. The European Division of a multinational manufacturing company.
9. The outpatient clinic in a profit-oriented hospital.
10. The mayor's office in a large city.

Exercise 11–34 Responsibility Accounting: Equipment Breakdown (LO1, 2)

How should a responsibility-accounting system handle each of the following scenarios?

1. Department A manufactures a component, which is then used by Department B. Department A recently experienced a machine breakdown that held up production of the component. As a result, Department B was forced to curtail its own production, thereby incurring large idle time costs. An investigation revealed that Department A's machinery had not been properly maintained.

2. Refer to the scenario above, but suppose the investigation revealed that the machinery in Department A had been properly maintained.

Exercise 11–35 Responsibility-Accounting Centres: Xerox Corporation **(LO1, 2)**

Xerox Corporation has been an innovator in its responsibility-accounting system. In one initiative, management changed the responsibility-centre orientation of its Logistics and Distribution Department from a cost centre to a profit centre. The department manages the inventories and provides other logistical services to the company's Business Systems Group. Formerly, the manager of the Logistics and Distribution Department was held accountable for adherence to an operating expense budget. Now the department "sells" its services to the company's other segments, and the department's manager is evaluated partially on the basis of the department's profit. Xerox Corporation's management feels that the change has been beneficial. The change has resulted in more innovative thinking in the department and has moved decision making down to lower levels in the company.

Required: Comment on the new responsibility-centre designation for the Logistics and Distribution Department.

Exercise 11–36 Performance Report: Hotel **(LO3)**

The following data pertain to the Waikiki Sands Hotel for the month of March:

	Flexible Budget for March (in thousands)*	Actual Results for March (in thousands)*
Banquets and catering	$ 650	$ 658
Restaurants	1,800	1,794
Kitchen staff wages	(85)	(86)
Food	(690)	(690)
Paper products	(125)	(122)
Variable overhead	(75)	(78)
Fixed overhead	(90)	(93)

*Numbers without parentheses denote profit; numbers with parentheses denote expenses.

Required: Prepare a March performance report similar to the lower portion of Exhibit 11–4. The report should have six numerical columns with headings analogous to those in Exhibit 11–4. Your performance report should cover only the Food and Beverage Department and the Kitchen. Draw arrows to show the relationships between the numbers in the report. Refer to Exhibit 11–4 for guidance. For the year-to-date columns in your report, use the data given in Exhibit 11–4. You will need to update those figures using the March data given above.

Exercise 11–37 Cost Allocation in a College **(LO4)**

Vancouver Community College has three divisions: Liberal Arts, Sciences, and Business Administration. The college's controller is trying to decide how to allocate the costs of the Admissions Department, the Registrar's Department, and the Computer Services Department. The controller has compiled the following data for the year just ended:

Department	Annual Cost
Admissions	$ 90,000
Registrar	150,000
Computer Services	320,000

Division	Budgeted Enrolment	Budgeted Credit Hours	Planned Courses Requiring Computer Work
Liberal Arts	1,000	30,000	12
Sciences	800	28,000	24
Business Administration	700	22,000	24

Required:

1. For each department, choose an allocation base and distribute the departmental costs to the college's three divisions. Justify your choice of an allocation base.

2. Would you have preferred a different allocation base than those available using the data compiled by the controller? Why?

3. *Build a spreadsheet:* Construct an Excel spreadsheet to solve requirement (1) above. Show how the solution will change if the following information changes: The costs incurred by the departments were $120,000, $160,000, and $360,000, for Admissions, Registrar, and Computer Services, respectively.

Exercise 11–38   Segmented Income Statement: TV Cable Company (LO5)

Tri-Cities Cable Services, Inc. is organized with three segments: Metro, Suburban, and Outlying. Data for these segments for the year just ended follow:

	Metro	Suburban	Outlying
Service revenue	$1,000,000	$800,000	$400,000
Variable expenses	200,000	150,000	100,000
Controllable fixed expenses	400,000	320,000	150,000
Fixed expenses controllable by others	230,000	200,000	90,000

In addition to the expenses listed above, the company has $95,000 of common fixed expenses. Income tax expense for the year is $145,000.

Required:

1. Prepare a segmented income statement for Tri-Cities Cable Services, Inc. Use the contribution format.

2. *Build a spreadsheet:* Construct an Excel spreadsheet to solve the preceding requirement. Show how the solution will change if the following information changes: The sales revenues were $950,000 and $815,000 for Metro and Suburban, respectively.

Exercise 11–39   Responsibility Accounting; Use of the Internet (LO1, 2)

Visit the website of one of the following companies, or a different company of your choosing:

Marriott Hotels	www.marriott.com	Pizza Hut	www.pizzahut.com
McDonald's Corporation	www.mcdonalds.com	Xerox Corporation	www.xerox.com

Required: Read about the company's activities and operations. Then do as good a job as you can in preparing an organization chart for the firm. For each subunit in the organization chart, indicate what type of responsibility accounting centre designation you believe would be most appropriate. (Refer to Exhibits 11–1 and 11–2 for guidance.)

Exercise 11–40   Components of ROI (LO6)

The following data pertain to Heritage Division's most recent year of operations:

Income	$ 4,000,000
Sales revenue	50,000,000
Average invested capital	20,000,000

Required: Compute Heritage Division's sales margin, capital turnover, and return on investment for the year.

Exercise 11–41   Improving ROI (LO7)

Refer to the preceding exercise.

Required: Demonstrate two ways Heritage Division's manager could improve the division's ROI to 25 percent.

Exercise 11–42   Residual Income (LO6)

Refer to the data for Exercise 11–40. Assume that the company's minimum desired rate of return on invested capital is 11 percent.

Required: Compute Heritage Division's residual income for the year.

Exercise 11–43   Calculate Weighted-Average Cost of Capital for EVA (LO6)

Coquitlam Construction Associates, a real estate developer and building contractor, has two sources of long-term capital: debt and equity. The cost to the company of issuing debt is the after-tax cost of the interest payments on the debt, taking into account the fact that the interest payments are tax-deductible. The cost of the company's equity capital is the investment opportunity rate of the company's investors, that is, the rate they could earn on investments of similar risk to that of investing in Coquitlam Construction Associates. The interest rate on the company's $60 million of long-term debt is 10 percent, and the company's tax rate is 40 percent. The cost of the company's equity capital is 15 percent. Moreover, the market value (and book value) of the company's equity is $90 million.

Required: Calculate Coquitlam Construction Associates' weighted-average cost of capital.

Exercise 11–44 Economic Value Added (EVA): Continuation of Preceding Exercise (LO6)

Refer to the data in the preceding exercise for Coquitlam Construction Associates. The company has two divisions: the real estate division and the construction division. The divisions' total assets, current liabilities, and before-tax operating income for the most recent year are as follows:

Division	Total Assets	Current Liabilities	Before-Tax Operating Income
Real estate	$100,000,000	$6,000,000	$20,000,000
Construction	60,000,000	4,000,000	18,000,000

Required: Calculate the economic value added (EVA) for each of Coquitlam Construction Associates' divisions. (You will need to use the weighted-average cost of capital, which was computed in the preceding exercise.)

Exercise 11–45 ROI; Residual Income (LO6)

Suburban Lifestyles, Inc. has manufactured prefabricated houses for over 20 years. The houses are constructed in sections to be assembled on customers' lots. Suburban Lifestyles expanded into the precut housing market when it acquired Fairmont Company, one of its suppliers. In this market, various types of lumber are precut into the appropriate lengths, banded into packages, and shipped to customers' lots for assembly. Suburban Lifestyles designated the Fairmont Division as an investment centre. Suburban Lifestyles uses return on investment (ROI) as a performance measure, with investment defined as average productive assets. Management bonuses are based in part on ROI. All investments are expected to earn a minimum return of 15 percent before income taxes. Fairmont's ROI has ranged from 19.3 to 22.1 percent since it was acquired. Fairmont had an investment opportunity in 20x1 that had an estimated ROI of 18 percent. Fairmont's management decided against the investment, because it believed the investment would decrease the division's overall ROI. The 20x1 income statement for Fairmont Division follows. The division's productive assets were $12,600,000 at the end of 20x1, a 5 percent increase over the balance at the beginning of the year.

FAIRMONT DIVISION
Income Statement
For the Year Ended December 31, 20x1
(in thousands)

Sales revenue		$24,000
Cost of goods sold		15,800
Gross margin		8,200
Operating expenses:		
Administrative	$2,140	
Selling	3,600	5,740
Income from operations before income taxes		$ 2,460

Required:

1. Calculate the following performance measures for 20x1 for the Fairmont Division:
   a. Return on investment
   b. Residual income
2. Would the management of Fairmont Division have been more likely to accept the investment opportunity it had in 20x1 if residual income was used as a performance measure instead of ROI? Explain your answer.
3. *Build a spreadsheet:* Construct an Excel spreadsheet to solve requirement (1) above. Show how the solution will change if income from operations was $2,700,000.

(CMA, adapted)

Exercise 11–46   ROI and Residual Income; Annual Reports; Use of the Internet **(LO6)**

Select one of the following companies (or any company of your choosing) and use the Internet to explore the company's most recent annual report.

Air Canada	www.aircanada.com
Deere & Company	www.deere.com
IBM	www.ibm.com
Pizza Hut	www.pizzahut.com
Ramada Inn	www.ramada.com
Walmart	www.walmart.com

Required:

1. Calculate the company's overall return on investment (ROI). Also, calculate the company's overall residual income. (Assume an imputed interest rate of 10 percent.) List and explain any assumptions you make.

2. Does the company include a calculation of ROI in its online annual report? If it does, do your calculations agree with those of the company? If not, what would be some possible explanations?

Exercise 11–47   Increasing ROI over Time **(LO6, 8, 9)**

Refer to Exhibit 11–10. Assume that you are a consultant who has been hired by Suncoast Food Centres.

Required: Write a memorandum to the company president explaining why the ROI based on net book value (in Exhibit 11–10) behaves as it does over the five-year time horizon.

Exercise 11–48   Improving ROI **(LO6, 7)**

The following data pertain to British Isles Aggregates Company, a producer of sand, gravel, and cement, for the year just ended. (£ denotes the British pound sterling, the national monetary unit of the United Kingdom.)

Sales revenue	£2,000,000
Cost of goods sold	1,100,000
Operating expenses	800,000
Average invested capital	1,000,000

Required:

1. Compute the company's sales margin, capital turnover, and ROI.

2. If the sales and average invested capital remain the same during the next year, to what level would total expenses have to be reduced in order to improve the firm's ROI to 15 percent?

3. Assume expenses are reduced, as calculated in requirement (2). Compute the firm's new sales margin. Show how the new sales margin and the old capital turnover together result in a new ROI of 15 percent.

Exercise 11–49   General Transfer Pricing Rule **(LO10)**

Metallurgy Corporation has two divisions. The Fabrication Division transfers partially completed components to the Assembly Division at a predetermined transfer price. The Fabrication Division's standard variable production cost per unit is $300. The division has no excess capacity, and it could sell all of its components to outside buyers at $380 per unit in a perfectly competitive market.

Required:

1. Determine a transfer price using the general rule.

2. How would the transfer price change if the Fabrication Division had excess capacity?

Exercise 11–50   Cost-Based Transfer Pricing **(LO11)**

Refer to the preceding exercise. The Fabrication Division's full (absorption) cost of a component is $340, which includes $40 of applied fixed-overhead costs. The transfer price has been set at $374, which is the Fabrication Division's full cost plus a 10 percent markup.

The Assembly Division has a special offer for its product of $465. The Assembly Division incurs variable costs of $100 in addition to the transfer price for the Fabrication Division's components. Both divisions currently have excess production capacity.

Required:

1. What is the Assembly Division's manager likely to do regarding acceptance or rejection of the special offer? Why?
2. Is this decision in the best interests of the company as a whole? Why?
3. How could the situation be remedied using the transfer price?

Problems

Problem 11–51 Create an Organization **(LO1, 2)**

Here is your chance to be a tycoon. Create your own company. You will be the president and chief executive officer. It can be a manufacturer, retailer, or service industry firm, but *not* a hotel or bank. Draw an organization chart for your company, similar to the one in Exhibit 11–1. Identify divisions and departments at all levels in the organization. Then prepare a companion chart similar to the one in Exhibit 11–2. This chart should designate the title of the manager of a subunit at each level in the organization. It also should designate the type of responsibility centre appropriate for each of these subunits. Finally, write a letter to your company's shareholders summarizing the major responsibilities of each of the managers you identified in your chart. For guidance, refer to the discussion of Exhibits 11–1 and 11–2 in the chapter. (Have fun, and be creative.)

Problem 11–52 Design Performance Reports: Continuation of Preceding Problem **(LO3)**

After designing your company, design a set of performance reports for the subunits you identified in your chart. Make up numbers for the performance reports, and show the relationship between the reports. Refer to Exhibit 11–4 for guidance.

Problem 11–53 Designating Responsibility Centres: Hotel **(LO2)**

The following partial organization chart is an extension of Exhibit 11–1 for Aloha Hotels and Resorts.

Each of the hotel's five main departments is managed by a director (e.g., director of Hospitality). The Front Desk subunit, which is supervised by the front desk manager, handles the hotel's reservations, room assignments, guest payments, and key control. The Bell Staff, managed by the bell captain, is responsible for greeting guests, front door service, assisting guests with their luggage, and delivering room-service orders. The Guest Services subunit, supervised by the manager of Guest Services, is responsible for assisting guests with local transportation arrangements, advising guests on tourist attractions, and such conveniences as valet and floral services.

Required: As an outside consultant, write a memo to the hotel's general manager suggesting a responsibility centre designation for each of the subunits shown in the organization chart above. Justify your choices.

Problem 11–54 Preparation of Performance Reports: Hospital **(LO3)**

Canadian Rockies General Hospital serves three regions in Alberta. The hospital is a nonprofit organization that is supported by government funding, patient billings, and private donations. The hospital's organization is shown in the following chart:

1. Canadian Rockies General Hospital, total cost, flexible budget, August: $582,700

The following cost information has been compiled for August:

	Budget		Actual	
	August	**Year to Date**	**August**	**Year to Date**
Cafeteria:				
Food servers' wages	$ 8,000	$ 64,000	$ 9,000	$ 72,000
Paper products	4,500	36,000	4,400	36,200
Utilities	1,000	8,000	1,050	8,100
Maintenance	400	3,200	100	1,100
Custodial	1,100	8,800	1,100	8,600
Supplies	1,200	9,600	900	9,600
Patient Food Service	17,000	136,000	18,500	137,000
Registered Dietitians' Section	7,500	60,000	7,500	60,000
Kitchen	31,000	248,000	29,400	246,000
Nursing Department	70,000	560,000	75,000	580,000
Radiology and Laboratory Department	18,000	144,000	18,100	144,000
Housekeeping Department	10,000	80,000	11,600	86,000
Maintenance Department	13,000	104,000	6,000	77,000
General Medicine Division	210,000	1,680,000	204,000	1,670,900
Surgical Division	140,000	1,120,000	141,000	1,115,800
Administrative Division	50,000	400,000	53,500	406,000

Required:

1. Prepare a set of cost performance reports similar to Exhibit 11–4. The report should have six columns, as in Exhibit 11–4. The first four columns will have the same headings as those used above. The last two columns will have the following headings: Variance—August and Variance—Year to Date.

Since all of the information in the performance reports for Canadian Rockies General Hospital is cost information, you do not need to show these data in parentheses. Use F or U to denote whether each variance in the reports is favourable or unfavourable.

2. Using arrows, show the relationships between the numbers in your performance reports for Canadian Rockies General Hospital. Refer to Exhibit 11–4 for guidance.

3. Put yourself in the place of the hospital's administrator. Which variances in the performance reports would you want to investigate further? Why?

Problem 11–55 Cost Distribution Using Allocation Bases: Hospital (LO4)

1. Facilities, General
Medicine: $71,250

Refer to the organization chart for Canadian Rockies General Hospital given in the preceding problem. Ignore the rest of the data in that problem. The following table shows the cost allocation bases used to distribute various costs among the hospital's divisions:

Cost Pool	Cost Allocation Base	Annual Cost
Facilities:		
Building depreciation	Square metres of space	$190,0000
Equipment depreciation		
Insurance		
Utilities:		
Electricity	Cubic metres of space	24,000
Waste disposal		
Water and sewer		
Cable TV and phone		
Heat		
General administration:		
Administrator	Budgeted number of employees	220,000
Administrative staff		
Office supplies		
Community outreach:		
Public education	Budgeted dollars of patient billings	40,000
School physical exams		

Shown below are the amounts of each cost allocation base associated with each division.

	Square Metres	Cubic Metres	Number of Employees	Patient Billings
General Medicine Division	15,000	135,000	30	$ 2,000,000
Surgical Division	8,000	100,000	20	1,250,000
Medical Support Division	9,000	90,000	20	750,000
Administrative Division	8,000	75,000	30	0
Total	40,000	400,000	100	$ 4,000,000

Required:

1. Prepare a table similar to Exhibit 11–5 that distributes each of the costs listed in the preceding table to the hospital's divisions.

2. Comment on the appropriateness of patient billings as the basis for distributing community outreach costs to the hospital's divisions. Can you suggest a better allocation base?

3. Is there any use in allocating utilities costs to the divisions? What purposes could such an allocation process serve?

4. *Build a spreadsheet:* Construct an Excel spreadsheet to solve requirement (1) above. Show how the solution will change if the following information changes: The costs incurred were $200,000, $25,000, $200,000, and $50,000, for facilities, utilities, general administration, and community outreach, respectively.

Problem 11–56 Segmented Income Statement; Responsibility Accounting (LO3, 5)

1. Segment profit margin,
Vancouver: $161,560

Show-Off, Inc. sells merchandise through three retail outlets—in Vancouver, Toronto, and Montreal—and operates a general corporate headquarters in Toronto. A review of the company's income statement indicates a record year in terms of sales and profits. Management, though, desires additional insights about the individual stores and has asked that Judson Wyatt, a newly hired intern, prepare a segmented income statement. The following information has been extracted from Show-Off's accounting records:

- The sales volume, sales price, and purchase price data are

	Vancouver	Toronto	Montreal
Sales volume	37,000 units	41,000 units	46,000 units
Unit selling price	$12.00	$11.00	$9.50
Unit purchase price	5.50	5.50	6.00

- The following expenses were incurred for sales commissions, local advertising, property taxes, management salaries, and other noncontrollable (but traceable) costs:

	Vancouver	Toronto	Montreal
Sales commissions	6%	6%	6%
Local advertising	$11,000	$22,000	$48,000
Local property taxes	4,500	2,000	6,000
Sales manager salary	—	—	32,000
Store manager salaries	31,000	39,000	38,000
Other noncontrollable costs	5,800	4,600	17,800

Local advertising decisions are made at the store manager level. The sales manager's salary in Montreal is determined by the Montreal store manager; in contrast, store manager salaries are set by Show-Off's vice-president.

- Nontraceable fixed corporate expenses total $192,300.
- The company uses a responsibility-accounting system.

Required:

1. Assume the role of Judson Wyatt and prepare a segmented income statement for Show-Off.
2. Determine the weakest-performing store and present an analysis of the probable causes of poor performance.
3. Assume that an opening has arisen at the Toronto corporate headquarters and the company's chief executive officer (CEO) desires to promote one of the three existing store managers. In evaluating the store managers' performance, should the CEO use a store's segment contribution margin, the profit margin controllable by the store manager, or a store's segment profit margin? Justify your answer.

Problem 11–57 Prepare Segmented Income Statement; Contribution-Margin Format: Retail (L05)

Buckeye Department Stores, Inc. operates a chain of department stores in British Columbia. The company's organization chart appears below. Operating data for 20x1 follow:

1. Profit margin traceable to segment, Trail store: $845,000

BUCKEYE DEPARTMENT STORES, INC.
Operating Data for 20x1
(in thousands)

| | Kootenays Division | | | |
	Trail Store	Nelson Store	Cranbrook Store	Cariboo Division (total for all stores)
Sales revenue	$5,000	$2,400	$11,000	$21,000
Variable expenses:				
Cost of merchandise sold	3,000	2,000	6,000	12,000
Sales personnel—salaries	400	300	750	1,600
Sales commissions	50	40	90	200
Utilities	80	60	150	300
Other	60	35	120	250
Fixed expenses:				
Depreciation—buildings	120	90	250	470
Depreciation—furnishings	80	50	140	290
Computing and billing	40	30	75	160
Warehouse	70	60	200	450
Insurance	40	25	90	200
Property taxes	35	20	80	170
Supervisory salaries	150	100	400	900
Security	30	30	80	210

The following fixed expenses are controllable at the divisional level: depreciation—furnishings, computing and billing, warehouse, insurance, and security. In addition to these expenses, each division annually incurs $50,000 of computing costs, which are not allocated to individual stores.

The following fixed expenses are controllable only at the company level: depreciation—building, property taxes, and supervisory salaries. In addition to these expenses, each division incurs costs for supervisory salaries of $100,000, which are not allocated to individual stores.

Buckeye Department Stores incurs common fixed expenses of $120,000, which are not allocated to the two divisions. Income tax expense for 20x1 is $1,950,000.

Required:

1. Prepare a segmented income statement similar to Exhibit 11–7 for Buckeye Department Stores, Inc. The statement should have the following columns:

	Segments of Company		Segments of Kootenays Division		
Buckeye Department Stores, Inc.	Cariboo Division	Kootenays Division	Trail Store	Nelson Store	Cranbrook Store Not Allocated

Prepare the statement in the contribution format, and indicate the controllability of expenses. Subtract all variable expenses, including cost of merchandise sold, from sales revenue to obtain the contribution margin.

2. How would the segmented income statement help the president of Buckeye Department Stores manage the company?

Problem 11–58 Responsibility Accounting; Participation; Behavioural Issues (LO1, 2, 3)
Building Services Co. (BSC) was started a number of years ago by Jim and Joan Forge to provide cleaning services to both large and small businesses in their home city. Over the years, as local businesses reduced underutilized building maintenance staffs, more and more cleaning services were subcontracted to BSC. BSC also expanded into other building services such as painting and local moving.

BSC maintains a pool of skilled workers who are contracted to perform the noncleaning services because these services do not recur on a day-to-day basis for the individual buildings. Many of BSC's full-time employees have been with the firm for a number of years. Five zone managers are each responsible for furnishing recurring nightly cleaning services to several businesses. In addition, the zone manager sells and schedules noncleaning service jobs for the company's central pool of skilled employees. Informal meetings are held periodically to discuss BSC's performance, personnel allocations, and scheduling problems. BSC's budgeting and planning have been done by the Forges, who also manage variations from budgets.

The Forges recently decided to retire and sold the business to Commercial Maintenance Inc. (CMI), which provides similar services in a number of metropolitan locations that surround BSC's business area. After news of the sale, several of BSC's long-term employees appeared resentful of the change in ownership and did not know what to expect.

CMI's senior management met with BSC's managers and announced that George Fowler would become president of BSC and that BSC would continue to operate as a separate subsidiary of CMI. Furthermore, in accordance with CMI's management philosophy, a responsibility-accounting system is to be implemented at BSC. Also, in line with other CMI subsidiaries, a participatory budgeting process is being considered. However, no decision will be made until an evaluation of BSC's existing policies, operational culture, and management is completed. In view of the significant change in management philosophy, CMI has taken considerable time in explaining how each system operates and assuring BSC's managers that they are expected and encouraged to participate in both the planning and implementation of any of the systems that are to be adopted.

Required: Two new systems are being considered at Building Services Co.:

- Responsibility-accounting system
- Participatory budgeting system

For each of these systems:

1. Identify at least two behavioural advantages that might arise.
2. Identify at least two potential problems that might arise.
3. Discuss the likelihood that the system will contribute to the alignment of organizational and personal goals.

(CMA, adapted)

Problem 11–59 Designing a Responsibility-Accounting System (LO1, 2)

Warriner Equipment Company, which is located in Ontario, manufactures heavy construction equipment. The company's primary product, an especially powerful bulldozer, is among the best produced in North America. The company operates in a very price-competitive industry, so it has little control over the price of its products. It must meet the market price. To do so, the firm has to keep production costs in check by operating as efficiently as possible. Mathew Basler, the company's president, has stated that, to be successful, the company must provide a very high-quality product and meet its delivery commitments to customers on time. Warriner Equipment Company is organized as shown below.

There is currently a disagreement between the company's two vice-presidents regarding the responsibility-accounting system. The vice-president for manufacturing claims that the 10 plants should be cost centres. He recently expressed the following sentiment: "The plants should be cost centres because the plant managers do not control the sales of our products. Designating the plants as profit centres would result in holding the plant managers responsible for something they can't control." A contrary view is held by the vice-president for marketing. He recently made the following remarks: "The plants should be profit centres. The plant managers are in the best position to affect the company's overall profit."

Required: As the company's new controller, you have been asked to make a recommendation to Mathew Basler, the company president, regarding the responsibility centre issue. Write a memo to the president making a recommendation and explaining the reasoning behind it. In your memo, address the following points.

1. Assuming that Warriner Equipment Company's overall goal is profitability, what are the company's critical success factors? A *critical success factor* is a variable that meets these two criteria: It is largely under the company's control and the company must succeed in this area in order to reach its overall goal of profitability.

2. Which responsibility-accounting arrangement is most consistent with achieving success on the company's critical success factors?

3. What responsibility-centre designation is most appropriate for the company's sales districts?

4. As a specific example, consider the rush-order problem illustrated in the chapter. Suppose that Warriner Equipment Company often experiences rush orders from its customers. Which of the two proposed responsibility-accounting arrangements is best suited to making good decisions about accepting or rejecting rush orders? Specifically, should the plants be cost centres or profit centres?

Problem 11–60 Comparing the Performance of Two Divisions (LO6, 8)

Long Beach Pharmaceutical Company has two divisions, which reported the following results for the most recent year:

	Division I	Division II
Income	$ 900,000	$ 200,000
Average invested capital	$6,000,000	$1,000,000
ROI	15%	20%

Required: Which was the more successful division during the year? Explain your answer.

Problem 11–61 ROI and Residual Income: Missing Data (LO6)

The following data pertain to three divisions of Aggregates, Inc. The company's required rate of return on invested capital is 8 percent.

Residual income, Division A: $240,000

	Division A	Division B	Division C
Sales revenue	?	$10,000,000	?
Income	$400,000	$2,000,000	?
Average investment	?	$2,500,000	?
Sales margin	20%	?	25%
Capital turnover	1	?	?
ROI	?	?	20%
Residual income	?	?	$120,000

Required: Fill in the blanks above.

Problem 11–62 Improving ROI (LO6, 7)

Refer to the preceding problem about Aggregates, Inc.

2. ROI: 25%

Required:

1. Explain three ways the Division B manager could improve her division's ROI. Use numbers to illustrate these possibilities.

2. Suppose Division A's sales margin increased to 25 percent, while its capital turnover remained constant. Compute the division's new ROI.

Problem 11–63 Residual Income (LO6, 8)

Refer to the data for Problem 11–60 regarding Long Beach Pharmaceutical Company.

Required: Compute each division's residual income for the year under each of the following assumptions about the firm's cost of acquiring capital:

1. 12 percent
2. 15 percent
3. 18 percent

Which division was more successful? Explain your answer.

Problem 11–64 Increasing ROI over Time; Accelerated Depreciation (L06, 8, 9)

Year 2, ROI based on net book value: 12.5%

Refer to Exhibit 11–10. Prepare a similar table of the changing ROI assuming the following accelerated depreciation schedule. Assume the same income before depreciation as shown in Exhibit 11–10. (If there is a loss, leave the ROI column blank.)

Year	Depreciation
1	$200,000
2	120,000
3	72,000
4	54,000
5	54,000
Total	$500,000

Required:

1. How does your table differ from the one in Exhibit 11–10? Why?
2. What are the implications of the ROI pattern in your table?

Problem 11–65 Increasing Residual Income over Time (L06, 8, 9)

Year 1, residual income (based on net book value): $5,000

Prepare a table similar to Exhibit 11–10, which focuses on residual income. Use a 10 percent rate to compute the imputed interest charge. The table should show the residual income on the investment during each year in its five-year life. Assume the same income before depreciation and the same depreciation schedule as shown in Exhibit 11–10.

Problem 11–66 ROI and Residual Income: Investment Evaluation (L06, 8)

3. Income: $150,000
5. Current residual income of the Northeastern Division: $148,000

Megatronics Corporation, a massive retailer of electronic products, is organized in four separate divisions. The four divisional managers are evaluated at year-end, and bonuses are awarded based on ROI. Last year, the company as a whole produced a 13 percent return on its investment.

During the past week, management of the company's Northeastern Division was approached about the possibility of buying a competitor that had decided to redirect its retail activities. (If the competitor is acquired, it will be acquired at its book value.) The data that follow relate to recent performance of the Northeastern Division and the competitor:

	Northeastern Division	Competitor
Sales	$8,400,000	$5,200,000
Variable costs	70% of sales	65% of sales
Fixed costs	$2,150,000	$1,670,000
Invested capital	$1,850,000	$625,000

Management has determined that in order to upgrade the competitor to Megatronics' standards, an additional $.375,000 of invested capital would be needed.

Required: As a group, complete the following requirements:

1. Compute the current ROI of the Northeastern Division and the division's ROI if the competitor is acquired.
2. What is the likely reaction of divisional management toward the acquisition? Why?
3. What is the likely reaction of Megatronics' corporate management toward the acquisition? Why?
4. Would the division be better off if it didn't upgrade the competitor to Megatronics' standards? Show computations to support your answer.

5. Assume that Megatronics uses residual income to evaluate performance and desires a 12 percent minimum return on invested capital. Compute the current residual income of the Northeastern Division and the division's residual income if the competitor is acquired. Will divisional management be likely to change its attitude toward the acquisition? Why?

Problem 11–67 ROI and Performance Evaluations (LO6, 8)

1. Capital turnover: 80%

Kenneth Washburn, head of the Sporting Goods Division of Reliable Products, has just completed a miserable nine months. "If it could have gone wrong, it did. Sales are down, income is down, inventories are bloated, and quite frankly, I'm beginning to worry about my job," he moaned. Washburn is evaluated on the basis of ROI. Selected figures for the past nine months follow.

Sales	$4,800,000
Operating income	360,000
Invested capital	6,000,000

In an effort to make something out of nothing and to salvage the current year's performance, Washburn was contemplating implementation of some or all of the following four strategies:

a. Write off and discard $60,000 of obsolete inventory. The company will take a loss on the disposal.

b. Accelerate the collection of $80,000 of overdue customer accounts receivable.

c. Stop advertising through year-end and drastically reduce outlays for repairs and maintenance. These actions are expected to save the division $150,000 of expenses and will conserve cash resources.

d. Acquire two competitors that are expected to have the following financial characteristics:

	Projected Sales	Projected Operating Expenses	Projected Invested Capital
Anderson Manufacturing	$3,000,000	$2,400,000	$5,000,000
Palm Beach Enterprises	4,500,000	4,120,000	4,750,000

Required:

1. Briefly define sales margin, capital turnover, and return on investment and then compute these amounts for the Sporting Goods Division over the past nine months.

2. Evaluate each of the first two strategies listed, with respect to its effect on the division's last nine months' performance, and make a recommendation to Washburn regarding which, if any, to adopt.

3. Are there possible long-term problems associated with strategy (c)? Briefly explain.

4. Determine the ROI of the investment in Anderson Manufacturing and do the same for the investment in Palm Beach Enterprises. Should Washburn reject both acquisitions, acquire one company, or acquire both companies? Assume that sufficient capital is available to fund investments in both organizations.

Problem 11–68 Weighted-Average Cost of Capital; Economic Value Added (EVA) (LO6)

1. Weighted-average cost of capital: 0.1056

Lobster Shacks, Inc. (LS) is a seafood restaurant chain. The company has two sources of long-term capital: debt and equity. The cost to LS of issuing debt is the after-tax cost of the interest payments on the debt, taking into account the fact that the interest payments are tax-deductible. The cost of LS's equity capital is the investment opportunity rate of LS's investors, that is, the rate they could earn on investments of similar risk to that of investing in Lobster Shacks, Inc. The interest rate on LS's $80 million of long-term debt is 9 percent, and the company's tax rate is 40 percent. The cost of LS's equity capital is 14 percent. Moreover, the market value (and book value) of LS's equity is $120 million.

Lobster Shacks, Inc. consists of two divisions, the Properties Division and the Food-Service Division. The divisions' total assets, current liabilities, and before-tax operating income for the most recent year are as follows:

Division	Total Assets	Current Liabilities	Before-Tax Operating Income
Properties	$145,000,000	$3,000,000	$29,000,000
Food-Service	64,000,000	6,000,000	15,000,000

Required:

1. Calculate the weighted-average cost of capital for Lobster Shacks, Inc.

2. Calculate the economic value added (EVA) for each of LS's divisions.

3. *Build a spreadsheet:* Construct an Excel spreadsheet to solve both of the preceding requirements. Show how the solution will change if the following information changes: Before-tax operating income was $30,000,000 and $14,000,000 for Properties and Food-Service, respectively.

Problem 11–69 Weighted-Average Cost of Capital; Economic Value Added (EVA) **(LO6)**

All-Canadian Ltd. is a multiproduct company with three divisions: Pacific Division, Plains Division, and Atlantic Division. The company has two sources of long-term capital: debt and equity. The interest rate on All-Canadian's $400 million debt is 9 percent, and the company's tax rate is 30 percent. The cost of All-Canadian's equity capital is 12 percent. Moreover, the market value of the company's equity is $600 million. (The *book value* of All-Canadian's equity is $430 million, but that amount does not reflect the current value of the company's assets or the value of intangible assets.)

The following data (in millions) pertain to All-Canadian's three divisions:

Division	Operating Income	Current Liabilities	Total Assets
Pacific..	$14	$6	$70
Plains...	45	5	300
Atlantic	48	9	480

Required:

1. Compute All-Canadian's weighted-average cost of capital (WACC).

2. Compute the economic value added (or EVA) for each of the company's three divisions.

3. What conclusions can you draw from the EVA analysis?

Problem 11–70 Comprehensive Transfer Pricing Problem; Ethics **(LO10, 11)**

Clearview Window Company manufactures windows for the home-building industry. The window frames are produced in the Frame Division. The frames are then transferred to the Glass Division, where the glass and hardware are installed. The company's best-selling product is a three-by-four, double-paned operable window.

The Frame Division also can sell frames directly to custom home builders, who install the glass and hardware. The sales price for a frame is $80. The Glass Division sells its finished windows for $190. The markets for both frames and finished windows exhibit perfect competition.

The standard variable cost of the window is detailed as follows:

	Frame Division	Glass Division
Direct material..	$15	$30*
Direct labour...	20	15
Variable overhead	30	30
Total...	$65	$75

*Not including the transfer price for the frame.

Required:

1. Assume that there is no excess capacity in the Frame Division.
   a. Use the general rule to compute the transfer price for window frames.
   b. Calculate the transfer price if it is based on standard variable cost with a 10 percent markup.

2. Assume that there is excess capacity in the Frame Division.
   a. Use the general rule to compute the transfer price for window frames.
   b. Explain why your answers to requirements (1*a*) and (2*a*) differ.
   c. Suppose the predetermined fixed-overhead rate in the Frame Division is 125 percent of direct-labour cost. Calculate the transfer price if it is based on standard full cost plus a 10 percent markup.
   d. Assume the transfer price established in requirement (2*c*) is used. The Glass Division has been approached by the Canadian Forces with a special order for 1,000 windows at $155. From the perspective of Clearview Window Company as a whole, should the special order be accepted or rejected? Why?
   e. Assume the same facts as in requirement (2*d*). Will an autonomous Glass Division manager accept or reject the special order? Why?
   f. Comment on any ethical issues you see in the questions raised in requirements (2*d*) and (2*e*).

3. Comment on the use of full cost as the basis for setting transfer prices.

Problem 11–71 Transfer Pricing; Negotiation **(LO11)**

4. Produce diode, sell externally, contribution margin: $275

Mitachlordion Technology, Inc. (MTI) has two divisions: Surrey and Burnaby. Surrey currently sells a diode reducer to manufacturers of aircraft navigation systems for $775 per unit. Variable costs amount to $500, and demand for this product currently exceeds the division's ability to supply the marketplace.

Despite this situation, MTI is considering another use for the diode reducer, namely, integration into a satellite positioning system that would be made by Burnaby. The positioning system has an anticipated selling price of $1,400 and requires an additional $670 of variable manufacturing costs. A transfer price of $750 has been established for the diode reducer.

Top management is anxious to introduce the positioning system; however, unless the transfer is made, an introduction will not be possible because of the difficulty of obtaining needed diode reducers. Surrey and Burnaby are in the process of recovering from previous financial problems, and neither division can afford any future losses. The company uses responsibility accounting and ROI in measuring divisional performance, and awards bonuses to divisional management.

Required:

1. How would Surrey's divisional manager likely react to the decision to transfer diode reducers to Burnaby? Show computations to support your answer.

2. How would Burnaby's divisional management likely react to the $750 transfer price? Show computations to support your answer.

3. Assume that a lower transfer price is desired. Should top management lower the price or should the price be lowered by another means? Explain.

4. From a contribution margin perspective, does MTI benefit more if it sells the diode reducers externally or transfers the reducers to Burnaby? By how much?

Problem 11–72 Setting a Transfer Price; International Setting; Differential Tax Rates **(LO10, 11)**

2. Canadian operation, income after tax: $24
3. German operation, income after tax: $36

Alpha Telecom, Inc., which produces telecommunications equipment in Canada, has a very strong local market for its circuit board. The variable production cost is $130, and the company can sell its entire supply domestically for $170. The Canadian tax rate is 40 percent.

Alternatively, Alpha can ship the circuit board to its division in Germany, to be used in a product that the German division will distribute throughout Europe. Information about the German product and the division's operating environment follows.

Selling price of final product	$360
Shipping fees to import circuit board	$ 20
Labour, overhead, and additional material costs of final product	$115
Import duties levied on circuit board (to be paid by the German division)..	10% of transfer price
German tax rate..	60%

Assume that Canadian and German tax authorities allow a transfer price for the circuit board set at either Canadian variable manufacturing cost or the Canadian market price. Alpha's management is in the process of exploring which transfer price is better for the firm as a whole.

Required:

1. Compute overall company profitability per unit if all units are transferred and Canadian variable manufacturing cost is used as the transfer price. Show separate calculations for the Canadian operation and the German division.

2. Repeat requirement (1), assuming the use of the Canadian market price as the transfer price. Which of the two transfer prices is better for the firm?

3. Assume that the German division can obtain the circuit board in Germany for $155.

   a. If you were the head of the German division, would you rather do business with your Canadian division or buy the circuit board locally? Why?

   b. Rather than proceed with the transfer, is it in the best interest of Alpha to sell its goods domestically and allow the German division to acquire the circuit board in Germany? Why? Show computations to support your answer.

4. Generally speaking, when tax rates differ between countries, what strategy should a company use in setting its transfer prices?

5. *Build a spreadsheet:* Construct an Excel spreadsheet to solve requirements (1) and (2) above. Show how the solution will change if the following information changes: The Canadian tax rate is 35 percent, the German tax rate is 55 percent, and the import duties are 8 percent of the transfer price.

2. Total contribution margin,
Mining Division: $15,200,000

Problem 11–73   Transfer Pricing; Management Behaviour (LO10, 11)

Redstone Industrial Resources Company (RIRC) has several divisions. However, only two divisions transfer products to other divisions. The Mining Division refines toldine, which is then transferred to the Metals Division. The toldine is processed into an alloy by the Metals Division, and the alloy is sold to customers at a price of $150 per unit. The Mining Division is currently required by RIRC to transfer its total yearly output of 400,000 units of toldine to the Metals Division at total actual manufacturing cost plus 10 percent. Unlimited quantities of toldine can be purchased and sold on the open market at $90 per unit. While the Mining Division could sell all the toldine it produces at $90 per unit on the open market, it would incur a variable selling cost of $5 per unit.

Brian Jones, manager of the Mining Division, is unhappy with having to transfer the entire output of toldine to the Metals Division at 110 percent of cost. In a meeting with the management of Redstone, he said, "Why should my division be required to sell toldine to the Metals Division at less than market price? For the year just ended in May, Metals' contribution margin was over $19 million on sales of 400,000 units, while Mining's contribution was just over $5 million on the transfer of the same number of units. My division is subsidizing the profitability of the Metals Division. We should be allowed to charge the market price for toldine when transferring to the Metals Division."

The following table shows the detailed unit cost structure for both the Mining and Metals Divisions during the most recent year:

	Mining Division	Metals Division
Transfer price from Mining Division	—	$ 66
Direct material	$12	6
Direct labour	16	20
Manufacturing overhead	32*	25†
Total cost per unit	$60	$117

*Manufacturing-overhead cost in the Mining Division is 25 percent fixed and 75 percent variable.

†Manufacturing-overhead cost in the Metals Division is 60 percent fixed and 40 percent variable.

Required:

1. Explain why transfer prices based on total actual costs are not appropriate as the basis for divisional performance measurement.

2. Using the market price as the transfer price, determine the contribution margin for both the Mining Division and the Metals Division.

3. If Redstone Industrial Resources Company was to institute the use of negotiated transfer prices and allow divisions to buy and sell on the open market, determine the price range for toldine that would be acceptable to both the Mining Division and the Metals Division. Explain your answer.

4. Use the general transfer pricing rule to compute the lowest transfer price that would be acceptable to the Mining Division. Is your answer consistent with your conclusion in requirement (3)? Explain.

5. Identify which one of the three types of transfer prices (cost-based, market-based, or negotiated) is most likely to elicit desirable management behaviour at RIRC. Explain your answer.

(CMA, adapted)

Cases

1. Net income, Victoria store:
$91,275
2. Net income for May, Surrey
store: $12,375

Case 11–74   Segmented Income Statement; Responsibility Accounting; Bonuses; Motivation; Ethics (LO1, 2, 5)

Elite Classic Clothes is a retailer that sells to professional women. The firm leases space for stores in upscale shopping centres, and the organizational structure consists of regions, districts, and stores. Each region consists of two or more districts; each district consists of three or more stores. Each store, district, and region has been established as a profit centre. At all levels, the company uses a responsibility-accounting system focusing on information and knowledge rather than blame and control. Every year, managers, in consultation with their supervisors, establish financial and nonfinancial goals, and these goals are integrated into the budget. Actual performance is measured each month.

The British Columbia Region consists of the Lower Mainland and the Inland District. The Lower Mainland District includes the Vancouver, Victoria, and Surrey stores. The Lower Mainland District's performance has not been up to expectations in the past. For the month of May, the district manager has set performance goals with the managers of the Vancouver and Victoria stores, who will receive bonuses if certain performance measures are exceeded. The manager in Surrey decided not to participate in the bonus scheme. Since the district manager is unsure what type of bonus will encourage better performance, the Vancouver manager will receive a bonus based on sales in excess of budgeted sales of $570,000, while the Victoria manager will receive a bonus based on net income in excess of budgeted net income. The company's net income goal for each store is 12 percent of sales. The budgeted sales revenue for the Victoria store is $530,000.

Other pertinent data for May are as follows:

- Lower Mainland District sales revenue was $1,500,000, and its cost of goods sold amounted to $633,750.
- The Lower Mainland District spent $75,000 on advertising.
- General and administrative expenses for the Lower Mainland District amounted to $180,000.
- At the Vancouver store, sales were 40 percent of Lower Mainland District sales, while sales at the Victoria store were 35 percent of district sales. The cost of goods sold in both Vancouver and Victoria was 42 percent of sales.
- Variable selling expenses (sales commissions) were 6 percent of sales for all stores, districts, and regions.
- Variable administrative expenses were 2.5 percent of sales for all stores, districts, and regions.
- Maintenance cost includes janitorial and repair services and is a direct cost for each store. The store manager has complete control over this outlay. Maintenance costs were incurred as follows: Vancouver, $7,500; Victoria, $600; and Surrey, $4,500.
- Advertising is considered a direct cost for each store and is completely under the control of the store manager. The Vancouver store spent two-thirds of the Lower Mainland District total outlay for advertising, which was 10 times the amount spent in Victoria on advertising.
- Lower Mainland District rental expense amounted to $150,000.
- The rental expenses at the Vancouver store were 40 percent of the Lower Mainland District's total, while the Victoria store incurred 30 percent of the district total.
- District expenses were allocated to the stores based on sales.
- British Columbia Region general and administrative expenses of $165,000 were allocated to the Lower Mainland District. These expenses were, in turn, allocated equally to the district's three stores.

Required:

1. Prepare the May segmented income statement for the Lower Mainland District and for the Vancouver and Victoria stores.
2. Compute the Surrey store's net income for May.
3. Discuss the impact of the responsibility-accounting system and bonus structure on the managers' behaviour and the effect of their behaviour on the financial results for the Vancouver store and the Victoria store.
4. The assistant controller for the British Columbia Region, Jack Isner, has been a close friend of the Vancouver store manager for over 20 years. When Isner saw the segmented income statement (as prepared in requirement [1]), he realized that the Vancouver store manager had really gone overboard on advertising expenditures. To make his friend look better to the regional management, he reclassified $25,000 of the advertising expenditures as miscellaneous expenses, and buried them in rent and other costs. Comment on the ethical issues in the assistant controller's actions. (Refer to specific ethical standards for management accountants that were given in Chapter 1.)

(CMA, adapted)

Case 11–75   Segmented Income Statement: International Operations **(LO1, 5)**

Pacific Rim Industries is a diversified company whose products are marketed both domestically and internationally. The company's major product lines are furniture, sports equipment, and household appliances. At a recent meeting of Pacific Rim's board of directors, there was a lengthy discussion on ways to improve overall corporate profitability. The members of the board decided that they required additional financial information about individual corporate operations in order to target areas for improvement.

Danielle Murphy, the controller, has been asked to provide additional data that would assist the board in its investigation. Murphy believes that income statements, prepared along both product lines and geographic areas, would provide the directors with the required insight into corporate operations. Murphy had several discussions with the division managers for each product line and compiled the following information from these meetings:

1, Operating income (loss), Canada: $421,000

eXcel

	Product Lines			
	Furniture	**Sports**	**Appliances**	**Total**
Production and sales in units......................................	160,000	180,000	160,000	500,000
Average selling price per unit.......................................	$8.00	$20.00	$15.00	
Average variable manufacturing cost per unit	4.00	9.50	$8.25	
Average variable selling expense per unit	2.00	2.50	$2.25	
Fixed manufacturing overhead, excluding depreciation				$ 500,000
Depreciation of plant and equipment..........................				400,000
Administrative and selling expense.............................				1,160,000

1. The division managers concluded that Murphy should allocate fixed manufacturing overhead to both product lines and geographic areas on the basis of the ratio of the variable costs expended to total variable costs.

2. Each of the division managers agreed that a reasonable basis for the allocation of depreciation on plant and equipment would be the ratio of units produced per product line (or per geographical area) to the total number of units produced.

3. There was little agreement on the allocation of administrative and selling expenses, so Murphy decided to allocate only those expenses that were traceable directly to a segment. For example, manufacturing staff salaries would be allocated to product lines, and sales staff salaries would be allocated to geographic areas. Murphy used the following data for this allocation:

Manufacturing Staff		**Sales Staff**	
Furniture	$120,000	United States..............................	$ 60,000
Sports.................................	140,000	Canada	100,000
Appliances	80,000	Asia	250,000

4. The division managers were able to provide reliable sales percentages for their product lines by geographical area:

	Percentage of Unit Sales		
	United States	**Canada**	**Asia**
Furniture	40%	10%	50%
Sports..	40%	40%	20%
Appliances	20%	20%	60%

Murphy prepared the following product-line income statement based on the data presented above:

PACIFIC RIM INDUSTRIES
Segmented Income Statement by Product Line
For the Fiscal Year Ended April 30, 20x4

	Product Line				
	Furniture	**Sports**	**Appliances**	**Unallocated**	**Total**
Sales in units..	160,000	180,000	160,000		
Sales	$1,280,000	$3,600,000	$2,400,000	—	$7,280,000
Variable manufacturing and selling costs ...	960,000	2,160,000	1,680,000	—	4,800,000
Contribution margin	$ 320,000	$1,440,000	$ 720,000	—	$2,480,000
Fixed costs:					
Fixed manufacturing overhead...........	$ 100,000	$ 225,000	$ 175,000	$ —	$ 500,000
Depreciation.....................................	128,000	144,000	128,000	—	400,000
Administrative and selling expenses...	120,000	140,000	80,000	820,000	1,160,000
Total fixed costs...........................	$ 348,000	$ 509,000	$ 383,000	$ 820,000	$2,060,000
Operating income (loss)........................	$ (28,000)	$ 931,000	$ 337,000	$(820,000)	$ 420,000

Required:

1. Prepare a segmented income statement for Pacific Rim Industries based on the company's geographical areas. The statement should show the operating income for each segment.

2. As a result of the information disclosed by both segmented income statements (by product line and by geographic area), recommend areas where Pacific Rim Industries should focus its attention in order to improve corporate profitability.

Case 11–76 ROI versus Residual Income: Incentive Effects (L01, 6, 8)

2. Residual income, RLI: $120,000

Holiday Entertainment Corporation (HEC), a subsidiary of New Age Industries, manufactures go-carts and other recreational vehicles. Family recreational centres that feature not only go-cart tracks but miniature golf, batting cages, and arcade games as well have increased in popularity. As a result, HEC has been receiving some pressure from New Age's management to diversify into some of these other recreational areas. Recreational Leasing, Inc. (RLI), one of the largest firms that leases arcade games to family recreational centres, is looking for a friendly buyer. New Age's top management believes that RLI's assets could be acquired for an investment of $3.2 million and has strongly urged Bill Grieco, division manager of HEC, to consider acquiring RLI.

Grieco has reviewed RLI's financial statements with his controller, Marie Donnelly, and they believe the acquisition may not be in the best interest of HEC. "If we decide not to do this, the New Age people are not going to be happy," said Grieco. "If we could convince them to base our bonuses on something other than return on investment, maybe this acquisition would look more attractive. How would we do if the bonuses were based on residual income, using the company's 15 percent cost of capital?"

New Age Industries traditionally has evaluated all of its divisions on the basis of return on investment. The desired rate of return for each division is 20 percent. The management team of any division reporting an annual increase in the ROI is automatically eligible for a bonus. The management of divisions reporting a decline in the ROI must provide convincing explanations for the decline in order to be eligible for a bonus. Moreover, this bonus is limited to 50 percent of the bonus paid to divisions reporting an increase in ROI.

In the following table are condensed financial statements for both HEC and RLI for the most recent year:

	RLI	HEC
Sales revenue	—	$ 9,500,000
Leasing revenue	$ 3,100,000	—
Variable expenses	(1,300,000)	(6,000,000)
Fixed expenses	(1,200,000)	(1,500,000)
Operating income	$ 600,000	$ 2,000,000
Current assets	$ 1,900,000	$ 2,300,000
Long-lived assets	1,100,000	5,700,000
Total assets	$ 3,000,000	$ 8,000,000
Current liabilities	$ 850,000	$1,4000,000
Long-term liabilities	1,200,000	3,800,000
Shareholders' equity	950,000	2,800,000
Total liabilities and shareholders' equity	$ 3,000,000	$ 8,000,000

Required:

1. If New Age Industries continues to use ROI as the sole measure of divisional performance, explain why HEC would be reluctant to acquire Recreational Leasing, Inc.

2. If New Age Industries could be persuaded to use residual income to measure the performance of HEC, explain why HEC would be more willing to acquire RLI.

3. Discuss how the behaviour of division managers is likely to be affected by the use of the following performance measures: (*a*) return on investment and (*b*) residual income.

(CMA, adapted)

1. Increase in net income before taxes: $132,000

3. Increase in net income before taxes for Interglobal Industries: $312,500

Case 11–77 Interdivisional Transfers: Pricing the Final Product (L010, 11)

InterGlobal Industries is a diversified corporation with separate operating divisions. Each division's performance is evaluated on the basis of profit and return on investment.

The Air Comfort Division manufactures and sells air-conditioner units. The coming year's budgeted income statement, which follows, is based on a sales volume of 15,000 units.

AIR COMFORT DIVISION
Budgeted Income Statement
(in thousands)

	Per Unit	Total
Sales revenue	$400	$ 6,000
Manufacturing costs:		
Compressor	70	1,050
Other direct material	37	555
Direct labour	30	450
Variable overhead	45	675
Fixed overhead	32	480
Total manufacturing costs	214	3,210
Gross margin	186	2,790
Operating expenses:		
Variable selling	18	270
Fixed selling	19	285
Fixed administrative	38	570
Total operating expenses	75	1,125
Net income before taxes	$111	$ 1,665

Air Comfort's division manager believes sales can be increased if the price of the air conditioners is reduced. A market research study by an independent firm indicates that a 5 percent reduction in the selling price would increase sales volume 16 percent, or 2,400 units. The division has sufficient production capacity to manage this increased volume with no increase in fixed costs.

The Air Comfort Division uses a compressor in its units, which it purchases from an outside supplier at a cost of $70 per compressor. The Air Comfort Division manager has asked the manager of the Compressor Division about selling compressor units to Air Comfort. The Compressor Division currently manufactures and sells a unit to outside firms that is similar to the unit used by the Air Comfort Division. The specifications of the Air Comfort Division compressor are slightly different, which would reduce the Compressor Division's direct material cost by $1.50 per unit. In addition, the Compressor Division would not incur any variable selling costs in the units sold to the Air Comfort Division. The manager of the Air Comfort Division wants all of the compressors it uses to come from one supplier and has offered to pay $50 for each compressor unit.

The Compressor Division has the capacity to produce 75,000 units. Its budgeted income statement for the coming year, which follows, is based on a sales volume of 64,000 units without considering Air Comfort's proposal.

COMPRESSOR DIVISION
Budgeted Income Statement
(in thousands)

	Per Unit	Total
Sales revenue	$100	$6,400
Manufacturing costs:		
Direct material	12	768
Direct labour	8	512
Variable overhead	10	640
Fixed overhead	11	704
Total manufacturing costs	41	2,624
Gross margin	59	3,776
Operating expenses:		
Variable selling	6	384
Fixed selling	4	256
Fixed administrative	7	448
Total operating expenses	17	1,088
Net income before taxes	$ 42	$ 2,688

Required:

1. Should the Air Comfort Division institute the 5 percent price reduction on its air-conditioner units even if it cannot acquire the compressors internally for $50 each? Support your conclusion with appropriate calculations.

2. Independently of your answer to requirement (1), assume the Air Comfort Division needs 17,400 units. Should the Compressor Division be willing to supply the compressor units for $50 each? Support your conclusions with appropriate calculations.

3. Independently of your answer to requirement (1), assume Air Comfort needs 17,400 units. Suppose InterGlobal's top management has specified a transfer price of $50. Would it be in the best interest of InterGlobal Industries for the Compressor Division to supply the compressor units at $50 each to the Air Comfort Division? Support your conclusions with appropriate calculations.

4. Is $50 a goal-congruent transfer price? (Refer to your answers for requirements [2] and [3].)

(CMA, adapted)

Case 11–78 Minimum and Maximum Acceptable Transfer Prices: Multinational **(LO10)**

2. Unit contribution margin, LDP: $6

5. Net savings, if TCH-320 is produced using an HDP: $112

General Instrumentation Company manufactures dashboard instruments for heavy construction equipment. The firm is based in Baltimore, but operates several divisions in the United States, Canada, and Europe. The Hudson Bay Division manufactures complex electrical panels that are used in a variety of the firm's instruments. There are two basic types of panels. The high-density panel (HDP) is capable of many functions and is used in the most sophisticated instruments, such as tachometers and pressure gauges. The low-density panel (LDP) is much simpler and is used in less-complicated instruments. Although there are minor differences among the different high-density panels, the basic manufacturing process and production costs are the same. The high-density panels require considerably more skilled labour than the low-density panels, but the unskilled labour needs are about the same. Moreover, the direct materials in the high-density panel cost substantially more than the materials in the low-density panels. Production costs are summarized as follows:

	LDP	HDP
Unskilled labour (5 hrs. @ $10)	$ 5	$ 5
Skilled labour:		
LDP (0.25 hrs. @ $20)	5	
HDP (1.5 hrs. @ $20)		30
Raw material	3	8
Purchased components	4	12
Variable overhead	5	15
Total variable cost	$22	$70

The annual fixed overhead in the Hudson Bay Division is $1,000,000. There is a limited supply of skilled labour available in the area, and the division must constrain its production to 40,000 hours of skilled labour each year. This has been a troublesome problem for Jacqueline Ducharme, the division manager. Ducharme has successfully increased demand for the LDP line to the point where it is essentially unlimited. Each LDP sells for $28. Business also has increased in recent years for the HDP, and Ducharme estimates the division could now sell anywhere up to 6,000 units per year at a price of $115.

On the other side of the Atlantic, General Instrumentation operates its Volkmar Tachometer Division in Berlin. A recent acquisition of General Instrumentation, the division was formerly a German company known as Volkmar Construction Instruments. The division's main product is a sophisticated tachometer used in heavy-duty cranes, bulldozers, and backhoes. The instrument, designated as a TCH-320, has the following production costs.

TCH–320

Unskilled labour (0.5 hr. @ $9)	$ 4.50
Skilled labour (3 hrs. @ $17)	51.00
Raw material	10.50
Purchased components	150.00
Variable overhead	12.00
Total variable cost	$228.00

The cost of purchased components includes a $145 control pack currently imported from Japan. Fixed overhead in the Volkmar Tachometer Division runs about $800,000 per year. Both skilled and unskilled labour are in abundant supply. The TCH-320 sells for $270.

Bertram Mueller, the division manager of the Volkmar Tachometer Division, recently attended a high-level corporate meeting in Baltimore. In a conversation with Jacqueline Ducharme, it was apparent that Hudson Bay's high-density panel might be a viable substitute for the control pack currently imported from Japan and used in Volkmar's TCH-320. On returning to Berlin, Mueller asked his chief engineer to look into the matter. Hans Schmidt obtained several HDP units from Hudson Bay, and a minor R&D project was mounted to determine if the HDP could replace the Japanese control pack. Several weeks later, the following conversation occurred in Mueller's office:

Schmidt: There's no question that Hudson Bay's HDP unit will work in our TCH-320. In fact, it could save us some money.

Mueller: That's good news. If we can buy our components within the company, we'll help Baltimore's bottom line without hurting ours. Also, it will look good to the brass at Corporate if they see us working hard to integrate our division into General Instrumentation's overall production program.

Schmidt: I've also been worried about the reliability of supply of the control pack. I don't like being dependent on such a critical supplier that way.

Mueller: I agree. Let's look at your figures on the HDP replacement.

Schmidt: I got together with the controller's people, and we worked up some numbers. If we replace the control pack with the HDP from Canada, we'll avoid the $145 control pack cost we're now incurring. In addition, I figure we'll save $5.50 on the basic raw materials. There is one catch, though. The HDP will require some adjustments in order to use it in the TCH-320. We can make the adjustments here in Berlin. I'm guessing it will require an additional two hours of skilled labour to make the necessary modifications. I don't think variable overhead would be any different. Then there is the cost of transporting the HDPs to Berlin. Let's figure on $4.50 per unit.

Mueller: Sounds good. I'll give Jacqueline Ducharme a call and talk this over. We can use up to 10,000 of the HDP units per year given the demand for the TCH-320. I wonder what kind of a transfer price Hudson Bay will want.

Required:

1. Draw a simple diagram depicting the two divisions and their products. Also show the two alternatives that the Volkmar Tachometer Division has in the production of its TCH-320.

2. From the perspective of General Instrumentation's top management, should any of the TCH-320 units be produced using the high-density panel? If so, how many?

3. Suppose Hudson Bay transfers 10,000 HDP units per year to Volkmar. From the perspective of General Instrumentation's top management, what effect will the transfer price have on the company's income?

4. What is the minimum transfer price that the Hudson Bay Division would find acceptable for the HDP?

5. What is the maximum transfer price that the Volkmar Tachometer Division would find acceptable for the HDP?

6. As the corporate controller for General Instrumentation, recommend a transfer price.

   Practise and learn online with Connect.

CHAPTER TWELVE

Decision Making: Relevant Costs and Benefits

FOCUS COMPANY

This chapter's focus company is Worldwide Airways, an international airline. Using this service industry company as our example, we will explore a variety of decisions that managers routinely make. Examples of such decisions are whether to accept a special offer for the company's services, whether to outsource a service, and whether to add or drop a service or department. We will find in this chapter that different kinds of cost information are relevant in these situations, depending on the type of decision to be made.

IN CONTRAST

In contrast to the transportation-services setting of Worldwide Airways, we will explore certain types of decisions that most often arise in a manufacturing setting. Our example will be the International Chocolate Company, which produces a variety of chocolate products. In addition to producing chocolate candy, the company processes cocoa beans into cocoa powder and cocoa butter. The cocoa powder can then be processed further into instant cocoa mix. We will explore a variety of decisions faced by the International Chocolate Company's management.

After completing this chapter, you should be able to

1 Describe seven steps in the decision-making process and the management accountant's role in that process.

2 Explain the relationship between quantitative and qualitative analyses in decision making.

3 Name and explain two criteria that must be satisfied by relevant information.

4 Identify relevant costs and benefits, giving proper treatment to sunk costs, opportunity costs, and unit costs.

5 Prepare analyses of various special decisions, properly identifying the relevant costs and benefits.

6 Analyze manufacturing decisions involving joint products and limited resources.

7 Explain the impact of an advanced manufacturing environment and activity-based costing on a relevant-cost analysis.

D ecision making is a fundamental part of management. Decisions about the acquisition of equipment, mix of products, methods of production, and pricing of products and services confront managers in all types of organizations. This chapter covers the role of managerial accounting information in a variety of common decisions. The next chapter examines pricing decisions.

The Management Accountant's Role in Decision Making

Management accountants are increasingly playing important roles as members of cross-functional management teams. These management teams face a broad array of decisions, including production, marketing, financial, and other decisions. All managers and management teams need information pertinent to their decisions. In support of the decision-making process, management accountants play a specific role in providing relevant information. This means that the management accountant must have a good understanding of the decisions faced by managers throughout the organization.

Steps in the Decision-Making Process

Learning Objective **1**

Describe seven steps in the decision-making process and the management accountant's role in that process.

Seven steps characterize the decision-making process:

1. ***Clarify the decision problem.*** Sometimes the decision to be made is clear-cut. For example, if a company receives a special order for its product at a price below the usual price, the decision problem is to accept or reject the order. But the decision problem is seldom so clear-cut. Perhaps demand for a company's most popular product is declining. What exactly is causing this problem? Increasing competition? Declining quality control? A new alternative product on the market? Before a decision can be made, the problem needs to be defined in more specific terms. Considerable managerial skill is required to define a decision problem in terms that can be addressed effectively.

2. ***Specify the criterion.*** Once a decision problem has been clarified, the manager should specify the criterion on which a decision will be made. Is the objective to maximize profit, increase market share, minimize cost, or improve public service? Sometimes objectives are in conflict, as in a decision problem where production cost is to be minimized but product quality must be maintained.

"We are looked upon as more business advisors than just accountants and that has a lot to do with the additional analysis and the forward-looking goals we are setting." (12a)

Caterpillar

In such cases, one objective is specified as the decision criterion—for example, cost minimization. The other objective is established as a constraint—for example, product quality must not be worse than one defective part in 1,000 manufactured units.

3. *Identify the alternatives.* A decision involves selecting between two or more alternatives. If a machine breaks down, what are the alternative courses of action? The machine can be repaired or replaced, or a replacement can be leased or bought. But perhaps repair will turn out to be more costly than replacement. Determining the possible alternatives is a critical step in the decision-making process.

4. *Develop a decision model.* A *decision model* is a simplified representation of the choice problem. Unnecessary details are stripped away, and the most important elements of the problem are highlighted. Thus, the decision model brings together the elements listed above: the criterion, the constraints, and the alternatives.

5. *Collect the data.* Although the management accountant often is involved in steps 1 through 4, he or she is mainly responsible for step 5. Selecting data pertinent to decisions is one of the management accountant's most important roles in an organization.

6. *Select an alternative.* Once the decision model is formulated and the pertinent data are collected, the appropriate manager makes a decision.

7. *Evaluate decision effectiveness.* After a decision has been implemented, the results of the decision are evaluated with the objective of improving future decisions.

Quantitative versus Qualitative Analysis

Decision problems involving accounting data are typically specified in quantitative terms. The criteria in such problems usually include objectives such as profit maximization or cost minimization. When a manager makes a final decision, however, the qualitative characteristics of the alternatives can be just as important as the quantitative measures. **Qualitative characteristics** are the factors in a decision problem that cannot be expressed effectively in numerical terms. To illustrate, suppose Worldwide Airways' top management is considering the elimination of its hub operation in London. Airlines establish hubs at airports where many of their routes intersect. Hub operations include facilities for in-flight food preparation, aircraft maintenance and storage, and administrative offices. A careful quantitative analysis indicates that Worldwide Airway's profit-maximizing alternative is to eliminate the London hub. In making its decision, however, the company's managers will consider such qualitative issues as the effect of the closing on its London employees and on the morale of its remaining employees in the airline's Paris, Toronto, and Tokyo hubs.

To clarify what is at stake in such qualitative analyses, quantitative analysis can allow the decision maker to put a "price" on the sum total of the qualitative characteristics. For example, suppose Worldwide Airways' controller gives top management a quantitative analysis showing that elimination of the London hub will increase annual profits by $2,000,000. However, the qualitative considerations favour the option of continuing the London operation. How important are these qualitative considerations to the top managers? If they decide to continue the London operation, the qualitative considerations must be worth at least $2,000,000 to them. Weighing the quantitative and qualitative considerations in making decisions is the essence of management. The skill, experience, judgment, and ethical standards of managers all come to bear on such difficult choices.

Exhibit 12–1 depicts the seven steps in the decision process, and the relationship between quantitative and qualitative analysis.

Learning Objective 2

Explain the relationship between quantitative and qualitative analyses in decision making.

Exhibit 12–1
The Decision-Making Process

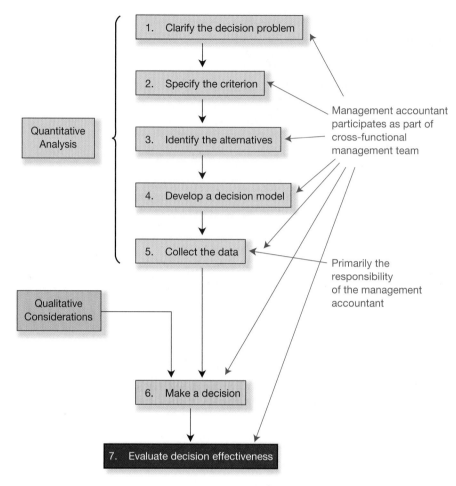

Criteria of Useful Information: Relevance, Accuracy, and Timeliness

What criteria should the management accountant use in designing the accounting information system that supplies data for decision making? Three characteristics of information determine its usefulness: relevance, accuracy, and timeliness.

Relevance   Information is **relevant** if it is *pertinent* to a decision problem. Different decisions will typically require different data. The primary theme of this chapter is how to decide what information is relevant to various common decision problems.

Accuracy   Information relevant to a decision problem must also be **accurate**, or it will be of little use. This means the information must be precise. For example, the cost incurred by Worldwide Airways to rent facilities at London's Heathrow Airport is relevant to a decision about eliminating the airline's London hub. However, if the rental cost data are imprecise, due to incomplete or misplaced records, the usefulness of the information will be diminished.

Timeliness   Relevant and accurate data are useful only if they are **timely**, that is, if the data are available in time to assist in decision making. However, some situations involve a trade-off between the accuracy and the timeliness of information. More accurate information may take longer to produce. Therefore, as accuracy improves, timeliness suffers, and vice versa.

To summarize, the management accountant's primary role in the decision-making process is twofold:

1. Decide what information is *relevant* to each decision problem.
2. Provide *accurate* and *timely* data, keeping in mind the proper balance between these often-conflicting criteria.

Relevant Information

What makes information relevant to a decision problem? Two criteria are important: It must involve a future event and it must involve costs or benefits that *differ among the alternatives.*

Learning Objective   3

Name and explain two criteria that must be satisfied by relevant information.

Impact on the Future   The consequences of decisions take place in the future, not in the past. To be relevant to a decision, therefore, cost or benefit information must involve a future event. The cost information relevant to Worldwide Airways' decision concerning its London operations involves the costs that *will be incurred in the future* under the airline's two alternatives. Costs incurred in the past in the airline's London operations will not change regardless of management's decision, and they are irrelevant to the decision at hand.

Since relevant information involves future events, the management accountant must predict the amounts of the relevant costs and benefits. In making these predictions, the accountant often will use estimates of cost behaviour based on historical data. There is an important and subtle issue here. *Relevant* information must involve costs and benefits to be realized in the *future.* However, the accountant's *predictions* of those costs and benefits are often based on data from the *past.*

Different Costs or Benefits among Competing Alternatives   Relevant information must involve costs or benefits that *differ among the alternatives.* Costs or benefits that are the same across all of the available alternatives have no impact on the decision. For example, suppose Worldwide Airways' management decides to keep its reservations and ticketing office in London regardless of whether its London hub is eliminated. Then the costs of the reservations and ticketing office will not differ between the two alternatives regarding elimination of the London hub. Hence, those costs are irrelevant to that decision.

"You have to try to summarize numbers. You can't just give numbers. People in marketing are going to make decisions based on your numbers. They have to understand what those numbers mean." (12b)
Abbott Laboratories

Unique versus Repetitive Decisions

Unique decisions arise infrequently or only once. Worldwide Airways' decision regarding its London hub is an example. Compiling data for unique decisions usually requires a special analysis by the management accountant. The relevant information often will be found in many diverse places in the organization's overall information system.

In contrast, *repetitive decisions* are made over and over again, at either regular or irregular intervals. For example, Worldwide Airways makes route-scheduling decisions every six months. Such a routine decision makes it worthwhile for the management accountant to keep a special file of the information relevant to the scheduling decision.

Cost predictions relevant to repetitive decisions typically can draw on a large amount of historical data. Since the decisions have been made repeatedly in the past, the data from those decisions should be readily available. Information relevant to unique decisions is harder to generate. The management accountant typically will have to give more thought to deciding which data are relevant, and will have less historical data available on which to base predictions.

Importance of Identifying Relevant Costs and Benefits

Why is it important for the management accountant to isolate the relevant costs and benefits in a decision analysis? First, generating information is a costly process. The relevant data must be sought, and this requires time and effort. By focusing on only the relevant information, the management accountant can simplify and shorten the data-gathering process.

Second, people can effectively use only a limited amount of information. Beyond this, they experience **information overload**, and their decision-making effectiveness declines. By routinely providing only information about relevant costs and benefits, the management accountant can reduce the likelihood of information overload.

Identifying Relevant Costs and Benefits

Learning Objective **4**

Identify relevant costs and benefits, giving proper treatment to sunk costs, opportunity costs, and unit costs.

To illustrate how management accountants determine relevant costs and benefits, we will consider several decisions faced by the management of Worldwide Airways. The airline flies routes between North America and Europe, between various cities in Europe, and between North America and several Asian cities.

Sunk Costs

Sunk costs are costs that have already been incurred. They do not affect any future cost and cannot be changed by any current or future action, so they are irrelevant to decision making. For example, a sunk cost to students is the amount of tuition fees they have already incurred in their studies. In deciding whether to continue or drop a course, the tuition fee already paid for the course (if nonrefundable) is irrelevant to the decision. Yet sunk costs often wrongly influence the decision made. A student at risk of failing a course will often stay in the course because of the money already spent on tuition fees when the better decision might be to drop the course and register again in a subsequent semester when more preparation will mitigate the risk of failure. In a game of chance, players who lose the most money will often continue to play to "recoup losses" (a sunk cost) as they are convinced that their chance of winning increases with each subsequent loss, even though the odds of winning remain constant. This phenomenon is referred to as the *gambler's fallacy*. The following two examples illustrate sunk costs in decisions to be made by Worldwide Airways.

Book Value of Equipment   At Charles de Gaulle Airport in Paris, Worldwide Airways has a three-year-old loader truck used to load in-flight meals onto airplanes. The box on the truck can be lifted hydraulically to the level of a jumbo jet's side doors. The *book value* of this loader, defined as the asset's acquisition cost less the accumulated depreciation to date, is computed as follows:

Acquisition cost of old loader	$100,000
Less: Accumulated depreciation	75,000
Book value	$ 25,000

The loader has one year of useful life remaining, after which its residual value will be zero. However, it could be sold now for $5,000. In addition to the annual depreciation of $25,000, Worldwide Airways annually incurs $80,000 in variable costs to operate the loader. These include the costs of operator labour, gasoline, and maintenance.

John Orville, Worldwide Airways' ramp manager at Charles de Gaulle Airport, faces a decision about replacement of the loader. A new kind of loader uses a conveyor belt to move meals into an airplane. The new loader is much cheaper than the old hydraulic loader and costs less to operate. However, the new loader would be operable for only one year before it would need to be replaced. Pertinent data about the new loader are as follows:

Acquisition cost of new loader	$15,000
Useful life	1 year
Residual value after one year	0
Annual depreciation	$15,000
Annual operating costs	$45,000

Orville's initial inclination is to continue using the old loader for another year. He exclaims, "We can't dump that equipment now. We paid $100,000 for it, and we've only used it for three years. If we get rid of that loader now, we'll lose $20,000 on the disposal." Orville reasons that the old loader's book value of $25,000, less its current residual value of $5,000, amounts to a loss of $20,000.

Fortunately, Orville's comment is overheard by Michelle Imbert, the management accountant in the company's Charles de Gaulle Airport administrative offices. She points out to Orville that the book value of the old loader is a *sunk cost*. It cannot affect any future cost the company might incur. To convince Orville that she is right, Imbert prepares the analysis shown in Exhibit 12–2.

Regardless of which alternative is selected, the $25,000 book value of the old loader will be an expense or loss in the next year. If the old loader is kept in service, the $25,000 will be recognized as depreciation expense; if replaced, the $25,000 cost will be incurred by the company as a write-off of the asset's book value. Thus, the current book value of the old loader is a *sunk cost* and irrelevant to the replacement decision.

Notice that the *relevant* data in the equipment-replacement decision are items (3), (4), and (5). Each of these items meets the two tests of relevant information:

1. The costs or benefits relate to the future
2. The costs or benefits differ between the alternatives

The proceeds from selling the old loader, item (3), will be received in the future only under the "replace" alternative. Similarly, the acquisition cost (depreciation) of the new loader, item (4), is a future cost incurred only under the "replace" alternative. The operating cost, item (5), is also a future cost that differs between the two alternatives.

Differential Costs Exhibit 12–2 includes a column entitled *Differential Cost*. A differential cost is the difference in a cost item under two decision alternatives. The computation of differential costs is a convenient way of summarizing the relative advantage of one alternative over the other. John Orville can make a correct equipment-replacement decision in either of two ways: (1) by comparing the total cost of the two alternatives,

> "[We are continually moving] from being the scorekeeper to being an active, involved participant in crafting business solutions." (12c)
> **Boeing**

		Costs of Two Alternatives		
		(a) **Do Not Replace Old Loader***	**(b)** **Replace Old Loader***	**(c)** **Differential Cost: (a) − (b)**
Sunk cost	(1) Depreciation of old loader	$ 25,000		
	OR			-0-
	(2) Write-off of old loader's book value		$25,000	
Relevant data	(3) Proceeds from disposal of old loader	-0-	(5,000)†	$ 5,000
	(4) Depreciation (cost) of new loader	-0-	15,000	(15,000)
	(5) Operating costs	80,000	45,000	35,000
	Total cost	$105,000	$80,000	$25,000

Exhibit 12–2

Equipment-Replacement
Decision: Worldwide Airways

*Since costs are the focus of the analysis in this exhibit, costs are shown in columns (a) and (b) without parentheses.

†Parentheses denote a cash inflow in this case.

shown in columns (a) and (b), or (2) by focusing on the total differential cost, shown in column (c), which favours the "replacement" option.

Cost of Inventory on Hand   The inventory of spare aircraft parts held by Worldwide Airways at Charles de Gaulle includes some obsolete parts that originally cost $20,000. The company no longer uses the planes for which the parts were purchased. The obsolete parts include spare passenger seats, luggage racks, and galley equipment. The spare parts might be sold to another airline for $17,000. However, with some modifications, the obsolete parts might still be used in the company's current fleet of aircraft. Using the modified parts would save Worldwide Airways the cost of purchasing new parts for its airplanes.

John Orville decides not to dispose of the obsolete parts, because doing so would entail a loss of $3,000. He reasons that the $20,000 book value of the parts, less the $17,000 proceeds from disposal, would result in a $3,000 loss on disposal. Michelle Imbert, the management accountant, comes to the rescue again, demonstrating that the right decision is to dispose of the parts. Imbert's analysis is shown in Exhibit 12–3.

Notice that the book value of the obsolete inventory is a *sunk cost*. If the parts are modified, the $20,000 book value will be an expense during the period when the parts are used. Otherwise, the $20,000 book value of the asset will be written off when the parts are sold. As a sunk cost, the book value of the obsolete inventory will not affect any future cash flow of the company.

As the management accountant's analysis reveals, the relevant data include the $17,000 proceeds from disposal, the $12,000 cost to modify the parts, and the $26,000 cost to buy new parts. All of these data meet the two tests of relevance: They affect future cash flows and they differ between the two alternatives. As Michelle Imbert's analysis shows, Worldwide Airways' cost will be $3,000 less if the obsolete parts are sold and new parts are purchased.

Exhibit 12–3
Obsolete Inventory Decision:
Worldwide Airways

		Costs of Two Alternatives		
		(a) Modify and Use Parts*	(b) Dispose of Parts*	(c) Differential Cost: (a) − (b)
Sunk cost	Book value of parts inventory: Asset value written off whether parts are used or not	$20,000	$20,000	$ –0–
Relevant data	Proceeds from disposal of parts	–0–	(17,000)†	17,000
	Cost to modify parts	12,000	–0–	12,000
	Cost incurred to buy new parts for current aircraft fleet	–0–	26,000	(26,000)
	Total cost	$32,000	$29,000	$ 3,000

*Since costs are the focus of the analysis in this exhibit, costs are shown in columns (a) and (b) without parentheses.
†Parentheses denote a cash inflow in this case.

Irrelevant Future Costs and Benefits

At Worldwide Airways' headquarters, Amy Earhart, manager of flight scheduling, is in the process of making a decision about the Atlanta-to-Honolulu route. The flight is currently nonstop, but she is considering a stop in San Francisco. She feels that the route would attract additional passengers if the stop is made, but there also would be additional variable costs. Her analysis appears in Exhibit 12–4.

The analysis indicates that the preferable alternative is the route that includes a stop in San Francisco. Notice that the cargo revenue (item [2]) and the aircraft maintenance

Exhibit 12–4
Flight-Route Decision:
Worldwide Airways

Relevant or Irrelevant		Revenues and Costs under Two Alternatives		
		(a) Nonstop Route*	(b) With Stop in San Francisco*	(c) Differential Amount:† (a) − (b)
Relevant	(1) Passenger revenue	$240,000	$258,000	$(18,000)
Irrelevant	(2) Cargo revenue	80,000	80,000	–0–
Relevant	(3) Landing fee in San Francisco	–0–	(5,000)	5,000
Relevant	(4) Use of airport gate facilities	–0–	(3,000)	3,000
Relevant	(5) Flight crew cost	(2,000)	(2,500)	500
Relevant	(6) Fuel	(21,000)	(24,000)	3,000
Relevant	(7) Meals and services	(4,000)	(4,600)	600
Irrelevant	(8) Aircraft maintenance	(1,000)	(1,000)	–0–
	Total revenue less costs	$292,000	$297,900	$ (5,900)

*In columns (a) and (b), parentheses denote costs and numbers without parentheses are revenues.
†In column (c), parentheses denote differential items favouring option (b).

cost (item [8]) are irrelevant to the flight-route decision. Although these data do affect future cash flows, they *do not differ between the two alternatives*. All of the other data in Exhibit 12–4 are relevant to the decision, because they differ between the two alternatives. The analysis in Exhibit 12–4 could have ignored the irrelevant data and the same decision would have been reached.

Opportunity Costs

Another decision confronting Amy Earhart is whether to add two daily round-trip flights between New York and Montreal. Her initial analysis of the relevant costs and benefits indicates that the additional revenue from the flights will exceed their costs by $30,000 per month, so she is ready to add the flights to the schedule. However, Chuck Lindbergh, Worldwide Airways' hangar manager in New York, points out that Earhart has overlooked an important consideration—a significant opportunity cost.

Worldwide Airways currently has excess space in its hangar. A commuter airline has offered to rent the hangar space for $40,000 per month. However, if the New York–Montreal flights are added to the schedule, the additional aircraft needed in New York will require the excess hangar space. If Worldwide Airways adds the New York–Montreal flights, it will forego the opportunity to rent the excess hangar space for $40,000 per month, so the $40,000 in rent foregone is an *opportunity cost* of the alternative to add the new flights.

An *opportunity cost* is the potential benefit given up when the choice of one action precludes a different action. For example, an opportunity cost for students is the amount of money they could have earned working instead of attending school. Although people tend to overlook or underestimate the importance of opportunity costs, they are just as relevant as out-of-pocket costs in evaluating decision alternatives. So, the cost of studying is made up of the tuition fees (out-of-pocket costs) and the amount of money that could have been earned instead of studying (opportunity costs). The opportunity costs in many decisions are often greater than the out-of-pocket costs. In Worldwide Airways' case, the best action is to rent the excess warehouse space to the commuter airline, rather than adding the new flights. The analysis in Exhibit 12–5 supports this conclusion.

It is a common mistake for people to overlook or undervalue opportunity costs. The $40,000 hangar rental, which will be foregone if the new flights are added, is an *opportunity cost* of the option to add the flights. It is a *relevant cost* of the decision, and it is just as important as any out-of-pocket expenditure.

Exhibit 12–5
Decision to Add Flights:
Worldwide Airways

	(a) **Add Flights**	(b) **Do Not Add Flights**	(c) **Differential Amount: (a) − (b)**
Additional revenue from new flights less additional costs	$30,000	–0–	$ 30,000
Rental of excess hangar space	–0–	$40,000	(40,000)*
Total	$30,000	$40,000	$(10,000)

*Parentheses denote that differential benefit favours option (b).

Summary: Relevant Costs and Benefits Basics

Relevant costs and benefits satisfy the following two criteria:

1. They affect the future.
2. They differ between alternatives.

Sunk costs are not relevant costs, because they do not affect the future. An example of a sunk cost is the book value of an asset, either equipment or inventory. *Future costs or benefits that are identical across all decision alternatives are not relevant.* They can be ignored when making a decision. *Opportunity costs are relevant costs.* Such costs deserve particular attention because many people tend to overlook them when making decisions.

Analysis of Special Decisions

What are the relevant costs and benefits when a manager must decide whether to add or drop a product or service? What data are relevant when deciding whether to produce or buy a service or component? These decisions and certain other nonroutine decisions merit special attention in our discussion of relevant costs and benefits.

Accept or Reject a Special Offer

Jim Wright, Worldwide Airways' vice-president of operations, has been approached by a Japanese tourist agency about flying chartered tourist flights from Japan to Hawaii. The tourist agency has offered Worldwide Airways $150,000 per round-trip flight on a jumbo jet. Given the airline's usual occupancy rate and air fares, a round-trip jumbo-jet flight between Japan and Hawaii typically brings in revenue of $250,000, so the tourist agency's price offer requires a special analysis by Jim Wright.

Wright knows that Worldwide Airways has two jumbo jets that are not currently being used. The airline has just eliminated several unprofitable routes, freeing these aircraft for other uses. The airline was not currently planning to add any new routes, and therefore the two jets were idle. To help in making his decision, Wright asks for cost data from the controller's office. The controller provides the information in Exhibit 12–6, which pertains to a typical round-trip jumbo-jet flight between Japan and Hawaii.

The variable costs cover aircraft fuel and maintenance, flight-crew costs, in-flight meals and services, and landing fees. The fixed costs allocated to each flight cover Worldwide Airways' fixed costs, such as aircraft depreciation, maintenance and depreciation of facilities, and fixed administrative costs.

If Jim Wright had not understood managerial accounting, he might have done the following *incorrect analysis*:

Special price for charter	$150,000
Total cost per flight	190,000
Loss on charter flight	$ (40,000)

Revenue:		
Passenger	$250,000	
Cargo	30,000	
Total revenue		$280,000
Expenses:		
Variable expenses of flight	$ 90,000	
Fixed expenses allocated to each flight	100,000	
Total expenses		190,000
Profit		$ 90,000

Exhibit 12–6

Data for Typical Flight between Japan and Hawaii: Worldwide Airways

Worldwide Airways

The calculation in the table at the bottom of the previous page suggests that the special charter offer should be rejected. What is the error in this analysis? The mistake is the inclusion of allocated fixed costs in the cost per flight. This is an error, because the *fixed costs will not increase in total* if the charter flight is added. Since the fixed costs will not change under either of the alternative choices, they are irrelevant.

Fortunately, Jim Wright does not make this mistake. He knows that only the variable costs of the proposed charter are relevant. Moreover, Wright determines that the variable cost of the charter would be lower than that of a typical flight, because Worldwide Airways would not incur the variable costs of reservations and ticketing. These variable expenses amount to $5,000 for a scheduled flight. Thus, Wright's analysis of the charter offer is as follows:

Assumes excess capacity (idle aircraft)	Special price for charter		$150,000
	Variable cost per routine flight	$90,000	
	Less: Savings on reservations and ticketing	5,000	
	Variable cost of charter		85,000
	Contribution from charter		$ 65,000

Wright's analysis shows that the special charter flight will contribute $65,000 toward covering the airline's fixed costs and generating profit. Since the airline has excess flight capacity, due to the existence of idle aircraft, the optimal decision is to accept the special charter offer.

No Excess Capacity Now let's consider how Wright's analysis would appear if Worldwide Airways had no idle aircraft. Suppose that in order to fly the charter between Japan and Hawaii, the airline would have to cancel its least profitable route, which is between Japan and Hong Kong. This route contributes $80,000 toward covering the airline's fixed costs and generating profit. So, if the charter offer is accepted, the airline will incur an opportunity cost of $80,000 from the foregone contribution of the Japan–Hong Kong route. Now Wright's analysis should appear as follows:

Assumes no excess capacity (no idle aircraft)	Special price for charter		$150,000
	Variable cost per routine flight	$90,000	
	Less: Savings on reservations and ticketing (no idle aircraft)	5,000	
	Variable cost of charter	85,000	
	Add: Opportunity cost, foregone contribution on cancelled Japan–Hong Kong route	80,000	165,000
	Loss from charter		$ (15,000)

So if Worldwide Airways has no excess flight capacity, Jim Wright should reject the special charter offer.

Summary The decision to accept or reject a specially priced order is common in both service industry and manufacturing firms. Manufacturers often are faced with decisions

> "I've seen it [managerial accounting] evolve to become more of a team player and being involved in major projects and being looked to as a business advisor or consultant to help leverage our expertise on profitability of certain products or sourcing decisions." (12e)
>
> **Caterpillar**

about selling products in a special order at less than full price. The correct analysis of such decisions focuses on the relevant costs and benefits. Fixed costs, which often are allocated to individual units of product or service, are usually irrelevant. Fixed costs typically will not change in total, whether the order is accepted or rejected.

When excess capacity exists, the only relevant costs usually will be the variable costs associated with the special order. When there is no excess capacity, the opportunity cost of using the firm's facilities for the special order is also relevant to the decision.

Outsource a Product or Service

Ellie Rickenbacker is Worldwide Airways' manager of in-flight services. She supervises the airline's flight attendants and all of its food and beverage operations. Rickenbacker currently faces a decision regarding the preparation of in-flight dinners at the airline's New York hub. In the New York flight kitchen, full-course dinners are prepared and packaged for long flights that pass through New York. In the past, all of the desserts were baked and packaged in the flight kitchen. However, Rickenbacker has received an offer from a New York bakery to bake the airline's desserts. Thus, her decision is whether to *outsource* the dessert portion of the in-flight dinners. An **outsourcing decision**, also called a **make-or-buy decision**, entails a choice between producing a product or service in-house or purchasing it from an outside supplier. To help in making her decision, Rickenbacker has assembled the cost information in Exhibit 12–7, which shows a total cost per dessert of 25 cents.

The New York bakery has offered to supply the desserts for 21 cents each. Rickenbacker's initial inclination is to accept the bakery's offer, since it appears that the airline would save 4 cents per dessert. However, the controller reminds Rickenbacker that not all of the costs listed in Exhibit 12–7 are relevant to the outsourcing decision. The controller modifies Rickenbacker's analysis as shown in Exhibit 12–8.

Exhibit 12–7
Cost of In-Flight Desserts: Worldwide Airways

	Cost per Dessert
Variable costs:	
Direct material (food and packaging)	$0.06
Direct labour	0.04
Variable overhead	0.04
Fixed costs (allocated to products):	
Supervisory salaries	0.04
Depreciation of flight-kitchen equipment	0.07
Total cost per dessert	$0.25

Exhibit 12–8
Cost Savings from Buying In-Flight Desserts: Worldwide Airways

	Cost per Dessert	Costs Saved by Purchasing Desserts
Variable costs:		
Direct material	$0.06	$ 0.06
Direct labour	0.04	0.04
Variable overhead	0.04	0.04
Fixed costs (allocated to products):		
Supervisory salaries	0.04	0.01
Depreciation of flight-kitchen equipment	0.07	–0–
Total cost per dessert	$0.25	$ 0.15
Cost of purchasing desserts (per dessert)		$ 0.21
Loss per dessert if desserts are purchased (savings per dessert minus purchase cost per dessert, or $0.15 − $0.21)		$(0.06)

OUTSOURCING

Northwest Airlines,
Air Canada, Apple,
HP, Motorola,
and Nokia

Outsourcing is widely used in a variety of businesses. The management at Northwest Airlines (which has since merged with Delta Airlines), for example, decided to outsource some of its flight attendants in order to reduce the cost of filling the most expensive of these positions. According to *The Wall Street Journal*, it was a sign "that Northwest, which has filed for bankruptcy protection, wants to become a 'virtual airline,' with all sorts of jobs previously claimed by organized labour outsourced to cheaper workers, some overseas."

Other airlines are outsourcing key maintenance operations. For example, Air Canada outsources full-service maintenance, repair, and overhaul of airframes and engines to facilities in El Salvador. "The agreement offers Air Canada a customized, flexible maintenance program with advantageous fixed price guarantees." After any required maintenance is performed, the jets will fly back to Canada. (Northwest Airlines flew its wide-body jets to Singapore and Hong Kong for service by outside contractors.)

BusinessWeek reports that many technology manufacturers are outsourcing research and development and product design to outside contractors in Taiwan and other countries. Among the companies outsourcing some of these key design functions are computer manufacturers Apple and HP, and cellphone manufacturers Motorola and Nokia.[1]

If Worldwide Airways stops making desserts, it will save all of the variable costs but only 1 cent of fixed costs. The 1-cent saving in supervisory salaries would result because the airline could get along with two fewer kitchen supervisors. The remainder of the fixed costs would be incurred even if the desserts were purchased. These remaining fixed costs of supervision and depreciation would have to be reallocated to the flight kitchen's other products. In light of the controller's revised analysis, Rickenbacker realizes that the airline should continue to make its own desserts. To outsource the desserts would require an expenditure of 21 cents per dessert, but only 15 cents (not 25 cents) per dessert would be saved.

To clarify her decision further, Rickenbacker asks the controller to prepare an analysis of the *total costs* per month of making or buying desserts. The controller's report, displayed in Exhibit 12–9, shows the total cost of producing 1,000,000 desserts, the flight kitchen's average monthly volume. The total-cost analysis confirmed Rickenbacker's decision to continue making desserts in the airline's flight kitchen.

	Cost per Month	Costs Saved by Purchasing Desserts
Variable costs:		
Direct material	$ 60,000	$ 60,000
Direct labour	40,000	40,000
Variable overhead	40,000	40,000
Fixed costs (allocated to products):		
Supervisory salaries	40,000	10,000*
Depreciation of flight-kitchen equipment	70,000	–0–
Total cost per month	$250,000	$150,000
Cost of purchasing desserts (per month)		$210,000
Total loss if desserts are purchased (total savings minus total cost of purchasing, or $150,000 − $210,000)		$ (60,000)

*Cost of monthly compensation for two kitchen supervisors, who will not be needed if desserts are purchased.

Exhibit 12–9
Total-Cost Analysis of Outsourcing Decision: Worldwide Airways

In today's global economy, more and more companies are outsourcing significant products and services. Gallo Winery, for example, buys a significant portion of its grapes from other vintners. Kodak outsources its entire data processing operation. Cummins Engine outsources many of its pistons, and Intel Corporation buys microchips. Chase Bank outsources its cafeteria and legal services. Many pharmaceutical companies, such as Japan's Yamanouchi Pharmaceutical, have outsourced much of their production to cut costs.[2] Pictured here are grape harvesting and pharmaceutical production.

Beware of Unit-Cost Data   Fixed costs often are allocated to individual units of product or service for product-costing purposes. For decision-making purposes, however, unitized fixed costs can be misleading. As the total-cost analysis in Exhibit 12–9 shows, only $10,000 in fixed monthly cost will be saved if the desserts are purchased. The remaining $100,000 in monthly fixed cost will continue whether the desserts are made or purchased. Ricken-backer's initial cost analysis in Exhibit 12–7 implies that each dessert costs the airline 25 cents, but that 25-cent cost includes 11 cents of unitized fixed costs. Most of these costs will remain unchanged regardless of the outsourcing decision. By allocating fixed costs to individual products or services, they are made to appear variable even though they are not.

Add or Drop a Service, Product, or Department

Worldwide Airways offers its passengers the opportunity to join its World Express Club. Club membership entitles a traveller to use the club facilities at the airport in Toronto. Club privileges include a private lounge and restaurant, discounts on meals and beverages, and use of a small health spa.

Jayne Wing, the president of Worldwide Airways, is worried that the World Express Club might not be profitable. Her concern is caused by the statement of monthly operating income shown in the Excel spreadsheet in Exhibit 12–10.

In her weekly staff meeting, Wing states her concern about the World Express Club's profitability. The controller responds by pointing out that not all of the costs on the club's income statement would be eliminated if the club was discontinued. The vice-president of sales adds that the club helps Worldwide Airways attract passengers whom it might otherwise lose to a competitor. As the meeting adjourns, Wing asks the controller to prepare an analysis of the relevant costs and benefits associated with the World Express Club. The controller's analysis is displayed in Exhibit 12–11.

	A	B	C	D	E	F	G
1	WORLDWIDE AIRWAYS: WORLD EXPRESS CLUB						
2	Monthly Operating Income Statement						
3							
4	Sales revenue					$ 200,000	
5	Less: Variable expenses:						
6	Food and beverages				$ 70,000		
7	Personnel				40,000		
8	Variable overhead				25,000	135,000	
9	Contribution margin					$ 65,000	
10	Less: Fixed expenses:						
11	Depreciation				$ 30,000		
12	Supervisory salaries				20,000		
13	Insurance				10,000		
14	Airport fees				5,000		
15	General overhead (allocated)				10,000	75,000	
16	Loss					$ (10,000)	

Exhibit 12–10

World Express Club Monthly Operating Income Statement: Worldwide Airways

	(a) Keep Club	(b) Eliminate Club	(c) Differential Amount: (a) − (b)
Part I:			
Sales revenue	$200,000	–0–	$200,000
Less: Variable expenses:			
Food and beverages	(70,000)	–0–	(70,000)
Personnel	(40,000)	–0–	(40,000)
Variable overhead	(25,000)	–0–	(25,000)
Contribution margin	65,000	–0–	65,000
Less: Fixed expenses:			
Depreciation	(30,000)	(30,000)	–0–
Supervisory salaries	(20,000)	–0–	(20,000)
Insurance	(10,000)	(10,000)	–0–
Airport fees	(5,000)	–0–	(5,000)
General overhead (allocated)	(10,000)	(10,000)	–0–
Total fixed expenses	(75,000)	(50,000)	(25,000)
Profit (loss)	$ (10,000)	$(50,000)	$ 40,000*
		Expenses in the column above are **unavoidable** expenses	Expenses in the column above are **avoidable** expenses
Part II:			
Contribution margin from general airline operations that will be foregone if club is eliminated	$ 60,000	–0–	$ 60,000

*The *positive* $40,000 differential amount reflects the fact that the company is $40,000 *better off* by keeping the club.

Exhibit 12–11

Relevant Costs and Benefits of World Express Club: Worldwide Airways

The controller's report contains two parts. Part I in Exhibit 12–11 focuses on the relevant costs and benefits of the World Express Club only, while ignoring any impact of the club on other airline operations. In column (a), the controller has listed the club's revenues and expenses from the income statement presented in Exhibit 12–10. Column (b) in Exhibit 12–11 lists the expenses that will continue if the club is eliminated. These expenses are called **unavoidable expenses**. In contrast, the expenses appearing in column (a) but not column (b) are shown in column (c) as **avoidable expenses**. The airline will no longer incur these expenses if the club is eliminated.

Notice that all of the club's variable expenses are avoidable. The depreciation expense, $30,000, is an allocated portion of the depreciation on a Worldwide Airways building, part of which is used by the World Express Club. If the club is discontinued, the airline will continue to own and use the building and the depreciation expense will continue, so this is an unavoidable expense. The fixed supervisory salaries are avoidable, since these employees will no longer be needed if the club is eliminated. The fixed insurance expense of $10,000 is not avoidable; the $5,000 fee paid to the airport for the privilege of operating the club is avoidable. Finally, the club's allocated portion of general overhead expenses, $10,000, is not avoidable. Worldwide Airways will incur these expenses regardless of its decision about the World Express Club.

The conclusion shown by Part I of the controller's report is that the club should not be eliminated. If the club is closed, the airline will lose more in contribution margin, $65,000, than it saves in avoidable fixed expenses, $25,000. So the club's $65,000 contribution margin is enough to cover the avoidable fixed expenses of $25,000 and still contribute $40,000 toward covering the overall airline's fixed expenses.

World Express Club's contribution margin	$65,000
Avoidable fixed expenses	25,000
Contribution of club toward covering overall airline's fixed expenses	$40,000

ADDING A SERVICE[3]

Managerial Accounting Practice

FedEx and Caterpillar

Changing business conditions can cause a company to rethink its business model and add new services. FedEx, for example, found that a sizable portion of its overnight letter delivery business had been eliminated by e-mail. Customers no longer needed to ship a hard-copy document overnight, when the same document could be sent instantaneously via e-mail. FedEx also found a decline in the need for overnight repair parts shipments. Many customers' improved supply-chain systems resulted in better spare-parts preparedness and less need for last-minute overnight shipments. FedEx responded by adding ground shipment services to compete more directly with UPS and Canada Post. While FedEx still excels when an overnight shipment is needed, its ground transport business has become a significant part of its operations.

Caterpillar has added heavy equipment overhaul services to its already successful manufacturing operations. The company uses available capacity in its manufacturing plants to disassemble and rebuild heavy diesel engines after cleaning, inspecting, and repairing them. This new service component of Caterpillar's operations has become the company's fastest-growing business unit, with annual revenue topping $1 billion.

Now consider Part II of the controller's analysis in Exhibit 12–11. As the vice-president of sales pointed out, the World Express Club is an attractive feature to many travellers. The controller estimates that if the club was discontinued, the airline would lose $60,000 each month in foregone contribution margin from general airline operations. This loss in contribution margin would result from losing to a competing airline current passengers who are attracted to Worldwide Airways by its World Express Club. This $60,000 in foregone contribution margin is an *opportunity cost* of the option to close down the club.

Considering both Parts I and II of the controller's analysis, Worldwide Airways' monthly profit will be greater by $100,000 if the club is kept open. Recognition of two issues is key to this conclusion:

1. Only the avoidable expenses of the club will be saved if it is discontinued.
2. Closing the club will adversely affect the airline's other operations.

Special Decisions in Manufacturing Firms

Some types of decisions are more likely to arise in manufacturing companies than in service industry firms. We will examine two of these decisions: to sell or process further, and use of limited resources.

Joint Products: Sell or Process Further

A **joint production process** results in two or more products, called *joint products*. An example is the processing of cocoa beans into cocoa powder and cocoa butter. Cocoa beans constitute the input to the joint production process, and the two joint products are cocoa powder and cocoa butter. The point in the production process where the joint products are identifiable as separate products is called the **split-off point**. Other examples of joint production processes include the processing of animals for various cuts of meat and of petroleum into various products, such as kerosene and gasoline.

Manufacturers with joint production processes sometimes must decide whether a joint product should be sold at the split-off point or processed further before being sold. Such a decision recently confronted Bill Candee, the president of the International Chocolate Company. Candee's firm imports cocoa beans and processes them into cocoa powder and cocoa butter. Only a portion of the cocoa powder is used by the International Chocolate Company in the production of chocolate candy. The remainder of the cocoa powder is sold to an ice cream producer. Candee is considering the possibility of processing his remaining cocoa powder into an instant cocoa mix to be marketed under the brand name ChocoTime. Data pertaining to Candee's decision are displayed in Exhibit 12–12.

Notice from the diagram that cocoa beans are processed in one-tonne batches. The total cost of the cocoa beans and the joint processing is $1,100. This is called the **joint cost**. The output of the joint process is 1,500 kilograms of cocoa butter and 500 kilograms of cocoa powder.

Exhibit 12–12

Joint Processing of Cocoa Beans: International Chocolate Company

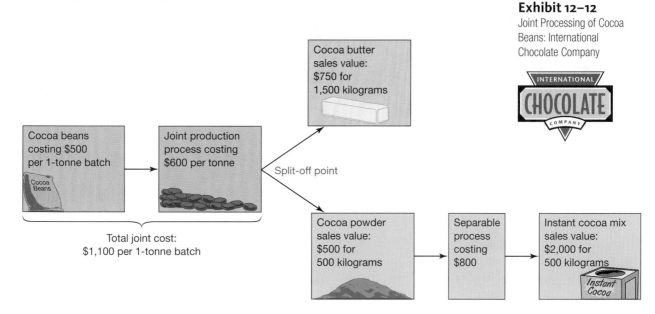

How should Bill Candee approach the decision about processing the cocoa powder into instant cocoa mix? What are the relevant costs and benefits? First, let's consider the joint cost of $1,100. Is this a relevant cost in the decision at hand? *The joint cost is not a relevant cost*, because it will not change regardless of the decision Candee makes.

Suppose the $1,100 joint cost had been allocated to the two joint products for product-costing purposes. A common method of allocating a joint cost is the **relative-sales-value method**, in which the joint cost is allocated between the joint products in proportion to their sales value at the split-off point. The International Chocolate Company would make the following joint cost allocation.

Joint Cost		Joint Products	Sales Value at Split-Off Point	Relative Proportion	Allocation of Joint Cost
	{	Cocoa butter	$750	0.60	$ 660
$1,100	{	Cocoa powder	500	0.40	440
		Total joint cost allocated			$1,100

Does this allocation of the $1,100 joint cost make it relevant to the decision about processing cocoa powder into instant cocoa mix? The answer is no. *The $1,100 joint cost still does not change in total*, whether the cocoa powder is processed further or not. The joint cost is irrelevant to the decision at hand.

The only costs and benefits relevant to Candee's decision are those that differ between the two alternatives. The proper analysis is shown in Exhibit 12–13.

There is a shortcut method that arrives at the same conclusion as Exhibit 12–13. In this approach, the incremental revenue from the further processing of cocoa powder is compared with the **incremental processing cost**, which is the cost incurred after the split-off point, as follows:

Sales value of instant cocoa mix	$2,000
Sales value of cocoa powder	500
Incremental revenue from further processing	$1,500
Less: Incremental processing cost	(800)
Net benefit from further processing	$ 700

Both analyses indicate that Bill Candee should process his excess cocoa powder into instant cocoa mix. The same conclusion is reached if the analysis is done on a per-unit

Exhibit 12–13
Decision to Sell or Process Further: International Chocolate Company

Relevant or Irrelevant			(a) Process Cocoa Powder into Instant Cocoa Mix	(b) Sell Cocoa Powder at Split-Off Point	(c) Differential Amount: (a) − (b)
		Sales revenue:			
	Irrelevant	Cocoa butter	$ 750	$ 750	–0–
Relevant		Instant cocoa mix	2,000		$1,500
Relevant		Cocoa powder		500	
		Less: Costs:			
	Irrelevant	Joint cost	(1,100)	(1,100)	–0–
Relevant		Incremental cost of processing cocoa powder into instant cocoa mix	(800)	–0–	(800)
		Total	$ 850	$ 150	$ 700

basis rather than a total basis: Once again, the analysis below shows that Bill Candee should decide to process the cocoa powder into instant cocoa mix:

Sales value of instant cocoa mix ($2,000 ÷ 500 kg)	$4.00 per kg
Sales value of cocoa powder ($500 ÷ 500 kg)	1.00 per kg
Incremental revenue from further processing	$3.00 per kg
Less: Incremental processing cost ($800 ÷ 500 kg)	(1.60) per kg
Net benefit from further processing	$1.40 per kg

Decisions Involving Limited Resources

Organizations typically have limited resources. Limited floor space, machine time, labour hours, or raw materials are common. Operating with limited resources, a firm often has to choose between sales orders, deciding which orders to fill and which to decline. In making such decisions, managers have to decide which product or service is the most profitable.

To illustrate, suppose the International Chocolate Company's plant makes two candy-bar products, Chewies and Chompos. The contribution margin for a case of each of these products is computed in Exhibit 12–14.

A glance at the contribution-margin data suggests that Chompos are more profitable than Chewies. It is true that a case of Chompos contributes more toward covering the company's fixed cost and profit. However, an important consideration has been ignored in the analysis so far. The plant's capacity is limited by its available machine time. Only 700 machine hours are available in the plant each month. The International Chocolate Company can sell as many cases of either candy bar as it can produce, so production is limited only by the constraint on machine time.

To maximize the plant's total contribution toward covering fixed cost and profit, management should strive to use each machine hour as effectively as possible. This realization alters the analysis of product profitability. The relevant question is *not* "Which candy bar has the highest contribution margin *per case*?" but "Which product has the highest contribution margin *per machine hour*?" This question is answered in the calculation in Exhibit 12–15.

A machine hour spent in the production of Chewies will contribute $50 toward covering fixed cost and profit, while a machine hour devoted to Chompos contributes only $40. So, when the plant's scarce resource is taken into account, the plant's most profitable product is Chewies.

	Chewies	Chompos
Sales price	$10.00	$14.00
Less: Variable costs:		
Direct material	3.00	3.75
Direct labour	2.00	2.50
Variable overhead	3.00	3.75
Variable selling and administrative costs	1.00	2.00
Total variable costs	9.00	12.00
Contribution margin per case	$ 1.00	$ 2.00

Exhibit 12–14
Contribution Margin per Case: International Chocolate Company

		Chewies	Chompos
(a)	Contribution margin per case	$ 1.00	$ 2.00
(b)	Machine hours required per case	0.02	0.05
(a) ÷ (b)	Contribution margin per machine hour	$50.00	$40.00

Exhibit 12–15
Contribution Margin per Machine Hour: International Chocolate Company

Suppose the International Chocolate Company's plant manager, Candace Barr, is faced with a choice between two sales orders, only one of which can be accepted. Only 100 hours of unscheduled machine time remains in the month, and it can be used to produce either Chewies or Chompos. The analysis in Exhibit 12–16 shows that Barr should devote the 100-hour block of machine time to filling the order for Chewies, since a decision about the best use of a limited resource should be made on the basis of the *contribution margin per unit of the scarce resource.*

Exhibit 12–16

Total Contribution from 100 Machine Hours: International Chocolate Company

	Chewies	Chompos
Contribution margin per case	$1.00	$2.00
Number of cases produced in 100 hours of machine time	× 5,000*	× 2,000†
Total contribution toward covering fixed cost and profit	$5,000	$4,000

*Chewies: 100 hours ÷ 0.02 hour per case = 5,000 cases.
†Chompos: 100 hours ÷ 0.05 hour per case = 2,000 cases.

Multiple Scarce Resources   Suppose the plant had a limited amount of *both* machine hours *and* labour hours. Now the analysis of product profitability is more complicated. The choice as to which product is most profitable typically will involve a trade-off between the two scarce resources. Solving such a problem requires a powerful mathematical tool called *linear programming*, which is covered in the online supplement to this chapter.

Theory of Constraints   As the previous analysis suggests, a binding constraint can limit a company's profitability. For example, a manufacturing company may have a *bottleneck operation*, through which every unit of a product must pass before moving on to other operations. The *theory of constraints* calls for identifying such limiting constraints and seeking ways to relax them. Also referred to as *managing constraints*, this management approach can significantly improve an organization's level of goal attainment. Among the ways that management can relax a constraint by expanding the capacity of a bottleneck operation are the following:

- *Outsourcing* (subcontracting) all or part of the bottleneck operation
- Investing in additional production equipment and using *parallel processing*, in which multiple product units undergo the same production operation simultaneously
- Working *overtime* at the bottleneck operation
- *Retraining* employees and shifting them to the bottleneck
- Eliminating any *non-value-added activities* at the bottleneck operation

Uncertainty

Our analyses of the decisions in this chapter assumed that all relevant data were known with certainty. In practice, of course, decision makers are rarely so fortunate. One common technique for addressing the impact of uncertainty is *sensitivity analysis*. Sensitivity analysis is a technique for determining what would happen in a decision analysis if a key prediction or assumption proved to be wrong.

To illustrate, let's return to Candace Barr's decision about how to use the remaining 100 hours of machine time in the International Chocolate Company's plant. The calculation in Exhibit 12–15 showed that Chewies have the higher contribution margin per machine hour. Suppose Barr is uncertain about the contribution margin per case of Chewies. A sensitivity analysis shows how sensitive her decision is to the value of this uncertain parameter. As Exhibit 12–17 shows, the Chewies contribution margin could decline to $0.80 per case of Chewies before Barr's decision would change. As long as the contribution margin per case of Chewies exceeds $0.80 per case, the 100 hours of available machine time should be devoted to Chewies.

		Chewies	Chompos
Original Analysis			
(a)	Contribution margin per case predicted	$ 1.00	$ 2.00
(b)	Machine hours required per case	0.02	0.05
(a) ÷ (b)	Contribution per machine hour	$ 50.00	$40.00
Sensitivity Analysis			
(c)	Contribution margin per case hypothesized in sensitivity analysis...	$ 0.80	
(d)	Machine hours required per case	0.02	Same
(c) ÷ (d)	Contribution per machine hour	$ 40.00	

Exhibit 12–17
Sensitivity Analysis: International Chocolate Company

Sensitivity analysis can help the management accountant decide which parameters in an analysis are most critical to estimate accurately. In this case, the management accountant knows that the contribution margin per case of Chewies could be as much as 20 percent lower than the original $1 prediction without changing the outcome of the analysis.

Expected Values   Another approach to dealing explicitly with uncertainty is to base the decision on expected values. The **expected value** of a random variable is equal to the sum of the possible values for the variable, each weighted by its probability. To illustrate, suppose the contribution margins per case for Chewies and Chompos are uncertain, as shown in Exhibit 12–18. As the exhibit shows, the choice as to which product to produce with excess machine time may be based on the *expected value* of the contribution per machine hour. Statisticians have developed many other methods for dealing with uncertainty in decision making, which are covered in statistics and decision analysis courses.

Chewies		**Chompos**	
Possible Values of Contribution Margin	**Probability**	**Possible Values of Contribution Margin**	**Probability**
$0.75	0.50	$1.50	0.30
1.25	0.50	2.00	0.40
		2.50	0.30
Expected value (0.50)($0.75) + (0.50)($1.25) = $1.00		(0.30)($1.50) + (0.40)($2.00) + (0.30)($2.50) = $2.00	
Machine hours required per case 0.02		0.05	
Expected value of contribution per machine hour $50.00	>	$40.00	

Exhibit 12–18
Use of Expected Values: International Chocolate Company

Activity-Based Costing and Today's Advanced Manufacturing Environment

In this chapter we have explored how to identify the relevant costs and benefits in various types of decisions. How will the relevant-costing approach change in a manufacturing environment characterized by JIT production methods and flexible manufacturing systems? How would a relevant-costing analysis change if a company used an activity-based costing (ABC) system?[4]

The *concepts* underlying a relevant-costing analysis continue to be completely valid in an advanced manufacturing setting and in a situation in which activity-based costing is used. The objective of the decision analysis is to determine the costs and benefits that

Learning Objective **7**

Explain the impact of an advanced manufacturing environment and activity-based costing on a relevant-cost analysis.

are relevant to the decision. As we found earlier in this chapter, relevant costs and benefits *have an impact on the future and differ among the decision alternatives.*

What *will* be different in a setting where activity-based costing is used is the decision maker's ability to determine what costs are relevant to a decision. Under ABC, the decision maker typically can associate costs with the activities that drive them much more accurately than under a conventional product-costing system. Let's explore these issues with an illustration.

Conventional Outsourcing (Make-or-Buy) Analysis

The International Chocolate Company makes fine chocolates in its Richmond plant. The chocolates are packaged in two-kilogram and five-kilogram gift boxes. The company also manufactures the gift boxes in the plant. Candace Barr, the plant manager, was approached recently by a packaging company with an offer to supply the gift boxes at a price of $0.45 each. Barr concluded that the offer should be rejected on the basis of the relevant-costing analysis in Exhibit 12–19. The International Chocolate Company's

Exhibit 12–19
Conventional Product-Costing Data and Outsourcing Analysis: International Chocolate Company

A. Manufacturing Overhead Budget for Richmond Plant	
Variable overhead:	
Electricity	$ 700,000
Oil and lubricants	120,000
Equipment maintenance	180,000
Total variable overhead	$1,000,000

Variable overhead rate: $1,000,000 ÷ 100,000 direct-labour hours = $10 per hour

Fixed overhead:	
Plant depreciation	$1,650,000
Product development	300,000
Supervisory salaries	600,000
Material handling	800,000
Purchasing	250,000
Inspection	300,000
Setup	400,000
Machinery depreciation	200,000
Total fixed overhead	$4,500,000

Fixed overhead rate: $4,500,000 ÷ 100,000 direct-labour hours = $45 per hour

B. Conventional Product-Costing Data: Gift Boxes	
Direct material	$ 100,000
Direct labour (10,000 hr. at $15 per hr.)	150,000
Variable overhead ($10 per direct-labour hr.)	100,000
Fixed overhead ($45 per direct-labour hr.)	450,000
Total cost	$ 800,000

Unit cost: $800,000 ÷ 1,000,000 boxes = $0.80 per box

C. Conventional Outsourcing Analysis: Gift Boxes	
Relevant costs (costs that will be avoided if the gift boxes are purchased):	
Direct material	$ 100,000
Direct labour	150,000
Variable overhead	100,000
Fixed overhead:	
Supervision	60,000
Machinery depreciation	20,000
Total costs to be avoided by purchasing	$ 430,000
Total cost of purchasing (1,000,000 boxes × $0.45 per box)	$ 450,000

traditional volume-based product-costing system showed a unit product cost of $0.80 per box, but Barr realized that not all of the costs would be avoided. She reasoned that all of the direct material, direct labour, and variable overhead would be avoided, but only a small part of the assigned fixed overhead would be saved. She concluded that $60,000 of supervisory salaries and $20,000 of machinery depreciation could be traced directly to gift package production. These costs would be avoided, she felt, but the remaining fixed costs would not. Barr concluded that only $430,000 of costs would be avoided by purchasing the gift boxes, while $450,000 would be spent to buy the boxes. The decision was clear: The supplier's offer should be rejected.

ABC Analysis of the Outsourcing Decision

At a staff meeting, Candace Barr mentioned her tentative decision to Dave Mint, the plant controller. Mint then explained to Barr that he was completing a pilot project using ABC. Mint offered to analyze the outsourcing decision using the new ABC database. Barr agreed, and Mint proceeded to do the ABC analysis shown in Exhibit 12–20.

In panel A of the ABC analysis, Mint designated 11 activity cost pools corresponding to the major items in the plant's overhead budget. These activity cost pools were categorized as facility-level, product-sustaining level, batch-level, or unit-level activities. In panel B of the ABC project, cost drivers were identified and pool rates were computed. The ABC analysis showed that $243,000 of overhead should be assigned to the

Exhibit 12–20
Activity-Based Costing Analysis of Outsourcing Decision: International Chocolate Company

A: Activity Cost Pools and Pool Rates

Activity Cost Pools	Budgeted Cost	Pool Rate and Cost Driver	Cost Assigned to Gift Boxes		
Facility level:					
Plant depreciation	$1,650,000	—			
Product-sustaining level:					
Product development	300,000	$600 per product spec	$600 ×	5* =	$ 3,000
Supervisory salaries	600,000	$40 per supervisory hr.	$40 ×	1,500 =	60,000
Batch level:					
Material handling	800,000	$8 per material-handling hour	$8 ×	5,000 =	40,000
Purchasing	250,000	$250 per purchase order	$250 ×	40 =	10,000
Inspection	300,000	$300 per inspection	$300 ×	20 =	6,000
Setup	400,000	$400 per setup	$400 ×	10 =	4,000
Unit level:					
Electricity	700,000	$1.40 per machine hour	$1.40 × 50,000 =		70,000
Oil and lubrication	120,000	$0.24 per machine hour	$0.24 × 50,000 =		12,000
Equipment maintenance	180,000	$0.36 per machine hour	$0.36 × 50,000 =		18,000
Machinery depreciation	200,000	$0.40 per machine hour	$0.40 × 50,000 =		20,000
Total overhead for Richmond plant	$5,500,000				
Total overhead assigned to gift box production					$243,000

*The numbers in this column are the quantities of each cost driver required for gift box production.

B: ABC Outsourcing Analysis: Gift Boxes

Relevant costs (costs that will be avoided if the gift boxes are purchased):

Direct material	$100,000
Direct labour	150,000
Overhead (from ABC analysis in panel A, above)	243,000
Total costs to be avoided by purchasing	$493,000
Total cost of purchasing (1,000,000 boxes × $0.45 per box)	$450,000

gift boxes, rather than $550,000 [$100,000 (variable) + $450,000 (fixed)] as the conventional product costing system had indicated.

Using the ABC database, Mint completed a new relevant-costing analysis of the outsourcing decision. Mint felt that all of the overhead costs assigned to the gift box operation could be avoided if the boxes were purchased. Notice that none of the facility-level costs are relevant to the analysis. They will not be avoided by purchasing the gift boxes. Mint's ABC analysis showed that a total of $493,000 of costs could be avoided by purchasing the boxes at a cost of $450,000. This would result in a net saving of $43,000.

Mint showed the ABC relevant-costing analysis to Barr. After some discussion, they agreed that various qualitative issues needed to be explored before a final decision was made. For example, would the new supplier be reliable, and would the gift boxes be of good quality? Nevertheless, Barr and Mint agreed that the ABC data cast an entirely different light on the decision.

The Key Point   What has happened here? Why did the conventional and ABC analyses of this decision reach different conclusions? Is the relevant-costing concept faulty?

The answer is no; both analyses sought to identify the relevant costs as those that would be avoided by purchasing the gift boxes. That approach is valid. The difference in the analyses lies in the superior ability of the ABC data to properly identify what the avoidable overhead costs are. This is the key point. The conventional analysis relied on a traditional volume-based product-costing system. That system lumps all of the fixed overhead costs together and assigns them using a single, unit-based cost driver (i.e., direct-labour hours). That analysis simply failed to note that many of the so-called fixed costs are *not* really fixed with respect to the appropriate cost driver. The more accurate ABC system correctly showed this fact, and identified additional costs that could be avoided by purchasing.

To summarize, under activity-based costing, the concepts underlying relevant costing analysis remain valid. However, the ABC system does enable the decision maker to apply the relevant-costing decision model more accurately.

Other Issues in Decision Making

Incentives for Decision Makers

In this chapter, we studied how managers should make decisions by focusing on the relevant costs and benefits. In previous chapters, we covered accounting procedures for evaluating managerial performance. There is an important link between *decision making* and *managerial performance evaluation*. Managers typically will make decisions that maximize their perceived performance evaluations and rewards. This is human nature. If we want managers to make optimal decisions by properly evaluating the relevant costs and benefits, then the performance evaluation system and reward structure had better be consistent with that perspective.

The proper treatment of sunk costs in decision making illustrates this issue. Earlier in this chapter, we saw that sunk costs should be ignored because they are irrelevant. For example, the book value of an outdated machine is irrelevant in making an equipment-replacement decision. Suppose, however, that a manager correctly ignores an old machine's book value and decides on early replacement of the machine he purchased a few years ago. Now suppose the hapless manager is criticized by his superior for "taking a loss" on the old machine, or for "buying a piece of junk" in the first place. What is our manager likely to do the next time he faces a similar decision? If he is like many people, he will tend to keep the old machine in order to justify his prior decision to purchase it. In so doing, he will be compounding his error. However, he also may be avoiding criticism from a superior who does not understand the importance of goal congruence.

The point is simply that if we want managers to make optimal decisions, we must give them incentives to do so. This requires that managerial performance be judged on the same factors that should be considered in making correct decisions.

Short-Run versus Long-Run Decisions

The decisions we have examined in this chapter were treated as short-run decisions. *Short-run decisions* affect only a short time period, typically a year or less. In reality, many of these decisions would have longer-term implications. For example, managers usually make a decision involving the addition or deletion of a product or service with a relatively long time frame in mind. The process of identifying relevant costs and benefits is largely the same whether the decision is viewed from a short-run or long-run perspective. One important factor that does change in a long-run analysis, however, is the *time value of money*. When several time periods are involved in a decision, the analyst should account for the fact that a $1 cash flow today is different from a $1 cash flow in five years. A dollar received today can be invested to earn interest, while the dollar received in five years cannot be invested over the intervening time period. The analysis of long-run decisions requires a tool called *capital budgeting*, which is discussed in Chapter 14, available on Connect.

Pitfalls to Avoid

Identification of the relevant costs and benefits is an important step in making any economic decision. However, analysts often overlook relevant costs or incorrectly include irrelevant data. In this section, we review four common mistakes to avoid in decision making:

1. ***Sunk costs.*** The book value of an asset, defined as its acquisition cost less the accumulated depreciation, is a sunk cost. Sunk costs cannot be changed by any current or future course of action, so they are irrelevant in decision making. Nevertheless, a common behavioural tendency is to give undue importance to book values in decisions that involve replacing an asset or disposing of obsolete inventory. People often seek to justify their past decisions by refusing to dispose of an asset, even if a better alternative has been identified. *Conclusion: Ignore sunk costs.*

2. ***Unitized fixed costs.*** For product-costing purposes, fixed costs often are divided by some activity measure and assigned to individual units of product. The result is to make a fixed cost appear variable. While there are legitimate reasons for this practice, from a *product-costing* perspective, it can create havoc in decision making. Therefore, in a decision analysis, it is usually wise to include a fixed cost in its total amount, rather than as a per-unit cost. *Conclusion: Beware of unitized fixed costs in decision making.*

3. ***Allocated fixed costs.*** It is also common to allocate fixed costs across divisions, departments, or product lines. A possible result is that a product or department may appear unprofitable when in reality it does make a contribution toward covering fixed costs and profit. Before deciding to eliminate a department, be sure to ask which costs will be *avoided* if a particular alternative is selected. A fixed cost that has been allocated to a department may continue, in total or in part, even after the department has been eliminated. *Conclusion: Beware of allocated fixed costs; identify the avoidable costs.*

4. ***Opportunity costs.*** People tend to overlook opportunity costs, or to treat such costs as less important than out-of-pocket costs. Yet opportunity costs are just as real and important to making a correct decision as are out-of-pocket costs. *Conclusion: Pay special attention to identifying and including opportunity costs in a decision analysis.*

Focus on Ethics

EFFECTS OF A DECISION TO CLOSE A DEPARTMENT AND OUTSOURCE

Outsourcing has become a common way of reducing costs in many organizations. Such decisions, though, often have repercussions that may not be captured "by the numbers." Employee morale, product quality, and vendor reliability are some of the issues that should be considered. Let's revisit the scenario described earlier at the International Chocolate Company. Recall that the plant manager, Candace Barr, was considering outsourcing the production of gift boxes for the company's fine chocolates. A conventional analysis of the decision pointed toward keeping the production operation in-house. Now let's change the scenario a bit, and consider the following conversation between Dave Mint, plant controller, and Jack Edgeworth, supervisor of the gift box production department. The conversation takes place after the two friends' weekly tennis game.

Mint: Well, you took me again, Jack. I'm starting to feel old.

Edgeworth: It was a close match, Dave. Always is. Fortunately, it looks like we'll be able to keep our matches up, too.

Mint: What do you mean?

Edgeworth: I'm talking about the outsourcing decision that is being considered. Fortunately, the analysis showed that we should keep making our own gift boxes. So my department stays in business. And I won't have to consider a transfer. My wife's very happy about that, with the twins in middle school and all.

Mint: Uh, Jack, I think there's something you need to know about.

Edgeworth: What's that?

Mint: I've been doing some preliminary studies using a technique called *activity-based costing*. I think it could improve our decision making in a lot of areas.

Edgeworth: So?

Mint: That outsourcing decision is one of the areas in which I tried out the new ABC approach. I just finished the analysis yesterday. I was going to schedule an appointment with you next week to discuss it.

Edgeworth: I'm getting queasy about where this is going, Jack. What did your analysis show?

Mint: It changes the conclusion—pretty dramatically, in fact. The ABC study shows that we'd save over $40,000 each year by outsourcing.

Edgeworth: Is that really all that much, Dave? Among friends, I mean?

Mint: It's not a trivial amount, Jack.

Edgeworth: Look, Dave, I don't think I've ever asked anything of you before. But can't you bury this one for me? Our family really doesn't need another move. And I've got people working for me who will probably lose their jobs. We've done a good job for the company. Our product is top-notch. Nobody's ever complained about a thing.

Mint: I don't see how I can withhold the analysis, Jack. Candace has a right to all the information I have.

Edgeworth: But you said you were just doing preliminary studies, Dave. Candace doesn't know anything about this one does she?

Mint: Not yet, Jack, but I've got a professional obligation to show it to her.

Edgeworth: You're opening a Pandora's box, Dave. What about employee morale if you close my department? And what about product quality, and reliability of the supply?

Mint: Those are valid issues, Jack. But they need to be addressed on their own merits, in a full and open discussion.

Edgeworth: Could you at least share this so-called ABC study with me before you show it to Candace? Maybe I'll see something you've missed.

Mint: I don't see why not, Jack. Come by my office tomorrow morning—say about 10.

Identify any ethical issues you see in this scenario. How would you resolve them? What should Mint, the controller, do?

Chapter Summary

LO1 Describe seven steps in the decision-making process and the management accountant's role in that process. The decision-making steps are (1) clarify the decision problem; (2) specify the criterion; (3) identify the alternatives; (4) develop a decision model; (5) collect the data; (6) select an alternative; and (7) evaluate decision effectiveness.

LO2 Explain the relationship between quantitative and qualitative analyses in decision making. The management accountant's key role in the decision-making process is to provide data relevant to the decision. Managers can then use these data in preparing a quantitative analysis of the decision. Qualitative factors also are considered in making the final decision.

LO3 Name and explain two criteria that must be satisfied by relevant information. In order to be relevant to a decision, a cost or benefit must (1) involve a future event and (2) involve costs or benefits that differ under the various decision alternatives.

LO4 Identify relevant costs and benefits, giving proper treatment to sunk costs, opportunity costs, and unit costs. Sunk costs, such as the book value of equipment or inventory, are not relevant to decisions. Such costs do not have any bearing on the future. Opportunity costs frequently are relevant to decisions, but they often are overlooked by decision makers. Unit costs bear particular scrutiny in decision-making situations. Fixed costs often are unitized and assigned to products or services for product-costing purposes. For decision-making purposes, however, unit costs can be misleading, since the total fixed cost will not increase as the total number of units produced increases.

LO5 Prepare analyses of various special decisions, properly identifying the relevant costs and benefits. To analyze any special decision, the proper approach is to determine all of the costs and benefits that will differ among the alternatives. Common decisions include the following: (1) accept or reject a special offer; (2) outsource a product or service; and (3) add or drop a service, product, or department.

LO6 Analyze manufacturing decisions involving joint products and limited resources. A common decision that arises in a joint-product environment is whether to sell a joint product at the split-off point or process it further. This decision should be based on the incremental costs and benefits occurring after the split-off point. A common decision involving limited resources is which of several products to produce. The correct decision is to produce the product with the highest contribution margin per unit of the scarce resource.

LO7 Explain the impact of an advanced manufacturing environment and activity-based costing on a relevant-cost analysis. The concepts underlying a relevant-cost analysis remain valid in an advanced manufacturing environment and in situations where activity-based costing is used. However, an ABC system typically enables a decision maker to estimate the relevant costs in a decision problem more accurately.

Review Problem on Relevant Costs

Lansing Camera Company has received a special order for photographic equipment it does not normally produce. The company has excess capacity, and the order could be manufactured without reducing production of the firm's regular products. Discuss the relevance of each of the following items in computing the cost of the special order.

1. Equipment to be used in producing the order has a book value of $2,000. The equipment has no other use for Lansing Camera Company. If the order is not accepted, the equipment will be sold for $1,500. If the equipment is used in producing the order, it can be sold in three months for $800.

2. If the special order is accepted, the operation will require some of the storage space in the company's plant. If the space is used for this purpose, the company will rent storage space temporarily in a nearby warehouse at a cost of $18,000. The building depreciation allocated to the storage space to be used in producing the special order is $12,000.

3. If the special order is accepted, it will require a subassembly. Lansing Camera can purchase the subassembly for $24 per unit from an outside supplier or make it for $30 per unit. The $30 cost per unit was determined as follows:

Direct material	$10
Direct labour	6
Variable overhead	6
Allocated fixed overhead	8
Total unit cost of subassembly	$30

Should Lansing Camera purchase or make the subassembly?

Solution to Review Problem

1. The book value of the equipment is a sunk cost, irrelevant to the decision. The relevant cost of the equipment is $700, determined as follows:

Sales value of equipment now	$1,500
Sales value after producing special order	800
Differential cost	$ 700

2. The $12,000 portion of building depreciation allocated to the storage space to be used for the special order is irrelevant. First, it is a sunk cost. Second, any costs relating to the company's factory building will continue whether the special order is accepted or not. The relevant cost is the $18,000 rent that will be incurred only if the special order is accepted.

3. Lansing Camera should make the subassembly. The subassembly's relevant cost is $22 per unit.

Relevant Cost of Making Subassembly (per unit)		Relevant Cost of Purchasing Subassembly (per unit)	
Direct material	$10	Purchase price	$24
Direct labour	6		
Variable overhead	6		
Total	$22		

Notice that the unitized fixed overhead, $8, is not a relevant cost of the subassembly. Lansing Camera Company's *total* fixed cost will not change, whether the special order is accepted or not.

Glossary

Review key terms and definitions on Connect.

Review Questions

12–1. List the seven steps in the decision-making process.

12–2. Describe the management accountant's role in the decision-making process.

12–3. Distinguish between qualitative and quantitative decision analyses.

12–4. Explain what is meant by the term *decision model*.

12–5. A quantitative analysis enables a decision maker to put a "price" on the sum total of the qualitative characteristics in a decision situation. Explain this statement, and give an example.

12–6. What is meant by each of the following potential characteristics of information: relevant, accurate, and timely? Is objective information always relevant? Accurate?

12–7. Name and explain two important criteria that must be satisfied in order for information to be relevant.

12–8. Explain why the book value of equipment is not a relevant cost.

12–9. Is the book value of inventory on hand a relevant cost? Why or why not?

12–10. Why might a manager exhibit a behavioural tendency to inappropriately consider sunk costs in making a decision?

12–11. Give an example of an irrelevant future cost. Why is it irrelevant?

12–12. Define the term *opportunity cost*, and give an example of one.

12–13. What behavioural tendency do people often exhibit with regard to opportunity costs?

12–14. How does the existence of excess production capacity affect the decision to accept or reject a special order?

12–15. What is meant by the term *differential cost analysis*?

12–16. Briefly describe the proper approach for making a decision about adding or dropping a product line.

12–17. What is a *joint production process*? Describe a special decision that commonly arises in the context of a joint production process. Briefly describe the proper approach for making this type of decision.

12–18. Are allocated joint processing costs relevant when making a decision to sell a joint product at the split-off point or process it further? Why or why not?

12–19. Briefly describe the proper approach to making a production decision when limited resources are involved.

12–20. What is meant by the term *contribution margin per unit of scarce resource?*

12–21. How is sensitivity analysis used to cope with uncertainty in decision making?

12–22. Explain the important link between decision making and managerial performance evaluation.

12–23. List four potential pitfalls in decision making that represent common errors.

12–24. Why can unitized fixed costs cause errors in decision making?

12–25. Give two examples of sunk costs and explain why they are irrelevant in decision making.

12–26. "Accounting systems should produce only relevant data and forget about the irrelevant data. Then I'd know what was relevant and what wasn't!" Comment on this remark by a company president.

12–27. Are the concepts underlying a relevant-cost analysis still valid in an advanced manufacturing environment? Are these concepts valid when activity-based costing is used? Explain.

12–28. List five ways in which management can seek to relax a constraint by expanding the capacity of a bottleneck operation.

Exercises

Exercise 12–29 Steps in the Decision-Making Process (LO1)

Choose an organization and a particular decision situation. Then give examples, using that decision context, of each step illustrated in Exhibit 12–1. For example, you might choose a decision that would be made by a retailer, such as Best Buy or Chapters. Or you might focus on a service provider, such as Hertz car rentals or Marriott Hotels. Alternatively, select a manufacturer, such as Nike or Nokia. Or consider a decision to be made by your school or home city or town.

Exercise 12–30 Irrelevant Future Costs and Benefits (LO4)

Required: Redo Exhibit 12–4 without the irrelevant data.

Exercise 12–31 Machine Replacement (LO4, 5)

Valley Pizza's owner bought his current pizza oven two years ago for $9,000, and it has one more year of life remaining. He is using straight-line depreciation for the oven. He could purchase a new oven for $1,900, but it would last only one year. The owner figures the new oven would save him $2,600 in annual operating expenses compared to operating the old one. Consequently, he has decided against buying the new oven, since doing so would result in a "loss" of $400 over the next year.

Required:

1. How do you suppose the owner came up with $400 as the loss for the next year if the new pizza oven was purchased? Explain.
2. Criticize the owner's analysis and decision.
3. Prepare a correct decision analysis for the owner.

Exercise 12–32 Joint Products (LO4, 6)

Lamont Industries produces chemicals for the swimming pool industry. In one joint process, 10,000 litres of GSX are processed into 7,000 litres of xenolite and 3,000 litres of banolide. The cost of the joint process, including the GSX, is $19,000. The firm allocates $13,300 of the joint cost to the xenolite and $5,700 of the cost to the banolide. The 3,000 litres of banolide can be sold at the split-off point for $2,500, or can be processed further into a product called *kitrocide*. The sales value of 3,000 litres of kitrocide is $10,000, and the additional processing cost is $8,100.

Required: Lamont's president has asked your consulting firm to make a recommendation as to whether the banolide should be sold at the split-off point or processed further. Write a letter providing an analysis and a recommendation.

Exercise 12–33 Drop Product Line (LO4, 5)

Day Street Deli's owner is disturbed by the poor profit performance of his ice cream counter. He has prepared the following profit analysis for the year just ended:

Sales	$45,000
Less: Cost of food	20,000
Gross profit	25,000
Less: Operating expenses:	
Wages of counter personnel $12,000	
Paper products (e.g., napkins) 4,000	
Utilities (allocated) 2,900	
Depreciation of counter equipment and furnishings 2,500	
Depreciation of building (allocated) 4,000	
Deli manager's salary (allocated) 3,000	
Total	28,400
Loss on ice cream counter	$ (3,400)

Required: Criticize and correct the owner's analysis.

Exercise 12–34 Outsourcing Decision; Use of the Internet (LO1, 2, 5)

Visit the website of one of the following companies, or a different company of your choice:

Tim Hortons	www.timhortons.com
Compaq	www.compaq.com
Corning	www.corning.com
Hudson's Bay Company	www.hbc.com
Kodak	www.kodak.com
CBC	www.cbc.ca

Required: Read about the company's activities and operations. Choose an activity that is necessary for the company's operations and then discuss the pros and cons of outsourcing that activity.

Exercise 12–35 Obsolete Inventory (LO4, 5)

Armstrong Corporation manufactures bicycle parts. The company currently has a $21,000 inventory of parts that have become obsolete due to changes in design specifications. The parts could be sold for $9,000, or modified for $12,000 and sold for $22,300.

Required:

1. Which of the data above are relevant to the decision about the obsolete parts?
2. Prepare a decision analysis.

Exercise 12–36 Special Order (LO4, 5)

Intercontinental Chemical Company, located in Buenos Aires, Argentina, recently received an order for a product it does not normally produce. Since the company has excess production capacity, management is considering accepting the order. In analyzing the decision, the assistant controller is compiling the relevant costs of producing the order. Production of the special order would require 8,000 kilograms of theolite. Intercontinental does not use theolite for its regular product, but the firm has 8,000 kilograms of the chemical on hand from the days when it used theolite regularly. The theolite could be sold to a chemical wholesaler for 14,500 p. (*p* denotes the peso, Argentina's national monetary unit.) The book value of the theolite is 2 p per kilogram. Intercontinental could buy theolite for 2.40 p per kilogram. (Many countries use the peso as their unit of currency. On the day this exercise was written, Argentina's peso was worth CDN$0.3274.)

Required:

1. What is the relevant cost of theolite for the purpose of analyzing the special-order decision? (Remember to express your answer in terms of Argentina's peso.)
2. Discuss each of the numbers given in the exercise with regard to its relevance in making the decision.

Exercise 12–37 Continuation of Preceding Exercise (LO4, 5)

Intercontinental's special order also requires 1,000 kilograms of genatope, a solid chemical regularly used in the company's products. The current stock of genatope is 8,000 kilograms at a book value of 8.10 p per kilogram. If the special order is accepted, the firm will be forced to restock genatope earlier than expected, at a predicted cost of 8.70 p per kilogram. Without the special order, the purchasing manager predicts that the price will be 8.30 p when normal restocking takes place. Any order of genatope must be in the amount of 5,000 kilograms.

Required:

1. What is the relevant cost of genatope?
2. Discuss each of the figures in the exercise in terms of its relevance to the decision.

(CMA, adapted)

Exercise 12–38   Closing a Department (LO4, 5)

Fusion Metals Company is considering the elimination of its Packaging Department. Management has received an offer from an outside firm to supply all of Fusion's packaging needs. To help her in making the decision, Fusion's president has asked the controller for an analysis of the cost of running Fusion's Packaging Department. Included in that analysis is $9,100 of rent, which represents the Packaging Department's allocation of the rent on Fusion's factory building. If the Packaging Department is eliminated, the space it used will be converted into storage space. Currently, Fusion rents storage space in a nearby warehouse for $11,000 per year. The warehouse rental would no longer be necessary if the Packaging Department was eliminated.

Required:

1. Discuss each of the figures given in the exercise with regard to its relevance in the department-closing decision.
2. What type of cost is the $11,000 warehouse rental from the viewpoint of the Packaging Department's costs?

Exercise 12–39   Continuation of Preceding Exercise (LO4, 5)

If Fusion Metals Company closes its Packaging Department, the department manager will be appointed manager of the Cutting Department with a similar salary. The Packaging Department manager makes $45,000 per year. To hire a new Cutting Department manager will cost Fusion $60,000 per year.

Required: Discuss the relevance of each of these salary figures to the department-closing decision.

Exercise 12–40   Joint Products; Relevant Costs; Cost–Volume–Profit Analysis (LO4, 6)

Zytel Corporation produces cleaning compounds and solutions for industrial and household use. While most of its products are processed independently, a few are related. Grit 337, a coarse cleaning powder with many industrial uses, costs $1.60 a kilogram to make and sells for $2 a kilogram. A small portion of the annual production of this product is retained for further processing in the Mixing Department, where it is combined with several other ingredients to form a paste that is marketed as a silver polish selling for $4 per jar. This further processing requires ¼ kilogram of Grit 337 per jar. Costs of other ingredients, labour, and variable overhead associated with this further processing amount to $2.50 per jar. Variable selling costs are $0.30 per jar. If the decision was made to cease production of the silver polish, $5,600 of Mixing Department fixed costs could be avoided. Zytel has limited production capacity for Grit 337, but unlimited demand for the cleaning powder.

Required: Calculate the minimum number of jars of silver polish that would have to be sold to justify further processing of Grit 337.

Exercise 12–41   Limited Resource (LO6)

Duo Company manufactures two products, Uno and Dos. Contribution-margin data follow.

	Uno	Dos
Unit sales price	$13.00	$31.00
Less variable cost:		
Direct material	7.00	5.00
Direct labour	1.00	6.00
Variable overhead	1.25	7.50
Variable selling and administrative cost	0.75	0.50
Total variable cost	10.00	19.00
Unit contribution margin	$ 3.00	$12.00

Duo Company's production process uses highly skilled labour, which is in short supply. The same employees work on both products and earn the same wage rate.

Required: Which of Duo Company's products is most profitable? Explain.

Problems

Problem 12–42 Production Decisions; Limited Capacity (LO5, 6)

Kitchen Magician, Inc. has assembled the following data pertaining to its two most popular products:

	Blender	Electric Mixer
Direct material	$6	$11
Direct labour	4	9
Manufacturing overhead @ $48 per machine hour	16	32
Cost if purchased from an outside supplier	20	38
Annual demand (units)	20,000	28,000

Past experience has shown that the fixed manufacturing overhead component included in the cost per machine hour averages $10. Kitchen Magician's management has a policy of filling all sales orders, even if it means purchasing units from outside suppliers.

Required:

1. If 50,000 machine hours are available, and management wants to follow an optimal strategy, how many units of each product should the firm manufacture? How many units of each product should be purchased?

2. With all other things constant, if management is able to reduce the direct material for an electric mixer to $6 per unit, how many units of each product should be manufactured? Purchased?

3. *Build a spreadsheet:* Construct an Excel spreadsheet to solve requirement (1) above. Show how the solution will change if the following information changes: The unit cost if purchased from an outside supplier is $22 for the blender and $40 for the electric mixer.

(CMA, adapted)

Problem 12–43 Special Order; Financial and Production Considerations (LO4, 5)

1. Net contribution margin to profit: $34,050

Jupiter Corporation manufactures skateboards. Several weeks ago, the firm received a special-order inquiry from Venus, Inc. Venus desires to market a skateboard similar to one of Jupiter's and has offered to purchase 11,000 units if the order can be completed in three months. The cost data for Jupiter's Model No. 43 skateboard follow.

Direct material	$ 8.20
Direct labour: 0.25 hr. @ $9	2.25
Total manufacturing overhead:	
0.5 hr. @ $20	10.00
Total	$20.45

Additional data:

* The normal selling price of the Model No. 43 is $26.50; however, Venus has offered Jupiter only $15.75 because of the large quantity it is willing to purchase.

* Venus requires a modification of the design that will allow a $2.10 reduction in direct-material cost.

* Jupiter's production supervisor notes that the company will incur $3,700 in additional setup costs and will have to purchase a $2,400 special device to manufacture these units. The device will be discarded once the special order is completed.

* Total manufacturing overhead costs are applied to production at the rate of $20 per machine hour. This figure is based, in part, on budgeted yearly fixed overhead of $750,000 and planned production activity of 60,000 machine hours (5,000 per month).

* Jupiter will allocate $1,800 of existing fixed administrative costs to the order as "part of the cost of doing business."

Required:

1. Assume that present sales will not be affected. Should the order be accepted from a financial point of view (i.e., is it profitable)? Why or why not? Show calculations.

2. Assume that Jupiter's current production activity consumes 70 percent of planned machine-hour activity. Can the company accept the order and meet Venus' deadline?

3. What options might Jupiter consider if management truly wanted to do business with Venus in hopes of building a long-term relationship with the firm?

Problem 12–44 Introducing a New Product (L04, 5)

1. Unit contribution margin, Enhanced Model: $200

Johnson, Inc. is a small firm involved in the production and sale of electronic business products. The company is well known for its attention to quality and innovation.

During the past 15 months, a new product has been under development that allows users hand-held access to e-mail and video images. Johnson code-named the product the Wireless Wizard and has been quietly designing two models: Basic and Enhanced. Development costs have amounted to $121,000 and $175,000, respectively. The total market demand for each model is expected to be 40,000 units, and management anticipates being able to obtain the following market shares: Basic, 25 percent; Enhanced, 20 percent. Forecasted data follow.

	Basic	Enhanced
Projected selling price	$ 250	$ 330
Per-unit production costs:		
Direct material	28	45
Direct labour	15	20
Variable overhead	24	32
Marketing and advertising	130,000	200,000
Sales salaries	57,000	57,000
Sales commissions*	10%	10%

*Computed on the basis of sales dollars.

Since the start of development work on the Wireless Wizard, advances in technology have altered the market somewhat, and management now believes that the company can introduce only one of the two models. Consultants confirmed this fact not too long ago, with Johnson paying $23,000 for an in-depth market study. The total fixed overhead is expected to be the same, regardless of which product is manufactured.

Required:

1. Compute the per-unit contribution margin for both models.
2. Which of the data in the table above should be ignored in making the product-introduction decision? For what reason?
3. Prepare a financial analysis and determine which of the two models should be introduced.
4. What other factors should Johnson, Inc. consider before a final decision is made?

Problem 12–45 Closing an Unprofitable Department (L05, 6)

1. Income (loss) from closure: $(12,800)

Tipton One-Stop Decorating sells paint and paint supplies, carpet, and wallpaper at a single store location in suburban Moncton. Although the company has been very profitable over the years, management has seen a significant decline in wallpaper sales and earnings. Much of this decline is attributable to the Internet and to companies that advertise deeply discounted prices in magazines and offer customers free shipping and toll-free telephone numbers. Recent figures follow.

	Paint and Supplies	Carpeting	Wallpaper
Sales	$380,000	$460,000	$140,000
Variable costs	228,000	322,000	112,000
Fixed costs	56,000	75,000	45,000
Total costs	284,000	397,000	157,000
Operating income (loss)	$ 96,000	$ 63,000	$ (17,000)

Management is studying whether to drop wallpaper because of the changing market and accompanying loss. If the line is dropped, the following changes are expected to occur:

- The vacated space will be remodelled at a cost of $12,400 and will be devoted to an expanded line of high-end carpet. Sales of carpet are expected to increase by $120,000, and the line's overall contribution margin ratio will rise by five percentage points.
- Tipton can cut wallpaper's fixed costs by 40 percent. Remaining fixed costs will continue to be incurred.
- Customers who purchased wallpaper often bought paint and paint supplies. Sales of paint and paint supplies are expected to fall by 20 percent.
- The firm will increase advertising expenditures by $25,000 to promote the expanded carpet line.

Required:

1. Should Tipton close its wallpaper operation? Show computations to support your answer.

2. Assume that Tipton's wallpaper inventory at the time of the closure decision amounted to $23,700. How would you have treated this additional information in making the decision?

3. What advantages might Internet and magazine-based firms have over Tipton that would allow these organizations to offer deeply discounted prices—prices far below what Tipton can offer?

4. *Build a spreadsheet:* Construct an Excel spreadsheet to solve requirement (1) above. Show how the solution will change if the following information changes: Sales were $400,000, $450,000, and $130,000, for paint and supplies, carpeting, and wallpaper, respectively.

Problem 12–46   Excess Production Capacity (LO5, 6)

2. Contribution margin per direct-labour hour, Deluxe Model: $12

Carpenter's Mate, Inc. manufactures electric carpentry tools. The Production Department has met all production requirements for the current month and has an opportunity to produce additional units of product with its excess capacity. Unit selling prices and unit costs for three different drill models are as follows:

	Basic Model	Deluxe Model	Pro Model
Selling price	$58	$65	$80
Direct material	16	20	19
Direct labour ($10 per hour)	10	15	20
Variable overhead	8	12	16
Fixed overhead	16	5	15

Variable overhead is applied on the basis of direct-labour dollars, while fixed overhead is applied on the basis of machine hours. There is sufficient demand for the additional production of any model in the product line.

Required:

1. If the company has excess machine capacity and can add more labour as needed (i.e., neither machine capacity nor labour is a constraint), the excess production capacity should be devoted to producing which product? (Assume that the excess capacity will be used for a single product line.)

2. If the company has excess machine capacity but a limited amount of labour time, the excess production capacity should be devoted to producing which product or products?

(CMA, adapted)

Problem 12–47   Make or Buy (LO4, 5)

Casting Technology Resources (CTR) has purchased 10,000 pumps annually from Kobec, Inc. Because the price keeps increasing and reached $68 per unit last year, CTR's management has asked for an estimate of the cost of manufacturing the pump in CTR's facilities. CTR makes stampings and castings and has little experience with products requiring assembly.

The engineering, manufacturing, and accounting departments have prepared a report for management that includes the following estimate for an assembly run of 10,000 pumps. Additional production employees would be hired to manufacture the pumps but no additional equipment, space, or supervision would be needed.

The report states that total costs for 10,000 units are estimated at $957,000, or $95.70 per unit. The current purchase price is $68 per unit, so the report recommends continued purchase of the product.

Components (outside purchases)	$120,000
Assembly labour*	300,000
Manufacturing overhead†	450,000
General and administrative overhead‡	87,000
Total costs	$957,000

*Assembly labour consists of hourly production workers.

†Manufacturing overhead is applied to products on a direct-labour-dollar basis. Variable-overhead costs vary closely with direct-labour dollars.

Fixed overhead	50% of direct-labour dollars
Variable overhead	100% of direct-labour dollars
Manufacturing-overhead rate	150% of direct-labour dollars

‡General and administrative overhead is applied at 10 percent of the total cost of material (or components), assembly labour, and manufacturing overhead.

Required: Was the analysis prepared by Casting Technology Resources' engineering, manufacturing, and accounting departments and their recommendation to continue purchasing the pumps correct? Explain your answer and include any supporting calculations you consider necessary.

(CMA, adapted)

Problem 12–48 Outsourcing Decision; Relevant Costs; Ethics **(LO3, 4, 5)**

Total cost to make: $575,040

The Western Division of the Paibec Corporation manufactures subassemblies that are used in the corporation's final products. Lynn Hardt of Western's Profit Planning Department has been assigned the task of determining whether a component, MTR-2000, should continue to be manufactured by the Western Division or purchased from Marley Company, an outside supplier. JY-65 is part of a subassembly manufactured by the Western Division.

Marley has submitted a bid to manufacture and supply the 32,000 units of MTR-2000 that Paibec will need for 20x1 at a unit price of $17.30. Marley has assured Paibec that the units will be delivered according to Paibec's production specifications and needs. While the contract price of $17.30 is applicable only in 20x1, Marley is interested in entering into a long-term arrangement beyond 20x1.

Hardt has gathered the following information regarding Western's cost to manufacture MTR-2000 in 20x0. These annual costs will be incurred to manufacture 30,000 units.

Direct material	$ 195,000
Direct labour	120,000
Factory space rental	84,000
Equipment leasing costs	36,000
Other manufacturing overhead	225,000
Total manufacturing costs	$ 660,000

Hardt has collected the following additional information related to manufacturing MTR-2000.

- Direct materials used in the production of MTR-2000 are expected to increase 8 percent in 20x1.

- Western's direct-labour contract calls for a 5 percent increase in 20x1.

- The facilities used to manufacture MTR-2000 are rented under a month-to-month rental agreement, so Western can withdraw from the rental agreement without any penalty. Western will have no need for this space if MTR-2000 is not manufactured.

- Equipment leasing costs represent special equipment that is used in the manufacture of MTR-2000. This lease can be terminated by paying the equivalent of one month's lease payment for each year left on the lease agreement. Western has two years left on the lease agreement, through the end of the year 20x2.

- Forty percent of the other manufacturing overhead is considered variable. Variable overhead changes with the number of units produced, and this rate per unit is not expected to change in 20x1. The fixed manufacturing overhead costs are not expected to change regardless of whether JY–65 is manufactured. Equipment other than the leased equipment can be used in Western's other manufacturing operations.

John Porter, divisional manager of Western stopped by Hardt's office to voice his concern regarding the outsourcing of MTR-2000. Porter commented, "I am really concerned about outsourcing MTR-2000. I have a son-in-law and a nephew, not to mention a member of our bowling team, who work on MTR-2000. They could lose their jobs if we buy that component from Marley. I really would appreciate anything you can do to make sure the cost analysis comes out right to show we should continue making MTR-2000. Corporate is not aware of the material increases and maybe you can leave out some of those fixed costs. I just think we should continue making MTR-2000!"

Required:

1. *a.* Prepare an analysis of relevant costs that shows whether the Western Division of Paibec Corporation should make MTR-2000 or purchase it from Marley Company for 20x1.

   b. Based solely on the financial results, recommend whether the 32,000 units of MTR-2000 for 20x1 should be made by Western or purchased from Marley.

2. Identify and briefly discuss three qualitative factors that the Western Division and Paibec Corporation should consider before agreeing to purchase MTR-2000 from Marley Company.

3. By referring to the standards of ethical conduct for management accountants given in Chapter 1, explain why Lynn Hardt would consider the request of John Porter to be unethical.

(CMA, adapted)

Problem 12–49 Joint Products: Sell or Process Further (LO6)

Connect Chemical Company is a diversified chemical processing company. The firm manufactures swimming pool chemicals, chemicals for metal processing, specialized chemical compounds, and pesticides.

Currently, the Norwood plant is producing two derivatives, RNA-1 and RNA-2, from the chemical compound VDB developed by the company's research labs. Each week, 1,200,000 kilograms of VDB are processed at a cost of $246,000 into 800,000 kilograms of RNA-1 and 400,000 kilograms of RNA-2. The proportion of these two outputs cannot be altered, because this is a joint process. RNA-1 has no market value until it is converted into a pesticide with the trade name Fastkil. Processing RNA-1 into Fastkil costs $240,000. Fastkil wholesales at $50 per 100 kilograms.

RNA-2 is sold as is for $80 per hundred kilograms. However, management has discovered that RNA-2 can be converted into two new products by adding 400,000 kilograms of compound LST to the 400,000 kilograms of RNA-2. This joint process would yield 400,000 kilograms each of DMZ-3 and Pestrol, the two new products. The additional direct-material and related processing costs of this joint process would be $120,000. DMZ-3 and Pestrol would each be sold for $57.50 per 100 kilograms. The company's management has decided not to process RNA-2 further based on the analysis presented in the following schedule.

	Sell as Is	Process Further		
	RNA–2	**DMZ–3**	**Pestrol**	**Total**
Production in kilograms	400,000	400,000	400,000	
Revenue	$320,000	$230,000	$230,000	$460,000
Costs:				
VDB costs	82,000*	61,500	61,500	123,000†
Additional direct materials (LST) and processing of RNA-2	—	60,000	60,000	120,000
Total costs	82,000	121,500	121,500	243,000
Weekly gross profit	$238,000	$108,500	$108,500	$217,000

*$82,000 is one-third of the $246,000 cost of processing VDB. When RNA-2 is not processed further, one-third of the final output is RNA-2 (400,000 out of a total of 1,200,000 kilograms).

†$123,000 is one-half of the $246,000 cost of processing VDB. When RNA-2 is processed further, one-half of the final output consists of DMZ-3 and Pestrol. The final products then are: 800,000 kilograms of RNA-1; 400,000 kilograms of DMZ-3; and 400,000 kilograms of Pestrol.

Required: Evaluate Connect Chemical Company's analysis, and make any revisions that are necessary. Your critique and analysis should indicate

a. Whether management made the correct decision

b. The gross savings or loss per week resulting from the decision not to process RNA-2 further, if different from management's analysis

(CMA, adapted)

Problem 12–50 Add a Product Line (LO4, 5)

Montreal Fashions, Inc., a high-fashion dress manufacturer, is planning to market a new cocktail dress for the coming season. Montreal Fashions supplies retailers in Quebec and Ontario.

Four metres of material are required to lay out the dress pattern. Some material remains after cutting, which can be sold as remnants. The leftover material also could be used to manufacture a matching handbag and a cape. However, if the leftover material is to be used for the cape and handbag, more care will be required in the cutting operation, which will increase the cutting costs.

The company expects to sell 1,250 dresses. Market research reveals that dress sales will be 20 percent higher if a matching cape and handbag are available. The market research indicates that the cape and handbag will be saleable only as accessories with the dress. The combinations of dresses, capes, and handbags expected to be sold by retailers are as follows:

	Percentage of Total
Complete sets of dress, cape, and handbag	70%
Dress and cape	6
Dress and handbag	15
Dress only	9
Total	100%

The material used in the dress costs $12.50 a metre, or $50 for each dress. The cost of cutting the dress if the cape and handbag are not manufactured is estimated at $20 a dress, and the resulting remnants can be sold for $5 per dress. If the cape and handbag are manufactured, the cutting costs will be increased by $9 per dress and there will be no saleable remnants. The selling prices and the costs to complete the three items once they are cut are as follows:

	Selling Price per Unit	Unit Cost to Complete (excludes costs of material and cutting operation)
Dress	$200.00	$80.00
Cape	27.50	19.50
Handbag	9.50	6.50

Required:

1. Calculate Montreal Fashions' incremental profit or loss from manufacturing the capes and handbags in conjunction with the dresses.
2. Identify any qualitative factors that could influence the company's management in its decision to manufacture capes and handbags to match the dresses.

(CMA, adapted)

Problem 12–51 Outsourcing Decision (LO4, 5)

Island Mechanical, Inc. has been producing two bearings, components T79 and B81, for use in production. Data regarding these two components follow.

1. Total variable cost per unit: $10.50
2. Quantity of component B81 to be purchased: 4,000 units

	T79	B81
Machine hours required per unit	2.5	3.0
Standard cost per unit:		
Direct material	$ 2.25	$ 3.75
Direct labour	4.00	4.50
Manufacturing overhead		
Variable*	2.00	2.25
Fixed†	3.75	4.50
Total	$12.00	$15.00

*Variable manufacturing overhead is applied on the basis of direct-labour hours.
†Fixed manufacturing overhead is applied on the basis of machine hours.

Island Mechanical's annual requirement for these components is 8,000 units of T79 and 11,000 units of B81. Recently, management decided to devote additional machine time to other product lines, leaving only 41,000 machine hours per year for producing the bearings. An outside company has offered to sell Island Mechanical its annual supply of bearings at prices of $11.25 for T79 and $13.50 for B81. Management wants to schedule the otherwise idle 41,000 machine hours to produce bearings so that the firm can minimize costs (maximize net benefits).

Required:

1. Compute the net benefit (loss) per machine hour that would result if Island Mechanical accepts the supplier's offer of $13.50 per unit for component B81.
2. Choose the correct answer. Island Mechanical will maximize its net benefits by
   a. Purchasing 4,800 units of T79 and manufacturing the remaining bearings
   b. Purchasing 8,000 units of T79 and manufacturing 11,000 units of B81
   c. Purchasing 11,000 units of B81 and manufacturing 8,000 units of T79
   d. Purchasing 4,000 units of B81 and manufacturing the remaining bearings
   e. Purchasing and manufacturing some amounts other than those given above
3. Suppose management has decided to drop component T79. Independently of requirements (1) and (2), assume that the company's idle capacity of 41,000 machine hours has a traceable, avoidable annual fixed cost of $44,000, which will be incurred only if the capacity is used. Calculate the maximum price Island Mechanical should pay a supplier for component B81.

(CMA, adapted)

Problem 12–52 Outsource a Component; Relevant Costs, Opportunity Costs, and Quality Control (LO4, 5)

Chenango Industries uses 10 units of Part JR63 every month in the production of dentistry equipment. The cost of manufacturing one unit of JR63 is as follows:

Direct material..	$ 1,000
Material handling (20% of direct-material cost)..	200
Direct labour...	8,000
Manufacturing overhead (150% of direct labour)	12,000
Total manufacturing cost..	$21,200

Material handling represents the direct variable costs of the Receiving Department that are applied to direct materials and purchased components on the basis of their cost. This is a separate charge in addition to manufacturing overhead. Chenango's annual manufacturing overhead budget is one-third variable and two-thirds fixed. Scott Supply, one of Chenango's reliable vendors, has offered to supply Part JR63 at a unit price of $15,000.

Required:

1. If Chenango purchases the JR63 units from Scott, the capacity Chenango used to manufacture these parts would be idle. If Chenango decides to purchase the parts from Scott, the unit cost of JR63 would increase (or decrease) by what amount?

2. Assume Chenango is able to rent out all of its idle capacity for $25,000 per month. If Chenango decides to purchase the 10 units from Scott Supply, Chenango's monthly cost for JR63 would increase (or decrease) by what amount?

3. Assume that Chenango does not want to commit to a rental agreement but could use its idle capacity to manufacture another product that would contribute $52,000 per month. If Chenango's management elects to manufacture JR63 in order to maintain quality control, what is the net amount of Chenango's cost from using the space to manufacture Part JR63?

(CMA, adapted)

Problem 12–53 Analysis of Special Order (LO3, 4, 5)

Excalibur, Inc. received an order for a piece of special machinery from Rex Company. Just as Excalibur completed the machine, Rex Company declared bankruptcy, defaulted on the order, and forfeited the 10 percent deposit paid on the selling price of $72,500.

Excalibur's manufacturing manager identified the costs already incurred in the production of the special machinery for Rex Company as follows:

Direct material		$16,600
Direct labour		21,400
Manufacturing overhead applied:		
Variable	$10,700	
Fixed	5,350	16,050
Fixed selling and administrative costs		5,405
Total		$59,455

Another company, Kaytell Corporation, will buy the special machinery if it is reworked to Kaytell's specifications. Excalibur, Inc. offered to sell the reworked machinery to Kaytell as a special order for $68,400. Kaytell agreed to pay the price when it takes delivery in two months. The additional identifiable costs to rework the machinery to Kaytell's specifications are as follows:

Direct materials	$ 6,200
Direct labour...	4,200
Total	$10,400

A second alternative available to Excalibur's management is to convert the special machinery into the standard model, which sells for $62,500. The additional identifiable costs for this conversion are as follows:

Direct materials..	$2,850
Direct labour..	3,300
Total	$6,150

A third alternative for Excalibur, Inc. is to sell the machine as is for a price of $52,000. However, the potential buyer of the unmodified machine does not want it for 60 days. This buyer has offered a $7,000 down payment, with the remainder due on delivery.

The following additional information is available regarding Excalibur's operations:

- The sales commission rate on sales of standard models is 2 percent, while the rate on special orders is 3 percent.
- Normal credit terms for sales of standard models are 2/10, net/30. This means that a customer receives a 2 percent discount if payment is made within 10 days, and payment is due no later than 30 days after billing. Most customers take the 2 percent discount. Credit terms for a special order are negotiated with the customer.
- The allocation rates for manufacturing overhead and fixed selling and administrative costs are as follows:

Manufacturing costs:

Variable	50% of direct-labour cost
Fixed	25% of direct-labour cost
Fixed selling and administrative costs	10% of the total of direct-material, direct-labour, and manufacturing-overhead costs

- Normal time required for rework is one month.

Required:

1. Determine the dollar contribution each of the three alternatives will add to Excalibur's before-tax profit.
2. If Kaytell makes Excalibur a counteroffer, what is the lowest price Exacalibur should accept for the reworked machinery from Kaytell? Explain your answer.
3. Discuss the influence that the fixed manufacturing-overhead cost should have on the sales price quoted by Excalibur, Inc. for special orders.

(CMA, adapted)

Problem 12–54 Special Order; Ethics **(LO3, 5)**

Winner's Circle, Inc. manufactures medals for winners of athletic events and other contests. Its manufacturing plant has the capacity to produce 10,000 medals each month. Current monthly production is 7,500 medals. The company normally charges $175 per medal. Variable costs and fixed costs for the current activity level of 75 percent of capacity are as follows:

2. Accepting the special order will result in a total additional contribution margin of $37,500.

Production Costs (at 75% of capacity)

Variable costs:		
Manufacturing:		
Direct labour	$ 375,000	
Direct material	262,500	
Marketing	187,500	
Total variable costs	825,000	
Fixed costs:		
Manufacturing	275,000	
Marketing	175,000	
Total fixed costs	450,000	
Total costs	$1,275,000	
Variable cost per unit	$ 110	
Fixed cost per unit	60	
Average unit cost	$ 170	

Winner's Circle has just received a special one-time order for 2,500 medals at $100 per medal. For this particular order, no variable marketing costs will be incurred. Cathy Donato, a management accountant with Winner's Circle, has been assigned the task of analyzing this order and recommending whether the company should accept or reject it. After examining the costs, Donato suggested to her supervisor, Gerard LePenn, who is the controller, that they request competitive bids from vendors for the raw material, as the current quote seems high. LePenn insisted that the prices are in line with those of other vendors, and told her that she was not to discuss her observations with anyone else. Donato later discovered that LePenn is a brother-in-law of the owner of the current raw-material supply vendor.

Required:

1. Identify and explain the costs that will be relevant to Cathy Donato's analysis of the special order being considered by Winner's Circle, Inc.
2. Determine if Winner's Circle should accept the special order. In explaining your answer, compute both the new average unit cost and the incremental unit cost for the special order.
3. Discuss any other considerations that Donato should include in her analysis of the special order.
4. What steps might Donato take to resolve the ethical conflict arising out of the controller's insistence that the company avoid competitive bidding?
5. *Build a spreadsheet:* Construct an Excel spreadsheet to solve requirements (1) and (2) above. Show how the solution will change if the sales price is $170 per medal.

(CMA, adapted)

---

2. Contribution margin, Product M07: $93

2. Total contribution margin: $113,250

Problem 12–55 Production Planning (LO5, 6)

Ozark Industries manufactures and sells three products, which are manufactured in a factory with four departments. Both labour and machine time are applied to the products as they pass through each department. The machines and labour skills required in each department are so specialized that neither machines nor labour can be switched from one department to another.

Ozark Industries' management is planning its production schedule for the next few months. The planning is complicated, because there are labour shortages in the community and some machines will be down for several months for repairs.

Management has assembled the following information regarding available machine and labour time by department and the machine hours and direct-labour hours required per unit of product. These data should be valid for the next six months.

	Department			
Monthly Capacity Availability	**1**	**2**	**3**	**4**
Normal machine capacity in machine hours	3,500	3,500	3,000	3,500
Capacity of machines being repaired in machine hours	(500)	(400)	(300)	(200)
Available machine capacity in machine hours	3,000	3,100	2,700	3,300
Available labour in direct-labour hours	3,700	4,500	2,750	2,600

Labour and Machine Specifications per Unit of Product					
Product	**Labour and Machine Time**				
M07	Direct-labour hours	2	3	3	1
	Machine hours	1	1	2	2
T28	Direct-labour hours	1	2	—	2
	Machine hours	1	1	—	2
B19	Direct-labour hours	2	2	2	1
	Machine hours	2	2	1	1

The sales department believes that the monthly demand for the next six months will be as follows:

Product	**Monthly Unit Sales**
M07	500
T28	400
B19	1,000

Inventory levels are satisfactory and need not be increased or decreased during the next six months. Unit price and cost data that will be valid for the next six months are as follows:

	Product		
	M07	**T28**	**B19**
Unit costs:			
Direct material	$ 7	$ 13	$ 17
Direct labour:			
Department 1	12	6	12
Department 2	21	14	14
Department 3	24	—	16
Department 4	9	18	9
Variable overhead	27	20	25
Fixed overhead	15	10	32
Variable selling expenses	3	2	4
Unit selling price	196	123	167

Required:

1. Calculate the monthly requirement for machine hours and direct-labour hours for the production of products M50, T79, and B81 to determine whether the monthly sales demand for the three products can be met by the factory.

2. What monthly production schedule should Ozark Industries select in order to maximize its dollar profits? Explain how you selected this production schedule, and present a schedule of the contribution to profit that would be generated by your production schedule.

3. Identify the alternatives Ozark Industries might consider so it can supply its customers with all the product they demand.

(CMA, adapted)

Problem 12–56 Conventional versus Activity-Based-Costing Analyses; Relevant Costs **(LO5, 7)**

In addition to fine chocolate, the International Chocolate Company also produces chocolate-covered pretzels in its plant. This product is sold in five-kilogram metal canisters, which also are manufactured at the facility. The plant manager, Marsha Mello, was recently approached by the Catawba Canister Company with an offer to supply the canisters at a price of $1 each. The International Chocolate's traditional product-costing system assigns the following costs to canister production:

2. Costs to be avoided by purchasing (ABC analysis), total: $810,750

Direct material...	$ 300,000
Direct labour (12,000 hrs. @ $15 per hr.)	180,000
Variable overhead ($10 per direct-labour hr.)..	120,000
Fixed overhead ($45 per direct-labour hr.)...	540,000
Total cost	$1,140,000

Unit costs: $1,140,000 ÷ 760,000 canisters = $1.50 per canister

Mello's conventional make-or-buy analysis indicated that Catawba's offer should be rejected, since only $708,000 of costs would be avoided (including $80,000 of supervisory salaries and $28,000 of machinery depreciation). In contrast, the firm would spend $760,000 buying the canisters. The controller, Dave Mint, came to the rescue with an activity-based costing analysis of the decision. Mint concluded that the cost driver levels associated with canister production are as follows:

10 product specs	30 inspections
2,000 supervisory hours...	15 setups
6,000 material-handling hours..	70,000 machine hours
55 purchase orders	

Additional conventional and ABC data for the plant are given in Exhibits 12–19 and 12–20.

Required:

1. Show how Mello arrived at the $708,000 of cost savings in her conventional make-or-buy analysis.
2. Determine the costs that will be saved by purchasing canisters, using Mint's ABC data.
3. Complete the ABC relevant-costing analysis of the make-or-buy decision. Should the firm buy from Catawba?
4. If the conventional and ABC analyses yield different conclusions, briefly explain why.

Cases

1. Contribution per hour, tackle boxes: $26.40

2. Improvement in contribution margin: $236,250

Case 12–57 Adding a Product Line (LO4, 5)

Bo Vonderweidt, the production manager for Sportway Corporation, had requested to have lunch with the company president. Vonderweidt wanted to put forward his suggestion to add a new product line. As they finished lunch, Meg Thomas, the company president, said, "I'll give your proposal some serious thought, Bo. I think you're right about the increasing demand for skateboards. What I'm not sure about is whether the skateboard line will be better for us than our tackle boxes. Those have been our bread and butter the past few years."

Vonderweidt responded with "Let me get together with one of the controller's people. We'll run a few numbers on this skateboard idea that I think will demonstrate the line's potential." Sportway is a wholesale distributor supplying a wide range of moderately priced sports equipment to large chain stores. About 60 percent of Sportway's products are purchased from other companies, while the remainder of the products are manufactured by Sportway. The company has a Plastics Department that is currently manufacturing moulded fishing tackle boxes. Sportway is able to manufacture and sell 8,000 tackle boxes annually, making full use of its direct-labour capacity at available workstations. The selling price and costs associated with Sportway's tackle boxes are as follows:

Selling price per box		$86.00
Costs per box:		
Moulded plastic	$ 8.00	
Hinges, latches, handle	9.00	
Direct labour ($15 per hr.)	18.75	
Manufacturing overhead	12.50	
Selling and administrative cost	17.00	65.25
Profit per box		$20.75

Because Sportway's sales manager believes the firm could sell 12,000 tackle boxes if it had sufficient manufacturing capacity, the company has looked into the possibility of purchasing the tackle boxes for distribution. Maple Products, a steady supplier of quality products, would be able to provide up to 9,000 tackle boxes per year at a price of $68.00 per box delivered to Sportway's facility.

Vonderweidt has come to the conclusion that the company could make better use of its Plastics Department by manufacturing skateboards and has a market study that indicates an expanding market for skateboards and a need for additional suppliers. Vonderweidt believes that Sportway could expect to sell 17,500 skateboards annually at a price of $45.00 per skateboard.

After his lunch with the company president, Vonderweidt worked out the following estimates with the assistant controller.

Selling price per skateboard		$45.00
Costs per skateboard:		
Moulded plastic	$5.50	
Wheels, hardware	7.00	
Direct labour ($15 per hr.)	7.50	
Manufacturing overhead	5.00	
Selling and administrative cost	9.00	34.00
Profit per skateboard		$11.00

In the Plastics Department, Sportway uses direct-labour hours as the application base for manufacturing overhead. Included in the manufacturing overhead for the current year is $50,000 of factorywide, fixed manufacturing overhead that has been allocated to the Plastics Department. For each unit of product that Sportway sells, regardless of whether the product has been purchased or is manufactured by Sportway, there is an allocated $6.00 fixed overhead cost per unit for distribution that is included in the selling and administrative cost for all products. Total selling and administrative costs for the purchased tackle boxes would be $10.00 per unit.

Required: In order to maximize the company's profitability, prepare an analysis that will show which product or products Sportway Corporation should manufacture or purchase.

1. First determine which of Sportway's options makes the best use of its scarce resources. How many skateboards and tackle boxes should be manufactured? How many tackle boxes should be purchased?

2. Calculate the improvement in Sportway's total contribution margin if it adopts the optimal strategy rather than continuing with the status quo.

(CMA, adapted)

Case 12–58 Drop a Product Line (LO4, 5)

Alberta Gauge Company, Ltd., a small manufacturing company in Alberta, manufactures three types of electrical gauges used in a variety of machinery. For many years the company has been profitable and has operated at capacity. However, in the last two years, prices on all gauges were reduced and selling expenses increased to meet competition and keep the plant operating at capacity. Second-quarter results for the current year, which follow, typify recent experience.

Unit contribution, E-gauge: $19

ALBERTA GAUGE COMPANY, LTD.
Income Statement
Second Quarter
(in thousands)

	Q-Gauge	E-Gauge	R-Gauge	Total
Sales	$1,600	$900	$ 900	$3,400
Cost of goods sold	1,048	770	950	2,768
Gross margin	$ 552	$130	$ (50)	$ 632
Selling and administrative expenses	370	185	135	690
Income before taxes	$ 182	$ (55)	$(185)	$ (58)

Alice Carlo, the company's president, is concerned about the results of the pricing, selling, and production prices. After reviewing the second-quarter results, she asked her management staff to consider the following three suggestions:

- Discontinue the R-Gauge line immediately. R-Gauges would not be returned to the product line unless the problems with the gauge can be identified and resolved.
- Increase quarterly sales promotion by $100,000 on the Q-Gauge product line in order to increase sales volume by 15 percent.
- Cut production on the E-Gauge line by 50 percent, and cut the traceable advertising and promotion for this line to $20,000 each quarter.

Jason Sperry, the controller, suggested a more careful study of the financial relationships to determine the possible effects on the company's operating results of the president's proposed course of action. The president agreed and assigned JoAnn Brower, the assistant controller, to prepare an analysis. Brower has gathered the following information:

- All three gauges are manufactured with common equipment and facilities.
- The selling and administrative expense is allocated to the three gauge lines based on average sales volume over the past three years.
- Special selling expenses (primarily advertising, promotion, and shipping) are incurred for each gauge as follows:

	Quarterly Advertising and Promotion	Shipping Expenses
Q-Gauge	$210,000	$10 per unit
E-Gauge	100,000	4 per unit
R-Gauge	40,000	10 per unit

- The unit manufacturing costs for the three products are as follows:

	Q-Gauge	E-Gauge	R-Gauge
Direct material	$ 31	$17	$ 50
Direct labour	40	20	60
Variable manufacturing overhead	45	30	60
Fixed manufacturing overhead	15	10	20
Total	$131	$77	$190

- The unit sales prices for the three products are

Q-Gauge $200
E-Gauge 90
R-Gauge 180

- The company is manufacturing at capacity and is selling all the gauges it produces.

Required:

1. JoAnn Brower says that Alberta Gauge Company's product-line income statement for the second quarter is not suitable for analyzing proposals and making decisions such as the ones suggested by Alice Carlo. Write a memo to Alberta Gauge's president that addresses the following points:

   a. Explain why the product-line income statement as presented is not suitable for analysis and decision making.

   b. Describe an alternative income statement format that would be more suitable for analysis and decision making, and explain why it is better.

2. Use the operating data presented for Alberta Gauge Company and assume that the president's proposed course of action had been implemented at the beginning of the second quarter. Then evaluate the president's proposal by specifically responding to the following points:

   a. Are each of the three suggestions cost-effective? Support your discussion with an analysis that shows the net impact on income before taxes for each of the three suggestions.

   b. Was the president correct in proposing that the R-Gauge line be eliminated? Explain your answer.

   c. Was the president correct in promoting the Q-Gauge line rather than the E-Gauge line? Explain your answer.

   d. Does the proposed course of action make effective use of the company's capacity? Explain your answer.

3. Are there any qualitative factors that Alberta Gauge Company's management should consider before it drops the R-Gauge? Explain your answer.

(CMA, adapted)

ONLINE SUPPLEMENT 12A   Linear Programming

 See Connect for a supplement to this chapter.

 Practise and learn online with Connect.

CHAPTER THIRTEEN

Target Costing and Cost Analysis for Pricing Decisions

FOCUS COMPANY

The focus company for this chapter is Sydney Sailing Supplies, a manufacturer of sailing supplies and equipment in Sydney, Australia. One of the company's most popular products is the Wave Darter, a two-person sailboat. In this chapter, we will explore a variety of issues surrounding how Sydney Sailing Supplies' management could set a price for the Wave Darter. We also will study a pricing method called *target costing*. Under this approach, management determines what consumers are willing to pay for a particular product. Then management has to find a way to produce that product at a low enough cost to justify the price the consumers are willing to pay.

IN CONTRAST

In contrast to the product-pricing setting explored in the first part of the chapter, we turn our attention to competitive bidding on projects, services, or products. In a competitive-bidding situation, two or more companies submit sealed bids for a job, and the buyer selects from among the bids. We will explore competitive bidding in the context of the focus company, Sydney Sailing Supplies' Marine Services Division. The company's Marine Services Division specializes in marina maintenance and construction, and its management is preparing a bid to build a new marina in Sydney Harbour.

After completing this chapter, you should be able to

1 List and describe the four major factors of pricing decisions.

2 Explain and use the economic, profit-maximizing pricing model.

3 Set prices using cost-plus pricing formulas.

4 Discuss the issues involved in the strategic pricing of new products.

5 List and discuss the key principles of target costing.

6 Explain the role of activity-based costing in setting a target cost.

7 Explain how product-cost distortion can undermine a firm's pricing strategy.

8 Explain the process of value engineering and its role in target costing.

9 Determine prices using the time and material pricing approach.

10 Set prices in competitive-bidding situations.

11 Describe the legal restrictions on setting prices.

S etting the price for an organization's product or service is one of the most important decisions a manager faces. It is also one of the most difficult, due to the number and variety of factors that must be considered. The pricing decision arises in virtually all types of organizations. Manufacturers set prices for the products they manufacture; merchandising companies set prices for their goods; service firms set prices for such services as insurance policies, train tickets, theme park admissions, and bank loans. Nonprofit organizations often set prices also. For example, government units price vehicle registrations, park-use fees, and utility services. The optimal approach to pricing often depends on the situation. Pricing a mature product or service that a firm has sold for a long time may be quite different from pricing a new product or service. Public utilities and telephone companies face political considerations in pricing their products and services, since their prices often must be approved by a government commission.

In this chapter, we will study pricing decisions that emphasize the role of managerial accounting information. The setting for our discussion is Sydney Sailing Supplies, a manufacturer of sailing supplies and equipment located in Sydney, Australia.

Major Influences on Pricing Decisions

Learning Objective **1**

List and describe the four major factors of pricing decisions.

Four major factors influence the prices set by Sydney Sailing Supplies:

1. Customer demand
2. Actions of competitors
3. Costs
4. Political, legal, and image-related issues

Customer Demand

The demands of customers are of paramount importance in all phases of business operations, from the design of a product to the setting of its price. Product-design issues and pricing considerations are interrelated, so they must be examined simultaneously. For example, if customers want a high-quality sailboat, more production time and more expensive raw materials are required. The result almost certainly will be a higher price. On the other hand, management must be careful not to price its product out of the market. Discerning customer demand is a critically important and continuous process. Companies routinely obtain information from market research, such as customer surveys and test-marketing campaigns, and through feedback from sales personnel. To be successful, Sydney Sailing Supplies must provide the products its customers want at a price they perceive to be appropriate.

Actions of Competitors

Although Sydney Sailing Supplies' managers would like the company to have the sailing market to itself, they are not so fortunate. Domestic and foreign competitors are striving to sell their products to the same customers. So, as Sydney Sailing Supplies' management designs products and sets prices, it must keep a watchful eye on the firm's competitors. If a competitor reduces its price on sailboats of a particular type, Sydney Sailing Supplies may have to follow suit to avoid losing its market share. Yet the company cannot follow its competitors blindly, either. Predicting competitive reactions to its product-design and pricing strategy is a difficult but important task for Sydney Sailing Supplies' management.

In considering the reactions of customers and competitors, management must be careful to properly define its product. Should Sydney Sailing Supplies' management define its product narrowly as sailing supplies, or more broadly as boating supplies? For example, if the company raises the price of its two-person sailboat, will this encourage potential customers to switch to canoes, rowboats, and small motorboats? Or will most potential sailboat customers react to a price increase only by price-shopping among competing sailboat manufacturers? The way in which Sydney Sailing Supplies' management answers these questions can profoundly affect its marketing and pricing strategies.

Costs

The role of costs in price setting varies widely among industries. In some industries, prices are determined almost entirely by market forces. An example is the agricultural industry, where grain and meat prices are market-driven. Farmers must meet the market price. To make a profit, they must produce at a cost below the market price. This is not always possible, so some periods of loss inevitably result. In other industries, managers set prices at least partially on the basis of production costs. For example, cost-based pricing is used in the aircraft, household appliance, and gasoline industries. Prices are set by adding a markup to production costs. Managers have some latitude in determining the markup, so market forces influence prices as well. In public utilities, such as electricity and natural gas companies, prices generally are set by a regulatory agency. Production costs are of prime importance in justifying utility rates. Typically, a public utility will make a request to a provincial utility commission or board for a rate increase on the basis of its current and projected production costs.

Balance of Market Forces and Cost-Based Pricing   In most industries, both market forces and cost considerations heavily influence prices. No organization or industry can price its products below their production costs (i.e., the floor price) indefinitely. And no company's management can set prices blindly at cost plus a markup without keeping an eye on the market (i.e., the ceiling price). In most cases, pricing can be viewed in either of the ways shown in the following illustration.

How Are Prices Set?

Prices are determined by the market, subject to the constraint that costs must be covered in the long run.

Prices are based on costs, subject to the constraint that the reactions of customers and competitors must be heeded.

In our example of Sydney Sailing Supplies' pricing policies, we will assume the company responds to both market forces and costs.

Political, Legal, and Image-Related Issues

Beyond the important effects on prices of market forces and costs are a range of environmental considerations. In the *legal* area, managers must adhere to certain laws. The law generally prohibits companies from discriminating among their customers in setting prices. Also prohibited is collusion in price setting, where the major firms in an industry all agree to set their prices at high levels. The Canadian *Competition Act* is a federal law that is intended to, among other things, "maintain and encourage competition in Canada" and "provide consumers with competitive prices and product choices."

Political considerations also can be relevant. For example, if the firms in an industry are *perceived* by the public as reaping unfairly large profits, there may be political pressure on legislators to tax those profits differentially or to intervene in some way to regulate prices.

Companies also consider their *public image* in the price-setting process. A firm with a reputation for very-high-quality products may set the price of a new product high to be consistent with its image. As we have all discovered, the same brand-name product may be available in a discount store at half the price charged in a more exclusive store.

Setting prices requires a balance between cost considerations and market forces. A good example is provided by the airlines, which keep a close eye on the fares of their competitors, while striving to cover operating costs. Large airlines, such as Air Canada, are increasingly finding it necessary to cut fares to compete with discounters such as WestJet.

Economic Profit-Maximizing Pricing

Learning Objective **2**

Explain and use the economic, profit-maximizing pricing model.

A company is sometimes a **price taker**, which means that its products' prices are determined totally by the market. Some agricultural commodities and precious metals are examples of such products. In most cases, however, firms have some flexibility in setting prices. Generally speaking, as the price of a product or service is increased, the quantity demanded declines, and vice versa.

Total Revenue, Demand, and Marginal Revenue Curves

The trade-off between a higher price and a higher sales quantity can be shown in the shape of the firm's **total revenue curve**, which graphs the relationship between total sales revenue and quantity sold. Sydney Sailing Supplies' total revenue curve for its two-person sailboat, the Wave Darter, is displayed in Exhibit 13–1, panel A. The total revenue curve increases throughout its range, but the rate of increase declines as monthly sales quantity increases. To see this, notice that the increase in total revenue when the sales quantity increases from zero to a units is greater than the increase in total revenue when the sales quantity increases from a units to b units.

A. Total Revenue Curve

Exhibit 13–1
Total Revenue, Demand, and
Marginal Revenue Curves

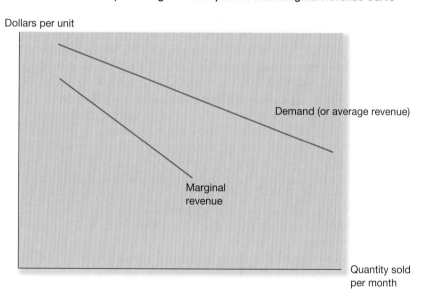

Dollars

Total revenue

Curve is increasing throughout its range, but at a declining rate

Quantity sold per month

0   a   b

B. Demand (or Average Revenue) Curve and Marginal Revenue Curve

Dollars per unit

Demand (or average revenue)

Marginal revenue

Quantity sold per month

C. Tabulated Price, Quantity, and Revenue Data

Quantity Sold per Month	Unit Sales Price	Total Revenue per Month	Changes in Total Revenue
10	$1,000	$10,000	
			$9,500
20	975	19,500	
			9,000
30	950	28,500	
			8,500
40	925	37,000	
			8,000
50	900	45,000	
			7,500
60	875	52,500	

Related to demand curve

Related to total revenue curve

Related to marginal revenue curve

Closely related to the total revenue curve are two other curves, which are graphed in panel B of Exhibit 13–1. The **demand curve** shows the relationship between the sales price and the quantity of units demanded. The demand curve decreases throughout its range, because any decrease in the sales price brings about an increase in the monthly sales quantity. The demand curve is also called the **average revenue curve**, since it shows the average price at which any particular quantity can be sold.

The **marginal revenue curve** shows the change in total revenue that accompanies a change in the quantity sold. The marginal revenue curve is decreasing throughout its range to show that total revenue increases at a declining rate as monthly sales quantity increases.

A tabular presentation of the price, quantity, and revenue data for Sydney Sailing Supplies is displayed in panel C of Exhibit 13–1. Study this table carefully to see how the data relate to the graphs shown in panels A and B of the exhibit. No matter what approach a manager takes to the pricing decision, a good understanding of the relationships shown in Exhibit 13–1 will lead to better decisions. Before we can fully use the revenue data, however, we must examine the cost side of Sydney Sailing Supplies' business.

Total Cost and Marginal Cost Curves

Understanding cost behaviour is important in many business decisions, and pricing is no exception. How does total cost behave as the number of Wave Darters produced and sold by Sydney Sailing Supplies changes? Panel A of Exhibit 13–2 displays the firm's **total cost curve**, which graphs the relationship between total cost and the quantity produced and sold each month.[1] Total cost increases throughout its range. The rate of increase in total cost declines as quantity increases from zero to c units. To verify this, notice that the increase in total costs when quantity increases from zero to a units is greater than the increase in total costs when quantity increases from a units to b units.

The rate of increase in total costs increases as quantity increases from c units upward. To verify this, notice that the increase in total costs as quantity increases from c units to d units is less than the increase in total costs as quantity increases from d units to e units.

Closely related to the total cost curve is the **marginal cost curve**, which is graphed in panel B of Exhibit 13–2. The marginal cost curve shows the change in total cost that accompanies a change in quantity produced and sold. Marginal cost declines as quantity increases from zero to c units, then it increases as quantity increases beyond c units.

A tabular presentation of the cost and quantity data for Sydney Sailing Supplies is displayed in panel C of Exhibit 13–2. Examine this table carefully, and trace the relationships between the data and the graphs shown in panels A and B of the exhibit.

Profit-Maximizing Price and Quantity

Now we have the tools we need to determine the profit-maximizing price and quantity. In Exhibit 13–3, we combine the revenue and cost data presented in Exhibits 13–1 and 13–2. Sydney Sailing Supplies' profit-maximizing sales quantity for the Wave Darter is determined by the intersection of the marginal cost and marginal revenue curves (see panel B of Exhibit 13–3). This optimal quantity is denoted by q^* on the graph. The profit-maximizing price, denoted by p^*, is determined from the demand curve for the quantity, q^*.

Examine the total revenue and total cost curves in panel A of Exhibit 13–3. At the profit-maximizing quantity (and price), the distance between these curves, which is equal to total profit, is maximized.

A tabular presentation of the revenue, cost, and profit data is shown in panel C of Exhibit 13–3. Notice that monthly profit is maximized when the price is set at $925 and 40 Wave Darters are produced and sold each month.

A. Total Cost Curve

Exhibit 13-2
Total Cost and Marginal
Cost Curves

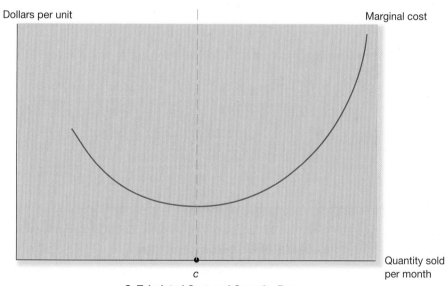

B. Marginal Cost Curve

C. Tabulated Cost and Quantity Data

Quantity Produced and Sold per Month	Average Cost per Unit	Total Cost per Month	Changes in Total Cost
10	$1,920	$19,200	
			$5,600
20	1,240	24,800	
			4,300
30	970	29,100	
			2,900
40	800	32,000	
			9,000
50	820	41,000	
			15,400
60	940	56,400	

Related to total cost curve   Related to marginal cost curve

Exhibit 13-3
Determining the Profit-
Maximizing Price and Quantity

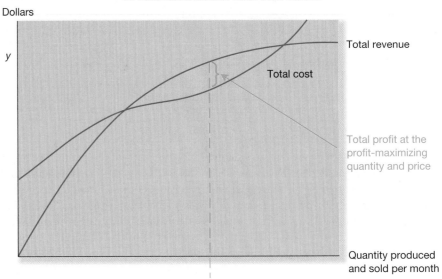

A. Total Revenue and Total Cost Curves

Dollars

y

Total revenue

Total cost

Total profit at the
profit-maximizing
quantity and price

Quantity produced
and sold per month

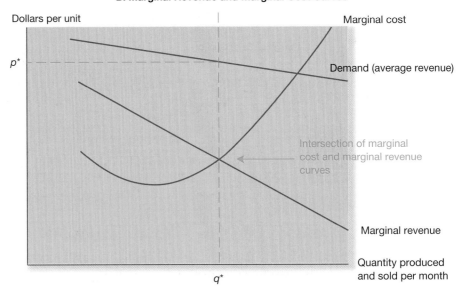

B. Marginal Revenue and Marginal Cost Curves

Dollars per unit

Marginal cost

*p**

Demand (average revenue)

Intersection of marginal
cost and marginal revenue
curves

Marginal revenue

Quantity produced
and sold per month

*q**

C. Tabulated Revenue, Cost, and Profit Data

	Quantity Produced and Sold per Month		Unit Sales Price	Total Revenue per Month	Total Cost per Month	Profit (Loss) per Month
	10	....	$1,000	$10,000	$19,200	$(9,200)
	20	....	975	19,500	24,800	(5,300)
Profit-maximizing quantity and price	30	....	950	28,500	29,100	(600)
	40	....	925	37,000	32,000	5,000
	50	....	900	45,000	41,000	4,000
	60	....	875	52,500	56,400	(3,900)

Price Elasticity

The impact of price changes on sales volume is called the **price elasticity**. Demand is *elastic* if a price increase has a large negative impact on sales volume, and vice versa. Demand is *inelastic* if price changes have little or no impact on sales quantity. **Cross-elasticity** refers to the extent to which a change in a product's price affects the demand for other *substitute products*. For example, if Sydney Sailing Supplies raises the price of its two-person sailboat, there may be an increase in demand for substitute recreational craft, such as small power-boats, canoes, or windsurfers.

Measuring price elasticity and cross-elasticity is an important objective of market research. Having a good understanding of these economic concepts helps managers to determine the profit-maximizing price.

Limitations of the Profit-Maximizing Model

The economic model of the pricing decision serves as a useful framework for approaching a pricing problem. However, it does have several limitations. First, the firm's demand and marginal revenue curves are difficult to discern with precision. Although market research is designed to gather data about product demand, it rarely enables management to predict completely the effects of price changes on the quantity demanded. Many other factors affect product demand in addition to price. Product design and quality, advertising and promotion, and company reputation also significantly influence consumer demand for a product.

Second, the marginal revenue, marginal cost paradigm is not valid for all forms of market organization. In an **oligopolistic market**, where a small number of sellers compete among themselves, the simple economic pricing model is no longer appropriate. In an *oligopoly*, such as the automobile industry, the reactions of competitors to a firm's pricing policies must be taken into account. While economists have studied oligopolistic pricing, the state of the theory is not sufficient to provide a thorough understanding of the impact of prices on demand.

The third limitation of the economic pricing model involves the difficulty of measuring marginal cost. Cost accounting systems are not designed to measure the marginal changes in cost incurred as production and sales increase unit by unit. To measure marginal costs would entail a very costly information system. Most managers believe that any improvements in pricing decisions made possible by marginal cost data would not be sufficient to defray the cost of obtaining the information.

Costs and Benefits of Information

Management accountants always face a cost–benefit trade-off in the production of cost information for pricing and other decisions. As Exhibit 13–4 shows, only a sophisticated information system can collect marginal cost data. However, such information is more costly to obtain. The result is that the optimal approach to pricing and other decisions is

Exhibit 13–4
Cost–Benefit Trade-Off in Information Production

Optimal Decisions

Economic model of pricing

Sophisticated decision model and information requirements

Marginal cost and marginal revenue data

More Costly Approach

Suboptimal Decisions

Cost-based approach to pricing

Simplified decision model and information requirements

Accounting product-cost data

Less Costly Approach

Best approach, in terms of costs and benefits, typically lies between the extremes.

likely to lie between the extremes shown in Exhibit 13–4. For this reason, most managers make pricing decisions based on a combination of economic considerations and accounting product-cost information.

In spite of its limitations, the marginal revenue, marginal cost paradigm of pricing serves as a useful conceptual framework for the pricing decision. Within this overall framework, managers typically rely heavily on a cost-based pricing approach, as we will see next.

Role of Accounting Product Costs in Pricing

Most managers base prices on accounting product costs, at least to some extent. There are several reasons for this. First, most companies sell many products or services. There simply is not time enough to do an economic pricing analysis for every product or service. Managers must rely on a quick and straightforward method for setting prices, and cost-based pricing formulas provide it. Second, even though market consider-ations ultimately may determine the final product price, a cost-based pricing formula gives the manager a place to start. Finally, and most importantly, the cost of a product or service provides a floor below which the price cannot be set in the long-run. Although a product may be "given away" initially, at a price below cost, a product's price ultimately must cover its costs in order for the firm to remain in business. Even a nonprofit organization, unless it is heavily subsidized, cannot forever price products or services below their costs.

Cost-Plus Pricing

Learning Objective **3**

Set prices using cost-plus pricing formulas.

Cost-based pricing formulas typically have the following general form:

$$\text{Price} = \text{Cost} + (\text{Markup percentage} \times \text{Cost})$$

Such a pricing approach often is called **cost-plus pricing**, because the price is equal to *cost plus a markup*. Depending on how cost is defined, the markup percentage may differ. Several different definitions of cost, each combined with a different markup per-centage, can result in the same price for a product or service.

Exhibit 13–5 illustrates how Sydney Sailing Supplies' management could use several different cost-plus pricing formulas and arrive at a price of $925 for the Wave Darter. Cost-plus formula (1) is based on variable manufacturing cost. Formula (2) is based on absorption (or full) manufacturing cost, which includes an allocated portion of fixed manufacturing costs. Formula (3) is based on all costs: both variable and fixed costs of the manufacturing, selling, and administrative functions. Formula (4) is based on all variable costs, including variable manufacturing, selling, and administrative costs. Notice that all four formulas are based on a linear representation of the cost function, in which all costs are categorized as fixed or variable.

As Sydney Sailing Supplies includes more costs in the cost base of the pricing formula, the required markup percentage declines. This reflects the fact that, one way or another, the price must cover all costs as well as a normal profit margin. If only variable manufacturing costs are included explicitly in the cost base, as in formula (1), then all of the other costs (and the firm's profit) must be covered by the markup. However, if the cost base used in the pricing formula includes all costs, as in formula (3), the markup can be much lower, since it needs to cover only the firm's normal profit margin.

A company typically uses only one of the four cost-plus pricing formulas illustrated in Exhibit 13–5. Which formula is best? Let's examine the advantages and disadvantages of each approach.

Each of the following cost-plus pricing formulas yields the same $925 price for the Wave Darter.

Price and Cost Data		Cost-Plus Pricing Formulas
Variable manufacturing cost	$400	**1** $925 = \$400 + (131.25\% \times \$400) = \begin{matrix}\text{Variable} \\ \text{manufacturing} \\ \text{cost}\end{matrix} + \left(\begin{matrix}\text{Markup} \\ \text{percentage}\end{matrix} \times \begin{matrix}\text{Variable} \\ \text{manufacturing} \\ \text{cost}\end{matrix}\right)$
Applied fixed manufacturing cost	250*	
Absorption manufacturing cost	650	**2** $925 = \$650 + (42.3\%^{\dagger} \times \$650) = \begin{matrix}\text{Absorption} \\ \text{manufacturing} \\ \text{cost}\end{matrix} + \left(\begin{matrix}\text{Markup} \\ \text{percentage}\end{matrix} \times \begin{matrix}\text{Absorption} \\ \text{manufacturing} \\ \text{cost}\end{matrix}\right)$
Variable selling and administrative cost	50	
Allocated fixed selling and administrative cost	100*	
Total cost	$800	**3** $925 = \$800 + (15.63\%^{\dagger} \times \$800) = \begin{matrix}\text{Total} \\ \text{cost}\end{matrix} + \left(\begin{matrix}\text{Markup} \\ \text{percentage}\end{matrix} \times \begin{matrix}\text{Total} \\ \text{cost}\end{matrix}\right)$
Variable manufacturing cost	$400	
Variable selling and administrative cost	50	
Total variable cost	$450	**4** $925 = \$450 + (105.56\%^{\dagger} \times \$450) = \begin{matrix}\text{Total} \\ \text{variable} \\ \text{cost}\end{matrix} + \left(\begin{matrix}\text{Markup} \\ \text{percentage}\end{matrix} \times \begin{matrix}\text{Total} \\ \text{variable} \\ \text{cost}\end{matrix}\right)$

*Based on planned monthly production of 40 units (or 480 units per year).

† Rounded.

Exhibit 13–5
Alternative Cost-Plus Pricing Formulas

Absorption-Cost Pricing Formulas

Most companies that use cost-plus pricing use either absorption manufacturing cost or total cost as the basis for pricing products or services. (See formulas (2) and (3) in Exhibit 13–5.) The reasons generally given for this tendency are as follows:

1. In the long run, the price must cover *all* costs and a normal profit margin. Basing the cost-plus formula on only variable costs might encourage managers to set too low a price in order to boost sales. This will not happen if managers understand that a variable cost-plus pricing formula requires a higher markup to cover fixed costs and profit. Nevertheless, many managers argue that people tend to view the cost base in a cost-plus pricing formula as the floor for setting prices. If prices are set too close to variable manufacturing cost, the firm will fail to cover its fixed costs. Ultimately, such a practice could result in the failure of the business.

2. Absorption-cost or total-cost pricing formulas provide a justifiable price that tends to be perceived as equitable by all parties. Consumers generally understand that a company must make a profit on its product or service in order to remain in business. Justifying a price as the total cost of production, sales, and administrative activities, plus a reasonable profit margin, seems reasonable to buyers.

3. When a company's competitors have similar operations and cost structures, cost-plus pricing based on full costs gives management an idea of how competitors may set prices.

4. Absorption-cost information is provided by a firm's cost accounting system, because it is required for external financial reporting under generally accepted accounting principles. Since absorption-cost information already exists, it is

cost-effective to use it for pricing. The alternative would involve preparing special product-cost data specifically for the pricing decision. In a firm with hundreds of products, such data could be expensive to produce.

The primary disadvantage of absorption-cost or total-cost pricing formulas is that they obscure the cost behaviour pattern of the firm. Since absorption-cost and total-cost data include allocated fixed costs, it is not clear from these data how the firm's total costs will change as volume changes. Another way of stating this criticism is that absorption-cost data are not consistent with cost–volume–profit analysis. CVP analysis emphasizes the distinction between fixed and variable costs. This approach enables managers to predict the effects of changes in prices and sales volume on profit. Absorption-cost and total-cost information obscures the distinction between variable and fixed costs.

> "An indemnity [insurance] company prices products by looking at existing costs and at what the trends have been. The company then predicts, or forecasts, costs for the next year and uses this information to set the price." (13c)
>
> **BlueCross**

Variable-Cost Pricing Formulas

To avoid blurring the effects of cost behaviour on profit, some managers prefer to use cost-plus pricing formulas based on either variable manufacturing costs or total variable costs. (See formulas (1) and (4) in Exhibit 13–5.) Three advantages are attributed to this pricing approach:

1. Variable-cost data do not obscure the cost behaviour pattern by unitizing fixed costs and making them appear to be variable. Thus, variable-cost information is more consistent with cost–volume–profit analysis often used by managers to see the profit implications of changes in price and volume.
2. Variable-cost data do not require allocation of common fixed costs to individual product lines. For example, the annual salary of Sydney Sailing Supplies' vice-president of sales is a cost that must be borne by all of the company's product lines. Arbitrarily allocating a portion of her salary to the Wave Darter product line is not meaningful.
3. Variable-cost data are exactly the type of information managers need when facing certain decisions, such as whether to accept a special order. This decision, examined in detail in the preceding chapter, often requires an analysis that separates fixed and variable costs.

The primary disadvantage of the variable-cost pricing formula was described earlier. If managers perceive the variable cost of a product or service as the floor for the price, they might tend to set the price too low for the firm to cover its fixed costs. Eventually this can spell disaster. Therefore, if variable-cost data are used as the basis for cost-plus pricing, managers must understand the need for higher markups to ensure that all costs are covered.

Determining the Markup

Regardless of which cost-plus formula is used, Sydney Sailing Supplies must determine its markup on the Wave Darter. If management uses a variable-cost pricing formula, the markup must cover all fixed costs and a reasonable profit. If management uses an absorption-costing formula, the markup still must be sufficient to cover the firm's profit on the Wave Darter product line. What constitutes a reasonable or normal profit margin?

Return-on-Investment Pricing   A common approach to determining the profit margin in cost-plus pricing is to base profit on the firm's target return on investment (ROI). To illustrate **return-on-investment pricing**, suppose Sydney Sailing Supplies' production plan calls for 480 Wave Darters to be manufactured during the year. Based on the cost data shown in Exhibit 13–5, this production plan will result in the following total costs:

Variable costs:		
Manufacturing	$192,000	
Selling and administrative	24,000	
Total variable costs		$216,000
Fixed costs:		
Manufacturing	$120,000	
Selling and administrative	48,000	
Total fixed costs		168,000
Total costs		$384,000

Suppose the year's average amount of capital invested in the Wave Darter product line is $300,000. If Sydney Sailing Supplies' target return on investment for the Wave Darter line is 20 percent, the required annual profit is computed as follows:

$$\text{Average invested capital} \times \text{Target ROI} = \text{Target profit}$$
$$\$300,000 \qquad \times \quad 20\% \quad = \quad \$60,000$$

The markup percentage required to earn Sydney Sailing Supplies a $60,000 profit on the Wave Darter line depends on the cost-plus formula used. We will compute the markup percentage for two cost-plus formulas:

1. *Cost-plus pricing based on total costs.* The total cost of a Wave Darter is $800 per unit (Exhibit 13–5). To earn a profit of $60,000 on annual sales of 480 sailboats, the company must make a profit of $125 per boat ($125 = $60,000 ÷ 480). This entails a markup percentage of 15.63 percent above total cost of $800:

$$15.63\% = \frac{\$925}{\$800} - 100\%$$

A shortcut to the same conclusion uses the following formula:

$$\frac{\text{Markup percentage}}{\text{on total cost}} = \frac{\text{Target profit}}{\text{Annual volume} \times \text{Total cost per unit}}$$

$$15.63\% \quad = \quad \frac{\$60,000}{480 \times \$800}$$

2. *Cost-plus pricing based on total variable costs.* The total variable cost of a Wave Darter is $450 per unit (Exhibit 13–5). The markup percentage applied to variable cost must be sufficient to cover *both* annual profit of $60,000 *and* total annual fixed costs of $168,000. The required markup percentage is computed as follows:

$$\frac{\text{Markup percentage}}{\text{on total variable cost}} = \frac{\text{Target profit} + \text{Total annual fixed cost}}{\text{Annual volume} \times \text{Total variable cost per unit}}$$

$$105.56\% \quad = \quad \frac{\$60,000 + \$168,000}{480 \times \$450}$$

General Formula The general formula for computing the markup percentage in cost-plus pricing to achieve a target ROI is as follows:

$$
\begin{array}{l}
\text{Markup percentage} \\
\text{applied to cost base in} \\
\text{cost-plus pricing formula}
\end{array}
=
\dfrac{
\begin{array}{l}
\text{Profit required to} \\
\text{achieve target ROI}
\end{array}
+
\begin{array}{l}
\text{Total annual costs } not \\
\text{included in cost base}
\end{array}
}{
\begin{array}{l}
\text{Annual} \\
\text{volume}
\end{array}
\times
\begin{array}{l}
\text{Cost base per unit} \\
\text{used in cost-plus} \\
\text{pricing formula}
\end{array}
}
$$

Cost-Plus Pricing: Summary and Evaluation

We have examined two different approaches to setting prices: (1) the economic, profit-maximizing approach and (2) cost-plus pricing. Although the techniques involved in these methods are quite different, the methods complement each other. In setting prices, managers cannot ignore the market (i.e., the ceiling price), nor can they ignore costs (i.e., the floor price). Cost-plus pricing is used widely in practice to establish a starting point in the process of determining a price. Cost-plus formulas are simple; they can be applied mechanically without taking the time of top management. They make it possible for a company with hundreds of products or services to cope with the tasks of updating prices for existing products and setting initial prices for new products.

Cost-plus pricing formulas can be used effectively with a variety of cost definitions, but the markup percentage has to be appropriate for the type of cost used. It is imperative that price-setting managers understand that ultimately the price must cover all costs and a normal profit margin. Absorption-cost-plus or total-cost-plus pricing has the advantage of keeping the manager's attention focused on covering total costs. The variable-cost-plus formulas have the advantage of not obscuring important information about cost behaviour.

Rogers
Communications,
Bell Canada,
TELUS, Fido, General
Motors, and Toyota

PRICE COMPETITION AND COST MANAGEMENT

Intense price competition, sometimes referred to as a *price war*, can occur in just about any industry. Rogers Communications, Bell Canada, and TELUS are among the telecom carriers currently being forced to lower their rates. In order to survive in a price war, though, a company must aggressively manage its costs. Fido, for example, is relaunching its discount brand with new plans and doing away with the much-hated system access fees, forcing telecom giants to follow suit.[2]

BusinessWeek reports that the auto insurance industry is entering such a period of price competition. Price competition is always intense in the auto industry. According to *The Wall Street Journal*, "In an attempt to rewrite pricing rules in the highly competitive U.S. auto market, General Motors will slash the price on most of its new vehicles. The move is the automaker's latest attempt to settle on a pricing strategy that is both profitable for the company and compelling for customers." In order to cut prices, though, GM will have to aggressively manage its production costs.[3]

Toyota's response to increased price competition is an aggressive cost-cutting campaign. In recent years, Toyota has reduced its procurement costs by nearly a third. The automaker's next move is to reduce the average "number of steel parts in cars from 610 to 500 to deal with the soaring cost of steel."[4]

Meeting competitive prices and effectively managing costs go hand in hand in any business.

Cost-plus pricing formulas establish a starting point in setting prices. Then the price setter must weigh market conditions, likely actions of competitors, and general business conditions. Effective price setting requires a constant interplay of market considerations and cost awareness.

Strategic Pricing of New Products

Learning Objective   **4**

Discuss the issues involved in the strategic pricing of new products.

Pricing a new product is an especially challenging decision problem. The newer the concept of the product, the more difficult the pricing decision is. For example, if Sydney Sailing Supplies comes out with a new two-person sailboat, its pricing problem is far easier than the pricing problem of a company that first markets products using a radically new technology. Genetic engineering, superconductivity, artificial hearts, and space-grown crystals are all examples of such frontier technologies.

Pricing a new product is harder than pricing a mature product because of the magnitude of the uncertainties involved. New products entail many uncertainties. For example, what obstacles will be encountered in manufacturing the product, and what will be the costs of production? Moreover, after the product is available, will anyone want to buy it, and at what price? If Sydney Sailing Supplies decides to market a new two-person sailboat, management can make a good estimate of both the production costs and the potential market for the product. The uncertainties here are far smaller than the uncertainties facing a company developing artificial hearts.

In addition to the production and demand uncertainties, new products pose another sort of challenge. There are two widely differing strategies that a manufacturer of a new product can adopt. One strategy is called **skimming pricing**, in which the initial product price is set high, and short-term profits are reaped on the new product. The initial market will be small, due in part to the high initial price. This pricing approach often is used for unique products, where there are people who "must have it" whatever the price. As the product gains acceptance and its appeal broadens, the price is lowered gradually. Eventually the product is priced in a range that appeals to several kinds of buyers. An example of a product for which skimming pricing was used is high-definition television. Initially, HDTVs were quite expensive and only a few buyers could afford them. Eventually the price was lowered, and HDTVs were purchased by a wide range of consumers.

An alternative initial pricing strategy is called **penetration pricing**, in which the initial price is set relatively low. By setting a low price for a new product, management hopes to penetrate a new market deeply, quickly gaining a large market share. This pricing approach often is used for products that are of good quality but do not stand out as vastly better than competing products.

The decision between skimming and penetration pricing depends on the type of product and involves trade-offs of price versus volume. Skimming pricing results in much slower acceptance of a new product, but higher unit profits. Penetration pricing results in greater initial sales volume, but lower unit profits.

Regardless of the pricing strategy used, companies must closely monitor and manage costs in order to remain price-competitive.

Target Costing

Learning Objective   **5**

List and discuss the key principles of target costing.

Earlier in this chapter, we described product pricing as a process whereby the cost of the product is determined, and then an appropriate price is chosen. Increasingly, the opposite approach is being taken. The company first uses market research to determine the price at which a new product can be sold. Given the likely sales price, management computes the cost for which the product must be manufactured in order to provide the firm with an acceptable profit margin. Finally, engineers and cost analysts work together to design a

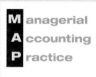

PRICING ON THE INTERNET BY "E-TAILERS"[5]

One of the most difficult issues in building an online retail business has proven to be pricing. "Many Internet merchants are still struggling to find ways to set prices to attract as many customers as possible, while fattening up their razor-thin profit margins. What these retailers do know is what *hasn't* worked."

As the dot-com industry struggles, flawed pricing strategies have taken much of the blame. "Too many merchants raced for the bottom with deep discounts that made profits all but impossible to achieve—especially when the stock market bottomed out and funding for dot-coms froze. Others have felt the consumer backlash to so-called price discrimination, as the Internet has given shoppers the ability to better detect price discrepancies and bargains. The survivors must now figure out if it is even possible to take advantage of the Internet's unique capabilities to set dynamic prices, which would better reflect a customer's willingness to pay more under different circumstances. 'Before the Internet existed, retail was a very competitive, difficult, low-margin business,' says economist Austan Goolsbee. 'With the advent of Internet retailers, there was a brief moment in which they and others believed they had broken the iron chain of low margins and high competition in retail by introducing the Internet. Now, retail online is starting to look like retail offline—very competitive, with squeezed profit margins. In all, a very tough place to be.'"

Pricing on the Internet "was expected to offer retailers a number of advantages." First, "it would be far easier to raise or lower prices in response to demand, without the need of a clerk running through a store with a pricing gun. Online prices could be changed in far smaller increments—even by just a penny or two—as frequently as a merchant desired, making it possible to fine-tune pricing strategies."

The real payoff, though, "was supposed to be better information on exactly how price-conscious customers are. For instance, knowing that customer A doesn't care whether the 'Gladiator' DVD in her shopping basket costs $21.95 or $25.95 would leave an enterprising merchant free to charge the higher price on the spot. By contrast, knowing that customer B is going to put author John le Carré's latest thriller back on the shelf unless it's priced at $20, instead of $28, would open an opportunity for a bookseller to make the sale by cutting the price in real time." However, putting this concept "into practice online has turned out to be exceptionally difficult, in part because the Internet also has empowered consumers to compare prices to find out if other merchants are offering a better deal or if other consumers are getting a bigger break." It has also made it easier for consumers to register a complaint. For example, "Amazon.com raised a furor . . . when customers learned they were paying different prices for the same DVD movies, the result of a marketing test in which the retailer varied prices to gauge the effect on demand." After receiving many complaints from irate consumers, "Amazon.com announced it would refund the difference between the highest and lowest prices in the test."

product that can be manufactured for the allowable cost. This process, called **target costing**, is used widely by companies in the development stages of new products. A new product's **target cost** is the projected long-run cost that will enable a firm to enter and remain in the market for the product and compete successfully with the firm's competitors.

A Strategic Profit and Cost Management Process

Target costing can be a critical tool for management as it seeks to strategically manage the company's costs and profits. By ensuring that products are designed so that they can be produced at a low enough cost to be priced competitively, management can achieve and maintain a sustainable competitive position in the market.

Key Principles of Target Costing Target costing involves seven key principles:[6]

- *Price-led costing.* Target costing sets the target cost by *first* determining the price at which a product can be sold in the marketplace. Subtracting the *target profit margin* from this *target price* yields the *target cost*, that is, the cost at which the product must be manufactured. This simple, but strategically important, relationship can be expressed in the following equation:

  Target cost = Target price − Target profit

  Notice that in a target costing approach, the price is set *first*, and *then* the target product cost is determined. This is opposite from the order in which the product cost and selling price are determined under traditional cost-plus pricing.

- *Focus on the customer.* To be successful at target costing, management must listen to the company's customers. What products do they want? What features are important? How much are they willing to pay for a certain level of product quality? Management needs to aggressively seek customer feedback, and then products must be designed to satisfy customer demand and be sold at a price they are willing to pay. In short, the target costing approach is market-driven.

- *Focus on product design.* Design engineering is a key element in target costing. Engineers must design a product from the ground up so that it can be produced at its target cost. This design activity includes specifying the raw materials and components to be used as well as the labour, machinery, and other elements of the production process. In short, a product must be designed for manufacturability.

Design engineers play a crucial role in target costing by designing a product that can be manufactured at its target cost and sold at its target price.

- *Focus on process design.* As indicated in the preceding point, every aspect of the production process must be examined to make sure that the product is produced as efficiently as possible. The use of touch labour, technology, global sourcing in procurement, and every aspect of the production process must be designed with the product's target cost in mind.

- *Cross-functional teams.* Manufacturing a product at or below its target cost requires the involvement of people from many different functions in an organization: market research, sales, design engineering, procurement, production engineering, production scheduling, material handling, and cost management. Individuals from all of these diverse areas of expertise can make key contributions to the target costing process. Moreover, "a cross-functional team is not a set of specialists who contribute their expertise and then leave; they are responsible for the entire product."[7]

- *Life-cycle costs.* In specifying a product's target cost, analysts must be careful to incorporate all of the product's *life-cycle costs.* These include the costs of product planning and concept design, preliminary design, detailed design and testing, production, distribution, and customer service. Traditional cost accounting systems have tended to focus only on the production phase and have not paid enough attention to the product's other life-cycle costs. A more detailed discussion of the budgeting for life-cycle costs was covered in Chapter 8.
- *Value-chain orientation.* Sometimes the projected cost of a new product is above the target cost. Then efforts are made to eliminate *non-value-added costs* to bring the projected cost down. In some cases, a close look at the company's entire value chain can help managers identify opportunities for cost reduction. For example, Procter & Gamble placed order-entry computers in Walmart stores. This resulted in substantial savings in order-processing costs for both companies.[8]

Price-led costing
Customer focus
Product design
Process design
Cross-functional teams
Life-cycle costing
Value-chain orientation

Activity-Based Costing and Target Costing

An activity-based costing (ABC) system can be particularly helpful as product design engineers try to achieve a product's target cost. ABC enables designers to break down the production process for a new product into its component activities. Then designers can attempt cost improvement in particular activities to bring a new product's projected cost into line with its target cost.

To illustrate, Sydney Sailing Supplies' Marine Services Division wants to introduce a new depth finder. Target costing studies indicate that a target cost of $340 must be met in order to successfully compete in this market. Exhibit 13–6 shows how ABC was used to bring the depth finder's initial cost estimate of $399 down to $337, just below the target cost. The company's design engineers were able to focus on key activities in the production process, such as material handling and inspection, and reduce the projected costs.

Computer-Integrated Manufacturing   When a computer-integrated manufacturing system is used, the process of target costing sometimes is computerized. A manufacturer's computer-aided design and cost accounting software are interconnected. An engineer can try out many different design features and immediately see the product-cost implications without ever leaving the computer terminal.

A. Activity-Based Costing System

Activity Cost Pool	Cost Driver	Pool Rate
Purchasing	Number of parts	$1 per part
Material handling	Dollar value of parts	$0.20 per direct-material dollar
Inspection	Inspection hours	$28 per inspection hour

B. Cost Projections for a New Product: Depth Finder

	Original Cost Projection	Improved Cost Projection
Direct material	$200	$190
Direct labour	100	70
Purchasing:		
$1 per part (45 parts)	45	
$1 per part (32 parts)		32
Material handling:		
$0.20 per direct-material dollar ($200)	40	
$0.20 per direct-material dollar ($190)		38
Inspection:		
$28 per inspection hour (0.5 hour)	14	
$28 per inspection hour (0.25 hour)		7
Total projected cost	$399	$337
Target cost		$340

Exhibit 13–6
Target Costing and Cost Improvement for a New Product

SYDNEY SAILING SUPPLIES

Product-Cost Distortion and Pricing: The Role of Activity-Based Costing

Use of a traditional volume-based product-costing system may result in significant cost distortion among product lines. In many cases, high-volume and relatively simple products are overcosted, while low-volume and complex products are undercosted. This results from the fact that high-volume and relatively simple products require proportionately less activity per unit for various manufacturing-support activities than do low-volume and complex products. Yet a traditional product-costing system, in which all overhead is assigned on the basis of a single unit-level activity like direct-labour hours, fails to capture the cost implications of product diversity. In contrast, an activity-based costing (ABC) system does measure the extent to which each product line drives costs in the key production-support activities.

Managers should be aware that cost distortion can result in overpricing high-volume and relatively simple products, while low-volume and complex products are undercosted. This can undermine any effort to set prices competitively, even under the target costing approach. The competitive implications of such strategic pricing errors can be disastrous.

Learning Objective 7

Explain how product-cost distortion can undermine a firm's pricing strategy.

Value Engineering and Target Costing

Target costing is an outgrowth of the concept of **value engineering**, which is a cost-reduction and process-improvement technique that utilizes information collected about a product's design and production processes and then examines various attributes of the design and processes to identify candidates for improvement efforts. The attributes examined include such characteristics as part diversity and process complexity. Examples of value engineering in the area of direct materials include changing the quality or grade

Learning Objective 8

Explain the process of value engineering and its role in target costing.

of materials, reducing the number of bolts in a part, using a component common to other products instead of a unique or specialized component, and changing the method of painting.

Much of the historical development of the target costing approach has taken place in Japanese industry, where "more than 80 percent of all assembly industries in Japan use target costing. Some of the best practitioners of target costing are leading Japanese companies."[9] In recent years, however, many other companies, including Caterpillar, Chrysler, Boeing, and Kodak, have made significant contributions to target costing theory and practice.

Isuzu Motors, Ltd. is a leading Japanese manufacturer of automobiles, buses, and both light and heavy-duty trucks. "At Isuzu, value engineering (VE) has been developed to cover all stages of product design and manufacture. Indeed, three different stages of VE—zeroth, first, and second 'looks'—are used in the design phase to increase the functionality of new products."[10]

- *Zeroth-look VE* is applied at the earliest stages of new product design—"the concept proposal stage, when the basic concept of the product is developed and its preliminary quality, cost, and investment targets are established."
- *First-look VE* is applied during the last half of the concept proposal stage and throughout the product planning phase. During this stage, a product's quality, functionality, and selling price are determined; a design plan is submitted; and target costs are determined for each of the new vehicle's major functions (e.g., engine and transmission). Also, the degree of component commonality is set. "First-look VE is used at this stage to increase the value of the product by increasing its functionality without increasing its cost."
- *Second-look VE* is applied during the last half of the product planning stage and the first half of the product development and preparation stage. "The components of the vehicle's major functions are identified, and hand-made prototypes are assembled. At this stage, VE works to improve the value and functionality of existing components, not to create new ones."

In addition, various *tear-down methods* are used by Isuzu, and many other companies, "to analyze competitive products in terms of materials they contain, parts they use, ways they function, and ways they are manufactured." At Isuzu, for example, dynamic tear-down focuses on reducing the number of vehicle assembly operations or the time required to perform them. *Cost tear-down* examines ways to reduce the cost of the components used in a vehicle. *Material tear-down* compares the materials and surface treatments of the components used by Isuzu with those of its competitors. *Static tear-down* disassembles a competitor's product into its components to enable Isuzu's engineers to compare Isuzu's components with those used in the competitor's product.

Although the Isuzu approach is illustrative of target costing methods, many different approaches are used by the thousands of companies now engaged in target costing programs. However, the Isuzu target costing and value-engineering process is indicative of the seriousness with which companies approach the problem of reducing costs in order to meet a product's target cost and remain competitive in an increasingly difficult market.

> "An old Japanese saying states that 'there are many ways to the top of a mountain.' Analogously, there is no one right way to do target costing." (13f)
>
> **Honda**

Time and Material Pricing

Learning Objective **9**

Determine prices using the time and material pricing approach.

Another cost-based approach to pricing is called **time and material pricing**. Under this approach, the company determines one charge for the labour used on a job and another charge for the materials. The labour typically includes the direct cost of the employee's time and a charge to cover various overhead costs. The material charge generally includes the direct cost of the materials used in a job plus a charge for material handling and storage. Time and material pricing is used widely by construction companies, printers, repair shops, and professional firms, such as engineering, law, and public accounting firms.

To illustrate, we will examine a special job undertaken by Sydney Sailing Supplies. The company's vice-president of sales, Richard Moby, was approached by a successful local physician about refurbishing her yacht. She wanted an engine overhaul, complete refurbishment and redecoration of the cabin facilities, and stripping and repainting of the hull and deck. The work would be done in the Repair Department of the company's Yacht Division.

Data regarding the operations of the Repair Department are as follows:

Labour rate, including fringe benefits	$18 per hour
Hourly charge to cover profit margin	$7 per hour
Annual labour hours	10,000 hours
Annual overhead costs:	
Material handling and storage	$40,000
Other overhead costs (supervision, utilities, insurance, and depreciation)	$200,000
Annual cost of materials used in Repair Department	$1,000,000

Based on these data, the Repair Department computed its time and material prices as follows:

The effect of the material-charge formula is to include a charge for the costs incurred in the handling and storage of materials.

Richard Moby estimates that the yacht refurbishment job will require 200 hours of labour and $8,000 in materials. Moby's price quotation for the job is shown in the Excel spreadsheet in Exhibit 13–7. Included in the $17,320 price quotation for the yacht refurbishment are charges for labour costs, overhead, material costs, material handling and storage costs, and a normal profit margin. Some companies also charge an additional markup on the materials used in a job in order to earn a profit on that component of their services. Sydney Sailing Supplies' practice is to charge a high enough profit charge on its labour to earn an appropriate profit for the Repair Department.

Exhibit 13–7
Time and Material Pricing

	A	B	C	D	E	F	G	H
1			SYDNEY SAILING SUPPLIES					
2			Price Quotation					
3			Yacht Division: Repair Department					
4								
5	Time charges	Labour time					200	hours
6		x Rate				x	$ 45	per hour
7		Total					$ 9,000	
8								
9	Material charges	Cost of materials for job					$ 8,000	
10		+ Charge for material handling and storage*					320	
11		Total					$ 8,320	
12								
13	Total price of job	Time					$ 9,000	
14		Material					8,320	
15		Total					$ 17,320	
16								
17	*Charge for material handling and storage:							
18	($8,000 material cost) x ($0.04 per dollar of material cost) = $320							

Competitive Bidding

Learning Objective   **10**

Set prices in competitive-bidding situations.

In a **competitive bidding** situation, two or more companies submit sealed bids (or prices) for a project, service, or product to a potential buyer. The buyer selects one of the companies for the job on the basis of the bid price and the design specifications for the job. Competitive bidding complicates a manager's pricing problem, because now the manager is in direct competition with one or more competitors. If all of the companies submitting bids offer a roughly equivalent product or service, the bid price becomes the sole criterion for selecting the contractor. The higher the price that is bid, the greater will be the profit on the job, if the firm gets the contract. However, a higher price also lowers the probability of obtaining the contract to perform the job. So there is a trade-off between bidding high, to make a good profit, and bidding low, to land the contract. Some say there is a "winner's curse" in competitive bidding, meaning that the company bidding low enough to beat out its competitors probably bid too low to make an acceptable profit on the job. Despite the winner's curse, competitive bidding is a common form of selecting contractors in many types of businesses.

Richard Moby was approached recently by the City of Sydney about building a new marina for moderate-sized sailing vessels. Moby decided that his company's Marine Services Division should submit a bid on the job. The Marine Services Division specializes in marina maintenance and construction. The City announced that three other firms also would be submitting bids. Since all four companies were equally capable of building the marina to the City's specifications, Moby assumed that the bid price would be the deciding factor in selecting the contractor.

Moby consulted with the controller and chief engineer of the Marine Services Division, and the following data were compiled:

Estimated direct-labour requirements, 1,500 hrs. @ $12 per hr.	$18,000
Estimated direct-material requirements	30,000
Estimated variable overhead (allocated on the basis of direct labour), 1,500 direct-labour hrs. @ $5 per hr.	7,500
Total estimated variable costs	55,500
Estimated fixed overhead (allocated on the basis of direct labour), 1,500 direct-labour hrs. @ $8 per hr.	12,000
Estimated total cost	$67,500

The Marine Services Division allocates variable-overhead costs to jobs on the basis of direct-labour hours. These costs consist of indirect-labour costs, such as the wages of equipment-repair personnel, gasoline and lubricants, and incidental supplies such as rope, chains, and drill bits. Fixed-overhead costs, also allocated to jobs on the basis of direct-labour hours, include such costs as Workers' Compensation insurance, depreciation on vehicles and construction equipment, depreciation of the division's buildings, and supervisory salaries.

It was up to Richard Moby to decide on the bid price for the marina. In his meeting with the divisional controller and the chief engineer, Moby argued that the marina job was important to the company for two reasons. First, the Marine Services Division had been operating well below capacity for several months. The marina job would not preclude the firm from taking on any other construction work, so it would not entail an opportunity cost. Second, the marina job would be good advertising for Sydney Sailing Supplies. City residents would see the firm's name on the project, and this would promote sales of the company's boats and sailing supplies.

Based on these arguments, Moby pressed for a bid price that just covered the firm's variable costs and allowed for a modest contribution margin. The chief engineer was obstinate, however, and argued for a higher bid price that would give the division a good profit on the job. "My employees work hard to do an outstanding job, and their work is worth a premium to the City" was the engineer's final comment on the issue. After the threesome tossed the problem around all morning, the controller agreed with Moby. A bid price of $60,000 was finally agreed on.

This is a typical approach to setting prices for competitively bid contracts. When a firm has excess capacity, a price that covers the incremental costs incurred because of the job will contribute toward covering the company's fixed cost and profit. None of the Marine Services Division's fixed costs will increase as a result of taking on the marina job. Therefore, a bid price of $60,000 will cover the $55,500 of variable costs on the job and contribute $4,500 toward covering the division's fixed costs.

Bid price	$60,000
Variable costs of marina job (incremental costs incurred only if job is done)	55,500
Contribution from marina job (contribution to covering the division's fixed costs)	$ 4,500

Naturally, Sydney Sailing Supplies' management would like to make a larger profit on the marina job, but bidding a higher price means running a substantial risk of losing the job to a competitor.

No Excess Capacity What if the Marine Services Division has no excess capacity? If management expects to have enough work to fully occupy the division, a different approach is appropriate in setting the bid price. The fixed costs of the division are capacity-producing costs, which are costs incurred in order to create productive capacity. Depreciation of buildings and equipment, supervisory salaries, insurance, and property taxes are examples of fixed costs incurred to give a company the capacity to carry on its operations. When such costs are allocated to individual jobs, the cost of each job reflects an estimate of the opportunity cost of using limited capacity to do that particular job. For this reasoning to be valid, however, the organization must be at full capacity. If there is excess capacity, there is no opportunity cost in using that excess capacity.

If the Marine Services Division has no excess capacity, it would be appropriate to focus on the estimated full cost of the marina job, $67,500, which includes an allocation of the division's fixed capacity-producing costs. Now Richard Moby might legitimately argue for a bid price in excess of $67,500. If the division is awarded the marina contract by the City, a price above $67,500 will cover all of the costs of the job and make a contribution toward the division's profit.

However, as Richard Moby pointed out, there will be valuable promotional benefits to Sydney Sailing Supplies if its Marine Services Division builds the marina. This is a qualitative factor, because these potential benefits are difficult to quantify. Moby will have to make a judgment regarding just how important the marina job is to the company. The greater the perceived qualitative benefits, the lower the bid price should be set to maximize the likelihood that the company will be awarded the contract.

Summary of Competitive-Bidding Analysis The Marine Services Division's pricing problem is summarized in Exhibit 13–8. As you can see, the final pricing decision requires managerial judgment to fully consider the quantitative cost data, the qualitative promotional benefits, and the trade-off between a higher profit and a greater likelihood of getting the marina contract.

Accept or Reject a Special Order In the preceding chapter, we examined in detail the decision as to whether a special order should be accepted or rejected. The analysis focused on identifying the relevant costs of the special order. The existence of excess capacity was an important factor in that analysis. Accepting a special order when excess capacity exists

Exhibit 13–8

Summary of Competitive-Bidding Analysis

entails no opportunity cost. But when there is no excess capacity, one relevant cost of accepting a special order is the opportunity cost incurred by using the firm's limited capacity for the special order instead of for some other job. After all relevant costs of the order have been identified, the decision maker compares the total relevant cost of the order with the price offered. If the price exceeds the relevant cost, the order generally should be accepted.

The decision is conceptually very similar to the bid-pricing problem discussed in this chapter. Setting a price for a special order or competitive bid also entails an analysis of the relevant costs of the job. Whether the decision maker is setting a price or has been offered a price, she or he must identify the relevant costs of providing the product or service requested.

Effect of Regulations on Pricing

Companies are not free to set any price they want for their products or services. The Canadian *Competition Act*—enacted in 1889, one year before the U.S.'s *Sherman Act*, making it the oldest antitrust statute in the Western world—restricts certain types of pricing behaviour. These laws prohibit **price discrimination**, which means quoting different prices to different customers for the same product or service. Such price differences are unlawful unless they can be clearly justified by differences in the costs incurred to produce, sell, or deliver the product or service. Managers should keep careful records justifying such cost differences when they exist, because the records may be vital to a legal defence if price differences are challenged in court.

Another pricing practice prohibited by law is **predatory pricing**. This practice involves temporarily cutting a price to broaden demand for a product with the intention of later restricting the supply and raising the price again. In determining whether a price is predatory, the courts examine a business's cost records. If the product is sold below cost, the pricing is deemed to be predatory. The laws and court cases are ambiguous as to the appropriate definition of cost. However, various court decisions make it harder to prove predatory pricing. Nevertheless, this is one area where a price-setting decision maker is well advised to have an accountant on the left and a lawyer on the right before setting prices that could be deemed predatory.

Learning Objective **11**

Describe the legal restrictions on setting prices.

Chapter Summary

LO1 List and describe the four major factors of **pricing decisions.** Many factors affect pricing decisions. Chief among these are customer demand; the actions of competitors; the costs of the products or services; and political, legal, and image-related issues.

LO2 Explain and use the economic, profit-maximizing pricing model. Under this approach to pricing, the profit-maximizing quantity is determined by the intersection of the marginal revenue and marginal cost curves. At this optimal sales quantity level, the profit-maximizing price is determined from the demand (or average revenue) curve.

LO3 Set prices using cost-plus pricing formulas. Cost-plus pricing formulas are commonly based on four product-cost measures: (1) variable manufacturing cost; (2) absorption manufacturing cost; (3) total cost; and (4) total variable cost. Markups often are set to earn the company a target profit on its products, based on a target rate of return on investment.

LO4 Discuss the issues involved in the strategic pricing of new products. Strategic pricing of new products is a particularly challenging problem for management. Various pricing approaches, such as skimming pricing or penetration pricing, may be appropriate, depending on the product.

LO5 List and discuss the key principles of target costing. Target costing often is used to design a new product that can be produced at a cost that will enable the firm to sell it at a competitive price. Value engineering and activity-based costing are valuable tools used in the target costing process.

LO6 Explain the role of activity-based costing in setting a target cost. Activity-based costing helps to avoid product-cost distortion, in which relatively high-volume and relatively simple products tend to be overcosted by traditional product-costing systems, and relatively low-volume and relatively complex products tend to be undercosted.

LO7 Explain how product-cost distortion can undermine a firm's pricing strategy. Product-cost distortion occurs when relatively high-volume and relatively simple products tend to be overcosted by traditional product-costing systems, and relatively low-volume and relatively complex products tend to be undercosted. This phenomenon can lead a company to lose sales by overpricing certain products and lose profit by selling other products at too low a price.

LO8 Explain the process of value engineering and its role in target costing. Value engineering analyzes a product's design and production process to identify areas for cost reduction and process improvement. By reducing a product's cost, management can bring a product's production cost down to meet its target cost.

LO9 Determine prices using the time and material pricing approach. In industries such as construction, repair, printing, and professional services, time and material pricing often is used. Under this approach, the price is determined as the sum of a labour-cost component and a material-cost component. Either or both of these components may include a markup to ensure that the company earns a profit on its services.

LO10 Set prices in competitive-bidding situations. Determining competitive bid prices entails an analysis of the relevant costs to be incurred in completing the job. The relevant-cost analysis should incorporate the existence of excess capacity or the lack of it.

LO11 Describe the legal restrictions on setting prices. The law prohibits price discrimination, which means quoting different prices to different customers for the same product or service. Also outlawed is predatory pricing, which involves temporarily cutting a price to broaden demand for a product with the intention of later restricting the supply and raising the price again.

Review Problem on Cost-Plus Pricing

Kitchenware Corporation manufactures high-quality copper pots and pans. Greta Cooke, one of the company's price analysts, is involved in setting a price for the company's new Starter Set. This set consists of seven of the most commonly used pots and pans. During the next year, the company plans to produce 10,000 Starter Sets, and the controller has provided Cooke with the following cost data:

	Predicted Costs of 10,000 Starter Sets
Direct material per set	$60
Direct labour per set, 2 hrs. @ $10 per hr.	20
Variable selling cost per set	5
Total	$85
Variable-overhead rate	$8 per direct-labour hour
Fixed-overhead rate	$12 per direct-labour hour

In addition, the controller indicated that the Accounting Department would allocate $20,000 of fixed administrative expenses to the Starter Set product line.

Required:

1. Compute the cost of a Starter Set using each of the four cost definitions commonly used in cost-plus pricing formulas.

2. Determine the markup percentage required for the Starter Set product line to earn a target profit of $317,500 before taxes during the next year. Use the total cost as the cost definition in the cost-plus formula.

Solution to Review Problem

1.

Variable manufacturing cost*	$ 96	[1]
Applied fixed-overhead cost†	24	
Absorption manufacturing cost	120	[2]
Variable selling cost	5	
Allocated fixed administrative cost‡	2	
Total cost	$127	[3]
Variable manufacturing cost	$ 96	
Variable selling cost	5	
Total variable cost	$101	[4]
*Direct material	$ 60	
Direct labour	20	
Variable overhead	16 (2 × $8 per hr.)	
Total variable manufacturing cost	$ 96	

*Variable manufacturing cost, $96 [$60 + $20 + (2 × $8 per hr.).
†Applied fixed overhead cost, $24 (2 × $12 per hr.).
‡Allocated fixed administrative cost, $2 ($20,000 ÷ 10,000 sets).

2. Markup percentage on total cost $= \dfrac{\$317{,}500}{10{,}000 \times \$127} = 25\%$

Proof:
Price = Total cost + (0.25 × Total cost) = $127 + (0.25)($127) = $158.75

Income Statement

Sales revenue (10,000 × $158.75)		$1,587,500
Less: Variable costs:		
Direct material	$600,000	
Direct labour	200,000	
Variable overhead	160,000	
Variable selling cost	50,000	
Total variable costs		1,010,000
Contribution margin		577,500
Less: Fixed costs:		
Manufacturing overhead	$240,000	
Administrative cost	20,000	
Total fixed costs		260,000
Profit		$ 317,500

Glossary

Review key terms and definitions on Connect.

Review Questions

13–1. Comment on the following remark made by a bank president: "The prices of our banking services are determined by the financial services market. Costs are irrelevant."

13–2. "All of this marginal revenue and marginal cost stuff is just theory. Prices are determined by production costs." Evaluate this assertion.

13–3. List and briefly describe four major factors of pricing decisions.

13–4. Explain what is meant by the following statement: "In considering the reactions of competitors, it is crucial to define your product."

13–5. Explain the following assertion: "Price setting generally requires a balance between market forces and cost considerations."

13-6. Briefly explain the concept of economic, profit-maximizing pricing. It may be helpful to use graphs in your explanation.

13–7. Define the following terms: *total revenue, marginal revenue, demand curve, price elasticity,* and *cross-elasticity.*

13–8. Briefly define *total cost* and *marginal cost.*

13–9. Describe three limitations of the economic, profit-maximizing model of pricing.

13–10. Determining the best approach to pricing requires a cost–benefit trade-off. Explain.

13–11. Write the general formula for cost-plus pricing, and briefly explain its use.

13–12. List the four common cost bases used in cost-plus pricing. How can they all result in the same price?

13–13. List four reasons often cited for the widespread use of absorption cost as the cost base in cost-plus pricing formulas.

13–14. What is the primary disadvantage of basing the cost-plus pricing formula on absorption cost?

13–15. List three advantages of pricing based on variable cost.

13–16. Explain the behavioural problem that can result when cost-plus prices are based on variable cost.

13–17. Briefly explain the concept of *return-on-investment pricing.*

13–18. Explain the phrase *price-led costing.*

13–19. Why is a focus on the customer such a key principle of target costing?

13–20. Explain the role of value engineering in target costing.

13–21. Can *tear-down* methods be used effectively for target pricing in a service industry company, such as a hotel or an airline? Explain.

13–22. Briefly describe the *time and material pricing approach.*

13–23. Explain the importance of the excess-capacity issue in setting a competitive bid price.

13–24. The decision to accept or reject a special order and the selection of a price for a special order are very similar decisions. Explain.

13–25. Describe the following approaches to pricing new products: skimming pricing, penetration pricing, and target costing.

13–26. Explain what is meant by *unlawful price discrimination* and *predatory pricing.*

13–27. Briefly explain the potential negative consequences in pricing decisions from using a traditional volume-based product-costing system.

Exercises

Exercise 13–28 Demand and Revenue Data (LO2)

Spectrum Sound, Inc. manufactures DVD players with unusual features in its Mississauga Division. The divisional sales manager has estimated the following demand-curve data:

Quantity Sold per Month	Unit Sales Price
20	$1,000
40	950
60	900
80	850
100	800

Required:

1. Prepare a table similar to panel C of Exhibit 13–1 summarizing Spectrum Sound's price, quantity, and revenue data.
2. Draw a graph similar to panel A of Exhibit 13–1 reflecting the data tabulated in requirement (1).

Exercise 13–29 Continuation of Preceding Exercise: Cost Data (LO2)

Refer to the preceding exercise. The divisional controller at Spectrum Sound's Mississauga Division has estimated the following cost data for the division's DVD players. (Assume there are no fixed costs.)

Quantity Produced and Sold per Month	Average Cost per Unit
20	$900
40	850
60	820
80	860
100	890

Required:

1. Prepare a table similar to panel C of Exhibit 13–2 summarizing Spectrum Sound's cost relationships.
2. Draw a graph similar to the panel A of Exhibit 13–2 reflecting the data tabulated in requirement (1).

Exercise 13–30 Continuation of Preceding Two Exercises: Profit-Maximizing Price (L02)

Refer to the data given in the preceding two exercises.

Required:

1. Prepare a table of Spectrum Sound's revenue, cost, and profit relationships. For guidance, refer to panel C of Exhibit 13–3.
2. Draw a graph similar to the one in Exhibit 13–3 reflecting the data tabulated in requirement (1).
3. To narrow down the pricing decision, the Mississauga Division's sales manager has decided to price the DVD player at one of the following prices: $800, $850, $900, $950 or $1,000. Which price do you recommend? Why?

Exercise 13–31 Marginal Revenue and Marginal Cost Curves (L02)

The marginal cost, marginal revenue, and demand curves for Houston Home and Garden's deluxe wheelbar-row are shown in the graph below.

Dollars per unit

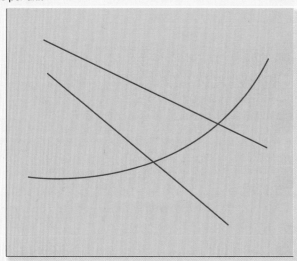

Quantity produced
and sold per month

Required:

1. Trace the graph onto a blank piece of paper, and label all parts of the graph.
2. Draw a companion graph directly above the traced graph. Use this graph to draw the firm's total revenue and total cost curves.
3. Show the company's profit-maximizing price on the lower graph and its profit-maximizing quantity on both graphs.

Exercise 13–32 Pricing, Advertising, and Special-Order Decisions (L010)

Corrientes Company produces a single product in its Buenos Aires plant that currently sells for 5.00 p per unit. (p denotes the peso, Argentina's national currency.) Fixed costs are expected to amount to 60,000 p for the year, and all variable manufacturing and administrative costs are expected to be incurred at a rate of 3.00 p per unit. Corrientes has two salespeople who are paid strictly on a commission basis. Their commission is 10 percent of the sales revenue they generate. (Ignore income taxes.) (Many countries use the peso as their national currency. On the day this exercise was written, 1 Argentina peso was worth $0.2244 in Canadian currency.)

Required:

1. Suppose management alters its current plans by spending an additional 5,000 p on advertising and increases the selling price to 6.00 p per unit. Calculate the profit on 60,000 units.
2. The Sorde Company has just approached Corrientes to make a special one-time purchase of 10,000 units. These units would not be sold by the sales personnel and, therefore, no commission would have to be paid. What is the price Corrientes would have to charge per unit on this special order to earn additional profit of 20,000 p?

(CMA, adapted)

Exercise 13–33 Target Costing for a New Product; Use of the Internet **(LO5, 6)**

Visit the website of one of the following companies, or a different company of your choice.

Research In Motion (RIM)	www.rim.com
Procter & Gamble	www.pg.com
Carnival Cruise Lines	www.carnival.com
TD Canada Trust	www.tdcanadatrust.com
General Electric Company	www.ge.com
Hewlett-Packard	www.hp.com
Intel Corporation	www.intel.com

Required: Read about a new product or service to be offered by the company. Then explain how the firm could use target costing to price the new product or service.

Exercise 13–34 Determining Markup Percentage; Target ROI **(LO3)**

Refer to the cost and production data for the Wave Darter in Exhibit 13–5. The target profit is $60,000.

Required: Use the general formula for determining a markup percentage to compute the required markup percentages with the following two cost-plus formulas:

1. Variable manufacturing costs: formula (1) in Exhibit 13–5.
2. Absorption manufacturing cost: formula (2) in Exhibit 13–5.

Exercise 13–35 Cost-Plus Pricing Formulas; Missing Data **(LO3)**

The following data pertain to Lawn Master Corporation's top-of-the-line lawn mower:

Variable manufacturing cost	$250
Applied fixed manufacturing cost	50
Variable selling and administrative cost	60
Allocated fixed selling and administrative cost	?

To achieve a target price of $450 per lawn mower, the markup percentage is 12.5 percent on total unit cost.

Required:

1. What is the fixed selling and administrative cost allocated to each unit of Lawn Master's top-of-the-line mower?
2. For each of the following cost bases, develop a cost-plus pricing formula that will result in a target price of $450 per mower: (*a*) variable manufacturing cost, (*b*) absorption manufacturing cost, and (*c*) total variable cost.

Exercise 13–36 Cost-Plus Pricing Formulas **(LO3)**

The following data pertain to Royal Lighting Company's oak-clad, contemporary chandelier:

Variable manufacturing cost	$200
Applied fixed manufacturing cost	70
Variable selling and administrative cost	30
Allocated fixed selling and administrative cost	50

Required: For each of the following cost bases, develop a cost-plus pricing formula that will result in a price of $400 for the oak chandelier.

    a. Variable manufacturing cost

    b. Absorption manufacturing cost

    c. Total cost

    d. Total variable cost

Exercise 13–37 Time and Material Pricing **(LO7)**

Refer to Exhibit 13–7. Suppose the Repair Department of Sydney Sailing Supplies adds a markup of 5 percent on the material charges of a job (including the cost of material handling and storage).

Required:

1. Rewrite the material component of the time and material pricing formula to reflect the markup on material cost.
2. Compute the new price to be quoted on the yacht refurbishment described in Exhibit 13–7.

Problems

Problem 13–38 Pricing a Special Order (LO10)

Badger Valve and Fitting Company, located in southern Ontario, manufactures a variety of industrial valves and pipe fittings. Currently, the company is operating at about 70 percent capacity and is earning a satisfactory return on investment. Management has been approached by Glasgow Industries Ltd. of Scotland with an offer to buy 120,000 units of a pressure valve. Glasgow Industries manufactures a valve that is almost identical to Badger's pressure valve; however, a fire in Glasgow Industries' valve plant has shut down its manufacturing operations. Glasgow needs the 120,000 valves over the next four months to meet commitments to its regular customers. Glasgow is prepared to pay $19 each for the valves. Badger's total product cost for the pressure valve is $20, based on current attainable standards and calculated as follows:

Direct material	$ 5
Direct labour	6
Manufacturing overhead	9
Total product cost	$20

Manufacturing overhead is applied to production at the rate of $18 per direct-labour hour. This overhead rate is made up of the following components:

Variable manufacturing overhead	$ 6
Fixed manufacturing overhead (traceable)	8
Fixed manufacturing overhead (allocated)	4
Applied manufacturing-overhead rate	$18

Additional costs incurred in connection with sales of the pressure valve include sales commissions of 5 percent and freight expense of $1 per unit. However, the company does not pay sales commissions on orders that come directly to management. In determining selling prices, Badger adds a 40 percent markup to total product cost. This provides a $28 suggested selling price for the pressure valve. The Marketing Department, however, has set the current selling price at $27 in order to maintain market share. Production management believes that it can handle the Glasgow Industries order without disrupting its scheduled production. The order would, however, require additional fixed factory overhead of $12,000 per month in the form of supervision and clerical costs. If management wins the bid, 30,000 pressure valves will be manufactured and shipped to Glasgow Industries each month for the next four months. Glasgow's management has agreed to pay the shipping charges for the valves.

Required:

1. Determine how many direct-labour hours would be required each month to fill the Glasgow Industries order.
2. Prepare an analysis showing the impact of winning the bid.
3. Calculate the minimum unit price that Badger Valve and Fitting Company's management could bid without reducing net income.
4. Identify the factors, other than price, that Badger's management should consider before bidding on the Glasgow Industries order.
5. *Build a spreadsheet:* Construct an Excel spreadsheet to solve requirements (2) and (3) above. Show how the solution will change if the following information changes: The direct material and direct labour per unit are $4.90 and $6.10, respectively.

eXcel

(CMA, adapted)

Problem 13–39 Cost-Plus Pricing; Bidding (LO3, 10)

North American Pharmaceuticals, Inc. specializes in packaging bulk drugs in standard dosages for local hospitals. The company has been in business for seven years and has been profitable since its second year of operation. Don Greenway, assistant controller, installed a standard costing system after joining the company three years ago.

Vancouver General Hospital (VGH) has asked North American Pharmaceuticals to bid on the packaging of one million doses of medication at total cost plus a return on total cost of no more than 15 percent. VGH defines total cost as including all variable costs of performing the service, a reasonable amount of fixed overhead, and reasonable administrative costs. The hospital will supply all packaging materials and ingredients. VGH's administrator has indicated that any bid over $0.015 per dose will be rejected.

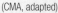

Greenway has accumulated the following information prior to the preparation of the bid:

Direct labour	$8 per direct-labour hour (DLH)
Variable overhead	$6 per DLH
Fixed overhead	$10 per DLH
Incremental administrative costs	$1,000 for the order
Production rate	2,000 doses per DLH

Required:

1. Calculate the minimum price per dose that North American Pharmaceuticals could bid for the VGH job that would not reduce the pharmaceutical company's income.

2. Calculate the bid price per dose using total cost and the maximum allowable return specified by VGH.

3. Independent of your answer to requirement (2), suppose that the price per dose that North American Pharmaceuticals, Inc. calculated using the cost-plus criterion specified by VGH is greater than the maximum bid of $0.015 per dose allowed by VGH. Discuss the factors that the pharmaceutical company's management should consider before deciding whether to submit a bid at the maximum price of $0.015 per dose that VGH allows.

(CMA, adapted)

Problem 13–40 Target Costing (LO1, 5, 6, 8)

4. Target profit: $2,520,000

MPE, Inc. will soon enter a very competitive marketplace in which it will have limited influence over the prices that are charged. Management and consultants are currently working to fine-tune the company's sole service, which hopefully will generate a 12 percent first-year return (profit) on the firm's $18,000,000 asset investment. Although the normal return in MPE's industry is 14 percent, executives are willing to accept the lower figure because of various start-up inefficiencies. The following information is available for first-year operations:

Hours of service to be provided	25,000
Anticipated variable cost per service hour	$22
Anticipated fixed cost	$1,900,000 per year

Required:

1. Assume that management is contemplating what price to charge in the first year of operation. The company can take its cost and add a markup to achieve a 12 percent return; alternatively, it can use target costing. Given MPE's marketplace, which approach is probably more appropriate? Why?

2. How much profit must MPE generate in the first year to achieve a 12 percent return?

3. Calculate the revenue per hour that MPE must generate in the first year to achieve a 12 percent return.

4. Assume that prior to the start of business in Year 1, management conducted a planning exercise to determine if MPE could attain a 14 percent return in Year 2. Can the company achieve this return if (*a*) competitive pressures dictate a maximum selling price of $175 per hour and (*b*) service hours and the variable cost per service hour are the same as the amounts anticipated in Year 1? Show your calculations.

5. If your answer to requirement (4) is no, suggest and briefly describe a procedure that MPE might use to achieve the desired results.

Problem 13–41 Cost-Plus Pricing versus Target Costing (LO1, 3, 5, 6, 8)

3. Required cost reduction: $24

For many years, Leno Corporation has used a straightforward cost-plus pricing system, marking its goods up approximately 25 percent of total cost. The company has been profitable; however, it has recently lost considerable business to foreign competitors that have become very aggressive in the marketplace. These firms appear to be using target costing.

An example of Leno's problem is typified by item #8976, which has the following unit-cost characteristics:

Direct material	$ 30
Direct labour	75
Manufacturing overhead	50
Selling and administrative expenses	25

The going market price for an identical product of comparable quality is $195, which is significantly below what Leno is charging.

Required:

1. Contrast cost-plus pricing and target costing. Which of the two approaches could be aptly labelled as *price-led costing*? Why?

2. What is Leno's current selling price of item #8976?

3. If Leno used target costing for item #8976, by how much must costs change if the company wants to meet the market price and maintain its current rate of profit *on sales*?

4. Would the identification of value-added and non-value-added costs assist Leno in this situation? Briefly explain.

5. Suppose that by previous cost-cutting drives, costs had already been "pared to the bone" on item #8976 What might Leno be forced to do with its markup on cost to remain competitive? By how much must the markup change?

6. Early in this chapter, it was noted that, in most industries, both market forces and cost considerations heavily influence prices. Explain what is meant by this statement.

7. *Build a spreadsheet:* Construct an Excel spreadsheet to solve requirements (2) and (3) above. Show how the solution will change if the following information changes: The direct material and direct labour per unit are $25 and $85, respectively.

Problem 13–42 Target Costing; Selection of Product Features **(LO5, 8)**

Danish Furniture (DF) manufactures easy-to-assemble wooden furniture for home and office. The firm is considering modification of a table to make it more attractive to individuals and businesses that buy products through outlets such as Staples. The table is small, can be used to hold a computer printer or fax machine, and has several shelves for storage.

The company's marketing department surveyed potential buyers of the table regarding five proposed modifications. The 200 survey participants were asked to evaluate the modifications by using a five-point scale that ranged from 1 (strongly disagree) to 5 (strongly agree). Their responses, along with DF's related unit costs for the modifications, follow:

3. Maximum allowable cost: $76

Proposed Modification	1 Strongly Disagree	2 Disagree	3 Neutral	4 Agree	5 Strongly Agree
Add cabinet doors in storage area ($6.00)	10	20	30	60	80
Expand storage area ($2.50)	10	40	70	50	30
Add security lock to storage area ($1.65)	30	60	50	40	20
Give table top a more rich, marble appearance ($4.25)	10	20	50	60	60
Extend warranty to five years ($5.10)	40	70	30	35	25

The table currently costs $64 to produce and distribute, and DF's selling price for this unit averages $80. An analysis of competitive tables in the marketplace revealed a variety of features, with some models having all of the features that management is considering and other models having only a few. The current manufacturers' selling prices for these tables averages $95.

Required:

1. Why is there a need in target costing to (*a*) focus on the customer and (*b*) have a marketing team become involved with product design?

2. DF's marketing team will evaluate the survey responses by computing a weighted-average rating of each of the modifications. This will be accomplished by weighting (multiplying) the point values (1, 2, etc.) by the frequency of responses, summing the results, and dividing by 200. Rank the popularity of the five modifications using this approach.

3. Management wants to earn approximately the same rate of profit on sales that is being earned with the current design.

   a. If DF uses target costing and wants to meet the current competitive selling price, what is the maximum cost of the modified table?

   b. Which of the modifications should management consider?

4. Assume that DF wanted to add a modification or two that you excluded in your answer to requirement (3*b*). What process might management adopt to allow the company to make its target profit for the table? Briefly explain.

1. The order will boost
Graydon's net income
by: $27,900

Problem 13–43   Pricing of a Special Order **(LO10)**

Graydon, Inc. manufactures food-blending machinery according to customer specifications. The company operated at 75 percent of practical capacity during the year just ended, with the following results (in thousands):

Sales revenue	$25,000
Less: Sales commissions (10%)	2,500
Net sales	22,500
Expenses:	
Direct material	6,000
Direct labour	7,500
Manufacturing overhead—variable	2,250
Manufacturing overhead—fixed	1,500
Corporate administration—fixed	750
Total costs	18,000
Income before taxes	4,500
Income taxes (40%)	1,800
Net income	$ 2,700

Graydon, which expects continued operations at 75 percent of capacity, recently submitted a bid of $165,000 on some custom-designed machinery for Premier Foods, Inc. Graydon used a pricing formula in deriving the bid amount, the formula being based on last year's operating results. The formula follows:

Estimated direct material	$ 29,200
Estimated direct labour	56,000
Estimated manufacturing overhead at 50% of direct labour	28,000
Estimated corporate overhead at 10% of direct labour	5,600
Estimated total costs excluding sales commissions	118,800
Add 25% for profit and taxes	29,700
Suggested price (with profit) before sales commissions	$148,500
Suggested total price: $148,500 ÷ 0.09 to adjust for 10% commission	$165,000

Required:

1. Calculate the impact the order would have on Graydon's net income if the $165,000 bid was accepted by Premier Foods, Inc.
2. Assume that Premier has rejected Graydon's bid but has stated it is willing to pay $127,000 for the machinery. Should Graydon manufacture the machinery for the counteroffer of $127,000? Explain your answer and show calculations.
3. At what bid price will Graydon break even on the order?
4. Explain how the profit performance in the coming year would be affected if Graydon accepted all of its work at prices similar to Premier's $127,000 counteroffer described in requirement (2).

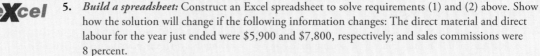

5. *Build a spreadsheet:* Construct an Excel spreadsheet to solve requirements (1) and (2) above. Show how the solution will change if the following information changes: The direct material and direct labour for the year just ended were $5,900 and $7,800, respectively; and sales commissions were 8 percent.

(CMA, adapted)

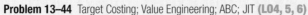

Problem 13–44   Target Costing; Value Engineering; ABC; JIT **(LO4, 5, 6)**

3. Pharsalia Electronics'
current profit on sales is
10 percent.

Alexis Kunselman, president of Pharsalia Electronics (PE), is concerned about the prospects of one of its major products. The president has been reviewing a marketing report with Jeff Keller, marketing product manager, for the company's 10-disc car CD changer. The report indicates another price reduction is needed to meet anticipated competitors' reductions in sales prices. The current selling price for their 10-disc car CD changers is $350 per unit. It is expected that within three months, PE's two major competitors will be selling their 10-disc car CD changers for $300 per unit. This concerns Kunselman because her company's current cost of producing the CD changers is $315, which yields a $35 profit on each unit sold.

The situation is especially disturbing because PE implemented an activity-based costing (ABC) system about two years ago. The ABC system helped the company to better identify costs, cost pools, cost drivers, and cost-reduction opportunities. Changes made when adopting ABC reduced costs on this product by approximately 15 percent during the last two years. Now it appears that costs will need to be reduced considerably more for the company to remain competitive and to earn a profit on the 10-disc car CD changers. Total costs to produce, sell, and service the CD changer units are as follows:

10-Disc Car CD Changer

		Per Unit
Material	Purchased components	$110
	All other material	40
Labour	Manufacturing, direct	65
	Setups	9
	Material handling	18
	Inspection	23
Machining	Cutting, shaping, and drilling	21
	Bending and finishing	14
Other	Finished-goods warehousing	5
	Warranty	10
	Total unit cost	$315

Kunselman has decided to hire Donald Collins, a consultant, to help her decide how to proceed. After two weeks of review, discussion, and value engineering analysis, Collins suggested that PE adopt a just-in-time (JIT) cell manufacturing process to help reduce costs. He also suggested that using target costing would help in meeting the new target price.

By changing to a JIT cell manufacturing system, PE expects that manufacturing direct labour will increase by $15 per finished unit. However, setup, material handling, inspection, and finished goods warehousing will all be eliminated. Machine costs will be reduced from $35 to $30 per unit, and warranty costs are expected to be reduced by 40 percent.

Required:

1. Define *target costing*.
2. Define *value engineering*.
3. Determine Pharsalia Electronics' unit target cost at the $300 competitive sales price while maintaining the same percentage of profit on sales as is earned on the current $350 sales price.
4. If the just-in-time cell manufacturing process is implemented with the changes in costs noted, will Pharsalia Electronics meet the unit target cost you determined in requirement (3)? Prepare a schedule detailing cost reductions and the unit cost under the proposed JIT cell manufacturing process.

(CMA, adapted)

Problem 13–45   Time and Material Pricing **(LO9)**

2. Total price of job: $77,600

Southern Tier Heating, Inc. installs heating systems in new homes built in Metro Vancouver. Jobs are priced using the time and materials method. The president of Southern Tier Heating, B. T. Ewing, is pricing a job involving the heating systems for six houses to be built by a local developer. He has made the following estimates:

Material cost	$60,000
Labour hours	400

The following predictions pertain to the company's operations for the next year:

Labour rate, including fringe benefits	$16 per hour
Annual labour hours	12,000 hours
Annual overhead costs:	
Material handling and storage	$25,000
Other overhead costs	$108,000
Annual cost of materials used	$250,000

Required: Southern Tier Heating adds a markup of $4 per hour on its time charges, but there is no markup on material costs.

1. Develop formulas for the company's (*a*) time charges and (*b*) material charges.
2. Compute the price for the job described above.
3. What would be the price of the job if Southern Tier Heating also added a markup of 10 percent on all material charges (including material handling and storage costs)?

Problem 13–46   Bidding on a Special Order (LO10)

Surrey Synthetic Fibres Inc. specializes in the manufacture of synthetic fibres that the company uses in many products such as blankets, coats, and uniforms for police and firefighters. The company applies overhead on the basis of direct-labour hours. Management has recently received a request to bid on the manufacture of 800,000 blankets scheduled for delivery to several military bases. The bid must be stated at full cost per unit plus a return on full cost of no more than 15 percent before income taxes. Full cost has been defined as including all variable costs of manufacturing the product, a reasonable amount of fixed overhead, and reasonable incremental administrative costs associated with the manufacture and sale of the product. The contractor has indicated that bids in excess of $25 per blanket are not likely to be considered.

In order to prepare the bid for the 800,000 blankets, Andrea Lightner, director of cost management, has gathered the following information about the costs associated with the production of the blankets:

Direct material	$1.50 per kilogram of fibres
Direct labour	$7.00 per hour
Direct machine costs*	$10.00 per blanket
Variable overhead	$3.00 per direct-labour hour
Fixed overhead	$8.00 per direct-labour hour
Incremental administrative costs	$2,500 per 1,000 blankets
Special fee†	$0.50 per blanket
Material usage	6 kilograms per blanket
Production rate	4 blankets per direct-labour hour

*Direct machine costs consist of items such as special lubricants, replacement of needles used in stitching, and maintenance costs. These costs are not included in the normal overhead rates.

†Surrey Synthetic Fibres recently developed a new blanket fibre at a cost of $750,000. In an effort to recover this cost, management has instituted a policy of adding a $0.50 fee to the cost of each blanket using the new fibre. To date, the company has recovered $125,000. Lightner knows that this fee does not fit within the definition of full cost as it is not a cost of manufacturing the product.

Required:

1. Calculate the minimum price per blanket that Surrey Synthetic Fibres Inc. could bid without reducing the company's net income.
2. Using the full cost criteria and the maximum allowable return specified, calculate Surrey Synthetic Fibres Inc.'s bid price per blanket.
3. Independently of your answer to requirement (2), assume that the price per blanket that Surrey Synthetic Fibres Inc. calculated using the cost-plus criteria specified is greater than the maximum bid of $25 per blanket allowed. Discuss the factors that management should consider before deciding whether to submit a bid at the maximum acceptable price of $25 per blanket.

(CMA, adapted)

Problem 13–47   Product Cost Distortion and Product Pricing; Departmental Overhead Rates (LO7)

Sounds Fine, Inc. manufactures two models of stereo speakers. Cost estimates for the two models for the coming year are as follows:

	Basic Model	Advanced Model
Direct material	$160	$260
Direct labour (10 hours at $14 per hour)	140	140
Manufacturing overhead*	100	100
Total cost	$400	$500

*The predetermined overhead rate is $10 per direct-labour hour.

Each stereo speaker requires 10 hours of direct labour. Each Basic Model unit requires two hours in Department I and eight hours in Department II. Each unit of the Advanced Model requires eight hours in Department I and two hours in Department II. The manufacturing overhead costs expected during the coming year in Departments I and II are as follows:

	Department I	Department II
Variable overhead	$8 per direct-labour hour	$4 per direct-labour hour
Fixed overhead	$150,000	$150,000

The expected operating activity for the coming year is 37,500 direct-labour hours in each department.

Required:

1. Show how Sounds Fine, Inc. derived its predetermined overhead rate.
2. What will be the price of each model stereo speaker if the company prices its products at absorption manufacturing cost plus 15 percent?
3. Suppose Sounds Fine, Inc. was to use departmental overhead rates. Compute these rates for Departments I and II for the coming year.
4. Compute the absorption cost of each model stereo speaker using the departmental overhead rates computed in requirement (3).
5. Suppose management sticks with its policy of setting prices equal to absorption cost plus 15 percent. Compute the new price for each speaker model using the product costs developed in requirement (4).
6. Should Sounds Fine, Inc. use plantwide or departmental overhead rates? Explain your answer.

Cases

Case 13–48 Pricing in a Tight Market; Possible Plant Closing (LO1, 10)

Gargantuan Industries is a multiproduct company with several manufacturing plants. The Richmond Plant manufactures and distributes two household cleaning and polishing compounds, standard and commercial, under the Super Clean label. The forecasted operating results for the first six months of the current year, when 100,000 cases of each compound are expected to be manufactured and sold, are presented in the following statement.

2(a). Contribution margin, Standard: $150

SUPER CLEAN COMPOUNDS—RICHMOND PLANT
Forecasted Results of Operations
For the Six-Month Period Ending June 30
(in thousands)

	Standard	Commercial	Total
Sales	$ 2,000	$3,000	$5,000
Cost of goods sold	1,600	1,900	3,500
Gross profit	400	1,100	1,500
Selling and administrative expenses:			
Variable	400	700	1,100
Fixed*	240	360	600
Total selling and administrative expenses	640	1,060	1,700
Income (loss) before taxes	$ (240)	$ 40	$ (200)

*The fixed selling and administrative expenses are allocated between the two products on the basis of dollar sales volume.

The standard compound sold for $20 a case and the commercial compound sold for $30 a case during the first six months of the year. The manufacturing costs, by case of product, are presented in the schedule below. Each product is manufactured on a separate production line. Annual normal manufacturing capacity is 200,000 cases of each product. However, the plant is capable of producing 250,000 cases of standard compound and 350,000 cases of commercial compound annually.

	Cost per Case	
	Standard	**Commercial**
Direct material...	$ 7	$ 8
Direct labour..	4	4
Variable manufacturing overhead...........................	1	2
Fixed manufacturing overhead*.............................	4	5
Total manufacturing cost..................................	$16	$19
Variable selling and administrative costs..................	$ 4	$ 7

*Depreciation charges are 50 percent of the fixed manufacturing overhead of each line.

The following schedule reflects the consensus of top management regarding the price–volume alternatives for the Super Clean products for the last six months of the current year. These are essentially the same alternatives management had during the first six months of the year.

Standard Compound		Commercial Compound	
Alternative Prices (per case)	**Sales Volume (in cases)**	**Alternative Prices (per case)**	**Sales Volume (in cases)**
$18	120,000	$25	175,000
20	100,000	27	140,000
21	90,000	30	100,000
22	80,000	32	55,000
23	50,000	35	35,000

Gargantuan's top management believes the loss for the first six months reflects a tight profit margin caused by intense competition. Management also believes that many companies will leave this market by next year and profit should improve.

Required:

1. What unit selling price should management select for each of the Super Clean compounds for the remaining six months of the year? Support your selection with appropriate calculations.

2. Independently of your answer to requirement (1), assume the optimum alternatives for the last six months were as follows: a selling price of $23 and volume of 50,000 cases for the standard compound, and a selling price of $35 and volume of 35,000 cases for the commercial compound.

    a. Should management consider closing down its operations until January 1 of the next year in order to minimize its losses? Support your answer with appropriate calculations.

    b. Identify and discuss the qualitative factors that should be considered in deciding whether the Richmond Plant should be closed down during the last six months of the current year.

(CMA, adapted)

Case 13–49 Bidding on a Special Order; Ethics **(LO10)**

2. Variable overhead rate: $5.40

Zylar Industries is a manufacturer of standard and custom-designed bottling equipment. Early in December 20x0, Lyan Company asked Zylar to quote a price for a custom-designed bottling machine to be delivered in April. Lyan intends to make a decision on the purchase of such a machine by January 1, so Zylar would have the entire first quarter of 20x1 to build the equipment.

Zylar's pricing policy for custom-designed equipment is 50 percent markup on absorption manufacturing cost. Lyan's specifications for the equipment have been reviewed by Zylar's Engineering and Cost Management Departments, which made the following estimates for direct material and direct labour.

Direct material...	$256,000
Direct labour (11,000 hours @ $15)	165,000

Manufacturing overhead is applied on the basis of direct-labour hours. Zylar normally plans to run its plant at a level of 15,000 direct-labour hours per month and assigns overhead on the basis of 180,000 direct-labour hours per year. The overhead application rate for 20x1 of $9 per hour is based on the following budgeted manufacturing overhead costs for 20x1:

Variable manufacturing overhead	$ 972,000
Fixed manufacturing overhead	648,000
Total manufacturing overhead	$1,620,000

Zylar's production schedule calls for 12,000 direct-labour hours per month during the first quarter. If Zylar is awarded the contract for the Lyan equipment, production of one of its standard products would have to be reduced. This is necessary because production levels can be increased to only 15,000 direct-labour hours each month on short notice. Furthermore, Zylar's employees are unwilling to work overtime.

Sales of the standard product equal to the reduced production would be lost, but there would be no permanent loss of future sales or customers. The standard product for which the production schedule would be reduced has a unit sales price of $12,000 and the following cost structure:

Direct material	$ 2,000
Direct labour (250 hours @ $15)	3,750
Manufacturing overhead (250 hours @ $9)	2,250
Total cost	$ 8,000

Lyan Company needs the custom-designed equipment to increase its bottle-making capacity so that it will not have to buy bottles from an outside supplier. Lyan requires 5,000,000 bottles annually. Its present equipment has a maximum capacity of 4,500,000 bottles, with a directly traceable cash outlay cost of 15 cents per bottle. Thus, Lyan has had to purchase 500,000 bottles from a supplier at 40 cents each. The new equipment would allow Lyan to manufacture its entire annual demand for bottles at a direct-material cost savings of 1 cent per bottle. Zylar estimates that Lyan's annual bottle demand will continue to be 5,000,000 bottles over the next five years, the estimated life of the special-purpose equipment.

Required: Zylar Industries plans to submit a bid to Lyan Company for the manufacture of the special-purpose bottling equipment.

1. Calculate the bid Zylar would submit if it follows its standard pricing policy for special-purpose equipment.
2. Calculate the minimum bid Zylar would be willing to submit on the Lyan equipment that would result in the same total contribution margin as planned for the first quarter of 20x1.
3. Suppose Zylar Industries has submitted a bid slightly above the minimum calculated in requirement (2). On receiving Zylar's bid, Lyan's assistant purchasing manager telephoned his friend at Tygar Corporation: "Hey Joe, we just got a bid from Zylar Industries on some customized equipment. I think Tygar would stand a good chance of beating it. Stop by the house this evening, and I'll show you the details of Zylar's bid and the specifications on the machine."
   Is Lyan Company's assistant purchasing manager acting ethically? Explain.

(CMA, adapted)

 Practise and learn online with Connect.

Photo Credits

Chapter One

Page 1: © Mike Clark/AFP/Getty Images; **page 2:** Courtesy of Roots Canada; **page 7 (left):** © PhotoLink/Getty Images/DIL; **page 7 (right):** © Susan Van Etten/PhotoEdit; **page 17:** Courtesy of Roots Canada; **page 18 (top left):** matt/Shutterstock; **page 18 (top middle):** © Royalty-Free/CORBIS; **page 18 (bottom left):** krsmanovic/Shutterstock; **page 18 (bottom middle):** Steve White/CPI/The Canadian Press; **page 18 (bottom right):** Kevin Van Paassen/The Globe and Mail.

Chapter Two

Page 28 (top): © Dmitry Rukhlenko/iStockphoto.com; **page 28 (bottom):** © Luti/Shutterstock; **page 32:** Courtesy of WestJet; **page 33:** Courtesy of Walmart Canada; **page 34 (top):** 20th Century Fox. All rights reserved/Courtesy Everett Collection; **page 34 (top middle):** © Michael Abramson/Woodfin Camp & Associates; **page 34 (middle):** Royalty-Free/CORBIS; **page 34 (bottom middle):** © The McGraw-Hill Companies, Inc./Jill Braaten, photographer; **page 34 (bottom):** © Malcolm Fife/Getty Images; **page 40:** © PhotoLink/Getty Images

Chapter Three

Page 68 (top): © Comstock images/Alamy; **page 68 (bottom left):** © Dynamic Graphics/PunchStock; **page 68 (bottom right):** © image 100/PunchStock; **page 72 (left):** © Creatas Images/Jupiter Images; **page 72 (middle):** © Christopher Kerrigan; **page 72 (right):** © Radius Images/Getty Images; **page 77:** © Dean Abramson/Stock Boston.

Chapter Four

Page 117 (top): © Erin Riley/Getty Images; **page 117 (bottom):** © Rim Light/PhotoLink/Getty Images; **page 122 (left):** Royalty-Free/CORBIS; **page 122 (right):** © Eric Martin, photographer/Iconotec.

Chapter Five

Page 150 (top): © Digital Vision/Getty Images; **page 150 (bottom):** © Masterfile Royalty-Free; **page 154 (left):** © Royalty-Free/CORBIS; **page 154 (right):** © Monty Rakusen/Getty Images; **page 164 (left):** © Flying Colours Ltd./Getty Images; **page 164 (right):** © Ronald Hilton.

Chapter Six

Page 207 (top): © PhotoDisc/PunchStock; **page 207 (bottom):** © PhotoDisc/Getty Images; **page 217:** © Bloomberg/Getty Images.

Chapter Seven

Page 248 (top): © Siri Stafford/Getty Images; **page 248 (bottom):** Dynamic Graphics/JupiterImages; **page 251 (left):** © Cultura RF/Getty Images; **page 251 (right):** © The McGraw-Hill Companies, Inc./Jill Braaten, photographer; **page 268:** Lonnie Duka/Getty Images.

Chapter Eight

Page 306 (top): © Ingram Publishing/SuperStock; **page 306 (bottom):** © JupiterImages; **page 308:** © Karen Bleier/AFP/Getty Images; **page 332:** © The McGraw-Hill Companies, Inc./Barry Barker, photographer.

Chapter Nine

Page 362: © PhotoDisc/Getty Images; **page 363:** © Royalty-Free/CORBIS; **page 378 (left):** © Elmer Marinez/AFP/Getty Images; **page 378 (right):** © Andreas Rentz/Getty Images; **page 388:** © Digital Vision/Getty Images; **page 396:** Courtesy of Texas Instruments.

Chapter Ten

Page 433 (top): © PhotoDisc/SuperStock; **page 433 (bottom):** © Royalty-Free/CORBIS; **page 438:** © Digital Vision/PunchStock; **page 454:** Dave Chidley/Canadian Press.

Chapter Eleven

Page 473 (top): © Chris Caldicott/Getty Images; **page 473 (bottom):** © Royalty-Free/CORBIS; **page 476 (top left):** © Jim West/The Image Images; **page 476 (top right):** © Scott Olson/Getty Images; **page 476 (bottom left):** © BananaStock/Iconotec; **page 476 (bottom right):** © Brand X Pictures/PunchStock; **page 489:** © Royalty-Free/CORBIS; **page 496:** © Kevin Horan/Stone/Getty Images; **page 505:** Courtesy of Simon Fraser University.

Chapter Twelve

Page 533 (top): © Steve Allen/Getty Images; **page 533 (bottom):** © BananaStock/PunchStock; **page 546 (left):** © PhotoLink/Getty Images; **page 546 (right):** © vario images GmbH & Co. KG/Alamy.

Chapter Thirteen

Page 577 (top): © PhotoLink/Getty Images; **page 577 (bottom):** © Dennis MacDonald/PhotoEdit; **page 580:** Stockbyte/PunchStock Image; **page 593:** © Kevin Horan/Stone/Getty Images.

Chapter Fourteen (Online)

Page 1 (top): © Scenics of America/PhotoLink/Getty Images; **page 1 (bottom):** © Digital Vision/SuperStock; **page 12:** © Maximilian Stock Ltd./Getty Images; **page 22:** © Bob Pool/Getty Images.

Chapter Fifteen (Online)

Page 1 (top): © Mark Thornton/Getty Images; **page 1 (bottom):** © Bloomberg/Getty Images; **page 13:** © Lester Lefkowitz/CORBIS.

Endnotes

Chapter One

1. Gary Siegel, "The Image of Corporate Accountants," *Strategic Finance* 82/2 (August 2000), p. 71.

2. This is, of course, a very simple illustration, because it focuses on a single resource, i.e., the cost of one employee's labour. Even a business as simple as a pizza shop involves many resources, such as pizza ingredients, multiple employees, buildings and equipment, and advertising. Imagine how much more complicated capacity issues are for a major airline or a large manufacturer. Nevertheless, by exploring the concepts of capacity and the cost of capacity in a very simple scenario, you should have an initial understanding of this critical issue. For a useful article about managing capacity, see David Welch and Ian Rowley, "Risky Business at Nissan," *BusinessWeek*, November 2, 2009, p. 34.

3. Ravi Kalakota and Andrew B. Whinston, *Electronic Commerce: A Manager's Guide* (Reading, MA: Addison-Wesley, 1997), p. 287; and Ravi Kalakota and Marcia Robinson, *E-Business: Road Map for Success* (Reading, MA: Addison-Wesley, 1999), p. 4.

4. The information and quotations for Canadian Direct Insurance, London Drugs, Viewtrak Technologies, and PropertyGuys.com in this feature are from Michael Favere-Marchesi and the respective companies' websites.

5. Excel® is a registered trademark of Microsoft Corporation.

6. James Vicini, "Top Court Hears Appeal by Enron's Skilling," *Reuters,* March 1, 2010; and Allan Sloan, "Laying Enron to Rest," *Newsweek 147/23* (June 5, 2006), pp. 25–30.

7. Joann Lublin and Kara Scannell, "Critics See Some Good from Sarbanes-Oxley," *The Wall Street Journal*, July 30, 2007, p. B1; and John Hodowanitz and Steven A. Solieri, "Guarding the Guardians," *Strategic Finance* 87/2 (August 2005), pp. 47–53.

Chapter Two

1. Based on the well-known and widely used Hayes-Wheelwright production process matrix, with the exception of mass customization, which postdates the Hayes-Wheelwright formulation. See Robert H. Hayes and Steven C. Wheelwright, *Restoring Our Competitive Edge* (New York: John Wiley and Sons, 1984), p. 209.

2. Thaddeus Herrick, "Dell's Profit Soars," *The Wall Street Journal*, February 17, 2006, p. A3; Louise Lee and Spencer Ante, "Can the PC King Excel in Services: Dell Is on a Tear, but Maintaining That Clip Could Be Tough," *BusinessWeek*, May 30, 2005, pp. 70–73; and Andy Serwer, "Dell Does Domination," *Fortune*, January 21, 2002, pp. 70–75.

3. "The Best Little Factory in Texas," *Forbes*, June 10, 2002, p. 110.

4. Louise Lee and Emily Thornton, "Hanging Up on Dell: Gripes about Tech Support Are on the Rise, and the PC King Is Scrambling to Upgrade," *BusinessWeek*, October 10, 2005, pp. 80–81; and Steve Lohr, "On a Roll, Dell Enters Uncharted Territory," *The New York Times*, August 25, 2002, Section 3, p. 1.

5. As mentioned at the beginning of Chapter 1, the focus organizations around which Chapters 2 through 15 are built are not real organizations. They are, however, realistic settings in which to discuss business and managerial accounting issues, and in most cases they are based on real organizations. These illustrations are intended to help students connect to everyday life the business and managerial accounting issues discussed in this book.

6. The description of the manufacturing process is based on that used by Dell Inc.

7. Such cost driver teams have been established by many companies. For descriptions of such efforts at Deere & Company and Hewlett-Packard Corporation, see the management cases "John Deere Component Works" and "Hewlett-Packard: Queensferry Telecommunications Division" (Harvard Business School).

8. LuAnn LaSalle, "WestJet Raises Dividend and Adds New Regional Airline to Take Flight in 2013," *The Canadian Press*, February 8, 2012; and Melanie Trottman and Scott McCartney, "The Age of Wal-Mart Airlines Crunches the Biggest Carriers," *The Wall Street Journal*, June 18, 2002, pp. A1, A8. For further reading, see Christopher Conkey, "Airports May Boost Runway Fees in Peak Hours," *The Wall Street Journal*, January 15, 2008, p. A33; and Alan Cowell, "Low-Cost Airlines Grow and Compete in Europe," *The New York Times*, July 28, 2002, p. 3.

9. The outsourcing decision, as well as several other common management decisions, is covered in detail in Chapter 12.

10. In professional American football, the Super Bowl is the championship game of the National Football League (NFL) in the United States.

11. The details of the outsourcing decision, including its relevant costs and the role of opportunity costs, are covered in Chapter 12.

12. Marginal cost of the 101st laptop computer is $995 (from Exhibit 2–11). Average cost per unit when 101 laptops are produced is $1,495 ($150,995 ÷ 101).

13. Jared Sandberg, Rebecca Blumenstein, and Shawn Young, "WorldCom Admits $3.8 Billion Error in Its Accounting—Firm Ousts Financial Chief and Struggles for Survival; SEC Probe Likely to Widen," *The Wall Street Journal*, June 26, 2002, p. A1; Jared Sandberg, Deborah Solomon, and Rebecca Blumenstein, "Disconnected: Inside WorldCom's Unearthing of a Vast Accounting Scandal," *The Wall Street Journal*, June 27, 2002, p. A1; and Jared Sandberg, "Leading the News: Was Ebbers Aware of Accounting Move at His WorldCom?," *The Wall Street Journal*, July 1, 2002, p. A3.

14. Devlin Barrett, "Ex-WorldCom Exec Pleads Guilty," Associated Press, September 27, 2002 (as it appeared in the *Ithaca Journal*). See also Kurt Eichenwald and Simon Romero, "Plea Deals Are Seen for Three WorldCom Executives," *The New York Times*, August 29, 2002, pp. C1, C4.

15. T. Richardson, "Worldcom CFO Lied, He Admits in Court," *The Register*, February 17, 2005, www.theregister.co.uk.

16. A. Latour, S. Young, and L. Yuan, "Ebbers Is Convicted in Massive Fraud," *The Wall Street Journal*, March 16, 2005, p. A1.

Chapter Three

1. One might legitimately ask why this is called "two-stage" cost allocation, when three types of allocation are involved, but the term is entrenched in the literature and in practice. It stems from the fact that there are two *cost objects*, or entities, to which costs are assigned: production *departments* in Stage 1 and production *jobs* in Stage 2.

2. C. T. Stambaugh and F. W. Carpenter, "RFID: Wireless Innovations in Inventory Monitoring and Accounting," *Strategic Finance*, December 2009, pp. 35–40; and Ariel Markelevich and Ronal Bell, "RFID: The Changes It Will Bring," *Strategic Finance*, August 2006, pp. 46–49.

3. Stanley Holmes and Mike France, "Boeing's Secret: Did the Aircraft Giant Exploit Accounting Rules to Conceal a Huge Factory Snafu?" *BusinessWeek*, May 20, 2002, pp. 110–120. Also see Andy Pasztor and Anne Soueo, "Boeing Could Pay Large Penalty to Settle Probes, Avoid Prosecution," *The Wall Street Journal*, September 17, 2005, pp. A1, A8. For more recent information on Boeing, see P. Sanders and A. Keeton, "Boeing Reports Signs of Recovery as It Shakes Off a Troubling Year," *The Wall Street Journal*, January 28, 2010, p. B1.

Chapter Four

1. The FIFO method of process costing is covered in Supplement 4A to this text entitled *Process Costing: The First-In, First-Out Method*. This supplement is available on ▓ connect.

2. Based on R. W. Hilton's research.
3. Sequential production operations are covered in Supplement 4B to this textbook entitled *Process Costing in Sequential Production Departments*. This supplement is available on ▣ **connect**
4. The budgeted amount for the cost driver is based on the company's practical capacity for production.

Chapter Five

1. The 230,000 machine hours used to compute the pool rate for the machine-related cost pool is also equal to management's estimate of the company's practical capacity of production, as expressed in terms of machine hours.
2. See the DHL website; S. Kranz, "Sitting Pretty in Prague: DHL's Tech Triumph," *BusinessWeek*, December 12, 2005, p. 56; and S. Player and C. Cobble, *Cornerstones of Decision Making: Profiles of Enterprise ABM* (Greensboro, NC: Oakhill Press, 1999), pp. 131–144.
3. This section draws on Lewis J. Soloway, "Using Activity-Based Management in Aerospace and Defense Companies," *Journal of Cost Management 6/4* (Winter 1993), pp. 56–66, and Peter B. B. Turney, "What an Activity-Based Cost Model Looks Like," *Journal of Cost Management 5/4* (Winter 1992), pp. 54–60.
4. This definition, as well as other material in this section, is drawn from James A. Brimson, "Improvement and Elimination of Non-Value-Added Costs," *Journal of Cost Management 2/2* (Summer 1988), pp. 62–65.
5. An important point that could be overlooked here is that activity-based costing analysis can be used in a very specific, targeted manner to address a particular management problem. In this case, the ABC focus is customer-profitability analysis. This is the essence of activity-based management—using the results of an ABC analysis to manage an enterprise more effectively.
6. "Alienating Customers Isn't Always a Bad Idea, Many Firms Discover," *The Wall Street Journal*, January 7, 1999.
7. In a conversation with a vice-president of a large consumer-products manufacturer, one of the authors was struck by the executive's statement "You can bet we pay a lot of attention to the needs and desires of the 'Mart Brothers,' K and Wal."
8. "Why Tech Bows to Best Buy," *BusinessWeek*, December 21, 2009, and recent Best Buy annual reports.
9. G. McWilliams, "Analyzing Customers: Best Buy Decides Not All Are Welcome," *The Wall Street Journal*, November 8, 2004.
10. Ibid.
11. Ibid.
12. Angela Norkiewicz, "Nine Steps to Implementing ABC," *Management Accounting 75/10* (April 1994), pp. 28–33.
13. For a more elaborate example of activity-based costing in a hospital's primary-care unit, see V. G. Narayanan, R. Moore, and L. Brem, "Cambridge Hospital Community Health Care Network—The Primary Care Unit" (Boston: The President and Fellows of Harvard College, 2000). In this case, minutes of time with a health-care professional is a key cost driver.
14. In a hospital setting, residents are doctors who have completed medical school and are currently doing in-hospital training in a specialty area (e.g., neurology, oncology). Interns are brand-new doctors in their first year of residency, who are not yet specialized and do rotations through all of the major units in a hospital.
15. The scenario described here, while fictitious, is based on several real-world events described in the ABC literature. Anecdotes in various ABC cases and other sources, as well as personal research, form the basis for the events described. A key source is the well-known "Schrader-Bellows" case, by R. Cooper (Boston: President and Fellows of Harvard College), which remains a classic, describing issues surrounding activity-based costing.
16. James B. Dilworth, *Production and Operations Management*, 3rd ed. (New York: Random House, 1996), pp. 354–361.
17. You might find it helpful to review Exhibit 1–3, which depicts the pull method of the JIT system.
18. Toyota's groundbreaking JIT system originally was referred to as *Kanban*, a Japanese word meaning "signboard." See Takeo Tanaka, "Kaizen Budgeting: Toyota's Cost Control System under TQC," *Journal of Cost Management 8/3* (Fall 1994), p. 57.
19. Robert Adams and Ray Carter, "United Technologies' Activity-Based Accounting Is a Catalyst for Success," *As Easy as ABC 18*, p. 4. United Technologies uses the term "*structural*-level activity," instead of "*facility*-level activity" as we have done in the chapter and in the table presented here.

Chapter Six

1. P. Coy, M. Conlin, and M. Herbst, "The Disposable Worker," *Businessweek*, January 18, 2010, pp. 33-45; and Clare Ansberry, "In the New Workplace, Jobs Morph to Suit Rapid Change of Pace," *The Wall Street Journal*, March 3, 2002, pp. A1, A7.
2. Ibid., pp. A1, A7.
3. Jonathan Eig, "Do Part-Time Workers Hold Key to When the Recession Breaks?" *The Wall Street Journal*, January 3, 2002, p. A1.
4. Michelle Conlin, "The Big Squeeze on Workers," *BusinessWeek*, May 13, 2002, pp. 96–98; and Michelle Conlin, "The Software Says You're Just Average," *BusinessWeek*, February 25, 2002, p. 126.
5. The budgeting process is covered in Chapter 8.
6. The information and quotations in this box are from Michelle Conlin, "The Big Squeeze on Workers," *BusinessWeek*, May 13, 2002, pp. 96, 97. See also P. Coy, M. Conlin, and M. Herbst, "The Disposable Worker," *Businessweek*, January 18, 2010, pp. 33–39.

Chapter Seven

1. The effect of income taxes on CVP analysis is covered in Supplement 7A to this text, entitled *Effect of Income Taxes on CVP Analysis*. This supplement is available on ▣ **connect**. In all of the examples in this chapter, income taxes will be ignored.
2. Susan Carey, "JetBlue, One of the Few U.S. Airlines to Buck the Downturn, Files for $125 Million IPO," *The Wall Street Journal*, February 13, 2002, p. B4. Also see "British Air's Net Soars Amid Strong Demand," *The Wall Street Journal*, February 4, 2008, p. A6.
3. Daniel Michaels, "Kinshasa Is Poor, Scary, and a Boon for Air France," *The Wall Street Journal*, April 30, 2002, pp. A1, A8.
4. This approach assumes that the predetermined fixed-overhead rate per unit does not change across time periods.
5. "Section 12: Inventory Valuation," *Income Tax Interpretations Bulletin IT-473R*.
6. See Chapter 5 for a thorough discussion of the concept of unit-level costs and cost hierarchies in the context of an activity-based-costing system.
7. This form of income statement, in which each item on the statement is expressed as a percentage of sales revenue, is often called a *common-size income statement*.
8. Timothy J. Mullaney and Robert D. Hof, "Finally, the Pot of Gold," *BusinessWeek*, June 24, 2002, p. 106.
9. This scenario is based on the case "I Enjoy Challenges," originally written by Michael W. Maher. It is used here with permission.

Chapter Eight

1. Activity-based costing (ABC) is covered in depth in Chapter 5.
2. This section is based on the following references: James A. Brimson and John Antos, *Driving Value Using Activity-Based Budgeting* (New York: John Wiley & Sons, 1999); Sofia Börjesson, "A Case Study on Activity-Based Budgeting," *Journal of Cost Management 10/4* (Winter 1997), pp. 7–18; and Robert S. Kaplan and Robin Cooper, *Cost and Effect* (Boston: Harvard Business School Press, 1998), pp. 301–315.

3. David M. Aldea and David E. Bullinger, "Using ABC for Shared Services, Charge-Outs, Activity-Based Budgeting, and Benchmarking," in *Activity-Based Management: Arthur Andersen's Lessons from the ABM Battlefield*, eds. Steve Player and David E. Keys (New York: John Wiley & Sons, 1999), pp. 138–145.

4. Jay Collins, "Advanced Use of ABM: Using ABC for Target Costing, Activity-Based Budgeting, and Benchmarking," in *Activity-Based Management: Arthur Andersen's Lessons from the ABM Battlefield*, eds. Steve Player and David E. Keys (New York: John Wiley & Sons, 1999), pp. 152–158.

5. A unit-level cost is one that must be incurred each time a unit is produced.

6. Just-in-time production and inventory control systems are covered in Chapter 5.

7. It is often desirable to have a buffer inventory just before a bottleneck manufacturing operation.

8. Further discussion of inventory management can be found in the appendix to Chapter 10.

9. A typical cost hierarchy includes costs incurred at the unit level, batch level, product-sustaining level, customer level, and facility or general-operations level. Cost hierarchies are discussed in detail in Chapter 5.

10. Ibid.

11. These two presidents' management consulting firms specialize in ABC, ABM, ABB, and cost management systems.

12. The direct and indirect methods of preparing the statement of cash flows are covered in financial accounting texts.

13. Steve Hornyak, "Budgeting Made Easy," *Management Accounting 80/4* (October 1998), pp. 18–23.

14. This section draws on Norm Raffish, "How Much Does That Product Really Cost?" in *Readings in Management Accounting*, 3rd ed., ed. S. Mark Young (Upper Saddle River, NJ: Prentice Hall, 2001), pp. 61, 62; Callie Berliner and James A. Brimson, eds., *Cost Management for Today's Advanced Manufacturing* (Boston: Harvard Business School Press, 1988).

Chapter Nine

1. David Johnsen and Parvez Sopariwala, "Standard Costing Is Alive and Well at Parker Brass," *Management Accounting Quarterly 1/2* (Winter 2000), pp. 12–20.

2. Kip R. Krumwiede, "Rewards and Realities of German Cost Accounting," *Strategic Finance 86/10* (April 2005), pp. 27–34; Carl S. Smith, "Going for GPK," *Strategic Finance 86/10* (April 2005), pp. 36–39; and Bernd Gaiser, "German Cost Management Systems," *Journal of Cost Management 11/5* (September/October 1997), pp. 35–41.

3. Activity-based costing is explored in detail in Chapter 5.

4. Key cost drivers used in activity-based flexible budgeting at Simon Fraser University include the number of students enrolled and the number of student credit hours. For further reading on activity-based budgeting, see Jay Collins, "Advanced Use of ABM: Using ABC for Target Costing, Activity-Based Budgeting, and Benchmarking," in *Activity-Based Management: Arthur Andersen's Lessons from the ABM Battlefield*, eds. Steve Player and David E. Keys (New York: John Wiley & Sons, 1999), pp. 152–158.

5. "Scoville: NuTone Housing Group" (a management accounting case) (Boston: President and Fellows of Harvard College).

6. L. Carr and C. Ittner. "Measuring the Cost of Ownership," *Journal of Cost Management 6/3* (Fall 1992), pp. 42–51

7. The sources for this material are Robert S. Kaplan, "Limitations of Cost Accounting in Advanced Manufacturing Environments," in *Measures for Manufacturing Excellence*, ed. Robert S. Kaplan (Boston: Harvard Business School Press, 1990), pp. 1–14; H. Thomas Johnson, "Performance Measurement for Competitive Excellence," in *Measures for Manufacturing Excellence*, ed. Robert S. Kaplan (Boston: Harvard Business School Press, 1990), pp. 63–90; Robert A. Bonsack, "Does Activity-Based Costing Replace Standard Costing?" *Journal of Cost Management 4/4* (Winter 1991), pp. 46, 47; and Michiharu Sukurai,

"The Influence of Factory Automation on Management Accounting Practices: A Study of Japanese Companies," in *Measures for Manufacturing Excellence*, ed. Robert S. Kaplan (Boston: Harvard Business School Press, 1990), pp. 39–62.

8. Activity-based management and the elimination of non-value-added costs are covered in Chapter 5.

9. Some companies have developed cost of ownership reporting systems. Among them are Northrop Aircraft Division, Texas Instruments, and Black & Decker. See L. Carr and C. Ittner, "Measuring the Cost of Ownership," *Journal of Cost Management 6/3* (Fall 1992), pp. 42–51. The information about Texas Instruments is based on R. W. Hilton's research.

Chapter Ten

1. The balanced scorecard concept was developed by Robert S. Kaplan and David D. Norton. See Robert S. Kaplan and David D. Norton, *The Strategy-Focused Organization: How Balanced Scorecard Companies Thrive in the New Business Environment* (Boston: Harvard Business School Press, 2001).

2. Raef Lawson, William Stratton, and Toby Hatch, "Scorecarding Goes Global," *Strategic Finance 87/9* (March 2006), pp. 35–41; and Thomas Wunder, "New Strategy Alignment in Multinational Corporations," *Strategic Finance 87/5* (November 2005), pp. 35–41.

3. Robert S. Kaplan and David D. Norton, *The Strategy-Focused Organization: How Balanced Scorecard Companies Thrive in the New Business Environment* (Boston: Harvard Business School Press, 2001); and Bruce Stanley, "UPS Battles Traffic Jams to Gain Ground in India," *The Wall Street Journal*, January 25, 2008, p. B1.

4. Many banking institutions have developed a balanced scorecard. The one shown in Exhibit 10–2 is an amalgamation of bank scorecards from a number of sources, including the author's research and the following resources: Robert S. Kaplan and David P. Norton, *The Strategy-Focused Organization: How Balanced Scorecard Companies Thrive in the New Business Environment* (Boston: Harvard Business School Press, 2001); Robert S. Kaplan, "Wells Fargo Online Financial Services," a Harvard Business School (HBS) management case (Boston: President and Fellows of Harvard College, 1998); and Norman Klein and Robert S. Kaplan, "Chemical Bank: Implementing the Balanced Scorecard," an HBS management case (Boston: President and Fellows of Harvard College, 1995).

5. Robert S. Kaplan and David P. Norton, *The Strategy-Focused Organization: How Balanced Scorecard Companies Thrive in the New Business Environment* (Boston: Harvard Business School Press, 2001).

6. Robert S. Kaplan and David P. Norton, *The Strategy-Focused Organization: How Balanced Scorecard Companies Thrive in the New Business Environment* (Boston: Harvard Business School Press, 2001); and Raef Lawson, William Stratton, and Toby Hatch, "Scorecarding Goes Global," *Strategic Finance 87/9* (March 2006), pp. 35–41.

7. This material is based on "Putting Strategy into the Balanced Scorecard," *Strategic Finance 83/7* (January 2002), pp. 44–52, and Robert S. Kaplan and David P. Norton, *The Strategy-Focused Organization: How Balanced Scorecard Companies Thrive in the New Business Environment* (Boston: Harvard Business School Press, 2001).

8. This section draws on Howard M. Armitage and Anthony A. Atkinson, "The Choice of Productivity Measures in Organizations," in *Measures for Manufacturing Excellence*, ed. Robert S. Kaplan (Boston: Harvard Business School Press, 1990), pp. 91–128; and Robert S. Kaplan and David P. Norton, *The Strategy-Focused Organization: How Balanced-Scorecard Companies Thrive in the New Business Environment* (Boston: Harvard Business School Press, 2001).

9. Eliyahu M. Goldratt, *Theory of Constraints* (Croton-on-Hudson, NY: North River Press, 1990).

10. Yasuhiro Monden and John Lee, "How a Japanese Auto Maker Reduces Costs," *Management Accounting 75/2* (August 1993), p. 24.

11. Takao Tanaka, "Target Costing at Toyota," *Journal of Cost Management 7/1* (Spring 1993), p. 4.

12. Peter B. B. Turney and James M. Reeve, "The Impact of Continuous Improvement on the Design of Activity-Based Cost Systems," *Journal of Cost Management 4/2* (Summer 1990), p. 44.

13. Takao Tanaka, "Kaizen Budgeting: Toyota's Cost Control System under TQC," *Journal of Cost Management 8/3* (Fall 1994), p. 62.

14. C. Kevin Cherry, "Re-Engineering: Harnessing Creativity and Innovation," *Journal of Cost Management 8/2* (Summer 1994), p. 49.

15. John B. MacArthur, "Theory of Constraints and Activity-Based Costing: Friends or Foes?" *Journal of Cost Management 7/2* (Summer 1993), p. 51.

16. For further information on cost of quality, see Zafar U. Khan, "Cost of Quality," in Barry J. Brinker, ed., *Guide to Cost Management* (New York: John Wiley & Sons, 2000), pp. 319–344. For examples of quality-cost reporting, see Lawrence Carr, "Cost of Quality: Making It Work," *Journal of Cost Management 9/1* (Spring 1995), pp. 61–65, and S. Brinkman and M. Applebaum, "The Quality Cost Report: It's Alive and Well," *Management Accounting 76/3* (September 1994), pp. 61–65.

17. This discussion is based on the following sources: Wayne J. Morse, Harold P. Roth, and Kay M. Poston, *Measuring, Planning and Controlling Quality Costs* (Montvale, NJ: National Association of Accountants, 1987); Jack Campanella, ed., *Principles of Quality Costs* (Milwaukee, WI: ASQC Quality Press, 1990); and Alahassane Diallo, Zafar V. Kahn, and Curtis F. Vail, "Cost of Quality in the New Manufacturing Environment," *Management Accounting 77/2* (August 1993), pp. 20–25.

18. R. Crockett, C. Edwards, and S. Ante, "How Motorola Got Its Groove Back," *BusinessWeek*, August 8, 2005, pp. 68–70; and M. Arndt, "Quality Isn't Just for Widgets," *BusinessWeek*, July 22, 2002, pp. 72, 73.

19. M. Arndt, "Quality Isn't Just for Widgets," *BusinessWeek*, July 22, 2002, pp. 72, 73.

20. Tad Leahy, "In Search of Perfection with Six Sigma," *Business Finance 5/1* (January 2000), pp. 73–76.

21. Amy Barrett and Diane Brady, "At Honeywell, It's Larry the Knife," *BusinessWeek*, November 26, 2001, pp. 98–100.

22. Tad Leahy, "In Search of Perfection with Six Sigma," *Business Finance 5/1* (January 2000), pp. 73–76. See also Gregory T. Lucier and Sridhar Seshadri, "GE Takes Six Sigma beyond the Bottom Line," *Strategic Finance 82/11* (May 2001), pp. 41–46.

23. The ISO standards are available on the Internet at www.iso.org.

24. Based on the discussion in German Böer, Margaret Curtin, and Louis Hoyt, "Environmental Cost Management," *Management Accounting 80/3* (September 1998), pp. 28–38. See also Ramona Dzinkowski, "Saving the Environment," *Strategic Finance 89/1* (July 2007), pp. 51–53.

25. Based on Satish Joshi, Ranjani Krishnan, and Lester Lave, "Estimating the Hidden Costs of Environmental Regulation," *The Accounting Review 76/2* (April 2001), pp. 171–198. See also Kathryn Kranhold, "GE's Environmental Push Hits Business Realities," *The Wall Street Journal*, September 14, 2007, p. A1.

26. Ibid.

27. Ibid.

28. Ibid.

29. German Böer, Margaret Curtin, and Louis Hoyt, "Environmental Cost Management," *Management Accounting 80/3* (September 1998), pp. 28–38.

30. Ibid.

Chapter Eleven

1. Although there is an important conceptual difference between profit centres and investment centres, the latter term is not always used in practice. Some managers use the term *profit centre* to refer to both types of responsibility centres., so when businesspeople use the term *profit centre*, they may be referring to a true profit centre (as defined in this chapter) or to an investment centre.

2. Activity-based costing and the elimination of non-value-added activities are covered in Chapter 5.

3. The *book value* of Suncoast Food Centres' equity is $41 million, but that amount does not reflect the current value of the company's assets or the value of intangible assets, such as the Suncoast Food Centres name.

4. Karra Seannell and Joann Lublin, "SEC Unhappy with Answers on Executive Pay," *The Wall Street Journal*, January 29, 2008, p. 31; Louis Lavelle, "The Gravy Train Just Got Derailed—'Pay for Performance' Is Back in Vogue," *BusinessWeek*, November 19, 2001; and Tad Leahy, "All the Right Moves," *Business Finance 6/1* (April 2000), p. 32.

5. Maheudra Gujarathi, "GlaxoSmithkline Plc.: International Transfer Pricing and Taxation," *Issues in Accounting Education 22/4* (November 2007), pp. 749–759; and Eric Krell, "Scrutiny of Transfer Pricing Grows," *Business Finance 6/4* (August 2000), p. 12.

6. Steven C. Wrappe, Ken Milani, and Julie Joy, "The Transfer Price Is Right," *Strategic Finance 81/1* (July 1999), p. 40.

Chapter Twelve

1. The sources for these anecdotes are S. Carey, "Northwest Targets Flight Attendants for Outsourcing," *The Wall Street Journal*, October 26, 2005, pp. A1, A8; S. Carey and A. Frangos, "Airlines, Facing Cost Pressure, Outsource Crucial Safety Tasks," *The Wall Street Journal*, January 21, 2005, pp. A1, A5; and P. Engardio and B. Einhorn, "Outsourcing Innovation," *BusinessWeek*, March 21, 2005, pp. 82–94.

2. Peter Landers, "Japan's Local Drug Makers to Outsource to Suppliers," *The Wall Street Journal*, March 26, 2002, p. A20.

3. "Delivering the Goods at FedEx," *BusinessWeek*, June 13, 2005, pp. 60–62; D. Foust, "The Ground War at FedEx," *BusinessWeek*, November 28, 2005, pp. 42, 43; "Overnight, Everything Changed for FedEx; Can It Reinvent Itself?" *The Wall Street Journal*, November 4, 1999, p. A1; and M. Arndt, "Cat Sinks Its Claws into Services," *BusinessWeek*, December 5, 2005, pp. 56–59.

4. Activity-based costing (ABC) is thoroughly explored in Chapter 5. This section can be studied most effectively after completing Chapter 5.

Chapter Thirteen

1. Notice that the demand and revenue curves are based on the quantity sold, while the cost curves are based on the quantity produced. We will assume for simplicity that Sydney Sailing Supplies' monthly sales and production quantities are the same. This assumption tends to be true in the pleasure boat industry.

2 P. Nowak, "Goodbye to Cellphone System Access Fees?" *CBCNews.ca*, November 4, 2008.

3. L. Hawkins, "GM Cuts Prices on Most Vehicles: Latest Bid to Restore Profits May Spark Price War," *The Wall Street Journal*, January 11, 2006, pp. D1, D3.

4. C. Dawson, "A China Price for Toyota," *BusinessWeek*, February 21, 2005, pp. 50, 51.

5. David P. Hamilton, "The Price Isn't Right: Internet Pricing Has Turned Out to Be a Lot Trickier Than Retailers Expected," *The Wall Street Journal*, February 12, 2001, p. R8.

6. This section is based on Shahid L. Ansari, Jan E. Bell, and the CAM-I Target Cost Core Group, *Target Costing: The Next Frontier in Strategic Cost Management* (Burr Ridge, IL: Irwin, 1997).

7. Ibid., p. 15.

8. J. Shank and V. Govindarajan, "Strategic Cost Management and the Value Chain," *Journal of Cost Management 5/4* (Winter 1992), p. 10. See also T. Tanaka, "Target Costing at Toyota," *Journal of Cost Management 7/1* (Spring 1993), pp. 4–12.

9. Shahid L. Ansari, Jan E. Bell, and the CAM-I Target Cost Core Group, *Target Costing: The Next Frontier in Strategic Cost Management* (Burr Ridge, IL: Irwin, 1997). See also Y. Kato, "Target Costing Support Systems: Lessons from Leading Japanese Companies," *Management Accounting Research 4* (1992), pp. 33–47; and T. Tani, H. Okano, N. Shimizu, Y. Iwabuchi, J. Fukuda, and S. Cooray, "Target Cost Management in Japanese Companies: Current State of the Art," *Management Accounting Research 6* (1994), pp. 67–81.

10. This description of Isuzu's target costing and value-engineering methods is drawn from Robin Cooper, *When Lean Enterprises Collide* (Boston, MA: Harvard Business School Press, 1995), pp. 165–183.

Chapter Fourteen (Online)

1. Based on S. Hensley, R. Winslow, and W. Mathews, "FDA Approves Pfizer Drug for Two Cancers," *The Wall Street Journal*, January 27, 2006, pp. 31, 34; J. Carey and A. Barrett, "Drug Prices: What's Fair?" *BusinessWeek*, December 10, 2001, pp. 61–70; and R. W. Hilton's discussions with pharmaceutical company personnel.

2. This section is based on discussions in R. Kaplan, "Must CIM Be Justified by Faith Alone?" *Harvard Business Review* 64/2 (March 1986), pp. 87–95; Callie Berliner and James A. Brimson, eds., *Cost Management for Today's Advanced Manufacturing* (Boston: Harvard Business School Press, 1988), pp. 16–18, 36–38, 150; and Jean L. Noble, "A New Approach for Justifying Computer-Integrated Manufacturing," *Journal of Cost Management 3*/4 (Winter 1990), pp. 14–19.

3. Using formula (1): $F = \$800 (1 + 0.12)^{10}$. From Table I, $(1 + 0.12)^{10} = 3.106$. (Note that the values in Table I are rounded.) So the future value of the investment is $(\$800)(3.106) = \$2,484.80$. Compound interest will more than triple the original $800 investment in 10 years.

4. Using formula (1): $F = \$18,000 (1 + 0.12)^{10}$. From Table III, $(1 + 0.08)^4 = 0.735$. (Note that the values in Table III are rounded.) So the future value of the investment is $(\$18,000)(0.735) = \$13,230$. An investment of $13,230 made now, earning annual interest at 8 percent, will accumulate to $18,000 at the end of four years.

Chapter Fifteen (Online)

1. A tie occurs when two or more service departments serve the same number of other service departments. Then the sequence among the tied service departments usually is an arbitrary choice.

2. Simultaneous equations are more quickly solved by computers than by people. Numerous software packages are available for this purpose.

References for "In Their Own Words"*

Chapter One

(1a) Gary Siegel and James E. Sorensen, principal investigators for the Gary Siegel Organization, *Counting More, Counting Less: Transformations in the Management Accounting Profession* (Montvale, NJ: Institute of Management Accountants, 1999).

(1b) Ibid.

(1c) Ibid.

(1d) Ibid.

(1e) Ibid.

(1f) Ibid.

(1g) Ibid.

(1h) Ibid.

(1i) Ibid.

(1j) Ibid.

Chapter Two

(2a) Gary Siegel and James E. Sorensen, principal investigators for the Gary Siegel Organization, *Counting More, Counting Less: Transformations in the Management Accounting Profession* (Montvale, NJ: Institute of Management Accountants, 1999).

(2b) Gary Siegel, project director, *The Practice Analysis of Management Accounting* (Montvale, NJ: Institute of Management Accountants, 1996), pp. 17, 18.

(2c) Ibid., p. 14.

(2d) Ibid., p. 19.

(2e) *Activity-Based Management: Part I*, a management education video (Boston: President and Fellows of Harvard College, 1993).

(2f) Gary Siegel, project director, *The Practice Analysis of Management Accounting* (Montvale, NJ: Institute of Management Accountants, 1996), p. 18.

(2g) Interview with a Delta Air Lines accountant conducted during research by Ronald W. Hilton.

(2h) Gary Siegel and James E. Sorensen, principal investigators for the Gary Siegel Organization, *Counting More, Counting Less: Transformations in the Management Accounting Profession* (Montvale, NJ: Institute of Management Accountants, 1999).

Chapter Three

(3a) *The Management Accounting Video,* a management education video (New York: McGraw-Hill, 1997). *Note:* Since this video was made, MiCRUS was sold to Philips.

(3b) Gary Siegel and James E. Sorensen, principal investigators for the Gary Siegel Organization, *Counting More, Counting Less: Transformations in the Management Accounting Profession* (Montvale, NJ: Institute of Management Accountants, 1999).

(3c) *The Management Accounting Video*, a management education video (New York: McGraw-Hill, 1997). *Note:* Since this video was made, MiCRUS was sold to Phillips.

(3d) Interview with a Chrysler accountant conducted during research by Ronald W. Hilton.

(3e) Interview with an accountant for The Walt Disney Company conducted during research by Ronald W. Hilton.

(3f) Interview with a Chrysler accountant conducted during research by Ronald W. Hilton.

(3g) Gary Siegel, project director, *The Practice Analysis of Management Accounting* (Montvale, NJ: Institute of Management Accountants, 1996), p. 17.

(3h) Office of Research Services, Simon Fraser University, *Guidelines for Indirect Cost (Overhead)*.

(3i) *The Management Accounting Video,* a management education video (New York: McGraw-Hill, 1997).

Chapter Four

(4a) Steve Player and Carol Cobble, *Cornerstones of Decision Making: Profiles of Enterprise ABM* (Greensboro, NC: Oakhill Press, 1999), p. 161.

(4b) Ibid., p. 12.

(4c) Ibid., p. 168.

Chapter Five

(5a) *Activity-Based Management: Part I*, a management education video (Boston: The President and Fellows of Harvard College, 1993).

(5b) Joyce R. Ochs and Kenneth L. Parkinson, "Moving to Activity-Based Cost Analysis," *Business Finance* 5/11 (November 1999), p. 101.

(5c) Steve Player and Carol Cobble, *Cornerstones of Decision Making: Profiles of Enterprise ABM* (Greensboro, NC: Oakhill Press, 1999), p. 167.

(5d) Ibid., p. 119.

(5e) Tad Leahy, "The A to Z of ABC Dictionaries," *Business Finance* 5/12 (December 1999), p. 82.

(5f) Steve Player and Carol Cobble, *Cornerstones of Decision Making: Profiles of Enterprise ABM* (Greensboro, NC: Oakhill Press, 1999), p. 151.

(5g) Ibid., p. 226.

(5h) Scott Smith, in Steve Player and Carol Cobble, *Cornerstones of Decision Making: Profiles of Enterprise ABM* (Greensboro, NC: Oakhill Press, 1999), p. 187.

(5i) BMO Financial Group, *Review of Operating Groups Performance, 1st Quarter of 2005.*

Chapter Six

(6a) Paulo Salgado, Margarida Bajanca, and Nuno Belo, in Steve Player and Carol Cobble, *Cornerstones of Decision Making: Profiles of Enterprise ABM* (Greensboro, NC: Oakhill Press, 1999), p. 172.

(6b) Steve Player and Carol Cobble, *Cornerstones of Decision Making: Profiles of Enterprise ABM* (Greensboro, NC: Oakhill Press, 1999), p. 214.

(6c) Interview with a Ford Motor Company accountant conducted during research by Ronald W. Hilton.

(6d) Steve Player and Carol Cobble, *Cornerstones of Decision Making: Profiles of Enterprise ABM* (Greensboro, NC: Oakhill Press, 1999), p. 78.

(6e) Interview with a Cornell University administrator conducted during research by Ronald W. Hilton.

---

*The references are organized by chapter, so reference (1a) relates to the first quote in Chapter 1, and so forth.

Chapter Seven

(7a) Gary Siegel and James E. Sorensen, principal investigators for the Gary Siegel Organization, *Counting More, Counting Less: Transformations in the Management Accounting Profession* (Montvale, NJ: Institute of Management Accountants, 1999).

(7b) Interview with a Cornell University accountant conducted during research by Ronald W. Hilton.

(7c) Interview with a Delta Air Lines accountant conducted during research by Ronald W. Hilton.

(7d) Gary Siegel and James E. Sorensen, principal investigators for the Gary Siegel Organization, *Counting More, Counting Less: Transformations in the Management Accounting Profession* (Montvale, NJ: Institute of Management Accountants, 1999).

(7e) Steve Player and Carol Cobble, *Cornerstones of Decision Making: Profiles of Enterprise ABM* (Greensboro, NC: Oakhill Press, 1999), p. 168.

(7f) Ibid, p. 78.

Chapter Eight

(8a) *The Management Accounting Video,* a management education video (New York: McGraw-Hill, 1997). Best Foods introduced several well-known brands, such as Skippy peanut butter, Hellmann's mayonnaise, and Thomas' English Muffins. Best Foods has been acquired by Unilever.

(8b) Ibid.

(8c) Gary Siegel and James E. Sorensen, principal investigators for the Gary Siegel Organization, *Counting More, Counting Less: Transformations in the Management Accounting Profession* (Montvale, NJ: Institute of Management Accountants, 1999).

(8d) Jay Collins, "Advanced Use of ABM: Using ABC for Target Costing, Activity-Based Budgeting, and Benchmarking," in *Activity-Based Management: Arthur Andersen's Lessons from the ABM Battlefield,* eds. Steve Player and David E. Keys (New York: John Wiley & Sons, 1999), p. 153.

(8e) James A. Brimson and John Antos, *Driving Value Using Activity-Based Budgeting* (New York: John Wiley & Sons, 1999), p. 10.

(8f) Steve Hornyak, "Budgeting Made Easy," *Management Accounting* 80/4 (October 1998), pp. 18–23.

Chapter Nine

(9a) *The Management Accounting Video,* a management education video (New York: McGraw-Hill, 1997).

(9b) Gary Siegel and James E. Sorensen, principal investigators for the Gary Siegel Organization, *Counting More, Counting Less: Transformations in the Management Accounting Profession* (Montvale, NJ: Institute of Management Accountants, 1999).

(9c) *The Management Accounting Video,* a management education video (New York: McGraw-Hill, 1997).

(9d) Interview with an A. T. Kearney consultant conducted during research by Ronald W. Hilton.

(9e) Steve Player and Carol Cobble, *Cornerstones of Decision Making: Profiles of Enterprise ABM* (Greensboro, NC: Oakhill Press, 1999), p. 79.

(9f) Cynthia Beier Greeson and Mehmet C. Kocakulah, "Implementing an ABC Pilot at Whirlpool," *Journal of Cost Management 11*/2 (March/April 1997), pp. 16–21.

(9g) Interview with an A. T. Kearney consultant conducted during research by Ronald W. Hilton.

(9h) *The Management Accounting Video,* a management education video (New York: McGraw-Hill, 1997).

Chapter Ten

(10a) Robert S. Kaplan, *City of Charlotte,* a management case (Boston: The President and Fellows of Harvard College, 1998).

(10b) Gary Siegel and James E. Sorensen, principal investigators for the Gary Siegel Organization, *Counting More, Counting Less: Transformations in the Management Accounting Profession* (Montvale, NJ: Institute of Management Accountants, 1999).

(10c) Susan Savage and Peter Neufeld, *Case Study: From Business Strategy to the Front Line at CIBC,* for HR conference, Toronto, April 19–21, 2004.

(10d) Mark Green, Jeanine Garrity, Andra Gumbus, and Bridget Lyons, "Pitney Bowes Calls for New Metrics," *Strategic Finance* 83/11 (May 2002), p. 34.

(10e) *The Management Accounting Video*, a management education video (New York: McGraw-Hill, 1997).

(10f) Gary Siegel and James E. Sorensen, principal investigators for the Gary Siegel Organization, *Counting More, Counting Less: Transformations in the Management Accounting Profession* (Montvale, NJ: Institute of Management Accountants, 1999).

(10g) Michael Arndt, "Quality Isn't Just for Widgets," *BusinessWeek,* July 22, 2002, p. 72.

Chapter Eleven

(11a) Interview with a Chrysler accountant conducted during research by Ronald W. Hilton.

(11b) Gary Siegel and James E. Sorensen, principal investigators for the Gary Siegel Organization, *Counting More, Counting Less: Transformations in the Management Accounting Profession* (Montvale, NJ: Institute of Management Accountants, 1999).

(11c) Ibid.

(11d) Interview with an American Management Systems consultant conducted during research by Ronald W. Hilton.

(11e) Gary Siegel and James E. Sorensen, principal investigators for the Gary Siegel Organization, *Counting More, Counting Less: Transformations in the Management Accounting Profession* (Montvale, NJ: Institute of Management Accountants, 1999).

(11f) Ibid.

(11g) Thomas P. Kunes, "Environmental Cost Management," *Strategic Finance,* February 2001, p. 83.

(11h) *Current Practices, Perceptions and Trends: Transfer Pricing—1997 Global Survey* (Chicago: Ernst & Young, 1997), p. 1.

(11i) Ibid., p. 4.

(11j) Ibid., p. 11.

(11k) Ibid., p. 11.

Chapter Twelve

(12a) Gary Siegel and James E. Sorensen, principal investigators for the Gary Siegel Organization, *Counting More, Counting Less: Transformations in the Management Accounting Profession* (Montvale, NJ: Institute of Management Accountants, 1999).

(12b) Ibid.

(12c) Ibid.

(12d) Ibid.

(12e) Ibid.

Chapter Thirteen

(13a) Gary Siegel and James E. Sorensen, principal investigators for the Gary Siegel Organization, *Counting More, Counting Less: Transformations in the Management Accounting Profession* (Montvale, NJ: Institute of Management Accountants, 1999).

(13b) Ibid.

(13c) Steve Player and Carol Cobble, *Cornerstones of Decision Making: Profiles of Enterprise ABM* (Greensboro, NC: Oakhill Press, 1999), p. 80.

(13d) Presentation by the U.S. Navy Acquisition Center, *The Second Annual International Conference on Target Costing*, sponsored by the Consortium for Advanced Manufacturing—International, Arthur Andersen, Ernst & Young, and the University of Akron (Washington, DC: CAM-I, 1998).

(13e) Presentation by Honda of America, *The Second Annual International Conference on Target Costing*, sponsored by the Consortium for Advanced Manufacturing—International, Arthur Andersen, Ernst & Young, and the University of Akron (Washington, DC: CAM-I, 1998).

(13f) Ibid.

Chapter Fourteen (Online)

(14a) Interview with a Ford Motor Company accountant conducted during research by Ronald W. Hilton.

(14b) Interview with a Hewlett-Packard accountant conducted during research by Ronald W. Hilton.

(14c) Letter from Cheryl Wenezenki-Yolland, Comptroller General for the Province of British Columbia to the International Federation of Accountants (IFAC), commenting on the *International Management Accounting Statement Exposure Draft: Project Appraisal Using Discounted Cash Flow*, September 2007.

(14d) Interview with a Boeing Company accountant conducted during research by Ronald W. Hilton.

(14e) Interview with an A. T. Kearney consultant conducted during research by Ronald W. Hilton.

Chapter Fifteen (Online)

(15a) Interview with a Chrysler accountant conducted during research by Ronald W. Hilton.

(15b) Interview with a Cornell University accountant conducted during research by Ronald W. Hilton.

(15c) Interview with an A. T. Kearney consultant conducted during research by Ronald W. Hilton.

Index of Companies and Organizations

Index of Subjects